W9-CBQ-080

See what students love about LearningCurve.

Macmillan Education
LearningCurve   **learningcurveworks.com**

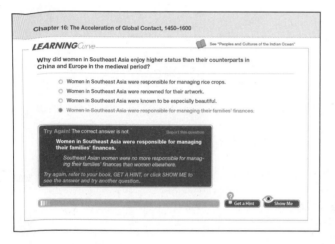

Students using LaunchPad receive access to LearningCurve for *A History of World Societies*.

Each chapter-based LearningCurve activity gives students **multiple chances to understand key concepts**, return to the narrative textbook if they need to reread, and answer questions correctly.

Over 90% of students report satisfaction with LearningCurve's **fun and accessible game-like interface**.

Assigning LearningCurve in place of reading quizzes is easy for instructors, and the **reporting features help instructors track overall class trends** and spot topics that are giving students trouble so that they can adjust lectures and class activities.

> "With LearningCurve, students engage with the content and retain it better."
>
> — Melissa Walker, *Converse College*

To learn more about LearningCurve, visit **learningcurveworks.com**.

LearningCurve: Everyone's got a learning curve — what's yours?

VALUE EDITION

A History of World Societies

Tenth Edition

John P. McKay
University of Illinois at Urbana-Champaign

Bennett D. Hill
Late of Georgetown University

John Buckler
Late of University of Illinois at Urbana-Champaign

Patricia Buckley Ebrey
University of Washington

Roger B. Beck
Eastern Illinois University

Clare Haru Crowston
University of Illinois at Urbana-Champaign

Merry E. Wiesner-Hanks
University of Wisconsin–Milwaukee

Jerry Dávila
University of Illinois at Urbana-Champaign

BEDFORD/ST. MARTIN'S

Boston • New York

FOR BEDFORD/ST. MARTIN'S

Director of Development for History: Jane Knetzger
Senior Developmental Editor: Sara Wise
Senior Production Editor: Christina M. Horn
Production Supervisor: Samuel Jones
Executive Marketing Manager: Sandra McGuire
Associate Editor: Robin Soule
Editorial Assistant: Arrin Kaplan
Production Assistant: Erica Zhang
Copy Editor: Jennifer Brett Greenstein
Indexer: Leoni Z. McVey
Cartography: Mapping Specialists, Ltd.
Photo Researcher: Bruce Carson
Senior Art Director: Anna Palchik
Text Design: Jonathon Nix
Cover Design: William Boardman
Cover Art: Portrait of an African Slave Woman, attributed to Annibale Carracci, ca. 1580. Courtesy
     Tomasso Brothers Fine Art, Leeds, England.
Composition: Jouve
Printing and Binding: RR Donnelley and Sons

Copyright © 2015 by Bedford/St. Martin's

All rights reserved. No part of this book may be reproduced, stored in a retrieval system, or
transmitted in any form or by any means, electronic, mechanical, photocopying, recording, or
otherwise, except as may be expressly permitted by the applicable copyright statutes or in writing
by the Publisher.

Manufactured in the United States of America.

9   8   7   6
f   e   d

For information, write: Bedford/St. Martin's, 75 Arlington Street, Boston, MA 02116
     (617-399-4000)

ISBN 978-1-4576-8526-2 (Combined Edition)
ISBN 978-1-4576-8532-3 (Volume 1)
ISBN 978-1-4576-8533-0 (Volume 2)

ACKNOWLEDGMENTS
*Acknowledgments and copyrights appear on the same page as the text and art selections they cover;
these acknowledgments and copyrights constitute an extension of the copyright page. It is a violation
of the law to reproduce these selections by any means whatsoever without the written permission of the
copyright holder.*

Preface
Why This Book This Way

WE ARE PLEASED TO INTRODUCE THE FIRST VALUE EDITION OF our popular textbook *A History of World Societies.* The Value Edition provides the social and cultural focus, comprehensive regional organization, and global perspective that have long been hallmarks of *A History of World Societies* in a two-color, trade-sized format at a low price. Featuring the full narrative of the thoroughly revised tenth edition of the parent text and select images, maps, features, and pedagogical tools, the Value Edition continues to incorporate the latest and best scholarship in the field in an accessible, student-friendly manner. It also reflects the contributions of the newest member of the author team, Jerry Dávila from the University of Illinois, who brings expertise in Latin America and the twentieth century. A renowned scholar of Brazil whose work focuses on race and social policy, Jerry offers a fresh perspective to our coverage of Latin America and to the final chapters in the books, which he has completely reconceptualized. Thus we continue to benefit from a collaborative team of regional experts with deep experience in the world history classroom.

New Tools for the Digital Age

We know that many students today are on a budget and that instructors want greater flexibility and more digital options in their choice of course materials. We are proud to offer a low-cost text that offers the engaging and readable narrative with a rich abundance of digital tools designed to help students think historically and master the material. Free when packaged with the book or heavily discounted when used standalone, **LaunchPad**'s course space and interactive e-book are ready to use as is (or can be edited and customized with your own material) and can be assigned right away. Developed with extensive feedback from history instructors and students, LaunchPad includes the complete narrative e-book, as well as abundant primary documents, maps, images, assignments, and activities. The aims of key learning outcomes are addressed via formative and summative assessments, short-answer and essay questions, multiple-choice quizzing, and **LearningCurve**, an adaptive learning tool designed to get students to read before they come to class. Available with training and support, LaunchPad can help you take your teaching into a new era. To learn more about the benefits of LearningCurve and LaunchPad, see "Versions and Supplements" on page xv.

What Makes *A History of World Societies* Special

In this age of global connections, with their influence on the global economy, global migration patterns, popular culture, and global warming, among other aspects of life, the study of world history is more vital and urgent than ever before. An understanding of the broad sweep of the human past helps us comprehend today's dramatic changes and enduring continuities. People now migrate enormous distances and establish new lives far from their places of birth, yet migration has been a constant in history since the first humans walked out of Africa. Satellites and cell phones now link nearly every inch of the planet, yet the expansion of communication networks is a process that is thousands of years old. Children who speak different languages at home now sit side by side in schools and learn from one another, yet intercultural encounters have long been a source of innovation, transformation, and at times, unfortunately, conflict.

This book is designed for twenty-first-century students who will spend their lives on this small interconnected planet and for whom an understanding of only local or national history will no longer be sufficient. We believe that the study of world history in a broad and comparative context is an exciting, important, and highly practical pursuit. It is our conviction, based on considerable experience in introducing large numbers of students to world history, that a book reflecting current trends in scholarship can excite readers and inspire an enduring interest in the long human experience.

Our strategy has been twofold. First, we have made social and cultural history the core elements of our narrative. We seek to re-create the lives of ordinary people in appealing human terms and also to highlight the interplay between men's and women's lived experiences and the ways they reflect on these to create meaning. Thus, in addition to foundational works of philosophy and literature, we include popular songs and stories. We present objects along with texts as important sources for studying history, and this has allowed us to incorporate the growing emphasis on material culture in the work of many historians. At the same time, we have been mindful of the need to give great economic, political, and intellectual developments the attention they deserve. We want to give individual students and instructors an integrated perspective so that they can pursue—on their own or in the classroom—the themes and questions that they find particularly exciting and significant.

Second, we have made every effort to strike an effective global and regional balance. The whole world interacts today, and to understand the interactions and what they mean for today's citizens, we must study the whole world's history. Thus we have adopted a comprehensive regional organization with a global perspective that is clear and manageable for students. For example, Chapter 7 introduces students in depth to East Asia, and at the same time the chapter highlights the cultural connections that occurred via the Silk Road and the spread of Buddhism. We study all geographical areas, conscious of the separate histories of many parts of the world, particularly in the earliest millennia of human development. We also stress the links among cultures, political units, and economic systems, for these connections have made the world what it is today. We make comparisons and connections across time as well as space, for understanding the unfolding of the human story in time is the central task of history.

Better-Prepared Students

Every instructor knows it can be a challenge to get students to complete assigned readings and then fully understand what is important once they have done the reading. *A History of World Societies*, Value Edition, addresses this challenge head-on with a suite of tools in **LaunchPad** that instructors can choose from.

To help students fully understand their reading and come to class prepared, instructors who adopt LaunchPad for *A History of World Societies*, Value Edition, can assign the **LearningCurve** formative assessment activities. This online learning tool is popular with students because it helps them rehearse content at their own pace in a nonthreatening, gamelike environment. LearningCurve is also popular with instructors because the reporting features allow them to track overall class trends and spot topics that are giving their students trouble so they can adjust their lectures and class activities. When LearningCurve is assigned, students come to class better prepared and instructors can better evaluate and adjust their classes.

Encouraging active reading is another way to make content memorable and highlight what is truly important. To help students read actively and understand the central idea of the chapter, instructors who use LaunchPad can also assign our **Guided Reading Exercises**. This new exercise, which appears at the start of each chapter, prompts students to collect information to be used to answer a broad analytic question central to the chapter as a whole.

To further encourage students to read and fully assimilate the text, as well as to measure how well they do this, instructors can assign the **new multiple-choice summative quizzes** in LaunchPad, where they are automatically graded. Not only do these secure tests encourage students to study the book, but they can be assigned at specific intervals as high-stakes testing and thus provide another means for analyzing class performance.

Primary Sources for Teaching Critical Thinking and Analysis

For those who are using LaunchPad, *A History of World Societies* offers an extensive program of primary source assignments to help students master a number of key learning outcomes, among them **critical thinking**, **historical thinking**, **analytical thinking**, and **argumentation**, as well as learning about the **diversity of world cultures**. When assigned in LaunchPad, all primary source features that appear in the full-sized version of *A History of World Societies* are accompanied by multiple-choice quizzes that help you ensure that students come to class prepared.

In LaunchPad, each chapter includes two Viewpoints features: sets of paired primary documents on a topic that illuminate the human experience and allow us to provide more concrete examples of differences in the ways people thought. Anyone teaching world history has to emphasize larger trends and developments, but students sometimes get the wrong impression that everyone in a society thought alike. We hope that teachers who adopt LaunchPad can use these passages to get students thinking about diversity within and across societies. The **66 Viewpoints assignments**—two in each LaunchPad unit—introduce students to working with sources, encourage critical analysis, and extend the narrative while giving voice to the people of the past. Each includes a brief introduction, questions for analysis, and multiple-choice questions. Carefully chosen for accessibility, each pair of documents presents views on a diverse range of topics. Viewpoints topics include "Addressing the Gods in Mesopotamia and Egypt"; "The Inglorious Side of War in the *Book of Songs* and the *Patirruppattu*"; "Hellenistic and Chinese Spells"; "Freeing Slaves in Justinian's *Code* and the Qur'an"; early Chinese and Portuguese accounts of Africa; Protestant and Neo-Confucian ideas on behavior; "Jahangir and Louis XIV on Priorities for Monarchs"; "Jean-Jacques

Rousseau and Mary Wollstonecraft on Women's Nature and Education"; perspectives on Indian cotton manufacturing in India and Britain; "African Views of the Scramble for Africa"; the abolition of slavery in the Americas; and women activists in Mexico.

Each LaunchPad unit also includes a longer primary source feature titled **Listening to the Past**, chosen to extend and illuminate a major historical issue considered in each chapter. The feature presents a single original source or several voices on the subject to help instructors teach the important skills of **critical thinking** and **analysis**. Each opens with an introduction and closes with questions for analysis that invite students to evaluate the evidence as historians would, and multiple-choice questions are provided. Selected for their interest and significance and carefully placed within their historical context, these sources, we hope, allow students to "hear the past" and to observe how history has been shaped by individuals. Topics include "The Teachings of Confucius"; "Gregory of Tours on the Veneration of Relics"; "Courtly Love Poetry"; "Stefan Zweig on Middle-Class Youth and Sexuality" (in early-twentieth-century Europe); "Reyita Castillo Bueno on Slavery and Freedom in Cuba"; "C. L. R. James on Pan-African Liberation"; and lyrics from a Brazilian band on globalization.

In addition to using documents as part of our special feature program in LaunchPad, we have quoted extensively from a wide variety of **primary sources within the narrative**, demonstrating in our use of these quotations that they are the "stuff" of history. Thus primary sources appear as an integral part of the narrative as well as in extended form in the Listening to the Past and expanded Viewpoints chapter features.

Assignable **Online Document Projects** in LaunchPad offer students more practice in interpreting primary sources. Each project, based on the Individuals in Society feature described in the next section, prompts students to explore a key question through analysis of multiple sources. Chapter 22's project, for example, asks students to analyze documents on the complexities of the Haitian Revolution and the conditions that made Toussaint L'Ouverture's story possible. Auto-graded multiple-choice questions based on the documents help students analyze the sources.

Finally, we have revised our **primary source documents collection**, *Sources for World Societies*, to add more visual sources and to closely align the readings with the chapter topics and themes of the tenth edition. The documents are now available in a fully assignable and assessable electronic format within each LaunchPad unit, and the accompanying multiple-choice questions measure comprehension and hold students accountable for their reading.

Student Engagement with Biography

In our years of teaching world history, we have often noted that students come alive when they encounter stories about real people in the past. To give students a chance to see the past through ordinary people's lives, each chapter includes one of the popular **Individuals in Society biographical essays**, each of which offers a brief study of an individual or group, informing students about the societies in which the individuals lived. This feature grew out of our long-standing focus on people's lives and the varieties of historical experience, and we believe that readers will empathize with these human beings who themselves were seeking to define their own identities. The spotlighting of individuals, both famous and obscure, perpetuates the book's continued attention to cultural and intellectual developments, highlights human agency, and reflects changing interests within the historical profession as well as the development of "microhistory." The Value Edition includes essays on Sudatta, a lay follower of the Buddha; Cosimo and Lorenzo de' Medici; Malintzin; and Sieng, a Mnong refugee living in the United States.

Assignable **Online Document Projects** in LaunchPad offer students more practice in interpreting primary sources. Each project, based on the Individuals in Society feature, prompts students to explore a key question through analysis of multiple sources. Auto-graded multiple-choice questions based on the documents help students analyze the sources.

Connecting History to Real-World Applications

In LaunchPad, we include **Global Trade** features from the full-sized text, essays that focus on a particular commodity, exploring the world trade, social and economic impact, and cultural influence of that commodity. Each essay is accompanied by a detailed map showing the trade routes of the commodity. We believe that careful attention to all these essays will enable students to appreciate the complex ways in which trade has connected and influenced various parts of the world. All the Global Trade features are fully assignable and assessable in LaunchPad.

Geographic and Visual Literacy

To address students' difficulties with geography and visual analysis, throughout the textbook and online more than **80 full-size maps** illustrate major developments in the chapter. We have also included **Mapping the Past map activities** and **Picturing the Past visual activities** in each LaunchPad unit. These activities ask students to analyze a map or visual and make connections to the larger processes discussed in the narrative, giving them valuable practice in reading and interpreting maps and images. In LaunchPad, these activities are assignable and students can submit their work.

Chronological Reasoning

To help students make comparisons, understand changes over time, and see relationships among contemporaneous events, each chapter ends with a **chapter chronology** that reviews major developments discussed in the chapter. **A unified timeline** available from every page in LaunchPad allows students to compare developments over the centuries.

Active Reading

With the goal of making the Value Edition as student centered as possible, we paid sharp attention to the book's reading and study aids:

- **Focus questions** at the start of each main heading help guide students in their reading. These questions are repeated in the chapter review section.

- In LaunchPad, instructors can assign the **Guided Reading Exercise** for each chapter, which prompts students to read actively to collect information that answers a broad analytic question central to the chapter as a whole.
- The chapter-closing **Connections** feature synthesizes main developments and makes connections and comparisons between countries and regions to explain how events relate to larger global processes, such as the influence of the Silk Road, the effects of the transatlantic slave trade, and the ramifications of colonialism.
- A **Chapter Summary** reinforces key chapter events and ideas for students.
- A **Chapter Review** at the end of each chapter includes a list of **key terms**, chapter **focus questions**, and **Make Connections** questions that prompt students to assess larger developments across chapters.
- **Key terms** are bolded in the text and listed in the chapter review to promote clarity and comprehension, and **phonetic spellings** are located directly after terms that readers are likely to find hard to pronounce.

Acknowledgments

It is a pleasure to thank the many instructors who read and critiqued the previous edition of *A History of World Societies* to make suggestions for the new edition of the parent text and this Value Edition:

Stewart Anderson, *Brigham Young University*
Brian Arendt, *Lindenwood University*
Stephen Auerbach, *Georgia College*
Michael Bardot, *Lincoln University*
Natalie Bayer, *Drake University*
Michael Bazemore, *William Peace University*
Brian Becker, *Delta State University*
Rosemary Bell, *Skyline College*
Chris Benedetto, *Granite State College*
Wesley L. Bishop, *Pitt Community College*
Robert Blackey, *California State University–San Bernardino*
Edward Bond, *Alabama A&M University*
Nathan Brooks, *New Mexico State University*
Jurgen Buchenau, *The University of North Carolina at Charlotte*
Paul Buckingham, *Morrisville State College*
Steven B. Bunker, *University of Alabama*
Kate Burlingham, *California State University, Fullerton*
David Bush, *The College of the Siskiyous*
Laura M. Calkins, *Texas Tech University*
Robert Caputi, *Erie Community College–North Campus*
Lucia Carter, *Mars Hill College*
Lesley Chapel, *Saginaw Valley State University*
Nevin Crouse, *Chesapeake College*
Everett Dague, *Benedictine College*
Jeffrey Demsky, *San Bernardino Valley College*
Peter de Rosa, *Bridgewater State University*

Nicholas Di Liberto, *Newberry College*
Randall Dills, *University of Louisville*
Shawn Dry, *Oakland Community College*
Roxanne Easley, *Central Washington University*
John Fielding, *Mount Wachusett Community College*
Barbara Fuller, *Indian River State College*
Dolores Grapsas, *New River Community College*
Emily Fisher Gray, *Norwich University*
Gayle Greene-Aguirre, *Mississippi Gulf Coast Community College*
Neil Greenwood, *Cleveland State Community College*
Christian Griggs, *Dalton State College*
W. Scott Haine, *Cañada College*
Irwin Halfond, *McKendree University*
Alicia Harding, *Southern Maine Community College*
Jillian Hartley, *Arkansas Northeastern College*
Robert Haug, *University of Cincinnati*
John Hunt, *Utah Valley University*
Fatima Imam, *Lake Forest College*
Rashi Jackman, *De Anza College*
Jackie Jay, *Eastern Kentucky University*
Timothy Jenks, *East Carolina University*
Andrew Kellett, *Harford Community College*
Christine Kern, *Edinboro University*
Christopher Killmer, *St. Johns River State College*
Mark Klobas, *Scottsdale Community College*
Chris Laney, *Berkshire Community College*
Erick D. Langer, *Georgetown University*
Mary Jean Lavery, *Delaware County Community College*
Mark Lentz, *University of Louisiana, Lafayette*
Darin Lenz, *Fresno Pacific University*
Yi Li, *Tacoma Community College*
Jonas Liliequist, *Umeå University*
Ron Lowe, *University of Tennessee at Chattanooga*
Mary Lyons-Carmona, *University of Nebraska at Omaha*
Elizabeth S. Manley, *Xavier University of Louisiana*
Brandon D. Marsh, *Bridgewater College*
Sean F. McEnroe, *Southern Oregon University*
John McLeod, *University of Louisville*
Brendan McManus, *Bemidji State University*
Christina Mehrtens, *University of Massachusetts–Dartmouth*
Charlotte Miller, *Middle Georgia State College*
Robert Montgomery, *Baldwin Wallace University*
Curtis Morgan, *Lord Fairfax Community College*
Richard Moss, *Harrisburg Area Community College*
Larry Myers, *Butler Community College*
Erik Lars Myrup, *University of Kentucky*
April Najjaj, *Mount Olive College*

Katie Nelson, *Weber State University*
Lily Rhodes Novicki, *Virginia Western Community College*
Monica Orozco, *Westmont College*
Neal Palmer, *Christian Brothers University*
Jenifer Parks, *Rocky Mountain College*
Melinda Pash, *Fayetteville Technical Community College*
Tao Peng, *Minnesota State University–Mankato*
Patricia Perry, *St. Edward's University*
William Plants, *University of Rio Grande/Rio Grande Community College*
Joshua Pollock, *Modesto Junior College*
Fabrizio Prado, *College of William & Mary*
Daniel Prosterman, *Salem College*
Tracie Provost, *Middle Georgia College*
Melissa Redd, *Pulaski Technical College*
Charles Reed, *Elizabeth City State University*
Leah Renold, *Texas State University*
Kim Richardson, *Front Range Community College*
David Ruffley, *Colorado Mountain College*
Martina Saltamacchia, *University of Nebraska at Omaha*
Karl Schmidt, *South Dakota State University*
Kimberly Schutte, *SUNY–The College at Brockport*
Eva Seraphin, *Irvine Valley College*
Courtney Shah, *Lower Columbia College*
Jeffrey Shumway, *Brigham Young University*
David Simonelli, *Youngstown State University*
James Smith, *Southwest Baptist University*
Kara D. Smith, *Georgia Perimeter College*
Ilicia Sprey, *Saint Joseph's College*
Rachel Standish, *San Joaquin Delta College*
Kate Staples, *West Virginia University*
Brian Strayer, *Andrews University*
Sonia Chandarana Tandon, *Forsyth Technical Community College*
James Todesca, *Armstrong Atlantic State University*
Elisaveta Todorova, *University of Cincinnati*
Dianne Walker, *Baton Rouge Community College*
Kenneth Wilburn, *East Carolina University*
Carol Woodfin, *Hardin-Simmons University*
Laura Zeeman, *Red Rocks Community College*

It is also a pleasure to thank the many editors who have assisted us over the years, first at Houghton Mifflin and now at Bedford/St. Martin's. At Bedford/St. Martin's, these include senior development editors Sara Wise and Laura Arcari; associate editor Robin Soule; editorial assistant Arrin Kaplan; executive editor Traci Mueller Crowell; director of development Jane Knetzger; publisher for history Mary Dougherty; photo researcher Bruce Carson; text permissions editor Eve Lehmann; and senior production editor Christina Horn, with the assistance of Erica Zhang and the guidance of Sue Brown, director of editing and design, and managing editor Michael Granger. Other key contributors were copy editor Jennifer Brett Greenstein, proofreaders Susan Moore and Susan Zorn, indexer Leoni McVey, and cover designer William Boardman. We would also like to thank former vice president for editorial humanities Denise Wydra and former president Joan E. Feinberg.

Many of our colleagues at the University of Illinois, the University of Washington, the University of Wisconsin–Milwaukee, and Eastern Illinois University continue to provide information and stimulation, often without even knowing it. We thank them for it. The authors recognize John P. McKay, Bennett D. Hill, and John Buckler, the founding authors of this textbook, whose vision set a new standard for world history textbooks. The authors also thank the many students over the years with whom we have used earlier editions of this book. Their reactions and opinions helped shape our revisions to this edition, and we hope it remains worthy of the ultimate praise that they bestowed on it, that it is "not boring like most textbooks." Merry Wiesner-Hanks would, as always, like to thank her husband, Neil, without whom work on this project would not be possible. Clare Haru Crowston thanks her husband, Ali, and her children, Lili, Reza, and Kian, who are a joyous reminder of the vitality of life that we try to showcase in this book. Roger Beck thanks Ann for supporting him while she was completing her Ph.D. He is also grateful to the World History Association for all past, present, and future contributions to his understanding of world history. Jerry Dávila thanks Liv, Ellen, and Alex, who are reminders of why history matters.

Each of us has benefited from the criticism of his or her coauthors, although each of us assumes responsibility for what he or she has written and revised. Merry Wiesner-Hanks has written and revised Chapters 1, 2, 5, 6, 8, 14, and 15; Patricia Buckley Ebrey has written and revised Chapters 3, 4, 7, 9, 12, 13, 17, 21, and 26; Roger B. Beck has written and revised Chapters 10, 20, 25, and 28–30; Clare Haru Crowston has written and revised Chapters 16, 18, 19, and 22–24. Jerry Dávila has completely rewritten Chapters 11, 27, and 31–33.

Versions and Supplements

Adopters of *A History of World Societies*, Value Edition, and their students have access to abundant print and digital resources and tools, including documents, assessment and presentation materials, the acclaimed Bedford Series in History and Culture volumes, and much more. And for the first time, the full-featured LaunchPad course space provides access to the narrative with all assignment and assessment opportunities at the ready. See below for more information, visit the book's catalog site at **bedfordstmartins.com/mckayworldvalue/catalog**, or contact your local Bedford/ St. Martin's sales representative.

Get the Right Version for Your Class

To accommodate different course lengths and course budgets, *A History of World Societies*, Value Edition, is available in several different formats, including low-priced PDF e-books, such as the *Bedford e-Book to Go for A History of World Societies*, Value Edition, from our Web site and other PDF e-books from other commercial sources. And for the best value of all, package a new print book with LaunchPad at no additional charge to get the best each format offers—a print version for easy portability and reading with a LaunchPad interactive e-book and course space with loads of additional assignment and assessment options.

- **Combined Volume** (Chapters 1–33): available in paperback and e-book formats and in LaunchPad
- **Volume 1, To 1600** (Chapters 1–16): available in paperback and e-book formats and in LaunchPad
- **Volume 2, Since 1450** (Chapters 16–33): available in paperback and e-book formats and in LaunchPad

As noted below, any of these volumes can be packaged with additional titles for a discount. To get ISBNs for discount packages, see the online catalog at **bedfordstmartins .com/mckayworldvalue/catalog** or contact your Bedford/St. Martin's representative.

▶ NEW Assign LaunchPad—a Content-Rich and Assessment-Ready Interactive e-Book and Course Space

Available for discount purchase on its own or for packaging with new books at no additional charge, LaunchPad is a breakthrough solution for today's courses. Intuitive and easy to use for students and instructors alike, LaunchPad is ready to use as is, and can be edited, customized with your own material, and assigned in seconds. *LaunchPad for A History of World Societies*, Value Edition, includes Bedford/St. Martin's high-quality content all in one place, including the full interactive e-book and the *Sources of World Societies* documents collection, plus LearningCurve formative quizzing, guided reading activities designed to help students read actively for key concepts, additional primary sources, images, videos, chapter summative quizzes, and more.

Through a wealth of formative and summative assessments, including short-answer and essay questions, multiple-choice quizzing, and the adaptive learning program of LearningCurve (see the full description ahead), students gain confidence and get into their reading *before* class. Map and visual activities engage students with visual analysis and critical thinking as they work through each unit, while special boxed features become more meaningful through automatically graded multiple-choice exercises and short-answer questions that prompt students to analyze their reading.

LaunchPad easily integrates with course management systems, and with fast ways to build assignments, rearrange chapters, and add new pages, sections, or links, it lets teachers build the courses they want to teach and hold students accountable. For more information, visit launchpadworks.com or contact us at history@bedfordstmartins .com to arrange a demo.

✅ Assign LearningCurve So Your Students Come to Class Prepared

Students using LaunchPad receive access to LearningCurve for *A History of World Societies*, Value Edition. Assigning LearningCurve in place of reading quizzes is easy for instructors, and the reporting features help instructors track overall class trends and spot topics that are giving students trouble so they can adjust their lectures and class activities. This online learning tool is popular with students because it was designed to help them rehearse content at their own pace in a nonthreatening, gamelike environment. The feedback for wrong answers provides instructional coaching and sends students back to the book for review. Students answer as many questions as necessary to reach a target score, with repeated chances to revisit material they haven't mastered. When LearningCurve is assigned, students come to class better prepared.

Take Advantage of Instructor Resources

Bedford/St. Martin's has developed a rich array of teaching resources for this book and for this course. They range from lecture and presentation materials and assessment tools to course management options. Most can be found in LaunchPad or can be downloaded or ordered at bedfordstmartins.com/mckayworldvalue/catalog.

Instructor's Resource Manual. The instructor's manual offers both experienced and first-time instructors tools for preparing lectures and running discussions. It includes chapter content learning objectives, teaching strategies, and a guide to chapter-specific supplements available for the text, plus suggestions on how to get the most out of LearningCurve and a survival guide for first-time teaching assistants.

Guide to Changing Editions. Designed to facilitate an instructor's transition from the previous edition of *A History of World Societies* to the Value Edition, this guide presents an overview of major changes as well as changes in each chapter.

Computerized Test Bank. The test bank includes a mix of fresh, carefully crafted multiple-choice, short-answer, and essay questions for each chapter. All questions appear in Microsoft Word format and in easy-to-use test bank software that allows instructors to add, edit, re-sequence, and print questions and answers. Instructors can also export questions into a variety of formats, including Blackboard, Desire2Learn, and Moodle.

The Bedford Lecture Kit. PowerPoint Maps and Images. Look good and save time with ***The Bedford Lecture Kit***. These presentation materials are downloadable individually from the Instructor Resources tab at bedfordstmartins.com/mckayworldvalue /catalog. They include all maps, figures, and images from the textbook in JPEG and PowerPoint formats.

Package and Save Your Students Money

For information on free packages and discounts up to 50 percent, visit bedfordstmartins .com/mckayworldvalue/catalog, or contact your local Bedford/St. Martin's sales representative. The products that follow all qualify for discount packaging.

The Bedford Series in History and Culture. More than 100 titles in this highly praised series combine first-rate scholarship, historical narrative, and important primary documents for undergraduate courses. Each book is brief, inexpensive, and focused on a specific topic or period. For a complete list of titles, visit bedfordstmartins.com /history/series.

Rand McNally Atlas of World History. This collection of almost 70 full-color maps illustrates the eras and civilizations in world history from the emergence of human societies to the present.

The Bedford Glossary for World History. This handy supplement for the survey course gives students historically contextualized definitions for hundreds of terms — from *abolitionism* to *Zoroastrianism* — that they will encounter in lectures, reading, and exams.

World History Matters: A Student Guide to World History Online. Based on the popular "World History Matters" Web site produced by the Center for History and New Media, this unique resource, edited by Kristin Lehner (The Johns Hopkins University), Kelly Schrum (George Mason University), and T. Mills Kelly (George Mason University), combines reviews of 150 of the most useful and reliable world history Web sites with an introduction that guides students in locating, evaluating, and correctly citing online sources.

Trade Books. Titles published by sister companies Hill and Wang; Farrar, Straus and Giroux; Henry Holt and Company; St. Martin's Press; Picador; and Palgrave Macmillan are available at a 50 percent discount when packaged with Bedford/St. Martin's textbooks. For more information, visit bedfordstmartins.com/tradeup.

A Pocket Guide to Writing in History. This portable and affordable reference tool by Mary Lynn Rampolla provides reading, writing, and research advice useful to students in all history courses. Concise yet comprehensive advice on approaching typical history assignments, developing critical reading skills, writing effective history papers, conducting research, using and documenting sources, and avoiding plagiarism — enhanced with practical tips and examples throughout — has made this slim reference a bestseller.

A Student's Guide to History. This complete guide to success in any history course provides the practical help students need to be successful. In addition to introducing students to the nature of the discipline, author Jules Benjamin teaches a wide range of skills from preparing for exams to approaching common writing assignments, and explains the research and documentation process with plentiful examples.

Brief Contents

Contents

 ⊫ ✓ Access the interactive content online. See inside the front cover for more information.

CHAPTER 7

East Asia and the Spread of Buddhism 221 B.C.E.–800 C.E.   174

CHAPTER 8

Continuity and Change in Europe and Western Asia 250–850   202

CHAPTER 14

Europe in the Middle Ages 800–1450   387

CHAPTER 17

The Islamic World Powers 1300–1800   489

CHAPTER 22

Revolutions in the Atlantic World 1775–1825   653

CHAPTER 28

World War and Revolution 1914–1929   860

Maps, Figures, and Tables

Special Features

INDIVIDUALS IN SOCIETY

1

✓ LearningCurve
After reading the chapter, go online
and use LearningCurve to retain what
you've read.

The Earliest
Human Societies

TO 2500 B.C.E.

WHEN DOES HISTORY BEGIN? PREVIOUS GENERATIONS OF HISTORIANS
generally answered that question with "when writing begins." Thus they
started their histories with the earliest known invention of writing, which
happened about 3200 B.C.E. in the Tigris and Euphrates River Valleys of Mesopotamia, in what is now Iraq. Anything before that was "prehistory." That
focus on only the last five thousand years leaves out most of the human
story, however, and today historians no longer see writing as such a sharp
dividing line. They explore all eras of the human past through many different
types of sources, and some push the beginning of history back to the formation of the universe, when time itself began. This very new conceptualization of "big history" is actually similar in scope to the world's oldest histories,
because for thousands and perhaps tens of thousands of years many peoples
have narrated histories of their origins that also begin with the creation of
the universe.

Exploring the entire human past means beginning in Africa, where millions of years ago humans evolved from a primate ancestor. They migrated
out of Africa in several waves, walking along coasts and over land, eventually spreading across much of the earth. Their tools were initially multi-
purpose sharpened stones and sticks, but gradually they invented more
specialized tools that enabled them to obtain food more easily, make clothing, build shelters, and decorate their surroundings. Environmental changes,
such as the advance and retreat of the glaciers, shaped life dramatically and
may have led to the most significant change in all of human history, the
domestication of plants and animals.

Evolution and Migration

How did humans evolve, and where did they migrate?

Studying the earliest era of human history involves methods that seem simple — looking carefully at an object — as well as new high-tech procedures, such as DNA analysis. Through such research, scholars have examined early human evolution, traced the expansion of the human brain, and studied migration out of Africa and across the planet. Combined with spoken language, that larger brain enabled humans to adapt to many different environments and to be flexible in their responses to new challenges.

Understanding the Early Human Past

People throughout the world have developed systems of classification that help them understand things: earth and sky; seen and unseen; animal, vegetable, and mineral; past, present, and future. Among these systems of classification was one invented in eighteenth-century Europe that divided all living things on earth into groups. Each of these divisions — such as that between plants and animals — is further subdivided into smaller and smaller groups, such as class, order, family, and genus. The final important division is the species, which is generally defined as a group of organisms that can interbreed with one another and produce fertile offspring of both sexes.

In their natural state, members of a species resemble one another, but over time they can become increasingly dissimilar. (Think of Chihuahuas and Great Danes, both members of the same species.) Ever since humans began shaping the world around them, this process has often been the result of human action. But in the long era before humans, the increasing dissimilarity resulted, in the opinion of most scientists, from the process of natural selection. Small variations within individuals in one species enabled them to acquire more food and better living conditions and made them more successful in breeding, thus allowing them to pass their genetic material on to the next generation. When a number of individuals within a species became distinct enough that they could no longer interbreed successfully with others, they became a new species. Species also become extinct, particularly during periods of mass extinctions such as the one that killed the dinosaurs about 65 million years ago. Natural processes of species formation and extinction continue, although today changes in the biosphere — the living matter in the world — result far more from human action than from natural selection.

The scientists who developed this system of organizing the world placed humans within it, using the same means of classification that they used for all other living things. Humans were in the animal kingdom, the order of Primates, the family Hominidae, and the genus *Homo*. Like all classifications, this was originally based on externally visible phenomena: humans were placed in the Primates order because, like other primates, they have hands that can grasp, eyes facing forward to allow better depth perception, and relatively large brains; they were placed in the **hominid** family along with chimpanzees, gorillas, and orangutans because they shared even more features with these great apes. Over 98 percent of human DNA is the same as that of chimpanzees, which indicates to most scientists that humans and chimpanzees share a common ancestor. That common ancestor probably lived between 5 million and 7 million years ago.

Genetic analysis is one of many types of technology used by scholars who study early humans. They often use chemical and physical tests to evaluate bones and other body parts left by humans and the animals they ate, and to study the material surrounding these remains. One of the most important of these tests is the analysis of the radioactive isotope of carbon, C-14, which appears in all things that were once alive. C-14 breaks down at a rate that is known, so that measuring the amount of C-14 that remains in an object allows scientists to determine how old the object is.

Physical remains were the earliest type of evidence studied to learn about the distant human past, and scholars used them to develop another system of classification, one that distinguished between periods of time rather than types of living creatures. (Constructing models of time is called "periodization.") They gave labels to eras according to the primary materials out of which tools that survived were made. Thus the earliest human era became the Stone Age, the next era the Bronze Age, and the next the Iron Age. They further divided the Stone Age into the Old Stone Age, or **Paleolithic era**, during which people used stone, bone, and other natural products to make tools and gained food largely by **foraging** — that is, by gathering plant products, trapping or catching small animals and birds, and hunting larger prey. This was followed by the New Stone Age, or **Neolithic era**, which saw the beginning of agricultural and animal domestication. People around the world adopted agriculture at various times, and some never did, but the transition between the Paleolithic and the Neolithic is usually set at about 9000 B.C.E., the point at which agriculture was first developed.*

Geologists refer to the last twelve thousand years as the Holocene (meaning very recent) epoch, a period so short given the 4.5 billion years of the solar system that it often does not show up on geologic timelines. The entire history of the human species fits well within the Holocene and the previous geologic epoch, the Pleistocene (PLIGH-stuh-seen), which began about 2.5 million years ago.

The Pleistocene was marked by repeated advances in glaciers and continental ice sheets. Glaciers tied up huge quantities of the earth's water, leading to lower sea levels, making it possible for animals and eventually humans to walk between places that were separated by oceans during interglacial times. Animals and humans were also prevented from migrating to other places by the ice sheets themselves, however, and the colder climate made large areas unfit to live in. Climate thus dramatically shaped human cultures.

Genetic analysis can indicate many things about the human family, and physical remains can provide some evidence about how people lived in the distant past, but the evidence is often difficult to interpret. By themselves, tools and other objects generally do not reveal who made or used them (though sometimes this can be determined from the location in which they were found), nor do they indicate what the objects meant to their creators or users. Thus, to learn about the early human past,

*A note on dates: This book generally uses **B.C.E.** (Before the Common Era) and **C.E.** (Common Era) when giving dates, a system of chronology based on the Christian calendar and now used widely around the world. Scholars who study the very earliest periods of hominid and human history usually use the phrase "years ago" to date their subjects, as do astrophysicists and geologists; this is often abbreviated as **B.P.** (Before the Present). Because the scale of time covered in Chapter 1 is so vast, a mere 2,000 years does not make much difference, and so **B.C.E.** and "years ago" have similar meaning.

scholars often also study groups of people from more recent times whose technology and way of life offer parallels with those of people in the distant past. They read written reports of conquerors, government officials, and missionaries who encountered groups that lived by foraging, and they directly observe the few remaining groups that maintain a foraging lifestyle today. Such evidence is also problematic, however. Outsiders had their own perspectives, generally regarded those who lived by foraging as inferior, and often misinterpreted what they were seeing. Contemporary foragers are not fully cut off from the modern world, nor is it correct to assume that their way of living has not changed for thousands of years, particularly because adaptability is a key feature of the foraging way of life. Thus evidence from more recent groups must be used carefully, but it can provide valuable clues.

Hominid Evolution

Using many different pieces of evidence from all over the world, archaeologists, paleontologists, and other scholars have developed a view of human evolution whose basic outline is widely shared, though there are disagreements about details. Most primates, including other hominids such as chimpanzees and gorillas, have lived primarily in trees, but at some point a group of hominids in East Africa began to spend more time on the ground, and between 6 and 7 million years ago they began to walk upright at least some of the time. Very recently, scientists have determined that skeletal remains from the genus *Ardipithecus*, which probably date from 4.4 million years ago, indicate a combination of two-limbed movement on land and four-limbed movement in trees. *Ardipithecus* also had smaller canine teeth than do modern chimpanzees, and male and female canine teeth were equal in size, which suggests that there was less male-male combat and perhaps closer male-female relations than among earlier hominids.

Over many generations, the skeletal and muscular structure of some hominids evolved to make upright walking easier, and they gradually became fully bipedal. The earliest fully bipedal hominids, whom paleontologists place in the genus *Australopithecus*, lived in southern and eastern Africa between 2.5 and 4 million years ago. Here they left bones, particularly in the Great Rift Valley that stretches from Ethiopia to Tanzania. Walking upright allowed australopithecines to carry and use things, which allowed them to survive better and may have also spurred brain development.

About 3.4 million years ago, some hominids began to use naturally occurring objects as tools, and sometime around 2.5 million years ago, one group of australopithecines in East Africa began to make and use simple tools, evolving into a different type of hominid that later paleontologists judged to be the first in the genus *Homo*. Called *Homo habilis* ("handy human"), they made sharpened stone pieces, which archaeologists call hand axes, and used them for various tasks. This suggests greater intelligence, and the skeletal remains support this, for *Homo habilis* had a larger brain than did the australopithecines.

About 2 million years ago, another species, called *Homo erectus* ("upright human"), evolved in East Africa. *Homo erectus* had still larger brains and made tools that were slightly specialized for various tasks, such as handheld axes, cleavers, and scrapers. Archaeological remains indicate that *Homo erectus* lived in larger groups than had earlier hominids and engaged in cooperative gathering, hunting, and food preparation. The location and shape of the larynx suggest that members of this species were

Fossil Footprints from Laetoli in Tanzania
About 3.5 million years ago, several australopithecines walked in wet ash from a volcanic eruption. Their footprints, discovered by the archaeologist Mary Leakey, indicate that they walked fully upright and suggest that they were not solitary creatures, for they walked close together. (John Reader/Science Source)

able to make a wider range of sounds than were earlier hominids, so they may have relied more on vocal sounds than on gestures to communicate ideas to one another.

One of the activities that *Homo erectus* carried out most successfully was moving (Map 1.1). Gradually small groups migrated out of East Africa onto the open plains of central Africa, and from there into northern Africa. From 1 million to 2 million years ago, the earth's climate was in a warming phase, and these hominids ranged still farther, moving into western Asia by as early as 1.8 million years ago. Bones and other materials from China and the island of Java in Indonesia indicate that *Homo erectus* had reached there by about 1.5 million years ago, migrating over large landmasses as well as along the coasts. (Sea levels were lower than they are today, and Java could be reached by walking.) *Homo erectus* also walked north, reaching what is now Spain by at least 800,000 years ago and what is now Germany by 500,000 years ago. In each of these places, *Homo erectus* adapted gathering and hunting techniques to the local environment, learning how to find new sources of plant food and how to best catch local animals. Although the climate was warmer than it is today, central Europe was not balmy, and these hominids may have used fire to provide light and heat, cook food, and keep away predators. Many lived in the open or in caves, but some built simple shelters, another indication of increasing flexibility and problem solving.

Homo Sapiens, "Thinking Humans"

Homo erectus was remarkably adaptable, but another hominid proved still more so: *Homo sapiens* ("thinking human"). A few scientists think that *Homo sapiens* evolved from *Homo erectus* in a number of places in Afroeurasia, but the majority think that, like hominid evolution from earlier primates, this occurred only in East Africa. The evidence is partly archaeological, but also genetic. One type of DNA, called mitochondrial DNA, indicates that modern humans are so similar genetically that they cannot have been evolving for the last 1 million or 2 million years. This evidence suggests that the evolution of *Homo sapiens* has instead taken place for only about 250,000 years. Because there is greater human genetic variety today in Africa than in other parts of the world, the evidence also suggests that *Homo sapiens* have lived there the longest,

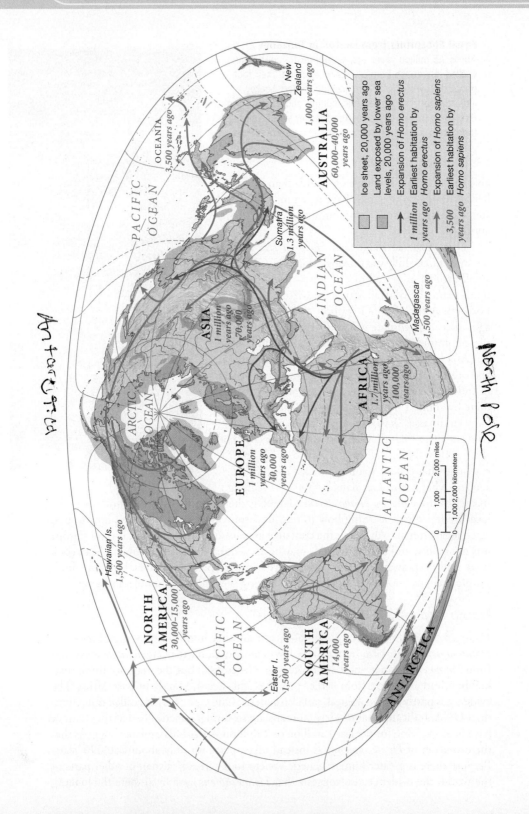

◄ MAP 1.1   Human Migration in the Paleolithic and Neolithic Eras

so that Africa is where they first emerged. According to this hypothesis, all modern humans are descended from a relatively small group in East Africa.

Although there is some debate about where and when *Homo sapiens* emerged, there is little debate about what distinguished these humans from earlier hominids: a bigger brain, in particular a bigger forebrain, the site of conscious thought. The ability to think reflectively allowed for the creation of symbolic language, that is, for language that follows certain rules and that can refer to things or states of being that are not necessarily present. Greater intelligence allowed *Homo sapiens* to better understand and manipulate the world around them, and symbolic language allowed this understanding to be communicated within a group and passed from one generation to the next. Through spoken language *Homo sapiens* began to develop collective explanations for the world around them that we would now call religion, science, and philosophy. Spoken language also enabled *Homo sapiens* to organize socially into larger groups, thus further enhancing their ability to affect the natural world.

The advantages of a larger brain seem evident to us, so we may not think to ask why hominids evolved this way. Large brains also bring disadvantages, however. They take more energy to run than other parts of the body, so that large-brained animals have to eat more than small-brained ones. Large brains create particular problems for bipedal mammals, for the narrow pelvic structure that works best for upright walking makes giving birth to a large-headed infant difficult and painful.

The question of why hominids developed ever-larger brains might best be answered by looking at how paleontologists think it happened. As *Homo habilis*, *Homo erectus*, and *Homo sapiens* made and used tools, the individuals whose mental and physical abilities allowed them to do so best were able to obtain more food and were more likely to mate and have children who survived. Thus bigger brains led to better tools, but the challenges of using and inventing better tools also created selective pressure that led to bigger brains.

The same thing may have happened with symbolic language and thought. A slightly bigger brain allowed for more complex thought and better language skills (aided by anatomical changes in the vocal tract and larynx that allowed for a greater range of sounds). These thinking and speaking skills enabled individuals to better attract mates and fend off rivals, which meant a greater likelihood of passing on the enhanced brain to the next generation. As we know from contemporary research on the brain, learning language promotes the development of specific areas of the brain.

The growth in brain size and complexity may also have been linked to social organization. Individuals who had better social skills were more likely to mate than those who did not — this has been observed in chimpanzees and, of course, in modern humans — and thus to pass on their genetic material. Social skills were particularly important for females, because the combination of bipedalism and growing brain size led to selective pressure for hominid infants to be born at an even earlier stage in their development than other primate infants. Thus the period when human infants are dependent on others is very long, and mothers with good social networks to assist them were more likely to have infants who survived. Humans are unique in the duration and complexity of their care for children, and cooperative child rearing, along with the development of social skills and the adaptability this encouraged, may have been an impetus to brain growth.

All these factors operated together in processes that promoted bigger and better brains. In the Paleolithic period, *Homo sapiens'* brains invented highly specialized tools made out of a variety of materials that replaced the more general-purpose stone tools made by *Homo erectus*: barbed fishhooks and harpoons, snares and traps for catching small animals, bone needles for sewing clothing, awls for punching holes in leather, nets for catching fish, sharpened flint pieces bound to wooden or bone handles for hunting or cutting, and slings for carrying infants. By 25,000 years ago, and perhaps earlier, humans in some parts of the world were weaving cloth and baskets, and by 17,000 years ago they were using bows and atlatls (AHT-lah-tuhlz) — notched throwing sticks made of bone, wood, or antler — to launch arrows and barbs with flint points bound to wooden shafts. The archaeological evidence for increasingly sophisticated language and social organization is less direct than that for tool use, but it is hard to imagine how humans could have made the tools they did — or would have chosen to decorate so many of them — without both of these.

Migration and Differentiation

Like *Homo erectus* had earlier, groups of *Homo sapiens* moved. By 200,000 years ago they had begun to spread across Africa, and by 120,000 years ago they had begun to migrate out of Africa to Eurasia (see Map 1.1). They most likely walked along the coasts of India and Southeast Asia, and then migrated inland. At the same time, further small evolutionary changes led to our own subspecies of anatomically modern humans, *Homo sapiens sapiens* (which literally translates as "thinking thinking humans"). *Homo sapiens sapiens* moved into areas where there were already *Homo erectus* populations, eventually replacing them, leaving *Homo sapiens* as the only survivors and the ancestors of all modern humans.

The best-known example of interaction between *Homo erectus* and *Homo sapiens sapiens* is that between Neanderthals (named after the Neander Valley in Germany, where their remains were first discovered) and a group of anatomically modern humans called Cro-Magnons. **Neanderthals** lived throughout Europe and western Asia beginning about 150,000 years ago, had brains as large as those of modern humans, and used tools, including spears and scrapers for animal skins, that enabled them to survive in the cold climate of Ice Age central Europe and Russia. They built freestanding houses, and they decorated objects and themselves with red ochre, a form of colored clay. They sometimes buried their dead carefully with tools, animal bones, and perhaps flowers, which suggests that they understood death to have a symbolic meaning. These characteristics led them to be originally categorized as a branch of *Homo sapiens*, but DNA evidence from Neanderthal bones now indicates that they were a separate branch of highly developed *Homo erectus*.

Cro-Magnon peoples moved into parts of western Asia where Neanderthals lived by about 70,000 years ago, and into Europe by about 45,000 years ago. The two peoples appear to have lived side by side for millennia, hunting the same types of animals and gathering the same types of plants. In 2010 DNA evidence demonstrated that they also had sex with one another, for between 1 and 4 percent of the DNA in modern humans living outside of Africa likely came from Neanderthals. The last evidence of Neanderthals as a separate species comes from about 30,000 years ago, and it is not clear exactly how they died out. They may have been killed by Cro-Magnon peoples, or they simply may have lost the competition for food as the climate worsened around 30,000 years ago and the glaciers expanded.

Until very recently Neanderthals were thought to be the last living hominids that were not *Homo sapiens*, but in 2003 archaeologists on the Indonesian island of Flores discovered bones and tools of three-foot-tall hominids that dated from only about 18,000 years ago. A few scientists view them as very small or malformed *Homo sapiens*, but most see them as a distinct species, probably descended from *Homo erectus* as were Neanderthals. Nicknamed "hobbits," the Flores hominids or their ancestors appear to have lived on the island for more than 800,000 years.

Homo erectus migrated great distances, but *Homo sapiens sapiens* made use of greater intelligence and better toolmaking capabilities to migrate still farther. They used simple rafts to reach Australia by at least 50,000 years ago, and by 35,000 years ago had reached New Guinea. By at least 15,000 years ago, humans had walked across the land bridges then linking Siberia and North America at the Bering Strait and had crossed into the Americas. Because by 14,000 years ago humans were already in southern South America, ten thousand miles from the land bridges, many scholars now think that people came to the Americas much earlier. They think humans came from Asia to the Americas perhaps as early as 20,000 or even 30,000 years ago, walking or using rafts along the coasts. (See Chapter 11 for a longer discussion of this issue.)

With the melting of glaciers sea levels rose, and parts of the world that had been linked by land bridges, including North America and Asia as well as many parts of Southeast Asia, became separated by water. This cut off migratory paths but also spurred innovation. Humans designed and built ever more sophisticated boats and learned how to navigate by studying wind and current patterns, bird flights, and the position of the stars. They sailed to increasingly remote islands, including those in the Pacific, the last parts of the globe to be settled. The western Pacific Islands were inhabited by about 2000 B.C.E., Hawaii by about 500 C.E., and New Zealand by about 1000 C.E. (For more on the settlement of the Pacific Islands, see page 355.)

Once humans had spread out over much of the globe, groups often became isolated from one another, and people mated only with other members of their own group or those who lived nearby, a practice anthropologists call endogamy. Thus, over thousands of generations, although humans remained one species, *Homo sapiens sapiens* came to develop differences in physical features, including skin and hair color, eye and body shape, and amount of body hair. Language also changed over generations, so that thousands of different languages were eventually spoken. Groups created widely varying cultures and passed them on to their children, further increasing diversity among humans.

Beginning in the eighteenth century, European natural scientists sought to develop a system that would explain human differences at the largest scale. They divided people into very large groups by skin color and other physical characteristics and termed these groups "races," a word that had originally meant lineage. They first differentiated these races by continent of origin — Americanus, Europaeus, Asiaticus, and Africanus — and then by somewhat different geographic areas. The word *Caucasian* was first used by the German anatomist and naturalist Johann Friedrich Blumenbach (1752–1840) to describe light-skinned people of Europe and western Asia because he thought that their original home was most likely the Caucasus Mountains on the border between Russia and Georgia. He thought that they were the first humans and the most attractive. This meaning of *race* has had a long life, though biologists and anthropologists today do not use it, as it has no scientific meaning or explanatory value. All humans are one species with less genetic variety than chimpanzees.

Paleolithic Society, 250,000–9000 B.C.E.

What were the key features of Paleolithic society?

Eventually human cultures became widely diverse, but in the Paleolithic period people throughout the world lived in ways that were similar to one another. Archaeological evidence and studies of modern foragers suggest that people lived in small groups of related individuals and moved throughout the landscape in search of food. Most had few material possessions, only what they could carry, although in areas where food resources were especially rich, such as along seacoasts, they built structures and lived more permanently in one place. In the later Paleolithic, people in many parts of the world created art and music and developed religious ideas that linked the natural world to a world beyond.

Foraging for Food

Paleolithic peoples have often been called hunter-gatherers, but recent archaeological and anthropological research indicates that both historical and contemporary hunter-gatherers have depended much more on gathered foods than on hunted meat. Thus it would be more accurate to call them "gatherer-hunters," and most scholars now call them foragers, a term that highlights the flexibility and adaptability in their search for food. Most of what foragers ate were plants, and much of the animal protein in their diet came from foods gathered or scavenged rather than hunted directly: insects, shellfish, small animals caught in traps, fish and other sea creatures caught in weirs and nets, and animals killed by other predators. Gathering and hunting probably varied in importance from year to year depending on environmental factors and the decisions of the group.

Paleolithic peoples did hunt large game. Groups working together forced animals over cliffs, threw spears, and, beginning about 15,000 B.C.E., used bows and atlatls to shoot projectiles so that they could stand farther away from their prey while hunting. The final retreat of the glaciers also occurred between 10,000 and 15,000 years ago, and the warming climate was less favorable to the very large mammals that had roamed the open spaces of many parts of the world. Woolly mammoths, mastodons, and woolly rhinos all died out in Eurasia in this **megafaunal extinction**, as did camels, horses, and sloths in the Americas and giant kangaroos and wombats in Australia. In many places, these extinctions occurred just about the time that modern humans appeared, and increasing numbers of scientists think that they were at least in part caused by human hunting.

Most foraging societies that exist today or did so until recently have some type of **division of labor** by sex, and also by age, with children and older people responsible for different tasks than adult men and women. Men are more often responsible for hunting, through which they gained prestige as well as meat, and women for gathering

Paleolithic Hand Axes Like most Paleolithic stone tools, these two hand axes from Libya in northern Africa were made by chipping flakes off stone to form a sharpened edge. Although they are traditionally called axes, they were used for a variety of purposes, including skinning, cutting, and chopping. (Robert Harding Images/Masterfile)

plant and animal products. This has led scholars to assume that in Paleolithic society men were also responsible for hunting, and women for gathering. Such a division of labor is not universal, however: in some of the world's foraging cultures, such as the Agta of the Philippines, women hunt large game, and in many they participate in group hunts. The stone and bone tools that remain from the Paleolithic period give no clear evidence of who used them, and the division of labor may have been somewhat flexible, particularly during periods of scarcity.

Obtaining food was a constant preoccupation, but it was not a constant job. Studies of recent foragers indicate that, other than in times of environmental disasters such as prolonged droughts, people need only about ten to twenty hours a week to gather food and carry out the other tasks needed to survive, such as locating water and building shelters. The diet of foragers is varied and nutritious: low in fat and salt, high in fiber, and rich in vitamins and minerals. The slow pace of life and healthy diet did not mean that Paleolithic life spans approached those of the modern world, however. People avoided such contemporary killers as heart disease and diabetes, but they often died at young ages from injuries, infections, animal attacks, and interpersonal violence. Mothers and infants died in childbirth, and many children died before they reached adulthood.

Total human population thus grew very slowly during the Paleolithic. Scholars can make rough estimates only, but one of them proposes that there were perhaps 500,000 humans in the world about 30,000 years ago. By about 10,000 years ago this number had grown to 5 million—ten times as many people. This was a significant increase, but it took twenty thousand years. (By contrast, the earth's population today is more than 7 billion; it was slightly under 1 billion a mere 300 years ago.) The low population density meant that human impact on the environment was relatively small, although still significant. In addition to contributing to the extinction of some large animals, Paleolithic people may have also shaped their environments by setting fires, which encouraged the growth of new plants and attracted animals that fed on them, making hunting or snaring game easier. This practice was a factor in the spread of plants that thrived best with occasional burning, such as the eucalyptus in Australia.

Family and Kinship Relationships

Small bands of humans—twenty or thirty people was a standard size for foragers in harsh environments—were scattered across broad areas, but this did not mean that each group lived in isolation. Their travels in search of food brought them into contact with one another, not simply for talking and celebrating, but also for providing opportunities for the exchange of sexual partners, which was essential to group survival. Today we understand that having sexual relations with close relatives is disadvantageous because it creates greater risk of genetic disorders. Earlier societies did not have knowledge of genetics, but most of them developed rules against sexual relations among immediate family members. Mating arrangements varied in their permanence, but many groups seem to have developed a somewhat permanent arrangement whereby a man or woman left his or her original group and joined the group of his or her mate, what would later be termed marriage.

Within each band, and within the larger kin groups, individuals had a variety of identities; they were simultaneously fathers, sons, husbands, and brothers, or mothers, daughters, wives, and sisters. Each of these identities was relational (parent to child, sibling to sibling, spouse to spouse), and some of them, especially parent to child, gave one power over others. In many areas kin groups remained significant power structures for millennia, and in some areas they still have influence over major aspects of life, such as an individual's job or marital partner. Paleolithic people were not differentiated by wealth, for in a foraging society accumulating material goods was not advantageous. But they were differentiated by such factors as age, gender, and position in a family, and no doubt by personal qualities such as intelligence, courage, and charisma.

Stereotypical representations of Paleolithic people often portray a powerful fur-clad man holding a club and dragging off a (usually attractive) fur-clad woman by her hair, or men going off to hunt while women and children crouched around a fire, waiting for the men to bring back great slabs of meat. Studies of the relative importance of gathering to hunting, women's participation in hunting, and gender relations among contemporary foraging peoples have led some analysts to turn these stereotypes on their heads. They see Paleolithic bands as egalitarian groups in which the contributions of men and women to survival were recognized and valued, and in which both men and women had equal access to the limited amount of resources held by the group. Other scholars argue that this is also a stereotype, overly romanticizing Paleolithic society. They note that although social relations among foragers were not as hierarchical as they were in other types of societies, many foraging groups had one person who held more power than others, and that person was almost always a man. This debate about gender relations is often part of larger discussions about whether Paleolithic society—and by implication, "human nature"—was primarily peaceful and nurturing or violent and brutal, and whether these qualities are gender related. Like much else about the Paleolithic, sources about gender and about violence are fragmentary and difficult to interpret; there may simply have been a diversity of patterns, as there is among more modern foragers.

Whether peaceful and egalitarian or violent and hierarchical, heterosexual relations produced children, who were cared for as infants by their mothers or other women who had recently given birth. Breast milk was the only food available that infants could easily digest, so mothers nursed their children for several years. Along with providing food for infants, extended nursing brings a side benefit: it suppresses ovulation and thus acts as a contraceptive. Foraging groups needed children to survive, but too many could tax scarce food resources. Many groups may have practiced selective infanticide or abandonment. They may also have exchanged children of different ages with other groups, which further deepened kinship connections between groups. Other than for feeding, children were most likely cared for by other male and female members of the group as well as by their mothers during the long period of human childhood.

Cultural Creations and Spirituality

Early human societies are often described in terms of their tools, but this misses a large part of the story. Beginning in the Paleolithic, human beings have expressed themselves through what we would now term the arts or culture: painting and decorating walls and objects, making music with their voices and a variety of instruments, imagining and telling stories, dancing alone or in groups. Evidence from the Paleolithic, particularly from after about 50,000 years ago, includes flutes, carvings, jewelry, and paintings done on cave walls and rock outcroppings that depict animals, people, and symbols. In many places these paintings show the outline of a human hand—often done by blowing pigment around it—or tracings of the fingers, a simple art form that allowed individuals to say "I was here."

Some cultural creations appear to have had a larger purpose: they may have been created to honor and praise ancestors or leaders, help people remember events and traditions, or promote good hunting or safe childbirth. Some were easy to do, and everyone in a culture was expected to participate in some way: to dance in order to bring rain or give thanks, to listen when stories were told, to take part in ceremonies. Other creations required particular talents or training and were probably undertaken only by specialists.

At the same time that people marked and depicted the world around them, they also appear to have developed ideas about supernatural forces that controlled some aspects of the natural world and the place of humans in it, what we now term spirituality or religion. The Neanderthals' careful burial of their dead suggests to some scholars that they had ideas about an afterlife or at least something beyond the visible world, and there is no doubt that this was the case for Paleolithic *Homo sapiens*. Paleolithic burials, paintings, and objects suggest that people may have thought of their world as extending beyond the visible. People, animals, plants, natural occurrences, and other things around them had spirits, an idea called **animism**. The only evidence of Paleolithic animism that survives is physical, of course, but more recent animist traditions carry on this understanding of the spiritual nature and interdependence of all things, as in this contemporary Chinook blessing from northwestern North America:

> We call upon the Earth, our planet home, with its beautiful depths and soaring heights, its vitality and abundance of life, and together we ask that it *Teach us, and show us the Way.* . . .

> We call upon the creatures of the fields and the forests and the seas, our brothers
> and sisters the wolves and the deer, the eagle and dove, the great whales and the
> dolphin, the beautiful orca and salmon who share our Northwest home, and ask
> them to *Teach Us and show us the Way.*[1]

Death took people from the realm of the living, but for Paleolithic groups people
continued to inhabit an unseen world, along with spirits and deities, after death; thus
kin groups included deceased as well as living members of a family. The unseen world
regularly intervened in the visible world, for good and ill, and the actions of dead
ancestors, spirits, and gods could be shaped by living people. Concepts of the supernatural pervaded all aspects of life; hunting, birth, death, and natural occurrences such
as eclipses, comets, and rainbows all had religious meaning. Supernatural forces were
understood to determine the basic rules for human existence, and upsetting these rules
could lead to chaos.

Ordinary people learned about the unseen world through dreams and portents,
and messages and revelations were also sent more regularly to **shamans**, spiritually
adept men and women who communicated with the unseen world. Shamans created
complex rituals through which they sought to ensure the health and prosperity of an
individual, family, or group. Many cave paintings show herds of prey animals, and
several include a masked human figure usually judged to be a shaman performing
some sort of ritual. Objects understood to have special power, such as carvings or
masks in the form of an animal or person, could give additional protection, as could
certain plants or mixtures eaten, sniffed, or rubbed on the skin. Shamans thus also
operated as healers, with cures that included what we would term natural medicines
and religious healing.

Judging by practices from later periods, the rituals and medicines through which
shamans and healers operated were often closely guarded secrets, but they were passed
orally from one spiritually adept individual to another, so that gradually a body of
knowledge developed around the medicinal properties of local plants and other natural materials. By observing natural phenomena and testing materials for their usable
qualities, Paleolithic people began to invent what would later be called science.

The Development of Agriculture in the Neolithic Era, ca. 9000 B.C.E.

**How did plant and animal domestication develop, and what effects did it
have on human society?**

Foraging remained the basic way of life for most of human history, and for groups
living in extreme environments, such as tundras or deserts, it was the only possible
way to survive. In a few especially fertile areas, however, the natural environment
provided enough food that people could become more settled. As they remained in
one place, they began to plant seeds as well as gather wild crops, to raise certain animals
instead of hunting them, and to selectively breed both plants and animals to make
them more useful to humans. This seemingly small alteration was the most important
change in human history; because of its impact it is often termed the **Agricultural
Revolution**. Plant and animal domestication marked the transition from the Paleolithic

to the Neolithic. It allowed the human population to grow far more quickly than did foraging, but it also required more labor, which became increasingly specialized.

The Development of Horticulture

Areas of the world differed in the food resources available to foragers. In some, acquiring enough food to sustain a group was difficult, and groups had to move constantly. In others, moderate temperatures and abundant rainfall allowed for verdant plant growth; or seas, rivers, and lakes provided substantial amounts of fish and shellfish. Groups in such areas were able to become more settled. About 15,000 years ago, the earth's climate entered a warming phase, and the glaciers began to retreat. As the earth became warmer, the climate became wetter, and more parts of the world were able to support sedentary or semi-sedentary groups of foragers.

In several of these places, foragers began planting seeds in the ground along with gathering wild grains, roots, and other foodstuffs. By observation, they learned the optimum times and places for planting. They removed unwanted plants through weeding and selected the seeds they planted in order to get crops that had favorable characteristics, such as larger edible parts. For grain crops, people chose plants with larger kernels clustered together that ripened all at one time and did not just fall on the ground, qualities that made harvesting more efficient. Through this human intervention, certain crops became **domesticated**, that is, modified by selective breeding so as to serve human needs, in this case to provide a more reliable source of food. Archaeologists trace the development and spread of plant raising by noting when the seeds and other plant parts they discover show evidence of domestication.

This early crop planting was done by individuals using hoes and digging sticks, and it is often termed **horticulture** to distinguish it from the later agriculture using plows. In some places, digging sticks were weighted with stones to make them more effective (earlier archaeologists thought these stones were the killing parts of war clubs).

Neolithic Tools from Lakes in Switzerland These highly specialized tools include arrow points, awls, chisels, scrapers, stone ax blades in antler sockets, sickle blades, and round spindle whorls, designed to twist fibers into thread. The people who made and used them lived in wooden houses on stilts over the water, and the mud of the lake bed preserved even the bone and antler. (Courtesy of Peter A. Bostrom)

Intentional crop planting developed first in the area archaeologists call the Fertile Crescent, which runs from present-day Lebanon, Israel, and Jordan north to Turkey and then south to the Iran-Iraq border. About 9000 B.C.E. people there began to plant seeds of the wild wheat and barley they had already been harvesting, along with seeds of legume crops, such as peas and lentils, and of the flax with which they made linen cloth. They then modified these crops through domestication. By about 8000 B.C.E. people were growing sorghum and millet in parts of the Nile River Valley, and perhaps yams in western Africa. By about 7000 B.C.E. they were growing domesticated rice, millet, and legumes in China; yams and taro in Papua New Guinea; and perhaps squash in Mesoamerica. In each of these places, the development of horticulture occurred independently, and it may have happened in other parts of the world as well. Archaeological evidence does not survive well in tropical areas like Southeast Asia and the Amazon Basin, which may have been additional sites of plant domestication.

Nowhere do archaeological remains alone answer the question of who within any group first began to cultivate crops, but the fact that, among foragers, women were primarily responsible for gathering plant products suggests that they may also have been the first to plant seeds in the ground. In many parts of the world, crops continued to be planted with hoes and digging sticks for millennia, and crop raising remained primarily women's work, while men hunted or later raised animals.

Why, after living successfully as foragers for tens of thousands of years, did humans in so many parts of the world all begin raising crops at about the same time? The answer to this question is not clear, but crop raising may have resulted from population pressures in those parts of the world where the warming climate provided more food. More food meant lower child mortality and longer life spans, which allowed communities to grow. Naturally occurring and then planted foods included cereal crops, which were soft enough for babies to eat, so that women could stop nursing their children at a younger age. Women lost the contraceptive effects of breast-feeding, so children may have been born at more frequent intervals, further speeding up population growth. Thus people had a choice: they could move to a new area—the solution that foragers had relied on when faced with the problem of food scarcity—or they could develop ways to increase the food supply to keep up with population growth, a solution that the warming climate was making possible. They chose the latter and began to plant more intensively, beginning cycles of expanding population and intensification of land use that have continued to today.

A recent archaeological find at Göbekli Tepe in present-day Turkey, at the northern edge of the Fertile Crescent, suggests that cultural factors may have played a role in the development of agriculture. Here, around 9000 B.C.E. hundreds of people came together to build rings of massive, multi-ton, elaborately carved limestone pillars and then covered them with dirt and built more. The people who created this site lived some distance away, where archaeological evidence indicates they first carved the pillars. The evidence also reveals that they ate wild game and plants, not crops. The project may have unintentionally spurred the development of new methods of food production that would allow the many workers to be fed efficiently. Indeed, it is very near here that evidence of the world's oldest domesticated wheat has been discovered. Archaeologists speculate that the symbolic, cultural, or perhaps religious importance of the structure can help explain why the people building it changed from foraging to agriculture.

Whatever the reasons for the move from foraging to crop raising, within several centuries of initial crop planting, people in the Fertile Crescent, parts of China, and the Nile Valley were relying on domesticated food products alone. They built permanent houses near one another in villages surrounded by fields, and they invented new ways of storing foods, such as in pottery made from clay. Villages were closer together than were the camps of foragers, so population density as well as total population grew.

A field of planted and weeded crops yields ten to one hundred times as much food — measured in calories — as the same area of naturally occurring plants, a benefit that would have been evident to early crop planters. It also requires much more labor, however, which was provided both by the greater number of people in the community and by those people working longer hours. In contrast to the twenty hours a week foragers spent on obtaining food, farming peoples were often in the fields from dawn to dusk, particularly during planting and harvest time, but also during the rest of the growing year because weeding was a constant task. Early farmers were also less healthy than foragers were. Their narrower range of foodstuffs made them more susceptible to disease and nutritional deficiencies such as anemia.

Foragers who lived at the edge of horticultural communities appear to have recognized the negative aspects of crop raising, for they did not immediately adopt this new way of life. Instead farming spread when a village became too large and some residents moved to a new area, cleared land, planted seeds, and built a new village, sometimes intermarrying with the local people. Because the population of farming communities grew so much faster than that of foragers, however, horticulture quickly spread into fertile areas. By about 6500 B.C.E. farming had spread northward from the Fertile Crescent into Greece, and by 4000 B.C.E. farther northward all the way to Britain; by 4500 B.C.E. it had spread southward into Ethiopia. At the same time, crop raising spread out from other areas in which it was first developed, and slowly larger and larger parts of China, South and Southeast Asia, and East Africa became home to horticultural villages.

People adapted crops to their local environments, choosing seeds that had qualities that were beneficial, such as drought resistance. They also domesticated new kinds of crops. In the Americas, for example, by about 3000 B.C.E. corn was domesticated in southern Mexico and potatoes and quinoa in the Andes region of South America, and by about 2500 B.C.E. squash and beans in eastern North America. These crops then spread, so that by about 1000 B.C.E. people in much of what is now the western United States were raising corn, beans, and squash. In the Indus Valley of South Asia, people were growing dates, mangoes, sesame seeds, and cotton along with grains and legumes by 4000 B.C.E. Accordingly, crop raising led to dramatic human alteration of the environment.

Certain planted crops eventually came to be grown over huge areas of land, so that some scientists describe the Agricultural Revolution as a revolution of codependent domestication: humans domesticated crops, but crops also "domesticated" humans so that they worked long hours spreading particular crops around the world. Of these, corn has probably been the most successful; more than half a million square miles around the world are now planted in corn.

In some parts of the world horticulture led to a dramatic change in the way of life, but in others it did not. Horticulture can be easily combined with gathering and hunting, as plots of land are usually small; many cultures, including some in Papua New Guinea and North America, remained mixed foragers and horticulturists for thousands of years. Especially in deeply wooded areas, people cleared small plots by chopping and burning the natural vegetation, and planted crops in successive years until the soil eroded or lost its fertility, a method termed "slash and burn." They then moved to another area and began the process again, perhaps returning to the first plot many years later, after the soil had rejuvenated itself. Groups using shifting slash-and-burn cultivation remained small and continued to rely on the surrounding forest for much of their food.

Animal Domestication and the Rise of Pastoralism

At roughly the same time that they domesticated certain plants, people also domesticated animals. The earliest animal to be domesticated was the dog, which separated genetically as a subspecies from wolves at least 15,000 years ago and perhaps much earlier. The mechanism of dog domestication is hotly debated: did it result only from human action, as foragers chose and bred animals that would help them with the hunt rather than attack them, or was it also caused by selective pressure resulting from wolf action, as animals less afraid of human contact came around campsites and then bred with one another? However it happened, the relationship provided both with benefits: humans gained dogs' better senses of smell and hearing and their body warmth, and dogs gained new food sources and safer surroundings. Not surprisingly, humans and domestic dogs migrated together, including across the land bridges to the Americas and on boats to Pacific Islands.

Dogs fit easily into a foraging lifestyle, but humans also domesticated animals that led them to completely alter their way of life. In about 9000 B.C.E., at the same time they began to raise crops, people in the Fertile Crescent domesticated wild goats and sheep, probably using them first for meat, and then for milk, skins, and eventually fleece. They learned from observation and experimentation that traits are passed down from generation to generation, and they began to breed the goats and sheep selectively for qualities that they wanted, including larger size, greater strength, better coats, increased milk production, and more even temperaments. Sometimes they trained dogs to assist them in herding, and then selectively bred the dogs for qualities that were advantageous for this task. The book of Genesis in the Bible, written in the Fertile Crescent sometime in the first millennium B.C.E., provides an early example of selective breeding. Jacob makes a deal with his father-in-law to take only those goats and sheep that are spotted, but he secretly increases the number of spotted animals in the flock by placing a spotted stick "before the eyes . . . of the strongest of the flocks . . . whenever they were breeding" so that more and stronger spotted animals were born (Genesis 30:41). This method was based on the idea—accepted for a very long time—that what a pregnant animal or woman saw during pregnancy would influence the outcome; although this notion has been firmly rejected in modern science, the Bible notes that the scheme was successful and that Jacob "grew exceedingly rich, and had large flocks."

Sometime after goats and sheep, pigs were domesticated in both the Fertile Crescent and China, as were chickens in southern Asia. Like domesticated crops, domesticated animals eventually far outnumbered their wild counterparts. For example, in the United

States today (excluding Alaska), there are about 77 million dogs, compared to about 6,000 wolves. (Including Alaska would add about 150,000 dogs and 10,000 wolves.) There are more than 1.5 billion cattle, with enormous consequences for the environment. Animal domestication also shaped human evolution; groups that relied on animal milk and milk products for a significant part of their diet tended to develop the ability to digest milk as adults, while those that did not remained lactose intolerant as adults, the normal condition for mammals.

Sheep and goats allow themselves to be herded, and people developed a new form of living, **pastoralism**, based on herding and raising livestock. In areas with sufficient rainfall and fertile soil, pastoralism can be relatively sedentary and thus is easily combined with horticulture; people built pens for animals, or in colder climates constructed special buildings or took them into their houses. They learned that animal manure increases crop yields, so they gathered the manure from enclosures and used it as fertilizer.

Increased contact with animals and their feces also increased human contact with various sorts of disease-causing pathogens, including minor illnesses such as the common cold and deadly killers such as influenza, bubonic plague, and smallpox. This was particularly the case where humans and animals lived in tight quarters. Thus pastoralists and agriculturalists developed illnesses that had not plagued foragers, and the diseases became endemic, that is, widely found within a region without being deadly. Ultimately people who lived with animals developed resistance to some of these illnesses, but foragers' lack of resistance to many illnesses meant that they died more readily after coming into contact with new endemic diseases, as was the case when Europeans brought smallpox to the Americas in the sixteenth century.

In drier areas, flocks need to travel long distances from season to season to obtain enough food, so some pastoralists became nomadic. Nomadic pastoralists often gather wild plant foods as well, but they tend to rely primarily on their flocks of animals for food. Pastoralism was well suited to areas where the terrain or climate made crop planting difficult, such as mountains, deserts, dry grasslands, and tundras. Eventually other grazing animals, including cattle, camels, horses, yak, and reindeer, also became the basis of pastoral economies in Central and West Asia, many parts of Africa, and far northern Europe.

Plow Agriculture

Horticulture and pastoralism brought significant changes to human ways of life, but the domestication of certain large animals had an even bigger impact. Cattle and water buffalo were domesticated in some parts of Asia and North Africa in which they occurred naturally by at least 7000 B.C.E., and horses, donkeys, and camels by about 4000 B.C.E. All these animals can be trained to carry people or burdens on their backs and to pull loads dragged behind them, two qualities that are rare among the world's animal species. In many parts of the world, including North America and much of South America and sub-Saharan Africa, no naturally occurring large species could be domesticated. In the mountainous regions of South America, llamas and alpacas were domesticated to carry packs, but the steep terrain made it difficult to use them to pull loads. The domestication of large animals dramatically increased the power available to humans to carry out their tasks, which had both an immediate effect in the societies in which this happened and a long-term effect when these societies later encountered societies in which human labor remained the only source of power.

The pulling power of animals came to matter most, because it could be applied to food production. Sometime in the seventh millennium B.C.E., people attached wooden sticks to frames that animals dragged through the soil, thus breaking it up and allowing seeds to sprout more easily. These simple scratch plows were pulled first by cattle and water buffalo, and later by horses. Over millennia, moldboards—angled pieces that turned the soil over, bringing fresh soil to the top—were added, which reduced the time needed to plow and allowed each person to work more land.

Using plows, Neolithic people produced a significant amount of surplus food, which meant that some people in the community could spend their days performing other tasks, increasing the division of labor. Surplus food had to be stored, and some began to specialize in making products for storage, such as pots, baskets, bags, bins, and other kinds of containers. Others specialized in making tools, houses, and other items needed in village life, or for producing specific types of food, including alcoholic beverages made from fermented fruits and grains. Families and households became increasingly interdependent, trading food for other commodities or services. In the same way that foragers had continually improved their tools and methods, people improved the processes through which they made things. Sometime in the fifth millennium B.C.E., pot makers in Mesopotamia invented the potter's wheel, which by a millennium later had been adapted for use on carts and plows pulled by animals. Wheeled vehicles led to road building, and wheels and roads together made it possible for people and goods to travel long distances more easily, whether for settlement, trade, or conquest.

Stored food was also valuable and could become a source of conflict, as could other issues in villages where people lived close together. Villagers needed more complex rules than did foragers about how food was to be distributed and how different types of work were to be valued. Certain individuals began to specialize in the determination and enforcement of these rules, and informal structures of power gradually became more formalized as elites developed. These elites then distributed resources to their own advantage, often using force to attain and maintain their power.

Neolithic Pot, from China, ca. 2600–2300 B.C.E. This two-handled pot, made of baked ceramics in the Yellow River Valley, is painted in a swirling red and black geometric design. Neolithic agricultural communities produced a wide array of storage containers for keeping food and other commodities from one season to the next. (Museum purchase, Fowler McCormack, Class of 1921. Fund. y1979-94. Photo: Bruce M. White/ Princeton University Art Museum/Art Resource, NY)

Neolithic Society

How did growing social and gender hierarchies and expanding networks of trade increase the complexity of human society in the Neolithic period?

The division of labor that plow agriculture allowed led to the creation of social hierarchies, the divisions between rich and poor, elites and common people that have been a central feature of human society since the Neolithic era. Plow agriculture also strengthened differentiation based on gender, with men becoming more associated with the world beyond the household and women with the domestic realm. Social hierarchies were reinforced over generations as children inherited goods and status from their parents; even the gods were increasingly understood to be arranged in a hierarchy, and assuring fertility became the most important religious practice. People increasingly communicated ideas within local and regional networks of exchange, just as they traded foodstuffs, tools, and other products.

Social Hierarchies and Slavery

Archaeological finds from Neolithic villages, particularly burials, show signs of growing social differentiation. Some people were buried with significant amounts of jewelry, household goods, weapons, and other objects, while others were buried with very little. How were some people able to attain such power over their neighbors that they could even take valuable commodities with them to the grave? This is one of the key questions in all of human history. Written sources do not provide a clear answer, because social hierarchies were already firmly in place by the time writing was invented, so that scholars have largely relied on archaeological sources.

Within foraging groups, some individuals already had more authority because of their links with the world of gods and spirits, positions as heads of kin groups, or personal characteristics. These three factors gave individuals advantages in agricultural societies, and the advantages became more significant over time as there were more resources to control. Priests and shamans developed more elaborate rituals and became full-time religious specialists, exchanging their services in interceding with the gods for food. In many communities, religious specialists were the first to work out formal rules of conduct that later became oral and written codes of law, generally explaining that these represented the will of the gods. The codes threatened divine punishment for those who broke them, and they often required people to accord deference to priests as the representatives of the gods, so that they became an elite group with special privileges.

Individuals who were the heads of large families or kin groups had control over the labor of others, and this power became more significant when that labor brought material goods that could be stored. Material goods — plows, sheep, cattle, sheds, pots, carts — gave one the ability to amass still more material goods, and the gap between those who had them and those who did not widened. Storage also allowed wealth to be retained over long periods of time and handed down from one family member to another, so that over generations small differences in wealth grew larger. The ability to control the labor of others could also come from physical strength, a charismatic personality, or leadership talents, and such traits may have also led to greater wealth.

Wealth itself could command labor, as individuals or families could buy the services of others to work for them or impose their wishes through force, hiring soldiers to threaten or carry out violence. Eventually some individuals bought others outright. As with social hierarchies in general, slavery predates written records, but it developed in almost all agricultural societies. Like animals, slaves were a source of physical power for their owners, providing them an opportunity to amass still more wealth and influence. In the long era before the invention of fossil fuel technology, the ability to exploit animal and human labor was the most important mark of distinction between elites and the rest of the population. As we will see in later chapters, landownership was often what distinguished elites from others, but that land was valuable only if there were people living on it who were required to labor for the owner.

Gender Hierarchies and Inheritance

Along with hierarchies based on wealth and power, the development of agriculture was intertwined with a hierarchy based on gender. The system in which men have more power and access to resources than women and some men are dominant over other men is called **patriarchy**. Every society in the world that has left written records has been patriarchal, but patriarchy came before writing, and searching for its origins involves interpreting many different types of sources. Some scholars see the origins of gender inequality in the hominid past, noting that male chimpanzees form alliances to gain status against other males and engage in cooperative attacks on females, which might have also happened among early hominids. Other scholars see the origins in the Paleolithic, with the higher status of men in lineage groups.

Plow agriculture heightened patriarchy. Although farming with a hoe was often done by women, plow agriculture came to be a male task, perhaps because of men's upper-body strength or because plow agriculture was more difficult to combine with care for infants and small children than was horticulture. The earliest depictions of plowing are on Mesopotamian cylinder seals, and they invariably show men with the cattle and plows. At the same time that cattle began to be raised for pulling plows and carts rather than for meat, sheep began to be raised primarily for wool. Spinning thread and weaving cloth became primarily women's work; the earliest Egyptian hieroglyph for weaving is, in fact, a seated woman with a shuttle, and a Confucian moral saying from ancient China asserts that "men plow and women weave." Spinning and weaving were generally done indoors and involved simpler and cheaper tools than plowing; they could also be taken up and put down easily, and so could be done at the same time as other tasks.

Though in some ways this arrangement seems complementary, with each sex doing some of the necessary labor, plow agriculture increased gender hierarchy. Men's responsibility for plowing and other agricultural tasks took them outside the household more often than women's duties did, enlarging their opportunities for leadership. This role may have led to their being favored as inheritors of family land and the right to farm communally held land, because when inheritance systems were established in later millennia, they often favored sons when handing down land. In some places inheritance was traced through the female line, but in such systems women themselves did not necessarily inherit goods or property; instead a man inherited from his mother's brother rather than from his father. Accordingly, over generations, women's independent access to resources decreased, and it became increasingly difficult for women to survive without male support.

As inherited wealth became more important, men wanted to make sure that their sons were theirs, so they restricted their wives' movements and activities. This was especially the case among elite families. Among foragers and horticulturalists, women needed to be mobile for the group to survive; their labor outdoors was essential. Among agriculturalists, the labor of animals, slaves, and hired workers could substitute for that of women in families that could afford them. Thus in some Neolithic societies, there is evidence that women spent more and more of their time within the household, either indoors or behind walls and barriers that separated the domestic realm from the wider world. Social norms and ideals gradually reinforced this pattern, so that by the time written laws and other records emerged in the second millennium B.C.E., elite women were expected to work at tasks that would not take them beyond the household or away from male supervision. Non-elite women also tended to do work that could be done within or close by the household, such as cooking, cloth production, and the care of children, the elderly, and small animals. A special program set up under the third-century-B.C.E. Indian emperor Ashoka, for example, supported poor women by paying them to spin and weave in their own homes.

Social and gender hierarchies were enhanced over generations as wealth was passed down unequally, and they were also enhanced by rules and norms that shaped sexual relationships, particularly heterosexual ones. However their power originated, elites began to think of themselves as a group set apart from the rest by some element that made them distinctive — such as military prowess, natural superiority, or connections with a deity. They increasingly understood this distinctive quality to be hereditary and developed traditions — later codified as written laws — that stipulated which hetero-sexual relationships would pass this quality on, along with passing on wealth. Relationships between men and women from elite families were formalized as marriage, through which both status and wealth were generally passed down. Relationships between elite men and non-elite women generally did not function in this way, or did so to a lesser degree; the women were defined as concubines or mistresses, or simply as sexual outlets for powerful men. The 1780 B.C.E. Code of Hammurabi, for example, one of the world's earliest law codes, sets out differences in inheritance for the sons a man had with his wife and those he had with a servant or slave, while not mentioning daughters at all:

> If his wife bear sons to a man, [and] his maid-servant [has] also borne sons, [but] the father while still living . . . did not say to the sons of the maid-servant: "My sons," and then the father dies, then the sons of the maid-servant shall not share with the sons of the wife, but the freedom of the maid and her sons shall be granted.[2]

Relations between an elite woman and a non-elite man generally brought shame and dishonor to the woman's family and sometimes death to the man. (Early rules and laws about sex generally did not pay much attention to same-sex relations because these did not produce children that could threaten systems of inheritance.)

Thus, along with the distinctions among human groups that resulted from migration and were enhanced by endogamy, distinctions developed within groups that were reinforced by social endogamy, what we might think of as the selective breeding of people. Elite men tended to marry elite women, which in some cases resulted in actual physical differences over generations, as elites had more access to food and were able to become taller and stronger. By 1800 C.E., for example, men in the highest level of the English aristocracy were five inches taller than the average height of all English people.

No elite can be completely closed to newcomers, however, because the accidents of life and death, along with the genetic problems caused by repeated close intermarriage, make it difficult for any small group to survive over generations. Thus mechanisms were developed in many cultures to adopt boys into elite families, to legitimate the children of concubines and slave women, or to allow elite girls to marry men lower on the social hierarchy. All systems of inheritance also need some flexibility. The inheritance patterns in some cultures favored male heirs exclusively, but in others close relatives were favored over those more distant, even if this meant allowing daughters to inherit. The drive to keep wealth and property within a family or kin group often resulted in women inheriting, owning, and in some cases managing significant amounts of wealth, a pattern that continues today. Hierarchies of wealth and power thus intersected with hierarchies of gender in complex ways, and in many cultures age and marital status also played roles. In many European and African cultures, for example, widows were largely able to control their own property, while unmarried sons were often under their father's control even if they were adults.

Trade and Cross-Cultural Connections

The increase in food production brought by the development of plow agriculture allowed Neolithic villages to grow ever larger. By 7000 B.C.E. or so, some villages in the Fertile Crescent may have had as many as ten thousand residents. One of the best known of these, Çatal Hüyük in what is now modern Turkey, shows evidence of trade as well as of the specialization of labor. Çatal Hüyük's residents lived in mud-brick houses whose walls were covered in white plaster and whose interiors were kept very clean, for all trash was taken outside the town. The houses were built next to one another with no lanes or paths separating them, and people seem to have entered through holes in the roofs; the rooftops may have also served as a place for people to congregate, for there is no sign of large public buildings. The men and women of the town grew wheat, barley, peas, and almonds and raised sheep and perhaps cattle, though they also seem to have hunted. They made textiles, pots, figurines, baskets, carpets, copper and lead beads, and other goods, and decorated their houses with murals showing animal and human figures. They gathered, sharpened, and polished obsidian, a volcanic rock that could be used for knives, blades, and mirrors, and then traded it with neighboring towns, obtaining seashells and flint. From here the obsidian was exchanged still farther away, for Neolithic societies slowly developed local and then regional networks of exchange and communication.

Among the goods traded in some parts of the world was copper. Pure copper occurs close to the surface in some areas, and people, including those at Çatal Hüyük, hammered it into shapes for jewelry and tools. More often, copper, like most metals, occurs mixed with other materials in a type of rock called ore, and by about 5500 B.C.E. people in the Balkans had learned that copper could be extracted from ore by heating it in a smelting process. Smelted copper was poured into molds and made into spear points, axes, chisels, beads, and other objects. (See "Individuals in Society: The Iceman," opposite.) Smelting techniques were discovered independently in many places around the world, including China, Southeast Asia, West Africa, and the Andes region. Pure copper is soft, but through experimentation artisans learned that it would become harder if they mixed it with other metals such as arsenic, zinc, or tin during heating, creating an alloy called bronze.

INDIVIDUALS IN SOCIETY • The Iceman

On September 19, 1991, two German vacationers climbing in the Italian Alps came upon a corpse lying facedown and covered in ice. Scientists determined that the Iceman, as the corpse is generally known, died 5,300 years ago. He was between twenty-five and thirty-five years old at the time of his death, and he stood about five feet two inches tall. An autopsy revealed much about the man and his culture. The bluish tinge of his teeth showed a diet of milled grain, which proves that he came from an environment where crops were grown. The Iceman hunted as well as farmed: he was found with a bow and arrows and shoes of straw, and he wore a furry cap and a robe of animal skins that had been stitched together with thread made from grass.

The equipment discovered with the Iceman demonstrates that his people mastered several technologies. He carried a hefty copper ax, made by someone with a knowledge of metallurgy. In his quiver were numerous wooden arrow shafts and two finished arrows. The arrows had sharpened flint heads and feathers attached to the ends of the shafts with resin-like glue. Apparently the people of his culture knew the value of feathers to direct the arrow and thus had mastered the basics of ballistics. His bow was made of yew, a relatively rare wood in central Europe that is among the best for archers.

Yet a mystery still surrounds the Iceman. When his body was first discovered, scholars assumed that he was a hapless traveler overtaken in a fierce snowstorm. But the autopsy found an arrowhead lodged under his left shoulder. The Iceman was not alone on his last day. Someone was with him, and that someone had shot him from below and behind. The Iceman is the victim in the first murder mystery in Europe, and the case will never be solved.

QUESTIONS FOR ANALYSIS

1. What does the autopsy of the corpse indicate about the society in which the Iceman lived?
2. How do the objects found with the Iceman support the generalizations about Neolithic society in this chapter?

LaunchPad
ONLINE DOCUMENT PROJECT

What can artifacts tell us about Neolithic society? Examine the objects found with the Iceman, and then complete a quiz and writing assignment based on the evidence and details from this chapter.
See inside the front cover to learn more.

Because it was stronger than copper, bronze had a far wider range of uses, so much so that later historians decided that its adoption marked a new period in human history, the Bronze Age. Like all new technologies, bronze arrived at different times in different places, so the dates of the Bronze Age vary. It began about 3000 B.C.E. in some places, and by about 2500 B.C.E. bronze technology was having an impact in many parts of the world, especially in weaponry. The end of the Bronze Age came with the adoption of

2

✓ LearningCurve
After reading the chapter, go online and use LearningCurve to retain what you've read.

The Rise of the State in Southwest Asia and the Nile Valley

3200–500 B.C.E.

FIVE THOUSAND YEARS AGO, HUMANS WERE LIVING IN MOST PARTS of the planet. They had designed technologies to meet the challenges presented by deep forests and jungles, steep mountains, and blistering deserts. As the climate changed, they adapted, building boats to cross channels created by melting glaciers and finding new sources of food when old sources were no longer plentiful. In some places the new sources included domesticated plants and animals, which allowed people to live in much closer proximity to one another than they had as foragers.

That proximity created opportunities, as larger groups of people pooled their knowledge to deal with life's challenges, but it also created problems. Human history from that point on can be seen as a response to these opportunities, challenges, and conflicts. As small villages grew into cities, people continued to develop technologies and systems to handle new issues. To control their more complex structures, people created systems of governance that were not based on the kin group, as well as military forces and taxation systems. In some places they invented writing to record taxes, inventories, and payments, and they later put writing to other uses. The first places where these new technologies and systems were introduced were the Tigris and Euphrates River Valleys of southwest Asia and the Nile Valley of northeast Africa, areas whose histories became linked through trade, military conquests, and migrations.

Writing, Cities, and States

How does writing shape what we can know about the past, and how did writing develop to meet the needs of cities and states?

The remains of buildings, burial sites, weapons, tools, artwork, and other handmade objects provide our only evidence of how people lived, thought, felt, and died during most of the human past. Beginning about 5,000 years ago, however, people in some parts of the world developed a new technology, writing, the surviving examples of which have provided a much wider range of information. Writing developed to meet the needs of more complex urban societies that are often referred to as "civilizations." In particular, writing met the needs of the state, a new political form that developed during the time covered in this chapter.

Written Sources and the Human Past

Writing is closely tied to the idea of history itself. The term *history* comes from the Greek word *historia*, coined by Herodotus (hi-ROD-duh-tuhs) (ca. 484–ca. 425 B.C.E.) in the fifth century B.C.E. to describe his inquiry into the past. As Herodotus used them, the words *inquiry* and *history* are the same. Herodotus based his *Histories*, at their core a study of the origins of the wars between the Persians and the Greeks that occurred about the time he was born, on the oral testimony of people he had met as he traveled. Many of these people had been participants in the wars, and Herodotus was proud that he could rely so much on the eyewitness accounts of the people involved. Today we call this methodology "oral history," and it remains a vital technique for studying the recent past. Following the standard practice of the time, Herodotus most likely read his *Histories* out loud at some sort of public gathering. Herodotus also wrote down his histories and consulted written documents. From his day until quite recently, this aspect of his methods has defined history and separated it from prehistory: history came to be regarded as the part of the human past for which there are written records. In this view, history began with the invention of writing in the fourth millennium B.C.E. in a few parts of the world.

As noted in Chapter 1, this line between history and prehistory has largely broken down. Historians who study human societies that developed systems of writing continue to use many of the same types of physical evidence as do those who study societies without writing. For some cultures, the writing or record-keeping systems have not yet been deciphered, so our knowledge of these people also depends largely on physical evidence. Scholars can read the writing of a great many societies, however, adding greatly to what we can learn about them.

Much ancient writing survives only because it was copied and recopied, sometimes years after it was first produced. The oldest known copy of Herodotus's *Histories*, for example, dates from about 900 C.E., nearly a millennium and a half after he finished this book. The survival of a work means that someone from a later period — and often a long chain of someones — judged it worthy of the time, effort, and resources needed to produce copies. The copies may not be completely accurate, either because the scribe made an error or because he (or, much less often, she) decided to change something. Historians studying ancient works thus often try to find as many early copies as they can and compare them to arrive at the version they think is closest to the original.

The works considered worthy of copying tend to be those that, like the *Histories*, are about the political and military events involving major powers, those that record religious traditions, or those that come from authors who were later regarded as important. By contrast, written sources dealing with the daily life of ordinary men and women were few to begin with and were rarely saved or copied because they were not considered significant.

Some early written texts survive in their original form because people inscribed them in stone, shells, bone, or other hard materials, intending them to be permanent. Stones with inscriptions were often erected in the open in public places for all to see, so they include text that leaders felt had enduring importance, such as laws, religious proclamations, decrees, and treaties. (The names etched in granite on the Vietnam Veterans Memorial in Washington, D.C., are perhaps the best-known modern example, but inscriptions can be found on nearly every major public building.) Sometimes this permanence was accidental: in ancient Mesopotamia (in the area of modern Iraq), all writing was initially made up of indentations on soft clay tablets, which then hardened. Hundreds of thousands of these tablets have survived, the oldest dating to about 3200 B.C.E., and from them historians have learned about many aspects of everyday life. By contrast, writing in Egypt at the same time was often done in ink on papyrus sheets, made from a plant that grows abundantly in Egypt. Some of these papyrus sheets have survived, but papyrus is much more fragile than hardened clay, so most have disintegrated. In China, the oldest surviving writing is on bones and turtle shells from about 1200 B.C.E., but it is clear that writing was done much earlier on less permanent materials such as silk and bamboo. (For more on the origins of Chinese writing, see page 94.)

However they have survived and however limited they are, written records often become scholars' most important original sources for investigating the past. Thus the discovery of a new piece of written evidence from the ancient past — such as the Dead Sea Scrolls, which contain sections of the Hebrew Bible and were first seen by scholars in 1948 — is always a major event. But reconstructing and deciphering what are often crumbling documents can take decades, and disputes about how these records affect our understanding of the past can go on forever.

Cities and the Idea of Civilization

Along with writing, the growth of cities has often been a way that scholars mark the increasing complexity of human societies. In the ancient world, residents of cities generally viewed themselves as more advanced and sophisticated than rural folk — a judgment still made today. They saw themselves as more "civilized," a word that comes from the Latin adjective *civilis*, which refers to a citizen either of a town or of a larger political unit such as an empire.

This depiction of people as either civilized or uncivilized was gradually extended to whole societies. Beginning in the eighteenth century European scholars described those societies in which political, economic, and social organizations operated on a large scale, not primarily through families and kin groups, as "civilizations." Civilizations had cities; laws that governed human relationships; codes of manners and social conduct that regulated how people were to behave; and scientific, philosophical, and theological ideas that explained the larger world. Generally only societies that used writing were judged to be civilizations, for writing allowed more permanent expression of thoughts, ideas, and feelings. Human societies in which people were nomadic or lived in small villages without formal laws, and in which traditions and ideas were passed down orally, were generally not regarded as civilizations.

Until the middle of the twentieth century, historians often referred to the earliest places where writing and cities developed as the "cradles of civilization," proposing a model of development for all humanity patterned on that of an individual person. However, the idea that all human societies developed (or should develop) in a uniform process from a "cradle" to a "mature" civilization has now been largely discredited, and some world historians choose not to use the word *civilization* at all because it could imply that some societies are superior to others. But they have not rejected the idea that about 5,000 years ago a new form of human society appeared.

The Rise of States, Laws, and Social Hierarchies

Cities concentrated people and power, and they required more elaborate mechanisms to make them work than had small agricultural villages and foraging groups. These mechanisms were part of what political scientists call "the state," an organization distinct from a tribe or kinship group in which a small share of the population is able to coerce resources out of everyone else in order to gain and then maintain power. In a state, the interest that gains power might be one particular family, a set of religious leaders, or even a charismatic or talented individual able to handle the problems of dense urban communities.

However they are established, states coerce people through violence, or the threat of violence, and develop permanent armies for this purpose. Using armed force every time they need food or other resources is not very efficient, however, so states also establish bureaucracies and systems of taxation. States also need to keep track of people and goods, so they sometimes develop systems of recording information and accounting, usually through writing, though not always. In the Inca Empire of the Andes, for example, information about money, goods, and people was recorded on collections of colored knotted strings called *khipus* (see page 298). Systems of recording information allow the creation of more elaborate rules of behavior, often written down in the form of law codes, which facilitate further growth in state power, or in the form of religious traditions, which specify what sort of behavior is pleasing to the gods or other supernatural forces.

Written laws and traditions generally create more elaborate social hierarchies, in which divisions between elite groups and common people are established more firmly. They also generally heighten gender hierarchies. Those who gain power in states are most often men, so they tend to establish laws and norms that favor males in marriage, property rights, and other areas.

Whether we choose to call the process "the birth of civilization" or "the growth of the state," in the fourth millennium B.C.E., Neolithic agricultural villages expanded into cities that depended largely on food produced by the surrounding countryside while people living in cities carried out other tasks. The organization of a more complex division of labor was undertaken by an elite group, which enforced its will through laws, taxes, and bureaucracies backed up by armed force or the threat of it. Social and gender hierarchies became more complex and rigid. All this happened first in Mesopotamia, then in Egypt, and then in India and China.

Mesopotamia from Sumer to Babylon

How did the peoples of Mesopotamia form states and develop new technologies and institutions?

States first developed in Mesopotamia, where sustained agriculture reliant on irrigation from the Euphrates and Tigris Rivers resulted in larger populations, a division of labor, and the growth of cities. Priests and rulers developed ways to control and organize these complex societies, including armies, taxation systems, and written records. Conquerors from the north unified Mesopotamian city-states into larger empires and spread Mesopotamian culture over a large area.

Environmental Challenges, Irrigation, and Religion

Mesopotamia was part of the Fertile Crescent, where settled agriculture first developed (see page 16). The earliest agricultural villages in Mesopotamia were in the northern, hilly parts of the river valleys, where there is abundant rainfall for crops. Farmers had brought techniques of crop raising southward by about 5000 B.C.E., to the southern part of Mesopotamia known as Sumer (SOO-mer). In this arid climate farmers developed large-scale irrigation, which required organized group effort but allowed the population to grow. By about 3800 B.C.E. one of these agricultural villages, Uruk (OO-rook), had expanded significantly, becoming what many historians view as the world's first city, with a population that eventually numbered more than fifty thousand. Over the next thousand years, other cities emerged in Sumer, trading with one another and creating massive hydraulic projects including reservoirs, dams, and dikes to prevent major floods. These cities built defensive walls, marketplaces, and large public buildings; each came to dominate the surrounding countryside, becoming city-states independent from one another, though not very far apart.

The city-states of Sumer relied on irrigation systems that required cooperation and at least some level of social and political cohesion. The authority to run this system was, it seems, initially assumed by Sumerian priests. Encouraged and directed by their religious leaders, people built temples on tall platforms in the center of their cities. Temples grew into elaborate complexes of buildings with storage space for grain and other products and housing for animals. (Much later, by about 2100 B.C.E., some of the major temple complexes were embellished with a huge stepped pyramid, called a ziggurat, with a shrine on the top.) Surrounding the temple and other large buildings were the houses of ordinary citizens, each constructed around a central courtyard.

To Sumerians, and to later peoples in Mesopotamia as well, many different gods and goddesses controlled the world, a religious idea later scholars called **polytheism**. Each deity represented cosmic forces such as the sun, moon, water, and storms. The gods judged good and evil and would punish humans who lied or cheated. Gods themselves suffered for their actions, sometimes for no reason at all, just as humans did. People believed that humans had been created to serve the gods and generally anticipated being well treated by the gods if they served them well. The best way to honor the gods was to make any temple built for them as grand and impressive as possible, because the temple's size demonstrated the strength of the community and the power of its chief deity. Once it was built, the temple itself, along with the shrine on the top of the ziggurat, was often off-limits to ordinary people. Instead the temple was staffed by priests and priestesses who carried out rituals to honor the god or goddess.

Sumerian Politics and Society

Exactly how kings emerged in Sumerian society is not clear. Scholars have suggested that during times of crisis, a chief priest or sometimes a military leader assumed what was supposed to be temporary authority over a city. He established an army, trained it, and led it into battle, making increasing use of bronze weaponry that became more common after 2500 B.C.E. Temporary power gradually became permanent kingship, and kings in some Sumerian city-states began to hand down the kingship to their sons, establishing patriarchal hereditary dynasties in which power was handed down through the male line. This is the point at which written records of kingship begin to appear. The symbol of royal status was the palace, which came to rival the temple in its grandeur.

Kings made alliances with other powerful individuals, often through marriage. Royal family members were responsible for many aspects of government. Kings worked closely with religious authorities and relied on ideas about their connections with the gods, as well as the kings' military might, for their power. Royal children, both sons and daughters, were sometimes priests and priestesses in major temples. Acting together, priests, nobles, and kings in Sumerian cities used force, persuasion, and threats of higher taxes to maintain order, keep the irrigation systems working, and keep food and other goods flowing.

The king and the nobles held extensive tracts of land, as did the temple; these lands were worked by the palace's or the temple's clients — free men and women who were dependent on the palace or the temple. They received crops and other goods in return for their labor. Although this arrangement assured the clients of a livelihood, the land they worked remained the possession of the palace or the temple. Some individuals and families owned land outright and paid their taxes in the form of agricultural products or items they made.

At the bottom rung of society were slaves. Slavery, like many other aspects of society, predates written records, so we are not sure exactly how and when people first began to own other people. Like animals, slaves were a source of physical power for their owners, providing them an opportunity to amass more wealth and influence.

Each of these social categories included both men and women, but their experiences were not the same, for Sumerian society made distinctions based on gender. Most elite landowners were male, but women who held positions as priestesses or as queens ran their own estates independently of their husbands and fathers. Some women owned businesses and took care of their own accounts. They could own property and distribute it to their offspring. Sons and daughters inherited from their parents, although a daughter received her inheritance in the form of a dowry, which technically remained hers but was managed by her husband or husband's family after marriage. The Sumerians established the basic social, economic, and intellectual patterns of Mesopotamia and influenced their neighbors to the north and east.

Writing, Mathematics, and Poetry

The origins of writing probably date back to the ninth millennium B.C.E., when people in southwest Asia used clay tokens as counters for record keeping. By the fourth millennium people had realized that impressing the tokens on soft clay, or drawing pictures of the tokens on clay, was simpler than making tokens. This breakthrough in turn suggested that more information could be conveyed by adding pictures of other objects, and slowly the new technology of writing developed. The result was a complex system of pictographs in which each sign pictured an object, such as "star" (line A of Figure 2.1). These pictographs were the forerunners of the Sumerian form of writing known as **cuneiform** (kyou-NEE-uh-form), from the Latin term for "wedge shaped," used to describe the indentations made by a sharpened stylus in clay.

Scribes could combine pictograms to express meaning. For example, the sign for "woman" (line B) and the sign for "mountain" (line C) were combined, literally, into "mountain woman" (line D), which meant "slave woman" because the Sumerians regularly obtained their slave women from wars against enemies in the mountains. Pictographs were initially limited in that they could not represent abstract ideas, but the development of ideograms—signs that represented ideas—made writing more versatile. Thus the sign for "star" could also be used to indicate "heaven," "sky," or even "god." The real breakthrough came when scribes started using signs to represent sounds. For instance, the symbol for "water" (two parallel wavy lines) could also be used to indicate "in," which sounded the same as the spoken word for "water" in Sumerian.

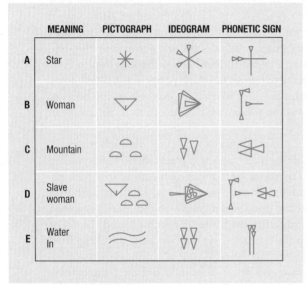

FIGURE 2.1 Sumerian Writing (Source: S. N. Kramer, *The Sumerians: Their History, Culture, and Character.* Copyright © 1963 by the University of Chicago Press. Reproduced with permission of UNIVERSITY OF CHICAGO PRESS in the format Republish in a book via Copyright Clearance Center.)

The development of the Sumerian system of writing was piecemeal, with scribes making changes and additions as they were needed. The system became so complicated that the Sumerians established scribal schools, which by 2500 B.C.E. flourished throughout the region. Students at the schools were all male, and most came from families in the middle range of urban society. Each school had a master, a teacher, and monitors. Discipline was strict, and students were caned for sloppy work and misbehavior. One graduate of a scribal school had few fond memories of the joy of learning:

> My headmaster read my tablet, said:
> "There is something missing," caned me.
> . . .

> The fellow in charge of silence said:
> "Why did you talk without permission," caned me.
> The fellow in charge of the assembly said:
> "Why did you stand at ease without permission," caned me.[1]

Scribal schools were primarily intended to produce individuals who could keep records of the property of temple officials, kings, and nobles. Thus writing first developed as a way to enhance the growing power of elites, not to record speech.

Sumerians wrote numbers as well as words on clay tablets, and some surviving tablets show multiplication and division problems. Mathematics was not just a theoretical matter to the people living in Mesopotamia, because the building of cities, palaces, temples, and canals demanded practical knowledge of geometry and trigonometry. The Sumerians and later Mesopotamians made significant advances in mathematics using a numerical system based on units of sixty, ten, and six, from which we derive our division of hours into sixty minutes and minutes into sixty seconds. They also developed the concept of place value—that the value of a number depends on where it stands in relation to other numbers.

Written texts were not an important part of Sumerian religious life, nor were they central to the religious practices of most of the other peoples in this region. Stories about the gods circulated orally and traveled with people when they moved up and down the rivers, so that gods often acquired new names and new characteristics over the centuries. Sumerians also told stories about heroes and kings, many of which were eventually reworked into the world's first **epic poem**, the *Epic of Gilgamesh* (GIL-guh-mesh), which was later written down. An epic poem is a narration of the achievements, labors, and sometimes failures of heroes that embodies people's ideas about themselves. Historians can use epic poems to learn about various aspects of a society, and to that extent epics can be used as historical sources. The epic recounts the wanderings of Gilgamesh—the semihistorical king of Uruk—and his search for eternal life, and it grapples with enduring questions about life and death, friendship, humankind and deity, and immortality.

Empires in Mesopotamia

The wealth of Sumerian cities also attracted conquerors from the north. Around 2300 B.C.E. Sargon, the king of a region to the north of Sumer, conquered a number of Sumerian cities with what was probably the world's first permanent army and created a large state. The symbol of his

Sargon of Akkad   This bronze head, with elaborately worked hair and beard, might portray the great conqueror Sargon of Akkad (though his name does not appear on it). The eyes were originally inlaid with precious jewels, which have since been gouged out. Produced about 2300 B.C.E., this head was found in the Assyrian capital of Nineveh, where it had been taken as loot. (© Interfoto/Alamy)

MAP 2.1   Spread of Cultures in Southwest Asia and the Nile Valley, ca. 3000–1640 B.C.E. This map illustrates the spread of the Mesopotamian and Egyptian cultures through the semicircular stretch of land often called the Fertile Crescent. From this area, the knowledge and use of agriculture spread throughout western Asia, northern Africa, and Europe.

triumph was a new capital, the city of Akkad (AH-kahd). Sargon also expanded the Akkadian empire westward to northern Syria, which became the breadbasket of the empire. He encouraged trading networks that brought in goods from as far away as the Indus River in South Asia and what is now Turkey (Map 2.1). Sargon spoke a different language than did the Sumerians, one of the many languages that scholars identify as belonging to the Semitic language family, which includes modern-day Hebrew and Arabic. Akkadians adapted cuneiform writing to their own language, and Akkadian became the diplomatic language used over a wide area.

Sargon tore down the defensive walls of Sumerian cities and appointed his own sons as their rulers to help him cement his power. He also appointed his daughter, Enheduana (2285–2250 B.C.E.), as high priestess in the city of Ur. Here she wrote a number of hymns, especially those in praise of the goddess Inanna, becoming the world's first author to put her name to a literary composition.

Sargon's dynasty appears to have ruled Mesopotamia for about 150 years, and then collapsed, in part because of a period of extended drought. Various city-states then rose to power, one of which was centered on the city of Babylon. Babylon was in an excellent position to dominate trade on both the Tigris and Euphrates Rivers, and it was fortunate in having a very able ruler in Hammurabi (hahm-moo-RAH-bee)

(r. 1792–1750 B.C.E.). Initially a typical king of his era, he unified Mesopotamia later in his reign by using military force, strategic alliances with the rulers of smaller territories, and religious ideas. As had earlier rulers, Hammurabi linked his success with the will of the gods. He connected himself with the sun-god Shamash, the god of law and justice, and encouraged the spread of myths that explained how Marduk, the primary god of Babylon, had been elected king of the gods by the other deities in Mesopotamia. Marduk later became widely regarded as the chief god of Mesopotamia, absorbing the qualities and powers of other gods. Babylonian ideas and beliefs thus became part of the cultural mixture of Mesopotamia, which spread far beyond the Tigris and Euphrates Valleys to the shores of the Mediterranean Sea and the Harappan cities of the Indus River Valley (see pages 61–64).

Life Under Hammurabi

Hammurabi's most memorable accomplishment was the proclamation of an extensive law code, introduced about 1755 B.C.E. Hammurabi's was not the first law code in Mesopotamia; the earliest goes back to about 2100 B.C.E. Like the codes of the earlier lawgivers, **Hammurabi's law code** proclaimed that he issued his laws on divine authority "to establish law and justice in the language of the land, thereby promoting the welfare of the people." Hammurabi's code set a variety of punishments for breaking the law, including fines and physical punishment such as mutilation, whipping, and burning. It demanded that the punishment fit the crime, calling for "an eye for an eye and a tooth for a tooth," at least among social equals, although higher-ranking people could pay a fine to lower-ranking victims instead of having an arm broken or losing an eye.

Hammurabi's code provides a wealth of information about daily life in Mesopotamia, although, like all law codes, it prescribes what the lawgivers hope will be the situation rather than providing a description of real life. We cannot know if its laws were enforced, but we can use it to see what was significant to people in Hammurabi's society. Because of farming's fundamental importance, the code dealt extensively with agriculture. Tenants faced severe penalties for neglecting the land or not working it at all. Since irrigation was essential to grow crops, tenants had to keep the canals and ditches in good repair. Anyone whose neglect of the canals resulted in damaged crops had to either bear the cost of losses or be sold into slavery. The code also regulated other trades, and artisans had to guarantee the quality of their goods and services to consumers. Hammurabi gave careful attention to marriage and

Law Code of Hammurabi Hammurabi ordered his code to be inscribed on stone pillars and set up in public throughout the Babylonian empire. At the top of the pillar Hammurabi (left) is depicted receiving the rod and ring of authority from Shamash, the god of law and justice. (© RMN–Grand Palais/Art Resource, NY)

the family. As elsewhere in the area, marriage had aspects of a business agreement. The groom or his father offered the prospective bride's father a gift, and if this was acceptable, the bride's father provided his daughter with a dowry, which technically remained hers. The penalty for adultery, defined as sex between a married woman and a man not her husband, was death, but a husband had the power to spare his wife by obtaining a pardon for her from the king. (Sex between a married man and a woman who was not his wife was not defined as adultery and carried no penalty.) A father could not disinherit a son without just cause, and the code ordered the courts to forgive a son for his first offense. On family matters and other issues, Hammurabi's code influenced other law codes, including those later written down in Hebrew Scripture (see page 49).

The Egyptians

How did the Egyptians create a prosperous and long-lasting society?

At about the same time that Sumerian city-states expanded and fought with one another in the Tigris and Euphrates Valleys, a more cohesive state under a single ruler grew in the valley of the Nile River in North Africa. This was Egypt, which for long stretches of history was prosperous and secure. At various times groups invaded and conquered Egypt or migrated into Egypt seeking better lives. Often these newcomers adopted aspects of Egyptian religion, art, and politics, and Egyptians also carried their traditions with them when they established an empire and engaged in trade.

The Nile and the God-King

The Greek historian and traveler Herodotus called Egypt the "gift of the Nile," and no other single geographical factor had such a fundamental and profound impact on Egyptian life, society, and history as this river (see Map 2.2, page 44). The Nile flooded once a year for a period of several months, bringing fertile soil and moisture for farming. In contrast to the violent and destructive floods of the Tigris and Euphrates, Nile floods were relatively gentle, and Egyptians praised the Nile primarily as a creative and comforting force:

> Hail to thee, O Nile, that issues from the earth and comes to keep Egypt alive! . . .
> He that waters the meadows which Ra created,
> He that makes to drink the desert . . .
> He who makes barley and brings emmer [wheat] into being . . .
> He who brings grass into being for the cattle . . .
> He who makes every beloved tree to grow . . .
> O Nile, verdant art thou, who makest man and cattle to live.[2]

Through the fertility of the Nile and their own hard work, Egyptians produced an annual agricultural surplus, which in turn sustained a growing and prosperous population. The Nile also unified Egypt, serving as a highway that promoted easy communication.

The political power structures that developed in Egypt came to be linked with the Nile. Somehow the idea developed that a single individual, a king, was responsible for the rise and fall of the Nile. The king came to be viewed as a descendant of the gods and thus a god himself. This belief came about before the development of writing in Egypt, so the precise details of its origins have been lost. Political unification most likely proceeded slowly, but stories told about early kings highlighted one who had united Upper Egypt—the upstream valley in the south—and Lower Egypt—the delta area of the Nile that empties into the Mediterranean Sea—into a single kingdom around 3100 B.C.E. Historians later divided Egyptian history into dynasties, or families, of kings, and more recently into periods with distinctive characteristics. The political unification of Egypt in the Archaic Period (3100–2660 B.C.E.) ushered in the period known as the Old Kingdom (2660–2180 B.C.E.), an era of prosperity, artistic flowering, and the evolution of religious beliefs.

The focal point of religious and political life in the Old Kingdom was the king, who commanded the wealth, resources, and people of Egypt. The king's surroundings had to be worthy of a god, and only a magnificent palace was suitable for his home; in fact, the word **pharaoh**, which during the New Kingdom (1570–1070 B.C.E.) came to be used for the king, originally meant "great house." Just as the kings occupied a great house in life, so they reposed in great pyramids after death. Built during the Old Kingdom, these massive stone tombs contained all the things needed by the king in his afterlife and also symbolized the king's power and his connection with the sun-god.

Like the Mesopotamians, the Egyptians were polytheistic, worshipping many gods of all types, some mightier than others. They developed complex ideas of their gods that reflected the world around them, and these views changed over the many centuries of Egyptian history as gods took on new attributes and often merged with one another. During the Old Kingdom, Egyptians considered the sun-god Ra the creator of life. Much later, during the New Kingdom (see page 44), the pharaohs of a new dynasty favored the worship of a different sun-god, Amon, whom they described as creating the entire cosmos by his thoughts. As his cult grew, Amon came to be identified with Ra, and eventually the Egyptians combined them into one sun-god, Amon-Ra.

The Egyptians likewise developed views of an afterlife that reflected the world around them and that changed over time. During the later part of the Old Kingdom, the walls of kings' tombs were carved with religious texts that provided spells that would bring the king back to life and help him ascend to heaven. Toward the end of the Old Kingdom, the tombs of powerful nobles also contained such inscriptions, an indication that more people expected to gain everlasting life. In the Middle Kingdom (2080–1640 B.C.E.), new types of spells appeared on the coffins of even more people, a further expansion in admissions to the afterlife. During the New Kingdom, a time when Egypt came into greater contact with the cultures of the Fertile Crescent, Egyptians developed even more complex ideas about the afterlife, recording these in written funerary manuscripts that have come to be known as the *Book of the Dead*. These texts explained that the soul left the body to become part of the divine after death and told of the god Osiris (oh-SIGH-ruhs), who died each year and was then brought back to life by his wife Isis (IGH-suhs) when the Nile flooded. Osiris eventually became king of the dead, weighing dead humans' hearts to determine whether they had lived justly enough to deserve everlasting life. Egyptians also believed that proper funeral rituals, in which the physical body was mummified, were essential for life after death, so Osiris was assisted by Anubis, the jackal-headed god of mummification.

To ancient Egyptians, the king embodied justice and order—harmony among people, nature, and the divine. Kings did not always live up to this ideal, of course.

The two parts of Egypt were difficult to hold together, and several times in Egypt's long history there were periods of civil war and political fragmentation, which scholars term the First (2180–2080 B.C.E.) and Second (1640–1570 B.C.E.) Intermediate Periods. Yet the monarchy survived, and in each period a strong warrior-king arose to restore order and expand Egyptian power.

Egyptian Society and Work

Egyptian society reflected the pyramids that it built. At the top stood the pharaoh, who relied on a circle of nobles, officials, and priests to administer his kingdom. All of them were assisted by scribes, who used a writing system perhaps adapted from Mesopotamia or perhaps developed independently. Egyptian scribes actually created two writing systems: one called hieroglyphics for engraving important religious or political texts on stone or writing them on papyrus made from reeds growing in the Nile Delta, and a much simpler system called hieratic that allowed scribes to write more quickly and was used for the documents of daily life. Students learned hieratic first, and only those from well-off families or whose families had high aspirations took the time to learn hieroglyphics. The cities of the Nile Valley were also home to artisans of all types, along with merchants and other tradespeople. A large group of farmers made up the broad base of the social pyramid.

For Egyptians, the Nile formed an essential part of daily life. During the flooding season — from June to October — farmers worked on the pharaoh's building programs

Egyptian Home Life   This grave painting depicts an intimate moment in the life of an aristocratic family, with the father and mother in the center and their children around them. (Giraudon/The Bridgeman Art Library)

and other tasks away from their fields. When the water began to recede, they diverted some of it into ponds for future irrigation and began planting wheat and barley for bread and beer, using plows pulled by oxen or people. From October to February, farmers planted and tended crops, and from February until the next flood, they harvested them. As in Mesopotamia, common people paid their obligations to their superiors in products and in labor. People's labor obligations in the Old Kingdom may have included forced work on the pyramids and canals, although recent research suggests that most people who built the pyramids were paid for their work. Some young men were drafted into the pharaoh's army, which served as both a fighting force and a labor corps.

The lives of all Egyptians centered around the family. Just as in Mesopotamia, marriage was a business arrangement. A couple's parents arranged the marriage, which seems to have taken place at a young age. Once couples were married, having children, especially sons, was a high priority, as indicated by surviving charms to promote fertility and prayers for successful childbirth. Boys continued the family line, and only they could perform the proper burial rites for their father. Most Egyptian men had only one wife, but among the wealthy some had several wives or concubines. Ordinary women were expected to obey their fathers, husbands, and other men, but they possessed considerable economic and legal rights. They could own land in their own names, operate businesses, and testify in court. Literature and art depict a world in which ordinary husbands and wives enjoyed each other's company.

Migrations, Revivals, and Collapse

While Egyptian civilization flourished in the Nile Valley, various groups migrated throughout the Fertile Crescent and then accommodated themselves to local cultures (Map 2.2). Some settled in the Nile Delta, including a group the Egyptians called Hyksos, meaning "rulers of the uplands." Although they were later portrayed as a conquering horde, the Hyksos were actually migrants looking for good land, and their entry into the delta, which began around 1800 B.C.E., was probably gradual and generally peaceful. The newcomers began to worship Egyptian deities and modeled their political structures on those of the Egyptians.

The Hyksos brought with them methods of making bronze (see Chapter 1) and casting it into weapons that became standard in Egypt. They thereby brought Egypt fully into the Bronze Age culture of the Mediterranean world. The Hyksos also introduced horse-drawn chariots and the composite bow, made of multiple materials for greater strength, which along with bronze weaponry revolutionized Egyptian warfare. The migration of the Hyksos, combined with a series of famines and internal struggles for power, led Egypt to fragment politically in what later came to be known as the Second Intermediate Period.

In about 1570 B.C.E. a new dynasty of pharaohs arose, pushing the Hyksos out of the delta and conquering territory to the south and northeast. These warrior-pharaohs inaugurated what scholars refer to as the New Kingdom, a period characterized not only by enormous wealth and conscious imperialism but also by a greater sense of insecurity because of new contacts and military engagements. By expanding Egyptian power beyond the Nile Valley, the pharaohs created the first Egyptian empire, and they celebrated their triumphs with monuments on a scale unparalleled since the pyramids of the Old Kingdom. Their giant statues and rich tombs might also indicate an

MAP 2.2 Empires and Migrations in the Eastern Mediterranean The rise and fall of empires in the eastern Mediterranean were shaped by internal developments, military conflicts, and the migration of peoples to new areas.

expansion of imported slave labor, although some scholars are rethinking the extent of slave labor in the New Kingdom.

The New Kingdom pharaohs include a number of remarkable figures. Among these was Hatshepsut (haht-SHEP-soot) (r. ca. 1479–ca. 1458 B.C.E.), one of the few female pharaohs in Egypt's long history who seized the throne for herself and used her reign to promote building and trade. (See "Individuals in Society: Hatshepsut and Nefertiti," page 46.) Amenhotep III (ah-men-HOE-tep) (r. ca. 1388–ca. 1350 B.C.E.) corresponded with other powerful kings in Babylonia and other kingdoms in the Fertile Crescent, sending envoys, exchanging gifts, making alliances, and in some cases marrying their daughters. Amenhotep III was succeeded by his son, who took the name Akhenaten (ah-keh-NAH-tuhn) (r. 1351–1334 B.C.E.). He renamed himself as a mark of his changing religious ideas, choosing to worship a new sun-god, Aten, instead of the traditional Amon or Ra. He was not a monotheist—someone who worships only one god — but he did order the erasure of the names of other sun-gods from the walls of buildings, the transfer of taxes from the traditional priesthood of Amon-Ra, and the building of huge new temples to Aten. Akhenaten's wife Nefertiti (nehf-uhr-TEE-tee) supported his religious ideas, but this new religion, imposed from above, failed to find a place among the people, and after his death traditional religious practices returned.

One of the key challenges facing the pharaohs after Akhenaten was the expansion of the kingdom of the Hittites. At about the same time that the Sumerians were establishing city-states, speakers of Indo-European languages migrated into Anatolia, modern-day Turkey. Indo-European is a large family of languages that includes English, most of the languages of modern Europe, ancient Greek, Latin, Persian, Hindi, Bengali, and Sanskrit (for more on Sanskrit, see page 64). It also includes Hittite, the language of one of the peoples who migrated into this area. Information about the Hittites comes from archaeological sources and also from written cuneiform tablets that provide details about politics and economic life. These records indicate that beginning about 1600 B.C.E., Hittite kings began to conquer more territory (see Map 2.2). As the Hittites expanded southward, they came into conflict with the Egyptians, who were establishing their own larger empire. There were a number of battles, but both sides seem to have recognized the impossibility of defeating the other, and in 1258 the Egyptian king Ramesses II (r. ca. 1290–1224 B.C.E.) and the Hittite king Hattusili III (r. ca. 1267–1237 B.C.E.) concluded a peace treaty, which was recorded in both Egyptian hieroglyphics and Hittite cuneiform.

The treaty brought peace between the Egyptians and the Hittites for a time, but this stability did not last. Within several decades of the treaty, groups of seafaring peoples whom the Egyptians called "Sea Peoples" raided, migrated, and marauded in the eastern Mediterranean, disrupting trade and in some cases looting and destroying cities. Just who these people were and where they originated is much debated among scholars, but their raids, combined with the expansion of the Assyrians (see page 52), led to the collapse of the Hittite Empire and the fragmentation of the Egyptian empire in what historians later termed the Third Intermediate Period (1100–653 B.C.E.). There is evidence of drought, and some scholars have suggested that a major volcanic explosion in Iceland cooled the climate for several years, leading to a series of poor harvests. All of these developments are part of a general "Bronze Age Collapse" in the period around 1200 B.C.E. that historians see as a major turning point.

The political and military story of battles, waves of migrations, and the rise and fall of empires can mask striking continuities in the history of Egypt and its neighbors. Disrupted peoples and newcomers shared practical concepts of agriculture and metallurgy with one another, and wheeled vehicles allowed merchants to transact business over long distances. Merchants, migrants, and conquerors carried their gods and goddesses with them, and religious beliefs and practices blended and changed. Cuneiform tablets, wall inscriptions, and paintings testify to commercial exchanges and cultural accommodation, adoption, and adaptation.

The Emergence of New States

The Bronze Age Collapse was a time of massive political and economic disruption, but it was also a period of the spread of new technologies, especially iron. Iron appears to have been smelted in Anatolia as early as 2500 B.C.E., but it was too brittle to be of

INDIVIDUALS IN SOCIETY • Hatshepsut and Nefertiti

Egyptians understood the pharaoh to be the living embodiment of the god Horus, the source of law and morality, and the mediator between gods and humans. His connection with the divine stretched to members of his family, so his siblings and children were also viewed as in some ways divine. Because of this, a pharaoh often took his sister or half-sister as one of his wives. This concentrated divine blood set the pharaonic family apart from other Egyptians (who did not marry close relatives) and allowed the pharaohs to imitate the gods, who in Egyptian mythology often married their siblings. A pharaoh chose one of his wives to be the "Great Royal Wife," or principal queen. Often this was a relative, though sometimes it was one of the foreign princesses who married pharaohs to establish political alliances.

The familial connection with the divine allowed a handful of women to rule in their own right in Egypt's long history. We know the names of four female pharaohs, of whom the most famous was Hatshepsut. She was the sister and wife of Thutmose II and, after he died, served as regent—as adviser and co-ruler—for her young stepson Thutmose III, who was the son of another woman. Hatshepsut sent trading expeditions and sponsored artists and architects, ushering in a period of artistic creativity and economic prosperity. She built one of the world's great buildings, an elaborate terraced temple at Deir el Bahri, which eventually served as her tomb. Hatshepsut's status as a powerful female ruler was difficult for Egyptians to conceptualize, and she is often depicted in male dress or with a false beard, thus looking more like the male rulers who were the norm. After her death, Thutmose III tried to destroy all evidence that she had ever ruled, smashing statues and scratching her name off inscriptions, perhaps because of personal animosity and perhaps because he wanted to erase the fact that a woman had once been pharaoh. Only within recent decades have historians and archaeologists begun to (literally) piece together her story.

Though female pharaohs were very rare, many royal women had power through their position as Great Royal Wives. The most famous was Nefertiti (ca. 1370–1330 B.C.E.), the wife of Akhenaten. Her name means "the perfect (or beautiful) woman has come," and inscriptions give her many other titles.

much use until about 1100 B.C.E., when techniques improved and iron weapons gradually became stronger and cheaper than their bronze counterparts. Thus, in the schema of dividing history into periods according to the main material out of which tools are made (see Chapter 1), the Iron Age began in about 1100 B.C.E. Iron weapons became important items of trade around the Mediterranean and throughout the Tigris and Euphrates Valleys, and the technology for making them traveled as well.

The decline of Egypt allowed new powers to emerge. South of Egypt along the Nile was a region called Nubia, which as early as 2000 B.C.E. served as a conduit of trade through which ivory, gold, ebony, and other products flowed north from sub-Saharan Africa. Small kingdoms with large buildings and rich tombs arose in this area. As Egypt expanded during the New Kingdom, it took over northern Nubia, incorpo-

Nefertiti used her position to spread the new religion of the sun-god Aten. Together she and Akhenaten built a new palace at Akhetaten, the present-day Amarna, away from the old centers of power. There they developed the cult of Aten to the exclusion of the traditional deities. Nearly the only literary survivor of their religious belief is the "Hymn to Aten," which declares Aten to be the only god. It describes Nefertiti as "the great royal consort whom he, Akhenaten, loves. The mistress of the Two Lands, Upper and Lower Egypt."

Nefertiti is often shown as being the same size as her husband, and in some inscriptions she is performing religious rituals that would normally have been carried out only by the pharaoh. The exact details of her power are hard to determine, however. An older theory held that her husband removed her from power, though there is also speculation that she may have ruled secretly in her own right after his death. Her tomb has long since disappeared, though some scholars believe that an unidentified mummy discovered in 2003 in Egypt's Valley of the Kings may be Nefertiti's.

QUESTIONS FOR ANALYSIS

1. Why might it have been difficult for Egyptians to accept a female ruler?
2. What opportunities do hereditary monarchies such as that of ancient Egypt provide for women? How does this fit with gender hierarchies in which men are understood as superior?

▶LaunchPad
ONLINE DOCUMENT PROJECT

Considering Egyptian views of gender roles, what complexities did Egyptian writers and artists face in depicting Hatshepsut? Analyze written and visual representations of Hatshepsut, and then complete a quiz and writing assignment based on the evidence and details from this chapter.

See inside the front cover to learn more.

rating it into the growing Egyptian empire. The Nubians adopted many features of Egyptian culture, including Egyptian gods, the use of hieroglyphs, and the building of pyramids. Many Nubians became officials in the Egyptian bureaucracy and officers in the army, and there was significant intermarriage between the two groups.

With the contraction of the Egyptian empire, an independent kingdom, Kush, rose to power in Nubia, with its capital at Napata in what is now Sudan. The Kushites conquered southern Egypt, and in 727 B.C.E. the Kushite king Piye (r. ca. 747–716 B.C.E.) swept through the entire Nile Valley to the delta in the north. United once again, Egypt enjoyed a brief period of peace during which the Egyptian culture continued to influence that of its conquerors. In the seventh century B.C.E. invading Assyrians pushed the Kushites out of Egypt, and the Kushite rulers moved their capital

Nubian Cylinder Sheath   This small silver sheath made about 520 B.C.E., perhaps for a dagger, shows a winged goddess on one side and the Egyptian god Amon-Ra (not visible in this photograph) on the other. It and others like it were found in the tombs of the king of Kush and suggest ways that Egyptian artistic styles and religious ideas influenced cultures farther up the Nile. (Cylinder sheath of Amani-natake-lebte, Nubian, Napatan Period, reign of King Amani-natake-lebte, 538–519 B.C.E. Findspot: Sudan, Nubia, Nuri, Pyramid 10. Gilded silver, colored paste inclusions. Height by diameter: 12 x 3.1 cm. (4¾ x 1¼ in.). Museum of Fine Arts, Boston. Harvard University–Museum of Fine Arts Expedition, 20.275. Photograph © 2014 Museum of Fine Arts, Boston)

farther up the Nile to Meroë, where they built hundreds of pyramids. Meroë became a center of iron production, its iron products the best in the world, smelted using wood from the vast forests in the area. Meroë traded iron goods to much of Africa and across the Red Sea and the Indian Ocean to India. Gold and cotton textiles also provided wealth to the Kushite kingdom, which in the third century B.C.E. developed its own alphabet. It was simpler than the Egyptian alphabet, but Meroitic script has not yet been deciphered.

While Kush expanded in the southern Nile Valley, another group rose to prominence along the Mediterranean coast of modern Lebanon. These people established the prosperous commercial centers of Tyre, Sidon, and Byblos, all cities still thriving today. These peoples were master shipbuilders, and from about 1100 B.C.E. to 700 B.C.E. many of the residents of these cities became the seaborne merchants of the Mediterranean. Their most valued products were purple and blue textiles, from which originated their Greek name, Phoenicians, meaning "Purple People." They also worked bronze and iron, which they shipped processed or as ore, and made and traded glass products. Phoenician ships often carried hundreds of jars of wine, and the Phoenicians introduced grape growing to new regions around the Mediterranean, dramatically increasing the amount of wine available for consumption and trade. They imported rare goods and materials, including hunting dogs, gold, and ivory, from Persia in the east and from their neighbors to the south.

The variety and quality of the Phoenicians' trade goods generally made them welcome visitors. They established colonies and trading posts throughout the Mediterranean and as far west as the Atlantic coast of modern-day Portugal. In the ninth century B.C.E. they founded the city of Carthage in modern-day Tunisia, which became the leading city in the western Mediterranean, although it would one day struggle with Rome for domination of the region (see pages 150–152). The Phoenicians' voyages brought them into contact with the Greeks, to whom they introduced many aspects of the older and more urbanized cultures of Mesopotamia and Egypt.

The Phoenicians' overwhelming cultural achievement was the spread of a completely phonetic system of writing—that is, an alphabet. Writers of cuneiform and hieroglyphics had developed signs that were used to represent sounds, but these were always used with a much larger number of ideograms. Sometime around 1800 B.C.E., workers in the Sinai Peninsula, which was under Egyptian control, began to use only phonetic signs to write, with each sign designating one sound. This system vastly simplified writing and reading and spread among common people as a practical means of record keeping and communication. Egyptian scribes and officials continued to use hieroglyphics, but the Phoenicians adapted the simpler system for their own language and spread it around the Mediterranean. The Greeks modified this alphabet for their own language, and the Romans later based their alphabet — the script we use to write English today — on Greek. Alphabets based on the Phoenician alphabet were also created in the Persian Empire and formed the basis of Hebrew, Arabic, and various alphabets of South and Central Asia. The system invented by ordinary people and spread by Phoenician merchants is the origin of most of the world's phonetic alphabets in use today.

The Hebrews

How did the Hebrews create an enduring written religious tradition?

The legacy of another people who took advantage of Egypt's collapse to found an independent state may have been even more far-reaching than that of the Phoenicians. For a period of several centuries, the Hebrews controlled first one and then two small states on the western end of the Fertile Crescent. Politically unimportant when compared with the Egyptians or Babylonians, the Hebrews created a new form of religious belief, a monotheism based on the worship of an all-powerful god they called **Yahweh** (YAH-way). Beginning in the late seventh century B.C.E. the Hebrews began to write down their religious ideas, traditions, laws, advice literature, prayers, hymns, history, and prophecies in a series of books. These were gathered together centuries later to form the Hebrew Bible, which Christians later adopted and termed the "Old Testament" to parallel specific Christian writings in the "New Testament." These writings later became the core of the Hebrews' religion, Judaism, named after Judah, the southern of the two Hebrew kingdoms. Jews today revere these texts, as do many Christians, and Muslims respect them, all of which gives them particular importance.

The Hebrew State

Most of the information about the Hebrews comes from the Bible, which, like all ancient documents, must be used with care as a historical source. Archaeological evidence has supported many of its details, and because it records a living religious tradition, extensive textual and physical research into everything it records continues, with enormous controversies among scholars about how to interpret findings.

The Hebrews were nomadic pastoralists who may have migrated into the Nile Delta from the east seeking good land for their herds of sheep and goats. According to the Hebrew Bible, they were enslaved by the Egyptians but were led out of Egypt by a charismatic leader named Moses. The Hebrews settled in the area between the Mediterranean and the Jordan River known as Canaan and were organized into tribes, each tribe consisting of numerous families who thought of themselves as related to one another. They slowly adopted agriculture and, not surprisingly, at times worshipped the agricultural gods of their neighbors, including Baal, an ancient fertility god represented as a golden calf. In this they followed the common historical pattern of newcomers by adapting the culture of an older, well-established people.

The Bible reports that the greatest danger to the Hebrews came from a group known as the Philistines (FIH-luh-steenz), who migrated to and established a kingdom in Canaan. The Philistines' superior technology and military organization at first made them invincible, but the Hebrews found a leader in Saul, who with his men fought the Philistines. Saul subsequently established a monarchy over the Hebrew tribes, an event conventionally dated to about 1025 B.C.E. Saul's work was carried on by David of Bethlehem, who captured the city of Jerusalem, which he made the religious and political center of the realm. His military successes enlarged the kingdom and his reign was a period of vitality. David's son Solomon (r. ca. 965–925 B.C.E.) launched a building program that the biblical narrative describes as including cities, palaces, fortresses, and roads. The most symbolic of these projects was the Temple of Jerusalem, which became the home of the Ark of the Covenant, the chest that contained the holiest Hebrew religious articles. The Temple of Jerusalem was intended to be the religious heart of the kingdom, a symbol of Hebrew unity and of Yahweh's approval of the Hebrew state.

This state did not last long. At Solomon's death his kingdom broke into political halves. The northern part became Israel, with its capital at Samaria, and the southern half was Judah, with Jerusalem remaining its center. War broke out between the northern and southern halves, and the Assyrians wiped out the northern kingdom in 722 B.C.E. Judah survived numerous invasions until the Babylonians crushed it in 587 B.C.E. The survivors were sent into exile in Babylonia, a period commonly known as the Babylonian Captivity. In 538 B.C.E. the Persian king Cyrus the Great conquered the Babylonians and permitted some forty thousand exiles to return to Jerusalem (see page 54). They rebuilt the temple, although politically the area was simply part of the Persian Empire.

The Jewish Religion

During and especially after the Babylonian Captivity, the most important Hebrew texts of history, law, and ethics were edited and brought together in the Torah, the first five books of the Hebrew Bible. Here the exiles redefined their beliefs and practices, establishing what they believed to be the law of Yahweh. Fundamental to an understanding of the Jewish religion is the concept of the Covenant, an agreement that people believed to exist between themselves and Yahweh. According to the Bible, Yahweh appeared to the tribal leader Abraham, promising him that he would be blessed, as would his descendants, if they followed Yahweh. (Because Judaism, Christianity, and Islam all regard this event as foundational, they are referred to as the "Abrahamic religions.") Yahweh next appeared to Moses when he was leading the Hebrews out of Egypt, and Yahweh made a covenant with the Hebrews: if they worshipped Yahweh as their only god, he would consider them his chosen people and protect them from their enemies. Individuals such as Abraham and Moses who acted as intermediaries between Yahweh and the Hebrew people were known as "prophets." Much of the Hebrew Bible consists of writings in the prophets' voices, understood as messages from Yahweh to the Hebrews.

Worship was embodied in a series of rules of behavior, the Ten Commandments, which Yahweh gave to Moses; these required certain kinds of religious observances and forbade the Hebrews to steal, kill, lie, or commit adultery, thus creating a system of ethical absolutes. From the Ten Commandments a complex system of rules of conduct was created and later written down as Hebrew law. Like the followers of other religions, Jews engaged in rituals through which they showed their devotion. They were to please Yahweh by living up to high moral standards and by worshipping him above all other gods. Increasingly this was understood to be a commandment to worship Yahweh alone. The later prophets such as Isaiah created a system of ethical monotheism, in which goodness was understood to come from a single transcendent god, and in which religious obligations included fair and just behavior toward other people as well as rituals.

Like Mesopotamian deities, Yahweh punished people, but the Hebrews also believed he would protect them all, not simply kings and powerful priests, and make them prosper if they obeyed his commandments. A hymn recorded in the Hebrew Bible's book of Psalms captures this idea:

> Blessed is every one who fears the Lord, who walks in his ways!
> You shall eat the fruit of the labor of your hands;
> you shall be happy, and it shall be well with you.
> Your wife will be like a fruitful vine without your house;
> your children will be like olive shoots around your table.
> Lo, thus shall the man be blessed who fears the Lord. (Psalms 128:1–4)

The religion of the Hebrews was thus addressed to not only the elites but also the individual. Because kings or other political leaders were not essential to its practice, the rise or fall of a kingdom was not crucial to the religion's continued existence. Religious leaders were important in Judaism, but personally following the instructions of Yahweh was the central task for observant Jews in the ancient world.

Hebrew Society

The Hebrews were originally nomadic, but they adopted settled agriculture in Canaan, and some lived in cities. Over time, communal use of land gave way to family or private ownership, and devotions to the traditions of Judaism replaced tribal identity.

Family relationships reflected evolving circumstances. Marriage and the family were fundamentally important in Jewish life. Celibacy was frowned upon, and almost all major Jewish thinkers and priests were married. As in Mesopotamia and Egypt, marriage was a family matter, too important to be left solely to the whims of young people. Although specific rituals may have been expected to ensure ritual purity in sexual relations, sex itself was viewed as part of Yahweh's creation and the bearing of children was seen in some ways as a religious function. Sons were especially desired because they maintained the family bloodline while keeping ancestral property in the family. A firstborn son became the head of the household upon his father's death. Mothers oversaw the early education of the children, but as boys grew older, their fathers provided more of their education.

The development of urban life among Jews created new economic opportunities, especially in crafts and trade. People specialized in certain occupations, such as milling flour, baking bread, making pottery, weaving, and carpentry. As in most ancient societies, these crafts were family trades.

The Assyrians and Persians

How did the Assyrians and the Persians consolidate their power and control the subjects of their empires?

Small kingdoms like those of the Phoenicians and the Jews could exist only in the absence of a major power. In the ninth century B.C.E. one major power arose in the form of the Assyrians, who starting in northern Mesopotamia created an empire through often-brutal military conquests. And from a base in what is now southern Iran, the Persians established an even larger empire, developing effective institutions of government.

Assyria, the Military Monarchy

Starting from a base in northern Mesopotamia around 900 B.C.E., the Assyrians began a campaign of expansion and domination, conquering, exacting tribute, and building new fortified towns, palaces, and temples. Over the next several centuries, Babylonia, Syria, Phoenicia, Israel, and many other states fell. By means of almost constant warfare, the Assyrians created an empire that stretched from their capital of Nineveh on the Tigris River to central Egypt. Revolt against the Assyrians inevitably promised the rebels bloody battles and cruel sieges followed by surrender, accompanied by systematic torture and slaughter, and sometimes deportations.

Assyrian methods were certainly harsh, but in practical terms Assyria's success was due primarily to the size of its army of infantrymen, archers, and charioteers and to the army's sophisticated and effective military organization. In addition, the Assyrians developed a wide variety of siege machinery and techniques, including excavations to undermine city walls and battering rams to knock down walls and gates. Never before in this area had anyone applied such technical knowledge to warfare. The Assyrians even invented the concept of a corps of engineers who bridged rivers with pontoons or provided soldiers with inflatable skins for swimming. The Assyrians also knew how to coordinate their efforts, both in open battle and in siege warfare. Not only did the Assyrians know how to win battles but they also knew how to take advantage of their victories. As early as the eighth century B.C.E., the Assyrian kings began to organize their conquered territories into an empire. The lands closest to Assyria became provinces governed directly by Assyrian officials. Kingdoms beyond the provinces were not annexed but became dependent states that followed Assyria's lead and also paid Assyria a hefty tribute.

By the seventh century B.C.E. Assyrian power seemed firmly established. Yet the downfall of Assyria was swift and complete. Babylon won its independence in 626 B.C.E. and joined forces with a new group, the Medes, an Indo-European-speaking people from Persia. Together the Babylonians and the Medes destroyed the Assyrian Empire in 612 B.C.E., paving the way for the rise of the Persians. The Hebrew prophet Nahum spoke for many when he asked: "Nineveh is laid waste: who will bemoan her?" (Nahum 3:7). Their cities destroyed and their power shattered, the Assyrians seemed to disappear from history.

Modern archaeology has brought the Assyrians out of obscurity. In the nineteenth century archaeologists unearthed huge sculpted figures of winged bulls, human-headed lions, and sphinxes, along with cuneiform tablets that recounted everything from military campaigns to business relationships. For the kings' palaces, Assyrian artists

Assyrian Warriors Attack a City   In this Assyrian carving from a royal throne room made about 865 B.C.E., warriors cross a river on inflated skins, which both support them and provide air for breathing underwater. Such innovative techniques, combined with a large army and effective military organization, allowed the Assyrians to establish a large empire. (Werner Forman Archive/British Museum, London. Location: 10. © 2004 Werner Forman/TopFoto/The Image Works)

carved reliefs that showed scenes of war as a series of episodes that progressed from the time the army marched out until the enemy was conquered. In doing so, they created a visual narrative of events, a form still favored by comic-book artists and the authors of graphic novels.

The Rise and Expansion of the Persian Empire

As we have seen, Assyria rose to power from a base in the Tigris and Euphrates River Valleys of Mesopotamia, which had seen many earlier empires. The Assyrians were defeated by a coalition that included not only a Mesopotamian power—Babylon—but also a people with a base of power in a part of the world that had not been the site of earlier urbanized states: Persia (modern-day Iran), a stark land of towering mountains and harsh deserts with a broad central plateau in the heart of the country (Map 2.3).

Iran's geographical position and topography explain its traditional role as the highway between western and eastern Asia. Nomadic peoples migrating south from the broad steppes of Russia and Central Asia have streamed into Iran throughout much of history. (For an in-depth discussion of these groups, see Chapter 12.) Confronting the uncrossable salt deserts, most have turned either westward or eastward, moving on until they reached the advanced and wealthy urban centers of Mesopotamia and India. Cities did emerge along these routes, however, and Iran became the area where nomads met urban dwellers.

Among these nomads were Indo-European-speaking peoples who migrated into this area about 1000 B.C.E. with their flocks and herds. They were also horse breeders, and the horse gave them a decisive military advantage over those who already lived in the area. One of these groups was the Medes, who settled in northern Iran and built

MAP 2.3 The Assyrian and Persian Empires, ca. 1000–500 B.C.E. The Assyrian Empire at its height around 650 B.C.E. included almost all of the old centers of power in the ancient Near East. By 500 B.C.E., however, the Persian Empire was far larger, extending from the Mediterranean Sea to the Indus River.

their capital city at Ecbatana, the modern Hamadan. With the rise of the Medes, the balance of power in western Asia shifted east of Mesopotamia for the first time.

In 550 B.C.E. Cyrus the Great (r. 559–530 B.C.E.), king of the Persians (another Indo-European-speaking group) and one of the most remarkable statesmen of antiquity, conquered the Medes. Cyrus then set out to win control of the shore of the Mediterranean and thus of the terminal ports of the great trade routes that crossed Iran and Anatolia and to secure eastern Iran from the threats of nomadic invasions. In a series of major campaigns Cyrus achieved both goals. He conquered the various kingdoms of the Tigris and Euphrates Valleys and swept into Anatolia, easily overthrowing the young kingdom of Lydia. His generals subdued the Greek cities along the coast of Anatolia and the Phoenician cities south of these, thus gaining him flourishing ports on the Mediterranean. From Lydia, Cyrus marched to the far eastern corners of Iran and conquered the regions of Parthia and Bactria in Central Asia, though he ultimately died on the battlefield there.

After his victories, Cyrus made sure the Persians were portrayed as liberators, and in some cases he was more benevolent than most conquerors. According to later Greek sources, he spared the life of the conquered king of Lydia, Croesus, who then became his adviser. According to his own account, he freed all the captive peoples, including the Hebrews, who were living in forced exile in Babylon. He returned the Hebrews' sacred objects to them and allowed those who wanted to do so to return to Jerusalem, where he paid for the rebuilding of their temple.

Cyrus's successors continued the Persian conquests, creating the largest empire the world had yet seen. Darius (r. 521–486 B.C.E.) conquered Scythia in Central Asia, along with much of Thrace and Macedonia, areas north of the Aegean Sea. Thus, within forty years the Persians had transformed themselves from a subject people to the rulers of a vast empire that included all the oldest kingdoms and peoples of the region (see Map 2.3, opposite). Darius began to call himself "King of Kings." Invasions of Greece by Darius and his son Xerxes were unsuccessful, but the Persian Empire lasted another two hundred years, until it became part of the empire of Alexander the Great (see page 129).

The Persians also knew how to preserve the peace they had won on the battlefield. To govern the empire, they created an efficient administrative system based in their newly built capital city of Persepolis, near modern Shiraz, Iran. Under Darius, they divided the empire into districts and appointed either Persian or local nobles as administrators called satraps to head each one. The satrap controlled local government, collected taxes, heard legal cases, and maintained order. He was assisted by a council and also by officials and army leaders sent from Persepolis who made sure that he knew the will of the king and that the king knew what was going on in the provinces. This system decreased opposition to Persian rule by making local elites part of the system of government, although sometimes satraps used their authority to build up independent power. The Persians allowed the peoples they conquered to maintain their own customs and beliefs as long as they paid the proper amount of taxes and did not rebel. Their rule resulted in an empire that brought people together in a new political system, with a culture that blended older and newer religious traditions and ways of seeing the world.

Communication and trade were eased by a sophisticated system of roads linking the empire from the coast of Asia Minor to the valley of the Indus River. These roads meant that the king was usually in close touch with officials and subjects, and they simplified the defense of the empire by making it easier to move Persian armies. The roads also aided the flow of trade, which Persian rulers further encouraged by building canals, including one that linked the Red Sea and the Nile.

The Persians made significant contributions to art and culture. In art they transformed the Assyrian tradition of realistic monumental sculpture from one that celebrated gory details of slaughter to one that showed both the Persians and their subjects as dignified. Because they depicted both themselves and non-Persians realistically, Persian art is an excellent source of information about the weapons, tools, clothing, and even hairstyles of many peoples of the area.

The Religion of Zoroaster

Persian religion was originally polytheistic and tied to nature, with Ahuramazda (ah-HOOR-uh-MAZ-duh) as the chief god. Around 600 B.C.E. the ideas of Zoroaster (zoh-roh-ASS-tuhr), a thinker and preacher whose dates are uncertain, began to gain prominence. Zoroaster is regarded as the author of key religious texts, which were later gathered together in a collection of sacred texts called the Avesta. He introduced new spiritual concepts, stressing devotion to Ahuramazda alone and emphasizing the individual's responsibility to choose between the forces of creation, truth, and order and those of nothingness, chaos, falsehood, and disorder. Zoroaster taught that people possessed free will and that they must rely on their own consciences to guide them through an active life in which they focused on "good thoughts, good words, and good deeds." Their decisions were crucial, he warned, for there would come a time of reckoning. At the end of time, the forces of order would win, and the victorious Ahuramazda, like the Egyptian god Osiris, would preside over a last judgment to determine each person's eternal fate.

Scholars—and contemporary Zoroastrians—debate whether Zoroaster saw the forces of disorder as a malevolent deity named Angra Mainyu who was co-eternal with and independent from Ahuramazda, or whether he was simply using this term to mean "evil thoughts" or "a destructive spirit." Later forms of **Zoroastrianism** followed each of these lines of understanding. Most Zoroastrians believed that Ahuramazda and Angra Mainyu were locked together in a cosmic battle for the human race, a religious conceptualization that scholars call dualism. Some, however, had a more monotheistic interpretation and saw Ahuramazda as the only uncreated god.

Whenever he actually lived, Zoroaster's writings were communicated by teachers, and King Darius began to use Zoroastrian language and images. Under the protection of the Persian kings, Zoroastrian ideas spread throughout Iran and the rest of the Persian Empire, and then into central China. Zoroastrianism became the official religion of the later Persian Empire ruled by the Sassanid dynasty, and much later Zoroastrians migrated to western India, where they became known as Parsis and still live today. Zoroastrianism survived the fall of the Persian Empire to influence Christianity, Islam, and Buddhism, largely because of its belief in a just life on earth and a happy afterlife. Good behavior in the world, even though unrecognized at the time, would receive ample reward in the hereafter. Evil, no matter how powerful a person had been in life, would be punished after death. In some form or another, Zoroastrian concepts still pervade many modern religions and Zoroastrianism still exists as a religion.

Chapter Summary

Beginning about 5,000 years ago, people in some parts of the world invented writing, in large part to meet the needs of the state, a new structure of governance in which leaders gained and maintained power through organized violence, bureaucracies, systems of taxation, social and gender hierarchies, and often written laws. States first developed in the southern part of Mesopotamia known as Sumer, where priests and rulers invented ways to control and organize people who lived in cities reliant on irrigation. Conquerors from the north unified Mesopotamian city-states into larger empires and spread Mesopotamian culture over a large area.

During the third millennium B.C.E. Egypt grew into a cohesive state under a single ruler in the Nile River Valley that provided rich farmland and an avenue of communication. For long stretches of history, Egypt was prosperous and secure in the Nile Valley, although at times various groups migrated into or invaded and conquered this kingdom. During the period known as the New Kingdom, warrior-kings created a large Egyptian empire. Newcomers and Egyptians often adopted aspects of each other's cultures. After the collapse of the New Kingdom, the Nubian rulers of Kush conquered Egypt, and another group, the Phoenicians, came to dominate trade in the Mediterranean, spreading a letter alphabet. Another group, the Hebrews, created a new form of religious belief based on the worship of a single all-powerful god. The Hebrews wrote down their religious laws and traditions in a series of books, which became the core of the Hebrews' religion, Judaism.

In the ninth century B.C.E. the Assyrians used a huge army and sophisticated military tactics to create an empire from a base in northern Mesopotamia. The Persians established an even larger empire, developing effective institutions of government and building roads. The Persians generally allowed their subjects to continue their own customs, traditions, and religions. Around 600 B.C.E. a new religion grew in Persia based on the teachings of the prophet Zoroaster, who emphasized the individual's responsibility to choose between good and evil.

Notes

1. *The Sumerians: Their History, Culture, and Character* by Samuel Noah Kramer, p. 238. Reproduced with permission of UNIVERSITY OF CHICAGO PRESS in the format Republish in a book via Copyright Clearance Center.
2. James B. Pritchard, ed., *Ancient Near Eastern Texts Relating to the Old Testament — Third Edition with Supplement.* © 1950, 1955, 1969, renewed 1978 by Princeton University Press. Reprinted by permission of Princeton University Press.

CONNECTIONS

"History is written by the victors" goes a common saying often incorrectly attributed to Winston Churchill. This is not always true; people who have been vanquished in wars or devastated by oppression have certainly made their stories known. But in other ways it is always true, for writing created records and therefore was the origin of what many people understand as history. Writing was invented to serve the needs of people who lived close to one another in cities and states, and almost everyone who could write lived in states. Because most history, including this book, concentrates on areas with states, the next two chapters examine the states that were developing in India and China during the period discussed in this chapter. In Chapter 5 we pick up on developments in the Mediterranean that link to those in Mesopotamia, Egypt, and Persia discussed in this chapter.

It is important to remember that, as was the spread of agriculture, the growth of the state was a slow process. States became the most powerful and most densely populated forms of human society, and today almost everyone on the planet is at least hypothetically a citizen of a state (or sometimes of more than one, if he or she has dual citizenship). Just 300 years ago, however, only about a third of the world was governed by states; in the rest of the world, people lived in bands of foragers, villages led by kin leaders, family groups of pastoralists, chiefdoms, confederations of tribes, or other forms of social organization. In 500 B.C.E. perhaps only a little over 5 percent of the world's population lived in states. In his *Histories*, Herodotus pays primary attention to the Persians and the Greeks, both of whom had writing and states, but he also discusses many peoples who had neither. In their attempts to provide a balanced account of all the world's peoples, historians today are also looking beyond written sources. Those sources invariably present only part of the story, as Winston Churchill—a historian as well as a political leader—noted in something he actually *did* say: "History will bear me out, particularly as I shall write that history myself."

Chapter Review

MAKE IT STICK

✓ LearningCurve
Go online and use LearningCurve to retain what you've read.

IDENTIFY KEY TERMS

Identify and explain the significance of each item below.

polytheism (p. 34)

cuneiform (p. 36)

epic poem (p. 37)

Hammurabi's law code (p. 39)

pharaoh (p. 41)

Indo-European languages (p. 45)

Iron Age (p. 46)

Phoenicians (p. 48)

Yahweh (p. 49)

Zoroastrianism (p. 56)

REVIEW THE MAIN IDEAS

Answer the focus questions from each section of the chapter.

1. How does writing shape what we can know about the past, and how did writing develop to meet the needs of cities and states? (p. 31)

2. How did the peoples of Mesopotamia form states and develop new technologies and institutions? (p. 34)

3. How did the Egyptians create a prosperous and long-lasting society? (p. 40)

4. How did the Hebrews create an enduring written religious tradition? (p. 49)

5. How did the Assyrians and the Persians consolidate their power and control the subjects of their empires? (p. 52)

MAKE CONNECTIONS

Analyze the larger developments and continuities within and across chapters.

1. What aspects of life in the Neolithic period continued with little change in the states of Mesopotamia and Egypt? What were the most important differences?

2. How were the empires that developed in Mesopotamia, Egypt, and Persia similar to one another? Which of the characteristics you have identified as a similarity do you predict will also be found in later empires, and why?

3. Most peoples in the ancient world gained influence over others and became significant in history through military conquest and the establishment of empires. By contrast, how did the Phoenicians and the Hebrews shape the development of world history?

▷LaunchPad
ONLINE DOCUMENT PROJECT

Depicting a Goddess-King
Considering Egyptian views of gender roles, what complexities did Egyptian writers and artists face in depicting Hatshepsut?

Analyze written and visual representations of Hatshepsut, and then complete a quiz and writing assignment based on the evidence and details from this chapter.

See inside the front cover to learn more.

CHRONOLOGY

ca. 3800 B.C.E.	• Establishment of first cities in Sumeria
ca. 3200 B.C.E.	• Earliest surviving cuneiform writing
2660–2180 B.C.E.	• Period of the Old Kingdom in Egypt
2500 B.C.E.	• Bronze weaponry becomes common in Mesopotamia
ca. 2300 B.C.E.	• Establishment of Akkadian empire
1792–1750 B.C.E.	• Hammurabi rules Babylon
ca. 1600 B.C.E.	• Hittites begin to expand their empire
ca. 1570–1070 B.C.E.	• Period of the New Kingdom in Egypt
ca. 1200 B.C.E.	• Bronze Age Collapse; destruction and drought
ca. 1100 B.C.E.	• Iron technology improves; beginning of the Iron Age; Phoenicians begin to trade in the Mediterranean
ca. 965–925 B.C.E.	• Hebrew kingdom ruled by Solomon
ca. 900–612 B.C.E.	• Assyrian Empire
722 B.C.E.	• Kingdom of Israel destroyed by the Assyrians
587 B.C.E.	• Kingdom of Judah destroyed by the Babylonians
550 B.C.E.	• Cyrus the Great consolidates the Persian Empire

3

LearningCurve
After reading the chapter, go online and use LearningCurve to retain what you've read.

The Foundation of Indian Society

TO 300 C.E.

DURING THE CENTURIES WHEN THE PEOPLES OF ANCIENT MESOPO-
tamia and Egypt were developing urban civilizations, people in India were wrestling with the same challenges—food production, building of cities, political administration, and questions about human life and the cosmos. Like the civilizations of the Nile River Valley and southwestern Asia, the earliest Indian civilization centered on a great river, the Indus. From about 2800 B.C.E. to 1800 B.C.E., the Indus Valley, or Harappan, culture thrived and expanded over a huge area.

A very different Indian society emerged after the decline of this civilization. It was dominated by the Aryans, warriors who spoke an early version of Sanskrit. The Indian caste system and the Hindu religion, key features of Indian society that continued into modern times, had their origins in early Aryan society. By the middle of the first millennium B.C.E., the Aryans had set up numerous small kingdoms throughout north India. This was the great age of Indian religious creativity, when Buddhism and Jainism were founded and the early Brahmanic religion of the Aryans developed into Hinduism.

The first major Indian empire, the Mauryan Dynasty, emerged in the wake of the Greek invasion of north India in 326 B.C.E. This dynasty reached its peak under King Ashoka, who actively promoted Buddhism both within his realm and beyond it. Not long after his reign, however, the empire broke up, and for several centuries India was politically divided. Although India never had a single language and only periodically had a centralized government, cultural elements dating back to the ancient period—the core ideas of Brahmanism, the caste system, and the early epics—spread through trade and other contact, even when the subcontinent was divided into competing kingdoms.

60

The Land and Its First Settlers, ca. 3000–1500 B.C.E.

What does archaeology tell us about the Harappan civilization in India?

The subcontinent of India, a landmass as large as western Europe, juts southward into the warm waters of the Indian Ocean. Today this region is divided into the separate countries of Pakistan, Nepal, India, Bangladesh, and Sri Lanka, but these divisions are recent, and for this discussion of premodern history, the entire subcontinent will be called India.

In India, as elsewhere, the possibilities for both agriculture and communication have always been shaped by geography. Some regions of the subcontinent are among the wettest on earth; others are arid deserts and scrubland. Most areas in India are warm all year, with high temperatures over 100°F; average temperatures range from 79°F in the north to 85°F in the south. Monsoon rains sweep northward from the Indian Ocean each summer. The lower reaches of the Himalaya Mountains in the northeast are covered by dense forests that are sustained by heavy rainfall. Immediately to the south are the fertile valleys of the Indus and Ganges Rivers. These lowland plains, which stretch all the way across the subcontinent, were tamed for agriculture over time, and India's great empires were centered there. To their west are the deserts of Rajasthan and southeastern Pakistan, historically important in part because their flat terrain enabled invaders to sweep into India from the northwest. South of the great river valleys rise the jungle-clad Vindhya Mountains and the dry, hilly Deccan Plateau. Only along the western coast of this part of India do the hills give way to narrow plains where crop agriculture flourished (see Map 3.2, page 79). India's long coastlines and predictable winds fostered maritime trade with other countries bordering the Indian Ocean.

Neolithic settlement of the Indian subcontinent occurred somewhat later than in the Nile River Valley and southwestern Asia, but agriculture followed a similar pattern of development and was well established by about 7000 B.C.E. Wheat and barley were the early crops, probably having spread in their domesticated form from what is today

MAP 3.1 Harappan Civilization, ca. 2500 B.C.E. The earliest civilization in India developed in the Indus River Valley in the west of the subcontinent.

the Middle East. Farmers also domesticated cattle, sheep, and goats and learned to make pottery.

The story of the first civilization in India is one of the most dramatic in the ancient world. From the Bible, people knew about ancient Egypt and Sumer for centuries, but it was not until 1921 that archaeologists found astonishing evidence of a thriving and sophisticated Bronze Age urban culture dating to about 2500 B.C.E. at Mohenjo-daro in what is now Pakistan.

This civilization is known today as the Indus Valley or the **Harappan** (huh-RAH-puhn) civilization, from the modern names of the river and city near where the first ruins were discovered. Archaeologists have discovered some three hundred Harappan cities and many more towns and villages in both Pakistan and India, making it possible to see both the vast regional extent of the Harappan civilization and its evolution over a period of nearly a millennium (Map 3.1). It was a literate civilization, like those of Egypt and Mesopotamia, but no one has been able to decipher the more than four hundred symbols inscribed on stone seals and copper tablets. It is even possible that these symbols are not words but rather names or even nonlinguistic symbols. The civilization flourished most from 2500 B.C.E. to 2000 B.C.E.

The Harappan civilization extended over nearly five hundred thousand square miles in the Indus Valley, making it more than twice as large as ancient Egypt or Sumer. Yet Harappan civilization was marked by striking uniformity. Throughout the region, for instance, even in small villages, bricks were made to the same standard proportion (4:2:1). Figurines of pregnant women have been found throughout the area, suggesting common religious ideas and practices.

Like Mesopotamian cities, Harappan cities were centers for crafts and trade and were surrounded by extensive farmland. Craftsmen produced ceramics decorated with geometric designs. The Harappans were the earliest known manufacturers of cotton cloth, and this cloth was so abundant that goods were wrapped in it for shipment. Trade was extensive. As early as the reign of Sargon of Akkad in the third millennium B.C.E. (see page 37), trade between India and Mesopotamia carried goods and ideas between the two cultures, probably by way of the Persian Gulf. The Harappan port of Lothal had a stone dock 700 feet long, next to which were massive granaries and bead-making factories. Hundreds of seals were found there, some of Persian Gulf origin, indicating that Lothal was a major port of exit and entry.

The cities of Mohenjo-daro in southern Pakistan, and Harappa, some 400 miles to the north, were huge for this period, more than 3 miles in circumference, with populations estimated at 35,000 to 40,000. Both were defended by great citadels that towered 40 to 50 feet above the surrounding plain. The cities had obviously been planned and built before being settled—they were not the outcomes of villages that grew and sprawled haphazardly. Large granaries stored food. Streets were straight and varied from 9 to 34 feet in width. The houses were substantial, many two stories tall, some perhaps three. The focal point of a house was a central courtyard onto which the rooms opened, much like many houses today in both rural and urban India.

Perhaps the most surprising aspect of the elaborate planning of these cities was their complex system of drainage, which at Mohenjo-daro is well preserved. Each house had a bathroom with a drain connected to brick-lined sewers located under the major streets. Openings allowed the refuse to be collected, probably to be used as fertilizer on nearby fields. No other ancient city had such an advanced sanitation system.

Mohenjo-daro

Mohenjo-daro was a planned city built of fired mud brick. Its streets were straight, and covered drainpipes were installed to carry away waste. From sites like this, we know that the early Indian political elite had the power and technical expertise to organize large, coordinated building projects. (© M. Kenoyer/Harrapa.com. Courtesy, Department of Archeology and Museums, Government of Pakistan)

Both Mohenjo-daro and Harappa also contained numerous large structures, which archaeologists think were public buildings. One of the most important was the large ventilated storehouse for the community's grain. Mohenjo-daro also had a marketplace or place of assembly, a palace, and a huge pool some 39 feet long by 23 feet wide by 8 feet deep. Like the later Roman baths, it had spacious dressing rooms for the bathers. Because the Great Bath at Mohenjo-daro resembles the ritual purification pools of later India, some scholars have speculated that power was in the hands of a priest-king and that the Great Bath played a role in the religious rituals of the city. In contrast to ancient Egypt and Mesopotamia, no great tombs have been discovered in Harappa, making it more difficult to envision the life of the elite.

The prosperity of the Indus civilization depended on constant and intensive cultivation of the rich river valley. Although rainfall seems to have been greater then than in recent times, the Indus, like the Nile, flowed through a relatively dry region made fertile by annual floods and irrigation. And as in Egypt, agriculture was aided by a long, hot growing season and near-constant sunshine.

Because no one has yet deciphered the written language of the Harappan people, their political, intellectual, and religious life is largely unknown. There clearly was a political structure with the authority to organize city planning and facilitate trade, but we do not even know whether there were hereditary kings. There are clear similarities between Harappan and Sumerian civilization, but the differences are just as clear. For instance, the Harappan script, like the Sumerian, was incised on clay tablets and seals, but it has no connection to Sumerian cuneiform, and the artistic style of the Harappan seals is distinct.

Soon after 2000 B.C.E., the Harappan civilization mysteriously declined. The port of Lothal was abandoned by about 1900 B.C.E., and other major centers came to house only a fraction of their earlier populations. Scholars have proposed many explanations for the mystery of the abandonment of these cities. The decline cannot be attributed to the arrival of powerful invaders, as was once thought. Rather it was internally generated. Environmental theories include an earthquake that led to a shift in the course of the river, or a severe drought. Perhaps the long-term practice of irrigation led to the buildup of salt and alkaline in the soil until they reached levels toxic to plants, forcing the Harappan people to move in search of arable land. Some scholars speculate that long-distance commerce collapsed, leading to an economic depression. Others theorize that the population fell prey to diseases, such as malaria, that caused people to flee the cities.

Even though the Harappan people apparently lived on after scattering to villages, the large urban centers were abandoned, and key features of their high culture were lost. For the next thousand years, India had no large cities, no kiln-fired bricks, and no written language. There are, however, many signs of continuity with later Indian civilization, ranging from the sorts of pottery ovens used to some of the images of gods. Some scholars speculate that the people of Harappa were the ancestors of the Tamils and other Dravidian-speaking peoples of modern south India.

The Aryans During the Vedic Age, ca. 1500–500 B.C.E.

What kind of society and culture did the Indo-European Aryans create?

After the decline of the Harappan civilization, a people who called themselves **Aryans** became dominant in north India. They were speakers of an early form of Sanskrit, an Indo-European language closely related to ancient Persian and more distantly related to Latin, Greek, Celtic, and their modern descendants, such as English. For example, the Sanskrit *nava*, "ship," is related to the English word *naval*; *deva*, "god," to *divine*; and *raja*, "ruler," to *regal*. The word *Aryan* itself comes from *Arya*, "noble" or "pure" in Sanskrit, and has the same linguistic root as *Iran* and *Ireland*. The Aryans flourished during the Vedic Age (ca. 1500–500 B.C.E.). Named for the Vedas, a large and significant body of ancient sacred works written in Sanskrit, this period witnessed the Indo-Aryan development of the caste system and the Brahmanic religion and the writing of the great epics that represent the earliest form of Indian literature.

Aryan Dominance in North India

Until relatively recently, the dominant theory was that the Aryans came into India from outside, perhaps as part of the same movements of people that led to the Hittites occupying parts of Anatolia, the Achaeans entering Greece, and the Kassites conquering Sumer—all in the period from about 1900 B.C.E. to 1750 B.C.E. Some scholars, however, have proposed that the Indo-European languages spread to this area much earlier; to them it seems possible that the Harappan people were speakers of an early Indo-European language. If that was the case, the Aryans would be one of the groups descended from this early population.

Modern politics complicates analysis of the appearance of the Aryans and their role in India's history. Europeans in the eighteenth and nineteenth centuries developed the concept of Indo-European languages, and they did so in an age both highly conscious of race and in the habit of identifying races with languages. The racist potential of the concept was exploited by the Nazis, who glorified the Aryans as a superior race. Even in less politicized contexts, the notion of a group of people who entered India from outside and made themselves its rulers is troubling to many. Does it mean that the non-Aryans are the true Indians? Does it add legitimacy to those who in later times conquered India from outside? Does it justify or undermine the caste system? One of the difficulties faced by scholars who wish to take a dispassionate view of these issues is that the evidence for the earlier Harappan culture is entirely archaeological, while the evidence for the Aryans is almost entirely based on linguistic analysis of modern languages and orally transmitted texts of uncertain date.

The central source of information on the early Aryans is the *Rig Veda*, the earliest of the Vedas, originally an oral collection of hymns, ritual texts, and philosophical treatises composed in Sanskrit between 1500 B.C.E. and 500 B.C.E. Like Homer's epics in Greece, written in this same period (see page 117), these texts were transmitted orally and are in verse. The *Rig Veda* portrays the Aryans as warrior tribes who glorified military skill and heroism; loved to drink, hunt, race, and dance; and counted their wealth in cattle. The Aryans did not sweep across India in a quick campaign, nor were they a disciplined army led by one conqueror. Rather they were a collection of tribes that frequently fought with each other and only over the course of several centuries came to dominate north India.

The key to the Aryans' success probably lay in their superior military technology. Those they fought often lived in fortified towns and put up a strong defense against them, but Aryan warriors had superior technology, including two-wheeled chariots, horses, and bronze swords and spears. Their epics present the struggle for north India in religious terms, describing their chiefs as godlike heroes and their opponents as irreligious savages who did not perform the proper sacrifices. In time, however, the Aryans clearly absorbed much from those they conquered, such as agricultural techniques and foods.

At the head of each Aryan tribe was a chief, or raja (RAH-juh), who led his followers in battle and ruled them in peacetime. The warriors in the tribe elected the chief for his military skills. Next in importance to the chief was the priest. In time, priests evolved into a distinct class possessing precise knowledge of the complex rituals and of the invocations and formulas that accompanied them, rather like the priest classes in ancient Egypt, Mesopotamia, and Persia. Below them in the pecking order was a warrior nobility who rode into battle in chariots and perhaps on horseback. The warrior class met at assemblies to reach decisions and advise the raja. The common tribesmen tended herds and worked the land. To the conquered non-Aryans fell the drudgery of menial tasks. It is difficult to define precisely their social status. Though probably not slaves, they were certainly subordinate to the Aryans and worked for them in return for protection.

Bronze Sword   This bronze sword, with a rib in the middle of the blade for strength, is a striking example of the quality of Aryan arms. Superior weapons gave the Aryans military advantage.
(© The Trustees of the British Museum/Art Resource, NY)

Over the course of several centuries, the Aryans pushed farther east into the valley of the Ganges River, at that time a land of thick jungle populated by aboriginal forest peoples. The tremendous challenge of clearing the jungle was made somewhat easier by the introduction of iron around 1000 B.C.E., probably by diffusion from Mesopotamia. Iron made it possible to produce strong axes and knives relatively cheaply.

The Aryans did not gain dominance over the entire Indian subcontinent. South of the Vindhya range, people speaking Dravidian languages maintained their control. In the great Aryan epics the *Ramayana* and *Mahabharata*, the people of the south and Sri Lanka are spoken of as dark-skinned savages and demons who resisted the Aryans' conquests. Nevertheless, these epics would become part of the common cultural heritage of all of India.

As Aryan rulers came to dominate large settled populations, the style of political organization changed from tribal chieftainship to territorial kingship. In other words, the ruler now controlled an area with people living in permanent settlements, not a nomadic tribe that moved as a group. Moreover, kings no longer needed to be elected by the tribe; it was enough to be invested by priests and to perform the splendid royal ceremonies they designed. The priests, or **Brahmins**, supported the growth of royal power in return for royal confirmation of their own power and status. The Brahmins also served as advisers to the kings. In the face of this royal-priestly alliance, the old tribal assemblies of warriors withered away. By the time Persian armies reached the Indus around 513 B.C.E., there were sixteen major Aryan kingdoms in north India.

Life in Early India

Caste was central to the social life of these north Indian kingdoms. Early Aryan society had distinguished among the warrior elite, the priests, ordinary tribesmen, and conquered subjects. These distinctions gradually evolved into the **caste system**, which divided society into strictly defined hereditary groups. Society was conceived of as four hierarchical strata whose members did not eat with or marry each other. These strata, or varnas, were Brahmin (priests), Kshatriya (warriors and officials), Vaishya (merchants), and Shudra (peasants and laborers). The Shudra stratum, which encompassed most of the conquered people, was the largest. By contrast, the three upper varnas probably accounted for no more than 30 percent of the population. The caste system thus allowed the numerically outnumbered Aryans to maintain dominance over their subjects and not be culturally absorbed by them.

Social and religious attitudes supported the caste system. Aryans considered the work of artisans impure. They left all such work to the local people, who were probably superior to them in these arts anyway. Trade, by contrast, was not viewed as demeaning. Brahmanic texts of the period refer to trade as equal in value to farming, serving the king, or being a priest.

In the *Rig Veda*, the caste system is attributed to the gods:

> When they divided [the primeval man], into how many different portions did they arrange him? What became of his mouth, what of his two arms? What were his two thighs and his two feet called?
> His mouth became the brahman, his two arms was made into the [kshatriya]; his two thighs became the vaishyas, of his two feet the shudra was born.[1]

As priests, the Brahmins were expected to memorize every syllable and tone of the Vedas so that their rituals would please the gods. They not only conducted the traditional ceremonies but also developed new ones for new circumstances. As agriculture became more important to the Aryans, for example, Brahmins acted as agents of Agni, the god of fire, to purify the land for crops. The Brahmins also knew the formulas and spells that were effective against diseases and calamities.

Those without places in the four varnas — that is, newly conquered peoples and those who had lost their caste status through violations of ritual — were outcastes. That simply meant that they belonged to no caste. In time, some of them became "untouchables" because they were "impure." They were scorned because they earned their living by performing such "polluting" jobs as slaughtering animals and dressing skins.

Slavery was a feature of early social life in India, as it was in Egypt, Mesopotamia, and elsewhere in antiquity. People captured in battle often became slaves, but captives could also be ransomed by their families. Later, slavery was less connected with warfare and became more of an economic and social institution. A free man might sell himself and his family into slavery because he could not pay his debts. At the same time, he could, if clever, hard-working, or fortunate, buy his and his family's way out of slavery. At birth, slave children automatically became the slaves of their parents' masters. Indian slaves could be bought, used as collateral, or given away.

Women's lives in early India varied according to their social status, much as men's did. Like most nomadic tribes, the Aryans were patrilineal and patriarchal (tracing descent through males and placing power in the senior men of the family). Thus the roles of women in Aryan society probably were more subordinate than were the roles of women in local Dravidian groups, many of which were matrilineal (tracing descent through females). But even in Aryan society women were treated somewhat more favorably than in later Indian society. They were not yet given in child-marriage, and widows had the right to remarry. In epics such as the *Ramayana*, women are often portrayed as forceful personalities, able to achieve their goals both by using feminine ploys to cajole men and by direct action.

Brahmanism

The Aryans recognized a multitude of gods who shared some features with the gods of other early Indo-European societies such as the Persians and Greeks. Some of them were great brawling figures, such as Agni, the god of fire, a particularly important god; Indra, wielder of the thunderbolt and god of war, who each year slew a dragon to release the monsoon rains; and Rudra, the divine archer who spread disaster and disease by firing his arrows at people. Others were shadowy figures, such as Dyaus, the father of the gods, related to the Greek Zeus. Varuna, the god of order in the universe, was a hard god, quick to punish those who sinned and thus upset the balance of nature. Ushas, the goddess of dawn, was a gentle deity who welcomed the birds, gave delight to human beings, and warded off evil spirits.

Ordinary people dealt with these gods through priests who made animal sacrifices to them. By giving valued things to the gods, people strengthened both the power of the gods and their own relationships with them. Gradually, under the priestly monopoly of the Brahmins, correct sacrifice and proper ritual became so important that most Brahmins believed that a properly performed ritual would force a god to grant a worshipper's wish. Ordinary people could watch a ceremony, such as a fire ritual, which was often held outdoors, but could not perform the key steps in the ritual.

The *Upanishads* (oo-PAH-nih-shadz), composed between 750 B.C.E. and 500 B.C.E., record speculations about the mystical meaning of sacrificial rites and about cosmological questions of man's relationship to the universe. They document a gradual shift from the mythical worldview of the early Vedic Age to a deeply philosophical one. Associated with this shift was a movement toward asceticism (uh-SEH-tuh-sihz-uhm) — severe self-discipline and self-denial. In search of wisdom, some men (but not women) retreated to the forests. These ascetics concluded that disciplined meditation on the ritual sacrifice could produce the same results as the physical ritual itself. Thus they reinterpreted ritual sacrifices as symbolic gestures with mystical meanings.

Ancient Indian cosmology (theories of the universe) focused not on a creator who made the universe out of nothing, but rather on endlessly repeating cycles. Key ideas were samsara, the reincarnation of souls by a continual process of rebirth, and karma, the tally of good and bad deeds that determined the status of an individual's next life. Good deeds led to better future lives, evil deeds to worse future lives — even to reincarnation as an animal. The wheel of life included human beings, animals, and gods. Reward and punishment worked automatically; there was no all-knowing god who judged people and could be petitioned to forgive a sin, and each individual was responsible for his or her own destiny in a just and impartial world.

To most people, especially those on the low end of the economic and social scale, these ideas were attractive. By living righteously and doing good deeds, people could improve their lot in the next life. Yet there was another side to these ideas: the wheel of life could be seen as a treadmill, giving rise to a yearning for release from the relentless cycle of birth and death. One solution offered in the *Upanishads* was moksha, or release from the wheel of life. Brahmanic mystics claimed that life in the world was actually an illusion and that the only way to escape the wheel of life was to realize that ultimate reality was unchanging.

The unchanging ultimate reality was called brahman. This important concept has been translated many ways. Scholars have offered both brief phrases — "the cosmic principle," "the principle of religious reality," "absolute reality," "eternal truth," and "universal soul" — and somewhat longer descriptions: "holy or sacred power that is the source and sustainer of the universe," "the ultimate unchanging reality, composed of pure being and consciousness," and "eternal, unchanging, infinite, and transcendent reality that is the divine ground of everything in this universe." Brahman was contrasted to the multitude of fleeting phenomena that people consider important in their daily lives. The individual soul or self was ultimately the same substance as the universal brahman, in the same way that each spark is in substance the same as a large fire.

The *Upanishads* gave the Brahmins a high status to which the poor and lowly could aspire in a future life. Consequently, the Brahmins greeted the concepts presented in these works and those who taught them with tolerance and understanding and made a place for them in traditional religious practice. The rulers of Indian society also encouraged the new trends, since the doctrines of samsara and karma encouraged the poor and oppressed to labor peacefully and dutifully. Thus, although the new doctrines were intellectually revolutionary, in social and political terms they supported the existing power structure.

India's Great Religions

What ideas and practices were taught by the founders of Jainism, Buddhism, and Hinduism?

By the sixth and fifth centuries B.C.E., cities had reappeared in India, and merchants and trade were thriving. Bricks were again baked in kilns and used to build ramparts around cities. One particular kingdom, Magadha, had become much more powerful than any of the other states in the Ganges plain, defeating its enemies by using war elephants and catapults for hurling stones. Written language had also reappeared.

This was a period of intellectual ferment throughout Eurasia—the period of the early Greek philosophers, the Hebrew prophets, Zoroaster in Persia, and Confucius and the early Daoists in China. In India it led to numerous sects that rejected various elements of Brahmanic teachings. The two most influential were Jainism and Buddhism. Their founders were contemporaries living in the Ganges plain. Hinduism emerged in response to these new religions but at the same time was the most direct descendant of the old Brahmanic religion.

Jainism

The key figure of Jainism, Vardhamana Mahavira (fl. ca. 520 B.C.E.), was the son of the chief of a small state and a member of the warrior class. Like many ascetics of the period, he left home to become a wandering holy man. For twelve years, from ages thirty to forty-two, he traveled through the Ganges Valley until he found enlightenment and became a "completed soul." Mahavira taught his doctrines for about thirty years, founding a disciplined order of monks and gaining the support of many lay followers, male and female.

Mahavira accepted the Brahmanic doctrines of karma and rebirth but developed these ideas in new directions, founding the religion referred to as Jainism. He asserted that human beings, animals, plants, and even inanimate objects all have living souls enmeshed in matter, accumulated through the workings of karma. Even a rock has a soul locked inside it, enchained by matter but capable of suffering if someone kicks it. The souls conceived by the Jains have finite dimensions. They float or sink depending on the amount of matter with which they are enmeshed. The ascetic, who willingly undertakes suffering, can dissipate some of the accumulated karma and make progress toward liberation. If a soul at last escapes from all the matter weighing it down, it becomes lighter than ordinary objects and floats to the top of the universe, where it remains forever in bliss.

Mahavira's followers pursued such liberation by living ascetic lives and avoiding evil thoughts and actions. The Jains considered all life sacred and tried to live without destroying other life. Some early Jains went to the extreme of starving themselves to death, since it is impossible to eat without destroying at least plants, but most took the less extreme step of distinguishing between different levels of life. The most sacred life-forms were human beings, followed by animals, plants, and inanimate objects. A Jain who wished to avoid violence to life became a vegetarian and took pains not to kill any creature, even tiny insects in the air and soil. Farming was impossible for Jains, who tended instead to take up trade. Among the most conservative Jains, priests practiced nudity, for clinging to clothes, even a loincloth, was a form of attachment. Lay Jains could pursue Jain teachings by practicing nonviolence and not eating meat. The Jains' radical nonviolence was motivated by a desire to escape the karmic consequences of causing harm to a life. In other words, violence had to be avoided above all because it harms the person who commits it.

For the first century after Mahavira's death, the Jains were a comparatively small and unimportant sect. Jainism began to flourish under the Mauryan Dynasty (ca. 322–185 B.C.E.; see pages 78–80), and Jain tradition claims the Mauryan Empire's founder, Chandragupta, as a major patron. About 300 B.C.E. the Jain scriptures were recorded, and the religion split into two sects, one maintaining the tradition of total nudity, the other choosing to wear white robes on the grounds that clothes were an insignificant external sign, unrelated to true liberation. Over the next few centuries, Jain monks were particularly important in spreading northern culture into the Deccan and Tamil regions of south India.

Although Jainism never took hold as widely as Hinduism and Buddhism (discussed below), it has been an influential strand in Indian thought and has several million adherents in India today. Fasting and nonviolence as spiritual practices in India owe much to Jain teachings. In the twentieth century Mohandas Gandhi, leader of the Indian independence movement, was influenced by these ideas through his mother, and the American civil rights leader Dr. Martin Luther King, Jr., was influenced by Gandhi.

Siddhartha Gautama and Buddhism

Siddhartha Gautama (fl. ca. 500 B.C.E.), also called Shakyamuni ("sage of the Shakya tribe"), is best known as the Buddha ("enlightened one"). He was a contemporary of Mahavira and came from the same warrior social class. He was born the son of a chief of one of the tribes in the Himalayan foothills in what is now Nepal. At age twenty-nine, unsatisfied with his life of comfort and troubled by the suffering he saw around him, he left home to become a wandering ascetic. He traveled south to the kingdom of Magadha, where he studied with yoga masters, but later took up extreme asceticism. According to tradition, while meditating under a bo tree at Bodh Gaya, he reached enlightenment—that is, perfect insight into the processes of the universe. After several weeks of meditation, he preached his first sermon, urging a "middle way" between asceticism and worldly life. For the next forty-five years, the Buddha traveled through the Ganges Valley, propounding his ideas, refuting his adversaries, and attracting followers. To reach as wide an audience as possible, the Buddha preached in the local language, Magadhi, rather than in Sanskrit, which was already becoming a priestly language. Probably because he refused to recognize the divine authority of the Vedas and dismissed sacrifices, he attracted followers mostly from among merchants, artisans, and farmers, rather than Brahmins.

In his first sermon the Buddha outlined his main message, summed up in the **Four Noble Truths** and the **Eightfold Path**. The Four Noble Truths are as follows: (1) pain and suffering, frustration, and anxiety are ugly but inescapable parts of human life; (2) suffering and anxiety are caused by human desires and attachments; (3) people can understand these weaknesses and triumph over them; and (4) this triumph is made possible by following a simple code of conduct, the Eightfold Path. The basic insight

Gandharan Frieze Depicting the Buddha This carved stone from ca. 200 C.E. is one in a series portraying scenes from the life of the Buddha. From the Gandharan kingdom (located in modern Pakistan), this frieze depicts the Buddha seated below the bo tree, where he was first enlightened. (Scenes from the life of the Buddha, Kushan Dynasty [stone]/Freer Gallery, Smithsonian Institution, Washington, D.C., U.S.A./The Bridgeman Art Library)

of Buddhism is thus psychological. The deepest human longings can never be satisfied, and even those things that seem to give pleasure cause anxiety because we are afraid of losing them. Attachment to people and things causes sorrow at their loss.

The Buddha offered an optimistic message in that all people can set out on the Eightfold Path toward liberation. All they have to do is take a series of steps, beginning with recognizing the universality of suffering ("right knowledge"), deciding to free themselves from it ("right purpose"), and then choosing "right conduct" (including abstaining from taking life), "right speech," "right livelihood," and "right endeavor." The seventh step is "right awareness," constant contemplation of one's deeds and words, giving full thought to their importance and whether they lead to enlightenment. "Right contemplation," the last step, entails deep meditation on the impermanence of everything in the world. Those who achieve liberation are freed from the cycle of birth and death and enter the state called nirvana, a kind of blissful nothingness and freedom from reincarnation.

Buddhism differed from Brahmanism and later Hinduism in that it ignored the caste system. Everyone, noble and peasant, educated and ignorant, male and female, could follow the Eightfold Path. Moreover, the Buddha was extraordinarily non-dogmatic. Convinced that each person must achieve enlightenment on his or her own, he emphasized that the path was important only because it led the traveler to enlightenment, not for its own sake. He compared it to a raft, essential to cross a river but useless once the traveler reaches the far shore. There was no harm in honoring local gods or observing traditional ceremonies, as long as one remembered the goal of enlightenment and did not let sacrifices become snares or attachments. The willingness of Buddhists to tolerate a wide variety of practices aided the spread of the religion.

Like Mahavira, the Buddha formed a circle of disciples, primarily men but including some women as well. He continually reminded them that each person must reach ultimate fulfillment by individual effort, but he also recognized the value of a group of people striving together for the same goal.

INDIVIDUALS IN SOCIETY • Sudatta, Lay Follower of the Buddha

During the decades when the Buddha traveled around north India spreading his teachings, he attracted both disciples and lay followers. Stories of the Buddha's interactions with them were passed down orally for centuries, and undoubtedly were elaborated over time. Still, these accounts give us a sense of what life was like in early India. The wealthy banker or merchant Sudatta is a good example of an ardent lay follower. He was so generous to others that he is normally referred to by his epithet, Anathapindada, which means "benefactor of the needy."

Sudatta met the Buddha in the first year after his enlightenment. In one early conversation with him, Sudatta asks if he must leave the world to attain nirvana:

> Now, I have heard thy disciples praise the bliss of the hermit and denounce the unrest of the world. "The Holy One," they say, "has given up his kingdom and his inheritance, and has found the path of righteousness, thus setting an example to all the world how to attain Nirvana." My heart yearns to do what is right and to be a blessing unto my fellows. Let me then ask you, Must I give up my wealth, my home, and my business enterprises, and, like you, go into homelessness in order to attain the bliss of a religious life?

The Buddha replied that the crucial issue was the way an individual looked on wealth. Anyone who cleaves to wealth needs to cast it aside, but anyone who "possessing riches, uses them rightly, will be a blessing unto his fellows." It is cleaving to wealth and power that enslaves people, not the mere possession of wealth. Artisans, merchants, or officers of the king who stay in the world should concentrate on performing their duties well. "If they live in the world not a life of self but a life of truth, then surely joy, peace, and bliss will dwell in their minds."*

Sudatta purchased a large park to provide a place where the Buddha and his disciples could live during the rainy season and had many buildings built there. The Buddha returned to this Jetavana Monastery many times and frequently gave sermons there. Sudatta also provided food for monks and gave generously to the poor and needy. As a result of his generosity, Sudatta was gradually reduced to poverty himself. Then, through divine intervention, those who owed him money returned it, making him wealthy once again.

Stories recounted that Sudatta's family, including his three daughters, became pious followers. Although Sudatta's son initially resisted the Buddha, he eventu-

---

*Paul Carus, *The Gospel of Buddha* (Chicago: Open Court, 1894/1915), pp. 61–63, slightly modified.

The Buddha's followers transmitted his teachings orally until they were written down in the second or first century B.C.E. These scriptures are called sutras. The form of monasticism that developed among the Buddhists was less strict than that of the Jains. Buddhist monks moved about for eight months of the year (except the rainy season), begging for their one meal a day, but they could bathe and wear clothes. Within a few centuries Buddhist monks began to overlook the rule that they should travel. They set up permanent monasteries, generally on land donated by kings or other patrons. Orders of nuns also appeared, giving women the opportunity to seek ally became a generous patron himself. The Buddha himself helped convert Sudatta's unpleasant daughter-in-law. Once when the Buddha was preaching at Sudatta's home, he was disrupted by the sounds of Sudatta's son's wife scolding the servants. The Buddha asked to have her brought to him, and he instructed her on the proper conduct of wives. There were three types of bad wives, he told her: the destructive wife, who is pitiless, fond of other men, and contemptuous of her husband; the thievish wife, who squanders the family wealth; and the mistress wife, who is rude, lazy, and domineering. These he contrasted with the four kinds of good wives: the motherly wife, who cares for her husband as a mother for her son; the sisterly wife, who defers to her husband in the same affectionate way that a younger sister defers to her older brother; the friend wife, who loves her husband as if he were her best friend; and the handmaiden wife, who is calm, patient, and obedient. Deeply moved by these teachings, the daughter-in-law determined to be a handmaiden wife.

Sudatta died before the Buddha. A sutra that survives purports to be the sermon that two of the Buddha's chief disciples preached to him on his deathbed. They counseled Sudatta on how to face his situation by training himself to decide not to cling to what is seen, heard, sensed, thought, attained, sought after, or pondered by the intellect.

QUESTIONS FOR ANALYSIS

1. What can you infer about the circumstances of the early followers of the Buddha from the life of Sudatta?

2. What insights does the life of Sudatta provide into the ways faith in Buddhism was spread?

▷LaunchPad
ONLINE DOCUMENT PROJECT

What made Buddhism accessible to everyone? Read a selection of Buddhist parables, and then complete a quiz and writing assignment based on the evidence and details from this chapter.

See inside the front cover to learn more.

truth in ways men had traditionally used. The main ritual that monks and nuns performed in their monastic establishments was the communal recitation of the sutras. Lay Buddhists could aid the spread of the Buddhist teachings by providing food for monks and support for their monasteries, and they could pursue their own spiritual progress by adopting practices such as abstaining from meat and alcohol. (See "Individuals in Society: Sudatta, Lay Follower of the Buddha," above.)

Because Buddhism had no central ecclesiastical authority like the Christian papacy, early Buddhist communities developed several divergent traditions and came to stress different sutras. One of the most important of these, associated with the monk-philosopher Nagarjuna (fl. ca. 100 C.E.), is called **Mahayana**, or "Great Vehicle," because it was a more inclusive form of the religion. It drew on a set of discourses allegedly given by the Buddha and kept hidden by his followers for centuries. One branch of Mahayana taught that reality is empty (that is, nothing exists independently of itself). Another branch held that ultimate reality is consciousness, that everything is produced by the mind.

Just as important as the metaphysical literature of Mahayana Buddhism was its devotional side, influenced by the religions then prevalent in Central Asia, such as Zoroastrianism (see page 55). The Buddha became deified and was placed at the head of an expanding pantheon of other Buddhas and **bodhisattvas** (boh-dih-SUHT-vuhz). Bodhisattvas were Buddhas-to-be who had stayed in the world after enlightenment to help others on the path to salvation. The Buddhas and bodhisattvas became objects of veneration, especially the Buddha of Infinite Light, Amitabha, and the bodhisattva of infinite compassion and mercy, Avalokitesvara (uh-vuh-lohk-ih-TAYSH-veh-ruh). With the growth of Mahayana, Buddhism attracted more and more laypeople.

Buddhism remained an important religion in India until about 1200 C.E. By that time it had spread widely through East, Central, and Southeast Asia. After 1200 C.E. Buddhism declined in India, losing out to both Hinduism and Islam, and the number of Buddhists in India today is small. Buddhism never lost its hold in Nepal and Sri Lanka, however, and today it is also a major religion in Southeast Asia, Tibet, China, Korea, and Japan.

Hinduism

Both Buddhism and Jainism were direct challenges to the old Brahmanic religion. Both rejected animal sacrifice, which by then was a central element in the rituals performed by Brahmin priests. Even more important, both religions tacitly rejected the caste system, accepting people of any caste into their ranks. Over the next several centuries (ca. 400 B.C.E.–200 C.E.), in response to this challenge, the Brahmanic religion evolved in a more devotional direction, developing into the religion commonly called Hinduism. In Hinduism Brahmins retained their high social status, but it became possible for individual worshippers to have more direct contact with the gods, showing their devotion without using priests as intermediaries.

The bedrock of Hinduism is the belief that the Vedas are sacred revelations and that a specific caste system is implicitly prescribed in them. Hinduism is a guide to life, the goal of which is to reach union with brahman, the unchanging ultimate reality. There are four steps in this search, progressing from study of the Vedas in youth to complete asceticism in old age. In their quest for brahman, people are to observe **dharma** (DAHR-muh), the moral law. Dharma stipulates the legitimate pursuits of Hindus: material gain, as long as it is honestly and honorably achieved; pleasure and love for the perpetuation of the family; and moksha, release from the wheel of life and unity with brahman. Because it recognizes the need for material gain and plea-sure, Hinduism allows a joyful embracing of life. This certainly was part of its appeal.

Hinduism assumes that there are innumerable legitimate ways of worshipping brahman, including devotion to personal gods. After the third century B.C.E. Hinduism began to emphasize the roles and personalities of thousands of powerful gods. Brahma, the creator; Shiva, the cosmic dancer who both creates and destroys; and Vishnu, the preserver and sustainer of creation, were three of the main male deities. Important female deities included Lakshmi, goddess of wealth, and Saraswati, goddess of learning and music. These gods were usually represented by images, either small ones in homes or larger ones in temples. People could show devotion to their personal gods by reciting hymns or scriptures and by making offerings of food or flowers before these images. A worshipper's devotion to one god did not entail denial of other deities; ultimately all were manifestations of brahman, the ultimate reality. Hinduism's embrace of a large pantheon of gods enabled it to incorporate new sects, doctrines, beliefs, rites, and deities.

A central ethical text of Hinduism is the *Bhagavad Gita* (BAH-guh-vahd GEE-tuh), a part of the world's longest ancient epic, the *Mahabharata*. The *Bhagavad Gita* offers guidance on the most serious problem facing a Hindu — how to live in the world and yet honor dharma and thus achieve release from the wheel of life. The heart of the *Bhagavad Gita* is the spiritual conflict confronting Arjuna, a human hero about to ride into battle against his kinsmen. As he surveys the battlefield, struggling with the grim notion of killing his relatives, Arjuna voices his doubts to his charioteer, none other than the god Krishna. When at last Arjuna refuses to spill his family's blood, Krishna instructs him on the true meaning of Hinduism:

> You grieve for those beyond grief,
> and you speak words of insight;
> but learned men do not grieve
> for the dead or the living.
> Never have I not existed,
> nor you, nor these kings;
> and never in the future
> shall we cease to exist.
> Just as the embodied self
> enters childhood, youth, and old
>   age,
> so does it enter another body;
> this does not confound a steadfast
>   man.
> Contacts with matter make us feel
> heat and cold, pleasure and pain.

The God Vishnu Vishnu is depicted here coming to the rescue of an elephant in the clutches of a crocodile. It comes from the fifth-century-C.E. Dasavatara Temple in Uttar Pradesh. (© akg-images/Jean-Louis Nou/The Image Works)

> Arjuna, you must learn to endure
> fleeting things — they come and go!
> When these cannot torment a man,
> when suffering and joy are equal
> for him and he has courage,
> he is fit for immortality.
> Nothing of nonbeing comes to be,
> nor does being cease to exist;
> the boundary between these two
> is seen by men who see reality.
> Indestructible is the presence
> that pervades all this;
> no one can destroy
> this unchanging reality.
> Our bodies are known to end,
> but the embodied self is enduring,
> indestructible, and immeasurable;
> therefore, Arjuna, fight the battle!
> He who thinks this self a killer
> and he who thinks it killed,
> both fail to understand;
> it does not kill, nor is it killed.
> It is not born,
> it does not die;
> having been,
> it will never not be;
> unborn, enduring,
> constant, and primordial,
> it is not killed
> when the body is killed.[2]

Krishna then clarifies the relationship between human reality and the eternal spirit. He explains compassionately to Arjuna the duty to act — to live in the world and carry out his duties as a warrior. Indeed, the *Bhagavad Gita* emphasizes the necessity of action, which is essential for the welfare of the world. For Arjuna the warrior's duty is to wage war in compliance with his dharma. Only those who live within the divine law without complaint will be released from rebirth. One person's dharma may be different from another's, but both individuals must follow their own dharmas.

Hinduism provided a complex and sophisticated philosophy of life and a religion of enormous emotional appeal that was attractive to ordinary Indians. Over time it grew to be the most common religion in India. Hinduism validated the caste system, adding to the stability of everyday village life, since people all knew where they stood in society. Hinduism also inspired the preservation of literary masterpieces in Sanskrit and the major regional languages of India. Among these are the *Puranas*, which are stories of the gods and great warrior clans, and the *Mahabharata* and *Ramayana*, which are verse epics of India's early kings.

Western Contact and the Mauryan Unification of North India, ca. 513–185 B.C.E.

What was the result of Indian contact with the Persians and Greeks, and what were the consequences of unification under the Mauryan Empire?

In the late sixth century B.C.E., with the creation of the Persian Empire that stretched from the west coast of Anatolia to the Indus River (see pages 53–55), west India was swept up in events that were changing the face of the ancient Near East. A couple of centuries later, by 322 B.C.E., the Greeks had supplanted the Persians in northwest India. Chandragupta saw this as an opportunity to expand his territories, and he successfully unified all of north India. The Mauryan (MAWR-ee-uhn) Empire that he founded flourished under the reign of his grandson, Ashoka, but after Ashoka's death the empire declined.

Encounters with the West

India became involved in the turmoil of the sixth century B.C.E. when the Persian emperor Darius conquered the Indus Valley and Kashmir about 513 B.C.E. Persian control did not reach eastward beyond the Punjab, but even so it fostered increased contact between India and the Near East and led to the introduction of new ideas, techniques, and materials into India. From Persian administrators Indians learned more about how to rule large tracts of land and huge numbers of people. They also learned the technique of minting silver coins, and they adopted the Persian monetary standard to facilitate trade with other parts of the empire. Even states in the Ganges Valley, which were never part of the Persian Empire, adopted the use of coinage.

Another result of contact with Persia was introduction of the Aramaic script, used to write the official language of the Persian Empire. To keep records and publish proclamations just as the Persians did, Indians in northwest India adapted the Aramaic script for writing several local languages (elsewhere, Indians developed the Brahmi script, the ancestor of the script used for modern Hindi). In time the sacred texts of the Buddhists and the Jains, as well as epics and other literary works, came to be recorded using Aramaic script to write down Indian languages.

The Persian Empire in turn succumbed to Alexander the Great, and in 326 B.C.E. Alexander led his Macedonian and Greek troops through the Khyber Pass into the Indus Valley (discussed in Chapter 5 on page 130). The India that Alexander encountered was composed of many rival states. He defeated some of these states in the northwest and heard reports of others. Porus, king of west Punjab, fought Alexander with a battalion of two thousand war elephants. After being defeated, he agreed to become a subordinate king under Alexander.

The Greeks were intrigued by the Indian culture they encountered. Alexander had heard of the sophistication of Indian philosophers and summoned some to instruct him or debate with him. The Greeks were also impressed with Indian cities, most notably Taxila, a major center of trade in the Punjab. The Greeks described it as "a city great and prosperous, the biggest of those between the Indus River and the Hydaspes [the modern Jhelum River]—a region not inferior to Egypt in size, with especially good pastures and rich in fine fruits."[3] From Taxila, Alexander followed

Hellenistic Influences in Gandharan Art
Because Alexander the Great's army had reached Gandhara and Hellenistic states subsequently controlled it for more than a century, the art of this region was strongly influenced by Greek artistic styles. This stucco figure was excavated from a site in eastern Afghanistan where some twenty-three thousand Greco-Buddhist sculptures were found. Hellenistic influence, as evidenced by the drape of the clothing and the modeling of the head, is particularly easy to recognize in this piece. (Erich Lessing/Art Resource, NY)

the Indus River south, hoping to find the end of the world. His men, however, mutinied and refused to continue. When Alexander turned back, he left his general Seleucus (suh-LOO-kuhs) in charge of his easternmost region.

Chandragupta and the Founding of the Mauryan Empire

The one to benefit most from Alexander's invasion was Chandragupta, the ruler of a growing state in the Ganges Valley. He took advantage of the crisis caused by Alexander's invasion to expand his territories, and by 322 B.C.E. he had made himself sole master of north India (Map 3.2). In 304 B.C.E. he defeated the forces of Seleucus.

With stunning effectiveness, Chandragupta applied the lessons learned from Persian rule. He adopted the Persian practice of dividing the area into provinces. Each province was assigned a governor, usually drawn from Chandragupta's own family. He established a complex bureaucracy to see to the operation of the state and a bureaucratic taxation system that financed public services through taxes on agriculture. He also built a regular army, complete with departments for everything from naval matters to the collection of supplies.

For the first time in Indian history, one man governed most of the subcontinent, exercising control through delegated power. From his capital at Pataliputra in the Ganges Valley, Chandragupta sent agents to the provinces to oversee the workings of government and to keep him informed of conditions in his realm. In designing his bureaucratic system, Chandragupta enjoyed the able assistance of his great minister Kautilya, who wrote a treatise called the *Arthashastra* on how a king should seize, hold, and manipulate power, rather like the Legalist treatises produced in China later that century (discussed in Chapter 4 on pages 107–108). Kautilya urged the king to use propaganda to gain support, for instance, to disguise secret agents to look like gods so that people would be awed when they saw him in their company. He stressed the importance of seeking the enemies of his enemies, who would make good allies. When a neighboring prince was in trouble, that was the perfect time to attack him. Interstate relations were likened to the law of the fish: the large swallow the small.

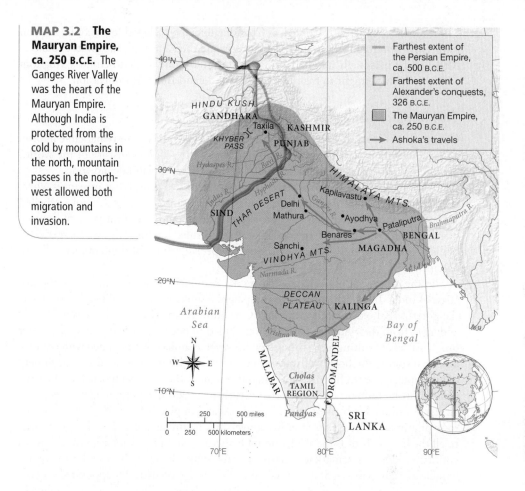

MAP 3.2 The Mauryan Empire, ca. 250 B.C.E. The Ganges River Valley was the heart of the Mauryan Empire. Although India is protected from the cold by mountains in the north, mountain passes in the north-west allowed both migration and invasion.

Megasthenes, a Greek ambassador sent by Seleucus, spent fourteen years in Chandragupta's court. He left a lively description of life there. He described the city as square and surrounded by wooden walls, twenty-two miles on each side, with 570 towers and 64 gates. It had a university, a library, and magnificent palaces, temples, gardens, and parks. The king personally presided over court sessions where legal cases were heard and petitions received. The king claimed for the state all mines and forests, and there were large state farms, granaries, shipyards, and spinning and weaving factories. Even prostitution was controlled by the state. Only a portion of the empire was ruled so directly, according to Megasthenes. In outlying areas, local kings were left in place if they pledged loyalty. Megasthenes described Chandragupta's fear of treachery and assassination attempts:

> Nor does the king sleep during the day, and at night he is forced at various hours to change his bed because of those plotting against him. . . . When he leaves to hunt, he is thickly surrounded by a circle of women, and on the outside by spear-carrying bodyguards. The road is fenced off with ropes, and to anyone who passes within the ropes as far as the women death is the penalty.[4]

Those measures apparently worked, as Chandragupta lived a long life. According to Jain tradition, Chandragupta became a Jain ascetic and died a peaceful death in 298 B.C.E. Although he personally adopted a nonviolent philosophy, he left behind a kingdom with the military might to maintain order and defend India from invasion.

The Reign of Ashoka, ca. 269–232 B.C.E.

Chandragupta's grandson Ashoka proved to be one of India's most remarkable figures. The era of Ashoka was enormously important in the religious history of the world, because Ashoka embraced Buddhism and promoted its spread beyond India.

As a young prince, Ashoka served as governor of two prosperous provinces where Buddhism flourished. At the death of his father about 274 B.C.E., Ashoka rebelled against his older brother, who had succeeded as king, and after four years of fighting won his bid for the throne. Crowned king, Ashoka ruled intelligently and energetically. He was equally serious about his pleasures, especially those of the banquet hall and harem.

In the ninth year of his reign, 261 B.C.E., Ashoka conquered Kalinga, on the east coast of India. In a grim and savage campaign, Ashoka reduced Kalinga by wholesale slaughter. As Ashoka himself admitted, "One hundred and fifty thousand were forcibly abducted from their homes, 100,000 were killed in battle, and many more died later on."[5] Instead of exulting like a conqueror, however, Ashoka was consumed with remorse and revulsion at the horror of war. He embraced Buddhism and used the machinery of his empire to spread Buddhist teachings throughout India. He supported the doctrine of not hurting humans or animals that was then spreading among religious people of all sects in India. He banned animal sacrifices, and in place of hunting expeditions he took pilgrimages. Two years after his conversion, he undertook a 256-day pilgrimage to all the holy sites of Buddhism, and on his return he sent missionaries to all known countries. Ashoka's remarkable crisis of conscience changed the way he ruled. He emphasized compassion, nonviolence, and adherence to dharma. He appointed officials to oversee the moral welfare of the realm and required local officials to govern humanely. He may have perceived dharma as a kind of civic virtue, a universal ethical model capable of uniting the diverse peoples of his extensive empire. Ashoka erected stone pillars, on the Persian model, with inscriptions to inform the people of his policies. He also had long inscriptions carved into large rock surfaces near trade routes. In his last important inscription he spoke of his efforts to encourage his people toward the path of righteousness:

> I have had banyan trees planted on the roads to give shade to man and beast; I have planted mango groves, and I have had ponds dug and shelters erected along the roads at every eight kos. Everywhere I have had wells dug for the benefit of man and beast. But his benefit is but small, for in many ways the kings of olden time have worked for the welfare of the world; but what I have done has been done that men may conform to righteousness.[6]

These inscriptions are the earliest fully dated Indian texts. (Until the script in which they were written was deciphered in 1837, nothing was known of Ashoka's achievements.) The pillars on which they are inscribed are also the first examples of Indian art to survive since the end of the Indus civilization.

The North Gate at Sanchi
This is one of four ornately carved gates guarding the stupa at Sanchi in the state of Madhya Pradesh in India. Containing the relics of the Buddha, this Buddhist memorial shrine was originally commissioned by Ashoka, but the gateways were added later. (Jean-Louis Nou/akg-images)

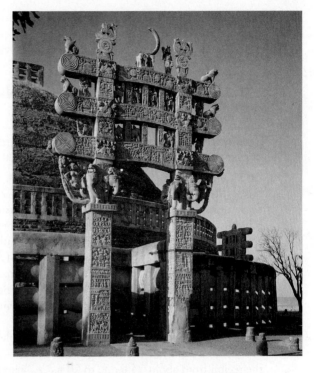

Ashoka felt the need to protect his new religion and to keep it pure. He warned Buddhist monks that he would not tolerate schism — divisions based on differences of opinion about doctrine or ritual. According to Buddhist tradition, a great council of Buddhist monks was held at Pataliputra, where the earliest canon of Buddhist texts was codified. At the same time, Ashoka honored India's other religions, even building shrines for Hindu and Jain worshippers. In one edict he banned rowdy popular fairs, allowing only religious gatherings.

Despite his devotion to Buddhism, Ashoka never neglected his duties as emperor. He tightened the central government of the empire and kept a close check on local officials. He built roads and rest spots to improve communication within the realm. These measures also facilitated the march of armies and the armed enforcement of Ashoka's authority. Ashoka described his work: "Whatever good I have done has indeed been accomplished for the progress and welfare of the world. By these shall grow virtues namely: proper support of mother and father, regard for preceptors and elders, proper treatment of Brahmins and ascetics, of the poor and the destitute, slaves and servants."[7]

Ashoka's inscriptions indirectly tell us much about the **Mauryan Empire**. He directly administered the central part of the empire, focusing on Magadha. Beyond it were four large provinces under princes who served as viceroys, each with its own sets of smaller districts and officials. The interior of south India was described as inhabited by undefeated forest tribes. Farther south, along the coasts, were peoples that Ashoka maintained friendly relations with but did not rule, such as the Cholas and Pandyas. Relations with Sri Lanka were especially close under Ashoka, and the king sent a branch of the tree under which the Buddha gained enlightenment to the Sri Lankan king. According to Buddhist legend, Ashoka's son Mahinda traveled to Sri Lanka to convert the people there.

Ashoka ruled for thirty-seven years. After he died in about 232 B.C.E., the Mauryan Dynasty went into decline, and India broke up into smaller units, much like those in existence before Alexander's invasion. Even though Chandragupta had instituted bureaucratic methods of centralized political control and Ashoka had vigorously pursued the political and cultural integration of the empire, the institutions they created were not entrenched enough to survive periods with weaker kings.

Small States and Trading Networks, 185 B.C.E.–300 C.E.

How was India shaped by political disunity and contacts with other cultures during the five centuries from 185 B.C.E. to 300 C.E.?

After the Mauryan Dynasty collapsed in 185 B.C.E., and for much of subsequent Indian history, political unity would be the exception rather than the rule. By this time, however, key elements of Indian culture—the caste system; the religious traditions of Hinduism, Buddhism, and Jainism; and the great epics and legends—had given India a cultural unity strong enough to endure even without political unity.

In the years after the fall of the Mauryan Dynasty, a series of foreign powers dominated the Indus Valley and adjoining regions. The first were hybrid Indo-Greek states ruled by the inheritors of Alexander's defunct empire stationed in what is now Afghanistan. The city of Taxila became a major center of trade, culture, and education, fusing elements of Greek and Indian culture.

The great, slow movement of nomadic peoples out of East Asia that brought the Scythians to the Near East brought the Shakas to northwest India. They controlled the region from about 94 B.C.E. to 20 B.C.E., when they were displaced by a new nomadic invader, the Kushans, who ruled the region of today's Afghanistan, Pakistan, and west India as far south as Gujarat. Buddhist sources refer to their king Kanishka (r. ca. 78–ca. 103 C.E.) as not only a powerful ruler but also a major patron of Buddhism. The famous silk trade from China to Rome passed through his territory.

During the Kushan period, Greek culture had a considerable impact on Indian art. Indo-Greek artists and sculptors working in India adorned Buddhist shrines, modeling the earliest representation of the Buddha on Hellenistic statues of Apollo. Another contribution from the Indo-Greek states was coin cast with images of the king, which came to be widely adopted by Indian rulers, aiding commerce and adding evidence of rulers' names and sequence to the historical record. Places where coins are found also show patterns of trade.

Cultural exchange also went in the other direction. Old Indian animal folktales were translated into Syriac and Greek and these translated versions eventually made their way to Europe. South India in this period was also the center of active seaborne trade, with networks reaching all the way to Rome. Indian sailing technology was highly advanced, and much of this trade was in the hands of Indian merchants. Roman traders based in Egypt followed the routes already used by Arab traders, sailing with the monsoon from the Red Sea to the west coast of India in about two weeks, and returning about six months later when the direction of the winds reversed. In the first century C.E. a Greek merchant involved in this trade reported that the traders sold coins, topaz, coral, crude glass, copper, tin, and lead and bought pearls, ivory, silk (probably originally from China), jewels of many sorts (probably many from Southeast Asia), and above all cinnamon and pepper. More Roman gold coins of the first and second centuries C.E. have been found near the southern tip of India than in any other area. The local rulers had slits made across the image of the Roman emperor to show that his sovereignty was not recognized, but they had no objection to the coins' circulating. (By contrast, the Kushan rulers in the north had Roman coins melted down to make coins with their own images on them.)

Even after the fall of Rome, many of the traders on the southwest coast of India remained. These scattered communities of Christians and Jews lived in the coastal cities into modern times. When Vasco da Gama, the Portuguese explorer, reached Calicut in 1498, he found a local Jewish merchant who was able to interpret for him.

During these centuries there were significant advances in science, mathematics, and philosophy. Indian astronomers charted the movements of stars and planets and recognized that the earth was spherical. In the realm of physics, Indian scientists, like their Greek counterparts, conceived of matter in terms of five elements: earth, air, fire, water, and ether. This was also the period when Indian law was codified. The *Code of Manu*, which lays down family, caste, and commercial law, was compiled in the second or third century C.E., drawing on older texts.

Regional cultures tend to flourish when there is no dominant unifying state, and the Tamils of south India were one of the major beneficiaries of the collapse of the Mauryan Dynasty. The period from 200 B.C.E. to 200 C.E. is considered the classical period of Tamil culture, when many great works of literature were written under the patronage of the regional kings. Some of the poems written then provide evidence of lively commerce, mentioning bulging warehouses, ships from many lands, and complex import-export procedures. From contact of this sort, the south came to absorb many cultural elements from the north, but also retained differences. Castes were present in the south before contact with the Sanskrit north, but took distinct forms, as the Kshatriya (warrior) and Vaishya (merchant) varnas were hardly known in the far south.

Chapter Summary

Civilization first emerged in the Indus River Valley of India in the third millennium B.C.E. The large cities of this Harappan civilization were carefully planned, with straight streets and sewers; buildings were of kiln-dried brick. Harappan cities were largely abandoned by 1800 B.C.E. for unknown reasons.

A few centuries later, the Aryans, speakers of an early form of the Indo-European language Sanskrit, rose to prominence in north India, marking the beginning of the Vedic Age. Aryan warrior tribes fought using chariots and bronze swords and spears, gradually expanding into the Ganges River Valley. The first stages of the Indian caste system date to this period, when warriors and priests were ranked above merchants, artisans, and farmers. The Vedas document the religious ideas of this age, such as the importance of sacrifice and the notions of karma and rebirth.

Beginning around 500 B.C.E. three of India's major religions emerged. Mahavira, the founder of the Jain religion, taught his followers to live ascetic lives, avoid harming any living thing, and renounce evil thoughts and actions. The founder of Buddhism, Siddhartha Gautama, or the Buddha, similarly taught his followers a path to liberation that involved freeing themselves from desires, avoiding violence, and gaining insight. Hinduism developed in response to the popularity of Jainism and Buddhism, both of which rejected animal sacrifice and ignored the caste system. Hindu traditions validated sacrifice and caste and developed devotional practice, giving individuals a more personal relationship with the gods they worshipped.

From contact with the Persians and Greeks in the sixth century B.C.E. and fourth century B.C.E., respectively, new political techniques, ideas, and art styles and the use of money entered the Indian repertoire. Shortly after the arrival of the Greeks, much of north India was politically unified by the Mauryan Empire under Chandragupta. His grandson Ashoka converted to Buddhism, promoted its spread inside and outside of India, and had stone monuments inscribed with his proclamations.

After the decline of the Mauryan Empire, India was politically fragmented for several centuries. Indian cultural identity remained strong, however, because of shared literature and religious ideas. In the northwest, new nomadic groups, the Shakas and the Kushans, emerged. Cultural interchange was facilitated through trade both overland and by sea.

Notes

1. *Rig Veda 10.90*, in *Sources of Indian Tradition* by Ainslie Thomas Embree, Stephen N. Hay, and William Theodore. Reproduced with permission of COLUMBIA UNIVERSITY PRESS in the format Book via Copyright Clearance Center.
2. Excerpt from Barbara Miller, *The Bhagavad-Gita* (New York: Columbia University Press), pp. 31–32, translation copyright © 1986 by Barbara Stoler Miller. Used by permission of Bantam Books, an imprint of Random House, a division of Random House LLC. All rights reserved. Any third-party use of this material, outside of this publication, is prohibited. Interested parties must apply directly to Random House LLC for permission.
3. Arrian, *Anabasis* 5.8.2; Plutarch, *Alexander* 59.1; trans. John Buckler.
4. *Strabo* 15.1.55, trans. John Buckler.
5. Quoted in H. Kulke and D. Rothermund, *A History of India*, 3d ed. (London: Routledge, 1998), p. 62.
6. Embree et al., *Sources of Indian Tradition*, p. 148. Reproduced with permission of COLUMBIA UNIVERSITY PRESS in the format Book via Copyright Clearance Center.
7. Quoted in B. G. Gokhale, *Asoka Maurya* (New York: Twayne Publishers, 1966), p. 169.

CONNECTIONS

India was a very different place in the third century C.E. than it had been in the early phase of Harappan civilization more than two thousand years earlier. The region was still divided into many different polities, but people living there in 300 shared much more in the way of ideas and traditions. The great epics such as the *Mahabharata* and the *Ramayana* provided a cultural vocabulary for groups that spoke different languages and had rival rulers. New religions had emerged, notably Buddhism and Jainism, and Hinduism was much more a devotional religion. Contact with ancient Mesopotamia, Persia, Greece, and Rome had brought new ideas, practices, and products.

During this same time period, civilization in China underwent similar expansion and diversification. China was farther away than India from other Eurasian centers of civilization, and its developments were consequently not as closely linked. Logographic writing appeared with the Bronze Age Shang civilization and was preserved into modern times, in striking contrast to India and lands to its west, which developed alphabetical writing systems. Still, some developments affected both India and China, such as the appearance of chariots and horseback riding. The next chapter takes up the story of these developments in early China. In Chapter 12, after considering early developments in Europe, Asia, Africa, and the Americas, we return to the story of India.

Chapter Review

MAKE IT STICK

 LearningCurve
Go online and use LearningCurve to retain what you've read.

IDENTIFY KEY TERMS

Identify and explain the significance of each item below.

Harappan (p. 62)

Aryans (p. 64)

Rig Veda (p. 65)

Brahmins (p. 66)

caste system (p. 66)

samsara (p. 68)

karma (p. 68)

brahman (p. 68)

Jainism (p. 69)

Four Noble Truths (p. 70)

Eightfold Path (p. 70)

Mahayana (p. 74)

bodhisattvas (p. 74)

dharma (p. 74)

Mauryan Empire (p. 81)

Code of Manu (p. 83)

REVIEW THE MAIN IDEAS

Answer the focus questions from each section of the chapter.

1. What does archaeology tell us about the Harappan civilization in India? (p. 61)

2. What kind of society and culture did the Indo-European Aryans create? (p. 64)

3. What ideas and practices were taught by the founders of Jainism, Buddhism, and Hinduism? (p. 69)

4. What was the result of Indian contact with the Persians and Greeks, and what were the consequences of unification under the Mauryan Empire? (p. 77)

5. How was India shaped by political disunity and contacts with other cultures during the five centuries from 185 B.C.E. to 300 C.E.? (p. 82)

MAKE CONNECTIONS

Analyze the larger developments and continuities within and across chapters.

1. In what ways did ancient India follow patterns of development similar to those seen elsewhere?

2. What are the similarities and differences between the religious ideas and practices of early India and those that emerged in the Nile River Valley and southwest Asia?

3. How was the development of India's material culture affected by developments elsewhere?

LaunchPad
ONLINE DOCUMENT PROJECT

Accessible Enlightenment
What made Buddhism accessible to everyone?

Read a selection of Buddhist parables, and then complete a quiz and writing assignment based on the evidence and details from this chapter.

See inside the front cover to learn more.

CHRONOLOGY

2800–2000 B.C.E.	• Height of Harappan civilization
ca. 1500–500 B.C.E.	• Vedic Age; flourishing of Aryan civilization; *Rig Veda*
ca. 1000 B.C.E.	• Introduction of iron
750–500 B.C.E.	• *Upanishads*
ca. 513 B.C.E.	• Persians conquer the Indus Valley and Kashmir
ca. 500 B.C.E.	• Founding of Buddhism and Jainism
ca. 400 B.C.E.–200 C.E.	• Gradual evolution of the Brahmanic religion into Hinduism
326 B.C.E.	• Alexander the Great enters Indus Valley
ca. 322–185 B.C.E.	• Mauryan Empire
ca. 300 B.C.E.	• Jain religion splits into two sects
ca. 269–232 B.C.E.	• Reign of Ashoka
ca. 150 B.C.E.–250 C.E.	• Classical period of Tamil culture
ca. 100 C.E.	• More inclusive Mahayana form of Buddhism emerges
ca. 200 C.E.	• *Code of Manu*

4

✓ LearningCurve
After reading the chapter, go online and use LearningCurve to retain what you've read.

China's Classical Age

TO 221 B.C.E.

IN COMPARISON TO INDIA AND MESOPOTAMIA, CHINA
developed in relative isolation. Communication with West and South Asia was very difficult, impeded by high mountains and vast deserts. Though there was some trade, the distances were so great that they did not allow the kind of cross-fertilization that occurred in western Eurasia. Moreover, there were no cultural breaks comparable to the rise of the Aryans in India or the Assyrians in Mesopotamia to introduce new peoples and languages. The impact of early China's relative isolation is found in many distinctive features of its culture. Perhaps the most important is its writing system; unlike the other major societies of Eurasia, China retained a logographic writing system with a symbol for each word. This writing system shaped not only Chinese literature and thought but also key social and political processes, such as the nature of the ruling class and interactions with non-Chinese peoples.

Chinese history is commonly discussed in terms of a succession of dynasties. The Shang Dynasty (ca. 1500–1050 B.C.E.) was the first to have writing, metalworking, cities, and chariots. The Shang kings played priestly roles, serving as intermediaries with both their royal ancestors and the high god Di. The Shang were overthrown by one of their vassal states, which founded the Zhou Dynasty (ca. 1050–256 B.C.E.). The Zhou rulers set up a decentralized feudal governmental structure that evolved over centuries into a multistate system. As warfare between the states intensified in the sixth century B.C.E., social and cultural change quickened. Aristocratic privileges declined, and China entered one of its most creative periods, when the philosophies of Confucianism, Daoism, and Legalism were developed.

87

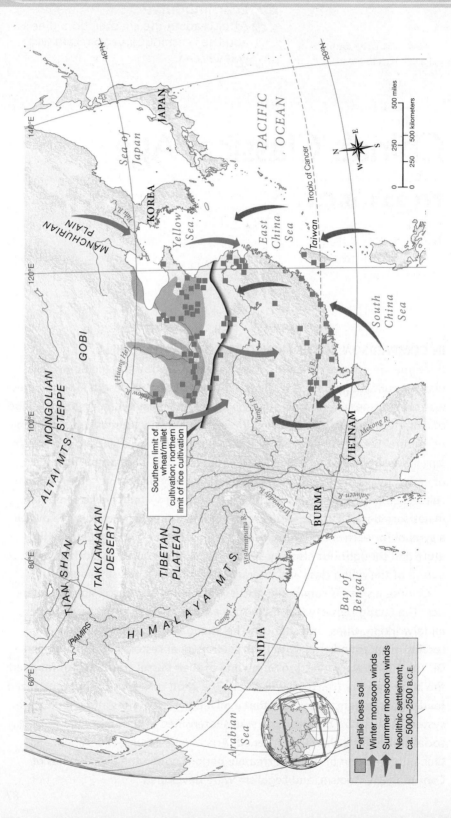

Southern limit of wheat/millet cultivation; northern limit of rice cultivation

PACIFIC OCEAN

Tropic of Cancer

JAPAN

Sea of Japan

KOREA

Yalu R.

MANCHURIAN PLAIN

Yellow Sea

East China Sea

Taiwan

South China Sea

GOBI

MONGOLIAN STEPPE

ALTAI MTS.

(Huang He)

Yellow R.

Yangzi R.

Xi R.

VIETNAM

Mekong R.

TIAN SHAN

TAKLAMAKAN DESERT

TIBETAN PLATEAU

BURMA

Salween R.

Irrawaddy R.

Brahmaputra R.

HIMALAYA MTS.

Ganges R.

PAMIRS

INDIA

Bay of Bengal

Arabian Sea

N E S W

500 miles
250
500 kilometers
250
0
0

Fertile loess soil
Winter monsoon winds
Summer monsoon winds
Neolithic settlement, ca. 5000–2500 B.C.E.

◀ **MAP 4.1** **The Geography of Historical China** Chinese civilization developed in the temperate regions drained by the Yellow and Yangzi Rivers.

The Emergence of Civilization in China

What was the impact of China's geography on the development of Chinese societies?

The term *China*, like the term *India*, does not refer to the same geographical entity at all points in history. The historical China, also called China proper, was smaller than present-day China, not larger like the historical India. The contemporary People's Republic of China includes Tibet, Inner Mongolia, Turkestan, Manchuria, and other territories that in premodern times were neither inhabited by Chinese nor ruled directly by Chinese states.

The Impact of Geography

As in most areas of the world, the geography of the region has had an impact on the development of Chinese civilization from ancient times to the present. China proper, about a thousand miles north to south and east to west, occupies much of the temperate zone of East Asia (Map 4.1). The northern part, drained by the Yellow River, is colder, flatter, and more arid than the south. Rainfall in many areas is less than twenty inches a year, making the land well suited to crops like wheat and millet. The dominant soil is loess—fine wind-driven earth that is fertile and easy to work even with simple tools. The soil gives the Yellow River its characteristic color, and because so much of the loess ends up as silt in the river, the riverbed rises and easily floods unless diked. Drought is another perennial problem for farmers in the north. The Yangzi (YANG-zuh) River is the dominant feature of the warmer, wetter, and more lush south, a region well suited to rice cultivation. Farmers in recent centuries have been able to get two rice crops a year from the land around the Yangzi River and farther south. The Yangzi and its many tributaries are navigable, so boats were traditionally the preferred means of transportation in the south.

Mountains, deserts, and grasslands separated China proper from other early civilizations. Between China and India lay Tibet, with its vast mountain ranges and high plateaus. North of Tibet are great expanses of desert where nothing grows except in rare oases, and north of the desert, grasslands stretch from Ukraine to eastern Siberia. Chinese civilization did not spread into any of these Inner Asian regions, above all because they were not suited to growing crops. Inner Asia, where raising animals is a more productive use of land than planting crops, became the heartland of China's traditional enemies, such as the nomadic tribes of the Xiongnu (SHUHNG-noo) and Mongols.

Early Agricultural Societies of the Neolithic Age

From about 10,000 B.C.E. agriculture was practiced in China. It apparently originated independently of somewhat earlier developments in Egypt and Mesopotamia but was perhaps influenced by developments in Southeast Asia, where rice was also cultivated

Neolithic Jade Plaque   This small plaque (2½ inches by 3¼ inches), dating from about 2000 B.C.E., is similar to others of the Liangzhu area near modern Shanghai. It is incised to depict a human figure that merges into a monster mask. The lower part could be interpreted as his arms and legs but at the same time resembles a monster mask with bulging eyes, prominent nostrils, and a large mouth. (Zhejiang Provincial Institute of Cultural Relics and Archeology/Uniphoto Press, Japan/ Ancient Art & Architecture Collection, Ltd.)

very early. By 5000 B.C.E. there were Neolithic village settlements in several regions of China. The primary Neolithic crops were drought-resistant millet, grown in the loess soils of the north, and rice, grown in the wetlands of the lower reaches of the Yangzi River, where inhabitants supplemented their diet with fish. In both areas pigs, dogs, and cattle were domesticated, and by 3000 B.C.E. sheep had become important in the north and water buffalo in the south. Silk production can also be traced back to this period.

Over the course of the fifth to third millennia B.C.E., many distinct regional Neolithic cultures emerged. One such culture emerged in the northwest during the fourth and third millennia B.C.E. These people are known for their fine red pottery vessels decorated in black pigment with bold designs, including spirals, sawtooth lines, and zoomorphic stick figures. At the same time in the east, a different culture made pottery that was rarely painted but had distinctive shapes, including three-legged, deep-bodied tripods. Jade ornaments, blades, and ritual objects, sometimes of extraordinary craftsmanship, have been found in several eastern sites but are rare in western ones.

These Neolithic societies left no written records, but we know from the material record that over time they came to share more social and cultural practices. Many practices related to the treatment of the dead spread to other groups from their original area, including use of coffins, large numbers of grave goods, and divination aimed at communicating with ancestors or gods based on interpreting cracks in cattle bones. Fortified walls made of rammed earth were built around settlements in many places, suggesting not only increased contact between Neolithic societies but also increased conflict. (For more on life in Neolithic societies, see Chapter 1.)

The Shang Dynasty, ca. 1500–1050 B.C.E.

What was life like during the Shang Dynasty, and what effect did writing have on Chinese culture and government?

Archaeological evidence indicates that after 2000 B.C.E. a Bronze Age civilization appeared in north China that shared traits with Bronze Age civilizations elsewhere in Eurasia, such as Mesopotamia, Egypt, and Greece. These traits included writing, metalworking, domestication of the horse, class stratification, and cult centers. The archaeological findings are linked to the Shang Dynasty, long known from early texts.

Shang Society

Shang civilization was not as densely urban as that of Mesopotamia, but Shang kings ruled from large settlements (Map 4.2). The best excavated is **Anyang**, from which the Shang kings ruled for more than two centuries. At the center of Anyang were large palaces, temples, and altars. These buildings were constructed on rammed-earth foundations (a feature of Chinese building practice that would last for centuries). Outside the central core were industrial areas where bronzeworkers, potters, stone carvers, and other artisans lived and worked. Many homes were built partly below ground level, probably as a way to conserve heat. Beyond these urban settlements were farming areas and large forests. Deer, bears, tigers, wild boars, elephants, and rhinoceros were still plentiful in north China in this era.

Texts found in the Shang royal tombs at Anyang show that Shang kings were military chieftains. The king regularly sent out armies of three thousand to five thousand men on campaigns, and when not at war they would go on hunts lasting for months. They fought rebellious vassals and foreign tribes, but the situation constantly changed as vassals became enemies and enemies accepted offers of alliance. War booty was an important source of the king's revenue, especially the war captives who could be made into slaves. Captives not needed as slaves might end up as sacrificial victims—or perhaps the demands of the gods and ancestors for sacrifices were a motive for going to war.

Bronze-tipped spears and battle axes were widely used by Shang warriors, giving them an advantage over less technologically advanced groups. Bronze was also used for the fittings of the chariots that came into use around 1200 B.C.E. Chariot technology apparently spread by diffusion across Asia, passing from one society to the next. The chariot provided commanders with mobile stations from which they could supervise their troops; it also gave archers and soldiers armed with long battle axes increased mobility.

MAP 4.2 The Shang and Early Zhou Dynasties, ca. 1500–400 B.C.E. The early Zhou government controlled larger areas than the Shang did, but the independent states of the Warring States Period were more aggressive about pushing out their frontiers, greatly extending the geographical boundaries of Chinese civilization.

Royal Burials at Anyang   Eleven large tombs and more than a thousand small graves have been excavated at the royal burial ground at Anyang. In 2005 seven pits were discovered in which horses and chariots had been buried to accompany a king in the afterlife. (© CHINA NEWSPHOTO/ Reuters/Corbis)

Shang power did not rest solely on military supremacy. The Shang king was also the high priest, the one best qualified to offer sacrifices to the royal ancestors and the high god Di. Royal ancestors were viewed as able to intervene with Di, send curses, produce dreams, assist the king in battle, and so on. The king divined his ancestors' wishes by interpreting the cracks made in heated cattle bones or tortoise shells prepared for him by professional diviners.

The Shang royal family and aristocracy lived in large houses built on huge platforms of rammed earth similar to those used in the Neolithic period. Shang palaces were undoubtedly splendid but were constructed of perishable material like wood, and nothing of them remains today, giving China none of the ancient stone buildings and monuments so characteristic of the West. What has survived are the lavish underground tombs built for Shang kings and their consorts.

The one royal tomb not robbed before it was excavated was for Lady Hao, one of the many wives of the king Wu Ding (ca. 1200 B.C.E.). The tomb was filled with almost 500 bronze vessels and weapons, over 700 jade and ivory ornaments, and 16 people who would tend to Lady Hao in the afterlife. Human sacrifice did not occur only at funerals. Inscribed bones report sacrifices of war captives in the dozens and hundreds. Some of those buried with kings were not sacrificial victims but followers or servants. The bodies of people who voluntarily followed their ruler to the grave were generally buried with their own ornaments and grave goods such as weapons.

Shang society was marked by sharp status distinctions. The king and other noble families had family and clan names transmitted along patrilineal lines, from father to son. Kingship similarly passed along patrilineal lines, from elder to younger brother and from father to son, but never to or through sisters or daughters. The kings and the aristocrats owned slaves, many of whom had been captured in war. In the urban centers there were substantial numbers of craftsmen who worked in stone, bone, and bronze.

Shang farmers were obligated to work for their lords (making them essentially serfs). Their lives were not that different from the lives of their Neolithic ancestors, and they worked the fields with similar stone tools. They usually lived in small, compact villages surrounded by fields. Some new crops became common in Shang times, most notably wheat, which had spread from western Asia. Farmers probably also raised silkworms, from whose cocoons fine silk garments could be made for the ruling elite.

Bronze Metalworking

As in Egypt, Mesopotamia, and India, the development of more complex forms of social organization in Shang China coincided with the mastery of metalworking, specifically bronze. The bronze industry required the coordination of a large labor force and skilled artisans. Bronze was used more for ritual than for war in Shang times. Most surviving Shang bronze objects are vessels such as cups, goblets, steamers, and cauldrons that would have originally been used during sacrificial ceremonies. They were beautifully formed in a great variety of shapes and sizes.

The decoration on Shang bronzes seems to say something interesting about Shang culture, but scholars do not agree about what that is. In the art of ancient Egypt, Assyria, and Babylonia, representations of agriculture (domesticated plants and animals) and of social hierarchy (kings, priests, scribes, and slaves) are very common, matching our understandings of the social, political, and economic development of those societies. In Shang China, by contrast, images of wild animals predominate. Some animal images readily suggest possible meanings. Jade cicadas were sometimes found in the mouths of the dead, and images of cicadas on bronzes are easy to interpret as images evocative of rebirth in the realm of ancestral spirits, as cicadas spend years underground before emerging. Birds, similarly, suggest to many the idea of messengers that can communicate with other realms, especially realms in the sky. More problematic is the most common image, the stylized animal face called the **taotie** (taow-tyeh). To some it is a monster—a fearsome image that would scare away evil forces. Others imagine a dragon—an animal whose vast powers had more positive associations. Some hypothesize that it reflects masks used in rituals. Others associate it with animal sacrifices, totemism, or shamanism. Still others see these images as hardly more than designs. Without new evidence, scholars can only speculate.

Bronze technology spread beyond Shang territories into areas the Shang would have considered enemy lands. In 1986, in the western province of Sichuan, discovery was made of a bronze-producing culture contemporaneous with the late Shang but very different from it. Two sacrificial pits contained the burned remains of elephant tusks and a wide range of gold, bronze, jade, and stone objects. Among them were life-size statues and many life-size bronze heads, all with angular facial features and enormous eyes. No human sacrifices were found, leading some scholars to speculate that the masks were used to top wood or clay statues buried in place of humans in a sacrificial ceremony. Archaeologists are continuing to excavate in this region, and new discoveries are gradually providing fuller understanding of the religion of the people who lived there.

The Development of Writing

The survival of divination texts inscribed on bones from Shang tombs demonstrates that writing was already a major element in Chinese culture by 1200 B.C.E. Writing must have been developed earlier, but the early stages cannot be traced, probably because writing was done on wood, bamboo, silk, or other perishable materials.

WORD	ox	goat, sheep	tree	moon	earth
SHANG SYMBOL					
MODERN CHARACTER	牛	羊	木	月	土

WORD	water	to show, declare	then (men and bowl)	heaven	to pray
SHANG SYMBOL					
MODERN CHARACTER	水	示	就	天	祝

FIGURE 4.1 The Origins of Chinese Writing The modern Chinese writing system (bottom row) evolved from the script employed by diviners in the Shang period (top row). (Source: Adapted from Patricia Buckley Ebrey, *The Cambridge Illustrated History of China* [Cambridge: Cambridge University Press, 1996], p. 26. Reprinted by permission of Cambridge University Press.)

The invention of writing had profound effects on China's culture and government. A written language made possible a bureaucracy capable of keeping records and corresponding with commanders and governors far from the palace. Hence literacy became the ally of royal rule, facilitating control over a wide realm. Literacy also preserved the learning, lore, and experience of early Chinese society and facilitated the development of abstract thought.

Like ancient Egyptian and Sumerian scripts, the Chinese script was **logographic**: each word was represented by a single symbol. In the Chinese case, some of the symbols were pictures, but for the names of abstract concepts other methods were adopted. Sometimes the symbol for a different word was borrowed because the two words were pronounced alike. Sometimes two different symbols were combined; for instance, to represent different types of trees, the symbol for "tree" could be combined with another symbol borrowed for its pronunciation (Figure 4.1).

In western Eurasia logographic scripts were eventually modified or replaced by phonetic scripts, but that never happened in China (although, because of changes in the spoken language, today many words are represented by two or three characters rather than a single one). Because China retained its logographic writing system, many years were required to gain full mastery of reading and writing, which added to the prestige of education.

Why did China retain a logographic writing system even after encounters with phonetic ones? Although phonetic systems have many real advantages, especially with respect to ease of learning to read, there are some costs to dropping a logographic system. Since characters did not change when the pronunciation changed, educated Chinese could read texts written centuries earlier without the need for translation.

Moreover, as the Chinese language developed regional variants, readers of Chinese could read books and letters by contemporaries whose oral language they could not comprehend. Thus the Chinese script played a large role in holding China together and fostering a sense of connection with the past. In addition, many of China's neighbors (Japan, Korea, and Vietnam, in particular) adopted the Chinese script, allowing communication through writing between people whose languages were totally unrelated. In this regard, Chinese characters were like Arabic numerals, which have the same meaning however they are pronounced (Table 4.1).

TABLE 4.1 Pronouncing Chinese Words

Phonetic equivalents for the vowels and especially perplexing consonants are given here.

LETTER	PHONETIC EQUIVALENT IN CHINESE
a	ah
e	uh
i	ee; except after *z*, *c*, and *ch*, when the sound is closer to *i* in *it*
u	oo; as in English *food*
c	ts (*ch*, however, is like English *ch*)
q	ch
z	dz
zh	j
x	sh

The Early Zhou Dynasty, ca. 1050–400 B.C.E.

How was China governed, and what was life like during the Zhou Dynasty?

The Shang campaigned constantly against enemies in all directions. To the west of the Shang were the fierce Qiang (chyang), considered barbarian tribesmen by the Shang and perhaps speaking an early form of Tibetan. Between the Shang capital and the Qiang were the Zhou (joe), who seem to have both inherited cultural traditions from the Neolithic cultures of the northwest and absorbed most of the material culture of the Shang. In about 1050 B.C.E. the Zhou rose against the Shang and defeated them in battle. Their successors maintained the cultural and political advances that the Shang rulers had introduced.

Zhou Politics

The early Zhou period is the first one for which transmitted texts exist in some abundance. The *Book of Documents* (ca. 900 B.C.E.) describes the Zhou conquest of the Shang as the victory of just and noble warriors over decadent courtiers led by an irresponsible and sadistic king. These documents also show that the Zhou recognized the Shang as occupying the center of the known world, were eager to succeed them in that role, and saw history as a major way to legitimate power.

Like the Shang kings, the Zhou kings sacrificed to their ancestors, but they also sacrificed to Heaven. The *Book of Documents* assumes a close relationship between Heaven and the king, who was called the Son of Heaven. According to the documents, Heaven gives the king a mandate to rule only as long as he rules in the interests of the people. Because the last king of the Shang had been decadent and cruel, Heaven took the mandate away from him and entrusted it to the virtuous Zhou kings. Because this theory of the **Mandate of Heaven** does not seem to have had any place in Shang cosmology, it may have been developed by the early Zhou rulers as a kind of propaganda

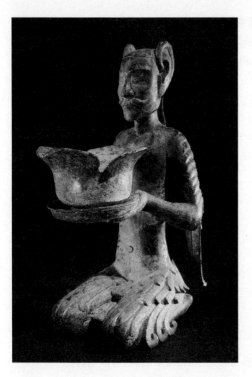

Winged Immortal   Less than 8 inches tall, this bronze candelabra is in the shape of an immortal. Those who mastered the secrets of not dying were thought to be able to fly through the heavens. (Werner Forman/akg-images)

to win over the former subjects of the Shang. Whatever its origins, it remained a central feature of Chinese political ideology from the early Zhou period on.

Rather than attempt to rule all their territories directly, the early Zhou rulers set up a decentralized feudal system. They sent relatives and trusted subordinates with troops to establish walled garrisons in the conquered territories. Such a vassal was generally able to pass his position on to a son, so that in time the domains became hereditary. By 800 B.C.E. there were about two hundred lords with domains large and small. Each lord appointed officers to serve him in ritual, administrative, or military capacities. These posts and their associated titles tended to become hereditary as well.

The decentralized rule of the early Zhou period carried within it the danger that the regional lords would become so powerful that they would no longer obey the commands of the king. As generations passed and ties of loyalty and kinship grew more distant, this happened. In 771 B.C.E. the Zhou king was killed by an alliance of non-Chinese tribesmen and Zhou vassals. One of his sons was put on the throne, and then for safety's sake the capital was moved east out of the Wei River Valley to modern Luoyang, just south of the Yellow River in the heart of the central plains (see Map 4.2, page 91).

The revived Zhou Dynasty never fully regained control over its vassals, and China entered a prolonged period without a strong central authority. For a few centuries a code of chivalrous or sportsmanlike conduct still regulated warfare between the states: one state would not attack another that was in mourning for its ruler; during battles one side would not attack before the other side had time to line up; ruling houses were not wiped out, so that successors could continue to sacrifice to their ancestors; and so on. Thereafter, however, such niceties were abandoned, and China entered a period of nearly constant conflict.

Life During the Zhou Dynasty

During the early Zhou period, aristocratic attitudes and privileges were strong. Inherited ranks placed people in a hierarchy ranging downward from the king to the rulers of states with titles like duke and marquis, to the hereditary great officials of the states, to the lower ranks of the aristocracy — men who could serve in either military or civil capacities, known as shi — and finally to the ordinary people (farmers, craftsmen, and traders). Patrilineal family ties were very important in this society, and at the upper reaches, at least, sacrifices to ancestors were one of the key rituals used to forge social ties.

Glimpses of what life was like at various social levels in the early Zhou Dynasty can be found in the *Book of Songs* (ca. 900 B.C.E.), which contains the earliest Chinese poetry. Some of the songs are hymns used in court religious ceremonies, such as offerings to ancestors. Others clearly had their origins in folk songs. The seasons set the pace for rural life, and the songs contain many references to seasonal changes, such as the appearance of insects like grasshoppers and crickets. Some of these songs depict farmers clearing fields, plowing and planting, gathering mulberry leaves for silkworms, and spinning and weaving. Farming life involved not merely cultivating crops like millet, hemp (for cloth), beans, and vegetables but also hunting small animals and collecting grasses and rushes to make rope and baskets.

Many of the folk songs are love songs that depict a more informal pattern of courtship than the one that prevailed in later China. One stanza reads:

> Please, Zhongzi,
> Do not leap over our wall,
> Do not break our mulberry trees.
> It's not that I begrudge the mulberries,
> But I fear my brothers.
> You I would embrace,
> But my brothers' words—those I dread.[1]

There were also songs of complaint, such as this one in which the ancestors are rebuked for failing to aid their descendants:

> The drought has become so severe
> That it cannot be stopped.
> Glowing and burning,
> We have no place.
> The great mandate is about at an end.
> Nothing to look forward to or back upon.
> The host of dukes and past rulers
> Does not help us.
> As for father and mother and the ancestors,
> How can they bear to treat us so?[2]

Other songs in this collection are court odes that reveal attitudes of the aristocrats. One such ode expresses a deep distrust of women's involvement in politics:

> Clever men build cities,
> Clever women topple them.
> Beautiful, these clever women may be
> But they are owls and kites.
> Women have long tongues
> That lead to ruin.
> Disorder does not come down from heaven;
> It is produced by women.[3]

Part of the reason for distrust of women in politics was the practice of concubinage. Rulers regularly demonstrated their power and wealth by accumulating large numbers of concubines (legal spouses who ranked lower than the wife) and by having children by several women. In theory, succession went to the eldest son of the wife, then to younger sons by her, and only in their absence to sons of concubines; but in actual practice, the ruler of a state or the head of a powerful ministerial family could select a son of a concubine to be his heir if he wished. This led to much scheming for favor among the various sons and their mothers and the common perception that women were incapable of taking a disinterested view of the larger good.

Social and economic change quickened after 500 B.C.E. Cities began appearing all over north China. Thick earthen walls were built around the palaces and ancestral temples of the ruler and other aristocrats, and often an outer wall was added to protect the artisans, merchants, and farmers who lived outside the inner wall. Accounts of sieges launched against these walled citadels, with scenes of the scaling of walls and the storming of gates, are central to descriptions of military confrontations in this period.

The development of iron technology in the early Zhou Dynasty promoted economic expansion and allowed some people to become very rich. By the fifth century B.C.E. iron was being widely used for both farm tools and weapons. In the early Zhou, inherited status and political favor had been the main reasons some people had more power than others. Beginning in the fifth century wealth alone was also an important basis for social inequality. Late Zhou texts frequently mention trade across state borders in goods such as furs, copper, dyes, hemp, salt, and horses. People who grew wealthy from trade or industry began to rival rulers for influence. Rulers who wanted trade to bring prosperity to their states welcomed traders and began making coins to facilitate trade.

Social mobility increased over the course of the Zhou period. Rulers often sent out their own officials rather than delegate authority to hereditary lesser lords. This trend toward centralized bureaucratic control created opportunities for social advancement for the shi on the lower end of the old aristocracy. Competition among such men guaranteed rulers a ready supply of able and willing subordinates, and competition among rulers for talent meant that ambitious men could be selective in deciding where to offer their services. (See "Individuals in Society: Lord Mengchang," page 100.)

Religion in Zhou times was not simply a continuation of Shang practices. The practice of burying the living with the dead—so prominent in the royal tombs of the Shang—steadily declined in the middle Zhou period. Still, a ruler who died in 433 B.C.E. had his female musicians buried with him, evidence that some rulers still had their servants accompany them in death. The musicians and their instruments also testify to the role that music played in court entertainment. New deities and cults also appeared, especially in the southern state of Chu, where areas that had earlier been considered barbarian were being incorporated into the cultural sphere of the Central States, as the core region of China was called. The state of Chu expanded rapidly in the Yangzi Valley, defeating and absorbing fifty or more small states as it extended its reach north to the heartland of Zhou and east to absorb the old states of Wu and Yue. By the late Zhou period, Chu was on the forefront of cultural innovation and produced the greatest literary masterpiece of the era, the *Songs of Chu*, a collection of fantastical poems full of images of elusive deities and shamans who can fly through the spirit world. Images found in Chu tombs, painted on coffins or pieces of silk, show both fearsome deities and spirit journeys.

The Warring States Period, 403–221 B.C.E.

How did advances in military technology contribute to the rise of independent states?

By 400 B.C.E. advances in military technology were undermining the old aristocratic social structure of the Zhou. Large, well-drilled infantry armies able to withstand and defeat chariot-led forces became potent military forces in the **Warring States Period**, which lasted from 403 B.C.E. to 221 B.C.E. Fueled by the development of new weaponry and war tactics, the Chinese states destroyed each other one by one until only one state was left standing—the state of Qin (chin). In response to the human and economic costs of war, rulers sought ways to increase population and expand trade even while they destroyed one another.

New Technologies for War

By 300 B.C.E. states were sending out armies of a few hundred thousand drafted foot soldiers, usually accompanied by horsemen. Adding to their effectiveness was the development of the **crossbow** around 350 B.C.E. The intricate bronze trigger of the crossbow allowed a foot soldier to shoot farther than could a horseman carrying a light bow. One text of the period reports that a skilled soldier with a powerful crossbow and a sharp sword was the match of a hundred ordinary men. To defend against crossbows, soldiers began wearing armor and helmets. Most of the armor was made of leather strips tied with cords. Helmets were sometimes made of iron.

The introduction of cavalry in this period further reduced the need for a chariot-riding aristocracy. Shooting bows and arrows from horseback was first perfected by non-Chinese peoples to the north of China proper, who at that time were making the transition to a nomadic pastoral economy. The northern state of Jin developed its own cavalry to defend itself from the attacks of these horsemen. Once it started using cavalry against other Chinese states, they too had to master the new technology. From this time on, acquiring and pasturing horses was a key component of military preparedness.

Because of these developments, rulers wanted to increase their populations, to have more commoners to serve as foot soldiers and more craftsmen to supply more weapons. To increase agricultural output, they brought new land into cultivation, drained marshes, and dug irrigation channels. Rulers began surveying their land and taxing farmers. They wanted to undermine the power of lords over their subjects in order to get direct access to the peasants' labor power. Serfdom thus gradually declined. Registering populations led to the extension of family names to commoners at an earlier date than anywhere else in the world.

The development of infantry armies also created the need for a new type of general, and rulers became less willing to let men lead troops merely because of aristocratic birth. In *The Art of War* (453–403 B.C.E.), Sun Wu described the ideal general as a master of maneuver, illusion, and deception. He argued that heroism is a useless virtue that leads to needless deaths. Discipline, however, is essential, and he insisted that the

INDIVIDUALS IN SOCIETY • Lord Mengchang

During the Warring States Period, men could rise to high rank on the basis of talent. Lord Mengchang rose on the basis of his people skills: he treated his retainers so well that he attracted thousands of talented men to his service, enabling him to rise to prime minister of his native state of Qi (chee) in the early third century B.C.E.

Lord Mengchang's beginnings were not promising. His father, a member of the Qi royal family, already had more than forty sons when Mengchang was born, and he ordered the mother, one of his many concubines, to leave the baby to die. She, however, secretly reared him, and while still a child he was able to win his father's approval through his cleverness.

At his father's death Mengchang succeeded him. Because Mengchang would provide room and board to men who sought to serve him, he soon attracted a few thousand retainers, many of humble background, some fleeing justice. Every night, we are told, he ate with them all in his hall, treating them equally no matter what their social origins.

Most of the stories about Mengchang revolve around retainers who solved his problems in clever ways. Once, when Mengchang had been sent as an envoy to Qin, the king of Qin was persuaded not to let so talented a minister return to help Qi. Under house arrest, Mengchang was able to ask one of the king's consorts to help him, but in exchange she wanted a fur coat kept in the king's treasury. A former thief among Mengchang's retainers stole it for him, and Mengchang was soon on his way. By the time he reached the barrier gate, Qin soldiers were pursuing him, and he knew that he had to get through quickly. One of his retainers imitated the crowing of a cock, which got the other cocks to crow, making the guards think it was dawn, so they opened the gates and let his party through.

When Mengchang served as prime minister of Qi, his retainers came up with many clever stratagems that convinced the nearby states of Wei and Han to join Qi in resisting Qin. Several times, one of his retainers of modest origins, Feng Xuan (schwan), helped Mengchang withstand the political vicissitudes of the day. When sent to collect debts owed to Mengchang in his fief of Xue, Feng Xuan instead forgave all the debts of those too poor to repay their loans. Later, when Lord Mengchang lost his post at court and returned to his fief, most of his retainers

entire army had to be trained to follow the orders of its commanders without questioning them. He also explicitly called for use of deceit:

> War is the Way of deceit. Thus one who is competent pretends to be incompetent; one who uses [his army] pretends not to use it; one who draws near pretends to be distant; one who is distant pretends to draw near. If [the enemy desires] some advantage, entice him [with it]. If he is in disorder, seize him. If he is substantial, be prepared for him. If he is strong, evade him. If he is enraged, irritate him [further]. If he is humble, make him haughty. If he is rested, make him toil. If he is intimate [with his ranks], separate them. Attack where he does not expect it and go where he has not imagined. This is how military experts are victorious.[4]

deserted him, but he found himself well loved by the local residents, all because of Feng Xuan's generosity in his name. After Mengchang reattained his court post and was traveling back to Qi, he complained to Feng Xuan about those who had deserted him. Feng Xuan, we are told, got down from the carriage and bowed to Lord Mengchang, and when pressed said that the lord should accept the retainers' departures as part of the natural order of things:

> Wealth and honor attract while poverty and lowliness repel; such is the nature of things. Think of it like the market. In the morning it is crowded and in the evening it is deserted. This is not because people prefer the morning to the evening, but rather because what they want can not be found there [in the evening]. Do not let the fact that your retainers left when you lost your position lead you to bar them from returning. I hope that you will treat them just the way you did before.*

QUESTIONS FOR ANALYSIS

1. How did Mengchang attract his many retainers, and how did their service benefit him?
2. Who in this story benefited from hereditary privilege, and who advanced because of ability? What does this suggest about social mobility during the Warring States Period?
3. Many of the stories about Mengchang are included in *Intrigues of the Warring States*, a book that Confucians disapproved of. What do you think they found objectionable?

Shi ji 75.2362. Translated by Patricia Ebrey.

LaunchPad
ONLINE DOCUMENT PROJECT

How did rulers and their subordinates interact during the Warring States Period? Read a selection of stories from the Warring States Period, and then complete a quiz and writing assignment based on the evidence and details from this chapter.

See inside the front cover to learn more.

The Victorious States

During the Warring States Period, states on the periphery of the Zhou realm had more room to expand than states in the center. With access to more resources, they were able to pick off their neighbors, one after the other. Still, for two centuries the final outcome was far from clear, as alliances among states were regularly made and nearly as regularly broken.

By the third century B.C.E. there were only seven important states remaining. These states were much more centralized than their early Zhou predecessors. Their kings had eliminated indirect control through vassals and in their place dispatched royal officials to remote cities, controlling them from a distance through the transmission of documents and dismissing them at will. Before the end of the third century B.C.E. one state, Qin, conquered all of the others, a development discussed in Chapter 7.

Confucius and His Followers

What ideas did Confucius teach, and how were they spread after his death?

The Warring States Period was the golden age of Chinese philosophy, the era when the "Hundred Schools of Thought" contended. During the same period in which Indian sages and mystics were developing religious speculation about karma, souls, and ultimate reality (see Chapter 3), Chinese thinkers were arguing about the ideal forms of social and political organization and man's connections to nature.

Confucius

Confucius (traditional dates: 551–479 B.C.E.) was one of the first men of ideas. As a young man, he had served in the court of his home state of Lu without gaining much influence. After leaving Lu, he set out with a small band of students and wandered through neighboring states in search of a ruler who would take his advice. We know what he taught from the *Analects*, a collection of his sayings put together by his followers after his death.

The thrust of Confucius's thought was ethical rather than theoretical or metaphysical. He talked repeatedly of an ideal age in the early Zhou Dynasty when everyone was devoted to fulfilling his or her role: superiors looked after those dependent on them; inferiors devoted themselves to the service of their superiors; parents and children, husbands and wives all wholeheartedly embraced what was expected of them. Confucius saw five relationships as the basis of society: between ruler and subject; between father and son; between husband and wife; between elder brother and younger brother; and between friend and friend. Mutual obligations of a hierarchical sort underlay the first four of these relationships — the senior leads and protects; the junior supports and obeys. The exception was the relationship between friends, which was conceived in terms of mutual obligations between equals.

A man of moderation, Confucius was an earnest advocate of gentlemanly conduct. He redefined the term *gentleman* (*junzi*) to mean a man of moral cultivation rather than a man of noble birth. He repeatedly urged his followers to aspire to be gentlemen rather than petty men intent on personal gain. Confucius did not advocate social equality, but his teachings minimized the importance of class distinctions and opened the way for intelligent and talented people to rise in the social scale. The Confucian gentleman found his calling in service to the ruler. Loyal advisers should encourage their rulers to govern through ritual, virtue, and concern for the welfare of their subjects, and much of the *Analects* concerns the way to govern well. To Confucius the ultimate virtue was **ren** (humanity). A person of humanity cares about others and acts accordingly:

> [The disciple] Zhonggong asked about humanity. Confucius said, "When you go out, treat everyone as if you were welcoming a great guest. Employ people as though you were conducting a great sacrifice. Do not do unto others what you would not have them do unto you. Then neither in your country nor in your family will there be complaints against you."[5]

In the Confucian tradition, studying texts came to be valued over speculation, meditation, and mystical identification with deities. Confucius encouraged the men who came to study with him to master the poetry, rituals, and historical traditions that we know today as Confucian classics.

The Spread of Confucian Ideas

The eventual success of Confucian ideas owes much to Confucius's followers in the three centuries following his death. The most important of them were Mencius (ca. 370–300 B.C.E.) and Xunzi (ca. 310–215 B.C.E.).

Mencius, like Confucius, traveled around offering advice to rulers of various states. Over and over he tried to convert them to the view that the ruler able to win over the people through benevolent government would succeed in unifying "all under Heaven." Mencius proposed concrete political and financial measures to ease tax burdens and otherwise improve the people's lot. Men willing to serve an unworthy ruler earned his contempt, especially when they worked hard to fill the ruler's coffers or expand his territory. In one conversation, the king of Qi asked if it was true that the founder of the Zhou Dynasty had taken up arms against his lord, the last king of Shang. Mencius replied that that was what the histories said. The king then asked, "Then is it permissible for a subject to assassinate his lord?" Mencius replied:

> Someone who does violence to the good we call a villain; someone who does violence to the right we call a criminal. A person who is both a villain and a criminal we call a scoundrel. I have heard that the scoundrel Zhou [the last Shang king] was killed, but have not heard that a lord was killed.[6]

With his disciples and fellow philosophers, Mencius also discussed other issues in moral philosophy, arguing strongly, for instance, that human nature is fundamentally good, as everyone is born with the capacity to recognize what is right and act on it. Anyone who saw a baby about to fall into a well would immediately come to its rescue. This would not be "because he wanted to improve his relations with the child's parents, nor because he wanted a good reputation among his friends and neighbors, nor because he disliked hearing the child cry."[7] Rather it would be because he has an inborn feeling of commiseration from which other virtues can grow.

Xunzi, a half century later, took the opposite view of human nature, arguing that people are born selfish and that only through education and ritual do they learn to put moral principle above their own interest. Much of what is desirable is not inborn but must be taught:

> When a son yields to his father, or a younger brother yields to his elder brother, or when a son takes on the work for his father or a younger brother for his elder brother, their actions go against their natures and run counter to their feelings. And yet these are the way of the filial son and the principles of ritual and morality.[8]

Neither Confucius nor Mencius had had much actual political or administrative experience, but Xunzi had worked for many years in the court of his home state. Not surprisingly, he showed more consideration than either Confucius or Mencius for the difficulties a ruler might face in trying to rule through ritual and virtue. Xunzi was also a more rigorous thinker than his predecessors and developed the philosophical

Serving Parents with Filial Piety   This twelfth-century-C.E. illustration of a passage in the *Classic of Filial Piety* shows how commoners should serve their parents: by working hard at productive jobs such as farming and tending to their parents' daily needs. The married son and daughter-in-law offer food or drink to the older couple as their own children look on, thus learning how they should treat their own parents after they become aged. (National Palace Museum, Taiwan/The Art Archive at Art Resource, NY)

foundations of many ideas merely outlined by Confucius and Mencius. Confucius, for instance, had declined to discuss gods, portents, and anomalies and had spoken of sacrificing as if the spirits were present. Xunzi went further and explicitly argued that Heaven does not intervene in human affairs.

Still, Xunzi did not propose abandoning traditional rituals. In contrast to Daoists (discussed in the next section), who saw rituals as unnatural or extravagant, Xunzi saw them as an efficient way to attain order in society. Rulers and educated men should continue traditional ritual practices such as complex funeral protocols because the rites themselves have positive effects on performers and observers. Not only do they let people express feelings and satisfy desires in an orderly way, but because they specify graduated ways to perform the rites according to social rank, ritual traditions sustain the social hierarchy. Xunzi compared and contrasted ritual and music: music shapes people's emotions and creates feelings of solidarity, while ritual shapes people's sense of duty and creates social differentiation.

The Confucian vision of personal ethics and public service found a small but ardent following during the Warring States Period. In later centuries rulers came to see men educated in Confucian virtues as ideal advisers and officials. Neither revolutionaries nor flatterers, Confucian scholar-officials opposed bad government and upheld the best ideals of statecraft. Confucian political ideals shaped Chinese society into the twentieth century.

The Confucian vision also provided a moral basis for the Chinese family that continues into modern times. Repaying parents and ancestors came to be seen as a sacred duty. Because people owe their very existence to their parents, they should reciprocate by respecting their parents, making efforts to please them, honoring their memories, and placing the interests of the family line above personal preferences, all of which were aspects of **filial piety**. Since the family line is a patrilineal line from father to son to grandson, placing great importance on it has had the effect of devaluing women.

Daoism, Legalism, and Other Schools of Thought

How did the teachings of Daoism, Legalism, and other schools of thought differ from Confucianism?

During the Warring States Period, rulers took advantage of the destruction of states to recruit newly unemployed men to serve as their advisers and court assistants. Lively debate often resulted as these strategists proposed policies and refuted opponents. Followers took to recording their teachers' ideas, and the circulation of these "books" (rolls of silk, or strips of wood or bamboo tied together) served to stimulate further debate.

Many of these schools of thought directly opposed the ideas of Confucius and his followers. Most notable were the Daoists, who believed that the act of striving to improve society only made it worse, and the Legalists, who argued that a strong government depended not so much on moral leadership as on effective laws and procedures.

Daoism

Confucius and his followers believed in moral action. They thought men of virtue should devote themselves to making the government work to the benefit of the people. Those who came to be labeled Daoists disagreed. They thought striving to make things better generally made them worse. Daoists defended private life and wanted the rulers to leave the people alone. They sought to go beyond everyday concerns and to let their minds wander freely. Rather than making human beings and human actions the center of concern, they focused on the larger scheme of things, the whole natural order identified as the Way, or **Dao**.

Early Daoist teachings are known from two surviving books, the *Laozi* and the *Zhuangzi*, both dating to the third century B.C.E. Laozi, the putative author of the *Laozi*, may not be a historical figure, but the text ascribed to him has been of enduring importance. A recurrent theme in this brief, aphoristic text is the mystical superiority of yielding over assertion and silence over words: "The Way that can be discussed is not the constant Way."[9] The highest good is like water: "Water benefits all creatures but does not compete. It occupies the places people disdain and thus comes near to the Way."[10]

Because purposeful action is counterproductive, the ruler should let people return to a natural state of ignorance and contentment:

> Do not honor the worthy,
> And the people will not compete.
> Do not value rare treasures,
> And the people will not steal.

> Do not display what others want,
> And the people will not have their hearts confused.
> A sage governs this way:
> He empties people's minds and fills their bellies.
> He weakens their wills and strengthens their bones.
> Keep the people always without knowledge and without desires,
> For then the clever will not dare act.
> Engage in no action and order will prevail.[11]

In the philosophy of the *Laozi*, the people would be better off if they knew less, gave up tools, renounced writing, stopped envying their neighbors, and lost their desire to travel or engage in war.

Zhuangzi (369–286 B.C.E.), the author of the book of the same name, shared many of the central ideas of the *Laozi*. He was proud of his disinterest in politics. In one of his many anecdotes, he reported that the king of Chu once sent an envoy to invite him to take over the government of his realm. In response Zhuangzi asked the envoy whether a tortoise that had been held as sacred for three thousand years would prefer to be dead with its bones venerated or alive with its tail dragging in the mud. When the envoy agreed that life was preferable, Zhuangzi told the envoy to leave. He preferred to drag his tail in the mud.

The *Zhuangzi* is filled with parables, flights of fancy, and fictional encounters between historical figures, including Confucius and his disciples. A more serious strain of Zhuangzi's thought concerned death. He questioned whether we can be sure life is better than death. People fear what they do not know, the same way a captive girl will be terrified when she learns she is to become the king's concubine. Perhaps people will discover that death has as many delights as life in the palace.

When a friend expressed shock that Zhuangzi was not weeping at his wife's death but rather singing, Zhuangzi explained:

> When she first died, how could I have escaped feeling the loss? Then I looked back to the beginning before she had life. Not only before she had life, but before she had form. Not only before she had form, but before she had vital energy. In this confused amorphous realm, something changed and vital energy appeared; when the vital energy was changed, form appeared; with changes in form, life began. Now there is another change bringing death. This is like the progression of the four seasons of spring and fall, winter and summer. Here she was lying down to sleep in a huge room and I followed her, sobbing and wailing. When I realized my actions showed I hadn't understood destiny, I stopped.[12]

Zhuangzi was similarly iconoclastic in his political philosophy. In one parable a wheelwright insolently tells a duke that books are useless because all they contain are the dregs of men long dead. The duke, offended, threatens execution unless the wheelwright can explain his remark. The wheelwright replies:

> I see things in terms of my own work. When I chisel at a wheel, if I go slow, the chisel slides and does not stay put; if I hurry, it jams and doesn't move properly. When it is

neither too slow nor too fast, I can feel it in my hand and respond to it from my heart. My mouth cannot describe it in words, but there is something there. I cannot teach it to my son, and my son cannot learn it from me. So I have gone on for seventy years, growing old chiseling wheels. The men of old died in possession of what they could not transmit. So it follows that what you are reading are their dregs.[13]

To put this another way, truly skilled craftsmen respond to situations spontaneously; they do not analyze or reason or even keep in mind the rules they have mastered. This strain of Daoist thought denies the validity of verbal reasoning and the sorts of knowledge conveyed through words.

Daoism can be seen as a response to Confucianism, a rejection of many of its basic premises. Nevertheless, over the course of Chinese history, many people felt the pull of both Confucian and Daoist ideas and studied the writings of both schools. Even Confucian scholars who had devoted much of their lives to public service might find that the teachings of the *Laozi* or *Zhuangzi* helped to put their frustrations in perspective. Whereas Confucianism often seems sternly masculine, Daoism is more accepting of feminine principles and even celebrates passivity and yielding. Those drawn to the arts were also often drawn to Daoism, with its validation of spontaneity and freedom. Rulers, too, were drawn to the Daoist notion of the ruler who can have great power simply by being himself without instituting anything.

Legalism

Over the course of the fourth and third centuries B.C.E., one small state after another was conquered, and the number of surviving states dwindled. Rulers fearful that their states might be next were ready to listen to political theorists who claimed expertise in the accumulation of power. These theorists, labeled **Legalists** because of their emphasis on the need for rigorous laws, argued that strong government depended not on the moral qualities of the ruler and his officials, as Confucians claimed, but on establishing effective laws and procedures. Legalism, though eventually discredited, laid the basis for China's later bureaucratic government.

In the fourth century B.C.E. the state of Qin radically reformed itself along Legalist lines. The king of Qin abolished the aristocracy. Social distinctions were to be based on military ranks determined by the objective criterion of the number of enemy heads cut off in battle. In place of the old fiefs, the Qin king created counties and appointed officials to govern them according to the laws he decreed at court. To increase the population, Qin recruited migrants from other states with offers of land and houses. To encourage farmers to work hard and improve their land, they were allowed to buy and sell it. Ordinary farmers were thus freed from serf-like obligations to the local nobility, but direct control by the state could be even more onerous. Taxes and labor service obligations were heavy. Travel required a permit, and vagrants could be forced into penal labor service. All families were grouped into mutual responsibility groups of five and ten families; whenever anyone in the group committed a crime, all the others were equally liable unless they reported it.

Legalism found its greatest exponent in Han Feizi (ca. 280–233 B.C.E.), who had studied with the Confucian master Xunzi but had little interest in Confucian values of goodness or ritual. In his writings he warned rulers of the political pitfalls awaiting them. They had to be careful where they placed their trust, for "when the ruler trusts someone, he falls under that person's control."[14] This is true even of wives and concubines, who think of the interests of their sons. Given subordinates' propensities to pursue their own selfish interests, the ruler should keep them ignorant of his intentions and control them by manipulating competition among them. Warmth, affection, or candor should have no place in his relationships with others.

Han Feizi saw the Confucian notion that government could be based on virtue as naive. Even parents, he argued, treat their sons and daughters differently based on their assessment of long-term advantage. That is, they celebrate when a son is born, because he will be able to continue the family, but are dejected when a daughter is born, since she will eventually leave. In Han Feizi's view, it is unrealistic to expect people with no close kinship tie to treat each other more altruistically than parents treat their children. If rulers would make the laws and prohibitions clear and the rewards and punishments automatic, then the officials and common people would be easy to govern. Uniform laws get people to do things they would not otherwise be inclined to do, such as work hard and fight wars; such laws are thus essential to the goal of establishing hegemony over all the other states.

The laws of the Legalists were designed as much to constrain officials as to regulate the common people. The third-century-B.C.E. tomb of a Qin official has yielded statutes detailing the rules for keeping accounts, supervising subordinates, managing penal labor, conducting investigations, and many other responsibilities of officials. Infractions were generally punishable through the imposition of fines.

Legalism saw no value in intellectual debate or private opinion. Divergent views of right and wrong lead to weakness and disorder. The ruler should not allow others to undermine his laws by questioning them. In Legalism, there were no laws above or independent of the wishes of the rulers, no laws that might set limits on rulers' actions in the way that natural or divine laws did in Greek thought (see Chapter 5).

Rulers of several states adopted some Legalist ideas, but only the state of Qin systematically followed them. The extraordinary but brief success Qin had with these policies is discussed in Chapter 7.

Yin and Yang

Confucians, Daoists, and Legalists had the greatest long-term impact on Chinese civilization, but the Hundred Schools of Thought also included everyone from logicians, hedonists, and utopians to natural philosophers who analyzed the workings of nature.

A key idea developed by the natural philosophers was the concept of **yin and yang**, first described in the divination manual called the *Book of Changes* (ca. 900 B.C.E.), and developed into much more elaborate theories by late Zhou theorists. Yin is the feminine, dark, receptive, yielding, negative, and weak; yang is the masculine, bright, assertive, creative, positive, and strong. Yin and yang are complementary poles rather than distinct entities or opposing forces. The movement of yin and yang accounts for the transition from day to night and from summer to winter. These models based on observation of nature were extended to explain not only phenomena we might classify as natural, such as illness, storms, and earthquakes, but also social

Phoenix and Tigers Divine animals, such as dragons and phoenixes, are often portrayed in the art of the Warring States Period, especially in the south, where the art of lacquered wood was perfected. (Werner Forman/akg-images)

phenomena, such as the rise and fall of states and conflict in families. In all these realms, unwanted things happen when the balance between yin and yang gets disturbed.

In recent decades archaeologists have further complicated our understanding of early Chinese thought by unearthing records of the popular religion of the time—astrological manuals, handbooks of lucky and unlucky days, medical prescriptions, exercises, and ghost stories. The tomb of an official who died in 316 B.C.E., for example, has records of divinations showing that illness was seen as the result of unsatisfied spirits or malevolent demons, best dealt with through performing exorcisms or offering sacrifices to the astral god Taiyi (Grand One).

Chapter Summary

After several thousand years of Neolithic cultures, beginning after 2000 B.C.E., Bronze Age civilization developed in China, with cities, writing, and sharp social distinctions. Shang kings led armies and presided at sacrifices to the high god Di and the imperial ancestors. The Shang armies' bronze-tipped weapons and chariots gave them technological superiority over their neighbors. War booty, including slaves who were often sacrificed to the gods, provided the Shang king with revenue.

The Zhou Dynasty, which overthrew the Shang in about 1050 B.C.E., parceled out its territory to hereditary lords. The earliest Chinese books date to this period. The *Book of Documents* provides evidence of the belief in the Mandate of Heaven, which justified Zhou rule. Because the last Shang king had not ruled in the interests of the people, Heaven took the mandate away from him and conferred it on a worthier person. The *Book of Songs* offers glimpses into what life was like for elites and ordinary people alike in the early Zhou.

By the Warring States Period, which began in 403 B.C.E., the old domains had become independent states. As states destroyed each other, military technology made many advances, including the introduction of cavalry, infantry armies, and the crossbow. Despite its name, the Warring States Period was the golden age of Chinese philosophy. Confucius and his followers promoted the virtues of sincerity, loyalty, benevolence, filial piety, and duty. Mencius urged rulers to rule through goodness and argued that human nature is good. Xunzi stressed the power of ritual and argued that human nature is selfish and must be curbed through education. Daoists and Legalists rejected all these ideas. The Daoists Laozi and Zhuangzi looked beyond the human realm to the entire cosmos and spoke of the relativity of concepts such as good and bad and life and death. Legalists heaped ridicule on the Confucian idea that a ruler could get his people to be good by being good himself and proposed instead rigorous laws with strict rewards and punishments. Natural philosophers explained the changes of seasons and health and illness in terms of the complementary forces of yin and yang.

Notes

1. Reprinted with the permission of Simon & Schuster Publishing Group from the Free Press edition of *Chinese Civilization: A Sourcebook*, 2nd Edition, by Patricia Buckley Ebrey, p. 11. Copyright © 1993 by Patricia Buckley Ebrey. All rights reserved.
2. Edward Shaughnessy, "Western Zhou History," in *The Cambridge History of Ancient China*, ed. M. Loewe and E. Shaughnessy (New York: Cambridge University Press, 1999), p. 336. Reprinted with the permission of Cambridge University Press.
3. Patricia Buckley Ebrey, *Cambridge Illustrated History of China* (Cambridge: Cambridge University Press, 1996), p. 34.
4. Victor H. Mair, Nancy S. Steinhardt, and Paul Goldin, ed., *Hawai'i Reader in Traditional Chinese Culture* (Honolulu: University of Hawai'i Press, 2005), p. 117.
5. Reprinted with the permission of Simon & Schuster Publishing Group from Ebrey, *Chinese Civilization*, p. 19.
6. Reprinted with the permission of Simon & Schuster Publishing Group from ibid., p. 23.
7. Reprinted with the permission of Simon & Schuster Publishing Group from ibid.
8. Reprinted with the permission of Simon & Schuster Publishing Group from ibid., p. 26.
9. Reprinted with the permission of Simon & Schuster Publishing Group from ibid., p. 27.
10. Reprinted with the permission of Simon & Schuster Publishing Group from ibid., p. 28, modified.
11. Reprinted with the permission of Simon & Schuster Publishing Group from ibid., p. 28.
12. Reprinted with the permission of Simon & Schuster Publishing Group from ibid., p. 31.
13. Reprinted with the permission of Simon & Schuster Publishing Group from ibid.
14. Reprinted with the permission of Simon & Schuster Publishing Group from ibid, p. 33.

CONNECTIONS

China's transition from Neolithic farming villages to a much more advanced civilization with writing, metalworking, iron coinage, crossbows, philosophical speculation, and competing states occurred centuries later than in Mesopotamia or India, but by the Warring States Period China was at much the same stage of development as other advanced societies in Eurasia. Although many elements of China's civilization were clearly invented in China—such as its writing system, its method of casting bronze, and its Confucian philosophy—it also adopted elements that diffused across Asia, such as the cultivation of wheat, the horse-driven chariot, and riding horseback.

Greece, the subject of the next chapter, is located very close to the ancient Near Eastern civilizations, so its trajectory was quite different from China's. It was also much smaller than China, yet in time had enormous impact on the wider world. With India and China in mind, the originality of the political forms and ideas of early Greece will stand out more clearly. We return to China's history in Chapter 7, after looking at Greece and Rome.

Chapter Review

MAKE IT STICK

 LearningCurve
Go online and use LearningCurve to retain what you've read.

IDENTIFY KEY TERMS

Identify and explain the significance of each item below.

loess (p. 89)	**Mandate of Heaven**	**crossbow** (p. 99)
Anyang (p. 91)	(p. 95)	**ren** (p. 102)
taotie (p. 93)	**shi** (p. 96)	**filial piety** (p. 105)
logographic (p. 94)	***Book of Songs*** (p. 97)	**Dao** (p. 105)
Book of Documents	**Warring States Period**	**Legalists** (p. 107)
(p. 95)	(p. 99)	**yin and yang** (p. 108)

REVIEW THE MAIN IDEAS

Answer the focus questions from each section of the chapter.

1. What was the impact of China's geography on the development of Chinese societies? (p. 89)
2. What was life like during the Shang Dynasty, and what effect did writing have on Chinese culture and government? (p. 90)
3. How was China governed, and what was life like during the Zhou Dynasty? (p. 95)
4. How did advances in military technology contribute to the rise of independent states? (p. 99)
5. What ideas did Confucius teach, and how were they spread after his death? (p. 102)
6. How did the teachings of Daoism, Legalism, and other schools of thought differ from Confucianism? (p. 105)

MAKE CONNECTIONS

Analyze the larger developments and continuities within and across chapters.

1. Which features of early China's history seem closest to developments in other early civilizations, such as Mesopotamia, Egypt, and India?
2. Why do we refer to the ideas developed in India in the second half of the first millennium B.C.E. as religion and those developed in China as philosophy? Is this a useful distinction? Why or why not?

⊳LaunchPad

ONLINE DOCUMENT PROJECT

The Limits of Loyalty

How did rulers and their subordinates interact during the Warring States Period?

Read a selection of stories from the Warring States Period, and then complete a quiz and writing assignment based on the evidence and details from this chapter.

See inside the front cover to learn more.

CHRONOLOGY

ca. 5000 B.C.E.	• Emergence of regional Neolithic settlements
ca. 1500–1050 B.C.E.	• Shang Dynasty
ca. 1200 B.C.E.	• Evidence of writing found in royal tombs; chariots come into use
ca. 1050–256 B.C.E.	• Zhou Dynasty
ca. 900 B.C.E.	• *Book of Songs, Book of Changes, Book of Documents*
551–479 B.C.E.	• Confucius
ca. 500 B.C.E.	• Iron technology in wide use; cities spread across the central Zhou states
500–200 B.C.E.	• Golden age of Chinese philosophy
453–403 B.C.E.	• *The Art of War*
403–221 B.C.E.	• Warring States Period; decline of the Zhou Dynasty
ca. 370–300 B.C.E.	• Mencius
ca. 350 B.C.E.	• Infantry armed with crossbows
ca. 310–215 B.C.E.	• Xunzi
ca. 300–200 B.C.E.	• Early Daoist teachings outlined in the *Laozi* and the *Zhuangzi*

5

✓ LearningCurve
After reading the chapter, go online
and use LearningCurve to retain what
you've read.

The Greek Experience

3500–30 B.C.E.

HUMANS CAME INTO GREECE OVER MANY THOUSANDS OF YEARS,
in waves of migrants whose place of origin and cultural characteristics have
been the source of much scholarly debate. The people of ancient Greece built
on the traditions and ideas of earlier societies to develop a culture that fundamentally shaped the civilization of the western part of Eurasia much as
the Chinese culture shaped the civilization of the eastern part. The Greeks
were the first in the Mediterranean and neighboring areas to explore many
of the questions about the world around them and the place of humans
in it that continue to concern thinkers today. Drawing on their day-to-day
experiences as well as logic and empirical observation, they developed ways
of understanding and explaining the world around them, which grew into
modern philosophy and science. They also created new political forms and
new types of literature and art.

Historians, archaeologists, and classicists divide the history of the Greeks
into three broad periods: the Helladic period, which covered the Bronze Age,
roughly 3000 B.C.E. to 1200 B.C.E.; the Hellenic period, from the Bronze Age
Collapse to the conquest of Greece by Macedonia in 338 B.C.E.; and the Hellenistic period, stretching from the death of Alexander the Great, the ruler of
Macedonia, in 323 B.C.E. to the Roman conquest in 30 B.C.E. of the kingdom
established in Egypt by Alexander's successors. During the Hellenic period,
Greeks developed a distinctive form of city-state known as the polis and
made lasting cultural and intellectual achievements. During the Hellenistic
period, Macedonian and Greek armies defeated the Persian Empire and
built new cities and kingdoms, spreading Greek ideas as far as India (see
Chapter 3). During their conquests they blended their ideas and traditions
with those of the societies they encountered, creating a vibrant culture.

Greece in the Bronze Age, ca. 3000–800 B.C.E.

How did the geography of Greece shape its earliest history?

Hellas, as the Greeks call their land, encompasses the Greek peninsula with its southern peninsular extension, known as the Peloponnesus (peh-luh-puh-NEE-suhs), and the islands surrounding it, an area known as the Aegean (ah-JEE-uhn) basin (Map 5.1). In ancient times this basin included the Greek settlements in Ionia, the western coast of the area known as Anatolia in modern western Turkey. During the Bronze Age, which for Greek history is called the "Helladic period," early settlers in Greece began establishing small communities contoured by the mountains and small plains that shaped the land. The geographical fragmentation of Greece encouraged political fragmentation. Early in Greek history several kingdoms did emerge—the Minoan on the island of Crete and the Mycenaean on the mainland—but the rugged terrain prohibited

MAP 5.1 Classical Greece, ca. 450 B.C.E. In antiquity the home of the Greeks included the islands of the Aegean and the western shore of Turkey as well as the Greek peninsula itself. Crete, the home of Minoan civilization, is the large island at the bottom of the map. The Peloponnesian peninsula, where Sparta is located, is connected to the rest of mainland Greece by a very narrow isthmus at Corinth.

the growth of a great empire like those of Mesopotamia and Egypt. The Minoan and Mycenaean societies flourished for centuries until the Bronze Age Collapse, when Greece entered a period of decline known as the Dark Age (ca. 1100–800 B.C.E.).

The Minoans and Mycenaeans

On the large island of Crete, Bronze Age farmers and fishermen began to trade their surpluses with their neighbors, and cities grew, housing artisans and merchants. Beginning about 2000 B.C.E. Cretans voyaged throughout the eastern Mediterranean and the Aegean, carrying the copper and tin needed to make bronze as well as many other goods. Social hierarchies developed, and in many cities certain individuals came to hold power, although exactly how this happened is not clear. The Cretans began to use writing about 1900 B.C.E., in a form later scholars called Linear A, but this script has not been deciphered. What we can know about the culture of Crete thus depends on archaeological and artistic evidence, and of this there is a great deal. At about the same time that writing began, rulers in several cities of Crete began to build large structures with hundreds of interconnected rooms. The largest of these, at Knossos (NOH-suhs), has over a thousand rooms along with pipes for bringing in drinking water and sewers to get rid of waste. The archaeologists who discovered these huge structures called them palaces, and they named the flourishing and vibrant culture of this era Minoan, after the mythical king of Crete, Minos.

Few specifics are known about Minoan political life except that a king and a group of nobles stood at its head. Minoan society was long thought to have been relatively peaceful, but new excavations are revealing more and more walls around cities, which has called the peaceful nature of Minoan society into question, although there is no doubt that it was wealthy. In terms of their religious life, Minoans appear to have worshipped goddesses far more than gods. Whether this translated into more egalitarian gender roles for real people is unclear, but surviving Minoan art, including frescoes and figurines, shows women as well as men leading religious activities, watching entertainment, and engaging in athletic competitions, such as leaping over bulls.

Beginning about 1700 B.C.E. Minoan society was disrupted by a series of earthquakes and volcanic eruptions on nearby islands, some of which resulted in large tsunamis. But new settlements and palaces were often built following these disasters.

As Minoan culture was flourishing on Crete, a different type of society developed on the mainland. This society was founded by groups who had migrated in during the period after 2000 B.C.E., and its members spoke an early form of Greek. By about 1650 B.C.E. one group of these immigrants had raised palaces and established cities at Thebes, Athens, Mycenae (migh-SEE-nee), and elsewhere. These palace-centers ruled by local kings formed a loose hegemony under the authority of the king of Mycenae, and the archaeologists who first discovered traces of this culture called it the Mycenaean (migh-see-NEE-ahn).

As in Crete, the political unit was the kingdom, and the king and his warrior aristocracy stood at the top of society. The seat and symbol of the king's power was his palace, which was also the economic center of the kingdom. Within the palace's walls, royal artisans fashioned gold jewelry and rich ornaments, made and decorated fine pottery, forged weapons, prepared hides and wool for clothing, and manufactured the other goods needed by the king and his supporters.

Mycenaean Dagger Blade   This scene in gold and silver on the blade of an iron dagger depicts hunters armed with spears and protected by shields defending themselves against charging lions. The Mycenaeans were a robust, warlike people who enjoyed the thrill and the danger of hunting. (From the Royal Tomb IV, Mycenae, found by H. Schliemann. National Archeological Museum, Athens, Greece/Ancient Art & Architecture Collection, Ltd./The Bridgeman Art Library)

Palace scribes kept records with a script known as Linear B, which has been deciphered, so that information on Mycenaean culture comes from inscriptions and other forms of written records as well as buildings and other objects. All of these point to a society in which war was common. Mycenaean cities were all fortified by thick stone walls, and graves contain spears, javelins, swords, helmets, and the first examples of metal armor known in the world.

Contacts between the Minoans and Mycenaeans were originally peaceful, and Minoan culture and trade goods flooded the Greek mainland. But most scholars think that around 1450 B.C.E., possibly in the wake of an earthquake that left Crete vulnerable, the Mycenaeans attacked Crete, destroying many towns and occupying Knossos. For about the next fifty years, the Mycenaeans ruled much of the island. The palaces at Knossos and other cities of the Aegean became grander as wealth gained through trade and tribute flowed into the treasuries of various Mycenaean kings. Prosperity, however, did not bring peace, and between about 1300 B.C.E. and 1000 B.C.E. various kingdoms in and beyond Greece fought one another in a savage series of wars that destroyed both the Minoan and Mycenaean civilizations.

The fall of the Minoans and Mycenaeans was part of what some scholars see as a general collapse of Bronze Age civilizations in the eastern Mediterranean, including the end of the Egyptian New Kingdom and the fall of the Hittite Empire (see Chapter 2). This collapse appears to have had a number of causes: internal economic and social problems, including perhaps slave revolts; invasions and migrations by outsiders, who destroyed cities and disrupted trade and production; changes in warfare and weaponry, particularly the adoption of iron weapons, which made foot soldiers the most important factor in battles and reduced the power of kings and wealthy nobles fighting from chariots; and natural disasters such as volcanic eruptions, earthquakes, and droughts, which reduced the amount of food and contributed to famines.

The "Dark Age"

In Greece these invasions, migrations, disasters, and social problems worked together to usher in a period of poverty and disruption that historians have traditionally called the "Dark Age" of Greece (ca. 1100–800 B.C.E.). Cities were destroyed, population declined, villages were abandoned, and trade decreased. Pottery became simpler, and jewelry and other grave goods became less ornate. Even writing, which was not widespread before this period, was a casualty of the chaos.

The Bronze Age Collapse led to the widespread and prolonged movement of Greek peoples, both within Greece itself and beyond. They dispersed beyond mainland Greece farther south to the islands of the Aegean Sea and in greater strength across the Aegean to the shores of Anatolia (see Map 5.1), arriving at a time when traditional states and empires had collapsed. By the conclusion of the Dark Age, the Greeks had spread their culture throughout the Aegean basin, and like many other cultures around the Mediterranean and the Near East, they had adopted iron.

Archaeological sources from the Dark Age are less rich than those from the periods that came after, so they are often used in conjunction with literary sources written in later centuries to give us a more complete picture of the era. These included tales of the heroic deeds of legendary heroes similar to the epic poems of Mesopotamia and the *Ramayana* in India. Sometime in the eighth or seventh century B.C.E. many of these were gathered together in two long epic poems: the *Iliad*, which tells the story of the Trojan War, a war similar to those fought by Mycenaean kings, and the *Odyssey*, which records the adventures of one of the heroes of that war. These poems were recited orally, and once writing was reintroduced to Greece, they were written down and attributed to a poet named Homer, though scholars debate whether Homer was an actual historical individual. The two poems present human and divine characters who are larger than life but also petty, vindictive, pouting, and deceitful, flaws that drive the action forward, usually with tragic results. The heart of the *Iliad* concerns the quarrel between the Mycenaean king, Agamemnon, and the stormy hero of the poem, Achilles (uh-KIHL-eez), and how this brought suffering to the Mycenaeans, whom Homer calls Achaeans. The first lines of the *Iliad* capture both the anger and the anguish:

> Sing, O goddess, the anger of Achilles son of Peleus, that brought countless ills upon the Achaeans. Many a brave soul did it send hurrying down to Hades [Hell], and many a hero did it yield as prey to dogs and vultures.[1]

The Development of the Polis in the Archaic Age, ca. 800–500 B.C.E.

What was the role of the polis in Greek society?

Homer lived in the era after the Dark Age, which later historians have termed the Archaic age (800–500 B.C.E.). The most important political change in this period was the development of the **polis** (PAH-luhs; plural *poleis*), a word generally translated as "city-state." With the polis, the Greeks established a new type of political structure. During the Archaic period, poleis established colonies throughout much of the Mediterranean, spreading Greek culture, and two particular poleis, each with a distinctive system of government, rose to prominence on the Greek mainland: Sparta and Athens.

Organization of the Polis

The Greek polis was not the first form of city-state to emerge. The earliest states in Sumer were also city-states, as were many of the small Mycenaean kingdoms. What differentiated the new Greek model from older city-states was that the polis was more

Spartan Hoplite   This bronze figurine portrays an armed foot soldier about to strike an enemy. His massive helmet with its full crest gives his head nearly complete protection, while a metal corselet covers his chest and back, and greaves (similar to today's shin guards) protect his shins. In his right hand he carries a thrusting spear (now broken off), and in his left a large round shield. (bpk, Berlin/Antikensammlung, Staatliche Museen, Berlin, Germany/Photo: Johannes Laurentius/Art Resource, NY)

than a political institution — it was a community of citizens with their own customs and laws. With one exception, the poleis that emerged after 800 B.C.E. did not have kings but instead were self-governing. The physical, religious, and political forms of the polis varied from place to place, but everywhere it was relatively small, reflecting the fragmented geography of Greece. The very smallness of the polis enabled Greeks to see how they fit individually into the overall system, and thus how the individual parts made up the social whole. This notion of community was fundamental to the polis and was the very badge of Greekness.

The polis included a city and its surrounding countryside. The countryside was essential to the economy of the polis and provided food to sustain the entire population. The people of the polis typically lived in a compact group of houses within the city, which by the fifth century B.C.E. was generally surrounded by a wall. Many left the city each morning to work their fields or tend their flocks of sheep and goats, and they returned at night. Another feature was a usually elevated area called the acropolis, where the people erected temples, altars, public monuments, and various dedications to the gods of the polis. The polis also contained a public square or marketplace, the agora, where there were porticoes, shops, public buildings, and courts. Originally the place where the warrior assembly met, the agora became the political center of the polis.

All poleis, with one exception, did not have standing armies. Instead they relied on their citizens for protection. Very rich citizens often served as cavalry, which was, however, never as important as the heavily armed infantrymen known as **hoplites**. These commoners were the backbone of the army, just as foot soldiers were in China during the Warring States Period (see Chapter 4). Hoplites wore bronze helmets and leather and bronze body armor, which they purchased themselves.

Greek poleis had several different types of government. Sporadic periods of violent political and social upheaval often led to the seizure of power by one man, a type of government the Greeks called tyranny. Tyrants generally came to power by using their wealth or by negotiating to win a political following that toppled the existing legal government. Tyrants were not always oppressive rulers, however, and sometimes used their power to benefit average citizens.

Democracy translates as "the power of the people" but was actually rule by citizens, not the people as a whole. Almost all Greek cities defined a citizen as an adult man with at least one citizen parent (or at some times and places, two citizen parents). Thus citizens shared ancestry as well as a place of residence. Women were citizens for religious and reproductive purposes, but their citizenship did not give them the right to participate in government. Free men who were not children of a citizen, known as resident foreigners, and slaves were not citizens and had no political voice. Thus ancient Greek democracy did not reflect the modern concept that all people are created equal, but it did permit male citizens to share equally in determining the diplomatic and military policies of the polis without respect to wealth.

Oligarchy, which literally means "the rule of the few," was government by a small group of wealthy citizens. Many Greeks preferred oligarchy because it provided more political stability than did democracy. Although oligarchy was the government of the prosperous, it left the door open for political and social advancement. If members of the polis could meet property or money qualifications, they could enter the governing circle.

Overseas Expansion

The development of the polis coincided with the growth of the Greek world in both wealth and numbers, bringing new problems. The increase in population created more demand for food than the land could supply. The resulting social and political tensions drove many people to seek new homes outside of Greece (Map 5.2).

Greeks traveled throughout the Mediterranean, sailing in great numbers to Sicily and southern Italy, where there was ample space for expansion. Here they established

MAP 5.2 Greek Colonization, ca. 750–550 B.C.E. The Greeks established colonies along the shores of the Mediterranean and Black Seas, spreading Greek culture and creating a large trading network.

prosperous cities and often intermarried with local people. Some adventurous Greeks sailed farther west to Sardinia, France, Spain, and perhaps even the Canary Islands. In Sardinia they first established trading stations, and then permanent towns. From these new outposts Greek influence extended to southern France.

In contrast to earlier military invasions and migrations of peoples, these were very often intentional colonizing ventures, organized and planned by a specific polis seeking new land for its residents, or by the losers in a political conflict within a polis who were forced to leave. Colonization changed the entire Greek world, both at home and abroad. In economic terms the expansion of the Greeks created a much larger market for agricultural and manufactured goods.

The Growth of Sparta

Many different poleis developed during the Archaic period, but Sparta became the leading military power in Greece. To expand their polis, the Spartans did not establish colonies but instead conquered Messenia (muh-SEE-nee-uh), a rich, fertile region in the southwestern Peloponnesus. They turned the Messenians into helots (HEH-luhts), unfree residents forced to work state lands. The helots soon rose in a revolt that took the Spartans thirty years to crush. Afterward, non-nobles who had shared in the fighting as foot soldiers appear to have demanded rights equal to those of the nobility and a voice in the government. (In more recent history, similar demands in the United States during the Vietnam War led to a lowering of the voting age to eighteen, to match the age at which soldiers were drafted.) Under intense pressure the aristocrats agreed to remodel the state into a new system.

The plan for the new system in Sparta was attributed to the lawgiver Lycurgus (ligh-KUHR-guhs), who may or may not have been an actual person. According to later Greek sources, political distinctions among Spartan men were eliminated, and all citizens became legally equal. Two kings, who were primarily military leaders, and a council of nobles shared executive power with five ephors (EH-fuhrs), overseers elected by the citizens. Helots worked the land, while Spartan citizens devoted their time to military training, and Sparta became extremely powerful.

In the system attributed to Lycurgus, every citizen owed primary allegiance to Sparta. Suppression of the individual along with an emphasis on military prowess led to a barracks state. Even family life was sacrificed to the polis. After long, hard military training that began at age seven, citizens became lifelong soldiers, the best in Greece. In battle Spartans were supposed to stand and die rather than retreat. Because men often did not see their wives or other women for long periods, not only in times of war but also in times of peace, their most meaningful relations were same-sex ones. The Spartan military leaders may have viewed such relationships as militarily advantageous because they believed that men would fight even more fiercely for lovers and comrades. An anecdote frequently repeated about one Spartan mother sums up Spartan military values. As her son was setting off to battle, the mother handed him his shield and advised him to come back either victorious and carrying the shield, or dead and being carried on it. Spartan men were expected to train vigorously, do with little, and like it, qualities reflected even today in the word *spartan*.

Spartans expected women in citizen families to be good wives and strict mothers of future soldiers. Xenophon, a later Athenian admirer of the Spartans, commented:

> [Lycurgus] insisted on the training of the body as incumbent no less on the female than the male; and in pursuit of the same idea instituted rival contests in running and feats of strength for women as for men. His belief was that where both parents were strong their progeny would be found to be more vigorous.[2]

With men in military service much of their lives, women in citizen families ran the estates and owned land in their own right, and they were not physically restricted or secluded.

The Evolution of Athens

Like Sparta, Athens faced pressing social and economic problems during the Archaic period, but the Athenian response was far different from that of the Spartans. Instead of creating a state devoted to the military, the Athenians created a state that became a democracy. For Athens, the late seventh century B.C.E. was a time of turmoil, the causes of which are unclear. In 621 B.C.E. Draco (DRAY-koh), an Athenian aristocrat, under pressure from small landholders and with the consent of the nobles, published the first law code of the Athenian polis. His code was harsh — and for this reason was the origin of the word *draconian* — but it embodied the ideal that the law belonged to all citizens. Yet the aristocracy still governed Athens oppressively, and the social and economic situation remained dire. Despite Draco's code, noble landholders continued to force small farmers and artisans into economic dependence. Many families were sold into slavery as settlement for debts, while others were exiled and their land mortgaged to the rich.

One person who recognized these problems was Solon (SOH-luhn), an aristocrat and a poet. Reciting his poems in the Athenian agora, where anyone could hear his call for justice and fairness, Solon condemned his fellow aristocrats for their greed and dishonesty. According to later sources, Solon's sincerity and good sense convinced other aristocrats that he was no crazed revolutionary. Moreover, he gained the trust of the common people, whose problems provoked them to demand access to political life, much as commoners in Sparta had. Around 594 B.C.E. the nobles elected him *archon* (AHR-kahn), chief magistrate of the polis, and gave him extraordinary power to reform the state.

Solon immediately freed all people enslaved for debt, recalled all exiles, canceled all debts on land, and made enslavement for debt illegal. Solon allowed non-nobles into the old aristocratic assembly, where they could vote in the election of magistrates. Later sixth-century-B.C.E. leaders further broadened the opportunities for commoners to take part in government, transforming Athens into a democracy.

The democracy functioned on the ideal that all full citizens should play a role in government. In 487 B.C.E. the election of the city's nine archons was replaced by reappointment by lot, which meant that any citizen with a certain amount of property had a chance of becoming an archon. This system gave citizens prestige, although the power of the archons gradually dwindled as military leaders called *strategoi* became increasingly important. Making laws was the responsibility of two bodies, the *boule* (BOO-lee), or council, composed of five hundred members, and the *ecclesia* (ee-KLEE-zhee-uh), the assembly of all citizens. By supervising the various committees of government and proposing bills and treaties to the ecclesia, the boule guided Athenian political life. Nonetheless, the ecclesia, open to all male citizens over eighteen years of age, had the final word through its votes.

Turmoil and Culture in the Classical Period, 500–338 B.C.E.

In the classical period, how did war influence Greece, and how did the arts, religion, and philosophy develop?

From the time of the Mycenaeans, violent conflict was common in Greek society, and this did not change in the fifth century B.C.E., the beginning of what scholars later called the classical period of Greek history, which they date from about 500 B.C.E. to the conquest of Greece by Philip of Macedon in 338 B.C.E. First, the Greeks beat back the armies of the Persian Empire. Then, turning their spears against one another, they destroyed their own political system in a century of warfare that began with the Peloponnesian War. Some thoughtful Greek historians recorded these momentous events. Despite the violence or to some degree because of it, playwrights and thinkers pondered the meaning of the universe and the role of humans in it, and artists and architects created new styles to celebrate Greek achievements. Thus, although warfare was one of the hallmarks of the classical period, intellectual and artistic accomplishments were as well.

The Deadly Conflicts, 499–404 B.C.E.

In 499 B.C.E. the Greeks who lived in Ionia unsuccessfully rebelled against the Persian Empire, which had ruled the area for fifty years (see Chapter 2). The Athenians provided halfhearted help to the Ionians, and in retaliation the Persians struck at Athens, only to be surprisingly defeated by the Athenian hoplites at the Battle of Marathon. (According to legend, a Greek runner carried the news of the victory to Athens. When the modern Olympics began in 1896, they included a long-distance running race between Marathon and Athens, a distance of about twenty-five miles, designed to honor the ancient Greeks.) In 480 B.C.E. the Persian king Xerxes (ZUHRK-seez) personally led a massive invasion of Greece. Under the leadership of Sparta, many Greek poleis, though not all, united to fight the Persians, and they engaged in major battles at the pass of Thermopylae and in the waters off Artemisium. The larger Persian army was victorious and occupied Athens, but only a month or so later the Greeks defeated the Persian navy in the decisive Battle of Salamis, an island across from Athens, and in 479 B.C.E. they overwhelmed the Persian army at Plataea.

The victorious Athenians and their allies then formed the Delian League, a military alliance intended to liberate Ionia from Persian rule and keep the Persians out of Greece. While driving the Persians out of Asia Minor, the Athenians also turned the league into an Athenian empire. They reduced their allies to the status of subjects, often collecting tribute by force and taking control of their economic resources. Athenian ideas of freedom and democracy did not extend to the citizens of other cities, and cities that objected to or revolted over Athenian actions were put down.

Under their great leader Pericles (PEHR-uh-kleez) (ca. 494–429 B.C.E.), the Athenians grew so powerful and aggressive that they alarmed Sparta and its allies. In 431 B.C.E. Athenian imperialism finally drove Sparta into the conflict known as the Peloponnesian War. The Peloponnesian War lasted a generation (431–404 B.C.E.) and brought in its wake disease, widespread civil wars, destruction, famine, and huge loss of life. With thousands of soldiers, Athens launched an attack on the island of Sicily, which ended in disaster. The Spartans encouraged revolts in cities that were subject to Athens and defeated the once-mighty Athenian fleet in naval battles. In 404 B.C.E. the Athenians finally surrendered, and Sparta stripped it of its empire. Conflicts among the states of Greece continued, however.

Writers at the time described and analyzed these wars, seeking to understand their causes and consequences. Herodotus (ca. 484–425 B.C.E.) traveled the Greek world to piece together the course of the Persian wars. Although he consulted documents when he could find them, he relied largely on the memories of the participants, and he presented all sides if there were conflicting views. Thucydides (ca. 460–ca. 399 B.C.E.) was an Athenian general in the Peloponnesian War but was banished early in the conflict because of a defeat; he traveled throughout Greece seeking information about the war from all sides. His account of the war saw human greed and desire for power as the root of the conflict, and he viewed the war itself as a disaster. As he told it, at the outbreak a Spartan ambassador warned the Athenians: "This day will be the beginning of great evils for the Greeks."[3] Thucydides agreed.

Athenian Arts in the Age of Pericles

In the midst of the warfare of the fifth century B.C.E., Pericles turned Athens into the showplace of Greece. He appropriated Delian League money to pay for a huge building program to rebuild the city that had been destroyed during the Persian occupation in 480 B.C.E. and to display to all Greeks the glory of the Athenian polis. Workers erected temples and other buildings as patriotic memorials housing statues and carvings, often painted in bright colors, showing the gods in human form and celebrating the Athenian victory over the Persians. (The paint later washed away, leaving the generally white sculpture that we think of as "classical.") The Acropolis in the center of the city was crowned by the Parthenon, a temple that celebrated the greatness of Athens and its patron goddess, Athena, who was represented by a huge statue.

Other aspects of Athenian culture were also rooted in the life of the polis. The development of drama was tied to the religious festivals of the city, especially those to the god of wine, Dionysus. The polis sponsored plays as part of the city's religious festivals and required wealthy citizens to pay the expenses of their production. Many plays were highly controversial, with overt political and social commentary, but they were neither suppressed nor censored. Not surprisingly, given the incessant warfare, conflict was a constant element in Athenian drama, and playwrights used their art in attempts to portray, understand, and resolve life's basic conflicts.

Aeschylus (EHS-kuh-luhs) (525–456 B.C.E.) was the first dramatist to explore such basic questions as the rights of the individual, the conflict between the individual and society, and the nature of good and evil. In his trilogy of plays, *The Oresteia*, he treats the themes of betrayal, murder, and reconciliation, urging the use of reason and justice to reconcile fundamental conflicts. The final play concludes with a prayer that civil dissension never be allowed to destroy Athens.

The plays of Sophocles (SAH-fuh-kleez) (496–406 B.C.E.) also deal with matters personal, political, and divine. In *Antigone*—which tells of how a king's mistakes in judgment lead to the suicides of his son, his son's fiancée, and his wife—Sophocles emphasizes the precedence of divine law over political law and family custom. In the closing lines he writes:

Good sense is by far the chief part of happiness; and we must not be impious towards the gods. The great words of boasters are always punished with great blows, and as they grow old teach them wisdom.[4]

In *Oedipus the King*, Sophocles tells the story of a good man doomed by the gods to kill his father and marry his mother. When Oedipus fails to avoid his fate, he blinds himself in despair and flees into exile. In *Oedipus at Colonus*, Sophocles treats the last days of the broken man, whose patient suffering and uncomplaining piety ultimately win the blessings and honor of the gods.

Euripides (yoo-RIH-puh-deez) (ca. 480–406 B.C.E.) likewise explored the theme of personal conflict within the polis and sounded the depths of the individual. With Euripides drama entered a new and more personal phase. To him the gods mattered far less than people.

Aeschylus, Sophocles, and Euripides are considered writers of tragedies: the stories of flawed people who bring disaster on themselves because their passions overwhelm reason. Athens also produced writers of comedies, who used humor as political commentary in an effort to suggest and support the best policies for the polis. Although comedies treated the affairs of the polis bawdily and often coarsely, they too were performed at religious festivals. Best known of the comedians is Aristophanes (eh-ruh-STAH-fuh-neez) (ca. 445–386 B.C.E.), a merciless critic of cranks, quacks, and fools. He used his art of sarcasm to dramatize his ideas on the right conduct of citizens and their leaders for the good of the polis.

Families and Sexual Relations

The Athenians, like other Greeks, lived with comparatively few material possessions in houses that were rather simple. A typical Athenian house consisted of a series of rooms opening onto a central courtyard that contained a well, an altar, and a washbasin. Larger houses often had a front room where the men of the family ate and entertained guests, as well as women's quarters at the back. Meals consisted primarily of various grains, especially wheat and barley, as well as lentils, olives, figs, grapes, fish, and a little meat, foods that are now part of the highly touted "Mediterranean diet."

In the city a man might support himself as a craftsman, potter, bronze-smith, or tanner, or he could contract with the polis to work on public buildings. Certain crafts, including spinning and weaving, were generally done by women. Men and women without skills worked as paid laborers. Slavery was commonplace in Greece, as it was throughout the ancient world. Slaves, who were paid for their work, were usually foreigners and often "barbarians," people whose native language was not Greek.

The social conditions of Athenian women have been the subject of much debate, in part because the sources are fragmentary. The available sources suggest that women rarely played notable roles in public affairs, and we know the names of no female poets, artists, or philosophers from classical Athens. The status of a free woman was strictly protected by law. Only her sons could be citizens. Only she was in charge of the household and the family's possessions, yet the law gave her these rights primarily to protect her husband's interests. Women in Athens and elsewhere in Greece, like those in Mesopotamia, brought dowries to their husbands upon marriage, which went back to their fathers in cases of divorce.

Hetaera and Young Man   In this scene painted on the inside of a drinking cup, a hetaera holds the head of a young man who has clearly had too much to drink. Sexual and comic scenes were common on Greek pottery, particularly on objects that would have been used at a private dinner party hosted by a citizen, known as a symposium. Wives did not attend symposia, but hetaerae and entertainers were often hired to perform for the male guests. (© Martin Von Wagner Museum der Universitat Wurzburg. Foto: P. Neckermann, courtesy of E. Oehrlein)

In ancient Athens the main function of women from citizen families was to bear and raise children. The ideal for Athenian citizen women was a secluded life in which the only men they usually saw were relatives and tradesmen. How far this ideal was actually a reality is impossible to know, but women in citizen families probably spent most of their time at home, leaving the house only to attend religious festivals, and perhaps occasionally plays, although this is debated. In their quarters of the house they oversaw domestic slaves and hired labor, and together with servants and friends worked wool into cloth. Women from noncitizen families lived freer lives, although they worked harder and had fewer material comforts. They performed manual labor in the fields or sold goods and services in the agora, going about their affairs much as men did. Among the services women and men sold was sex. Women who sold sexual services ranged from poor streetwalkers to sophisticated courtesans known as hetaerae, who added intellectual accomplishments to physical beauty. Hetaerae accompanied men in public settings where their wives would not have been welcome, serving men as social as well as sexual partners.

Same-sex relations were generally accepted in all of ancient Greece, not simply in Sparta. In classical Athens part of a male adolescent citizen's training might entail a hierarchical sexual and tutorial relationship with an older man, who most likely was married and may have had female sexual partners as well. These relationships between young men and older men were often celebrated in literature and art, in part because Athenians regarded perfection as possible only in the male. Women were generally seen as inferior to men, dominated by their bodies rather than their minds.

How often actual sexual relations between men or between men and women approached the ideal in Athens is very difficult to say, as most of our sources are prescriptive, idealized, or fictional. A small number of sources refer to female-female sexual desire, the most famous of which are a few of the poems of Sappho (SA-foh), a female poet of the sixth century B.C.E. The Greeks praised her skills as a lyric poet, but over the last century she has become better known for her sexuality than for her writing.

Today the English word *lesbian* is derived from Sappho's home island of Lesbos in the northern Aegean Sea.

Same-sex relations did not mean that people did not marry, for Athenians saw the continuation of the family line as essential. Sappho, for example, appears to have been married and had a daughter. Sexual desire and procreation were both important aspects of life, but ancient Greeks did not necessarily link them.

Public and Personal Religion

Like most peoples of the ancient world, the Greeks were polytheists, worshipping a variety of gods and goddesses who were immortal but otherwise acted just like people. As elsewhere, Greek religion was primarily a matter of ritual, with rituals designed to appease the divinities believed to control the forces of the natural world. Processions, festivals, and sacrifices offered to the gods were frequently occasions for people to meet together socially, times of cheer or even drunken excess. Migration, invasion, and colonization brought the Greeks into contact with other peoples and caused their religious beliefs to evolve.

By the classical era, the primary gods were understood to live metaphorically on Mount Olympus, the highest mountain in Greece. Zeus was the king of the gods and the most powerful of them, and he was married to Hera, who was also his sister (just as, in Egypt, Isis was Osiris's wife and sister; see Chapter 2). Zeus and Hera had several children, including Ares, the god of war, and Zeus's children with other women included gods such as Apollo and Athena and heroes such as Hercules and Perseus. Apollo represented the epitome of youth, beauty, and athletic skill, and he served as the patron god of music and poetry. His half-sister Athena was a warrior-goddess who had been born from the head of Zeus.

Besides these Olympian gods, each polis had its own minor deities, each with his or her own local group of worshippers. The polis administered the cults and religious festivals, and everyone was expected to participate in these civic rituals, which were similar to today's patriotic parades or ceremonies. In contrast to Mesopotamia, Egypt, and Vedic India, priests held little power in Greece; their purpose was to care for temples and sacred property and to conduct the proper rituals, but not to make religious or political rules or doctrines, much less to enforce them. Much religion was local and domestic, and individual families honored various deities privately in their homes. Many people also believed that magic rituals and spells were effective and sought the assistance of individuals reputed to have special knowledge or powers to cure disease, drive away ghosts, bring good weather, or influence the actions of others.

Along with public and family forms of honoring the gods, some Greeks also participated in what later historians have termed **mystery religions**, in which participants underwent an initiation ritual and gained secret knowledge that they were forbidden to reveal to the uninitiated. One of these was the religion of Dionysus (digh-uh-NIGH-suhs), the god of wine and powerful emotions. He was killed and then reborn and became the center of a mystery religion offering rebirth. As the god of wine, Dionysus also represented freedom from the normal constraints of society, and his worshippers were reported to have danced ecstatically.

The Greeks also shared some Pan-Hellenic festivals, the chief of which were held at Olympia to honor Zeus and at Delphi to honor Apollo. The festivities at Olympia included athletic contests that inspired the modern Olympic games. Held every four years after they started in 776 B.C.E., the contests attracted visitors from all over the Greek world and lasted until the fourth century C.E., when they were banned by a Christian emperor because they were pagan. The Pythian games at Delphi were also held every four years, and these contests included musical and literary competitions.

The Flowering of Philosophy

Just as the Greeks developed rituals to honor gods, they spun myths and epics to explain the origins of the universe. Over time, however, as Greeks encountered other peoples with different beliefs, some of them began to question their old gods and myths, and they sought rational rather than supernatural explanations for natural phenomena. These Greek thinkers, based in Ionia, are called the Pre-Socratics because their rational efforts preceded those of the better-known Socrates. Taking individual facts, they wove them into general theories that led them to conclude that, despite appearances, the universe is actually simple and subject to natural laws. Although they had little impact on the average Greek, the Pre-Socratics began an intellectual revolution with their idea that nature was predictable, creating what we now call philosophy and science.

Drawing on their observations, the Pre-Socratics speculated about the basic building blocks of the universe, and most decided that all things were made of four simple substances: fire, air, earth, and water. Democritus (dih-MAW-kruh-tuhs) (ca. 460 B.C.E.) broke this down further and created the atomic theory that the universe is made up of invisible, indestructible particles. The stream of thought started by the Pre-Socratics branched into several directions. Hippocrates (hih-PAW-kruh-teez) (ca. 470–400 B.C.E.) became the most prominent physician and teacher of medicine of his time. He sought natural explanations for diseases and natural means to treat them. Illness was caused not by evil spirits, he asserted, but by physical problems in the body, particularly by imbalances in what he saw as four basic bodily fluids: blood, phlegm, black bile, and yellow bile. In a healthy body these fluids, called humors, were in perfect balance, and medical treatment of the ill sought to help the body bring them back into balance. Hippocrates seems to have advocated letting nature take its course and not intervening too much, though later medicine based on the humoral theory would be much more interventionist, with bloodletting emerging as the central treatment for many illnesses.

The Sophists (SOFF-ihsts), a group of thinkers in fifth-century-B.C.E. Athens, applied philosophical speculation to politics and language, questioning the beliefs and laws of the polis to understand their origin. They believed that excellence in both politics and language could be taught, and they provided lessons for the young men of Athens who wished to learn how to persuade others in the often-tumultuous Athenian democracy. Their later opponents criticized them for charging fees and also accused them of using rhetoric to deceive people instead of presenting the truth. (Today the word *sophist* is usually used in this sense, describing someone who deceives people with clever-sounding but false arguments.)

Socrates (SOK-ruh-teez) (ca. 470–399 B.C.E.), whose ideas are known only through the works of others, also applied philosophy to politics and to people. He seemed to many Athenians to be a Sophist because he also questioned Athenian traditions, although he never charged fees. His approach when exploring ethical issues and defining concepts was to start with a general topic or problem and to narrow the matter to its essentials. He did so by continuously questioning participants in a discussion or argument rather than lecturing, a process known as the Socratic method. Because he posed questions rather than giving answers, it is difficult to say exactly what Socrates thought about many things, although he does seem to have felt that through knowledge people could approach the supreme good and thus find happiness. He clearly thought that Athenian leaders were motivated more by greed and opportunism than by a desire for justice in the war with Sparta, and he criticized Athenian democracy openly. Many Athenians viewed Socrates with suspicion because he challenged the traditional beliefs and values of Athens. His views brought him into conflict with the government. The leaders of Athens tried him for corrupting the youth of the city, and for impiety, that is, for not believing in the gods honored in the city. In 399 B.C.E. they executed him.

Most of what we know about Socrates comes from his student Plato (427–347 B.C.E.), who wrote dialogues in which Socrates asks questions and who also founded the Academy, a school dedicated to philosophy. Plato developed the theory that there are two worlds: the impermanent, changing world that we know through our senses, and the eternal, unchanging realm of "forms" that constitute the essence of true reality. According to Plato, true knowledge and the possibility of living a virtuous life come from contemplating ideal forms — what later came to be called **Platonic ideals** — not from observing the visible world. Thus, if you want to understand justice, asserted Plato, you should think about what would make perfect justice instead of studying the imperfect examples of justice around you. Plato believed that the ideal polis could exist only when its leaders were well educated.

Plato's student Aristotle (384–322 B.C.E.) also thought that true knowledge was possible, but he believed that such knowledge came from observation of the world, analysis of natural phenomena, and logical reasoning, not contemplation. Aristotle thought that everything had a purpose, so that to know something, one also had to know its function. The range of Aristotle's thought is staggering. His interests embraced logic, ethics, natural science, physics, politics, poetry, and art. He studied the heavens as well as earth and judged the earth to be the center of the universe, with the stars and planets revolving around it.

Plato's idealism profoundly shaped Western philosophy, but Aristotle came to have an even wider influence. For many centuries in Europe, the authority of his ideas was second only to the Bible's, and his ideas had a great impact in the Muslim world as well. His works — which are actually a combination of his lecture notes and those of his students, copied and recopied many times — were used as the ultimate proof that something was true, even if closer observation of the phenomenon indicated that it was not. Thus, ironically, Aristotle's authority was sometimes invoked in a way that contradicted his own ideas. Despite these limitations, the broader examination of the universe and the place of humans in it that Socrates, Plato, and Aristotle engaged in is widely regarded as Greece's most important intellectual legacy.

The philosophers of ancient Athens lived at roughly the same time as major thinkers in religious and philosophical movements in other parts of the world, including Mahavira (the founder of Jainism), the Buddha, Confucius, and several prophets in Hebrew Scripture. All of these individuals thought deeply about how to live a moral life, and all had tremendous influence on later intellectual, religious, and social developments. There is no evidence that they had any contact with one another, but the parallels among them are strong enough that some historians describe the period from about 800 B.C.E. to 200 B.C.E. as the "Axial Age," by which they mean that this was a pivotal period of intellectual and spiritual transformation.

Hellenistic Society, 323–30 B.C.E.

How did Alexander the Great's conquests shape society in the Hellenistic period?

The Greek city-states wore themselves out fighting one another, and Philip II, the ruler of Macedonia, a kingdom in the north of Greece, gradually conquered one after another and took over their lands. He then turned against the Persian Empire but was killed by an assassin. His son Alexander continued the fight. A brilliant military leader, Alexander conquered the entire Persian Empire from Libya in the west to Bactria in the east (see Map 5.3, page 130). He also founded new cities in which Greek and local populations mixed, although he died while planning his next campaign. Alexander left behind an empire that quickly broke into smaller kingdoms, but more importantly, his death in 323 B.C.E. ushered in an era, the Hellenistic, in which Greek culture, the Greek language, and Greek thought spread as far as India, blending with local traditions. The end of the Hellenistic period is generally set at 30 B.C.E., the Roman conquest of the Hellenistic kingdom of Egypt, but many aspects of Hellenistic culture continued to flourish under Roman governance.

From Polis to Monarchy, 404–200 B.C.E.

Immediately after the Peloponnesian War, Sparta began striving for empire over all of the Greeks but could not maintain its hold. In 371 B.C.E. an army from the polis of Thebes destroyed the Spartan army, but the Thebans were unable to bring peace to Greece. Philip II, ruler of the kingdom of Macedonia on the northern border of Greece (r. 359–336 B.C.E.), turned the situation to his advantage. By clever use of his wealth and superb army, Philip won control of the northern Aegean, and in 338 B.C.E. he defeated a combined Theban-Athenian army, conquering Greece. Because the Greek city-states could not put aside their quarrels with one another, they fell to an invader, an event that historians see as marking the end of the classical period.

After his victory, Philip united the Greek states with his Macedonian kingdom and got the states to cooperate in a crusade to liberate the Ionian Greeks from Persian rule. Before he could launch his crusade, Philip fell to an assassin's dagger in 336 B.C.E. His young son Alexander, who had been tutored by Aristotle, vowed to carry on Philip's mission and led an army of Macedonians and Greeks into western Asia. He won major battles against the Persians and seized Egypt from them without a fight. After honoring the priestly class, Alexander was proclaimed pharaoh, the legitimate ruler of Egypt. He ordered the building of a new city where the Nile meets the Mediterranean, a city that would soon be called Alexandria and that within a century would grow into an enormous city, rivaling Chang-an in China and Pataliputra in the Mauryan Empire of India. He also took the principal Persian capital of Persepolis and performed a symbolic act of retribution by burning the buildings of Xerxes, the invader of Greece during the Persian wars 150 years earlier.

By 330 B.C.E. the Persian Empire had fallen, but Alexander had no intention of stopping, and he set out to conquer much of the rest of Asia. He plunged eastward into lands completely unknown to the Greek world. After four years of fighting his soldiers crossed the Indus River (in the area that is now Pakistan), and finally, at the Hyphasis River, the troops refused to go farther. Alexander was enraged by the mutiny, but the army stood firm. Still eager to explore the limits of the world, Alexander turned south to the Arabian Sea and then back west (Map 5.3).

He never saw Macedonia again, however, as he died in Babylon in 323 B.C.E. from fever, wounds, and excessive drinking. He was only thirty-two, but in just thirteen years he had created an empire that stretched from his homeland of Macedonia to India, gaining the title "the Great" along the way. Alexander was instrumental in changing the face of politics in the eastern Mediterranean. His campaign swept away the Persian Empire, and in its place he established a Macedonian monarchy, although this fell apart with his death. Several of the chief Macedonian generals aspired to become sole ruler, which led to a civil war that lasted for decades and tore Alexander's empire apart. By the end of this conflict, the most successful generals had carved out their own smaller monarchies, although these continued to be threatened by internal splits and external attacks.

MAP 5.3 Alexander's Conquests, 336–324 B.C.E. Alexander's campaign of conquest was extensive and speedy. More important than the great success of his military campaigns was his founding of Hellenistic cities.

Ptolemy (TAH-luh-mee) seized Egypt, and his descendants, the Ptolemies, ruled Egypt for nearly three hundred years, until the death of the last Ptolemaic ruler, Cleopatra VII, in 30 B.C.E. Antigonus and his descendants, the Antigonids (an-TIH-guh-nuhds), gained control of the Macedonian kingdom in Europe, which they held until they were overthrown by the Romans in 168 B.C.E. (see Chapter 6). Seleucus won the bulk of Alexander's empire, his monarchy extending from western Asia to India (see below), but this Seleucid (SUH-loo-suhd) kingdom gradually broke into smaller states. In terms of political stability and peace, these monarchies were no improvement on the Greek polis.

To encourage obedience, Hellenistic kings often created ruler cults that linked the king's authority with that of the gods, or they adopted ruler cults that already existed, as Alexander did in Egypt. This created a symbol of unity within kingdoms ruling different peoples who at first had little in common; however, these kingdoms never won the deep emotional loyalty that Greeks had once felt for the polis. Kings sometimes gave the cities in their territory all the external trappings of a polis, such as a council or an assembly of citizens, but these had no power. The city was not autonomous, as the polis had been, but had to follow royal orders. Hellenistic rulers generally relied on paid professionals to staff their bureaucracies and on trained, paid, full-time soldiers rather than citizen hoplites to fight their wars.

Building a Hellenized Society

Alexander's most important legacy was clearly not political unity. Instead it was the spread of Greek ideas and traditions across a wide area, a process scholars later called Hellenization. To maintain contact with the Greek world as he moved farther eastward, Alexander founded new cities and military colonies and settled Greek and Macedonian troops and veterans in them. This practice continued after his death, with more than 250 new cities founded in North Africa, West and Central Asia, and southeastern Europe. These cities and colonies became powerful instruments in the spread of Hellenism and in the blending of Greek and other cultures. Wherever it was established, the Hellenistic city resembled a modern city. It was a cultural center with theaters, temples, and libraries—a seat of learning and a place for amusement. The Hellenistic city was also an economic center—a marketplace and a scene of trade and manufacturing.

The ruling dynasties of the Hellenistic world were Macedonian in origin, and Greeks and Macedonians initially filled all important political, military, and diplomatic positions. The prevailing institutions and laws were Greek, and Greek became the common spoken language of the entire eastern Mediterranean. Instead of the different dialects spoken in Greece itself, a new Greek dialect called the koine (kaw-NAY), which means common, became the spoken language of traders, the royal court, the bureaucracy, and the army across the Hellenistic world. Everyone, Greek or easterner, who wanted to find an official position or compete in business had to learn it. Those who did gained an avenue of social mobility, and as early as the third century B.C.E. local people in some Greek cities began to rise in power and prominence. Cities granted citizenship to Hellenized natives, although there were fewer political benefits of citizenship than there had been in the classical period because real power was held by monarchs, not citizens. Cultural influences in the other direction occurred less frequently because they brought fewer advantages. Few Greeks learned a non-Greek language unless they were required to because of their official position. Greeks did begin to worship local deities, but often these were somewhat Hellenized and their qualities blended with those of an existing Greek god or goddess.

In the booming city of Alexandria, the Ptolemies generally promoted Greek culture over that of the local Egyptians. This favoritism eventually led to civil unrest, but it also led the Ptolemies to support anything that enhanced Greek learning or traditions. Ptolemaic kings established what became the largest library in the ancient world, where scholars copied works loaned from many places onto papyrus scrolls, translating them into Greek if they were in other languages. They also studied the newest discoveries in science and mathematics. Alexandria was home to the largest Jewish community in the ancient world, and here Jewish scholars translated the Hebrew Bible into Greek for the first time.

The kings of Bactria and Parthia spread Greek culture far to the east, and their kingdoms became outposts of Hellenism, from which the rulers of China and India learned of sophisticated societies other than their own. Some Bactrian and Parthian rulers converted to Buddhism, and the Buddhist ruler of the Mauryan Empire in northern India, Ashoka, may have ordered translations of his laws into Greek for the Greek-speaking residents of Bactria and Parthia. In the second century B.C.E., after the collapse of the Mauryan Empire, Bactrian armies conquered part of northern India, establishing several small Indo-Greek states where the mixing of religious and artistic traditions was particularly pronounced (see Chapter 3).

The Bactrian city of Ay Khanoum on the Oxus River, on the border of modern Afghanistan, is a good example of a brand-new city where cultures met. It had Greek temples and administration buildings, and on a public square was a long inscription carved in stone in Greek verse relating Greek ideals:

> In childhood, learn good manners
> In youth, control your passions
> In middle age, practice justice
> In old age, be of good counsel
> In death, have no regrets.[5]

The city also had temples to local deities and artwork that blended Greek and local styles (for an example, see page 78).

Yet the spread of Greek culture was wider than it was deep, as it generally did not extend far beyond the reaches of the cities. Many urban residents adopted the aspects of Hellenism that they found useful, but people in the countryside generally did not embrace it, nor were they encouraged to.

The Growth of Trade and Commerce

Not only did Alexander's conquests change the political face of the ancient world, but the spread of Greeks eastward also created new markets, causing trade to flourish. The economic connections of the Hellenistic world later proved valuable to the Romans, allowing them to trade products and ideas more easily over a broad area.

When Alexander conquered the Persian Empire, he found the royal treasury filled with vast sums of gold and silver and other valuables. The victors used this wealth to

Metal Plate from Ay Khanoum　This spectacular metal plate, made in the Bactrian city of Ay Khanoum in the second century B.C.E., probably depicts the goddess Cybele being pulled in a chariot by lions with the sun-god above. Worship of Cybele, an earth-mother goddess, spread into Greece from Turkey and was then spread by her Greek followers as they traveled and migrated. (Photo by Thierry Olivier/Musée Guimet/Getty Images)

finance the building of roads, the development of harbors, and especially, as noted earlier, the founding of new cities. These cities opened whole new markets to merchants who eagerly took advantage of the unforeseen opportunities. Whenever possible, merchants sent their goods by water, but overland trade also became more prominent in the Hellenistic era. Overland trade with India was organized by Asian merchants and conducted by camel caravans through the harsh terrain of western Asia. Once goods reached the Hellenistic monarchies, Greek merchants took a hand in the trade. Commerce from the east arrived at Egypt and the harbors of Palestine, Phoenicia, and Syria. From these ports goods flowed to Greece, Italy, and Spain. This period also saw the development of standardized business customs, so that merchants of different nationalities, aided especially by the koine, communicated in a way understandable to them all. Trade was further facilitated by the coining of money, which provided merchants with a standard way to value goods as well as a convenient method of payment.

The increased volume of trade helped create prosperity that made luxury goods affordable to more people. As a result, overland traders brought easily transportable luxuries such as gold, silver, and precious stones to market. They extended their networks into China, from which the most prominent good in terms of volume was silk. The trade in silk later gave the major east-west route its name: the Great Silk Road. In return the peoples of the eastern Mediterranean sent east manufactured or extracted goods, especially metal weapons, cloth, wine, and olive oil. (For more on the Silk Road in East Asia, see Chapter 7.)

More economically important than trade in exotic goods were commercial dealings in essential commodities like raw materials and grain and industrial products such as pottery. The Hellenistic monarchies usually raised enough grain for their own needs as well as a surplus for export. For the cities of Greece and the Aegean the trade in grain was essential, because many of them could not grow enough in their mountainous terrain. Fortunately for them, abundant wheat supplies were available nearby in Egypt and in the area north of the Black Sea.

The Greek cities often paid for their grain by exporting olive oil, wine, honey, dried fruit, nuts, and vegetables. Another significant commodity supplied by the Greeks was fish, which for export was salted, pickled, or dried. This trade was doubly important because fish provided poor people with protein, an essential element of their diet.

Slaves were a staple of Hellenistic trade, traveling in all directions on both land and sea routes. Ancient authors cautioned against having too many slaves from one area together, as this might encourage them to revolt. War provided prisoners for the slave market; to a lesser extent, so did kidnapping and capture by pirates, although the origin of most slaves is unknown. Both old Greek states and new Hellenistic kingdoms were ready slave markets, and throughout the Mediterranean world slaves were almost always in demand for work in shops, fields, farms, mines, and the homes of wealthier people.

Most trade in bulk commodities like grain and wood was seaborne, and Hellenistic merchant ships were the workhorses of the day. A merchant ship had a broad beam, which made it more stable and allowed large cargoes, and it relied on sails for propulsion. Such ships were far more seaworthy than Hellenistic warships, which were long, narrow, and built for speed. A small crew of experienced sailors easily handled the merchant vessels. Aside from providing work for sailors, maritime trade presented opportunities for shipbuilders, dockworkers, teamsters, and pirates. Piracy was a constant factor in the Hellenistic world and remained so until Rome cleared it from the seas.

Despite the increase in trade, the Hellenistic period did not see widespread improvements in the way most people lived and worked. Cities flourished, but many people who lived in rural areas were actually worse off than they had been before, because of higher levels of rents and taxes. Technology was applied to military needs, but not to the production of food or other goods. Manual labor, not machinery, continued to turn out the agricultural produce, raw materials, and manufactured goods the Hellenistic world used. The Greek historian Diodorus gives a picture of this hard labor, commenting on life in the gold mines owned by the Ptolemy rulers of Egypt:

> The kings of Egypt condemn [to the mines] those found guilty of wrong-doing and those taken prisoner in war, those who are victims of false accusations and were put into jail because of royal anger. . . . The condemned — and they are very many — all of them are put in chains, and they work persistently and continually, both by day and throughout the night, getting no rest and carefully cut off from escape.[6]

The Ptolemies even condemned women and children to work in the mines. Besides gold and silver, used primarily for coins and jewelry, bronze continued to be used for shields, and iron for weapons and tools.

Hellenistic Religion, Philosophy, and Science

How did religion, philosophy, and science develop in the Hellenistic world?

The mixing of peoples in the Hellenistic era influenced religion, philosophy, and science. The Hellenistic kings built temples to the old Olympian gods and promoted rituals and ceremonies like those in earlier Greek cities, but new deities also gained prominence. More people turned to mystery religions that blended Greek and non-Greek elements. Others turned to practical philosophies that provided advice on how to live a good life. In the scholarly realm, Hellenistic thinkers made advances in mathematics, astronomy, and mechanical design. Additionally, physicians used observation and dissection to better understand the way the human body works.

Religion in the Hellenistic World

When Hellenistic kings founded cities, they also built temples — staffed by priests and supported by taxes — for the old Olympian gods. In this way they spread Greek religious beliefs throughout the Hellenistic world. The transplanted religions, like those in Greece itself, sponsored literary, musical, and athletic contests, which were staged in beautiful surroundings among splendid Greek-style buildings. Greeks and non-Greeks in the Hellenistic world also honored and worshipped deities that had not been important in the Hellenic period or that were a blend of imported Greek and indigenous gods and goddesses. Tyche (TIGH-kee), for example, was a new deity, the goddess and personification of luck, fate, chance, and fortune. Temples to her were built in major cities of the eastern Mediterranean, including Antioch and Alexandria, and her image was depicted on coins and bas-reliefs. Contemporaries commented that when no other cause could be found for an event, Tyche was responsible.

Increasingly, many people were attracted to mystery religions, which in the Hellenic period had been linked to specific gods in particular places, so that people who wished to become members had to travel. But new mystery religions, like Hellenistic culture in general, were not tied to a particular place; instead they were spread throughout the Hellenistic world, and temples of the new deities sprang up wherever Greeks lived.

Mystery religions incorporated aspects of both Greek and non-Greek religions and claimed to save their adherents from the worst that fate could do. Most taught that by the rites of initiation, in which the secrets of the religion were shared, devotees became united with a deity who had also died and risen from the dead. The sacrifice of the god and his victory over death saved the devotee from eternal death. Similarly, mystery religions demanded a period of preparation in which the converts strove to become

Isis and Horus   In this small statue from Egypt, the goddess Isis is shown suckling her son, Horus. Worship of Isis spread throughout the Hellenistic world; her followers believed that Isis offered them life after death, just as she had brought Horus's father, Osiris, back to life. (Louvre, Paris, France/Peter Willi/The Bridgeman Art Library) pure and holy, that is, to live by the religion's precepts. Once aspirants had prepared themselves, they went through the initiation, usually a ritual of great emotional intensity symbolizing the entry into a new life.

Among the mystery religions the Egyptian cult of Isis took the Hellenistic world by storm. In Egyptian mythology Isis brought her husband, Osiris, back to life (see page 41), and during the Hellenistic era this power came to be understood by her followers as extending to them as well. She promised to save any mortal who came to her, and her priests asserted that she had bestowed on humanity the gift of civilization and founded law and literature. Isis was understood to be a devoted mother as well as a devoted wife, and she became the goddess of marriage, conception, and childbirth. She became the most important goddess of the Hellenistic world. Devotion to Isis, and to many other mystery religions, spread to the Romans as well as the Greeks when the two civilizations came into greater contact.

Philosophy and Its Guidance for Life

While some people turned to mystery religions to overcome Tyche and provide something permanent in a world that seemed unstable, others turned to philosophy. Several new schools of philosophical thought emerged and caught the minds and hearts of many Greeks and some non-Greeks. One of these was **Epicureanism**, a practical philosophy of serenity in an often-tumultuous world. Epicurus (340–270 B.C.E.) used observation and logic to study the world and also to examine the human condition. He decided that the principal goods of human life were contentment and pleasure, which he defined as the absence of pain, fear, and suffering. By encouraging the pursuit of pleasure, he was not advocating drunken revels or sexual excess, which he thought caused pain, but promoting moderation in food, clothing, and shelter. Epicurus also taught that individuals could most easily attain peace and serenity by ignoring the outside world and looking instead into their personal feelings. His followers ignored politics because it led to tumult, which would disturb the soul.

Zeno (335–262 B.C.E.), a philosopher from Cyprus, advanced a different concept of human beings and the universe. Zeno first came to Athens to form his own school, the Stoa, named after the covered walkways where he preferred to teach. His philosophy, **Stoicism** (STOH-uh-sih-zuhm), in turn, came to be named for his school. Zeno and his followers considered nature an expression of divine will; in their view, people could be happy only when living in accordance with nature. They stressed the unity of humans and the universe, stating that all people were obliged to help one another.

The Stoics' most lasting practical achievement was the creation of the concept of natural law. They concluded that as all people were kindred, partook of divine reason, and were in harmony with the universe, one natural law governed them all.

Hellenistic Science and Medicine

In the scholarly realm, Hellenistic thinkers made advances in mathematics, astronomy, and mechanical design. The most notable of the Hellenistic astronomers was Aristarchus of Samos (ca. 310–230 B.C.E.). Aristarchus rightly concluded that the sun is far larger than the earth and that the stars are enormously distant from the earth. He also argued against Aristotle's view that the earth is the center of the universe, instead propounding the heliocentric theory—that the earth and planets revolve around the sun. His theory was discussed for several centuries, then forgotten, and was resurrected in the sixteenth century C.E. by the brilliant Polish astronomer Nicolaus Copernicus.

In geometry Euclid (YOO-kluhd) (fl. ca. 300 B.C.E.), a mathematician living in Alexandria, compiled a valuable textbook of existing knowledge. His *The Elements of Geometry* became the standard introduction to the subject. Generations of students from antiquity to the present have learned the essentials of geometry from it.

The greatest thinker of the Hellenistic period was Archimedes (ahr-kuh-MEE-deez) (ca. 287–212 B.C.E.). A clever inventor, he devised new artillery for military purposes. In peacetime he created the water screw to draw water from a lower to a higher level. (See "Individuals in Society: Archimedes, Scientist and Inventor," page 138.) He also invented the compound pulley to lift heavy weights. His chief interest, however, lay in pure mathematics. He founded the science of hydrostatics (the study of fluids at rest) and discovered the principle that the weight of a solid floating in a liquid is equal to the weight of the liquid displaced by the solid.

Archimedes willingly shared his work with others, among them Eratosthenes (ehr-uh-TOSS-thuh-neez) (285–ca. 204 B.C.E.), who was the librarian of the vast Ptolemaic royal library in Alexandria. Eratosthenes used mathematics to further the geographical studies for which he is most famous. He concluded that the earth is a spherical globe and calculated the circumference of the earth geometrically, estimating it at about 24,675 miles. He was not wrong by much: the earth is actually 24,860 miles in circumference.

As the new artillery devised by Archimedes indicates, Hellenistic science was used for purposes of war as well as peace. Theories of mechanics were applied to build military machines. Fully realizing the practical possibilities of the first effective artillery in Western history, Philip of Macedonia had introduced the machines to the broader world in the middle of the fourth century B.C.E. The catapult became the most widely used artillery piece. As the Assyrians had earlier, engineers built siege towers, large wooden structures that served as artillery platforms, and put them on wheels so that soldiers could roll them up to a town's walls. Generals added battering rams to bring down large portions of walls. If these new engines made warfare more efficient, they also added to the misery of the people, as war often directly involved the populations of cities. War and illness fed the need for medical advances, and doctors as well as scientists combined observation with theory during the Hellenistic period. Herophilus, who lived in the first half of the third century B.C.E., worked in Alexandria and studied the writings attributed to Hippocrates. He approached the study of medicine in a systematic, scientific fashion: he dissected dead bodies and measured what he observed. He was the first to accurately describe the nervous system and studied the liver, lungs, uterus, and brain, which he considered the center of intelligence. His students carried on his work, searching for the causes and nature of illness and pain.

Medical study did not lead to effective cures for the infectious diseases that were the leading cause of death for most people, however, and people used a variety of ways to attempt to combat illness. Medicines prescribed by physicians or prepared at home often included natural products blended with materials understood to work magically. People in the Hellenistic world may have thought that fate determined what would happen, but they also actively sought to make their lives longer and healthier.

INDIVIDUALS IN SOCIETY • Archimedes, Scientist and Inventor

Archimedes was born in the Greek city of Syracuse in Sicily, an intellectual center in which he pursued scientific interests. He was the most original thinker of his time and a practical inventor. In his book *On Plane Equilibriums*, he dealt for the first time with the basic principles of mathematics, including the principle of the lever. He once said that if he were given a lever and a suitable place to stand, he could move the world. He also demonstrated how easily his compound pulley could move huge weights with little effort:

> A three-masted merchant ship of the royal fleet had been hauled on land by hard work and many hands. Archimedes put aboard her many men and the usual freight. He sat far away from her; and without haste, but gently working a compound pulley with his hand, he drew her towards him smoothly and without faltering, just as though she were running on the surface.*

He likewise invented the Archimedian screw, a pump to bring subterranean water up to irrigate fields, which quickly came into common use. In his treatise *On Floating Bodies*, Archimedes founded the science of hydrostatics. He concluded that an object will float if it weighs less than the water it displaces, and that whenever a solid floats in a liquid, the weight of the solid equals the weight of the liquid displaced. This discovery and his reaction to it have become famous:

> When he was devoting his attention to this problem, he happened to go to a public bath. When he climbed down into the bathtub there, he noticed that water in the tub equal to the bulk of his body flowed out. Thus, when he observed this method of solving the problem, he did not wait. Instead, moved with joy, he sprang out of the tub, and rushing home naked he kept indicating in a loud voice that he had indeed discovered what he was seeking. For while running he was shouting repeatedly in Greek, "Eureka, eureka" ("I have found it, I have found it").†

War between Rome and Syracuse unfortunately interrupted Archimedes's scientific life. In 213 B.C.E., during the Second Punic War, the Romans besieged the city. Hiero, its king and Archimedes's friend, asked the scientist for help in repulsing Roman attacks. Archimedes began to build remarkable devices that served as artil-

---

*Plutarch, *Life of Marcellus*.
†Vitruvius, *On Architecture*, 9 Preface, 10.

Chapter Summary

Greece's mountainous terrain encouraged the development of small, independent communities and political fragmentation. Sometime after 2000 B.C.E. two kingdoms—the Minoan on Crete and the Mycenaean on the mainland—did emerge, but these remained smaller than the great empires of Mesopotamia, India, and China. The fall of these kingdoms led to a period of disruption and decline known as the Greek Dark Age (ca. 1100–800 B.C.E.). However, Greek culture survived, and Greeks developed the independent city-state, known as the polis. Greeks also established lery. One weapon shot missiles to break up infantry attacks. Others threw huge masses of stones that fell on the enemy with incredible speed and noise. They tore gaping holes in the Roman lines and broke up attacks. For use against Roman warships he is said to have designed a machine with beams from which large claws dropped onto the hulls of enemy warships, hoisted them into the air, and dropped them back into the sea. Later Greek authors reported that he destroyed Roman ships with a series of polished mirrors that focused sunlight and caused the ships to catch fire. Modern experiments re-creating Archimedes's weapons have found that the claw may have been workable, but the mirrors probably were not, as they required a ship to remain stationary for the fire to ignite. It is not certain whether his war machines were actually effective, but later people recounted tales that the Romans became so fearful that whenever they saw a bit of rope or a stick of timber projecting over one of the walls protecting Syracuse, they shouted, "There it is. Archimedes is trying some engine on us," and fled. After many months the Roman siege was successful, however, and Archimedes was killed by a Roman soldier.

QUESTIONS FOR ANALYSIS

1. How did Archimedes combine theoretical mathematics and practical issues in his work?

2. What applications do you see in the world around you of the devices Archimedes improved or invented, such as the lever, the pulley, and artillery?

LaunchPad
ONLINE DOCUMENT PROJECT

What advances in technological warfare occurred during the Hellenistic period? Read accounts of the siege of Syracuse, and then complete a quiz and writing assignment based on the evidence and details from this chapter.

See inside the front cover to learn more.

colonies and traveled and traded as far east as the Black Sea and as far west as the Atlantic Ocean. Two poleis became especially powerful: Sparta, which created a military state in which men remained in the army most of their lives, and Athens, which created a democracy in which male citizens had a direct voice. In the classical period, between 500 B.C.E. and 338 B.C.E., Greeks engaged in war with the Persians and with one another, but they also created drama, philosophy, and magnificent art and architecture.

In the middle of the fourth century B.C.E. the Greek city-states were conquered by the Macedonians under King Philip II and his son Alexander. A brilliant military leader, Alexander conquered the entire Persian Empire and founded new cities in which Greek and local populations mixed. His successors continued to build cities and colonies, which were centers of trade and spread Greek culture over a broad area, extending as far east as India. The mixing of peoples in the Hellenistic era influenced religion, philosophy, and science. New deities gained prominence, and many people turned to mystery religions that blended Greek and non-Greek elements as they offered followers secret knowledge and eternal life. Others turned to practical philosophies that provided advice on how to live a good life. Advances were made in technology, mathematics, science, and medicine, but these were applied primarily to military purposes, not to improving the way ordinary people lived and worked.

Notes

1. Homer, *Iliad*, trans. Samuel Butler, Book 1, lines 1–5.
2. *The Works of Xenophon*, trans. Henry G. Dakyns (London: Macmillan and Co., 1892), p. 296.
3. Thucydides 2.12, trans. J. Buckler.
4. Sophocles, *Antigone*, ed. and trans. Hugh Lloyd-Jones (Cambridge, Mass.: Harvard University Press, 1994), p. 127.
5. Ahmad Hasan Dani et al., *History of Civilizations of Central Asia* (Paris: UNESCO, 1992), p. 107.
6. Diodoros 3.12.2–3, trans. J. Buckler.

CONNECTIONS

The ancient Greeks built on the achievements of earlier societies in the eastern Mediterranean, but they also added new elements, including history, drama, philosophy, science, and realistic art. The Greek world was largely conquered by the Romans, as you will learn in the following chapter, and the various Hellenistic monarchies became part of the Roman Empire. In cultural terms the lines of conquest were reversed: the Romans derived their alphabet from the Greek alphabet, though they changed the letters somewhat. Roman statuary was modeled on Greek and was often, in fact, made by Greek sculptors, who found ready customers among wealthy Romans. Furthermore, the major Roman gods and goddesses were largely the same as Greek ones, though they had different names. Although the Romans did not seem to have been particularly interested in the speculative philosophy of Socrates and Plato, they were drawn to the more practical philosophies of the Epicureans and Stoics. And like the Hellenistic Greeks, many Romans turned to mystery religions that offered secret knowledge and promised eternal life.

The influence of the ancient Greeks was not limited to the Romans, of course. As discussed in Chapter 3, art and thought in northern India was shaped by the blending of Greek and Buddhist traditions. And as you will see in Chapter 15, European thinkers and writers made conscious attempts to return to classical ideals in art, literature, and philosophy during the Renaissance. In America political leaders from the Revolutionary era on decided that important government buildings should be modeled on the Parthenon or other temples, complete with marble statuary of their own heroes. In some ways, capitol buildings in the United States are good symbols of the legacy of Greece — gleaming ideals of harmony, freedom, democracy, and beauty that (as with all ideals) do not always correspond with realities.

Chapter Review

MAKE IT STICK

✓ LearningCurve
Go online and use LearningCurve to retain what you've read.

IDENTIFY KEY TERMS

Identify and explain the significance of each item below.

polis (p. 117)

hoplites (p. 118)

democracy (p. 119)

oligarchy (p. 119)

mystery religions (p. 126)

Platonic ideals (p. 128)

Hellenistic (p. 129)

Hellenization (p. 131)

Epicureanism (p. 136)

Stoicism (p. 136)

REVIEW THE MAIN IDEAS

Answer the focus questions from each section of the chapter.

1. How did the geography of Greece shape its earliest history? (p. 114)

2. What was the role of the polis in Greek society? (p. 117)

3. In the classical period, how did war influence Greece, and how did the arts, religion, and philosophy develop? (p. 122)

4. How did Alexander the Great's conquests shape society in the Hellenistic period? (p. 129)

5. How did religion, philosophy, and science develop in the Hellenistic world? (p. 134)

MAKE CONNECTIONS

Analyze the larger developments and continuities within and across chapters.

1. Philosophers and religious thinkers in ancient India, China, and Greece, such as Mahavira and the Buddha (Chapter 3), Confucius and Zhuangzi (Chapter 4), and Socrates and Zeno (this chapter), all developed ideas about the ultimate aim of human life. What similarities and differences do you see among them?

2. The Persian Empire (Chapter 2) first brought India and the Mediterranean in contact with one another, and these contacts increased with the conquests of Alexander (Chapter 3 and this chapter). What were the major results of these contacts in terms of politics, culture, and economics?

3. Looking at your own town or city, what evidence do you find of the cultural legacy of ancient Greece?

▷LaunchPad
ONLINE DOCUMENT PROJECT

Technological Warfare
What advances in technological warfare occurred during the Hellenistic period?

Read accounts of the siege of Syracuse, and then complete a quiz and writing assignment based on the evidence and details from this chapter.

See inside the front cover to learn more.

CHRONOLOGY

ca. 3000–1200 B.C.E.	• Helladic period
ca. 2000–1100 B.C.E.	• Minoan and Mycenaean civilizations
ca. 1200–323 B.C.E.	• Hellenic period
ca. 1100–800 B.C.E.	• Greece's Dark Age; population declines, trade decreases, writing disappears
ca. 800–500 B.C.E.	• Archaic age; rise of the polis; Greek colonization of the Mediterranean
ca. 700–500 B.C.E.	• Sparta and Athens develop distinctive political institutions
ca. 500–338 B.C.E.	• Classical period; development of drama, philosophy, and major building projects in Athens
499–404 B.C.E.	• Persian and Peloponnesian wars
336–324 B.C.E.	• Alexander the Great's military campaigns
323–30 B.C.E.	• Hellenistic period
323–ca. 300 B.C.E.	• Civil wars lead to the establishment of the Ptolemaic, Antigonid, and Seleucid dynasties
168 B.C.E.	• Roman overthrow of the Antigonid dynasty
30 B.C.E.	• Roman conquest of Egypt; Ptolemaic dynasty ends

✓ LearningCurve
After reading the chapter, go online
and use LearningCurve to retain what
you've read.

The World of Rome

ca. 1000 B.C.E.–400 C.E.

LIKE THE PERSIANS UNDER CYRUS, THE MAURYANS UNDER
Chandragupta, and the Macedonians under Alexander, the Romans conquered vast territories. With a republican government under the leadership
of the Senate, a political assembly whose members were primarily wealthy
landowners, the Romans conquered all of Italy, then the western Mediterranean basin, and then areas in the East that had been part of Alexander
the Great's empire. As they did, they learned about and incorporated Greek
art, literature, philosophy, and religion, but the wars of conquest also led
to serious problems that the Senate proved unable to handle. After a grim
period of civil war that ended in 31 B.C.E., the emperor Augustus restored
peace and expanded Roman power and law as far east as the Euphrates
River, creating the institution that the modern world calls the "Roman
Empire." Later emperors extended Roman authority farther still, so that
at its largest the Roman Empire stretched from England to Egypt and from
Portugal to Persia.

Roman history is generally divided into three periods: the monarchical
period, traditionally dated from 753 B.C.E. to 509 B.C.E., in which the city of
Rome was ruled by kings; the republic, traditionally dated from 509 B.C.E. to
27 B.C.E., in which it was ruled by the Senate; and the empire, from 27 B.C.E.
to 476 C.E., in which Roman territories were ruled by an emperor.

The Romans in Italy

How did the Romans come to dominate Italy, and what political institutions did they create?

The colonies established by Greek poleis (city-states) in the Hellenic era included a number along the coast of southern Italy and Sicily, an area already populated by a variety of different groups that farmed, fished, and traded. So many Greek settlers came to this area that it later became known as Magna Graecia—Greater Greece. Although Alexander the Great created an empire that stretched from his homeland of Macedonia to India, his conquests did not reach as far as southern Italy and Sicily. Thus the Greek colonies there remained independent, and they transmitted much of their culture to people who lived farther north in the Italian peninsula. These included the Etruscans (ih-TRUHS-kuhns), who built the first cities north of Magna Graecia, and then the Romans, who eventually came to dominate the peninsula. In addition to allying with conquered peoples and granting them citizenship, the Romans established a republic ruled by a Senate. However, social conflicts over the rights to power eventually erupted and had to be resolved.

The Etruscans

The culture that is now called Etruscan developed in north-central Italy about 800 B.C.E. Recent studies of DNA evidence have indicated that the Etruscans most likely originated in Turkey or elsewhere in southwest Asia, although when they migrated to Italy is not clear. The Etruscans spoke a language that was very different from Greek and Latin, but they adopted the Greek alphabet to write their language. We know they wrote letters, records, and literary works, but once the Romans conquered them, knowledge of how to read and write Etruscan died out. Also, the writings themselves largely disappeared, other than inscriptions on stone or engravings in metal. Modern scholars have learned to read Etruscan again to some degree, but most of what we

Sarcophagus of Seianti Hanunia Tlesnasa The woman portrayed on this lavish sarcophagus is the wealthy Etruscan Seianti Hanunia Tlesnasa. Although she is portrayed as a lovely young woman, analysis of the teeth on the body indicates that she was about fifty when she died. The influence of Hellenistic Greek art on Etruscan art is apparent in almost every feature of the sarcophagus. (© The Trustees of the British Museum/Art Resource, NY)

know about their civilization comes from archaeological evidence and from the writings of other peoples who lived around them at the same time.

The Etruscans established permanent settlements that evolved into cities resembling the Greek city-states (see page 117) and thereby built a rich cultural life, full of art and music, that became the foundation of civilization in much of Italy. They spread their influence over the surrounding countryside, which they farmed and mined for its rich mineral resources. From an early period the Etruscans began to trade natural products, especially iron, with their Greek neighbors to the south and with other peoples throughout the Mediterranean in exchange for luxury goods. Etruscan cities appear to have been organized in leagues, and beginning about 750 B.C.E. the Etruscans expanded southward into central Italy through military actions on land and sea and through the establishment of colony cities. In the process they encountered a small collection of villages subsequently called Rome.

The Founding of Rome

Archaeological evidence indicates that the ancestors of the Romans began to settle on the hills east of the Tiber during the early Iron Age, around 1000 B.C.E. to 800 B.C.E. Archaeological sources provide the most important information about this earliest period of Roman history, but later Romans told a number of stories about the founding of Rome. These mix legend and history, but they illustrate the traditional ethics, morals, and ideals of Rome.

The Romans' foundation myths were told in a number of different versions. In the most common of these, Romulus and Remus founded the city of Rome, an event later Roman authors dated precisely to 753 B.C.E. These twin brothers were the sons of the war god Mars, and their mother, Rhea Silvia, was a descendant of Aeneas, a brave and pious Trojan who left Troy after it was destroyed by the Greeks in the Trojan War. The brothers, who were left to die by a jealous uncle, were raised by a female wolf. When they were grown they decided to build a city in the hills that became part of Rome, but they quarreled over which hill should be the site of the city; Romulus killed Remus and named the city after himself. He also established a council of advisers later called the Senate, which means "council of old men." He and his mostly male followers expanded their power over neighboring peoples, in part by abducting and marrying their women. The women then arranged a peace by throwing themselves between their brothers and their husbands, convincing them that killing kin would make the men cursed. The Romans, favored by the gods, continued their rise to power. Despite its tales of murder and kidnapping, this founding myth ascribes positive traits to the Romans: they are descended from gods and heroes, can thrive in wild and tough settings, will defend their boundaries at all costs, and mix with other peoples rather than simply conquering them. Also, the story portrays women who were ancestors of Rome as virtuous and brave.

Later Roman historians continued the story by describing a series of kings after Romulus—the traditional number is seven—each elected by the Senate. According to tradition, the last three kings were Etruscan, and another tale about female virtue was told to explain why the Etruscan kings were overthrown. In this story, of which there are several versions, the son of King Tarquin, the Etruscan king who ruled Rome, raped Lucretia, a virtuous Roman wife, in her own home. She demanded that her husband and father seek vengeance and then committed suicide in front of them. Her father and husband and the other Roman nobles swore on the bloody knife to avenge Lucretia's death by throwing out the Etruscan kings, and they did. Whether any of this story was true can never be known, but Romans generally accepted it as history and dated the expulsion of the Etruscan kings to 509 B.C.E. They thus saw this year as marking the end of the monarchical period and the dawn of the republic, which had come about because of a wronged woman and her demands.

Most historians today view the idea that Etruscan kings ruled the city of Rome as legendary, but they stress the influence of the Etruscans on Rome. The Etruscans transformed Rome into a real city with walls, temples, a drainage system, and other urban structures. The Romans adopted the Etruscan alphabet, which the Etruscans themselves had adopted from the Greeks. Even the toga, the white woolen robe worn by citizens, came from the Etruscans, as did gladiatorial combat honoring the dead. In engineering and architecture the Romans adopted some design elements and the basic plan of their temples, along with paved roads, from the Etruscans.

In this early period the city of Rome does appear to have been ruled by kings, as were most territories in the ancient world. A hereditary aristocracy also developed — again, an almost universal phenomenon — which advised the kings and may have played a role in choosing them. And sometime in the sixth century B.C.E. a group of aristocrats revolted against these kings and established a government in which the main institution of power would be the Senate, an assembly of aristocrats, rather than a single monarch. Executive power was in the hands of leaders called **consuls**, but there were always two of them and they were elected for one-year terms only, not for life. Rome thereby became a republic, not a monarchy. Thus at the core of the myths is a bit of history.

The Roman Conquest of Italy

In the years following the establishment of the republic, the Romans fought numerous wars with their neighbors on the Italian peninsula. The Roman army was made up primarily of citizens of Rome, who were organized for military campaigns into legions; those who could afford it bought their own weapons and armor. War also involved diplomacy, at which the Romans became masters. At an early date they learned the value of alliances, which became a distinguishing feature of Roman expansion in Italy.

In 387 B.C.E. the Romans suffered a major setback when the Celts — or Gauls, as the Romans called them — invaded the Italian peninsula from the north, swept aside a Roman army, and sacked the city of Rome. More intent on loot than land, the Celts agreed to abandon Rome in return for a thousand pounds of gold. In the century that followed, the Romans rebuilt their city and recouped their losses. They brought Latium and their Latin allies fully under their control and conquered Etruria. In a series of bitter wars the Romans also subdued southern Italy, including much of Magna Graecia, and then turned north. Their superior military institutions, organization, and manpower allowed them to conquer or bring under their influence most of Italy by about 265 B.C.E. (Map 6.1).

As they expanded their territory, the Romans spread their religious traditions throughout Italy, blending them with local beliefs and practices. Religion for the Romans was largely a matter of honoring the state and the family. The main goal of religion was to secure the peace of the gods, what was termed *pax deorum*, and to harness divine power for public and private enterprises. Religious rituals were an important way of expressing common values, which for Romans meant those evident in their foundation myths: bravery, morality, seriousness, family, and home. In the city of Rome the shrine of Vesta, the goddess of hearth and home, was tended by six "vestal virgins" chosen from patrician families. Roman military losses were sometimes blamed on inattention by the vestal virgins, another link between female honor and the Roman state. Victorious generals made sure to honor the gods of people they had conquered and by doing so transformed them into gods they could also call on for assistance in their future campaigns. As the Romans conquered the cities of Magna Graecia, the Greek deities were absorbed into the Roman pantheon.

Once they had conquered an area, the Romans did what the Persians had earlier done to help cement their new territory: they built roads. Roman roads facilitated the flow of communication, trade, and armies from the capital to outlying areas. They were the tangible sinews of unity, and many were marvels of engineering, as were the stone bridges the Romans built over Italy's many rivers.

In politics the Romans shared full Roman citizenship with many of their oldest allies, particularly the inhabitants of the cities of Latium. In other instances they granted citizenship without the franchise, that is, without the right to vote or hold Roman office. These allies were subject to Roman taxes and calls for military service but ran their own local affairs.

The Roman State

Along with citizenship, the republican government was another important institution of Roman political life. The Romans summed up their political existence in a single phrase: *senatus populusque Romanus*, "the Senate and the Roman people," which they abbreviated "SPQR." This sentiment reflects the republican ideal of shared government rather than power concentrated in a monarchy. It stands for the beliefs, customs, and laws of the republic—its unwritten constitution that evolved over two centuries to meet the demands of the governed.

In the early republic, social divisions determined the shape of politics. Political power was in the hands of a hereditary aristocracy—the **patricians**, whose privileged legal status was determined by their birth as members of certain families. Patrician men dominated the affairs of state, provided military leadership in time of war, and monopolized knowledge of law and legal procedure. The common people of Rome, the **plebeians** (plih-BEE-uhns), were free citizens with a voice in politics, but they had few of the patricians' political and social advantages. While some plebeian merchants rivaled the patricians in wealth, most plebeians were poor artisans, small farmers, and landless urban dwellers.

The Romans created several assemblies through which men elected high officials and passed ordinances. The most important of these was the Senate, a political assembly that by tradition was established by Romulus and in reality most likely originated in the monarchical period as a council of the heads of powerful families who advised the king. During the republic, the Senate advised the consuls and other officials about military and political matters and handled government finances. Because the Senate sat year after year with the same members, while the consuls changed annually, it

Rome

Hills of Rome

FIELD OF MARS

Quirinal Hill
Viminal Hill
Esquiline Hill
Caelian Hill
Senate House
Forum
Regia
Capitoline Hill
Palatine Hill
Temple of Jupiter
Circus Maximus
Aventine Hill
Servian Wall
Tiber Island
Tiber R.

1,000 meters
3,000 feet
500
1,500
0
0

Legend:
- Roman territory (full citizens)
- Roman territory (citizens without suffrage)
- Roman allies
- Latin colonies
- Carthaginian possessions
- Greek city
- Major roads by 100 B.C.E.
- Roman territory added by 218 B.C.E.

EPIRUS
ILLYRIA
Epidamnus
Apollonia
Brundisium
CALABRIA
Barium
Tarentum
Gulf of Tarentum
Appian Way
Thurii
Croton
LUCANIA
BRUTTIUM
Locri
Rhegium
Messana
Syracuse
Sicily
Lilybaeum
Venusia
APENNINES
APULIA
Beneventum
Aesinum
CAMPANIA
SAMNIUM
Capua
Misenum
Neapolis
Paestum
Aquileia
Verona
Cremona
Placentia
Genua
PO VALLEY
Adige R.
Po R.
CISALPINE GAUL
ALPS
Bononia
Florentia
Pisae
Arno R.
Populonia
Elba
ETRURIA
Arretium
Saturnia
Veii
Rome
Appian Way
Tiber R.
Reate
UMBRIA
PICENUM
Ariminum
Fanum Fortunae
Ancona
Castrum Truentinum
Castrum Novum
Corfinium
LATIUM
Tarracina
Ligurian Sea
Corsica
Aleria
Sardinia
Neapolis
Mediterranean Sea
Tyrrhenian Sea
NORTH AFRICA
Hippo Regius
Carthage
Utica
Cape Bon

N E W S

100 miles
100 kilometers
50
50
0
0

45°N
40°N
20°E
15°E
10°E

◀ **MAP 6.1   Roman Italy and the City of Rome, ca. 218 B.C.E.** As Rome expanded, it built roads linking major cities and offered various degrees of citizenship to the territories it conquered or with which it made alliances. The territories outlined in green that are separate from the Italian peninsula were added by 218 B.C.E., largely as a result of the Punic Wars.

provided stability, and its advice came to have the force of law. Another responsibility of the Senate was to handle relations between Rome and other powers, as Polybius, a Greek politician and historian writing in the middle of the second century B.C.E., reported:

> If it is necessary to send an embassy to reconcile warring communities, or to remind them of their duty, or sometimes to impose requisitions upon them, or to receive their submission, or finally to proclaim war against them — this too is the business of the Senate.[1]

The highest officials of the republic were the two consuls, positions initially open only to patrician men. The consuls commanded the army in battle, administered state business, and supervised financial affairs. When the consuls were away from Rome, praetors (PREE-tuhrz) could act in their place; they could also command armies, interpret law, and administer justice. After the age of overseas conquests (see below), the Romans divided their lands in the Mediterranean into provinces governed by ex-consuls and ex-praetors. Because of these officials' experience in Roman politics, they were suited to administer the affairs of the provinces and to adapt Roman law and customs to new contexts. Other officials worked with the Senate to oversee the public treasury, register citizens, and supervise the city of Rome.

A lasting achievement of the Romans was their development of law. Roman civil law, the *ius civile*, consisted of statutes, customs, and forms of procedure that regulated the lives of citizens. As the Romans came into more frequent contact with foreigners, the praetors applied a broader *ius gentium*, the "law of the peoples," to such matters as peace treaties, the treatment of prisoners of war, and the exchange of diplomats. In the ius gentium, all sides were to be treated the same regardless of their nationality. By the late republic, Roman jurists had widened this still further into the concept of *ius naturale*, "natural law" based in part on Stoic beliefs (see page 136). Natural law, according to these thinkers, is made up of rules that govern human behavior that come from applying reason rather than customs or traditions, and so apply to all societies. In reality, Roman officials generally interpreted the law to the advantage of Rome, of course, at least to the extent that the strength of Roman armies allowed them to enforce it. But Roman law came to be seen as one of Rome's most important legacies.

Social Conflict in Rome

Inequality between plebeians and patricians led to a conflict known as the Struggle of the Orders. In this conflict the plebeians sought to increase their power by taking advantage of the fact that Rome's survival depended on its army, which needed plebeians to fill the ranks of the infantry. According to tradition, in 494 B.C.E. the plebeians literally walked out of Rome and refused to serve in the army. Their general strike worked, and the patricians made important concessions. They allowed the plebeians to elect their own officials, the tribunes, who could bring plebeian grievances to the Senate for resolution and could also veto the decisions of the consuls. Thus, as in Archaic age Greece (see page 117), political rights were broadened because of military needs for foot soldiers.

The law itself was the plebeians' primary target. As noted above, only the patricians knew what the law was, and only they could argue cases in court. All too often they used the law for their own benefit. The plebeians wanted the law codified and published. After much struggle, in 449 B.C.E. the patricians surrendered their legal monopoly and codified and published the Laws of the Twelve Tables, so called because they were inscribed on twelve bronze plaques. The Laws of the Twelve Tables covered many legal issues, including property ownership, guardianship, inheritance, and punishments for various crimes. The patricians also made legal procedures public so that plebeians could argue cases in court. Several years later the patricians passed a law that for the first time allowed patricians and plebeians to marry one another.

After a ten-year battle, the Licinian-Sextian laws passed in 367 B.C.E. gave wealthy plebeians access to all the offices of Rome, including the right to hold one of the two consulships. Once plebeians could hold the consulship, they could also sit in the Senate and advise on policy. Though decisive, this victory did not automatically end the Struggle of the Orders. That happened only in 287 B.C.E. with the passage of the *lex Hortensia*, which gave the resolutions of the *concilium plebis*, the plebeian assembly, the force of law for patricians and plebeians alike. This compromise established a new elite of wealthy plebeians and patricians. Yet the Struggle of the Orders had made all citizens equal before the law, resulting in a Rome stronger and more united than before.

Roman Expansion and Its Repercussions

How did Rome expand its power beyond Italy, and what were the effects of this expansion?

As the republican government was developing, Roman territory continued to expand. In a series of wars the Romans conquered lands all around the Mediterranean, creating an overseas empire that brought them unheard-of power and wealth. As a result, many Romans became more cosmopolitan and comfortable, and they were especially influenced by the culture of one conquered land: Greece. Yet social unrest also came in the wake of the wars, opening unprecedented opportunities for ambitious generals who wanted to rule Rome like an empire. Civil war ensued, which was quelled briefly by the great politician and general Julius Caesar. His grandnephew Octavian, better known to history as Augustus, finally restored peace and order to Rome.

Overseas Conquests and the Punic Wars, 264–133 B.C.E.

The Romans did not map out grandiose strategies to conquer the world, as had Alexander the Great. Rather they responded to situations as they arose. This meant that they sought to eliminate any state they saw as a military threat.

Their presence in southern Italy brought the Romans to the island of Sicily, where they confronted another great power in the western Mediterranean, Carthage (CAHR-thij). The city of Carthage had been founded by Phoenicians as a trading colony in the eighth century B.C.E. (see page 48). It commanded one of the best harbors on the northern African coast and was supported by a fertile inland. By the fourth century B.C.E. the Carthaginians began to expand their holdings, and they engaged in war with the Etruscans and Greeks. At the end of a long string of wars, the Carthaginians had created and defended a mercantile empire that stretched from western Sicily to beyond Gibraltar.

The conflicting ambitions of the Romans and Carthaginians led to the first of the three Punic Wars. During the course of the first war, which lasted from 264 B.C.E. to 241 B.C.E., Rome built a navy and defeated Carthage in a series of sea battles. Sicily became Rome's first province, but despite a peace treaty, the conflict was not over.

Carthaginian armies moved into Spain, where Rome was also claiming territory. The brilliant Carthaginian general Hannibal (ca. 247–183 B.C.E.) marched an army of tens of thousands of troops—and, more famously, several dozen war elephants—from Spain across what is now France and over the Alps into Italy, beginning the Second Punic (PYOO-nik) War (218–201 B.C.E.). Hannibal won three major victories, including a devastating blow at Cannae in southeastern Italy in 216 B.C.E. There he inflicted perhaps fifty thousand casualties on the Romans. He then spread devastation throughout Italy, and a number of cities in central and southern Italy rebelled against Rome because it appeared to them that Hannibal would be victorious. Yet Hannibal was not able to win areas near Rome in central Italy. His allies, who included Philip V, the Antigonid king of Macedonia (see page 131), did not supply him with enough food and supplies to sustain his troops, and Rome fought back.

The Roman general Scipio Africanus (ca. 236–ca. 183 B.C.E.) copied Hannibal's methods of mobile warfare and guerrilla tactics and made more extensive use of cavalry than had earlier Roman commanders. He took Spain from the Carthaginians and then struck directly at Carthage itself, prompting the Carthaginians to recall Hannibal from Italy to defend the homeland. In 202 B.C.E., near the town of Zama, Scipio defeated Hannibal in one of the world's truly decisive battles. Scipio's victory meant that the world of the western Mediterranean would henceforth be Roman. Roman language, law, and culture, fertilized by Greek influences, would in time permeate this entire region.

The Second Punic War contained the seeds of still other wars. Unabated fear of Carthage led to the Third Punic War (149–146 B.C.E.), a needless, unjust, and savage conflict that ended when Scipio Aemilianus, a grandson by adoption of Scipio Africanus, destroyed the hated rival and burned Carthage to the ground.

After the Second Punic War, the Romans turned east. The Roman legions were victorious over Macedonian troops, and the Romans made Antigonid Macedonia into a Roman province. Then they moved farther east and defeated the Seleucid monarchy. In 133 B.C.E. the king of Pergamum in Asia Minor willed his kingdom to Rome when he died. The Ptolemies of Egypt retained formal control of their kingdom, but they obeyed Roman wishes in terms of trade policy. Declaring the Mediterranean *mare nostrum*, "our sea," the Romans began to create a political and administrative machinery to hold the Mediterranean together under a mutually shared cultural and political system of provinces ruled by governors sent from Rome.

Not all Romans were joyful over Rome's conquest of the Mediterranean world; some considered that victory a misfortune. The historian Sallust (86–34 B.C.E.), writing from hindsight, complained that the acquisition of an empire was the beginning of Rome's troubles:

> But when through labor and justice our Republic grew powerful . . . then fortune began to be harsh and to throw everything into confusion. The Romans had easily borne labor, danger, and hardship. To them leisure, riches—otherwise desirable—proved to be burdens and torments. So at first money, then desire for power, grew great. These things were a sort of cause of all evils.[2]

New Influences and Old Values in Roman Culture

With the conquest of the Mediterranean world, Rome became a great city. The spoils of war went to build theaters, stadiums, and other places of amusement, and Romans and Italian townspeople began to spend more of their time in leisure pursuits. This new urban culture reflected Hellenistic influences. Romans developed a liking for Greek literature, and it became common for an educated Roman to speak both Latin and Greek. Furthermore, the Roman conquest of the Hellenistic East resulted in wholesale confiscation of Greek paintings and sculpture to grace Roman temples, public buildings, and private homes.

The Greek custom of bathing also gained popularity in the Roman world. Increasingly, Romans built large public buildings containing pools supplied by intricate systems of aqueducts, which by the early empire became essential parts of the Roman city. These structures were more than just places to bathe. Baths included gymnasia where men exercised, snack bars and halls where people chatted and read, and even libraries and lecture halls. Women had opportunities to bathe, generally in separate facilities or at separate times, and both women and men went to the baths to see and be seen. Conservative commentators objected to these new pastimes as a corruption of traditional Roman values, but most Romans saw them as a normal part of urban life.

New customs did not change the core Roman social structures. The male head of the household was called the **paterfamilias**, and he had great power over his children. Initially this seems to have included power over life and death, but by the second century B.C.E. his authority had been limited by law and custom. Fathers continued to have the power to decide how family resources should be spent, however, and sons did not inherit until after their fathers had died. Women could inherit and own property, though they generally received a smaller portion of any family inheritance than their brothers. The Romans praised women, like Lucretia of old, who were virtuous and loyal to their husbands and devoted to their children. Very young children were under their mother's care, and most children learned the skills they needed from their own parents. For children from wealthier urban families, opportunities for formal education increased in the late republic. Boys and girls might be educated in their homes by tutors, who were often Greek slaves, and boys also might go to a school, paid for by their parents.

Most Romans continued to work long days, but an influx of slaves from Rome's conquests provided labor for the fields, mines, and cities. To the Romans slavery was a misfortune that befell some people, but it did not entail any racial theories. For loyal slaves the Romans always held out the possibility of freedom, and manumission—the freeing of individual slaves by their masters—became common. Nonetheless, slaves rebelled from time to time in large-scale revolts put down by Roman armies.

Membership in a family did not end with death, as the spirits of the family's ancestors were understood to remain with the family. They and other gods regarded as protectors of the household—collectively these were called the *lares* and *penates*—were represented by small statues that stood in a special cupboard, were honored at family celebrations, and were taken with the family when they moved.

The Late Republic and the Rise of Augustus, 133–27 B.C.E.

The wars of conquest eventually created serious political problems for the Romans. When the soldiers returned home, they found their farms practically in ruins. Many were forced to sell their land to ready buyers who had grown rich from the wars. These wealthy men created huge estates called latifundia. Now landless, veterans moved to the cities, especially Rome, but could not find work. These developments not only created unrest in the city but also threatened Rome's army by reducing its ranks. The Romans had always believed that only landowners should serve in the army, for only they had something to fight for. Landless men, even if they were Romans and lived in Rome, were forbidden to serve. The landless veterans were willing to follow any leader who promised help. The leader who answered their call was Tiberius Gracchus (163–133 B.C.E.), an aristocrat who was appalled by the situation. Elected tribune in 133 B.C.E., he proposed dividing public land among the poor. But a group of wealthy senators murdered him, launching a long era of political violence that would destroy the republic. Still, Tiberius's brother Gaius Gracchus (153–121 B.C.E.) passed a law providing the urban poor with cheap grain and urged practical reforms. Once again senators tried to stem the tide of reform by murdering him.

The next reformer, Gaius Marius (ca. 157–86 B.C.E.), recruited landless men into the army to put down a rebel king in Africa. He promised them land for their service. But after his victory, the Senate refused to honor his promise. From then on, Roman soldiers looked to their commanders, not to the Senate or the state, to protect their interests. Rome was also dividing into two political factions, both of which wanted political power. Both factions named individuals as supreme military commander, and each led Roman troops against an external enemy but also against each other. One of these generals, Sulla, gained power in Rome, and in 81 B.C.E. the Senate made him dictator, an official office in the Roman Republic given to a man who was granted absolute power temporarily to handle emergencies such as war. Dictators were supposed to step down after six months—and more than eighty dictators had done so in Roman history—but Sulla held this position for nine years, and after that it was too late to restore the republican constitution. Sulla's abuse of political office became the blueprint for later leaders.

The history of the late republic is the story of power struggles among many famous Roman figures against a background of unrest at home and military campaigns abroad. Pompey (PAHM-pee), who had been one of Sulla's officers, used military victories in Spain to force the Senate to allow him to run for consul. In 59 B.C.E. he was joined in a political alliance called the First Triumvirate by Crassus, another ambitious politician and the wealthiest man in Rome, and by Julius Caesar (100–44 B.C.E.). Born of a noble family, Caesar, an able general, was also a brilliant politician with unbridled ambition and a superb orator with immense literary ability. Recognizing that military success led to power, he led his troops to victory in Spain and Gaul, modern France. The First Triumvirate fell apart after Crassus was killed in battle in 53 B.C.E. while trying to conquer Parthia, leaving Caesar and Pompey in competition with each other

INDIVIDUALS IN SOCIETY • Queen Cleopatra

Cleopatra VII (69–30 B.C.E.) was a Ptolemy, a member of the dynasty of Hellenistic rulers of Egypt who had established power in the third century B.C.E. Although she was a Greek, she was passionately devoted to her Egyptian subjects and was the first in her dynasty who could speak Egyptian as well as Greek. Just as ancient pharaohs had linked themselves with the gods, she had herself portrayed as the goddess Isis and may have seen herself as a reincarnation of Isis (see page 41).

At the same time that civil war was raging in the late Roman Republic, Cleopatra and her brother Ptolemy XIII were in a dispute over who would be supreme ruler in Egypt. Julius Caesar captured the Egyptian capital of Alexandria, Cleopatra arranged to meet him, and the two became lovers, although Cleopatra was much younger and Caesar was married. The two apparently had a son, Caesarion, and Caesar's army defeated Ptolemy's army, ending the power struggle. In 46 B.C.E. Cleopatra arrived in Rome, where Caesar put up a statue of her as Isis in one of the city's temples. The Romans hated her because they saw her as a decadent Eastern queen and a threat to what were considered traditional Roman values.

After Caesar's assassination, Cleopatra returned to Alexandria. There she became involved in the continuing Roman civil war that now pitted Octavian, Caesar's heir, against Marc Antony, who commanded the Roman army in the East. When Antony visited Alexandria in 41 B.C.E. he met Cleopatra, and though he was already married to Octavian's sister, he became her lover. He abandoned (and later divorced) his Roman wife, married Cleopatra in 37 B.C.E., and changed his will to favor his children by Cleopatra. Antony's wedding present to Cleopatra was a huge grant of territory, much of it Roman, that greatly increased her power and that of all her children, including Caesarion. Antony also declared Caesarion to be Julius Caesar's rightful heir.

Octavian used the wedding gift as the reason to declare Antony a traitor. He and other Roman leaders described Antony as a romantic fool captivated by the seductive Cleopatra. Roman troops turned against Antony and joined with Octavian, and at the Battle of Actium in 31 B.C.E. Octavian defeated the army and navy of Antony and Cleopatra. Antony committed suicide, as did Cleopatra shortly after-

for power. The result was civil war. The Ptolemaic rulers of Egypt became mixed up in this war, particularly Cleopatra VII, who allied herself with Caesar and had a son by him. (See "Individuals in Society: Queen Cleopatra," above.) Although the Senate backed Pompey, Caesar was victorious. The Senate then began appointing Caesar to various offices, including that of consul, dictator, and imperator (ihm-puh-RAH-tuhr), a title given to victorious commanders. Caesar began to make a number of legal and economic reforms, acting on his own authority, though often with the approval of the Senate, which he packed with his supporters. He issued laws about debt, the collection of taxes, and the distribution of grain and land. Roman allies in Italy were to have full citizenship. He founded new colonies, which were to be populated by veterans and the poor.

improved i
land in the
He encour
bond betw
Augustus (
and becam
ing alongsi
military vi
buildings c

In the
changes th
from male
and womer
of property
money or
prostitution

Aside f
aged poets
age" of Lati
ments in v
conception

Rome'
(uh-NEE-i
(see page 1
of Rome ar
Trojan herc
at the fall c

Arms a
predest
to Italy
Smitter
by viol
stern Ju
he suff
the city
to safe
the Lat
and fro

As Vir
queen of C
ing the des
enmity hel
the good o
and the rea
Making th
an ancestor

ward. Octavian ordered the teenage Caesarion killed, but the young children of Antony and Cleopatra were allowed to go back to Rome, where they were raised by Antony's widow. In another consequence of Octavian's victory, Egypt became a Roman province.

Roman sources are viciously hostile to Cleopatra, and she became the model of the alluring woman whose sexual attraction led men to their doom. Stories about her beauty, sophistication, lavish spending, desire for power, and ruthlessness abounded and were retold for centuries. The most dramatic story was that she committed suicide through the bite of a poisonous snake, which may have been true and which has been the subject of countless paintings. Her tumultuous relationships with Caesar and Antony have been portrayed in plays, novels, movies, and television programs.

QUESTIONS FOR ANALYSIS

1. How did Cleopatra benefit from her relationships with Caesar and Antony? How did they benefit from their relationships with her?

2. How did ideas about gender and Roman suspicion of the more sophisticated Greek culture combine to shape Cleopatra's fate and the way she is remembered?

3. "Individuals in Society: Hatshepsut and Nefertiti" in Chapter 2 (see page 46) also focuses on leading female figures in Egypt, but these two women lived more than a thousand years before Cleopatra. How would you compare their situation with hers?

◗LaunchPad
ONLINE DOCUMENT PROJECT

What do Roman depictions of Cleopatra reveal about the attitudes and values of her time? Explore Roman accounts of Cleopatra to see what light they shed on political, social, and cultural values in the late republic and early empire, and then complete a quiz and writing assignment based on the evidence and details from this chapter.
See inside the front cover to learn more.

Caesar was wildly popular with most people in Rome, but some senators opposed his rise to what was becoming absolute power. In 44 B.C.E. a group of conspirators assassinated him and set off another round of civil war. His grandnephew and heir, the eighteen-year-old Octavian (63 B.C.E.–14 C.E.), joined with two of Caesar's followers, Marc Antony and Lepidus, in the Second Triumvirate. After defeating Caesar's murderers, they had a falling-out. Octavian forced Lepidus out of office and waged war against Antony, who had now also become allied with Cleopatra. In 31 B.C.E., with the might of Rome at his back, Octavian defeated the combined forces of Antony and Cleopatra at the Battle of Actium in Greece. His victory ended the age of civil war. For his success, in 27 B.C.E. the Senate gave Octavian the name Augustus, meaning "revered one." Although the Senate did not mean this to be a decisive break, that

date is g
Roman

The Su

After Au
tion. He
welfare o
Augustu

Aug
forming
fit his o
himself
held by

The
imperato
nization
pontifex
civitatis,
had beer
the word
what Au

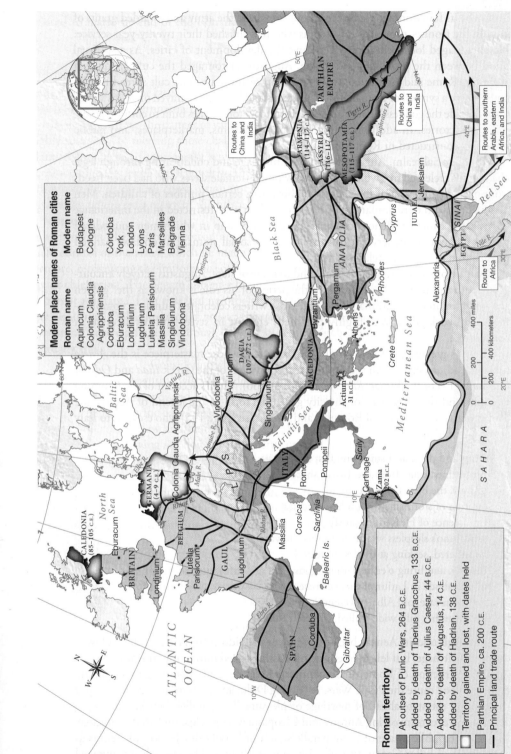

Modern place names of Roman cities

Roman name	Modern name
Aquincum	Budapest
Colonia Claudia Agrippinensis	Cologne
Corduba	Córdoba
Eburacum	York
Londinium	London
Lugdunum	Lyons
Lutetia Parisiorum	Paris
Massilia	Marseilles
Singidunum	Belgrade
Vindobona	Vienna

Routes to China and India

Routes to China and India

Routes to southern Arabia, eastern Africa, and India

Route to Africa

PARTHIAN EMPIRE

ARMENIA (114–117 C.E.)

ASSYRIA (116–117 C.E.)

MESOPOTAMIA (115–117 C.E.)

Tigris R.

Euphrates R.

Red Sea

Jerusalem

JUDAEA

Cyprus

EGYPT

SINAI

Nile R.

Black Sea

ANATOLIA

Pergamum

Rhodes

Alexandria

Dnieper R.

Byzantium

MACEDONIA

Athens

Crete

Mediterranean Sea

400 miles

400 kilometers

DACIA (107–272 C.E.)

Aquincum

Singidunum

Actium 31 B.C.E.

Adriatic Sea

SAHARA

Baltic Sea

Vistula R.

Vindobona

Danube R.

ALPS

ITALY

Rome

Pompeii

Sicily

Carthage

Zama 202 B.C.E.

Corsica

Sardinia

Massilia

Balearic Is.

GERMANIA (4–9 C.E.)

Colonia Claudia Agrippinensis

Elbe R.

Rhine R.

Main R.

BELGIUM

GAUL

Lugdunum

Lutetia Parisiorum

Rhone R.

North Sea

CALEDONIA (85–105 C.E.)

Eburacum

BRITAIN

Londinium

ATLANTIC OCEAN

SPAIN

Corduba

Gibraltar

Ebro R.

N E S W

Roman territory

- At outset of Punic Wars, 264 B.C.E.
- Added by death of Tiberius Gracchus, 133 B.C.E.
- Added by death of Julius Caesar, 44 B.C.E.
- Added by death of Augustus, 14 C.E.
- Added by death of Hadrian, 138 C.E.
- Territory gained and lost, with dates held
- Parthian Empire, ca. 200 C.E.
- Principal land trade route

◀ **MAP 6.2   Roman Expansion, 262 B.C.E.–180 C.E.** Rome expanded in all directions, eventually controlling every shore of the Mediterranean and vast amounts of land.

Virgil to write the *Aeneid* and made sure it was circulated widely immediately after Virgil died.

One of the most significant aspects of Augustus's reign was Roman expansion into northern and western Europe (Map 6.2). Augustus completed the conquest of Spain, founded twelve new towns in Gaul, and saw that the Roman road system linked new settlements with one another and with Italy. After hard fighting, he made the Rhine River the Roman frontier in Germania (Germany). Meanwhile, generals conquered areas as far as the Danube River, and Roman legions penetrated the areas of modern Austria, southern Bavaria, and western Hungary. The regions of modern Serbia, Bulgaria, and Romania also fell. Within this area the legionaries built fortified camps. Roads linked these camps with one another, and settlements grew up around the camps, eventually becoming towns. Traders began to frequent the frontier and to do business with the people who lived there; as a result, for the first time, central and northern Europe came into direct and continuous contact with Mediterranean culture.

Romans did not force their culture on native people in Roman territories. However, just as earlier ambitious people in the Hellenistic world knew that the surest path to political and social advancement lay in embracing Greek culture and learning to speak Greek (see page 131), those determined to get ahead now learned Latin and adopted aspects of Roman culture.

Rome and the Provinces

What was life like in Rome, and what was it like in the provinces?

In the late eighteenth century the English historian Edward Gibbon dubbed the stability and relative peace within the empire that Augustus created the **pax Romana**, the "Roman peace," which he saw as lasting about two hundred years, until the end of the reign of the emperor Marcus Aurelius in 180 C.E. People being conquered by the Romans might not have agreed that things were so peaceful, but during this time the growing city of Rome saw great improvements, and trade and production flourished in the provinces. Rome also expanded eastward and came into indirect contact with China.

Political and Military Changes in the Empire

For fifty years after Augustus's death in 14 C.E. the dynasty that he established — known as the Julio-Claudians because all were members of the Julian and Claudian clans — provided the emperors of Rome. Some of the Julio-Claudians, such as Tiberius and Claudius, were sound rulers and created a bureaucracy of able administrators to help them govern. Others, including Caligula and Nero, were weak and frivolous.

In 68 C.E. Nero's inept rule led to military rebellion and widespread disruption. Yet only two years later Vespasian (r. 69–79 C.E.), who established the Flavian dynasty, restored order. He also turned Augustus's principate into a hereditary monarchy and expanded the emperor's powers. The Flavians (69–96 C.E.) restored discipline in the army and carried on Augustus's work in Italy and on the frontiers. During the brief reign of Vespasian's son Titus, Mount Vesuvius in southern Italy erupted, destroying Pompeii and other cities and killing thousands of people. The Flavians paved the way for the Antonines (96–192 C.E.), a dynasty of emperors under whose leadership the Roman Empire experienced a long period of prosperity and the height of the pax Romana. Wars generally ended victoriously and were confined to the frontiers. Second-century emperors made further changes in government. Hadrian (HAY-dree-uhn), who became emperor in 117 C.E., made the imperial bureaucracy created by Claudius more organized. He established imperial administrative departments and separated civil service from military service. In addition, he demanded professionalism from members of the bureaucracy. These innovations helped the empire run more efficiently while increasing the authority of the emperor.

The Roman army also saw changes, transforming from a mobile unit to a much larger defensive force, with more and more troops who were noncitizens. Because army service could lead to citizenship, men from the provinces and even from beyond the borders of the Roman Empire joined the army willingly to gain citizenship, receive a salary, and learn a trade. The frontiers became firmly fixed and were defended by a system of forts and walls, some of which, such as sections of Hadrian's Wall in England, are still standing today. Behind these walls, the network of roads was expanded and improved, both to supply the forts and to reinforce them in times of trouble. The Roman road system eventually grew to over fifty thousand miles, longer than the current interstate highway system in the United States; some of those roads are still usable today.

Life in Imperial Rome

The expansion and stabilization of the empire created great wealth, much of which flowed into Rome. The city, with a population of over a million, may have been the largest city in the world at that time. Although Rome could boast of stately palaces, noble buildings, and beautiful residential areas, most people lived in shoddily constructed houses. They took whatever work was available, making food, clothing, construction materials, and the many other items needed by the city's residents, or selling these products from small shops or at the city's many marketplaces. Many residents of the city of Rome were slaves, who ranged from highly educated household tutors or government officials or widely sought sculptors to workers who engaged in hard physical tasks.

Fire and crime were perennial problems even in Augustus's day, and sanitation was poor. In the second century urban planning and new construction greatly improved the situation. For example, engineers built an elaborate system that collected sewage from public baths, the ground floors of buildings, and public latrines. They also built hundreds of miles of aqueducts, most of them underground, to bring fresh water into the city from the surrounding hills. The aqueducts, powered entirely by gravity, were a sophisticated system that required regular maintenance. Building aqueducts required thousands and sometimes tens of thousands of workers, who were generally paid out of the imperial treasury.

Rome grew so large that it became ever more difficult to feed its residents. Emperors solved the problem by providing citizens with free oil, wine, and grain for bread. By doing so, they also stayed in favor with the people. They and other sponsors also entertained the people with gladiatorial contests in which participants fought using swords and other weapons. Games were advertised on billboards, and spectators were given a program with the names and sometimes the fighting statistics of the pairs, so that they could bet more easily. Some gladiators were criminals or prisoners of war, but by the imperial period increasing numbers were volunteers, often poor immigrants who saw gladiatorial combat as a way to support themselves. All gladiators were trained in gladiatorial schools and were legally slaves, although they could keep their winnings and a few became quite wealthy. The Hollywood portrayal of gladiatorial combat has men fighting to their death, but this was increasingly rare, as the owners of especially skilled fighters wanted them to continue to compete. The Romans were even more addicted to chariot racing than to gladiatorial shows. Winning charioteers were idolized just as sports stars are today.

Prosperity in the Roman Provinces

As the empire grew and stabilized, many Roman provinces grew prosperous through the growth of agriculture, trade, and industry, among other factors. Peace and security opened Britain, Gaul, and the lands of the Danube to settlers from other parts of the Roman Empire. Veterans were given small parcels of land in the provinces, becoming

Roman Architecture   The Pont du Gard at Nîmes in France is a bridge over a river that carried an aqueduct supplying millions of gallons of water per day to the Roman city of Nîmes in Gaul; the water flowed in a channel at the very top. Although this bridge was built largely without mortar or concrete, many Roman aqueducts and bridges relied on concrete and sometimes iron rods for their strength. (De Agostini Picture Library/O. Geddo/The Bridgeman Library)

This apocalyptic belief was an old one among Jews, but by the first century C.E. it had become more widespread than ever.

The pagan world also played its part in the story of early Christianity. The term **pagan**, which originally referred to those who lived in the countryside, came to refer to those who practiced religions other than Judaism or Christianity. This included religions devoted to the traditional Roman gods of the hearth, home, and countryside. Known as syncretistic religions, these religions blended Roman and indigenous deities. The cult of the emperor spread through the erection of statues, temples, and monuments, and mystery religions offered the promise of life after death (see Chapter 5). Many people in the Roman Empire practiced all of these religions, combining them in whatever way seemed most beneficial or satisfying to them.

The Life and Teachings of Jesus

Into this climate of Messianic hope and Roman religious blending came Jesus of Nazareth (ca. 3 B.C.E.–29 C.E.). According to Christian Scripture, he was born to deeply religious Jewish parents and raised in Galilee, stronghold of the Zealots and a trading center where Greeks and Romans interacted with Jews. His ministry began when he was about thirty, and he taught by preaching and telling stories.

Like Socrates and the Buddha, Jesus left no writings. Accounts of his sayings and teachings first circulated orally among his followers and were later written down. The principal evidence for his life and deeds are the four Gospels of the Bible (Matthew, Mark, Luke, and John), books that are part of what Christians later termed the New Testament. These Gospels — the name means "good news" — are records of Jesus's teachings, written sometime in the late first century to build a community of faith. The Gospels include certain details of Jesus's life, but they were not meant to be biographies. Their authors had probably heard many different people talk about what Jesus said and did, and there are discrepancies among the four accounts. These differences indicate that early followers had a diversity of beliefs about Jesus's nature and purpose. This diversity of beliefs about Jesus continues today. Some see him as a moral teacher, some as a prophet, and many as the son of God who rose from the dead and is himself divine.

However, almost all the early sources agree on certain aspects of Jesus's teachings: he preached of a heavenly kingdom of eternal happiness in a life after death and of the importance of devotion to God and love of others. His teachings were based on Hebrew Scripture and reflected a conception of God and morality that came from Jewish tradition. Jesus's orthodoxy enabled him to preach in the synagogue and the temple, but he deviated from orthodoxy in insisting that he taught in his own name, not in the name of Yahweh (the Hebrew name for God). The Greek translation of the Hebrew word *Messiah* is *Christos*, the origin of the English word *Christ*. Was Jesus the Messiah, the Christ? A small band of followers thought so, and Jesus claimed that he was. Yet Jesus had his own conception of the Messiah. He would establish a spiritual kingdom, not an earthly one. As recounted in one of the Gospels, he commented:

> Do not lay up for yourselves treasures on earth, where moth and rust consume and where thieves break in and steal, but lay up for yourselves treasures in heaven, where neither moth nor rust consumes and where thieves do not break in and steal. For where your treasure is, there will your heart be also. (Matthew 6:19–21)

The Roman official Pontius Pilate knew little about Jesus's teachings. He was concerned with maintaining peace and order. According to the New Testament, crowds followed Jesus into Jerusalem at the time of Passover, a highly emotional point in the Jewish year that marked the Jewish people's departure from Egypt under the leadership of Moses (see page 49). The prospect that these crowds would spark violence alarmed Pilate. Some Jews believed that Jesus was the long-awaited Messiah. Others hated and feared him because they thought him religiously dangerous. To avert riot and bloodshed, Pilate condemned Jesus to death, and his soldiers carried out the sentence. On the third day after Jesus's crucifixion, some of his followers claimed that he had risen from the dead. For his earliest followers and for generations to come, the resurrection of Jesus became a central element of faith.

The Spread of Christianity

The memory of Jesus and his teachings survived and flourished. Believers in his divinity met in small assemblies or congregations, often in one another's homes, to discuss the meaning of Jesus's message and to celebrate a ritual (later called the Eucharist or Lord's Supper) commemorating his last meal with his disciples before his arrest. Because they expected Jesus to return to the world very soon, they regarded earthly life and institutions as unimportant. Only later did these congregations evolve into what came to be called the religion of Christianity, with a formal organization and set of beliefs.

The catalyst in the spread of Jesus's teachings and the formation of the Christian Church was Paul of Tarsus, a well-educated Hellenized Jew who was comfortable in both the Roman and the Jewish worlds. The New Testament reports that at first Paul persecuted members of the new sect, but on the road to the city of Damascus in Syria he was converted to belief in Jesus and became a vigorous promoter of Jesus's ideas. Paul traveled all over the Roman Empire and wrote letters of advice to many groups. These letters were copied and widely circulated, transforming Jesus's ideas into more specific moral teachings. As a result of his efforts, Paul became the most important figure in changing Christianity from a Jewish sect into a separate religion, and many of his letters became part of Christian Scripture.

The breadth of the Roman Empire was another factor behind the spread of Christianity. If all roads led to Rome, they also led outward to the provinces. This enabled early Christians to spread their faith easily throughout the world known to them, as Jesus had told his followers to do in the Gospels, thus making his teachings universal.

Christian Oil Lamp   When Christianity spread in the Roman Empire, many believers purchased household goods with Christian symbols. This pottery lamp for an ordinary home, dating from the fourth century C.E., is marked with a common symbol for Jesus, the letters *XP* (chi rho), the first two letters in Greek for *Christos,* "Christ." (photo by Z. Radovan, Jerusalem/Bible Land Pictures/ akg-images)

The Romans also considered their empire universal, and the early Christians combined the two concepts of universalism.

Though most of the earliest converts seem to have been Jews, or Greeks and Romans who were already interested in Jewish moral teachings, Paul urged that Gentiles, or non-Jews, be accepted on an equal basis. The earliest Christian converts included people from all social classes. These people were reached by missionaries and others who spread the Christian message through family contacts, friendships, and business networks. Many women were active in spreading Christianity. Paul greeted male and female converts by name in his letters and noted that women often provided financial support for his activities. The growing Christian communities differed over the extent to which women should participate in the workings of the religion; some favored giving women a larger role in church affairs, while others were more restrictive.

People were attracted to Christian teachings for a variety of reasons. It was in many ways a mystery religion, offering its adherents special teachings that would give them immortality. But in contrast to traditional mystery religions, Christianity promised this immortality widely, not only to a select few. Christianity also offered the possibility of forgiveness, for believers accepted that human nature is weak and that even the best Christians could fall into sin. But Jesus loved sinners and forgave those who repented. Christianity was also attractive to many because it gave the Roman world a cause. Instead of passivity, Christians stressed the ideal of striving for a goal. By spreading the word of Christ, Christians played their part in God's plan for the triumph of Christianity on earth. They were not discouraged by temporary setbacks, believing Christianity to be invincible. Christianity likewise gave its devotees a sense of identity and community, which was very welcome in the often highly mobile world of the Roman Empire. To stress the spiritual kinship of this new type of community, Christians often called one another brother and sister. Also, many Christians took Jesus's commandment to love one another as a guide and provided support for widows, orphans, and the poor, just as they would for family members.

The Growing Acceptance and Evolution of Christianity

At first, most Roman officials largely ignored the followers of Jesus, viewing them simply as one of the many splinter groups within Judaism, but slowly some came to oppose Christian practices and beliefs. They considered Christians to be subversive dissidents because they stopped practicing traditional rituals and they objected—often publicly or in writing—to the cult of the emperor. Some Romans thought that Christianity was one of the worst of the mystery cults, with immoral and indecent rituals. Pagans also feared that the Greco-Roman gods would withdraw their favor from the Roman Empire because of the Christian insistence that the pagan gods either did not exist or were evil spirits. And many worried that Christians were trying to destroy the Roman family with their insistence on a new type of kinship and pointed to Jesus's words in the Gospels saying that salvation was far more important than family relationships.

Persecutions of Christians, including torture and executions, were organized by governors of Roman provinces and sometimes by the emperor, beginning with Nero. Most persecutions were local and sporadic in nature, however, and some of the gory stories about the martyrs are later inventions, designed to strengthen believers with accounts of earlier heroes. Responses to Christianity on the part of Roman emperors varied. Some left Christians in peace, while others ordered them to sacrifice to the emperor and the Roman gods or risk death.

By the second century Christianity was changing. The belief that Jesus was soon coming again gradually waned, and as the number of converts increased, permanent institutions were established instead of simple house churches. These included buildings and a hierarchy of officials often modeled on those of the Roman Empire. **Bishops**, officials with jurisdiction over a certain area, became especially important. They began to assert that they had the right to determine the correct interpretation of Christian teachings and to choose their successors.

Christianity also began to attract more highly educated individuals who developed complex theological interpretations of issues that were not clear in scripture. Often drawing on Greek philosophy and Roman legal traditions, they worked out understandings of such issues as how Jesus could be both divine and human and how God could be both a father and a son (and later a spirit as well, a Christian doctrine known as the Trinity). Bishops and theologians often modified teachings that seemed upsetting to Romans, such as Jesus's harsh words about wealth and family ties. Given all these changes, Christianity became more formal in the second century, with power more centralized.

Turmoil and Reform

How did the emperors respond to political, economic, and religious issues in the third and fourth centuries?

The prosperity and stability of the second century gave way to a period of domestic upheaval and foreign invasion in the Roman Empire that historians have termed the "crisis of the third century." Trying to repair the damage was the major work of the emperors Diocletian (r. 284–305) and Constantine (r. 306–337), both of whom rose to leadership through the ranks of the military. They enacted political and religious reforms that dramatically changed the empire.

Political Measures

During the crisis of the third century the Roman Empire was stunned by civil war, as different individuals, generally military commanders from the border provinces, claimed rights to leadership of the empire. Beginning in 235, emperors often ruled for only a few years or even months. Army leaders in the provinces declared their loyalty to one faction or another, or they broke from the empire entirely, thus ceasing to supply troops or taxes. Non-Roman groups on the frontiers took advantage of the chaos to invade Roman-held territory along the Rhine and Danube, occasionally even crossing the Alps to maraud in Italy. In the East, Sassanid armies advanced all the way to the Mediterranean. By the time peace was restored, the empire's economy was shattered, cities had shrunk in size, and many farmers had left their lands.

Diocletian, who had risen through the ranks of the military to become emperor in 284, ended the period of chaos. Under Diocletian the princeps became *dominus*, "lord," reflecting the emperor's claim that he was "the elect of god," ruling because of along the northern border between the Qin realm and the land controlled by the nomadic Xiongnu. After Li Si complained that scholars (especially Confucians) used records of the past to denigrate the emperor's achievements and undermine popular support, the emperor had all writings other than useful manuals on topics such as agriculture, medicine, and divination collected and burned. As a result of this massive book burning, many ancient texts were lost.

Assassins tried to kill the First Emperor three times, and perhaps as a consequence he became obsessed with discovering the secrets of immortality. He spent lavishly on a tomb designed to protect him in the afterlife. Although the central chambers have not yet been excavated, in nearby pits archaeologists have unearthed thousands of life-size terra-cotta figures of armed soldiers and horses lined up to protect him.

Like Ashoka in India a few decades earlier (see page 80), the First Emperor erected many stone inscriptions to inform his subjects of his goals and accomplishments. He had none of Ashoka's modesty, however. On one stone he described the conquest of the other states this way:

> The six states, insatiable and perverse, would not make an end of slaughter, until, pitying the people, the emperor sent troops to punish the wicked and display his might. His penalties were just, his actions true, his power spread far, all submitted to his rule. He wiped out tyrants, rescued the common people, brought peace to the four corners of the earth. His enlightened laws spread far and wide as examples to All Under Heaven until the end of time. Great is he indeed! The whole universe obeys his sagacious will; his subjects praise his achievements and have asked to inscribe them on stone for posterity.[1]

After the First Emperor died in 210 B.C.E., the Qin state unraveled. The Legalist institutions designed to concentrate power in the hands of the ruler made the stability of the government dependent on his strength and character, and his heir proved ineffective. The heir was murdered by his younger brother, and uprisings soon followed.

The Han Dynasty, 206 B.C.E.–220 C.E.

The eventual victor in the struggle for power that ensued in the wake of the collapse of the Qin Dynasty was Liu Bang, known in history as Emperor Gaozu (r. 202–195 B.C.E.). The First Emperor of Qin was from the Zhou aristocracy. Gaozu was, by contrast, from a modest family of commoners, so his elevation to emperor is evidence of how thoroughly the Qin Dynasty had destroyed the old order.

Gaozu did not disband the centralized government created by the Qin, but he did remove its most unpopular features. Harsh laws were canceled, taxes were sharply reduced, and a policy of noninterference was adopted in an effort to promote economic recovery. With policies of this sort, relative peace, and the extension of China's frontiers, the Chinese population grew rapidly (Map 7.1). The census of 2 C.E. recorded a population of 58 million, the earliest indication of China's large population. Few other societies kept such good records, making comparisons difficult, but high-end estimates for the Roman Empire are in a similar range (50–70 million).

The Han government was largely supported by the taxes and forced labor demanded of farmers, but this revenue regularly fell short of the government's needs. To pay for his military campaigns, Emperor Wu, the "Martial Emperor" (r. 141–87 B.C.E.), took

MAP 7.1 **The Han Empire, 206 B.C.E.–220 C.E.** The Han Dynasty asserted sovereignty over vast regions from Korea in the east to Central Asia in the west and Vietnam in the south. Once garrisons were established, traders were quick to follow, leading to considerable spread of Chinese material culture in East Asia. Chinese goods, especially silk, were in demand far beyond East Asia, promoting long-distance trade across Eurasia.

over the minting of coins, confiscated the land of nobles, sold offices and titles, and increased taxes on private businesses. A widespread suspicion of commerce as an un-productive exploitation of the true producers made it easy to levy especially heavy assessments on merchants. The worst blow to businessmen, however, was the govern-ment's decision to enter into market competition with them by selling the commodities that had been collected as taxes. In 119 B.C.E. government monopolies were established in the production of iron, salt, and liquor. These enterprises had previously been sources of great profit for private entrepreneurs. Large-scale grain dealing also had been a profitable business, and the government now took that over as well. Grain was to be bought where it was plentiful and its price low and to be either stored in granaries or transported to areas of scarcity. This procedure was supposed to eliminate speculation in grain, provide more constant prices, and bring profit to the government.

Han Intellectual and Cultural Life

In contrast to the Qin Dynasty, which favored Legalism, the Han came to promote Confucianism and recruit officials on the basis of their Confucian learning or Confucian moral qualities. The Han government's efforts to recruit men trained in the Confucian classics marked the beginning of the Confucian scholar-official system, one of the most distinctive features of imperial China.

However, the Confucianism that made a comeback during the Han Dynasty was a changed Confucianism. Although Confucian texts had fed the First Emperor's bonfires, some dedicated scholars had hidden their books, and others had memorized whole works: one ninety-year-old man was able to recite two long books almost in their entirety. The ancient books recovered in this way—called the **Confucian classics**—were revered as repositories of the wisdom of the past. Confucian scholars treated these classics with piety and attempted to make them more useful as sources of moral guidance by writing commentaries on them. Many Confucian scholars specialized in a single classic, and teachers passed on to their disciples their understanding of each sentence in the work. Other Han Confucians went to the opposite extreme, developing comprehensive cosmological theories that explained the world in terms of cyclical flows of yin and yang (see page 108) and the five phases (fire, water, earth, metal, and wood). Some used these theories to elevate the role of the emperor, who alone had the capacity to link the realms of Heaven, earth, and man. Natural disasters such as floods or earthquakes were viewed as portents that the emperor had failed in his role of maintaining the proper balance among the forces of Heaven and earth.

Han art and literature reveal a fascination with omens, portents, spirits, immortals, and occult forces. Emperor Wu tried to make contact with the world of gods and immortals through elaborate sacrificial offerings of food and wine, and he welcomed astrologers, alchemists, seers, and shamans to his court. He marveled at stories of deities such as the Queen Mother of the West and the Yellow Emperor, who took his entire court with him when he ascended to the realm of the immortals. Much of this interest in immortality and communicating with the spirit world was absorbed into the emerging religion of Daoism, which also drew on the philosophical ideas of Laozi and Zhuangzi (see pages 105–107).

Bronze Mirror The backs of bronze mirrors were frequently decorated with images of deities and animals and with auspicious words. As viewers turned the mirrors, they saw different scenes. This Han mirror features an outer border with semicircles decorated with cloud patterns and squares with words written on them. In the center are deities. (Mirror Featuring Deities and Kings in Three Sections Surrounded by Rings of Squares and Semicircles [bronze]. Eastern Han Dynasty [25–220]/Cleveland Museum of Art, Ohio, U.S.A./Gift of Drs. Thomas and Martha Carter in Honor of Sherman E. Lee/The Bridgeman Art Library)

A major intellectual accomplishment of the Han Dynasty was history writing. Sima Qian (145–ca. 85 B.C.E.) wrote a comprehensive history of China from the time of the mythical sage-kings of high antiquity to his own day, dividing his account into a chronology recounting political events, biographies of key individuals, and treatises on subjects such as geography, taxation, and court rituals. As an official of the emperor, he had access to important people and documents and to the imperial library. Like the Greek historians Herodotus and Thucydides (see page 123), Sima Qian believed fervently in visiting the sites where history was made, examining artifacts, and questioning people about events. He was also interested in China's geography and local history. The result of his research, ten years or more in the making, was *Records of the Grand Historian*, a massive work of literary and historical genius. In the chapter devoted to moneymakers, he described how the Ping family made its fortune:

> Lu people are customarily cautious and miserly, but the Ping family of Cao were particularly so. They started out by smelting iron and in time accumulated a fortune of a hundred million cash. All the members of the family from the father and elder brothers down to the sons and grandsons, however, made a promise that they would "Never look down without picking up something useful; never look up without grabbing something of value." They traveled about to all the provinces and kingdoms, selling goods on credit, lending money and trading. It was because of their influence that so many people in Zou and Lu abandoned scholarship and turned to the pursuit of profit.[2]

From examples like these, Sima Qian concluded that wealth has no permanent master: "It finds its way to the man of ability like the spokes of a wheel converging upon the hub, and from the hands of the worthless it falls like shattered tiles."[3] For centuries to come, Sima Qian's work set the standard for Chinese historical writing, although most of the histories modeled after it covered only a single dynasty. The first of these was the work of three members of the Ban family in the first century C.E. (See "Individuals in Society: The Ban Family," page 180.)

The circulation of books like Sima Qian's was made easier by the invention of paper, which the Chinese traditionally date to 105 C.E. Scribes had previously written on strips of bamboo and wood or rolls of silk. Cai Lun, to whom the Chinese attribute the invention of paper, worked the fibers of rags, hemp, bark, and other scraps into sheets of paper. Paper, thus, was somewhat similar to the papyrus made from pounded reeds in ancient Egypt. Though much less durable than wood, paper was far cheaper than silk and became a convenient means of conveying the written word. Compared to papyrus, it depended less on a specific source of plant fiber and so could be produced in many areas.

Inner Asia and the Silk Road

The difficulty of defending against the nomadic pastoral peoples to the north in the region known as Inner Asia is a major reason China came to favor a centralized bureaucratic form of government. Resources from the entire subcontinent were needed to maintain control of the northern border.

Chinese civilization did not spread easily to the grasslands north of China proper, because those lands were too dry and cold to make good farmland. Herding sheep,

INDIVIDUALS IN SOCIETY ◆ The Ban Family

Ban Biao (3–54 C.E.), a successful official from a family with an envied library, had three highly accomplished children: his twin sons, the general Ban Chao (32–102) and the historian Ban Gu (32–92); and his daughter, Ban Zhao (ca. 45–120). After distinguishing himself as a junior officer in campaigns against the Xiongnu, Ban Chao was sent in 73 C.E. to the western regions to see about the possibility of restoring Chinese overlordship there, which had been lost several decades earlier. Ban Chao spent most of the next three decades in Central Asia. Through patient diplomacy and a show of force, he re-established Chinese control over the oasis cities of Central Asia, and in 92 he was appointed protector general of the area.

His twin brother, Ban Gu, was one of the most accomplished writers of his age, excelling in a distinctive literary form known as the rhapsody (*fu*). His "Rhapsody on the Two Capitals" is in the form of a dialogue between a guest from Chang'an and his host in Luoyang. It describes the palaces, spectacles, scenic spots, local products, and customs of the two great cities. Emperor Zhang (r. 76–88) was fond of literature and often had Ban Gu accompany him on hunts or travels. He also had him edit a record of the court debates he held on issues concerning the Confucian classics.

Ban Biao was working on the *History of the Former Han Dynasty* when he died in 54. Ban Gu took over this project, modeling it on Sima Qian's *Records of the Grand Historian*. He added treatises on law, geography, and bibliography, the last a classified list of books in the imperial library.

Because of his connection to a general out of favor, Ban Gu was sent to prison in 92, where he soon died. At that time the *History of the Former Han Dynasty* was still incomplete. The emperor called on Ban Gu's widowed sister, Ban Zhao, to finish it. She came to the palace, where she not only worked on the history but also became a teacher of the women of the palace. According to the *History of the Later Han*, she taught them the classics, history, astronomy, and mathematics. In 106 an infant succeeded to the throne, and the widow of an earlier emperor became regent. This empress frequently turned to Ban Zhao for advice on government policies.

horses, camels, and other animals made better economic use of those lands. By the third century B.C.E. several different peoples practicing nomadic pastoralism lived in those regions, moving with their herds north in summer and south in winter. Families lived in tents that could be taken down and moved to the next camp. Herds were tended on horseback, and everyone learned to ride from a young age. Especially impressive from the Chinese perspective was the ability of nomad horsemen to shoot arrows while riding horseback. Chinese farmers and Inner Asian herders had such different modes of life that it is not surprising that they had little respect for each other. For most of the imperial period, Chinese farmers looked on the northern non-Chinese horsemen as gangs of bullies who thought robbing was easier than working for a living. The nomads identified glory with military might and viewed farmers as contemptible weaklings.

Ban Zhao credited her own education to her learned father and cultured mother and became an advocate of the education of girls. In her *Admonitions for Women*, Ban Zhao objected that many families taught their sons to read but not their daughters. She did not claim girls should have the same education as boys; after all, "just as yin and yang differ, men and women have different characteristics." Women, she wrote, will do well if they cultivate womanly virtues such as humility. "Humility means yielding and acting respectful, putting others first and oneself last, never mentioning one's own good deeds or denying one's own faults, enduring insults and bearing with mistreatment, all with due trepidation."* In subsequent centuries Ban Zhao's *Admonitions* became one of the most commonly used texts for the education of Chinese girls.

QUESTIONS FOR ANALYSIS

1. What inferences can you draw from the fact that a leading general had a brother who was a literary man?

2. What does Ban Zhao's life tell us about women in her society? How do you reconcile her personal accomplishments with the advice she gave for women's education?

*Patricia Buckley Ebrey, ed., *Chinese Civilization: A Sourcebook*, 2d ed., revised and expanded (New York: Free Press, 1993), p. 75.

◗LaunchPad
ONLINE DOCUMENT PROJECT

What do Ban Zhao's writings reveal about attitudes toward women during her time? Read sources by and about Ban Zhao, and then complete a quiz and writing assignment based on the evidence and details from this chapter.

See inside the front cover to learn more.

In the late third century B.C.E. the Xiongnu (possibly the same group that was known in the West as the Huns) formed the first great confederation of nomadic tribes (see Map 7.1). The Qin's Great Wall was built to defend against the Xiongnu, and the Qin sent out huge armies in pursuit of them. The early Han emperors tried to make peace with them, offering generous gifts of silk, rice, cash, and even imperial princesses as brides. But these policies were controversial, since critics thought they merely strengthened the enemy. Xiongnu power did not wane, and in 166 B.C.E. 140,000 Xiongnu raided to within a hundred miles of the Chinese capital.

Emperor Wu then decided that China had to push the Xiongnu back. He sent several armies of 100,000 to 300,000 troops deep into Xiongnu territory. These costly campaigns were of limited value because the Xiongnu were a moving target: fighting nomads was not like attacking walled cities. If the Xiongnu did not want to fight the

Chinese troops, they simply moved their camps. To try to find allies and horses, Emperor Wu turned his attention west, toward Central Asia. From an envoy he sent into Bactria, Parthia, and Ferghana in 139 B.C.E., the Chinese learned for the first time of other civilized states comparable to China. The envoy described Ferghana as an urban society 10,000 *li* (about 3,000 miles) west of China, where grapes were grown for wine and the horses were particularly fine. In Parthia he was impressed by the use of silver coins stamped with the image of the king's face. These regions, he reported, were familiar with Chinese products, especially silk, and did a brisk trade in them.

In 114 B.C.E. Emperor Wu sent an army into Ferghana and gained recognition of Chinese overlordship in the area, thus obtaining control over the trade routes across Central Asia commonly called the **Silk Road** (see Map 7.1). The city-states along this route could carry out the trade on which they depended more conveniently with Chinese garrisons to protect them.

At the same time, Emperor Wu sent troops into northern Korea to establish military districts that would flank the Xiongnu on their eastern border. By 111 B.C.E. the Han government also had extended its rule south into Nam Viet, which extended from south China into what is now northern Vietnam. Thus, during Emperor Wu's reign, the territorial reach of the Han state was vastly extended.

During the Han Dynasty, China developed a **tributary system** to regulate contact with foreign powers. States and tribes beyond its borders sent envoys bearing gifts and received gifts in return. Over the course of the dynasty, the Han government's outlay on these gifts was huge, perhaps as much as 10 percent of state revenue. In 25 B.C.E., for instance, the government gave tributary states twenty thousand rolls of silk cloth and about twenty thousand pounds of silk floss. Although the tributary system was a financial burden to the Chinese, it reduced the cost of defense and offered China confirmation that it was the center of the civilized world.

The silk given to the Xiongnu and other northern tributaries often entered the trading networks of Persian, Parthian, and Indian merchants, who carried it by caravans across Asia. There was a market both for skeins of silk thread and for silk cloth woven in Chinese or Syrian workshops. Caravans returning to China carried gold, horses, and occasionally handicrafts of West Asian origin, such as glass beads and cups. Through the trade along the Silk Road, the Chinese learned of new foodstuffs, including walnuts, pomegranates, sesame, and coriander, all of which came to be grown in China. This trade was largely carried by the two-humped Bactrian camel, which had been bred in Central Asia since the first century B.C.E. With a heavy coat of hair to withstand the bitter cold of winter, each camel could carry about five hundred pounds of cargo.

Maintaining a military presence so far from the center of China was expensive. To cut costs, the government set up self-supporting military colonies, recruited Xiongnu tribes to serve as auxiliary forces, and established vast government horse farms. Still, military expenses threatened to bankrupt the Han government.

Life in Han China

How were ordinary people's lives affected by the creation of a huge Han bureaucratic empire? The lucky ones who lived in Chang'an or Luoyang, the great cities of the empire, got to enjoy the material benefits of increased long-distance trade and a boom in the production of luxury goods.

Ceramic Model of a Pigsty
Chinese farmers regularly raised pigs, keeping them in walled-off pens and feeding them scraps. This Han Dynasty model of such a pigsty was placed in a tomb to represent the material goods one hoped the deceased would enjoy in the afterlife. (Funerary model of a pigsty [earthenware], Western Han Dynasty [206 B.C.–A.D. 24]/Minneapolis Institute of Arts, Minnesota, U.S.A./Gift of Alan and Dena Naylor in memory of Thomas E. Leary/ The Bridgeman Art Library)

The government did not promote trade per se. The Confucian elite, like ancient Hebrew wise men, considered trade necessary but lowly. Agriculture and crafts were more honorable because they produced something, but merchants merely took advantage of others' shortages to make profits as middlemen. In a debate conducted in 81 B.C.E., the Confucian scholars argued: "If a country possesses a wealth of fertile land and yet its people are underfed, the reason is that merchants and workers have prospered while agriculture has been neglected."[4] This attitude justified the government's takeover of the grain, iron, and salt businesses. Still, the government indirectly promoted commerce by building roads and defending cities.

Markets were the liveliest places in the cities. Besides stalls selling goods of all kinds, markets offered fortune-tellers and entertainers. People flocked to puppet shows and performances of jugglers and acrobats. The markets were also used for the execution of criminals, to serve as a warning to onlookers.

Government patronage helped maintain the quality of craftsmanship in the cities. By the beginning of the first century C.E. China also had about fifty state-run iron-working factories. Chinese metalworking was the most advanced in the world at the time. In contrast to Roman blacksmiths, who hammered heated iron to make wrought iron tools, the Chinese knew how to liquefy iron and pour it into molds, producing tools with a higher carbon content that were harder and more durable. Han workmen turned out iron plowshares, agricultural tools with wooden handles, and weapons and armor.

Iron was replacing bronze in tools, but bronzeworkers still turned out a host of goods. Bronze was prized for jewelry, mirrors, and dishes. Bronze was also used for minting coins and for precision tools such as carpenters' rules and adjustable wrenches. Surviving bronze gear-and-cog wheels bear eloquent testimony to the sophistication of Han machinery. Han metal-smiths were mass-producing superb crossbows long before the crossbow was dreamed of in Europe.

The bulk of the population in Han times and even into the twentieth century consisted of peasants living in villages of a few hundred households. Because the Han empire, much like the contemporaneous Roman Empire, drew its strength from a large population of free peasants who contributed both taxes and labor services to the state, the government had to try to keep peasants independent and productive. The economic insecurity of smallholders was described by one official in 178 B.C.E. in terms that could well have been repeated in most later dynasties:

> They labour at plowing in the spring and hoeing in the summer, harvesting in the autumn and storing foodstuff in winter, cutting wood, performing labour service for the local government, all the while exposed to the dust of spring, the heat of summer, the storms of autumn, and the chill of winter. Through all four seasons they never get a day off. They need funds to cover such obligations as entertaining guests, burying the dead, visiting the sick, caring for orphans, and bringing up the young. No matter how hard they work they can be ruined by floods or droughts, or cruel and arbitrary officials who impose taxes at the wrong times or keep changing their orders. When taxes fall due, those with produce have to sell it at half price [to raise the needed cash], and those without [anything to sell] have to borrow [at such high rates] they will have to pay back twice what they borrowed. Some as a consequence sell their lands and houses, even their children and grandchildren.[5]

To fight peasant poverty, the government kept land taxes low (one-thirtieth of the harvest), provided relief in time of famine, and promoted up-to-date agricultural methods. Still, many hard-pressed peasants were left to choose between migration to areas where new lands could be opened and quasi-servile status as the dependents of a magnate. Throughout the Han period, Chinese farmers in search of land to till pushed into frontier areas, expanding Chinese domination at the expense of other ethnic groups, especially in central and south China.

The Chinese family in Han times was much like Roman (see page 153) and Indian (see page 67) families. In all three societies senior males had great authority, parents arranged their children's marriages, and brides normally joined their husbands' families. Other practices were more distinctive to China, such as the universality of patrilineal family names, the practice of dividing land equally among the sons in a family, and the great emphasis placed on the virtue of filial piety. The brief *Classic of Filial Piety*, which claimed that filial piety was the root of all virtue, gained wide circulation in Han times. The virtues of loyal wives and devoted mothers were extolled in the *Biographies of Exemplary Women*, which told the stories of women from China's past who were notable for giving their husbands good advice, knowing how to educate their sons, and sacrificing themselves when forced to choose between their fathers and husbands. The book also contained a few cautionary tales of scheming, jealous, manipulative women who brought destruction to all around them. One of the most commonly used texts for the education of women is Ban Zhao's *Admonitions for Women*, in which she extols the feminine virtues, such as humility. (See "Individuals in Society: The Ban Family," page 180.)

China and Rome

The empires of China and Rome (discussed in Chapter 6) were large, complex states governed by monarchs, bureaucracies, and standing armies. Both reached the people directly through taxation and conscription policies, and both invested in infrastructure such as roads and waterworks. The empires faced the similar challenge of having to work hard to keep land from becoming too concentrated in the hands of hard-to-tax wealthy magnates. In both empires people in neighboring areas that came under political domination were attracted to the conquerors' material goods, productive techniques, and other cultural products, resulting in gradual cultural assimilation. China and Rome also had similar frontier problems and tried similar solutions, such as recruiting "barbarian" soldiers and settling soldier-colonists.

Nevertheless, the differences between Rome and Han China are worth as much notice as the similarities. The Roman Empire was linguistically and culturally more diverse than China. In China there was only one written language; people in the Roman Empire still wrote in Greek and several other languages, and people in the eastern Mediterranean could claim more ancient civilizations. China did not have comparable cultural rivals. Politically the dynastic principle was stronger in China than in Rome. Han emperors were never chosen by the army or by any institution comparable to the Roman Senate, nor were there republican ideals in China. In contrast to the graduated forms of citizenship in Rome, Han China drew no distinctions between original and added territories. The social and economic structures also differed in the two empires. Slavery was much more important in Rome than in China, and merchants were more favored. Over time these differences put Chinese and Roman social and political development on different trajectories.

The Fall of the Han and the Age of Division

In the second century C.E. the Han government suffered a series of blows. A succession of child emperors required regents to rule in their place until they reached maturity, allowing the families of empresses to dominate the court. Emperors, once grown, turned to eunuchs (castrated palace servants) for help in ousting the empresses' families, only to find that the eunuchs were just as difficult to control. In 166 and 169 scholars who had denounced the eunuchs were arrested, killed, or banished from the capital and official life. Then in 184 a millenarian religious sect rose in massive revolt. The armies raised to suppress the rebels soon took to fighting among themselves. In 189 one general slaughtered two thousand eunuchs in the palace and took the Han emperor captive. After years of fighting, a stalemate was reached, with three warlords each controlling distinct territories in the north, the southeast, and the southwest. In 220 one of them forced the last of the Han emperors to abdicate, formally ending the Han Dynasty.

The period after the fall of the Han Dynasty is often referred to as the Age of Division (220–589). A brief reunification from 280 to 316 came to an end when non-Chinese who had been settling in north China since Han times seized the opportunity afforded by the political turmoil to take power. For the next two and a half centuries, north China was ruled by one or more non-Chinese dynasties (the Northern Dynasties), and the south was ruled by a sequence of four short-lived Chinese dynasties (the Southern Dynasties) centered in the area of the present-day city of Nanjing.

In the south a hereditary aristocracy entrenched itself in the higher reaches of officialdom. These families intermarried only with families of equivalent pedigree and compiled lists and genealogies of the most eminent families. They saw themselves as maintaining the high culture of the Han and looked on the emperors of the successive dynasties as upstarts—as military men rather than men of culture. In this aristocratic culture the arts of poetry and calligraphy flourished, and people began collecting writings by famous calligraphers.

Establishing the capital at Nanjing, south of the Yangzi River, had a beneficial effect on the economic development of the south. To pay for an army and to support the imperial court and aristocracy in a style that matched their pretensions, the government had to expand the area of taxable agricultural land, whether by settling migrants or converting the local inhabitants into taxpayers. The south, with its temperate climate and ample supply of water, offered nearly unlimited possibilities for such development.

The Northern Dynasties are interesting as the first case of alien rule in China. Ethnic tensions flared from time to time. In the late fifth century the Northern Wei (way) Dynasty (386–534) moved the capital from near the Great Wall to the ancient city of Luoyang, adopted Chinese-style clothing, and made Chinese the official language. But the armies remained in the hands of the non-Chinese Xianbei tribesmen. Soldiers who saw themselves as marginalized by the pro-Chinese reforms rebelled in 524. For the next fifty years north China was torn apart by struggles for power. It had long been the custom of the northern pastoral tribes to enslave those they captured; sometimes the residents of entire cities were enslaved. In 554, when the city of Jiangling was taken, a hundred thousand civilians were enslaved and distributed to generals and officials.

The Spread of Buddhism Out of India

How did Buddhism find its way into East Asia, and what was its appeal and impact?

In much the same period that Christianity was spreading out of its original home in ancient Israel, Buddhism was spreading beyond India. Buddhism came to Central, East, and Southeast Asia with merchants and missionaries along the overland Silk Road, by sea from India and Sri Lanka, and also through Tibet. Like Christianity, Buddhism was shaped by its contact with cultures in the different areas into which it spread, leading to several distinct forms.

Buddhism's Path Through Central Asia

Central Asia is a loose term used to refer to the vast area between the ancient civilizations of Persia, India, and China. Modern political borders are a product of competition for empire among the British, Russians, and Chinese in the mid-nineteenth century and have relatively little to do with the earlier history of the region. Through most of recorded history, the region was ethnically and culturally diverse; it was home to urban centers, especially at the oases along the Silk Road, and to animal herders in the mountains and grasslands.

Under Ashoka in India (see pages 80–82), Buddhism began to spread to Central Asia. This continued under the Kushan empire (ca. 50–250 C.E.), especially under the greatest Kushan king, Kanishka I (ca. 100 C.E.). In this region, where the influence of Greek art was strong, artists began to depict the Buddha in human form. Over the next several centuries most of the city-states of Central Asia became centers of Buddhism, from Bamiyan northwest of Kabul, to Kucha, Khotan, Loulan, Turfan, and Dunhuang. Because the remarkable Buddhist civilization of Central Asia was later supplanted by

Islam, it was not until early in the twentieth century that European archaeologists discovered its traces. The main sites yielded not only numerous Buddhist paintings but also thousands of texts in a variety of languages. In Khotan, for instance, an Indian language was used for administrative purposes long after the fall of the Kushan empire. Other texts were in various Persian languages, showing the cultural mix of the region.

The form of Buddhism that spread from Central Asia to China, Japan, and Korea was called Mahayana, which means "Great Vehicle" (see page 74), reflecting the claims of its adherents to a more inclusive form of the religion. Influenced by the Iranian religions then prevalent in Central Asia, Buddhism became more devotional. The Buddha came to be treated as a god, the head of an expanding pantheon of other Buddhas and bodhisattvas (Buddhas-to-be). With the growth of this pantheon, Buddhism became as much a religion for laypeople as for monks and nuns.

The first translators of Buddhist texts into Chinese were not Indians but Parthians, Sogdians, and Kushans from Central Asia. One of the most important interpreters of Buddhism in China was the eminent Central Asian monk Kumarajiva (350–413) from Kucha, who settled in Chang'an and directed several thousand monks in the translation of Buddhist texts.

The Appeal and Impact of Buddhism in China

Why did Buddhism find so many adherents in China during the three centuries after the fall of the Han Dynasty in 220? There were no forced conversions, but still the religion spread rapidly. In the unstable political environment, many people were open to new ideas. To Chinese scholars the Buddhist concepts of the reincarnation of souls, karma, and nirvana posed a stimulating intellectual challenge. To rulers the Buddhist religion offered a source of magical power and a political tool to unite Chinese and non-Chinese. In a rough and tumultuous age Buddhism's emphasis on kindness, charity, and eternal bliss was deeply comforting. As in India, Buddhism posed no threat to the social order, and the elite who were drawn to Buddhism encouraged its spread to people of all classes.

The monastic establishment grew rapidly in China. Like their Christian counterparts in medieval Europe, Buddhist monasteries played an active role in social, economic, and political life. By 477 there were said to be 6,478 Buddhist temples and 77,258 monks and nuns in the north. Some decades later south China had 2,846 temples and 82,700 clerics. Given the importance of family lines in China, becoming a monk was a major decision, since a man had to give up his surname and take a vow of celibacy, thus cutting himself off from the ancestral cult. Those not ready to become monks or nuns could pursue Buddhist goals as pious laypeople by performing devotional acts and making contributions to monasteries. Among the most generous patrons were rulers in both the north and south.

In China women turned to Buddhism as readily as men. Although birth as a female was considered lower than birth as a male, it was also viewed as temporary, and women were encouraged to pursue salvation on terms nearly equal to those of men. Joining a nunnery became an alternative for a woman who did not want to marry or did not want to stay with her husband's family in widowhood. Later, the only woman ruler of China, Empress Wu, invoked Buddhist principles to justify her role (see page 189), further evidence of how Buddhism brought new understandings of gender.

Meditating Monk   This monk, wearing the traditional patchwork robe, sits in the crossed-legged meditation position. His small niche is to the left of the main image of the Buddha in cave 285 at Dunhuang, a cave completed in 539 C.E. under the patronage of a prince of the Northern Wei imperial house who was then the local governor. (Photo: Lois Conner. Courtesy, Dunhuang Academy)

Buddhism had an enormous impact on the visual arts in China, especially sculpture and painting. Before Buddhism, Chinese had not set up statues of gods in temples, but now they decorated temples with a profusion of images. Inspired by the cave temples of India and Central Asia, Buddhists in China, too, carved caves into rock faces to make temples.

Not everyone was won over by Buddhist teachings. Critics of Buddhism labeled it immoral, unsuited to China, and a threat to the state since monastery land was not taxed and monks did not perform labor service. Twice in the north orders were issued to close monasteries and force monks and nuns to return to lay life, but these suppressions did not last long. No attempt was made to suppress belief in Buddhism, and the religion continued to thrive in the subsequent Sui and Tang periods.

The Chinese Empire Re-created: Sui (581–618) and Tang (618–907)

What were the lasting accomplishments of the Sui and Tang Dynasties?

Political division was finally overcome when the Sui Dynasty conquered its rivals to reunify China in 581. Although the dynasty lasted only thirty-seven years, it left a lasting legacy in the form of political reform, the construction of roads and canals, and the institution of written merit-based exams for the appointment of officials. The Tang Dynasty that followed would last for centuries and would build upon the Sui's accomplishments to create an era of impressive cultural creativity and political power.

The Sui Dynasty, 581–618

In the 570s and 580s the long period of division in China was brought to an end under the leadership of the Sui (sway) Dynasty. Yang Jian, who both founded the Sui Dynasty and oversaw the reunification of China, was from a Chinese family that had intermarried with the non-Chinese elite of the north. His conquest of the south involved naval as well as land battles, with thousands of ships on both sides contending for control of the Yangzi River. The Sui reasserted Chinese control over northern Vietnam and campaigned into Korea and against the new force on the steppe, the Turks. The Sui strengthened central control of the government by curtailing the power of local officials to appoint their own subordinates and by instituting in 605 C.E. competitive written examinations for the selection of officials. Preparing for such exams would come to dominate the lives of educated men in later centuries.

The crowning achievement of the Sui Dynasty was the construction of the **Grand Canal**, which connected the Yellow and Yangzi River regions. The canal facilitated the shipping of tax grain (that is, grain paid as tax) from the prosperous Yangzi Valley to the centers of political and military power in north China. Henceforth the rice-growing Yangzi Valley and south China played an ever more influential role in the country's economic and political life, strengthening China's internal cohesion and facilitating maritime trade with Southeast Asia, India, and areas farther west.

Despite these accomplishments, the Sui Dynasty lasted for only two reigns. The ambitious projects of the two Sui emperors led to exhaustion and unrest, and in the ensuing warfare Li Yuan, a Chinese from the same northwest aristocratic circles as the founder of the Sui, seized the throne.

The Tang Dynasty, 618–907

The dynasty founded by Li Yuan, the Tang, was one of the high points of traditional Chinese civilization. Especially during this dynasty's first century, its capital, Chang'an, was the cultural center of East Asia, drawing in merchants, pilgrims, missionaries, and students to a degree never matched before or after. This position of strength gave the Chinese the confidence to be open to learning from the outside world, leading to a more cosmopolitan culture than in any other period before the twentieth century.

The first two Tang rulers, Gaozu (Li Yuan, r. 618–626) and Taizong (r. 626–649), were able monarchs. Adding to their armies auxiliary troops composed of Turks, Tanguts, Khitans, and other non-Chinese led by their own chieftains, they campaigned into Korea, Vietnam, and Central Asia. In 630 the Chinese turned against their former allies, the Turks, gaining territory from them and winning for Taizong the title of Great Khan, so that for a short period he was simultaneously head of both the Chinese and the Turkish empires.

In the civil sphere Tang accomplishments far outstripped anything known in Europe until the growth of national states in the seventeenth century. Tang emperors subdivided the administration of the empire into departments, much like the numerous agencies of modern governments. They built on the Sui precedent of using written examinations to select officials. Although only about thirty men were recruited this way each year, the prestige of passing the examinations became so great that more and more men attempted them. Candidates had to master the Confucian classics and the rules of poetry, and they had to be able to analyze practical administrative and political matters. Government schools were founded to prepare the sons of officials and other young men for service as officials.

The mid-Tang Dynasty saw two women — Empress Wu and Consort Yang Guifei — rise to positions of great political power. Empress Wu was the consort of the weak and sickly Emperor Gaozong. After Gaozong suffered a stroke in 660, she took full charge. She continued to rule after Gaozong's death, summarily deposing her own two sons and dealing harshly with all opponents. In 690 she proclaimed herself emperor, the only woman who took that title in Chinese history. To gain support, she circulated a Buddhist sutra that predicted the imminent reincarnation of the Buddha Maitreya as a female monarch, during whose reign the world would be free of illness, worry, and disaster. Although despised by later Chinese historians as an evil usurper, Empress Wu was an effective leader. It was not until she was over eighty that members of the court were able to force her out in favor of her son.

Her grandson, the emperor Xuanzong (r. 713–756), presided over a brilliant court and patronized leading poets, painters, and calligraphers in his early years. In his later years, however, after he became enamored of his consort Yang Guifei, he did not want to be bothered by the details of government. In this period ample and rounded proportions were much admired in women, and Yang was said to be such a full-figured beauty. The emperor allowed her to place friends and relatives in important positions in the government. One of her favorites was the general An Lushan, who, after getting into a quarrel with Yang's brother over control of the government, rebelled in 755. Xuanzong had to flee the capital, and the troops that accompanied him forced him to have Yang Guifei executed.

The rebellion of An Lushan was devastating to the Tang Dynasty. Peace was restored only by calling on the Uighurs (WEE-gurz), a Turkish people allied with the Tang, who looted the capital after taking it from the rebels. After the rebellion was finally suppressed in 763, the central government had to keep meeting the extortionate demands of the Uighurs. Many military governors came to treat their provinces as hereditary kingdoms and withheld tax returns from the central government. In addition, eunuchs gained increasing power at court and were able to prevent both the emperors and the Confucian officials from doing much about them.

Tang Culture

The reunification of north and south led to cultural flowering. The Tang capital cities of Chang'an and Luoyang became great metropolises; Chang'an and its suburbs grew to more than 2 million inhabitants (probably making it the largest city in the world at the time). The cities were laid out in rectangular grids and contained a hundred-odd walled "blocks" inside their walls. Like the gates of the city, the gates of each block were locked at night.

In these cosmopolitan cities, knowledge of the outside world was stimulated by the presence of envoys, merchants, pilgrims, and students who came from neighboring states in Central Asia, Japan, Korea, Tibet, and Southeast Asia. Because of the presence of foreign merchants, many religions were practiced, including Nestorian Christianity, Manichaeism, Zoroastrianism, Judaism, and Islam, although none of them spread into the Chinese population the way Buddhism had a few centuries earlier. Foreign fashions in hair and clothing were often copied, and foreign amusements such as the Persian game of polo found followings among the well-to-do. The introduction of new musical instruments and tunes from India, Iran, and Central Asia brought about a major transformation in Chinese music.

The Tang Dynasty was the great age of Chinese poetry. Skill in composing poetry was tested in the civil service examinations, and educated men had to be able to com-

Five-Stringed Pipa/Biwa   This musical instrument, decorated with fine wood marquetry, was probably presented by the Tang court to a Japanese envoy. It was among the objects placed in a Japanese royal storage house (Shōsōin) in 756. (Kyodo News International, Inc.)

pose poems at social gatherings. The pain of parting, the joys of nature, and the pleasures of wine and friendship were all common poetic topics. One of Li Bo's (701–762) most famous poems describes an evening of drinking with only the moon and his shadow for company:

> A cup of wine, under the flowering trees;
> I drink alone, for no friend is near.
> Raising my cup I beckon the bright moon,
> For he, with my shadow, will make three men.
> The moon, alas, is no drinker of wine;
> Listless, my shadow creeps about at my side.
> . . .
> Now we are drunk, each goes his way.
> May we long share our odd, inanimate feast,
> And we meet at last on the cloudy River of the sky.[6]

The poet Bo Juyi (772–846) often wrote of more serious subjects. At times he worried about whether he was doing his job justly and well:

> From these high walls I look at the town below
> Where the natives of Pa cluster like a swarm of flies.
> How can I govern these people and lead them aright?
> I cannot even understand what they say.
> But at least I am glad, now that the taxes are in,
> To learn that in my province there is no discontent.[7]

In Tang times Buddhism fully penetrated Chinese daily life. Stories of Buddhist origin became widely known, and Buddhist festivals, such as the festival for feeding hungry ghosts in the summer, became among the most popular holidays. Buddhist monasteries became an important part of everyday life. They ran schools for children. In remote areas they provided lodging for travelers. Merchants entrusted their money and wares to monasteries for safekeeping, in effect transforming the monasteries into banks and warehouses. The wealthy often donated money or land to support temples and monasteries, making monasteries among the largest landlords.

At the intellectual and religious level, Buddhism was developing in distinctly Chinese directions. Two schools that thrived were Pure Land and Chan. **Pure Land** appealed to laypeople because its simple act of calling on the Buddha Amitabha and his chief helper, the compassionate bodhisattva Guanyin, could lead to rebirth in Amitabha's paradise, the Pure Land. Among the educated elite the **Chan** school (known in Japan as Zen) also gained popularity. Chan teachings rejected the authority of the sutras and claimed the superiority of mind-to-mind transmission of Buddhist truths.

The "northern" Chan tradition emphasized meditation and monastic discipline. The "southern" tradition was even more iconoclastic, holding that enlightenment could be achieved suddenly through insight into one's own true nature, even without prolonged meditation.

Opposition to Buddhism re-emerged in the late Tang period. In addition to concerns about the fiscal impact of removing so much land from the tax rolls and so many men from government labor service, there were concerns about Buddhism's foreign origins. As China's international position weakened, xenophobia surfaced. During the persecution of 845, more than 4,600 monasteries and 40,000 temples and shrines were destroyed, and more than 260,000 Buddhist monks and nuns were forced to return to secular life. Although this ban was lifted after a few years, the monastic establishment never fully recovered. Buddhism retained a strong hold among laypeople, and basic Buddhist ideas like karma and reincarnation had become fully incorporated into everyday Chinese thinking. But Buddhism was never again as central to Chinese life.

The East Asian Cultural Sphere

What elements of Chinese culture were adopted by Koreans, Vietnamese, and Japanese, and how did they adapt them to their own circumstances?

During the millennium from 200 B.C.E. to 800 C.E., China exerted a powerful influence on its immediate neighbors, who began forming states of their own. By Tang times China was surrounded by independent states in Korea, Manchuria, Tibet, the area that is now Yunnan province, Vietnam, and Japan. All of these states were much smaller than China in area and population, making China by far the dominant force politically and culturally until the nineteenth century. Nevertheless, each of these separate states developed a strong sense of its independent identity. In the case of Tibet, cultural borrowing was more often from neighboring India than from China.

The earliest information about each of these countries is found in Chinese sources. Han armies brought Chinese culture to Korea and Vietnam, but even in those cases much cultural borrowing was entirely voluntary as the elite, merchants, and craftsmen adopted the techniques, ideas, and practices they found appealing. In Japan much of the process of absorbing elements of Chinese culture was mediated via Korea. In Korea, Japan, and Vietnam the fine arts—painting, architecture, and ceramics in particular—were all strongly influenced by Chinese models. Tibet, though a thorn in the side of Tang China, was as much in the Indian sphere of influence as in the Chinese and thus followed a somewhat different trajectory. Most significantly, it never adopted Chinese characters as its written language, nor was it as influenced by Chinese artistic styles as were other areas. Moreover, the form of Buddhism that became dominant in Tibet came directly from India, not through Central Asia and China.

In each area Chinese-style culture was at first adopted by elites, but in time many Chinese products and ideas, ranging from written language to chopsticks and soy sauce, became incorporated into everyday life. By the eighth century the written Chinese language was used by educated people throughout East Asia. Educated Vietnamese, Koreans, and Japanese could communicate in writing when they could not understand each other's spoken languages, and envoys to Chang'an could in this way carry out "brush conversations" with each other. The books that educated people read included the Chinese classics, histories, and poetry, as well as Buddhist sutras translated into Chinese. The great appeal of Buddhism known primarily through Chinese translation was a powerful force promoting cultural borrowing.

Vietnam

Vietnam is today classed with the countries to its west as part of Southeast Asia, but its ties are at least as strong to China, and its climate is much like that of southernmost China—subtropical, with abundant rain and rivers. The Vietnamese first appear in Chinese sources as a people of south China called the Yue, who gradually migrated farther south as the Chinese state expanded. The people of the Red River Valley in northern Vietnam had achieved a relatively advanced level of Bronze Age civilization by the first century B.C.E. The bronze heads of their arrows were often dipped in poison to facilitate killing large animals such as elephants, whose tusks were traded to China for iron. Power was held by hereditary tribal chiefs who served as civil, religious, and military leaders, with the king as the most powerful chief.

The collapse of the Qin Dynasty in 206 B.C.E. had an impact on this area because a former Qin general, Zhao Tuo (Trieu Da in Vietnamese), finding himself in the far south, set up his own kingdom of Nam Viet (Nan Yue in Chinese). This kingdom covered much of south China and was ruled by Trieu Da from his capital near the present site of Guangzhou. Its population consisted chiefly of the Viet people. After killing all officials loyal to the Chinese emperor, Trieu Da adopted the customs of the Viet and made himself the ruler of a vast state that extended as far south as modern-day Da Nang.

After almost a hundred years of diplomatic and military duels between the Han Dynasty and Trieu Da and his successors, Nam Viet was conquered in 111 B.C.E. by Chinese armies. Chinese administrators were assigned to replace the local nobility. Chinese political institutions were imposed, and Confucianism was treated as the official ideology. The Chinese language was introduced as the medium of official and literary expression, and Chinese characters were adopted as the written form for the Vietnamese spoken language. The Chinese built roads, waterways, and harbors to facilitate communication within the region and to ensure that they maintained administrative and military control over it. Chinese art, architecture, and music had a powerful impact on their Vietnamese counterparts.

Chinese innovations that were beneficial to the Vietnamese were readily integrated into the indigenous culture, but the local elite were not reconciled to Chinese political domination. The most famous early revolt took place in 39 C.E., when two widows of local aristocrats, the Trung sisters, led an uprising against foreign rule. After overwhelming Chinese strongholds, they declared themselves queens of an independent Vietnamese kingdom. Three years later a powerful army sent by the Han emperor re-established Chinese rule.

China retained at least nominal control over northern Vietnam through the Tang Dynasty, and there were no real borders between China proper and Vietnam during this time. The local elite became culturally dual, serving as brokers between the Chinese governors and the native people.

Korea

Korea is a mountainous peninsula some 600 miles long extending south from Man-churia and Siberia. At its tip it is about 120 miles from Japan (Map 7.2). Archaeological, linguistic, and anthropological evidence indicates that the Korean people share a com-mon ethnic origin with other peoples of North Asia, including those of Manchuria, Siberia, and Japan. Linguistically, Korean is not related to Chinese.

Korea began adopting elements of technology from China in the first millennium B.C.E., including bronze and iron technology. Chinese-Korean contact expanded during the Warring States Period, when the state of Yan extended into part of Korea. In about 194 B.C.E. Wiman, an unsuccessful rebel against the Han Dynasty, fled to Korea and set up a state called Choson in what is now northwest Korea and southern Manchuria. In 108 B.C.E. this state was overthrown by Han armies. Four prefectures were established there, and Chinese officials were dispatched to govern them.

The impact of the Chinese prefectures in Korea was similar to that of the con-temporaneous Roman colonies in Britain in encouraging the spread of culture and political forms. The prefectures survived not only through the Han Dynasty but also for nearly a century after the fall of the dynasty, until 313 C.E. The Chinese never controlled the entire Korean peninsula, however. The Han commanderies coexisted with the native Korean kingdom of Koguryŏ, founded in the first century B.C.E. Chi-nese sources describe this kingdom as a society of aristocratic tribal warriors who had under them a mass of serfs and slaves, mostly from conquered tribes. After the Chinese colonies were finally over-thrown, the kingdoms of Paekche and Silla emerged farther south on the penin-sula in the third and fourth centuries C.E., leading to what is called the Three Kingdoms Period (313–668 C.E.). In all three Korean kingdoms Chi-nese was used as the language of government and learning. Each of the three kingdoms had hereditary kings, but their power was curbed by the existence of very strong hereditary elites.

MAP 7.2 Korea and Japan, ca. 600 C.E. Korea and Japan are of similar lati-tude, but Korea's climate is more continental, with harsher winters. Of Japan's four islands, Kyushu is closest to Korea and mainland Asia.

Buddhism was officially introduced in Koguryŏ from China in 372 and in the other states not long after. Buddhism connected Korea to societies across Asia. Buddhist monks went back and forth between China and Korea. One even made the journey to India and back, and others traveled on to Japan to aid in the spread of Buddhism there.

When the Sui Dynasty finally reunified China in 589, it tried to establish control of at least a part of Korea. But the Korean kingdoms were much stronger than their predecessors in Han times, and they repeatedly repulsed Chinese attacks. The Tang government then tried allying itself with one state, Silla, to fight the others. Silla and Tang jointly destroyed Paekche in 660 and Koguryŏ in 668. With its new resources Silla was able to repel Tang efforts to make Korea a colony but agreed to vassal status. The unification under Silla marked the first political unification of Korea.

For the next century Silla embarked on a policy of wholesale borrowing of Chinese culture and institutions. Annual embassies were sent to Chang'an, and large numbers of students studied in China. The Silla government was modeled on the Tang, although modifications were made to accommodate Korea's more aristocratic social structure.

Japan

Japan does not touch China as do Korea, Tibet, and Vietnam. The heart of Japan is four mountainous islands off the coast of Korea (see Map 7.2). Since the land is rugged and lacking in navigable waterways, the Inland Sea, like the Aegean in Greece, was the easiest avenue of communication in early times. Hence the land bordering the Inland Sea — Kyushu, Shikoku, and Honshu — developed as the political and cultural center of early Japan. Geography also blessed Japan with a moat — the Korea Strait and the Sea of Japan. Consequently, the Japanese for long periods were free to develop their way of life without external interference.

Japan's early development was closely tied to that of the mainland, especially to Korea. Physical anthropologists have discerned several major waves of immigrants into Japan. People of the Jōmon culture, established by about 10,000 B.C.E., after an influx of people from Southeast Asia, practiced hunting and fishing and fashioned clay pots. New arrivals from northeast Asia brought agriculture and a distinct culture called Yayoi (ca. 300 B.C.E.–300 C.E.). Later Yayoi communities were marked by complex social organization with rulers, soldiers, artisans, and priests. During the Han Dynasty, objects of Chinese and Korean manufacture found their way into Japan, an indication that people were traveling back and forth as well. In the third century C.E. Chinese histories begin to report on the land called Wa made up of mountainous islands. It had numerous communities with markets, granaries, tax collection, and class distinctions. The people ate with their fingers, used body paint, purified themselves by bathing after a funeral, and liked liquor.

One of the most distinctive features of early Japan was its female rulers. A Chinese historian wrote:

> The country formerly had a man as ruler. For some seventy or eighty years after that there were disturbances and warfare. Thereupon the people agreed upon a woman for their ruler. Her name was Pimiko. She occupied herself with magic and sorcery, bewitching the people. Though mature in age, she remained unmarried. She had a younger brother who assisted her in ruling the country. After she became the ruler,

there were few who saw her. She had one thousand women as attendants, but only one man. He served her food and drink and acted as a medium of communication. . . .

When Pimiko passed away, a great mound was raised, more than a hundred paces in diameter. Over a hundred male and female attendants followed her to the grave. Then a king was placed on the throne, but the people would not obey him. Assassination and murder followed; more than one thousand were thus slain.

A relative of Pimiko named Iyo, a girl of thirteen, was then made queen and order was restored.[8]

During the fourth through sixth centuries new waves of migrants from Korea brought the language that evolved into Japanese. They also brought sericulture (silkmaking), bronze swords, crossbows, iron plows, and the Chinese written language. In this period a social order similar to Korea's emerged, dominated by a warrior aristocracy organized into clans. Clad in helmet and armor, these warriors wielded swords, battle-axes, and often bows, and some rode into battle on horseback. Those vanquished in battle were made slaves. Each clan had its own chieftain, who marshaled clansmen for battle and served as chief priest. Over time the clans fought with each other, and their numbers were gradually reduced through conquest and alliance. By the fifth century the chief of the clan that claimed descent from the sun-goddess, located in the Yamato plain around modern Osaka, had come to occupy the position of Great King—or Queen, for as the quotation above shows, female rulers were not uncommon in this period.

The Yamato rulers used their religion to subordinate the gods of their rivals, much as Hammurabi had used Marduk in Babylonia (see page 39). They established the chief shrine of the sun-goddess near the seacoast, where she could catch the first rays of the rising sun. Cults to other gods were also supported as long as they were viewed as subordinate to the sun-goddess. This native religion was later termed **Shinto**, the Way of the Gods. Buddhism was formally introduced in 538 C.E. and coexisted with the Shinto reverence for the spirits of ancestors and all living things.

In the sixth century Prince Shōtoku (574–622) undertook a sweeping reform of the state designed to strengthen Yamato rule by adopting Chinese-style bureaucratic practices (though not the recruitment of officials by examination). His Seventeen Principles of 604 drew from both Confucian and Buddhist teachings. In it he likened the ruler to Heaven and instructed officials to put their duty to the ruler above the interest of their families. He instituted a ladder of official ranks similar to China's, admonished the nobility to avoid strife and opposition, and urged adherence to Buddhist precepts. Near his seat of government, Prince Shōtoku built the magnificent Hōryūji Temple and staffed it with monks from Korea. He also opened direct relations with China, sending four missions during the brief Sui Dynasty.

State-building efforts continued through the seventh century and culminated in the establishment in 710 of Japan's first long-term true city, the capital at **Nara**, north of modern Osaka. Nara, which was modeled on the Tang capital of Chang'an, gave its name to an era that lasted until 794 and was characterized by the avid importation of Chinese ideas and methods. Seven times missions with five hundred to six hundred men were sent on the dangerous sea crossing and long overland journey to Chang'an. As Buddhism developed a stronghold in Japan, it inspired many trips to China to

Hōryūji Temple   Japanese Buddhist temples, like those in China and Korea, consisted of several buildings within a walled compound. The buildings of the Hōryūji Temple (built between 670 and 711, after Prince Shōtoku's original temple burned down) include the oldest wooden structures in the world and house some of the best early Buddhist sculpture in Japan. The three main buildings depicted here are the pagoda, housing relics; the main hall, with the temple's principal images; and the lecture hall, for sermons. The five-story pagoda could be seen from far away, much like the steeples of cathedrals in medieval Europe. (Michael Hitoshi/The Image Bank/Getty Images)

acquire sources and to study at Chinese monasteries. Chinese and Korean craftsmen were often brought back to Japan, especially to help with the decoration of the many Buddhist temples then under construction. Musical instruments and tunes were imported as well, many originally from Central Asia. Chinese practices were instituted, such as the compilation of histories and law codes, the creation of provinces, and the appointment of governors to collect taxes from them. By 750 some seven thousand men staffed the central government.

Increased contact with the mainland had unwanted effects as well. In contrast to China and Korea, both part of the Eurasian landmass, Japan had been relatively isolated from many deadly diseases, so when diseases arrived with travelers, people did not have immunity. The great smallpox epidemic of 735–737 is thought to have reduced the population of about 5 million by 30 percent.

The Buddhist monasteries that ringed Nara were both religious centers and wealthy landlords, and the monks were active in the political life of the capital. Copying the policy of the Tang Dynasty in China, the government ordered every province to establish a Buddhist temple with twenty monks and ten nuns to chant sutras and perform other ceremonies on behalf of the emperor and the state. When an emperor abdicated in 749 in favor of his daughter, he became a Buddhist monk, a practice many of his successors would later follow.

Many of the temples built during the Nara period still stand, the wood, clay, and bronze statues in them exceptionally well preserved. The largest of these temples was the Tōdaiji, with its huge bronze statue of the Buddha, which stood fifty-three feet tall and was made from more than a million pounds of metal. When the temple and statue were completed in 752, an Indian monk painted the eyes, and the ten thousand monks present for the celebration had a magnificent vegetarian feast. Objects from the dedication ceremony were placed in a special storehouse, the Shōsōin, and about ten thousand of them are still there, including books, weapons, mirrors, screens, and objects of gold, lacquer, and glass, most made in China but some coming from Central Asia and Persia via the Silk Road.

Chapter Summary

After unifying China in 221 B.C.E., the Qin Dynasty created a strongly centralized government that did away with noble privilege. The First Emperor standardized script, coinage, weights, and measures. He also built roads, the Great Wall, and a huge tomb for himself. During the four centuries of the subsequent Han Dynasty, the harsher laws of the Qin were lifted, but the strong centralized government remained. The Han government promoted internal peace by providing relief in cases of floods, droughts, and famines and by keeping land taxes low for the peasantry. The Han government sent huge armies against the nomadic Xiongnu, whose confederation threatened them in the north, but the Xiongnu remained a potent foe. Still, Han armies expanded Chinese territory in many directions. For nearly four centuries after the fall of the Han Dynasty, China was divided among contending states. After 316 the north was in the hands of non-Chinese rulers, while the south had Chinese rulers.

In the first and second centuries C.E. merchants and missionaries brought Buddhism to China. Many elements of Buddhism were new to China—a huge body of scriptures, celibate monks and nuns, traditions of depicting Buddhas and bodhisattvas in statues and paintings, and a strong proselytizing tradition. Rulers became major patrons in both north and south.

Unlike the Roman Empire, China was successfully reunified in 589 C.E. The short Sui Dynasty was followed by the longer Tang Dynasty. Tang China regained overlordship of the Silk Road cities in Central Asia. The Tang period was one of cultural flowering, with achievements in poetry especially notable. Music was enriched with instruments and tunes from Persia. Tang power declined after 755, when a powerful general turned his army against the government. Although the rebellion was suppressed, the government was not able to regain its strong central control. Moreover, powerful states were formed along Tang's borders. At court, eunuchs gained power at the expense of civil officials.

Over the ten centuries covered in Chapter 7, Korea, Japan, and Vietnam developed distinct cultures while adopting elements of China's material, political, and religious culture, including the Chinese writing system. During the Tang era, ambitious Korean and Japanese rulers sought Chinese expertise and Chinese products, including Chinese-style centralized governments and the Chinese written language.

Notes

1. Li Yuning, ed., *The First Emperor of China* (White Plains, N.Y.: International Arts and Sciences Press, 1975), pp. 275–276, slightly modified.
2. Burton Watson, trans., *Records of the Grand Historian of China*, vol. 2 (New York: Columbia University Press, 1961), p. 496.
3. Ibid., p. 499.
4. Patricia Buckley Ebrey, ed., *Chinese Civilization: A Sourcebook*, 2d ed., revised and expanded (New York: Free Press, 1993), p. 62.
5. Patricia Buckley Ebrey, *Cambridge Illustrated History of China* (Cambridge: Cambridge University Press, 1996), p. 74.
6. Arthur Waley, trans., *More Translations from the Chinese* (New York: Knopf, 1919), p. 27.
7. Ibid., p. 71.
8. *Sources of Japanese Tradition*, by William Theodore de Bary, Donald Keene, George Tanabe, and Paul Varley, eds. Reproduced with permission of COLUMBIA UNIVERSITY PRESS in the format Book via Copyright Clearance Center.

CONNECTIONS

East Asia was transformed in the millennium between the Qin unifi-cation in 221 B.C.E. and the end of the eighth century C.E. The Han Dynasty and four centuries later the Tang Dynasty proved that a cen-tralized, bureaucratic monarchy could bring peace and prosperity to populations of 50 million or more spread across China proper. By 800 C.E. neighboring societies along China's borders, from Korea and Japan on the east to the Uighurs and Tibetans to the west, had followed China's lead, forming states and building cities. Buddhism had transformed the lives of all of these societies, bringing new ways of thinking about life and death and new ways of pursuing spiritual goals.

In the same centuries that Buddhism was adapting to and simultaneously trans-forming the culture of much of eastern Eurasia, comparable processes were at work in western Eurasia, where Christianity continued to spread. The spread of these religions was aided by increased contact between different cultures, facilitated in Eurasia by the merchants traveling the Silk Road or sailing the Indian Ocean. Where contact between cultures wasn't as extensive, as in Africa (discussed in Chapter 10), religious beliefs were more localized. The collapse of the Roman Empire in the West during this period was not unlike the collapse of the Han Dynasty, but in Europe the empire was never put back together at the level that it was in China, where the Tang Dynasty by many measures was more splendid than the Han. The story of these centuries in western Eurasia is taken up in the next two chapters, which trace the rise of Christianity and Islam and the movement of peoples throughout Europe and Asia. Before returning to the story of East Asia after 800 in Chapter 13, we will also examine the empires in Africa (Chapter 10) and the Americas (Chapter 11).

◄ **MAP 8.1   The Byzantine and Sassanid Empires, ca. 600** Both the Byzantine and Sassanid Empires included territory that had earlier been part of the Roman Empire. The Sassanid Persians fought Roman armies before the founding of the Byzantine Empire. Later Byzantium and the Sassanids engaged in a series of wars that weakened both and brought neither lasting territorial acquisitions.

depended on agriculture for its economic prosperity, but its location also proved well suited for commerce (see Map 8.1). A lucrative caravan trade linked the Sassanid empire to the Silk Road and China. Persian metalwork, textiles, and glass were exchanged for Chinese silks, and this trade brought about considerable cultural contact between the Sassanids and the Chinese.

Whereas the Parthians had tolerated many religions, the Sassanid Persians made Zoroastrianism the official state religion. Religion and the state were inextricably tied together. The king's power rested on the support of nobles and Zoroastrian priests who monopolized positions in the court and in the imperial bureaucracy. A highly elaborate court ceremonial and ritual exalted the status of the king and emphasized his semidivine pre-eminence over his subjects. (The Byzantine monarchy, the Roman papacy, and the Muslim caliphate subsequently copied aspects of this Persian ceremonial.)

Adherents to religions other than Zoroastrianism, such as Jews and Christians, faced discrimination. The Jewish population in the Sassanid empire was sizable because the Romans had forced many Jews out of Israel and Judaea after a series of revolts against Roman rule, a dispersal later termed the diaspora. Jews suffered intermittent persecution under the Sassanids, as did Christians, whom followers of Zoroastrianism saw as being connected to Rome and Constantinople.

An expansionist foreign policy brought Persia into frequent conflict with Rome and then with Byzantium. Neither side was able to achieve a clear-cut victory until the early seventh century, when the Sassanids advanced all the way to the Mediterranean and even took Egypt in 621. Their victory would be very short-lived, however, as the taxes required to finance the wars and conflicts over the succession to the throne had weakened the Persians. Under Emperor Heraclius I (r. 610–641), the Byzantines crushed the Persians in a series of battles ending with one at Nineveh in 627. Just five years later, the first Arabic forces inspired by Islam entered Persian territories, and by 651 the Sassanid dynasty had collapsed (see page 236).

Justinian's Code of Law

Byzantine emperors organized and preserved Roman law, making a lasting contribution to the medieval and modern worlds. Roman law had developed from many sources—decisions by judges, edicts of emperors, legislation passed by the Senate, and opinions of jurists expert in the theory and practice of law. By the fourth century Roman law had become a huge, bewildering mass. Its sheer bulk made it almost unusable.

Sweeping and systematic codification took place under the emperor Justinian. He appointed a committee of eminent jurists to sort through and organize the laws. The result was the *Corpus Juris Civilis* (Body of Civil Law), a multipart collection of laws and legal commentary issued from 529 to 534 that is often simply termed **Justinian's**

Code. The first part of this work, the *Codex*, brought together all the existing imperial laws into a coherent whole, eliminated outmoded laws and contradictions, and clarified the law itself. The second part of Justinian's compilation, the *Digest*, is a collection of the opinions of the foremost Roman jurists on complex legal problems. The third part, the *Institutes*, is a handbook of civil law designed for students and beginning jurists. All three parts were given the force of law and formed the backbone of Byzantine jurisprudence from that point on. Like so much of classical culture, Justinian's *Code* was lost in western Europe with the end of the Roman Empire, but it was rediscovered in the eleventh century and came to form the foundation of law for nearly every modern European nation.

Byzantine Intellectual Life

Just as they valued the law, the Byzantines prized education. As a result, many masterpieces of ancient Greek literature survived to influence the intellectual life of the modern world. The literature of the Byzantine Empire was predominantly Greek, although politicians, scholars, and lawyers also spoke and wrote Latin. Among members of the large reading public, history was a favorite subject.

The most remarkable Byzantine historian was Procopius (ca. 500–ca. 562), who left a rousing account of Justinian's reconquest of North Africa and Italy, but also wrote the *Secret History*, a vicious and uproarious attack on Justinian and his wife, the empress Theodora. (See "Individuals in Society: Theodora of Constantinople," page 208.)

Although the Byzantines discovered little that was new in mathematics and geometry, they made advances in military applications. For example, they invented an

Greek Fire   In this illustration from a twelfth-century manuscript, sailors shoot Greek fire toward an attacking ship from a pressurized tube that looks strikingly similar to a modern flamethrower. The exact formula for Greek fire has been lost, but it was probably made from a petroleum product because it continued burning on water. Greek fire was particularly important in Byzantine defenses of Constantinople from Muslim forces in the late seventh century. (Prado, Madrid, Spain/The Bridgeman Art Library)

explosive liquid that came to be known as "Greek fire." The liquid was heated and propelled by a pump through a bronze tube, and as the jet left the tube, it was ignited—somewhat like a modern flamethrower. Greek fire saved Constantinople from Arab assault in 678 and was used in both land and sea battles for centuries, although modern military experts still do not know the exact nature of the compound.

The Byzantines devoted a great deal of attention to medicine, and their general level of medical competence was far higher than that of western Europeans. Yet their physicians could not cope with the terrible disease, often called "the Justinian plague," that swept through the Byzantine Empire and parts of western Europe between 542 and 560. Probably originating in northwestern India and carried to the Mediterranean region by ships, the disease was similar to the bubonic plague. Characterized by high fevers, chills, delirium, and enlarged lymph nodes, or by inflammation of the lungs that caused hemorrhages of black blood, the plague claimed the lives of tens of thousands of people. The epidemic had profound political as well as social consequences. It weakened Justinian's military resources, thus hampering his efforts to restore unity to the Mediterranean world.

Life in Constantinople

By the seventh century Constantinople was the greatest city in the Christian world: a large population center, the seat of the imperial court and administration, and the pivot of a large volume of international trade. Given that the city was a natural geographical connecting point between East and West, its markets offered goods from many parts of the world. Furs and timber flowed across the Black Sea from the Rus (Russia) to the capital, as did slaves across the Mediterranean from northern Europe and the Balkans via Venice. Spices, silks, jewelry, and other luxury goods came to Constantinople from India and China by way of Arabia, the Red Sea, and the Indian Ocean. In return, the city exported glassware, mosaics, gold coins, silk cloth, carpets, and a host of other products, with much foreign trade in the hands of Italian merchants. At the end of the eleventh century Constantinople may have been the world's third-largest city, with only Córdoba in Spain and Kaifeng in China larger.

Although merchants could become fabulously wealthy, the landed aristocracy always held the dominant social position, as in western Europe and China. By contrast, merchants and craftsmen, even when they acquired considerable wealth, never won social prominence. Aristocrats and monasteries usually invested their wealth in real estate, which involved little risk but brought little gain.

Constantinople did not enjoy constant political stability. Between the accession of Emperor Heraclius in 610 and the fall of the city to Western Crusaders in 1204 (see page 400), four separate dynasties ruled at Constantinople. Imperial government involved such intricate court intrigue, assassination plots, and military revolts that the word *byzantine* is sometimes used in English to mean extremely entangled and complicated politics.

What do we know about private life in Constantinople? Research has revealed a fair amount about the Byzantine *oikos* (OI-kohs), or household. The typical household in the city included family members and servants, some of whom were slaves. Artisans lived and worked in their shops, while clerks, civil servants, minor officials, and business people—those who today would be called middle class—commonly dwelled in

(The Christian Church headed by the pope in Rome was generally called the Roman Church in this era, and later the Roman Catholic Church. The word *catholic* derives from a Greek word meaning "general," "universal," or "worldwide.")

The popes also expanded the church's secular authority. They made treaties with barbarian leaders, charged taxes, enforced laws, and organized armies. The Western Christian Church headed by the pope in Rome would become the most enduring nongovernmental institution in world history.

By contrast, in the East the emperor's jurisdiction over the church was fully acknowledged, even though the bishops of Antioch, Alexandria, Jerusalem, and Constantinople had more power than other bishops. As in Rome, there was a head of the church in Constantinople, called the patriarch, but he did not develop the same powers that the pope did in the West because there was never a similar power vacuum into which he needed to step. He and other high church officials were appointed by the emperor. The Eastern emperors looked on religion as a branch of the state, and they considered it their duty to protect the faith not only against heathen outsiders but also against heretics within the empire. Following the pattern set by Constantine, the emperors summoned councils of bishops and theologians to settle doctrinal disputes. They and the Eastern bishops did not accept Rome's claim to primacy, and gradually the Byzantine Christian Church, generally called the **Orthodox Church**, and the Roman Church began to diverge. (*Orthodoxy* with a capital *O* refers to the Eastern Church, and *orthodoxy* with a lowercase *o* means correct doctrine as defined by church leaders.) In addition, other branches of Christianity in the East, including the Nestorians, Maronites, and Copts, developed their own distinctive theological ideas and patterns of organization. Some of these later joined with Roman Catholicism and affirmed the primacy of the pope, but many remain independent branches of Christianity today. About 20 percent of the population of Lebanon in 2010, for example, was Maronite Christian, and about 10 percent of the population of Egypt was Coptic Christian.

Christian Monasticism

Christianity began and spread as a city religion. With time, however, some especially pious Christians started to feel that a life of asceticism (extreme material sacrifice, including fasting and the renunciation of sex) was a better way to show their devotion to Christ's teachings, just as followers of Mahavira or the Buddha had centuries earlier in South Asia (see Chapter 3). Asceticism was—and is—a common part of many religious traditions, either as a temporary practice during especially holy times or as a permanent way of life.

Ascetics often separate themselves from their families and normal social life, and this is what Christian ascetics did. Individuals and small groups withdrew from cities and moved to the Egyptian desert, where they sought God through prayer in caves and shelters in the desert or mountains. These individuals were called hermits (from the Greek word *eremos*, meaning "desert") or monks (from the Greek word *monos*, meaning "alone"). Gradually, large groups of monks emerged in the deserts of Upper Egypt, creating a style of life known as monasticism. Many devout women were also attracted to this eremitical type of monasticism, becoming nuns. Although monks and nuns led isolated lives, ordinary people soon recognized them as holy people and sought them as spiritual guides.

Church leaders did not really approve of eremitical life. Hermits sometimes claimed to have mystical experiences—direct communications with God. If hermits could communicate directly with the Lord, what need had they for priests, bishops, and the institutional church? The church hierarchy instead encouraged those who wanted to live ascetic lives of devotion to do so in communities. Communal living in a monastery, they argued, provided an environment for training the aspirant in the virtues of charity, poverty, and freedom from self-deception. Consequently, in the fourth, fifth, and sixth centuries many different kinds of communal monasticism developed in Gaul, Italy, Spain, Anglo-Saxon England, and Ireland.

In 529 Benedict of Nursia (ca. 480–547), who had experimented with both the eremitical and the communal forms of monastic life, wrote a brief set of regulations for the monks who had gathered around him at Monte Cassino, between Rome and Naples. Benedict's guide for monastic life, known as *The Rule of Saint Benedict*, slowly replaced all others, and it has influenced all forms of organized religious life in the Roman Church. The guide outlined a monastic life of regularity, discipline, and moderation in an atmosphere of silence. Under Benedict's regulations, monks spent part of each day in formal prayer, chanting psalms and other prayers from the Bible. The rest of the day was passed in manual labor, study, and private prayer. The monastic life as conceived by Saint Benedict provided opportunities for men of different abilities and talents—from mechanics to gardeners to literary scholars. The Benedictine form of religious life also appealed to women, because it allowed them to show their devotion and engage in study. Benedict's twin sister, Scholastica (480–543), adapted the *Rule* for use by her community of nuns.

Benedictine monasticism also succeeded partly because it was so materially successful. In the seventh and eighth centuries Benedictine monasteries pushed back forests and wastelands, drained swamps, and experimented with crop rotation, making a significant contribution to the agricultural development of Europe. In the process they sometimes earned immense wealth. Monasteries also conducted schools for local young people. Some learned about prescriptions and herbal remedies and went on to provide medical treatment for their localities. Others copied manuscripts and wrote books. Local and royal governments drew on the services of the literate men and able administrators the monasteries produced.

Because all monasteries followed rules, men who lived a communal monastic life came to be called regular clergy, from the Latin word *regulus* (rule). In contrast, priests and bishops who staffed churches in which people worshipped and who were not cut off from the world were called secular clergy. According to official church doctrine, women were not members of the clergy, but this distinction was not clear to most people.

Monasticism in the Orthodox world differed in fundamental ways from the monasticism that evolved in western Europe. First, while *The Rule of Saint Benedict* gradually became the universal guide for all western European monasteries, each monastic house in the Byzantine world developed its own set of rules for organization and behavior. Second, education never became a central feature of the Orthodox houses. Monks and nuns had to be literate to perform the services of the choir, and children destined for the monastic life were taught to read and write, but no monastery assumed responsibility for the general training of the local young. Since bishops and patriarchs of the Orthodox Church were recruited only from the monasteries, however, these institutions did exercise cultural influence.

Christian Ideas and Practices

How did Christian thinkers adapt classical ideas to Christian teachings, and what new religious concepts and practices did they develop?

The growth of Christianity was tied not just to institutions such as the papacy and monasteries but also to ideas. Initially, Christians rejected Greco-Roman culture. Gradually, however, Christian leaders and thinkers developed ideas that drew on classical influences, though there were also areas of controversy that differed in the Western and Eastern Churches.

Christianity and Classical Culture

In the first century Christians believed that Christ would soon fulfill his promise to return and that the end of the world was near; therefore, they saw no point in devoting time to learning. By the second century, however, these apocalyptic expectations were diminishing, and church leaders began to incorporate elements of Greek and Roman philosophy and learning into Christian teachings (see page 167). They found support for this incorporation in the written texts that circulated among Christians. In the third and fourth centuries these texts were brought together as the New Testament of the Bible, with general agreement about most of what should be included but sharp disputes about some books. Although some of Jesus's sermons as recorded in the Gospels (see page 164) urged followers to avoid worldly attachments, other parts of the Bible advocated acceptance of existing social, economic, and political structures. Christian thinkers built on these, adapting Christian teachings to fit with Roman realities and Roman ideas to fit with Christian aims, just as Buddhist thinkers adapted Buddhist teachings when they spread them to Central Asia, China, Korea, and Japan (see Chapter 7).

Saint Jerome (340–419), a distinguished theologian and linguist regarded as a father of the church, translated the Old Testament and New Testament from Hebrew and Greek, respectively, into vernacular Latin. Called the Vulgate, his edition of the Bible served as the official translation until the sixteenth century, and scholars rely on it even today. Familiar with the writings of classical authors such as Cicero and Virgil, Saint Jerome believed that Christians should study the best of ancient thought because it would direct their minds to God. He maintained that the best ancient literature should be interpreted in light of the Christian faith.

Christian attitudes toward gender and sexuality provide a good example of the ways early Christians first challenged and then largely adopted the views of their contemporary world. In his plan of salvation Jesus considered women the equal of men. Women were among the earliest converts to Christianity and took an active role in its spread, preaching, acting as missionaries, being martyred alongside men, and perhaps even baptizing believers. Because early Christians believed that the second coming of Christ was imminent, they devoted their energies to their new spiritual family of co-believers. Also, they often met in people's homes and called one another brother and sister, a metaphorical use of family terms that was new to the Roman Empire. Some women embraced the ideal of virginity and either singly or in monastic communities declared themselves "virgins in the service of Christ." All this initially made Christianity seem dangerous to many Romans, who viewed marriage as the foundation of society and the proper patriarchal order.

The Marys at Jesus's Tomb This late-fourth-century ivory panel tells the biblical story of Mary Magdalene and another Mary who went to Jesus's tomb to anoint the body (Matthew 28:1–7). At the top guards collapse when an angel descends from Heaven, and at the bottom the Marys listen to the angel telling them that Jesus has risen. Here the artist uses Roman artistic styles to convey Christian subject matter, synthesizing classical form and Christian teaching. (Castello Sforzesco, Milan, Italy/Scala/Art Resource, NY)

Not all Christian teachings about gender were radical, however. In the first century male church leaders began to place restrictions on female believers. Women were forbidden to preach and were gradually excluded from holding official positions in Christianity other than in women's monasteries. In so limiting the activities of female believers, Christianity was following well-established social patterns, just as it modeled its official hierarchy after that of the Roman Empire.

Christian teachings about sexuality also built on and challenged classical models. The rejection of sexual activity involved an affirmation of the importance of a spiritual life, but it also incorporated hostility toward the body found in some Hellenistic philosophies. Just as spirit was superior to matter, the thinking went, the mind was superior to the body. Though Christian teachings affirmed that God had created the material world and sanctioned marriage, most Christian thinkers also taught that celibacy was the better life and that anything that distracted one's attention from the spiritual world performed an evil function. For most clerical writers (who were themselves male), this temptation came from women, and in some of their writings women themselves are portrayed as evil, the "devil's gateway." Thus the writings of many church fathers contain a strong streak of misogyny (hatred of women), which was passed down to later Christian thinkers.

Saint Augustine on Sin, Grace, and Redemption

One thinker had an especially strong role in shaping Christian views about sexual activity and many other issues: Saint Augustine of Hippo (354–430), the most influential church father in the West. Augustine was born into an urban family in what is now Algeria in North Africa. His father, a minor civil servant, was a pagan; his mother, Monica, was a devout Christian. He gained an excellent education, fathered a son, and experimented with various religious ideas. In adulthood he converted to his mother's religion, eventually becoming bishop of the city of Hippo Regius. Augustine gained renown as a preacher, a vigorous defender of orthodox Christianity, and the author of more than ninety-three books and treatises.

Augustine's autobiography, *The Confessions*, is a literary masterpiece and one of the most influential books in Western history. Written in the rhetorical style and language of late Roman antiquity, it marks a synthesis of Greco-Roman forms and Christian thought. *The Confessions* describes Augustine's moral struggle, the conflict between his spiritual aspirations and his sensual self. Many Greek and Roman philosophers had taught that knowledge would lead to virtue. Augustine came to reject this idea, claiming that people do not always act on the basis of rational knowledge. Instead the basic or dynamic force in any individual is the will. When Adam ate the fruit forbidden by God in the Garden of Eden (Genesis 3:6), he committed the "original sin" and corrupted the will, wrote Augustine. Adam's sin did not simply remain his own but was passed on to all later humans through sexual intercourse; even infants were tainted. Original sin thus became a common social stain, in Augustine's opinion, transmitted by sexual desire. By viewing sexual desire as the result of Adam and Eve's disobedience to divine instructions, Augustine linked sexuality even more clearly with sin than had earlier church fathers. According to Augustine, because Adam disobeyed God, all human beings have an innate tendency to sin: their will is weak. But Augustine held that God restores the strength of the will through grace, which is transmitted in certain rituals that the church defined as **sacraments**. Augustine's ideas on sin, grace, and redemption became the foundation of all subsequent Western Christian theology, Protestant as well as Catholic.

The Iconoclastic Controversy

Augustine's ideas about original sin did not become important in the Eastern Orthodox Church, where other issues seemed more significant. In the centuries after Constantine, the most serious dispute within the Orthodox Church concerned icons—images or representations of God the Father, Jesus, and the saints in painting, bas-relief, or mosaic. Since the third century the church had allowed people to venerate icons. Although all prayer was to be directed to God the Father, Christian teaching held that icons representing the saints fostered reverence and that Jesus and the saints could most effectively plead a cause to God the Father. (For more about the role of saints, see page 224.) Iconoclasts, those who favored the destruction of icons, argued that people were worshipping the image itself rather than what it signified. This, they claimed, constituted idolatry, a violation of one of the Ten Commandments, the religious and moral code found in Hebrew Scripture that was also sacred to Christians.

The result of this dispute was a terrible theological conflict, the **iconoclastic controversy**, that split the Byzantine world for a century. In 730 the emperor Leo III (r. 717–741) ordered the destruction of icons. The removal of these images from Byzantine churches provoked a violent reaction: entire provinces revolted, and the Byzantine Empire and the Roman papacy severed relations. Since Eastern monasteries were the fiercest defenders of icons, Leo's son Constantine V (r. 741–775), nicknamed Copronymous ("Dung-name") by his enemies, took the war to the monasteries. He seized their property, executed some of the monks, and forced other monks into the army. Theological disputes and civil disorder over the icons continued intermittently until 843, when the icons were restored.

The implications of the iconoclastic controversy extended far beyond strictly theological issues. Iconoclasm raised the question of the right of the emperor to intervene in religious disputes—a central problem in the relations between church and state. Iconoclasm antagonized the pope and served to encourage him in his quest for an alliance with the Frankish monarchy (see page 227). This further divided the two parts of Christendom, and in 1054 a theological disagreement led the pope in Rome and the patriarch of Constantinople to declare each other a heretic. The outcome was a continuing schism between the Roman Catholic and the Orthodox Churches.

From a cultural perspective, the ultimate acceptance of icons profoundly influenced subsequent religious art within Christianity. The Greco-Roman tradition of giving divine figures human forms continued in both Eastern and Western Christianity, in contrast to Judaism and Islam, in which images of divine figures were often prohibited. These images became important tools in conversion and in people's devotional lives.

Migrating Peoples

How did the barbarians shape social, economic, and political structures in Europe and western Asia?

Along with *The Confessions*, Augustine's other major work was *The City of God*, a work that develops a Christian view of history and was written in direct response to what many people in Rome thought was a disaster: the capture of the city in 410 by Visigothic forces. The Visigoths were one of the many peoples moving west and south from Central Asia and northern Europe that the Romans—and later historians—labeled "barbarians" (Map 8.2). The word *barbarian* comes from the Greek *barbaros*, meaning someone who did not speak Greek. (To the Greeks, others seemed to be speaking nonsense syllables; *barbar* is the Greek equivalent of "blah-blah" or "yada-yada.") The Greeks used this word to include people such as the Egyptians, whom the Greeks respected. The Romans usually used the Latin version of *barbarian* to mean the peoples who lived beyond the northeastern boundary of Roman territory, whom they regarded as unruly, savage, and primitive. That value judgment is generally also present when we use *barbarian* in English, but there really is no other word to describe the many different peoples who lived to the north of the Roman Empire. Thus historians of late antiquity use the word *barbarian* to designate these peoples, who spoke a variety of languages but had similarities in their basic social, economic, and political structures. Many of these historians find much to admire in barbarian society.

Barbarians included many different ethnic groups with social and political structures, languages, laws, and beliefs developed in central and northern Europe and western Asia over many centuries. Among the largest barbarian groups were the Celts (whom the Romans called Gauls) and Germans; Germans were further subdivided into various tribes, such as Ostrogoths, Visigoths, Burgundians, and Franks. *Celt* and *German* are often used as ethnic terms, but they are better understood as linguistic terms, a Celt being a person who spoke a Celtic language, an ancestor of the modern Gaelic or Breton languages, and a German one who spoke a Germanic language, an ancestor of modern German, Dutch, Danish, Swedish, and Norwegian. Celts, Germans,

Europe. Churches could be built, and people could be required to attend services and belong to parishes, but the process of conversion was a gradual one.

How did missionaries and priests get masses of pagan and illiterate peoples to understand Christian ideals and teachings? They did it through preaching, assimilation of pagan customs, the ritual of penance, and veneration of the saints. Those who preached aimed to present the basic teachings of Christianity and strengthen the newly baptized in their faith through stories about the lives of Christ and the saints.

Deeply ingrained pagan customs and practices, however, could not be stamped out by words alone or even by imperial edicts. Thus Christian missionaries often pursued a policy of assimilation, easing the conversion of pagan men and women by stressing similarities between their customs and beliefs and those of Christianity. In the same way that classically trained scholars such as Jerome and Augustine blended Greco-Roman and Christian ideas, missionaries and converts mixed barbarian pagan ideas and practices with Christian ones. For example, bogs and lakes sacred to Germanic gods became associated with saints, as did various aspects of ordinary life, such as traveling, planting crops, and worrying about a sick child. Aspects of existing midwinter celebrations, which often centered on the return of the sun as the days became longer, were assimilated into celebrations of Christmas. Spring rituals involving eggs and rabbits (both symbols of fertility) were added to celebrations of Easter.

The ritual of **penance** was also instrumental in teaching people Christian ideas. Christianity taught that certain actions and thoughts were sins, meaning that they were against God's commands. Only by confessing sins and asking forgiveness could a sinning believer be reconciled with God. Confession was initially a public ritual, but by the fifth century individual confession to a parish priest was more common. During this ritual the individual knelt before the priest, who questioned him or her about sins he or she might have committed. The priest then set a penance such as fasting or saying specific prayers to allow the person to atone for the sin. Penance gave new converts a sense of the behavior expected of Christians, encouraged the private examination of conscience, and offered relief from the burden of sinful deeds.

Although confession became mostly a private affair, most religious observances continued to be community matters, as they had been in the ancient world. People joined with family members, friends, and neighbors to celebrate baptisms and funerals, presided over by a priest.

Veneration of **saints**, people who had lived (or died) in a way that was spiritually heroic or noteworthy, was another way that Christians formed stronger connections with their religion. Saints were understood to provide protection and assistance to worshippers, and parish churches often housed saints' relics, that is, bones, articles of clothing, or other objects associated with them. The relics served as links between the material world and the spiritual, and miracle stories about saints and their relics were an important part of Christian preaching and writing.

Christians came to venerate the saints as powerful and holy. They prayed to saints or to the Virgin Mary to intercede with God, or they simply asked the saints to assist and bless them. The entire village participated in processions marking saints' days or important points in the agricultural year, often carrying images of saints or their relics around the houses and fields. The decision to adopt Christianity was often made first by an emperor or king, but actual conversion was a local matter, as people came to feel that the parish priest and the saints provided them with benefits in this world and the world to come.

Frankish Rulers and Their Territories

How did the Franks build and govern a European empire?

Most barbarian kingdoms did not last very long, but one that did—and that came to have a decisive role in history—was that of the Franks. The Franks were a confederation of Germanic peoples who came from the marshy lowlands north and east of the northernmost part of the Roman Empire. In the fourth and fifth centuries they settled within the empire and allied with the Romans, some attaining high military and civil positions. Though at that time the Frankish kingdom was simply one barbarian kingdom among many, rulers after the influential Clovis used a variety of tactics to expand their holdings, enhance their authority, and create a stable system. Charles the Great (r. 768–814), generally known by the French version of his name, Charlemagne (SHAHR-luh-mayne), created the largest state in western Europe since the Roman Empire.

The Merovingians and Carolingians

The Franks believed that Merovech, a semi-legendary figure, founded their ruling dynasty, which was thus called Merovingian (mehr-uh-VIHN-jee-uhn). The reign of Clovis (r. ca. 481–511) was decisive in the development of the Franks as a unified people. Through military campaigns, Clovis acquired the central provinces of Roman Gaul and began to conquer southern Gaul from other Germanic tribes. His wife, Clotild, a Roman Christian, pressured him to convert, but he refused. His later biographer Gregory of Tours, a bishop in the Frankish kingdom in the sixth century, attributed his conversion to a battlefield vision, just as Emperor Constantine's biographers had reported about his conversion. Gregory wrote:

> Queen Clotild continued to pray that her husband might recognize the true God and give up his idol-worship. Nothing could persuade him to accept Christianity. Finally war broke out against the Alemanni and in this conflict he was forced by necessity to accept what he had refused of his own free will. It so turned out that when the two armies met on the battlefield there was a great slaughter and the troops of Clovis were rapidly being annihilated. He raised his eyes to heaven when he saw this, felt compunction in his heart and was moved to tears. "Jesus Christ," he said, "you who Clotild maintains to be the Son of the living God, you who deign to give help to those in travail and victory to those who trust in you, in faith I beg the glory of your help. If you will give me victory over my enemies, and if I may have evidence to that miraculous power which the people dedicated to your name say that they have experienced, then I will believe in you and I will be baptized in your name." . . . Even as he said this the Alemanni turned their backs and began to run away. As soon as they saw that their King was killed, they submitted to Clovis. "We beg you," they said, "to put an end to this slaughter. We are prepared to obey you." Clovis stopped the war. He made a speech in which he called for peace. Then he went home. He told the Queen how he had won a victory by calling on the name of Christ.[4]

Most historians today conclude that Clovis's conversion to Roman Christianity was a pragmatic choice: it brought him the crucial support of the bishops of Gaul in his campaigns against tribes that were still pagan or had accepted the Arian version of Christianity. As the defender of Roman Christianity against heretical tribes, Clovis went on to conquer the Visigoths, extending his domain to include much of what is now France and southwestern Germany.

Following Frankish traditions in which property was divided among male heirs, at Clovis's death his kingdom was divided among his four sons. For the next two centuries rulers of the various kingdoms fought one another in civil wars, and other military leaders challenged their authority. So brutal and destructive were these wars that at one time the term "Dark Ages" was used to apply to the entire Merovingian period, although more recently historians have noted that the Merovingians also developed new political institutions, so the era was not uniformly bleak.

Merovingian kings based some aspects of their government on Roman principles. For example, they adopted the Roman concept of the *civitas* — Latin for a city and its surrounding territory. A count presided over the civitas, raising troops, collecting royal revenues, and providing justice. Many counts were not conquerors from outside, but came from families that had been administrators in Gaul when it was ruled by the Romans. Within the royal household, Merovingian politics provided women with opportunities, and some queens not only influenced but occasionally also dominated events. Because the finances of the kingdom were merged with those of the royal family, queens often had control of the royal treasury just as more ordinary women controlled household expenditures.

At the king's court — that is, wherever the king was present — an official called the mayor of the palace supervised legal, financial, and household officials; the mayor of the palace also governed in the king's absence. In the seventh century the position as mayor was held by members of an increasingly powerful family, the **Carolingians** (ka-ruh-LIHN-jee-uhns), who advanced themselves through advantageous marriages, a well-earned reputation for military strength, and the help of the church.

Eventually the Carolingians replaced the Merovingians as rulers of the Frankish kingdom, cementing their authority when the Carolingian Charles Martel defeated Muslim invaders in 732 at the Battle of Poitiers (PWAH-tee-ay) in central France. Muslims and Christians have interpreted the battle differently. Muslims considered it a minor skirmish and attributed the Frankish victory to Muslim difficulties in maintaining supply lines over long distances and to ethnic conflicts and unrest in Islamic Spain. Charles Martel and later Carolingians used the victory to portray themselves as defenders of Christendom against the Muslims.

The Battle of Poitiers helped the Carolingians acquire more support from the church, perhaps their most important asset. They further strengthened their ties to the church by supporting the work of missionaries who preached Christian principles — including the duty to obey secular authorities — to pagan peoples and by allying themselves with the papacy against other Germanic tribes.

The Warrior-Ruler Charlemagne

The most powerful of the Carolingians was Charlemagne, who fought more than fifty campaigns and became the greatest warrior of the early Middle Ages. Through brutal military expeditions that brought wealth — lands, booty, slaves, and tribute — and by peaceful travel, personal appearances, shrewd marital alliances, and the sheer force of his personality, Charlemagne sought to awe newly conquered peoples and rebellious domestic enemies. By around 805 the Frankish kingdom included all of

Charlemagne and His Wife This illumination from a ninth-century manuscript portrays Charlemagne with one of his wives Marriage was an important tool of diplomacy for Charlemagne, and he had a number of wives and concubines. (Erich Lessing/ Art Resource, NY)

continental Europe except Spain, Scandinavia, southern Italy, and the Slavic fringes of the East.

For administrative purposes, Charlemagne divided his entire kingdom into counties. Each of the approximately six hundred counties was governed by a count, who had full military and judicial power and held his office for life but could be removed by the emperor for misconduct. As a link between local authorities and the central government, Charlemagne appointed officials called *missi dominici*, "agents of the lord king." Each year beginning in 802 two missi, usually a count and a bishop or abbot, visited assigned districts. They checked up on the counts and their districts' judicial, financial, and clerical activities.

In the autumn of the year 800 Charlemagne visited Rome, where on Christmas Day Pope Leo III crowned him emperor. The event had momentous consequences. In taking as his motto *Renovatio romani imperi* (Revival of the Roman Empire), Charlemagne was deliberately perpetuating old Roman imperial ideas while identifying with the new Rome of the Christian Church. From Baghdad, the Abbasid Empire's caliph, Harun al-Rashid (r. 786–809), congratulated Charlemagne on his coronation with the gift of an elephant. The elephant survived for nearly a decade, though like everyone else at Charlemagne's capital of Aachen (on the western border of modern Germany), it lived in a city that was far less sophisticated, healthy, and beautiful than Abbasid Baghdad. Although the Muslim caliph recognized Charlemagne as a fellow sovereign, the Byzantines regarded his papal coronation as rebellious and Charlemagne as a usurper. His crowning as emperor thus marked a decisive break between Rome and Constantinople and gave church authorities in the West proof that the imperial title could only be granted by the pope.

As he built an empire through conquest and strategic alliances, Charlemagne also set in motion a cultural revival that later historians called the "Carolingian Renaissance." The Carolingian Renaissance was a rebirth of interest in, study of, and preservation of the language, ideas, and achievements of classical Greece and Rome. Scholars at Aachen copied Greco-Roman and Christian books and manuscripts and created libraries housed in churches and monasteries. Furthermore, Charlemagne urged monasteries to promote Christian learning, and both men's and women's houses produced beautiful illustrated texts, preserving Christian and classical works for subsequent generations.

Charlemagne left his vast empire to his sole surviving son, Louis the Pious (r. 814–840), who attempted to keep the empire intact. This proved to be impossible. Members of the nobility engaged in plots and open warfare against the emperor, often allying themselves with one of Louis's three sons. In 843, shortly after Louis's death, those sons agreed to the **Treaty of Verdun**, which divided the empire into three parts: Charles the Bald received the western part, Lothair the middle and the title of emperor, and Louis the eastern part, from which he acquired the title "the German." Though of course no one knew it at the time, this treaty set the pattern for political boundaries in Europe that have been maintained through today. Other than brief periods under Napoleon and Hitler, Europe would never again see as large a unified state as it had under Charlemagne, which is one reason he has become a symbol of European unity in the twenty-first century.

The weakening of central power was hastened by invasions and migrations from the north, south, and east. Thus Charlemagne's empire ended in much the same way that the Roman Empire had earlier, from a combination of internal weakness and external pressure.

Chapter Summary

During the sixth and seventh centuries the Byzantine Empire survived waves of attacks, owing to effective military leadership and to fortifications around Constantinople. Byzantine emperors organized and preserved Roman institutions, and the Byzantine Empire survived until 1453. The emperor Justinian oversaw creation of a new uniform code of Roman law. The Byzantines prized education, and because of them many aspects of ancient Greek thought survived to influence the intellectual life of the Muslim world and eventually that of western Europe.

Christianity gained the support of the fourth-century emperors, and the church gradually adopted the Roman system of hierarchical organization. The church possessed able administrators and leaders. Bishops expanded their activities, and in the fifth century the bishops of Rome, taking the title "pope," began to stress their supremacy over other Christian communities. Monasteries offered opportunities for individuals to develop deeper spiritual devotion and also provided a model of Christian living and places for education and learning. Christian thinkers reinterpreted the classics in a Christian sense, incorporating elements of Greek and Roman philosophy into Christian teachings.

Barbarian groups migrated throughout Europe and Central Asia beginning in the second century. Among barbarians, the basic social unit was the tribe, made up of kin groups and led by a tribal chieftain. Missionaries and priests persuaded pagan and illiterate peoples to accept Christianity by stressing similarities between pagan customs and beliefs and those of Christianity, and introducing the ritual of penance and the veneration of saints. Most barbarian kingdoms were weak and short-lived, though the kingdom of the Franks was relatively more unified and powerful. Rulers first in the Merovingian dynasty, and then in the Carolingian, used military victories, carefully calculated marriage alliances, and the help of the church to enhance their authority.

Carolingian government reached the peak of its power under Charlemagne, who brought much of Europe under his authority through military conquest and strategic alliances.

Notes

1. Quoted in E. Patlagean, "Byzantium in the Tenth and Eleventh Centuries," in *A History of Private Life.* Vol. 1: *From Pagan Rome to Byzantium*, ed. P. Ariès and G. Duby (Cambridge, Mass.: Harvard University Press, 1987), p. 573.
2. R. C. Petry, ed., *A History of Christianity: Readings in the History of Early and Medieval Christianity* (Englewood Cliffs, N.J.: Prentice-Hall, 1962), p. 70.
3. E. F. Henderson, ed., *Select Historical Documents of the Middle Ages* (London: G. Bell and Sons, 1912), pp. 176, 189.
4. Gregory of Tours, *The History of the Franks*, trans. with an introduction by Lewis Thorpe (London: Penguin Books, 1974), pp. 141–144. Copyright © Lewis Thorpe, 1974, London. Reproduced by permission of Penguin Books Ltd.

CONNECTIONS

For centuries the end of the Roman Empire in the West was seen as a major turning point in history, the fall of the sophisticated and educated classical world to uncouth and illiterate tribes. Over the last several decades, however, many historians have put a greater emphasis on continuities. Barbarian kings relied on officials trained in Roman law, and Latin remained the language of scholarly communication and the Christian Church. Greco-Roman art and architecture still adorned the land, and people continued to use Roman roads, aqueducts, and buildings. In eastern Europe and western Asia, the Byzantine Empire preserved the traditions of the Roman Empire and protected the intellectual heritage of Greco-Roman culture for another millennium.

Very recently, however, some historians and archaeologists have returned to an emphasis on change. They note that people may have traveled on Roman roads after the end of the Roman Empire, but the roads were rarely maintained, and travel itself was much less secure than during the empire. Merchants no longer traded over long distances, so people's access to goods produced outside their local area plummeted. Knowledge about technological processes such as the making of glass and roof tiles declined or disappeared. Although intermarriage and cultural assimilation occurred among Romans and barbarians, violence and great physical destruction also existed, even in Byzantium.

In the middle of the era covered in this chapter, a new force emerged that had a dramatic impact on much of Europe and western Asia—Islam. In the seventh and eighth centuries Sassanid Persia, much of the Byzantine Empire, and the barbarian kingdoms in the Iberian Peninsula fell to Arab forces carrying this new religion. As we have seen in this chapter, a reputation as victors over Islam helped the Franks establish the most powerful state in Europe. As we will see when we pick up the story of Europe again in Chapter 14, Islam continued to shape European culture and politics in subsequent centuries. In terms of world history, the expansion of Islam may have been an even more dramatic turning point than the fall of the Roman Empire. Here, too, however, there were continuities, as the Muslims adopted and adapted Greek, Byzantine, and Persian political and cultural institutions.

followers were forced to flee to Medina. This *hijra* (hih-JIGH-ruh), or emigration, occurred in 622, and Muslims later dated the beginning of their era from it.

At Medina, Muhammad attracted increasing numbers of believers, many of whom were Bedouins who supported themselves by raiding caravans en route to Mecca, setting off a violent conflict between Mecca and Medina. After eight years of strife, Mecca capitulated. In this way, by the time Muhammad died in 632, he had welded together all the Bedouin tribes.

Muhammad displayed genius as both a political strategist and a religious teacher. He gave Arabs the idea of a unique and unified umma (UH-muh), or community, that consisted of all those whose primary identity and bond was a common religious faith, not a tribal tie. The umma was to be a religious and political community led by Muhammad for the achievement of God's will on earth. In the early seventh century the southern Arab tribal confederations lacked cohesiveness and were constantly warring. The Islamic notion of an absolute higher authority transcended the boundaries of individual tribal units and fostered political consolidation. All authority came from God through Muhammad.

Islam's Spread Beyond Arabia

After the Prophet's death, Islam quickly spread far beyond Arabia. In the sixth century two powerful empires divided the Middle East: the Greek-Byzantine empire centered at Constantinople and the Persian-Sassanid empire concentrated at Ctesiphon (near Baghdad in present-day Iraq). The Byzantine Empire stood for Hellenistic culture and championed Christianity (see Chapter 8). The Sassanid empire espoused Persian cultural traditions and favored the religious faith known as Zoroastrianism (see pages 55–56). Although each empire maintained an official state religion, neither possessed religious unity. Both had sizable Jewish populations, and within Byzantium sects that Orthodox Greeks considered heretical — Monophysites and Nestorians — were politically divisive forces. From the fourth through sixth centuries the Byzantines and Sassanids fought each other fiercely, each trying to expand its territories at the expense of the other and to control and tax the rich trade coming from Arabia and the Indian Ocean region. Many peripheral societies were drawn into the conflict. The resulting disorder facilitated the growth of Muslim states.

The second and third successors of Muhammad, Umar (r. 634–644) and Uthman (r. 644–656), launched a two-pronged attack against the Byzantine and Sassanid Empires. One force moved north from Arabia against the Byzantine provinces of Syria and Palestine (see page 203). From Syria, the Muslims conquered the rich province of Egypt, taking the commercial and intellectual hub of Alexandria in 642. Simultaneously, Arab armies swept into the Sassanid empire. The Muslim defeat of the Persians at Nihawand in 642 signaled the collapse of this empire (Map 9.1).

The Muslims continued their drive eastward and in the mid-seventh century occupied the province of Khurasan, where the city of Merv became the center of Muslim control over eastern Persia and the base for campaigns farther east. By 700 the Muslims had crossed the Oxus River and swept toward Kabul, today the capital of Afghanistan. They then penetrated Kazakhstan and seized Tashkent, one of the oldest cities in Central Asia. The clash of Muslim horsemen with a Chinese army at the Talas River in 751 marked the farthest Islamic penetration into Central Asia. From southern Persia, a Muslim force marched into the Indus Valley in northwest India and in 713 founded an Islamic community there. Beginning in the eleventh century Muslim dynasties from Ghazni in Afghanistan carried Islam deeper into the Indian subcontinent (see page 345).

To the west, Arab forces moved across North Africa and crossed the Strait of Gibraltar. In 711 at the Guadalete River they easily defeated the Visigothic kingdom of Spain. A few Christian princes supported by Merovingian rulers held out in the Cantabrian Mountains, but the Muslims controlled most of Spain until the thirteenth century. Advances into France were stopped in 732 when the Franks defeated Arab armies in a battle near the city of Tours, and Muslim occupation of parts of southern France did not last long.

Reasons for the Spread of Islam

By the beginning of the eleventh century the crescent of Islam had flown from the Iberian heartlands to northern India. How can this rapid and remarkable expansion be explained? The internal view of Muslim historians was that God supported the Islamic faith and aided its spread. The external, especially European, view was that the Muslim concept of jihad (JEE-hahd), or struggle, was the key element. The Qur'an does not precisely explain jihad. Some Muslim scholars hold that it signifies the individual struggle against sin and toward perfection on "the straight path" of Islam. Others claim that jihad has a social and communal implication—a militancy as part of a holy war against unbelievers living in territories outside the control of the Muslim community.

Today, few historians emphasize religious zeal alone but rather point to a combination of the Arabs' military advantages and the political weaknesses of their opponents. The Byzantine and Sassanid Empires had just fought a grueling century-long war and had also been weakened by the plague, which hit urban, stationary populations harder than nomadic populations. Equally important are the military strength and tactics of the Arabs. For example, rather than scattering as landlords of peasant farmers over conquered lands, Arab soldiers remained together in garrison cities, where their Arab ethnicity, tribal organization, religion, and military success set them apart. All soldiers were registered in the **diwān** (dih-WAHN), an administrative organ adopted from the Persians or Byzantines. Soldiers received a monthly ration of food for themselves and their families and an annual cash stipend. In return, they had to be available for military service. Fixed salaries, regular pay, and the lure of battlefield booty attracted rugged tribesmen from Arabia.

The Arab commanders recognized the economic benefits of capturing the major cities of the region. Arab caravans frequented the market towns of southern Syria and the rich commercial centers of the north, such as Edessa, Aleppo, and Damascus. Syria's economic prosperity probably attracted the Muslims, and perhaps Muhammad saw the land as a potential means of support for the poor who flooded into Medina. Syria also contained sites important to the faith: Jerusalem, where Jesus and other prophets mentioned in the Qur'an had lived and preached, and Hebron, the traditional burial place of Abraham, the father of monotheism.

prime targets for Muslim slave raids, as they made good slave soldiers. Once the Turks understood that Muslims could not be captured for slaves, more and more of them converted to Sunni Islam and often became *ghazi*, frontier raiders, who attacked un-converted Turks to capture slaves.

In the 1020s and 1030s Seljuk Turks overran Persia and then pushed into Iraq and Syria. Baghdad fell to them on December 18, 1055, and the caliph became a puppet of the Turkish sultan—literally, "he with authority." The Turkish elite rapidly gave up pastoralism and took up the sedentary lifestyle of the people they governed.

The Turks brought badly needed military strength to the Islamic world. They played a major part in recovering Jerusalem after it was held for nearly a century, from 1099 to 1187, by the European Crusaders (who had fought to take Christian holy lands back from the Muslims; see page 400). They also were important in preventing the later Crusades from accomplishing much. Moreover, the Turks became staunch Sunnis and led a campaign against the Shi'a.

The influx of Turks from 950 to 1100 also helped provide a new expansive dy-namic. At the Battle of Manzikert in 1071, Seljuk Turks broke through Byzantine border defenses, opening Anatolia to Turkish migration. Over the next couple of centuries, perhaps a million Turks entered the area—including bands of ghazis and dervishes (Sufi brotherhoods; see page 259). Seljuk Turks set up the Sultanate of Rum in Anatolia, which lasted until the Mongols invaded in 1243. With the Turks came many learned men from the Persian-speaking East. Over time, many of the Christians in Anatolia converted to Islam and became fluent in Turkish.

The Mongol Invasions

In the early thirteenth century the Mongols arrived in the Middle East. Originally from the grasslands of Mongolia, in 1206 they proclaimed Chinggis Khan (ca. 1162–1227) as their leader, and he welded Mongol, Tartar, and Turkish tribes into a strong confederation that rapidly subdued neighboring settled societies (see pages 334–337). After conquering much of north China, the Mongols swept westward, leaving a trail of blood and destruction. They used terror as a weapon, and out of fear many cities surrendered without a fight.

In 1219–1221, when the Mongols first reached the Islamic lands, the areas from Persia through the Central Asian cities of Herat and Samarkand were part of the kingdom of Khwarizm. The ruler—the son of a Turkish slave who had risen to gov-ernor of a province—was a conqueror himself, having conquered much of Persia. He had the audacity to execute Chinggis's envoy, and Chinggis retaliated with a force of a hundred thousand soldiers that sacked city after city, often slaughtering the residents or enslaving them and sending them to Mongolia. Millions are said to have died. The irrigation systems that were needed for agriculture in this dry region had been neglected for some time, and with the Mongol invasions they suffered a fatal blow.

Not many Mongol forces were left in Persia after the campaign of 1219–1221, and another army, sent in 1237, captured the Persian city of Isfahan. In 1251 the deci-sion was taken to push farther west. Chinggis Khan's grandson Hülegü (1217–1265) led an attack on the Abbasids in Baghdad, sacking and burning the city and killing the last Abbasid caliph in 1258. The fall of Damascus followed in 1260. Mamluk soldiers from Egypt, however, were able to withstand the Mongols and win a major victory at Ayn Jalut in Syria, which has been credited with saving Egypt and the Muslim lands in North Africa and perhaps Spain. At any rate, the desert ecology of the region did not provide suitable support for the Mongol armies, which required five horses for each soldier. Moreover, in 1260 the Great Khan (ruler of Mongolia and China) died, and the top Mongol generals withdrew to Mongolia for the selection of the next Great Khan.

Hülegü and his descendants ruled the central Muslim lands (referred to as the Il-khanate) for eighty years. In 1295 his descendant Ghazan embraced Islam and worked for the revival of Muslim culture. As the Turks had done earlier, the Mongols, once converted, injected new vigor into the faith and spirit of Islam. In the Il-khanate the Mongols governed through Persian viziers and native financial officials.

Muslim Society: The Life of the People

What social distinctions were important in Muslim society?

When the Prophet appeared, Arab society consisted of independent Bedouin tribal groups loosely held together by loyalty to a strong leader and by the belief that all members of a tribe were descended from a common ancestor. Heads of families elected the sheik, or tribal chief. He was usually chosen from among elite warrior families who believed their bloodlines made them superior. According to the Qur'an, however, birth counted for nothing; piety was the only criterion for honor: "O ye folk, verily we have created you male and female. . . . Verily the most honourable of you in the sight of God is the most pious of you."[1] The idea of social equality was a basic Muslim doctrine.

When Muhammad defined social equality, he was thinking about equality among Muslims alone. But even among Muslims, a sense of pride in ancestry could not be destroyed by a stroke of the pen. Claims based on birth remained strong among the first Muslims, and after Islam spread outside of Arabia, full-blooded Arab tribesmen regarded themselves as superior to foreign converts.

The Social Hierarchy

In the Umayyad period, Muslim society was distinctly hierarchical. At the top of the hierarchy were the caliph's household and the ruling Arab Muslims. Descended from Bedouin tribespeople and composed of warriors, veterans, governing officials, and townsmen, this class constituted the ruling elite. It was a relatively small group, greatly outnumbered by Muslim villagers and country people.

Converts constituted the second class in Islamic society, one that grew slowly over time. Converts to Islam had to attach themselves to one of the Arab tribes in a subordinate capacity. Many resented having to do this, since they believed they represented a culture superior to that of Arab tribespeople. From the Muslim converts eventually came the members of the commercial and learned professions—merchants, traders, teachers, doctors, artists, and interpreters of the shari'a. Second-class citizenship led some Muslim converts to adopt Shi'ism (see page 240). Even so, over the centuries, Berber, Copt, Persian, Aramaean, and other converts to Islam intermarried with their Muslim conquerors. Gradually, assimilation united peoples of various ethnic backgrounds.

silver, and copper for Asian spices, dyes, and drugs and for Chinese silks and porcelains. Muslim and Jewish merchants dominated the trade with India, and all spoke and wrote Arabic. Their commercial practices included the *sakk* (the Arabic word is the root of the English *check*), an order to a banker to pay money held on account to a third party; the practice can be traced to Roman Palestine. Muslims also developed other business innovations, such as the bill of exchange, a written order from one person to another to pay a specified sum of money to a designated person or party, and the idea of the joint stock company, an arrangement that lets a group of people invest in a venture and share its profits (and losses) in proportion to the amount each has invested.

Trade also benefited from improvements in technology. The adoption from the Chinese of the magnetic compass, an instrument for determining directions at sea by means of a magnetic needle turning on a pivot, greatly helped navigation of the Arabian Sea and the Indian Ocean. The construction of larger ships led to a shift in long-distance cargoes from luxury goods such as pepper, spices, and drugs to bulk goods such as sugar, rice, and timber. Venetian galleys sailing the Mediterranean came to carry up to 250 tons of cargo, but the Arab and Persian ships plying the Indian Ocean were built to carry up to 400 tons. The teak forests of western India supplied the wood for Arab ships.

In this period Egypt became the center of Muslim trade, benefiting from the decline of Iraq caused by the Mongol capture of Baghdad and the fall of the Abbasid caliphate (see page 244). Beginning in the late twelfth century Persian and Arab seamen sailed down the east coast of Africa and established trading towns between Somalia and Sofala (see pages 286–290). These thirty to fifty urban centers—each merchant-controlled, fortified, and independent—linked Zimbabwe in southern Africa with the Indian Ocean trade and the Middle Eastern trade.

A private ninth-century list mentions a great variety of commodities transported into and through the Islamic world by land and by sea:

> Imported from India: tigers, leopards, elephants, leopard skins, red rubies, white sandal-wood, ebony, and coconuts
>
> From China: aromatics, silk, porcelain, paper, ink, peacocks, fiery horses, saddles, felts, cinnamon
>
> From the Byzantines: silver and gold vessels, embroidered cloths, fiery horses, slave girls, rare articles in red copper, strong locks, lyres, water engineers, specialists in plowing and cultivation, marble workers, and eunuchs
>
> From Egypt: ambling donkeys, fine cloths, papyrus, balsam oil, and, from its mines, high-quality topaz
>
> From the Khazars [a people living on the northern shore of the Black Sea]: slaves, slave women, armor, helmets, and hoods of mail
>
> From Ahwaz [a city in southwestern Persia]: sugar, silk brocades, castanet players and dancing girls, kinds of dates, grape molasses, and candy.[5]

Did Muslim economic activity amount to a kind of capitalism? If capitalism is defined as private (not state) ownership of the means of production, the production of goods for sale, profit as the main motive for economic activity, competition, and a money economy, then, unquestionably, the medieval Muslim economy had capitalistic features. Until the sixteenth century much more world trade went through Muslim than European hands.

One byproduct of the extensive trade through Muslim lands was the spread of useful plants. Cotton, sugarcane, and rice spread from India to other places with suitable climates. Citrus fruits made their way to Muslim Spain from Southeast Asia and India. The value of this trade contributed to the prosperity of the Abbasid era.

Cultural Developments

What new ideas and practices emerged in the arts, sciences, education, and religion?

Long-distance trade provided the wealth that made possible a gracious and sophisticated culture in the cities of the Muslim world. (See "Individuals in Society: Ibn Battuta," page 254.) Education helped foster achievements in the arts and sciences, and Sufism brought a new spiritual and intellectual tradition.

The Cultural Centers of Baghdad and Córdoba

Although cities and mercantile centers dotted the entire Islamic world, the cities of Baghdad and Córdoba, at their peak in the tenth century, stand out as the finest examples of cosmopolitan Muslim civilization. On Baghdad's streets thronged a kaleidoscope of races, creeds, costumes, and cultures, an almost infinite variety of peoples: returning travelers, administrative officials, slaves, visitors, and merchants from Asia, Africa, and Europe. Shops and marketplaces offered a dazzling and exotic array of goods from all over the world.

The caliph Harun al-Rashid presided over a glamorous court. He invited writers, dancers, musicians, poets, and artists to live in Baghdad, and he is reputed to have rewarded one singer with 100,000 silver pieces for a single song. This brilliant era provided the background for the tales that appear in *The Thousand and One Nights*.

The central story of this fictional collection concerns the attempt of a new bride, Scheherazade, to keep her husband, Shahyar, legendary king of Samarkand, from killing her out of certainty that she will be unfaithful like his first wife. In efforts to delay her execution, she entertains him with one tale a night for 1,001 nights. In the end, Scheherazade's efforts succeed, and her husband pardons her. Among the tales she tells him are such famous ones as "Aladdin and His Lamp," "Sinbad the Sailor," and "Ali Baba and the Forty Thieves." Though filled with folklore, the *Arabian Nights* (as it is also called) has provided many of the images through which Europeans have understood the Islamic world.

Córdoba in southern Spain competed with Baghdad for the cultural leadership of the Islamic world. In the tenth century no city in Asia or Europe could equal dazzling Córdoba. Its streets were well paved and lighted, and the city had an abundant supply of fresh water. With a population of about 1 million, Córdoba contained 1,600 mosques, 900 public baths, 213,177 houses for ordinary people, and 60,000 mansions for generals, officials, and the wealthy. In its 80,455 shops, 13,000 weavers produced silks, woolens, and brocades that were internationally famous. Córdoba was also a great educational center with 27 free schools and a library containing 400,000 volumes. (By contrast, the renowned Benedictine abbey of Saint-Gall in Switzerland had about

INDIVIDUALS IN SOCIETY • Ibn Battuta

In 1354 the sultan of Morocco appointed a scribe to write an account of the travels of Abu 'Abdallah Ibn Battuta (1304–1368), who between 1325 and 1354 had traveled through most of the Islamic world. The two men collaborated. The result was a travel book written in Arabic and later hailed as the richest eyewitness account of fourteenth-century Islamic culture. It has often been compared to the slightly earlier *Travels* of the Venetian Marco Polo (see page 342).

Ibn Battuta was born in Tangiers to a family of legal scholars. As a youth, he studied Muslim law, gained fluency in Arabic, and acquired the qualities considered essential for a civilized Muslim gentleman: courtesy, manners, and the social polish that eases relations among people.

At age twenty-one he left Tangiers to make the hajj (pilgrimage) to Mecca. He crossed North Africa and visited Alexandria, Cairo, Damascus, and Medina. Reaching Mecca in October 1326, he immediately praised God for his safe journey, kissed the Holy Stone at the Ka'ba, and recited the ritual prayers. There he decided to see more of the world.

In the next four years Ibn Battuta traveled to Iraq and to Basra and Baghdad in Persia, then returned to Mecca before sailing down the coast of Africa as far as modern Tanzania. On the return voyage he visited Oman and the Persian Gulf region, then traveled by land across central Arabia to Mecca. Strengthened by his stay in the holy city, he decided to go to India by way of Egypt, Syria, and Anatolia; across the Black Sea to the plains of western Central Asia, detouring to see Constantinople; back to the Asian steppe; east to Khurasan and Afghanistan; and down to Delhi in northern India.

For eight years Ibn Battuta served as a judge in the service of the sultan of Delhi. In 1341 the sultan chose him to lead a diplomatic mission to China. After the expedition was shipwrecked off the southeastern coast of India, Ibn Battuta traveled through southern India, Sri Lanka, and the Maldive Islands. Then he went to China, stopping in Bengal and Sumatra before reaching the southern coast of China, then under Mongol rule. Returning to Mecca in 1346, he set off for home, getting to Morocco in 1349. After a brief trip across the Strait of Gibraltar to Granada, he

600 books.) Moreover, Córdoba's scholars made contributions in chemistry, medicine and surgery, music, philosophy, and mathematics. It was through Córdoba and Persia that the Indian game of chess entered western Europe. The contemporary Saxon nun Hrosthwita of Gandersheim (d. 1000) described Córdoba as the "ornament of the world."[6]

Education and Intellectual Life

Muslim culture valued learning, especially religious learning, because knowledge provided the guidelines by which men and women should live. Parents thus established elementary schools for the training of their children. After the caliph Uthman (see page 293) ordered the preparation of an approved text of the Qur'an and had copies of it made, the Qur'an became the basic text. From the eighth century onward, formal undertook his last journey, by camel caravan across the Sahara to Mali in the West African Sudan (see page 280), returning home in 1354. Scholars estimate that he had traveled about seventy-five thousand miles.

Ibn Battuta had a driving intellectual curiosity to see and understand the world. At every stop, he sought the learned jurists and pious men at the mosques and madrasas. He marveled at the Lighthouse of Alexandria, then in ruins; at the vast harbor at Kaffa (in southern Ukraine on the Black Sea), whose two hundred Genoese ships were loaded with silks and slaves for the markets at Venice, Cairo, and Damascus; and at the elephants in the sultan's procession in Delhi, which carried machines that tossed gold and silver coins to the crowds.

Ibn Battuta must have had an iron constitution. Besides walking long distances on his land trips, he endured fevers, dysentery, malaria, the scorching heat of the Sahara, and the freezing cold of the steppe. His thirst for adventure was stronger than his fear of nomadic warriors and bandits on land and the dangers of storms and pirates at sea.

Source: R. E. Dunn, *The Adventures of Ibn Battuta: A Muslim Traveler of the Fourteenth Century* (Berkeley: University of California Press, 1986).

QUESTIONS FOR ANALYSIS

1. Trace the routes of Ibn Battuta's travels on Map 9.2 (page 250).

2. How did a common Muslim culture facilitate Ibn Battuta's travels?

LaunchPad
ONLINE DOCUMENT PROJECT

How did Ibn Battuta describe his travels? Read parts of Ibn Battuta's account of his travels, and then complete a quiz and writing assignment based on the evidence and details from this chapter.

See inside the front cover to learn more.

education for young men involved reading, writing, and the study of the Qur'an, believed essential for its religious message and for its training in proper grammar and syntax.

Islam is a religion of the law, taught at madrasas (muh-DRA-suhs), schools for the study of Muslim law and religion. Many madrasas were founded between 1000 and 1350. By 1193 thirty madrasas existed in Damascus, with sixty more established there between 1200 and 1250. Aleppo, Jerusalem, Alexandria, and above all Cairo also witnessed the foundation of madrasas.

Schools were urban phenomena. Wealthy merchants endowed them, providing salaries for teachers, stipends for students, and living accommodations for both. All Islamic higher education rested on a close relationship between teacher and students, so in selecting a teacher, the student (or his father) considered the character and

Teachers Disputing in a Madrasa Although Islamic education relied heavily on memorization of the Qur'an, religious scholars frequently debated the correct interpretation of a particular text. Listening to this lively disputation, the students illustrated in this 1222 book are learning to think critically and creatively. (From *The Schefer Magamat*, Ms. Arabe 5847, fol. 118v/R. and S. Michaud/akg-images)

intellectual reputation of the teacher, not that of the institution. Students built their subsequent careers on the reputation of their teachers.

Learning depended heavily on memorization. In primary school, which was often attached to an institution of higher learning, a boy began his education by memorizing the entire Qur'an. Normally, he achieved this feat by the time he was seven or eight. In adolescence a student learned by heart an introductory work in one of the branches of knowledge, such as jurisprudence or grammar. Later he analyzed the texts in detail. Memorizing four hundred to five hundred lines a day was considered outstanding. Every class day, the teacher examined the student on the previous day's learning and determined whether the student fully understood what he had memorized. Students, of course, learned to write, for they had to record the teacher's commentary on a particular text. But the overwhelming emphasis was on the oral transmission of knowledge.

Because Islamic education focused on particular books, when the student had mastered a text to his teacher's satisfaction, the teacher issued the student a certificate stating that he had studied the book or collection of traditions with his teacher. The certificate allowed the student to transmit a text to the next generation on the authority of his teacher.

As the importance of books suggests, the Muslim transmission and improvement of papermaking techniques had special significance to education. For centuries the Chinese had been making paper from rags and from the fibers of hemp, jute, bamboo, and other plants. After these techniques spread westward, Muslim papermakers improved on them by adding starch to fill the pores in the surfaces of the sheets. Muslims carried this new method to Baghdad in Iraq, Damascus in Syria, Cairo in Egypt, and the Maghrib (North Africa), from which it entered Spain. Even before the invention of printing, papermaking had a revolutionary impact on the collection and diffusion of knowledge.

Muslim higher education, apart from its fundamental goal of preparing men to live wisely and in accordance with God's law, aimed at preparing them to perform religious and legal functions as Qur'an—or hadith—readers; as preachers in the mosques; as professors, educators, or copyists; and especially as judges. Judges issued fatwas, or legal opinions, in the public courts; their training was in the Qur'an, hadith, or some text forming part of the shari'a.

On the issue of female education, Islamic culture was ambivalent. Tradition holds that Muhammad said, "The seeking of knowledge is a duty of every Muslim," but, because of the basic Islamic principle that "men are the guardians of women, because God has set the one over the other," the law excluded women from participating in the legal, religious, or civic occupations for which the madrasa prepared young men. Moreover, educational theorists insisted that men should study in a sexually isolated environment because feminine allure would distract them. Nevertheless, many young women received substantial educations at home. The daughter of Ali Ibn Muhammad al-Diruti al-Mahalli, for example, memorized the Qur'an, learned to write, and received instruction in several sacred works. According to one biographical dictionary covering the lives of 1,075 women, 411 of them had memorized the Qur'an, studied with a particular teacher, and received a certificate.

In comparing Islamic higher education during the twelfth through fourteenth centuries with that available in Europe or China at the same time (see pages 408, 367), there are some striking similarities and some major differences. In both Europe and the Islamic countries religious authorities ran most schools, while in China the government, local villages, and lineages ran schools, and private tutoring was very common. In the Islamic world, as in China, the personal relationship of teacher and student was seen as key to education. In Europe the reward for satisfactorily completing a course of study was a degree granted by the university. In China, at the very highest levels, the state ran a civil service examination system that rewarded achievement with appointments in the state bureaucracy. In Muslim culture, by contrast, it was not the school or the state but the individual teacher whose evaluation mattered and who granted certificates.

Still, there were also some striking similarities in the practice of education. Students in all three cultures had to master a sacred language (Latin, Arabic, or classical Chinese). In all three cultures education rested heavily on the study of basic religious, legal, or philosophical texts: the Old and New Testaments or the Justinian *Code* in Europe; the Confucian classics and commentaries in China; the Qur'an, hadith, and legal texts deriving from them in the Muslim world. Also, in all three cultures memorization played a large role in the acquisition and transmission of learning. Furthermore, teachers in all three societies lectured on particular passages, and leading teachers might disagree fiercely about the correct interpretations of a particular text, forcing students to question, to think critically, and to choose among divergent opinions. All these similarities in educational practice contributed to cultural cohesion and ties among the educated living in scattered localities.

In the Muslim world the spread of the Arabic language, not only among the educated classes but also among all the people, was the decisive element in the creation of a common culture. Recent scholarship demonstrates that after the establishment of the Islamic empire, the spread of the Arabic language was more important than religion in fostering cultural change. Whereas conversion to Islam was gradual, linguistic conversion went much faster. Arabic became the official language of the state and its bureaucracies in former Byzantine and Sassanid territories, and Muslim conquerors

722–1492), polemical anti-Christian writings appeared. In other periods, Muslim views were more positive.

In the Middle Ages, Christians and Muslims met frequently in business and trade. Commercial contacts, especially when European merchants resided for a long time in the Muslim East, gave Europeans, notably the Venetians, familiarity with Muslim art and architecture. Likewise, when in the fifteenth century Muslim artists in the Ottoman Empire and in Persia became acquainted with Western artists, such as Gentile Bellini, they admired and imitated them. Also, Christians very likely borrowed aspects of their higher education system from Islam.

In the Christian West, Islam had the greatest cultural impact in Andalusia in southern Spain. Between roughly the eighth and twelfth centuries Muslims, Christians, and Jews lived in close proximity in Andalusia, and some scholars believe the period represents a remarkable era of interfaith harmony. Many Christians adopted Arabic patterns of speech and dress, gave up the practice of eating pork, and developed a special appreciation for Arabic music and poetry. Some Christian women of elite status chose the Muslim practice of going out in public with their faces veiled. Records describe Muslim and Christian youths joining in celebrations and merrymaking. These assimilated Christians, called **Mozarabs** (moh-ZAR-uhbz), did not attach much importance to the doctrinal differences between the two religions.

However, Mozarabs soon faced the strong criticism of both Muslim scholars and Christian clerics. Muslim teachers feared that close contact between people of the two religions would lead to Muslim contamination and become a threat to the Islamic faith. Christian bishops worried that a knowledge of Islam would lead to confusion about essential Christian doctrines. Both Muslim scholars and Christian theologians argued that assimilation led to moral decline.

Playing Chess
This page from a thirteenth-century book on chess and other games depicts a Moor and a Christian playing chess together.
(Biblioteca Monasterio del Escorial, Madrid, Spain/Index/The Bridgeman Art Library)

Thus, beginning in the late tenth century, Muslim regulations closely defined what Christians and Muslims could do. A Christian, however much assimilated, remained an unbeliever, a word that carried a pejorative connotation. Mozarabs had to live in special sections of cities; could not learn the Qur'an, employ Muslim workers or servants, or build new churches; and had to be buried in their own cemeteries. A Muslim who converted to Christianity was sentenced to death. By about 1250 the Christian reconquest of Muslim Spain had brought most of the Iberian Peninsula under Christian control. With their new authority, Christian kings set up schools that taught both Arabic and Latin to train missionaries.

Beyond Andalusian Spain, mutual animosity limited contact between people of the two religions. The Muslim assault on Christian Europe in the eighth and ninth centuries—with villages burned, monasteries sacked, and Christians sold into slavery—left a legacy of bitter hostility. Christians felt threatened by a faith that acknowledged God as creator of the universe but denied the Trinity and that accepted Jesus as a prophet but denied his divinity. Europeans' perception of Islam as a menace helped inspire the Crusades of the eleventh through thirteenth centuries (see pages 399–402).

Despite the conflicts between the two religions, Muslim scholars often wrote sympathetically about Jesus. For example, the great historian al-Tabari (d. 923), relying on Arabic sources, wrote positively of Jesus's life, focusing on his birth and crucifixion. Also, Ikhwan al-Safa, an eleventh-century Islamic brotherhood, held that in his preaching Jesus deliberately rejected the harsh punishments reflected in the Jewish Torah and tried to be the healing physician, teaching by parables and trying to touch people's hearts by peace and love. The prominent theologian and qadi (judge) of Teheran, Abd al-Jabbar (d. 1024), though not critical of Jesus, argued that Christians had rejected Jesus's teachings: they failed to observe the ritual purity of prayer, substituting poems by Christian scholars for scriptural prayers; they gave up circumcision, the sign of their covenant with God and Abraham; they moved the Sabbath from Saturday to Sunday; they allowed the eating of pork and shellfish; and they adopted a Greek idea, the Trinity, defending it by quoting Aristotle. Thus, al-Jabbar maintained—and he was followed later by many other Muslim theologians and scholars—that Christians failed to observe the laws of Moses and Jesus and distorted Jesus's message.

In the Christian West, both positive and negative views of Islam appeared in literature. The Bavarian knight Wolfram von Eschenbach's *Parzival* and the Englishman William Langland's *Piers the Plowman*—two medieval poems that survive in scores of manuscripts, suggesting that they circulated widely—reveal broad-mindedness and tolerance toward Muslims. Some travelers in the Middle East were impressed by the kindness and generosity of Muslims and with the strictness and devotion with which Muslims observed their faith. Frequently, however, Christian literature portrayed Muslims as the most dreadful of Europe's enemies, guilty of every kind of crime. In his *Inferno*, for example, the great Florentine poet Dante (1265–1321) placed the Muslim philosophers Avicenna and Averroës with other virtuous "heathens," among them Socrates and Aristotle, in the first circle of Hell, where they endured only moderate punishment. Muhammad, however, Dante consigned to the ninth circle, near Satan himself, where he was condemned as a spreader of discord and scandal and suffered perpetual torture.

Even when they rejected each other most forcefully, the Christian and Muslim worlds had a significant impact on each other. Art styles, technology, and even institutional practices spread in both directions. During the Crusades Muslims adopted Frankish weapons and methods of fortification. Christians in contact with Muslim scholars recovered ancient Greek philosophical texts that survived only in Arabic translation.

Chapter Summary

Muhammad, born in the Arabian peninsula, experienced a religious vision, after which he preached to the people to give up their idols and submit to the one indivisible God. He believed in the same God as the Christians and Jews and taught strict monotheism. Islam, the religion based on Muhammad's teachings, appropriated much of the Old and New Testaments of the Bible. After Muhammad's death, his followers gathered his revelations, eventually producing the Qur'an.

Within the span of a century, Muslims carried their faith from the Arabian peninsula through the Middle East, to North Africa and Spain, and to the borders of China and India. Successors to Muhammad established the caliphate, which through two successive dynasties coordinated rule over Muslim lands. A key challenge faced by the caliphate was a fundamental division in Muslim theology between the Sunnis and the Shi'a.

Over time, many parts of the Muslim empire gained considerable local independence. Far-flung territories such as Spain began to break away from the Baghdad-centered caliphate. By the tenth century Turks played a more important role in the armies and came to be the effective rulers in much of the Middle East. They were succeeded by the Mongols, who invaded the Middle East in the thirteenth century and ruled the central Muslim lands for eighty years.

Muslim society was distinctly hierarchical. In addition to a structure that privileged the ruling Arab Muslims over converts to Islam, then over Jews, Christians, and Zoroastrians, there were also a substantial number of slaves, generally war captives. Slaves normally were converted to Islam and might come to hold important positions, especially in the army. Distinctions between men and women in Islamic society were strict. Over time, the seclusion and veiling of women became common practices, especially among the well-to-do.

Islam did not discourage trade and profitmaking. By land and sea Muslim merchants transported a rich variety of goods across Asia, the Middle East, Africa, and western Europe. As trade thrived, innovations such as money orders to bankers, bills of exchange, and joint stock companies aided the conduct of business.

Wealth from trade made possible a gracious and sophisticated culture in the cities of the Muslim world, especially Baghdad and Córdoba. During this period Muslim scholars produced important work in many disciplines, especially mathematics, medicine, and philosophy. A new spiritual and intellectual tradition arose in the mystical practices of Sufism. Muslims, Christians, and Jews interacted in many ways during this period. At the time of the Crusades and of the Christian reconquest of Muslim Spain, polemical anti-Christian writings appeared, but in other periods Muslim views were more positive. Many Christians converted in the early centuries of the spread of Islam. Others such as the Mozarabs assimilated into Muslim culture while retaining their religion.

Notes

1. Quoted in R. Levy, *The Social Structure of Islam*, 2d ed. (Cambridge: Cambridge University Press, 1957), p. 56.
2. Quoted in B. F. Stowasser, "The Status of Women in Early Islam," in *Muslim Women*, ed. F. Hussain (New York: St. Martin's Press, 1984), p. 25.
3. F. E. Peters, *A Reader on Classical Islam* (Princeton, N.J.: Princeton University Press, 1994), p. 250.
4. Quoted in B. Lewis, ed. and trans., *Islam from the Prophet Muhammad to the Capture of Constantinople*. Vol. 2: *Religion and Society*, 35w from p. 126. © 1974 by Bernard Lewis. Used by permission of Oxford University Press, USA, www.oup.com.
5. Ibid., pp. 154–157.
6. R. Hillenbrand, "Cordoba," in *Dictionary of the Middle Ages*, vol. 3, ed. J. R. Strayer (New York: Scribner's, 1983), pp. 597–601.
7. Margaret Smith, *Readings from the Mystics of Islam* (London: Luzac and Co., 1950), p. 11.

CONNECTIONS

During the five centuries that followed Muhammad's death, his teachings came to be revered in large parts of the world, from Spain to Afghanistan. Although in some ways similar to the earlier spread of Buddhism out of India and Christianity out of Palestine, the spread of Islam occurred largely through military conquests that extended Muslim lands. Still, conversion was never complete; both Christians and Jews maintained substantial communities within Muslim lands. Moreover, cultural contact among Christians, Jews, and Muslims was an important element in the development of each culture.

Muslim civilization in these centuries drew from many sources, including Persia and Byzantium, and in turn had broad impact beyond its borders. Muslim scholars preserved much of early Greek philosophy and science through translation into Arabic. Trade connected the Muslim lands both to Europe and to India and China.

During the first and second centuries after Muhammad, Islam spread along the Mediterranean coast of North Africa, which had been part of the Roman world. The next chapter explores other developments in the enormous and diverse continent of Africa during this time. Many of the written sources that tell us about the African societies of these centuries were written in Arabic by visitors from elsewhere in the Muslim world. Muslim traders traveled through many of the societies in Africa north of the Congo, aiding the spread of Islam to the elites of many of these societies. Ethiopia was an exception, as Christianity spread there from Egypt before the time of Muhammad and retained its hold in subsequent centuries. Africa's history is introduced in the next chapter.

elders and the commoners. Among the Yoruba in modern Nigeria, the Queen Mother held the royal insignia and could refuse it if the future king did not please her. She also placed the royal beaded crown on the king's head. The institutions of female chiefs, known as *iyalode* among the Yoruba and *omu* among the Igbo in modern Nigeria, were established to represent women in the political process. The *omu* was even considered a female co-ruler with the male chief.

Western Sudanese religious practices, like African religions elsewhere, were animistic and polytheistic. Most people believed that a supreme being had created the universe and was the source of all life. Most African religions also recognized ancestral spirits, which might seek God's blessings for families' and communities' prosperity and security as long as these groups behaved appropriately. If not, the ancestral spirits might not protect them from harm, and illness and misfortune could result. Some African religions believed as well that nature spirits lived in such things as the sky, forests, rocks, and rivers. These spirits controlled natural forces and had to be appeased. During the annual agricultural cycle, for example, all the spirits had to be propitiated from the time of clearing the land through sowing the seed to the final harvest. Because special ceremonies were necessary to satisfy the spirits, special priests with the knowledge and power to communicate with them through sacred rituals were needed. Family and village heads were often priests. Each family head was responsible for ceremonies honoring the family's dead and living members.[2]

In some West African societies, oracles who spoke for the gods were particularly important. Some of the most famous were the Ibo oracles in modern Nigeria. These were female priestesses who were connected with a particular local deity that resided in a sacred cave or other site. Inhabitants of surrounding villages would come to the priestess to seek advice about such matters as crops and harvests, war, marriage, legal issues, and religion. Clearly, these priestesses held much power and authority, even over the local male rulers.

Kinship patterns and shared religious practices helped to bind together the early western Sudan kingdoms. Islam's spread across the Sahara by at least the ninth century C.E., however, created a north-south religious and cultural divide in the western Sudan. Islam advanced across the Sahel into modern Mauritania, Mali, Burkina Faso, Niger, northern Nigeria, and Chad but halted when it reached the West African savanna and forest zones. Societies in these southern zones maintained their traditional animistic religious practices. Muslim empires along the Niger River's great northern bend evolved into formidable powers ruling over sizable territory as they seized control of the southern termini of the trans-Saharan trade. What made this long-distance trade possible was the "ship of the desert," the camel.

The Trans-Saharan Trade

What characterized trans-Saharan trade, and how did it affect West African society?

"Trans-Saharan trade" refers to the north-south trade across the Sahara (Map 10.1). The camel had an impact on this trade comparable to the very important impact of horses and oxen on European agriculture. Although scholars dispute exactly when the

MAP 10.1 **African Kingdoms and Trade, ca. 800–1500** Throughout world history powerful kingdoms have generally been closely connected to far-flung trade networks.

camel was introduced from Central Asia—first into North Africa, then into the Sahara and the Sudan—they agree that it was before 200 C.E. Camels can carry about five hundred pounds as far as twenty-five miles a day and can go for days without drinking, living on the water stored in their stomachs. Temperamental and difficult to work with, camels had to be loaded on a daily, sometimes twice-daily, basis, and much of the cargo for a long trip was made up of provisions for the journey itself. Nevertheless, camels proved more efficient for desert transportation than horses or oxen. The trans-Saharan trade brought lasting economic and social change to Africa, facilitating the spread of Islam via Muslim Arab traders, and affected the development of world commerce.

The Berbers of North Africa

Sometime in the fifth century C.E. the North African Berbers fashioned a saddle for use on the camel. This saddle had no direct effect on commercial operations, for a merchant usually walked and guided the camel on foot. But the saddle gave the Berbers and later the region's Arabian inhabitants maneuverability on the animal and thus a powerful political and military advantage: they came to dominate the desert and to create lucrative routes across it. The Berbers determined who could enter the desert, and they extracted large sums of protection money from merchant caravans in exchange for a safe trip.

Between 700 C.E. and 900 C.E. the Berbers developed a network of caravan routes between the Mediterranean coast and the Sudan (see Map 10.1). The long expedition across the Sahara testifies to the traders' spirit and to their passion for wealth. Because of the blistering sun and daytime temperatures reaching 110°F, caravan drivers preferred night travel, when temperatures might drop to the low 20s. Ibn Battuta, an Arab traveler in the fourteenth century, when the trade was at its height, left one of the best descriptions of the trans-Saharan traffic. (See "Individuals in Society: Ibn Battuta," page 254.) It took Ibn Battuta twenty-five days to travel from Sijilmasa to the oasis of Taghaza and another sixty-five days to travel from Taghaza to the important market town of Walata.

Nomadic raiders, the Tuareg (TWAH-rehg), posed a serious threat to trans-Saharan traders. The Tuareg were Berbers who lived in the desert uplands and preyed on the caravans as a way of life. To avoid being victimized, merchants made safe-conduct agreements with them and selected guides from among them. Large numbers of merchants crossed the desert together to discourage attack; caravans of twelve thousand camels were reported in the fourteenth century. Blinding sandstorms often separated part of a line of camels and on at least one recorded occasion buried alive some camels and drivers. Water was the biggest problem. To satisfy normal thirst and to compensate for constant sweating, each person required a gallon of water per day. Desperate thirst sometimes forced the traders to kill camels and drink the foul, brackish water in their stomachs. The Tuareg used this problem to their advantage, sometimes poisoning wells to wipe out caravans and steal their goods.

Berber merchants from North Africa controlled the caravan trade that carried dates, salt (essential in tropical climates to replace the loss from perspiration) from the Saharan salt mines, and some manufactured goods—silk and cotton cloth, beads, mirrors—to the Sudan. These products were exchanged for the much-coveted commodities of the West African savanna—gold, ivory, gum, kola nuts (eaten as a stimulant), and enslaved West African men and women who were sold to Muslim slave markets in Morocco, Algiers, Tripoli, and Cairo.

Effects of Trade on West African Society

The steady growth of trans-Saharan trade had three important effects on West African society. First, trade stimulated gold mining. Parts of modern-day Senegal, Nigeria, and Ghana contained rich veins of gold. Both sexes shared in mining it. Men hacked out gold-bearing rocks and crushed them, separating gold from soil. Women washed the gold in gourds. Alluvial gold (mixed with soil, sand, or gravel) was separated from the soil by panning. Scholars estimate that by the eleventh century nine tons of gold were exported to the Mediterranean coast and Europe annually — a prodigious amount for the time, since even with modern machinery and sophisticated techniques, total gold exports from the same region in 1937 amounted to only twenty-one tons. Some of this metal went to Egypt. From there it was transported down the Red Sea and eventually to India (see Map 9.2, page 250) to pay for the spices and silks demanded by Mediterranean commerce. In this way, African gold linked the entire world, exclusive of the Western Hemisphere.

Second, trade in gold and other goods created a desire for slaves. Slaves were West Africa's second-most valuable export (after gold). Slaves worked the gold and salt mines, and in Muslim North Africa, southern Europe, and southwestern Asia there was a high demand for household slaves among the elite. African slaves, like their early European and Asian counterparts, seem to have been peoples captured in war. Recent research suggests, moreover, that large numbers of black slaves were also recruited for Muslim military service through the trans-Saharan trade. Manumission (the freeing of individual slaves), high death rates from disease, and the assimilation of some blacks into Muslim society meant that the demand for slaves remained high for centuries. Table 10.1 shows the scope of the trans-Saharan slave trade. The total number of blacks enslaved over an 850-year period may be tentatively estimated at more than 4 million.[3]

Slavery in Muslim societies, as in European and Asian countries before the fifteenth century, was not based on skin color. Muslims also enslaved Caucasians who had been purchased, seized in war, or kidnapped from Europe. Wealthy Muslim households in Córdoba, Alexandria, and Tunis often included slaves of a number of races, all of whom had been completely cut off from their cultural roots. Likewise, West African kings who sold blacks to northern traders also bought a few white slaves — Slavic, British, and Turkish — for their own domestic needs. Race had little to do with the phenomenon of slavery.

TABLE 10.1 Estimated Magnitude of Trans-Saharan Slave Trade, 650–1500

YEARS	ANNUAL AVERAGE OF SLAVES TRADED	TOTAL
650–800	1,000	150,000
800–900	3,000	300,000
900–1100	8,700	1,740,000
1100–1400	5,500	1,650,000
1400–1500	4,300	430,000

Source: R. A. Austen, "The Trans-Saharan Slave Trade: A Tentative Census," in *The Uncommon Market: Essays in the Economic History of the Atlantic Slave Trade*, ed. H. A. Gemery and J. S. Hogendorn (New York: Academic Press, 1979). Used with permission.

The third important effect of trans-Saharan trade on West African society was its role in stimulating the development of urban centers. Scholars date the growth of African cities from around the early ninth century. Families that had profited from trade tended to congregate in the border zones between the savanna and the Sahara. They acted as middlemen between the miners to the south and the Muslim merchants from the north. By the early thirteenth century these families had become powerful merchant dynasties. Muslim traders from the Mediterranean settled permanently in the trading depots, from which they organized the trans-Saharan caravans. The concentration of people stimulated agriculture and the craft industries. Gradually cities of sizable population emerged. Jenne, Gao, and Timbuktu, which enjoyed commanding positions on the Niger River bend, became centers of the export-import trade. Sijilmasa grew into a thriving market center. Koumbi Saleh, with between fifteen thousand and twenty thousand inhabitants, was probably the largest city in the western Sudan in the twelfth century. (By European standards, Koumbi Saleh was a metropolis; London and Paris achieved this size only in the late thirteenth century.) Between 1100 and 1400 these cities played a dynamic role in West Africa's commercial life and became centers of intellectual creativity.

The Spread of Islam in Africa

Perhaps the most influential consequence of the trans-Saharan trade was the introduction of Islam to West Africa. In the eighth century Arab invaders overran all of coastal North Africa. They introduced the Berbers living there to Islam, and gradually the Berbers became Muslims. As traders, these Berbers carried Islam to sub-Saharan West Africa. From the eleventh century onward militant Almoravids, a coalition of fundamentalist western Saharan Berbers, preached Islam to the rulers of Ghana, Mali, Songhai, and Kanem-Bornu. These rulers, admiring Muslim administrative techniques and wanting to protect their kingdoms from Muslim Berber attacks, converted to Islam. Some merchants also sought to preserve their elite mercantile status with the Berbers by adopting Islam. By the tenth century Muslim Berbers controlled the north-south trade routes to the savanna. By the eleventh century African rulers of Gao and Timbuktu had accepted Islam. The king of Ghana was also influenced by Islam. Muslims quickly became integral to West African government and society. Hence, from roughly 1000 to 1400, Islam in West Africa was a class-based religion with conversion inspired by political or economic motives. Rural people in the Sahel region and the savanna and forest peoples farther south, however, largely retained their traditional animism.

Conversion to Islam introduced West Africans to a rich and sophisticated culture. By the late eleventh century Muslims were guiding the ruler of Ghana in the operation of his administrative machinery. Ghana's king adopted the Muslim diwān, the agency for keeping financial records (see page 237). Because efficient government depends on keeping and preserving records, Islam's arrival in West Africa marked the advent of written documents there. Arab Muslims also taught Ghana's rulers how to manufacture bricks, and royal palaces and mosques began to be built of brick. African rulers corresponded with Arab and North African Muslim architects, theologians, and other intellectuals, who advised them on statecraft and religion. Islam accelerated the development of the West African empires of the ninth through fifteenth centuries.

After the Muslim conquest of Egypt in 642 (see page 236), Islam spread southward from Egypt up the Nile Valley and west to Darfur and Wadai. This Muslim penetration came not suddenly by military force but, as in the trans-Saharan trade routes in West Africa, gradually through commercial networks.

Muslim expansion from the Arabian peninsula across the Red Sea to the Horn of Africa, then southward along the coast of East Africa, represents a third direction of Islam's growth in Africa. From ports on the Red Sea and the Gulf of Aden, maritime trade carried the Prophet's teachings to East Africa and the Indian Ocean. Muslims founded the port city of Mogadishu between the eighth and tenth centuries, today Somalia's capital. In the twelfth century Mogadishu developed into a Muslim sultanate, a monarchy that employed a slave military corps against foreign and domestic enemies. Archaeological evidence, confirmed by Arabic sources, reveals a rapid Islamic expansion along Africa's east coast in the thirteenth century as far south as Kilwa, where Ibn Battuta visited a center for Islamic law in 1331.

African Kingdoms and Empires, ca. 800–1500

How were the East African city-states, Aksum, and Great Zimbabwe different from and similar to the kingdoms of the western Sudan?

All African societies shared one basic feature: a close relationship between political and social organization. Ethnic or blood ties bound clan members together. What scholars call stateless societies were culturally homogeneous ethnic societies, generally organized around kinship groups. The smallest ones numbered fewer than a hundred people and were nomadic hunting groups. Larger stateless, or decentralized, societies, such as the Tiv in modern central Nigeria, consisted of perhaps several thousand people who lived a settled and often agricultural and/or herding life. These societies lacked a central authority figure, such as a king, capital city, or military. A village or group of villages might recognize a chief who held very limited powers and whose position was not hereditary, but more commonly they were governed by local councils, whose members were either elders or persons of merit. Although stateless societies functioned successfully, their weakness lay in their inability to organize and defend themselves against attack by the powerful armies of neighboring kingdoms or by the European powers of the colonial era.

While stateless societies were relatively common in Africa, the period from about 800 to 1500 is best known as the age of Africa's great empires (see Map 10.1). This period witnessed the flowering of several powerful African states. In the western Sudan the large empires of Ghana, Mali, and Songhai developed, complete with sizable royal bureaucracies. On the east coast emerged thriving city-states based on sophisticated mercantile activities and, like the western Sudan, heavily influenced by Islam. In Ethiopia, in central East Africa, kings relied on their peoples' Christian faith to strengthen political authority. In southern Africa the empire of Great Zimbabwe, built on the gold trade with the east coast, flourished.

The Kingdom of Ghana, ca. 900–1100

So remarkable was the kingdom of Ghana during the age of Africa's great empires that Arab and North African visitors praised it as a model for other rulers. Even in modern times, ancient Ghana holds a central place in Africa's historical consciousness. When the Gold Coast colony gained its independence from British colonial rule in 1957, its new political leaders paid tribute to their heritage by naming their new country Ghana. Although modern Ghana lies far from the site of the old kingdom, the name was selected to signify the rebirth of ancient Ghana's illustrious past.

The Soninke people inhabited the nucleus of the territory that became the Ghanaian kingdom. They called their ruler *ghana*, or war chief. By the late eighth century Muslim traders and other foreigners applied the king's title to the region where the Soninke lived, the kingdom south of the Sahara. The Soninke themselves called their land Wagadou (WAH-guh-doo). Only the southern part of Wagadou received enough rainfall to be agriculturally productive, and it was here that the civilization of Ghana developed (see Map 10.1). Skillful farming and efficient irrigation systems led to abundant crop production, which eventually supported a population of as many as two hundred thousand.

INDIVIDUALS IN SOCIETY • Amda Siyon

Scholars consider Amda Siyon (r. 1314–1344) the greatest ruler of Ethiopia's Solomonic dynasty. Yet we have no image or representation of him. We know nothing of his personal life, though if he followed the practice of most Ethiopian kings, he had many wives and children. Nor do we know anything about his youth and education. The evidence of what he did, however, suggests a tough military man who personified the heroic endurance and physical pain expected of warriors. According to a chronicle of Siyon's campaign against the Muslim leader of Ifat,

> [Siyon] clove the ranks of the rebels and struck so hard that he transfixed two men as one with the blow of his spear, through the strength of God. Thereupon the rebels scattered and took to flight, being unable to hold their ground in his presence.

Amda Siyon reinforced control over his kingdom's Christian areas. He then expanded into the neighboring regions of Shewa, Gojam, and Damot. Victorious there, he gradually absorbed the Muslim states of Ifat and Hedya to the east and southeast. These successes gave him effective control of the central highlands and also the Indian Ocean trade routes to the Red Sea (see Map 10.1). He governed in a quasi-feudal fashion. Theoretically the owner of all land, he assigned *gults*, or fiefs, to his ablest warriors. In return for nearly complete authority in their regions, these warrior-nobles conscripted soldiers for the king's army, required agricultural services from the farmers working on their land, and collected taxes in kind.

Ethiopian rulers received imperial coronation at Aksum, but their kingdom had no permanent capital. Rather, the ruler and court were peripatetic. They constantly traveled around the country to crush revolts, to check the warrior-nobles' management of the gults, and to impress ordinary people with royal dignity.

Territorial expansion had important economic and religious consequences. Amda Siyon concluded trade agreements with Muslims by which they were allowed to trade with his country in return for Muslim recognition of his authority and their promise to accept his administration and pay taxes. Economic growth followed. As a result of these agreements, the flow of Ethiopian gold, ivory, and slaves to Red Sea ports for export to the Islamic heartlands and to South Asia accelerated. Profits from commercial exchange improved people's lives, or at least the lives of the upper classes.

most striking feature of Ethiopian society from 500 to 1500 was the close relationship between the church and the state. Christianity inspired fierce devotion and equated doctrinal heresy with political rebellion, thus reinforcing central monarchical power.

The East African City-States

Like Ethiopia, the East African city-states were shaped by their proximity to the trade routes of the Red Sea and Indian Ocean. In the first century C.E. a merchant seaman from Alexandria in Egypt sailed down the Red Sea and out into the Indian Ocean, where he stopped at seaports along the coasts of East Africa, Arabia, and India. He took

Monk-missionaries from traditional Christian areas flooded newly conquered regions, stressing that Ethiopia was a new Zion, or a second Israel—a Judeo-Christian nation defined by religion. Ethiopian Christianity focused on the divinity of the Old Testament Yahweh, rather than on the humanity of the New Testament Jesus. Jewish dietary restrictions, such as the avoidance of pork and shellfish, shaped behavior, and the holy Ark of the Covenant had a prominent place in the liturgy. But the monks also taught New Testament values, especially the importance of charity and spiritual reform. Following the Byzantine pattern, the Ethiopian priest-king claimed the right to summon church councils and to issue doctrinal degrees. Christianity's stress on monogamous marriage, however, proved hard to enforce. As in other parts of Africa (and in Islamic lands, China, and South Asia), polygyny remained common, at least among the upper classes.

Sources: G. W. B. Huntingford, ed., *The Glorious Victories of Amda Seyon* (Oxford: Oxford University Press, 1965), pp. 89–90; H. G. Marcus, *A History of Ethiopia*, updated ed. (Berkeley: University of California Press, 2002); J. Iliffe, *Africans: The History of a Continent*, 2d ed. (New York: Cambridge University Press, 2007).

QUESTIONS FOR ANALYSIS

1. What features mark Ethiopian culture as unique and distinctive among early African societies?
2. Referring to Solomonic Ethiopia, assess the role of legend in history.

▷LaunchPad
ONLINE DOCUMENT PROJECT

What role did religion play in the formation of Ethiopian identity?
Explore early Ethiopian chronicles, and then complete a quiz and writing assignment based on the evidence and details from this chapter.
See inside the front cover to learn more.

careful notes on all he observed, and the result, *Periplus of the Erythraean Sea* (*erythraean* comes from the Greek word meaning "red" that was used to designate the Red Sea as well as the Indian Ocean), is the earliest surviving literary evidence of the city-states of the East African coast. Although primarily preoccupied with geography and navigation, the *Periplus* includes accounts of the local East African peoples and their commercial activities. Since the days of the Roman emperors, the *Periplus* testifies, the East African coast had strong commercial links with India and the Mediterranean.

Greco-Roman ships sailed from Adulis on the Red Sea around the tip of the Gulf of Aden and down the portion of the East African coast that the Greeks called Azania, in modern-day Kenya and Tanzania (see Map 10.1). These ships carried manufactured goods—cotton cloth, copper and brass, iron tools, and gold and silver plate. At the African coastal emporiums, Mediterranean merchants exchanged these goods for cinnamon, myrrh and frankincense, captive slaves, and animal byproducts such as ivory, rhinoceros horns, and tortoise shells. The ships then headed back north and, somewhere around Cape Guardafui on the Horn of Africa, caught the monsoon winds eastward to India, where ivory was in great demand.

In the early centuries of the Common Era many merchants and seamen from the Mediterranean settled in East African coastal towns. Succeeding centuries saw the arrival of more traders. The great emigration from Arabia after the death of Muhammad accelerated Muslim penetration of the area, which the Arabs called the Zanj, "land of the blacks," a land inhabited by Bantu-speaking peoples whom they also called the Zanj. Along the coast, Arabic Muslims established small trading colonies whose local peoples were ruled by kings and practiced various animistic religions. Eventually—whether through Muslim political hegemony or gradual assimilation—the coastal peoples slowly converted to Islam. Indigenous African religions, however, remained strong in the continent's interior.

Migrants from the Arabian peninsula and the Malay Archipelago had a profound influence on the lives of the East African coastal people. Beginning in the late twelfth century fresh waves of Arabs and of Persians from Shiraz poured down the coast, first settling at Mogadishu, then pressing southward to Kilwa. Everywhere they landed, they introduced Islamic culture to the indigenous population. Similarly, from the first to the fifteenth centuries Indonesians crossed the Indian Ocean and settled on the African coast and on the large island of Madagascar, or Malagasy, an Indonesian name. All these immigrants intermarried with Africans, and the resulting society combined Asian, African, and especially Islamic traits. The East African coastal culture was called **Swahili**, after a Bantu language whose vocabulary and poetic forms exhibit a strong Arabic influence. The thirteenth-century Muslim mosque at Mogadishu and the fiercely Muslim populations of Mombasa and Kilwa in the fourteenth century attest to strong Muslim influences.

By the late thirteenth century **Kilwa** had become the most powerful coastal city, exercising political hegemony as far north as Pemba and as far south as Sofala (see Map 10.1). In the fourteenth and fifteenth centuries the coastal cities were great commercial empires, comparable to the Italian city-state of Venice (discussed in Chapter 14). Like Venice, Swahili cities such as Kilwa, Mombasa, and Pemba were situated on offshore islands. The tidal currents that isolated them from the mainland also protected them from landside attack.

Much current knowledge about life in the East African trading societies rests on the account of Ibn Battuta. When he arrived at Kilwa, he found "a large city on the seacoast, most of whose inhabitants are Zinj, jet-black in colour. They have tattoo marks on their faces. . . . The city of Kilwa is one of the finest and most substantially built towns; all the buildings are of wood, and the houses are roofed with al-dis [reeds]."[14] On the mainland were fields and orchards of rice, millet, oranges, mangoes, and bananas and pastures and yards for cattle, sheep, and poultry. Yields were apparently high; Ibn Battuta noted that the rich enjoyed three enormous meals a day and were very fat.

From among the rich mercantile families that controlled the coastal cities arose rulers who governed both the main city and surrounding territory. Such was the case

Great Mosque at Kilwa Built between the thirteenth and fifteenth centuries to serve the Muslim commercial aristocracy of Kilwa on the Indian Ocean, the mosque attests to the wealth and power of the East African city-states. (© Ulrich Doering/Alamy)

with the island city of Kilwa and the nearby mainland. These rulers took various titles, including king, sultan, and sheik.

Approaching the East African coastal cities in the late fifteenth century, Portuguese traders were astounded at their enormous wealth and prosperity. This wealth rested on the ruler's monopolistic control of all trade in the area. Some coastal cities manufactured goods for export: Mogadishu produced cloth for the Egyptian market, Mombasa and Malindi processed iron tools, and Sofala made cottons for the interior trade. The bulk of the cities' exports, however, consisted of animal products—leopard skins, tortoise shell, ambergris, ivory—and gold. The gold originated in the Mutapa region south of the Zambezi River, where the Bantu mined it. As in tenth-century Ghana, gold was a royal monopoly in the fourteenth-century coastal city-states. The Mutapa kings received it as annual tribute, prohibited outsiders from entering the mines or participating in the trade, and controlled shipments down the Zambezi to the coastal markets. Kilwa's prosperity rested on its traffic in gold.

African goods satisfied the global aristocratic demand for luxury goods. In Arabia leopard skins were made into saddles, shells were made into combs, and ambergris was used in the manufacture of perfumes. Because African elephants' tusks were larger and more durable than those of Indian elephants, African ivory was in great demand in India for sword and dagger handles, carved decorative objects, and the ceremonial bangles used in Hindu marriage rituals. Wealthy Chinese also valued African ivory for use in sedan chair construction.

In exchange for these natural products, the Swahili cities brought in, among many other items, incense, glassware, glass beads, and carpets from Arabia; textiles, spices, rice, and cotton from India; and grains, fine porcelain, silk, and jade from China. Swahili kings imposed enormous duties on imports, perhaps more than 80 percent of the value of the goods themselves. Even so, traders who came to Africa made fabulous profits.

Slaves were another export from the East African coast. Reports of East African slave trading began with the publication of the *Periplus*. The trade accelerated with the establishment of Muslim settlements in the eighth century and continued up through the arrival of the Portuguese in the late fifteenth century, which provided a market for African slaves in the New World (discussed in Chapter 15). In fact, the global slave market fueled the East African coastal slave trade until at least the beginning of the twentieth century.

Copper Coin from Mogadishu, Twelfth Century Islamic proscriptions against representation of the human form prevented the use of rulers' portraits on coinage, unlike the practice of the Romans, Byzantines, and Sassanids. Instead Islamic coins since the Umayyad period were decorated exclusively with writing. Sultan Haran Ibn Suleiman of Kilwa on the East African coast minted this coin, a symbol of the region's Muslim culture and of its rich maritime trade. (© The Trustees of the British Museum/Art Resource, NY)

As in West Africa, traders obtained slaves primarily through raids and kidnapping. As early as the tenth century Arabs from Oman enticed hungry children with dates. When the children accepted the sweet fruits, they were abducted and enslaved.

The Arabs called the northern Somalia coast *Ras Assir* (Cape of Slaves). From there, Arab traders transported slaves northward up the Red Sea to the markets of Arabia and Persia. Muslim dealers also shipped blacks from the Zanzibar region across the Indian Ocean to markets in India. Rulers of the Deccan Plateau in central India used large numbers of black slave soldiers in their military campaigns. Slaves also worked on the docks and dhows (typical Arab lateen-rigged ships) in the Muslim-controlled Indian Ocean and as domestic servants and concubines throughout South and East Asia.

As early as the tenth century sources mention persons with "lacquer-black bodies" in the possession of wealthy families in Song China.[15] In 1178 a Chinese official noted in a memorial to the emperor that Arab traders were shipping thousands of blacks from East Africa to the Chinese port of Guangzhou (Canton) by way of the Malay Archipelago. The Chinese employed these slaves as household servants, as musicians, and, because East Africans were often expert swimmers, as divers to caulk leaky ship seams below the waterline.

By the thirteenth century Africans living in many parts of South and East Asia had made significant economic and cultural contributions to their societies. It appears, however, that in Indian, Chinese, and East African markets, slaves were never as valuable a commodity as ivory. Thus the volume of the Eastern slave trade did not approach that of the trans-Saharan slave trade.[16]

Southern Africa and Great Zimbabwe

Southern Africa, bordered on the northwest by the Kalahari Desert and on the northeast by the Zambezi River (see Map 10.1), enjoys a mild and temperate climate. Desert conditions prevail along the Atlantic coast, which gets less than five inches of annual rainfall. Eastward toward the Indian Ocean rainfall increases, amounting to fifty to ninety inches a year in some places. Temperate grasslands characterize the interior highlands. Considerable variations in climate occur throughout much of southern Africa from year to year.

Southern Africa has enormous mineral resources: gold, copper, diamonds, platinum, and uranium. Preindustrial peoples mined some of these deposits in open excavations down several feet, but fuller exploitation required modern technology. (Today, gold-mining operations can penetrate two miles below the surface.)

Located at the southern extremity of the Afroeurasian landmass, southern Africa has a history that is very different from those of West Africa, the Nile Valley, and the East African coast. Unlike the rest of coastal Africa, southern Africa remained far removed from the outside world until the Portuguese arrived in the late fifteenth century—with one important exception. Bantu-speaking people reached southern Africa in the eighth century. They brought skills in ironworking and mixed farming (settled crop production plus cattle and sheep raising) and immunity to the kinds of diseases that later decimated the Amerindians of South America (discussed in Chapter 16).

The earliest residents of southern Africa were hunters and gatherers. In the first millennium C.E. new farming techniques from the north arrived. Lack of water and timber (both needed to produce the charcoal used in iron smelting) slowed the spread of iron technology and tools and thus of crop production in southwestern Africa. These advances reached the western coastal region by 1500. By that date, Khoisan-speakers were tending livestock in the arid western regions. The area teemed with wild game—elephants, buffalo, lions, hippopotamuses, leopards, zebras, and many varieties of antelope. To the east, descendants of Bantu-speaking immigrants grew sorghum, raised cattle and sheep, and fought with iron-headed spears. However, disease-bearing insects such as the tsetse fly, which causes sleeping sickness, attacked the cattle and sheep and retarded their domestication.

The nuclear family was the basic social unit among early southern African peoples, who practiced polygyny and traced descent in the male line. Several families formed bands numbering between twenty and eighty people. Such bands were not closed entities; people in neighboring territories identified with bands speaking the same language. As in most preindustrial societies, a division of labor existed whereby men hunted and women cared for children and raised edible plants. People lived in caves or in camps made of portable material, and they moved from one watering or hunting region to another as seasonal or environmental needs required.

In 1871 a German explorer came upon the ruined city of **Great Zimbabwe** southeast of what is now Masvingo in Zimbabwe. Archaeologists consider Great Zimbabwe the most impressive monument in Africa south of the Nile Valley and the Ethiopian highlands. The ruins consist of two vast complexes of dry-stone buildings, a fortress, and an elliptically shaped enclosure commonly called the Temple. Stone carvings, gold and copper ornaments, and Asian ceramics once decorated the buildings. The ruins extend over sixty acres and are encircled by a massive wall. The entire city was built from local granite between the eleventh and fifteenth centuries without any outside influence.

These ruins tell a remarkable story. Great Zimbabwe was the political and religious capital of a vast empire. During the first millennium C.E. settled crop cultivation, cattle raising, and work in metal led to a steady buildup in population in the Zambezi-Limpopo region. The area also contained a rich gold-bearing belt. Gold ore lay near the surface; alluvial gold lay in the Zambezi River tributaries. In the tenth century the inhabitants collected the alluvial gold by panning and washing; after the year 1000 the gold was worked in open mines with iron picks. Traders shipped the gold eastward to Sofala (see Map 10.1). Great Zimbabwe's wealth and power rested on this gold trade.

Great Zimbabwe declined in the fifteenth century, perhaps because the area had become agriculturally exhausted and could no longer support the large population.

Some people migrated northward and settled in the Mazoe River Valley, a tributary of the Zambezi. This region also contained gold, and the settlers built a new empire in the tradition of Great Zimbabwe. This empire's rulers were called Mwene Mutapa, and their power was also based on the gold trade down the Zambezi River to Indian Ocean ports. It was this gold that the Portuguese sought when they arrived on the East African coast in the late fifteenth century.

Chapter Summary

Africa is a huge continent with many different climatic zones and diverse geography. The African peoples are as varied as the topography. North African peoples were closely connected with the Middle Eastern and European civilizations of the Mediterranean basin. New crops introduced from Asia and the adoption of agriculture profoundly affected early societies across western and northeastern Africa as they transitioned from hunting and gathering in small bands to settled farming communities. Beginning in modern Cameroon and Nigeria, Bantu-speakers spread across central and southern Africa over a two-thousand-year period. Possessing iron tools and weapons, domesticated livestock, and a knowledge of agriculture, these Bantu-speakers assimilated, killed, or drove away the region's previous inhabitants.

Africans in the West African Sahel participated in the trans-Saharan trade, which affected West African society in three important ways: it stimulated gold mining; it increased the demand for West Africa's second-most important commodity, slaves; and it stimulated the development of large urban centers in West Africa.

Similarly, the Swahili peoples along the East African coast organized in city-states, such as Kilwa and Mogadishu, and traded with Arabia, the Persian Gulf, India, China, and the Malay Archipelago. They depended on Indian Ocean commercial networks, which they used to trade African products for luxury items from Arabia, Southeast Asia, and East Asia. Great Zimbabwe, in southern Africa's interior, traded gold to the coast for the Indian Ocean trade.

The Swahili city-states and the western Sudan kingdoms were both part of the Islamic world. Arabian merchants brought Islam with them as they settled along the East African coast, and Berber traders brought Islam to West Africa. Differing from its neighbors, Ethiopia formed a unique enclave of Christianity in the midst of Islamic societies. The Bantu-speaking peoples of Great Zimbabwe, and central and southern Africa generally, were neither Islamic nor Christian.

Notes

1. T. Spear, "Bantu Migrations," in *Problems in African History: The Precolonial Centuries*, ed. R. O. Collins et al. (New York: Markus Weiner Publishing, 1994), p. 98.
2. J. S. Trimingham, *Islam in West Africa* (Oxford: Oxford University Press, 1959), pp. 6–9.
3. R. A. Austen, "The Trans-Saharan Slave Trade: A Tentative Census," in *The Uncommon Market: Essays in the Economic History of the Atlantic Slave Trade*, ed. H. A. Gemery and J. S. Hogendorn (New York: Academic Press, 1979), pp. 1–71, esp. p. 66.
4. Quoted in J. O. Hunwick, "Islam in West Africa, A.D. 1000–1800," in *A Thousand Years of West African History*, ed. J. F. Ade Ajayi and I. Espie (New York: Humanities Press, 1972), pp. 244–245.
5. Quoted in A. A. Boahen, "Kingdoms of West Africa, c. A.D. 500–1600," in *The Horizon History of Africa* (New York: American Heritage, 1971), p. 183.
6. Al-Bakri, *Kitab al-mughrib fdhikr bilad Ifriqiya wa'l-Maghrib (Description de l'Afrique Septentrionale)*, trans. De Shane (Paris: Adrien-Maisonneuve, 1965), pp. 328–329.

7. Quoted in R. Oliver and C. Oliver, eds., *Africa in the Days of Exploration* (Englewood Cliffs, N.J.: Prentice-Hall, 1965), p. 10.

8. Quoted in Boahen, "Kingdoms of West Africa," p. 184.

9. This quotation and the next appear in E. J. Murphy, *History of African Civilization* (New York: Delta, 1972), pp. 109, 111.

10. Pekka Masonen and Humphrey J. Fisher, "Not Quite Venus from the Waves: The Almoravid Conquest of Ghana in the Modern Historiography of Western Africa," *History in Africa* 23 (1996): 197–232.

11. Quoted in Murphy, *History of African Civilization*, p. 120.

12. Quoted in Oliver and Oliver, *Africa in the Days of Exploration*, p. 18.

13. See H. G. Marcus, *A History of Ethiopia*, updated ed. (Berkeley: University of California Press, 2002), pp. 17–20.

14. Ibn Battuta, *The Travels of Ibn Battuta, A.D. 1325–1354*, vol. 1, ed. H. A. R. Gibb (London: University Press, 1972), pp. 379–380.

15. Austen, "The Trans-Saharan Slave Trade," p. 65; J. H. Harris, *The African Presence in Asia* (Evanston, Ill.: Northwestern University Press, 1971), pp. 3–6, 27–30; P. Wheatley, "Analecta Sino-Africana Recensa," in Neville Chittick and Robert Rotberg, *East Africa and the Orient* (New York: Africana Publishing, 1975), p. 109.

16. I. Hrbek, ed., *General History of Africa*. Vol. 3: *Africa from the Seventh to the Eleventh Century* (Berkeley: University of California Press; New York: UNESCO, 1991), pp. 294–295, 346–347.

CONNECTIONS

Because our ancestors first evolved in Africa, Africa's archaeological record is rich with material artifacts, such as weapons, tools, ornaments, and eating utensils. But its written record is much less complete, and thus the nonmaterial dimensions of human society—human interaction in all its facets—is much more difficult to reconstruct. The only exception is in Egypt, where hieroglyphic writings give us a more complete picture of Egyptian society than of nearly any other ancient culture.

Not until the Phoenicians, Greeks, and Romans were there written accounts of the peoples of North and East Africa. These accounts document Africa's early connections and contributions to the vast trans-Saharan and Indian Ocean trading networks that stretched from Europe to China. This trade brought wealth to the kingdoms, empires, and city-states that developed alongside the routes. But the trade in ideas more profoundly connected the growing African states to the wider world, most notably through Islam, which had arrived by the seventh century, and Christianity, which developed a foothold in Ethiopia.

Prior to the late fifteenth century Europeans had little knowledge about African societies. All this would change during the European Age of Discovery. Chapter 16 traces the expansion of Portugal from a small, poor European nation to an overseas empire, as it established trading posts and gained control of the African gold trade. Portuguese expansion led to competition, spurring Spain and then England to strike out for gold of their own in the Americas. The acceleration of this conquest would forever shape the history of Africa and the Americas (discussed in Chapters 11 and 15) and intertwine them via the African slave trade that fueled the labor needs of the colonies in the Americas.

Chapter Review

MAKE IT STICK

✓ **LearningCurve**
Go online and use LearningCurve to retain what you've read.

IDENTIFY KEY TERMS

Identify and explain the significance of each item below.

Bantu (p. 269)

Sudan (p. 271)

Berbers (p. 274)

Mogadishu (p. 276)

stateless societies (p. 277)

Ghana (p. 277)

Koumbi Saleh (p. 278)

Timbuktu (p. 282)

Aksum (p. 283)

Swahili (p. 288)

Kilwa (p. 288)

Great Zimbabwe (p. 291)

REVIEW THE MAIN IDEAS

Answer the focus questions from each section of the chapter.

1. How did Africa's geography shape its history and contribute to its diverse population? (p. 267)

2. How did agriculture affect life among the early societies in the western Sudan and among the Bantu-speaking societies of central and southern Africa? (p. 268)

3. What characterized trans-Saharan trade, and how did it affect West African society? (p. 272)

4. How were the East African city-states, Aksum, and Great Zimbabwe different from and similar to the kingdoms of the western Sudan? (p. 277)

MAKE CONNECTIONS

Analyze the larger developments and continuities within and across chapters.

1. How did the geography and size of Africa affect African societies and their contact with the rest of the world?

2. What different cultures influenced the African people living along the continent's eastern coast?

3. How did Islam influence the different societies of West and East Africa?

LaunchPad

ONLINE DOCUMENT PROJECT

Creating an Ethiopian National Identity
What role did religion play in the formation of Ethiopian identity?

Explore early Ethiopian chronicles, and then complete a quiz and writing assignment based on the evidence and details from this chapter.

See inside the front cover to learn more.

CHRONOLOGY

ca. 1000 B.C.E.–1500 C.E.	• Bantu-speakers expand across central and southern Africa
ca. 600 C.E.	• Christian missionaries convert Nubian rulers
639–642 C.E.	• Islam introduced to Africa
642 C.E.	• Muslim conquest of Egypt
650–1500 C.E.	• Slave trade from sub-Saharan Africa to the Mediterranean
700–900 C.E.	• Berbers develop caravan routes
ca. 900–1100 C.E.	• Kingdom of Ghana; bananas and plantains arrive in Africa from Asia
ca. 1100–1400 C.E.	• Great Zimbabwe is built, flourishes
ca. 1200–1450 C.E.	• Kingdom of Mali
ca. 1312–1337 C.E.	• Reign of Mansa Musa in Mali
1314–1344 C.E.	• Reign of Amda Siyon in Ethiopia
1324–1325 C.E.	• Mansa Musa's pilgrimage to Mecca

11

LearningCurve
After reading the chapter, go online
and use LearningCurve to retain what
you've read.

The Americas

2500 B.C.E.–1500 C.E.

WHEN PEOPLES OF THE AMERICAS FIRST CAME INTO SUSTAINED
contact with peoples from Europe, Africa, and Asia at the turn of the sixteenth century, their encounters were uneven. Thousands of years of isolation
from other world societies made peoples of the Americas vulnerable to diseases found elsewhere in the world. When indigenous peoples were first
exposed to these diseases through contact with Europeans, the devastating
effects of epidemics facilitated European domination and colonization. But
this exchange also brought into global circulation the results of thousands of
years of work by peoples of the Americas in plant domestication that
changed diets worldwide, making corn, potatoes, and peppers into the daily
staples of many societies.

The ancient domestication of these crops intensified agriculture across the
Americas that sustained increasingly complex societies. At times these societies grew into vast empires built on trade, conquest, and tribute. Social stratification and specialization produced lands not just of kings but of priests,
merchants, artisans, scientists, and engineers who achieved extraordinary
feats.

In Mesoamerica—the region stretching from present-day Nicaragua to California—the dense urban centers of Maya, Teotihuacan, Toltec, and Mexica
city-states and empires featured great monuments, temples, and complex
urban planning. Roadways and canals extended trade networks that reached
from South America to the Great Lakes region of North America. Sophisticated
calendars guided systems of religious, scientific, medical, and agricultural
knowledge.

296

These achievements were rivaled only in the Andes, the mountain range that extends from southernmost present-day Chile north to Colombia and Venezuela. Andean peoples adapted to the mountain range's stark vertical stratification of climate and ecosystems to produce agricultural abundance similar to that of Mesoamerica. The technological, agricultural, and engineering innovations of ancient Andean civilizations allowed people to make their difficult mountain terrain a home rather than a boundary.

Societies of the Americas in a Global Context

How did ancient peoples of the Americas adapt to, and adapt, their environment?

Ancient societies of the Americas shared many characteristics that were common to other premodern societies around the world that stretched from the Pacific Rim to the Mediterranean. But many elements were also unique to the ancient peoples of the Americas, and we must consider these on their own terms. Since societies of the Americas developed in isolation, their history offers a counterpoint to premodern histories of other parts of the world. Like people everywhere, civilizations of the Americas interpreted the meaning of the world and their place in the cosmos. They organized societies stratified not just by gender, class, and ethnicity but also by professional roles and wealth, and they adapted to and reshaped their physical and natural world. But they did all this on their own, without outside influences and within a distinct environment.

If the differences between civilizations in the Americas and other world regions are remarkable, the similarities are even more so. By studying the peoples of the Americas before their encounters with other world societies, we gain a clearer view of universal aspects of the human experience.

Trade and Technology

The domestication of crops and animals created an abundance of food and livestock, which allowed people to take on new social roles and to develop specialized occupations. As cities emerged, they became hubs of a universal human activity: trade. These cities were home to priests who interpreted the nature of our world, as well as a nobility from which kings emerged, some of whom forged vast empires based on their ability to coordinate conquest, trade, tribute from conquered subjects, and systems of religious beliefs.

The differences in the development and application of three different kinds of technologies — the wheel, writing and communications systems, and calendars — capture this essential nature of human adaptability.

Before their encounters with other world peoples that began in 1492, societies in Mesoamerica and the Andes did not use wheeled transportation. Had they failed to invent one of the basic technologies used elsewhere in the world? No: wheels were used in children's toys, just not for transportation. Tools emerged (or did not emerge) from specific needs. In Mesoamerica there were no large animals like horses or oxen to domesticate as beasts of burden, so there was no way to power wagons or chariots.

In the Andes, domesticated llamas and alpacas served as pack animals and were a source of wool and meat. But in the most densely settled, cultivated, and developed areas, the terrain was too difficult for wheeled transportation. Instead Andean peoples developed extensive networks of roads that navigated steep changes in altitude, supported by elaborate suspension bridges made from woven vegetable fibers.

Peoples of the Americas also did not develop an alphabet or character-based writing systems, but this did not mean they did not communicate or record information. If we separate our understanding of the alphabetical reading you are doing right now from its functions—communicating and storing of information—we can appreciate the ways in which Andean and Mesoamerican civilizations accomplished both. Peoples of the Americas spoke thousands of languages (hundreds are still spoken today). Mesoamericans, beginning with the Olmecs (1500–400 B.C.E.), used pictographic glyphs similar to those of ancient Egyptian writing to record and communicate information. Later civilizations continued to adapt these systems. The Aztecs produced hieroglyphic books written on paper and deerskin.

The Andean innovation for recording information was particularly remarkable. The khipu (KEY-pooh) was an assemblage of colored and knotted strings. The differences in color, arrangement, and type of knot, as well as the knots' order and placement, served as a binary system akin to a contemporary computer database. As archaeologists and linguists struggle to decode khipus, they have discerned their role in recording demographic, economic, and political information that allowed imperial rulers and local leaders to understand and manage complex data.

Mesoamerican peoples used a sophisticated combination of calendars. These were based on a Calendar Round that combined a 365-day solar calendar with a 260-day calendar based on the numbers thirteen and twenty, which were sacred to peoples of Mesoamerica. Annual cycles were completed when twenty 13-day bundles converged with thirteen 20-day bundles. Together with the solar calendar, these formed a fifty-two-year cycle whose precision was unsurpassed in the premodern world. It also provided an incredibly intricate mechanism not only for following the solar and lunar years but also for connecting these to aspects of daily life and religion, helping users of the calendar to interpret their world.

Settlement and Environment

Ancient settlers in the Americas adapted to and adapted diverse environments ranging from the high plateau of the Andes and central plateau of Mesoamerica to the tropical rain forest and river systems of the Amazon and Caribbean, as well as the prairies of North and South America. But, given the isolation of these societies, where did the first peoples to settle the continent come from?

The first settlers migrated from Asia, though their timing and their route are debated. One possibility is that the first settlers migrated across the Bering Strait from what is now Russia to Alaska and gradually migrated southward sometime between 15,000 and 13,000 B.C.E. But archaeological excavations have identified much earlier settlements along the Andes in South America, perhaps dating to over 40,000 years ago, than they have for Mesoamerica or North America. These findings suggest that the original settlers in the Americas arrived instead (or also) as fishermen circulating the Pacific Ocean.

Like early settlers elsewhere in the world, populations of the Americas could be divided into three categories: nomadic peoples, semi-sedentary farming communities, and dense agricultural communities capable of sustaining cities. Urban settlement and empire formation centered around two major regions. The first area, Lake Titicaca, located at the present-day border between Peru and Bolivia, is the highest lake in the world (12,500 feet high) and the largest lake in South America (3,200 square miles). The second area was in the Valley of Mexico on the central plateau of Mesoamerica, where empires emerged from the cities around Lake Texcoco. Access to these large freshwater lakes allowed settlers to expand agriculture through irrigation, which in turn supported growing urban populations.

The earliest farming settlements emerged around 5000 B.C.E. These farming communities began the long process of domesticating and modifying plants, including maize (corn) and potatoes. Farmers also domesticated other crops native to the Americas such as peppers, beans, squash, and avocados.

The origins of maize in Mesoamerica are unclear, though it became a centerpiece of the Mesoamerican diet and spread across North and South America. Unlike other grains such as wheat and rice, the kernels of maize—which are the seeds as well as the part that is eaten for food—are wrapped in a husk, so the plant cannot propagate itself easily, meaning that farmers had to intervene to cultivate the crop. In addition, no direct ancestor of maize has been found. Biologists believe that Mesoamerican farmers identified a mutant form of a related grass called teosinte and gradually adapted it through selection and hybridization. Eaten together with beans, maize provided Mesoamerican peoples with a diet sufficient in protein despite the scarcity of meat. Mesoamericans processed kernels through **nixtamalization**, boiling the maize in a solution of water and mineral lime. The process broke down compounds in the kernels, increasing their nutritional value, while enriching the resulting *masa*, or paste, with dietary minerals including calcium, potassium, and iron.

The masa could then be cooked with beans, meat, or other ingredients to make tamales. It could also be rolled flat on a stone called a *metate* and baked into tortillas. Tortillas played roles similar to bread in wheat-producing cultures: they could be stored,

Making Tortillas
A mother teaches her daughter to roll tortillas on a metate. The dough at the right of the metate was masa made with maize and lime. The preparation process, known as nixtamalization, enriched the maize paste by adding calcium, potassium, and iron. (Page from the *Codex Mendoza*, Mexico, c. 1541–42 [pen and ink on paper], Bodleian Library, Oxford, UK/The Bridgeman Art Library)

they were light and easy to transport, and they were used as the basic building block of meals. Aztec armies of the fifteenth century could travel long distances because they carried tortillas for sustenance. Along their route, communities were obligated to provide tribute in tortillas. The rapid military expansion of the Aztec Empire was sustained in part by the versatility of the tortilla, which gave soldiers the ability to fight far from home.

Andean peoples cultivated another staple of the Americas, the potato. Potatoes first grew wild, but selective breeding produced many different varieties. For Andean peoples, potatoes became an integral part of a complex system of cultivation at varying altitudes. Communities created a system of "vertical archipelagos" through which they took advantage of the changes of climate along the steep escarpments of the Andes. Different crops could be cultivated at different altitudes, allowing communities to engage in intense and varied farming in what would otherwise have been inhospitable territory.

The settlement of communities, including what would become the largest cities, often took place at an altitude of nearly two miles (about 10,000 feet), in a temperate region at the boundary between ecological zones for growing maize and potatoes. The notable exception was the Lake Titicaca basin, at an elevation of 12,500 feet, where the abundance of fresh water tempered the climate and made irrigation possible. Communities raised multiple crops and engaged in year-round farming by working at different altitudes located within a day's journey from home. Some of these zones of cultivation were so distant—sometimes over a week's journey—that they were tended by temporary or permanent colonies, called *mitmaq*, of the main settlement.

At higher elevations, members of these communities cultivated potatoes. Arid conditions across much of the altiplano, or high-plains plateau, meant that crops of potatoes could sometimes be planted only every few years. But the climate—dry with daily extremes of heat and cold—could be used to freeze-dry potatoes that could be stored indefinitely. Above the potato-growing zone, shepherds tended animals such as llamas and alpacas, which provided wool and dried meat, or *ch'arki* (the origin of the word *jerky*). They also served as pack animals that helped farmers bring in the crops from their high- and low-altitude plots. The animals' manure served as fertilizer for farming at lower altitudes.

At middle altitudes, communities used terraces edged by stone walls to extend cultivation along steep mountainsides to grow corn. In the lowlands, they cultivated the high-protein grain quinoa, as well as beans, peppers, and coca. Farmers chewed coca (the dried leaves of a plant native to the Andes from which cocaine is derived) to alleviate the symptoms of strenuous labor at extremely high altitudes. Coca also added nutrients such as calcium to the Andean diet and played an important role in religious rituals. In the lowlands communities also grew cotton, and in coastal areas they harvested fish and mussels. Fishermen built inflatable rafts made of sealskin.

Ancient Societies

What patterns established by early societies shaped civilization in Mesoamerica and the Andes?

Between 1500 and 1200 B.C.E. emerging civilizations in Mesoamerica and the Andes established lasting patterns of production, culture, and social organization that would long influence societies of the Americas. In Mesoamerica, Olmec civilization brought together practices of farming and trade, as well as religious and technological innovations that served future empires. The imprint of Olmec civilization spread across long networks of trade that would one day extend from Central America to the Mississippi Valley and the Great Lakes of North America. In the Andes, Chavín and Moche civilizations formed the early part of a long cycle of centralization and decentralization. This political and economic centralization helped spread technology, culture, and religion.

Olmec Agriculture, Technology, and Religion

The Olmecs were an early civilization that shaped the religion, trade practices, and technology of later civilizations in Mesoamerica. They flourished in the coastal lowlands of Mexico along a region stretching from Veracruz to the Yucatán from 1500 to 300 B.C.E. The Olmecs formed the first cities of Mesoamerica, and these cities served as centers of agriculture, trade, and religion. Through long-distance trade, the Olmecs spread their culture and technology across Mesoamerica, establishing beliefs and practices that became common to the civilizations that followed.

The Olmecs settled and farmed along rivers in coastal lowlands, where they cultivated maize, squash, beans, and other plants and supplemented their diet with wild game and fish. But they lacked many other resources. In particular, they carried stone for many miles for the construction of temples and for carving massive monuments, many in the shape of heads. Across far-flung networks the Olmecs traded rubber, cacao (from which chocolate is made), pottery, clay figures, and jaguar pelts, as well as the services of artisans such as painters and sculptors, in exchange for obsidian, a volcanic glass that could be carved to a razor-sharp edge and used for making knives, tools, spear tips, and other weapons.

These ties between the Olmecs and other communities spread religious practices, creating a shared framework of beliefs among later civilizations. These practices included the construction of large pyramid temples, as well as acts that ranged from blood sacrifice, in which nobles ritually cut and bled themselves but did not die, to human sacrifice, in which the subject died. In addition to the manner of worship, archaeologists can trace the nature of the deities common in Mesoamerica. Olmec deities, like those of their successors, were combinations of gods and humans, included merged animal and human forms, and had both male and female identities. People practicing later religions based their gods on the fusion of human and spirit traits along the lines of the Olmec were-jaguar: a half-man, half-jaguar figure.

The Olmecs also used a Long Count solar calendar—a calendar based on a 365-day year. This calendar begins with the year 3114 B.C.E., though its origins and the significance of this date are unclear. Archaeologists presume that the existence of the Long Count calendar meant that the Calendar Round combining the 260-day and 365-day years already existed as well. All the later Mesoamerican civilizations used at least one of these calendars, and most used both of them.

Hohokam, Hopewell, and Mississippian Societies

Mesoamerican trading networks extended into southwestern North America, where by 300 B.C.E. the Hohokam people and other groups were using irrigation canals, dams, and terraces to enhance their farming of arid lands. Like the Olmecs and other

Pan-Andean cultures re-emerged during the Middle Horizon (500–1000 C.E.), centered to the south in Tiwanaku, near Lake Titicaca, and to the north at Wari, near present-day southern Peru. The city-state of Wari's dominion stretched from the altiplano north of Lake Titicaca to the Pacific coast, drawing on Moche cultural influences. Its reach between mountain and coastal regions led to extensive exchanges of goods and beliefs between ecologically different farming zones. The city-state of Tiwanaku extended its influence in the other direction, south of the lake. Both Wari and Tiwanaku practiced ancestor worship, and Tiwanaku religion centered on the figure of Viracocha, the god creator and father of humanity, who was identified with the sun and storms.

Storms and climate shifts were central to Andean people's worldview because changes in climate, particularly abrupt changes brought by El Niño, could devastate whole civilizations. El Niño disrupted Moche culture and contributed to the decline of Wari and Tiwanaku. The remains of elaborate projects designed to extend irrigation and reclaim land for farming along Lake Titicaca reveal the social and political impact of drought in already-arid Andean environments. As the Middle Horizon ended, the cities of Tiwanaku and Wari endured on a smaller scale, but between 1000 and 1200 C.E. they lost their regional influence. The eras between the Early, Middle, and Late Horizon, known as Intermediate Periods, were times of decentralization in which local cultures and practices re-emerged. It was out of these local developments that new centralizing empires would over time emerge.

The Incas

What were the sources of strength and prosperity, and of problems, for the Incas?

Inca was the name of a ruling family that settled in the basin of Cuzco and formed the largest and last Andean empire. The empire, whose people we will call the Incas, was called Tawantinsuyu (TAH-want-een-soo-you), meaning "from the four parts, one," expressing the idea of a unified people stretching in all directions.

The Inca Model of Empire

In the Late Intermediate Period (1200–1470), the Pan-Andean influences of Wari and Tiwanaku waned. City-states around Lake Titicaca competed and fought with each other. The strongest ones to emerge again followed the division between the region north of the lake and toward the coast, and south of the lake and across the altiplano. To the north, the Chimu claimed the legacy of the Moche and Wari. To the south, the city of Cuzco became the hub of a growing kingdom under the hereditary control of the Inca (Map 11.1). *Inca* refers to the empire's ruler, while the empire was called Tawantinsuyu. According to their religious beliefs, the Inca rulers invented civilization. In reality, they inherited it from the civilizations of the Titicaca basin and the Chimu on the northern coast.

From the 1420s until 1438 Viracocha Inca emerged as the first Inca leader to attempt permanent conquest. Unlike the *sinchis* (SEEN-cheese), or kings, of earlier and rival city-states, Viracocha Inca fashioned himself an emperor and, in adopting the name Viracocha, connected himself to the god of creation. In 1438 rivals invaded

MAP 11.1 The Inca Empire, 1532 Andean peoples turned their stark mountain landscape to their advantage by settling and farming in vertical archipelagos. Settlements were located at temperate altitudes, while farming and herding took place at higher and lower altitudes.

Viracocha Inca's territories and he fled. His son, Pachacuti, remained in Cuzco and fended off the invaders. He crowned himself emperor and embarked on a campaign of conquest. Pachacuti Inca (r. 1438–1471) conquered the Chimu near the end of his reign, and he incorporated beliefs and practices from this northern civilization.

After conquering the Chimu, Pachacuti instituted practices that quickly expanded the empire across the Andes. He combined Andean ancestor worship with the Chimu system of a split inheritance, a combination that drove swift territorial expansion and transformed Tawantinsuyu into one of the largest empires in the world within less than fifty years. Under the system of ancestor worship, the Incas believed the dead emperor's spirit was still present, and they venerated him through his mummy. Split inheritance meant that the dead emperor retained all the lands he had conquered, commanded the loyalty of all his subjects, and continued to receive tribute. A *panaqa* (pan-AH-kah), a trust formed by his closest relatives, managed both the cult of his mummy and his temporal affairs. Chimu split inheritance became the political structure that determined the Inca emperor's authority.

When the ruler died, his corpse was preserved as a mummy in elaborate clothing and housed in a sacred and magnificent chamber. A sixteenth-century account of the death of Pachacuti Inca in 1471 described the practices for burying and honoring him:

> He was buried by putting his body in the earth in a large new clay urn, with him very well dressed. Pachacuti Inca [had] ordered that a golden image made to resemble him be placed on top of his tomb. And it was to be worshiped in place of him by the people who went there. . . . [He had] ordered those of his own lineage to bring this statue out for the feasts that were held in Cuzco. When they brought it out like

this, they sang about the things that the Inca did in his life, both in the wars and in his city. Thus they served and revered him, changing its garments as he used to do, and serving it as he was served when he was alive.[1]

The panaqa of descendants of each dead ruler managed his lands and used his income to care for his mummy, maintain his cult, and support themselves, all at great expense. When a ruler died, one of his sons was named the new Inca emperor. He received the title, but not the lands and tribute—nor, for that matter, the direct allegiance of the nobility, bound as it was to the deceased ruler. The new emperor built his own power and wealth by conquering new lands.

Inca Imperial Expansion

The combination of ancestor worship and split inheritance provided the logic and impulse for expanding Inca power. The desire for conquest provided incentives for courageous (or ambitious) nobles: those who succeeded in battle and gained new territories for the state could expect to receive lands, additional wives, servants, herds of llamas, gold, silver, fine clothes, and other symbols of high status. Even common soldiers who distinguished themselves in battle could be rewarded with booty and raised to noble status. Under Pachacuti Inca and his successors, Inca domination was extended by warfare to the frontier of present-day Ecuador and Colombia in the north and to the Maule River in present-day Chile in the south, an area of about 350,000 square miles. Eighty provinces, scores of ethnic groups, and 16 million people came under Inca control.

The Incas pursued the integration of regions they conquered by imposing their language and their gods. Magnificent temples scattered throughout the expanding empire housed images of these gods. Priests led prayers and elaborate rituals, and during occasions such as terrible natural disasters or great military victories they sacrificed humans. The Incas forced conquered peoples to adopt **Quechua** (KEH-chuh-wuh), the official language of the empire, which extinguished many regional languages, although another major Andean language, Aymara, endured. Though Quechua did not exist in written form until the Spanish in Peru adopted it as a second official language, it is still spoken by millions in Peru and Bolivia, as well as in regions of Ecuador, Argentina, and Chile.

The pressure for growth strained the Inca Empire. Open lands became scarce, so the Incas tried to penetrate the tropical Amazon forest east of the Andes—an effort that led to repeated military disasters. Traditionally, the Incas waged war with highly trained armies drawn up in massed formation and fought pitched battles on level ground, often engaging in hand-to-hand combat. But in dense jungles the troops could not maneuver or maintain order against enemies, who used guerrilla tactics against them. Another source of stress came from revolts among subject peoples in conquered territories. Even the system of roads and message-carrying runners couldn't keep up with the administrative needs of the empire. The average runner could cover about 175 miles per day—a remarkable feat of physical endurance, especially at a high altitude—but the larger the empire became, the greater the distances to be covered grew. The round trip from the capital at Cuzco to Quito in Ecuador, for example, took from ten to twelve days, so an emperor might have to base urgent decisions on incomplete or out-of-date information. The empire was overextended.

Machu Picchu The Inca ruins of Machu Picchu rise spectacularly above the steep valley of the Urubamba River. The site was built around 1450 as a royal estate and abandoned after the Spanish conquest. (Tony Camacho/Photo Researchers, Inc.)

Imperial Needs and Obligations

At its height, the Inca Empire extended over 2,600 miles. The challenges of sustaining an empire with that reach, not to mention one built so fast, required extraordinary resourcefulness. The Inca Empire met these demands by adapting aspects of local culture to meet imperial needs. For instance, the empire demanded that the ayllus, the local communities with shared ancestors, include imperial tribute in the rotation of labor and the distribution of harvested foods.

As each new Inca emperor conquered new lands and built his domain, he mobilized people and resources by drawing on local systems of labor and organization. Much as ayllus had developed satellite communities called mitmaq, populated by settlers from the ayllu in order to take advantage of remote farming areas, the emperor relocated families or even whole villages over long distances to consolidate territorial control or quell unrest. What had been a community practice became a tool of imperial expansion. The emperor sent mitmaq settlers, known as *mitmaquisuna*, far and wide, creating diverse ethnic enclaves. The emperor also consolidated the empire by regulating marriage, using maternal lines to build kinship among conquered peoples. Inca rulers and nobles married the daughters of elite families among the peoples they conquered. Very high-ranking Inca men sometimes had many wives, but marriage among commoners was generally monogamous.

The reciprocal labor carried out within ayllus expanded into a labor tax called the *mit'a* (MEE-tuh), which rotated among households in an ayllu throughout the year.

Tribute paid in labor provided the means for building the infrastructure of empire. Rotations of laborers carried out impressive engineering feats, allowing the vast empire to extend over the most difficult and inhospitable terrain. An excellent system of roads—averaging three feet in width, some paved and others not—facilitated the transportation of armies and the rapid communication of royal orders by runners. Like Persian and Roman roads, these great feats of Inca engineering linked an empire. The government also made an ayllu responsible for maintaining state-owned granaries, which distributed grain in times of shortage and famine and supplied assistance in natural disasters.

On these roads Inca officials, tax collectors, and accountants traveled throughout the empire, using elaborate khipus to record financial and labor obligations, the output of fields, population levels, land transfers, and other numerical records. Khipus may also have been used to record narrative history, but this is speculation, as knowledge of how to read them died out after the Spanish conquest. Only around 650 khipus are known to survive today, because colonial Spaniards destroyed them, believing khipus might contain religious messages that would encourage people to resist Spanish authority.

The Maya and Teotihuacan

How did the Maya and Teotihuacan develop prosperous and stable societies in the classical era?

In Mesoamerica the classical period (300 C.E. to 900 C.E.) saw major advances in religion, art, architecture, and farming, akin to those of the classical civilizations of the Mediterranean (see Chapters 5 and 6). It saw the rise of many city-states, and although the Maya city-states, which peaked between 600 C.E. and 900 C.E., were the longest lasting, others were significant as well. The city of Teotihuacan in the Valley of Mexico emerged as a major center of trade (300–650 C.E.). It was followed by the postclassical Toltec Empire (900–1200 C.E.), which adapted the cultural, ritual, and aesthetic practices that influenced later empires like the Aztecs.

Maya Agriculture and Trade

The Maya inhabited the highlands of Guatemala and the Yucatán peninsula in present-day Mexico and Belize. Their physical setting shaped two features of Maya society. First, the abundance of high-quality limestone allowed them to build monumental architecture. Second, limestone formations created deep natural wells called *cenotes* (say-NOH-tehs), which became critical sources of water in an often-arid environment. Cenotes were essential to farming and also became important religious and spiritual sites. The staple crop of the Maya was maize, often raised in small remote plots called *milpas* in combination with other foodstuffs, including beans, squash, chili peppers, some root crops, and fruit trees. They farmed on raised narrow rectangular plots that they built above the seasonally flooded low-lying land bordering rivers.

The entire Maya region may have had as many as 14 million inhabitants. Sites like Uxmal, Uaxactún, Copán, Piedras Negras, Tikal, Palenque, and Chichén Itzá (Map 11.2) emerged as independent city-states, each ruled by a hereditary king. These cities produced polychrome pottery and featured altars, engraved pillars, masonry

MAP 11.2 The Maya World, 300–900 C.E. The Maya built dozens of cities linked together in trading networks of roads and rivers. Only the largest of them are shown here.

temples, palaces for nobles, pyramids where nobles were buried, and courts for ball games. The largest site, Tikal, may have had forty thousand people and served as a religious and ceremonial center. A hereditary nobility owned land, waged war, traded, exercised political power, and directed religious rituals. Artisans and scribes made up the social level below. Other residents were farmers, laborers, and slaves, the latter including prisoners of war.

At Maya markets, jade, obsidian, beads of red spiny oyster shell, lengths of cloth, and cacao beans — all in high demand in the Mesoamerican world — served as media of exchange. The extensive trade among Maya communities, plus a common language, promoted unity among the peoples of the region. Merchants traded beyond Maya regions, particularly with the Zapotecs of Monte Albán, in the Valley of Oaxaca, and with the Teotihuacanos of the central valley of Mexico. Since this long-distance trade played an important part in international relations, the merchants conducting it were high nobles or even members of the royal family.

Maya Science and Religion

The Maya developed the most complex writing system in the Americas, a script with nearly a thousand glyphs. They recorded important events and observations in books made of bark paper and deerskin, on pottery, on stone pillars called steles, and on temples and other buildings. Archaeologists and anthropologists have demonstrated that the inscriptions are historical documents that record major events in the lives of Maya kings and nobles. As was common for elites everywhere, Maya leaders stressed the ancient ancestry of their families. "In the year 3114 B.C.E. my forefathers were present, during the Creation of the World," reads one stele in the city of Tikal, recording the lineage of the Maya lord Kan Boar.[2]

Learning about Maya religion through written records is difficult. In the sixteenth century Spanish religious authorities viewed Maya books as demonic and ordered them destroyed. Only a handful survived, offering a window into religious rituals and practices, as well as Maya astronomy. From observation of the earth's movements around the sun, the Maya used a calendar of eighteen 20-day months and one 5-day month, for a total of 365 days, along with the 260-day calendar based on 20 weeks of 13 days.

the challenge of reinvigorating the empire through renewed displays of strength. He had little margin for failure. To symbolize the restoration of Tenochtitlan's power, he waged wars of conquest that defied precedence in their scale, culminating in two coronation ceremonies, the second of which incorporated sacrificing over eighty thousand captive warriors.

Blood sacrifice was not new to the Aztecs. For centuries Mesoamerican peoples had honored their gods this way. For instance, the cult honoring Xipe Totec, the god of spring renewal, involved two emblematic sacrifices. Priests wore the skin of a sacrificial victim to symbolize the shedding of leaves and new growth, and they greeted the arrival of spring by binding a human sacrifice to a post and shooting his body full of arrows with slits carved along their shafts. Blood channeled off the arrows and dripped to the ground, symbolizing the spring rains.

The Aztecs elevated the warrior cult as the central observance. They were the chosen people, who faced a bleak struggle to stave off the apocalypse. The Mexica believed the earth had been destroyed and re-created four times. The end of creation loomed after their age, the fifth sun. Since this apocalypse might be forestalled through divine intervention, their sacrifice could show that humans were worthy of divine intervention. If ancient deities had given their lives to save the sun, how could mortals refuse to do the same? Their service to the gods culminated on the altar of the temple to Huitzilopochtli, where priests cut into the chests of warriors with their obsidian knives to pull out their beating hearts and raise them in sacrifice to the sun.

Such sacrifice evoked the power of Aztec rulers, but the ceremony observing the end of each fifty-two-year bundle better reflected the Mexica worldview. Had humans sacrificed enough for the gods to intercede and ensure the sun would rise again? In preparation for the end, families broke their earthenware vessels, cleansed their homes, and extinguished all fires. As the new day came, priests made a fire on the chest of a living, powerful captive warrior. Noble warriors lit torches from this new fire and relayed the flame of creation into each hearth in the empire. For the next fifty-two years, all would know the fire in their hearth, like the rising of the sun itself, was the fruit of a sacred warrior sacrifice.

The need for sacrifice, as well as the glorification of the warriors who provided it through battle, was a powerful rationale for the expansion of the Aztec Empire. The role of the Aztecs' sacrifice-based religious system is the subject of scholarly debate: Did the religious system guide imperial expansion? Or did imperial expansion guide the religious system? These views are by no means incompatible: for the Aztecs, the peoples who came under their rule, and the peoples who resisted them, the twin goals of empire building and service to the gods were inseparable.

American Empires and the Encounter

What did the European encounter mean for peoples of the major American empires?

By 1500 the Incas and Aztecs strained under the burdens of managing the largest empires the Americas had seen. Both faced the challenges of consolidating their gains, bearing the costs of empire and of the swelling nobility, and waging war in increasingly distant and difficult conditions.

The Fall of the Aztecs

In 1502 Moctezuma II, the last Mexica to rule before the arrival of the Spaniards, was named tlatoani. His reign presents a paradox. On one hand, we know the most about it because it was narrated in detail both by Spanish chroniclers and by indigenous informants (the defeated Mexica continued to create books narrating their history for decades after the conquest). On the other hand, we interpret this information knowing that between 1519 and 1521 the Aztec Empire fell to the Spanish conquistador Hernán Cortés, and our tendency is to analyze Moctezuma II's reign with the knowledge that six hundred foreigners could topple the most powerful empire ever seen in Mesoamerica. Was the Aztecs' loss the result of an empire in crisis? Was it a technological failure? A political failure? A mismatch between a more advanced and a less advanced civilization?

Moctezuma inherited a strained empire. His predecessors had expanded the empire's reach from the Caribbean coast to the Pacific. At the margins of the empire the Aztecs encountered peoples who were seminomadic or who, like the Maya, abandoned their cities to resist conquest. An empire that had expanded rapidly through conquest found itself with little room to grow.

Aztec leaders had sought targets for conquest that were easy to overpower, were strategic for trade, or that possessed resources or produced goods that made for valuable tribute. This created an empire riddled with independent enclaves that had resisted conquest. The most powerful of these was Tlaxcala, at the edge of the Valley of Mexico. In addition, even those areas nominally under Aztec rule retained local leadership and saw themselves as subjected peoples, not as Aztecs. An Aztec army en route to conquer new lands frequently had to reconquer cities along its path.

Finally, the costs of expanding and sustaining the empire had become onerous. Generations of social mobility through distinction in combat had produced a bloated nobility both exempt from and sustained by tribute. Tenochtitlan became dependent on tributary maize in order to feed itself. Materially, the lack of new peoples to conquer meant the empire had little promise of increased prosperity. Spiritually, the dwindling flow of sacrificial victims meant the Mexica might be losing the great cosmic struggle to keep creation from ending.

Faced with these challenges, Moctezuma II reformed the empire. His predecessors had formalized social stratification and defined both the classes of nobility and the means by which to ascend into them. Moctezuma reduced the privileges (and thus the costs to the empire) of the lesser nobility and narrowed the pathways of social mobility. The austerity he imposed in the imperial capital caused unrest. He also pressed the consolidation of territory by seeking to conquer the autonomous enclaves left by his predecessors. As Moctezuma targeted these enclaves, Aztec ability to resist sapped their resources and strained their morale without producing a corresponding reward for the empire in sacrifice or tribute.

Would Moctezuma have been able to consolidate these reforms and help the empire make the transition from expansion to stable maturity? Or was he a modern version of Tizoc, whose failures led to his assassination and a successor who responded to his predecessor's weakness with a surge of human sacrifice? The Aztec Empire had no real military or political rivals. As a result, the empire was well poised to continue despite its limitations, but it was also vulnerable to disruption upon the arrival of Europeans.

Past and Present Meet in Mexico City   Construction for the Pino Suárez metro station unearthed the Aztec ceremonial altar of Ehecatl, the Aztec god of wind. (David Hiser/National Geographic/SuperStock)

By the time he reached the gates of Tenochtitlan in 1519, Hernán Cortés had forged alliances with foes of the Aztec Empire, particularly Tlaxcala, which had so ably resisted conquest. The Tlaxcalans saw in the foreigners an opportunity that could aid their struggle against the Mexica and formed an alliance with the Spanish. Cortés's band of six hundred Spaniards arrived in Tenochtitlan accompanied by tens of thousands of Tlaxcalan soldiers. In Tlaxcala the defeat of Tenochtitlan would be seen as the Tlaxcalans' victory, not that of the handful of Spaniards.

Mexica accounts from after the Spanish conquest are filled with prophecies that foretold the conquest of Tenochtitlan and the fall of the Aztec Empire. One of the most evocative was the myth of the return of Quetzalcoatl. Surely Moctezuma could not resist a man he believed to be a powerful god descended from the Toltecs. Whatever he made of the strangers, he received them as guests, probably because he sought to understand the nature of this encounter and its significance for his empire. Perhaps Moctezuma hesitated, losing the opportunity to act against them. Perhaps he concluded that he had no chance of defeating them, since at that moment most of the men he could count on in battle were tending to their crops and the capital had been so riddled with division and resentment of his reforms that he was powerless to act.

Either way, Cortés and his men managed the encounter skillfully and succeeded in taking Moctezuma prisoner. When the residents of Tenochtitlan rose up to expel the Spaniards, Moctezuma was killed, either at the hands of the Spaniards or by his own subjects, depending on the account. Though the Spaniards were cast out of the city, they left an unwelcome guest, smallpox. The first epidemic of the disease swept through the city in 1520, killing Moctezuma's successor, Cuitlahuac, within a matter of months. Cuauhtemoc, the last tlatoani of the Mexica, was named that same year.

The Aztec Empire and the Mexica people were not defeated by technology, cultural superiority, or a belief that the Europeans were gods. Instead the Mexica suffered a political defeat: they fell because of ruptures in their leadership due to the death of Moctezuma and his successor, as well as the willingness of allies and enemies alike to join with the Spaniards against them when they perceived an opportunity.

Through the lens of history, the destruction of the Aztec Empire seems sudden and swift, but Tenochtitlan resisted for two years, surrendering only in 1521. During this time the Spaniards and Tlaxcalans brokered alliances across the Valley of Mexico and beyond, leaving the Mexica virtually alone in their fight. In this sense, the end of the Aztec Empire looked a lot like its beginning: people who had obeyed the Mexica now took advantage of the opportunity to defeat them, just as the Mexica had done with the Tepanec Alliance. Even so, abandoned by their allies, the besieged Mexica fought on through famine and disease, defending their city street by street until they were finally vanquished.

The Fall of the Incas

In 1525 Huayna Capac Inca, the grandson of Pachacuti Inca, became ill while carrying out a military campaign in present-day Ecuador, at the northern frontier of the empire. Campaigns of conquest always take place at frontiers (even if these frontiers are between enclaves within an empire, as was the case for the Aztecs). But in this case, because of split inheritance, Huayna Capac's entire dominion would have to be created by expanding outward beyond the frontiers of his father's empire. His illness was plague, introduced by Europeans waging wars of conquest in Mesoamerica, and it would kill him. But as he waged war, he also received news of the foreigners in the north and anticipated that they would come southward. From his deathbed, he urged his successor to make peace with them.

But peace did not follow Huayna Capac's death. Instead civil war erupted between two of his sons over succession to the throne. Huascar claimed it as the firstborn. His half-brother Atahualpa, Huayna Capac's favorite and an experienced military commander who had accompanied him in his Ecuadorean campaign, claimed it as well. Atahualpa asserted that Huayna Capac's dying wish was that Atahualpa succeed him. The brothers fought for seven years, turning the empire's armies against each other. In 1532 Atahualpa vanquished and imprisoned his brother and consolidated his rule in Cuzco. That same year a group of Spaniards led by Francisco Pizarro landed on the Peruvian coast, pursuing rumors of a city of gold in the mountains.

Atahualpa agreed through emissaries to meet the Spaniards at the city of Cajamarca in northern Peru. In a demonstration of his imperial authority, he entered Cajamarca carried on a golden litter, accompanied by four military squadrons of eight thousand men each. Other members of the nobility followed, carried on their own litters. Their procession was preceded by a multitude of servants who cleared the ground, removing all stones, pebbles, and even bits of straw. Atahualpa met the Spanish intending not to fight a battle, but to understand them and hear them out. The meeting between Atahualpa and Pizarro reflected two deeply different worldviews.

In the scuffle that ensued at the meeting, the Spaniards took Atahualpa prisoner, and they eventually executed him. The Spaniards named a new indigenous leader, Manco Capac, whom they hoped to control. But Manco Capac turned against the Spaniards. He, and later his son Tupac Amaru, led resistance against the Spaniards until 1567. Each time the Inca forces besieged a Spanish-controlled city or town, however, their proximity to the Spaniards exposed them to European diseases. They were more successful in smaller-scale attacks, which delayed and limited Spanish colonization, but did not undo it.

Chapter Summary

The Inca and Aztec Empires that encountered Spanish conquerors were short-lived products of the cycle of centralization and decentralization that had characterized the Andes and Mesoamerica for thousands of years. In this sense, there was nothing new in the toppling of these empires. The empires preceding those of the Incas and Aztecs had been undone when their own people turned against them, when climate changes disrupted them, or when they faced outside competition. What was new in the sixteenth century was that this outside competition came from Europeans.

The civilizations of the Andes and Mesoamerica from which the Incas and Aztecs emerged had remarkable similarities with and differences from other ancient and premodern civilizations in other regions of the world. Without being influenced by developments in Africa, Asia, or Europe, indigenous societies of the Americas developed extensive networks of trade. In Mesoamerica and the Andes, the domestication of crops led to the kind of bountiful production that allowed for diversification of labor among farmers, priests, nobles, merchants, and artisans. In these environments, cycles of centralization occurred in which powerful city-states emerged and embarked on campaigns of conquest, bringing vast regions under their political, religious, and cultural influence.

But civilizations of the Americas developed in unique ways as well. This was particularly true in the Andes, where peoples developed specialized patterns of farming in vertical archipelagos in their inhospitable mountain environment. Similarly, though Andean peoples did not develop writing, they instead developed the khipu into a sophisticated system of recording and communicating information.

Ultimately, the history of the peoples of the Americas was defined by their diverse experiences as they coped with varied climates, ecology, and geography. Chinampa agriculture in the Valley of Mexico and raised-bed farming practiced by the Maya are examples. And peoples' experiences of adapting to their environments, and of transforming those environments to meet their needs, shaped the ways they understood their world. These experiences led them to produce precise calendars, highly detailed readings of the stars, and an elaborate architecture of religious beliefs through which they interpreted their relationships to their world and their place in the cosmos.

Notes

1. *Narrative of the Incas by Juan de Betanzos*, trans. and ed. Roland Hamilton and Dana Buchanan from the Palma de Mallorca manuscript, p. 138.
2. "Maya Writing," Authentic Maya, http://www.authenticmaya.com/maya_writing.htm.
3. Michael Coe, *Mexico from the Olmecs to the Aztecs*, 5th ed. (New York: Thames and Hudson, 2002), p. 107.
4. Ross Hassig, *War and Society in Ancient Mesoamerica* (Berkeley: University of California Press, 1992), p. 56.

5. Ibid., p. 49.

6. Ibid., pp. 81, 85.

7. Bernal Díaz, *The Conquest of New Spain*, trans. J. M. Cohen (New York: Penguin Books, 1978), p. 214.

8. Ross Hassig, *Aztec Warfare* (Norman: University of Oklahoma Press, 1988), p. 143.

9. Miguel León-Portilla, "Mexico to 1519," in *Cambridge History of Latin America*, ed. Leslie Bethell, vol. 1 (Cambridge: Cambridge University Press, 1984), p. 14.

CONNECTIONS

 Though we often think of history unfolding along differences between peoples (Spaniards versus Aztecs, for instance), a more common division is often evident: rural versus urban experiences. The disruption of American societies and cultures after the encounter with Europeans occurred in both rural and urban areas, but there were deep differences in the effects of colonization upon urban and rural peoples of the Americas.

The early sixteenth century marked the end of independent empires of the Americas and the gradual integration of American peoples into global empires seated in Europe. Spaniards were the most motivated and had their greatest success when they encountered dense, organized urban areas. Here they displaced existing overlords as the recipients of tribute in goods and labor. The Spanish were less interested in sparsely settled areas that did not have well-established systems of trade and tribute and were harder to subdue. As a result, European conquest was a surprisingly drawn-out process. Peoples of the Americas resisted conquest until well into the nineteenth century.

The incidental companion of conquest—disease—was also uneven in its effects. Over the course of the sixteenth century, epidemic diseases decimated the population of the Americas, which fell from 50 million to just 5 million. But epidemics of diseases that are spread through human contact, such as measles and smallpox, are primarily urban phenomena: these diseases emerged as ancient cities grew large enough that the diseases could spread quickly among dense populations. As a result, the impact of the diseases brought by Europeans was the most severe and the most destructive in the cities of the Americas.

Since cities faced the brunt of both disease and wars of conquest, the disruptions caused by the encounter were disproportionally felt there. Whole systems of knowledge, sets of artisanal skills, political cultures, and religious thought resided in cities. As epidemics erupted, as besieging armies tore down buildings stone by stone, and as survivors dispersed, many of the most remarkable aspects of American civilizations were lost. Rural peoples and cultures were much more resilient. It was in rural areas that languages, foodways, farming practices, and approaches to healing—indeed whole worldviews—endured and evolved. This process occurred either in isolation from or in dialogue with European cultures, but local practices in rural regions were not obliterated, as they were in major cities. In the end, the European encounter destroyed the urban cultures and systems of knowledge in the Americas.

Chapter Review

MAKE IT STICK

✓ LearningCurve
Go online and use LearningCurve to retain what you've read.

IDENTIFY KEY TERMS

Identify and explain the significance of each item below.

Mesoamerica (p. 296)   Moche (p. 303)   Teotihuacan (p. 308)
khipu (p. 298)   Inca (p. 304)   Nahuatl (p. 312)
nixtamalization (p. 299) Quechua (p. 306)   Mexica (p. 312)
Olmecs (p. 301)   Maya (p. 308)   Tenochtitlan (p. 313)

REVIEW THE MAIN IDEAS

Answer the focus questions from each section of the chapter.

1. How did ancient peoples of the Americas adapt to, and adapt, their environment? (p. 297)
2. What patterns established by early societies shaped civilization in Mesoamerica and the Andes? (p. 300)
3. What were the sources of strength and prosperity, and of problems, for the Incas? (p. 304)
4. How did the Maya and Teotihuacan develop prosperous and stable societies in the classical era? (p. 308)
5. How did the Aztecs build on the achievements of earlier Mesoamerican cultures and develop new traditions to create their large empire? (p. 312)
6. What did the European encounter mean for peoples of the major American empires? (p. 320)

MAKE CONNECTIONS

Analyze the larger developments and continuities within and across chapters.

1. Why didn't societies of the Americas adopt the wheel for transportation, as peoples of other world regions did?
2. How does the connection between religion and imperial expansion among the Aztecs and Incas resemble the role of religion in other societies?
3. Much of what we know of ancient societies of the Americas is based on archaeological data rather than written sources. How does the reliance on archaeological data shape our understanding of history? What does it help us understand? What is hard for us to interpret from it?

LaunchPad
ONLINE DOCUMENT PROJECT

The Making and Remaking of Aztec History
Why did Tlacaelel believe the Aztec Empire needed a new history?

Read documents that examine Aztec history and culture, and then complete a quiz and writing assignment based on the evidence and details from this chapter.

See inside the front cover to learn more.

CHRONOLOGY

ca. 40,000–13,000 B.C.E.	• Initial human migration to the Americas
ca. 5000 B.C.E.	• Intensification of agriculture
ca. 2000 B.C.E.	• Earliest mound building in North America
ca. 1500–300 B.C.E.	• Olmec culture
ca. 1200 B.C.E.	• Emergence of Chavín culture in the Andes
ca. 100–800 C.E.	• Moche culture
ca. 300–650 C.E.	• Peak of Teotihuacan's influence
ca. 600–900 C.E.	• Peak of Maya culture
ca. 1050–1250 C.E.	• Construction of mounds at Cahokia
ca. 1325 C.E.	• Construction of Aztec city of Tenochtitlan begins
ca. 1428–1521 C.E.	• Aztec Empire dominates Mesoamerica
ca. 1438–1532 C.E.	• Inca Empire dominates the Andes

Manichaean Priests   Many religions spread through Central Asia before it became predominantly Muslim after 1300. This fragment of a tenth- to twelfth-century illustrated document, found at the Silk Road city of Turfan, is written in the Uighur language and depicts Manichaean priests. (Archives Charmet/ The Bridgeman Art Library)

The three most wide-ranging and successful confederations were those of the Xiongnu—Huns, as they were known in the West—who emerged in the third century B.C.E. in the area near China; the Turks, who had their origins in the same area in the fourth and fifth centuries C.E.; and the Mongols, who did not become important until the late twelfth century. In all three cases, the entire steppe region was eventually swept up in the movement of peoples and armies.

The Turks

The Turks were the first of the Inner Asian peoples to have left a written record in their own language; the earliest Turkish documents date from the eighth century. Turkic languages may have already been spoken in dispersed areas of the Eurasian steppe when the Turks first appeared; today these languages are spoken by the Uighurs in western China; the Uzbeks, Kazakhs, Kyrghiz (KIHR-guhz), and Turkmens of Central Asia; and the Turks of modern Turkey. The original religion of the Turks was shamanistic and involved worship of Heaven, making it similar to the religions of many other groups in the steppe region.

In 552 a group called Turks who specialized in metalworking rebelled against their overlords, the Rouruan, whose empire dominated the region from the eastern Silk Road cities of Central Asia through Mongolia. The Turks quickly supplanted the Rouruan as overlords of the Silk Road in the east. When the first Turkish khagan (ruler) died a few years later, the Turkish empire was divided between his younger brother, who took the western part (modern Central Asia), and his son, who took the eastern part (modern Mongolia). Sogdians—who were influential merchants along the Silk Road—convinced the Turks to send a delegation to both the Persian (see Chapter 9) and the Byzantine courts (see Chapter 8). Repeated diplomatic overtures in both directions did not prevent hostilities, however, and in 576 the Western Turks captured the Byzantine city of Bosporus in the Crimea.

The Eastern Turks frequently raided China and just as often fought among themselves. The Chinese history of the Sui Dynasty, written in the seventh century, records that "the Turks prefer to destroy each other rather than to live side-by-side. They have a thousand, nay ten thousand clans who are hostile to and kill one another. They mourn their dead with much grief and swear vengeance."[1] In the early seventh century the empire of the Eastern Turks ran up against the growing military might of the Tang Dynasty in China and soon broke apart.

In the eighth century a Turkic people called the Uighurs (Wee-gurs) formed a new empire based in Mongolia that survived about a century. It had close ties to Tang China, providing military aid but also extracting large payments in silk. During this period many Uighurs adopted religions then current along the Silk Road, notably Buddhism, Nestorian Christianity, and Manichaeism. In the ninth century this Uighur empire was destroyed by another Turkic people from north of Mongolia called the Kyrghiz. Some Uighurs fled to what is now western China. Setting up their capital city in Kucha, the Uighurs created a remarkably stable and prosperous kingdom that lasted four centuries (ca. 850–1250). Because of the dry climate of the region, many buildings, wall paintings, and manuscripts written in a variety of languages have been preserved from this era. They reveal a complex urban civilization in which Buddhism, Manichaeism, and Christianity existed side by side, practiced by Turks as well as by Tokharians, Sogdians, and other Iranian peoples.

Farther west in Central Asia other groups of Turks, such as the Karakhanids, Ghaznavids, and Seljuks, rose to prominence. Often local Muslim forces would try to capture them, employ them as slave soldiers, and convert them. By the mid- to late tenth century many were serving in the armies of the Abbasid caliphate. Also in the tenth century Central Asian Turks began converting to Islam (which protected them from being abducted as slaves). Then they took to raiding unconverted Turks.

In the mid-eleventh century Turks had gained the upper hand in the caliphate, and the caliphs became little more than figureheads. From there Turkish power was extended into Syria, Palestine, and Asia Minor. (Asia Minor is now called Turkey because Turks migrated there by the thousands over several centuries.) In 1071 Seljuk Turks inflicted a devastating defeat on the Byzantine army in eastern Anatolia (see page 243). Other Turkish confederations established themselves in Afghanistan and extended their control into north India (see page 346).

In India, Persia, and Anatolia the formidable military skills of nomadic Turkish warriors made it possible for them to become overlords of settled societies. Just as the Uighurs developed a hybrid urban culture along the eastern end of the Silk Road, adopting many elements from the mercantile Sogdians, the Turks of Central and West Asia created an Islamic culture that drew from both Turkish and Iranian sources. Often Persian was used as the administrative language of the states they formed. Nevertheless, despite the presence of Turkish overlords all along the southern fringe of the steppe, no one group of Turks was able to unite them all into a single political unit. That feat had to wait for the next major power on the steppe, the Mongols.

The Mongols

In the twelfth century ambitious Mongols did not aspire to match the Turks or other groups that had migrated west, but rather wanted to be successors to the Khitans and Jurchens, nomadic groups that had stayed in the east and mastered ways to extract resources from China, the largest and richest country in the region. The Khitans and Jurchens had formed hybrid nomadic-urban states, with northern sections where tribesmen continued to live in the traditional way and southern sections politically controlled by the non-Chinese rulers but settled largely by taxpaying Chinese. The Khitans and Jurchens had scripts created to record their languages and adopted many Chinese governing practices. They built cities in pastoral areas that served as trading centers and places to enjoy their newly acquired wealth. In both the Khitan and Jurchen cases, their elite became culturally dual, adept in Chinese ways as well as in their own traditions.

The Mongols lived north of these hybrid nomadic-settled societies and maintained their traditional ways. Chinese, Persian, and European observers have all left descriptions of the daily life of the Mongols, which they found strikingly different from their own. They lived in tents called **yurts** rather than in houses. The yurts, about twelve to fifteen feet in diameter, were constructed of light wooden frames covered by layers of wool felt, greased to make them waterproof. Yurts were round, since this shape held up better against the strong winds that blew across the treeless grasslands. The floor of a yurt was covered first with dried grass or straw, then with felt, skins, or rugs. In the center, directly under the smoke hole, was the hearth. The master's bed was on the north. Goat horns attached to the frame of the yurt were used as hooks to hang joints of meat, cooking utensils, bows, quivers of arrows, and the like. A group of families traveling together would set up their yurts in a circle open to the south and draw up their wagons in a circle around the yurts for protection.

The Mongol diet consisted mostly of animal products. The most common meat was mutton, supplemented with wild game. When grain or vegetables could be obtained through trade, they were added to the diet. Wood was scarce, so dried animal dung or grasses fueled the cook fires.

The Mongols milked sheep, goats, cows, and horses and made cheese and fermented alcoholic drinks from the milk. A European visitor to Mongolia in the 1250s described how they milked mares, a practice unfamiliar to Europeans:

> They fasten a long line to two posts standing firmly in the ground, and to the line they tie the young colts of the mares which they mean to milk. Then come the mothers who stand by their foals, and allow themselves to be milked. And if any of them be too unruly, then one takes her colt and puts it under her, letting it suck a while, and presently taking it away again, and the milker takes its place.[2]

He also described how they made the alcoholic drink koumiss from the milk, a drink that "goes down very pleasantly, intoxicating weak brains."[3]

Because of the intense cold of the winter, the Mongols made much use of furs and skins for clothing. Both men and women usually wore silk trousers and tunics (the silk obtained from China). Over these they wore robes of fur, for the very coldest times in two layers—an inner layer with the hair on the inside and an outer layer with the hair on the outside. Hats were of felt or fur, boots of felt or leather. Men wore leather belts to which their bows and quivers could be attached. Women of high rank wore elaborate headdresses decorated with feathers.

Mongol women had to work very hard and had to be able to care for the animals when the men were away hunting or fighting. They normally drove the carts and set up and dismantled the yurts. They also milked the sheep, goats, and cows and made the butter and cheese. In addition, they made the felt, prepared the skins, and sewed the clothes. Because water was scarce, clothes were not washed with water, nor were dishes. Women, like men, had to be expert riders, and many also learned to shoot. They participated actively in family decisions, especially as wives and mothers. In *The Secret History of the Mongols*, a work written in Mongolian in about 1240, the mother and wife of the Mongol leader Chinggis Khan frequently make impassioned speeches on the importance of family loyalty.

Mongol men kept as busy as the women. They made the carts and wagons and the frames for the yurts. They also made harnesses for the horses and oxen, leather saddles, and the equipment needed for hunting and war, such as bows and arrows. Men also had charge of the horses, and they milked the mares. Young horses were allowed to run wild until it was time to break them in. Catching them took great skill in the use of a long springy pole with a noose at the end. One specialist among the nomads was the blacksmith, who made stirrups, knives, and other metal tools.

Kinship underlay most social relationships among the Mongols. Normally each family occupied a yurt, and groups of families camping together were usually related along the male line (brothers, uncles, nephews, and so on). More distant patrilineal relatives were recognized as members of the same clan and could call on each other for aid. People from the same clan could not marry each other, so men had to get wives from other clans. When a woman's husband died, she would be inherited by another male in the family, such as her husband's brother or his son by another woman. Tribes were groups of clans, often distantly related. Both clans and tribes had chiefs who would make decisions on where to graze and when to retaliate against another tribe that had stolen animals or people. Women were sometimes abducted for brides. When tribes stole men from each other, they normally made them into slaves, and slaves were forced to do much of the heavy work. They would not necessarily remain slaves their entire lives, however, as their original tribes might be able to recapture them or make exchanges for them, or their masters might free them.

Even though population was sparse in the regions where the Mongols lived, conflict over resources was endemic, and each camp had to be on the alert for attacks. Defending against attacks and retaliating against raids was as much a part of the Mongols' daily life as caring for their herds and trading with nearby settlements.

Mongol children learned to ride at a young age, first on goats. The horses they later rode were short and stocky, almost like ponies, but nimble and able to endure long journeys and bitter cold. Even in the winter the horses survived by grazing, foraging beneath the snow. The prime weapon boys had to learn to use was the compound bow, which had a pull of about 160 pounds and a range of more than 200 yards; it was well suited for using on horseback, giving Mongol soldiers an advantage in battle. Other commonly used weapons were small battle-axes and lances fitted with hooks to pull enemies off their saddles.

Hunting was a common form of military training among the Mongols. Each year tribes would organize one big hunt; mounted hunters would form a vast ring perhaps ten or more miles in circumference, then gradually shrink it down, trapping all the animals before killing them. On military campaigns a Mongol soldier had to be able to ride for days without stopping to cook food; he ate from a supply of dried milk curd and cured meat, which could be supplemented by blood let from the neck of his horse. When time permitted, the soldiers would pause to hunt, adding dogs, wolves, foxes, mice, and rats to their food.

As with the Turks and other steppe nomads, religious practices centered around the shaman, a religious expert believed to be able to communicate with the gods. The high god of the Mongols was Heaven/Sky, but they recognized many other gods as well. Some groups of Mongols, especially those closer to settled communities, converted to Buddhism, Nestorian Christianity, or Manichaeism.

Chinggis Khan and the Mongol Empire

How did Chinggis Khan and his successors conquer much of Eurasia, and how did the Mongol conquests change the regions affected?

In the mid-twelfth century the Mongols were just one of many peoples in the eastern grasslands, neither particularly numerous nor especially advanced. Why then did the Mongols suddenly emerge as an overpowering force on the historical stage? One explanation is ecological. A drop in the mean annual temperature created a subsistence crisis. As pastures shrank, the Mongols and other nomads had to look beyond the steppe to get more of their food from the agricultural world. A second reason for their sudden rise was the appearance of a single individual, the brilliant but utterly ruthless Temujin (ca. 1162–1227), later and more commonly called Chinggis Khan (sometimes spelled Genghis or Ghengis).

Chinggis Khan

What we know of Temujin's early career was recorded in *The Secret History of the Mongols*, written within a few decades of his death. In Temujin's youth, his father had built a modest tribal following. When Temujin's father was poisoned by a rival, his followers, not ready to follow a boy of twelve, drifted away, leaving Temujin and his mother and brothers in a vulnerable position. Temujin slowly collected followers. In 1182 Temujin was captured and carried in a cage to a rival's camp. After a daring midnight escape, he led his followers to join a stronger chieftain whom his father had once aided. With the chieftain's help, Temujin began avenging the insults he had received.

Temujin proved to be a natural leader, and as he subdued the Tartars, Kereyids, Naimans, Merkids, and other Mongol and Turkish tribes, he built up an army of loyal followers. He mastered the art of winning allies through displays of personal courage in battle and generosity to his followers. To those who opposed him, he could be merciless. He once asserted that nothing gave more pleasure than massacring one's enemies, seizing their horses and cattle, and ravishing their women. Sometimes Temujin would kill all the men in a defeated tribe to prevent later vendettas. At other times he would take them on as soldiers in his own armies. Courage impressed him. One of his leading generals, Jebe, first attracted his attention when he held his ground against overwhelming opposition and shot Temujin's horse out from under him. Another prominent general, Mukhali, became Temujin's personal slave at age twenty-seven after his tribe was defeated by Temujin in 1197. Within a few years he was leading a corps of a thousand men from his own former tribe.

In 1206, at a great gathering of tribal leaders, Temujin was proclaimed Chinggis Khan, or Great Ruler. Chinggis decreed that Mongol, until then an unwritten language, be written down in the script used by the Uighur Turks. With this script a record was

The Tent of Chinggis Khan   In this fourteenth-century Persian illustration from Rashid al-Din's *History of the World*, two guards stand outside while Chinggis is in his tent. (From a book by Rashid al-Din [1247–1318] [vellum], Persian School [14th century]/Bibliothèque Nationale, Paris, France/ The Bridgeman Art Library)

made of the Mongol laws and customs, ranging from the rules for the annual hunt to punishments of death for robbery and adultery. Another measure adopted at this assembly was a postal relay system to send messages rapidly by mounted courier, suggesting that Chinggis already had ambitions to rule a vast empire.

With the tribes of Mongolia united, the energies previously devoted to infighting and vendettas were redirected to exacting tribute from the settled populations nearby, starting with the Jurchen (Jin) state that extended into north China (see Map 13.1, page 366). Because of his early experiences with intertribal feuding, Chinggis mistrusted traditional tribal loyalties, and as he fashioned a new army, he gave it a new, nontribal decimal structure (based on units of ten). He conscripted soldiers from all the tribes and assigned them to units that were composed of members from different tribes. He selected commanders for each unit whom he could remove at will, although he allowed commanders to pass their posts on to their sons.

After Chinggis subjugated a city, he would send envoys to cities farther out to demand submission and threaten destruction. Those who opened their city gates and submitted without fighting could join the Mongols, but those who resisted faced the prospect of mass slaughter. He despised city dwellers and would sometimes use them as living shields in the next battle. After the Mongol armies swept across north China in 1212–1213, ninety-odd cities lay in rubble. Beijing, captured in 1215, burned for more than a month. Not surprisingly many governors of cities and rulers of small states hastened to offer submission.

Chinggis preferred conquest to administration and did not stay in north China to set up an administrative structure. He left that to subordinates and turned his

◀ **MAP 12.1** **The Mongol Empire** The creation of the vast Mongol Empire facilitated communication across Eurasia and led to both the spread of deadly plagues and the transfer of technical and scientific knowledge. After the death of Chinggis Khan in 1227, the empire was divided into four khanates ruled by different lines of his successors. In the 1270s the Mongols conquered southern China, but most of their subsequent campaigns did not lead to further territorial gains.

attention westward, to Central Asia and Persia, then dominated by different groups of Turks. In 1218 Chinggis proposed to the Khwarizm shah of Persia that he accept Mongol overlordship and establish trade relations. The shah, to show his determination to resist, ordered the envoy and the merchants who had accompanied him killed. The next year Chinggis led an army of one hundred thousand soldiers west to retaliate. Mongol forces destroyed the shah's army and sacked one Persian city after another, demolishing buildings and massacring hundreds of thousands of people.

After returning from Central Asia, Chinggis died in 1227 during the siege of a city in northwest China. Before he died, he instructed his sons not to fall out among themselves but instead to divide the spoils.

Chinggis's Successors

Although Mongol leaders traditionally had had to win their positions, after Chinggis died the empire was divided into four states called khanates, with one of the lines of his descendants taking charge of each (Map 12.1). Chinggis's third son, Ögödei, assumed the title of khan, and he directed the next round of invasions.

In 1237 representatives of all four lines led 150,000 Mongol, Turkish, and Persian troops into Europe. During the next five years, they gained control of Moscow and Kievan Russia and looted cities in Poland and Hungary. They were poised to attack deeper into Europe when they learned of the death of Ögödei in 1241. To participate in the election of a new khan, the army returned to the Mongols' new capital city, Karakorum.

Once Ögödei's son was certified as his successor, the Mongols turned their attention to Persia and the Middle East. In 1256 a Mongol army took northwest Iran, then pushed on to the Abbasid capital of Baghdad. When it fell in 1258, the last Abbasid caliph was murdered, and the population was put to the sword. The Mongol onslaught was successfully resisted, however, by both the Delhi sultanate (see page 346) and the Mamluk rulers in Egypt (see page 244).

Under Chinggis's grandson Khubilai Khan (r. 1260–1294), the Mongols completed their conquest of China. South China had never been captured by non-Chinese, in large part because horses were of no strategic advantage in a land of rivers and canals. Proceeding deliberately, the Mongols first surrounded the Song empire in central and south China (discussed in Chapter 13) by taking its westernmost province in 1252, as well as Korea to its east in 1258; destroying the Nanzhao kingdom in modern Yunnan in 1254; and then continuing south and taking Annam (northern Vietnam) in 1257. A surrendered Song commander advised the Mongols to build a navy to attack the great Song cities located on rivers. During the five-year siege of a central Chinese river port, both sides used thousands of boats and tens of thousands of troops. The Mongols employed experts in naval and siege warfare from all over their empire—Chinese, Korean, Jurchen, Uighur, and Persian. Catapults designed by Muslim engineers launched a barrage of rocks weighing up to a hundred pounds each. During their advance toward the Chinese capital of Hangzhou, the Mongols ordered the total slaughter of the people of the major city of Changzhou, and in 1276 the Chinese empress dowager surrendered in hopes of sparing the people of the capital a similar fate.

Having overrun China and Korea, Khubilai turned his eyes toward Japan. In 1274 a force of 30,000 soldiers and support personnel sailed from Korea to Japan. In 1281 a combined Mongol and Chinese fleet of about 150,000 made a second attempt to conquer Japan. On both occasions the Mongols managed to land but were beaten back by Japanese samurai armies. Each time fierce storms destroyed the Mongol fleets. The Japanese claimed that they had been saved by the *kamikaze*, the "divine wind" (which later lent its name to the thousands of Japanese aviators who crashed their airplanes into American warships during World War II). Twelve years later, in 1293, Khubilai tried sending a fleet to the islands of Southeast Asia, including Java, but it met with no more success than the fleets sent to Japan.

Why were the Mongols so successful against so many different types of enemies? Even though their population was tiny compared to the populations of the large agricultural societies they conquered, their tactics, their weapons, and their organization all gave them advantages. Like other nomads before them, they were superb horsemen and excellent archers. Their horses were extremely nimble, able to change direction quickly, thus allowing the Mongols to maneuver easily and ride through infantry forces armed with swords, lances, and javelins. Usually only other nomadic armies, like the Turks, could stand up well against the Mongols.

The Mongols were also open to trying new military technologies. To attack walled cities, they learned how to use catapults and other engines of war. At first they employed Chinese catapults, but when they learned that those used by the Turks in Afghanistan were more powerful, they adopted the better model. The Mongols also used exploding arrows and gunpowder projectiles developed by the Chinese.

The Mongols made good use of intelligence and tried to exploit internal divisions in the countries they attacked. Thus in north China they appealed to the Khitans, who had been defeated by the Jurchens a century earlier, to join them in attacking the Jurchens. In Syria they exploited the resentment of Christians against their Muslim rulers.

The Mongols as Rulers

The success of the Mongols in ruling vast territories was due in large part to their willingness to incorporate other ethnic groups into their armies and governments. Whatever their original country or religion, those who served the Mongols loyally were rewarded. Uighurs, Tibetans, Persians, Chinese, and Russians came to hold powerful positions in the Mongol governments. Chinese helped breach the walls of Baghdad in the 1250s, and Muslims operated the catapults that helped reduce Chinese cities in the 1270s.

Since, in Mongol eyes, the purpose of fighting was to gain riches, the Mongols would regularly loot the settlements they conquered, taking whatever they wanted, including the residents. Land would be granted to military commanders, nobles, and army units to be governed and exploited as the recipients wished. Those working the land would be given to them as serfs. The Mongols built a capital city called Karakorum in modern Mongolia, and to bring it up to the level of the cities they conquered, they transported skilled workers from those cities. For instance, after Bukhara and Samarkand were captured in 1219–1220, some thirty thousand artisans were enslaved and transported to Mongolia. Sometimes these slaves gradually improved their status. A French goldsmith from Budapest named Guillaume Boucher was captured by the Mongols in 1242 and taken to Karakorum, where he gradually won favor and was put in charge of fifty workers to make gold and silver vessels for the Mongol court.

The traditional nomad disdain for farmers led some commanders to suggest turning north China into a gigantic pasture after it was conquered. In time, though, the Mongols came to realize that simply appropriating the wealth and human resources of the settled lands was not as good as extracting regular revenue from them. A Chinese-educated Khitan who had been working for the Jurchens in China explained to the Mongols that collecting taxes from farmers would be highly profitable: they could extract a revenue of 500,000 ounces of silver, 80,000 bolts of silk, and more than 20,000 tons of grain from the region by taxing it. The Mongols gave this a try, but soon political rivals convinced the khan that he would gain even more by letting Central Asian Muslim merchants bid against each other for licenses to collect taxes any way they could, a system called **tax-farming**. Ordinary Chinese found this method of tax collecting much more oppressive than traditional Chinese methods, since there was little to keep the tax collectors from seizing everything they could.

By the second half of the thirteenth century there was no longer a genuine pan-Asian Mongol Empire. Much of Asia was in the hands of Mongol successor states, but these were generally hostile to each other. Khubilai was often at war with the khanate of Central Asia, then held by his cousin Khaidu, and he had little contact with the khanate of the Golden Horde in south Russia. The Mongols adapted their methods of government to the existing traditions of each place they ruled, and the regions went their separate ways.

In China the Mongols resisted assimilation and purposely avoided many Chinese practices. The rulers conducted their business in the Mongol language and spent their summers in Mongolia. Khubilai discouraged Mongols from marrying Chinese and took only Mongol women into the palace. Some Mongol princes preferred to live in yurts erected on the palace grounds rather than in the grand palaces constructed at Beijing. Chinese were treated as legally inferior not only to the Mongols but also to all other non-Chinese. In cases of assault the discrepancy was huge, as a Mongol who murdered a Chinese could get off with a fine, but a Chinese who hit a Mongol to defend himself would face severe penalties.

In Central Asia, Persia, and Russia the Mongols tended to merge with the Turkish groups already there and, like them, converted to Islam. Russia in the thirteenth century was not a strongly centralized state, and the Mongols allowed Russian princes and lords to continue to rule their territories as long as they turned over adequate tribute (thus adding to the burden on peasants). The city of Moscow became the center of Mongol tribute collection and grew in importance. In the Middle East the Mongol Il-khans (as they were known in Persia) were more active as rulers, again continuing the traditions of the caliphate. In Mongolia itself, however, Mongol traditions were maintained.

Mongol control in each of the khanates lasted about a century. In the mid-fourteenth century the Mongol dynasty in China deteriorated into civil war, and in the 1360s the Mongols withdrew back to Mongolia. There was a similar loss of Mongol power in Persia and Central Asia. Only on the south Russian steppe did the Golden Horde maintain its hold for another century.

As Mongol rule in Central Asia declined, a new conqueror emerged, Timur, also known as Tamerlane (Timur the Lame). Not a nomad but a highly civilized Turkish noble, Timur in the 1360s struck out from his base in Samarkand into Persia, north India (see page 347), southern Russia, and beyond. His armies used the terror tactics that the Mongols had perfected, massacring the citizens of cities that resisted. In the decades after his death in 1405, however, Timur's empire went into decline.

East-West Communication During the Mongol Era

How did the Mongol conquests facilitate the spread of ideas, religions, inventions, and diseases?

The Mongol governments did more than any earlier political entities to encourage the movement of people and goods across Eurasia. With these vast movements came cultural accommodation as the Mongols, their conquered subjects, and their trading partners learned from one another. This cultural exchange involved both physical goods and the sharing of ideas, including the introduction of new religious beliefs and the adoption of new ways to organize and rule the Mongol Empire. It also facilitated the spread of the plague and the unwilling movement of enslaved captives.

The Movement of Peoples

The Mongols had never looked down on merchants the way the elites of many traditional states did, and they welcomed the arrival of merchants from distant lands. Even when different groups of Mongols were fighting among themselves, they usually allowed caravans to pass without harassing them.

The Mongol practice of transporting skilled people from the lands they conquered also brought people into contact with each other in new ways. Besides those forced to move, the Mongols recruited administrators from all over. Especially prominent were the Uighur Turks of Chinese Central Asia, whose familiarity with Chinese civilization and fluency in Turkish were extremely valuable in facilitating communication. Literate Uighurs staffed much of the Mongol administration.

One of those who served the Mongols was Rashid al-Din (ca. 1247–1318). A Jew from Persia and the son of an apothecary, Rashid al-Din converted to Islam at the age of thirty and entered the service of the Mongol Il-khan of Persia as a physician. He rose in government service, traveled widely, and eventually became prime minister. Rashid al-Din became friends with the ambassador from China, and together they arranged for translations of Chinese works on medicine, agronomy, and statecraft. Aware of the great differences between cultures, he believed that the Mongols should try to rule in accord with the moral principles of the majority in each land. On that basis he convinced the Mongol khan of Persia to convert to Islam. Rashid al-Din undertook to explain the great variety of cultures by writing a world history more comprehensive than any previously written.

The Mongols were remarkably open to religious experts from all the lands they encountered. More Europeans made their way as far as Mongolia and China in the Mongol period than ever before. Popes and kings sent envoys to the Mongol court in the hope of enlisting the Mongols on their side in their long-standing conflict with Muslim forces over the Holy Land. European visitors were also interested in finding Christians who had been cut off from the West by the spread of Islam, and in fact there were considerable numbers of Nestorian Christians in Central Asia. In 1245 Pope Innocent IV wrote two letters to the "King and people of the Tartars" asking him to become a Christian and cease attacks against Europe. They were delivered to a Mongol general in Armenia. The next year another envoy, Giovanni di Pian de Carpine, reached the Volga River and the camp of Batu, the khan of the Golden Horde. Batu sent him on to the new Great Khan in Karakorum with two Mongol guides, riding so fast that they had to change horses five to seven times a day. Their full journey of more than three thousand miles took a remarkably short five and a half months. Carpine spent four months at the Great Khan's court but never succeeded in convincing the khan to embrace Christianity or drop his demand that the pope appear in person to tender his submission to the khan. When Carpine returned home, he wrote a report that urged preparation for a renewed Mongol attack on Europe. The Mongols had to be resisted "because of the harsh, indeed intolerable, and hitherto unheard-of slavery seen with our own eyes, to which they reduce all peoples who have submitted to them."[4]

Planting Trees　　The illustrations in early copies of Marco Polo's book show the elements that Europeans found most interesting. This page illustrates Khubilai's order that trees be planted along the main roads. (Illumination from *Le Livre des Merveilles du Monde* [Travels of Marco Polo], by the Paris studio of the Boucicaut Master, c. 1412/Bibliothèque Nationale, Paris/akg-images)

A few years later, in 1253, Flemish friar William of Rubruck set out with the permission of King Louis IX of France as a missionary to convert the Mongols. He too made his way to Karakorum, where he found many Europeans. At Easter, Hungarians, Russians, Georgians, Armenians, and Alans all took communion in a Nestorian church.

The most famous European visitor to the Mongol lands was the Venetian Marco Polo (ca. 1254–1324). In his famous *Travels*, Marco Polo described all the places he visited or learned about during his seventeen years away from home. He reported being warmly received by Khubilai, who impressed him enormously. He was also awed by the wealth and splendor of Chinese cities and spread the notion of Asia as a land of riches. In Marco Polo's lifetime some skeptics did not believe his tale, and even today some scholars speculate that he may have learned about China from Persian merchants he met in the Middle East without actually going to China. But Mongol scholars staunchly defend Marco Polo, even though they admit that he stretched the truth to make himself look good in several places.

The Spread of Disease, Goods, and Ideas

The rapid transfer of people and goods across Central Asia spread more than ideas and inventions. It also spread diseases, the most deadly of which was the plague known in Europe as the Black Death, which scholars identify today as the bubonic plague. In the early fourteenth century, transmitted by rats and fleas, the plague began to spread from Central Asia into West Asia, the Mediterranean, and western Europe. When the Mongols were assaulting the city of Kaffa in the Crimea in 1346, they were infected by the plague and had to withdraw. In retaliation, they purposely spread the disease to their enemy by catapulting the bodies of victims into the city of Kaffa. Soon the disease was carried from port to port throughout the Mediterranean by ship. The confusion of the mid-fourteenth century that led to the loss of Mongol power in China, Iran, and Central Asia undoubtedly owes something to the effect of the spread of the plague and other diseases. (For more on the Black Death, see Chapter 14.)

Traditionally, the historians of each of the countries conquered by the Mongols portrayed them as a scourge. Russian historians, for instance, saw this as a period of bondage that set Russia back and cut it off from western Europe. Among contemporary Western historians, it is now more common to celebrate the genius of the Mongol military machine and treat the spread of ideas and inventions as an obvious good, probably because we see global communication as a good in our own world. There is no reason to assume, however, that people benefited equally from the improved communications and the new political institutions of the Mongol era. Merchants involved in long-distance trade prospered, but those enslaved and transported hundreds or thousands of miles from home would have seen themselves not as the beneficiaries of opportunities to encounter cultures different from their own but rather as the most pitiable of victims.

The places that were ruled by Mongol governments for a century or more—China, Central Asia, Persia, and Russia—do not seem to have advanced at a more rapid rate during that century than they did in earlier centuries, either economically or culturally. By Chinese standards, Mongol imposition of hereditary status distinctions was a step backward from a much more mobile and open society, and placing Persians, Arabs, or Tibetans over Chinese did not arouse interest in foreign cultures. Many more styles of foreign music, clothing, art, and furnishings were integrated into Chinese civilization in Tang times than in Mongol times.

In terms of the spread of technological and scientific ideas, Europe seems to have been by far the main beneficiary of increased communication, largely because in 1200 it lagged farther behind than the other areas. Chinese inventions such as printing, gunpowder, and the compass spread westward. Persian and Indian expertise in astronomy and mathematics also spread. In terms of the spread of religions, Islam probably gained the most. It came to dominate in Chinese Central Asia, which had previously been Buddhist.

India, Islam, and the Development of Regional Cultures, 300–1400

What was the result of India's encounters with Turks, Mongols, and Islam?

South Asia, although far from the heartland of the steppe, still felt the impact of the arrival of the Turks in Central Asia. Over the course of many centuries, horsemen from both the east and the west (Scythians, Huns, Turks, and Mongols) all sent armies south to raid or invade north India. After the Mauryan Empire broke apart in 185 B.C.E. (see page 82), India was politically divided into small kingdoms for several centuries. Only the Guptas in the fourth century would emerge to unite much of north India, though their rule was cut short by the invasion of the Huns in about 450. A few centuries later, India was profoundly shaped by Turkish nomads from Central Asia who brought their culture and, most important, Islam to India. Despite these events, the lives of most Indians remained unchanged, with the majority of the people living in villages in a society defined by caste.

The Gupta Empire, ca. 320–480

In the early fourth century a state emerged in the Ganges plain that was able to bring large parts of north India under its control. The rulers of this Indian empire, the Guptas, consciously modeled their rule after that of the Mauryan Empire, and the founder took the name of the founder of that dynasty, Chandragupta. Although the Guptas never controlled as much territory as the Mauryans had, they united north India and received tribute from states in Nepal and the Indus Valley, thus giving large parts of India a period of peace and political unity.

The Guptas' administrative system was not as centralized as that of the Mauryans. In the central regions they drew their revenue from a tax on agriculture of one-quarter of the harvest and maintained monopolies on key products such as metals and salt (reminiscent of Chinese practice). They also exacted labor service for the construction and upkeep of roads, wells, and irrigation systems. More distant areas were assigned to governors who were allowed considerable leeway, and governorships often became hereditary. Areas still farther away were encouraged to become vassal states, able to participate in the splendor of the capital and royal court in subordinate roles and to engage in profitable trade, but not required to turn over much in the way of revenue.

The Gupta kings were patrons of the arts. Poets composed epics for the courts of the Gupta kings, and other writers experimented with prose romances and popular tales. India's greatest poet, Kalidasa (ca. 380–450), like Shakespeare, wrote poems as well as plays in verse. His most highly esteemed play, *Shakuntala*, concerns a daughter of a hermit who enthralls a king who is out hunting. The king sets up house with her, then returns to his court and, owing to a curse, forgets her. Only much later does he acknowledge their child as his true heir. Equally loved is Kalidasa's one-hundred-verse poem "The Cloud Messenger" about a demigod who asks a passing cloud to carry a message to his wife, from whom he has long been separated. At one point he instructs the cloud to tell her: "I see your body in the sinuous creeper, your gaze in the startled eyes of deer, your cheek in the moon, your hair in the plumage of peacocks, and in the tiny ripples of the river I see your sidelong glances, but alas, my dearest, nowhere do I see your whole likeness."[5]

In mathematics, too, the Gupta period could boast of impressive intellectual achievements. The so-called Arabic numerals are actually of Indian origin. Indian mathematicians developed the place-value notation system, with separate columns for ones, tens, and hundreds, as well as a zero sign to indicate the absence of units in a given column. This system greatly facilitated calculation and had spread as far as Europe by the seventh century.

The Gupta rulers were Hindus, but they tolerated all faiths. Buddhist pilgrims from other areas of Asia reported that Buddhist monasteries with hundreds or even thousands of monks and nuns flourished in the cities. The success of Buddhism did not hinder Hinduism with its many gods, which remained popular among ordinary people.

The great crisis of the Gupta Empire was the invasion of the Huns in about 450. Mustering his full might, the Gupta ruler Skandagupta (r. ca. 455–467) threw back the invaders, but they had dealt the dynasty a fatal blow.

India's Medieval Age and the First Encounter with Islam

After the decline of the Gupta Empire, India once again broke into separate kingdoms that were frequently at war with each other. Most of the dynasties of India's medieval age (ca. 500–1400) were short-lived, but a balance of power was maintained between the major regions of India, with none gaining enough of an advantage to conquer the others. Particularly notable are the Cholas, who dominated the southern tip of the peninsula, Sri Lanka, and much of the eastern Indian Ocean to the twelfth century (Map 12.2).

Political division fostered the development of regional cultures. Literature came to be written in India's regional languages, among them Marathi, Bengali, and Assamese. Commerce continued as before, and the coasts of India remained important in the sea trade of the Indian Ocean.

The first encounters with Islam occurred in this period. In 711, after pirates had plundered a richly laden Arab ship near the mouth of the Indus, the Umayyad governor of Iraq sent a force with six thousand horses and six thousand camels to seize the Sind area in western India (modern Pakistan). The western part of India remained part of the caliphate for centuries, but Islam did not spread much beyond this foothold. During the ninth and tenth centuries Turks from Central Asia moved into the region of

MAP 12.2 **South and Southeast Asia in the Thirteenth Century** The extensive coastlines of South and Southeast Asia and the predictable monsoon winds aided seafaring in this region. Note the Strait of Malacca, through which most east-west sea trade passed.

today's northeastern Iran and western Afghanistan, then known as Khurasan. Converts to Islam, they first served as military forces for the caliphate in Baghdad, but as its authority weakened (see page 338), they made themselves rulers of an effectively in-dependent Khurasan and frequently sent raiding parties into north India. Beginning in 997 Mahmud of Ghazni (r. 997–1030) led seventeen annual forays into India from his base in modern Afghanistan. His goal was plunder to finance his wars against other Turkish rulers in Central Asia. Toward this end, he systematically looted Indian palaces and temples, viewing religious statues as infidels' idols. Eventually the Arab conquerors of the Sind fell to the Turks. By 1030 the Indus Valley, the Punjab, and the rest of northwest India were in the grip of the Turks.

The new rulers encouraged the spread of Islam, but the Indian caste system (see page 66) made it difficult to convert higher-caste Indians. Al-Biruni (d. 1048), a Persian scholar who spent much of his later life at the court of Mahmud and learned Sanskrit, wrote of the obstacles to Hindu-Muslim communication. The most basic barrier was language, but the religious gulf was also fundamental:

> They totally differ from us in religion, as we believe in nothing in which they believe, and vice versa. On the whole, there is very little disputing about theological topics among them; at the utmost they fight with words, but they will never stake their soul or body or property on religious controversy. . . . They call foreigners impure and forbid having any connection with them, be it by intermarriage or any kind of relationship, or by sitting, eating, and drinking with them, because thereby, they think, they would be polluted.[6]

After the initial period of raids and destruction of temples, the Muslim Turks came to an accommodation with the Hindus, who were classed as a **protected people**, like the Christians and Jews, and allowed to follow their religion. They had to pay a special tax but did not have to perform military service. Local chiefs and rajas were often allowed to remain in control of their domains as long as they paid tribute. Most Indians looked on the Muslim conquerors as a new ruling caste, capable of governing and taxing them but otherwise peripheral to their lives. The myriad castes largely governed themselves, isolating the newcomers.

Nevertheless, over the course of several centuries Islam gained a strong hold on north India, especially in the Indus Valley (modern Pakistan) and in Bengal at the mouth of the Ganges River (modern Bangladesh). Moreover, the sultanate seems to have had a positive effect on the economy. Much of the wealth confiscated from temples was put to more productive use, and India's first truly large cities emerged. The Turks also were eager to employ skilled workers, giving new opportunities to low-caste manual and artisan labor.

The Muslim rulers were much more hostile to Buddhism than to Hinduism, seeing Buddhism as a competitive proselytizing religion. In 1193 a Turkish raiding party destroyed the great Buddhist university at Nalanda in Bihar. Buddhist monks were killed or forced to flee to Buddhist centers in Southeast Asia, Nepal, and Tibet. Buddhism, which had thrived for so long in peaceful and friendly competition with Hinduism, subsequently went into decline in its native land.

Hinduism, however, remained as strong as ever. South India was largely unaffected by these invasions, and traditional Hindu culture flourished there under native kings ruling small kingdoms. (See "Individuals in Society: Bhaskara the Teacher," page 348.) Devotional cults and mystical movements flourished. This was a great age of religious art and architecture in India. Extraordinary temples covered with elaborate bas-relief were built in many areas. Sexual passion and the union of men and women were frequently depicted, symbolically representing passion for and union with the temple god.

The Delhi Sultanate

In the twelfth century a new line of Turkish rulers arose in Afghanistan, led by Muhammad of Ghur (d. 1206). Muhammad captured Delhi and extended his control nearly throughout north India. When he fell to an assassin in 1206, one of his generals, the former slave Qutb-ud-din, seized the reins of power and established a government at Delhi, separate from the government in Afghanistan. This sultanate of Delhi lasted for three centuries, even though dynasties changed several times.

The North African Muslim world traveler Ibn Battuta (see "Individuals in Society: Ibn Battuta," page 254) served for several years as a judge at the court of one of the Delhi sultans. He praised the sultan for his insistence on the observance of ritual prayers and many acts of generosity to those in need, but he also considered the sultan overly violent. Here is just one of many examples he offered of how quick the sultan was to execute:

> During the years of the famine, the Sultan had given orders to dig wells outside the capital, and have grain crops sown in those parts. He provided the cultivators with the seed, as well as with all that was necessary for cultivation in the way of money and supplies, and required them to cultivate these crops for the [royal] grain-store. When the jurist 'Afif al-Din heard of this, he said, "This crop will not produce what is hoped for." Some informer told the Sultan what he had said, so the Sultan jailed him, and said to him, "What reason have you to meddle with the government's business?" Some time later he released him, and as 'Afif al-Din went to his house he was met on the way by two friends of his, also jurists, who said to him, "Praise be to God for your release," to which our jurist replied, "Praise be to God who has delivered us from the evildoers." They then separated, but they had not reached their houses before this was reported to the Sultan, and he commanded all three to be fetched and brought before him. "Take out this fellow," he said, referring to 'Afif al-Din, "and cut off his head baldrickwise," that is, the head is cut off along with an arm and part of the chest, "and behead the other two." They said to him, "He deserves punishment, to be sure, for what he said, but in our case for what crime are you killing us?" He replied, "You heard what he said and did not disavow it, so you as good as agreed with it." So they were all put to death, God Most High have mercy on them.[7]

A major accomplishment of the Delhi sultanate was holding off the Mongols. Chinggis Khan and his troops entered the Indus Valley in 1221 in pursuit of the shah of Khurasan. The sultan wisely kept out of the way, and when Chinggis Khan left some troops in the area, the sultan made no attempt to challenge them. Two generations later, in 1299, a Mongol khan launched a campaign into India with two hundred thousand men, but the sultan of the time was able to defeat them. Two years later the Mongols returned and camped at Delhi for two months, but they eventually left without taking the sultan's fort. Another Mongol raid in 1306–1307 also was successfully repulsed.

Although the Turks by this time were highly cosmopolitan and no longer nomadic, they had retained their martial skills and understanding of steppe warfare. They were expert horsemen, and horses thrived in northwest India. The south and east of India, however, like the south of China, were less hospitable to raising horses. In India's case, though, the climate of the south and east was well suited to elephants, which had been used as weapons of war in India since early times. Rulers in the northwest imported elephants from more tropical regions. The Delhi sultanate is said to have had as many as one thousand war elephants at its height.

During the fourteenth century, however, the Delhi sultanate was in decline and proved unable to ward off the armies of Timur (see page 340), who took Delhi in

Easter Island Statues   Archaeologists have excavated and restored many of Easter Island's huge statues, which display remarkable stylistic consistency, with the heads disproportionately large and the legs not visible. (Jean-Pierre De Mann/Robert Harding World Imagery)

300 C.E., Easter Island in perhaps 1000, and New Zealand not until about 1000–1300. There even were groups who sailed west, eventually settling in Madagascar between 200 and 500.

In the more remote islands, such as Hawai'i, Easter Island, and New Zealand, the societies that developed were limited by the small range of domesticated plants and animals that the settlers brought with them and those that were indigenous to the place. Easter Island is perhaps the most extreme case. Only 15 miles wide at its widest point (only 63 square miles in total area), it is 1,300 miles from the nearest inhabited island (Pitcairn) and 2,240 miles from the coast of South America. At some point there was communication with South America, as sweet potatoes originally from there made their way to Easter Island. The community that developed on the island raised chickens and cultivated sweet potatoes, taro, and sugarcane. The inhabitants also engaged in deep-sea fishing, catching dolphins and tuna. Their tools were made of stone, wood, or bone. The population is thought to have reached about fifteen thousand at Easter Island's most prosperous period, which began about 1200 C.E. It was then that its people devoted remarkable efforts to fashioning and erecting the large stone statues that still dot the island.

What led the residents of such a small island to erect more than eight hundred statues, most weighing around ten tons and standing twenty to seventy feet tall? When the first Europeans arrived in 1722, no statues had been erected for several generations, and the local residents explained them as representing ancestors. One common theory is that they were central to the islanders' religion and that rival clans competed with each other to erect the most impressive statues. The effort they had to expend to carve them with stone tools, move them to the chosen site, and erect them would have been formidable.

After its heyday, Easter Island suffered severe environmental stress with the decline of its forests. Whether the rats that came with the original settlers ate too many of the trees' seeds or the islanders cut down too many of the trees to transport the stone statues, the impact of deforestation was severe. The islanders could not make boats to fish in the ocean, and bird colonies shrank as nesting areas decreased, also reducing the food supply. Scholars still disagree on how much weight to give the many different elements that contributed to the decline in the prosperity of Easter Island from the age when the statues were erected.

Certainly, early settlers of an island could have a drastic impact on its ecology. When Polynesians first reached New Zealand, they found large birds up to ten feet tall. They hunted them so eagerly that within a century the birds had all but disappeared. Hunting seals and sea lions also led to their rapid depletion. But the islands of New Zealand were much larger than Easter Island, and in time the Maori (the indigenous people of New Zealand) found more sustainable ways to feed themselves, depending more and more on agriculture.

Chapter Summary

The pastoral societies that stretched across Eurasia had the great military advantage of being able to raise horses in large numbers and support themselves from their flocks of sheep, goats, and other animals. Nomadic pastoralists generally were organized on the basis of clans and tribes that selected chiefs for their military talent. Much of the time these tribes fought with each other, but several times in history leaders formed larger confederations capable of coordinated attacks on cities and towns.

From the fifth to the twelfth centuries the most successful nomadic groups on the Eurasian steppes were Turks who gained ascendancy in many of the societies from the Middle East to northern India. In the early thirteenth century, through his charismatic leadership and military genius, the Mongol leader Chinggis Khan conquered much of Eurasia. Those who submitted without fighting could become vassals, but those who resisted faced the prospect of mass slaughter or enslavement.

After Chinggis's death, the empire was divided into four khanates ruled by four of Chinggis's descendants. For a century the Mongol Empire fostered unprecedented East-West contact. The Mongols encouraged trade and often moved craftsmen and other specialists from one place to another. They were tolerant of other religions. As more Europeans made their way east, Chinese inventions such as printing and the compass made their way west. Europe especially benefited from the spread of technical and scientific ideas. Diseases also spread, including the Black Death, carried by fleas and rats that found their way into the goods of merchants and other travelers.

India was invaded by the Mongols but not conquered. After the fall of the Gupta Empire in about 480, India was for the next millennium ruled by small kingdoms, which allowed regional cultures to flourish. For several centuries Muslim Turks ruled north India from Delhi. Over time Islam gained adherents throughout South Asia. Hinduism continued to flourish, but Buddhism declined.

Throughout the medieval period India continued to be the center of active sea-borne trade, and this trade helped carry Indian ideas and practices to Southeast Asia. Local rulers used experts from India to establish strong states, such as the Khmer kingdom and the Srivijayan kingdom. Buddhism became the dominant religion throughout the region, though Hinduism also played an important role. The Pacific islands east of Indonesia remained isolated culturally for centuries.

Notes

1. Trans. in Denis Sinor, "The Establishment and Dissolution of the Türk Empire," in *The Cambridge History of Early Inner Asia*, ed. Denis Sinor (Cambridge: Cambridge University Press, 1990), p. 307.
2. Manuel Komroff, ed., *Contemporaries of Marco Polo* (New York: Dorset Press, 1989), p. 65.
3. Ibid.
4. Cited in John Larner, *Marco Polo and the Discovery of the World* (New Haven, Conn.: Yale University Press, 1999), p. 22.
5. Quoted in A. L. Basham, *The Wonder That Was India*, 2d ed. (New York: Grove Press, 1959), p. 420. Copyright © Picador, A. L. Basham. Reprinted by permission of Pan Macmillan, London.
6. Edward C. Sachau, *Alberuni's India*, vol. 1 (London: Kegan Paul, 1910), pp. 19–20, slightly modified.
7. H. A. R. Gibb, *The Travels of Ibn Battuta* (Cambridge: Cambridge University Press for the Hakluyt Society, 1971), pp. 700–701. Reprinted by permission of David Higham Associates on behalf of the Hakluyt Society.
8. Guy le Strang, trans., *Clavijo, Embassy to Tamerlane, 1403–1406* (London: Routledge, 1928), pp. 265–266.
9. Quoted in Basham, *The Wonder That Was India*, p. 161. Copyright © Picador, A. L. Basham. Reprinted by permission of Pan Macmillan, London.

CONNECTIONS

The societies of Eurasia became progressively more connected to each other during the centuries discussed in this chapter. One element promoting connection was the military superiority of the nomadic warriors of the steppe: first the Turks, then the Mongols, who conquered many of the settled civilizations near them. Invading Turks brought Islam to India. Connection between societies also came from maritime trade across the Indian Ocean and East Asia. Maritime trade was a key element in the spread of Indian culture to both the mainland and insular Southeast Asia. Other elements connecting these societies included Sanskrit as a language of administration and missionaries who brought both Hinduism and Buddhism far beyond their homelands. Some societies did remain isolated, probably none more than the remote islands of the Pacific, such as Hawai'i, Easter Island, and New Zealand.

East Asia was a key element in both the empires created by nomadic horsemen and the South Asian maritime trading networks. As discussed in Chapter 13, before East Asia had to cope with the rise of the Mongols, it experienced one of its most prosperous periods, during which China, Korea, and Japan became more distinct culturally. China's economy boomed during the Song Dynasty, and the scholar-official class, defined through the civil service examination, came more and more to dominate culture. In Korea and Japan, by contrast, aristocrats and military men gained ascendancy. Although China, Korea, and Japan all drew on both Confucian and Buddhist teachings, they ended up with elites as distinct as the Chinese scholar-official, the Korean aristocrat, and the Japanese samurai.

Chapter Review

MAKE IT STICK

☑ LearningCurve
Go online and use LearningCurve to retain what you've read.

IDENTIFY KEY TERMS

Identify and explain the significance of each item below.

nomads (p. 329)

steppe (p. 329)

yurts (p. 332)

Chinggis Khan (p. 334)

khanates (p. 337)

tax-farming (p. 339)

protected people (p. 346)

jati (p. 351)

sati (p. 352)

Sanskrit (p. 353)

Srivijaya (p. 354)

REVIEW THE MAIN IDEAS

Answer the focus questions from each section of the chapter.

1. What aspects of nomadic life gave the nomads of Central Asia military advantages over nearby settled civilizations? (p. 329)

2. How did Chinggis Khan and his successors conquer much of Eurasia, and how did the Mongol conquests change the regions affected? (p. 334)

3. How did the Mongol conquests facilitate the spread of ideas, religions, inventions, and diseases? (p. 340)

4. What was the result of India's encounters with Turks, Mongols, and Islam? (p. 343)

5. How did states develop along the maritime trade routes of Southeast Asia and beyond? (p. 352)

MAKE CONNECTIONS

Analyze the larger developments and continuities within and across chapters.

1. How do the states established by Arabs in the seventh and eighth centuries compare to those established by Turks in the tenth and eleventh centuries?

2. What similarities and differences are there in the military feats of Alexander the Great and Chinggis Khan?

3. How does the slow spread of Buddhism and Indian culture to Southeast Asia compare to the slow spread of Christianity and Roman culture in Europe?

LaunchPad
ONLINE DOCUMENT PROJECT

Intellectual and Religious Life in India
What ideas and beliefs were central to Indian culture?

Read a Persian account of medieval India, and then complete a quiz and writing assignment based on the evidence and details from this chapter.

See inside the front cover to learn more.

CHRONOLOGY

ca. 320–480	• Gupta Empire in India
ca. 380–450	• Life of India's greatest poet, Kalidasa
ca. 450	• Huns invade northern India
ca. 500	• Srivijaya gains control of Strait of Malacca
ca. 500–1400	• India's medieval age; caste system reaches its mature form
552	• Turks rebel against Rouruan and rise to power in Central Asia
ca. 780	• Borobudur temple complex begun in Srivijaya
802–1432	• Khmer Empire of Cambodia
ca. 850–1250	• Kingdom of the Uighurs
1030	• Turks control north India
ca. 1100–1200	• Buddhism declines in India
ca. 1200–1300	• Easter Island society's most prosperous period
1206	• Temujin proclaimed Chinggis Khan; Mongol language recorded; Delhi sultanate established
ca. 1240	• *The Secret History of the Mongols*
1276	• Mongol conquest of Song China
ca. 1300	• Plague begins to spread throughout Mongol Empire
1398	• Timur takes control of the Delhi sultanate

13

✔ LearningCurve
After reading the chapter, go online and use LearningCurve to retain what you've read.

States and Cultures in East Asia

800–1400

DURING THE SIX CENTURIES BETWEEN 800 AND 1400, EAST ASIA WAS the most advanced region of the world. For several centuries the Chinese economy had grown spectacularly, and China's methods of production were highly advanced in fields as diverse as rice cultivation, the production of iron and steel, and the printing of books. Philosophy and the arts all flourished. China's system of government was also advanced for its time. In the Song period, the principle that the government should be in the hands of highly educated scholar-officials, selected through competitive written civil service examinations, became well established. Song China's great wealth and sophisticated government did not give it military advantage, however, and in this period China had to pay tribute to militarily more powerful northern neighbors, the Khitans, the Jurchens, and finally the Mongols, who conquered all of China in 1279.

During the previous millennium, basic elements of Chinese culture had spread beyond China's borders, creating the East Asian cultural sphere based on the use of Chinese as the language of civilization. Beginning around 800, however, the pendulum shifted toward cultural differentiation as Japan, Korea, and China developed in distinctive ways. In both Korea and Japan, for several centuries court aristocrats were dominant both politically and culturally, and then aristocrats lost out to military men with power in the countryside. By 1200 Japan was dominated by warriors—known as samurai—whose ethos was quite unlike that of China's educated elite. In both Korea and Japan, Buddhism retained a very strong hold, one of the ties that continued to link the countries of East Asia. In addition, China and Korea both had to deal with the same menacing neighbors to the north. Even Japan had to mobilize its resources to fend off two seaborne Mongol attacks.

The Medieval Chinese Economic Revolution, 800–1100

What made possible the expansion of the Chinese economy, and what were the outcomes of this economic growth?

Chinese historians traditionally viewed dynasties as following a standard cyclical pattern. Founders were vigorous men able to recruit capable followers to serve as officials and generals. Externally they would extend China's borders; internally they would bring peace. They would collect low but fairly assessed taxes. Over time, however, emperors born in the palace would get used to luxury and lack the founders' strength and wisdom. Families with wealth or political power would find ways to avoid taxes, forcing the government to impose heavier taxes on the poor. As a result, impoverished peasants would flee, the morale of those in the government and armies would decline, and the dynasty would find itself able neither to maintain internal peace nor to defend its borders.

Viewed in terms of this theory of the **dynastic cycle,** by 800 the Tang Dynasty (see pages 189–192) was in decline. It had ruled China for nearly two centuries, and its high point was in the past. A massive rebellion had wracked it in the mid-eighth century, and the Uighur Turks and Tibetans were menacing its borders. Many of the centralizing features of the government had been abandoned, with power falling more and more to regional military governors.

Historically, Chinese political theorists always assumed that a strong, centralized government was better than a weak one or than political division, but, if anything, the Tang toward the end of its dynastic cycle seems to have been both intellectually and economically more vibrant than the early Tang had been. Less control from the central government seems to have stimulated trade and economic growth.

A government census conducted in 742 shows that China's population was still approximately 50 million, very close to what it had been in 2 C.E. Over the next three centuries, with the expansion of wet-field rice cultivation in central and south China, the country's food supply steadily increased, and so did its population, which reached 100 million by 1100. China was certainly the largest country in the world at the time; its population probably already exceeded that of all the Islamic countries of the time or that of all the countries of Europe put together.

Agricultural prosperity and denser settlement patterns aided commercialization of the economy. Farmers in Song China no longer merely aimed at self-sufficiency. They had found that producing for the market made possible a better life. Farmers sold their surpluses and used their profits to buy charcoal, tea, oil, and wine. In many places farmers specialized in commercial crops, such as sugar, oranges, cotton, silk, and tea. The need to transport the products of interregional trade stimulated the inland and coastal shipping industries, providing employment for shipbuilders and sailors and business opportunities for enterprising families with enough capital to purchase a boat. Marco Polo, the Venetian merchant who wrote of his visit to China from about 1275 to 1292, was astounded at the boat traffic on the Yangzi River. He claimed to have seen no fewer than fifteen thousand vessels at one city on the river, but he commented, "And yet there are other towns where the number is still greater."[1]

As marketing increased, demand for money grew enormously, leading eventually to the creation of the world's first paper money. The decision by the late Tang government to abandon the use of bolts of silk as supplementary currency had increased the demand for copper coins. By 1085 the output of coins had increased tenfold to more than 6 billion coins a year. To avoid the weight and bulk of coins for large transactions, local merchants in late Tang times started trading receipts from deposit shops where they had left money or goods. The early Song authorities awarded a small set of these shops a monopoly on the issuing of these certificates of deposit, and in the 1120s the government took over the system, producing the world's first government-issued paper money.

With the intensification of trade, merchants became progressively more specialized and organized. They set up partnerships and joint stock companies, with a separation of owners (shareholders) and managers. In the large cities merchants were organized into guilds according to the type of product sold, and they arranged sales from wholesalers to shop owners and periodically set prices. When government officials wanted to requisition supplies or assess taxes, they dealt with the guild heads.

Foreign trade also flourished in the Song period. In 1225 the superintendent of customs at the coastal city of Quanzhou wrote an account of the foreign places Chinese merchants visited, with sketches of major trading cities from Srivijaya and Malabar in Southeast Asia to Cairo and Baghdad in the Middle East. Pearls were said to come from the Persian Gulf, ivory from the Red Sea port of Aden, pepper from the Indonesian islands of Java and Sumatra, and cotton from the various kingdoms of India. Chinese ships began to displace Indian and Arab merchants in the South Seas, and ship design was improved in several ways. Watertight bulkheads improved buoyancy and protected cargo. Stern-mounted rudders improved steering. Some of the ships were powered by both oars and sails and were large enough to hold several hundred men.

Also important to oceangoing travel was the perfection of the **compass**. The ability of a magnetic needle to point north had been known for some time, but in Song times the needle was reduced in size and attached to a fixed stem (rather than floated in water). In some instances it was put in a small protective case with a glass top, making it suitable for sea travel. The first reports of a compass used in this way date to 1119.

The Song also witnessed many advances in industrial techniques. Heavy industry, especially iron, grew astoundingly. With advances in metallurgy, iron production reached around 125,000 tons per year in 1078, a sixfold increase over the output in 800. At first charcoal was used in the production process, leading to deforestation of parts of north China. By the end of the eleventh century, however, bituminous coke had largely taken the place of charcoal. Much of the iron was put to military purposes. Mass-production methods were used to make iron armor in small, medium, and large sizes. High-quality steel for swords was made through high-temperature metallurgy. Huge bellows, often driven by water wheels, were used to superheat the molten ore. The needs of the army also brought Chinese engineers to experiment with the use of gunpowder. In the twelfth-century wars against the Jurchens (see page 331), those defending a besieged city used gunpowder to propel projectiles at the enemy.

Economic expansion fueled the growth of cities. Dozens of cities had 50,000 or more residents, and quite a few had more than 100,000, very large populations compared

Transplanting Rice To get the maximum yield per plot and to make it possible to grow two crops in the same field, Chinese farmers grew rice seedlings in a seedbed and then, when a field was free, transplanted the seedlings into the flooded field. Because the Song government wanted to promote up-to-date agricultural technology, in the twelfth century it commissioned a set of twelve illustrations of the steps to be followed. This painting comes from a later version of those illustrations. (*Tilling Rice*, Yuan Dynasty [ink and colour on paper], Qi, Cheng [13th century] [attr. to]/Freer Gallery of Art, Smithsonian Institution, Washington, D.C., U.S.A./ The Bridgeman Art Library)

to other places in the world at the time. China's two successive capitals, Kaifeng (kighfuhng) and Hangzhou (hahng-joh), each had an estimated 1 million residents. Marco Polo described Hangzhou as the finest and most splendid city in the world. He reported that it had ten marketplaces, each half a mile long, where 40,000 to 50,000 people would shop on any given day. There were also bathhouses; permanent shops selling items such as spices, drugs, and pearls; and innumerable courtesans, whom Marco Polo described as "adorned in much finery, highly perfumed, occupying well-furnished houses, and attended by many female domestics."[2]

The medieval economic revolution shifted the economic center of China south to the Yangzi River drainage area. This area had many advantages over the north China plain. Rice, which grew in the south, provides more calories per unit of land and therefore allows denser settlement. The milder temperatures often allowed two crops to be grown on the same plot of land, first a summer crop of rice and then a winter crop of wheat or vegetables. The abundance of rivers and streams facilitated shipping, which reduced the cost of transportation and thus made regional specialization economically more feasible. In the first half of the Song Dynasty, the capital was still at Kaifeng in the north, close to the Grand Canal (see page 189), which linked the capital to the rich south.

The economic revolution of Song times cannot be attributed to intellectual change, as Confucian scholars did not reinterpret the classics to defend the morality of commerce. But neither did scholar-officials take a unified stand against economic development. As officials they had to work to produce revenue to cover government expenses such as defense, and this was much easier to do when commerce was thriving.

Ordinary people benefited from the Song economic revolution in many ways. There were more opportunities for the sons of farmers to leave agriculture and find work in cities. Those who stayed in agriculture had a better chance of improving their situations by taking up sideline production of wine, charcoal, paper, or textiles. Energetic farmers who grew cash crops such as sugar, tea, mulberry leaves (for silk), and cotton (recently introduced from India) could grow rich. Greater interregional trade led to the availability of more goods at the rural markets held every five or ten days.

Of course, not everyone grew rich. Poor farmers who fell into debt had to sell their land, and if they still owed money they could be forced to sell their daughters as maids, concubines, or prostitutes. The prosperity of the cities created a huge demand for women to serve the rich in these ways, and Song sources mention that criminals would kidnap girls and women to sell in distant cities at huge profits.

China During the Song and Yuan Dynasties, 960–1368

How did the civil service examinations and the scholar-official class shape Chinese society and culture, and what impact did the Mongol conquest have on them?

In the tenth century Tang China broke up into separate contending states, some of which had non-Chinese rulers. The two states that proved to be long lasting were the Song, which came to control almost all of China proper south of the Great Wall, and the Liao, whose ruling house was Khitan and which held the territory of modern Beijing and areas north (Map 13.1). Although the Song Dynasty had a much larger population, the Liao was militarily the stronger of the two. In the early twelfth century the Liao state was defeated by the Jurchens, another non-Chinese people, who founded the Jin Dynasty and went on to conquer most of north China, leaving Song to control only the south. After a century the Jurchens' Jin Dynasty was defeated by the Mongols, who extended their Yuan Dynasty to control all of China by 1276.

The Song Dynasty

The founder of the Song Dynasty, Taizu (r. 960–976), was a general whose troops elevated him to emperor (somewhat reminiscent of Roman practice). Taizu worked to make sure that such an act could not happen in the future by placing the armies under central government control. To curb the power of his generals, he retired or rotated them and assigned civil officials to supervise them. In time these civil bureaucrats came to dominate every aspect of Song government and society. The civil service examination system established during the Sui Dynasty (see page 188) was greatly expanded to provide the dynasty with a constant flow of men trained in the Confucian classics.

Curbing the generals' power ended warlordism but did not solve the military problem of defending against the nomadic Khitans' Liao Dynasty to the north. After several attempts to push the Liao back beyond the Great Wall, the Song concluded a peace treaty with them. The Song agreed to make huge annual payments of gold and silk to the Khitans, in a sense paying them not to invade. Even so, the Song rulers had to maintain a standing army of more than a million men. By the middle of the eleventh century military expenses consumed half the government's revenues. Song had the industrial base to produce swords, armor, and arrowheads in huge quantities, but had difficulty maintaining enough horses and well-trained horsemen. Even though China was the economic powerhouse of the region, with by far the largest population, the

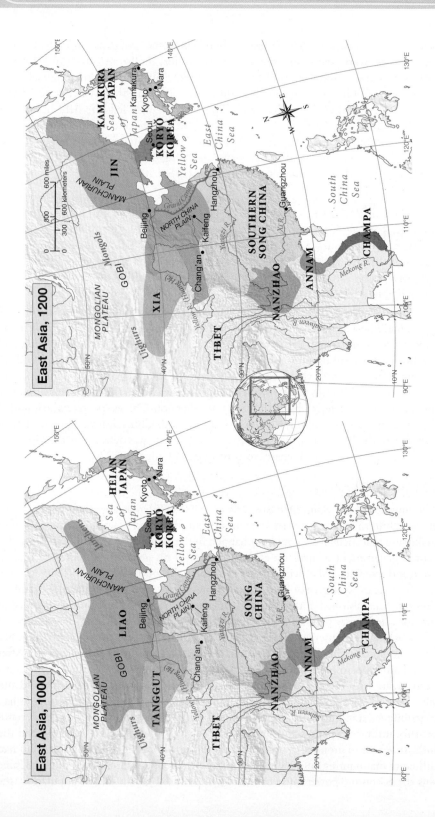

◀ **MAP 13.1**   **East Asia in 1000 and 1200** The Song empire did not extend as far as its predecessor, the Tang, and faced powerful rivals to the north—the Liao Dynasty of the Khitans and the Xia Dynasty of the Tanguts. Koryŏ Korea maintained regular contact with Song China, but Japan, by the late Heian period, was no longer deeply involved with the mainland. By 1200 military families dominated both Korea and Japan, but the borders were little changed. On the mainland the Liao Dynasty had been overthrown by the Jurchens' Jin Dynasty, which also seized the northern third of the Song empire. Because the Song relocated its capital to Hangzhou in the south, this period is called the Southern Song period.

horse was a major weapon of war in this period, and it was not easy to convert wealth to military advantage.

In the early twelfth century the military situation rapidly worsened when the Khitan state was destroyed by another tribal confederation led by the Jurchens. Although the Song allied with the Jurchens, the Jurchens quickly realized how easy it would be to defeat the Song. When they marched into the Song capital in 1126, they captured the emperor and former emperor and took them and the entire court into captivity. Song forces rallied around one of the emperor's sons who had escaped capture, and this prince re-established a Song court in the south at Hangzhou (see Map 13.1). This Southern Song Dynasty controlled only about two-thirds of the former Song territories, but the social, cultural, and intellectual life there remained vibrant until the Song fell to the Mongols in 1279.

The Scholar-Officials and Neo-Confucianism

The Song period saw the full flowering of one of the most distinctive features of Chinese civilization, the **scholar-official class** certified through highly competitive civil service examinations. This elite was both broader and better educated than the elites of earlier periods in Chinese history. Once the **examination system** was fully developed, aristocratic habits and prejudices largely disappeared. Ancestry did not matter as much when office depended more on study habits than on connections.

The examination system came to carry such prestige that the number of scholars entering each competition escalated rapidly, from fewer than 30,000 early in the eleventh century, to nearly 80,000 by the end of that century, to about 400,000 by the dynasty's end. To prepare for the examinations, men had to memorize the classics in order to be able to recognize even the most obscure passages. They also had to master specific forms of composition, including poetry, and be ready to discuss policy issues, citing appropriate historical examples. Those who became officials this way had usually tried the exams several times and were on average a little over thirty years of age when they succeeded. Because the competition was so fierce, the great majority of those who devoted years to preparing for the exams never became officials.

The invention of printing should be given some credit for the trend toward a better-educated elite. Tang craftsmen developed the art of carving words and pictures into wooden blocks, inking the blocks, and pressing paper onto them. Each block held an entire page of text. Such whole-page blocks were used for printing as early as the middle of the ninth century, and in the eleventh century **movable type** (one piece of type for each character) was invented, but it was rarely used because whole-block printing was cheaper. In China, as in Europe a couple of centuries later,

INDIVIDUALS IN SOCIETY • Shen Gua

In the eleventh century it was not rare for Chinese men of letters to have broad interests, but few could compare to Shen Gua (1031–1095), a man who tried his hand at everything from mathematics, geography, economics, engineering, medicine, divination, and archaeology to military strategy and diplomacy.

Shen Gua's father was an official, and Shen Gua often accompanied him on his assignments, which built up his knowledge of geography. In 1063 he passed the civil service examinations, and in 1066 he received a post in the capital. He eventually held high astronomical, ritual, and financial posts and became involved in waterworks and the construction of defense walls. He was sent as an envoy to the Khitans in 1075 to try to settle a boundary dispute. When a military campaign that he advised failed in 1082, he was demoted and later retired to write.

It is from his book of miscellaneous notes that we know the breadth of his interests. In one note Shen describes how, on assignment to inspect the frontier, he made a relief map of wood and glue-soaked sawdust to show the mountains, roads, rivers, and passes. The emperor was so impressed when he saw it that he ordered all the border prefectures to make relief maps. Elsewhere Shen describes the use of petroleum and explains how to make movable type from clay. Shen Gua often applied a mathematical approach to issues that his contemporaries did not think of in those terms. He once computed the total number of possible situations on a Go board, and another time he calculated the longest possible military campaign given the limits of human carriers, who had to carry their own food as well as food for the soldiers.

Shen Gua is especially known for his scientific explanations. He explained the deflection of the compass from due south. He identified petrified bamboo and from its existence argued that the region where it was found must have been much warmer and more humid in ancient times. He argued against the theory that tides are caused by the rising and setting of the sun, demonstrating that they correlate with the cycles of the moon. He proposed switching from a lunar calendar to a solar one of 365 days, saying that even though his contemporaries would reject his idea, "surely in the future some will adopt my idea." To convince his readers that

the introduction of printing dramatically lowered the price of books, thus aiding the spread of literacy.

Among the upper class the availability of cheaper books enabled scholars to amass their own libraries. Song publishers printed the classics of Chinese literature in huge editions to satisfy scholarly appetites. Works on philosophy, science, and medicine were also avidly consumed, as were Buddhist texts. Han and Tang poetry and historical works became the models for Song writers. One popular literary innovation was the encyclopedia, which first appeared in the Song period, at least five centuries before the publication of the first European encyclopedia.

The life of the educated man involved more than study for the civil service examinations and service in office. Many took to refined pursuits such as collecting antiques or old books and practicing the arts—especially poetry writing, calligraphy, the sun and the moon were spherical, not flat, he suggested that they cover a ball with fine powder on one side and then look at it obliquely. The powder was the part of the moon illuminated by the sun, and as the viewer looked at it obliquely, the white part would be crescent shaped, like a waxing moon. Shen Gua, however, did not realize that the sun and moon had entirely different orbits, and he explained why they did not collide by positing that both were composed of *qi* (vital energy) and had form but not substance.

Shen Gua also wrote on medicine and criticized his contemporaries for paying more attention to old treatises than to clinical experience. Yet he, too, was sometimes stronger on theory than on observation. In one note he argued that longevity pills could be made from cinnabar. He reasoned that if cinnabar could be transformed in one direction, it ought to be susceptible to transformation in the opposite direction as well. Therefore, since melted cinnabar causes death, solid cinnabar should prevent death.

QUESTIONS FOR ANALYSIS

1. How did Shen Gua's travels add to his curiosity about the material world?

2. In what ways could Shen Gua have used his scientific interests in his work as a government official?

3. How does Shen Gua's understanding of the natural world compare to that of the early Greeks? (See pages 136–137.)

▷LaunchPad
ONLINE DOCUMENT PROJECT

What cultural pursuits interested the scholar-official class? View images from the Song period, and then complete a quiz and writing assignment based on the evidence and details from this chapter.

See inside the front cover to learn more.

and painting. For many individuals these cultural interests overshadowed any philosophical, political, or economic concerns; others found in them occasional outlets for creative activity and aesthetic pleasure. In the Song period, the engagement of the elite with the arts led to extraordinary achievement in calligraphy and painting, especially landscape painting. A large share of the social life of upper-class men was centered on these refined pastimes, as they gathered to compose or criticize poetry, to view each other's art treasures, and to patronize young talents.

The new scholar-official elite produced some extraordinary men able to hold high court offices while pursuing diverse intellectual interests. (See "Individuals in Society: Shen Gua," above.) Ouyang Xiu spared time in his busy official career to write love songs, histories, and the first analytical catalogue of rubbings of ancient stone and bronze inscriptions. Sima Guang, besides serving as chancellor, wrote a narrative history of China from the Warring States Period (403–221 B.C.E.) to the founding of the Song Dynasty. Su Shi wrote more than twenty-seven hundred poems and eight hundred letters while active in opposition politics. He was also an esteemed painter, calligrapher, and theorist of the arts. Su Song, another high official, constructed an eighty-foot-tall mechanical clock. He adapted the water-powered clock invented in the Tang period by adding a chain-driven mechanism. The clock told not only the time of day but also the day of the month, the phase of the moon, and the position of certain stars and planets in the sky. As in Renaissance Europe a couple of centuries later (discussed in Chapter 15), gifted men made advances in a wide range of fields.

These highly educated men accepted the Confucian responsibility to aid the ruler in the governing of the country. Factional disputes often made government service stressful, especially during the period when the emperor supported the New Policies of the reformer Wang Anshi, which many leading men opposed.

Besides politics, scholars also debated issues in ethics and metaphysics. For several centuries Buddhism had been more vital than Confucianism. Beginning in the late Tang period, Confucian teachers began claiming that the teachings of the Confucian sages contained all the wisdom one needed and that a true Confucian would reject Buddhist teachings. During the eleventh century many Confucian teachers urged students to set their sights not on exam success but on the higher goals of attaining the wisdom of the sages. Metaphysical theories about the workings of the cosmos in terms of *li* (principle) and *qi* (vital energy) were developed in response to the challenge of the sophisticated metaphysics of Buddhism.

Neo-Confucianism, as this movement is generally termed, was more fully developed in the twelfth century by the immensely learned Zhu Xi (joo shee) (1130–1200). Besides serving in office, he wrote, compiled, or edited almost a hundred books; corresponded with dozens of other scholars; and still regularly taught groups of disciples, many of whom stayed with him for years at a time. Although he was treated as a political threat during his lifetime, within decades of his death his writings came to be considered orthodox, and in subsequent centuries candidates for the examinations had to be familiar with his commentaries on the classics.

Women's Lives in Song Times

Thanks to the spread of printing, more books survive from the Song period than from earlier periods, giving us more glimpses of women's lives. Stories, documents, and legal cases show us widows who ran inns, maids who were sent out by their mistresses to do errands, midwives who delivered babies, pious women who spent their days chanting Buddhist sutras, nuns who called on such women to explain Buddhist doctrine, girls who learned to read with their brothers, farmers' daughters who made money by weaving mats, childless widows who accused their nephews of stealing their property, wives who were jealous of the concubines their husbands brought home, and women who used part of their own large dowries to help their husbands' sisters marry well.

Families who could afford it usually tried to keep their wives and daughters within the walls of the house, rather than let them work in the fields or in shops or inns. At home there was plenty for them to do. Not only was there the work of tending children and preparing meals, but spinning, weaving, and sewing were considered women's work as well and took a great deal of time. Families that raised silkworms also needed women to do much of the work of coddling the worms and getting them to spin their cocoons. Within the home women generally had considerable say and took an active interest in issues such as the selection of marriage partners for their children.

Women tended to marry between the ages of sixteen and twenty. Their husbands were, on average, a couple of years older than they were. Marriages were arranged by their parents, who would have either called on a professional matchmaker (most often an older woman) or turned to a friend or relative for suggestions. Before a wedding took place, written agreements were exchanged, listing the prospective bride's and groom's birth dates, parents, and grandparents; the gifts that would be exchanged; and the dowry the bride would bring. The goal was to match families of approximately equal status, but a young man who had just passed the civil service exams would be considered a good prospect even if his family had little wealth.

A few days before the wedding, the bride's family sent her dowry to the groom's family, which at a minimum contained boxes full of clothes and bedding. In better-off families, the dowry also included items of substantial value, such as gold jewelry or deeds to land. On the day of the wedding, the groom and some of his friends and relatives went to the bride's home to get her. She would be elaborately dressed and would tearfully bid farewell to everyone in her family. She was carried to her new home in a fancy sedan chair to the sound of music, alerting everyone on the street that a wedding was taking place. Meanwhile, the groom's family's friends and relatives had gathered at his home, ready to greet the bridal party. The bride would kneel and bow to her new parents-in-law and later also to the tablets with the names of her husband's ancestors. A classical ritual still practiced was for the new couple to drink wine from the same cup. A ritual that had become popular in Song times was to attach a string to the bride and groom, literally tying them together. Later they were shown to their new bedroom, where the bride's dowry had already been placed, and people tossed beans or rice on the bed, symbolizing the desired fertility. After teasing them, the guests left them alone and went out to the courtyard for a wedding feast.

The young bride's first priority was to try to win over her mother-in-law, since everyone knew that mothers-in-law were hard to please. One way to do this was to quickly bear a son for the family. Within the patrilineal system, a woman fully secured her position in the family by becoming the mother of one of the men. Every community had older women skilled in midwifery

Woman Attendant   The Song emperors were patrons of a still-extant temple in northern China that enshrined a statue of the "holy mother," the mother of the founder of the ancient Zhou Dynasty. The forty-two maids who attend her, one of whom is shown here, seem to have been modeled on the palace ladies who attended Song emperors. (Taiyuan Jinci/Goddess Hall/Uniphoto Press International Japan/ Art and Architecture Collection Ltd.)

who were called to help when a woman went into labor. If the family was well-to-do, arrangements might be made for a wet nurse to help her take care of the newborn.

Women frequently had four, five, or six children, but likely one or more would die in infancy. If a son reached adulthood and married before the woman herself was widowed, she would be considered fortunate, for she would have always had an adult man who could take care of business for her—first her husband, then her grown son. But in the days when infectious diseases took many people in their twenties and thirties, it was not uncommon for a woman to be widowed while in her twenties, when her children were still very young.

A woman with a healthy and prosperous husband faced another challenge in middle age: her husband could bring home a concubine (and more than one if he could afford them). Moralists insisted that it was wrong for a wife to be jealous of her husband's concubines, but contemporary documents suggest that jealousy was very common. Wives outranked concubines and could give them orders in the house, but a concubine had her own ways of getting back through her hold on the husband. The children born to a concubine were considered just as much children of the family as the wife's children, and if the wife had had only daughters and the concubine had a son, the wife would find herself dependent on the concubine's son in her old age.

As a woman's children grew up, she would start thinking of suitable marriage partners. Many women liked the idea of bringing other women from their families of birth—perhaps a brother's daughter—to be their daughters-in-law. No matter who was selected, a woman's life became easier once she had a daughter-in-law to do the cooking and cleaning. Many found more time for religious devotions at this stage of their lives. Their sons, still living with them, could be expected to look after them and do their best to make their late years comfortable.

Neo-Confucianism is sometimes blamed for a decline in the status of women in Song times, largely because one of the best known of the Neo-Confucian teachers, Cheng Yi, once told a follower that it would be better for a widow to die of starvation than to lose her virtue by remarrying. In later centuries this saying was often quoted to justify pressuring widows, even very young ones, to stay with their husbands' families and not remarry. In Song times, however, widows frequently remarried.

It is true that foot binding began during the Song Dynasty, but it was not recommended by Neo-Confucian teachers; rather it was associated with the pleasure quarters and with women's efforts to beautify themselves. Mothers bound the feet of girls aged five to eight with long strips of cloth to keep them from growing and to bend the four smaller toes under to make the foot narrow and arched. The hope was that the girl would be judged more beautiful. Foot binding spread gradually during Song times but was probably still largely an elite practice. In later centuries it became extremely common in north and central China, eventually spreading to all classes. Women with bound feet were less mobile than women with natural feet, but only those who could afford servants bound their feet so tightly that walking was difficult.

China Under Mongol Rule

As discussed in Chapter 12, the Mongols conquered China in stages, gaining much of north China by 1215 and all of it by 1234, but not taking the south till the 1270s. The north suffered the most devastation. The non-Chinese rulers in the north, the

Jin Dynasty of the Jurchen—with 150,000 cavalry, mostly Jurchen, and more than 300,000 Chinese infantrymen—thought they had the strongest army known to history. Yet Mongol tactics frustrated them. The Mongols would take a city, plunder it, and then withdraw, letting the Jin take it back and deal with the resulting food shortages and destruction. Under these circumstances, Jurchen power rapidly collapsed.

Not until Khubilai was Great Khan was the Song Dynasty defeated and south China brought under the control of the Mongols' Yuan Dynasty. Non-Chinese rulers had gained control of north China several times in Chinese history, but none of them had been able to secure control of the region south of the Yangzi River, which required a navy. By the 1260s Khubilai had put Chinese shipbuilders to work building a fleet, crucial to his victory over the Song (see page 337).

Life in China under the Mongols was much like life in China under earlier alien rulers. Once order was restored, people did their best to get on with their lives. Some were deprived of their land, business, or freedom and suffered real hardship. Yet people still spoke Chinese, followed Chinese customary practices in dividing their family property, made offerings at local temples, and celebrated the new year and other customary festivals. Teachers still taught students the classics, scholars continued to write books, and books continued to be printed.

The Mongols, like other foreign rulers before them, did not see anything particularly desirable in the social mobility of Chinese society. Preferring stability, they assigned people hereditary occupations such as farmer, Confucian scholar, physician, astrologer, soldier, artisan, salt producer, miner, and Buddhist monk; the occupations came with obligations to the state. Besides these occupational categories, the Mongols classified the population into four grades, with the Mongols occupying the top grade. Next came various non-Chinese, such as the Uighurs and Persians. Below them were Chinese former subjects of the Jurchen, called the Han. At the bottom were the former subjects of the Song, called southerners.

The reason for codifying ethnic differences this way was to preserve the Mongols' privileges as conquerors. Chinese were not allowed to take Mongol names, and great efforts were made to keep them from passing as Mongols or marrying Mongols. To keep Chinese from rebelling, they were forbidden to own weapons or congregate in public. Khubilai even prohibited Chinese from dealing in bamboo because it could be used to make bows and arrows.

As the Mongols captured Chinese territory, they recruited Chinese into their armies and government. Although some refused to serve the Mongols, others argued that the Chinese would fare better if Chinese were the administrators and could shield Chinese society from the most brutal effects of Mongol rule. A few Confucian scholars devoted themselves to the task of patiently teaching Mongol rulers the principles of Confucian government.

Nevertheless, government service, which had long been central to the identity and income of the educated elite in China, was not as widely available under the Mongols. The Mongols reinstituted the civil service examinations in 1315, but filled only about 2 percent of the positions in the bureaucracy through them and reserved half of those places for Mongols.

The scholar-official elite without government employment turned to alternative ways to support themselves. Those who did not have land to live off of found work

Blue-and-White Jars of the Yuan Period Chinese ceramics had long been in demand outside of China, and an innovation of the Mongol period—decorating white porcelain with underglaze designs in blue—proved especially popular. Persia imported large quantities of Chinese blue-and-white ceramics, and Korean, Japanese, and Vietnamese potters took up versions of the style themselves. (© The Trustees of the British Museum/Art Resource, NY)

as physicians, fortune-tellers, children's teachers, Daoist priests, publishers, booksellers, or playwrights. Many took leadership roles at the local level, such as founding academies for Confucian learning or promoting local charitable ventures. Through such activities, scholars without government offices could assert the importance of civil over military values and see themselves as trustees of the Confucian tradition.

Since the Mongols wanted to extract wealth from China, they had every incentive to develop the economy. They encouraged trade both within China and beyond its borders and tried to keep paper money in circulation. They repaired the Grand Canal, which had been ruined during their initial conquest of north China. Chinese industries with strong foreign markets, such as porcelain, thrived. Nevertheless, the economic expansion of late Tang and Song times did not continue under the alien rule of the Jurchens and Mongols. The economy of north China, with its strong iron industry, contracted under the Jurchens, and the destruction of cities was extensive during the first five decades of Mongol rule of the north.

The Mongols' Yuan Dynasty began a rapid decline in the 1330s as disease, rebellions, and poor leadership led to disorder throughout the country. When a Chinese strongman succeeded in consolidating the south, the Mongol rulers retreated to Mongolia before he could take Beijing. By 1368 the Yuan Dynasty had given way to a new Chinese-led dynasty: the Ming.

Korea Under the Koryŏ Dynasty, 935–1392

How did Korean society and culture develop in an age when its northern neighbors were Khitans, Jurchens, and Mongols?

During the Silla period, Korea was strongly tied to Tang China and avidly copied China's model (see page 194). This changed along with much else in North Asia between 800 and 1400. In this period Korea lived more in the shadows of the powerful states of the Khitans, Jurchens, and Mongols than of the Chinese.

The Silla Dynasty began to decline after the king was killed in a revolt in 780. For the next 155 years the kings were selected from several collateral lines, and the majority of them met violent deaths. Rebellions and coups d'état followed one after the other, as different groups of nobles placed their candidates on the throne and killed as many of their opponents as they could. As conditions deteriorated, serfs absconded in large numbers, and independent merchants and seamen of humble origins came to dominate the three-way trade between China, Korea, and Japan.

The dynasty that emerged from this confusion was called Koryŏ (KAW-ree-oh) (935–1392). (The English word *Korea* derives from the name of this dynasty.) During this time Korea developed more independently of the China model than it had in Silla times, just as contemporary Japan was doing (see the next section). This was not because the Chinese model was rejected; the Koryŏ capital was laid out on the Chinese model, and the government was closely patterned on the Tang system. But despite Chinese influence, Korean society remained deeply aristocratic.

The founder of the dynasty, Wang Kon (877–943), was a man of relatively obscure maritime background, and he needed the support of the old aristocracy to maintain control. His successors introduced civil service examinations on the Chinese model, as well as examinations for Buddhist clergy, but because the aristocrats were the best educated and the government schools admitted only the sons of aristocrats, this system served primarily to solidify their control. Politics was largely the competition among aristocratic clans for influence at court and marriage of their daughters to the royal princes. Like the Heian aristocrats in Japan (see pages 377–379), the Koryŏ aristocrats wanted to stay in the capital and only reluctantly accepted posts in the provinces.

At the other end of the social scale, the number of people in the serf-slave stratum seems to have increased. This lowborn stratum included not only privately held slaves but also large numbers of government slaves as well as government workers in mines, porcelain factories, and other government industries. Sometimes entire villages or groups of villages were considered lowborn. There were occasional slave revolts, and some freed slaves did rise in status, but prejudice against anyone with slave ancestors was so strong that the law provided that "only if there is no evidence of lowborn status for eight generations in one's official household registration may one receive a position in the government."[3] In China and Japan, by contrast, slavery was a much more minor element in the social landscape.

The commercial economy declined in Korea during this period, showing that it was not closely linked to China's then-booming economy. Except for the capital, there were no cities of commercial importance, and in the countryside the use of money declined. One industry that did flourish was ceramics. Connoisseurs have long appreciated the elegance of the pale green Koryŏ celadon pottery, decorated with designs executed in inlaid white or gray clay.

Buddhism remained strong throughout Korea, and monasteries became major centers of art and learning. As in Song China and Kamakura Japan, Chan (Zen) and Tiantai (Tendai) were the leading Buddhist teachings (see pages 191, 382). The founder of the Koryŏ Dynasty attributed the dynasty's success to the Buddha's protection, and he and his successors were ardent patrons of the church. The entire Buddhist canon was printed in the eleventh century and again in the thirteenth. (The 81,258 individual woodblocks used to print it still survive in a Korean Buddhist monastery.) As in medieval Europe, aristocrats who entered the church occupied the major abbacies. Monasteries played the same roles as they did in China and Japan, such as engaging in money-lending and charitable works. As in Japan (but not China), some monasteries accumulated military power.

Not all cultural advances were connected to monasteries or Buddhism. The most important literary work of the Koryŏ period is *The History of the Three Kingdoms*, compiled in 1145 in Chinese. Modeled on Chinese histories, it is the best source of information on early Korean history.

The Koryŏ Dynasty was preserved in name long after the ruling family had lost most of its power. In 1170 the palace guards massacred the civil officials at court and placed a new king on the throne. The coup leaders scrapped the privileges that had kept the aristocrats in power and appointed themselves to the top posts. After incessant infighting among the generals and a series of coups, in 1196 the general Ch'oe Ch'ung-hon took control. Ch'oe had a private army of about three thousand warrior-retainers and an even larger number of slaves. The domination of Korea by the Ch'oe family was much like the contemporaneous situation in Japan, where warrior bands were seizing power. Moreover, because the Ch'oes were content to dominate the government while leaving the Koryŏ king on the throne, they had much in common with the Japanese shoguns, who followed a similar strategy.

Although Korea adopted many ideas from China, it could not so easily adopt the Chinese assumption that it was the largest, most powerful, and most advanced society in the world. Korea, from early times, recognized China as being in many ways senior to it, but when strong non-Chinese states emerged to its north in Manchuria, Korea was ready to accommodate them as well. Koryŏ's first neighbor to the north was the Khitan state of Liao, which in 1010 invaded and sacked the capital. To avoid destruction, Koryŏ acceded to vassal status, but Liao invaded again in 1018. This time Koryŏ was able to repel the nomadic Khitans. Afterward a defensive wall was built across the Korean peninsula south of the Yalu River. When the Jurchens and their Jin Dynasty supplanted the Khitans' Liao Dynasty, Koryŏ agreed to send them tribute as well.

As mentioned in Chapter 12, Korea was conquered by the Mongols, and the figurehead Koryŏ kings were moved to Beijing, where they married Mongol princesses, their descendants becoming more Mongol than Korean. This was a time of hardship for the Korean people. In the year 1254 alone, the Mongols enslaved two hundred thousand Koreans and took them away. Ordinary people in Korea suffered grievously when their land was used as a launching pad for the huge Mongol invasions of Japan: nine hundred ships and the provisions for the soldiers on them had to be procured from the Korean countryside. In this period Korea also suffered from frequent attacks by Japanese pirates, somewhat like the depredations of the Vikings in Europe a little earlier (see page 391). The Mongol overlords did little to provide protection, and the harried coastal people had little choice but to retreat inland.

When Mongol rule in China fell apart in the mid-fourteenth century, it declined in Korea as well. Chinese rebels opposing the Mongols entered Korea and even briefly captured the capital in 1361. When the Ming Dynasty was established in China in 1368, the Koryŏ court was unsure how to respond. In 1388 a general, Yi Song-gye, was sent to oppose a Ming army at the northwest frontier. When he saw the strength of the Ming, he concluded that making an alliance was more sensible than fighting, and he led his troops back to the capital, where in 1392 he usurped the throne, founding the Chosŏn Dynasty.

Japan's Heian Period, 794–1185

How did the Heian form of government contribute to the cultural flowering of Japan in this period?

As described in Chapter 7, during the seventh and eighth centuries the Japanese ruling house pursued a vigorous policy of adopting useful ideas, techniques, and policies from the more advanced civilization of China. The rulers built a splendid capital along Chinese lines in Nara and fostered the growth of Buddhism. Monasteries grew so powerful in Nara, however, that in less than a century the court decided to move away from them and encourage other sects of Buddhism.

The new capital was built about twenty-five miles away at Heian (HAY-ahn; modern Kyoto). Like Nara, Heian was modeled on the Tang capital of Chang'an (although neither of the Japanese capitals had walls, a major feature of Chinese cities). For the first century at Heian the government continued to follow Chinese models, but it turned away from them with the decline of the Tang Dynasty in the late ninth century. The last official embassy to China made the trip in 894. During the Heian period (794–1185), Japan witnessed a literary and cultural flowering under the rule of the Fujiwara family.

Fujiwara Rule

Only the first two Heian emperors were much involved in governing. By 860 political management had been taken over by a series of regents from the Fujiwara family, who supplied most of the empresses in this period. The emperors continued to be honored, even venerated, because of their presumed divine descent, but the Fujiwaras ruled. Fujiwara dominance represented the privatization of political power and a return to clan politics. Political history thus took a very different course in Japan than in China, where, when a dynasty weakened, military strongmen would compete to depose the emperor and found their own dynasties. In Japan for the next thousand years, political contenders sought to manipulate the emperors rather than supplant them.

The Fujiwaras reached the apogee of their glory under Fujiwara Michinaga (r. 995–1027). Like many aristocrats of the period, he was learned in Buddhism, music, poetry, and Chinese literature and history. He dominated the court for more than thirty years as the father of four empresses, the uncle of two emperors, and the grandfather of three emperors. He acquired great landholdings and built fine palaces for himself and his family. After ensuring that his sons could continue to rule, he retired to a Buddhist monastery, all the while continuing to maintain control.

By the end of the eleventh century several emperors who did not have Fujiwara mothers had found a device to counter Fujiwara control: they abdicated but continued to exercise power by controlling their young sons on the throne. This system of rule has been called cloistered government because the retired emperors took Buddhist orders, while maintaining control of the government from behind the scenes. Thus for a time the imperial house was a contender for political power along with other aristocratic groups.

Aristocratic Culture

A brilliant aristocratic culture developed in the Heian period. In the capital at Heian, nobles, palace ladies, and imperial family members lived a highly refined and leisured life. In their society, niceties of birth, rank, and breeding counted for everything. From their diaries we know of the pains aristocratic women took in their dress, selecting the color combinations of the kimonos they wore, layer upon layer. The elegance of one's calligraphy and the allusions in one's poems were matters of intense concern to both men and women at court. Courtiers did not like to leave the capital, and some like the court lady Sei Shonagon shuddered at the sight of ordinary working people. In her *Pillow Book*, she wrote of encountering a group of commoners on a pilgrimage: "They looked like so many basket-worms as they crowded together in their hideous clothes, leaving hardly an inch of space between themselves and me. I really felt like pushing them all over sideways."[4]

In this period a new script was developed for writing Japanese phonetically. Each symbol was based on a simplified Chinese character and represented one of the syllables used in Japanese (such as *ka, ki, ku, ke, ko*). Although "serious" essays, histories, and government documents continued to be written in Chinese, less formal works such as poetry and memoirs were written in Japanese. Mastering the new writing system took much less time than mastering writing in Chinese and aided the spread of literacy, especially among women in court society.

In the Heian period, women played important roles at all levels of society. Women educated in the arts and letters could advance at court as attendants to the ruler's empress and other consorts. Women could inherit property from their parents, and they would compete with their brothers for shares of the family property. In political life, marrying a daughter to an emperor or shogun (see page 380) was one of the best ways to gain power, and women often became major players in power struggles.

The literary masterpiece of this period is **The Tale of Genji**, written in Japanese by Lady Murasaki over several years (ca. 1000–1010). This long narrative depicts a cast of characters enmeshed in court life, with close attention to dialogue and personality. Murasaki also wrote a diary that is similarly revealing of aristocratic culture. In one passage she tells of an occasion when word got out that she had read the Chinese classics:

> Worried what people would think if they heard such rumors, I pretended to be unable to read even the inscriptions on the screens. Then Her Majesty asked me to read to her here and there from the collected works of [the Tang Chinese poet] Bo Juyi, and, because she evinced a desire to know much more about such things, we carefully chose a time when other women would not be present and, amateur that I was, I read with her the two books of Bo Juyi's New Ballads in secret; we started the summer before last.[5]

Despite the reluctance of Murasaki and the lady she served to let others know of their learning, there were, in fact, quite a few women writers in this period. The wife of a high-ranking court official wrote a poetic memoir of her unhappy twenty-year marriage to him and his rare visits. A woman wrote both an autobiography that related her father's efforts to find favor at court and a love story of a hero who travels to China. Another woman even wrote a history that concludes with a triumphal biography of Fujiwara Michinaga.

The Tale of Genji   In this scene from a twelfth-century painting illustrating *The Tale of Genji*, Genji has his inkstone and brushes ready to respond to the letter he is reading. (Tokugawa Reimeikai Foundation, Tokyo, Japan/Photo © AISA/The Bridgeman Art Library)

    Buddhism remained very strong throughout the Heian period. A mission sent to China in 804 included two monks in search of new texts. One of the monks, Saichō, spent time at the monasteries on Mount Tiantai and brought back the Buddhist teachings associated with that mountain (called Tendai in Japanese). Tendai's basic message is that all living beings share the Buddha nature and can be brought to salvation. Tendai practices include strict monastic discipline, prayer, textual study, and meditation. Once back in Japan, Saichō established a monastery on Mount Hiei outside Kyoto, which grew to be one of the most important monasteries in Japan. By the twelfth century this monastery and its many branch temples had vast lands and a powerful army of monk-soldiers to protect its interests. Whenever the monastery felt that its interests were at risk, it sent the monk-soldiers into the capital to parade its sacred symbols in an attempt to intimidate the civil authorities.

    Kūkai, the other monk on the 804 mission to China, came back with texts from another school of Buddhism — Shingon, "True Word," a form of **Esoteric Buddhism**. Esoteric Buddhism is based on the idea that teachings containing the secrets of enlightenment had been secretly transmitted from the Buddha. People can gain access to these mysteries through initiation into the mandalas (cosmic diagrams), mudras (gestures), and mantras (verbal formulas). On his return to Japan, Kūkai attracted many followers and was allowed to establish a monastery at Mount Kōya, south of Osaka. The popularity of Esoteric Buddhism was a great stimulus to Buddhist art.

The Samurai and the Kamakura Shogunate, 1185–1333

What were the causes and consequences of military rule in Japan?

The gradual rise of a warrior elite over the course of the Heian period finally brought an end to the domination of the Fujiwaras and other Heian aristocratic families. In 1156 civil war broke out between the Taira and Minamoto warrior clans based in western and eastern Japan, respectively. Both clans relied on skilled warriors, later called samurai, who were rapidly becoming a new social class. A samurai and his lord had a double bond: in return for the samurai's loyalty and service, the lord granted him land or income. From 1159 to 1181 a Taira named Kiyomori dominated the court, taking the position of prime minister and marrying his daughter to the emperor. His relatives became governors of more than thirty provinces, managed some five hundred tax-exempt estates, and amassed a fortune in the trade with Song China and Koryŏ Korea. Still, the Minamoto clan managed to defeat the Taira, and the Minamoto leader, Yoritomo, became **shogun**, or general-in-chief. With him began the Kamakura Shogunate (1185–1333). This period is often referred to as Japan's feudal period because it was dominated by a military class whose members were tied to their superiors by bonds of loyalty and supported by landed estates rather than salaries.

Military Rule

The similarities between military rule in Japan and feudalism in medieval Europe during roughly the same period have fascinated scholars, as have the very significant differences. In Europe feudalism emerged out of the fusion of Germanic and Roman social institutions and flowered under the impact of Muslim and Viking invasions. In Japan military rule evolved from a combination of the native warrior tradition and Confucian ethical principles of duty to superiors.

The emergence of the samurai was made possible by the development of private landholding. The government land allotment system, copied from Tang China, began breaking down in the eighth century (much as it did in China). By the ninth century local lords had begun escaping imperial taxes and control by commending (formally giving) their land to tax-exempt entities such as monasteries, the imperial family, and high-ranking officials. The local lord then received his land back as a tenant and paid his protector a small rent. The monastery or privileged individual received a steady income from the land, and the local lord escaped imperial taxes and control. By the end of the thirteenth century most land seems to have been taken off the tax rolls this way. Each plot of land could thus have several people with rights to shares of its produce, ranging from the cultivator, to a local lord, to an estate manager working for him, to a regional strongman, to a noble or temple in the capital. Unlike peasants in medieval Europe, where similar practices of commendation occurred, those working the land in Japan never became serfs. Moreover, Japanese lords rarely lived on the lands they had rights in, unlike English or French lords who lived on their manors.

Samurai resembled European knights in several ways. Both were armed with expensive weapons, and both fought on horseback. Just as the knight was supposed to live according to the chivalric code, so Japanese samurai were expected to live accord-

The Shogun Minamoto Yoritomo in Court Dress This wooden sculpture, 27.8 inches tall, was made about a half century after Yoritomo's death for use in a shrine dedicated to his memory. The bold shapes convey Yoritomo's dignity and power. (*Yoritomo [Minamotono-Yoritomo]*, wood with colored painting and quartz eyes, Kamakura Period, 1300/National Museum, Tokyo, Japan/akg-images)

ing to Bushido (or "way of the warrior"), a code that stressed military honor, courage, stoic acceptance of hardship, and, above all, loyalty. Physical hardship was accepted as routine, and soft living was despised as weak and unworthy. Disloyalty brought social disgrace, which the samurai could avoid only through *seppuku*, ritual suicide by slashing his belly.

The Kamakura Shogunate derives its name from Kamakura, a city near modern Tokyo that was the seat of the Minamoto clan. The founder, Yoritomo, ruled the country much the way he ran his own estates, appointing his retainers to newly created offices. To cope with the emergence of hard-to-tax estates, he put military land stewards in charge of seeing to the estates' proper operation. To bring order to the lawless countryside, he appointed military governors to oversee the military and enforce the law in the provinces. They supervised the conduct of the land stewards in peacetime and commanded the provincial samurai in war.

Yoritomo's wife, Masako, protected the interests of her own family, the Hōjōs, especially after Yoritomo died. She went so far as to force her first son to abdicate when he showed signs of preferring the family of his wife to the family of his mother. She later helped her brother take power away from her father. Thus the process of reducing power holders to figureheads went one step further in 1219 when the Hōjō family reduced the shogun to a figurehead. The Hōjō family held the reins of power for more than a century until 1333.

The Mongols' two massive seaborne invasions in 1274 and 1281 (see page 338) were a huge shock to the shogunate. The Kamakura government was hard-pressed to gather adequate resources for its defense. Temples were squeezed, farmers were taken away from their fields to build walls, and warriors were promised generous rewards in return for their service. Although the Hōjō regents, with the help of a "divine wind" (kamikaze), repelled the Mongols, they were unable to reward their vassals in the traditional way because little booty was found among the wreckage of the Mongol fleets. Discontent grew among the samurai, and by the fourteenth century the entire political system was breaking down. Both the imperial and the shogunate families were fighting among themselves. As land grants were divided, samurai became impoverished and took to plunder and piracy, or shifted their loyalty to local officials who could offer them a better living.

The factional disputes among Japan's leading families remained explosive until 1331, when the emperor Go-Daigo tried to recapture real power. His attempt sparked an uprising by the great families, local lords, samurai, and even Buddhist monasteries, which had thousands of samurai retainers. Go-Daigo destroyed the Kamakura Shogunate in 1333 but soon lost the loyalty of his followers. By 1338 one of his most important military supporters, Ashikaga Takauji, had turned on him and established the Ashikaga Shogunate, which lasted until 1573. Takauji's victory was also a victory for the samurai, who took over civil authority throughout Japan.

Cultural Trends

The cultural distance between the elites and the commoners narrowed a little during the Kamakura period. Buddhism was spread to ordinary Japanese by energetic preachers. Honen (1133–1212) propagated the Pure Land teaching, preaching that paradise could be reached through simple faith in the Buddha and repeating the name of the Buddha Amitabha. Neither philosophical understanding of Buddhist scriptures nor devotion to rituals was essential. His follower Shinran (1173–1263) taught that monks should not shut themselves off in monasteries but should marry and have children. A different path was promoted by Nichiren (1222–1282), a fiery and intolerant preacher who proclaimed that to be saved people had only to invoke sincerely the Lotus Sutra, one of the most important of the Buddhist sutras. These lay versions of Buddhism found a receptive audience among ordinary people in the countryside.

It was also during the Kamakura period that **Zen** came to flourish in Japan. Zen teachings originated in Tang China, where they were known as Chan (see page 191). Rejecting the authority of the sutras, Zen teachers claimed the superiority of mind-to-mind transmission of Buddhist truth. When Japanese monks went to China in the twelfth century looking for ways to revitalize Japanese Buddhism, they were impressed by the rigorous monastic life of the Chan/Zen monasteries. One school of Zen held that enlightenment could be achieved suddenly through insight into one's own true nature. This school taught rigorous meditation and the use of kōan riddles to unseat logic and free the mind for enlightenment. This teaching found eager patrons among the samurai, who were attracted to its discipline and strong master-disciple bonds.

Buddhism remained central to the visual arts. Many temples in Japan still house fine sculptures done in this period. In painting, narrative hand scrolls brought to life the miracles that faith could bring and the torments of Hell awaiting unbelievers. All forms of literature were depicted in these scrolls, including *The Tale of Genji*, war stories, and humorous anecdotes.

During the Kamakura period, war tales continued the tradition of long narrative prose works. *The Tale of the Heike* tells the story of the fall of the Taira family and the rise of the Minamoto clan. The tale reached a large and mostly illiterate audience because blind minstrels would chant sections to the accompaniment of a lute. The story is suffused with the Buddhist idea of the transience of life and the illusory nature of glory. Yet it also celebrates strength, courage, loyalty, and pride. The Minamoto warriors from the east are portrayed as the toughest. In one scene one of them dismisses his own prowess with the bow, claiming that other warriors from his region could pierce three sets of armor with their arrows. He then brags about the martial spirit of warriors from the east: "They are bold horsemen who never fall, nor do they let their horses stumble on the roughest road. When they fight they do not care if even their parents or children are killed; they ride over their bodies and continue the battle."[6] In this they stood in contrast to the warriors of the west, who in good Confucian fashion would retire from battle to mourn their parents.

After stagnating in the Heian period, agricultural productivity began to improve in the Kamakura period, and the population grew, reaching perhaps 8.2 million by 1333. Much like farmers in contemporary Song China, Japanese farmers adopted new strains of rice, often double-cropped in warmer regions, made increased use of fertilizers, and improved irrigation for paddy rice. Besides farming, ordinary people made their livings as artisans, traders, fishermen, and entertainers. Although trade in human beings was banned, those who fell into debt might sell themselves or their children, and professional slave traders kidnapped women and children. A vague category of outcastes occupied the fringes of society, in a manner reminiscent of India. Buddhist strictures against killing and Shinto ideas of pollution probably account for the exclusion of butchers, leatherworkers, morticians, and lepers, but other groups, such as bamboo whisk makers, were also traditionally excluded for no obvious reason.

Chapter Summary

The countries of East Asia—China, Japan, and Korea—all underwent major changes in the six centuries from 800 to 1400. In China the loosening of the central government's control of the economy stimulated trade and economic growth. Between 800 and 1100 China's population doubled to 100 million, reflecting in part the spread of wet-field rice cultivation, especially in the south. The economic center of China shifted from the north China plain to the south, the milder region drained by the Yangzi River.

In the Song period, the booming economy and the invention of printing allowed for expansion of the scholar-official class, which came to dominate government and society. Men who aspired to this life spent a decade or more studying for the highly competitive civil service examinations. Many educated men pursued interests in literature, antiquities, philosophy, and art. Repeatedly, the Song government chose to pay tribute to its militarily powerful neighbors—first the Khitans, then the Jurchens, then the Mongols—to keep the peace. Eventually, however, Song fell to the Mongols. The Mongols instituted hereditary occupations, ending much of the social mobility that characterized the Song Dynasty.

During the Koryŏ Dynasty, Korea evolved more independently of China than it had previously, in part because it had to placate powerful non-Chinese neighbors. The commercial economy declined, and an increasing portion of the population was unfree, working as slaves for aristocrats or the government. Military strongmen dominated the government, but their armies were no match for the much larger empires to their north. The period of Mongol domination was particularly difficult.

In Heian Japan, a tiny aristocracy dominated government and society. A series of regents, most of them from the Fujiwara family and fathers-in-law of the emperors, controlled political life. The aristocratic court society put great emphasis on taste and refinement. Women were influential at the court and wrote much of the best literature of the period. The Heian aristocrats had little interest in life in the provinces, which gradually came under the control of military clans.

After a civil war between the two leading military clans, a military government, called the shogunate, was established. The Kamakura Shogunate was dominated by a military class of samurais, who were bound to their lord by loyalty and service in return for land and income. Emperors had little power. Two invasions by the Mongols caused major crises in military control. Although both times the invaders were repelled, defense costs were high. During this period culture was less centered around the capital, and Buddhism spread to ordinary people.

Notes

1. *The Travels of Marco Polo, the Venetian*, ed. Manuel Komroff (New York: Boni and Liveright, 1926), p. 227.
2. Ibid., p. 235.
3. Peter H. Lee, ed., *Sourcebook of Korean Civilization* (New York: Columbia University Press, 1993), p. 327.
4. *The Pillow Book of Sei Shonagon*, edited and translated by Ivan Morris, p. 258. © Ivan Morris 1967. Copyright © 1991 Columbia University Press. Reprinted by permission of Columbia University Press and Oxford University Press.
5. Quoted in M. Collcott, M. Jansen, and I. Kumakura, *Cultural Atlas of Japan* (New York: Facts on File, 1988), p. 82, slightly modified.
6. Ibid., p. 101.

CONNECTIONS

East Asia faced many internal and external challenges between 800 and 1400, and the ways societies responded to them shaped their subsequent histories. In China the first four centuries of this period saw economic growth, urbanization, the spread of printing, and the expansion of the educated class. In Korea and Japan aristocratic dominance and military rule were more typical of the era. All three areas, but especially China and Korea, faced an unprecedented challenge from the Mongols, with Japan less vulnerable because it did not share a land border. The challenges of the period did not hinder creativity in the literary and visual arts; among the greatest achievements of this era are the women's writings of Heian Japan, such as *The Tale of Genji*, and landscape painting of both Song and Yuan China.

Europe during these six centuries, the subject of the next chapter, also faced invasions from outside; in its case, the pagan Vikings were especially dreaded. Europe had a social structure more like that of Korea and Japan than of China, with less centralization and a more dominant place in society for military men. The centralized church in Europe, however, was unlike anything known in East Asian history. These centuries in Europe saw a major expansion of Christendom, especially to Scandinavia and eastern Europe, through both conversion and migration. Although there were scares that the Mongols would penetrate deeper into Europe, the greatest challenge in Europe was the Black Death and the huge loss of life that it caused.

Chapter Review

MAKE IT STICK

 LearningCurve
Go online and use LearningCurve to retain what you've read.

IDENTIFY KEY TERMS

Identify and explain the significance of each item below.

dynastic cycle (p. 362)

compass (p. 363)

scholar-official class (p. 367)

examination system (p. 367)

movable type (p. 367)

Neo-Confucianism (p. 370)

concubine (p. 372)

foot binding (p. 372)

cloistered government (p. 377)

The Tale of Genji (p. 378)

Esoteric Buddhism (p. 379)

shogun (p. 380)

Bushido (p. 381)

Zen (p. 382)

REVIEW THE MAIN IDEAS

Answer the focus questions from each section of the chapter.

1. What made possible the expansion of the Chinese economy, and what were the outcomes of this economic growth? (p. 362)

2. How did the civil service examinations and the scholar-official class shape Chinese society and culture, and what impact did the Mongol conquest have on them? (p. 365)

3. How did Korean society and culture develop in an age when its northern neighbors were Khitans, Jurchens, and Mongols? (p. 374)

4. How did the Heian form of government contribute to the cultural flowering of Japan in this period? (p. 377)

5. What were the causes and consequences of military rule in Japan? (p. 380)

MAKE CONNECTIONS

Analyze the larger developments and continuities within and across chapters.

1. What elements in women's lives in Song China were common in other parts of the world as well? What elements were more distinctive?

2. How did the impact of Mongol rule on China compare to its impact on Muslim lands?

3. How did being an island country affect Japan's history? What other island countries make good comparisons?

⏻LaunchPad

ONLINE DOCUMENT PROJECT

Song Artwork
What cultural pursuits interested the scholar-official class?

View images from the Song period, and then complete a quiz and writing assignment based on the evidence and details from this chapter.

See inside the front cover to learn more.

CHRONOLOGY

794–1185	• Heian period in Japan
804	• Two Japanese Buddhist monks, Saichō and Kūkai, travel to China
935–1392	• Koryŏ Dynasty in Korea
960–1279	• Song Dynasty in China; emergence of scholar-official class; invention of movable type
995–1027	• Fujiwara Michinaga dominant at Heian court
ca. 1000–1010	• *The Tale of Genji*
1119	• First reported use of compass
1120s	• First government-issued paper money introduced by Song
1126	• Song loss of north China to the Jurchens; Song capital relocated to Hangzhou
1130–1200	• Zhu Xi, Neo-Confucian philosopher
1185–1333	• Kamakura Shogunate in Japan; Zen Buddhism flourishes
1234–1368	• Mongols' Yuan Dynasty in China
ca. 1275–1292	• Marco Polo travels in China

✓ LearningCurve
After reading the chapter, go online
and use LearningCurve to retain what
you've read.

Europe in the Middle Ages

800–1450

BY THE FIFTEENTH CENTURY SCHOLARS IN THE GROWING CITIES OF
northern Italy had begun to think that they were living in a new era, one in
which the glories of ancient Greece and Rome were being reborn. What separated their time from classical antiquity, in their opinion, was a long period
of darkness and barbarism, to which a seventeenth-century professor gave
the name "Middle Ages." In this conceptualization, the history of Europe was
divided into three periods—ancient, medieval, and modern—an organization
that is still in use today. Later, the history of other parts of the world was
sometimes fit into this three-period schema as well, with discussions of the
"classical" period in Maya history, of "medieval" India and China, and of
"modern" everywhere.

Today historians often question whether labels of past time periods for
one culture work on a global scale, and some scholars are uncertain about
whether "Middle Ages" is a just term even for European history. They assert
that the Middle Ages was not simply a period of stagnation between two
high points but rather a time of enormous intellectual energy and creative
vitality. While agrarian life continued to dominate Europe, political structures
that would influence later European history began to form, and Christianity
continued to spread. People at the time did not know that they were living
in an era that would later be labeled "middle" or sometimes even "dark,"
and we can wonder whether they would have shared this negative view
of their own times.

Political Developments

How did medieval rulers restore order and centralize political power?

Later scholars dated the beginning of the Middle Ages to the fifth century, the time of the fall of the Roman Empire in the West. However, the growth of Germanic kingdoms such as those of the Merovingians and the Carolingians (see Chapter 8) is generally viewed as the beginning of "medieval" politics in Europe, and that is why we begin this chapter with the ninth century. In 800 Charlemagne, the most powerful of the Carolingians, was crowned Holy Roman emperor. After his death his empire was divided among his grandsons, and their kingdoms were weakened by nobles vying for power. In addition, beginning around 800 western Europe was invaded by several different groups. Local nobles were the strongest power, and common people turned to them for protection. By the eleventh century, however, rulers in some parts of Europe had reasserted authority and were slowly building centralized states.

Invasions and Migrations

From the moors of Scotland to the mountains of Sicily, there arose in the ninth century the prayer "Save us, O God, from the violence of the Northmen." The feared Northmen were pagan Germanic peoples from Norway, Sweden, and Denmark who came to be known as Vikings. They began to make overseas expeditions, which they themselves called *vikings*, and the word came to be used for people who went on such voyages as well.

Viking assaults began around 800, and by the mid-tenth century the Vikings had brought large sections of continental Europe and Britain under their sway. In the east they sailed the rivers of Russia as far as the Black Sea. In the west they established permanent settlements in Iceland and short-lived ones in Greenland and Newfoundland in Canada (Map 14.1).

The Vikings were superb seamen with advanced methods of boatbuilding. Propelled either by oars or by sails, deckless, and about sixty-five feet long, a Viking ship could carry between forty and sixty men — enough to harass an isolated monastery or village. Against these ships navigated by experienced and fearless sailors, the Carolingian Empire, with no navy, was helpless. At first the Vikings attacked and sailed off laden with booty. Later, on returning, they settled down and colonized the areas they had conquered, often marrying local women and adopting the local languages and some of the customs.

Along with the Vikings, groups of central European steppe peoples known as Magyars (MAG-yahrz) also raided villages in the late ninth century, taking plunder and captives and forcing leaders to pay tribute in an effort to prevent further destruction. Moving westward, small bands of Magyars on horseback reached far into Europe. They subdued northern Italy, compelled Bavaria and Saxony to pay tribute, and penetrated into the Rhineland and Burgundy. Western Europeans thought of them as returning Huns, so the Magyars came to be known as Hungarians. They settled in the area that is now Hungary, became Christian, and in the eleventh century allied with the papacy.

From North Africa, the Muslims also began new encroachments in the ninth century. They already ruled most of Spain and now conquered Sicily, driving northward into central Italy and the south coast of France.

MAP 14.1 **Invasions and Migrations of the Ninth and Tenth Centuries** This map shows the Viking, Magyar, and Muslim invasions and migrations in the ninth and tenth centuries. Compare it with Map 8.2 (page 218) on the barbarian migrations of late antiquity.

From the perspective of those living in what had been Charlemagne's empire, Viking, Magyar, and Muslim attacks contributed to increasing disorder and violence. Italian, French, and English sources often describe this period as one of terror and chaos. People in other parts of Europe might have had a different opinion. In Muslim Spain and Sicily scholars worked in thriving cities, and new crops such as cotton and sugar enhanced ordinary people's lives. In eastern Europe states such as Moravia and Hungary became strong kingdoms. A Viking point of view might be the most positive, for by 1100 descendants of the Vikings not only ruled their homelands in Norway, Sweden, and Denmark but also ruled northern France (a province known as Normandy, or land of the Northmen), England, Sicily, Iceland, and Russia, with an outpost in Greenland and occasional voyages to North America.

"Feudalism" and Manorialism

The large-scale division of Charlemagne's empire into three parts in the ninth century led to a decentralization of power at the local level. Civil wars weakened the power and prestige of kings, who could do little about regional violence. Likewise, the invasions of the ninth century, especially those of the Vikings, weakened royal authority. The Frankish kings were unable to halt the invaders, and the local aristocracy had to assume responsibility for defense. Thus, in the ninth and tenth centuries, aristocratic families increased their authority in their local territories, and distant and weak kings could not interfere. Common people turned for protection to the strongest power, the local nobles.

The most powerful nobles were those who gained warriors' allegiance, often symbolized in an oath-swearing ceremony of homage and fealty that grew out of earlier Germanic oaths of loyalty. In this ceremony a warrior (knight) swore his loyalty as a **vassal**—from a Celtic term meaning "servant"—to the more powerful individual, who became his lord. In return for the vassal's loyalty, aid, and military assistance, the lord promised him protection and material support. This support might be a place in the lord's household but was more likely land of the vassal's own, called a **fief** (*feudum* in Latin). The fief, which might contain forests, churches, and towns, technically still belonged to the lord, and the vassal had only the use of it. Peasants living on a fief produced the food and other goods necessary to maintain the knight. Most legal scholars and historians have identified these personal ties of loyalty cemented by grants of land rather than allegiance to an abstract state as a political and social system they term **feudalism**. In the last several decades, however, increasing numbers of medieval historians have found the idea of "feudalism" problematic, because the word was a later invention and the system was so varied and changed over time. They still point to the personal relationship between lords and vassals as the key way political authority was organized and note that the church also received and granted land.

The economic power of the warrior class rested on landed estates, which were worked by peasants under a system of **manorialism**. Free farmers surrendered themselves and their land to the lord's jurisdiction in exchange for protection. The land was given back to them to farm, but they were tied to the land by various payments and services. Most significantly, a peasant lost his or her freedom and became a **serf**, part of the lord's permanent labor force. Unlike slaves, serfs were personally free, but they were bound to the land and unable to leave it without the lord's permission.

By the year 800 perhaps 60 percent of the population of western Europe had been reduced to serfdom. Over the next several centuries unstable conditions and insecurity further increased the need for protection, so that by around 1000 the majority of western Europeans were serfs. While serfs ranged from the highly prosperous to the desperately poor, all had lost their freedom. In eastern Europe the transition was slower but longer lasting. Western European peasants began to escape from serfdom in the later Middle Ages, at the very point that serfs were more firmly tied to the land in eastern Europe, especially in eastern Germany, Poland, and Russia.

The Restoration of Order

The eleventh century witnessed the beginnings of political stability in western Europe. Foreign invasions gradually declined, and in some parts of Europe lords in control of large territories built up their power even further, becoming kings over growing and slowly centralizing states. In a process similar to that occurring at the same time in the West African kingdom of Ghana (see pages 277–280), rulers expanded their territories and extended their authority by developing larger bureaucracies, armies, judicial systems, and other institutions to maintain control, as well as taxation systems to pay for them. These new institutions and practices laid the foundations for modern national states. Political developments in England, France, and Germany provide good examples of the beginnings of the national state in the central Middle Ages.

Throughout the ninth century the Vikings made a concerted effort to conquer and rule all of Anglo-Saxon England, and in the early eleventh century they succeeded. The Viking Canute (r. 1016–1035) made England the center of his empire, while promoting a policy of assimilation and reconciliation between Anglo-Saxons and Vikings. At the same time, England was divided into local shires, or counties, each under the jurisdiction of a sheriff appointed by the king. When Canute's heir Edward died childless, there were three claimants to the throne. One of these, Duke William of Normandy, crossed the Channel and won the English throne by defeating and killing his Anglo-Saxon rival, Harold II, at the Battle of Hastings in 1066. Later dubbed "the Conqueror," William (r. 1066–1087) limited the power of the nobles and church officials and built a unified monarchy. He retained the Anglo-Saxon institution of sheriff, but named Normans to the posts.

In 1085 William decided to conduct a systematic survey of the entire country to determine how much wealth there was and who had it. This process was described by a contemporary chronicler:

> He sent his men over all England into every shire and had them find out . . . what or how much everybody had who was occupying land in England, in land or cattle, and how much money it was worth. So very narrowly did he have it investigated, that there was no single . . . yard of land, nor indeed . . . one ox nor one cow nor one pig was there left out, and not put down in his record: and all these records were brought to him afterwards.[1]

The resulting record, called the *Domesday Book* (DOOMZ-day) from the Anglo-Saxon word *doom*, meaning "judgment," provided William and his descendants with vital information for governing the country. Completed in 1086, the book still survives, and it is an invaluable source of social and economic information about medieval England.

In 1128 William's granddaughter Matilda married a powerful French noble, Geoffrey of Anjou. Their son, who became Henry II of England, inherited provinces in northwestern France from his father. When Henry married the great heiress Eleanor of Aquitaine in 1152, he claimed lordship over Aquitaine and other provinces in southwestern France as well. The histories of England and France were thus closely intertwined in the Middle Ages.

In the early twelfth century France consisted of a number of nearly independent provinces, each governed by its local ruler. The work of unifying and enlarging France began under Philip II (r. 1180–1223), also known as Philip Augustus. By the end of his reign Philip was effectively master of northern France, and by 1300 most of the provinces of modern France had been added to the royal domain through diplomacy, marriage, war, and inheritance.

In central Europe the German king Otto I (r. 936–973) defeated many other lords to build up his power, based on an alliance with and control of the church. Otto asserted the right to control church appointments, and bishops and abbots had to perform feudal homage for the lands that accompanied their church positions. Under Otto I and his successors, a loose confederation stretching from the North Sea to the Mediterranean developed. In this confederation, later called the Holy Roman Empire, the emperor shared power with princes, dukes, counts, city officials, archbishops, and bishops.

Frederick Barbarossa (r. 1152–1190) of the house of Hohenstaufen tried valiantly to make the Holy Roman Empire a united state. He made alliances with the high nobles and even compelled the great churchmen to become his vassals. When he tried to enforce his authority over the cities of northern Italy, however, they formed a league against him in alliance with the pope, and infantrymen from the cities defeated Frederick's mounted knights. Frederick's absence from the German part of his empire allowed the princes and other rulers of independent provinces to consolidate their power there as well, and Germany did not become a unified state.

Law and Justice

Throughout Europe in the twelfth and thirteenth centuries, the law was a hodgepodge of customs, feudal rights, and provincial practices. Rulers wanted to blend these elements into a uniform system of rules acceptable and applicable to all their peoples, though their success in doing so varied.

The French king Louis IX (r. 1226–1270) was famous for his concern for justice. Each French province, even after being made part of the kingdom of France, retained its unique laws and procedures. But Louis IX created a royal judicial system, establishing the Parlement of Paris, a kind of supreme court that heard appeals from lower courts.

Under Henry II (r. 1154–1189), England developed and extended a common law—a law common to and accepted by the entire country, unique in medieval Europe. Henry's son John (r. 1199–1216), however, met with serious disappointment after taking the throne. He lost the French province of Normandy to Philip Augustus in 1204 and spent the rest of his reign trying to win it back. Saddled with heavy debt from his father and his brother Richard (r. 1189–1199), John tried to squeeze more money from nobles and town dwellers, creating an atmosphere of resentment. When John's military campaign failed in 1214, it was clear that the French lands that had once belonged to the English king were lost for good. A rebellion begun by northern barons grew, and in 1215 the barons forced him to attach his seal to the Magna Carta—the "Great Charter," which became the cornerstone of English justice and law.

The Magna Carta was simply meant to assert traditional rights enjoyed by certain groups, but in time it came to signify the broader principle that everyone, including the king and the government, must obey the law. Because later generations referred to the Magna Carta as a written statement of English liberties, it gradually came to have an almost sacred importance.

Statements of legal principles such as the Magna Carta were not how most people experienced the law in medieval Europe. Instead they were involved in actual cases. Judges determined guilt or innocence in a number of ways. In some cases, particularly those in which there was little clear evidence, they ordered a trial by ordeal, in which the accused might be tied hand and foot and dropped in a lake or river. People believed that water was a pure substance and would reject anything foul or unclean, although God could always affect the outcome. Thus a person who sank was considered innocent, while a person who floated was found guilty. Trials by ordeal were relatively rare, and courts increasingly favored more rational procedures, in which judges heard testimony, sought witnesses, and read written evidence if it was available. Violent crimes were often punished by public execution. Hanging was the most common method of execution, although nobles might be beheaded because hanging was seen as demeaning. Executioners were feared figures, but they were also well-paid public officials and were a necessary part of the legal structure.

The Christian Church

How did the Christian Church enhance its power and create new institutions and religious practices?

Kings and emperors were not the only rulers consolidating their power in the eleventh and twelfth centuries; the papacy did as well, although the popes' efforts were sometimes challenged by medieval kings and emperors. Despite such challenges, monasteries continued to be important places for learning and devotion, and new religious orders were founded. Christianity expanded into Europe's northern and eastern regions, and Christian rulers expanded their holdings in Muslim Spain.

Papal Reforms

During the ninth and tenth centuries the church came under the control of kings and feudal lords, who chose priests, bishops, abbots, and other church officials in their territories, granting them fiefs that provided an income and expecting loyalty and service in return. Church offices were sometimes sold outright—a practice called *simony*. Although the Roman Church encouraged clerical celibacy, many priests were married or living with women. Wealthy Roman families chose popes from among their members; thus popes paid more attention to their families' political fortunes or their own pleasures than to the church's institutional or spiritual health. Not surprisingly, clergy at all levels who had bought their positions or had been granted them for political reasons provided little spiritual guidance and were rarely models of high moral standards.

Serious efforts to reform the church began in the eleventh century. A series of popes believed that secular or lay control over the church was largely responsible for the lack of moral leadership, so they proclaimed the church independent from secular rulers. The Lateran Council of 1059 decreed that the authority and power to elect the pope rested solely in the college of cardinals, a special group of priests from the major churches in and around Rome. The college retains that power today.

Pope Gregory VII (pontificate 1073–1085) vigorously championed reform and the expansion of papal power. He ordered all priests to give up their wives and children or face dismissal, invalidated the ordination of church officials who had purchased their offices, and placed nuns under firmer control of male authorities. He believed that the pope, as the successor of Saint Peter, was the vicar of God on earth and that papal orders were the orders of God. He emphasized the political authority of the papacy, ordering that any church official selected or appointed by a layperson should be deposed, and any layperson, including rulers, who appointed a church official should be excommunicated — cut off from the sacraments and the Christian community.

European rulers immediately protested this restriction of their power, and the strongest reaction came from Henry IV, the ruler of Germany who later became the Holy Roman emperor. Henry continued to appoint officials, and Gregory responded by excommunicating bishops who supported Henry and threatening to depose him. In January 1077 Henry arrived at the pope's residence in Canossa in northern Italy and, according to a letter later sent by Gregory to his German allies, stood outside in the snow for three days seeking forgiveness. Gregory readmitted the emperor into the Christian community. Although Henry bowed before the pope, he actually won a victory, maintaining authority over his subjects and in 1084 being crowned emperor. This victory was temporary, however, for high nobles within the empire took advantage of further conflicts with the pope to enhance their position, siding with the church to gain power. They subordinated lesser nobles, expanded restrictions on peasants, and prevented later emperors such as Frederick Barbarossa from unifying the empire.

Monastic Life

Although they were in theory cut off from the world (see page 212), monasteries and convents were deeply affected by issues of money, rank, and power. By the eighth century monasteries and convents dotted the European landscape, and during the ninth and tenth centuries they were often the target of Viking attacks or raids by local looters seeking valuable objects. Some religious communities fled and dispersed, while others fell under the control and domination of local feudal lords. Powerful laymen appointed themselves or their relatives as abbots, took the lands and goods of monasteries, and spent monastic revenues.

Medieval monasteries also provided noble boys with education and opportunities for ecclesiastical careers. Although a few men who rose in the ranks of church officials were of humble origins, most were from high-status families. Social class also defined the kinds of religious life open to women. Kings and nobles usually established convents for their female relatives and other elite women, and the position of abbess, or head of a convent, became the most powerful position a woman could hold in medieval society. (See "Individuals in Society: Hildegard of Bingen," page 396.) People of lower social standing did live and work in monasteries, but as lay brothers and sisters who performed manual labor, not religious duties.

Routines within individual monasteries varied widely from house to house and from region to region. In every monastery, however, daily life centered on the liturgy or Divine Office, psalms, and other prayers, which monks and nuns said seven times a day and once during the night. Praying was looked on as a vital service, as crucial as the labor of peasants and the military might of nobles. Prayers were said for peace, rain, good harvests, the civil authorities, the monks' and nuns' families, and their benefactors. Monastic patrons in turn lavished gifts on the monasteries, which often became very wealthy, controlling large tracts of land and the peasants who farmed them.

The combination of lay control and wealth created problems for monasteries as monks and nuns concentrated on worldly issues and spiritual observance and intellectual activity declined. To counteract this problem, new religious orders, such as the Cistercians (sihs-TUHR-shuhnz), founded in 1098, established their houses in isolated areas, rejected the traditional feudal sources of income (such as the possession of mills and serfs), and lived very simply. Their innovative methods of farming, sheep raising, and cloth production brought financial success, however, and by the late twelfth century economic prosperity and political power had begun to compromise the original Cistercian ideals.

In the thirteenth century the growth of cities provided a new challenge for the church. Many urban people thought that the church did not meet their spiritual needs. They turned instead to heresies — that is, to versions of Christianity outside of those approved by the papacy, many of which called on the church to give up its wealth and power. Combating **heresy** became a principal task of new religious orders, most prominently the Dominicans and Franciscans, who preached and ministered to city dwellers; the Dominicans also staffed the papal Inquisition, a special court designed to root out heresy.

Popular Religion

Apart from the land, the weather, and local legal and social conditions, religion had the greatest impact on the daily lives of ordinary people in medieval Europe. Religious practices varied widely from country to country and even from province to province. But everywhere, religion permeated everyday life.

For Christians, the village church was the center of community life — social, political, and economic as well as religious — with the parish priest in charge of a host of activities. People gathered at the church for services on Sundays and holy days, breaking the painful routine of work. The feasts that accompanied baptisms, weddings, funerals, and other celebrations were commonly held in the churchyard. In everyday life people engaged in rituals and used

Statue of Saint Anne, the Virgin Mary, and the Christ Child   Nearly every church had at least one image of the Virgin Mary, the most important figure of Christian devotion in medieval Europe. In this thirteenth-century wooden sculpture, she is shown holding the infant Jesus, and is herself sitting on the lap of her mother, Anne. Statues such as this reinforced people's sense that the heavenly family was much like theirs, with grandparents who sometimes played important roles. (Museo Nazionale del Bargello, Florence, Italy/Scala/Art Resource, NY)

INDIVIDUALS IN SOCIETY • Hildegard of Bingen

The tenth child of a lesser noble family, Hildegard (1098–1179) was turned over to the care of an abbey in the Rhineland when she was eight years old. There she learned Latin and received a good education. She spent most of her life in various women's religious communities, two of which she founded herself. When she was a child, she began having mystical visions, often of light in the sky, but told few people about them. In middle age, however, her visions became more dramatic: "And it came to pass . . . when I was 42 years and 7 months old, that the heavens were opened and a blinding light of exceptional brilliance flowed through my entire brain. And so it kindled my whole heart and breast like a flame, not burning but warming . . . and suddenly I understood of the meaning of expositions of the books."* She wanted the church to approve of her visions and wrote first to Saint Bernard of Clairvaux, who answered her briefly and dismissively, and then to Pope Eugenius, who encouraged her to write them down. Her first work was *Scivias* (Know the Ways of the Lord), a record of her mystical visions that incorporates extensive theological learning.

Obviously possessed of leadership and administrative talents, Hildegard left her abbey in 1147 to found the convent of Rupertsberg near Bingen. There she produced *Physica* (On the Physical Elements) and *Causa et Curae* (Causes and Cures), scientific works on the curative properties of natural elements; poems; a religious play; and several more works of mysticism. She carried on a huge correspondence with scholars, prelates, and ordinary people. When she was over fifty, she left her community to preach to audiences of clergy and laity, and she was the only woman of her time whose opinions on religious matters were considered authoritative by the church.

*From *Scivias*, trans. Mother Columba Hart and Jane Bishop, *The Classics of Western Spirituality* (New York/Mahwah: Paulist Press, 1990).

language heavy with religious symbolism. Before planting began on local lands, the village priest customarily went out and sprinkled the fields with water, symbolizing renewal and life. Everyone participated in village processions to honor the saints and ask their protection. The entire calendar was designed with reference to Christmas, Easter, and Pentecost, events in the life of Jesus and his disciples.

The Christian calendar was also filled with saints' days. Saints were individuals who had lived particularly holy lives and were honored locally or more widely for their connection with the divine. Veneration of the saints had been an important tool of Christian conversion since late antiquity (see Chapter 8), and the cult of the saints was a central feature of popular culture in the Middle Ages. People believed that the saints possessed supernatural powers that enabled them to perform miracles, and each saint became the special property of the locality in which his or her relics—remains or possessions—rested. In return for the saint's healing powers and support, peasants

Hildegard's visions have been explored by theologians and also by neurologists, who judge that they may have originated in migraine headaches, as she reports many of the same phenomena that migraine sufferers do: auras of light around objects, areas of blindness, feelings of intense doubt and intense euphoria. The interpretations that she develops come from her theological insight and learning, however, not from her illness. That same insight also emerges in her music, which is what she is best known for today. Eighty of her compositions survive—a huge number for a medieval composer—most of them written to be sung by the nuns in her convent, so they have strong lines for female voices. Many of her songs and chants have been recorded recently by various artists and are available on compact disk, as downloads, and on several Web sites.

QUESTIONS FOR ANALYSIS

1. Why do you think Hildegard might have kept her visions secret at first? Why do you think she eventually sought church approval for them?

2. In what ways were Hildegard's accomplishments extraordinary given women's general status in the Middle Ages?

⏵LaunchPad
ONLINE DOCUMENT PROJECT

Why was Hildegard of Bingen considered a worthy instrument for the transmission of God's word? Read excerpts from Hildegard's correspondence, and then complete a quiz and writing assignment based on the evidence and details from this chapter.

See inside the front cover to learn more.

would offer prayers, loyalty, and gifts. The Virgin Mary, Christ's mother, became the most important saint, with churches built in her honor and special hymns, prayers, and ceremonies created.

Most people in medieval Europe were Christian, but there were small Jewish communities scattered through many parts of Europe, as well as Muslims in the Iberian Peninsula, Sicily, other Mediterranean islands, and southeastern Europe. Increasing suspicion and hostility marked relations among believers in different religions throughout the Middle Ages, but there were also important similarities in the ways that European Christians, Jews, and Muslims understood and experienced their faiths. In all three traditions, every major life transition was marked by a ceremony that involved religious officials or spiritual elements. In all three faiths, death was marked by religious rituals, and the living had obligations to the dead, including prayers and special mourning periods.

The Expansion of Christianity

The eleventh and twelfth centuries saw not only reforms in monasticism and the papacy but also an expansion of Christianity into Scandinavia, the Baltic lands, eastern Europe, and Spain that had profound cultural consequences. The expansion was accomplished through wars, the establishment of new bishoprics, and the vast migration of Christian colonists into non-Christian territories. As it occurred, more and more Europeans began to think of themselves as belonging to a realm of Christianity that was political as well as religious, a realm they called Christendom.

Christian influences entered Scandinavia and the Baltic lands primarily through the creation of dioceses (church districts headed by bishops). This took place in Denmark and Norway in the tenth and eleventh centuries, and then in Sweden and Finland. In all of these areas, Christian missionaries preached, baptized, and built churches. Royal power advanced institutional Christianity, and traditional Norse religions practiced by the Vikings were outlawed. In eastern Europe the German emperor Otto I (see page 392) planted a string of dioceses along his northern and eastern frontiers, hoping to pacify the newly conquered Slavs in eastern Europe. German nobles built castles and ruthlessly crushed revolts by Slavic peoples.

The church also moved into central Europe, first into Bohemia in the tenth century and from there into Poland and Hungary in the eleventh century. In the twelfth and thirteenth centuries thousands of settlers poured into eastern Europe from the west. These new immigrants, German in descent, name, language, and law, settled in Silesia, Mecklenburg, Bohemia, Poland, Hungary, and Transylvania, where they established towns.

The Iberian Peninsula was another area of Christian expansion. In about 950 Caliph Abd al-Rahman III (912–961) of the Umayyad Dynasty of Córdoba ruled most of the peninsula. Christian Spain consisted of the small kingdoms of Castile, León, Catalonia, Aragon, Navarre, and Portugal. In the eleventh century divisions and civil wars in the caliphate of Córdoba allowed Christian armies to conquer an increasingly large part of the Iberian Peninsula. By 1248 Christians held all of the peninsula save for the small state of Granada in the south. As the Christians advanced, they changed the face of Spanish cities, transforming mosques into cathedrals.

Fourteenth-century clerical writers would call the movement to expel the Muslims the **reconquista** (ray-kon-KEES-tah; reconquest)—a sacred and patriotic crusade to wrest the country from "alien" Muslim hands. This religious idea became part of Spanish political culture and of the national psychology. Rulers of the Christian kingdoms of Spain increasingly passed legislation discriminating against Muslims and Jews living under Christian rule, and they attempted to exclude anyone from the nobility who could not prove "purity of blood"—that is, that they had no Muslim or Jewish ancestors. As a consequence of the reconquista, the Spanish and Portuguese also learned how to administer vast tracts of newly acquired territory. In the sixteenth century they used their claims about the rightful dominance of Christianity to justify their colonization of new territories in Mexico, Brazil, Peru, Angola, and the Philippines and relied on their experiences at home to provide models of how to govern.

Spain was not the only place in Europe where "blood" became a way of understanding differences among people and a basis for discriminatory laws. When Germans moved into eastern Europe and English forces took over much of Ireland, they increasingly barred local people from access to legal courts and denied them positions in monasteries or craft guilds. They banned intermarriage between ethnic groups in an attempt to maintain ethnic purity, even though everyone was Christian. As Europeans later came into contact with people from Africa and Asia, and particularly as they developed colonial empires there, these notions of blood also became a way of conceptualizing racial categories.

The Crusades

What were the causes, course, and consequences of the Crusades?

The expansion of Christianity in the Middle Ages was not limited to Europe but extended to the eastern Mediterranean in what were later termed the **Crusades**. Occurring in the late eleventh and early twelfth centuries, the Crusades were wars sponsored by the papacy to recover the holy city of Jerusalem from the Muslims. The word *crusade* was not actually used at the time and did not appear in English until the late sixteenth century. It means literally "taking the cross," a vow to spread Christianity symbolized by the cross that soldiers sewed on their garments. Although people of all ages and classes participated in the Crusades, so many knights did that crusading became a distinctive feature of the upper-class lifestyle. In an aristocratic military society, men coveted reputations as Crusaders; the Christian knight who had been to Jerusalem enjoyed great prestige.

Background and Motives

In the eleventh century the papacy had strong reasons for wanting to launch an expedition against Muslims in the East. If the pope could muster a large army against the enemies of Christianity, his claim to be the leader of Christian society in the West would be strengthened. Moreover, in 1054 a serious theological disagreement had split the Greek Church of Byzantium and the Roman Church of the West. The pope believed that a crusade would lead to strong Roman influence in Greek territories and eventually the reunion of the two churches.

Popes and other church officials gained support for war in defense of Christianity by promising spiritual benefits to those who joined a campaign or died fighting. Church leaders said that these people would be forgiven for their sins without having to do penance, that is, without having to confess to a priest and carry out some action to make up for the sins. Preachers communicated these ideas widely and told stories about warrior-saints who slew hundreds of enemies.

Religious zeal led increasing numbers of people to go on pilgrimages to holy places, including Jerusalem. The Arab Muslims who had ruled Jerusalem and the surrounding territory for centuries allowed Christian pilgrims to travel freely, but in the late eleventh century the Seljuk Turks took over Palestine, defeating both Arab and Byzantine armies, and pilgrimage became more difficult. The Byzantine emperor at Constantinople appealed to western European Christians for support. The emperor's appeal fit well with papal aims, and in 1095 Pope Urban II called for a great Christian holy war against the infidels—a term Christians and Muslims both used to describe the other. Urban urged Christian knights who had been fighting one another to direct their energies against those he claimed were the true enemies of God, the Muslims.

The Course of the Crusades

Thousands of people of all classes responded to Urban's call, streaming southward and then toward Jerusalem in what became known as the First Crusade. The First Crusade was successful, mostly because of the dynamic enthusiasm of the participants, who had little more than religious zeal. They knew little of the geography or climate of the Middle East, and although there were several counts with military experience, the Crusaders could never agree on a leader. Adding to these disadvantages, supply lines were never set up, starvation and disease wracked the army, and the Turks slaughtered hundreds of noncombatants. Nevertheless, the army pressed on, besieging and taking several cities, including Antioch. After a monthlong siege, the Crusaders took Jerusalem in July 1099 (Map 14.2). Fulcher of Chartres, a chaplain on the First Crusade, described the scene:

> Amid the sound of trumpets and with everything in an uproar they attacked boldly, shouting "God help us!" . . . They ran with the greatest exultation as fast as they could into the city and joined their companions in pursuing and slaying their wicked enemies without cessation. . . . If you had been there your feet would have been stained to the ankles in the blood of the slain. What shall I say? None of them were left alive. Neither women nor children were spared.[2]

With Jerusalem taken, some Crusaders regarded their mission as accomplished and set off for home, but the appearance of more Muslim troops convinced other Crusaders that they needed to stay. Slowly institutions were set up to rule local territories and the Muslim population. Four small "Crusader states"—Jerusalem, Edessa, Tripoli, and Antioch—were established, and castles and fortified towns were built in these states to defend against Muslim reconquest. Reinforcements arrived in the form of pilgrims and fighters from Europe, so that there was constant coming and going by land and more often by sea after the Crusaders conquered port cities. Most Crusaders were men, but some women came along as well, assisting in the besieging of towns and castles by providing water to fighting men or foraging for food, working as washerwomen, and providing sexual services.

Between 1096 and 1270 the crusading ideal was expressed in eight papally approved expeditions, though none after the First Crusade accomplished very much. The Muslim states in the Middle East were politically fragmented when the Crusaders first came, and it took them about a century to reorganize. They did so dramatically under Saladin (Salah al-Din), who unified Egypt and Syria. In 1187 the Muslims retook Jerusalem, but the Christians held onto port towns, and Saladin allowed pilgrims safe passage to Jerusalem. From that point on, the Crusader states were more important economically than politically or religiously, giving Italian and French merchants direct access to Eastern products such as perfumes and silk.

After the Muslims retook Jerusalem, the crusading movement faced other setbacks. During the Fourth Crusade (1202–1204), Crusaders stopped in Constantinople, and when they were not welcomed, they sacked the city and grabbed thousands of relics, which were later sold in Europe. The Byzantine Empire splintered into three parts and soon consisted of little more than the city of Constantinople. Moreover, the assault of one Christian people on another—when one of the goals of the Crusades was reunion

MAP 14.2 The Crusades, 1096–1270 The Crusaders took many different sea and land routes on their way to Jerusalem, often crossing the lands of the Byzantine Empire, which led to conflict with Eastern Christians. The Crusader kingdoms in the East lasted only briefly.

of the Greek and Latin Churches—made the split between the churches permanent and discredited the entire crusading movement in the eyes of many Christians.

In the late thirteenth century Turkish armies, after gradually conquering all other Muslim rulers, turned against the Crusader states. In 1291 the Christians' last stronghold, the port of Acre, fell in a battle that was just as bloody as the first battle for Jerusalem two centuries earlier. Knights then needed a new battlefield for military actions, which some found in Spain, where the rulers of Aragon and Castile continued fighting Muslims until 1492.

Consequences of the Crusades

The Crusades testified to the religious enthusiasm of the High Middle Ages and the influence of the papacy, gave kings and the pope opportunities to expand their bureaucracies, and provided an outlet for nobles' dreams of glory. The Crusades also introduced some Europeans to Eastern luxury goods, but their immediate cultural impact on the West remains debatable. By the late eleventh century there were already strong economic and intellectual ties with the East; however, the Crusades were a boon to Italian merchants, who profited from outfitting military expeditions as well as from the opening of new trade routes and the establishment of trading communities in the Crusader states.

Despite these advantages, the Crusades had some seriously negative sociopolitical consequences. For one thing, they proved to be a disaster for Jewish-Christian relations. Inspired by the ideology of holy war, Christian armies on their way to Jerusalem on the First Crusade joined with local mobs to attack Jewish families and communities, sometimes burning people alive in the synagogue or Jewish section of town. Later Crusades brought similar violence, enhanced by accusations that Jews engaged in the ritual murder of Christians to use their blood in religious rites.

Legal restrictions on Jews gradually increased throughout Europe. Jews were forbidden to have Christian servants or employees, to hold public office, to appear in public on Christian holy days, or to enter Christian parts of town without a badge marking them as Jews. They were prohibited from engaging in any trade with Christians except money-lending and were banished from England and France.

The Crusades also left an inheritance of deep bitterness in Christian-Muslim relations. Each side dehumanized the other, viewing those who followed the other religion as unbelievers. Whereas Europeans perceived the Crusades as sacred religious movements, Muslims saw them as expansionist and imperialistic. The ideal of a sacred mission to conquer or convert Muslim peoples entered Europeans' consciousness and became a continuing goal. When in 1492 Christopher Columbus sailed west, he used the language of the Crusades in his diaries, and he hoped to establish a Christian base in India from which a new crusade against Islam could be launched (see page 468).

The Life of the People

How did the lives of common people, nobles, and townspeople differ, and what new commercial developments increased wealth?

In the late ninth century medieval intellectuals described Christian society as composed of those who pray (the monks), those who fight (the nobles), and those who work (the peasants). This image of society became popular in the Middle Ages, especially among people who were worried about the changes they saw around them. They asserted that the three categories of citizens had been established by God and that every person had been assigned a fixed place in the social order.

This three-category model does not fully describe medieval society—there were degrees of wealth and status within each group. Also, the model does not take townspeople and the emerging commercial classes into consideration, and it completely excludes those who were not Christian, such as Jews, Muslims, and pagans. Furthermore, those who used the model, generally bishops and other church officials, ignored the fact that each of these groups was made up of both women and men; they spoke only of warriors, monks, and farmers. Despite—or perhaps because of—these limitations, the model of the three categories was a powerful mental construct. Therefore, we can use it to organize our investigation of life in the Middle Ages, broadening it to include groups and issues that medieval authors did not. (See page 394 for a discussion of the life of monks and nuns—"those who pray.")

The Life and Work of Peasants

The men and women who worked the land in medieval Europe made up probably more than 90 percent of the population, as they did in China, India, and other parts of the world where agriculture predominated. The evolution of localized systems of authority into more centralized states had relatively little impact on the daily lives of these peasants except when it involved warfare. While only nobles fought, their battles often destroyed the houses, barns, and fields of ordinary people, who might also be killed either directly or as a result of the famine and disease that often accompanied war. Villagers might seek protection in the local castle during times of war, but typically they worked and lived without paying much attention to political developments within castle walls.

At the same time, since villagers did not perform what were considered "noble" deeds, the aristocratic monks and clerics who wrote the records that serve as historical sources did not spend time or precious writing materials on them. So it is more difficult to find information on the majority of Europeans who were peasants than on the small group at the top of society.

Medieval theologians lumped everyone who worked the land into the category of "those who work," but in fact there were many levels of peasants, ranging from slaves to free and sometimes very rich farmers. Most peasants were serfs, required to stay in the village and perform labor on the lord's land. The number of workdays varied, but serfs usually worked three days a week except in the planting or harvest seasons, when the number of days increased. Serfs were also often obliged to pay fees on common occurrences, such as marriage or inheritance of property. A free person had to do none of these things.

Serfdom was a hereditary condition. A person born a serf was likely to die a serf, though many serfs did secure their freedom, and the economic revival that began in

Agricultural Work In this scene from a German manuscript written about 1190, men and women of different ages are sowing seeds and harvesting grain. All residents of a village, including children, engaged in agricultural tasks. (Rheinisches Landesmuseum, Bonn, Germany/Giraudon/ The Bridgeman Art Library)

the eleventh century (see pages 405–406) allowed some to buy their freedom. Further opportunities for increased personal freedom came when lords organized groups of villagers to migrate to sparsely settled frontier areas or to cut down forests or fill in swamps so that there was more land available for farming. Those who took on this extra work often gained a reduction in traditional manorial obligations and an improvement of their social and legal conditions.

In the Middle Ages most European peasants, free and unfree, lived in family groups in small villages that were part of a manor, the estate of a lord (see page 390). The manor was the basic unit of medieval rural organization and the center of rural life. Within the manors of western and central Europe, villages were made up of small houses for individual families, a church, and perhaps the large house of the lord. Peasant households consisted of one married couple, their children (including stepchildren), and perhaps one or two other relatives, such as a grandparent or unmarried aunt. In southern and eastern Europe, extended families were more likely to live in the same household or very near one another. Between one-third and one-half of children died before age five, though many people lived into their sixties.

The arable land of the manor was divided between the lord and the peasantry, with the lord's portion known as the demesne (dih-MAYN) or home farm. A peasant family's land was not usually one particular field but a scattering of strips across many fields, some of which would be planted in grain, some in other crops, and some left unworked to allow the soil to rejuvenate. That way if one field yielded little, strips in a different field might be more bountiful.

The peasants' work was typically divided according to gender. Men and boys were responsible for clearing new land, plowing, and caring for large animals; women and girls were responsible for the care of small animals, spinning, and food preparation. Both sexes harvested and planted, though often there were gender-specific tasks within each of these major undertakings. Women and men worked in the vineyards and in the harvest and preparation of crops needed by the textile industry—flax and plants used for dyeing cloth. Beginning in the eleventh century water mills and windmills aided in some tasks, especially grinding grain, and an increasing use of horses rather than oxen speeded up plowing.

The mainstay of the diet for peasants everywhere—and for all other classes—was bread. Peasants also ate vegetables; animals were too valuable to be used for food on a regular basis, but weaker animals were often slaughtered in the fall so that they did not need to be fed through the winter, and their meat was preserved with salt and eaten on great feast days such as Christmas and Easter. Ale was the universal drink of common people, and it provided needed calories and some relief from the difficult and monotonous labor that filled people's lives.

The Life and Work of Nobles

The nobility, though a small fraction of the total population, influenced all aspects of medieval culture. Despite political, scientific, and industrial revolutions, nobles continued to hold real political and social power in Europe into the nineteenth century.

In the early Middle Ages noble status was limited to a very few families, but in the eleventh century knights in service to kings began to claim such status because it gave them special legal privileges. Nobles generally paid few taxes, and they had power over the people living on their lands. They maintained order, resolved disputes, and protected their dependents from attacks. They appointed officials who oversaw agricultural production. The liberty and privileges of the noble were inheritable, perpetuated by blood and not by wealth alone.

The nobles' primary obligation was warfare, just as it was for nobles among the Mexica (see pages 313–319) and the samurai in Japan (see page 380). Nobles were also obliged to attend the lord's court on important occasions when the lord wanted to put on great displays, such as on religious holidays or the wedding of a son or daughter.

Originally, most knights focused solely on military skills, but around 1200 a different ideal of knighthood emerged, usually termed chivalry. Chivalry was a code of conduct in which fighting to defend the Christian faith and protecting one's countrymen was declared to have a sacred purpose. Other qualities gradually became part of chivalry: bravery, generosity, honor, graciousness, mercy, and eventually gallantry toward women, which came to be called "courtly love." The chivalric ideal—and it was an ideal, not a standard pattern of behavior—created a new standard of masculinity for nobles, in which loyalty and honor remained the most important qualities, but graceful dancing and intelligent conversation were not considered unmanly.

Noblewomen played a large and important role in the functioning of the estate. They were responsible for managing the household's "inner economy"—cooking, brewing, spinning, weaving, and caring for yard animals. When the lord was away for long periods, his wife became the sole manager of the family properties. Often the responsibilities of the estate fell permanently to her if she became a widow.

Towns, Cities, and the Growth of Commercial Interests

Most people continued to live in villages in the Middle Ages, but the rise of towns and the growth of a new business and commercial class were central to Europe's recovery after the disorders of the tenth century. Several factors contributed to this growth: a rise in population; increased agricultural output, which provided an adequate food supply for new town dwellers; and enough peace and political stability to allow merchants to transport and sell goods.

Towns in Europe were generally enclosed by walls as were towns in China, India, and the Middle East. (The terms *burgher* and *bourgeois* derive from the Old English and Old German words *burg, burgh, borg,* and *borough* for "a walled or fortified place.") Most towns were first established as trading centers, with a marketplace in the middle, and they were likely to have a mint for coining money and a court for settling disputes. In each town, many people inhabited a small, cramped area. As population increased, towns rebuilt their walls, expanding the living space to accommodate growing numbers. Residents bargained with lords to make the town politically independent, which gave them the right to hold legal courts, select leaders, and set taxes.

Townspeople also tried to acquire liberties, above all personal freedom, for themselves. It gradually developed that an individual who lived in a town for a year and a day, and was accepted by the townspeople, was free of servile obligations and status. Thus serfs who fled their manors for towns and were able to find work and avoid recapture became free of personal labor obligations. In this way the growth of towns contributed to a slow decline of serfdom in western Europe, although the complete elimination of serfdom took centuries.

Merchants constituted the most powerful group in most towns, and they were often organized into merchant guilds, which prohibited nonmembers from trading, pooled members' risks, monopolized city offices, and controlled the economy of the town. Towns became centers of production as well, and artisans in particular trades formed their own **craft guilds**, including guilds of butchers, weavers, blacksmiths, bakers, silversmiths, and so on. Members of the craft guilds determined the quality, quantity, and price of the goods produced and the number of apprentices and journeymen affiliated with the guild. Formal membership in guilds was generally limited to men, but women often worked in guild shops without official membership.

Artisans generally made and sold products in their own homes, with production taking place on the ground floor. A window or door opened from the main workroom directly onto the street, and passersby could look in and see the goods being produced. The family lived above the business on the second or third floor. As the business and the family expanded, additional stories were added.

Most medieval towns and cities developed with little planning or attention to sanitation. Horses and oxen, the chief means of transportation and power, dropped tons of dung on the streets every year. It was universal practice in the early towns to dump household waste, both animal and human, into the road in front of one's house. The stench must have been abominable, as officials of the king noted in their order to the citizens of one English town in 1298:

> The air is so corrupted and infected by the pigsties situated in the king's highways and in the lanes of that town and by the swine feeding and frequently wandering about . . . and by dung and dunghills and many other foul things placed in the streets and lanes, that great repugnance overtakes the king's ministers staying in that town and . . . the advantage of more wholesome air is impeded. . . . [So] the king, being unwilling longer to tolerate such great and unbearable defects there, orders . . . the pigsties, aforesaid streets and lanes to be cleansed from all dung.[3]

Despite such unpleasant aspects of urban life, people wanted to get into medieval towns because they represented opportunities for economic advancement, social mobility, and improvement in legal status.

The Expansion of Trade and the Commercial Revolution

The growth of towns went hand in hand with a revival of trade as artisans and craftsmen manufactured goods for local and foreign consumption. As in the city-states of East Africa (see pages 286–290), most trade centered in towns and was controlled by merchants. They began to pool their money to finance trading expeditions, sharing the profits and also sharing the risks. If disaster struck the ship or caravan, an investor's loss was limited to the amount of that individual's investment, a legal concept termed "limited liability" that is essential to the modern capitalist economy.

Italian cities, especially Venice, led the West in trade in general and completely dominated trade with Asia and North Africa. Venetian ships carried salt from the Venetian lagoon; pepper and other spices from North Africa; and slaves, silk, and purple textiles from the East to northern and western Europe. Wealthy European consumers had greater access to foreign luxuries than they had earlier, and their tastes became more sophisticated. Merchants from Florence and Milan were also important traders, and they developed new methods of accounting and record keeping that facilitated the movement of goods and money. The towns of Bruges, Ghent, and Ypres in Flanders were leaders in long-distance trade and built up a vast industry in the manufacture of cloth, aided by ready access to wool from England, just across the Channel. The availability of raw wool also encouraged the development of cloth manufacture within England itself, and commercial families in manufacturing towns grew fabulously rich.

In much of northern Europe, the Hanseatic League (known as the Hansa for short), a mercantile association of towns formed to achieve mutual security and exclusive trading rights, controlled trade. During the thirteenth century perhaps two hundred cities from Holland to Poland joined the league. The ships of the Hansa cities carried furs, wax, copper, fish, grain, timber, and wine. These goods were exchanged for other products, mainly cloth and salt, from western cities. At cities such as Bruges and London, Hanseatic merchants secured special concessions exempting them from all tolls and allowing them to trade at local fairs. Hanseatic merchants also established foreign trading centers, which they called "factories," because the commercial agents within them were called "factors." (Later the word *factory* would be applied to centers of production as well.)

These developments added up to what historians of Europe have called the **commercial revolution**, a direct parallel to the economic revolution going on in Song Dynasty China at the same time (see pages 362–365). In giving the transformation this name, historians point not only to an increase in the sheer volume of trade and in the complexity and sophistication of business procedures but also to the new attitude toward business and making money. Some even detect a "capitalist spirit" in which making a profit was regarded as a good thing in itself.

The commercial revolution created a great deal of new wealth, which did not escape the attention of kings and other rulers. Wealth could be taxed, and through taxation kings could create strong and centralized states. Through the activities of merchants, Europeans again saw products from Africa and Asia in city marketplaces, as they had in Roman times. The commercial revolution also provided the opportunity for thousands of serfs in western Europe to improve their social position. There were also strong continuities: many people continued to live hand to mouth on low wages; most towns remained small; and the nobility and churchmen continued to determine the preponderant social attitudes, values, and patterns of thought and behavior.

Learning and Culture

What were the primary educational and cultural developments in medieval Europe?

The towns that became centers of trade and production in the High Middle Ages also developed into cultural and intellectual centers. Trade brought in new ideas as well as merchandise, and in many cities a new type of educational institution—the university—emerged, meeting the needs of the new bureaucratic states and the church for educated administrators. As universities emerged, so did other cultural advancements, such as new forms of architecture and literature.

Appearance of the plague

| | 1346 |
| | 1349 |

1347

1350

1348

After 1350

City or area partially
or totally spared

Major trade route

◀ **MAP 14.3   The Course of the Black Death in Fourteenth-Century Europe**
The plague followed trade routes as it spread into and across Europe. A few cities that took
strict quarantine measures were spared.

traveling from the Crimea in southern Russia brought the plague to Messina, from
which it spread across Sicily and into Italy. From Italy it traveled in all directions.

Most historians and almost all microbiologists identify the disease that spread in
the fourteenth century as the bubonic plague, caused by the bacillus *Yersinia pestis*.
The disease normally afflicts rats. Fleas living on the infected rats drink their blood
and pass the bacteria that cause the plague on to the next rat they bite. Usually the
disease is limited to rats and other rodents, but at certain points in history the fleas
have jumped from their rodent hosts to humans and other animals. The fourteenth-
century disease showed some differences from later outbreaks of bubonic plague; there
are no reports of massive rat die-offs, and the disease was often transmitted directly
from one person to another through coughing and sneezing. These differences have
led a few historians to ask whether the fourteenth-century outbreak was some disease
other than the bubonic plague — perhaps something like the Ebola virus. Debates
about the nature of the disease fuel continued study of medical aspects of the plague,
with scientists using innovative techniques such as studying the tooth pulp of bodies
in medieval cemeteries to see if it contains DNA from plague-causing agents.

Procession of Flagellants   In this manuscript illumination from 1349, shirtless flagellants,
men and women who whipped and scourged themselves as penance for their and society's
sins, walk through the Flemish city of Tournai, which had just been struck by the plague. Many
people believed that the Black Death was God's punishment for humanity's wickedness. (The
Flagellants at Doornik in 1349, copy of a miniature from the *Chronicle of Aegidius Li Muisis*/Private Collection/
The Bridgeman Art Library)

Whatever it was, the disease had dreadful effects on the body. The classic symptom was a growth the size of a nut or an apple in the armpit, in the groin, or on the neck. This was the boil, or *bubo*, that gave the disease its name and caused agonizing pain. If the bubo was lanced and the pus thoroughly drained, the victim had a chance of recovery. The secondary stage was the appearance of black spots or blotches caused by bleeding under the skin. Finally, the victim began to cough violently and spit blood. This stage, indicating the presence of millions of bacilli in the bloodstream, signaled the end, and death followed in two or three days. Physicians could sometimes ease the pain but had no cure.

Most people believed that the Black Death was caused by poisons or by "corrupted air" that carried the disease from place to place. They sought to keep poisons from entering the body by smelling or ingesting strong-smelling herbs, and they tried to remove the poisons through bloodletting. They also prayed and did penance. Anxiety and fears about the plague caused people to look for scapegoats, and they found them in the Jews, who they believed had poisoned the wells of Christian communities and thereby infected the drinking water. This charge led to the murder of thousands of Jews across Europe.

Because population figures for the period before the arrival of the plague do not exist for most countries and cities, only educated guesses can be made about mortality rates. Of a total English population of perhaps 4.2 million, probably 1.4 million died of the Black Death in its several visits. In Italy densely populated cities endured incredible losses. Florence lost between one-half and two-thirds of its population when the plague visited in 1348. The disease recurred intermittently in the 1360s and 1370s and reappeared many times, as late as the early 1700s in Europe. (It still continues to infect rodent and human populations sporadically today.)

In the short term the economic effects of the plague were severe because the death of many peasants disrupted food production. But in the long term the dramatic decline in population eased pressure on the land, and wages and per capita wealth rose for those who survived. The psychological consequences of the plague were profound. Some people sought release in wild living, while others turned to the severest forms of asceticism and frenzied religious fervor.

The Hundred Years' War

While the plague ravaged populations in Asia, North Africa, and Europe, a long international war in western Europe added further death and destruction. England and France had engaged in sporadic military hostilities from the time of the Norman Conquest in 1066 (see page 391), and in the middle of the fourteenth century these became more intense. From 1337 to 1453 the two countries intermittently fought one another in what was the longest war in European history, ultimately dubbed the Hundred Years' War, though it actually lasted 116 years.

The Hundred Years' War had a number of causes. Both England and France claimed the duchy of Aquitaine in southwestern France, and the English king Edward III argued that, as the grandson of an earlier French king, he should have rightfully inherited the French throne. Nobles in provinces on the borders of France who were worried about the growing power of the French king supported Edward, as did wealthy wool merchants and clothmakers in Flanders who depended on English wool. The

Siege of the Castle of Mortagne near Bordeaux This miniature of a battle in the Hundred Years' War shows the French besieging an English-held castle. Medieval warfare usually consisted of small skirmishes and attacks on castles. (From *The Coronation of Richard II to 1387* by Jean de Batard Wavrin/© British Library Board. All Rights Reserved./The Bridgeman Art Library)

governments of both England and France promised wealth and glory to those who fought, and each country portrayed the other as evil.

The war, fought almost entirely in France, consisted mainly of a series of random sieges and raids. During the war's early stages, England was successful, primarily through the use of longbows fired by well-trained foot soldiers against mounted knights and, after 1375, by early cannons. By 1419 the English had advanced to the walls of Paris. But the French cause was not lost. Though England scored the initial victories, France won the war.

The ultimate French success rests heavily on the actions of Joan, an obscure French peasant girl whose vision and military leadership revived French fortunes and led to victory. (Over the centuries, she acquired the name "of Arc"—*d'Arc* in French—based on her father's name; she never used this name for herself, but called herself "the maiden"—*la Pucelle* in French.) Born in 1412 to well-to-do peasants, Joan grew up in a pious household. During adolescence she began to hear voices, which she later said belonged to Saint Michael, Saint Catherine, and Saint Margaret. In 1428 these voices told her that the dauphin of France—Charles VII, who was uncrowned as king because of the English occupation—had to be crowned and the English expelled from France. Joan went to the French court disguised as a male for safety and secured the support of the dauphin to travel, dressed as a knight, with the French army to the besieged city of Orléans.

At Orléans, Joan inspired and led French attacks, and the English retreated. As a result of her successes, Charles made Joan co-commander of the entire army, and she led it to a string of military victories in the summer of 1429; many cities surrendered without a fight. Two months after the victory at Orléans, Charles VII was crowned king at Reims.

Joan and the French army continued their fight against the English. In 1430 England's allies, the Burgundians, captured Joan and sold her to the English, and the French did not intervene. The English wanted Joan eliminated for obvious political reasons, but the primary charge against her was heresy, and the trial was conducted by church authorities. She was interrogated about the angelic voices and about why she wore men's clothing. She apparently answered skillfully, but in 1431 the court condemned her as a heretic, and she was burned at the stake in the marketplace at Rouen. (A new trial in 1456 cleared her of all charges, and in 1920 she was canonized as a saint.) Joan continues to be a symbol of deep religious piety to some, of conservative nationalism to others, and of gender-bending cross-dressing to others. Beneath the pious and popular legends is a teenage girl who saved the French monarchy, which was the embodiment of France. The French army continued its victories without her, and demands for an end to the war increased among the English, who were growing tired of the mounting loss of life and the flow of money into a seemingly bottomless pit. Slowly the French reconquered Normandy and finally ejected the English from Aquitaine. At the war's end in 1453, only the town of Calais remained in English hands.

The long war had a profound impact on the two countries. In England and France the war promoted nationalism—the feeling of unity and identity that binds together a people. It led to technological experimentation, especially with gunpowder weaponry, whose firepower made the protective walls of stone castles obsolete. However, such weaponry also made warfare increasingly expensive. The war also stimulated the development of the English Parliament. Between 1250 and 1450 representative assemblies from several classes of society flourished in many European countries, but only the English Parliament became a powerful national body. Edward III's constant need for money to pay for the war compelled him to summon it many times, and its representatives slowly built up their powers.

Challenges to the Church

In times of crisis or disaster people of all faiths have sought the consolation of religion, but in the fourteenth century the official Christian Church offered little solace. While local clergy eased the suffering of many, a dispute over who was the legitimate pope weakened the church as an institution. In 1309 pressure by the French monarchy led the pope to move his permanent residence to Avignon in southern France, the location of the papal summer palace. This marked the start of seven successive papacies in Avignon. Not surprising, all these popes were French—a matter of controversy among church followers outside France. Also, the popes largely concentrated on bureaucratic and financial matters to the exclusion of spiritual objectives.

In 1376 one of the French popes returned to Rome, and when he died there several years later Roman citizens demanded an Italian pope who would remain in Rome. The cardinals elected Urban VI, but his tactless, arrogant, and bullheaded manner caused them to regret their decision. The cardinals slipped away from Rome and declared Urban's election invalid because it had come about under threats from the Roman mob. They elected a French cardinal who took the name Clement VII (pontificate 1378–1394) and set himself up at Avignon in opposition to Urban. There were thus two popes, a situation that was later termed the Great Schism.

The powers of Europe aligned themselves with Urban or Clement along strictly political lines. France recognized the Frenchman, Clement; England, France's historic enemy, recognized Urban. The rest of Europe lined up behind one or the other. In all European countries the common people — hard-pressed by inflation, wars, and plague — were thoroughly confused about which pope was legitimate. In the end the schism weakened the religious faith of many Christians and brought church leadership into serious disrepute.

A first attempt to heal the schism led to the installation of a third pope and a threefold split, but finally a church council meeting at Constance (1414–1418) successfully deposed the three schismatic popes and elected a new leader, who took the name Martin V (pontificate 1417–1431). The schism was over, but those who had hoped that the council would also reform problems in the church were disappointed. In the later fifteenth century the papacy concentrated on building up its wealth and political power in Italy rather than on the concerns of the whole church. As a result, many people decided that they would need to rely on their own prayers and pious actions rather than on the institutional church for their salvation.

Peasant and Urban Revolts

The difficult conditions of the fourteenth and fifteenth centuries spurred a wave of peasant and urban revolts across Europe. In 1358, when French taxation for the Hundred Years' War fell heavily on the poor, the frustrations of the French peasantry exploded in a massive uprising called the Jacquerie (zhah-kuh-REE), after a supposedly happy agricultural laborer, Jacques Bonhomme (Good Fellow). Adding to the anger over taxes was the toll taken by the plague and by the famine that had struck some areas. Crowds swept through the countryside, slashing the throats of nobles, burning their castles, raping their wives and daughters, and killing or maiming their horses and cattle. Artisans, small merchants, and parish priests joined the peasants, and residents of both urban and rural areas committed terrible destruction. For several weeks the nobles were on the defensive, until the upper class united to repress the revolt with merciless ferocity. Thousands of the "Jacques," innocent as well as guilty, were cut down.

Taxes and other grievances also led to the 1381 English Peasants' Revolt, involving tens of thousands of people. The Black Death had dramatically reduced the supply of labor, and peasants had demanded higher wages and fewer manorial obligations. Parliament countered with a law freezing wages and binding workers to their manors. Although the law was difficult to enforce, it contributed to an atmosphere of discontent, which was further enhanced by popular preachers who proclaimed that great disparities between rich and poor went against Christ's teachings. Moreover, decades of aristocratic violence, much of it perpetrated against the weak peasantry, had bred hostility and bitterness.

In 1380 Parliament imposed a poll tax on all citizens to fund the Hundred Years' War, requiring rich and poor to pay the same amount and ordering sheriffs to collect it. This tax imposed a greater burden on the poor than on wealthier citizens, and it sparked revolt. Beginning with assaults on the tax collectors, the uprising in England followed much the same course as had the Jacquerie in France. Castles and manors were sacked; manorial records were destroyed; nobles were murdered. Urban discontent merged with rural violence. Apprentices and journeymen, frustrated because the highest positions in the guilds were closed to them, rioted.

The boy-king Richard II (r. 1377–1399) met the leaders of the revolt, agreed to charters ensuring the peasants' freedom, tricked them with false promises, and then proceeded to crush the uprising with terrible ferocity. The nobility tried to use this defeat to restore the labor obligations of serfdom, but they were not successful, and the conversion to money rents continued. In Flanders, France, and England peasant revolts often blended with conflicts involving workers in cities. Unrest also occurred in Italian, Spanish, and German cities. In Florence in 1378 the *ciompi*, or poor propertyless wool workers, revolted and briefly shared government of the city with wealthier artisans and merchants. Rebellions and uprisings everywhere revealed deep peasant and worker frustration with the socioeconomic conditions of the time.

Chapter Summary

Invasions by Vikings, Magyars, and Muslims, along with civil wars, created instability in the ninth and tenth centuries. Local nobles became the strongest powers against external threats, establishing a form of decentralized government later known as feudalism. By the twelfth century rulers in some parts of Europe had reasserted authority and were beginning to develop new institutions of government and legal codes that enabled them to assert power over lesser lords and the general population. The papacy also consolidated its power, though these moves were sometimes challenged by kings and emperors. Monasteries continued to be important places for learning and devotion, and new religious orders were founded. A papal call to retake the holy city of Jerusalem led to the Crusades, nearly two centuries of warfare between Christians and Muslims. Many of the effects of the Crusades were disastrous, including attacks on Jewish communities and more uniformly hostile Christian-Muslim relations.

The vast majority of medieval Europeans were peasants who lived in small villages and worked their own and their lord's land. Most Europeans were Christian, and the village church was generally the center of community life. Nobles were a tiny fraction of the total population, but they exerted great power over all aspects of life. Medieval towns and cities grew initially as trading centers and then became centers of production.

Towns also developed into cultural and intellectual centers, as trade brought in new ideas as well as merchandise. Universities offered courses of study based on classical models, and townspeople built churches and cathedrals as symbols of their Christian faith and their civic pride. New types of vernacular literature arose in which poems, songs, and stories were written down in local dialects.

In the fourteenth century a worsening climate brought poor harvests, which contributed to an international economic depression and fostered disease. The Black Death caused enormous population losses and social, psychological, and economic consequences. Additional difficulties included the Hundred Years' War, a schism among rival popes that weakened the Western Christian Church, and peasant and worker frustrations that exploded into uprisings.

Notes

1. D. C. Douglas and G. E. Greenaway, eds., *English Historical Documents*, vol. 2 (London: Eyre & Spottiswoode, 1961), p. 853.
2. Fulcher of Chartres, *A History of the Expedition to Jerusalem, 1095–1127*, trans. Frances Rita Ryan, ed. Harold S. Fink (Knoxville: University of Tennessee Press, 1969), pp. 121–123.
3. H. Rothwell, ed., *English Historical Documents*, vol. 3 (London: Eyre & Spottiswoode, 1975), p. 854.
4. Erwin Panofsky, trans. and ed., *Abbot Suger on the Abbey Church of St.-Denis and Its Art Treasures* (Princeton, N.J.: Princeton University Press, 1946), p. 101.

CONNECTIONS

 Medieval Europe continues to fascinate us today. We go to medieval banquets, fairs, and even weddings; visit castle-themed hotels and amusement parks; watch movies about knights and their conquests; play video games in which we become warriors, trolls, or sorcerers; and read stories with themes of great quests, some set in the Middle Ages and some set in places that just seem medieval, with humble but brave villagers, beautiful ladies, powerful wizards, and gorgeous warriors on horseback. From all these amusements the Middle Ages emerges as a strange and wonderful time, when people's emotions were more powerful, challenges more dangerous, and friendships more lasting than in the safe, shallow, fast-paced modern world. Characters from other parts of the world often heighten the exoticism: a Muslim soldier joins the fight against a common enemy, a Persian princess rescues the hero and his sidekick, a Buddhist monk teaches martial arts techniques. These characters from outside Europe are fictional, but they also represent aspects of reality, because medieval Europe was not isolated, and political and social structures similar to those in Europe developed elsewhere.

In reality few of us would probably want to live in the real Middle Ages, when most people worked in the fields all day, a banquet meant a piece of tough old rooster instead of the usual meal of pea soup and black bread, and even wealthy lords lived in damp and drafty castles. We do not really want to return to a time when one-third to one-half of all children died before age five and alcohol was the only real pain reliever. But the contemporary appeal of the Middle Ages is an interesting phenomenon, particularly because it stands in such sharp contrast to the attitude of educated Europeans who lived in the centuries immediately afterward. They were the ones who dubbed the period "middle" and viewed the soaring cathedrals as dreadfully "Gothic." They saw their own era as the one to be celebrated, and the Middle Ages as best forgotten.

Chapter Review

MAKE IT STICK

 LearningCurve
Go online and use LearningCurve to retain what you've read.

IDENTIFY KEY TERMS

Identify and explain the significance of each item below.

vassal (p. 390)	**reconquista** (p. 398)	**Scholastics** (p. 408)
fief (p. 390)	**Crusades** (p. 399)	**Gothic** (p. 409)
feudalism (p. 390)	**chivalry** (p. 405)	**vernacular literature**
manorialism (p. 390)	**craft guilds** (p. 406)	(p. 410)
serf (p. 390)	**commercial revolution**	**Black Death** (p. 411)
heresy (p. 395)	(p. 407)	

REVIEW THE MAIN IDEAS

Answer the focus questions from each section of the chapter.

1. How did medieval rulers restore order and centralize political power? (p. 388)

2. How did the Christian Church enhance its power and create new institutions and religious practices? (p. 393)

3. What were the causes, course, and consequences of the Crusades? (p. 399)

4. How did the lives of common people, nobles, and townspeople differ, and what new commercial developments increased wealth? (p. 402)

5. What were the primary educational and cultural developments in medieval Europe? (p. 407)

6. Why have the later Middle Ages been seen as a time of calamity and crisis? (p. 411)

MAKE CONNECTIONS

Analyze the larger developments and continuities within and across chapters.

1. What similarities and differences do you see between the institutions and laws established by medieval European rulers and those of the Roman (Chapter 6), Byzantine (Chapter 8), and Chinese (Chapter 13) emperors?

2. What factors over the centuries enabled the Christian Church (Chapters 6, 8) to become the most powerful and wealthy institution in Europe, and what problems did this create?

▷LaunchPad

ONLINE DOCUMENT PROJECT

Hildegard of Bingen

Why was Hildegard of Bingen considered a worthy instrument for the transmission of God's word?

Read excerpts from Hildegard's correspondence, and then complete a quiz and writing assignment based on the evidence and details from this chapter.

See inside the front cover to learn more.

CHRONOLOGY

722–1492	• Reconquista, the Christian reconquest of Spain from Muslims
ca. 800–950	• Viking, Magyar, and Muslim attacks on Europe
1066–1087	• Reign of William the Conqueror
1086	• *Domesday Book*
1095–1270	• Crusades
1180–1270	• Height of construction of cathedrals in France
1215	• Magna Carta
1225–1274	• Life of Saint Thomas Aquinas, author of *Summa Theologica*
1309–1376	• Papacy in Avignon
1315–1322	• Famine in northern Europe
ca. 1337–1453	• Hundred Years' War
1347	• Black Death arrives in Europe
1358	• Jacquerie peasant uprising in France
1378–1417	• Great Schism
1381	• English Peasants' Revolt
1429	• Joan of Arc leads French troops to victory at Orléans

Henry VII revealed his distrust of the nobility: very few great lords were among the king's closest advisers, who instead were lesser landowners and lawyers. They were, in a sense, middle class. The royal council handled any business the king put before it—executive, legislative, and judicial.

Secretive, cautious, and thrifty, Henry VII rebuilt the monarchy. He encouraged the cloth industry and built up the English merchant marine. He crushed an invasion from Ireland, secured peace with Scotland through the marriage of his daughter Margaret to the Scottish king, and enhanced English prestige through the marriage of his eldest son, Arthur, to Catherine of Aragon, the daughter of Ferdinand and Isabella of Spain. (Several years after Arthur's death, Catherine became the wife of his younger brother and the next king of England, Henry VIII; see page 444.) When Henry VII died in 1509, he left a country at peace both domestically and internationally, a substantially augmented treasury, and the dignity and role of the Crown much enhanced.

Spain

While England and France laid the foundations of unified nation-states during the Renaissance, Spain remained a conglomerate of independent kingdoms. Even the wedding in 1469 of the dynamic and aggressive Isabella of Castile and the crafty and persistent Ferdinand of Aragon did not bring about administrative unity. Isabella and Ferdinand were, however, able to exert their authority in ways similar to the rulers of France and England. They curbed aristocratic power by excluding aristocrats and great territorial magnates from the royal council, and instead appointed only men of middle-class background. The council and various government boards recruited men trained in Roman law, which exalted the power of the Crown. They also secured from the Spanish pope Alexander VI the right to appoint bishops in Spain and in the Hispanic territories in America, enabling them to establish the equivalent of a national church. In 1492 their armies conquered Granada, the last territory held by Arabs in southern Spain.

Ferdinand and Isabella's rule also marked the start of greater persecution of the Jews. In the Middle Ages, the kings of France and England had expelled the Jews from their kingdoms, and many had sought refuge in Spain. During the long centuries of the reconquista (see page 398), Christian kings in Spain had renewed Jewish rights and privileges; in fact, Jewish industry, intelligence, and money had supported royal power. But while Christians of all classes borrowed from Jewish moneylenders and while all who could afford them sought Jewish physicians, a strong undercurrent of resentment of Jewish influence and wealth festered.

In the fourteenth century anti-Semitism in Spain was aggravated by fiery anti-Jewish preaching, by economic dislocation, and by the search for a scapegoat during the Black Death. Anti-Semitic pogroms, violent massacres and riots directed against Jews, swept the towns of Spain, and perhaps 40 percent of the Jewish population was killed or forced to convert. Those who converted were called *conversos* (kuhn-VEHR-sohz) or New Christians. Conversos were often well educated and held prominent positions in government, the church, medicine, law, and business.

Such successes bred resentment. Aristocrats resented their financial dependence on conversos, the poor hated the converso tax collectors, and churchmen doubted the sincerity of their conversions. Queen Isabella shared these suspicions, and she and Ferdinand received permission from Pope Sixtus IV to establish an Inquisition to "search out and punish converts from Judaism who had transgressed against Christianity by secretly adhering to Jewish beliefs and performing rites of the Jews."[3] Investigations and trials began immediately, with officials of the Inquisition looking for conversos who showed any sign of incomplete conversion, such as not eating pork.

Recent scholarship has carefully analyzed documents of the Inquisition. Most conversos identified themselves as sincere Christians; many came from families that had received baptism generations before. In response, officials of the Inquisition developed a new type of anti-Semitism. A person's status as a Jew, they argued, could not be changed by religious conversion, but was in the person's blood and was heritable, so Jews could never be true Christians. Under what were known as "purity of blood" laws, having "pure Christian blood" became a requirement for noble status. Ideas about Jews developed in Spain became important components in European concepts of race, and discussions of "Jewish blood" later expanded into discriminatory definitions of the "Jewish race."

In 1492, shortly after the conquest of Granada, Isabella and Ferdinand issued an edict expelling all practicing Jews from Spain. Of the community of perhaps 200,000 Jews, 150,000 fled. Absolute religious orthodoxy and "purity of blood" served as the theoretical foundation of the Spanish national state.

The Habsburgs

War and diplomacy were important ways that states increased their power in sixteenth-century Europe, but so was marriage. Because almost all of Europe was ruled by hereditary dynasties — the Papal States and a few cities being the exceptions — claiming and holding resources involved shrewd marital strategies, for it was far cheaper to gain land by inheritance than by war.

The benefits of an advantageous marriage stretched across generations, as can be seen most dramatically with the Habsburgs. The Holy Roman emperor Frederick III, a Habsburg who was the ruler of most of Austria, acquired only a small amount of territory — but a great deal of money — with his marriage to Princess Eleanore of Portugal in 1452. He arranged for his son Maximilian to marry Europe's most prominent heiress, Mary of Burgundy, in 1477; she inherited the Netherlands, Luxembourg, and the county of Burgundy in what is now eastern France. Through this union with the rich and powerful duchy of Burgundy, the Austrian house of Habsburg, already the strongest ruling family in the empire, became an international power. The marriage of Maximilian and Mary angered the French, who considered Burgundy French territory, and it inaugurated centuries of conflict between the Habsburgs and the kings of France. Within the empire, German principalities that resented Austria's pre-eminence began to see that they shared interests with France.

Maximilian learned the lesson of marital politics well, marrying his son and daughter to the children of Ferdinand and Isabella, the rulers of Spain, much of southern Italy, and eventually the Spanish New World empire. His grandson Charles V (1500–1558) fell heir to a vast and incredibly diverse collection of states and peoples, each governed in a different manner and held together only by the person of the emperor (Map 15.1). Charles was convinced that it was his duty to maintain the political and religious unity of Western Christendom. This conviction would be challenged far more than Charles ever anticipated.

Lands inherited by Charles V
Lands gained by Charles V, 1519–1556
States favorable to Charles V
Enemies of Charles V
Boundary of the Holy Roman Empire

Spanish holdings, 1550

◀ **MAP 15.1** **The Global Empire of Charles V, ca. 1556** Charles V exercised theoretical jurisdiction over more European territory than anyone since Charlemagne. He also claimed authority over large parts of North and South America, although actual Spanish control was weak in much of this area.

The Protestant Reformation

What were the central ideas of Protestant reformers, and why were they appealing to various groups across Europe?

Calls for reform in the church came from many quarters in early-sixteenth-century Europe—from educated laypeople such as Christian humanists and urban residents, from villagers and artisans, and from church officials themselves. This dissatisfaction helps explain why the ideas of Martin Luther, an obscure professor from a new and not very prestigious German university, found a ready audience. Within a decade of his first publishing his ideas (using the new technology of the printing press), much of central Europe and Scandinavia had broken with the Catholic Church in a movement that came to be known as the Protestant Reformation. In addition, even more radical concepts of the Christian message were being developed and linked to calls for social change.

Criticism of the Church

Sixteenth-century Europeans were deeply pious. Despite—or perhaps because of—the depth of their piety, many people were also highly critical of the Roman Catholic Church and its clergy. Papal conflicts with rulers and the Great Schism (see page 417) badly damaged the prestige of church leaders. Papal tax collection methods were also attacked, and some criticized the papacy itself as an institution. Court records, written descriptions of bishops' visitations of parishes, and even popular songs and printed images show widespread anticlericalism, or opposition to the clergy.

In the early sixteenth century, critics of the church concentrated their attacks on clerical immorality, ignorance, and absenteeism. Charges of immorality were aimed at a number of priests who were drunkards, neglected the rule of celibacy, gambled, or indulged in fancy dress. Charges of ignorance applied to barely literate priests who delivered poor-quality sermons and who were obviously ignorant of the Latin words of the Mass.

In regard to absenteeism, many clerics, especially higher ecclesiastics, held several benefices (offices) simultaneously—a practice termed pluralism. However, they seldom visited the communities served by the benefices, let alone performed the spiritual responsibilities those offices entailed. Instead, they collected revenues from all the benefices assigned to them and hired a poor priest to fulfill their spiritual duties, paying him just a fraction of the income.

There was also local resentment of clerical privileges and immunities. Priests, monks, and nuns were exempt from civic responsibilities, such as defending the city and paying taxes. Yet religious orders frequently held large amounts of urban property, in some cities as much as one-third. City governments were increasingly determined to integrate the clergy into civic life. This brought city leaders into opposition with bishops and the papacy, which for centuries had stressed the independence of the church from lay control and the distinction between members of the clergy and laypeople.

Martin Luther

By itself, widespread criticism of the church did not lead to the dramatic changes of the sixteenth century. Those resulted from the personal religious struggle of a German university professor, Martin Luther (1483–1546). Luther's father wanted him to be a lawyer, but a sense of religious calling led him to join the Augustinian friars, an order whose members often preached to, taught, and assisted the poor. Luther was ordained a priest in 1507 and after additional study earned a doctorate of theology. From 1512 until his death in 1546 he served as professor of the Scriptures at the new University of Wittenberg.

Martin Luther was a very conscientious friar, but his scrupulous observance of the religious routine, frequent confessions, and fasting gave him only temporary relief from anxieties about sin and his ability to meet God's demands. Through his study of Saint Paul's letters in the New Testament, he gradually arrived at a new understanding of Christian doctrine. His understanding is often summarized as "faith alone, grace alone, scripture alone." He believed that salvation and justification (righteousness in God's eyes) come through faith, and that faith is a free gift of God, not the result of human effort. God's word is revealed only in biblical scripture, not in the traditions of the church.

At the same time that Luther was engaged in scholarly reflections and professorial lecturing, Pope Leo X authorized a special Saint Peter's indulgence to finance his building plans in Rome. An **indulgence** was a document, signed by the pope or another church official, that substituted for penance. The archbishop who controlled the area in which Wittenberg was located, Albert of Mainz, also promoted the sale of indulgences, in his case to pay off a debt he had incurred to be named bishop of several additional territories. Albert's sales campaign, run by a Dominican friar who mounted an advertising blitz, promised that the purchase of indulgences would bring full forgiveness for one's own sins or buy release from purgatory for a loved one. One of the slogans — "As soon as coin in coffer rings, the soul from purgatory springs" — brought phenomenal success.

Luther was severely troubled that many people believed that they had no further need for repentance once they had purchased indulgences. He wrote a letter to Archbishop Albert on the subject and enclosed in Latin his "Ninety-five Theses on the Power of Indulgences." His argument was that indulgences undermined the seriousness of the sacrament of penance and competed with the preaching of the Gospel. After Luther's death, biographies reported that the theses were also posted on the door of the church at Wittenberg Castle on October 31, 1517. Such an act would have been very strange — they were in Latin and written for those learned in theology, not for normal churchgoers — but it has become a standard part of Luther lore. In any case, Luther intended the theses for academic debate, but by December 1517 they had been translated into German and were being read throughout central Europe. Luther

Ihr deutschen merckt mich recht/
    Des heiligen Vaters Papstes Knecht/
Bin ich/vnd br ingeuch jßt allein/
    Zehn taufent vnd neun hundert carein/
Jnad vnd Ablaß von einer Sünd/
    Vor euch/ewer Eltern/Weib vnd Kind/
Sol ein jeder gewehret fein
    So viel jhr legt ins Kästelein/
So bald der Gülden im Becken klingt/
    Im huy die Seel im Himel springt/

Selling Indulgences   A German single-page pamphlet shows a monk offering an indulgence, with the official seals of the pope attached, as people run to put their money in the box in exchange for his promise of heavenly bliss, symbolized by the dove above his head. Indulgences were sold widely in Germany, and they were the first Catholic practice that Luther criticized openly. This pamphlet also attacks the sale of indulgences, calling it devilish and deceitful, a point of view expressed in the woodcut by the peddler's riding on a donkey, an animal that had long been used as a symbol of ignorance. (akg-images)

was ordered to go to Rome, but he was able to avoid this because the ruler of the territory in which he lived protected him. The pope nonetheless ordered him to recant many of his ideas, and Luther publicly burned the letter containing the papal order. In this highly charged atmosphere, the twenty-one-year-old emperor Charles V summoned Luther to appear before the **Diet of Worms**, an assembly of representatives from the territories of the Holy Roman Empire meeting in the city of Worms in 1521. Luther refused to give in to demands that he take back his ideas:

> Unless I am convinced by the evidence of Scripture or by plain reason — for I do not accept the authority of the Pope or the councils alone, since it is established that they have often erred and contradicted themselves — I am bound by the Scriptures I have cited and my conscience is captive to the Word of God. I cannot and will not recant anything, for it is neither safe nor right to go against conscience.[4]

the reformation of the city of Geneva. There, beginning in 1541, Calvin worked assiduously to establish a Christian society ruled by God through civil magistrates and reformed ministers. Geneva thereby became the model of a Christian community for sixteenth-century Protestant reformers.

To understand Calvin's Geneva, it is necessary to understand Calvin's ideas. These he embodied in *The Institutes of the Christian Religion*, first published in 1536 and modified several times afterward. The cornerstone of Calvin's theology was his belief in the absolute sovereignty and omnipotence of God and the total weakness of humanity. Before the infinite power of God, he asserted, men and women are as insignificant as grains of sand.

Calvin did not ascribe free will to human beings, because that would detract from the sovereignty of God. According to his beliefs, men and women could not actively work to achieve salvation; rather, God decided at the beginning of time who would be saved and who damned. This viewpoint constitutes the theological principle called **predestination**. Many people consider the doctrine of predestination, which dates back to Saint Augustine and Saint Paul, to be a pessimistic view of the nature of God. But "this terrible decree," as even Calvin called it, did not lead to pessimism or fatalism. Instead, although Calvinists believed that one's own actions could do nothing to change one's fate, many came to believe that hard work, thrift, and moral conduct could serve as signs that one was among the "elect" chosen for salvation. Any occupation or profession could be a God-given "calling" and should be carried out with diligence and dedication.

Calvin transformed Geneva into a community based on his religious principles. The most powerful organization in the city became the Consistory, a group of laymen and pastors charged with investigating and disciplining deviations from proper doctrine and conduct.

Religious refugees from France, England, Spain, Scotland, and Italy visited Calvin's Geneva, which became the model of a Christian community for many. Subsequently, the Reformed Church of Calvin served as the model for the Presbyterian Church in Scotland, the Huguenot (HYOO-guh-naht) Church in France, and the Puritan Churches in England and New England. Calvinism became the compelling force in international Protestantism, first in Europe and then in many Dutch and English colonies around the world.

The Catholic Reformation

How did the Catholic Church respond to the new religious situation?

Between 1517 and 1547 Protestantism made remarkable advances. Nevertheless, the Roman Catholic Church made a significant comeback. After about 1540 no new large areas of Europe, other than the Netherlands, accepted Protestant beliefs (Map 15.2). Many historians see the developments within the Catholic Church after the Protestant Reformation as two interrelated movements, one a drive for internal reform linked to earlier reform efforts, and the other a Counter-Reformation that opposed Protestants intellectually, politically, militarily, and institutionally. In both movements, papal reforms and new religious orders were important agents.

Papal Reforms and the Council of Trent

Renaissance popes and advisers were not blind to the need for church reforms, but they resisted calls for a general council representing the entire church, fearing loss of power, revenue, and prestige. This changed beginning with Pope Paul III (pontificate 1534–1549), under whom the papal court became the center of the reform movement rather than its chief opponent.

In 1542 Pope Paul III established the Supreme Sacred Congregation of the Roman and Universal Inquisition, often called the Holy Office, with jurisdiction over the Roman Inquisition, a powerful instrument of the Catholic Reformation. The Inquisition was a committee of six cardinals with judicial authority over all Catholics and the power to arrest, imprison, and execute. Within the Papal States, the Inquisition effectively destroyed heresy (and some heretics).

Pope Paul III also called a general council, which met intermittently from 1545 to 1563 at Trent, an imperial city close to Italy. It was called not only to reform the church but also to secure reconciliation with the Protestants. Lutherans and Calvinists were invited to participate, but their insistence that the Scriptures be the sole basis for discussion made reconciliation impossible.

Nonetheless, the decrees of the Council of Trent laid a solid basis for the spiritual renewal of the Catholic Church. It gave equal validity to the Scriptures and to tradition as sources of religious truth and authority. It reaffirmed the seven sacraments and the traditional Catholic teaching on transubstantiation (the transformation of bread and wine into the body and blood of Christ in the Eucharist). It tackled the disciplinary matters that had disillusioned the faithful, requiring bishops to reside in their own dioceses, suppressing pluralism and the selling of church offices, and forbidding the sale of indulgences. Clerics who kept concubines were to give them up, and bishops were given greater authority. The council also required every diocese to establish a seminary for educating and training clergy. Seminary professors were to determine whether candidates for ordination had vocations, genuine callings to the priesthood. This was a novel idea, since from the time of the early church, parents had determined their sons' (and daughters') religious careers. Finally, great emphasis was placed on preaching to and instructing the laity, especially the uneducated. One decision had especially important social consequences for laypeople. The Council of Trent stipulated that for a marriage to be valid, consent (the essence of marriage) as given in the vows had to be made publicly before witnesses, one of whom had to be the parish priest. Trent thereby ended the widespread practice of secret marriages in Catholic countries. For four centuries the doctrinal and disciplinary legislation of Trent served as the basis for Roman Catholic faith, organization, and practice.

New Religious Orders

Just as seminaries provided education, so did new religious orders, which aimed to raise the moral and intellectual level of the clergy and people. The Ursuline (UHR-suh-luhn) order of nuns, founded by Angela Merici (1474–1540), attained enormous prestige for its education of women. The daughter of a country gentleman, Merici worked for many years among the poor, sick, and uneducated around her native Brescia in northern Italy. In 1535 she established the first women's religious order

Predominant religion in 1555

- Lutheran
- Calvinist (Reformed)
- Church of England
- Roman Catholic
- Eastern Orthodox
- Muslim
- Spread of Calvinism, from 1541
- Huguenot center
- Ottoman Empire, 1566

0   150   300 miles
0   150   300 kilometers

Augsburg
Peace of Augsburg
1555

Wittenberg
Martin Luther writes
Ninety-five Theses
1517

Trent
Council of Trent
1545–1563

Geneva
Calvin assists in
Reformation beginning
in 1541

Penetration of Calvinism
to England after 1558

Worms
Edict of Worms
1521

Nantes
Edict of Nantes
1598

◀ **MAP 15.2** **Religious Divisions in Europe, ca. 1555** The Reformation shattered the religious unity of Western Christendom. The situation was even more complicated than a map of this scale can show. Many cities within the Holy Roman Empire, for example, accepted a different faith than did the surrounding countryside; Augsburg, Basel, and Strasbourg were all Protestant, though surrounded by territory ruled by Catholic nobles.

concentrating exclusively on teaching young girls, with the goal of re-Christianizing society by training future wives and mothers. After receiving papal approval in 1565, the Ursulines rapidly spread to France and the New World.

Another important new order was the Society of Jesus, or Jesuits. Founded by Ignatius Loyola (1491–1556) in 1540, this order played a powerful international role in strengthening Catholicism in Europe and spreading the faith around the world. While recuperating from a severe battle wound in his legs, Loyola studied the life of Christ and other religious books and decided to give up his military career and become a soldier of Christ. The first Jesuits, whom Loyola recruited primarily from wealthy merchant and professional families, saw the causes and cures of church problems as related not to doctrinal issues but to people's spiritual condition. Reform of the church, as Luther and Calvin understood that term, played no role in the future the Jesuits planned for themselves. Instead their goal was "to help souls." The Society of Jesus developed into a highly centralized, tightly knit organization whose professed members vowed to go anywhere the pope said they were needed. They established schools that adopted the modern humanist curricula and that educated the sons of the nobility as well as the poor. The Jesuits attracted many recruits and achieved phenomenal success for the papacy and the reformed Catholic Church, carrying Christianity to much of South and Central America, India, and Japan before 1550 and to Brazil, North America, and the Congo in the 1600s. Within Europe the Jesuits brought almost all of southern Germany and much of eastern Europe back to Catholicism. Also, as confessors and spiritual directors to kings, Jesuits exerted great political influence.

Teresa of Ávila Teresa of Ávila (1515–1582) was a Spanish nun who experienced mystical visions, reformed her religious order, and founded new convents, seeing them as answers to the spread of Protestantism elsewhere in Europe. In this wood carving from 1625, the Spanish artist Gregorio Fernandez shows Saint Teresa book in hand, actively teaching. The influence of her ideas and actions led the pope to give Teresa the title "Doctor of the Church" in 1970, the first woman to be so honored. (Gregorio Fernandez [1576–1636], *Saint Teresa of Ávila*, 1625. Polychromatic Baroque carving on wood, Valladolid, Spain. National Museum of Sculpture/© P. Rotger/ Iberfoto/The Image Works)

Religious Violence

What were the causes and consequences of religious violence, including riots, wars, and witch-hunts?

In 1559 France and Spain signed the Treaty of Cateau-Cambrésis, which ended the long conflict known as the Habsburg-Valois wars. However, over the next century religious differences led to riots, civil wars, and international conflicts. Especially in France and the Netherlands, Protestants and Catholics opposed one another through preaching, teaching, and violence, for each side regarded the other as a poison in the community that would provoke the wrath of God. Catholics and Protestants alike feared people of other faiths, whom they often saw as agents of Satan. Even more, they feared those explicitly identified with Satan: people believed to be witches. This era saw the most virulent witch persecutions in European history, as both Protestants and Catholics tried to make their cities and states more godly.

French Religious Wars

The costs of the Habsburg-Valois wars, waged intermittently through the first half of the sixteenth century, forced the French to increase taxes and borrow heavily. King Francis I's treaty with the pope (see page 433) gave the French crown a rich supplement of money and offices and also a vested financial interest in Catholicism. Significant numbers of French people, however, were attracted to the "reformed religion," as Calvinism was called. Calvinism drew converts from among reform-minded members of the Catholic clergy, the industrious middle classes, and artisan groups. Additionally, some French nobles became Calvinist, either because of religious conviction or because this allowed them to oppose the monarchy. By the middle of the sixteenth century perhaps one-tenth of the French population had become **Huguenots**, the name given to French Calvinists.

Both Calvinists and Catholics believed that the others' books, services, and ministers polluted the community. Preachers communicated these ideas in sermons, triggering violence at the baptisms, marriages, and funerals of the other faith. Armed clashes between Catholic royalist nobles and Calvinist antimonarchical nobles occurred in many parts of France.

Calvinist teachings called the power of sacred images into question, and mobs in many cities destroyed statues, stained-glass windows, and paintings. Though it was often inspired by fiery Protestant sermons, this iconoclasm is an example of men and women carrying out the Reformation themselves, rethinking the church's system of meaning. Catholic mobs responded by defending the sacred images, and crowds on both sides killed their opponents, often in gruesome ways.

A savage Catholic attack on Calvinists in Paris on August 24, 1572 — Saint Bartholomew's Day — followed the usual pattern. The occasion was the marriage of the king's sister Margaret of Valois to the Protestant Henry of Navarre, which was intended to help reconcile Catholics and Huguenots. Instead Huguenot wedding guests in Paris were massacred, and other Protestants were slaughtered by mobs. Violence spread to the provinces, where thousands were killed. The Saint Bartholomew's Day massacre led to a civil war that dragged on for fifteen years. As a result, agriculture in many areas was destroyed, commercial life declined severely, and starvation and death haunted the land.

Massacre of the Huguenots, **1573** The Italian artist Giorgio Vasari depicts the Saint Bartholomew's Day massacre in Paris, one of many bloody events in the religious wars that accompanied the Reformation. Here Admiral Coligny, a leader of the French Protestants (called Huguenots), is hurled from a window while his followers are slaughtered. This fresco was commissioned by Pope Gregory XIII to decorate a hall in the Vatican Palace in Rome. Both sides used visual images to win followers and celebrate their victories. (Giorgio Vasari [1511–1574], Sala Regia, Apostolic Palace, Vatican City/De Agostini Picture Library/The Bridgeman Art Library)

What ultimately saved France was a small group of moderates of both faiths called **politiques** (POH-lee-teeks) who believed that only the restoration of a strong monarchy could reverse the trend toward collapse. The politiques also favored officially recognizing the Huguenots. The death of the French queen Catherine de' Medici, followed by the assassination of her son King Henry III, paved the way for the accession of Henry of Navarre (the unfortunate bridegroom of the Saint Bartholomew's Day massacre), a politique who became Henry IV (r. 1589–1610).

Henry's willingness to sacrifice religious principles to political necessity saved France. He converted to Catholicism but also, in 1598, issued the Edict of Nantes (nahnt), which granted liberty of conscience (freedom of thought) and liberty of public worship to Huguenots in 150 fortified towns. By helping restore internal peace in France, the reign of Henry IV and the Edict of Nantes paved the way for French kings to claim absolute power in the seventeenth century.

Civil Wars in the Netherlands

In the Netherlands a movement for church reform developed into a struggle for Dutch independence. The Catholic emperor Charles V had inherited the seventeen provinces that compose present-day Belgium and the Netherlands (see page 435). In the Netherlands, as elsewhere, corruption in the Roman Catholic Church and the critical spirit of the Renaissance provoked pressure for reform, and Lutheran ideas took root. Charles V had grown up in the Netherlands, however, and he was able to limit the impact of the new ideas. Charles V abdicated in 1556 and transferred power over the Netherlands to his son Philip II, who had grown up in Spain. Although Philip, like his father, opposed Protestantism, Protestant ideas spread in the Netherlands.

thousands of Chinese emigrated to the Philippines, where they acquired commercial dominance of the island of Luzon by 1600.

Another center of Indian Ocean trade was India, the crucial link between the Persian Gulf and the Southeast Asian and East Asian trade networks. The subcontinent had ancient links with its neighbors to the northwest: trade between South Asia and Mesopotamia dates back to the origins of human civilization. Trade among ports bordering the Indian Ocean was revived in the Middle Ages by Arab merchants who circumnavigated India on their way to trade in the South China Sea. The need for stopovers led to the establishment of trading posts at Gujarat and on the Malabar coast, where the cities of Calicut and Quilon became thriving commercial centers.

The inhabitants of India's Coromandel coast traditionally looked to Southeast Asia, where they had ancient trading and cultural ties. Hinduism and Buddhism arrived in Southeast Asia from India during the Middle Ages, and a brisk trade between Southeast Asian and Coromandel port cities persisted from that time until the arrival of the Portuguese in the sixteenth century. India itself was an important contributor of goods to the world trading system. Most of the world's pepper was grown in India, and Indian cotton and silk textiles, mainly from the Gujarat region, were also highly prized.

Peoples and Cultures of the Indian Ocean

Indian Ocean trade connected peoples from the Malay Peninsula (the southern extremity of the Asian continent), India, China, and East Africa, among whom there was an enormous variety of languages, cultures, and religions. In spite of this diversity, certain sociocultural similarities linked these peoples, especially in Southeast Asia.

For example, by the fifteenth century inhabitants of what we call Indonesia, Malaysia, the Philippines, and the many islands in between all spoke languages of the Austronesian family, reflecting continuing interactions among them. A common environment led to a diet based on rice, fish, palms, and palm wine. Rice, harvested by women, is probably indigenous to the region, and it formed the staple of the diet. The seas provided many varieties of fish, crabs, and shrimp, and fishing served as the chief male occupation, well ahead of agriculture. Also, sugarcane grew in profusion, and it was chewed as a confectionery and used as a sweetener.[3]

In comparison to India, China, or even Europe after the Black Death, Southeast Asia was sparsely populated. People were concentrated in port cities and in areas of intense rice cultivation. Another difference between Southeast Asia and India, China, and Europe was the higher status of women—their primary role in planting and harvesting rice gave them authority and economic power. At marriage, which typically occurred around age twenty, the groom paid the bride (or sometimes her family) a sum of money called bride wealth, which remained under her control. This practice was in sharp contrast to the Chinese, Indian, and European dowry, which came under the husband's control. Property was administered jointly, in contrast to the Chinese principle and Indian practice that wives had no say in the disposal of family property. All children, regardless of gender, inherited equally, and when Islam arrived in the region, the rule requiring sons to receive double the inheritance of daughters was never implemented.

Respect for women carried over to the commercial sphere. Women participated in business as partners and independent entrepreneurs, even undertaking long sea

The Port of Calicut in India   The port of Calicut, located on the west coast of India, was a center of the Indian Ocean spice trade during the Middle Ages. Vasco da Gama arrived in Calicut in 1498 and obtained permission to trade there, leading to hostilities between the Portuguese and the Arab traders who had previously dominated the port. (Private Collection/The Stapleton Collection/The Bridgeman Art Library)

voyages to accompany their wares. When Portuguese and Dutch men settled in the region and married local women, their wives continued to play important roles in trade and commerce.

In contrast to most parts of the world other than Africa, Southeast Asian peoples had an accepting attitude toward premarital sexual activity and placed no premium on virginity at marriage. Divorce carried no social stigma and was easily attainable if a pair proved incompatible. Either the woman or the man could initiate a divorce, and common property and children were divided.

Trade with Africa and the Middle East

On the east coast of Africa, Swahili-speaking city-states engaged in the Indian Ocean trade, exchanging ivory, rhinoceros horn, tortoise shells, copra (dried coconut), and slaves for textiles, spices, cowrie shells, porcelain, and other goods. The most important cities were Mogadishu, Mombasa, and Kilwa, which had converted to Islam by the eleventh century. Peopled by confident and urbane merchants, the cities were known for their prosperity and culture.

West Africa also played an important role in world trade. In the fifteenth century most of the gold that reached Europe came from the Sudan region in West Africa and, in particular, from the kingdom of Mali near present-day Ghana. Transported across the Sahara by Arab and African traders on camels, the gold was sold in the ports of

North Africa. Other trading routes led to the Egyptian cities of Alexandria and Cairo, where the Venetians held commercial privileges.

Inland nations that sat astride the north-south caravan routes grew wealthy from this trade. In the mid-thirteenth century the kingdom of Mali emerged as an important player on the overland trade route. In later centuries, however, the diversion of gold away from the trans-Sahara routes would weaken the inland states of Africa politically and economically.

Gold was one important object of trade; slaves were another. Slavery was practiced in Africa, as it was virtually everywhere else in the world, long before the arrival of Europeans. Arab and African merchants took West African slaves to the Mediterranean to be sold in European, Egyptian, and Middle Eastern markets and also brought eastern Europeans to West Africa as slaves. In addition, Indian and Arab merchants traded slaves in the coastal regions of East Africa.

The Middle East served as an intermediary for trade between Europe, Africa, and Asia and was also an important supplier of goods for foreign exchange, especially silk and cotton. Two great rival empires, the Persian Safavids and the Turkish Ottomans, dominated the region, competing for control over western trade routes to the East. By the mid-sixteenth century the Ottomans had established control over eastern Mediterranean sea routes to trading centers in Syria, Palestine, Egypt, and the rest of North Africa. Their power also extended into Europe as far west as Vienna.

Genoese and Venetian Middlemen

Compared to the riches and vibrancy of the East, Europe constituted a minor outpost in the world trading system, for European craftsmen produced few products to rival those of Asia. However, Europeans desired luxury goods from the East, and in the late Middle Ages such trade was controlled by the Italian city-states of Venice and Genoa. Venice had opened the gateway to Asian trade in 1304, when it established formal relations with the sultan of Mamluk Egypt and started operations in Cairo. In exchange for European products like Spanish and English wool, German metal goods, and Flemish textiles, the Venetians obtained luxury items like spices, silks, and carpets from middlemen in the eastern Mediterranean and Asia Minor. Because Eastern demand for European goods was low, Venetians funded their purchases through shipping and trade in firearms and slaves.

Venice's ancient trading rival was Genoa. By the time the Crusades ended around 1270, Genoa dominated the northern route to Asia through the Black Sea. From then until the fourteenth century, the Genoese expanded their trade routes as far as Persia and the Far East. In 1291 they sponsored a failed expedition into the Atlantic in search of India. This voyage reveals the early origins of Genoese interest in Atlantic exploration.

In the fifteenth century, with Venice claiming victory in the spice trade, the Genoese shifted focus from trade to finance and from the Black Sea to the western Mediterranean. Located on the northwestern coast of Italy, Genoa had always been active in the western Mediterranean, trading with North African ports, southern France, Spain, and even England and Flanders through the Strait of Gibraltar. When Spanish and Portuguese voyages began to explore the western Atlantic (see page 468), Genoese merchants, navigators, and financiers provided their skills and capital to the Iberian monarchs.

A major element of Italian trade was slavery. Merchants purchased slaves, many of whom were fellow Christians, in the Balkans of southeastern Europe. After the loss of the Black Sea trade routes—and thus the source of slaves—to the Ottomans, the Genoese sought new supplies of slaves in the West, eventually seizing or buying and selling the Guanches (indigenous peoples from the Canary Islands), Muslim prisoners and Jewish refugees from Spain, and, by the early 1500s, both black and Berber Africans. With the growth of Spanish colonies in the New World, Genoese and Venetian merchants became important players in the Atlantic slave trade.

Italian experience in colonial administration, slaving, and international trade served as a model for the Iberian states as they pushed European expansion to new heights. Mariners, merchants, and financiers from Venice and Genoa—most notably Christopher Columbus—played crucial roles in bringing the fruits of this experience to the Iberian Peninsula and to the New World.

The European Voyages of Discovery

Why and how did Europeans undertake ambitious voyages of expansion?

Europe was by no means isolated before the voyages of exploration and its "discovery" of the New World. But because Europeans did not produce many products desired by Eastern elites, they were modest players in the Indian Ocean trading world. As Europe recovered after the Black Death, new European players entered the scene with novel technology, eager to spread Christianity and to undo Italian and Ottoman domination of trade with the East. A century after the plague, Iberian explorers began the overseas voyages that helped create the modern world, with immense consequences for their own continent and the rest of the planet.

Causes of European Expansion

European expansion had multiple causes. The first was economic. By the middle of the fifteenth century Europe was experiencing a revival of population and economic activity after the lows of the Black Death. This revival created renewed demand for luxuries, especially spices, from the East. The fall of Constantinople and the subsequent Ottoman control of trade routes created obstacles to fulfilling these demands. European merchants and rulers eager for the profits of trade thus needed to find new sources of precious metal to exchange with the Ottomans or trade routes that bypassed the Ottomans.

Why were spices so desirable? Introduced into western Europe by the Crusaders in the twelfth century, pepper, nutmeg, ginger, mace, cinnamon, and cloves added flavor and variety to the monotonous European diet. Not only did spices serve as flavorings for food, but they were also used in anointing oil and as incense for religious rituals, and as perfumes, medicines, and dyes in daily life. Apart from their utility, the expense and exotic origins of spices meant that they were a high-status good, which European elites could use to demonstrate their social standing.

Religious fervor and the crusading spirit were another important catalyst for expansion. Just seven months separated Isabella and Ferdinand's conquest of the emirate of Granada, the last remaining Muslim state on the Iberian Peninsula, and Columbus's departure across the Atlantic. Overseas exploration thus transferred the militaristic religious fervor of the reconquista (reconquest) to new non-Christian territories. As they conquered indigenous empires, Iberians brought the attitudes and administrative practices developed during the reconquista to the Americas. Conquistadors fully expected to be rewarded with land, titles, and power over conquered peoples, just as the leaders of the reconquista had been.

A third motivation was the dynamic spirit of the Renaissance. Like other men of the Renaissance era, explorers sought to win glory for their amazing exploits and demonstrated a genuine interest in learning more about unknown waters. Scholars have frequently described the European discoveries as an outcome of Renaissance curiosity about the physical universe. The detailed journals kept by European voyagers attest to their fascination with the new peoples and places they visited.

Individual explorers often manifested all of these desires at once. Columbus, a devout Christian, aimed to discover new territories where Christianity could be spread while seeking a direct trade route to Asia. The motives of Portuguese explorer Bartholomew Diaz were, in his own words, "to serve God and His Majesty, to give light to those who were in darkness and to grow rich as all men desire to do." When the Portuguese explorer Vasco da Gama reached the port of Calicut, India, in 1498 and a native asked what he wanted, he replied, "Christians and spices."[4] The bluntest of the Spanish conquistadors (kahn-KEES-tuh-dawrz), or conquerors, Hernán Cortés, announced as he prepared to conquer Mexico, "I have come to win gold, not to plow the fields like a peasant."[5]

Ordinary seamen joined these voyages to escape poverty at home, to continue a family trade, or to win a few crumbs of the great riches of empire. Common sailors were ill-paid, and life at sea meant danger, unbearable stench, hunger, and overcrowding. For months at a time, 100 to 120 people lived and worked in a space of 1,600 to 2,000 square feet.

The people who stayed at home had a powerful impact on the voyages of discovery. Merchants provided the capital for many early voyages and had a strong say in their course. To gain authorization and financial support for their expeditions, they sought official sponsorship from the Crown. Competition among European monarchs for the prestige and profit of overseas exploration thus constituted another crucial factor in encouraging the steady stream of expeditions that began in the late fifteenth century.

The small number of Europeans who could read provided a rapt audience for tales of fantastic places and unknown peoples. Cosmography, natural history, and geography aroused enormous interest among educated people in the fifteenth and sixteenth centuries. One of the most popular books of the time was the fourteenth-century text *The Travels of Sir John Mandeville*, which purported to be a firsthand account of the author's travels in the Middle East, India, and China. Although we now know they were fictional, these fantastic tales of cannibals, one-eyed giants, men with the heads of dogs, and other marvels were believed for centuries. Columbus took a copy of Mandeville and the equally popular and more reliable *The Travels of Marco Polo* on his voyage in 1492.

Technology and the Rise of Exploration

Technological developments in shipbuilding, navigation, and weaponry enabled European expansion. Since ancient times, most seagoing vessels had been narrow, open boats called galleys, propelled by slaves or convicts manning the oars. Though well

Brass Astrolabe   Between 1500 and 1635 over nine hundred ships sailed from Portugal to ports on the Indian Ocean in annual fleets composed of five to ten ships. Portuguese sailors used astrolabes, such as the one pictured here, to accurately plot their position. (© The Trustees of the British Museum/Art Resource, NY)

suited to the placid waters of the Mediterranean, galleys could not withstand the rougher conditions in the Atlantic. The need for sturdier craft, as well as population losses caused by the Black Death, forced the development of a new style of ship that would not require much manpower. Over the course of the fifteenth century the Portuguese developed the **caravel**, a small, light, three-mast sailing ship with triangular lateen sails. The caravel was much more maneuverable than the galley. When fitted with cannon, it could dominate larger vessels.

This period also saw great strides in cartography and navigational aids. Around 1410 Arab scholars reintroduced Europeans to **Ptolemy's *Geography***. Written in the second century, the work synthesized the geographical knowledge of the classical world. It represented a major improvement over medieval cartography, showing the world as round and introducing the idea of latitude and longitude to plot a ship's position accurately. It also contained significant errors. Unaware of the Americas, Ptolemy showed the world as much smaller than it is, so that Asia appeared not very far to the west of Europe. Both the assets and the flaws of Ptolemy's work shaped the geographical knowledge that explorers like Christopher Columbus brought to their voyages.

The magnetic compass made it possible for sailors to determine their direction and position at sea. The astrolabe, an instrument invented by the ancient Greeks and perfected by Muslim navigators, was used to determine the altitude of the sun and other celestial bodies. It permitted mariners to plot their latitude, that is, their precise position north or south of the equator.

Like the astrolabe, much of the new technology that Europeans used on their voyages was borrowed from the East. Gunpowder, the compass, and the sternpost rudder were Chinese inventions. Advances in cartography also drew on the rich tradition of Judeo-Arabic mathematical and astronomical learning in Iberia. In exploring new territories, European sailors thus called on techniques and knowledge developed over centuries in China, the Muslim world, and trading centers along the Indian Ocean.

The Portuguese in Africa and Asia

For centuries Portugal was a small and poor nation on the margins of European life whose principal activities were fishing and subsistence farming. It would have been hard for a medieval European to predict Portugal's phenomenal success overseas after 1450. Yet Portugal had a long history of seafaring and navigation. Blocked from access to western Europe by Spain, the Portuguese turned to the Atlantic, whose waters they knew better than did other Europeans. Nature favored the Portuguese: winds blowing along their coast offered passage to Africa, its Atlantic islands, and, ultimately, Brazil. Once they had mastered the secret to sailing against the wind to return to Europe (by sailing farther west to catch winds from the southwest), they were ideally poised to lead Atlantic exploration.

In the early phases of Portuguese exploration, Prince Henry (1394–1460), a dynamic younger son of the king, played a leading role. A nineteenth-century scholar dubbed Henry "the Navigator" because of his support for the study of geography and navigation and for the annual expeditions he sponsored down the western coast of Africa. Although he never personally participated in voyages of exploration, Henry's involvement ensured that Portugal did not abandon the effort despite early disappointments.

Portugal's conquest of Ceuta, an Arab city in northern Morocco, in 1415 marked the beginning of European overseas expansion. In the 1420s, under Henry's direction, the Portuguese began to settle the Atlantic islands of Madeira (ca. 1420) and the Azores (1427). In 1443 they founded their first African commercial settlement at Arguin in North Africa. By the time of Henry's death in 1460, his support for exploration was vindicated—in Portuguese eyes—by thriving sugar plantations on the Atlantic islands, the first arrival of enslaved Africans in Portugal (see page 475), and new access to African gold.

Pepper Harvest   To break the monotony of their bland diet, Europeans had a passion for pepper, which—along with cinnamon, cloves, nutmeg, and ginger—was the main object of the Asian trade. We can appreciate the fifteenth-century expression "as dear as pepper": one kilo of pepper cost 2 grams of silver at the place of production in the East Indies and from 1 to 10 grams of silver in Alexandria, Egypt; 14 to 18 grams in Venice; and 20 to 30 grams at the markets of northern Europe. Here natives fill vats, and the dealer tastes a peppercorn for pungency. (Bibliothèque Nationale, Paris, France/Archives Charmet/The Bridgeman Art Library)

MAP 16.2 Overseas Exploration and Conquest in the Fifteenth and Sixteenth Centuries The voyages of discovery marked a dramatic new phase in the centuries-old migrations of European peoples. This map depicts the voyages of the most significant European explorers of the period.

The Portuguese next established fortified trading posts, called factories, on the gold-rich Guinea coast and penetrated into the African continent all the way to Timbuktu (Map 16.2). By 1500 Portugal controlled the flow of African gold to Europe. In contrast to the Spanish conquest of the Americas (see page 471), the Portuguese did not establish large settlements in West Africa or seek to control the political or cultural lives of those with whom they traded. Instead they sought easier and faster profits by inserting themselves into pre-existing trading systems. For the first century of their relations, African rulers were equal partners with the Portuguese, protected by their experienced armies and European vulnerability to tropical diseases.

In 1487 Bartholomew Diaz (ca. 1451–1500) rounded the Cape of Good Hope at the southern tip of Africa (see Map 16.2), but storms and a threatened mutiny

A New World Sugar Refinery in Brazil   Sugar was the most important and most profitable plantation crop in the New World. This image shows the processing and refinement of sugar on a Brazilian plantation. Sugarcane was grown, harvested, and processed by African slaves who labored under brutal and ruthless conditions to generate enormous profits for plantation owners. (Bibliothèque Nationale, Paris, France/Giraudon/The Bridgeman Art Library)

profitable to trade with African leaders, who were accustomed to dealing in enslaved people captured through warfare with neighboring powers. In 1483 the Portuguese established an alliance with the kingdom of Kongo. The royal family eventually converted to Christianity, and Portuguese merchants intermarried with Kongolese women, creating a permanent Afro-Portuguese community. From 1490 to 1530 Portuguese traders brought between three hundred and two thousand enslaved Africans to Lisbon each year. There they performed most of the manual labor and constituted 10 percent of the city's population.

In this stage of European expansion, the history of slavery became intertwined with the history of sugar. Originally sugar was an expensive luxury, but population increases and greater prosperity in the fifteenth century led to increasing demand. The establishment of sugar plantations on the Canary and Madeira Islands in the fifteenth century testifies to this demand.

Sugar was a particularly difficult crop to produce for profit. Seed-stems were planted by hand, thousands to the acre. When mature, the cane had to be harvested and processed rapidly to avoid spoiling. Moreover, sugarcane has a virtually constant growing season, meaning that there was no fallow period when workers could recuperate. The invention of roller mills to crush the cane more efficiently meant that yields could be significantly augmented, but only if a sufficient labor force was found to supply the mills. Europeans solved the labor problem by forcing first native islanders and then transported Africans to perform the backbreaking work.

The transatlantic slave trade that would ultimately result in the forced transport of over 12 million individuals began in 1518, when Spanish king Charles V authorized traders to bring enslaved Africans to New World colonies. The Portuguese brought the first slaves to Brazil around 1550; by 1600 four thousand were being imported annually. After its founding in 1621, the Dutch West India Company transported thousands of Africans to Brazil and the Caribbean, mostly to work on sugar planta- tions. In the late seventeenth century, with the chartering of the Royal African Company, the English began to bring slaves to Barbados and other English colonies in the Carib- bean and mainland North America.

Before 1700, when slavers decided it was better business to improve conditions, some 20 percent of slaves died on the voyage from Africa to the Americas.[10] The most common cause of death was dysentery induced by poor-quality food and water, lack of sanitation, and intense crowding. (To increase profits, slave traders packed several hundred captives on each ship.) Men were often kept in irons during the passage, while women and girls were subject to sexual abuse by sailors. On sugar plantations, death rates among enslaved people from illness and exhaustion were extremely high, leading to a constant stream of new human shipments from Africa. Driven by rising demands for sugar, cotton, tobacco, and other plantation crops, the tragic transatlantic slave trade reached its height in the eighteenth century.

The Birth of the Global Economy

With Europeans' discovery of the Americas and their exploration of the Pacific, the entire world was linked for the first time in history by seaborne trade. The opening of that trade brought into being three successive commercial empires: the Portuguese, the Spanish, and the Dutch.

The Portuguese were the first worldwide traders. In the sixteenth century they controlled the sea route to India. From their fortified bases at Goa on the Arabian Sea and at Malacca on the Malay Peninsula, ships carried goods to the Portuguese settlement at Macao, founded in 1557, in the South China Sea. From Macao Portuguese ships loaded with Chinese silks and porcelains sailed to the Japanese port of Nagasaki and to the Philippine port of Manila, where Chinese goods were exchanged for Spanish silver from New Spain. Throughout Asia the Portuguese traded in slaves. They also exported horses from Mesopotamia and copper from Arabia to India; from India they exported hawks and peacocks for the Chinese and Japanese markets. Back to Portugal they brought Asian spices that had been purchased with textiles produced in India and with gold and ivory from East Africa. They also shipped back sugar from their colony in Brazil, produced by African slaves whom they had transported across the Atlantic.

Becoming an imperial power a few decades later than the Portuguese, the Spanish were determined to claim their place in world trade. This was greatly facilitated by the discovery of immense riches in silver, first at Potosí in modern-day Bolivia and later in Mexico. Silver poured into Europe through the Spanish port of Seville, contributing to steep inflation across Europe. Demand for silver also created a need for slaves to work in the mines.

The Spanish Empire in the New World was basically land based, but across the Pacific the Spaniards built a seaborne empire centered at Manila in the Philippines. The city of Manila served as the transpacific bridge between Spanish America and China. In Manila Spanish traders used silver from American mines to purchase Chinese silk for European markets. The European demand for silk was so huge that in 1597, for example, 12 million pesos of silver, almost the total value of the transatlantic trade, moved from Acapulco in New Spain to Manila. After 1640, however, the Spanish silk trade declined in the face of stiff competition from Dutch imports.

In the seventeenth century the Dutch challenged the Spanish and Portuguese Empires. The Dutch East India Company was founded in 1602 with the stated intention of capturing the spice trade from the Portuguese. Drawing on their commercial wealth and long experience in European trade, by the end of the century the Dutch emerged as the most powerful worldwide seaborne trading power (see Chapter 19).

Changing Attitudes and Beliefs

How did new encounters shape cultural attitudes and beliefs in Europe and the New World?

The age of overseas expansion heightened Europeans' contacts with the rest of the world. These contacts gave birth to new ideas about the inherent superiority or inferiority of different races, in part to justify European participation in the slave trade. Religion became another means of cultural contact, as European missionaries aimed to spread Christianity in both the New World and East Asia, with mixed results. While Christianity was embraced in parts of the New World, it was met largely with suspicion in China and Japan. However, the East-West contacts led to exchanges of influential cultural and scientific ideas.

Religious Conversion

Converting indigenous people to Christianity was one of the most important justifications for European expansion. Jesuit missionaries were active in Japan and China in the sixteenth and seventeenth centuries, until authorities banned their teachings (see page 647). The first missionaries to the New World accompanied Columbus on his second voyage, and more than 2,500 Franciscans, Dominicans, Jesuits, and other friars crossed the Atlantic in the following century. Later French explorers were also accompanied by missionaries who preached to the Native American tribes who traded with the French.

Catholic friars were among the first Europeans to seek an understanding of native cultures and languages as part of their effort to render Christianity comprehensible to indigenous people. In Mexico they not only learned the Nahuatl language, but also taught it to non-Nahuatl-speaking groups to create a shared language for Christian teaching. They were also the most vociferous opponents of abuses committed by Spanish settlers.

Religion had been a central element of pre-Columbian societies, and many, if not all, indigenous people were receptive to the new religion that accompanied the victorious Iberians. It is estimated that missionaries had baptized between 4 and 9 million indigenous people in New Spain by the mid-1530s.[11] In addition to spreading Christianity, missionaries taught indigenous peoples European methods of agriculture and instilled obedience to colonial masters.

Despite the success of initial conversion efforts, authorities became suspicious about the thoroughness of native peoples' conversion and lingering belief in the old gods. They could not prevent, however, the melding together of Catholic teachings with elements of pagan beliefs and practices. For example, a sixteenth-century apparition of the Virgin Mary in Mexico City, known as the Virgin of Guadalupe, which became a central icon of New World Catholicism, seems to have been associated with the Aztec Mother Earth goddess, Tonantzin.

European Debates About Indigenous Peoples

Iberian exploitation of the native population of the Americas began from the moment of Columbus's arrival in 1492. Denunciations of this abuse by Catholic missionaries, however, quickly followed, inspiring vociferous debates in both Europe and the colonies about the nature of indigenous peoples and how they should be treated. Bartolomé de Las Casas (1474–1566), a Dominican friar and former encomienda holder, was one of the earliest and most outspoken critics of the brutal treatment inflicted on indigenous peoples. He wrote:

> To these quiet Lambs . . . came the Spaniards like most c(r)uel Tygres, Wolves and Lions, enrag'd with a sharp and tedious hunger; for these forty years past, minding nothing else but the slaughter of these unfortunate wretches, whom with divers kinds of torments neither seen nor heard of before, they have so cruelly and inhumanely butchered, that of three millions of people which Hispaniola itself did contain, there are left remaining alive scarce three hundred persons.[12]

Mounting criticism in Spain led King Charles V to assemble a group of churchmen and lawyers to debate the issue in 1550 in the city of Valladolid. One side of the **Valladolid debate**, led by Juan Ginés de Sepúlveda, argued that conquest and forcible conversion were both necessary and justified to save indigenous people from the horrors of human sacrifice, cannibalism, and idolatry. He described them as barbarians who belonged to a category of inferior beings identified by the ancient Greek philosopher Aristotle as naturally destined for slavery. To counter these arguments, Las Casas and his supporters depicted indigenous people as rational and innocent children, who deserved protection and tutelage from more advanced civilizations. Both sides claimed victory in the debate, but it had little effect on the situation in the Americas.

Elsewhere in Europe, audiences also debated these questions. Eagerly reading denunciations of Spanish abuses by critics like Las Casas, they derived the **Black Legend** of Spanish colonialism, the notion that the Spanish were uniquely brutal and cruel in their conquest and settlement of the Americas. This legend helped other European powers overlook their own record of colonial violence and exploitation.

New Ideas About Race

At the beginning of the transatlantic slave trade, most Europeans would have thought of Africans, if they thought of them at all, as savages in their social customs and religious practices. They grouped Africans into the despised categories of pagan heathens or Muslim infidels. As Europeans turned to Africa for new sources of slaves, they drew on beliefs about Africans' primitiveness and barbarity to defend slavery and even argue, like Sepúlveda with regard to indigenous Americans, that enslavement benefited Africans by bringing civilization and Christianity to heathen peoples. In 1444 an observer defended the enslavement of the first Africans by Portuguese explorers as necessary

Ispañol con India.
Mestizo.

Mestizo con Española.
Castizo.

5   6

Mulato con Española.
Morisco.

Morisco con Española.
Chino.

9   10

Lobo con China.
Cribaro.

Gibaro con Mulata.
Albarazado.

13   14

Sanbaigo con Loba.
Calpamulato.

Calpamulato con Canbuja.
Tenteen elAire.

Mixed Races The unprecedented mixing of peoples in the Spanish New World colonies inspired great fascination. An elaborate terminology emerged to describe the many possible combinations of indigenous, African, and European blood, which were known collectively as *castas*. This painting belongs to a popular genre of the eighteenth century depicting couples composed of individuals of different ethnic origin and the children produced of their unions. (Schalkwijk/Art Resource, NY)

"because they lived like beasts, without any of the customs of rational creatures, since they did not even know what were bread and wine, nor garments of cloth, nor life in the shelter of a house; and worse still was their ignorance, which deprived them of knowledge of good, and permitted them only a life of brutish idleness."[13]

Over time, the institution of slavery fostered a new level of racial inequality. Africans gradually became seen as utterly distinct from and wholly inferior to Europeans. In a transition from rather vague assumptions about Africans' non-Christian religious beliefs and general lack of civilization, Europeans developed increasingly rigid ideas of racial superiority and inferiority to safeguard the growing profits gained from plantation slavery. Black skin became equated with slavery itself as Europeans at home and in the colonies convinced themselves that blacks were destined by God to serve them as slaves in perpetuity.

Support for this belief went back to the Greek philosopher Aristotle's argument that some people are naturally destined for slavery and to biblical associations between darkness and sin. A more explicit justification was found in the story of Noah's curse upon the descendants of his disobedient son Ham to be the "servant[s] of servants." Biblical genealogies listing Ham's sons as those who peopled North Africa and Kush (which includes parts of modern Egypt and Sudan) were interpreted to mean that all inhabitants of those regions bore Noah's curse. From the sixteenth century onward, many defenders of slavery cited this story as justification.

After 1700 the emergence of new methods of observing and describing nature led to the use of science to define race. Although previously the term referred to a nation or an ethnic group, henceforth "race" would be used to describe supposedly biologically distinct groups of people whose physical differences produced differences in culture, character, and intelligence. Biblical justifications for inequality thereby gave way to allegedly scientific ones (see page 750).

Chapter Summary

Prior to Columbus's voyages, well-developed trade routes linked the peoples and products of Africa, Asia, and Europe. Overall, Europe played a minor role in the Afroeurasian trade world because it did not produce many products desired by Eastern elites. Nevertheless, Europeans — especially Venetian and Genoese merchants — sought to tap into the goods and wealth of Afroeurasian commerce. As the economy and population recovered from the Black Death, Europeans began to seek more direct and profitable access to the Afroeurasian trade world. Technological developments such as the invention of the caravel and the magnetic compass enabled men like Christopher Columbus and Ferdinand Magellan to undertake ever more ambitious voyages.

In the aftermath of their conquest of the Aztec and Inca Empires, the Spanish established new forms of governance to dominate native peoples and exploit their labor, including the encomienda system. The arrival of Europeans brought enormous population losses to native communities, primarily through the spread of infectious diseases. Disease was one element of the Columbian exchange, a complex transfer of germs, plants, and animals between the Old and New Worlds. Over time, the Columbian exchange brought new crops to both the New and Old Worlds — crops that eventually altered consumption patterns internationally. These exchanges contributed to the creation of the first truly global economy. Tragically, a major component of global trade was the transatlantic slave trade, in which Europeans transported, under horrific conditions, Africans to labor in the sugar plantations and silver mines of the New World. European nations vied for supremacy in global trade, with early Portuguese success in India and Asia being challenged first by the Spanish and then by the Dutch, who took control of trade with the East in the mid-seventeenth century.

Increased contact with the outside world led Europeans to develop new ideas about cultural and racial differences. Debates occurred in Spain and its colonies over the nature of the indigenous peoples of the Americas and how they should be treated. Europeans had long held negative attitudes about Africans; as the slave trade grew, they began to express more rigid notions of racial inequality and to claim that Africans were inherently suited for slavery. Most Europeans, with some important exceptions, shared such views. Religion became another means of cultural contact, as European missionaries aimed to spread Christianity in the New World.

Notes

1. Marco Polo, *The Book of Ser Marco Polo, the Venetian: Concerning the Kingdoms and Marvels of the East*, vol. 2, trans. and ed. Colonel Sir Henry Yule (London: John Murray, 1903), pp. 185–186.
2. Thomas Benjamin, *The Atlantic World: Europeans, Africans, Indians and Their Shared History, 1400–1900* (Cambridge: Cambridge University Press, 2009), p. 56.
3. A. Reid, *Southeast Asia in the Age of Commerce, 1450–1680*. Vol. 1: *The Land Under the Winds* (New Haven, Conn.: Yale University Press, 1988), pp. 3–20.
4. Quoted in C. M. Cipolla, *Guns, Sails, and Empires: Technological Innovation and the Early Phases of European Expansion, 1400–1700* (New York: Minerva Press, 1965), p. 132.

5. Quoted in F. H. Littell, *The Macmillan Atlas: History of Christianity* (New York: Macmillan, 1976), p. 75.

6. Quoted in J. Devisse, "Africa in Inter-Continental Relations," in *General History of Africa*. Vol. 4: *Africa from the Twelfth to the Sixteenth Century*, ed. D. T. Niane (Berkeley, Calif.: Heinemann Educational Books, 1984), p. 664.

7. Quoted in F. Maddison, "Tradition and Innovation: Columbus' First Voyage and Portuguese Navigation in the Fifteenth Century," in *Circa 1492: Art in the Age of Exploration*, ed. J. A. Levenson (Washington, D.C.: National Gallery of Art, 1991), p. 69.

8. Quoted in R. L. Kagan, "The Spain of Ferdinand and Isabella," in *Circa 1492: Art in the Age of Exploration*, ed. J. A. Levenson (Washington, D.C.: National Gallery of Art, 1991), p. 60.

9. Benjamin, *The Atlantic World*, p. 141.

10. Herbert S. Klein, "Profits and the Causes of Mortality," in *The Atlantic Slave Trade*, ed. David Northrup (Lexington, Mass.: D. C. Heath, 1994), p. 116.

11. David Carrasco, *The Oxford Encyclopedia of Mesoamerican Cultures* (Oxford: Oxford University Press, 2001), p. 208.

12. Quoted in C. Gibson, ed., *The Black Legend: Anti-Spanish Attitudes in the Old World and the New* (New York: Knopf, 1971), pp. 74–75.

13. Quoted in James H. Sweet, "The Iberian Roots of American Racist Thought," *The William and Mary Quarterly*, Third Series, 54 (January 1997): 155.

CONNECTIONS

Just three years separated Martin Luther's attack on the Catholic Church in 1517 and Ferdinand Magellan's discovery of the Pacific Ocean in 1520. Within a few short years western Europeans' religious unity and notions of terrestrial geography were shattered. Old medieval certainties about Heaven and earth collapsed. In the ensuing decades Europeans struggled to come to terms with religious differences among Protestants and Catholics at home and with the multitudes of new peoples and places they encountered abroad. While some Europeans were fascinated and inspired by this new diversity, too often the result was suffering and violence. Europeans endured decades of religious civil war, and indigenous peoples overseas underwent massive population losses as a result of European warfare, disease, and exploitation. Tragically, both Catholic and Protestant religious leaders condoned the trade in slaves that ultimately brought suffering and death to millions of Africans.

Even as the voyages of discovery contributed to the fragmentation of European culture, they also played a role in state centralization and consolidation in the longer term. Henceforth, competition to gain overseas colonies became an integral part of European politics. While Spain's enormous profits from conquest ultimately led to a weakening of its power, over time the Netherlands, England, and France used profits from colonial trade to help build modernized, centralized states.

Two crucial consequences emerged from this era of expansion. The first was the creation of enduring contacts among five of the seven continents of the globe—Europe, Asia, Africa, North America, and South America. From the sixteenth century onward, the peoples of the world were increasingly entwined in divergent forms of economic, social, and cultural exchange. The second was the growth of European power. Europeans controlled the Americas and gradually assumed control over existing trade networks in Asia and Africa. Although China remained the world's most powerful economy until at least 1800, the era of European dominance was born.

Chapter Review

MAKE IT STICK

✓ LearningCurve
Go online and use LearningCurve to retain what you've read.

IDENTIFY KEY TERMS

Identify and explain the significance of each item below.

bride wealth (p. 460)

conquistador (p. 464)

caravel (p. 465)

Ptolemy's *Geography* (p. 465)

Treaty of Tordesillas (p. 470)

Aztec Empire (p. 472)

Inca Empire (p. 474)

viceroyalties (p. 476)

captaincies (p. 476)

encomienda system (p. 476)

Columbian exchange (p. 478)

Valladolid debate (p. 483)

Black Legend (p. 483)

REVIEW THE MAIN IDEAS

Answer the focus questions from each section of the chapter.

1. What was the Afroeurasian trade world like prior to the era of European exploration? (p. 458)

2. Why and how did Europeans undertake ambitious voyages of expansion? (p. 463)

3. What was the impact of Iberian conquest and settlement on the peoples and ecologies of the Americas? (p. 471)

4. How was the era of global contact shaped by new commodities, commercial empires, and forced migrations? (p. 478)

5. How did new encounters shape cultural attitudes and beliefs in Europe and the New World? (p. 482)

MAKE CONNECTIONS

Analyze the larger developments and continuities within and across chapters.

1. What range of attitudes toward new and unknown peoples did you encounter in this chapter? How do you explain similarities and differences in attitudes toward such peoples?

2. How did European motivations for expansion compare to those of the Roman Empire, the Arab world under Islam, or the Mongols in Central Asia?

▷LaunchPad
ONLINE DOCUMENT PROJECT

Interpreting Conquest
How did Spanish and Amerindian artists depict Malintzin?

Examine Spanish and Amerindian representations of Malintzin's role in the conquest, and then complete a quiz and writing assignment based on the evidence and details from this chapter.

See inside the front cover to learn more.

CHRONOLOGY

1271–1295	• Marco Polo travels to China
1443	• Portuguese establish first African trading post at Arguin
1492	• Columbus lands on San Salvador
1494	• Treaty of Tordesillas ratified
1518	• Atlantic slave trade begins
1519–1522	• Magellan's expedition circumnavigates the world
1521	• Cortés conquers Aztec Empire
1533	• Pizarro conquers Inca Empire
1571	• Spanish establish port of Manila in the Philippines
1602	• Dutch East India Company founded

17

✓ LearningCurve
After reading the chapter, go online and use LearningCurve to retain what you've read.

The Islamic World Powers

1300–1800

AFTER THE DECLINE OF THE MONGOL EMPIRE IN THE MID-FOURTEENTH century, powerful new Islamic states emerged in south and west Eurasia. By the sixteenth century the Ottoman Empire, centered in Anatolia; the Safavid (sah-FAH-weed) Empire in Persia; and the Mughal (MOO-guhl) Empire in India controlled vast territories from West Africa to Central Asia, from the Balkans to the Bay of Bengal.

Lasting more than six centuries (1299–1922), the Ottoman Empire was one of the largest, best-organized, and most enduring political entities in world history. In Persia (now Iran) the Safavid Dynasty created a Shi'a state and presided over a brilliant culture. In India the Mughal leader Babur and his successors gained control of much of the Indian subcontinent. Mughal rule inaugurated a period of radical administrative reorganization in India and the flowering of intellectual and architectural creativity. Although these three states were often at war with each other, they shared important characteristics and challenges. For instance, their ruling houses all emerged from Turkish tribal organizations, and they all had to adapt their armies to the introduction of firearms. Over time, they became strongly linked culturally, as merchants, poets, philosophers, artists, and military advisers moved relatively easily across their political boundaries. Before the end of this period, Europeans were also active in trade in these empires, especially in India.

The Turkish Ruling Houses: The Ottomans, Safavids, and Mughals

How were the three Islamic empires established, and what sorts of governments did they set up?

Before the Mongols arrived in Central Asia and Persia, another nomadic people from the region of modern Mongolia, the Turks, had moved west, gained control over key territories from Anatolia to Delhi in north India, and contributed to the decline of the Abbasid caliphate in the thirteenth century. The Turks had been quick to join the Mongols and were important participants in the armies and administrations of the Mongol states in Persia and Central Asia. In these regions Turks far outnumbered ethnic Mongols.

As Mongol strength in Persia and Central Asia deteriorated in the late thirteenth to mid-fourteenth centuries, the Turks resumed their expansion. In the late fourteenth century the Turkish leader Timur (1336–1405), also called Tamerlane, built a Central Asian empire from his base in Samarkand that reached into India and through Persia to the Black Sea. Timur campaigned continuously from the 1360s until his death in 1405, aspiring to repeat the achievements of Chinggis Khan. He did not get involved in administering the new territories but rather appointed lords and let them make use of existing political structures. His conquests were exceptionally destructive and benefited only Samarkand, where craftsmen and other specialists were forced to move to work for the new rulers. After his death, his sons and grandson fought each other for succession. By 1450 his empire was in rapid decline, and power devolved to the local level. Meanwhile, Sufi orders (groups of Islamic mystics) thrived, and Islam became the most important force integrating the region. It was from the many small Turkish chiefs that the founders of the three main empires emerged.

The Expansion of the Ottoman Empire

The **Ottomans** took their name from Osman (r. 1299–1326), the chief of a band of seminomadic Turks that had migrated into western **Anatolia** while the Mongols still held Persia. The Ottomans gradually expanded at the expense of other small Turkish states and the Byzantine Empire (Map 17.1). The Ottoman ruler called himself "border chief," or leader of the *ghazis* (GAH-zeez), frontier raiders. Although temporarily slowed by defeat at the hands of Timur in 1402, the Ottomans quickly reasserted themselves after Timur's death in 1405.

Osman's campaigns were intended to subdue, not to destroy. The Ottomans built their empire by absorbing the Muslims of Anatolia and by becoming the protector of the Orthodox Church and of the millions of Greek Christians in Anatolia and the Balkans. In 1326 they took Bursa in western Anatolia, and in 1352 they gained a foothold in Europe by seizing Gallipoli. Their victories led more men, including recent converts, to join them as ghazis. In 1389 at Kosovo in the Balkans, the Ottomans defeated a combined force of Serbs and Bosnians. And in 1396 on the Danube River in modern Bulgaria, they crushed King Sigismund of Hungary, who was supported by French, German, and English knights. After the victories in the Balkans, the Ottomans made slaves of many captives and trained them as soldiers. These troops were outfitted with guns and artillery and trained to use them effectively.

Sultan Mehmet II   Mehmet was called "the Conqueror" because at age twenty-one he captured Constantinople and ended the Byzantine Empire, but he is also known for his patronage of the arts and appreciation of beauty. (Topkapi Palace Museum, Istanbul, Turkey/ Giraudon/The Bridgeman Art Library)

In 1453, during the reign of Sultan Mehmet II (r. 1451–1481), the Ottomans conquered Constantinople, capital of the Byzantine Empire, which had lasted a thousand years. The Byzantine emperor, with only about ten thousand men, relied on Constantinople's magnificent system of circular walls and the iron chains that spanned the city's harbor. In response, Mehmet's army carried boats over steep hills to come in behind the chains blocking the harbor and then bombarded the city from the rear. A Transylvanian cannonmaker who had deserted the Greeks for the Turks cast huge bronze cannon on the spot (bringing raw materials to the scene of military action was easier than moving guns long distances), and these guns were used to weaken the defensive walls.

Once Constantinople was theirs, the Ottoman sultans considered themselves successors to both the Byzantine and Seljuk Turk emperors, and they quickly absorbed the rest of the Byzantine Empire. In the sixteenth century they continued to expand through the Middle East and into North Africa.

To begin the transformation of Constantinople (renamed Istanbul) into an imperial Ottoman capital, Mehmet ordered wealthy residents to participate in building mosques, markets, fountains, baths, and other public facilities. To make up for the loss of population through war, Mehmet transplanted inhabitants of other territories to the city, granting them tax remissions and possession of empty houses. He wanted them to start businesses, make Istanbul prosperous, and transform it into a microcosm of the empire.

Gunpowder, which was invented by the Chinese and adapted to artillery use by the Europeans, played an influential role in the expansion of the Ottoman state. In the first half of the sixteenth century, thanks to the use of this technology, the Ottomans gained control of shipping in the eastern Mediterranean, eliminated the Portuguese from the Red Sea and the Persian Gulf, and supported Andalusian and North African Muslims in their fight against the Christian reconquest of Muslim Spain. In 1514, under the superb military leadership of Selim (r. 1512–1520), the Ottomans turned the Safavids back from Anatolia. In addition, the Ottomans added Syria and Palestine (1516) and Egypt (1517). Control of Syria gave them control of the holy cities of

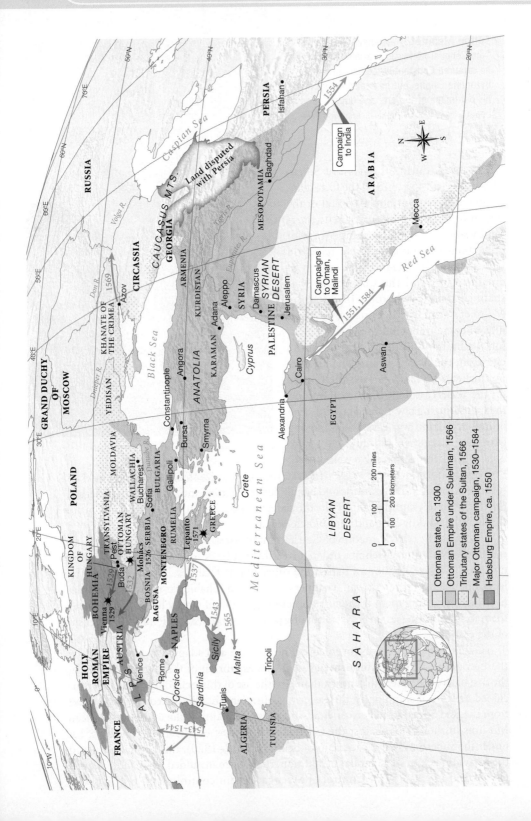

◀ **MAP 17.1   The Ottoman Empire at Its Height, 1566** The Ottomans, like their great rivals the Habsburgs, rose to rule a vast dynastic empire encompassing many different peoples and ethnic groups. The army and the bureaucracy served to unite the disparate territories into a single state.

Islam. Control of Egypt gave them access to the Indian Ocean, where they competed with the Portuguese for control of shipping. Before long the Ottomans had extended their rule across North Africa to Tunisia and Algeria. For the next four centuries a majority of Arabs lived under Ottoman rule.

Suleiman (r. 1520–1566) extended Ottoman dominion to its widest geographical extent (see Map 17.1). Suleiman's army crushed the Hungarians at Mohács in 1526, killing the king and thousands of his nobles. Three years later the Turks unsuccessfully besieged the Habsburg capital of Vienna. From the late fourteenth to the early seventeenth centuries, the Ottoman Empire was a key player in European politics. In 1525 Francis I of France and Suleiman struck an alliance; both believed that only their collaboration could prevent Habsburg domination of Europe. The Habsburg emperor Charles V retaliated by seeking an alliance with Safavid Persia. Suleiman renewed the French agreement with Francis's son, Henry II (r. 1547–1559), and this accord became the cornerstone of Ottoman policy in western Europe. Suleiman also allied with the German Protestant princes, forcing the Catholic Habsburgs to grant concessions to the Protestants. Ottoman pressure thus contributed to the official recognition of Lutheran Protestants at the Peace of Augsburg in 1555 and the consolidation of the national monarchy in France.

In eastern Europe to the north of Ottoman lands stood the Grand Duchy of Moscow. In the fifteenth century Ottoman rulers did not regard it as a threat; in 1497 they even gave Russian merchants freedom of trade within the empire. But in 1547 Ivan IV (the Terrible) brought the entire Volga region under Russian control (see Map 17.1). In 1557 Ivan's ally, the Cossack chieftain Dimitrash, tried to take Azov, the northernmost Ottoman fortress. Ottoman plans to recapture the area succeeded in uniting Russia, Persia, and the pope against the Turks.

Though usually victorious on land, the Ottomans did not enjoy complete dominion on the seas. Competition with the Habsburgs and pirates for control of the Mediterranean led the Ottomans to conquer Cyprus in 1570 and settle thousands of Turks from Anatolia there. (Thus began the large Turkish presence on Cyprus that continues to the present day.) In response, Pope Pius V organized a Holy League against the Turks, which won a victory in 1571 at Lepanto off the west coast of Greece with a squadron of more than two hundred Spanish, Venetian, and papal galleys. Still, the Turks remained supreme on land and quickly rebuilt their entire fleet.

To the east, war with Safavid Persia occupied the sultans' attention throughout the sixteenth century. Several issues lay at the root of the long and exhausting conflict: religious antagonism between the Sunni Ottomans and the Shi'a Persians, competition to expand at each other's expense in Mesopotamia, desire to control trade routes, and European alliances. (For more on the Shi'a faith, see page 495.) Finally, in 1638 the Ottomans captured Baghdad, and the treaty of Kasr-I-Shirim established a permanent border between the two powers.

The Ottoman political system reached its classic form under Suleiman I. All authority flowed from the sultan to his public servants: provincial governors, police officers, military generals, heads of treasuries, and **viziers**. In Turkish history Suleiman is known as "the Lawgiver" because of his profound influence on the civil law. He ordered Lütfi Paşa (d. 1562), a poet and juridical scholar of slave origin, to draw up a new general code of laws that prescribed penalties for routine criminal acts such as robbery, adultery, and murder. It also sought to reform bureaucratic and financial corruption, such as foreign merchants' payment of bribes to avoid customs duties, imprisonment without trial, and promotion in the provincial administration because of favoritism rather than ability. The legal code also introduced the idea of balanced government budgets. The head of the religious establishment was given the task of reconciling sultanic law with Islamic law. Suleiman's legal acts influenced many legal codes, including that of the United States. Today, Suleiman's image appears in the chamber of the U.S. House of Representatives, along with the images of the Athenian lawmaker Solon, Moses, and Thomas Jefferson.

The Ottomans ruled their more distant lands, such as those in North Africa, relatively lightly. Governors of distant provinces collected taxes and maintained trade routes, but their control did not penetrate deeply into the countryside.

The Ottoman Empire's Use of Slaves

The power of the Ottoman central government was sustained through the training of slaves. Slaves were purchased from Spain, North Africa, and Venice; captured in battle; or drafted through the system known as **devshirme**, by which the sultan's agents compelled Christian families in the Balkans to sell their boys. As the Ottoman frontier advanced in the fifteenth and sixteenth centuries, Albanian, Bosnian, Wallachian, and Hungarian slave boys filled Ottoman imperial needs. The slave boys were converted to Islam and trained for the imperial civil service and the standing army. The brightest 10 percent entered the palace school, where they learned to read and write Arabic, Ottoman Turkish, and Persian in preparation for administrative jobs. Other boys were sent to Turkish farms, where they acquired physical toughness in preparation for military service. Known as **janissaries** (Turkish for "recruits"), they formed the elite army corps. Thoroughly indoctrinated and absolutely loyal to the sultan, the janissary corps threatened the influence of fractious old Turkish families. They played a central role in Ottoman military affairs in the sixteenth century, adapting easily to the use of firearms. The devshirme system enabled the Ottomans to apply merit-based recruitment to military and administrative offices at little cost and provided a means of assimilating Christians living in Ottoman lands. Some Muslims, however, doubted whether janissary converts could be viewed as reliably Muslim.

The Ottoman ruling class consisted partly of descendants of Turkish families that had formerly ruled parts of Anatolia and partly of people of varied ethnic origins who rose through the bureaucratic and military ranks, many beginning as the sultan's slaves. All were committed to the Ottoman way: Islamic in faith, loyal to the sultan, and well versed in the Turkish language and the culture of the imperial court. In return for their services to the sultan, they held landed estates for the duration of their lives. Because all property belonged to the sultan and reverted to him on the holder's death, Turkish nobles, unlike their European counterparts, did not have a local base independent of the ruler. The absence of a hereditary nobility and private ownership of agricultural land differentiates the Ottoman system from European feudalism.

Another distinctive characteristic of the Ottomans was the sultan's failure to marry. From about 1500 on, the sultans did not contract legal marriages but perpetuated the ruling house through concubinage. A slave **concubine** could not expect to exert power the way a local or foreign noblewoman could. (For a notable exception, see "Individuals in Society: Hürrem," page 496.) When one of the sultan's concubines became pregnant, her status and her salary increased. If she delivered a boy, she raised him until the age of ten or eleven. Then the child was given a province to govern under his mother's supervision. She accompanied him there, was responsible for his good behavior, and worked through imperial officials and the janissary corps to promote his interests. Because succession to the throne was open to all the sultan's sons, fratricide often resulted upon his death, and the losers were blinded or executed.

Slave concubinage paralleled the Ottoman development of slave soldiers and slave viziers. All held positions entirely at the sultan's pleasure, owed loyalty solely to him, and thus were more reliable than a hereditary nobility. Great social prestige, as well as the opportunity to acquire power and wealth, was attached to being a slave of the imperial household. Suleiman even made it a practice to marry his daughters to top-ranking slave-officials.

The Safavid Empire in Persia

With the decline of Timur's empire after 1450, Persia was controlled by Turkish lords, with no single one dominant until 1501, when fourteen-year-old Isma'il (1487–1524) led a Turkish army to capture Tabriz and declared himself **shah** (king).

The strength of the early **Safavid** state rested on three crucial features. First, it had the loyalty and military support of nomadic Turkish Sufis known as **Qizilbash** (KIH-zihl-bahsh; a Turkish word meaning "redheads" that was applied to these people because of the red hats they wore). The shah secured the loyalty of the Qizilbash by granting them vast grazing lands, especially on the troublesome Ottoman frontier. In return, the Qizilbash supplied him with troops. Second, the Safavid state utilized the skills of urban bureaucrats and made them an essential part of the civil machinery of government.

The third source of Safavid strength was the Shi'a faith, which became the compulsory religion of the empire. The Shi'a believed that leadership among Muslims rightfully belonged to the Prophet Muhammad's descendants. Because Isma'il claimed descent from a line of twelve infallible imams (leaders) beginning with Ali (Muhammad's cousin and son-in-law), he was officially regarded as their representative on earth. Isma'il recruited Shi'a scholars outstanding in learning and piety from other lands to instruct and guide his people, and he persecuted and exiled Sunni **ulama**. To this day, Iran remains the only Muslim state in which Shi'ism is the official religion.

Safavid power reached its height under Shah Abbas (r. 1587–1629), who moved the capital from Qazvin to Isfahan. His military achievements, support for trade and commerce, and endowment of the arts earned him the epithet "the Great." In the

INDIVIDUALS IN SOCIETY • Hürrem

Hürrem (1505?–1558) was born in the western Ukraine (then part of Poland), the daughter of a Ruthenian priest, and was given the Polish name Aleksandra Lisowska. When Tartars raided, they captured and enslaved her. In 1520 she was given as a gift to Suleiman on the occasion of his accession to the throne. The Venetian ambassador (probably relying on secondhand or thirdhand information) described her as "young, graceful, petite, but not beautiful." She was given the Turkish name Hürrem, meaning "joyful."

Hürrem apparently brought joy to Suleiman. Their first child was born in 1521. By 1525 they had four sons and a daughter; sources note that by that year Suleiman visited no other woman. But he waited eight or nine years before breaking Ottoman dynastic tradition by making Hürrem his legal wife, the first slave concubine so honored. For the rest of her life, Hürrem played a highly influential role in the political, diplomatic, and philanthropic life of the Ottoman state. First, great power flowed from her position as mother of the prince, the future sultan Selim II (r. 1566–1574). Then, as the intimate and most trusted adviser of the sultan, she was Suleiman's closest confidant. During his frequent trips to the far-flung corners of his multiethnic empire, Hürrem wrote him long letters filled with her love and longing for him and her prayers for his safety in battle. She also shared political information about affairs in Istanbul, the activities of the grand vizier, and the attitudes of the janissaries. At a time when some people believed that the sultan's absence from the capital endangered his hold on the throne, Hürrem acted as his eyes and ears for potential threats.

Hürrem was the sultan's contact with her native Poland, which sent more embassies to Istanbul than any other power. Through her correspondence with King Sigismund I, peace between Poland and the Ottomans was maintained. When Sigismund II succeeded his father in 1548, Hürrem sent congratulations on his accession, along with two pairs of pajamas (originally a Hindu garment but commonly worn in southwestern Asia) and six handkerchiefs. Also, she sent the shah of Persia gold-embroidered sheets and shirts that she had sewn herself, seeking to display the wealth of the sultanate and to keep peace between the Ottomans and the Safavids.

---

military realm he adopted the Ottoman practice of building an army of slaves, primarily captives from the Caucasus (especially Armenians and Georgians), who could serve as a counterweight to the Qizilbash, who had come to be considered a threat. He also increased the use of gunpowder weapons and made alliances with European powers against the Ottomans and Portuguese. In his campaigns against the Ottomans, Shah Abbas captured Baghdad, Mosul, and Diarbakr in Mesopotamia (Map 17.2).

Conflict between the Ottomans and the Safavids was not an even match. The Safavids did not have as many people or as much wealth as the Ottomans and continually had to defend against encroachments on their western border. Still, they were able to attract some of the Turks in Ottoman lands who felt that their government had

The enormous stipend that Suleiman gave Hürrem permitted her to participate in his vast building program. In Jerusalem (in the Ottoman province of
Palestine) she founded a hospice for fifty-five pilgrims that included a soup
kitchen that fed four hundred pilgrims a day. In Istanbul Suleiman built and
Hürrem endowed the Haseki (meaning "royal favorite concubine") mosque
complex and a public bath for women near the Women's Market.

Perhaps Hürrem tried to fulfill two functions hitherto distinct in Ottoman
political theory: those of the sultan's favorite and of mother of the prince.
She also performed the conflicting roles of slave concubine and imperial wife.
Many Turks resented Hürrem's interference at court. They believed she was behind the execution of Suleiman's popular son Mustafa on a charge of treason
to make way for her own son to succeed as sultan.

Source: Leslie P. Peirce, *The Imperial Harem: Women and Sovereignty in the Ottoman Empire* (New
York: Oxford University Press, 1993).

QUESTIONS FOR ANALYSIS

1. How does Hürrem compare to powerful women in other places, such as Empress
   Wu in China, Isabella of Castile, Catherine de' Medici of France, Elizabeth I of
   England, or any other you know about?
2. What was Hürrem's "nationality"? What role did it play in her life?

LaunchPad
ONLINE DOCUMENT PROJECT

How did Europeans view the Ottoman Empire? Examine a Habsburg
ambassador's impressions of the Ottoman Empire, and then complete
a quiz and writing assignment based on the evidence and details from
this chapter.
See inside the front cover to learn more.

shifted too far from its nomadic roots. After Shah Abbas, Safavid power was sapped
by civil war between tribal factions vying for control of the court.

The Mughal Empire in India

Of the three great Islamic empires of the early modern world, the **Mughal** Empire of
India was the largest, wealthiest, and most populous. Extending over 1.2 million square
miles at the end of the seventeenth century, with a population between 100 and 150
million, and with fabulous wealth and resources, the Mughal Empire surpassed the
other two by a wide margin. In the sixteenth century only the Ming Dynasty in China
could compare.

MAP 17.2   The Safavid Empire, 1587–1629 In the late sixteenth century the power of the Safavid kingdom of Persia rested on its strong military force, its Shi'a Muslim faith, and its extraordinarily rich trade in rugs and pottery. Many of the cities on the map, such as Tabriz, Qum, and Shiraz, were great rug-weaving centers.

In 1504 Babur (r. 1483–1530), a Turkish ruler forced out of a small territory in Central Asia, captured Kabul and established a kingdom in Afghanistan. An adventurer who claimed descent from Chinggis Khan and Timur, Babur moved southward in search of resources to restore his fortunes. In 1526, with a force that was small (twelve thousand in number) but was equipped with firearms, Babur defeated the sultan of Delhi at Panipat. Babur's capture of the cities of Agra and Delhi, key fortresses of the north, paved the way for further conquests in northern India. Although many of his soldiers wished to return north with their spoils, Babur decided to stay in India. A gifted writer, Babur wrote an autobiography in Turkish that recounts his military campaigns, describes places and people he encountered, recounts his difficulties giving up wine, and shows his wide-ranging interests in everything from fruit and swimming to a Turkish general who excelled at leapfrog. He was not particularly impressed by India, as can be inferred from this description in his memoirs:

> Hindustan is a country which has few pleasures to recommend it. The people are
> not handsome. They have no idea of the charms of friendly society, of frankly mixing
> together, or familiar discourse. They have no genius, no comprehension of mind,
> no politeness of manner, no kindness or fellow-feeling, no ingenuity or mechanical
> invention in planning or executing their handicraft works, no skill or knowledge in
> design or architecture; they have no horses, no good flesh, no grapes or muskmelons,
> no good fruits, no ice or cold water, no good food or bread in their bazaars, no baths
> or colleges, no candles, no torches, not a candlestick.[1]

During the reign of Babur's son Humayun (r. 1530–1540 and 1555–1556), the
Mughals lost most of their territories in Afghanistan. Humayun went into temporary
exile in Persia, where he developed a deep appreciation for Persian art and literature.
The reign of Humayun's son Akbar (r. 1556–1605) may well have been the greatest
in the history of India. A boy of thirteen when he succeeded to the throne, Akbar
pursued expansionist policies. Under his dynamic leadership, the Mughal state took
definitive form and encompassed most of the subcontinent north of the Godavari
River. No kingdom or coalition of kingdoms could long resist Akbar's armies. The
once-independent states of northern India were forced into a centralized political
system under the sole authority of the Mughal emperor.

Akbar replaced Turkish with Persian as the official language of the Mughal Empire,
and Persian remained the official language until the British replaced it with English
in 1835. To govern this vast region, Akbar developed an administrative bureaucracy
centered on four co-equal ministers: finance and revenue; the army and intelligence;
the judiciary and religious patronage; and the imperial household, whose jurisdiction
included roads, bridges, and infrastructure throughout the empire. Under Akbar's
Hindu finance minister, Raja Todar Mal, a uniform system of taxes was put in place.
In the provinces imperial governors were appointed by and responsible solely to the
emperor. Whereas the Ottoman sultans and Safavid shahs made extensive use of slaves
acquired from non-Muslim lands for military and administrative positions, Akbar used
the services of royal princes, nobles, and warrior-aristocrats. Initially these men were
Muslims from Central Asia, but to reduce their influence, Akbar vigorously recruited
Persians and Hindus. No single ethnic or religious faction could challenge the
emperor.

Akbar's descendants extended the Mughal Empire further. His son Jahangir
(r. 1605–1628) lacked his father's military abilities and administrative genius, but
he did succeed in consolidating Mughal rule in Bengal. Jahangir's son Shah Jahan
(r. 1628–1658) launched fresh territorial expansion. Faced with dangerous revolts by
the Muslims in Ahmadnagar and the resistance of the newly arrived Portuguese in
Bengal, Shah Jahan not only crushed this opposition but also strengthened his northwestern frontier. Shah Jahan's son Aurangzeb (r. 1658–1707), unwilling to wait for
his father to die, deposed him and confined him for years in a small cell. A puritanically
devout and strictly orthodox Muslim, as well as a skillful general and a clever diplomat,
Aurangzeb ruled more of India than did any previous Mughal emperor, having extended
the realm deeper into south India. His reign, however, also marked the beginning of
the empire's decline. His non-Muslim subjects were not pleased with his religious
zealotry, and his military campaigns were costly. In the south resistance to Mughal rule
led to major uprisings. (For more on Aurangzeb's rule, see page 507.)

Cultural Flowering

What cultural advances occurred under the rule of the Ottoman, Safavid, and Mughal Empires?

All three Islamic empires presided over an extraordinary artistic and intellectual flowering in everything from carpetmaking to architecture and gardening, from geography and astronomy to medicine. At the same time, new religious practices (and conflicts) emerged, and new gathering places—coffeehouses—became popular outlets for socializing and exchanging ideas. Artistic and intellectual advances spread from culture to culture, probably because of the common Persian influence on the Turks since the tenth century. This exchange was also aided by common languages. Persian was used as the administrative language by the Mughals in India, and Arabic was a lingua franca of the entire region because of its centrality in Islam. In Ottoman lands both Persian and Arabic were literary languages, but Turkish slowly became the lingua franca of the realm.

The Arts

One of the arts all three empires shared was carpetmaking. Carpet designs and weaving techniques demonstrate both cultural integration and local distinctiveness. Turkic migrants carried their weaving traditions with them as they moved but also readily adopted new motifs, especially from Persia. In Safavid Persia, Shah Abbas was determined to improve his country's export trade and built the small cottage business of carpet weaving into a national industry. In the capital city of Isfahan alone, factories employed more than twenty-five thousand weavers who produced woolen carpets, brocades, and silks of brilliant color, design, and quality. Women and children were often employed as weavers, especially of the most expensive rugs, because their smaller hands could tie tinier knots.

Another art that spread from Persia to both Ottoman and Mughal lands was miniature painting, especially for book illustration. This tradition had been enriched by the many Chinese artists brought to Persia during the Mongol period. There was also an interplay between carpets and miniature painting. Naturalistic depictions of lotus blossoms, peonies, chrysanthemums, tulips, carnations, birds, and even dragons appear in both book illustrations and carpets.

In Mughal India, as throughout the Muslim world, books were regarded as precious objects. Time, talent, and expensive materials went into their production, and they were highly coveted because they reflected wealth, learning, and power. Akbar reportedly possessed twenty-four thousand books when he died. The historian Abu'l-Fazl described Akbar's library and love of books:

> His Majesty's library is divided into several parts. . . . Prose works, poetical works, Hindi, Persian, Greek, Kashmirian, Arabic, are all separately placed. In this order they are also inspected. Experienced people bring them daily and read them before His Majesty, who hears every book from beginning to end . . . and rewards the readers with presents of cash either in gold or silver, according to the number of leaves read out by them. . . . There are no historical facts of past ages, or curiosities of science, or interesting points of philosophy, with which His Majesty, a leader of impartial sages, is unacquainted.[2]

City and Palace Building

In all three empires strong rulers built capital cities and imperial palaces as visible expressions of dynastic majesty. Europeans called Suleiman "the Magnificent" because of the grandeur of his court. With annual state revenues of about $80 million (at a time when Elizabeth I of England could expect $150,000 and Francis I of France perhaps $1 million) and thousands of servants, he had a lifestyle no European monarch could begin to rival. He used his fabulous wealth to adorn Istanbul with palaces, mosques, schools, and libraries, and the city reached about a million in population. The building of hospitals, roads, and bridges and the reconstruction of the water systems of the great pilgrimage sites at Mecca and Jerusalem benefited his subjects. Safavid Persia and Mughal India produced rulers with similar ambitions.

The greatest builder under the Ottomans was Mimar Sinan (1491–1588), a Greek-born devshirme recruit who rose to become imperial architect under Suleiman. A contemporary of Michelangelo, Sinan designed 312 public buildings, including mosques, schools, hospitals, public baths, palaces, and burial chapels. His masterpieces, the Shehzade and Suleimaniye Mosques in Istanbul, which rivaled the Byzantine church of Hagia Sophia, were designed to maximize the space under the dome. His buildings expressed the discipline, power, and devotion to Islam that characterized the Ottoman Empire under Suleiman.

Shah Abbas made his capital, Isfahan, the jewel of the Safavid Empire. He had his architects place a polo ground in the center and surrounded it with palaces, mosques, and bazaars. A seventeenth-century English visitor described one of Isfahan's bazaars as "the surprisingest piece of Greatness in Honour of commerce the world can boast of." In addition to splendid rugs, stalls displayed pottery and fine china, metalwork of exceptionally high quality, and silks and velvets of stunning weave and design. A city of perhaps 750,000 people, Isfahan also contained 162 mosques, 48 schools where future members of the ulama learned the sacred Muslim sciences, 273 public baths, and the vast imperial palace. Mosques were richly decorated with blue tile. Private houses had their own garden courts, and public gardens, pools, and parks adorned the wide streets. Tales of the beauty of Isfahan circulated

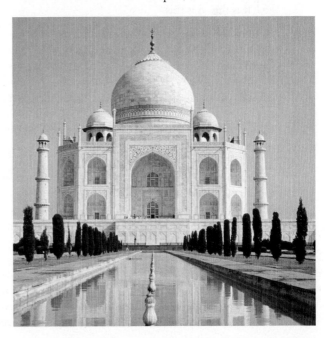

The Taj Mahal The Taj Mahal, built between 1631 and 1648 in Agra in northern India, is perhaps the finest example of Mughal architecture. Its white marble exterior is decorated with Arabic inscriptions and floral designs. (Dinodia/The Bridgeman Art Library)

worldwide, attracting thousands of tourists annually in the seventeenth and eighteenth centuries.

Akbar in India was also a great builder. The birth of a long-awaited son, Jahangir, inspired Akbar to build a new city, Fatehpur Sikri, to symbolize the regime's Islamic foundations. He personally supervised the construction of the city, which combined the Muslim tradition of domes, arches, and spacious courts with the Hindu tradition of flat stone beams, ornate decoration, and solidity. The historian Abu'l-Fazl reported, "His Majesty plans splendid edifices, and dresses the work of his mind and heart in the garment of stone and clay."[3] Completed in 1578, the city included an imperial palace, a mosque, lavish gardens, and a hall of worship, as well as thousands of houses for ordinary people. Unfortunately, because of its bad water supply, the city was soon abandoned.

Of Akbar's successors, Shah Jahan had the most sophisticated interest in architecture. Because his capital at Agra was cramped, in 1639 he decided to found a new capital city at Delhi. In the design and layout of the buildings, Persian ideas predominated, an indication of the number of Persian architects and engineers who had flocked to the subcontinent. The walled palace-fortress alone extended over 125 acres. Built partly of red sandstone, partly of marble, it included private chambers for the emperor; mansions for the wives, widows, and concubines of the imperial household; huge audience rooms for the conduct of public business (treasury, arsenal, and military); baths; and vast gardens filled with flowers, trees, and thirty silver fountains spraying water. In 1650, with living quarters for guards, military officials, merchants, dancing girls, scholars, and hordes of cooks and servants, the palace-fortress housed fifty-seven thousand people. It also boasted a covered public bazaar. The sight of the magnificent palace left contemporaries speechless. Shah Jahan had a Persian poetic couplet inscribed on the walls:

> If there is a paradise on the face of the earth,
> It is this, it is this.

Beyond the walls, princes and aristocrats built mansions and mosques on a smaller scale. With its fine architecture and its population of between 375,000 and 400,000, Delhi gained the reputation of being one of the great cities of the Muslim world.

For his palace, Shah Jahan ordered the construction of the Peacock Throne. This famous piece, encrusted with emeralds, diamonds, pearls, and rubies, took seven years to fashion and cost the equivalent of $5 million. It served as the imperial throne of India until 1739, when the Persian warrior Nadir Shah seized it as plunder and carried it to Persia.

Shah Jahan's most enduring monument is the Taj Mahal. Between 1631 and 1648 twenty thousand workers toiled over the construction of this memorial in Agra to Shah Jahan's favorite wife, who died giving birth to their fifteenth child. One of the most beautiful structures in the world, the Taj Mahal is both an expression of love and a superb architectural blending of Islamic and Indian culture.

Gardens

Many of the architectural masterpieces of this age had splendid gardens attached to them. Gardens represent a distinctive and highly developed feature of Persian culture. They commonly were walled, with a pool in the center and geometrically laid-out

Polo   Two teams of four on horse-back ride back and forth on a grass field measuring 200 by 400 yards, trying to hit a 4½-ounce wooden ball with a 4-foot mallet through the opponent's goal. Because a typical match involves many high-speed collisions among the horses, each player has to maintain a string of expensive ponies in order to change mounts several times during the game. Students of the history of sports believe the game originated in Persia, as shown in this eighteenth-century miniature, whence it spread to India, China, and Japan. Brought from India to England, where it became very popular among the aristocracy in the nineteenth century, polo is a fine example of cross-cultural influences. (Private Collection)

flowering plants, especially roses. Identified with paradise in Arab tradition, gardens served not only as centers of prayer and meditation but also as places of leisure and revelry. After the incorporation of Persia into the caliphate in the seventh century, formal gardening spread west and east through the Islamic world, as illustrated by the magnificent gardens of Muslim Spain, southern Italy, and, later, southeastern Europe. The Mongol followers of Timur took landscape architects from Persia back to Samarkand and adapted their designs to nomad encampments. When Babur established the Mughal Dynasty in India, he adapted the Persian garden to the warmer southern climate. Gardens were laid out near palaces, mosques, shrines, and mausoleums, including the Taj Mahal, which had four water channels symbolizing the four rivers of paradise.

Because it evoked paradise, the garden played a large role in Muslim literature. Some scholars hold that to understand Arabic poetry, one must study Arab gardening. The secular literature of Muslim Spain, rife with references such as "a garland of verses," influenced the lyric poetry of southern France, the troubadours, and the courtly love tradition.

Gardens, of course, are seasonal. To remind themselves of paradise during the cold winter months, rulers, city people, and nomads ordered Persian carpets, most of which use floral patterns and have formal garden designs.

Intellectual Advances and Religious Trends

Between 1400 and 1800 the culture of the Islamic empires developed in many directions. Particularly notable were new movements within Islam as well as advances in mathematics, geography, astronomy, and medicine. Building on the knowledge of earlier Islamic writers and stimulated by Ottoman naval power, the geographer and cartographer Piri Reis produced a map incorporating Islamic and Western knowledge that showed all the known world (1513); another of his maps detailed Columbus's third voyage to the New World. Piri Reis's *Book of the Sea* (1521) contained 129 chapters, each with a map incorporating all Islamic (and Western) knowledge of the seas and navigation and describing harbors, tides, dangerous rocks and shores, and storm areas. In the field of astronomy, Takiyuddin Mehmet (1521–1585), who served as the sultan's chief astronomer, built an observatory at Istanbul. He also produced *Instruments of the Observatory*, which catalogued astronomical instruments and described an astronomical clock that fixed the location of heavenly bodies with greater precision than ever before.

There were also advances in medicine. Under Suleiman the imperial palace itself became a center of medical science, and the large number of hospitals established in Istanbul and throughout the empire testifies to his support for medical research and his concern for the sick. Abi Ahmet Celebi (1436–1523), the chief physician of the empire, produced a study on kidney and bladder stones. Recurrent outbreaks of the plague posed a challenge for physicians in Muslim lands. Muhammad had once said not to go to a country where an epidemic existed but also not to leave a place because an epidemic broke out. As a consequence, when European cities began enforcing quarantines to control the spread of the plague, early Muslim rulers dismissed such efforts. By the sixteenth century, however, a better understanding of contagion led to a redefinition of the proper response to a plague epidemic and allowed for leaving the city in search of clean air.

In the realm of religion, the rulers of all three empires drew legitimacy from their support for Islam, at least among their Muslim subjects. The Sunni-Shi'a split between the Ottomans and Safavids led to efforts to define and enforce religious orthodoxy on both sides. For the Safavids this entailed suppressing Sufi movements and Sunnis, even marginalizing—sometimes massacring—the original Qizilbash warriors, who had come to be seen as politically disruptive. Sectarian conflicts within Islam were not as pronounced in Mughal lands, perhaps because even though the Mughals ruled over both Sunni and Shi'a subjects, these subjects were greatly outnumbered by non-Muslims, mostly Hindus.

Sufi fraternities thrived throughout the Muslim world in this era, even when the states tried to limit them. In India Sufi orders also influenced non-Muslims. The mystical Bhakti movement among Hindus involved dances, poems, and songs reminiscent of Sufi practice. The development of the new religion of the Sikhs (seeks) was also influenced by Sufis. The Sikhs traced themselves back to a teacher in the sixteenth century who argued that God did not distinguish between Muslims and Hindus but saw everyone as his children. Sikhs rejected the caste system (division of society into hereditary groups) and forbade alcohol and tobacco, and men did not cut their hair, covering it instead with a turban. The Sikh movement was most successful in northwest India, where Sikh men armed themselves to defend their communities.

Despite all the signs of cultural vitality in the three Islamic empires, none of them adopted the printing press or went through the sorts of cultural expansion associated with it in China and Europe. Until 1729 the Ottoman authorities prohibited printing books in Turkish or Arabic (Jews, Armenians, and Greeks could establish presses and print in their own languages). Printing was not banned in Mughal India, but neither did the technology spread, even after Jesuit missionaries printed Bibles in Indian languages beginning in the 1550s. The copying of manuscripts was a well-established practice, and those who made their living this way sometimes organized to keep competition at bay. It also needs to be noted that by the end of this period, scientific knowledge was not keeping up with advances made in Europe (see page 556).

Coffeehouses and Their Social Impact

In the mid-fifteenth century a new social convention spread throughout the Islamic world—drinking coffee. Arab writers trace the origins of coffee drinking to Yemen Sufis, who sought a trancelike concentration on God to the exclusion of everything else and found that coffee helped them stay awake (similarly, Buddhist monks drank tea to stay awake during long meditation sessions, a practice responsible for the spread of tea in East Asia). Most Sufis were not professional holy men but tradesmen or merchants. Therefore, the use of coffee for pious purposes led to its use as a business lubricant—an extension of hospitality to a potential buyer in a shop. Merchants carried the Yemenite practice to Mecca in about 1490. From Mecca, where pilgrims were introduced to it, coffee drinking spread to Egypt and Syria. In 1555 two Syrians opened a coffeehouse in Istanbul.

Coffeehouses provided a place for conversation and male sociability; there a man could entertain his friends cheaply and more informally than at home. But coffeehouses encountered religious and governmental opposition based on the following arguments: (1) because of its composition, coffee is intoxicating, making it analogous to wine, prohibited to Muslims; (2) coffee drinking was an innovation and therefore a violation of Islamic law; (3) coffeehouses encouraged political discussions, facilitating sedition; (4) coffeehouses attracted unemployed soldiers and other low types, encouraging immoral behavior, such as gambling, using drugs, and soliciting prostitutes; and (5) music at coffeehouses encouraged debauchery. Thus coffeehouses drew the attention of government officials, who considered themselves the guardians of public morality. On the other hand, the coffee trade was a major source of profit that local notables sought to control.

Although debate over the morality of coffeehouses continued through the sixteenth century, their eventual acceptance represented a revolution in Islamic life: socializing was no longer confined to the home. Ultimately, because the medical profession remained divided on coffee's harmful effects and because religious authorities could not prove that coffeehouses violated religious law, coffee drinking could not be forbidden. In the seventeenth century coffee and coffeehouses spread to Europe.

Non-Muslims Under Muslim Rule

How did Christians, Jews, Hindus, and other non-Muslims fare under these Islamic states?

Drawing on Qur'anic teachings, Muslims had long practiced a religious tolerance unknown in Christian Europe. Muslim rulers for the most part guaranteed the lives and property of Christians and Jews on their promise of obedience and the payment of a poll tax. In the case of the Ottomans, this tolerance was extended not only to the Christians and Jews who had been living under Muslim rule for centuries but also to the Serbs, Bosnians, Croats, and other Orthodox Christians in the newly conquered Balkans. The Ottoman conqueror of Constantinople, Mehmet, nominated the Greek patriarch as official representative of the Greek population. This and other such appointments recognized non-Muslims as functioning parts of the Ottoman society and economy. In 1454 Rabbi Isaac Sarfati sent a letter to the Jews in the Rhineland, Swabia, Moravia, and Hungary, urging them to move to Turkey because of the good conditions for Jews there. A massive migration to Ottoman lands followed. When Ferdinand and Isabella of Spain expelled the Jews in 1492 and later, many immigrated to the Ottoman Empire.

The Safavid authorities made efforts to convert Armenian Christians in the Caucasus, and many seem to have embraced Islam, some more voluntarily than others. Nevertheless, the Armenian Christian Church retained its vitality, and under the Safavids Armenian Christians were prominent merchants in long-distance trade (see page 510).

Babur and his successors acquired even more non-Muslim subjects with their conquests in India, which included not only Hindus but also substantial numbers of Jains, Zoroastrians, Christians, and Sikhs. Over time, the number of Indians who converted to Islam increased, but the Mughal rulers did not force conversion. When the first reliable census was taken in 1901, the Ganges plain, the area of the Indian subcontinent most intensely exposed to Mughal rule and for the longest span of time, had a Muslim population of only 10 to 15 percent. Accordingly, some scholars have argued that in the Indian subcontinent there was an inverse relationship between the degree of Muslim political penetration and conversion to Islam.

Akbar went the furthest in promoting Muslim-Hindu accommodation. He celebrated important Hindu festivals, such as Diwali, the festival of

Emperor Akbar in the City of Fatehpur Sikri   In 1569 Akbar founded the city of Fatehpur Sikri (the City of Victory) to honor the Muslim holy man Sheik Salim Chishti, who had foretold the birth of Akbar's son and heir Jahangir. Akbar is shown here seated on the cushion in the center overseeing the construction of the city. The image is contained in the *Akbarnama*, a book of illustrations Akbar commissioned to officially chronicle his reign. (Victoria & Albert Museum, London, UK/The Bridgeman Art Library)

lights, and he wore his uncut hair in a turban as a concession to Indian practice. Also, Akbar twice married Hindu princesses, one of whom became the mother of his heir, Jahangir, and he appointed the Spanish Jesuit Antonio Monserrate (1536–1600) as tutor to his second son, Prince Murad. Eventually, Hindus totaled 30 percent of the imperial bureaucracy. In 1579 Akbar abolished the **jizya**, the poll tax on non-Muslims that guaranteed their protection. These actions, especially the abolition of the jizya, infuriated the ulama, and serious conflict erupted between its members and the emperor. Ultimately, Akbar issued an imperial decree declaring that the Mughal emperor had supreme authority, even above the ulama, in all religious matters, to the dismay of the Muslim religious establishment.

Some of Akbar's successors, above all Aurangzeb, sided more with the ulama. Aurangzeb appointed censors of public morals in important cities to enforce Islamic laws against gambling, prostitution, drinking, and the use of narcotics. He forbade sati — the self-immolation of widows on their husbands' funeral pyres — and the castration of boys to be sold as eunuchs. He also abolished all taxes not authorized by Islamic law. To compensate for the loss of revenue, in 1679 Aurangzeb reimposed the tax on non-Muslims. Aurangzeb's reversal of Akbar's religious tolerance and cultural cosmopolitanism extended further. He ordered the destruction of some Hindu temples and tried to curb Sikhism. He also required Hindus to pay higher customs duties than Muslims. Out of fidelity to Islamic law, he even criticized his mother's tomb, the Taj Mahal: "The lawfulness of a solid construction over a grave is doubtful, and there can be no doubt about the extravagance involved."[4] Aurangzeb's attempts to enforce rigid Islamic norms proved highly unpopular and aroused resistance that weakened Mughal rule. Aurangzeb himself died on an unsuccessful military campaign in 1707 to suppress a rebellion by the Marathas in the southern highlands.

Shifting Trade Routes and European Penetration

How were the Islamic empires affected by the gradual shift toward trade routes that bypassed their lands?

It has widely been thought that a decline in the wealth and international importance of the Muslim empires could be directly attributed to the long-term shift in trading patterns that resulted from the discoveries of Columbus, Magellan, and other European explorers. The argument is that new sea routes enabled Europeans to acquire goods from the East without using Muslim intermediaries, so that the creation of European colonial powers beginning in the sixteenth century led directly and indirectly to the eclipse of the Ottomans, Safavids, and Mughals. Recent scholars have challenged these ideas as too simplistic. First, it was not until the eighteenth century that political decline became evident in the three Islamic empires. Second, Turkish, Persian, and Indian merchants remained very active as long-distance traders into the eighteenth century and opened up many new routes themselves. It is true that in the Islamic empires New World crops like potatoes and sweet potatoes fueled population increases less rapidly than in western Europe and East Asia. By 1800 the population of India was about 190 million, that of Safavid lands about 8 million, and that of Ottoman lands about 24 million. (By comparison, China's population stood at about 300 million in

1800 and Russia's about 35 million.) But economic growth does not always correlate with population increases.

Over the centuries covered in this chapter, the Islamic empires became not only more tied to European powers but also more connected to each other. Europeans gained deeper knowledge of Islamic lands, but so did residents of these lands, who more frequently traveled to other Islamic countries and wrote about their travels.

European Rivalry for Trade in the Indian Ocean

Shortly before Babur's invasion of India, the Portuguese had opened the subcontinent to Portuguese trade. In 1510 they established the port of Goa on the west coast of India as their headquarters and through an aggressive policy took control of Muslim shipping in the Indian Ocean and Arabian Sea, charging high fees to let ships through. The Portuguese historian Barrões attempted to justify Portugal's seizure of commercial traffic that the Muslims had long dominated:

> It is true that there does exist a common right to all to navigate the seas and in Europe we recognize the rights which others hold against us; but the right does not extend beyond Europe and therefore the Portuguese as Lords of the Sea are justified in con-fiscating the goods of all those who navigate the seas without their permission.[5]

In short, the Portuguese decided that Western principles of international law should not restrict them in Asia. As a result, they controlled the spice trade over the Indian Ocean for almost a century.

In 1602 the Dutch formed the Dutch East India Company with the stated goal of wresting the enormously lucrative spice trade from the Portuguese. In 1685 they supplanted the Portuguese in Ceylon (Sri Lanka). The scent of fabulous profits also attracted the English. With a charter signed by Queen Elizabeth, eighty London merchants organized the British East India Company. In 1619 Emperor Jahangir granted a British mission important commercial concessions. Soon, by offering gifts, medical services, and bribes to Indian rulers, the British East India Company was able to set up twenty-eight coastal forts/trading posts. By 1700 the company had founded the cities that became Madras and Calcutta (today called Chennai and Kolkata) and had taken over Bombay (today Mumbai), which had been a Portuguese possession (Map 17.3).

The British called their trading posts **factory-forts**. The term *factory* did not signify manufacturing; it designated the walled compound containing the residences, gardens, and offices of British East India Company officials and the warehouses where goods were stored before being shipped to Europe. The company president exercised political authority over all residents.

Factory-forts existed to make profits from Asian-European trade, which was robust due to the popularity of Indian and Chinese wares in Europe in the late seventeenth and early eighteenth centuries. The European middle classes wanted Indian textiles, which were colorful, durable, cheap, and washable. The upper classes desired Chinese wallpaper and porcelains and Indian silks and cottons. Other Indian goods in demand included pepper and other spices, sugar, and opium. To pay for these goods, the British East India Company sold silver, copper, zinc, lead, and fabrics to the Indians. Profits grew even larger after 1700, when the company began to trade with China.

MAP 17.3 India, 1707–1805 In the eighteenth century Mughal power gradually yielded to the Hindu Marathas and to the British East India Company.

Merchant Networks in the Islamic Empires

The shifting trade patterns associated with European colonial expansion brought no direct benefit to the Ottomans and the Safavids, whose merchants could now be bypassed by Europeans seeking goods from India, Southeast Asia, or China. Yet merchants from these Islamic empires often proved adaptable, finding ways to benefit from the new trade networks.

In the case of India, the appearance of European traders led to a rapid increase in overall trade, helping Indian merchants and the Indian economy. Some Indian merchants in Calcutta and Bombay, for instance, made gigantic fortunes from trade within Asia carried on European ships. Block-printed cotton cloth, produced by artisans

English Dress Made of Indian Printed Cotton Cloth Early British traders in India were impressed with the quality of the textiles made there and began ordering designs that would be popular with the English. This dress, created around 1770–1780 in England, is made of printed cotton (chintz) from the southeastern part of India. Chintz became so popular in England that it was eventually banned because it was threatening local textile industries. (Victoria & Albert Museum, London, UK/Art Resource, NY)

working at home, was India's chief export. Through an Islamic business device involving advancing payment to artisans, banker-brokers supplied the material for production and money for the artisans to live on while they worked; the cloth brokers specified the quality, quantity, and design of the finished products. This procedure resembles the later English "domestic" or "putting-out" system (see page 693), for the very good reason that the English took the idea from the Indians.

Within India the demand for cotton cloth, as well as for food crops, was so great that Akbar had to launch a wide-scale road-building campaign. From the Indian region of Gujarat, Indian merchant bankers shipped their cloth worldwide: across the Indian Ocean to Aden and the Muslim-controlled cities on the east coast of Africa; across the Arabian Sea to Muscat and Hormuz and up the Persian Gulf to the cities of Persia; up the Red Sea to the Mediterranean; by sea also to Malacca, Indonesia, China, and Japan; by land across Africa to Ghana on the west coast; and to Astrakhan, Poland, Moscow, and even the Russian cities on the distant Volga River. Indian businessmen had branch offices in many of these places, and all this activity produced fabulous wealth for some Indian merchants. Some scholars have compared India's international trade in the sixteenth century with that of Italian firms, such as the Medici. Indian trade actually extended over a far wider area, however. Indian merchants were often devout Hindus, Muslims, Buddhists, or Jains, evidence that undermines the argument of some Western writers, notably Karl Marx (see page 728), that religion retarded Asia's economic development.

Throughout Muslim lands both Jews and Christians were active in commerce. A particularly interesting case involves the Armenian Christians in the Safavid Empire in the sixteenth to eighteenth centuries. Armenian merchants had been trading from their base in Armenia for centuries and were especially known for their trade in Persian silk. When the Portuguese first appeared on the western coast of India in 1498 and began to settle in south India, they found many Armenian merchant communities already there. A few decades later Akbar invited Armenians to settle in his new capital, Agra. In 1603 Shah Abbas captured much of Armenia, taking it from the Ottomans. Because defending this newly acquired border area was difficult, he forced the Armenians to move more deeply into Persia. Among them was the merchant community of Julfa, which was moved to a new suburb of Isfahan that was given the name New Julfa. The old city of Julfa was burned down so that the residents could not return. Shah Abbas made use of the Armenian merchants as royal merchants and financiers, but their economic mainstay continued to be long-distance trade.

Surviving letters and account books have allowed scholars to reconstruct the expanding trading networks of the Armenian merchants — networks that stretched from Venice and Amsterdam in western Europe, Moscow in Russia, and Ottoman-controlled Aleppo and Smyrna to all the major trading cities of India and even regions farther east, including Guangzhou in southern China and Manila in the Philippines. Many Armenian communities in these cities became quite substantial, built churches, and recruited priests. Kinship connections were regularly used to cement commercial relations, and members of the community living in these scattered cities would return to New Julfa to marry, creating new kinship connections. Business, though, was conducted through contracts. The merchant about to take a journey would borrow a sum of money to purchase goods and would contract to pay it back with interest on his return. Using couriers, these Armenian merchants sent long letters describing the trade environment and the prices that could be realized for given goods. These letters were written in a dialect of Armenian known to few outside their community, making it easier to maintain confidentiality in reports on trade conditions.

The Armenian merchants would sail on whatever ships were available, including Dutch and Italian ones. The goods they dealt in included silver, gold, precious stones, indigo and other dyestuffs, silk, cotton cloth, and tea. The merchants could often speak half a dozen languages and were comfortable in both Islamic and Christian lands. In India Armenian merchants reached an agreement with the British East India Company that recognized their rights to live in company cities and observe their own religion. By the 1660s they had settled in Manila, and a few decades later they entered what is now Malaysia and Indonesia. By the end of the seventeenth century a small group of Armenian merchants had crossed the Himalayas from India and established themselves in Lhasa, Tibet. By the mid-eighteenth century they had also settled in the Dutch colony of Batavia (Indonesia). Clearly the Armenian merchants were able to operate profitably in cities European powers dominated.

In the mid-eighteenth century the Armenian community lost its center in New Julfa because of religious persecution by a zealous shah, and the community scattered. Still, Armenian merchants remained prominent in many trading centers, including Russia, the Mediterranean, and especially India, well into the nineteenth century.

From the British East India Company
to the British Empire in India

Britain's presence in India began with the British East India Company and its desire to profit from trade. Managers of the company in London discouraged all unnecessary expenses and financial risks and thus opposed missionary activities or interference in local Indian politics. Nevertheless, the company responded to political instability in India in the early eighteenth century by extending political control. When warlords appeared or an uprising occurred, people from the surrounding countryside flocked into the company's factory-forts, which gradually came to exercise political authority over the territories around them. The company's factories evolved into defensive installations manned by small garrisons of native troops—known as sepoys—trained in Western military weapons and tactics.

Britain eventually became the dominant foreign presence in India, despite challenges from the French. From 1740 to 1763 Britain and France were engaged in a tremendous global struggle, and India, like North America in the Seven Years' War, became a battlefield and a prize. The French won land battles, but English sea power proved decisive by preventing the landing of French reinforcements. The Treaty of Paris of 1763 recognized British control of much of India, marking the beginning of the British Empire in India.

How was Britain to govern so large a territory? Eventually, the East India Company was pushed out of its governing role because the English Parliament distrusted the company, believing it was corrupt. The Regulating Act of 1773 created the office of governor general to exercise political authority over the territory controlled by the company. The India Act of 1784 required that the governor general be chosen from outside the company, and it made company directors subject to parliamentary supervision.

Implementation of these reforms fell to three successive governors: Warren Hastings (r. 1774–1785), Lord Charles Cornwallis (r. 1786–1794), and the marquess Richard Wellesley (r. 1797–1805). Hastings sought allies among Indian princes, laid the foundations for the first Indian civil service, abolished tolls to facilitate internal trade, placed the salt and opium trades under government control, and planned a codification of Muslim and Hindu laws. Cornwallis introduced the British style of property relations, in effect converting a motley collection of former Mughal officers, tax collectors, and others into English-style landlords. The result was a new system of landholding in which the rents of tenant farmers supported the landlords. Wellesley was victorious over local rulers who resisted British rule, vastly extending British influence in India. Like most nineteenth-century British governors of India, Wellesley believed that British rule strongly benefited the Indians. With supreme condescension, he wrote that British power should be established over the Indian princes in order "to deprive them of the means of prosecuting any measure or of forming any confederacy hazardous to the security of the British empire, and to enable us to preserve the tranquility of India by exercising a general control over the restless spirit of ambition and violence which is characteristic of every Asiatic government."[6]

Political Decline

What common factors led to the decline of central power in the Islamic empires in the seventeenth and eighteenth centuries?

By the end of the eighteenth century all three of the major Islamic empires were on the defensive and losing territory. They faced some common problems—succession difficulties, financial strain, and loss of military superiority—but their circumstances differed in significant ways as well.

The first to fall was the Safavid Empire. Persia did not have the revenue base to maintain the sort of standing armies that the Ottomans and the Mughals had. Decline in the strength of the army encouraged increased foreign aggression. In 1722 the

Afghans invaded from the east, seized Isfahan, and were able to repulse an Ottoman invasion from the west. In Isfahan thousands of officials and members of the shah's family were executed. In the following century some potential leaders emerged, but none were able to reunite all of Persia. In this political vacuum, Shi'a religious institutions grew stronger.

The Ottoman Empire also suffered from poor leadership. Early Ottoman practice had guaranteed that the sultans would be forceful men. The sultan's sons gained administrative experience as governors of provinces and military experience on the battlefield as part of their education. After the sultan died, any son who wanted to succeed had to contest his brothers to claim the throne, after which the new sultan would have his defeated brothers executed. Although bloody, this system led to the succession of capable, determined men. After Suleiman's reign, however, the tradition was abandoned. To prevent threats of usurpation, sons of the sultan were brought up in the harem and confined there as adults, denied roles in government. The result was a series of rulers who were minor children or incompetent adults, leaving power in the hands of high officials and the mothers of the heirs. Political factions formed around viziers, military leaders, and palace women. In the contest for political favor, the devshirme was abandoned, and political and military ranks were filled by Muslims.

The Ottoman Empire's military strength also declined. The defeat of the Turkish fleet by the Spanish off the coast of Greece at Lepanto in 1571 marked the loss of Ottoman dominance in the Mediterranean. By the terms of a peace treaty with Austria signed at Karlowitz (1699), the Ottomans lost the major European provinces of Hungary and Transylvania, along with the tax revenues they had provided. Also, the Ottoman armies were depending more on mercenaries, and they did not keep up with the innovations in drill, command, and control that were then transforming European armies. From the late seventeenth century Ottoman armies began losing wars and territory along both northern and eastern borders. In 1774 the empire lost the lands on the northern bank of the Black Sea to Russia. In North Africa the local governors came to act more independently, sometimes starting hereditary dynasties.

In Mughal India the old Turkish practice of letting heirs fight for the throne persisted, leading to frequent struggles over succession, but also to strong rulers. Yet military challenges proved daunting there as well. After defeating his father and brothers, Aurangzeb made it his goal to conquer the south. The stiffest opposition came from the Marathas, a militant Hindu group centered in the western Deccan. From 1681 until his death in 1707, Aurangzeb led repeated sorties through the Deccan. He took many forts and won several battles, but total destruction of the Maratha guerrilla bands eluded him.

Aurangzeb's death led to thirteen years of succession struggles, shattering the empire. His eighteenth-century successors were less successful than the Ottomans in making the dynasty the focus of loyalty. Mughal provincial governors began to rule independently, giving only minimal allegiance to the throne at Delhi. Meanwhile, the Marathas pressed steadily northward, constituting the gravest threat to Mughal authority. Threats also came from the west. In 1739 the Persian adventurer Nadir Shah invaded India, defeated the Mughal army, looted Delhi, and, after a savage massacre, carried off a huge amount of treasure, including the Peacock Throne. Constant skirmishes between the Afghans and the Marathas for control of the Punjab and northern India ended in 1761 at Panipat, where the Marathas were crushed by the Afghans. At that point, India no longer had a state strong enough to impose order on the subcontinent or check the penetration of the Europeans. Not until 1857, however, did the Mughal Dynasty come to a formal end.

In all three empires fiscal difficulties contributed to strain on the state. A long period of peace in the late sixteenth century and again in the mid-eighteenth century, as well as a decline in the frequency of visits of the plague, led to a doubling of the population. Increased population, coupled with the "little ice age" of the mid-seventeenth century, meant that the land could not sustain so many people, nor could the towns provide jobs for the thousands of agricultural workers who fled to them. The return of demobilized soldiers aggravated the problem. Inflation, famine, and widespread revolts resulted. The economic center of gravity shifted from the capital to the provinces, and politically the empire began to decentralize as well. Power was seized by local notables and military strongmen at the expense of central government officials. There was a positive side to increasing provincial autonomy, however, because it drew more people into political participation, thus laying a foundation for later nationalism. At the time, however, central government officials perceived the growth in provincial power in negative terms.

Chapter Summary

After the decline of the Mongols in Central Asia and Persia, many small Turkic-ruled states emerged in the region from Anatolia through Afghanistan. Three of them went on to establish large empires: the Ottomans in Anatolia, the Safavids in Persia, and the Mughals in India. The Ottoman Empire's political system reached its classic form under Suleiman I. All authority flowed from the sultan to his public servants: provincial governors, police officers, military generals, heads of treasuries, and viziers. In Persia for some time Turkish lords competed for power, with no single one dominant until 1501, when a fourteen-year-old military leader declared himself shah. The strength of this Safavid state rested in part on the skills of urban bureaucrats, who were vital to the civil machinery of government. Babur, from his base in Afghanistan, founded the Mughal Empire in India. His grandson Akbar extended Mughal rule far into India. Whereas the Ottoman sultans and Safavid shahs used slaves acquired from non-Muslim lands for military and administrative positions, Akbar relied on the services of royal princes, nobles, and warrior-aristocrats. All three empires quickly adapted to new gunpowder technologies.

Each of the three Islamic empires presided over an extraordinary artistic and intellectual flowering in everything from carpetmaking and book illustration to architecture and gardening, from geography and astronomy to medicine. Each of these empires drew legitimacy from its support for Islam. There were, however, key differences: the Ottomans and Mughals supported the Sunni tradition, the Safavids the Shi'a tradition.

The three Islamic empires all had a substantial number of non-Muslim subjects. The Ottomans ruled over the Balkans, where most of the people were Christian, and Muslims in India were greatly outnumbered by Hindus.

European exploration opened new trade routes and enabled Europeans to trade directly with India and China, bypassing Muslim intermediaries in the Middle East.

Within India British merchants increased their political control in politically unstable areas, leading before the end of the eighteenth century to a vast colonial empire in India.

By the end of the eighteenth century all three of the major Islamic empires were losing territory. The first to fall was the Safavid Empire, which could not maintain the sizable standing armies of the Ottomans and the Mughals. From the late seventeenth century Ottoman armies began losing wars along the northern and eastern borders, resulting in substantial loss of territory. Military challenges proved daunting in Mughal India as well. In all three empires, as central power declined, local notables and military strongmen seized power.

Notes

1. *Memoirs of Zehir-Ed-Din Muhammed Baber: Emperor of Hindustan*, trans. John Leyden and William Erskine (London: Longman and Cadell, 1826), p. 333.
2. Quoted in M. C. Beach, *The Imperial Image: Paintings for the Mughal Court* (Washington, D.C.: Freer Gallery of Art, Smithsonian Institution, 1981), pp. 9–10.
3. Quoted in V. A. Smith, *The Oxford History of India* (Oxford: Oxford University Press, 1967), p. 398.
4. Quoted in S. K. Ikram, *Muslim Civilization in India* (New York: Columbia University Press, 1964), p. 202.
5. Quoted in K. M. Panikkar, *Asia and Western Domination* (London: George Allen & Unwin, 1965), p. 35.
6. Quoted in W. Bingham, H. Conroy, and F. W. Iklé, *A History of Asia*, vol. 2 (Boston: Allyn and Bacon, 1967), p. 74.

CONNECTIONS

From 1300 to 1800 and from North Africa to India, Islamic civilization thrived under three dynastic houses: the Ottomans, the Safavids, and the Mughals. All three empires had a period of expansion when territory was enlarged, followed by a high point politically and culturally, and later a period of contraction, when territories broke away. Two of the empires had large non-Muslim populations. India, even under Mughal rule, remained a predominantly Hindu land, and the Ottomans, in the process of conquering the Balkans, acquired a population that was largely Greek Orthodox Christians. Though all three states supported Islam, the Safavids took Shi'a teachings as orthodox, and the other two favored Sunni teachings. At the cultural level, the borders of these three states were porous, and people, ideas, art motifs, languages, and trade flowed back and forth.

In East Asia the fifteenth through eighteenth century also saw the creation of strong, prosperous, and expanding states, though in the case of China (under the Qing Dynasty) and Japan (under the Tokugawa Shogunate) the eighteenth century was a cultural high point, not a period of decline. The Qing emperors were Manchus, from the region northeast of China proper, reminiscent of the Mughals, who began in Afghanistan. As in the Islamic lands, during these centuries the presence of European powers became an issue in East Asia, though the details were quite different. Although one of the commodities that the British most wanted was the tea produced in China, Britain did not extend political control in China the way it did in India. Japan managed to refuse entry to most European traders after finding their presence and their support for missionary activity disturbing. The next chapter takes up these developments in East Asia.

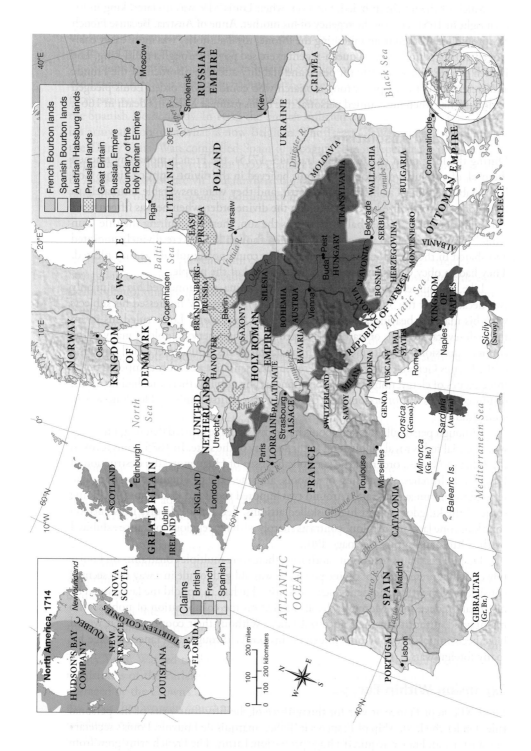

◀ **MAP 18.2   Europe After the Peace of Utrecht, 1715** The series of treaties commonly called the Peace of Utrecht ended the War of the Spanish Succession and redrew the map of Europe. A French Bourbon king succeeded to the Spanish throne. France surrendered the Spanish Netherlands (later Belgium), then in French hands, to Austria and recognized the Hohenzollern rulers of Prussia. Spain ceded Gibraltar to Great Britain, for which it has been a strategic naval station ever since. Spain also granted Britain the *asiento*, the contract for supplying African slaves to America.

roughly 125,000 men during the period of France's participation in the Thirty Years' War (1630–1648) to 250,000 during the Dutch War (1672–1678) and 340,000 during the War of the League of Augsburg (1688–1697).[5] Uniforms and weapons were standardized, and a system of training and promotion was devised. As in so many other matters, Louis's model was emulated across Europe, amounting to a continent-wide transformation in military capability scholars have referred to as a "military revolution."

During this long period of warfare, Louis's goal was to expand France to what he considered its natural borders. His armies extended French borders to include important commercial centers in the Spanish Netherlands and Flanders as well as the entire province of Franche-Comté between 1667 and 1678. In 1681 Louis seized the city of Strasbourg, and three years later he sent his armies into the province of Lorraine. At that moment the king seemed invincible. In fact, Louis had reached the limit of his expansion. The wars of the 1680s and 1690s brought no additional territories and placed unbearable strains on French resources.

Louis's last war was endured by a French people suffering high taxes, crop failure, and widespread malnutrition and death. This war resulted from a dispute over the rightful successor to the Spanish throne. In 1700 the childless Spanish king Charles II (r. 1665–1700) died. His will bequeathed the Spanish crown and its empire to Philip of Anjou, Louis XIV's grandson (Louis's wife, Maria-Theresa, had been Charles's sister). The will violated a prior treaty by which the European powers had agreed to divide the Spanish possessions between the king of France and the Holy Roman emperor, both brothers-in-law of Charles II. Claiming that he was following both Spanish and French interests, Louis broke with the treaty and accepted the will, thereby triggering the War of the Spanish Succession (1701–1713).

In 1701 the English, Dutch, Austrians, and Prussians formed the Grand Alliance against Louis XIV. War dragged on until 1713, when it was ended by the Peace of Utrecht. This series of treaties allowed Louis's grandson Philip to remain king of Spain on the understanding that the French and Spanish crowns would never be united. France surrendered large territories overseas to England (Map 18.2; see also page 545).

The Peace of Utrecht marked the end of French expansion. Thirty-three years of war had given France the rights to all of Alsace (on France's present-day border with Germany and Switzerland) and some commercial centers in the north. But at what price? In 1714 an exhausted France hovered on the brink of bankruptcy. It is no wonder that when Louis XIV died on September 1, 1715, many subjects felt as much relief as they did sorrow.

The Economic Policy of Mercantilism

France's ability to build armies and fight wars depended on a strong economy. Fortunately for Louis, his controller general, Jean-Baptiste Colbert (1619–1683), proved to be a financial genius. Colbert's central principle was that the wealth and the economy of France should serve the state. To this end, from 1665 to his death in 1683, Colbert rigorously applied mercantilist policies to France.

Mercantilism is a collection of governmental policies for the regulation of economic activities by and for the state. It derives from the idea that a nation's international power is based on its wealth, specifically its supply of gold and silver. To accumulate wealth, a country always had to sell more goods abroad than it bought. Thus, to reduce imports, Colbert insisted that French industry should produce everything needed by the French people.

To increase exports, Colbert supported old industries and created new ones. He enacted new production regulations, created guilds to boost quality standards, and encouraged foreign craftsmen to immigrate to France. To encourage the purchase of French goods, he abolished many domestic tariffs and raised tariffs on foreign products. In 1664 Colbert founded the Company of the East Indies with hopes of competing with the Dutch for Asian trade. Colbert also sought to increase France's control over and presence in New France (Canada), which was rich in untapped minerals and contained some of the best agricultural land in the world (see page 544).

During Colbert's tenure as controller general, Louis was able to pursue his goals without massive tax increases and without creating a stream of new offices. The constant pressure of warfare after Colbert's death, however, undid many of his economic achievements.

The Austrian Habsburgs

Absolutism was also the dominant form of monarchical rule among the many states that composed the Holy Roman Empire. Prussia, a minor power with scattered holdings, emerged in the seventeenth and eighteenth centuries under the Hohenzollern dynasty as a major rival to the Austrian Habsburg dynasty (see Chapter 19). Like all of central Europe, the Habsburgs emerged from the Thirty Years' War impoverished and exhausted. Their efforts to destroy Protestantism in the German lands and to turn the weak Holy Roman Empire into a real state had failed. Defeat in central Europe encouraged the Austrian Habsburgs to turn away from a quest for imperial dominance and to focus inward and eastward in an attempt to unify their diverse holdings.

Habsburg victory over Bohemia during the Thirty Years' War was an important step in this direction. Ferdinand II (r. 1619–1637) drastically reduced the power of the Bohemian Estates, the largely Protestant representative assembly. He also confiscated the landholdings of Protestant nobles and gave them to loyal Catholic nobles and to the foreign aristocratic mercenaries who led his armies. After 1650 a large portion of the Bohemian nobility was of recent origin and owed its success to the Habsburgs.

With the support of this new nobility, the Habsburgs established direct rule over Bohemia. Under their rule, the condition of the serfs worsened substantially. The Habsburgs also successfully eliminated Protestantism in Bohemia. These changes were important steps in creating absolutist rule.

Ferdinand III (r. 1637–1657) continued to build state power. He centralized the government in the empire's German-speaking provinces, which formed the core Habsburg holdings. For the first time, a permanent standing army was ready to put down any internal opposition. The Habsburg monarchy then turned east toward Hungary, which had been divided between the Ottomans and the Habsburgs in the early sixteenth century. Between 1683 and 1699 the Habsburgs pushed the Ottomans from most of Hungary and Transylvania. The recovery of all the former kingdom of Hungary was completed in 1718.

Despite its reduced strength, the Hungarian nobility effectively thwarted the full development of Habsburg absolutism. Throughout the seventeenth century Hungarian nobles periodically rose in revolt against the Habsburgs. They never triumphed decisively, but neither were they crushed. In 1703, with the Habsburgs bogged down in the War of the Spanish Succession, the Hungarians rose in one last patriotic rebellion under Prince Francis Rákóczy (RAH-coht-see). Rákóczy and his forces were eventually defeated, but the Habsburgs agreed to restore many of the traditional privileges of the Hungarian aristocracy in return for the country's acceptance of Habsburg rule. Thus Hungary was never fully integrated into a centralized, absolute Habsburg state.

Elsewhere, the Habsburgs made significant achievements in state-building by forging consensus with the church and the nobility. A sense of common identity and loyalty to the monarchy grew among elites in Habsburg lands, even to a certain extent in Hungary. German became the language of the state. As in France and Spain, rulers used Catholicism to fuse a collective identity. Vienna became the political and cultural center of the empire. By 1700 it was a thriving city with a population of one hundred thousand and a royal palace to rival that of Louis XIV in France.

The Absolutist Palace

Through most of the seventeenth century the French court had no fixed home, following the monarch to his numerous residences. In 1682 Louis moved his court and government to the newly renovated palace at Versailles, in the countryside southwest of Paris. The palace quickly became the center of political, social, and cultural life. The king required all great nobles to spend at least part of the year in attendance on him there. Since he controlled the distribution of state power and wealth, nobles had no choice but to obey and compete with each other for his favor at Versailles.

Elaborate formal gardens were a crucial component of the palace. The themes of the sculptures in the Versailles gardens hailed Louis's power, with images of Apollo, the Roman sun god, and Neptune, the sea god, making frequent appearances. The rational orderliness and symmetry of the gardens showed that Louis's force extended even to nature, while its terraces and waterworks served as showcases for the latest techniques in military and civil engineering. Exotic plants and elaborate designs testified to the sovereign's global trading networks and cultivated taste.

Louis further revolutionized court life by establishing an elaborate set of etiquette rituals to mark every moment of his day, from waking up and dressing in the morning to removing his clothing and retiring at night. These rituals may seem absurd, but they were far from meaningless or trivial. The king controlled immense resources and privileges; access to him meant favored treatment for government offices, military and religious posts, state pensions, honorary titles, and a host of other benefits.

Courtiers sought these rewards for themselves and their family members and followers. A system of patronage—in which a higher-ranked individual protected a lower-ranked one in return for loyalty and services—flowed from the court to the provinces. Through this mechanism Louis gained cooperation from powerful nobles. Although they were denied public offices and posts, women played a central role in the patronage system. At court the king's wife, mistresses, and other female relatives recommended individuals for honors, advocated policy decisions, and brokered alliances between noble factions.

With Versailles as the center of European politics, French culture grew in international prestige. French became the language of polite society and international diplomacy, gradually replacing Latin as the language of scholarship and learning. The royal courts of Sweden, Russia, Poland, and Germany all spoke French. France inspired a cosmopolitan European culture in the late seventeenth century that looked to Versailles as its center.

Louis's rival European monarchs soon followed his example, and palace building became a Europe-wide phenomenon. In 1693 Charles XI of Sweden, having reduced the power of the aristocracy, ordered the construction of his Royal Palace, which dominates the center of Stockholm to this day. Another such palace was Schönbrunn, an enormous Viennese Versailles begun in 1695 by Emperor Leopold to celebrate Austrian military victories and Habsburg might. As Frederick the Great of Prussia noted, every descendant of a princely family "imagines himself to be something like Louis XIV. He builds his Versailles, has his mistresses, and maintains his army."[6]

Constitutionalism and Empire in England and the Dutch Republic

Why and how did the constitutional state triumph in England and the Dutch Republic?

While most European nations developed absolutist states in the seventeenth century, England and the Netherlands evolved toward constitutionalism, which is the limitation of government by law. Constitutionalism also implies a balance between the authority and power of the government, on the one hand, and the rights and liberties of the subjects, on the other.

After decades of civil war and an experiment with republicanism, the English opted for a constitutional monarchy in 1688. Under this system of government, England retained a monarch as the titular head of government but vested sovereignty in an elected parliament. For their part, the Dutch rejected monarchical rule in 1648, when their independence from Spain was formally recognized. Instead they adopted a republican form of government in which elected Estates (assemblies) held supreme power.

Religious Divides and Civil War

In 1603 beloved Queen Elizabeth was succeeded by her Scottish cousin James Stuart, who ruled England as James I (r. 1603–1625). Like Louis XIV, James believed that a monarch had a divine right to his authority and was responsible only to God. James went so far as to lecture the English Parliament's House of Commons: "There are no privileges and immunities which can stand against a divinely appointed King." Such a view ran counter to the long-standing English tradition that a person's property could not be taken away without due process of law. James I and his son Charles I (r. 1625–1649) considered such constraints a threat to their divine-right prerogative. Consequently, at every meeting of Parliament between 1603 and 1640, bitter squabbles erupted between the Crown and the House of Commons.

Religious issues also embittered relations between the king and the House of Commons. In the early seventeenth century many English people felt dissatisfied with the Church of England established by Henry VIII. Calvinist **Puritans** wanted to take the Reformation further by "purifying" the Anglican Church of Roman Catholic elements — elaborate vestments and ceremonials, bishops, and even the giving and wearing of wedding rings. James I responded to such ideas by declaring, "No bishop, no king." For James, bishops were among the chief supporters of the throne. His son and successor, Charles I, further antagonized subjects by marrying a French Catholic princess and supporting the high-handed policies of archbishop of Canterbury William Laud (1573–1645).

Charles avoided direct confrontation by refusing to call Parliament into session from 1629 to 1640, financing his government through extraordinary stopgap levies considered illegal by most English people. However, when Scottish Calvinists revolted in anger against his religious policies, Charles was forced to summon Parliament to obtain funding for an army to put down the revolt. Angry with the king's behavior and sympathetic with the Scots' religious beliefs, the House of Commons passed the Triennial Act in 1641, which compelled the king to call Parliament every three years. The Commons also impeached Archbishop Laud and then threatened to abolish bishops. King Charles, fearful of a Scottish invasion — the original reason for summoning Parliament — reluctantly accepted these measures. The next act in the conflict was precipitated by the outbreak of rebellion in Ireland, where English governors and landlords had long exploited the people. In 1641 the Catholic gentry of Ireland led an uprising in response to a feared invasion by British anti-Catholic forces.

Without an army, Charles I could neither come to terms with the Scots nor respond to the Irish rebellion. After a failed attempt to arrest parliamentary leaders, Charles left London for the north of England, where he began to raise an army. In response, Parliament formed its own army, the New Model Army. During the spring of 1642 both sides prepared for war.

The English Civil War (1642–1649) pitted the power of the king against that of Parliament. After three years of fighting, Parliament's army defeated the king's forces at the Battles of Naseby and Langport in the summer of 1645. Charles refused to concede defeat, and both sides waited for a decisive event. This arrived in the form of the army under the leadership of Oliver Cromwell, a member of the House of Commons and a devout Puritan. In 1647 Cromwell's troops captured the king and dismissed members of the Parliament who opposed Cromwell's actions. In 1649 the remaining representatives, known as the Rump Parliament, put Charles on trial for high treason. Charles was found guilty and beheaded on January 30, 1649, an act that sent shock waves around Europe.

The Puritan Protectorate

With the execution of Charles, the monarchy was abolished. The question then became how the country would be governed. One answer was provided by philosopher Thomas Hobbes (1588–1679). Hobbes held a pessimistic view of human nature and believed that, left to themselves, humans would compete violently for power and wealth. The only solution, as he outlined in his 1651 treatise *Leviathan*, was a social contract in which all members of society placed themselves under the absolute rule of a monarch who would maintain peace and order. Hobbes imagined society as a human body in which the monarch served as head and individual subjects together made up the body. Just as the body cannot sever its own head, so Hobbes believed that society could not, having accepted the contract, rise up against its king.

Hobbes's longing for a benevolent absolute monarch was not widely shared in England. Instead a commonwealth, or republican government, was proclaimed. Theoretically, legislative power rested in the surviving members of Parliament, and executive power was lodged in a council of state. In fact, the army that had defeated the king controlled the government, and Oliver Cromwell controlled the army. Though called the Protectorate, the rule of Cromwell (1653–1658) was a form of military dictatorship. Reflecting Puritan ideas of morality, Cromwell's state forbade sports, kept the theaters closed, and rigorously censored the press.

On the issue of religion, Cromwell favored some degree of tolerance, and the Instrument of Government gave all Christians except Roman Catholics the right to practice their faiths. Cromwell had long associated Catholicism in Ireland with sedition and heresy, and he led an army there to reconquer the country in August 1649. Following Cromwell's reconquest, the English banned Catholicism in Ireland, executed priests, and confiscated land from Catholics for English and Scottish settlers. These brutal acts left a legacy of Irish hatred for England and did little to undermine Catholicism.

The Protectorate collapsed when Cromwell died in 1658 and his ineffectual son succeeded him. Fed up with military rule, the English longed for a return to civilian government and, with it, common law and social stability. By 1660 they were ready to restore the monarchy.

The Massacre at Drogheda   In September 1649 English forces under Oliver Cromwell laid siege to Drogheda, a town on the east coast of Ireland, and killed approximately three thousand soldiers and civilians when they entered the town. The Drogheda massacre long fostered hatred of Cromwell and English rule in Ireland. (Rue des Archives/The Granger Collection, NYC—All rights reserved.)

Constitutional Monarchy

The Restoration of 1660 brought to the throne Charles II (r. 1660–1685), the eldest son of Charles I. Both houses of Parliament were also restored, as was the Anglican Church. However, Charles was succeeded by his Catholic brother James II, arousing fears of a return of Catholicism. A group of eminent persons in Parliament and the Church of England offered the English throne to James's Protestant daughter Mary and her Dutch husband, Prince William of Orange. In December 1688 James II, his queen, and their infant son fled to France. Early in 1689 William and Mary were crowned king and queen of England.

The English called the events of 1688 and 1689 the Glorious Revolution because they believed it replaced one king with another with barely any bloodshed. In truth, William's arrival sparked riots and violence across the British Isles and in North American cities such as Boston and New York. Uprisings by supporters of James, known as Jacobites, occurred in 1689 in Scotland. In Ireland the two sides waged outright war from 1689 to 1691. William's victory at the Battle of the Boyne (1690) and the subsequent Treaty of Limerick (1691) sealed his accession to power.

In England the revolution represented the final destruction of the idea of divine-right monarchy. The men who brought about the revolution framed their intentions in the **Bill of Rights of 1689**, which was formulated in direct response to Stuart absolutism. Law was to be made in Parliament; once made, it could not be suspended by the Crown. Parliament had to be called at least once every three years. The Bill of Rights also established the independence of the judiciary and mandated that there be no standing army in peacetime. Protestants could possess arms, but the Catholic minority could not. Catholics could not inherit the throne. Additional legislation granted freedom of worship to Protestant dissenters but not to Catholics. William and Mary accepted these principles when they took the throne, and Parliament passed the Bill of Rights in December 1689.

The Glorious Revolution and the concept of representative government found its best defense in political philosopher John Locke's *Second Treatise of Civil Government* (1690). Locke (1632–1704) maintained that a government that oversteps its proper function — protecting the natural rights of life, liberty, and property — becomes a tyranny. By "natural rights," Locke meant rights basic to all men because all have the ability to reason. Under a tyrannical government, he argued, the people have the natural right to rebellion.

Although the events of 1688 and 1689 brought England closer to Locke's ideal, they did not constitute a democratic revolution. The Glorious Revolution placed sovereignty in Parliament, and Parliament represented the upper classes. Nondemocratic government lasted in England at least until 1832 and in many ways until 1928, when all women received voting rights.

The Dutch Republic

The independence of the Republic of the United Provinces of the Netherlands was recognized in 1648 in the treaty that ended the Thirty Years' War. Rejecting the rule of a monarch, the Dutch adopted a system of **republicanism**, whereby power rested in the hands of the people and was exercised through elected representatives. Other republics of the time included the Swiss Confederation and several autonomous city-states of Italy and the Holy Roman Empire. Among the Dutch, an oligarchy of wealthy businessmen called regents handled domestic affairs in each province's Estates, or assemblies. The provincial Estates held virtually all the power. A federal assembly, or States General, handled foreign affairs and war, but it did not possess sovereign authority. All issues had to be referred back to the local Estates for approval, and each of the seven provinces could veto any proposed legislation. Holland, the province with the largest navy and the most wealth, usually dominated the republic and the States General.

In each province, the Estates appointed an executive officer, known as the stadholder, who carried out ceremonial functions and was responsible for military defense. Although in theory freely chosen by the Estates, in practice the reigning prince of Orange usually held the office of stadholder in several of the seven provinces of the republic. Tensions persisted between supporters of the House of Orange and those of the staunchly republican Estates, who suspected the princes of harboring monarchical ambitions. When one of them, William III, took the English throne in 1689 with his wife, Mary, the republic simply continued without stadholders for several decades.

Global trade and commerce brought the Dutch the highest standard of living in Europe, perhaps in the world. Salaries were high, and all classes of society ate well. A scholar has described the Netherlands as "an island of plenty in a sea of want." Consequently, the Netherlands experienced very few of the food riots that characterized the rest of Europe.[7]

The moral and ethical bases of their commercial wealth were thrift, frugality, and religious tolerance. Jews enjoyed a level of acceptance and assimilation in Dutch business and general culture unique in early modern Europe. (See "Individuals in Society: Glückel of Hameln," page 542.) In the Dutch Republic tolerance not only seemed the right way, but also earned profits by attracting a great deal of foreign capital and investment. After Louis XIV revoked the Edict of Nantes, many Huguenots fled France for the Dutch Republic. They brought with them a high level of artisanal skill and business experience, as well as a loathing for state repression that would help inspire the political views of the Enlightenment (see page 567).

Colonial Expansion and Empire

How did European nations compete for global trade and empire in the Americas and Asia?

For almost a century after the fall of the Aztec capital of Tenochtitlan, the Spanish and Portuguese dominated European overseas trade and colonization (see Chapter 16). In the early seventeenth century, however, England, France, and the Netherlands challenged Spain's monopoly. They eventually succeeded in creating overseas empires, consisting of settler colonies in North America, slave plantations in the Caribbean, and scattered trading posts in West Africa and Asia.

The Dutch Trading Empire

The so-called golden age of the Dutch Republic in the seventeenth century was built on its commercial prosperity and its highly original republican system of government. The Dutch came to dominate the European shipping business by putting profits from their original industry—herring fishing—into shipbuilding. They then took aim at Portugal's immensely lucrative Asian trade empire.

In 1599 a Dutch fleet returned to Amsterdam from a voyage to Southeast Asia carrying 600,000 pounds of pepper and 250,000 pounds of cloves and nutmeg. Those who had invested in the expedition received a 100 percent profit. The voyage led to the establishment in 1602 of the Dutch East India Company, founded with the stated intention of capturing the spice trade from the Portuguese.

In return for assisting Indonesian princes in local squabbles and disputes with the Portuguese, the Dutch won broad commercial concessions. Through agreements, seizures, and outright military aggression, they gained control of the western access to the Indonesian archipelago in the first half of the seventeenth century. Gradually, they acquired political domination over the archipelago itself. The Dutch were willing to use force more ruthlessly than the Portuguese and had superior organizational efficiency. These factors allowed them to expel the Portuguese from Ceylon and other East Indian islands in the 1660s and henceforth dominate the production and trade of spices. The company also established the colony of Cape Town on the southern tip of Africa as a provisioning point for its Asian fleets.

Not content with challenging the Portuguese in the Indian Ocean, the Dutch also aspired to a role in the Americas. Founded in 1621, the Dutch West India Company aggressively sought to open trade with North and South America and capture Spanish territories there. The company captured or destroyed hundreds of Spanish ships, seized the Spanish silver fleet in 1628, and claimed portions of Brazil and the Caribbean. The Dutch also successfully interceded in the transatlantic slave trade, establishing a large number of trading stations on the west coast of Africa. Ironically, the nation that was known throughout Europe as a bastion of tolerance and freedom came to be one of the principal operators of the slave trade starting in the 1640s.

Colonial Empires of England and France

England and France followed the Dutch in challenging Iberian dominance overseas. Unlike the Iberian powers, whose royal governments financed exploration and directly ruled the colonies, England, France, and the Netherlands conducted the initial phase of colonization through chartered companies with monopolies over settlement and trade in a given area. These corporate bodies were granted extensive powers over faraway colonies, including the right to monopolize trade, make war, raise taxes, and administer justice.

After an unsuccessful first colony at Roanoke (in what is now North Carolina), the English colony of Virginia, founded at Jamestown in 1607, gained a steady hold by producing tobacco for a growing European market. Indentured servants obtained free passage to the colony in exchange for several years of work and the promise of greater opportunity than in England. In the 1670s English colonists from the Caribbean island of Barbados settled Carolina, where conditions were suitable for large rice plantations. During the late seventeenth century enslaved Africans replaced indentured servants as laborers on tobacco and rice plantations, and a harsh racial divide was imposed.

For the first settlers on the coast of New England, the reasons for seeking a new life in the colonies were more religious than economic. Many of these colonists were

INDIVIDUALS IN SOCIETY • Glückel of Hameln

In 1690 a Jewish widow in the small German town of Hameln in Lower Saxony sat down to write her autobiography. She wanted to distract her mind from the terrible grief she felt over the death of her husband and to provide her twelve children with a record. She told them that she was writing her memoirs "so you will know from what sort of people you have sprung, lest today or tomorrow your beloved children or grandchildren came and know naught of their family." Out of her pain and heightened consciousness, Glückel (1646–1724) produced an invaluable source for scholars.

She was born in Hamburg two years before the end of the Thirty Years' War. In 1649 the merchants of Hamburg expelled the Jews, who moved to nearby Altona, then under Danish rule. When the Swedes overran Altona in 1657–1658, the Jews returned to Hamburg "purely at the mercy of the Town Council." Glückel's narrative unfolds against a background of the constant harassment to which Jews were subjected—special papers, permits, bribes—and in Hameln she wrote, "And so it has been to this day and, I fear, will continue in like fashion."

When Glückel was "barely twelve," her father betrothed her to Chayim Hameln, and they married when she was fourteen. She describes him as "the perfect pattern of the pious Jew," a man who stopped his work every day for study and prayer, fasted, and was scrupulously honest in his business dealings. Only a few years older than Glückel, Chayim earned his living dealing in precious metals and in making small loans on pledges (pawned goods). This work required constant travel to larger cities, markets, and fairs, often in bad weather, always over dangerous roads. Chayim consulted his wife about all his business dealings. As he lay dying, a friend asked if he had any last wishes. "None," he replied. "My wife knows everything. She shall do as she has always done." For thirty years Glückel had been his friend, full business partner, and wife. They had thirteen children, twelve of whom survived their father, eight then unmarried. As Chayim had foretold, Glückel succeeded in launching the boys in careers and in providing dowries for the girls.

Glückel's world was her family, the Jewish community of Hameln, and the Jewish communities into which her children married. Her social and business activities took her across Europe, from Amsterdam to Berlin, from Danzig to Vienna; thus her

---

radical Protestants escaping Anglican repression. The small and struggling outpost of Plymouth Colony (1620) was followed by Massachusetts Bay Colony (1630), which grew into a prosperous settlement. Religious disputes in Massachusetts led to the dispersion of settlers into the new communities of Providence, Connecticut, Rhode Island, and New Haven. Because New England lacked the conditions for plantation agriculture, slavery was always a minor factor there.

English settlements hugged the Atlantic coastline, but this did not prevent conflicts with the indigenous inhabitants over land and resources. The haphazard nature of English colonization also led to conflicts of authority within the colonies. As the English crown grew more interested in colonial expansion, efforts were made to acquire the territory between New England in the north and Virginia in the south. The goal world was far from narrow or provincial. She took great pride that Prince Frederick of Cleves, later king of Prussia, danced at the wedding of her eldest daughter. The rising prosperity of Chayim's businesses allowed the couple to maintain up to six servants.

Glückel was deeply religious, and her culture was steeped in Jewish literature, legends, and mystical and secular works. Above all, she relied on the Bible. Her language, heavily sprinkled with scriptural references, testifies to a rare familiarity with the Scriptures.

Students who wish to learn about seventeenth-century business practices, the importance of the dowry in marriage, childbirth, Jewish life, birthrates, family celebrations, and even the meaning of life can gain a good deal from the memoirs of this extraordinary woman who was, in the words of one of her descendants, the poet Heinrich Heine, "the gift of a world to me."

Source: *The Memoirs of Glückel of Hameln* (New York: Schocken Books, 1977).

QUESTIONS FOR ANALYSIS

1. Consider the ways in which Glückel of Hameln was both an ordinary and an extraordinary woman of her times. Would you call her a marginal or a central person in her society? Why?

2. How might Glückel's successes be attributed to the stabilizing force of absolutism in the seventeenth century?

▶LaunchPad
ONLINE DOCUMENT PROJECT

What factors shaped life for European Jews in the early modern era?
Read excerpts from Glückel of Hameln's memoirs and other accounts of Jewish life, and then complete a quiz and writing assignment based on the evidence and details from this chapter.
See inside the front cover to learn more.

was to unify English holdings and minimize French and Dutch competition on the Atlantic seaboard. The results of these efforts were the mid-Atlantic colonies: the Catholic settlement of Maryland (1632); New York, captured from the Dutch in 1664; and the Quaker colony of Pennsylvania (1681).

Whereas English settlements were largely agricultural, the French established trading factories in present-day Canada, much like those in Asia and Africa. In 1608 Samuel de Champlain founded the first permanent French settlement at Quebec as a post for trading beaver pelts with local Algonquin and Huron peoples. The settlement of Ville-Marie, later named Montreal, followed in 1642. Louis XIV's capable controller general, Jean-Baptiste Colbert, established direct royal control over New France (Canada) and tried to enlarge its population by sending colonists.

The Fur Trade   In the early seventeenth century, European fur traders relied on Native Americans' expertise and experience, leading to the equal relations depicted in this scene from the colony of New Sweden (in modern-day Pennsylvania). The action in the background shows violence among indigenous groups, rivalries exacerbated by contact with Europeans and their trade goods. European demand for beaver hats, made from the felted pelts of beavers, drove the tremendous expansion of the North American fur trade in the beginning of the seventeenth century. (From *Geographia Americae with An Account of the Delaware Indians, Based on Surveys and Notes Made 1654–1656,* by Peter Lindestrom, published by The Swedish Colonial Society/Visual Connection Archive)

French immigration to New Canada remained small compared with the stream of settlers who came to British North America; nevertheless, the French were energetic and industrious traders and explorers. Following the waterways of the St. Lawrence River, the Great Lakes, and the Mississippi River, they ventured into much of North America in the 1670s and 1680s. In 1673 the Jesuit Jacques Marquette and the merchant Louis Joliet sailed down the Mississippi and claimed possession of the land on both sides of the river as far south as present-day Arkansas. In 1682 Robert de La Salle traveled the Mississippi to the Gulf of Mexico, opening the way for French occupation of Louisiana.

In the first decades of the seventeenth century, English and French captains also challenged Spain's hold over the Caribbean (see Map 19.2, page 580). The English seized control of Bermuda (1612), Barbados (1627), and a succession of other islands. The French took Cayenne (1604), St. Christophe (1625), Martinique and Guadeloupe (1635), and, finally, Saint-Domingue (1697) on the western half of Spanish-occupied Hispaniola. These islands acquired new importance after 1640, when the Portuguese brought sugar plantations to Brazil. Sugar and slaves quickly followed in the West

Indies (see pages 479–481), making the Caribbean plantations the most lucrative of all colonial possessions.

The northern European powers also expanded in Africa and Asia. In the 1600s France and England—along with Denmark and other northern European powers—established fortified trading posts, or factories, in West Africa as bases for purchasing slaves and in India and the Indian Ocean for spices and other luxury goods. Thus, by the end of the seventeenth century, a handful of European powers possessed overseas empires that truly spanned the globe.

Mercantilism and Colonial Wars

Trade to and among European overseas possessions was governed by mercantilist economic policy (see page 534). The acquisition of colonies was intended to favor the wealth and power of the mother country, and to that end, European states—starting with Spain in the sixteenth century—imposed trading monopolies on their overseas colonies and factories. The mercantilist notion of a "zero-sum game," in which any country's gain must come from another country's loss, led to hostile competition and outright warfare among European powers over their colonial possessions.

In England Oliver Cromwell established the first of a series of Navigation Acts in 1651, and the restored monarchy of Charles II extended them in 1660 and 1663. The acts required most goods imported into England and Scotland (Great Britain after 1707) to be carried on British-owned ships with British crews or on ships of the country producing the article. Moreover, these laws gave British merchants and shipowners a virtual monopoly on trade with British colonies. The colonists were required to ship their products on British (or American) ships and to buy almost all European goods from Britain. These economic regulations were intended to eliminate foreign competition and to encourage the development of a British shipping industry whose seamen could serve when necessary in the Royal Navy.

The Navigation Acts were a form of economic warfare against the Dutch, who were far ahead of the English in shipping and foreign trade in the mid-seventeenth century. In conjunction with three Anglo-Dutch wars between 1652 and 1674, the Navigation Acts seriously damaged Dutch shipping and commerce. By the late seventeenth century the Netherlands was falling behind England in shipping, trade, and settlement.

Thereafter France was England's most serious rival in the competition for overseas empire. Rich in natural resources and home to a population three or four times that of England, France was continental Europe's leading military power. It was already building a powerful fleet and a worldwide system of rigidly monopolized colonial trade. But the War of the Spanish Succession, the last of Louis XIV's many wars (see page 533), tilted the balance in favor of England. The 1713 Peace of Utrecht forced France to cede its North American holdings in Newfoundland, Nova Scotia, and the Hudson Bay territory to Britain. Spain was compelled to give Britain control of its West African slave trade—this contract was called the *asiento* (ah-SYEHN-toh)—and to let Britain send one ship of merchandise into the Spanish colonies annually. These acquisitions primed Britain to take a leading role in the growing Atlantic trade of the eighteenth century, including the transatlantic slave trade (discussed in Chapter 19).

People Beyond Borders

As they seized new territories, European nations produced maps proudly outlining their possessions. The situation on the ground, however, was often much more complicated than the lines on those maps would suggest. Many groups of people lived in the contested frontiers between empires, habitually crisscrossed their borders, or carved out niches within empires where they carried out their own lives in defiance of the official rules.

Restricted from owning land and holding many occupations in Europe, Jews were eager participants in colonial trade and established closely linked mercantile communities scattered across many different empires. Similarly, a community of Christian Armenians in Isfahan in the Safavid Empire formed the center of a trade network extending from London to Manila and Acapulco. Family ties and trust within these minority groups were a tremendous advantage in generating the financial credit and cooperation necessary for international commerce. Yet Jews and Armenians were minorities where they settled and vulnerable to persecution. For example, restrictions existed on the number of slaves Jews could own in Barbados in the early eighteenth century, and the end of Persian tolerance in the same period led to the dispersion of Armenians from Isfahan.

Other groups openly defied the law. The growth in world trade attracted smugglers who routinely violated colonial trade monopolies as well as bandits eager to profit from the vulnerability of fleets laden with precious silver or spices. During the seventeenth century piracy was endemic in the Caribbean islands, as well as in the South China Sea, in the western Indian Ocean, and along the north African coast. States often encouraged predatory attacks by authorizing privateers to raid the ships of countries with which they were at war. A thin line thus separated illegal piracy from legal privateering. Another important group of outlaw communities in the Caribbean islands were Maroons, runaway slaves who took advantage of the mountainous terrain to establish secret settlements where they could live in freedom.

The nomadic Cossacks and Tartars who inhabited the steppes of the Don River basin that bordered the Russian and Ottoman Empires are yet another example of "in-between" peoples. Often depicted as warring pawns of the two great powers whose clients they became, in fact the Cossacks and the Tartars maintained considerable political and cultural autonomy through the seventeenth century and enjoyed a degree of peaceful interaction. By the eighteenth century, however, both Ottoman and Russian rulers had expanded state control in their frontiers and had reined in the raiding and migration of nomadic steppe peoples. As their example suggests, the assertion of state authority in the seventeenth and eighteenth centuries made it progressively harder for all of these groups to retain autonomy from the grip of empire.

The Russian Empire

How did Russian rulers build a distinctive absolutist monarchy and expand into a vast and powerful empire?

Russia occupied a unique position among Eurasian states. With borders straddling eastern Europe and northwestern Asia, its development into a strong imperial state drew on elements from both continents. Like the Muslim empires in Central and South

Asia and the Ming Dynasty in China, the expansion of Russia was a result of the weakening of the great Mongol and Timurid Empires (see Chapters 16 and 17). After declaring independence from the Mongols, the Russian tsars conquered a vast empire, extending through North Asia all the way to the Pacific Ocean. State-building and territorial expansion culminated during the reign of Peter the Great, who turned Russia toward the West by intervening in western European wars and politics and forcing his people to adopt elements of Western culture.

Mongol Rule in Russia and the Rise of Moscow

In the thirteenth century the Mongols had conquered Kievan Rus, the medieval Slavic state centered first at Novgorod and then at Kiev, a city on the Dnieper River, which included most of present-day Ukraine, Belarus, and part of northwest Russia. For two hundred years the Mongols forced the Slavic princes to submit to their rule and to render tribute and slaves. The princes of the Grand Duchy of Moscow, also known as Muscovy, a principality within Kievan Rus, became particularly adept at serving the Mongols. They loyally put down uprisings and collected the khan's taxes. Eventually the Muscovite princes were able to destroy the other princes who were their rivals for power. Ivan III (r. 1462–1505), known as Ivan the Great, greatly expanded the principality of Moscow, claiming large territories in the north and east to the Siberian frontier.

By 1480 Ivan III was strong enough to refuse to pay tribute to the Mongols and declare the autonomy of Moscow. To legitimize his new position, Ivan and his successors borrowed elements of Mongol rule. They forced weaker Slavic principalities to render tribute previously paid to Mongols and adopted Mongol institutions such as the tax system, postal routes, and census. Loyalty from the highest-ranking nobles, or boyars, helped the Muscovite princes consolidate their power.

Another source of legitimacy lay in Moscow's claim to the political and religious inheritance of the Byzantine Empire. After the empire's capital, Constantinople, fell to the Ottomans in 1453, the princes of Moscow saw themselves as heirs of the Byzantine caesars (emperors) and guardians of the Orthodox Christian Church. Ivan III's marriage to the daughter of the last Byzantine emperor enhanced Moscow's claim to have inherited imperial authority. The title *tsar*, first taken by Ivan IV in 1547, is a contraction of *caesar*.

Building the Russian Empire

Developments in Russia took a chaotic turn with the reign of Ivan IV (r. 1533–1584), the famous Ivan the Terrible, who ascended to the throne at age three. His mother died, possibly poisoned, when he was eight, leaving Ivan to suffer insults and neglect from the boyars at court. At age sixteen he suddenly pushed aside his hated advisers and crowned himself tsar.

After the sudden death of his wife, however, Ivan began a campaign of persecution against those he suspected of opposing him. He executed members of leading boyar families, along with their families, friends, servants, and peasants. To replace them, Ivan created a new service nobility, whose loyalty was guaranteed by their dependence on the state for land and titles.

As landlords demanded more from the serfs who survived the persecutions, growing numbers of peasants fled toward recently conquered territories to the east and south. There they joined free groups and warrior bands known as Cossacks. Ivan responded by tying serfs ever more firmly to the land and to noble landholders. Simultaneously, he ordered that urban dwellers be bound to their towns and jobs so that he could tax them more heavily. The urban classes had no security in their property, and even the wealthiest merchants were dependent agents of the tsar. These restrictions checked the growth of the Russian middle classes and stood in sharp contrast to economic and social developments in western Europe.

Ivan's reign was successful in defeating the remnants of Mongol power, adding vast new territories to the realm, and laying the foundations for the huge multiethnic Russian empire. In the 1550s, strengthened by an alliance with Cossack bands, he conquered the Muslim khanates of Kazan and Astrakhan and brought the fertile steppe region around the Volga River under Russian control. In the 1580s Cossacks fighting for the Russian state crossed the Ural Mountains and began the long conquest of Siberia. Because of the size and distance of the new territories, the Russian state did not initially seek to impose the Orthodox religion and maintained local elites in positions of honor and leadership, buying their loyalty with grants of land. In relying on cooperation from local elites and ruthlessly exploiting the common people, the Russians followed the pattern of the Spanish and other early modern European imperial states.

Following Ivan's death, Russia entered a chaotic period known as the Time of Troubles (1598–1613). While Ivan's relatives struggled for power, the Cossacks and peasants rebelled against nobles and officials. This social explosion from below brought the nobles together. They crushed the Cossack rebellion and elected Ivan's grandnephew, Michael Romanov (r. 1613–1645), the new hereditary tsar. The Romanov dynasty would endure as one of the most successful European absolutist dynasties until the Russian Revolution of 1917.

Despite the turbulence of the period, the Romanov tsars, like their western European counterparts, made further achievements in territorial expansion and state-building. After a long war, Russia gained land to the west in Ukraine in 1667, after allying with Cossacks in rebellion against Poland. By the end of the century it had completed the conquest of Siberia to the east. This vast territorial expansion brought Russian power to the Pacific Ocean and was only checked by the powerful Qing Dynasty, which forced Russia to recognize China's northern border. The basis of Russian wealth in Siberia was furs, which the state collected by forced annual tribute payments from local peoples. Profits from furs and other natural resources, especially mining in the eighteenth century, funded expansion of the Russian bureaucracy and the army.

The growth of state power did nothing to improve the lot of the common people. In 1649 a new law code extended serfdom to all peasants in the realm, giving lords unrestricted rights over their serfs and establishing penalties for harboring runaways. The new code also removed the privileges that non-Russian elites had enjoyed within the empire and required conversion to Russian orthodoxy. Henceforth, Moscow maintained strict control of trade and administration throughout the empire.

The peace imposed by harsh Russian rule was disrupted in 1670 by a rebellion led by the Cossack Stenka Razin, who attracted a great army of urban poor and peasants. He and his followers killed landlords and government officials and proclaimed freedom from oppression, but their rebellion was defeated in 1671. The ease with which Moscow crushed the rebellion testifies to the success of the Russian state in unifying and consolidating its empire.

Peter the Great and Russia's Turn to the West

Heir to his predecessors' efforts at state-building, Peter the Great (r. 1682–1725) embarked on a tremendous campaign to accelerate and complete these processes. Possessing enormous energy and willpower, Peter built on the service obligations of Ivan the Terrible and his successors and continued their tradition of territorial expansion. Peter's ambitions hinged on gaining access to the sea by extending Russia's borders to the Black Sea (controlled by the Ottomans) and to the Baltic Sea (dominated by Sweden).

Peter embarked on his first territorial goal by conquering the Ottoman fort of Azov in 1696 and quickly built Russia's first navy base nearby. In 1697 the tsar led a group of 250 Russian officials and young nobles on an eighteen-month tour of western European capitals. Peter was fascinated by foreign technology, and he hoped to forge an anti-Ottoman alliance to strengthen his hold on the Black Sea. Traveling unofficially to avoid lengthy diplomatic ceremonies, Peter met with foreign kings, shipbuilders, and other experts. He failed to secure a military alliance, but he did learn his lessons from the growing power of the Dutch and the English.

To realize his second goal, Peter entered the Great Northern War (1700–1721) against Sweden. After a humiliating defeat at the Battle of Narva in 1700, Peter responded with measures designed to increase state power, strengthen his military, and gain victory. He required all nobles to serve in the army or in the civil administration — for life. Peter also created schools and universities to produce skilled technicians and experts. Furthermore, he established an interlocking military-civilian bureaucracy with fourteen ranks, and he decreed that all had to start at the bottom and work toward the top. Drawing on his experience abroad, Peter sought talented foreigners and placed them in his service. These measures gradually combined to make the army and government more powerful and efficient.

Peter also greatly increased the service requirements of commoners. In the wake of the Narva disaster, he established a regular standing army of more than two hundred thousand peasant-soldiers, drafted for life. He added an additional hundred thousand

Peter the Great This compelling portrait by Grigory Musikiysky captures the strength and determination of the warrior-tsar in 1723, after more than three decades of personal rule. In his hand Peter holds the scepter, symbol of royal sovereignty, and across his breastplate is draped an ermine fur, a mark of honor. In the background are the battleships of Russia's new Baltic fleet and the famous St. Peter and St. Paul Fortress that Peter built in St. Petersburg. (Hermitage, St. Petersburg, Russia/The Bridgeman Art Library)

MAP 18.3 **The Expansion of Russia, 1462–1689** In little more than two centuries, Russia expanded from the small principality of Muscovy to an enormous multiethnic empire, stretching from the borders of western Europe through northern Asia to the Pacific.

men in special regiments of Cossacks and foreign mercenaries. To fund the army, taxes on peasants increased threefold during Peter's reign. Serfs were also arbitrarily assigned to work in the growing number of factories and mines that supplied the military. Under Peter, Russia's techniques for governing its territories — including the policing of borders and individual identity documents — were far ahead of those of most other imperial powers.

In 1709 Peter's new war machine was able to crush Sweden's army in Ukraine at Poltava in one of the most significant battles in Russian history (Map 18.3). Russia's victory against Sweden was conclusive in 1721, and Estonia and present-day Latvia came under Russian rule for the first time. The cost was high: warfare consumed 80 to 85 percent of all revenues. But Russia became the dominant power in the Baltic and very much a great European power.

After his victory at Poltava, Peter channeled enormous resources into building a new Western-style capital on the Baltic to rival the great cities of Europe. Originally a desolate and swampy Swedish outpost, the magnificent city of St. Petersburg was designed to reflect modern urban planning with wide, straight avenues; buildings set in a uniform line; and large parks. Each summer, twenty-five thousand to forty thousand peasants were sent to provide construction labor in St. Petersburg without pay.

There were other important consequences of Peter's reign. For Peter, modernization meant westernization, and both Westerners and Western ideas flowed into Russia for the first time. He required nobles to shave their heavy beards and wear Western clothing. He also required them to attend parties where young men and women would mix together and freely choose their own spouses, in defiance of the traditional pattern of strictly controlled marriages. From these efforts a new elite class of Western-oriented Russians began to emerge.

Peter's reforms were unpopular with many Russians. For nobles, one of Peter's most detested reforms was the imposition of unigeniture—inheritance of land by one son alone—cutting off daughters and other sons from family property. For peasants, the reign of the tsar saw a significant increase in the bonds of serfdom, and the gulf between the serfs and the educated nobility increased. Despite the unpopularity of Peter's reforms, his modernizing and westernizing of Russia paved the way for it to move somewhat closer to the European mainstream in its thought and institutions during the Enlightenment, especially under Catherine the Great (see page 575).

Chapter Summary

Most parts of Europe experienced the first centuries of the early modern era as a time of crisis. Following the religious divides of the sixteenth-century Protestant and Catholic Reformations and the decades of bloodshed they unleashed, Europeans in the seventeenth century suffered from economic stagnation, social upheaval, and renewed military conflict. Despite these obstacles, both absolutist and constitutional European states emerged from the seventeenth century with increased powers and more centralized control. Whether they ruled through monarchical fiat or parliamentary negotiation, European governments increased the size and professionalism of their armies, strengthened their bureaucracies, and raised more taxes. The most successful acquired huge land- or sea-based empires.

Monarchs in Spain, France, and Austria used divine right to claim they possessed absolute power and were not responsible to any representative institutions. As Spain's economic weakness curtailed its role in European politics, Louis XIV's magnificent palace at Versailles became a center of European power and culture. Absolute monarchs overcame the resistance of the nobility both through military force and by affirming existing economic and social privileges. England and the Netherlands defied the general trend toward absolute monarchy, adopting distinctive forms of constitutional rule.

As Spain's power weakened in the early seventeenth century, the Netherlands, England, and France competed for access to overseas trade and territory. Mercantilist competition among these powers led to hostility and war. England emerged in the early eighteenth century with a distinct advantage over its rivals.

In Russia, Mongol conquest and rule set the stage for a harsh tsarist autocracy that was firmly in place by the time of the reign of Ivan the Terrible in the sixteenth century. The reign of Ivan and his successors saw a great expansion of Russian territory, laying the foundations for a huge multiethnic empire. Peter the Great forcibly turned Russia toward the West by adopting Western technology and culture.

Notes

1. Theodore K. Rabb, *The Struggle for Stability in Early Modern Europe* (Oxford: Oxford University Press, 1975), p. 10.
2. Quoted in Cecile Hugon, *Social France in the XVII Century* (London: McMillan, 1911), p. 189.
3. H. Kamen, "The Economic and Social Consequences of the Thirty Years' War," *Past and Present* 39 (April 1968): 44–61.

4. J. H. Elliott, *Imperial Spain, 1469–1716* (New York: Mentor Books, 1963), pp. 306–308.

5. John A. Lynn, "Recalculating French Army Growth," in *The Military Revolution Debate: Readings on the Military Transformation of Early Modern Europe*, ed. Clifford J. Rogers (Boulder, Colo.: Westview Press, 1995), p. 125.

6. Quoted in R. Ergang, *The Potsdam Führer: Frederick William I, Father of Prussian Militarism* (New York: Octagon Books, 1972), p. 13.

7. Simon Schama, *The Embarrassment of Riches: An Interpretation of Dutch Culture in the Golden Age* (New York: Alfred A. Knopf, 1987), pp. 165–170; quotation from p. 167.

CONNECTIONS

The seventeenth century represented a difficult passage between two centuries of dynamism and growth in Europe. On one side lay the sixteenth century's religious enthusiasm and strife, overseas discoveries, rising populations, and vigorous commerce. On the other side stretched the eighteenth century's renewed population growth, economic development, and cultural flourishing. The first half of the seventeenth century was marked by the spread of religious and dynastic warfare across Europe, resulting in death and widespread suffering. Recurring crop failure, famine, and epidemic disease contributed to a stagnant economy and population loss. In the middle decades of the seventeenth century, the very survival of the European monarchies established in the Renaissance appeared in doubt.

With the re-establishment of order in the second half of the century, maintaining stability was of paramount importance to European rulers. While a few nations placed their trust in constitutionally limited governments, many more were ruled by monarchs proclaiming their absolute and God-given authority. The ability to assume such power depended on cooperation from local elites, who acquiesced to state authority in exchange for privileges and payoffs. In this way, both absolutism and constitutionalism relied on political compromises forged from decades of strife.

As Spain's power weakened, other European nations bordering the Atlantic Ocean sought their own profits and glory from overseas empires. Henceforth, war among European powers would include high-stakes conflicts over territories and trade in the colonies. European rulers' increased control over their own subjects thus went hand in glove with the expansion of European power in the world.

The eighteenth century was to see these power politics thrown into question by new Enlightenment aspirations for human society, which themselves derived from the inquisitive and self-confident spirit of the Scientific Revolution. These movements — both of which would have tremendous worldwide influence — are explored in the next chapter. By the end of the eighteenth century demands for real popular sovereignty, colonial self-rule, and slave emancipation challenged the very bases of order so painfully achieved in the seventeenth century. Chapter 22 recounts the revolutionary movements that swept the late-eighteenth-century Atlantic world, while Chapters 25, 26, and 27 follow the story of European imperialism and the resistance of colonized peoples into the nineteenth century.

Chapter Review

MAKE IT STICK

✓ **LearningCurve**
Go online and use LearningCurve to retain what you've read.

IDENTIFY KEY TERMS

Identify and explain the significance of each item below.

Protestant Reformation (p. 519)
Jesuits (p. 522)
moral economy (p. 527)
Thirty Years' War (p. 527)
sovereignty (p. 528)
absolutism (p. 529)
divine right of kings (p. 531)

mercantilism (p. 534)
constitutionalism (p. 536)
Puritans (p. 537)
Bill of Rights of 1689 (p. 539)
republicanism (p. 539)
Navigation Acts (p. 545)
Cossacks (p. 548)

REVIEW THE MAIN IDEAS

Answer the focus questions from each section of the chapter.

1. How did the Protestant and Catholic Reformations change power structures in Europe and shape European colonial expansion? (p. 519)

2. How did seventeenth-century European states overcome social and economic crisis to build strong states? (p. 523)

3. How did absolutism evolve in the seventeenth century in Spain, France, and Austria? (p. 529)

4. Why and how did the constitutional state triumph in England and the Dutch Republic? (p. 536)

5. How did European nations compete for global trade and empire in the Americas and Asia? (p. 540)

6. How did Russian rulers build a distinctive absolutist monarchy and expand into a vast and powerful empire? (p. 546)

MAKE CONNECTIONS

Analyze the larger developments and continuities within and across chapters.

1. What common features did the Ming empire in China and the Muslim empires of the Middle East and India share with the Russian and other European empires? How would you characterize interaction among these Eurasian empires?

LaunchPad
ONLINE DOCUMENT PROJECT

Jewish Life in the Early Modern Era
What factors shaped life for European Jews in the early modern era?

Read excerpts from Glückel of Hameln's memoirs and other accounts of Jewish life, and then complete a quiz and writing assignment based on the evidence and details from this chapter.

See inside the front cover to learn more.

CHRONOLOGY

ca. 1500–1650	• Consolidation of serfdom in eastern Europe
1533–1584	• Reign of Ivan the Terrible in Russia
1589–1610	• Reign of Henry IV in France
1598–1613	• Time of Troubles in Russia
1612–1697	• Caribbean islands colonized by France, England, and the Netherlands
ca. 1620–1740	• Growth of absolutism in Austria and Prussia
1642–1649	• English Civil War, ending with the execution of Charles I
1643–1715	• Reign of Louis XIV in France
1651	• First of the Navigation Acts
1653–1658	• Oliver Cromwell's military rule in England (the Protectorate)
1660	• Restoration of English monarchy under Charles II
1665–1683	• Jean-Baptiste Colbert applies mercantilism to France
1670–1671	• Cossack revolt led by Stenka Razin
1682	• Louis XIV moves court to Versailles
1682–1725	• Reign of Peter the Great in Russia
1683–1718	• Habsburgs push the Ottoman Turks from Hungary
1685	• Edict of Nantes revoked
1688–1689	• Glorious Revolution in England
1701–1713	• War of the Spanish Succession

19

New Worldviews and Ways of Life

1540–1790

FROM THE MID-SIXTEENTH CENTURY ON, AGE-OLD PATTERNS OF knowledge and daily life were disrupted by a series of transformative developments. The same bold impetus toward exploring and conquering new territories that led Europeans across the Atlantic resulted in momentous new discoveries in astronomy and physics. Just as the authority of ancient models of the globe was overturned, so ancient frameworks for understanding the heavens were challenged and eventually discarded. The resulting conception of the universe and its laws remained in force until Albert Einstein's discoveries in the first half of the twentieth century. Along with new discoveries in botany, zoology, chemistry, and other domains, these developments constituted a fundamental shift in the basic framework for understanding the natural world and the methods for examining it known collectively as the "Scientific Revolution."

In the eighteenth century philosophers extended the use of reason from nature to human society. Self-proclaimed members of an "Enlightenment" movement, they wished to bring the same progress to human affairs that their predecessors brought to the understanding of the natural world. The Enlightenment created concepts of human rights, equality, progress, and tolerance that still guide Western societies. At the same time, some Europeans used their new understanding of reason to explain their own superiority, thus rationalizing attitudes now regarded as racist and sexist.

The expression of new ideas was encouraged by changes in the material world. With the growth of population, the revitalization of industry, and growing world trade, Europeans began to consume at a higher level.

Feeding the growth of consumerism was the expansion of transatlantic trade and lower prices for colonial goods, often produced by slaves. During the eighteenth century ships crisscrossing the Atlantic circulated commodities, ideas, and people to all four continents bordering the ocean. As trade became more integrated and communication intensified, an Atlantic world of mixed identities and vivid debates emerged.

The Scientific Revolution

What revolutionary discoveries were made in the sixteenth and seventeenth centuries, and why did they occur in Europe?

Building on developments in the Middle Ages and the Renaissance, tremendous advances in Europeans' knowledge of the natural world and techniques for establishing such knowledge took place between 1500 and 1700. Collectively known as the "Scientific Revolution," these developments were the result of many more people studying the natural world, who used new methods to answer fundamental questions about the universe and how it operated. The authority of ancient Greek texts was replaced by a conviction that knowledge should be acquired by observation and experimentation and that mathematics could be used to understand and represent the workings of the physical world. By 1700 precise laws governing physics and astronomy were known, and a new emphasis on the practical uses of knowledge had emerged.

For a long time, historians focused on the role of heroic individuals in the development of physics and astronomy. While the work of these scientists constituted highly significant milestones in the creation of modern science, their discoveries must be placed in the broader context of international trade, imperial expansion, and cultural contact. Alongside developments in natural philosophy, historians now emphasize the growth of natural history in this period, spurred by colonial empires and their competition over trade and territory.

Why Europe?

In 1500 scientific activity flourished in many parts of the world. With the expansion of Islam into the lands of the Byzantine Empire in the seventh and eighth centuries, Muslim scholars inherited ancient Greek learning, which itself was built on centuries of borrowing from older civilizations in Egypt, Babylonia, and India. The interaction of peoples and cultures across the vast Muslim world, facilitated by religious tolerance and the common scholarly language of Arabic, was highly favorable to advances in learning.

In a great period of cultural and intellectual flourishing from 1000 to 1500, Muslim scholars thrived in cultural centers such as Baghdad and Córdoba, the capital of Islamic Spain. They established the world's first universities in Constantinople, Fez (Morocco), and Cairo. In this fertile atmosphere, scholars surpassed the texts they had inherited in areas such as mathematics, physics, astronomy, and medicine. Arab and Persian mathematicians, for example, invented algebra, the concept of the algorithm, and decimal point notation, while Arab astronomers improved on measurements recorded in ancient works.

China was also a vital center of scientific activity, which reached a peak in the mid-fourteenth century. Among its many achievements, papermaking, gunpowder, and the use of the compass in navigation would be the most influential for the West. In Mesoamerica, civilizations such as the Maya and the Aztecs devised complex calendar systems based on astronomical observations and developed mathematics and writing.

Given the multiple world sites of learning and scholarship, it was by no means inevitable that Europe would take the lead in scientific thought or that "modern science" as we know it would emerge. In world history, periods of advancement produced by intense cultural interaction, such as those that occurred after the spread of Islam, are often followed by stagnation and decline during times of conflict and loss of authority. This is what happened in western Europe after the fall of the Western Roman Empire in the fifth century and in the Maya civilization after the collapse of its cultural and political centers around 900. The Muslim world successfully resisted a similar threat after the Mongol invasions.

The re-establishment of stronger monarchies and the growth of trade in the High Middle Ages contributed to a renewal of learning in western Europe. As Europeans began to encroach on Islamic lands in Iberia, Sicily, and the eastern Mediterranean, they became aware of the rich heritage of Greek learning in these regions and the ways scholars had improved upon ancient knowledge. In the twelfth century many ancient Greek texts—including works of Aristotle, Ptolemy, Galen, and Euclid previously unknown in the West—were translated into Latin, along with the commentaries of Arab scholars. A number of European cities created universities in which Aristotle's works dominated the curriculum.

As Europe recovered from the ravages of the Black Death in the late fourteenth and fifteenth centuries, the intellectual and cultural movement known as the Renaissance provided a crucial foundation for the Scientific Revolution. Scholars called humanists, working in the bustling mercantile city-states of Italy, emphasized the value of acquiring knowledge for the practical purposes of life. The quest to restore the glories of the ancient past led to the rediscovery of other classical texts such as Ptolemy's *Geography*, which was translated into Latin around 1410. An encyclopedic treatise on botany by Theophrastus was rediscovered in the 1450s moldering on the shelves of the Vatican library. The fall of Constantinople to the Ottomans in 1453 resulted in a great influx of little-known Greek works, as Christian scholars fled to Italy with their precious texts.

In this period, western European universities established new professorships of mathematics, astronomy, and natural philosophy. The prestige of the new fields was low, especially mathematics, which was reserved for practical problems such as accounting, surveying, and computing planetary tables but not used as a tool to understand the functioning of the physical world itself. Nevertheless, these professorships eventually enabled the union of mathematics with natural philosophy that was to be a hallmark of the Scientific Revolution.

European overseas expansion in the fifteenth and sixteenth centuries provided another catalyst for new thought about the natural world. In particular, the navigational problems of long oceanic voyages in the age of expansion stimulated scientific research and invention. To help solve these problems, inventors developed many new scientific instruments, such as the telescope, barometer, thermometer, pendulum clock,

microscope, and air pump. Better instruments, which permitted more accurate observations, often led to important new knowledge. Another crucial technology in this
period was printing, which provided a faster and less expensive way to circulate
knowledge.

Political and social conflicts were widespread in Eurasia in the sixteenth and early
seventeenth centuries, but they had different results. The three large empires of the
Muslim world (see Chapter 17) that arose in the wake of the Mongol Empire sought
to restore order and assert legitimacy in part by imposing Islamic orthodoxy. Their
failure to adopt the printing press (see page 504) can be seen as part of a wider reaction
against earlier traditions of innovation. Similarly, in China after the Manchu invasion
of 1644, the new Qing Dynasty legitimized its authority through stricter adherence
to Confucian tradition. By contrast, western Europe remained politically fragmented
into smaller competitive nations, divisions that were augmented by the religious frac-
turing of the Protestant Reformation. These conditions made it impossible for authorities to impose one orthodox set of ideas and thus allowed individuals to question
dominant patterns of thinking.

Scientific Thought to 1550

For medieval scholars, philosophy was the path to true knowledge about the world,
and its proofs consisted of the authority of ancients (as interpreted by Christian theologians) and their techniques of logical argumentation. Questions about the physical
nature of the universe and how it functioned belonged to a minor branch of philosophy,
called natural philosophy. Natural philosophy was based primarily on the ideas of
Aristotle, the great Greek philosopher of the fourth century B.C.E. According to the
Christianized version of Aristotle, a motionless earth stood at the center of the universe
and was encompassed by ten separate concentric crystal spheres in which were embedded the moon, sun, planets, and stars. Beyond the spheres was Heaven with the throne
of God and the souls of the saved. Angels kept the spheres moving in perfect circles.

Aristotle's views also dominated thinking about physics and motion on earth.
Aristotle had distinguished between the world of the celestial spheres and that of the
earth — the sublunar world. The sublunar realm was made up of four imperfect,
changeable elements: air, fire, water, and earth. Aristotle and his followers also believed
that a uniform force moved an object at a constant speed and that the object would
stop as soon as that force was removed.

Aristotle's cosmology made intellectual sense, but it could not account for the
observed motions of the stars and planets and, in particular, provided no explanation
for the apparent backward motion of the planets (which we now know occurs as planets
closer to the sun periodically overtake the earth on their faster orbits). The ancient
Greek scholar Ptolemy offered a theory for this phenomenon. According to Ptolemy,
the planets moved in small circles, called epicycles, each of which moved in turn along
a larger circle, or deferent. Ptolemaic astronomy was less elegant than Aristotle's neat
nested circles and required complex calculations, but it provided a surprisingly accurate
model for predicting planetary motion.

The work of Ptolemy also provided the basic foundation of knowledge about the
earth. Rediscovered around 1410, his *Geography* presented crucial advances on medieval
cartography by representing a round earth divided into 360 degrees with the major

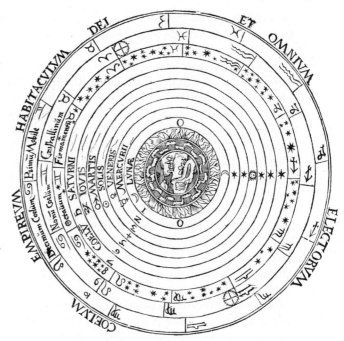

The Aristotelian Universe as Imagined in the Sixteenth Century
A round earth is at the center, surrounded by spheres of water, air, and fire. Beyond this small nucleus, the moon, the sun, and the five planets were embedded in their own rotating crystal spheres, with the stars sharing the surface of one enormous sphere. Beyond, the heavens were composed of unchanging ether. (Image Select/Art Resource, NY)

latitude marks. Ptolemy's work reintroduced the idea of using coordinates of latitude and longitude to plot points on the earth's surface, a major advantage for long-distance navigation. However, Ptolemy's map reflected the limits of ancient knowledge, showing only the continents of Europe, Africa, and Asia, with land covering three-quarters of the world. Lacking awareness of the Pacific Ocean and the Americas, Ptolemy vastly underestimated the distance west from Europe to Asia.

These two frameworks reveal the strengths and limitations of European knowledge on the eve of the Scientific Revolution. Overcoming the authority of the ancients to develop a new understanding of the natural world, derived from precise techniques of observation and experimentation, was a monumental achievement. Europeans were not the first to use experimental methods — of which there was a long tradition in the Muslim world and elsewhere — but they were the first to separate scientific knowledge decisively from philosophical and religious beliefs and to accord mathematics a fundamental role in understanding the natural world.

Astronomy and Physics

The first great departure from the medieval understanding of cosmology was the work of the Polish cleric Nicolaus Copernicus (1473–1543). Copernicus studied astronomy, medicine, and church law at the famed universities of Bologna, Padua, and Ferrara before taking up a church position in East Prussia. Copernicus came to believe that Ptolemy's cumbersome rules detracted from the majesty of a perfect creator. He preferred an idea espoused by some ancient Greek and Arab scholars: that the sun, rather than the earth, was at the center of the universe. Without questioning the Aristotelian belief in crystal spheres, Copernicus theorized that the stars and planets, including the earth, revolved around a fixed sun. Fearing the ridicule of other astronomers, Copernicus did not publish his *On the Revolutions of the Heavenly Spheres* until 1543, the year of his death.

One astronomer who agreed with the Copernican hypothesis was the Danish astronomer Tycho Brahe (TEE-koh BRAH-hee) (1546–1601). Brahe established himself as Europe's leading astronomer with his detailed observations of a new star that appeared suddenly in 1572 and shone very brightly for almost two years. The new star, which was actually a distant exploding star, challenged the idea that the heavenly spheres were unchanging and therefore perfect. Aided by grants from the king of Denmark, Brahe built the most sophisticated observatory of his day. Upon the king's death, Brahe acquired a new patron in the Holy Roman emperor Rudolph II and built an observatory in Prague. For twenty years Brahe observed the stars and planets with his naked eye in order to create new and improved tables of planetary motions, dubbed the *Rudolphine Tables* in honor of his patron.

Brahe's assistant, Johannes Kepler (1571–1630), carefully re-examined his predecessor's notations and came to believe that they could not be explained by Ptolemy's astronomy. Abandoning the notion of epicycles and deferents, Kepler developed three revolutionary laws of planetary motion. First, he demonstrated that the orbits of the planets around the sun are elliptical rather than circular. Second, he demonstrated that the planets do not move at a uniform speed in their orbits. When a planet is close to the sun it moves more rapidly, and it slows as it moves farther away from the sun. Finally, Kepler's third law stated that the time a planet takes to make its complete orbit is precisely related to its distance from the sun.

Kepler's contribution was monumental. Whereas Copernicus had speculated, Kepler used mathematics to prove the precise relations of a sun-centered (solar) system. His work demolished the old system of Aristotle and Ptolemy, and in his third law he came close to formulating the idea of universal gravitation (see page 561). In 1627 he also completed Brahe's *Rudolphine Tables*, which were used by astronomers for many years.

While Kepler was unraveling planetary motion, a young Florentine named Galileo Galilei (1564–1642) was challenging Aristotelian ideas about motion on earth. Like Kepler and so many early scientists, Galileo was a poor nobleman first marked for a religious career. Instead his fascination with mathematics led to a professorship in which he examined motion and mechanics in a new way. Galileo focused on deficiencies in Aristotle's theories of motion. He measured the movement of a rolling ball across a surface, repeating the action again and again to verify his results. In his famous acceleration experiment, he showed that a uniform force — in this case, gravity — produced a uniform acceleration. Through another experiment, he formulated the law of inertia. He found that rest was not the natural state of objects. Rather, an object continues in motion forever unless stopped by some external force. His discoveries proved Aristotelian physics wrong.

On hearing details about the invention of the telescope in Holland, Galileo made one for himself in 1609. He quickly discovered the first four moons of Jupiter, which clearly demonstrated that Jupiter could not possibly be embedded in an impenetrable crystal sphere as Aristotle and Ptolemy maintained. This discovery provided concrete evidence for the Copernican theory, in which Galileo already believed. Galileo then pointed his telescope at the moon. He wrote in 1610 in *Sidereus Nuncius*:

> By the aid of a telescope anyone may behold [the Milky Way] in a manner which so distinctly appeals to the senses that all the disputes which have tormented philosophers through so many ages are exploded by the irrefutable evidence of our eyes, and we are freed from wordy disputes upon the subject.[1]

Reading these famous lines, one feels a crucial corner in Western civilization being turned. No longer should one rely on established authority. A new method of learning and investigating was being developed, one that proved useful in any field of inquiry.

Newton's Synthesis

By about 1640 the work of Brahe, Kepler, and Galileo had been largely accepted by the scientific community despite opposition from religious leaders (see page 565). But the new findings failed to explain what forces controlled the movement of the planets and objects on earth. That challenge was taken up by English scientist Isaac Newton (1642–1727).

Born into the lower English gentry, Newton enrolled at Cambridge University in 1661. He arrived at some of his most basic ideas about physics in 1666 at age twenty-four but was unable to prove them mathematically. In 1684, after years of studying optics, Newton returned to physics for eighteen intensive months. The result was his towering accomplishment, a single explanatory system that integrated the astronomy of Copernicus, as corrected by Kepler's laws, with the physics of Galileo and his predecessors. Newton did this through a set of mathematical laws that explain motion and mechanics. These laws were published in 1687 in Newton's *Mathematical Principles of Natural Philosophy* (also known as the *Principia*). Because of their complexity, it took scientists and engineers two hundred years to work out all their implications.

The key feature of the Newtonian synthesis was the **law of universal gravitation**. According to this law, each body in the universe attracts every other body in a precise mathematical relationship, whereby the force of attraction is proportional to the quantity of matter of the objects and inversely proportional to the square of the distance between them. The whole universe—from Kepler's elliptical orbits to Galileo's rolling balls—was unified in one majestic system. Matter moved on earth and throughout the heavens according to the same laws, which could be understood and expressed in mathematical terms. Newton's synthesis prevailed until the twentieth century.

Natural History and Empire

At the same time that they made advances in astronomy and physics, Europeans embarked on the pursuit of knowledge about unknown geographical regions and the useful and valuable resources they contained. Because they were the first to acquire a large overseas empire, the Spanish pioneered these efforts. Following the conquest of the Aztec and Inca Empires (see Chapter 16), they sought to learn about and profit from their New World holdings. The Spanish crown sponsored many scientific expeditions to gather information and specimens, out of which emerged new discoveries that reshaped the fields of botany, zoology, cartography, and metallurgy, among others. These accomplishments have attracted less attention from historians in part because of the strict policy of secrecy imposed on scientific discoveries by the Spanish crown.

Plants were a particular source of interest because they offered tremendous profits in the form of spices, medicines, dyes, and cash crops. King Philip II of Spain sent his personal physician, Francisco Hernández, to New Spain for seven years in the 1560s. Hernández filled fifteen volumes with illustrations of three thousand plants previously unknown in Europe. He interviewed local healers about the plants' medicinal properties, thereby benefiting from centuries of Mesoamerican botanical knowledge. In the seventeenth century, for example, the Spanish obtained a monopoly on the world's supply of cinchona bark, which comes from a tree native to the high altitudes of the Andes and is used to treat malaria.

Other countries followed the Spanish example as their global empires expanded, relying on both official expeditions and the private initiative of merchants, missionaries, and settlers. Royal botanical gardens served as living laboratories for cultivating valuable foreign plants. The stream of new information about plant and animal species overwhelmed existing intellectual frameworks. Carl Linnaeus (1707–1778) of Sweden sent his students on exploratory voyages around the world and, based on their observations and the specimens they collected, devised a system of naming and classifying living organisms still used today (with substantial revisions).

New encyclopedias of natural history popularized this knowledge with realistic drawings and descriptions emphasizing the usefulness of animals and plants. Audiences at home eagerly read the accounts of naturalists, who braved the heat, insects, and diseases of tropical jungles to bring home exotic animal, vegetable, and mineral specimens (along with indigenous human subjects). They heard much less about the many local guides, translators, and practitioners of medicine and science who made these expeditions possible and who contributed rich knowledge about the natural world.

Magic and Alchemy

Recent historical research on the Scientific Revolution has focused on the contribution of ideas and practices that no longer belong to the realm of science, such as astrology and alchemy. For most of human history, interest in astronomy was inspired by the belief that the movement of heavenly bodies influenced events on earth. Many of the most celebrated astronomers were also astrologers. Used as a diagnostic tool in medicine, astrology formed a regular part of the curriculum of medical schools.

Centuries-old practices of magic and alchemy also remained important traditions for natural philosophers. Early modern practitioners of magic strove to understand and control hidden connections they perceived among different elements of the natural world, such as that between a magnet and iron. The idea that objects possessed hidden or "occult" qualities that allowed them to affect other objects was a particularly important legacy of the magical tradition. Belief in occult qualities — or numerology or cosmic harmony — was not antithetical to belief in God. On the contrary, adherents believed that only a divine creator could infuse the universe with such meaningful mystery.

Johannes Kepler exemplifies the interaction among these different strands of interest in the natural world. His duties as court mathematician included casting horoscopes for the royal family, and he based his own life on astrological principles. He also wrote at length on cosmic harmonies and explained elliptical motion through ideas about the beautiful music created by the combined motion of the planets. Kepler's fictional account of travel to the moon, written partly to illustrate the idea of a non-earth-centered universe, caused controversy and may have contributed to the arrest and trial of his mother as a witch in 1620. Kepler also suffered because of his unorthodox brand of Lutheranism, which led to his condemnation by both Lutherans and Catholics.

Another example of the interweaving of ideas and beliefs is Sir Isaac Newton, who was both intensely religious and also fascinated by alchemy, whose practitioners believed (among other things) that base metals could be turned into gold. Critics complained that his idea of universal gravitation was merely a restatement of old magical ideas about the innate sympathies between bodies; Newton himself believed that the attraction of gravity resulted from God's actions in the universe.

Important Changes in Scientific Thinking and Practice

What intellectual and social changes occurred as a result of the Scientific Revolution?

The Scientific Revolution was not accomplished by a handful of brilliant individuals working alone. Advancements occurred in many fields — medicine, chemistry, and botany, among others — as scholars developed new methods to seek answers to long-standing problems with the collaboration and assistance of skilled craftsmen who invented new instruments and helped conduct experiments. These results circulated in an international intellectual community from which women were usually excluded.

The Methods of Science

One of the keys to achieving a better understanding of the world was the development of better ways of obtaining knowledge. Two important thinkers, Francis Bacon (1561–1626) and René Descartes (day-KAHRT) (1596–1650), were influential in describing and advocating for improved scientific methods based, respectively, on experimentation and mathematical reasoning.

The English politician and writer Francis Bacon was the greatest early propagandist for the experimental method. Rejecting the Aristotelian and medieval method of using speculative reasoning to build general theories, Bacon argued that new knowledge had to be pursued through empirical research. The researcher who wants to learn more about leaves or rocks, for example, should not speculate about the subject but should rather collect a multitude of specimens and then compare and analyze them to derive general principles. Bacon's contribution was to formalize the empirical method, which had already been used by Brahe and Galileo, into the general theory of inductive reasoning known as **empiricism**.

On the continent more speculative methods retained support. In 1619, as a twenty-three-year-old soldier serving in the Thirty Years' War (1618–1648), the French philosopher René Descartes experienced a life-changing intellectual vision. Descartes saw that there was a perfect correspondence between geometry and algebra and that geometrical spatial figures could be expressed as algebraic equations and vice versa. A major step forward in mathematics, Descartes's discovery of analytic geometry provided scientists with an important new tool.

Descartes used mathematics to elaborate a highly influential vision of the workings of the cosmos. Drawing on ancient Greek atomist philosophies, Descartes developed the idea that matter was made up of identical "corpuscles" (tiny particles) that collided together in an endless series of motions, akin to the working of a machine. All occurrences in nature could be analyzed as matter in motion, and, according to Descartes, the total "quantity of motion" in the universe was constant. Descartes's mechanistic philosophy of the universe depended on the idea that a vacuum was impossible, which meant that every action had an equal reaction, continuing in an eternal chain reaction. Although Descartes's hypothesis about the vacuum proved wrong, his notion of a mechanistic universe intelligible through the physics of motion spread widely.

Descartes's greatest achievement was to develop his initial vision into a whole philosophy of knowledge and science. The Aristotelian cosmos was appealing in part because it corresponded with the evidence of the human senses. When experiments proved that sensory impressions could be wrong, Descartes decided it was necessary to doubt them and everything that could reasonably be doubted, and then, as in geometry, to use deductive reasoning from self-evident truths, which he called "first principles," to ascertain scientific laws. Descartes's reasoning ultimately reduced all substances to "matter" and "mind" — that is, to the physical and the spiritual. The devout Descartes believed that God had endowed man with reason for a purpose and that rational speculation could provide a path to the truths of creation. His view of the world as consisting of two fundamental entities is known as Cartesian dualism. Descartes's thought was particularly influential in France and the Netherlands but less so in England, where experimental philosophy won the day.

Both Bacon's inductive experimentalism and Descartes's deductive mathematical reasoning had flaws. Bacon's inability to appreciate the importance of mathematics and his obsession with practical results illustrated the limitations of antitheoretical empiricism. Likewise, some of Descartes's positions demonstrated the inadequacy of rigid, dogmatic rationalism. He believed, for example, that it was possible to deduce the whole science of medicine from first principles. Although insufficient on their own, Bacon's and Descartes's extreme approaches are combined in the modern scientific method, which began to crystallize in the late seventeenth century.

Medicine, the Body, and Chemistry

The Scientific Revolution, which began with the study of the cosmos, soon transformed understanding of the microcosm of the human body. For many centuries the ancient Greek physician Galen's explanation of the body carried the same authority as Aristotle's account of the universe. According to Galen, the body contained four humors: blood, phlegm, black bile, and yellow bile. Illness was believed to result from an imbalance of these humors.

Swiss physician and alchemist Paracelsus (1493–1541) was an early proponent of the experimental method in medicine and pioneered the use of chemicals and drugs to address what he saw as chemical, rather than humoral, imbalances. Another experimentalist, Flemish physician Andreas Vesalius (1514–1564), studied anatomy by dissecting human bodies. In 1543, the same year Copernicus published *On the Revolutions of the Heavenly Spheres*, Vesalius issued *On the Structure of the Human Body*. Its two hundred precise drawings revolutionized the understanding of human anatomy,

Frontispiece to *De Humani Corporis Fabrica* (*On the Structure of the Human Body*) The frontispiece to Vesalius's pioneering work, published in 1543, shows him dissecting a corpse before a crowd of students. This was a revolutionary new hands-on approach for physicians, who usually worked from a theoretical, rather than a practical, understanding of the body. Based on direct observation, Vesalius replaced ancient ideas drawn from Greek philosophy with a much more accurate account of the structure and function of the body. (© SSPL/Science Museum/The Image Works)

disproving Galen, just as Copernicus and his successors had disproved Aristotle and Ptolemy. The experimental approach also led English royal physician William Harvey (1578–1657) to discover the circulation of blood through the veins and arteries in 1628. Harvey was the first to explain that the heart worked like a pump and to explain the function of its muscles and valves.

Irishman Robert Boyle (1627–1691) was a key figure in the victory of experimental methods in England and helped create the Royal Society in 1660. Boyle's scientific work led to the development of modern chemistry. Following Paracelsus's lead, he undertook experiments to discover the basic elements of nature, which he believed was composed of infinitely small atoms. Boyle was the first to create a vacuum, thus disproving Descartes's belief that a vacuum could not exist in nature, and he discovered Boyle's law (1662), which states that the pressure of a gas varies inversely with volume.

Science and Religion

It is sometimes assumed that the relationship between science and religion is fundamentally hostile and that the pursuit of knowledge based on reason and proof is incompatible with faith. Yet during the Scientific Revolution most practitioners were devoutly religious and saw their work as contributing to the celebration of God's glory rather than undermining it. However, the concept of heliocentrism, which displaced the earth from the center of the universe, threatened the understanding of the place of mankind in creation as stated in Genesis. All religions derived from the Old Testament—Catholic, Protestant, Jewish, and Muslim—thus faced difficulties accepting the Copernican system. The Catholic Church was initially less hostile than Protestant and Jewish religious leaders, but in the first decades of the sixteenth century its attitude changed. In 1616 the Holy Office placed the works of Copernicus and his supporters, including Kepler, on a list of books Catholics were forbidden to read.

Out of caution Galileo Galilei silenced his views on heliocentrism for several years, until 1623 saw the ascension of Pope Urban VIII, a man sympathetic to the new science. However, Galileo's 1632 *Dialogue on the Two Chief Systems of the World* went too far. Published in Italian and widely read, it openly lampooned the Aristotelian view and defended Copernicus. In 1633 Galileo was tried for heresy by the papal Inquisition. Imprisoned and threatened with torture, the aging Galileo recanted, "renouncing and cursing" his Copernican errors.

Thereafter, the Catholic Church became more hostile to science, a change that helped account for the decline of science in Italy (but not in Catholic France) after 1640. At the same time, some Protestant countries, including the Netherlands, Denmark, and England, became quite "pro-science." This was especially true in countries without a strong religious authority capable of imposing religious orthodoxy on scientific questions.

Science and Society

The rise of modern science had many consequences. First, it led to the emergence of a new and expanding social group—the international scientific community. Members of this community were linked together by common interests and values as well as by journals and scientific societies. The personal success of scientists and scholars depended on making new discoveries, and as a result science became competitive. Second, as governments intervened to support and sometimes direct research, the new scientific community became closely tied to the state and its agendas. National academies of science were created under state sponsorship in London in 1662, Paris in 1666, Berlin in 1700, and later across Europe.

It was long believed that the Scientific Revolution was the work of exceptional geniuses and had little relationship to ordinary people and their lives until the late-eighteenth-century Industrial Revolution (see Chapter 23). More recently, historians have emphasized the importance of skilled craftsmen in the rise of science, particularly in the development of the experimental method. Many artisans developed a strong interest in emerging scientific ideas, and, in turn, the practice of science in the seventeenth century relied heavily on artisans' expertise in making instruments and conducting precise experiments.

Some things did not change in the Scientific Revolution. For example, scholars willing to challenge received ideas about the natural universe did not question traditional inequalities between the sexes. Instead, the emergence of professional science may have worsened the inequality in some ways. When Renaissance courts served as centers of learning, talented noblewomen could find niches in study and research. But the rise of a scientific community raised barriers for women because the universities and academies that furnished professional credentials refused them entry.

There were, however, a number of noteworthy exceptions. In Italy universities and academies did accept women. Across Europe women worked as makers of wax anatomical models and as botanical and zoological illustrators. They were also very much involved in informal scientific communities, attending salons (see page 583), conducting experiments, and writing learned treatises. Some female intellectuals became full-fledged participants in the philosophical dialogue. In England, Margaret Cavendish, Anne Conway, and Mary Astell all contributed to debates about Descartes's mind-body dualism, among other issues.

The Enlightenment

What new ideas about society and human relations emerged in the Enlightenment, and what new practices and institutions enabled these ideas to take hold?

The political, intellectual, and religious developments of the early modern period that gave rise to the Scientific Revolution further contributed to a series of debates about key issues in eighteenth-century Europe and the wider world that came to be known as the Enlightenment. By shattering the unity of Western Christendom, the conflicts of the Reformation brought old religious certainties into question; the strong states that emerged to quell the disorder soon inspired questions about political sovereignty and its limits. Increased movement of peoples, goods, and ideas within and among the states of Asia, Africa, Europe, and its colonies offered examples of shockingly different ways of life and values. Finally, the tremendous achievements of the Scientific Revolution inspired intellectuals to believe that answers to all the questions being asked could be found through observation and the use of reason. Progress was possible in human society as well as science.

The Early Enlightenment

Loosely united by certain key questions and ideas, the European Enlightenment (ca. 1690–1789) was a broad intellectual and cultural movement that gained strength gradually and did not reach its maturity until about 1750. Its origins in the late seventeenth century lie in a combination of developments, including political opposition to absolutist rule, religious conflicts between Protestants and Catholics and within Protestantism, and the attempt to apply principles and practices from the Scientific Revolution to human society.

A key crucible for Enlightenment thought was the Dutch Republic, with its proud commitments to religious tolerance and republican rule. When Louis XIV demanded that all Protestants convert to Catholicism, around two hundred thousand Huguenots fled the country, many destined for the Dutch Republic. From this haven of tolerance, French Huguenots and their supporters began to publish tracts denouncing religious intolerance and suggesting that only a despotic monarch, not a legitimate ruler, would deny religious freedom. Their challenge to authority thus combined religious and political issues.

These dual concerns drove the career of one important early Enlightenment writer, Pierre Bayle (1647–1706), a Huguenot who took refuge from government persecution in the Dutch Republic. Bayle critically examined the religious beliefs and persecutions of the past in his *Historical and Critical Dictionary* (1697). Demonstrating that human beliefs had been extremely varied and very often mistaken, he concluded that nothing can ever be known beyond all doubt, a view known as skepticism. His influential *Dictionary* was found in more private libraries of eighteenth-century France than any other book.

The Dutch Jewish philosopher Baruch Spinoza (1632–1677) was a key figure in the transition from the Scientific Revolution to the Enlightenment. Deeply inspired by advances in the Scientific Revolution — and in particular by debates about Descartes's thought — Spinoza sought to apply natural philosophy to thinking about human society. He borrowed Descartes's emphasis on rationalism and his methods of deductive reasoning but rejected the French thinker's mind-body dualism. Instead Spinoza came to espouse monism, the idea that mind and body are united in one substance and that God and nature were merely two names for the same thing. He envisioned a deterministic universe in which good and evil were merely relative values, and human actions were shaped by outside circumstances, not free will. Spinoza was excommunicated by the Jewish community of Amsterdam for his controversial religious ideas, but he was heralded by his Enlightenment successors as a model of personal virtue and courageous intellectual autonomy.

German philosopher and mathematician Gottfried Wilhelm von Leibniz (1646–1716), who had developed calculus independently of Isaac Newton, refuted both Cartesian dualism and Spinoza's monism. Instead he adopted the idea of an infinite number of substances, or "monads," from which all matter is composed according to a harmonious divine plan. His *Theodicy* (1710) declared that ours must be "the best of all possible worlds" because it was created by an omnipotent and benevolent God. Leibniz's optimism was later ridiculed by the French philosopher Voltaire in *Candide, or Optimism* (1759).

Out of this period of intellectual turmoil came John Locke's *Essay Concerning Human Understanding* (1690), perhaps the most important text of the early Enlightenment. In this work Locke (1632–1704) set forth a new theory about how human beings learn and form their ideas. Whereas Descartes based his deductive logic on the conviction that certain first principles, or innate ideas, are imbued in humans by God, Locke insisted that all ideas are derived from experience. According to Locke, the human mind at birth is like a blank tablet, or tabula rasa, on which understanding and beliefs are inscribed by experience. Human development is therefore determined by external forces, like education and social institutions, not innate characteristics. Locke's essay contributed to the theory of sensationalism, the idea that all human ideas and thoughts are produced as a result of sensory impressions.

Along with Newton's *Principia*, the *Essay Concerning Human Understanding* was one of the dominant intellectual inspirations of the early Enlightenment. Locke's equally important contribution to political theory, *Two Treatises of Civil Government* (1690), argued that real sovereignty rested with an elected Parliament, not in the authority of the Crown.

The Influence of the Philosophes

Divergences among the early thinkers of the Enlightenment show that, while they shared many of the same premises and questions, the answers they found differed widely. The spread of this spirit of inquiry and debate owed a great deal to the work of the philosophes, a group of influential intellectuals in France who proudly proclaimed that they were bringing the light of knowledge to their ignorant fellow creatures.

To appeal to the public and get around the censors, the philosophes wrote novels and plays, histories and philosophies, and dictionaries and encyclopedias, all filled with satire and double meanings to spread their message. One of the greatest philosophes, the baron de Montesquieu (mahn-tuhs-KYOO) (1689–1755) pioneered this approach in *The Persian Letters*, a social satire published in 1721. This work consists of letters supposedly written by two Persian travelers, Usbek and Rica, who as outsiders see European customs in unique ways and thereby allow Montesquieu a vantage point for criticizing existing practices and beliefs.

Disturbed by the growth in royal power under Louis XIV and inspired by the example of the physical sciences, Montesquieu set out to apply the critical method to the problem of government in *The Spirit of Laws* (1748). Arguing that forms of governments were shaped by history, geography, and customs, Montesquieu identified three main types: monarchies, republics, and despotisms. A great admirer of the English parliamentary system, Montesquieu argued for a separation of powers, with political power divided among different classes and legal estates holding unequal rights and privileges. Montesquieu was no democrat; he was apprehensive about the uneducated poor, and he did not question the sovereignty of the French monarch. But he was concerned that absolutism in France was drifting into tyranny and believed that strengthening the influence of intermediary powers was the best way to prevent it. Decades later, his theory of separation of powers had a great impact on the constitutions of the United States in 1789 and of France in 1791.

The most famous philosophe was François-Marie Arouet, known by the pen name Voltaire (1694–1778). In his long career, Voltaire wrote more than seventy witty volumes, hobnobbed with royalty, and died a millionaire because of shrewd business speculations. His early career, however, was turbulent, and he was twice arrested for insulting noblemen. To avoid a prison term, Voltaire moved to England for three years, and there he came to share Montesquieu's enthusiasm for English liberties and institutions.

Returning to France, Voltaire met Gabrielle-Emilie Le Tonnelier de Breteuil, marquise du Châtelet (1706–1749), a gifted noblewoman. Madame du Châtelet invited Voltaire to live in her country house at Cirey in Lorraine and became his long-time companion (under the eyes of her tolerant husband). Passionate about science, she studied physics and mathematics and published the first French translation of Newton's *Principia*, still in use today. Excluded from the Royal Academy of Sciences because she was a woman, Madame du Châtelet had no doubt that women's limited role in science was due to their unequal education. Discussing what she would do

Voltaire in Conversation
The French philosopher Voltaire is depicted here with his long-time companion, the writer and mathematician Gabrielle-Emilie Le Tonnelier de Breteuil, marquise du Châtelet. (Château de Breteuil/Gianni Dagli Orti/The Art Archive at Art Resource, NY)

if she were a ruler, she wrote, "I would reform an abuse which cuts off, so to speak, half the human race. I would make women participate in all the rights of humankind, and above all in those of the intellect."[2]

While living at Cirey, Voltaire wrote works praising England and popularizing English scientific progress. Yet, like almost all the philosophes, Voltaire was a reformer, not a revolutionary. He pessimistically concluded that the best form of government was a good monarch, since human beings "are very rarely worthy to govern themselves." Nor did Voltaire believe in social and economic equality. The only realizable equality, Voltaire thought, was that "by which the citizen only depends on the laws which protect the freedom of the feeble against the ambitions of the strong."[3]

Voltaire's philosophical and religious positions were much more radical. Voltaire believed in God, but he rejected Catholicism in favor of **deism**, belief in a distant, noninterventionist deity. Drawing on mechanistic philosophy, he envisioned a universe in which God acted like a great clockmaker who built an orderly system and then stepped aside and let it run. Above all, Voltaire and most of the philosophes hated religious intolerance, which they believed led to fanaticism and cruelty.

The strength of the philosophes lay in their number, dedication, and organization. Their greatest achievement was a group effort — the seventeen-volume *Encyclopedia: The Rational Dictionary of the Sciences, the Arts, and the Crafts*, edited by Denis Diderot (1713–1784) and Jean le Rond d'Alembert (1717–1783). The two men set out in 1751 to find coauthors who would examine the rapidly expanding whole of human knowledge and teach people to think critically about all matters.

Completed in 1765 despite opposition from the French state and the Catholic Church, the *Encyclopedia* contained hundreds of thousands of articles by leading scientists, writers, skilled workers, and progressive priests. Science and the industrial arts were exalted, religion and immortality questioned. Intolerance, legal injustice, and out-of-date social institutions were openly criticized. The *Encyclopedia* also included thousands of articles describing non-European cultures and societies, including acknowledgment of Muslim scholars' contribution to the development of Western science. Summing up the new worldview of the Enlightenment, the *Encyclopedia* was widely read, especially in less expensive reprint editions.

After about 1770 a number of thinkers and writers began to attack the philosophes' faith in reason and progress. The most famous of these was the Swiss intellectual Jean-Jacques Rousseau (1712–1778). Rousseau was both one of the most influential voices of the Enlightenment and, in his rejection of rationalism and social discourse, a harbinger of reaction against Enlightenment ideas. Like other Enlightenment thinkers, Rousseau was passionately committed to individual freedom. Unlike them, however, he attacked rationalism and civilization as destroying, rather than liberating, the individual. Warm, spontaneous feeling, Rousseau believed, had to complement and correct cold intellect. Moreover, he asserted, the basic goodness of the individual and the unspoiled child had to be protected from the cruel refinements of civilization. Rousseau's ideals greatly influenced the early romantic movement, which rebelled against the culture of the Enlightenment in the late eighteenth century.

Rousseau also called for a rigid division of gender roles, arguing that women and men were radically different beings. According to Rousseau, because women were destined by nature to assume a passive role in sexual relations, they should also be passive in social life and devote themselves to taking care of their husbands and children. Additionally, he believed that women's love for displaying themselves in public, attending salons, and pulling the strings of power was unnatural and had a corrupting effect on both politics and society.

Rousseau's contribution to political theory in *The Social Contract* (1762) was based on two fundamental concepts: the general will and popular sovereignty. According to Rousseau, the **general will** is sacred and absolute, reflecting the common interests of all people, who have displaced the monarch as the holder of sovereign power. The general will is not necessarily the will of the majority, however. At times the general will may be the authentic, long-term needs of the people as correctly interpreted by a farseeing minority. Little noticed before the French Revolution, Rousseau's concept of the general will appealed greatly to democrats and nationalists after 1789.

Cultural Contacts and Race

The Scientific Revolution and the political and religious conflicts of the late seventeenth century were not the only developments that influenced European thinkers. Europeans' increased interactions with non-European peoples and cultures also helped produce the Enlightenment spirit. In the wake of the great discoveries of the fifteenth and sixteenth centuries, the rapidly growing travel literature taught Europeans that the peoples of China, India, Africa, and the Americas had very different beliefs and customs. Europeans shaved their faces and let their hair grow. Ottomans shaved their heads and let their beards grow. In Europe a man bowed before a woman to show respect. In Siam a man turned his back on a woman when he met her because it was disrespectful to look directly at her. Countless similar examples discussed in travel accounts helped change the perspective of educated Europeans. They began to look at truth and morality in relative, rather than absolute, terms. If anything was possible, who could say what was right or wrong?

The powerful and advanced nations of Asia were obvious sources of comparison with the West. Seventeenth-century Jesuit missionaries served as a conduit for transmission of knowledge to the West about Chinese history and culture. The philosopher and mathematician Leibniz corresponded with Jesuits stationed in China, coming to believe that Chinese ethics and political philosophy were superior but that Europeans had equaled China in science and technology; some scholars believe his concept of monads was influenced by Confucian teaching on the inherent harmony between the cosmic order and human society.[4]

During the eighteenth century Enlightenment opinion on China was divided. Voltaire and some other philosophes revered China—without ever visiting or seriously studying it—as an ancient culture replete with wisdom and learning, ruled by benevolent absolutist monarchs. They enthusiastically embraced Confucianism as a natural religion in which universal moral truths were uncovered by reason. By contrast, Montesquieu and Diderot criticized China as a despotic land ruled by fear.

Attitudes toward Islam and the Muslim world were similarly mixed. As the Ottoman military threat receded at the end of the seventeenth century, some Enlightenment thinkers assessed Islam favorably. Some deists praised Islam as superior to Christianity and Judaism in its rationality, compassion, and tolerance. Others, including

Spinoza, saw Islamic culture as superstitious and favorable to despotism. In most cases, writing about Islam and Muslim cultures served primarily as a means to reflect on Western values and practices. Thus Montesquieu's *Persian Letters* used the Persian harem as a symbol of despotic rule that he feared his own country was adopting. Voltaire's play about the life of the Prophet portrayed Muhammad as the epitome of the religious fanaticism the philosophes opposed.

One writer with considerable personal experience in a Muslim country was Lady Mary Wortley Montagu, wife of the English ambassador to the Ottoman Empire. Her letters challenged prevailing ideas by depicting Turkish people as sympathetic and civilized. Montagu also disputed the notion that women were oppressed in Ottoman society.

Apart from debates about Asian and Muslim lands, the "discovery" of the New World and subsequent explorations in the Pacific Ocean also destabilized existing norms and values in Europe. One popular idea, among Rousseau and others, was that indigenous peoples of the Americas were living examples of "natural man," who embodied the essential goodness of humanity uncorrupted by decadent society. Other popular candidates for utopian natural men were the Pacific Island societies explored by Captain James Cook and others from the 1770s on (see pages 815–817).

As scientists developed taxonomies of plant and animal species in response to discoveries in the Americas, they also began to classify humans into hierarchically ordered "races" and to speculate on the origins of such races. The French naturalist Georges-Louis Leclerc, comte de Buffon (1707–1788), argued that humans originated with one species that then developed into distinct races due largely to climatic conditions. Enlightenment thinkers such as David Hume and Immanuel Kant (see page 573) helped popularize these ideas.

Using the word *race* to designate biologically distinct groups of humans was new in European thought. Previously, Europeans had grouped other peoples into "nations" based on their historical, political, and cultural affiliations, rather than on supposedly innate physical differences. Unsurprisingly, when thinkers drew up a hierarchical classification of human species, their own "race" was placed at the top. Europeans had long believed they were culturally superior. The new idea that racial difference was physical and innate rather than cultural taught them they were biologically superior as well. In turn, scientific racism helped legitimate and justify the tremendous growth of slavery that occurred during the eighteenth century by depicting Africans as belonging to a biologically inferior race that was naturally fit for enslavement.

Racist ideas did not go unchallenged. The abbé Raynal's *History of the Two Indies* (1770) fiercely attacked slavery and the abuses of European colonization. *Encyclopedia* editor Denis Diderot adopted Montesquieu's technique of criticizing European attitudes through the voice of outsiders in his dialogue between Tahitian villagers and their European visitors. Scottish philosopher James Beattie (1735–1803) responded directly to claims of white superiority by pointing out that Europeans had started out as savage as nonwhites supposedly were and that many non-European peoples in the Americas, Asia, and Africa had achieved high levels of civilization. Former slaves, like Olaudah Equiano (see Chapter 20) and Ottobah Cugoana, published eloquent memoirs testifying to the horrors of slavery and the innate equality of all humans. These challenges to racism, however, were in the minority. More often, Enlightenment thinkers, Thomas Jefferson among them, supported racial inequality.

The International Enlightenment

The Enlightenment was a movement of international dimensions, with thinkers traversing borders in a constant exchange of visits, letters, and printed materials. Voltaire alone wrote almost eighteen thousand letters to correspondents across Europe. The Republic of Letters, as this international group of scholars and writers was called, was a truly cosmopolitan set of networks stretching from western Europe to its colonies in the Americas, to Russia and eastern Europe, and along the routes of trade and empire to Africa and Asia.

Within this broad international conversation, scholars have identified regional and national particularities. Outside of France, many strains of Enlightenment thought—Protestant, Catholic, and Jewish—sought to reconcile reason with faith, rather than emphasizing the errors of religious fanaticism and intolerance. Some scholars point to a distinctive "Catholic Enlightenment" that aimed to renew and reform the church from within, looking to divine grace rather than human will as the source of social progress.

The Scottish Enlightenment, centered in Edinburgh, was marked by an emphasis on common sense and scientific reasoning. After the Act of Union with England in 1707, Scotland was freed from political crisis to experience a vigorous period of intellectual growth. Scottish intellectual revival was also stimulated by the creation of the first public educational system in Europe.

A central figure in Edinburgh was David Hume (1711–1776), whose civic morality and religious skepticism had a powerful impact at home and abroad. Hume strove to apply Newton's experimental methods to what he called the "science of man." Building on Locke's writings on learning, Hume argued that the human mind is really nothing but a bundle of impressions. These impressions originate only in sensory experiences and our habits of joining these experiences together. Since our ideas ultimately reflect only our sensory experiences, our reason cannot tell us anything about questions that cannot be verified by sensory experience (in the form of controlled experiments or mathematics), such as the origin of the universe or the existence of God. Hume further argued, in opposition to Descartes, that reason alone could not supply moral principles but that they derived instead from emotions and desires, such as feelings of approval or shame. Hume's rationalistic inquiry thus ended up undermining the Enlightenment's faith in the power of reason by emphasizing the superiority of the passions over reason in driving human behavior.

Hume's emphasis on human experience, rather than abstract principle, had a formative influence on another major figure of the Scottish Enlightenment, Adam Smith (1723–1790). In his *Theory of Moral Sentiments* (1759), Smith argued that social interaction produced feelings of mutual sympathy that led people to behave in ethical ways, despite inherent tendencies toward self-interest. By observing others and witnessing their feelings, individuals imaginatively experienced such feelings and learned to act in ways that would elicit positive sentiments and avoid negative ones. Smith believed that the thriving commercial life of the eighteenth century was likely to produce civic virtue through the values of competition, fair play, and individual autonomy. In *An Inquiry into the Nature and Causes of the Wealth of Nations* (1776), Smith attacked the laws and regulations created by mercantilist governments that, he argued, prevented commerce from reaching its full capacity (see Chapter 18). For Smith, ordinary people were capable of forming correct judgments based on their own experience and should therefore not be hampered by government regulations. Smith's economic liberalism became the dominant form of economic thought in the early nineteenth century.

Inspired by philosophers of moral sentiments, like Hume and Smith, as well as by physiological studies of the role of the nervous system in human perception, the celebration of sensibility became an important element of eighteenth-century culture. *Sensibility* referred to an acute sensitivity of the nerves and brains to outside stimulus that produced strong emotional and physical reactions. Novels, plays, and other literary genres depicted moral and aesthetic sensibility as a particular characteristic of women and the upper classes. The proper relationship between reason and the emotions (or between *Sense and Sensibility*, as Jane Austen put it in the title of her 1811 novel) became a key question.

After 1760 Enlightenment ideas were hotly debated in the German-speaking states, often in dialogue with Christian theology. Immanuel Kant (1724–1804), a professor in East Prussia, was the greatest German philosopher of his day. Kant posed the question of the age when he published a pamphlet in 1784 titled *What Is Enlightenment?* He answered, "*Sapere Aude* (dare to know)! 'Have the courage to use your own understanding' is therefore the motto of enlightenment." He argued that if intellectuals were granted the freedom to exercise their reason publicly in print, enlightenment would surely follow. Kant was no revolutionary; he also insisted that in their private lives, individuals must obey all laws, no matter how unreasonable, and should be punished for "impertinent" criticism. Like other Enlightenment figures in central and east-central Europe, Kant thus tried to reconcile absolutism and religious faith with a critical public sphere.

Northern Europeans often regarded the Italian states as culturally backward, yet important developments in Enlightenment thought also took place in the Italian peninsula. After achieving independence from Habsburg rule (1734), the kingdom of Naples entered a period of intellectual flourishing as reformers struggled to lift the heavy weight of church and noble power. In northern Italy a central figure was Cesare Beccaria (1738–1794), a nobleman educated at Jesuit schools and the University of Pavia. His *On Crimes and Punishments* (1764) was a passionate plea for reform of the penal system that decried the use of torture, arbitrary imprisonment, and capital punishment and advocated the prevention of crime over its punishment. The text was quickly translated into French and English and made an impact throughout Europe.

Enlightened Absolutism and Its Limits

Although Enlightenment thinkers were often critical of untrammeled despotism and eager for reform, their impact on politics was mixed. Outside of England and the Netherlands, especially in central and eastern Europe, most believed that political change could best come from above — from the ruler — rather than from below. Nevertheless, government officials' daily involvement in complex affairs of state made them naturally attracted to ideas for improving human society. Encouraged and instructed by these officials, some absolutist rulers tried to reform their governments in accordance with Enlightenment ideals. The result was what historians have called the

enlightened absolutism of the later eighteenth century. (Similar programs of reform in France and Spain will be discussed in Chapter 22.)

Influenced by the philosophes, Frederick II (r. 1740–1786) of Prussia, known as Frederick the Great, and Catherine the Great of Russia (r. 1762–1796) set out to rule in an enlightened manner. Frederick promoted religious tolerance and free speech and improved the educational system. Under his reign, Prussia's laws were simplified, torture of prisoners was abolished, and judges decided cases quickly and impartially. However, Frederick did not free the serfs of Prussia; instead he extended the privileges of the nobility over them.

Frederick's reputation as an enlightened prince was rivaled by that of Catherine the Great of Russia. When she was fifteen years old, Catherine's family ties to the Romanov dynasty made her a suitable bride for the heir to the Russian throne. Catherine profited from her husband's unpopularity and had him murdered so that she could be declared empress of Russia. Once in power, Catherine pursued three major goals. First, she worked hard to continue Peter the Great's efforts to bring the culture of western Europe to Russia (see page 549). To do so, she patronized Western architects, sculptors, musicians, and Enlightenment philosophes and encouraged Russian nobles to follow her example. Catherine's second goal was domestic reform. Like Frederick, she restricted the practice of torture, allowed limited religious tolerance, and tried to improve education and local government. The philosophes applauded these measures and hoped more would follow.

These hopes were dashed by a massive uprising of serfs in 1733 under the leadership of a Cossack soldier named Emelian Pugachev. Although Pugachev was ultimately captured and executed, his rebellion shocked Russian rulers and ended any reform programs Catherine might have intended to implement. After 1775 Catherine gave nobles absolute control of their serfs and extended serfdom into new areas. In 1785 she formally freed nobles from taxes and state service. Under Catherine the Russian nobility thus attained its most exalted position, and serfdom entered its most oppressive phase.

Catherine's third goal was territorial expansion, and in this respect she was extremely successful. Her armies subjugated the last descendants of the Mongols and the Crimean Tartars and began the conquest of the Caucasus on the border between Europe and Asia. Her greatest coup was the partition of Poland, which took place in stages from 1772 to 1795 (Map 19.1).

Joseph II (r. 1780–1790), the Austrian Habsburg emperor, was perhaps the most sincere proponent of enlightened absolutism. Joseph abolished serfdom in 1781, and in 1789 he decreed that peasants could pay landlords in cash rather than through compulsory labor. This measure was rejected not only by the nobility but also by the peasants it was intended to help, because they lacked the necessary cash. When Joseph died at forty-nine, the Habsburg empire was in turmoil. His brother Leopold II (r. 1790–1792) canceled Joseph's radical edicts in order to re-establish order.

Perhaps the best examples of the limitations of enlightened absolutism are the debates surrounding the possible emancipation of the Jews. For the most part, Jews in Europe were confined to tiny, overcrowded ghettos; were excluded by law from most occupations; and could be ordered out of a kingdom at a moment's notice. Still, a very few did manage to succeed and to obtain the right of permanent settlement, usually by performing some special service for the state, such as banking.

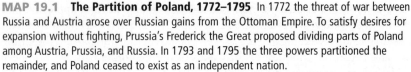

MAP 19.1   The Partition of Poland, 1772–1795   In 1772 the threat of war between Russia and Austria arose over Russian gains from the Ottoman Empire. To satisfy desires for expansion without fighting, Prussia's Frederick the Great proposed dividing parts of Poland among Austria, Prussia, and Russia. In 1793 and 1795 the three powers partitioned the remainder, and Poland ceased to exist as an independent nation.

In the eighteenth century an Enlightenment movement known as the **Haskalah** emerged from within the European Jewish community, led by the Prussian philosopher Moses Mendelssohn (1729–1786). Christian and Jewish Enlightenment philosophers, including Mendelssohn, began to advocate for freedom and civil rights for European Jews. In an era of growing reason and tolerance, they argued, restrictions on religious grounds could not stand. (See "Individuals in Society: Moses Mendelssohn and the Jewish Enlightenment," page 578.)

Arguments for tolerance won some ground, especially under Joseph II of Austria. Most monarchs, however, refused to entertain the idea of emancipation. In 1791 Catherine the Great established the Pale of Settlement, a territory encompassing modern-day Belarus, Lithuania, Latvia, Moldova, Ukraine, and parts of Poland, in which most Jews were required to live until the Russian Revolution of 1917.

Economic Change and the Atlantic World

How did economic and social change and the rise of Atlantic trade interact with Enlightenment ideas?

Enlightenment debates took place within a rapidly evolving material world. Agricultural reforms contributed to a rise in population that in turn fueled substantial economic growth in eighteenth-century Europe. A new public sphere emerged in the growing cities in which people exchanged opinions in cafés, bookstores, and other spaces. A consumer revolution brought fashion and imported foods into the reach of common people for the first time.

These economic and social changes were fed by an increasingly integrated Atlantic economy that circulated finished European products, raw materials from the colonies, and enslaved peoples from Africa. Over time, the peoples, goods, and ideas that criss-crossed the ocean created distinctive Atlantic communities and identities.

Economic and Demographic Change

The seventeenth century saw important gains in agricultural productivity in north-western Europe that slowly spread throughout the continent. Using new scientific techniques of observation and experimentation, a group of scientists, government officials, and a few big landowners devised agricultural practices and tools that raised crop yields dramatically, especially in England and the Netherlands. These included new forms of crop rotation, better equipment, and selective breeding of livestock. The controversial process of enclosure, fencing off common land to create privately owned fields, allowed a break with traditional methods but at the cost of reducing poor farm-ers' access to land.

Colonial plants also provided new sources of calories and nutrition. Introduced into Europe from the Americas—along with corn, squash, tomatoes, and many other useful plants—the humble potato provided an excellent new food source. Contain-ing a good supply of carbohydrates and vitamins A and C, the potato offset the lack of fresh vegetables and fruits in common people's winter diet. The potato had become an important dietary supplement in much of Europe by the end of the eighteenth century.

Increases in agricultural productivity and better nutrition, combined with the disappearance of bubonic plague after 1720 and improvements in sewage and water supply, contributed to the tremendous growth of the European population in the eighteenth century. Growth took place unevenly, with Russia growing very quickly after 1700 and France much more slowly. Nonetheless, the explosion of population was a major phenomenon in all European countries, leading to a doubling of the number of Europeans between 1700 and 1835.

Population growth increased the number of rural workers with little or no land, and this in turn contributed to the development of industry in rural areas. The poor in the countryside increasingly needed to supplement their agricultural earnings with other types of work, and urban capitalists were eager to employ them, at much lower wages than they paid urban workers. Cottage industry, which consisted of manufac-turing with hand tools in peasant cottages and work sheds, grew markedly in the eighteenth century and became a crucial feature of the European economy.

INDIVIDUALS IN SOCIETY • Moses Mendelssohn and the Jewish Enlightenment

I n 1743 a small, humpbacked Jewish boy with a stammer left his poor parents in Dessau in central Germany and walked eighty miles to Berlin, the capital of Frederick the Great's Prussia. According to one story, when the boy reached the Rosenthaler Gate, the only one through which Jews could pass, he told the inquiring watchman that his name was Moses and that he had come to Berlin "to learn." The watchman laughed and waved him through. "Go Moses, the sea has opened before you."*

In Berlin the young Mendelssohn studied Jewish law and eked out a living copying Hebrew manuscripts in a beautiful hand. But he was soon fascinated by an intellectual world that had been closed to him in the Dessau ghetto. There, like most Jews throughout central Europe, he had spoken Yiddish—a mixture of German, Polish, and Hebrew. Now, working mainly on his own, he mastered German; learned Latin, Greek, French, and English; and studied mathematics and Enlightenment philosophy. Word of his exceptional abilities spread in Berlin's Jewish community (the dwelling of 1,500 of the city's 100,000 inhabitants). He began tutoring the children of a wealthy Jewish silk merchant, and he soon became the merchant's clerk and later his partner. But his great passion remained the life of the mind and the spirit, which he avidly pursued in his off-hours.

Gentle and unassuming in his personal life, Mendelssohn was a bold thinker. Reading eagerly in works of Western philosophy dating back to antiquity, he was, as a pious Jew, soon convinced that Enlightenment teachings need not be opposed to Jewish thought and religion. He concluded that reason could complement and strengthen religion, although each would retain its integrity as a separate sphere.† Developing this idea in his first great work, "On the Immortality of the Soul" (1767), Mendelssohn used the neutral setting of a philosophical dialogue between Socrates and his followers in ancient Greece to argue that the human soul lived forever. In refusing to bring religion and critical thinking into conflict, he was strongly influ-

---

*H. Kupferberg, *The Mendelssohns: Three Generations of Genius* (New York: Charles Scribner's Sons, 1972), p. 3.
†D. Sorkin, *Moses Mendelssohn and the Religious Enlightenment* (Berkeley: University of California Press, 1996), pp. 8ff.

Rural manufacturing developed most successfully in England, particularly for the spinning and weaving of woolen cloth. By 1500 half of England's textiles were being produced in the countryside. By 1700 English industry was generally more rural than urban and heavily reliant on cottage industry. Most continental countries, with the exception of Flanders and the Dutch Republic, developed rural industry more slowly. The latter part of the eighteenth century witnessed a remarkable expansion of rural industry in certain densely populated regions of continental Europe.

Despite the rise in rural industry, life in the countryside was insufficient to support the rapidly growing population. Many people thus left their small villages to join the enced by contemporary German philosophers who argued similarly on behalf of Christianity. His thoughts reflected the way the German Enlightenment generally supported established religion, in contrast to the French Enlightenment, which attacked it.

Mendelssohn's treatise on the human soul captivated the educated German public, which marveled that a Jew could have written a philosophical masterpiece. In the excitement, a Christian zealot named Lavater challenged Mendelssohn in a pamphlet to accept Christianity or to demonstrate how the Christian faith was not "reasonable." Replying politely but passionately, the Jewish philosopher affirmed that his studies had only strengthened him in his faith, although he did not seek to convert anyone not born into Judaism. Rather, he urged tolerance in religious matters and spoke up courageously against oppression of Jews.

An Orthodox Jew and a German philosophe, Moses Mendelssohn serenely combined two very different worlds. He built a bridge from the ghetto to the dominant culture over which many Jews would pass, including his novelist daughter Dorothea and his famous grandson, the composer Felix Mendelssohn.

QUESTIONS FOR ANALYSIS

1. How did Mendelssohn seek to influence Jewish religious thought in his time?
2. How do Mendelssohn's ideas compare with those of the French Enlightenment?

LaunchPad
ONLINE DOCUMENT PROJECT

How did Moses Mendelssohn fit into the larger Enlightenment debate about religious tolerance? Examine primary sources written by Mendelssohn and his contemporaries, and then complete a quiz and writing assignment based on the evidence and details from this chapter.

See inside the front cover to learn more.

tide of migration to the cities, especially after 1750. London and Paris swelled to over five hundred thousand people, while Naples and Amsterdam had populations of more than one hundred thousand. It was in the bustling public life of these cities that the Enlightenment emerged and took root.

The Atlantic Economy

European economic growth in the eighteenth century was spurred by the expansion of trade across the Atlantic Ocean. Commercial exchange in the Atlantic is often referred to as the triangle trade, designating a three-way transport of goods: European

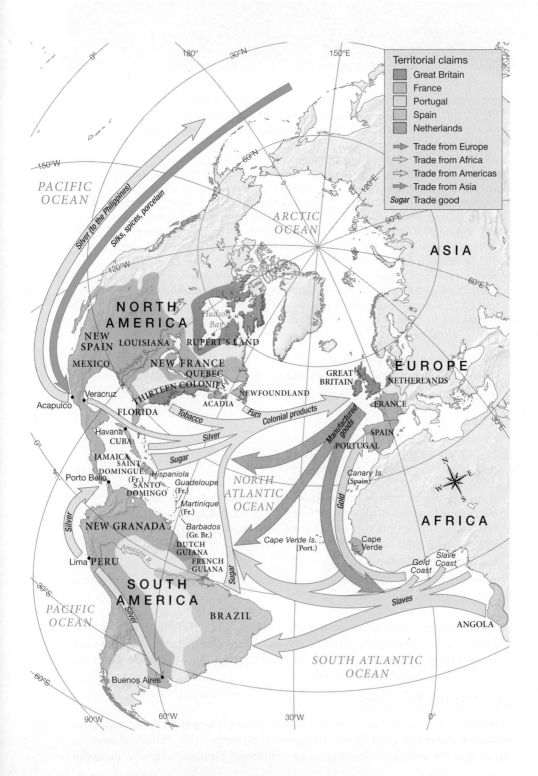

Territorial claims

- Great Britain
- France
- Portugal
- Spain
- Netherlands

- ⇒ Trade from Europe
- ⇒ Trade from Africa
- ⇒ Trade from Americas
- ⇒ Trade from Asia
- *Sugar* Trade good

PACIFIC OCEAN

Silver (to the Philippines)

Silks, spices, porcelain

ARCTIC OCEAN

ASIA

NORTH AMERICA

Hudson Bay

NEW SPAIN   LOUISIANA   RUPERT'S LAND

MEXICO   NEW FRANCE
QUEBEC

EUROPE

GREAT BRITAIN   NETHERLANDS

Veracruz   THIRTEEN COLONIES
Acapulco   FLORIDA   ACADIA   NEWFOUNDLAND

FRANCE

Mississippi

Tobacco   Furs   Colonial products

Manufactured goods

SPAIN

Havana   Silver

CUBA   PORTUGAL

JAMAICA   SAINT
DOMINGUE   Hispaniola
Porto Bello   (Fr.)   Guadeloupe
SANTO   (Fr.)
DOMINGO   Martinique
(Fr.)

Sugar

NORTH ATLANTIC OCEAN

Canary Is.
(Spain)

Gold

AFRICA

NEW GRANADA   Barbados
(Gr. Br.)
DUTCH
GUIANA

Cape Verde Is.
(Port.)

Cape Verde

Lima   PERU   FRENCH
GUIANA

Slave
Coast
Gold
Coast

Amazon R.

SOUTH AMERICA

BRAZIL

Slaves

ANGOLA

PACIFIC OCEAN

Silver

Buenos Aires

SOUTH ATLANTIC OCEAN

◀ **MAP 19.2** **The Atlantic Economy, 1701** The growth of trade encouraged both economic development and military conflict in the Atlantic basin. Four continents were linked together by the exchange of goods and slaves.

commodities, like guns and textiles, to Africa; enslaved Africans to the colonies; and colonial goods, such as cotton, tobacco, and sugar, back to Europe. This model highlights some of the most important flows of trade but significantly oversimplifies the picture. For example, a brisk intercolonial trade existed, with the Caribbean slave colonies importing food in the form of fish, flour, and livestock from the northern colonies and rice from the south, in exchange for sugar and slaves (Map 19.2).

Moreover, the Atlantic economy was inextricably linked to trade with the Indian and Pacific Oceans. For example, cowries, seashells originating in the Maldives in the Indian Ocean, served as a form of currency in West Africa. European traders obtained them in Asia, packing them alongside porcelains, spices, and silks for the journey home. They then brought the cowries from European ports to the West African coast to be traded for slaves. Indian cotton cloth was also prized in Africa and played a similar role in exchange. The rising economic and political power of Europeans in the eighteenth century thus drew on the connections they established between the long-standing Asian and Atlantic trade worlds.

Over the course of the eighteenth century the economies of European nations bordering the Atlantic Ocean relied more and more on colonial exports. In England sales to the mainland colonies of North America and the West Indian sugar islands — with an important assist from West Africa and Latin America — soared from £500,000 to £4 million. Exports to England's colonies in Ireland and India also rose substantially from 1700 to 1800.

At the core of this Atlantic world was the misery and profit of the Atlantic slave trade (see pages 605–612). The brutal practice intensified dramatically after 1700 and especially after 1750 with the growth of trade and demand for slave-produced goods. English dominance of the slave trade provided another source of large profits to the home country.

The French also profited enormously from colonial trade in the eighteenth century, even after losing their vast North American territories to England in 1763. The Caribbean colonies of Saint-Domingue (modern-day Haiti), Martinique, and Guadeloupe, which remained in French hands, provided immense fortunes from plantation agriculture. By 1789 the population of Saint-Domingue (sehn daw-MEHNG) included five hundred thousand slaves, whose labor had allowed the colony to become the world's leading producer of coffee and sugar and the most profitable plantation colony in the New World.[5] The wealth generated from colonial trade fostered the confidence of the merchant classes in Nantes, Bordeaux, and other large cities, and merchants soon joined other elite groups clamoring for more political power.

The third major player in the Atlantic economy, Spain, also saw its colonial fortunes improve during the eighteenth century. Its mercantilist goals were boosted by a recovery in silver production, which had dropped significantly in the seventeenth century. Spanish territory in North America expanded significantly in the second half of the eighteenth century. At the close of the Seven Years' War (1756–1763) (see page 657), Spain gained Louisiana from the French, and its influence extended westward all the way to northern California through the efforts of Spanish missionaries and ranchers.

Urban Life and the Public Sphere

Urban life in the Atlantic world gave rise to new institutions and practices that encouraged the spread of Enlightenment thought. From about 1700 to 1789 the production and consumption of books grew significantly, and the types of books people read changed dramatically. For example, the proportion of religious and devotional books published in Paris declined after 1750; history and law held constant; the arts and sciences surged. Lending libraries, bookshops, cafés, and Masonic lodges provided spaces in which urban people debated new ideas. Together these spaces and institutions helped create a new **public sphere** that celebrated open debate informed by critical reason. The public sphere was an idealized space where members of society came together to discuss the social, economic, and political issues of the day. Although Enlightenment thinkers addressed their ideas to educated and prosperous readers, even poor and illiterate people learned about such issues as they were debated at the marketplace or tavern.

The French Book Trade Book consumption surged in the eighteenth century and along with it, new bookstores. This appealing bookshop in France with its intriguing ads for the latest works offers to put customers "Under the Protection of Minerva," the Roman goddess of wisdom. Large packets of books sit ready for shipment to foreign countries. (Musée des Beaux-Arts, Dijon, France/Art Resource, NY)

Another important Enlightenment institution was the salon. In Paris from about 1740 to 1789, a number of talented, wealthy women presided over regular social gatherings named after their elegant private drawing rooms, or **salons**. There they encouraged the exchange of observations on literature, science, and philosophy with great aristocrats, wealthy middle-class financiers, high-ranking officials, and noteworthy foreigners.

Elite women also exercised great influence on artistic taste. Soft pastels, ornate interiors, sentimental portraits, and starry-eyed lovers protected by hovering cupids were all hallmarks of the style they favored. This style, known as rococo, was popular throughout Europe from 1720 to 1780. During this period, women were closely associated with the rise of the novel as a literary genre, as both authors and readers. The novel helped popularize the cult of sensibility, which celebrated strong emotions and intimate family love. Some philosophes championed greater rights and expanded education for women, claiming that the position and treatment of women were the best indicators of a society's level of civilization and decency.[6]

Economic growth in the second half of the eighteenth century also enabled a significant rise in the consumption of finished goods and new foodstuffs that historians have labeled a "consumer revolution." A boom in textile production and cheap reproductions of luxury items meant that the common people could afford to follow fashion for the first time, if only in a modest manner. Colonial trade made previously expensive and rare foodstuffs, such as sugar, tea, coffee, chocolate, and tobacco, widely available. By the end of the eighteenth century these products, which turned out to be mildly to extremely addictive, had become dietary staples for people of all social classes, especially in Britain.

The consumer revolution was concentrated in large cities in northwestern Europe and North America. This was not yet the society of mass consumption that emerged toward the end of the nineteenth century with the full expansion of the Industrial Revolution. The eighteenth century did, however, lay the foundations for one of the most distinctive features of modern Western life: societies based on the consumption of goods and services obtained through global markets in which many individuals' identities and self-worth are derived from the goods they consume.

Culture and Community in the Atlantic World

As contacts among the Atlantic coasts of the Americas, Africa, and Europe became more frequent, and as European settlements grew into well-established colonies, new identities and communities emerged. The term *Creole* referred to people of Spanish or other European ancestry born in the Americas. Wealthy Creoles throughout the Atlantic colonies prided themselves on following European ways of life. In addition to their agricultural estates, they maintained townhouses in colonial cities built on the European model, with theaters, plazas, churches, and coffeehouses. They purchased luxury goods made in Europe and sent their children to be educated in the home country.

Over time, however, the colonial elite came to feel that their circumstances gave them different interests and characteristics from people of their home countries. One observer explained that "a turn of mind peculiar to the planter, occasioned by a physical difference of constitution, climate, customs, and education, tends . . . to repress the

The Consumer Revolution From the mid-eighteenth century on, the cities of western Europe witnessed a new proliferation of consumer goods. Items once limited to the wealthy few—such as fans, watches, snuffboxes, umbrellas, ornamental containers, and teapots—were now reproduced in cheaper versions for middling and ordinary people. The fashion for wide hoopskirts was so popular that the armrests of the chairs of the day, known as Louis XV chairs, were specially designed to accommodate them. (© RMN–Grand Palais/Art Resource, NY)

remains of his former attachment to his native soil."[7] Creoles became "Americanized" by adopting native foods, like chocolate, chili peppers, and squash, and sought relief from tropical disease in native remedies. Also, they began to turn against restrictions from their home countries: Creole traders and planters, along with their counterparts in English colonies, increasingly resented the regulations and taxes imposed by colonial bureaucrats, and such resentment would eventually lead to revolutions against colonial powers (discussed in Chapter 22).

Not all Europeans in the colonies were wealthy or well educated. Numerous poor and lower-middle-class whites worked as clerks, shopkeepers, craftsmen, and laborers. With the exception of the English colonies of North America, white Europeans made up a minority of the population, outnumbered by indigenous peoples in Spanish America and by the growing numbers of enslaved people of African descent in the Caribbean. Since most European migrants were men, much of the colonial population of the Atlantic world descended from unions—forced or through consent—of European men and indigenous or African women. Colonial attempts to identify and control racial categories greatly influenced developing Enlightenment thought on racial differences.

In the Spanish and French Caribbean, as in Brazil, many slave masters acknowledged and freed their mixed-race children, leading to sizable populations of free people of color. Advantaged by their fathers, some became wealthy landowners and slaveholders in their own right. In the second half of the eighteenth century the prosperity of some free people of color brought a backlash from the white population of Saint-Domingue in the form of new race laws prohibiting nonwhites from marrying whites and forcing them to adopt distinctive attire. In the British colonies of the Caribbean and the southern mainland, by contrast, masters tended to leave their mixed-race progeny in slavery, maintaining a stark discrepancy between free whites and enslaved people of color.[8] British colonial law forbade marriage between Englishmen and -women and Africans or Native Americans.

Some mixed-race people sought to enter Creole society and obtain its many official and unofficial privileges by passing as white. Where they existed in any number, though, free people of color established their own proud social hierarchies based on wealth, family connections, occupation, and skin color.

Restricted from owning land and holding many occupations in Europe, Jews were eager participants in the new Atlantic economy and established a network of mercantile communities along its trade routes. As in the Old World, Jews in European colonies faced discrimination; for example, restrictions existed on the number of slaves they could own in Barbados in the early eighteenth century.[9] Jews were considered to be white Europeans and thus ineligible to be slaves, but they did not enjoy equal status with Christians. The status of Jews adds one more element to the complexity of Atlantic identities.

The Atlantic Enlightenment

Enlightenment ideas thrived in the colonies, although with as much diversity and disagreement as in Europe. The colonies of British North America were deeply influenced by the Scottish Enlightenment, with its emphasis on pragmatic approaches to the problems of life. Following the Scottish model, leaders in the colonies adopted a moderate, "commonsense" version of the Enlightenment that emphasized self-improvement and ethical conduct. In most cases, this version of the Enlightenment was perfectly compatible with religion and was chiefly spread through the growing colleges and universities of the colonies, which remained church-based institutions.

Some thinkers went even further in their admiration for Enlightenment ideas. Benjamin Franklin's writings and political career provide an outstanding example of the combination of the pragmatism and economic interests of the Scottish Enlightenment with the constitutional theories of Locke, Montesquieu, and Rousseau. Franklin was privately a deist, but he continued to attend church and respect religious proprieties, a cautious pattern followed by fellow deist Thomas Jefferson and other leading thinkers of the American Enlightenment.

Northern Enlightenment thinkers often depicted Spain and its American colonies as the epitome of the superstition and barbarity they contested. The Catholic Church strictly controlled the publication of books on the Iberian Peninsula and across the Atlantic. Nonetheless, the dynasty that took power in Spain in the early eighteenth century followed its own course of enlightened absolutism, just like its counterparts in the rest of Europe. Under King Carlos III (r. 1759–1788) and his son Carlos IV (r. 1788–1808), Spanish administrators attempted to strengthen colonial rule by posting a standing army in the colonies and increasing royal monopolies and taxes to pay for it. They also ordered officials to gather more accurate information about the colonies as a basis for improving the government. Enlightened administrators debated the status of indigenous peoples and whether it would be better for these peoples (and for the prosperity of Spanish America) if they maintained their distinct legal status or were integrated into Spanish society.

Educated Creoles were well aware of the new currents of thought, and the universities, newspapers, and salons of Spanish America produced their own reform ideas. The establishment of a mining school in Mexico City in 1792, the first in the Spanish colonies, illuminates the practical achievements of reformers. As in other European colonies, one effect of Enlightenment thought was to encourage Creoles to criticize the policies of the mother country and aspire toward greater autonomy.

Chapter Summary

Decisive breakthroughs in astronomy and physics in the seventeenth century demolished the medieval synthesis of Aristotelian philosophy and Christian theology. Among the most notable discoveries were that the sun, not the earth, was the center of the universe and Newton's universal law of gravitation. Bacon's inductive approach and Descartes's deductive reasoning eventually combined to form the modern scientific method, which relies on both experimentation and reason. The impact of these scientific breakthroughs on intellectual life was enormous, nurturing a new critical attitude in many disciplines. In addition, an international scientific community arose, and state-sponsored academies, which were typically closed to women, advanced scientific research.

Believing that all aspects of life were open to debate and skepticism, Enlightenment thinkers asked challenging questions about religious tolerance, representative government, and racial and sexual difference. Enlightenment thinkers drew inspiration from the new peoples and cultures encountered by Europeans and devised new ideas about race as a scientific and biological category. The ideas of the Enlightenment inspired absolutist rulers in central and eastern Europe, but real reforms were limited. For example, most rulers refused to support emancipation of the Jews.

In the second half of the eighteenth century agricultural reforms helped produce tremendous population growth. Economic growth and urbanization favored the spread of Enlightenment thought by producing a public sphere in which ideas could be debated. The expansion of transatlantic trade made economic growth possible, as did the lowering of prices on colonial goods due to the growth of slave labor. Atlantic trade involved the exchange of commodities among Europe, Africa, and the Americas, but it was also linked with trade in the Indian and Pacific Oceans. The movement of people and ideas across the Atlantic helped shape the identities of colonial inhabitants. At first colonial elites prided themselves on following European ways of life, but over time they developed customs and attitudes apart from those of their homeland.

Notes

1. H. Butterfield, *The Origins of Modern Science* (New York: Macmillan, 1951), p. 120.
2. L. Schiebinger, *The Mind Has No Sex? Women in the Origins of Modern Science* (Cambridge, Mass.: Harvard University Press, 1989), p. 64.
3. Quoted in G. L. Mosse et al., eds., *Europe in Review* (Chicago: Rand McNally, 1964), p. 156.
4. D. E. Mungello, *The Great Encounter of China and the West, 1500–1800*, 2d ed. (Lanham, Md.: Rowman & Littlefield, 2005), p. 98.
5. Laurent Dubois and John D. Garrigus, *Slave Revolution in the Caribbean, 1789–1904* (New York: Palgrave, 2006), p. 8.
6. See E. Fox-Genovese, "Women in the Enlightenment," in *Becoming Visible: Women in European History*, 2d ed., ed. R. Bridenthal, C. Koonz, and S. Stuard (Boston: Houghton Mifflin, 1987), esp. pp. 252–259, 263–265.
7. Pierre Marie François Paget, *Travels Round the World in the Years 1767, 1768, 1769, 1770, 1771*, vol. 1 (London, 1793), p. 262.
8. Orlando Patterson, *Slavery and Social Death* (Cambridge, Mass.: Harvard University Press, 1982), p. 255.
9. Erik R. Seeman, "Jews in the Early Modern Atlantic: Crossing Boundaries, Keeping Faith," in *The Atlantic in Global History, 1500–2000*, ed. Jorge Canizares-Esguerra and Erik R. Seeman (Upper Saddle River, N.J.: Pearson Prentice-Hall, 2007), p. 43.

CONNECTIONS

Hailed as the origin of modern thought, the Scientific Revolution must also be seen as a product of its past. Borrowing from Islamic cultural achievements, medieval universities gave rise to important new scholarship in mathematics and natural philosophy. In turn, the ambition and wealth of Renaissance patrons nurtured intellectual curiosity and encouraged scholarly research and foreign exploration. Natural philosophers starting with Copernicus pioneered new methods of explaining and observing nature while drawing on centuries-old traditions of astrology, alchemy, and magic. A desire to control and profit from empire led the Spanish, followed by their European rivals, to explore and catalogue the flora and fauna of their American colonies. These efforts resulted in new frameworks in natural history and constituted a crucial element of the Scientific Revolution.

Enlightenment ideas of the eighteenth century were a similar blend of past and present, progressive and traditional, homegrown and foreign-inspired. Enlightenment thinkers advocated universal rights and liberties but also preached the biological inferiority of non-Europeans and women. Their principles often served as much to bolster absolutist regimes as to inspire revolutionaries to fight for human rights.

New notions of progress and social improvement would drive Europeans to embark on world-changing revolutions in politics and industry (see Chapters 22 and 23) at the end of the eighteenth century. These revolutions provided the basis for modern democracy and unprecedented scientific advancement. Yet some critics have seen a darker side. For them, the mastery over nature enabled by the Scientific Revolution now threatens to overwhelm the earth's fragile equilibrium, and the Enlightenment belief in the universal application of reason can lead to intolerance of other people's spiritual, cultural, and political values. Ongoing debates about the legacy of these intellectual and scientific developments testify to their continuing importance in today's world.

As the era of European exploration and conquest gave way to empire building, the eighteenth century witnessed increased consolidation of global markets and bitter competition among Europeans. The eighteenth-century Atlantic world thus tied the shores of Europe, the Americas, and Africa in a web of commercial and human exchange, including the tragedy of slavery, discussed in Chapter 20. The Atlantic world maintained strong ties with trade in the Pacific and the Indian Ocean.

Chapter Review

MAKE IT STICK

☑ LearningCurve
Go online and use LearningCurve to retain what you've read.

IDENTIFY KEY TERMS

Identify and explain the significance of each item below.

Copernican hypothesis (p. 560)
law of inertia (p. 560)
law of universal gravitation (p. 561)
empiricism (p. 563)
Enlightenment (p. 567)
sensationalism (p. 568)
philosophes (p. 568)
deism (p. 570)

general will (p. 571)
economic liberalism (p. 574)
enlightened absolutism (p. 575)
Haskalah (p. 576)
enclosure (p. 577)
cottage industry (p. 577)
public sphere (p. 582)
salons (p. 583)

REVIEW THE MAIN IDEAS

Answer the focus questions from each section of the chapter.

1. What revolutionary discoveries were made in the sixteenth and seventeenth centuries, and why did they occur in Europe? (p. 556)

2. What intellectual and social changes occurred as a result of the Scientific Revolution? (p. 563)

3. What new ideas about society and human relations emerged in the Enlightenment, and what new practices and institutions enabled these ideas to take hold? (p. 567)

4. How did economic and social change and the rise of Atlantic trade interact with Enlightenment ideas? (p. 577)

MAKE CONNECTIONS

Analyze the larger developments and continuities within and across chapters.

1. How did the era of European exploration and discovery (Chapter 16) affect the ideas of scientists and philosophers discussed in this chapter? In what ways did contact with new peoples and places stimulate new forms of thought among Europeans?

2. What was the relationship between the Scientific Revolution and the Enlightenment? How did new ways of understanding the natural world influence thinking about human society?

LaunchPad
ONLINE DOCUMENT PROJECT

Moses Mendelssohn
How did Moses Mendelssohn fit into the larger Enlightenment debate about religious tolerance?

Examine primary sources written by Mendelssohn and his contemporaries, and then complete a quiz and writing assignment based on the evidence and details from this chapter.

See inside the front cover to learn more.

CHRONOLOGY

ca. 1500–1700	• Scientific Revolution
ca. 1690–1789	• Enlightenment
ca. 1700–1789	• Growth of book publishing
1720–1780	• Rococo style in art and decoration
1740–1786	• Reign of Frederick the Great of Prussia
ca. 1740–1789	• French salons led by elite women
1762–1796	• Reign of Catherine the Great of Russia
1765	• Philosophes publish *Encyclopedia: The Rational Dictionary of the Sciences, the Arts, and the Crafts*
1780–1790	• Reign of Joseph II of Austria
1791	• Establishment of the Pale of Settlement
1792	• Establishment of mining school in Mexico City as part of reforms

✓ LearningCurve
After reading the chapter, go online
and use LearningCurve to retain what
you've read.

20

Africa and the World

1400–1800

AFRICAN STATES AND SOCIETIES OF THE EARLY MODERN PERIOD— from the fifteenth through the eighteenth centuries—included a wide variety of languages, cultures, political systems, and levels of economic development. Kingdoms and stateless societies coexisted throughout Africa, from small Senegambian villages to the Songhai kingdom and its renowned city of Timbuktu in West Africa, and from the Christian state of Ethiopia to the independent Swahili city-states along the East Africa coast. By the fifteenth century Africans had developed a steady rhythm of contact and exchange. Across the vast Sahara, trade goods and knowledge passed back and forth from West Africa to North Africa, and beyond to Europe and the Middle East. The same was true in East Africa, where Indian Ocean traders touched up and down the African coast to deliver goods from Arabia, India, and Asia and to pick up the ivory, gold, spices, and other products representing Africa's rich natural wealth. In the interior as well, extensive trading networks linked African societies across the vast continent.

Modern European intrusion into Africa beginning in the fifteenth century profoundly affected these diverse societies and ancient trading networks. The intrusion led to the transatlantic slave trade, one of the greatest forced migrations in world history, through which Africa made a substantial, though involuntary, contribution to the building of the West's industrial civilization. In the seventeenth century an increasing desire for sugar in Europe resulted in an increasing demand for slave labor in South America and the West Indies, where sugar was produced. In the eighteenth century Western technological changes created a demand for cotton and other crops that required extensive human labor, thus intensifying the West's "need" for African slaves.

West Africa in the Fifteenth and Sixteenth Centuries

What types of economic, social, and political structures were found in the kingdoms and states along the west coast and in the Sudan?

In mid-fifteenth-century Africa, Benin and a number of other kingdoms flourished along the two-thousand-mile west coast between Senegambia and the northeastern shore of the Gulf of Guinea. Because much of that coastal region is covered by tropical rain forest, in contrast to the western Sudan (immediately south of the Sahara), it is called the West African Forest Region (Map 20.1). Further inland, in the region of the Sudan, the kingdoms of Songhai, Kanem-Bornu, and Hausaland benefited from the trans-Saharan caravan trade, which along with goods brought Islamic culture to the region. These West African kingdoms maintained their separate existences for centuries. Stateless societies such as those in the region of Senegambia (modern-day Senegal and the Gambia) existed alongside these more centralized states. Despite their political differences and whether they were agricultural, pastoral, or a mixture of both, West African cultures all faced the challenges presented by famine, disease, and the slave trade.

MAP 20.1   West African Societies, ca. 1500–1800 The coastal region of West Africa witnessed the rise of a number of kingdoms in the sixteenth century.

The West Coast: Senegambia and Benin

The Senegambian states possessed a homogeneous culture and a common history. For centuries Senegambia—named for the Senegal and Gambia Rivers—served as an important entrepôt for desert caravan contact with North African and Middle Eastern Islamic civilizations. Through the transatlantic slave trade, Senegambia came into contact with Europe and the Americas. Thus Senegambia felt the impact of Islamic culture to the north and of European influences from the maritime West.

The Senegambian peoples spoke Wolof, Serer, and Pulaar, which all belong to the West African language group. Both the Wolof-speakers and the Serer-speakers had clearly defined social classes: royalty, nobility, warriors, peasants, low-caste artisans such as blacksmiths and leatherworkers, and enslaved persons. The enslaved class consisted of individuals who were pawned for debt, house servants who could not be sold, and people who were acquired through war or purchase. Senegambian slavery varied from society to society but generally was not a benign institution. In some places slaves were considered chattel property and were treated as harshly as they would be later in the Western Hemisphere.

The word chattel originally comes from a Latin word meaning "head," as in "so many head of cattle." It reflects the notion that enslaved people are not human, but subhuman, like beasts of burden or other animals. Thus they can be treated like animals—whipped, beaten, worked to exhaustion, and forced to live in conditions no better than those provided for animals. But in Senegambia and elsewhere in Africa, many enslaved people were not considered chattel property. That is, unlike livestock or other common property, they could not be bought and sold. Some even served as royal advisers and enjoyed great power and prestige.[1] Unlike in the Americas, where slave status passed forever from one generation to the next, in Africa the enslaved person's descendants were sometimes considered free, although the stigma of slavery could attach to the family.

Senegambia was composed of stateless societies, culturally homogeneous ethnic populations where kinship and lineage groups tended to fragment communities. These societies comprised small groups of villages without a central capital. Among these stateless societies, age-grade systems evolved. Age-grades were groups of teenage males and females whom the society initiated into adulthood at the same time. Age-grades cut across family ties, created community-wide loyalties, and provided a means of local law enforcement, because each age-grade was responsible for the behavior of all its members.

The typical Senegambian community was a small, self-supporting agricultural village of closely related families. Fields were cut from the surrounding forest, and the average six- to eight-acre farm supported a moderate-size family. Millet and sorghum were the staple grains in northern Senegambia; farther south, forest dwellers cultivated yams as a staple. Senegambians supplemented their diet with plantains, beans, bananas, fish, oysters, and small game such as rabbits and monkeys. Village markets for produce exchange offered opportunities for receiving outside news and for social diversion. Social life centered on the family, and government played a limited role, interceding mostly to resolve family disputes and conflicts between families.

Alongside West African stateless societies like Senegambia were kingdoms and states ruled by kings who governed defined areas through bureaucratic hierarchies.

The Oba of Benin The oba's palace walls were decorated with bronze plaques that date from about the sixteenth to eighteenth centuries. This plaque vividly conveys the oba's power, majesty, and authority. The two attendants holding his arms also imply that the oba needs the support of his people. The oba's legs are mudfish, which represent fertility, peace, well-being, and prosperity, but their elongation, suggesting electric eels, relates the oba's terrifying and awesome power to the eel's jolting shock. (National Museum, Lagos, Nigeria/ photo: André Held/akg-images)

The great forest kingdom of Benin emerged in the fifteenth and sixteenth centuries in what is now southern Nigeria (see Map 20.1). Over time, the position of its **oba**, or king, was exalted, bringing stability to the state. In the later fifteenth century the oba Ewuare, a great warrior himself, strengthened his army and pushed Benin's borders as far as the Niger River in the east, westward into Yoruba country, and south to the Gulf of Guinea. During the late sixteenth and seventeenth centuries the office of the oba evolved from a warrior-kingship to a position of spiritual leadership.

At its height in the late sixteenth century, Benin controlled a vast territory, and European visitors described a sophisticated society. A Dutch visitor in the early 1600s, possibly Dierick Ruiters, described the capital, Benin City, as possessing a great, wide, and straight main avenue down the middle, with many side streets crisscrossing it. The visitor entered the city through a high, well-guarded gate framed on each side by a very tall earthen bulwark, or wall, with an accompanying moat. There was also an impressive royal palace, with at least four large courtyards surrounded by galleries leading up to it. William Bosman, another Dutch visitor writing a hundred years later, in 1702, described the prodigiously long and broad streets "in which continual Markets are kept, either of Kine [cattle], Cotton, Elephants Teeth, European Wares; or, in short, whatever is to be come at in this Country."[2] Visitors also noted that Benin City was kept scrupulously clean and had no beggars and that public security was so effective that theft was unknown. The period also witnessed remarkable artistic creativity in ironwork, carved ivory, and especially bronze portrait busts. Over nine hundred brass plaques survive, providing important information about Benin court life, military triumphs, and cosmological ideas.

In 1485 Portuguese and other Europeans began to appear in Benin in pursuit of trade, and over the next couple of centuries Benin grew rich from the profits made through the slave trade and the export of tropical products, particularly pepper and ivory. Its main European trading partners along this stretch of the so-called slave coast were the Dutch and Portuguese. In the early eighteenth century tributary states and stronger neighbors nibbled at Benin's frontiers, challenging its power. Benin, however, survived as an independent entity until the British conquered and burned Benin City in 1898 as part of the European imperialist seizure of Africa (discussed in Chapter 25).

The Sudan: Songhai, Kanem-Bornu, and Hausaland

The Songhai kingdom, a successor state of the kingdoms of Ghana (ca. 900–1100) and Mali (ca. 1200–1450), dominated the whole Niger region of the western and central Sudan (see Map 20.1). The imperial expansion of Songhai (song-GUY) began during the reign of the Songhai king Sonni Ali (r. ca. 1464–1492) and continued under his eventual successor, Muhammad Toure (r. 1493–1528). From his capital at Gao, Toure extended his rule as far north as the salt-mining center at **Taghaza** in the western Sahara and as far east as Agades and Kano. A convert to Islam, Toure returned from a pilgrimage to Mecca impressed by what he had seen there. He tried to bring about greater centralization in his own territories by building a strong army, improving taxation procedures, and replacing local Songhai officials with more efficient Arabs in an effort to substitute royal institutions for ancient kinship ties.

We know little about daily life in Songhai society because of the paucity of written records and surviving artifacts. Some information is provided by Leo Africanus (ca. 1465–1550), a Moroccan captured by pirates and given as a slave to Pope Leo X. Africanus became a Christian, taught Arabic in Rome, and in 1526 published an account of his many travels, including a stay in the Songhai kingdom.

As a scholar, Africanus was naturally impressed by Timbuktu, the second-largest city of the empire, which he visited in 1513. "Here [is] a great store of doctors, judges, priests, and other learned men, that are bountifully maintained at the King's court," he reported.[3] Many of these Islamic scholars had studied in Cairo and other Muslim learning centers. They gave Timbuktu a reputation for intellectual sophistication, religious piety, and moral justice.

Songhai under Muhammad Toure seems to have enjoyed economic prosperity. Leo Africanus noted the abundant food supply, which was produced in the southern savanna and carried to Timbuktu by a large fleet of canoes. The elite had immense wealth, and expensive North African and European luxuries—clothes, copperware, glass and stone beads, perfumes, and horses—were much in demand. The existence of many shops and markets implies the development of an urban culture. In Timbuktu merchants, scholars, judges, and artisans constituted a distinctive bourgeoisie, or middle class. The presence of many foreign merchants, including Jews and Italians, gave the city a cosmopolitan atmosphere. Jews largely controlled the working of gold.

Slavery played an important role in Songhai's economy. On the royal farms scattered throughout the kingdom, enslaved people produced rice—the staple crop—for the royal granaries. Slaves could possess their own slaves, land, and cattle, but they could not bequeath any of this property; the king inherited all of it. Muhammad Toure greatly increased the number of royal slaves. He bestowed slaves on favorite Muslim scholars, who thus gained a steady source of income. Slaves were also sold at the large market at Gao, where traders from North Africa bought them to resell later in Cairo, Constantinople, Lisbon, Naples, Genoa, and Venice.

Despite its considerable economic and cultural strengths, Songhai had serious internal problems. Islam never took root in the countryside, and Muslim officials alienated the king from his people. Muhammad Toure's reforms were a failure. He governed diverse peoples—Tuareg, Mandinka, and Fulani as well as Songhai—who were often hostile to one another, and no cohesive element united them. Finally, the Songhai never developed an effective method of transferring power. Revolts, conspiracies, and palace intrigues followed the death of every king, and only three of the nine rulers in the dynasty begun by Muhammad Toure died natural deaths. Muhammad Toure himself was murdered by one of his sons. His death began a period of political instability that led to the kingdom's slow disintegration.

In 1582 the Moroccan sultanate began to press southward in search of a greater share of the trans-Saharan trade. The Songhai people, lacking effective leadership and believing the desert to be sure protection against invasion, took no defensive precautions. In 1591 a Moroccan army of three thousand soldiers—many of whom were slaves of European origin equipped with European muskets—crossed the Sahara and inflicted a crushing defeat on the Songhai at Tondibi, spelling the empire's end.

East of Songhai lay the kingdoms of Kanem-Bornu and Hausaland (see Map 20.1). Under the dynamic military leader Idris Alooma (r. 1571–1603), Kanem-Bornu subdued weaker peoples and gained jurisdiction over an extensive area. Well drilled and equipped with firearms, his standing army and camel-mounted cavalry decimated warriors fighting with spears and arrows. Idris Alooma perpetuated a form of feudalism by granting land to able fighters in return for loyalty and the promise of future military assistance. Meanwhile, agriculture occupied most people, peasants and slaves alike. Kanem-Bornu shared in the trans-Saharan trade, shipping eunuchs and young girls to North Africa in return for horses and firearms. A devout Muslim, Idris Alooma elicited high praise from ibn-Fartura, who wrote a history of his reign called *The Kanem Wars*:

> So he made the pilgrimage and visited Medina with delight. . . . Among the benefits which God . . . conferred upon the Sultan Idris Alooma was the acquisition of Turkish musketeers and numerous household slaves who became skilled in firing muskets. . . .
>
> Among the most surprising of his acts was the stand he took against obscenity and adultery, so that no such thing took place openly in his time. Formerly the people had been indifferent to such offences. . . . In fact he was a power among his people and from him came their strength.
>
> The Sultan was intent on the clear path laid down by the Qur'an . . . in all his affairs and actions.[4]

Idris Alooma built mosques at his capital city of N'gazargamu and substituted Muslim courts and Islamic law for African tribunals and ancient customary law. His eighteenth-century successors lacked his vitality and military skills, however, and the empire declined.

Between Songhai and Kanem-Bornu were the lands of the Hausa, an agricultural people who lived in small villages. Hausa merchants carried on a sizable trade in slaves and kola nuts with North African communities across the Sahara. Obscure trading posts evolved into important Hausa city-states like Kano and Katsina, through which Islamic influences entered the region. Kano and Katsina became Muslim intellectual centers and in the fifteenth century attracted scholars from Timbuktu. The Muslim chronicler of the reign of King Muhammad Rimfa of Kano (r. 1463–1499) records that the king introduced the Muslim practices of purdah, or seclusion of women; *idal-fitr*, the festival after the fast of Ramadan; and the assignment of eunuchs to high state offices.[5] As in Songhai and Kanem-Bornu, however, Islam made no strong imprint on the Hausa masses until the nineteenth century.

The Lives of the People of West Africa

Wives and children were highly desired in African societies because they could clear and cultivate the land and because they brought prestige, social support, and security in old age. The results were intense competition for women, inequality of access to them, an emphasis on male virility and female fertility, and serious tension between male generations. Polygyny was almost universal; as recently as the nineteenth century two-thirds of rural wives were in polygynous marriages.

Men acquired wives in two ways. In some cases, couples simply eloped and began their union. More commonly, a man's family gave bride wealth to the bride's family as compensation for losing the fruits of her productive and reproductive abilities. She was expected to produce children, to produce food through her labor, and to pass on the culture in the raising of her children. Because it took time for a young man to acquire the bride wealth, all but the richest men delayed marriage until about age thirty. Women married at about the onset of puberty.

The easy availability of land in Africa reduced the kinds of generational conflict that occurred in western Europe, where land was scarce. Competition for wives between male generations, however, was fierce. On the one hand, myth and folklore stressed respect for the elderly, and the older men in a community imposed their authority over the younger ones through painful initiation rites into adulthood, such as circumcision. On the other hand, in West Africa and elsewhere, societies were not based on rule by elders, as few people lived much beyond forty. Young men possessed the powerful asset of their labor, which could easily be turned into independence where so much land was available.

"Without children you are naked" goes a Yoruba proverb, and children were the primary goal of marriage. Just as a man's virility determined his honor, so barrenness damaged a woman's status. A wife's infidelity was considered a less serious problem than her infertility. A woman might have six widely spaced pregnancies in her fertile years; the universal practice of breast-feeding infants for two, three, or even four years may have inhibited conception. Long intervals between births due to food shortages also may have limited pregnancies and checked population growth. Harsh climate, poor nutrition, and infectious diseases also contributed to a high infant mortality rate.

Both nuclear and extended families were common in West Africa. Nuclear families averaged only five or six members, but the household of a Big Man (a local man of power) included his wives, married and unmarried sons, unmarried daughters, poor relations, dependents, and scores of children. Extended families were common among the Hausa and Mandinka peoples. On the Gold Coast in the seventeenth century, a well-to-do man's household might number 150 people, in the Kongo region in west-central Africa, several hundred. In areas where one family cultivated extensive land, a large household of young adults, children, and slaves probably proved most efficient. Still, although many children might be born, many also died. Families rarely exceeded five or six people; high infant mortality rates and short life spans kept the household numbers low.

In agriculture men did the heavy work of felling trees and clearing the land; women then planted, weeded, and harvested. Between 1000 and 1400, cassava (manioc), bananas, and plantains came to West Africa from Asia. Cassava required little effort to grow and became a staple food, but it had little nutritional value. In the sixteenth century the Portuguese introduced maize (corn), sweet potatoes, and new varieties of yams from the Americas. Fish supplemented the diets of people living near bodies of water. According to former slave Olaudah Equiano, the Ibo people in the mid-eighteenth century ate plantains, yams, beans, and Indian corn, along with stewed poultry, goat, or bullock (castrated steer) seasoned with peppers.[6] However, such a protein-rich diet was probably exceptional.

Disease posed perhaps the biggest obstacle to population growth. Malaria, spread by mosquitoes and rampant in West Africa (except in cool, dry Cameroon), was the greatest killer, especially of infants. West Africans developed a relatively high degree of immunity to malaria and other parasitic diseases, including hookworm (which enters the body through shoeless feet and attaches itself to the intestines), yaws (contracted by nonsexual contact and recognized by ulcerating lesions), sleeping sickness (the parasite enters the blood through the bite of the tsetse [SEHT-see] fly; symptoms are enlarged lymph nodes and, at the end, a comatose state), and a mild nonsexual form of syphilis. Acute strains of smallpox introduced by Europeans certainly did not help population growth, nor did venereal syphilis, which possibly originated in Latin America. As in Chinese and European communities in the early modern period, the sick depended on folk medicine. African medical specialists, such as midwives, bone-setters, exorcists using religious rituals, and herbalists, administered a variety of treatments, including herbal medications like salves, ointments, and purgatives. Still, disease was common where the diet was poor and lacked adequate vitamins.

The devastating effects of famine, often mentioned in West African oral traditions, represented another major check on population growth. Drought, excessive rain, swarms of locusts, and rural wars that prevented land cultivation all meant later food shortages. In the 1680s famine extended from the Senegambian coast to the Upper Nile, and many people sold themselves into slavery for food. In the eighteenth century "slave exports" reached their peak in times of famine, and ships could fill their cargo holds simply by offering food. The worst disaster occurred from 1738 to 1756, when, according to one chronicler, the poor were reduced literally to cannibalism, also considered a metaphor for the complete collapse of civilization.[7]

Because the Americas had been isolated from the Eurasian-African landmass for thousands of years, parasitic diseases common in Europe, Africa, and Asia were unknown in the Americas before the Europeans' arrival. Enslaved Africans taken to the Americas brought with them the diseases common to tropical West Africa, such as yellow fever, dengue fever, malaria, and hookworm. Thus the hot, humid disease environment in the American tropics, where the majority of enslaved Africans lived and worked, became more "African." On the other hand, cold-weather European diseases, such as chicken pox, mumps, measles, and influenza, prevailed in the northern temperate zone in North America and the southern temperate zone in South America. This difference in disease environment partially explains why Africans made up the majority of the unskilled labor force in the tropical areas of the Americas, and

Europeans made up the majority of the unskilled labor force in the Western Hemisphere temperate zones, such as the northern United States and Canada.

Trade and Industry

As in all premodern societies, West African economies rested on agriculture. There was some trade and industry, but population shortages encouraged local self-sufficiency, slowed transportation, and hindered exchange. There were very few large markets, and their relative isolation from the outside world and failure to attract large numbers of foreign merchants limited technological innovation.

For centuries black Africans had exchanged goods with North African merchants in centers such as Gao and Timbuktu. This long-distance trans-Saharan trade was conducted and controlled by Muslim-Berber merchants using camels. The two primary goods exchanged were salt, which came from salt mines in North Africa, and gold, which came mainly from gold mines in modern-day Mali and, later, modern Ghana.

As elsewhere around the world, water was the cheapest method of transportation, and many small dugout canoes and larger trading canoes plied the Niger and its delta region (see Map 20.1). On land West African peoples used pack animals (camels or donkeys) rather than wheeled vehicles; only a narrow belt of land in the Sudan was suitable for animal-drawn carts. When traders reached an area infested with tsetse flies, they transferred each animal's load to human porters. Such difficulties in transport severely restricted long-distance trade, so most people relied on the regional exchange of local specialties.

West African communities had a well-organized market system. At informal markets on riverbanks, fishermen bartered fish for local specialties. More formal markets existed within towns and villages or on neutral ground between them. Markets also rotated among neighboring villages on certain days. People exchanged cotton cloth, thread, palm oil, millet, vegetables, and small household articles. Local sellers were usually women; traders from afar were men.

Salt had long been one of Africa's most critical trade items. Salt is essential to human health; the Hausa language has more than fifty words for it. The salt trade dominated the West African economies in the fifteenth, sixteenth, and seventeenth centuries. The main salt-mining center was at Taghaza (see Map 20.1) in the western Sahara. In the most wretched conditions, slaves dug the salt from desiccated lakes and loaded heavy blocks onto camels' backs. **Tuareg** warriors and later Moors (peoples of Berber and Arab descent) traded their salt south for gold, grain, slaves, and kola nuts, which were used by Muslims as stimulants or aphrodisiacs. **Cowrie shells**, imported from the Maldives in the Indian Ocean by way of Gujarat (see page 581) and North Africa, served as the medium of exchange (and continued to do so long after European intrusion). Gold continued to be mined and shipped from Mali until South American bullion flooded Europe in the sixteenth century. Thereafter, its production in Africa steadily declined. In the late twentieth and early twenty-first centuries gold mining revived in Mali, to the point that gold has been Mali's leading export since 1999. Mali is now Africa's fourth-largest gold producer, after South Africa, Ghana, and Tanzania, and ranked sixteenth in the world in 2011.

West African peoples engaged in many crafts, such as basket weaving and potterymaking. Ironworking, a specialized skill producing articles useful to hunters, farmers, and warriors, became hereditary in individual families; such expertise was regarded as family property. The textile industry had the greatest level of specialization. The earliest fabric in West Africa was made of vegetable fiber. Muslim traders introduced cotton and its weaving in the ninth century, as the fine-quality fabrics found in Mali reveal. By the fifteenth century the Wolof and Mandinka regions had professional weavers producing beautiful cloth, but this cloth was too expensive to compete in the Atlantic and Indian Ocean markets after 1500. Women who spun cotton used only a spindle and not a wheel, which slowed output. Women wove on inefficient broadlooms, men on less clumsy but narrow looms. Although the relatively small quantities of cloth produced on these narrow looms (one to two inches wide) could not compete in a world market, they are the source of the famous multicolored African kente cloth made from threads of cotton, or cotton and silk, by the Akan people of Ghana and the Ivory Coast. The area around Kano, in northern Nigeria, is famous for the deeply dyed blue cloth produced on the narrowest looms in the world and favored by the Tuareg Berber peoples of North Africa.

Cross-Cultural Encounters Along the East African Coast

How did the arrival of Europeans and other foreign cultures affect the East African coast, and how did Ethiopia and the Swahili city-states respond to these incursions?

East Africa in the early modern period faced repeated incursions from foreign powers. At the beginning of the sixteenth century Ethiopia faced challenges from the Muslim state of Adal, and then from Europeans. Jesuit attempts to substitute Roman Catholic liturgical forms for the Coptic Christian liturgies (see below) met with fierce resistance and ushered in a centuries-long period of hostility to foreigners. The wealthy Swahili city-states along the southeastern African coast also resisted European intrusions in the sixteenth century, with even more disastrous results. Cities such as Mogadishu, Kilwa, and Sofala used Arabic as the language of communication, and their commercial economies had long been tied to the trade of the Indian Ocean. The arrival of the Portuguese in 1498 proved catastrophic for those cities, and the Swahili coast suffered economic decline as a result.

Muslim and European Incursions in Ethiopia, ca. 1500–1630

At the beginning of the sixteenth century the powerful East African kingdom of Ethiopia extended from Massawa in the north to several tributary states in the south (Map 20.2), but the ruling Solomonic dynasty in Ethiopia, in power since the thirteenth century, faced serious external threats. Alone among the states in northeast and eastern Africa, Ethiopia was a Christian kingdom that practiced **Coptic Christianity**, an orthodox form of the Christian faith that originated in Egypt in 451. Christianity had first come to Ethiopia from Egypt when the archbishop in Alexandria appointed Saint Frumentius the first bishop of Ethiopia in 328. By the early 1500s Ethiopia was an island of Christianity surrounded by a sea of Muslim states.

Adal, a Muslim state along the southern base of the Red Sea, began incursions into Ethiopia, and in 1529 the Adal general Ahmad ibn-Ghazi inflicted a disastrous

MAP 20.2   East Africa in the Sixteenth Century In early modern times, the Christian kingdom of Ethiopia, first isolated and then subjected to Muslim and European pressures, played an insignificant role in world affairs. But the East African city-states, which stretched from Sofala in the south to Mogadishu in the north, had powerfully important commercial relations with Mughal India, China, the Ottoman world, and southern Europe.

defeat on the Ethiopian emperor Lebna Dengel (r. 1508–1540). Ibn-Ghazi followed up his victory with systematic devastation of the land; destruction of many Ethiopian artistic and literary works, churches, and monasteries; and the forced conversion of thousands to Islam. Lebna Dengel fled to the mountains and appealed to Portugal for assistance. A Portuguese force of four hundred men under Cristóvão da Gama came to his aid, but Dengel was killed in battle before the Portuguese arrived. The Muslim occupation of Christian Ethiopia, which began around 1531, ended in 1543, after a joint Ethiopian and Portuguese force defeated a larger Muslim army at the Battle of Wayna Daga, east of Lake Tana, on February 21. During the battle General ibn-Ghazi was killed by a Portuguese musketeer, but not before he had left a horrific legacy of destruction and death that continues to resonate in Ethiopia today.

In the late twelfth century tales of Prester John, rumored to be a powerful Christian monarch ruling a vast and wealthy African empire, reached western Europe. The search for Prester John, as well as for gold and spices, spurred the Portuguese to undertake a series of trans-African expeditions that reached Timbuktu and Mali in the 1480s and the Ethiopian court by 1508. Although Prester John was a mythical figure, Portuguese emissaries triumphantly but mistakenly identified the Ethiopian emperor as Prester John.[8] It was their desire to convert Ethiopians from Coptic Christianity to Roman Catholicism that motivated the Portuguese to aid the Ethiopians in defeating Adal's forces at Wayna Daga in 1543.

No sooner had the Muslim threat ended than Ethiopia encountered three more dangers. The Galla, now known as the Oromo, moved northward in great numbers in the 1530s, occupying portions of Harar, Shoa, and Amhara. The Ethiopians could not defeat them militarily, and the Galla were not interested in assimilation. For the next two centuries the two peoples lived together in an uneasy truce. Simultaneously, the Ottoman Turks seized Massawa and other coastal cities. Then the Jesuits arrived and attempted to force Roman Catholicism on a proud people whose Coptic form of Christianity long antedated the European version. The overzealous Jesuit missionary Alphonse Mendez tried to revamp the Ethiopian liturgy, rebaptize the people, and replace ancient Ethiopian customs and practices with Roman ones. Since Ethiopian national sentiment was closely tied to Coptic Christianity, violent rebellion and anarchy ensued.

In 1633 the Jesuit missionaries were expelled. For the next two centuries hostility to foreigners, weak political leadership, and regionalism characterized Ethiopia. Civil conflicts between Galla and Ethiopians erupted continually. The Coptic Church, though lacking strong authority, survived as the cornerstone of Ethiopian national identity.

Saint George in Ethiopian Art This wall painting of Saint George slaying a dragon resides in the stone-carved Church of Saint George in Lalibela, Ethiopia, and attests to the powerful and pervasive Christian influence on Ethiopian culture. (Galen R. Frysinger)

The Swahili City-States and the Arrival of the Portuguese, ca. 1500–1600

The word **Swahili** means "People of the Coast" and refers to the people living along the East African coast and on the nearby islands. Although predominantly a Bantu-speaking people, the Swahili have incorporated significant aspects of Arab culture. The Arabic alphabet was used for the first written works in Swahili (although the Latin alphabet is now standard), and roughly 35 percent of Swahili words come from Arabic. Surviving texts in Swahili—from the earliest known Swahili documents dating from 1711—provide historians with a glimpse of early Swahili history that is not possible when studying early nonliterate African societies. By the eleventh century the Swahili had accepted Islam, which provided a common identity and unifying factor for all the peoples along coastal East Africa. Living on the Indian Ocean coast, the Swahili also felt the influences of Indians, Indonesians, Persians, and even the Chinese.

Swahili civilization was overwhelmingly maritime. A fertile, well-watered, and intensely cultivated stretch of land extending down the coast yielded rice, grains, citrus fruit, and cloves. The region's considerable prosperity, however, rested on trade and commerce. The Swahili acted as middlemen in an Indian Ocean–East African economy that might be described as early capitalism. They exchanged ivory, rhinoceros horn, tortoise shells, inlaid ebony chairs, copra (dried coconut meat that yields coconut oil), and inland slaves for Arabian and Persian perfumes, toilet articles, ink, and paper; for Indian textiles, beads, and iron tools; and for Chinese porcelains and silks. In the fifteenth century the cosmopolitan city-states of Mogadishu, Pate, Lamu, Mombasa, and especially Kilwa enjoyed a worldwide reputation for commercial prosperity and high living standards.[9]

The arrival of the Portuguese explorer Vasco da Gama (see Map 16.2, page 467) in 1498 spelled the end of the Swahili cities' independence. Lured by the spice trade, da Gama wanted to build a Portuguese maritime empire in the Indian Ocean. Swahili rulers responded in different ways to Portuguese intrusion. Some, such as the sultan of Malindi, quickly agreed to a trading alliance with the Portuguese. Others, such as the sultan of Mombasa, were tricked into commercial agreements. Swahili rulers who rejected Portuguese overtures saw their cities bombarded and attacked. To secure alliances made between 1502 and 1507, the Portuguese erected forts at the southern port cities of Kilwa, Zanzibar, and Sofala. These fortified markets and trading posts served as the foundation of Portuguese commercial power on the Swahili coast. The better-fortified northern cities, such as Mogadishu, survived as important entrepôts for goods to India.

The Portuguese presence in the south did not yield the expected commercial fortunes. Rather than accept Portuguese commercial restrictions, the residents deserted the towns, and the town economies crumbled. Large numbers of Kilwa's people, for example, immigrated to northern cities. The gold flow from inland mines to Sofala slowed to a trickle. Swahili noncooperation successfully prevented the Portuguese from gaining control of the local coastal trade.

In 1589 Portugal finally won an administrative stronghold near Mombasa. Called Fort Jesus, it remained a Portuguese base for over a century. In the late seventeenth century pressures from the northern European maritime powers—the Dutch, French, and English, aided greatly by Omani Arabs—combined with local African rebellions to bring about the collapse of Portuguese influence in Africa. A Portuguese presence remained only at Mozambique in the far south and Angola on the west coast.

The Portuguese had no religious or cultural impact on the Swahili cities. Their sole effect was the cities' economic decline.

The African Slave Trade

What role did slavery play in African societies before the transatlantic slave trade began, and what was the effect of European involvement?

The exchange of peoples captured in local and ethnic wars within sub-Saharan Africa, the trans-Saharan slave trade with the Mediterranean Islamic world beginning in the seventh century, and the slave traffic across the Indian Ocean all testify to the long tradition and continental dimensions of the African slave trade before European intrusion. The enslavement of human beings was practiced in some form or another all over Africa — indeed, all over the world. Sanctioned by law and custom, enslaved people served critical and well-defined roles in the social, political, and economic organization of many African societies. Domestically these roles ranged from concubines and servants to royal guards and advisers. As was the case later in the Americas, some enslaved people were common laborers. Economically, slaves were commodities for trade, no more or less important than other trade items, such as gold and ivory.

Over time, the trans-Saharan slave trade became less important than the trans-atlantic trade, which witnessed an explosive growth during the seventeenth and eighteenth centuries. The millions of enslaved Africans forcibly exported to the Americas had a lasting impact on African society and led ultimately to a wider use of slaves within Africa itself.

The Institution of Slavery in Africa

Islamic practices strongly influenced African slavery. African rulers justified enslavement with the Muslim argument that prisoners of war could be sold and that captured people were considered chattel, or personal possessions, to be used any way the owner saw fit. Between 650 and 1600 black as well as white Muslims transported perhaps as many as 4.82 million black slaves across the trans-Saharan trade route.[10] In the fourteenth and fifteenth centuries the rulers and elites of Mali and Benin imported thousands of white Slavic slave women, symbols of wealth and status, who had been seized in slave raids from the Balkans and Caucasus regions of the eastern Mediterranean by Turks, Mongols, and others.[11] In 1444, when Portuguese caravels landed 235 slaves at Algarve in southern Portugal, a contemporary observed that they seemed "a marvelous (extraordinary) sight, for, amongst them, were some white enough, fair enough, and well-proportioned; others were less white, like mulattoes; others again were black as Ethiops."[12]

Meanwhile, the flow of black people to Europe, begun during the Renaissance, continued. In the seventeenth and eighteenth centuries as many as two hundred thousand Africans entered European societies. Some arrived as slaves, others as servants; the legal distinction was not always clear. Eighteenth-century London, for example, had more than ten thousand blacks, most of whom arrived as sailors on Atlantic crossings or as personal servants brought from the West Indies. In England most were free, not slaves. Initially, a handsome black person was a fashionable accessory, a rare status symbol. Later, English aristocrats considered black servants too ordinary. The duchess of Devonshire offered her mother an eleven-year-old boy, explaining that the duke did not want a Negro servant because "it was more original to have a Chinese page than to have a black one; everybody had a black one."[13] London's black population constituted a well-organized, self-conscious subculture, with black pubs, black churches, and black social groups assisting the black poor and unemployed. Some black people attained wealth and position, the most famous being Francis Barber, manservant of the sixteenth-century British literary giant Samuel Johnson and heir to Johnson's papers and to most of his sizable fortune. Barber had helped Johnson in revising Johnson's famous *Dictionary of the English Language*, published in 1755, and he is frequently mentioned in the celebrated biography of Johnson by James Boswell. He was a contemporary of another well-known African who lived in London for a while, Olaudah Equiano.

In 1658 the Dutch East India Company (see page 482) began to allow the importation of slaves into the Cape Colony, which the company had founded on the southern tip of Africa in 1652. Over the next century and a half about 75 percent of the slaves brought into the colony came from Dutch East India Company colonies in India and Southeast Asia or from Madagascar; the remaining 25 percent came from Africa. Some of those enslaved at the Cape served as domestic servants or as semiskilled artisans, but most worked long and hard as field hands and at any other menial or manual forms of labor needed by their European masters.

The Dutch East India Company was the single largest slave owner in the Cape Colony, employing its slaves on public works and company farms. Initially, individual company officials collectively owned the most slaves, working them on their wine and grain estates, but by about 1740 urban and rural free burghers (European settlers) owned the majority of the slaves. In 1780 half of all white men at the Cape had at least one slave, as slave ownership fostered a strong sense of racial and economic solidarity in the white master class.

The slave population at the Cape was never large, although from the early 1700s to the 1820s it outnumbered the European free burgher population. When the British ended slavery in the British Empire in 1834, there were around thirty-six thousand slaves in the Cape Colony. In comparison, over three hundred thousand enslaved Africans labored on the Caribbean island of Jamaica, also a British slaveholding colony at the time.

Although in the seventeenth and eighteenth centuries Holland enjoyed a Europe-wide reputation for religious tolerance and intellectual freedom (see page 540), in the Cape Colony the Dutch used a strict racial hierarchy and heavy-handed paternalism to maintain control over enslaved native and foreign-born peoples. Early accounts of slavery at the Cape often gave the impression that it was a relatively benign institution in comparison with slavery in the Americas. Modern scholars, however, consider slavery in the Cape Colony in many ways as oppressive as slavery in the Americas and the Muslim world. In Muslim society the offspring of a free man and an enslaved woman were free, but in southern Africa such children remained enslaved. Because enslaved males greatly outnumbered enslaved females in the Cape Colony, marriage and family life were almost nonexistent. Because there were few occupations requiring special skills, those enslaved in the colony lacked opportunities to earn manumission, or freedom. And in contrast with North and South America and with Muslim societies, in the Cape Colony only a very small number of those enslaved won manumission; most of them were women, suggesting they gained freedom through sexual or close personal relationships with their owners.[14]

The slave trade expanded greatly in East Africa's savanna and Horn regions in the late eighteenth century and the first half of the nineteenth century. Slave exports from these areas and from Africa's eastern coast amounted to perhaps thirty thousand a year. Why this demand? Merchants and planters wanted slaves to work the sugar plantations on the Mascarene Islands, located east of Madagascar; the clove plantations on Zanzibar and Pemba; and the food plantations along the Kenyan coast. The eastern coast also exported enslaved people to the Americas, particularly to Brazil. In the late eighteenth and early nineteenth centuries, precisely when the slave trade to North America and the Caribbean declined, the Arabian and Asian markets expanded. Only with colonial conquest of Africa by Great Britain, Germany, and Italy after 1870 did suppression of the trade begin. Enslavement, of course, persists even today.

The Transatlantic Slave Trade

Although the trade in African people was a worldwide phenomenon, the transatlantic slave trade involved the largest number of enslaved Africans. This forced migration of millions of human beings, extending from the early sixteenth to the late nineteenth centuries, represents one of the most inhumane, unjust, and shameful tragedies in human history. It also immediately provokes a troubling question: why Africa? Why, in the seventeenth and eighteenth centuries, did enslavement in the Americas become exclusively African?

European settlers first enslaved indigenous peoples, the Amerindians, to mine the silver and gold discovered in the New World (see page 476). When they proved ill suited to the harsh rigors of mining, the Spaniards brought in Africans. Although the Dutch had transported Indonesian peoples to work as slaves in the Cape Colony in South Africa, the cost of transporting Chinese or Pacific Island peoples to the Americas was far too great.

One scholar has argued that a pan-European insider-outsider ideology prevailed across Europe. This cultural attitude permitted the enslavement of outsiders but made the enslavement of white Europeans taboo. Europeans could not bear the sight of other Europeans doing plantation slave labor. According to this theory, a similar pan-African ideology did not exist, as Africans had no problem with selling Africans to Europeans.[15] Several facts argue against the validity of this theory. English landlords exploited their Irish peasants with merciless severity, French aristocrats often looked on their peasantry with cold contempt, and Russian boyars treated their serfs with casual indifference and harsh brutality. These and other possible examples contradict the existence of a pan-European ideology or culture that opposed the enslavement of white Europeans. Moreover, the flow of white enslaved Slavic peoples from the Balkans into the eastern Mediterranean continued unabated during the same period.

Another theory holds that in the Muslim and Arab worlds by the tenth century, an association had developed between blackness and menial slavery. The Arab word *abd*, or "black," had become synonymous with *slave*. Although the great majority of enslaved persons in the Islamic world were white, a racial element existed in Muslim perceptions: not all slaves were black, but blacks were identified with slavery. In Europe, after the arrival of tens of thousands of sub-Saharan Africans in the Iberian Peninsula during the fifteenth century, Christian Europeans also began to make a strong association between slavery and black Africans. Therefore, Africans seemed the "logical" solution to the labor shortage in the Americas.[16]

Another important question relating to the African slave trade is this: why were African peoples enslaved in a period when serfdom was declining in western Europe and when land was so widely available and much of the African continent had a labor shortage? The answer seems to lie in a technical problem related to African agriculture. Partly because of the tsetse fly, which causes sleeping sickness and other diseases, and partly because of easily leached lateritic soils (containing high concentrations of oxides), farmers had great difficulty using draft animals. Tropical soils responded poorly to plowing, and most work had to be done with the hoe. Productivity, therefore, was low. Economists maintain that in most societies the value of a worker's productivity determines the value of his or her labor. In precolonial Africa the individual's agricultural productivity was low, so his or her economic value to society was less than the economic value of a European peasant in Europe. Enslaved persons in the Americas were more productive than free producers in Africa. And European slave dealers were very willing to pay a price higher than the value of an African's productivity in Africa.

The incidence of disease in the Americas also helps explain African enslavement. Smallpox took a terrible toll on Native Americans, and between 30 and 50 percent of Europeans exposed to malaria succumbed to that sickness. Africans had developed some immunity to both diseases, and in the Americas they experienced the lowest mortality rate of any people, making them, ironically, the most suitable workers for the environment.

In 1500 a Portuguese fleet en route to India around Africa sailed too far west into the Atlantic and made landfall on the coast of modern Brazil. Although its commander, Pedro Álvares Cabral, did not know where he was, he followed the common practice (see page 466) and immediately claimed the land for King Manuel I, the Portuguese monarch. Colonization began in the early 1530s, and in 1551 the Portuguese founded a sugar colony at Bahia. Between 1551 and 1575, before the North American slave traffic began, the Portuguese delivered more African slaves to Brazil than ever reached British North America. Portugal essentially monopolized the slave trade until 1600 and continued to play a significant role in the seventeenth century, though the trade was increasingly taken over by the Dutch, French, and English. From 1690 until the British House of Commons abolished the slave trade in 1807, England was the leading carrier of African slaves.

Population density and supply conditions along the West African coast and the sailing time to New World markets determined the sources of slaves. As the demand for slaves rose, slavers moved down the West African coast from Senegambia to the more densely populated hinterlands of the Bight of Benin and the Bight of Biafra (a bight is a bend or curve in the coast). The abundant supply of Africans to enslave in Angola, the region south of the Congo River, and the quick passage from Angola to Brazil and the Caribbean established that region as the major coast for Portuguese slavers.

Transatlantic wind patterns partly determined exchange routes. Shippers naturally preferred the swiftest crossing — that is, from the African port nearest the latitude of the intended American destination. Thus Portuguese shippers carried their cargoes from Angola to Brazil, and British merchants sailed from the Bight of Benin to the

Caribbean. The great majority of enslaved Africans were intended for the sugar and coffee plantations extending from the Caribbean islands to Brazil. Angola produced 26 percent of all African slaves and 70 percent of all Portuguese slaves. Trading networks extending deep into the interior culminated at two major ports on the Angolan coast, Luanda and Benguela. The Portuguese acquired a few slaves through warfare but secured the vast majority through trade with African dealers. Whites did not participate in the inland markets, which were run solely by Africans.

Almost all Portuguese shipments went to satisfy the virtually insatiable Brazilian demand for slaves. The so-called **Middle Passage** was the horrific journey experienced by Africans from freedom to enslavement in the Americas. Here is an excerpt from a Portuguese doctor's 1793 report on conditions in Luanda before the voyage across the Atlantic had begun. Be sure to note in this and subsequent quotations how the enslaved peoples are clearly considered, and treated, as chattel:

> The dwelling place of the slave is simply the dirt floor of the compound, and he remains there exposed to harsh conditions and bad weather, and at night there are only a lean-to and some sheds . . . which they are herded into like cattle.
>
> Their food continues scarce as before . . . limited at times to badly cooked beans, at other times to corn. . . .
>
> And when they reach a port . . . , they are branded on the right breast with the coat of arms of the king and nation, of whom they have become vassals. . . . This mark is made with a hot silver instrument in the act of paying the king's duties, and this brand mark is called a *carimbo*. . . .
>
> In this miserable and deprived condition the terrified slaves remain for weeks and months, and the great number of them who die is unspeakable. With some ten or twelve thousand arriving at Luanda each year, it often happens that only six or seven thousand are finally transported to Brazil.[17]

Conditions during the Middle Passage were even worse. Olaudah Equiano (see "Individuals in Society: Olaudah Equiano," page 608) describes the experience of his voyage as a captured slave from Benin to Barbados in the Caribbean:

> At last, when the ship we were in had got in all her cargo [of slaves], they made ready with many fearful noises, and we were all put under deck so that we could not see how they managed the vessel. . . . The stench of the hold while we were on the coast was so intolerably loathsome that it was dangerous to remain there for any time, and some of us had been permitted to stay on the deck for the fresh air; but now that the whole ship's cargo were confined together it became absolutely pestilential. The closeness of the place and the heat of the climate, added to the number in the ship, which was so crowded that each had scarcely room to turn himself, almost suffocated us. This produced copious perspirations, so that the air soon became unfit for respiration from a variety of loathsome smells, and brought on a sickness among the slaves, of which many died, thus falling victims to the improvident avarice, as I may call it, of their purchasers. This wretched situation was again aggravated by the galling of the chains, now become insupportable, and the filth of the necessary tubs [of human waste], into which the children often fell and were almost suffocated. The shrieks of the women and the groans of the dying rendered the whole a scene of horror almost inconceivable.[18]

INDIVIDUALS IN SOCIETY • Olaudah Equiano

The transatlantic slave trade was a mass movement involving millions of human beings. It was also the sum of individual lives spent partly or entirely in slavery. Most of those lives remain hidden to us. Olaudah Equiano (1745–1797) represents a rare window into the slaves' obscurity; he is probably the best-known African slave.

In his autobiography, *The Interesting Narrative of the Life of Olaudah Equiano* (1789), Equiano says that he was born in Benin (modern Nigeria) of Ibo ethnicity.* His father, one of the village elders (or chieftains), presided over a large household that included "many slaves," prisoners captured in local wars. All people, slave and free, shared in the cultivation of family lands. One day, when all the adults were in the fields, two strange men and a woman broke into the family compound, kidnapped the eleven-year-old Olaudah and his sister, tied them up, and dragged them into the woods. Brother and sister were separated, and Olaudah was sold several times to various dealers before reaching the coast. As it took six months to walk there, his home must have been far inland. The sea, the slave ship, and the strange appearance of the white crew terrified the boy (see page 607). Equiano's master took him to Jamaica, to Virginia, and then to England, where he placed him in the custody of a kind family. They gave him the rudiments of an education, and he was baptized a Christian.

Equiano soon went to sea as a captain's boy (servant), serving in the Royal Navy during the Seven Years' War (see page 657).On shore at Portsmouth, England, after one battle, Equiano was urged by his master to read, study, and learn basic mathematics. This education served him well, for after a voyage to the West Indies, his master sold him to a Philadelphia Quaker, Robert King, who was a rum and sugar merchant. Equiano worked as a clerk in King's warehouse, as a longshoreman loading and unloading cargo ships, and at sea where he developed good navigational skills; King paid him for his work. Equiano became an entrepreneur himself, buying and selling small goods in the islands and mainland ports. Determined to buy his freedom, Equiano had amassed enough money by 1766, and King signed the deed of manumission. Equiano was twenty-one years old; he had been a slave for ten years.

Equiano returned to London and used his remaining money to hire tutors to teach him hairdressing, mathematics, and how to play the French horn. When

---

*Recent scholarship has re-examined Equiano's life and raised some questions about his African origins and his experience of the Middle Passage. To explore the debate over Equiano's authorship of the African and Middle Passage portions of his autobiography, see Vincent Carretta, *Equiano, the African: Biography of a Self-Made Man* (New York: Penguin, 2007).

Although the demand was great, Portuguese merchants in Angola and Brazil sought to maintain only a steady trickle of slaves from the African interior to Luanda and across the ocean to Bahia and Rio de Janeiro: a flood of slaves would have depressed the American market. Rio, the port capital through which most enslaved Africans money was scarce, he found work as a merchant seaman, traveling to Portugal, Nice, Genoa, Naples, and Turkey. He even participated in an Arctic expedition.

Equiano's *Narrative* reveals a complex and sophisticated man. He had a strong constitution and an equally strong character. His Christian faith undoubtedly sustained him. On the title page of his book, he cited a verse from Isaiah (12:2): "The Lord Jehovah is my strength and my song." The very first thought that came to his mind the day he was freed was a passage from Psalm 126: "I glorified God in my heart, in whom I trusted."

Equiano loathed the brutal slavery he saw in the West Indies and the vicious racism he experienced in the North American colonies. He respected the fairness of Robert King, admired British navigational and industrial technologies, and had many close white friends. He once described himself as "almost an Englishman." He was also involved in the black communities in the West Indies and in London. Equiano's *Narrative* is a well-documented argument for the abolition of slavery and a literary classic that went through nine editions before his death.

Olaudah Equiano's *Narrative*, with its horrific descriptions of slavery, proved influential, and after its publication Equiano became active in the abolition movement. He spoke to large crowds in the industrial cities of Manchester and Birmingham in England, arguing that it was in the business interests of manufacturers to support abolition, as Africa was a huge, virtually untapped market for English cloth. Though he died in 1797, ten years before its passage, Equiano significantly advanced the abolitionist cause that led to the Slave Trade Act of 1807.

Source: *Equiano's Travels: The Interesting Narrative of the Life of Olaudah Equiano*, ed. Paul Edwards (Portsmouth, N.H.: Heinemann, 1996).

QUESTIONS FOR ANALYSIS

1. How typical was Olaudah Equiano's life as a slave? How atypical?
2. Describe Equiano's culture and his sense of himself.

ᕫLaunchPad
ONLINE DOCUMENT PROJECT

What role did slave accounts play in antislavery activism? Read several first-person accounts of slavery, and then complete a quiz and writing assignment based on the evidence and details from this chapter.

See inside the front cover to learn more.

passed, commanded the Brazilian trade. Planters and mine operators from the provinces traveled to Rio to buy slaves. Between 1795 and 1808 approximately 10,000 Angolans per year stood in the Rio slave market. In 1810 the figure rose to 18,000; in 1828 it reached 32,000.[19]

Peddlers in Rio de Janeiro   A British army officer sketched this early-nineteenth-century scene of everyday life in Rio de Janeiro, Brazil. The ability to balance large burdens on the head meant that the person's hands were free for other use. Note the player (on the left) of a musical instrument originating in the Congo. On the right a woman gives alms to the man with the holy image in return for being allowed to kiss the image as an act of devotion. We do not know whether the peddlers were free and self-employed or were selling for their owners. (From "Views and Costumes of the City and Neighborhood of Rio de Janeiro, Brazil," in *Drawings Taken by Lieutenant Henry Chamberlain, During the Years 1819 and 1820* [London: Columbian Press, 1822]/Visual Connection Archive)

The English ports of London, Bristol, and particularly Liverpool dominated the British slave trade. In the eighteenth century Liverpool was the world's greatest slave-trading port. In all three cities, small and cohesive merchant classes exercised great public influence. The cities also had huge stores of industrial products for export, growing shipping industries, and large amounts of ready cash for investment abroad. Merchants generally formed partnerships to raise capital and to share the risks; each voyage was a separate enterprise or venture.

Slaving ships from Bristol plied back and forth along the Gold Coast, the Bight of Benin, Bonny, and Calabar looking for African traders who were willing to supply them with slaves. Liverpool's ships drew enslaved people from Gambia, the Windward Coast, and the Gold Coast. British ships carried textiles, gunpowder and flint, beer and spirits, British and Irish linens, and woolen cloth to Africa. A collection of goods was grouped together into what was called the **sorting**. An English sorting might include bolts of cloth, firearms, alcohol, tobacco, and hardware; this batch of goods was traded for an enslaved individual or a quantity of gold, ivory, or dyewood.[20]

European traders had two systems for exchange. First, especially on the Gold Coast, they established factory-forts. (For more on factory-forts, see page 508.) These fortified trading posts were expensive to maintain but proved useful for fending off European rivals. Second, they used **shore trading**, in which European ships sent boats ashore or invited African dealers to bring traders and enslaved Africans out to the ships. The English captain John Adams, who made ten voyages to Africa between 1786 and 1800, described the shore method of trading at Bonny:

This place is the wholesale market for slaves, as not fewer than 20,000 are annually sold here; 16,000 of whom are natives of one nation called Ibo. . . . Fairs where the slaves of the Ibo nation are obtained are held every five or six weeks at several villages, which are situated on the banks of the rivers and creeks in the interior, and to which the African traders of Bonny resort to purchase them.

. . . The traders augment the quantity of their merchandise, by obtaining from their friends, the captains of the slave ships, a considerable quantity of goods on credit. . . . Evening is the period chosen for the time of departure, when they proceed in a body, accompanied by the noise of drums, horns, and gongs. At the expiration of the sixth day, they generally return bringing with them 1,500 or 2,000 slaves, who are sold to Europeans the evening after their arrival, and taken on board the ships. . . .

It is expected that every vessel, on her arrival at Bonny, will fire a salute the instant the anchor is let go, as a compliment to the black monarch who soon afterwards makes his appearance in a large canoe, at which time, all those natives who happen to be alongside the vessel are compelled to proceed in their canoes to a respectful distance, and make way for his Majesty's barge. After a few compliments to the captain, he usually enquires after brother George, meaning the King of England, George III, and hopes he and his family are well. He is not pleased unless he is regaled with the best the ship affords. . . . His power is absolute; and the surrounding country, to a considerable distance, is subject to his dominion.[21]

The shore method of buying slaves allowed the ship to move easily from market to market. The final prices of those enslaved depended on their ethnic origin, their availability when the shipper arrived, and their physical health when offered for sale in the West Indies or the North or South American colonies.

The supply of slaves for the foreign market was controlled by a small, wealthy African merchant class or by a state monopoly. By contemporary standards, slave raiding was a costly operation: gathering a band of raiders and the capital for equipment, guides, tolls, and supplies involved considerable expense. Only black African entrepreneurs with sizable capital and labor could afford to finance and direct raiding drives. They exported enslaved men and women because the profits on exports were greater than the profits to be made from using labor in the domestic economy.

The transatlantic slave trade that the British, as well as the Dutch, Portuguese, French, Americans, and others, participated in was part of a much larger trading network that is known as the triangle trade. European merchants sailed to Africa on the first leg of the voyage to trade European manufactured goods for enslaved Africans. When they had filled their ships' holds with enslaved peoples, they headed across the Atlantic on the second leg of the voyage, the Middle Passage. When they reached the Americas, the merchants unloaded and sold their human cargoes and used the profits to purchase raw materials—such as cotton, sugar, and indigo—that they then transported back to Europe, completing the third leg of the commercial triangle.

Enslaved African people had an enormous impact on the economies and cultures of the Portuguese and Spanish colonies of South America and the Dutch, French, and British colonies of the Caribbean and North America. For example, on the sugar plantations of Mexico and the Caribbean; on the North American cotton, rice, and tobacco plantations; and in Peruvian and Mexican silver and gold mines, enslaved

The African Slave Trade   Enslaved African men, women, and children, captured in the interior, are marched to the coast by their African captors. The guards carry guns obtained from Europeans in the slave trade. The enslaved men are linked together by heavy wooden yokes, making it impossible to escape. (The Granger Collection, NYC—All rights reserved)

Africans not only worked in the mines and fields but also filled skilled, supervisory, and administrative positions and performed domestic service. In the United States enslaved Africans and their descendants influenced many facets of American culture, such as language, music (ragtime and jazz), dance, and diet. Even the U.S. White House and Capitol building, where Congress meets, were built partly by slave labor.[22] But the importance of the slave trade extended beyond the Atlantic world. Both the expansion of capitalism and the industrialization of Western societies, Egypt, and the nations of West, Central, and South Africa were related in one way or another to the traffic in African people.

Impact on African Societies

What economic impact did European trade have on African societies? Africans possessed technology well suited to their environment. Over the centuries they had cultivated a wide variety of plant foods; developed plant and animal husbandry techniques; and mined, smelted, and otherwise worked a great variety of metals. Apart from firearms, American tobacco and rum, and the cheap brandy brought by the Portuguese, European goods presented no novelty to Africans. They found foreign products desirable because of their low prices. Traders of handwoven Indian cotton textiles, Venetian imitations of African beads, and iron bars from European smelters could undersell African manufacturers. Africans exchanged slaves, ivory, gold, pepper, and animal skins for those goods. African states eager to expand or to control commerce bought European firearms, although the difficulty of maintaining guns often gave gun owners only marginal superiority over skilled bowmen.[23] The kingdom of Dahomey (modern-day Benin in West Africa), however, built its power on the effective use of firearms.

The African merchants who controlled the production of exports gained the most from foreign trade. Dahomey's king, for example, had a gross income in 1750 of £250,000 (almost U.S. $33 million today) from the overseas export of his fellow Africans. A portion of his profit was spent on goods that improved his people's living standard. Slave-trading entrepôts, which provided opportunities for traders and for farmers who supplied foodstuffs to towns, caravans, and slave ships, prospered. But such economic returns did not spread very far.[24] International trade did not lead to Africa's economic development. Africa experienced neither technological growth nor the gradual spread of economic benefits in early modern times.

As in the Islamic world, women in sub-Saharan Africa also engaged in the slave trade. In Guinea these women slave merchants and traders were known as *nhara*, a corruption of the Portuguese term *senhora*, a title used for a married woman. They acquired considerable riches, often by marrying the Portuguese merchants and serving as go-betweens for these outsiders who were not familiar with the customs and languages of the African coast. One of them, Mae Aurélia Correia (1810?–1875?), led a life famous in the upper Guinea coastal region for its wealth and elegance. Between the 1820s and 1840s she operated her own trading vessels and is said to have owned several hundred slaves. Some of them she hired out as skilled artisans and sailors. She and her sister (or aunt) Julia amassed a fortune in gold, silver jewelry, and expensive cloth while living in European-style homes. Julia and her husband, a trader from the Cape Verde Islands, also owned their own slave estates where they produced peanuts.

The intermarriage of French traders and Wolof women in Senegambia created a métis, or mulatto, class. In the emerging urban centers at Saint-Louis, members of this small class adopted the French language, the Roman Catholic faith, and a French manner of life, and they exercised considerable political and economic power. However, European cultural influences did not penetrate West African society beyond the seacoast.

Sapi-Portuguese Saltcellar   Contact with the Sapi people of present-day Sierra Leone in West Africa led sixteenth-century Portuguese traders to commission this ivory saltcellar, for which they brought Portuguese designs. But the object's basic features—a spherical container and separate lid on a flat base, with men and/or women supporting, or serving as, beams below—are distinctly African. Here a Portuguese caravel sits on top with a man in the crow's nest. Four men stand below: two finely carved, regally dressed, and fully armed noblemen facing forward and two attendants in profile. (© akg-images/The Image Works)

The political consequences of the slave trade varied from place to place. The trade enhanced the power and wealth of some kings and warlords in the short run but promoted conditions of instability and collapse over the long run. In the Kongo kingdom, which was located in parts of modern Angola, the Republic of the Congo, and the Democratic Republic of the Congo, the perpetual Portuguese search for Africans to enslave undermined the monarchy, destroyed political unity, and led to constant disorder and warfare; power passed to the village chiefs. Likewise in Angola, which became a Portuguese proprietary colony (a territory granted to one or more individuals by the Crown for them to govern at their will), the slave trade decimated and scattered the population and destroyed the local economy. By contrast, the military kingdom of Dahomey, which entered into the slave trade in the eighteenth century and made it a royal monopoly, prospered enormously. Dahomey's economic strength rested on the slave trade. The royal army raided deep into the interior, and in the late eighteenth century Dahomey became one of the major West African sources of slaves. When slaving expeditions failed to yield sizable catches and when European demand declined, the resulting depression in the Dahomean economy caused serious political unrest. Iboland, inland from the Niger Delta, from whose great port cities of Bonny and Brass the British drained tens of thousands of enslaved Africans, experienced minimal political effects. A high birthrate kept pace with the incursions of the slave trade, and Ibo societies remained demographically and economically strong.

What demographic impact did the slave trade have on Africa? Between approximately 1501 and 1866 more than 12 million Africans were forcibly exported to the Americas, 6 million were traded to Asia, and 8 million were retained as slaves within Africa.

The early modern slave trade involved a worldwide network of relationships among markets in the Middle East, Africa, Asia, Europe, and the Americas. But Africa was the crucible of the trade. There is no small irony in the fact that Africa, which of all the continents was most desperately in need of population because of its near total dependence on labor-intensive agriculture and pastoralism, lost so many millions to the trade. Although the British Parliament abolished the slave trade in 1807 and traffic in Africans to Brazil and Cuba gradually declined, within Africa the trade continued at the levels of the peak years of the transatlantic trade, 1780–1820. In the later nineteenth century developing African industries, using slave labor, produced a variety of products for domestic consumption and export. Again, there is irony in the fact that in the eighteenth century European demand for slaves expanded the trade (and wars) within Africa, yet in the nineteenth century European imperialists defended territorial aggrandizement by arguing that they were "civilizing" Africans by abolishing slavery. But after 1880 European businessmen (and African governments) did not push abolition; they wanted cheap labor.

Markets in the Americas generally wanted young male slaves. Consequently, two-thirds of those exported to the Americas were male, one-third female. Asian and African markets preferred young females. Women were sought for their reproductive value, as sex objects, and because their economic productivity was not threatened by the possibility of physical rebellion, as might be the case with young men. As a result, the population on Africa's western coast became predominantly female; the population in the East African savanna and Horn regions was predominantly male. The slave trade therefore had significant consequences for the institutions of marriage, the local trade in enslaved people (as these local populations became skewed with too many males or too many females), and the sexual division of labor. Although Africa's overall population may have shown modest growth from roughly 1650 to 1900, that growth was offset by declines in the Horn and on the eastern and western coasts. While Europe and Asia experienced considerable demographic and economic expansion in the eighteenth century, Africa suffered a decline.[25]

The political and economic consequences of the African slave trade are easier to measure than the human toll taken on individuals and societies. While we have personal accounts from many slaves, ships' captains and crews, slave masters, and others of the horrors of the slave-trading ports along Africa's coasts, the brutality of the Middle Passage, and the inhuman cruelty enslaved Africans endured once they reached the Americas, we know much less about the beginning of the slave's journey in Africa. Africans themselves carried out much of the "man stealing," the term used by Africans to describe capturing enslaved men, women, and children and marching them to the coast, where they were traded to Arabs, Europeans, or others. Therefore, we have few written firsthand accounts of the pain and suffering these violent raids inflicted, either on the person being enslaved or on the families and societies they left behind.

Chapter Summary

In the early modern world, West African kingdoms and stateless societies existed side by side. Both had predominantly agricultural economies. Stateless societies revolved around a single village or group of villages without a central capital or ruler. Kings ruled over defined areas through bureaucratic hierarchies. The Sudanic empires controlled the north-south trans-Saharan trade in gold, salt, and other items. Led by predominantly Muslim rulers, these kingdoms belonged to a wider Islamic world, allowing them access to vast trade networks and some of the most advanced scholarship in the world. Still, Muslim culture affected primarily the royal and elite classes, seldom reaching the masses.

Europeans believed a wealthy (mythical) Christian monarch named Prester John ruled the Christian kingdom of Ethiopia. This fable attracted Europeans to Ethiopia for centuries, and partly explains why the Portuguese helped the Ethiopians fight off Muslim incursions. Jesuit missionaries tried to convert Ethiopians to Roman Catholicism but were fiercely resisted and expelled in 1633.

Swahili city-states on Africa's southeastern coast possessed a Muslim and mercantile culture. The Swahili acted as middlemen in the East African–Indian Ocean trade network, which, in the late fifteenth and early sixteenth centuries, Portugal sought to conquer and control. Swahili rulers who refused to form trading alliances with the Portuguese were attacked. The Portuguese had little influence on Swahili culture or religion, but their presence caused the economic decline and death of many Swahili cities.

Slavery existed across Africa before Europeans arrived. Enslaved people were treated relatively benignly in some societies but elsewhere as chattel possessions, suffering harsh and brutal treatment. European involvement in the slave trade began around 1550, when the Portuguese purchased Africans to work in Brazil. The Dutch East India Company used enslaved Africans and Southeast Asians in their Cape Colony.

African entrepreneurs and merchants partnered in the trade, capturing people in the interior and exchanging them for firearms, liquor, and other goods with European slave ships. Though some kingdoms experienced a temporary rise of wealth and power, over time the slave trade was largely destabilizing. The individual suffering and social disruption in Africa caused by the enslavement of millions of Africans is impossible to estimate.

Notes

1. P. D. Curtin, *Economic Change in Precolonial Africa: Senegambia in the Era of the Slave Trade* (Madison: University of Wisconsin Press, 1975), pp. 34–35; J. A. Rawley, *The Transatlantic Slave Trade: A History* (Lincoln: University of Nebraska Press, 2005).
2. Pieter de Marees, *Description of the Gold Kingdom of Guinea*, trans. and ed. Albert van Dantzig and Adam Jones (1602; repr., Oxford: Oxford University Press, 1987), pp. 226–228; William Bosman, *A New Description of the Coast of Guinea*, ed. John Ralph Willis (London: Frank Cass, 1967), p. 461.
3. Quoted in R. Hallett, *Africa to 1875* (Ann Arbor: University of Michigan Press, 1970), p. 151.
4. A. ibn-Fartura, "The Kanem Wars," in *Nigerian Perspectives*, ed. T. Hodgkin (London: Oxford University Press, 1966), pp. 111–115.
5. "The Kano Chronicle," quoted in *Nigerian Perspectives*, ed. T. Hodgkin (London: Oxford University Press, 1966), pp. 89–90.
6. *Equiano's Travels: The Interesting Narrative of the Life of Olaudah Equiano*, ed. P. Edwards (Portsmouth, N.H.: Heinemann, 1996), p. 4.
7. J. Iliffe, *Africans: The History of a Continent* (Cambridge: Cambridge University Press, 2007), p. 68.
8. See A. J. R. Russell-Wood, *The Portuguese Empire: A World on the Move* (Baltimore: Johns Hopkins University Press, 1998), pp. 11–13.
9. Ibid., pp. 35–38.
10. P. E. Lovejoy, *Transformations in Slavery: A History of Slavery in Africa* (Cambridge: Cambridge University Press, 1992), p. 25, Table 2.1, "Trans-Saharan Slave Trade, 650–1600."
11. Iliffe, *Africans*, p. 77.
12. Quoted in H. Thomas, *The Slave Trade* (New York: Simon and Schuster, 1997), p. 21.
13. G. Gerzina, *Black London: Life Before Emancipation* (New Brunswick, N.J.: Rutgers University Press, 1995), pp. 29–66 passim; quotation from p. 53.
14. R. Shell, *Children of Bondage: A Social History of the Slave Society at the Cape of Good Hope, 1652–1838* (Hanover, N.H.: University Press of New England, 1994), pp. 285–289.
15. See D. Eltis, *The Rise of African Slavery in the Americas* (Cambridge: Cambridge University Press, 2000), chap. 3; and the review/commentary by J. E. Inikori, *American Historical Review* 106.5 (December 2001): 1751–1753.
16. R. Blackburn, *The Making of New World Slavery: From the Baroque to the Modern, 1492–1800* (New York: Verso, 1998), pp. 79–80.
17. R. E. Conrad, *Children of God's Fire: A Documentary History of Black Slavery in Brazil* (Princeton, N.J.: Princeton University Press, 1983), pp. 20–23.
18. *Equiano's Travels*, pp. 23–26.
19. Rawley, *The Transatlantic Slave Trade*, pp. 45–47.
20. Robert W. July, *A History of the African People* (Prospect Heights, Ill.: Waveland Press, 1998), p. 171.
21. J. Adams, "Remarks on the Country Extending from Cape Palmas to the River Congo," in *Nigerian Perspectives*, ed. T. Hodgkin (London: Oxford University Press, 1966), pp. 178–180.
22. J. Thornton, *Africa and Africans in the Making of the Atlantic World* (New York: Cambridge University Press, 1992), pp. 138–142.
23. Robert W. July, *Precolonial Africa: An Economic and Social History* (New York: Scribner's, 1975), pp. 269–270.
24. A. G. Hopkins, *An Economic History of West Africa* (New York: Columbia University Press, 1973), p. 119.
25. P. Manning, *Slavery and African Life: Occidental, Oriental, and African Slave Trades* (New York: Cambridge University Press, 1990), pp. 22–23 and chap. 3, pp. 38–59.

CONNECTIONS

During the period from 1400 to 1800 many parts of Africa experienced a profound transition with the arrival of Europeans all along Africa's coasts. Ancient trade routes, such as those across the Sahara Desert or up and down the East African coast, were disrupted. In West Africa trade routes that had been purely internal now connected with global trade networks at European coastal trading posts. Along Africa's east coast the Portuguese attacked Swahili city-states in their effort to take control of the Indian Ocean trade nexus.

The most momentous consequence of the European presence along Africa's coast, however, was the introduction of the transatlantic slave trade. For more than three centuries Europeans, with the aid of African slave traders, enslaved millions of Africa's healthiest and strongest men and women. Although many parts of Africa were untouched by the transatlantic slave trade, at least directly, areas where Africans were enslaved experienced serious declines in agricultural production, little progress in technological development, and significant increases in violence.

As we saw in Chapter 17 and will see in Chapter 21, early European commercial contacts with the empires of the Middle East and of South and East Asia were similar in many ways to those with Africa. Initially, the Portuguese, and then the English, Dutch, and French, did little more than establish trading posts at port cities and had to depend on the local people to bring them trade goods from the interior. Tropical diseases, particularly in India and Southeast Asia, took heavy death tolls on the Europeans, as they did in tropical Africa. What is more, while it was possible for the Portuguese to attack and conquer the individual Swahili city-states, Middle Eastern and Asian empires—such as the Ottomans in Turkey, the Safavids in Persia, the Mughals in India, and the Ming and Qing Dynasties in China—were, like the West African kingdoms, economically and militarily powerful enough to dictate terms of trade with the Europeans.

Resistance to enslavement took many forms on both sides of the Atlantic. In Haiti, as discussed in Chapter 22, resistance led to revolution and independence, marking the first successful uprising of non-Europeans against a colonial power. At the end of the nineteenth century, as described in Chapter 25, Europeans used the ongoing Arab-Swahili slave raids from Africa's eastern coast far into the interior as an excuse to invade and eventually colonize much of central and eastern Africa. The racial discrimination that accompanied colonial rule in Africa set the stage for a struggle for equality that led to eventual independence after World War II.

Chapter Review

MAKE IT STICK

✓ LearningCurve
Go online and use LearningCurve to retain what you've read.

IDENTIFY KEY TERMS

Identify and explain the significance of each item below.

chattel (p. 592)

age-grade systems (p. 592)

oba (p. 593)

Taghaza (p. 594)

Tuareg (p. 598)

cowrie shells (p. 598)

Coptic Christianity (p. 599)

Swahili (p. 602)

Middle Passage (p. 607)

sorting (p. 610)

shore trading (p. 610)

REVIEW THE MAIN IDEAS

Answer the focus questions from each section of the chapter.

1. What types of economic, social, and political structures were found in the kingdoms and states along the west coast and in the Sudan? (p. 591)

2. How did the arrival of Europeans and other foreign cultures affect the East African coast, and how did Ethiopia and the Swahili city-states respond to these incursions? (p. 599)

3. What role did slavery play in African societies before the transatlantic slave trade began, and what was the effect of European involvement? (p. 603)

MAKE CONNECTIONS

Analyze the larger developments and continuities within and across chapters.

1. In what ways did Islam enrich the Sudanic empires of West Africa?

2. Discuss the ways in which Africa came into greater contact with a larger world during the period discussed in this chapter.

3. How did the transatlantic slave trade affect West African society?

ⓟLaunchPad
ONLINE DOCUMENT PROJECT

African Voices in the Antislavery Movement
What role did slave accounts play in antislavery activism?

Read several first-person accounts of slavery, and then complete a quiz and writing assignment based on the evidence and details from this chapter.

See inside the front cover to learn more.

CHRONOLOGY

1400–1600s	• Salt trade dominates West African economy
ca. 1464–1591	• Songhai kingdom dominates the western Sudan
1485	• Portuguese and other Europeans first appear in Benin
1493–1528	• Muhammad Toure governs and expands kingdom of Songhai
1498	• Portuguese explorer Vasco da Gama sails around Africa
ca. 1500–1900	• Era of transatlantic slave trade
1502–1507	• Portuguese erect forts at Kilwa, Zanzibar, and Sofala on Swahili coast
1529	• Adal defeats Ethiopian emperor and begins systematic devastation of Ethiopia
1543	• Joint Ethiopian and Portuguese force defeats Muslims in Ethiopia
1571–1603	• Idris Alooma governs kingdom of Kanem-Bornu
1591	• Moroccan army defeats Songhai
1658	• Dutch East India Company allows importation of slaves into Cape Colony
1680s	• Famine from Senegambian coast to Upper Nile
1738–1756	• Major famine in West Africa
1789	• Olaudah Equiano publishes autobiography

✓ LearningCurve
After reading the chapter, go online
and use LearningCurve to retain what
you've read.

Continuity and Change in East Asia

1400–1800

THE FOUR CENTURIES FROM 1400 TO 1800 WERE A TIME OF GROWTH
and dynamic change throughout East Asia. Although both China and Japan
suffered periods of war, each ended up with expanded territories. The age of
exploration brought New World crops to the region, leading to increased agricultural output and population growth. It also brought new opportunities
for foreign trade and new religions. Another link between these countries
was the series of massive Japanese invasions of Korea in the late sixteenth
century, which led to war between China and Japan.

In China the native Ming Dynasty (1368–1644) brought an end to Mongol
rule. Under the Ming, China saw agricultural reconstruction, commercial
expansion, and the rise of a vibrant urban culture. In the early seventeenth
century, after the Ming Dynasty fell into disorder, the non-Chinese Manchus
founded the Qing Dynasty (1644–1911) and added Taiwan, Mongolia, Tibet,
and Xinjiang to their realm. The Qing Empire thus was comparable to the
other multiethnic empires of the early modern world, such as the Ottoman,
Russian, and Habsburg Empires. In China itself the eighteenth century was
a time of peace and prosperity.

In the Japanese islands the fifteenth century saw the start of civil war that
lasted a century. At the end of the sixteenth century the world seemed to
have turned upside down when a commoner, Hideyoshi (HEE-deh-YOH-shee),
became the supreme ruler. He did not succeed in passing on his power to an
heir, however. Power was seized by Tokugawa Ieyasu (toh-koo-GAH-wuh ee-
eh-YAH-soo). Under the Tokugawa Shogunate (1603–1867), Japan restricted
contact with the outside world and social mobility among its own people.
Yet Japan thrived, as agricultural productivity increased and a lively urban
culture developed.

Ming China, 1368–1644

What sort of state and society developed in China after the Mongols were ousted?

The story of Ming China begins with a poor boy who rose to become emperor of a new dynasty. This individual, Zhu Yuanzhang (JOO yoowan-JAHNG), proved to be one of the most despotic emperors in Chinese history. Still, peace brought prosperity and a lively urban culture. By the beginning of the seventeenth century, however, the Ming government was beset by fiscal, military, and political problems.

The Rise of Zhu Yuanzhang and the Founding of the Ming Dynasty

The founder of the **Ming Dynasty**, Zhu Yuanzhang (1328–1398), began life in poverty during the last decades of the Mongol Yuan Dynasty. His home region was hit by drought and then plague in the 1340s, and when he was only sixteen years old, his father, oldest brother, and that brother's wife all died, leaving two penniless boys with three bodies to bury. With no relatives to turn to, Zhu Yuanzhang asked a monastery to accept him as a novice. The monastery itself was short of funds, and the monks soon sent Zhu out to beg for food. For three or four years he wandered through central China. Only after he returned to the monastery did he learn to read.

A few years later, in 1351, members of a religious sect known as the Red Turbans rose in rebellion against the government. Red Turban teachings drew on Manichaean ideas about the incompatibility of the forces of good and evil as well as on the cult of the Maitreya Buddha, who according to believers would in the future bring his paradise to earth to relieve human suffering. The Red Turbans met with considerable success, even defeating Mongol cavalry. When the temple where Zhu Yuanzhang was living was burned down in the fighting, Zhu joined the rebels and rose rapidly.

Zhu and his followers developed into brilliant generals, and gradually they defeated one rival after another. In 1356 Zhu took the city of Nanjing and made it his base. In 1368 his armies took Beijing, which the Mongol emperor and his closest followers had vacated just days before. Then forty years old, Zhu Yuanzhang declared himself emperor of the Ming (Bright) Dynasty. As emperor, he is known as Taizu (TIGH-dzoo) or the Hongwu emperor.

Taizu started his reign wanting to help the poor. To lighten the weight of government taxes and compulsory labor, he ordered a full-scale registration of cultivated land and population so that these burdens could be assessed more fairly. He also tried persuasion. He issued instructions to be read aloud to villagers, telling them to be obedient to their parents, live in harmony with their neighbors, work contentedly at their occupations, and refrain from evil.

Although in many ways anti-Mongol, Taizu retained some Yuan practices. One was setting up provinces as the administrative layer between the central government and the prefectures (local governments a step above counties). Another was the hereditary service obligation for both artisan and military households. Any family classed as a military household had to provide a soldier at all times, replacing those who were injured, who died, or who deserted.

Garrisons were concentrated along the northern border and near the capital at Nanjing. Each garrison was allocated a tract of land that the soldiers took turns cultivating to supply their own food. Although in theory this system should have provided the Ming with a large but inexpensive army, the reality was less satisfactory. Garrisons were rarely self-sufficient. Furthermore, men compelled to become soldiers did not necessarily make good fighting men, and desertion was difficult to prevent. Consequently, like earlier dynasties, the Ming turned to non-Chinese northerners for much of its armed forces. Many of the best soldiers in the Ming army were Mongols in Mongol units. Taizu did not try to conquer the Mongols, and Ming China did not extend into modern Inner Mongolia.

Taizu had deeply ambivalent feelings about men of education and sometimes brutally humiliated them in open court, even having them beaten. His behavior was so erratic that it is most likely that he suffered from some form of mental illness. As Taizu became more literate, he realized that scholars could criticize him in covert ways, using phrases that had double meanings or that sounded like words for "bandit," "monk," or the like. Even poems in private circulation could be used as evidence of subversive thoughts. When literary men began to avoid official life, Taizu made it illegal to turn down appointments or to resign from office. He began falling into rages that only the empress could stop, and after her death in 1382 no one could calm him. In 1376 Taizu had thousands of officials killed because they were found to have taken shortcuts in their handling of paperwork for the grain tax. In 1380 Taizu concluded that his chancellor was plotting to assassinate him, and thousands only remotely connected to the chancellor were executed. From then on, Taizu acted as his own chancellor, dealing directly with the heads of departments and ministries.

The next important emperor, called Chengzu or the Yongle emperor (r. 1403–1425), was also a military man. One of Taizu's younger sons, he took the throne by force from his nephew and often led troops into battle against the Mongols. Like his father, Chengzu was willing to use terror to keep government officials in line.

Early in his reign, Chengzu decided to move the capital from Nanjing to Beijing, which had been his own base as a prince and the capital during Mongol times. Constructed between 1407 and 1420, Beijing was a planned city. Like Chang'an in Sui-Tang times (581–907), it was arranged like a set of boxes within boxes and built on a north-south axis. The main outer walls were forty feet high and nearly fifteen miles around, pierced by nine gates. Inside was the Imperial City, with government offices, and within that the palace itself, called the Forbidden City, with close to ten thousand rooms. Because the Forbidden City survives today, people can still see the series of audience halls with vast courtyards between them where attending officials would stand or kneel.

The areas surrounding Beijing were not nearly as agriculturally productive as those around Nanjing. To supply Beijing with grain, the Yuan Grand Canal connecting the city to the rice basket of the Yangzi River regions was broadened, deepened, and supplied with more locks and dams. The 15,000 boats and the 160,000 soldiers of the transport army who pulled loaded barges from the towpaths along the canal became the lifeline of the capital.

Problems with the Imperial Institution

Taizu had decreed that succession should go to the eldest son of the empress or to the son's eldest son if the son predeceased his father, the system generally followed by earlier dynasties. In Ming times, the flaws in this system became apparent as one mediocre, obtuse, or erratic emperor followed another. There were emperors who refused to hold audiences, who fell into irrational fits, and who let themselves be manipulated by palace ladies.

Because Taizu had abolished the position of chancellor, emperors turned to secretaries and eunuchs to manage the paperwork. Eunuchs were essentially slaves. Many boys and young men were acquired by dubious means, often from non-Chinese areas in the south, and after they were castrated they had no option but to serve the imperial family. Zheng He, for instance (see page 644), was taken from Yunnan as a boy of ten by a Ming general assigned the task of securing boys to be castrated. Society considered eunuchs the basest of servants, and Confucian scholars heaped scorn on them. Yet Ming emperors, like rulers in earlier dynasties, often preferred the always-compliant eunuchs to high-minded, moralizing civil service officials.

In Ming times, the eunuch establishment became huge. By the late fifteenth century the eunuch bureaucracy had grown as large as the civil service, with each having roughly twelve thousand positions. After 1500 the eunuch bureaucracy grew even more rapidly, and by the mid-sixteenth century seventy thousand eunuchs were in service throughout the country, with ten thousand in the capital. Tension between the two bureaucracies was high. In 1420 Chengzu set up a eunuch-run secret service to investigate cases of suspected corruption and sedition in the regular bureaucracy. Eunuch control over vital government processes, such as appointments, became a severe problem.

In hope of persuading emperors to make reforms, many Ming officials risked their careers and lives by speaking out. In 1376, when Taizu asked for criticism, one official criticized harsh punishment of officials for minor lapses. Incensed, Taizu had him brought to the capital in chains and let him starve to death in prison. In 1519, when an emperor announced plans to make a tour of the southern provinces, over a hundred officials staged a protest by kneeling in front of the palace. The emperor ordered the officials to remain kneeling for three days, then had them flogged; eleven died. The Confucian tradition celebrated these acts of political protest as heroic. Rarely, however, did they succeed in moving an emperor to change his mind.

Although the educated public complained about the performance of emperors, no one proposed or even imagined alternatives to imperial rule. High officials were forced to find ways to work around uncooperative emperors, but they were not able to put in place institutions that would limit the damage an emperor could do. Knowing that strong emperors often acted erratically, many high officials came to prefer weak emperors who let them take care of the government. Emperors, of course, resented the way officials tried to keep them busy doing harmless activities.

The Mongols and the Great Wall

The early Ming emperors held Mongol fighting men in awe and feared they might form another great military machine of the sort Chinggis Khan (ca. 1162–1227) had put together two centuries earlier. Although in Ming times the Mongols were never united in a pan-Mongol federation, groups of Mongols could and did raid. Twice they threatened the dynasty: in 1449 the khan of the western Mongols captured the Chinese emperor, and in 1550 Beijing was surrounded by the forces of the khan of the Mongols in Inner Mongolia. Fearful of anything that might strengthen the Mongols, Ming officials were reluctant to grant any privileges to Mongol leaders, such as trading posts along the borders. Instead they wanted the different groups of Mongols to trade only through the formal tribute system. When trade was finally liberalized in 1570, friction was reduced.

Two important developments shaped Ming-Mongol relations: the construction of the Great Wall, and closer relations between Mongolia and Tibet. The Great Wall, much of which survives today, was built as a compromise when Ming officials could agree on no other way to manage the Mongol threat. The wall extends about 1,500 miles from northeast of Beijing into Gansu province. In the eastern 500 miles, the wall averages about 35 feet high and 20 feet across, with lookout towers every half mile. Much of the way, the wall is faced with brick, which gives it an imposing appearance that greatly impressed the first Westerners who saw it.

Whether the wall did much to protect Ming China from the Mongols is still debated. Perhaps of more significance was the spread of Tibetan Buddhism among the Mongols. Tibet in this period was largely ruled by the major Buddhist monasteries. When Tibetan monasteries needed military assistance, they asked competing Mongol leaders for help, and many struggles were decided by Mongol military intervention. The Tibetan Buddhist Tsong-kha-pa (1357–1419) founded the Yellow Hat, or Gelug-pa, sect, whose heads later became known as the Dalai Lamas. In 1577 the third Dalai Lama accepted the invitation of Altan Khan to visit Mongolia, and the khan declared Tibetan Buddhism to be the official religion of all the Mongols. The Dalai Lama gave the khan the title "King of Religion," and the khan swore that the Mongols would renounce blood sacrifice. When the third Dalai Lama's reincarnation was found to be the great-grandson of Altan Khan, the ties between Tibet and Mongolia, not surprisingly, became even stronger. From the perspective of Ming China, the growing influence of Buddhism among the Mongols seemed a positive development, as Buddhist emphasis on nonviolence was expected to counter the Mongols' love of war.

The Examination Life

In sharp contrast to Europe in this era, Ming China had few social barriers. It had no hereditary aristocracy that could have limited the emperor's absolute power. Although China had no titled aristocracy, it did have an elite whose status was based above all on government office acquired through education. Agricultural land remained the most highly prized form of wealth, but antiques, books, paintings and calligraphies, and urban real estate also brought status. Unlike in many European countries of the era, China's merchants did not become a politically articulate bourgeoisie. Instead the politically active class was that of the scholars who Confucianism taught should aid the ruler in running the state. With the possible exception of the Jewish people, no people have respected learning as much as the Chinese. Merchants tried to marry into the scholar class in order to rise in the world.

Thus, despite the harsh and arbitrary ways in which the Ming emperors treated their civil servants, educated men were eager to enter the government. Reversing the

Portrait of a Scholar-Official

The official Jiang Shunfu arranged to have his portrait painted wearing an official robe and hat and followed by two boy attendants, one holding a lute wrapped in cloth. During Ming and Qing times, the rank of an official was made visible by the badges he wore on his robes. The pair of cranes on Jiang's badge shows he held a first-rank post in the civil service hierarchy. (From *Mingqing renwuxiaoxiang huaxuan* [Nanjing: Nanjing Bowuguan], pl 16/Visual Connection Archive)

policies of the Mongol Yuan Dynasty, the Ming government recruited almost all its officials through **civil service examinations.** Candidates had to study the Confucian classics and the interpretations of them by the twelfth-century Neo-Confucian scholar Zhu Xi (joo shee) (1130–1200), whose teachings were declared orthodox. To become officials, candidates had to pass examinations at the prefectural, the provincial, and the capital levels. To keep the wealthiest areas from dominating the exams, quotas were established for the number of candidates that each province could send on to the capital.

Of course, boys from well-to-do families had a significant advantage because their families could start their education with tutors at age four or five, though less costly schools were becoming increasingly available as well. Families that for generations had pursued other careers—for example, as merchants or physicians—had more opportunities than ever for their sons to become officials through the exams. (See "Individuals in Society: Tan Yunxian, Woman Doctor," page 626.) Clans sometimes operated schools for their members because the clan as a whole would enjoy the prestige of a successful clansman. Most of those who attended school stayed only a few years, but students who seemed most promising moved on to advanced schools where they practiced essay writing and studied the essays of men who had succeeded in the exams.

The examinations at the prefecture level lasted a day and drew hundreds if not thousands of candidates. The government compound would be taken over to give all candidates places to sit and write. The provincial and capital examinations were given in three sessions spread out over a week. In the first session, candidates wrote essays on passages from the classics. In the second and third sessions, candidates had to write essays on practical policy issues and on a passage from the *Classic of Filial Piety* (a brief text celebrating devotion to parents and other superiors). In addition, they had to show that they could draft state papers such as edicts, decrees, and judicial rulings. Reading the dynastic histories was a good way to prepare for policy questions and state paper exercises.

INDIVIDUALS IN SOCIETY • Tan Yunxian, Woman Doctor

The grandmother of Tan Yunxian (1461–1554) was the daughter of a physician, and her husband had married into her home to learn medicine himself. At least two of their sons—including Yunxian's father—passed the civil service examination and became officials, raising the social standing of the family considerably. The grandparents wanted to pass their medical knowledge down to someone, and because they found Yunxian very bright, they decided to teach it to her.

Tan Yunxian married and raised four children but also practiced medicine, confining her practice to women. At age fifty she wrote an autobiographical account, *Sayings of a Female Doctor*. In the preface she described how, under her grandmother's tutelage, she had first memorized the *Canon of Problems* and the *Canon of the Pulse*. Then when her grandmother had time, she asked her granddaughter to explain particular passages in these classic medical treatises.

Tan Yunxian began the practice of medicine by treating her own children, asking her grandmother to check her diagnoses. When her grandmother was old and ill, she gave Yunxian her notebook of prescriptions and her equipment for making medicines, telling her to study them carefully. Later, Yunxian herself became seriously ill and dreamed of her grandmother telling her on what page of which book to find the prescription that would cure her. When she recovered, she began her medical career in earnest.

Tan Yunxian's book records the cases of thirty-one patients she treated, most of them women with chronic complaints rather than critical illnesses. Many of the women had what the Chinese classed as women's complaints, such as menstrual irregularities, repeated miscarriages, barrenness, and postpartum fatigue. Some had ailments that men too could suffer, such as coughs, nausea, insomnia, diarrhea, rashes, and swellings. Like other literati physicians, Yunxian regularly prescribed herbal medications. She also practiced moxibustion, the technique of burning moxa (dried artemisia) at specified points on the body with the goal of stimulating the circulation of qi (life energy). Because the physician applying the moxa had to touch the patient, male physicians could not perform moxibustion on women.

Yunxian's patients included working women, and Yunxian seems to have thought that their problems often sprang from overwork. One woman came to her because she had had vaginal bleeding for three years. When questioned, the

The provincial examinations were major local events. From five thousand to ten thousand candidates descended on the city and filled up its hostels. Candidates would show up a week in advance to present their credentials and gather the paper, ink, brushes, candles, blankets, and food they needed to survive in their small exam cells. To prevent cheating, no written material could be taken into the cells, and candidates were searched before being admitted. Anyone caught wearing a cheat-sheet (an inner gown covered with the classics in minuscule script) was thrown out of the exam and banned from the next session as well. Clerks used horns and gongs to begin and end each two-day session. During the sessions candidates had time to write rough drafts of their essays, correct them, and then copy neat final versions. Throughout this time, woman told Yunxian that she worked all day with her husband at their kiln making bricks and tiles. Yunxian's diagnosis was overwork, and she gave the woman pills to replenish her yin energies. A boatman's wife came to her complaining of numbness in her hands. When the woman told Yunxian that she worked in the wind and rain handling the boat, the doctor advised some time off. In another case Yunxian explained to a servant girl that she had gone back to work too soon after suffering a wind damage fever.

By contrast, when patients came from upper-class families, Tan Yunxian believed negative emotions were the source of their problems, particularly if a woman reported that her mother-in-law had scolded her or that her husband had recently brought a concubine home. Yunxian told two upper-class women who had miscarried that they lost their babies because they had hidden their anger, causing fire to turn inward and destabilize the fetus.

Tan Yunxian herself lived a long life, dying at age ninety-three.

Source: Based on Charlotte Furth, *A Flourishing Yin: Gender in China's Medical History, 960–1665* (Berkeley: University of California Press, 1999), pp. 285–295.

QUESTIONS FOR ANALYSIS

1. Why do you think Tan Yunxian treated only women? Why might she have been more effective with women patients than a male physician would have been?

2. What do you think of Yunxian's diagnoses? Do you think she was able to help many of her patients?

⯈LaunchPad
ONLINE DOCUMENT PROJECT

What kinds of treatments did Chinese doctors employ? Examine artwork depicting Chinese medical practices, and then complete a quiz and writing assignment based on the evidence and details from this chapter.

See inside the front cover to learn more.

tension was high. Sometimes rumors that the examiners had been bribed to leak the questions led to riots in the exam quarters, and knocked-over candles occasionally caused fires.

After the papers were handed in, clerks recopied them and assigned them numbers to preserve anonymity. Proofreaders checked the copying before handing the papers to the assembled examiners, who divided them up to grade. The grading generally took about twenty days, and most candidates stayed in the vicinity to await the results. Those few who passed (generally from 2 to 10 percent) were invited to the governor's compound for a celebration. By the time they reached home, most of their friends, neighbors, and relatives had already heard their good news. They could not spend long celebrating, however, because they had to begin preparing for the capital exams, less than a year away.

Everyday Life in Ming China

For civil servants and almost everyone else, everyday life in Ming China followed patterns established in earlier periods. The family remained central to most people's lives, and almost everyone married. Beyond the family, people's lives were shaped by the type of work they did and where they lived.

Large towns and cities proliferated in Ming times and became islands of sophistication in the vast sea of rural villages. In these urban areas small businesses manufactured textiles, paper, and luxury goods such as silks and porcelains. The southeast became a center for the production of cotton and silks; other areas specialized in the grain and salt trades and in silver. Merchants could make fortunes moving these goods across the country.

Printing was invented in Tang times (618–907) and had a great impact on the life of the educated elite in Song times (960–1279), but not until Ming times did it transform the culture of the urban middle classes. By the late Ming period, publishing houses were putting out large numbers of books aimed at general audiences. These included fiction, reference books of all sorts, and popular religious tracts, such as ledgers for calculating the moral value of one's good deeds and subtracting the demerits from bad deeds. To make their books attractive in the marketplace, entrepreneurial book publishers commissioned artists to illustrate them. By the sixteenth century more and more books were being published in the vernacular language (the language people spoke), especially short stories, novels, and plays. Ming vernacular short stories depicted a world much like that of their readers, full of shop clerks and merchants, monks and prostitutes, students and matchmakers.

The full-length novel made its first appearance during the Ming period. The plots of the early novels were heavily indebted to story cycles developed by oral storytellers over the course of several centuries. *Water Margin* is the episodic tale of a band of bandits, while *The Romance of the Three Kingdoms* is a work of historical fiction based on the exploits of the generals and statesmen contending for power at the end of the Han Dynasty. *The Journey to the West* is a fantastic account of the Tang monk Xuanzang's travels to India; in this book he is accompanied by a pig and a monkey with supernatural powers. *Plum in the Golden Vase* is a novel of manners about a lustful merchant with a wife and five concubines. Competing publishers brought out their own editions of these novels, sometimes adding new illustrations or commentaries.

The Chinese found recreation and relaxation in many ways besides reading. The affluent indulged in an alcoholic drink made from fermented and distilled rice, and once tobacco was introduced from the Americas, both men and women took up pipes. Plays were also very popular. The Jesuit missionary Matteo Ricci, who lived in China from 1583 to 1610, described resident troupes in large cities and traveling troupes that "journey everywhere throughout the length and breadth of the country" putting on plays. The leaders of the troupes would purchase young children and train them to sing and perform. Ricci thought too many people were addicted to these performances:

These groups of actors are employed at all imposing banquets, and when they are called they come prepared to enact any of the ordinary plays. The host at the banquet is usually presented with a volume of plays and he selects the one or several he may like. The guests, between eating and drinking, follow the plays with so much satisfaction that the banquet at times may last for ten hours.[1]

People not only enjoyed play performances but also avidly read the play scripts. The love stories and social satires of Tang Xianzu, the greatest of the Ming playwrights, were very popular. One of his plays tells the story of a young man who falls asleep while his meal is cooking. In his dream he sees his whole life: he comes in first in the civil service examinations, rises to high office, is unfairly slandered and condemned to death, and then is cleared and promoted. At the point of death, he wakes up, sees that his dinner is nearly ready, and realizes that life passes as quickly as a dream.

More than bread in Europe, rice supplied most of the calories of the population in central and south China. (In north China, wheat, made into steamed or baked bread or into noodles, served as the dietary staple.) In the south, terracing and irrigation of mountain slopes, introduced in the eleventh century, had increased rice harvests. Other innovations also brought good results. Farmers began to stock the rice paddies with fish, which continuously fertilized the rice fields, destroyed malaria-bearing mosquitoes, and enriched the diet. Farmers also grew cotton, sugarcane, and indigo as commercial crops. New methods of crop rotation allowed for continuous cultivation and for more than one harvest per year from a single field.

The Ming rulers promoted the repopulation and colonization of war-devastated regions through reclamation of land and massive transfers of people. Immigrants to these areas received large plots and exemption from taxation for many years. Reforestation played a dramatic role in the agricultural revolution. In 1391 the Ming government ordered 50 million trees planted in the Nanjing area to produce lumber for the construction of a maritime fleet. In 1392 each family holding a land grant in Anhui province had to plant two hundred mulberry, jujube, and persimmon trees. In 1396 peasants in the present-day provinces of Hunan and Hubei in central China planted 84 million fruit trees. Historians have estimated that 1 billion trees were planted during Taizu's reign.

Increased food production led to steady population growth and the multiplication of markets, towns, and small cities. Larger towns had permanent shops; smaller towns had periodic markets — some every five days, some every ten days, some only once a month. They sold essential goods — such as pins, matches, oil for lamps, candles, paper, incense, and tobacco — to country people from the surrounding hamlets. Markets usually included moneylenders, pawnbrokers, a tearoom, and sometimes a wine shop where tea and rice wine were sold and entertainers performed. Tradesmen carrying their wares on their backs and craftsmen — carpenters, barbers, joiners, locksmiths — moved constantly from market to market. Itinerant salesmen depended on the city market for their wares.

Ming Decline

Beginning in the 1590s the Ming government was beset by fiscal, military, and political problems. The government went nearly bankrupt helping defend Korea against a Japanese invasion (see pages 644–646). Then came a series of natural disasters: floods, droughts, locusts, and epidemics ravaged one region after another. At the same time, a "little ice age" brought a drop in average temperatures that shortened the growing season and reduced harvests. In areas of serious food shortages, gangs of army deserters and laid-off soldiers began scouring the countryside in search of food. Once the gangs had stolen all their grain, hard-pressed farmers joined them just to survive. The Ming government had little choice but to try to increase taxes to deal with these threats, but the last thing people needed was heavier taxes.

Adding to the hardship was a sudden drop in the supply of silver. In place of the paper money that had circulated in Song and Yuan times, silver ingots came into general use as money in Ming times. Even agricultural taxes came to be paid in silver rather than in grain. Much of this silver originated in either Japan or the New World and entered China as payment for the silk and porcelains exported from China. When events in Japan and the Philippines led to disruption of trade, silver imports dropped. This led to deflation in China, which caused real rents to rise. Soon there were riots among urban workers and tenant farmers. In 1642 a group of rebels cut the dikes on the Yellow River, causing massive flooding. A smallpox epidemic soon added to the death toll. In 1644 the last Ming emperor, in despair, took his own life when rebels entered Beijing, opening the way for the start of a new dynasty.

The Manchus and Qing China, to 1800

Did the return of alien rule with the Manchus have any positive consequences for China?

The next dynasty, the **Qing Dynasty** (1644–1911), was founded by the Manchus, a non-Chinese people who were descended from the Jurchens who had ruled north China during the Jin Dynasty (1127–1234), when south China was controlled by the Song. Manchu men shaved the front of their heads and wore the rest of their hair in a long braid called a queue. In the late sixteenth century the Manchus began expanding their territories, and in 1644 they founded the Qing Dynasty, which brought peace and in time prosperity. Successful Qing military campaigns extended the borders into Mongol, Tibetan, and Uighur regions, creating a multiethnic empire that was larger than any earlier Chinese dynasty.

The Rise of the Manchus

In the Ming period, the Manchus lived in dispersed communities in what is loosely called Manchuria (the northeast of modern-day China). In the more densely populated southern part of Manchuria, the Manchus lived in close contact with Mongols, Koreans, and Chinese (Map 21.1). They were not nomads but rather hunters, fishers, and farmers. Like the Mongols, they also were excellent horsemen and archers and had a strongly hierarchical social structure, with elites and slaves. Slaves, often Korean or Chinese, were generally acquired through capture. A Korean visitor described many small Manchu settlements, most no larger than twenty households, supported by fishing, hunting for pelts, collecting pine nuts or ginseng, or growing crops such as wheat, millet, and barley. Villages were often at odds with each other over resources, and men did not leave their villages without arming themselves with bows and arrows or swords.

Interspersed among these Manchu settlements were groups of nomadic Mongols who lived in tents.

The Manchus credited their own rise to Nurhaci (1559–1626). Over several decades, he united the Manchus and expanded their territories. Like Chinggis Khan, who had reorganized the Mongol armies to reduce the importance of tribal affiliations, Nurhaci created a new social basis for his armies in units called **banners**. Each banner was made up of a set of military companies and included the families and slaves of the soldiers. Each company had a hereditary captain, often from Nurhaci's own lineage. Over time new companies and new banners were formed, and by 1644 there were eight each of Manchu, Mongol, and Chinese banners. When new groups were defeated, their members were distributed among several banners to lessen their potential for subversion.

The Manchus entered China by invitation of the distinguished Ming general Wu Sangui, himself a native of southern Manchuria, who was near the eastern end of the Great Wall when he heard that the rebels had captured Beijing. The Manchus proposed to Wu that they join forces and liberate Beijing. Wu opened the gates of the Great Wall to let the Manchus in, and within a couple of weeks they occupied Beijing. When the Manchus made clear that they intended to conquer the rest of the country and take the throne themselves, Wu and many other Chinese generals joined forces with them. Before long, China was again under alien rule.

In the summer of 1645 the Manchus ordered all Chinese serving in Manchu armies to shave the front of their heads in the Manchu fashion, presumably to make it easier to recognize whose side they were on. Soon this order was extended to all Chinese men. Because so many of those newly conquered by the Qing refused to shave off their hair, Manchu commanders felt justified in ordering the slaughter of defiant cities. After quelling resistance, the Qing put in place policies and institutions that gave China a respite from war and disorder. Most of the political institutions of the Ming Dynasty were taken over relatively unchanged, including the examination system.

After peace was achieved, population growth took off. Between 1700 and 1800 the Chinese population seems to have nearly doubled, from about 150 million to over 300 million. Population growth during the eighteenth century has been attributed to many factors: global warming that extended the growing season, expanded use of New World crops, slowing of the spread of new diseases that had accompanied the sixteenth-century expansion of global traffic, and the efficiency of the Qing government in providing relief in times of famine.

Some scholars have recently argued that China's overall standard of living in the mid-eighteenth century was comparable to Europe's and that the standards of China's most developed regions, such as the lower Yangzi region, compared favorably to the most developed regions of Europe at the time, such as England and the Netherlands. Life expectancy, food consumption, and even facilities for transportation were at similar levels.

Competent and Long-Lived Emperors

For more than a century, China was ruled by only three rulers, each of them hard-working, talented, and committed to making the Qing Dynasty a success. Two, the Kangxi and Qianlong emperors, had exceptionally long reigns.

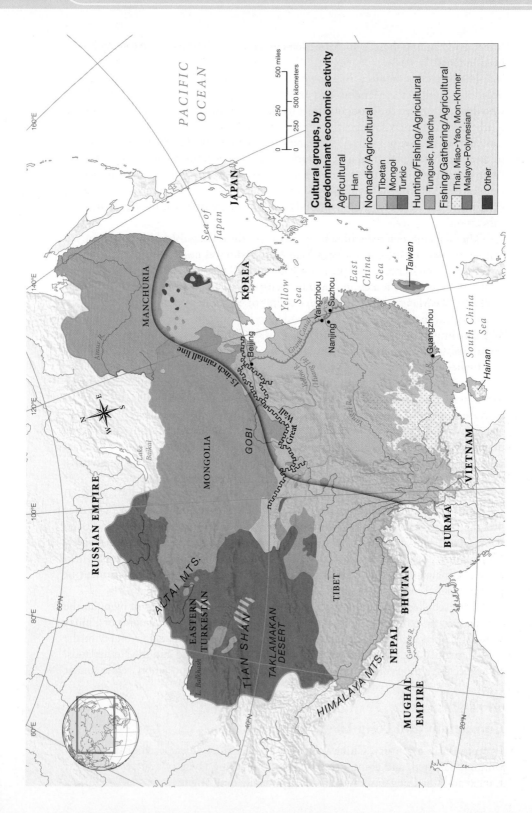

◄ **MAP 21.1** **The Qing Empire, ca. 1800** The sheer size of the Qing Empire in China almost inevitably led to its profound cultural influence on the rest of Asia.

Kangxi (r. 1661–1722) proved adept at meeting the expectations of both the Chinese and the Manchu elites. At age fourteen he announced that he would begin ruling on his own and had his regent imprisoned. Kangxi (KAHNG-shee) could speak, read, and write Chinese and made efforts to persuade educated Chinese that the Manchus had a legitimate claim to rule, even trying to attract Ming loyalists who had been unwilling to serve the Qing. He undertook a series of tours of the south, where Ming loyalty had been strongest, and he held a special exam to select men to compile the official history of the Ming Dynasty.

Kangxi's son and heir, the Yongzheng emperor (r. 1722–1735), was also a hard-working ruler who took an interest in the efficiency of the government. Because his father had lived so long, he did not come to the throne until his mid-forties and reigned only thirteen years. His successor, however, the Qianlong emperor (r. 1736–1796), like Kangxi had a reign of sixty years, with the result that China had only three rulers in 135 years.

Qianlong (chyan-loong) put much of his energy into impressing his subjects with his magnificence. He understood that the Qing's capacity to hold the multiethnic empire together rested on their ability to appeal to all those they ruled. Besides speaking Manchu and Chinese, Qianlong learned to converse in Mongolian, Uighur, Tibetan, and Tangut, and he addressed envoys in their own languages. He became as much a patron of Tibetan Buddhism as of Chinese Confucianism. He initiated a massive project to translate the Tibetan Buddhist canon into Mongolian and Manchu and had huge multilingual dictionaries compiled.

To demonstrate to the Chinese scholar-official elite that he was a sage emperor, Qianlong worked on affairs of state from dawn until early afternoon and then turned

Presenting a Horse to the Emperor This detail from a 1757 hand scroll shows the Qianlong emperor, seated, receiving envoys from the Kazakhs. Note how the envoy, presenting a pure white horse, is kneeling to the ground performing the kowtow, which involved lowering his head to the ground as an act of reverence. The artist was Giuseppe Castiglione, an Italian who worked as a painter in Qianlong's court. (by Father Giuseppe Castiglione [1688–1766]; Musée des Arts Asiatiques-Guimet/© RMN–Grand Palais/Art Resource, NY)

to reading, painting, and calligraphy. He was ostentatious in his devotion to his mother, visiting her daily and tending to her comfort with all the devotion of the most filial Chinese son. He took several tours down the Grand Canal to the southeast, in part to emulate his grandfather, in part to entertain his mother, who accompanied him on these tours.

Despite these displays of Chinese virtues, the Qianlong emperor was not fully confident that the Chinese supported his rule, and he was quick to act on any suspicion of anti-Manchu thoughts or actions. During a project to catalogue nearly all the books in China, he began to suspect that some governors were holding back books with seditious content. He ordered full searches for books with disparaging references to the Manchus or to previous alien conquerors like the Jurchens and Mongols. Sometimes passages were deleted or rewritten, but when an entire book was offensive, it was destroyed. So thorough was this book burning that no copies survive of more than two thousand titles.

Through Qianlong's reign, China remained an enormous producer of manufactured goods and led the way in assembly-line production. The government operated huge textile factories, but some private firms were even larger. Hangzhou had a textile firm that gave work to 4,000 weavers, 20,000 spinners, and 10,000 dyers and finishers. The porcelain kilns at Jingdezhen employed the division of labor on a large scale and were able to supply porcelain to much of the world. The growth of the economy benefited the Qing state, and the treasury became so full that the Qianlong emperor was able to cancel taxes on several occasions. When he abdicated in 1796, his treasury had 400 million silver dollars in it.

Imperial Expansion

The Qing Dynasty put together a multiethnic empire that was larger than any earlier Chinese dynasty. Taiwan was acquired in 1683 after Qing armies pursued a rebel there. Mongolia was acquired next. In 1696 Kangxi led an army of eighty thousand men into Mongolia, and within a few years Manchu supremacy was accepted there. Cannon and muskets gave Qing forces military superiority over the Mongols, who were armed only with bows and arrows. Thus the Qing could dominate the steppe cheaply, effectively ending two thousand years of Inner Asian military advantage.

In the 1720s the Qing established a permanent garrison of banner soldiers in Tibet. By this time, the expanding Qing and Russian Empires were nearing each other. In 1689 the Manchu and the Russian rulers approved a treaty—written in Russian, Manchu, Chinese, and Latin—defining their borders in Manchuria and regulating trade. Another treaty in 1727 allowed a Russian ecclesiastical mission to reside in Beijing and a trade caravan to make a trip from Russia to Beijing once every three years.

The last region to be annexed was Chinese Turkestan (the modern province of Xinjiang). Both the Han and the Tang Dynasties had stationed troops in the region, exercising loose overlordship, but neither the Song nor the Ming had tried to control the area. The Qing won the region in the 1750s through a series of campaigns against Uighur and Dzungar Mongol forces.

Both Tibet and Turkestan were ruled lightly. The local populations kept their own religious leaders and did not have to wear the queue.

Japan's Middle Ages, ca. 1400–1600

How did Japan change during this period of political instability?

In the twelfth century Japan entered an age dominated by military men, an age that can be compared to Europe's feudal age. The Kamakura Shogunate (1185–1333) had its capital in the east, at Kamakura. It was succeeded by the Ashikaga Shogunate (1338–1573), which returned the government to Kyoto (KYOH-toh) and helped launch, during the fifteenth century, the great age of Zen-influenced Muromachi culture. The sixteenth century brought civil war over succession to the shogunate, leading to the building of massive castles and the emergence of rulers of obscure origins who eventually unified the realm.

Muromachi Culture

The headquarters of the Ashikaga shoguns were on Muromachi Street in Kyoto, and the refined and elegant style that they promoted is often called Muromachi culture. The shoguns patronized Zen Buddhism, the school of Buddhism associated with meditation and mind-to-mind transmission of truth. Because Zen monks were able to read and write Chinese, they often assisted the shoguns in handling foreign affairs. Many of the Kyoto Zen temples in this period had rock gardens, seen as aids to Zen meditation.

Zen ideas of simplicity permeated the arts. The Silver Pavilion built by the shogun Yoshimasa (r. 1449–1473) epitomizes Zen austerity. A white sand cone constructed in the temple garden was designed to reflect moonlight. Yoshimasa was also influential in the development of the tea ceremony, practiced by warriors, aristocrats, and priests, but not by women. Aesthetes celebrated the beauty of imperfect objects, such as plain or misshapen cups or pots. Spare monochrome paintings fit into this aesthetic, as did simple asymmetrical flower arrangements.

The shoguns were also patrons of the **Nō theater**. Nō drama originated in popular forms of entertainment, including comical skits and dances directed to the gods. It was transformed into high art by Zeami (1363–1443), an actor and playwright who also wrote on the aesthetic theory of Nō. Nō was performed on a bare stage with a pine tree painted across the backdrop. One or two actors wearing brilliant brocade robes performed, using stylized gestures and stances. One actor wore a mask indicating whether the character he was portraying was male or female, old or young, a god, a ghost, or a demon. The actors were accompanied by a chorus and a couple of musicians playing drums and flute. Many of the stories concerned ghosts consumed by jealous passions or the desire for revenge. Zeami argued that the most meaningful moments came during silence, when the actor's spiritual presence allowed the audience to catch a glimpse of the mysterious and inexpressible.

Civil War

Civil war began in Kyoto in 1467 as a struggle over succession to the shogunate. Rival claimants and their followers used arson as their chief weapon and burned down temples and mansions, destroying much of the city and its treasures. In the early phases defeated opponents were exiled or allowed to retire to monasteries. As the conflict continued, violence escalated; hostages and prisoners were slaughtered and corpses mutilated. Once Kyoto was laid waste, war spread to outlying areas. When the shogun could no longer protect cities, merchants banded together to hire mercenaries. In the political vacuum, the Lotus League, a commoner-led religious sect united by faith in the saving power of the Lotus Sutra, set up a commoner-run government that collected taxes and settled disputes. In 1536, during eight days of fighting, the powerful Buddhist monastery Enryakuji attacked the League and its temples, burned much of the city, and killed men, women, and children thought to be believers.

In these confused and violent circumstances, power devolved to the local level, where warlords, called **daimyo** (DIGH-myoh), built their power bases. Unlike earlier power holders, these new lords were not appointed by the court or shogunate and did not send taxes to absentee overlords. Instead they seized what they needed and used it to build up their territories and recruit more samurai. To raise revenues, they surveyed the land and promoted irrigation and trade. Many of the most successful daimyo were self-made men who rose from obscurity.

The violence of the period encouraged castle building. The castles were built not on mountaintops but on level plains, and they were surrounded by moats and walls made from huge stones. Inside a castle was a many-storied keep, which could be elegantly decorated with painted sliding doors and screens. Though relatively safe from incendiary missiles, the keeps were vulnerable to Western-style cannon, introduced in the 1570s.

The Victors: Nobunaga and Hideyoshi

The first daimyo to gain a predominance of power was Oda Nobunaga (1534–1582). A samurai of the lesser daimyo class, he recruited followers from masterless samurai who had been living by robbery and extortion. After he won control of his native province in 1559, he immediately set out to extend his power through central Japan. A key step was destroying the military power of the great monasteries. To increase revenues, he minted coins, the first government-issued money in Japan since 958. Also to raise revenues, he promoted trade by eliminating customs barriers and opening the little fishing village of Nagasaki to foreign commerce; it soon became Japan's largest port.

In 1582, in an attempted coup, Nobunaga was forced by one of his vassals to commit suicide. His general and staunchest adherent, Toyotomi Hideyoshi (1537–1598), avenged him and continued the drive toward unification of the daimyo-held lands.

Like the Ming founder, Hideyoshi was a peasant's son who rose to power through military talent. Hideyoshi succeeded in bringing northern and western Japan under his control. In 1582 he attacked the great fortress at Takamatsu. When direct assault failed, his troops flooded the castle to force its surrender. A successful siege of the town of Kagoshima then brought the southern island of Kyushu (KYOO-shoo) under his domination. Hideyoshi soothed the vanquished daimyo as Nobunaga had done—with lands and military positions—but he also required them to swear allegiance and to obey him down to the smallest particular. For the first time in over two centuries, Japan had a single ruler.

Hideyoshi did his best to ensure that future peasants' sons would not be able to rise as he had. His great sword hunt of 1588 collected weapons from farmers, who were no longer allowed to wear swords. Restrictions were also placed on samurai; they were prohibited from leaving their lord's service or switching occupations. To improve

Matsumoto Castle
Hideyoshi built Matsumoto Castle between 1594 and 1597. Designed to be impregnable, it was surrounded by a moat and had a base constructed of huge stones. In the sixteenth and early seventeenth centuries Spanish and Portuguese missionaries compared Japanese castles favorably to European castles of the period. (Adina Tovy/Robert Harding World Imagery)

tax collection, Hideyoshi ordered a survey of the entire country. His agents collected detailed information about each daimyo's lands and about towns, villages, agricultural produce, and industrial output all over Japan. His surveys not only tightened tax collection, but also registered each peasant household and tied the peasants to the land. With the country pacified, Hideyoshi embarked on an ill-fated attempt to conquer Korea and China that ended only with his death, discussed below (see page 644).

The Tokugawa Shogunate, to 1800

What was life like in Japan during the Tokugawa peace?

On his deathbed, Hideyoshi set up a council of regents to govern during the minority of his infant son. The strongest regent was Hideyoshi's long-time supporter Tokugawa Ieyasu (1543–1616), who ruled vast territories around Edo (AY-doh; modern-day Tokyo). In 1600 at Sekigahara, Ieyasu smashed a coalition of daimyo defenders of the heir and began building his own government. In 1603 he took the title "shogun." The Tokugawa Shogunate that Ieyasu fashioned lasted until 1867. This era is also called the Edo period after the location of the shogunate, starting Tokyo's history as Japan's most important city (Map 21.2). Peace brought many benefits. Towns and cities thrived and became centers for the theater and publishing.

Tokugawa Government

Over the course of the seventeenth century the Tokugawa shoguns worked to consolidate relations with the daimyo. In a scheme resembling the later residency requirements imposed by Louis XIV in France (see page 535) and Peter the Great in Russia (see page 550), Ieyasu set up the alternate residence system, which compelled the lords to live in Edo every other year and to leave their wives and sons there—essentially as hostages. This arrangement had obvious advantages: the shogun could keep tabs on the daimyo, control them through their wives and children, and weaken them financially with the burden of maintaining two residences.

MAP 21.2   Tokugawa Japan, 1603–1867 The lands that the shogunate directly controlled were concentrated near its capital at Edo. The daimyo of distant places, such as the island of Kyushu, were required to make long journeys to and from Edo every year.

The peace imposed by the Tokugawa Shogunate brought a steady rise in population to about 30 million people by 1800 (making Tokugawa Japan about one-tenth the size of Qing China). To maintain stability, the early Tokugawa shoguns froze social status. Laws rigidly prescribed what each class could and could not do. Nobles, for example, were strictly forbidden to go sauntering, whether by day or by night, through the streets or lanes in places where they had no business to be. Daimyo were prohibited from moving troops outside their frontiers, making alliances, and coining money. As intended, these rules protected the Tokugawa shoguns from daimyo attack and helped ensure a long era of peace.

The early Tokugawa shoguns also restricted the construction and repair of castles—symbols, in Japan as in medieval Europe, of feudal independence. Continuing Hideyoshi's policy, the Tokugawa regime enforced a policy of complete separation of samurai and peasants. Samurai were defined as those permitted to carry swords. They had to live in castles (which evolved into castle-towns), and they depended on stipends from their lords, the daimyo. Samurai were effectively prevented from establishing ties to the land, so they could not become landholders. Likewise, merchants and artisans had to live in towns and could not own land. Japanese castle-towns evolved into bustling, sophisticated urban centers.

After 1639 Japan limited its contacts with the outside world because of concerns both about the loyalty of subjects converted to Christianity by European missionaries and about the imperialist ambitions of European powers (discussed below). However, China remained an important trading partner and source of ideas. For example, Neo-Confucianism gained a stronger hold among the samurai-turned-bureaucrats, and painting in Chinese styles enjoyed great popularity. The Edo period also saw the development of a school of native learning that rejected Buddhism and Confucianism as alien and tried to identify a distinctly Japanese sensibility.

Commercialization and the Growth of Towns

During the civil war period, warfare seems to have promoted social and economic change, much as it had in China during the Warring States Period (403–221 B.C.E.). Trade grew, and greater use was made of coins imported from Ming China. Markets began appearing at river crossings, at the entrances to temples and shrines, and at other places where people congregated. Towns and cities sprang up all around the country, some of them around the new castles. Traders and artisans dealing in a specific product — such as comb makers, sesame oil producers, or metalworkers — began forming guilds. Money-lending was a very profitable business — annual interest rates reached 300 percent. In Kyoto the powerful monastery Enryakuji licensed the money-lenders, in essence running a lucrative protection racket. Foreign trade also flourished, despite chronic problems with pirates who raided the Japanese, Korean, and Chinese coasts (see pages 644–645).

Recent scholarship demonstrates that the Tokugawa era witnessed the foundations of modern Japanese capitalism: the development of a cash economy, the use of money to make more money, the accumulation of large amounts of capital for investment in factory or technological enterprises, the growth of business ventures operating over a national network of roads, and the expansion of wage labor. That these developments occurred simultaneously with, but entirely independent of, similar changes in Europe fascinates and challenges historians.

In most cities, merchant families with special privileges from the government controlled the urban economy. Frequently, a particular family dominated the trade in a particular product and then branched out into other businesses. The family of Kōnoike Shinroku is an example. In 1600 he established a sake (SAH-kay) brewery in the village of Kōnoike (sake is an alcoholic beverage made from fermented rice). By 1604 he had opened a branch office in Edo, and in 1615 he opened an office in Osaka and began shipping taxes paid in rice from western Japan to Osaka. In 1656 one of Shinroku's sons founded a banking or money-changing business in Osaka. Forty years later the Kōnoike family was doing business in thirty-two daimyo domains. Eventually, the Kōnoike banking house made loans to and handled the tax-rice for 110 daimyo families. In 1705, with the interest paid from daimyo loans, the Kōnoike bought a tract of ponds and swampland, turned the land into rice paddies, and settled 480 households on the land. (Land reclamation under merchant supervision became a typical feature of Tokugawa business practices.) Involved by this time in five or six business enterprises, the house of Kōnoike had come a long way from brewing sake.

Japanese merchant families also devised distinct patterns and procedures for their business operations. What today is called "family-style management principles" determined the age of apprenticeship (between eleven and thirteen); the employee's detachment from past social relations and adherence to the norms of a particular family business; salaries; seniority as the basis of promotion, although job performance at the middle rungs determined who reached the higher ranks; and the time for retirement. All employees in a family business were expected to practice frugality, resourcefulness, self-denial, and careful accounting. These values formed the basis of what has been called the Japanese "industrious revolution." They help to explain how, after the Meiji (MAY-jee) Restoration of 1867 (see page 810), Japan was able to industrialize rapidly and compete successfully with the West. (In both Japan and China there was a market for books giving advice on how to get ahead.)

In the seventeenth century underemployed farmers and samurai, not to mention the ambitious and adventurous, thronged to the cities. As a result, Japan's cities grew tremendously. Kyoto became the center for the manufacture of luxury goods like lacquer, brocade, and fine porcelain. Osaka was the chief market, especially for rice. Edo was a center of consumption by the daimyo, their vassals, and government bureaucrats. Both Osaka and Edo reached about a million residents.

Two hundred fifty towns came into being in this period. Most ranged in size from 3,000 to 20,000 people, but a few, such as Hiroshima, Kagoshima, and Nagoya, had populations of between 65,000 and 100,000. In addition, perhaps two hundred towns along the main road to Edo emerged to meet the needs of men traveling on the alternate residence system. In the eighteenth century perhaps 4 million people, 15 percent of the Japanese population, resided in cities or towns.

The Life of the People in the Edo Period

The Tokugawa shoguns brought an end to civil war by controlling the military. Stripped of power and required to spend alternate years at Edo, many of the daimyo and samurai passed their lives in idle pursuit of pleasure. They spent extravagantly on fine silks, paintings, concubines, boys, the theater, and the redecoration of their castles. These temptations, as well as more sophisticated pleasures and the heavy costs of maintaining alternate residences at Edo, gradually bankrupted the warrior class.

All major cities contained places of amusement for men — teahouses, theaters, restaurants, and houses of prostitution. Desperately poor parents sometimes sold their daughters to entertainment houses (as they did in China and medieval Europe), and the most attractive or talented girls, trained in singing, dancing, and conversational arts, became courtesans, later called geishas (GAY-shahz), "accomplished persons."

Another form of entertainment in the cities was **kabuki theater**, patronized by both merchants and samurai. An art form created by townspeople, kabuki originated in crude, bawdy skits dealing with love and romance. Performances featured elaborate costumes, song, dance, and poetry. Because actresses were thought to corrupt public morals, the Tokugawa government banned them from the stage in 1629. From that time on, men played all the parts. Male actors in female dress and makeup performed as seductively as possible to entice the burly samurai who thronged the theaters. Homosexuality, long accepted in Japan, was widely practiced among the samurai, who pursued the actors and spent profligately on them. Some moralists and bureaucrats complained from time to time, but the Tokugawa government decided to accept kabuki and prostitution as necessary evils.

Cities were also the center for commercial publishing. As in contemporary China, the reading public eagerly purchased fiction and the scripts for plays. Ihara Saikaku (1642–1693) wrote stories of the foibles of townspeople in such books as *Five Women Who Loved Love* and *The Life of an Amorous Man*. One of the puppet plays of Chikamatsu Monzaemon (1653–1724) tells the story of the son of a business owner who, caught between duty to his family and love of a prostitute, decides to resolve the situation by double suicide. The art of color woodblock printing also was perfected during this period. Many of the surviving prints, made for a popular audience, depict the theater and women of the entertainment quarters.

Almost as entertaining as attending the theater was watching the long processions of daimyo, their retainers, and their luggage as they passed back and forth to and from Edo twice a year. The shogunate prohibited travel by commoners, but they could get passports to take pilgrimages, visit relatives, or seek the soothing waters of medicinal hot springs. Setting out on foot, groups of villagers would travel to such shrines as Ise, often taking large detours to visit Osaka or Edo to sightsee or attend the theater. Older women with daughters-in-law to run their households were among the most avid pilgrims.

According to Japanese tradition, farmers deserved respect. In practice, however, peasants were often treated callously. In 1649 every village in Japan received these regulations:

> Peasants are people without sense or forethought. Therefore they must not give rice to their wives and children at harvest time, but must save food for the future. They should eat millet, vegetables, and other coarse food instead of rice. Even the fallen leaves of plants should be saved as food against famine. . . . During the seasons of planting and harvesting, however, when the labor is arduous, the food taken may be a little better. . . .
>
> They must not buy tea or sake to drink nor must their wives. The husband must work in the fields, the wife must work at the loom. Both must do night work. However good-looking a wife may be, if she neglects her household duties by drinking tea or sightseeing or rambling on the hillsides, she must be divorced.
>
> Peasants must wear only cotton or hemp — no silk. They may not smoke tobacco. It is harmful to health, it takes up time, and costs money. It also creates a risk of fire.[2]

During the seventeenth and eighteenth centuries daimyo and upper-level samurai paid for their extravagant lifestyles by raising taxes on their subordinate peasants from 30 or 40 percent of the rice crop to 50 percent. Not surprisingly, this angered peasants, and peasant protests became chronic during the eighteenth century. For example, oppressive taxation provoked eighty-four thousand farmers in the province of Iwaki to revolt in 1739; after widespread burning and destruction, their demands for lower taxes were met. Natural disasters also added to the peasants' misery. In 1783 Mount Asama erupted, spewing volcanic ash that darkened the skies all summer; the resulting crop failures led to famine. When famine recurred again in 1787, commoners rioted for five days in Edo, smashing merchants' stores and pouring sake and rice into the muddy streets. The shogunate responded by trying to control the floating population of day laborers without families in the city. At one point they were rounded up and transported to work the gold mines in an island off the north coast, where most of them died within two or three years.

Edo Craftsman at Work   Less than 3 inches tall, this ivory figure shows a parasol maker seated on the floor (the typical Japanese practice) eating his lunch, his tools by his side. (Photo © Boltin Picture Library/The Bridgeman Art Library)

This picture of peasant hardship tells only part of the story. Agricultural productivity increased substantially during the Tokugawa period. Peasants who improved their lands and increased their yields continued to pay the same assessed tax and could pocket the surplus as profit. As those without land drifted to the cities, peasants left in the countryside found ways to improve their livelihoods. At Hirano near Osaka, for example, 61.7 percent of all arable land was sown in cotton. The peasants ginned the cotton locally before transporting it to wholesalers in Osaka. In many rural places, as many peasants worked in the manufacture of silk, cotton, or vegetable oil as in the production of rice.

In comparison to farmers, merchants had a much easier life, even if they had no political power. By contemporary standards anywhere in the world, the Japanese mercantile class lived well. In 1705 the shogunate confiscated the property of a merchant in Osaka "for conduct unbecoming a member of the commercial class." In fact, the confiscation was at the urging of influential daimyo and samurai who owed the merchant gigantic debts. The government seized 50 pairs of gold screens, 360 carpets, several mansions, 48 granaries and warehouses scattered around the country, and hundreds of thousands of gold pieces. Few merchants possessed such fabulous wealth, but many lived very comfortably.

Within a village, some families would be relatively well-off, others barely able to get by. The village headman generally came from the richest family, but he consulted a council of elders on important matters. Women in better-off families were much more likely to learn to read than women in poor families. Daughters of wealthy peasants studied penmanship, the Chinese classics, poetry, and the proper forms of correspondence, and they rounded out their education with travel. By contrast, girls from middle-level peasant families might have had from two to five years of formal schooling, but they were thought incapable of learning the difficult Chinese characters, so their education focused on moral instruction intended to instill virtue.

By the fifteenth and sixteenth centuries Japan's family and marriage systems had evolved in the direction of a patrilocal, patriarchal system more like China's, and Japanese women had lost the prominent role in high society that they had occupied during the Heian period. It became standard for women to move into their husbands' homes, where they occupied positions subordinate to both their husbands and their mothers-in-law. In addition, elite families stopped dividing their property among all their children; instead they retained it for the sons alone or increasingly for a single son who would continue the family line. Marriage, which now had greater consequence, also had a more public character and was marked by greater ceremony. Wedding rituals involved both the exchange of betrothal gifts and the movement of the bride from her parents' home to her husband's home. She brought with her a trousseau that provided her with clothes and other items she would need for daily life, but not with land, which would have given her economic autonomy. On the other hand, her position within her new family was more secure, for it became more difficult for a husband to divorce his wife. She also gained authority within the family. If her husband was away, she managed family affairs. If her husband fathered children with concubines, she was their legal mother.

A peasant wife shared responsibility for the family's economic well-being with her husband. If of poor or middling status, she worked alongside her husband in the fields, doing the routine work while he did the heavy work. If they were farm hands and worked for wages, the wife invariably earned a third or a half less than her husband. Wives of prosperous farmers never worked in the fields, but they reeled silk, wove cloth, helped in any family business, and supervised the maids. When cotton growing spread to Japan in the sixteenth century, women took on the jobs of spinning and weaving it. Whatever their economic status, Japanese women, like women everywhere in the world, tended the children. Families were growing smaller in this period in response to the spread of single-heir inheritance. From studies of household registers, demographic historians have shown that Japanese families restricted the number of children they had by practicing abortion and infanticide, turning to adoption when no heir survived.

How was divorce initiated, and how frequent was it? Among the elite, the husband alone could initiate divorce; all he had to do was order his wife to leave or send her possessions to her parents' home. For the wife, divorce carried a stigma, but she could not prevent it or insist on keeping her children. Widows and divorcées of the samurai elite — where female chastity was the core of fidelity — were not expected to remarry. Among the peasant classes, by contrast, divorce seems to have been fairly common — the divorce rate was at least 15 percent in the villages near Osaka in the eighteenth century. A poor woman wanting a divorce could simply leave her husband's home. It was also possible to secure divorce through a temple. If a married woman entered the temple and performed rites there for three years, her marriage bond was dissolved. Sometimes Buddhist temple priests served as divorce brokers: they went to the village headman and had him force the husband to agree to a divorce. News of the coming of temple officials was usually enough to produce a letter of separation.

Maritime Trade, Piracy, and the Entry of Europe into the Asian Maritime Sphere

How did the sea link the countries of East Asia, and what happened when Europeans entered this maritime sphere?

In the period 1400–1800 maritime trade and piracy connected China and Japan to each other and also to Korea, Southeast Asia, and Europe. All through the period China and Japan traded extensively with each other as well as with Korea. Both Korea and Japan relied on Chinese coinage, and China relied on silver from Japan. During the fifteenth century China launched overseas expeditions. Japan was a major base for pirates. In the sixteenth century European traders appeared, eager for Chinese porcelains and silks. Christian missionaries followed, but despite initial successes, they were later banned, first by the Japanese government and then by the Chinese government. Political changes in Europe changed the international makeup of the European traders in East Asia, with the dominant groups first the Portuguese, next the Dutch, and then the British.

Zheng He's Voyages

Early in the Ming period, the Chinese government tried to revive the tribute system of the Han (206–220 c.e.) and Tang (618–907) Dynasties, when China had dominated East Asia and envoys had arrived from dozens of distant lands. To invite more countries to send missions, the third Ming emperor (Chengzu, or Yongle) authorized an extraordinary series of voyages to the Indian Ocean under the command of the Muslim eunuch Zheng He (1371–1433).

Zheng He's father had made the trip to Mecca, and the seven voyages that Zheng led between 1405 and 1433 followed old Arab trade routes. The first of the seven was made by a fleet of 317 ships, of which 62 were huge, 440 feet long. Each expedition involved from twenty thousand to thirty-two thousand men. Their itineraries included stops in Vietnam, Malaysia, Indonesia, Sri Lanka, India, and, in the later voyages, Hormuz (on the coast of Persia) and East Africa (see Map 16.1, page 459). At each stop Zheng He went ashore to visit rulers, transmit messages of China's peaceful intentions, and bestow lavish gifts. Rulers were invited to come to China or send envoys and were offered accommodation on the return voyages. Near the Straits of Malacca, Zheng He's fleet battled Chinese pirates, bringing them under control. Zheng He made other shows of force as well, deposing rulers deemed unacceptable in Java, Sumatra, and Sri Lanka.

On the return of these expeditions, the Ming emperor was delighted by the exotic things the fleet brought back, such as giraffes and lions from Africa, fine cotton cloth from India, and gems and spices from Southeast Asia. Ma Huan, an interpreter who accompanied Zheng He, collected data on the plants, animals, peoples, and geography that they encountered and wrote a book titled *The Overall Survey of the Ocean's Shores*. Still, these expeditions were not voyages of discovery; they followed established routes and pursued diplomatic rather than commercial goals.

Why were these voyages abandoned? Officials complained about their cost and modest returns. As a consequence, after 1474 all the remaining ships with three or more masts were broken up and used for lumber. Chinese did not pull back from trade in the South China Sea and Indian Ocean, but the government no longer promoted trade, leaving the initiative to private merchants and migrants.

Piracy and Japan's Overseas Adventures

One goal of Zheng He's expeditions was to suppress piracy, which had become a problem all along the China coast. Already in the thirteenth century social disorder and banditry in Japan had expanded into seaborne banditry, some of it within the Japanese islands around the Inland Sea (Map 21.3), but also in the straits between Korea and Japan. Japanese "sea bandits" would raid the Korean coast, seizing rice and other goods to take home. In the sixteenth century bands several hundred strong would

MAP 21.3   East Asia, ca. 1600 Pirates and traders often plied the same waters as sea-borne trade grew in the sixteenth century. The Portuguese were especially active in setting up trading ports.

attack and loot Chinese coastal cities or hold them hostage for ransom. As maritime trade throughout East Asia grew more lively, sea bandits also took to attacking ships to steal their cargo. Although the pirates were called the "Japanese pirates" by both the Koreans and the Chinese, pirate gangs in fact recruited from all countries. The Ryūkyū (ryoo-kyoo) Islands and Taiwan became major bases.

Possibly encouraged by the exploits of these bandits, Hideyoshi, after his victories in unifying Japan, decided to extend his territory across the seas. In 1590, after receiving congratulations from Korea on his victories, Hideyoshi sent a letter asking the Koreans to allow his armies to pass through their country, declaring that his real target was China: "Disregarding the distance of the sea and mountain reaches that lie in between, I shall in one fell swoop invade Great Ming. I have in mind to introduce Japanese customs and values to the four hundred and more provinces of that country and bestow upon it the benefits of imperial rule and culture for the coming hundred million years."[3] He also sent demands for submission to countries of Southeast Asia and to the Spanish governor of the Philippines.

In 1592 Hideyoshi mobilized 158,000 soldiers and 9,200 sailors for his invasion and equipped them with muskets and cannon, which had recently been introduced into Japan. His forces overwhelmed Korean defenders and reached Seoul within three weeks and Pyongyang in two months. A few months later, in the middle of winter, Chinese armies arrived to help defend Korea, and Japanese forces were pushed back from Pyongyang. A stalemate lasted till 1597, when Hideyoshi sent new troops. This time the Ming army and the Korean navy were more successful in resisting the Japanese. In 1598, after Hideyoshi's death, the Japanese army withdrew, but Korea was left devastated.

After recovering from the setbacks of these invasions, Korea began to advance socially and economically. During the Chosŏn Dynasty (1392–1910), the Korean elite (the yangban) turned away from Buddhism and toward strict Neo-Confucian orthodoxy. As agricultural productivity improved, the population grew from about 4.4 million in 1400 to about 8 million in 1600, 10 million in 1700, and 14 million in 1810 (or about half the size of Japan's population and one-twentieth of China's). With economic advances, slavery declined. When slaves ran away, landowners found that it was less expensive to replace them with sharecroppers than to recapture them. Between 1750 and 1790 the slave population dropped from 30 percent to 5 percent of the population. The hold of the yangban elite, however, remained strong. Through the eighteenth century about two dozen yangban families dominated the civil service examinations, leaving relatively few slots for commoners to rise to through study.

Europeans Enter the Scene

In the sixteenth century Portuguese, Spanish, and Dutch merchants and adventurers began to participate in the East Asian maritime world (see Chapter 16). The trade between Japan, China, and Southeast Asia was very profitable, and the European traders wanted a share of it. They also wanted to develop trade between Asia and Europe.

The Portuguese and Dutch were not reluctant to use force to gain control of trade, and they seized many outposts along the trade routes, including Taiwan. Moreover, they made little distinction between trade, smuggling, and piracy. In 1521 the Ming tried to ban the Portuguese from China. Two years later an expeditionary force commissioned by the Portuguese king to negotiate a friendship treaty defeated its mission by firing on Chinese warships near Guangzhou. In 1557, without informing Beijing, local Chinese officials decided that the way to regulate trade was to allow the Portuguese to build a trading post on uninhabited land near the mouth of the Pearl River. The city they built there—Macao—became the first destination for Europeans going to China until the nineteenth century, and it remained a Portuguese possession until 1999.

European products were not in demand in China, but silver was. Japan had supplied much of China's silver, but with the development of silver mines in the New World, European traders began supplying large quantities of silver to China, allowing the expansion of China's economy.

Chinese were quick to take advantage of the new trading ports set up by European powers. In Batavia harbor (now Jakarta, Indonesia) Chinese ships outnumbered those from any other country by two or three to one. Manila, under Spanish control, and Taiwan and Batavia, both under Dutch control, all attracted thousands of Chinese colonists. Local people felt the intrusion of Chinese more than of Europeans, and riots against Chinese led to massacres on several occasions.

Dutch in Japan   The Japanese were curious about the appearance, dress, and habits of the Dutch who came to the enclave of Deshima to trade. In this detail from a long hand scroll, Dutch traders are shown interacting with a Japanese samurai in a room with Japanese tatami mats on the floor. Note also the Western musical instrument. (Private Collection/The Bridgeman Art Library)

A side benefit of the appearance of European traders was New World crops. Sweet potatoes, maize, peanuts, tomatoes, chili peppers, tobacco, and other crops were quickly adopted in East Asia. Sweet potatoes and maize in particular facilitated population growth because they could be grown on land previously thought too sandy or too steep to cultivate. Sweet potatoes became a common poor people's food.

Christian Missionaries

The Spanish and Portuguese kings supported missionary activity, and merchant vessels soon brought Catholic missionaries to East Asia. The first to come were Jesuits, from the order founded by Ignatius Loyola in 1540 to promote Catholic scholarship and combat the Protestant Reformation.

The Jesuit priest Francis Xavier had worked in India and the Indies before China and Japan attracted his attention. In 1549, after many misadventures, he landed on Kyushu, Japan's southernmost island (see Map 21.2). After he was expelled by the local lord, he traveled throughout western Japan as far as Kyoto, proselytizing wherever warlords allowed. He soon made many converts among the poor and even some among the daimyo. Xavier then set his sights on China but died on an uninhabited island off the China coast in 1552.

Other missionaries carried on his work, and by 1600 there were three hundred thousand baptized Christians in Japan. Most of them lived on Kyushu, where the shogun's power was weakest and the loyalty of the daimyo most doubtful. In 1615

The call for liberty was also a call for a new kind of government. Reformers believed that the people had sovereignty — that is, that the people alone had the authority to make laws limiting an individual's freedom of action. In practice, this system of government meant choosing legislators who represented the people and were accountable to them. Monarchs might retain their thrones, but their rule should be constrained by the will of the people.

Equality was a more ambiguous idea. Eighteenth-century liberals argued that, in theory, all citizens should have identical rights and liberties and that the nobility had no right to special privileges based on birth. However, they accepted a number of distinctions. First, most eighteenth-century liberals were men of their times, and they generally believed that equality between men and women was neither practical nor desirable. Women played an important informal role in the Atlantic revolutions, but in each case male legislators limited formal political rights — the right to vote, to run for office, to participate in government — to men. Second, few questioned the superiority of people of European descent over those of indigenous or African origin. Even those who believed that the slave trade was unjust and should be abolished, such as Thomas Jefferson, usually felt that emancipation was so socially and economically dangerous that it needed to be indefinitely postponed.

Finally, liberals never believed that everyone should be equal economically. Great differences in wealth and income between rich and poor were perfectly acceptable, so long as every free white male had a legally equal chance at economic gain. However limited they appear to modern eyes, these demands for liberty and equality were revolutionary, given that a privileged elite had long existed with little opposition.

The two most important Enlightenment references for late-eighteenth-century liberals were John Locke and the baron de Montesquieu. Locke maintained that England's long political tradition rested on "the rights of Englishmen" and on representative government through Parliament. He argued that if a government oversteps its proper function of protecting the natural rights of life, liberty, and private property, it becomes a tyranny. Montesquieu was also inspired by English constitutional history and the Glorious Revolution of 1688–1689, which placed sovereignty in Parliament (see page 539). He, too, believed that powerful "intermediary groups" — such as the judicial nobility of which he was a proud member — offered the best defense of liberty against despotism.

The belief that representative institutions could defend their liberty and interests appealed powerfully to the educated middle classes. Yet liberal ideas about individual rights and political freedom also appealed to some progressive members of the hereditary nobility. Representative government did not mean democracy, which liberal thinkers tended to equate with mob rule. Rather, they envisioned voting for representatives as being restricted to men who owned property — those with "a stake in society." The blurring of practical distinctions between landed aristocrats and wealthy commoners meant that there was no clear-cut opposition between nobles and non-nobles on political issues.

The Atlantic revolutions began with aspirations for equality and liberty among the social elite. Soon, however, dissenting voices emerged as some revolutionaries became frustrated with the limitations of liberal notions of equality and liberty and clamored for a fuller realization of these concepts. Depending on location, their demands included political rights for women and free people of color, the emancipation of slaves, better treatment of indigenous people, and government regulations to reduce economic inequality. The age of revolution was thus characterized by bitter conflicts over how far reform should go and to whom it should apply.

The Seven Years' War

The roots of revolutionary ideology could be found in Enlightenment texts, but it was by no means inevitable that such ideas would result in revolution. Many members of the educated elite were satisfied with the status quo or too intimidated to challenge it. Instead events—political, economic, and military—created crises that opened the door for radical action. One of the most important was the global conflict known as the Seven Years' War (1756–1763).

The war's battlefields stretched from central Europe to India to North America (where the conflict was known as the French and Indian War), pitting a new alliance of England and Prussia against the French, Austrians, and, later, Spanish. Its origins were in conflicts left unresolved at the end of the War of the Austrian Succession in 1748, during which Prussia had seized the Austrian territory of Silesia. In central Europe, Austria's monarch Maria Theresa vowed to win back Silesia and to crush Prussia, thereby re-establishing the Habsburgs' traditional leadership in German affairs. By the end of the Seven Years' War, Maria Theresa had almost succeeded, but Prussia survived with its boundaries intact.

Unresolved tensions also lingered in North America, particularly regarding the border between the French and British colonies. The encroachment of English settlers into territory claimed by the French in the Ohio Valley resulted in skirmishes that soon became war. Although the inhabitants of New France were greatly outnumbered—Canada counted 55,000 inhabitants, compared to 1.2 million in the thirteen English colonies—French forces achieved major victories until 1758. Both sides relied on the participation of Native American tribes with whom they had long-standing trade contacts and actively sought new indigenous allies during the conflict. The tide of the conflict turned when the British diverted resources from the war in Europe, using superior sea power to destroy the French fleet and choke French commerce around the world. In 1759 the British laid siege to Quebec for four long months, finally defeating the French in a battle that sealed the fate of France in North America.

British victory on all colonial fronts was ratified in the 1763 **Treaty of Paris**. Canada and all French territory east of the Mississippi River passed to Britain, and France ceded Louisiana to Spain as compensation for Spain's loss of Florida to Britain. France also gave up most of its holdings in India, opening the way to British dominance on the subcontinent.

By 1763 Britain had realized its goal of monopolizing a vast trading and colonial empire, but at a tremendous cost in war debt. France emerged from the conflict humiliated and broke, but with its profitable Caribbean colonies intact. In the aftermath of war, British, French, and Spanish governments had to increase taxes to repay loans, raising a storm of protest and demands for political reform. Since the Caribbean colony of Saint-Domingue remained French, revolutionary turmoil in the mother country would directly affect its population. The seeds of revolutionary conflict in the Atlantic world were thus sown.

The American Revolutionary Era, 1775–1789

Why and how did American colonists forge a new, independent nation?

Increased taxes and government control sparked colonial protests in the New World, where the era of liberal political revolution began. After revolting against their home country, the thirteen mainland colonies of British North America succeeded in establishing a new unified government. Participants in the revolution believed they were demanding only the traditional rights of English men and women. But those traditional rights were liberal rights, and in the American context they had strong democratic and popular overtones. In founding a government firmly based on liberal principles, the Americans set an example that would have a forceful impact on France and its colonies. Yet the revolution was a grievous disappointment to the one-fifth of the American population living in slavery who were denied freedom under the new government despite its liberal principles.

The Origins of the Revolution

The high cost of the Seven Years' War doubled the British national debt. Anticipating further expenses to defend newly conquered territories, the British government broke with tradition and announced that it would maintain a large army in North America and tax the colonies directly. In 1765 Parliament passed the Stamp Act, which levied taxes on a long list of commercial and legal documents, diplomas, newspapers, almanacs, and playing cards. These measures seemed perfectly reasonable to the British, for a much heavier stamp tax already existed in Britain, and proceeds from the tax were to fund the defense of the colonies. Nonetheless, the colonists vigorously protested the Stamp Act by rioting and by boycotting British goods. Thus Parliament reluctantly repealed it.

This dispute raised important political questions. To what extent could the British government reassert its power while limiting the authority of elected colonial bodies? Who had the right to make laws for Americans? The British government replied that Americans were represented in Parliament, albeit indirectly (like most British people), and that Parliament ruled throughout the empire. Many Americans felt otherwise. In the words of John Adams, a major proponent of colonial independence, "A Parliament of Great Britain can have no more rights to tax the colonies than a Parliament of Paris." Thus British colonial administration and parliamentary supremacy came to appear as grave threats to existing American liberties.

Americans' resistance to these threats was fed by the great degree of independence they had long enjoyed. In British North America, unlike in England and Europe, no powerful established church existed, and religious freedom was taken for granted. Colonial assemblies made the important laws, which were seldom overturned by the British government. Also, the right to vote was much more widespread than in England. In many parts of colonial Massachusetts, for example, as many as 95 percent of adult males could vote.

Moreover, greater political equality was matched by greater social and economic equality, at least for the free population. No hereditary nobility exercised privileges over peasants and other social groups. Instead independent farmers dominated colonial society. This was particularly true in the northern colonies, where the revolution originated.

In 1773 disputes over taxes and representation flared up again. Under the Tea Act of that year, the British government permitted the financially hard-pressed East India Company to ship tea from China directly to its agents in the colonies rather than through London middlemen, who sold to independent merchants in the colonies. Thus the company secured a profitable monopoly on the tea trade, and colonial merchants were excluded. The price on tea was actually lowered for colonists, but the act generated a great deal of opposition because of its impact on local merchants.

In protest, Boston men disguised as Native Americans held a rowdy Tea Party in which they boarded East India Company ships and threw tea from them into the harbor. In response, the so-called Coercive Acts of 1774 instated a series of harsh measures. The acts closed the port of Boston, curtailed local elections, and expanded the royal governor's power. County conventions in Massachusetts urged that the acts be "rejected as the attempts of a wicked administration to enslave America." Other colonial assemblies joined in the denunciations. In September 1774 the First Continental Congress — consisting of colonial delegates who sought at first to peacefully resolve conflicts with Britain — met in Philadelphia. The more radical members of this assembly argued successfully against concessions to the English crown. The British Parliament also rejected compromise, and in April 1775 fighting between colonial and British troops began at Lexington and Concord.

Independence from Britain

As fighting spread, the colonists moved slowly toward open calls for independence. The uncompromising attitude of the British government and its use of German mercenaries did much to dissolve loyalties to the home country and to unite the separate colonies. *Common Sense* (1775), a brilliant attack by the recently arrived English radical Thomas Paine (1737–1809), also mobilized public opinion in favor of independence. A runaway bestseller with sales of 120,000 copies in a few months, Paine's tract ridiculed the idea of a small island ruling a great continent. In his call for freedom and republican government, Paine expressed Americans' growing sense of separateness and moral superiority.

On July 4, 1776, the Second Continental Congress adopted the Declaration of Independence. Written by Thomas Jefferson and others, this document boldly listed the tyrannical acts committed by George III (r. 1760–1820) and confidently proclaimed the natural rights of mankind and the sovereignty of the American states. The Declaration of Independence in effect universalized the traditional rights of English people and made them the rights of all mankind.

After the Declaration of Independence, the conflict often took the form of a civil war pitting patriots against Loyalists, those who maintained an allegiance to the Crown. The Loyalists, who numbered up to 20 percent of the total white population, tended to be wealthy and politically moderate. They were few in number in New England and Virginia, but more common in the Deep South and on the western frontier. British commanders also recruited Loyalists from enslaved people by promising freedom to any slave who left his master to fight for the mother country.

Many wealthy patriots — such as John Hancock and George Washington — willingly allied themselves with farmers and artisans in a broad coalition. This coalition harassed the Loyalists and confiscated their property to help pay for the war, causing sixty thousand to eighty thousand of them to flee, mostly to Canada. State governments extended the right to vote to many more men, including free African American men in some cases, but not to women.

On the international scene, the French wanted revenge against the British for the humiliating defeats of the Seven Years' War. Thus they sympathized with the rebels and supplied guns and gunpowder from the beginning of the conflict. By 1777 French volunteers were arriving in Virginia, and a dashing young nobleman, the marquis de Lafayette (1757–1834), quickly became one of the most trusted generals of George Washington, who was commanding American troops. In 1778 the French government offered a formal alliance to the American ambassador in Paris, Benjamin Franklin, and in 1779 and 1780 the Spanish and Dutch declared war on Britain. Catherine the Great of Russia helped organize the League of Armed Neutrality to protect neutral shipping rights and succeeded in hampering Britain's naval power.

Thus by 1780 Britain was engaged in an imperial war against most of Europe as well as the thirteen colonies. In these circumstances, and in the face of severe reverses in India, in the West Indies, and at Yorktown in Virginia, a new British government decided to cut its losses and end the war. American officials in Paris were receptive to negotiating a deal with England alone, for they feared that France wanted a treaty that would bottle up the new United States east of the Allegheny Mountains and give British holdings west of the Alleghenies to France's ally, Spain. Thus the American negotiators deserted their French allies and accepted the extraordinarily favorable terms Britain offered.

Under the Treaty of Paris of 1783, Britain recognized the independence of the thirteen colonies and ceded all its territory between the Allegheny Mountains and the Mississippi River to the Americans. Out of the bitter rivalries of the Old World, the Americans snatched dominion over a vast territory.

Framing the Constitution

The liberal program of the American Revolution was consolidated by the federal Constitution, the Bill of Rights, and the creation of a national republic. Assembling in Philadelphia in the summer of 1787, the delegates to the Constitutional Convention were determined to end the period of economic depression, social uncertainty, and leadership under a weak central government that had followed independence. The delegates thus decided to grant the federal, or central, government important powers: regulation of domestic and foreign trade, the right to tax, and the means to enforce its laws.

Strong rule would be placed squarely in the context of representative self-government. Senators and congressmen would be the lawmaking delegates of the voters, and the president of the republic would be an elected official. The central government would operate in Montesquieu's framework of checks and balances, under which authority was distributed across three different branches—the executive, legislative, and judicial branches—which would prevent one interest from gaining too much power. The power of the federal government would in turn be checked by that of the individual states.

When the results of the Constitutional Convention were presented to the states for ratification, a great public debate began. The opponents of the proposed Constitution—the **Antifederalists**—charged that the framers of the new document had taken too much power from the individual states and made the federal government too strong. Moreover, many Antifederalists feared for the individual freedoms for which they had fought. To overcome these objections, the Federalists promised to spell out these basic freedoms as soon as the new Constitution was adopted. The result was the first ten amendments to the Constitution, which the first Congress passed shortly after it met in New York in March 1789. These amendments, ratified in 1791, formed an effective Bill of Rights to safeguard the individual. Most of them — trial by jury, due process of law, the right to assemble, freedom from unreasonable search — had their origins in English law and the English Bill of Rights of 1689. Other rights — the freedoms of speech, the press, and religion — reflected natural-law theory and the strong value colonists had placed on independence from the start.

Limitations of Liberty and Equality

The American Constitution and the Bill of Rights exemplified the strengths and the limits of what came to be called classical liberalism. Liberty meant individual freedoms and political safeguards. Liberty also meant representative government, but it did not mean democracy, with its principle of one person, one vote. Equality meant equality before the law, not equality of political participation or wealth. It did not mean equal rights for slaves, Native Americans, or women.

A vigorous abolitionist movement during the 1780s led to the passage of emancipation laws in all northern states, but slavery remained prevalent in the South, and discord between pro- and antislavery delegates roiled the Constitutional Convention of 1787. The result was a compromise stipulating that an enslaved person would count as three-fifths of a person in tallying population numbers for taxation and proportional representation in the House of Representatives. This solution levied higher taxes on the South, but also guaranteed slaveholding states greater representation in Congress, which they used to oppose emancipation. Congress did ban participation in the international slave trade from 1808, but did not prohibit the sale of enslaved people between states.

The new republic also failed to protect the Native American tribes whose lands fell within or alongside the territory ceded by Britain at the Treaty of Paris. The 1787 Constitution promised protection to Native Americans and guaranteed that their land would not be taken without consent. Nonetheless, the federal government forced tribes to concede their land for meager returns; state governments and the rapidly expanding population paid even less heed to the Constitution and often simply seized Native American land for new settlements.

Although lacking the voting rights enjoyed by so many of their husbands and fathers in the relatively democratic colonial assemblies, women played a vital role in the American Revolution. As household provisioners, women were essential participants in boycotts of British goods, like tea, which squeezed profits from British merchants and fostered the revolutionary spirit. After the outbreak of war, women raised funds for the Continental Army and took care of homesteads, workshops, and other businesses when their men went off to fight. Yet despite Abigail Adams's plea to her husband, John Adams, that the framers of the Declaration of Independence should "remember the ladies," women did not receive the right to vote in the new Constitution, an omission confirmed by a clause added in 1844.

Revolution in France, 1789–1791

How did the events of 1789 result in a constitutional monarchy in France, and what were the consequences?

No country felt the consequences of the American Revolution more deeply than France. Hundreds of French officers served in America and were inspired by the experience. French intellectuals and publicists engaged in passionate analysis of the federal Constitution as well as the constitutions of the various states of the new United States. Yet the French Revolution did not mirror the American example. It was more radical and more complex, more influential and more controversial, more loved and more hated. For Europeans and most of the rest of the world, it was the great revolution of the eighteenth century, the revolution that opened the modern era in politics.

Breakdown of the Old Order

As did the American Revolution, the French Revolution had its immediate origins in the financial difficulties of the government. The efforts of the ministers of King Louis XV (r. 1715–1774) to raise taxes to meet the expenses of the War of the Austrian Succession and the Seven Years' War were thwarted by the high courts, known as the parlements. The noble judges of the parlements resented this threat to their exemption from taxation and decried the government's actions as a form of royal despotism.

When renewed efforts to reform the tax system similarly failed in 1776, the government was forced to finance its enormous expenditures during the American war with borrowed money. As a result, the national debt soared. In 1786 the finance minister informed King Louis XVI (r. 1774–1792) that the nation was on the verge of bankruptcy. Fully 50 percent of France's annual budget went to interest payments on the ever-increasing debt. Another 25 percent went to maintain the military, while 6 percent was absorbed by the royal family and the court. Less than 20 percent of the national budget served the productive functions of the state, such as transportation and general administration.

Spurred by a depressed economy and falling tax receipts, Louis XVI's minister of finance revived old proposals to impose a general tax on all landed property as well as to form provincial assemblies to help administer the tax. He convinced the king to call an assembly of notables in 1787 to gain support for the idea. The assembled notables, mainly important noblemen and high-ranking clergy, declared that such sweeping tax changes required the approval of the **Estates General**, the representative body of all three estates, which had not met since 1614. Louis XVI's efforts to reject their demands failed, and in July 1788 he reluctantly called the Estates General into session.

The National Assembly

As its name indicates, the Estates General was a legislative body with representatives from the three orders of society: the clergy, nobility, and commoners. On May 5, 1789, the twelve hundred newly elected delegates of the three estates gathered in Versailles for the opening session of the Estates General. They met in an atmosphere of deepening crisis. A poor grain harvest in 1788 caused sharp increases in the price of bread, and inflation spread quickly through the economy. As a result, demand for manufactured goods collapsed, and thousands of artisans and small traders lost work.

The Estates General was almost immediately deadlocked by arguments about voting procedures. Controversy had begun during the electoral process itself when the government confirmed that, following precedent, each estate should meet and vote separately. Critics had demanded instead a single assembly dominated by the third estate. In his famous pamphlet "What Is the Third Estate?" the abbé Emmanuel Joseph Sieyès argued that the nobility was a tiny, overprivileged minority and that commoners constituted the true strength of the French nation. The government granted the third estate as many delegates as the clergy and the nobility combined, but then nullified the reform by granting one vote per estate, meaning that the two privileged estates could always outvote the third. The issue came to a crisis in June 1789 when delegates of the third estate refused to meet until the king ordered the clergy and nobility to sit with them in a single body. On June 20 the delegates of the third estate, excluded from their hall because of "repairs," moved to a large indoor tennis court where they swore the famous Oath of the Tennis Court, pledging not to disband until they had been recognized as a **National Assembly** and had written a new constitution.

The king's response was disastrously ambivalent. Although he made a conciliatory speech accepting the deputies' demands, he called a large army toward the capital to bring the Assembly under control, and on July 11 he dismissed his finance minister and other liberal ministers. On July 14, 1789, several hundred common people, angered by the king's actions and fearing he would use violence to disband the National Assembly, stormed the Bastille (ba-STEEL), a royal prison, to obtain weapons for the city's defense. Ill-judged severity on the part of the Crown thus led to the first episodes of popular violence, just as the Coercive Acts of 1774 had pushed British colonists toward the fight for independence.

Uprisings also rocked the countryside. In the summer of 1789 throughout France peasants began to rise in insurrection against their lords, ransacking manor houses and burning feudal documents that recorded their obligations. In some areas peasants reoccupied common lands enclosed by landowners and seized forests. Fear of marauders and vagabonds hired by vengeful landlords—called the Great Fear by contemporaries—seized the rural poor and fanned the flames of rebellion.

The National Assembly responded to the swell of popular anger with a surprise maneuver on the night of August 4, 1789. By a decree of the Assembly, all the old noble privileges—peasant serfdom where it still existed, exclusive hunting rights, fees for having legal cases judged in the lord's court, the right to make peasants work on the roads, and a host of other dues—were abolished along with tithes paid to the church. From this point on, French peasants would seek mainly to protect and consolidate this victory. On August 27, 1789, the Assembly further issued the Declaration of the Rights of Man and of the Citizen. This clarion call of the liberal revolutionary ideal guaranteed equality before the law, representative government for a sovereign people, and individual freedom. It was quickly disseminated throughout France, the rest of Europe, and around the world.

The National Assembly's declaration had little practical effect for the poor and hungry people of Paris. The economic crisis worsened after the fall of the Bastille, as aristocrats fled the country and the luxury market collapsed. Foreign markets also shrank, and unemployment among the urban working class grew. In addition, women—the traditional managers of food and resources in poor homes—could no longer look to the church, which had been stripped of its tithes, for aid.

Constitutional Monarchy

The next two years, until September 1791, saw the consolidation of the liberal revolution. In June 1790 the National Assembly abolished the nobility, and in July the king swore to uphold the as-yet-unwritten constitution, effectively enshrining a constitutional monarchy. The king remained the head of state, but all lawmaking power now resided in the National Assembly, elected by the wealthiest half of French males. The constitution finally passed in September 1791 was the first in French history. It legalized divorce and broadened women's rights to inherit property and to obtain financial support for illegitimate children from fathers, but excluded women from political office and voting.

This decision was attacked by a small number of men and women who believed that the rights of man should be extended to all French citizens. Olympe de Gouges (1748–1793), a self-taught writer and woman of the people, protested the evils of slavery as well as the injustices done to women. In September 1791 she published her "Declaration of the Rights of Woman." This pamphlet echoed its famous predecessor, the Declaration of the Rights of Man and of the Citizen, proclaiming, "Woman is born free and remains equal to man in rights." De Gouges's position found little sympathy among leaders of the Revolution, however.

In addition to ruling on women's rights, the National Assembly replaced the complicated patchwork of historic provinces with eighty-three departments of approximately equal size, a move toward more rational and systematic methods of administration. The deputies prohibited monopolies, guilds, and workers' associations and abolished barriers to trade within France in the name of economic liberty. Thus the National Assembly applied the spirit of the Enlightenment in a thorough reform of France's laws and institutions.

The National Assembly also imposed a radical reorganization on religious life. It granted religious freedom to the small minority of French Jews and Protestants. Furthermore, in November 1789 it nationalized the property of the Catholic Church and abolished monasteries. The government used all former church property as collateral to guarantee a new paper currency, the assignats (A-sihg-nat), and then sold the property in an attempt to put the state's finances on a solid footing.

Imbued with the rationalism and skepticism of the eighteenth-century Enlightenment philosophes, many delegates distrusted popular piety and "superstitious religion." Thus, in July 1790, with the Civil Constitution of the Clergy, they established a national church with priests chosen by voters. The National Assembly then forced the Catholic clergy to take an oath of loyalty to the new government. The pope formally condemned this measure, and only half the priests of France swore the oath. Many sincere Christians, especially those in the countryside, were also upset by these changes in the religious order. The attempt to remake the Catholic Church, like the abolition of guilds and workers' associations, sharpened the conflict between the educated classes and the common people that had been emerging in the eighteenth century.

The National Convention

The outbreak and progress of revolution in France produced great excitement and a sharp division of opinion in Europe and the United States. Liberals and radicals saw a triumph of liberty over despotism, while conservative leaders were deeply troubled by the aroused spirit of reform. In 1790 Edmund Burke published *Reflections on the Revolution in France*, one of the great expressions of European conservatism. He derided abstract principles of "liberty" and "rights" and insisted on the importance of inherited traditions and privileges as a bastion of social stability. He predicted that reform like that occurring in France would lead only to chaos and tyranny. Burke's work intensified the international debate over the French Revolution.

The kings and nobles of continental Europe, who had at first welcomed the revolution in France as weakening a competing power, now feared its impact. In June 1791 the royal family was arrested and returned to Paris after a failed attempt to escape France. To the monarchs of Austria and Prussia, the arrest of a crowned monarch was unacceptable. Two months later they issued the Declaration of Pillnitz, proclaiming their willingness to intervene in France to restore Louis XVI's rule, if necessary.

The new French representative body, called the Legislative Assembly, was dominated by members of the Jacobin Club. Political clubs had proliferated in Parisian neighborhoods since the beginning of the Revolution, drawing men and women to debate the issues of the day. The Jacobins and other deputies reacted with patriotic fury to the Declaration of Pillnitz. They said that if the kings of Europe were attempting to incite war against France, then "we will incite a war of people against kings."[1] In April 1792 France declared war on Francis II of Austria, the Habsburg monarch.

France's crusade against tyranny went poorly at first. Prussian forces joined Austria against the French, who broke and fled at their first military encounter with this First Coalition of antirevolutionary foreign powers. The Legislative Assembly declared the country in danger, and volunteers rallied to the capital. In August the Assembly suspended the king from all his functions, imprisoned him, and called for a legislative and constitutional assembly to be elected by universal male suffrage.

The fall of the monarchy marked a rapid radicalization of the Revolution. In late September 1792 a new assembly, called the National Convention, was elected by universal manhood suffrage. The Convention proclaimed France a republic, a nation in which the people, instead of a monarch, held sovereign power. Under the leadership of the Mountain, the radical faction of the Jacobin Club led by Maximilien Robespierre and Georges Jacques Danton, the Convention tried the king for treason. By a narrow majority, it found him guilty, and on January 21, 1793, Louis was executed by the guillotine, a recent invention intended to provide quick, humane executions. His wife, Marie Antoinette, suffered the same fate later that year.

In February 1793 the National Convention declared war on Britain, the Dutch Republic, and Spain. Republican France was now at war with almost all of Europe, and it faced mounting internal opposition. Peasants in western France revolted against being drafted into the army, with the Vendée region of Brittany emerging as the epicenter of revolt. Devout Catholics, royalists, and foreign agents encouraged their rebellion, and the counter-revolutionaries recruited veritable armies to fight for their cause.

By March 1793 the National Convention was locked in a life-and-death political struggle between two factions of the Jacobin Club, the radical Mountain and the more moderate Girondists. With the middle-class delegates so bitterly divided, the laboring poor of Paris once again emerged as the decisive political factor. The laboring poor and the petty traders were often known as the sans-culottes (san-koo-LAHT; "without breeches") because their men wore trousers instead of the knee breeches of the aristocracy and the bourgeoisie. They demanded radical political action to guarantee them their daily bread. The Mountain, sensing an opportunity to outmaneuver the Girondists, joined with sans-culotte activists to engineer a popular uprising. On June 2, 1793, armed sans-culottes invaded the Convention and forced its deputies to arrest twenty-nine Girondist deputies for treason. All power passed to the Mountain.

This military and political crisis led to the most radical period of the Revolution, which lasted from spring 1793 until summer 1794. To deal with threats from within and outside France, the Convention formed the Committee of Public Safety in April 1793. Led by Robespierre, the Committee held dictatorial power to deal with the national emergency, allowing it to use whatever force necessary to defend the Revolution. Robespierre and the Committee of Public Safety advanced on several fronts in 1793 and 1794. First, they collaborated with the sans-culottes, who continued pressing the common people's case for fair prices and a moral economic order. In September 1793 Robespierre and his coworkers established a planned economy with egalitarian social overtones. Rather than let supply and demand determine prices, the government set maximum allowable prices for key products. Though the state was too weak to enforce all its price regulations, it did fix the price of bread in Paris at levels the poor could afford.

The government also put the people to work producing arms, munitions, and uniforms for the war effort. The government told craftsmen what to produce, nationalized many small workshops, and requisitioned raw materials and grain. These economic reforms amounted to an emergency form of socialism, which thoroughly frightened Europe's propertied classes and greatly influenced the subsequent development of socialist ideology.

Second, while radical economic measures supplied the poor with bread and the armies with weapons, the **Reign of Terror** (1793–1794) enforced compliance with republican beliefs and practices. Special revolutionary courts tried "enemies of the nation" for political crimes. As a result, some forty thousand French men and women were executed or died in prison. Presented as a necessary measure to save the republic, the Terror was a weapon directed against all suspected of opposing the revolutionary government. As Robespierre himself put it, "Terror is nothing more than prompt, severe inflexible justice."[2] For many Europeans of the time, however, the Reign of Terror represented a frightening perversion of the ideals of 1789.

In their efforts to impose unity, the Jacobins also took actions to suppress women's participation in political debate, which they perceived as disorderly and a distraction from women's proper place in the home. On October 30, 1793, the National Convention declared, "The clubs and popular societies of women, under whatever denomination are prohibited." Among those convicted of sedition was writer Olympe de Gouges, who was sent to the guillotine in November 1793.

The third element of the Committee's program was to bring about a cultural revolution that would transform former royal subjects into republican citizens. The government sponsored revolutionary art and songs as well as secular holidays and open-air festivals to celebrate republican virtues. It also attempted to rationalize daily life by adopting the decimal system for weights and measures and a new calendar based on ten-day weeks. A campaign of de-Christianization aimed to eliminate Catholic symbols and beliefs. Fearful of the hostility aroused in rural France, however, Robespierre called for a halt to de-Christianization measures in mid-1794.

The final element in the program of the Committee of Public Safety was its appeal to a new sense of national identity and patriotism. With a common language and a common tradition reinforced by the revolutionary ideals of popular sovereignty and democracy, many French people developed an intense emotional attachment to the nation, and they saw the war against foreign opponents as a life-and-death struggle between good and evil. This was the birth of modern nationalism, the strong identification with one's nation, which would have a profound effect on subsequent European history.

To defend the nation, a decree of August 1793 imposed a draft on all unmarried young men. By January 1794 French armed forces outnumbered those of their enemies almost four to one.[3] Well trained, well equipped, and constantly indoctrinated, the enormous armies of the republic were led by young, impetuous generals. These generals often had risen from the ranks, and they personified the opportunities the Revolution offered gifted sons of the people. By spring 1794 French armies were victorious on all fronts and domestic revolt was largely suppressed. The republic was saved.

The Directory

The success of French armies led the Committee of Public Safety to relax emergency economic controls, but they extended the political Reign of Terror. The revolutionary tribunals sent many critics to the guillotine, including long-standing collaborators who Robespierre believed had turned against him. A group of radicals and moderates in the Convention, knowing that they might be next, organized a conspiracy. They howled down Robespierre when he tried to speak to the National Convention on July 27, 1794 — a date known as 9 Thermidor according to France's newly adopted republican calendar. The next day it was Robespierre's turn to be guillotined.

The respectable middle-class lawyers and professionals who had led the liberal Revolution of 1789 then reasserted their authority. This period of **Thermidorian reaction**, as it was called, harkened back to the beginnings of the Revolution, rejecting the radicalism of the sans-culottes in favor of moderate policies that favored

The Execution of Robespierre
Completely wooden except for the heavy iron blade, the guillotine was devised by a French revolutionary doctor named Guillotin as a humane method of execution. The guillotine was painted red for Robespierre's execution, a detail not captured in this black-and-white engraving of the 1794 event. Large crowds witnessed the execution in a majestic public square in central Paris, then known as the Place de la Revolution and now called the Place de la Concorde (Harmony Square). (Photo © Tarker/The Bridgeman Art Library)

property owners. In 1795 the National Convention abolished many economic controls, let prices rise sharply, and severely restricted local political organizations through which the sans-culottes exerted their strength. In addition, the middle-class members of the National Convention wrote a new constitution restricting eligibility to serve as a deputy to men of substantial means. Real power lay with a new five-man executive body, called the Directory. France's new rulers continued to support military expansion abroad, but war was no longer so much a crusade as a response to economic problems. Large, victorious armies reduced unemployment at home. However, the French people quickly grew weary of the corruption and ineffectiveness that characterized the Directory. This general dissatisfaction revealed itself clearly in the national elections of 1797, which returned a large number of conservative and even monarchist deputies. Fearing for their survival, the Directory used the army to nullify the elections and began to govern dictatorially. Two years later Napoleon Bonaparte ended the Directory in a coup d'état (koo day-TAH) and substituted a strong dictatorship for a weak one. While claiming to uphold revolutionary values, Napoleon would install authoritarian rule.

Napoleon's Europe, 1799–1815

How did Napoleon Bonaparte assume control of France and much of Europe, and what factors led to his downfall?

For almost fifteen years, from 1799 to 1814, France was in the hands of a keen-minded military dictator of exceptional ability. Napoleon Bonaparte (1769–1821) realized the need to put an end to civil strife in France in order to create unity and consolidate his rule. And he did. But Napoleon saw himself as a man of destiny, and the glory of war and the dream of universal empire proved irresistible.

Napoleon's Rule of France

Born on the Mediterranean island of Corsica into an impoverished noble family, Napoleon left home and became a lieutenant in the French artillery in 1785. Rising rapidly in the new army, Napoleon was placed in command of French forces in Italy and won brilliant victories there in 1796 and 1797. His next campaign, in Egypt, was a failure, but Napoleon returned to France before the fiasco was generally known, and his reputation remained intact. French aggression in Egypt and elsewhere provoked the British to organize a new alliance in 1798, the Second Coalition, which included Austria and Russia.

Napoleon soon learned that some prominent members of the legislature were plotting against the Directory. The dissatisfaction of these plotters stemmed not so much from the fact that the Directory was a dictatorship as from the fact that it was a weak dictatorship. To these disillusioned revolutionaries, ten years of upheaval and uncertainty had made firm rule much more appealing than liberty and popular politics.

The young Napoleon, nationally revered for his heroism, was an ideal figure of authority. On November 9, 1799, Napoleon and his conspirators ousted the Directors, and the following day soldiers disbanded the legislature. Napoleon was named first consul of the republic, and a new constitution consolidating his position was overwhelmingly approved in a plebiscite in December 1799. Republican appearances were maintained, but Napoleon became the real ruler of France.

The Coronation of Napoleon, 1804   In this detail from a grandiose painting by Jacques-Louis David, Napoleon, instead of the pope, prepares to crown his wife, Josephine, in an elaborate ceremony in Notre Dame Cathedral. Napoleon, the ultimate upstart, also crowned himself. Pope Pius VII, seated glumly behind the emperor, is reduced to being a spectator. (Jacques-Louis David [1748–1825]/Louvre, Paris, France/The Bridgeman Art Library)

Napoleon's domestic policy centered on using his popularity and charisma to maintain order and end civil strife. He did so by appeasing powerful groups in France, offering them favors in return for loyal service. Napoleon's bargain with the middle class was codified in the famous Civil Code of March 1804, also known as the **Napoleonic Code**, which reasserted two of the fundamental principles of the Revolution of 1789: equality of all male citizens before the law and absolute security of wealth and private property. Napoleon and the leading bankers of Paris established the privately owned Bank of France in 1800, which served the interests of both the state and the financial oligarchy. Napoleon won over peasants by defending the gains in land and status they had won during the Revolution.

At the same time, Napoleon consolidated his rule by recruiting disillusioned revolutionaries for the network of government officials; they depended on him and came to serve him well. Nor were members of the old nobility slighted. In 1800 and again in 1802 Napoleon granted amnesty to one hundred thousand noble émigrés on the condition that they return to France and take a loyalty oath. Members of this returning elite soon occupied high posts in the expanding centralized state. Napoleon also created a new imperial nobility to reward his most talented generals and officials.

Furthermore, Napoleon sought to restore the Catholic Church in France so that it could serve as a bulwark of social stability. Napoleon and Pope Pius VII (pontificate 1800–1823) signed the Concordat of 1801. Under this agreement the pope gained the right for French Catholics to practice their religion freely, but Napoleon gained political power: his government now nominated bishops, paid the clergy, and exerted great influence over the church in France.

The domestic reforms of Napoleon's early years were his greatest achievement. Much of his legal and administrative reorganization has survived in France to this day, but order and unity had a price: authoritarian rule. Women lost many of the gains they had made in the 1790s. Under the Napoleonic Code, women were dependents of either their fathers or their husbands, and they could not make contracts or have bank accounts in their own names. Napoleon aimed at re-establishing a family monarchy, where the power of the husband and father was as absolute over the wife and the children as that of Napoleon over his subjects. He also curtailed free speech and freedom of the press and manipulated voting in the occasional elections. After 1810 political suspects were held in state prisons, as they had been during the Terror.

Napoleon's Expansion in Europe

Napoleon was above all a great military man. After coming to power in 1799, he sent peace feelers to Austria and Britain, the dominant powers of the Second Coalition. When these overtures were rejected, French armies led by Napoleon decisively defeated the Austrians. Subsequent treaties with Austria in 1801 and Britain in 1802 consolidated France's hold on the territories its armies had won up to that point.

In 1802 Napoleon was secure but still driven to expand his power. Aggressively redrawing the map of German-speaking lands so as to weaken Austria and encourage the secondary states of southwestern Germany to side with France, Napoleon tried to restrict British trade with all of Europe. He then plotted to attack Britain, but his Mediterranean fleet was destroyed by Lord Nelson at the Battle of Trafalgar on October 21, 1805. Renewed fighting had its advantages, however, for the first consul used his high status as a military leader to have himself proclaimed emperor in late 1804.

Austria, Russia, and Sweden joined with Britain to form the Third Coalition against France shortly before the Battle of Trafalgar. Yet the Austrians and the Russians were no match for Napoleon, who scored a brilliant victory over them at the Battle of Austerlitz in December 1805. Russia decided to pull back, and Austria accepted large territorial losses in return for peace as the Third Coalition collapsed.

Napoleon then reorganized the German states to his liking. In 1806 he abolished many tiny German states as well as the Holy Roman Empire and established by decree the German Confederation of the Rhine, a union of fifteen German states minus Austria, Prussia, and Saxony. Naming himself "protector" of the confederation, Napoleon firmly controlled western Germany.

Napoleon's intervention in German affairs alarmed the Prussians, who mobilized their armies. In October 1806 Napoleon attacked them and won two more brilliant victories at Jena and Auerstädt, where the Prussians were outnumbered two to one. The war with Prussia, now joined by Russia, continued into the following spring. After Napoleon's larger armies won another victory, Alexander I of Russia was ready to negotiate for peace. In the treaties of Tilsit in 1807, Prussia lost half its population through land concessions, while Russia accepted Napoleon's reorganization of western and central Europe and promised to enforce Napoleon's economic blockade against British goods.

The Grand Empire and Its End

Increasingly, Napoleon saw himself as the emperor of Europe, not just of France. The so-called **Grand Empire** he built had three parts. The core, or first part, was an ever-expanding France, which by 1810 included Belgium, Holland, parts of northern Italy, and much German territory on the east bank of the Rhine (Map 22.1). The second part consisted of a number of dependent satellite kingdoms. The third part comprised the independent but allied states of Austria, Prussia, and Russia. After 1806 both satellites and allies were expected to support Napoleon's **Continental System**, a blockade in which no ship coming from Britain or its colonies was permitted to dock at any port that was controlled by the French. The blockade was intended to halt all trade between Britain and continental Europe, thereby destroying the British economy and its military force.

The impact of the Grand Empire on the peoples of Europe was considerable. In the areas incorporated into France and in the satellites, Napoleon abolished feudal dues and serfdom. Yet he had to put the prosperity and special interests of France first in order to safeguard his power base. Levying heavy taxes in money and men for his armies, Napoleon came to be regarded more as a conquering tyrant than as an enlightened liberator. Thus French rule sparked patriotic upheavals and encouraged the growth of reactive nationalism.

The first great revolt occurred in Spain. In 1808 Napoleon deposed Spanish king Ferdinand VII and placed his own brother Joseph on the throne. A coalition of Catholics, monarchists, and patriots rebelled against this attempt to turn Spain into a satellite of France. French armies occupied Madrid, but the foes of Napoleon fled to the hills and waged uncompromising guerrilla warfare. Events in Spain sent a clear warning: resistance to French imperialism was growing.

Yet Napoleon pushed on. In 1810, when the Grand Empire was at its height, Britain still remained at war with France, helping the guerrillas in Spain and Portugal. The Continental System was a failure. Instead of harming Britain, the system provoked the British to set up a counter-blockade, which created hard times for French consumers. Perhaps looking for a scapegoat, Napoleon turned on Alexander I of Russia, who in 1811 openly repudiated Napoleon's prohibitions against British goods.

Napoleon's invasion of Russia began in June 1812 with a force that eventually numbered 600,000, probably the largest force yet assembled in a single army. Only one-third of this army was French, however; nationals of all the satellites and allies were drafted into the operation. Originally planning to winter in the Russian city of Smolensk, Napoleon recklessly pressed on toward Moscow (see Map 22.1). The Battle of Borodino that followed was a draw. Alexander ordered the evacuation of Moscow, which the Russians then burned in part, and he refused to negotiate. Finally, after five weeks in the scorched city, Napoleon ordered a disastrous retreat. The Russian army, the Russian winter, and starvation cut Napoleon's army to pieces. When the frozen remnants staggered into Poland and Prussia in December, 370,000 men had died and another 200,000 had been taken prisoner.[4]

Leaving his troops to their fate, Napoleon raced to Paris to raise another army. Meanwhile, Austria and Prussia deserted Napoleon and joined Russia and Britain in the Treaty of Chaumont in March 1814, by which the four powers formed the Quadruple Alliance to defeat the French emperor. Less than a month later, on April 4, 1814,

MAP 22.1 Napoleonic Europe in 1812 At the height of the Grand Empire in 1810, Napoleon had conquered or allied with every major European power except Britain. But in 1812, angered by Russian repudiation of his ban on trade with Britain, Napoleon invaded Russia with disastrous results. Compare this map with Map 18.2 (page 532), which shows the division of Europe in 1715.

a defeated Napoleon abdicated his throne. After this unconditional abdication, the victorious allies exiled Napoleon to the island of Elba off the coast of Italy.

In February 1815 Napoleon staged a daring escape from Elba. Landing in France, he issued appeals for support and marched on Paris. French officers and soldiers who had fought so long for their emperor responded to the call. But Napoleon's gamble was a desperate long shot, for the allies were united against him. At the end of a frantic period known as the Hundred Days, they crushed his forces at Waterloo on June 18, 1815, and imprisoned him on the island of St. Helena, off the western coast of Africa. The restored Bourbon dynasty took power under Louis XVIII, a younger brother of Louis XVI.

The Haitian Revolution, 1791–1804

How did slave revolt on colonial Saint-Domingue lead to the creation of the independent nation of Haiti in 1804?

The events that led to the creation of the independent nation of Haiti constitute the third, and perhaps most extraordinary, chapter of the revolutionary era in the Atlantic world. Prior to 1789 Saint-Domingue, the French colony that was to become Haiti, reaped huge profits through a ruthless system of slave-based plantation agriculture. News of revolution in France lit a powder keg of contradictory aspirations among white planters, free people of color, and slaves. While revolutionary authorities debated how far to extend the rights of man on Saint-Domingue, free people of color and, later, the enslaved took matters into their own hands, rising up to claim their freedom. They succeeded, despite invasion by the British and Spanish and Napoleon Bonaparte's bid to reimpose French control. In 1804 Haiti became the only nation in history to claim its freedom through slave revolt.

Revolutionary Aspirations in Saint-Domingue

On the eve of the French Revolution, Saint-Domingue — the most profitable of all Caribbean colonies — was even more rife with social tensions than France itself. The colony, which occupied the western third of the island of Hispaniola, was inhabited by a variety of social groups who resented and mistrusted one another. The European population included French colonial officials, wealthy plantation owners and merchants, and poor artisans and clerks. Vastly outnumbering the white population were the colony's five hundred thousand enslaved people, along with a sizable population of some forty thousand free people of African and mixed African and European descent. Members of this last group referred to themselves as "free people of color."

Legal and economic conditions on Saint-Domingue vastly favored the white population. Most of the island's enslaved population performed grueling toil in the island's sugar plantations. The highly outnumbered planters used extremely harsh methods, such as beating, maiming, and executing slaves, to maintain their control. The 1685 Code Noir (Black Code) that legally regulated slavery was intended to provide minimal standards of humane treatment, but its tenets were rarely enforced. Masters calculated that they could earn more by working slaves ruthlessly and purchasing new ones when they died than by providing the food, rest, and medical care needed to allow the enslaved population to reproduce naturally. This meant that a constant inflow of newly enslaved people from Africa was necessary to work the plantations.

Saint-Domingue Slave Life   Although the brutal conditions of plantation slavery left little time or energy for leisure, slaves on Saint-Domingue took advantage of their day of rest on Sunday to engage in social and religious activities. The law officially prohibited slaves of different masters from mingling together, but such gatherings were often tolerated if they remained peaceful. This image depicts a fight between two slaves, precisely the type of unrest and violence feared by authorities. (Musée du Nouveau Monde, La Rochelle, France/Scala/White Images/Art Resource, NY)

Despite their brutality, slaveholders on Saint-Domingue freed a certain number of their slaves, mostly their own mixed-race children, thereby producing one of the largest populations of free people of color in any slaveholding colony. The Code Noir had originally granted free people of color the same legal status as whites: they could own property, live where they wished, and pursue any education or career they desired. From the 1760s on, however, colonial administrators began rescinding these rights, and by the time of the French Revolution many aspects of the lives of free people of color were ruled by discriminatory laws.

The political and intellectual turmoil of the 1780s, with its growing rhetoric of liberty, equality, and fraternity, raised new challenges and possibilities for each of Saint-Domingue's social groups. For enslaved people, who constituted approximately 90 percent of the population, news of abolitionist movements in France led to hopes that the mother country might grant them freedom. Free people of color looked to reforms in Paris as a means of gaining political enfranchisement and reasserting equal status with whites. The white elite, however, was determined to protect its way of life, including slaveholding. They looked to revolutionary ideals of representative government for the chance to gain control of their own affairs, as had the American colonists before them.

The National Assembly frustrated the hopes of all these groups. Cowed by colonial representatives who claimed that support for free people of color would result in slave insurrection, the Assembly refused to extend French constitutional safeguards to the colonies. After dealing this blow to the aspirations of nonwhites, the Assembly also reaffirmed French monopolies over colonial trade, thereby angering planters as well. Like the American settlers did earlier, the colonists chafed under the rule of the mother country.

In July 1790 Vincent Ogé (aw-ZHAY) (ca. 1750–1791), a free man of color, returned to Saint-Domingue from Paris determined to win rights for his people. He raised an army of several hundred and sent letters to the new Provincial Assembly of Saint-Domingue demanding political rights for all free citizens. When Ogé's demands were flatly refused, he and his followers turned to armed insurrection. After initial victories, his army was defeated, and Ogé was tortured and executed by colonial officials. Revolutionary leaders in Paris were more sympathetic to Ogé's cause. In May 1791, responding to what it perceived as partly justified grievances, the National Assembly granted political rights to free people of color born to two free parents who possessed sufficient property. When news of this legislation arrived in Saint-Domingue, the white elite was furious, and the colonial governor refused to enact it. Violence then erupted between groups of whites and free people of color in parts of the colony.

The Outbreak of Revolt

Just as the sans-culottes helped push forward more radical reforms in France, the second stage of revolution in Saint-Domingue also resulted from decisive action from below. In August 1791 slaves, who had witnessed the confrontation between whites and free people of color for over a year, took events into their own hands. Groups of slaves held a series of nighttime meetings to plan a mass insurrection. In doing so, they drew on their own considerable military experience; the majority of slaves had been born in Africa, and many had served in the civil wars of the kingdom of Kongo and other conflicts before being taken into slavery.[5] They also drew on a long tradition of slave resistance prior to 1791, which had ranged from work slowdowns, to running away, to taking part in African-derived religious rituals and dances known as *vodou* (or voodoo). According to some sources, the August 1791 pact to take up arms was sealed by such a voodoo ritual.

Revolts began on a few plantations on the night of August 22. Within a few days the uprising had swept much of the northern plain, creating a slave army estimated at around 2,000 individuals. By August 27 it was described by one observer as "10,000 strong, divided into 3 armies, of whom 700 or 800 are on horseback, and tolerably well-armed."[6] During the next month enslaved combatants attacked and destroyed hundreds of sugar and coffee plantations.

On April 4, 1792, as war loomed with the European states, the National Assembly issued a decree extending full citizenship rights, including the right to vote, to free people of color. As in France, voting rights and the ability to hold public office applied to men only. The Assembly hoped this measure would win the loyalty of free men of color and their aid in defeating the slave rebellion.

Warfare in Europe soon spread to Saint-Domingue (Map 22.2). Since the beginning of the slave insurrection, the Spanish colony of Santo Domingo, on the eastern

MAP 22.2   **The War of Haitian Independence, 1791–1804**   Neighbored by the Spanish colony of Santo Domingo, Saint-Domingue was the most profitable European colony in the Caribbean. In 1791 slave revolts erupted in the north near Le Cap, which had once been the capital. In 1770 the French had transferred the capital to Port-au-Prince, which in 1804 became capital of the newly independent Haiti.

side of the island of Hispaniola, had supported rebel slaves. In early 1793 the Spanish began to bring slave leaders and their soldiers into the Spanish army. Toussaint L'Ouverture (TOO-sahn LOO-vair-toor) (1743–1803), a freed slave who had joined the revolt, was named a Spanish officer. In September the British navy blockaded the colony, and invading British troops captured French territory on the island. For the Spanish and British, revolutionary chaos provided a tempting opportunity to capture a profitable colony.

Desperate for forces to oppose France's enemies, commissioners sent by the newly elected National Convention promised freedom to slaves who fought for France. By October 1793 the commissioners had abolished slavery throughout the colony. On February 4, 1794, the Convention ratified the abolition of slavery and extended it to all French territories, including the Caribbean colonies of Martinique and Guadeloupe.

The tide of battle began to turn when Toussaint L'Ouverture switched sides, bringing his military and political skills, along with four thousand well-trained soldiers, to support the French war effort. By 1796 the French had regained control of the colony, and L'Ouverture had emerged as a key military leader. (See "Individuals in Society: Toussaint L'Ouverture," page 678.) In May 1796 he was named commander of the western province of Saint-Domingue (see Map 22.2). The increasingly conservative nature of the French government during the Thermidorian reaction, however, threatened to undo the gains made by former slaves and free people of color.

The War of Haitian Independence

With Toussaint L'Ouverture acting increasingly as an independent ruler of the western province of Saint-Domingue, another general, André Rigaud (1761–1811), set up his own government in the southern peninsula. Tensions mounted between L'Ouverture and Rigaud. While L'Ouverture was a freed slave of African descent, Rigaud belonged to an elite group of free people of color. This elite resented the growing power of former slaves like L'Ouverture, who in turn accused the elite of adopting the prejudices of white settlers. Civil war broke out between the two sides in 1799, when L'Ouverture's forces, led by his lieutenant, Jean Jacques Dessalines (1758–1806), invaded the south. Victory over Rigaud in 1800 gave L'Ouverture control of the entire colony.

This victory was soon challenged by Napoleon, who had his own plans for using the profits from a re-established system of plantation slavery as a basis for expanding the French empire. Napoleon ordered his brother-in-law, General Charles-Victor-Emmanuel Leclerc (1772–1802), to lead an expedition to the island to crush the new regime. In 1802 Leclerc landed in Saint-Domingue and ordered the arrest of Toussaint L'Ouverture. The rebel leader was deported to France, along with his family, where he died in 1803.

It was left to L'Ouverture's lieutenant, Jean Jacques Dessalines, to unite the resistance, and he led it to a crushing victory over French forces. On January 1, 1804, Dessalines formally declared the independence of Saint-Domingue and the creation of the new sovereign nation of Haiti, the name used by the pre-Columbian inhabitants of the island.

Haiti, the second independent state in the Americas and the first in Latin America, was born from the only successful large-scale slave revolt in history. This event spread shock and fear through slaveholding societies in the Caribbean and the United States, bringing to life their worst nightmares of the utter reversal of power and privilege. Fearing the spread of slave rebellion to the United States, President Thomas Jefferson refused to recognize Haiti. The liberal proponents of the American Revolution thus chose to protect slavery at the expense of revolutionary ideals of universal human rights. Yet Haitian independence had fundamental repercussions for world history, helping spread the idea that liberty, equality, and fraternity must apply to all people. The next phase of Atlantic revolution soon opened in the Spanish-American colonies.

Revolution in the Spanish Empire

Why and how did the Spanish and Portuguese colonies of North and South America shake off European domination and develop into national states?

In 1800 the Spanish Empire in the Americas stretched from the headwaters of the Mississippi River in present-day Minnesota to the tip of Cape Horn in the Antarctic (see Map 22.3, page 682). Spain believed that the great wealth of the Americas existed for its benefit, a stance that fostered bitterness and the desire for independence in the

INDIVIDUALS IN SOCIETY • Toussaint L'Ouverture

Little is known of the early life of Saint-Domingue's brilliant military and political leader Toussaint L'Ouverture. He was born in 1743 on a plantation outside Le Cap owned by the Count de Bréda. According to tradition, L'Ouverture was the eldest son of a captured African prince from modern-day Benin. Toussaint Bréda, as he was then called, occupied a privileged position among slaves. Instead of performing backbreaking labor in the fields, he served his master as a coachman and livestock keeper. He also learned to read and write French and some Latin, but he was always more comfortable with the Creole dialect.

During the 1770s the plantation manager emancipated L'Ouverture, who subsequently leased his own small coffee plantation, worked by slaves. He married Suzanne Simone, who already had one son, and the couple had another son during their marriage. In 1791 he joined the slave uprisings that swept Saint-Domingue, and he took on the *nom de guerre* (war name) L'Ouverture, meaning "the opening." L'Ouverture rose to prominence among rebel slaves allied with Spain and by early 1794 controlled his own army. A devout Catholic who led a frugal and ascetic life, L'Ouverture impressed others with his enormous physical energy, intellectual acumen, and air of mystery. In 1794 he defected to the French side and led his troops to a series of victories against the Spanish. In 1795 the National Convention promoted L'Ouverture to brigadier general.

Over the next three years L'Ouverture successively eliminated rivals for authority on the island. First he freed himself of the French commissioners sent to govern the colony. With a firm grip on power in the northern province, L'Ouverture defeated General André Rigaud in 1800 to gain control in the south. His army then marched on the capital of Spanish Santo Domingo on the eastern half of the island, meeting little resistance. The entire island of Hispaniola was now under his command.

With control in his hands, L'Ouverture was confronted with the challenge of building a post-emancipation society, the first of its kind. The task was made even more difficult by the chaos wreaked by war, the destruction of plantations, and

colonies. Between 1806 and 1825 the Spanish colonies in Latin America were convulsed by upheavals that ultimately resulted in their separation from Spain. Until 1898 Spain did, however, retain its Caribbean colonies of Cuba and Puerto Rico.

The Origins of the Revolutions Against Colonial Powers

The Latin American movements for independence drew strength from unfair taxation and trade policies, Spain's declining control over its Latin American colonies, racial and class discrimination, and the spread of revolutionary ideas. By the eighteenth century the Spanish colonies had become self-sufficient producers of foodstuffs, wine, textiles, and consumer goods, though Spain maintained monopolies on alcohol and tobacco and the colonies traded with each other. In Peru, for example, domestic agriculture supported the large mining settlements, and the colony did not have to import food. Craft workshops owned by the state or by private individuals produced consumer bitter social and racial tensions. For L'Ouverture the most pressing concern was to re-establish the plantation economy. Without revenue to pay his army, the gains of the rebellion could be lost. He therefore encouraged white planters to return and reclaim their property. He also adopted harsh policies toward former slaves, forcing them back to their plantations and restricting their ability to acquire land. When they resisted, he sent troops across the island to enforce submission. L'Ouverture's 1801 constitution reaffirmed his draconian labor policies and named L'Ouverture governor for life, leaving Saint-Domingue as a colony in name alone. In June 1802 French forces arrested L'Ouverture and jailed him at Fort de Joux in France's Jura Mountains near the Swiss border. He died of pneumonia on April 7, 1803, leaving his lieutenant, Jean Jacques Dessalines, to win independence for the new Haitian nation.

QUESTIONS FOR ANALYSIS

1. Toussaint L'Ouverture was both slave and slave owner. How did each experience shape his life and actions?

2. What did L'Ouverture and Napoleon Bonaparte have in common? How did they differ?

LaunchPad
ONLINE DOCUMENT PROJECT

How did the French Revolution affect France's Caribbean colonies? Examine reactions of slaves and free men of color to the French Revolution, and then complete a quiz and writing assignment based on the evidence and details from this chapter.

See inside the front cover to learn more.

goods for the working class; what was not manufactured locally was bought from Mexico and transported by the Peruvian merchant marine.

Spain's humiliating defeat in the War of the Spanish Succession (1701–1713; see page 545) prompted demands for sweeping reform of all of Spain's institutions, including its colonial policies and practices. The new Bourbon dynasty, descended from the ruling house of France, initiated a decades-long effort known as the Bourbon reforms, which aimed to improve administrative efficiency and increase central control. Reform took on new urgency after Spain's expensive and lackluster participation in the Seven Years' War. Under Charles III (r. 1759–1788), Spanish administrators drew on Enlightenment ideals of rationalism and progress to strengthen colonial rule and thereby increase the fortunes and power of the Spanish state. They created a permanent standing army and enlarged colonial militias. To bring the church under tighter control, they expelled the powerful and wealthy Jesuit order (which had already been exiled from Portugal, Brazil, and France). They also ceased the appointment of Creoles to state posts and followed the Bourbon tradition of dispatching intendants (government commissioners) from the mother country with extensive new powers over justice, administration, tax collection, and military affairs.

Additionally, Spain ended its centuries-old policy of insisting on monopoly over trade with its colonies. Instead it adopted a policy of free trade in order to compete with Great Britain and Holland in the struggle for empire. In Latin America these actions stimulated the production of agricultural commodities that were in demand in Europe, such as coffee, sugar, leather, and salted beef. Between 1778 and 1788 the volume of Spain's trade with the colonies soared, possibly by as much as 700 percent.[7] Colonial manufacturing, however, which had been growing steadily, suffered a heavy blow under free trade. Colonial textiles and china, for example, could not compete with cheap Spanish products.

Madrid's tax reforms also aggravated discontent. Like Great Britain, Spain believed its colonies should bear some of the costs of their own defense. Accordingly, Madrid raised the prices of its monopoly products — tobacco and liquor — and increased sales taxes on many items. War with revolutionary France in the 1790s led to additional taxes and forced loans. As a result, protest movements in Latin America, like those in British North America in the 1770s, claimed that the colonies were being unfairly taxed. Moreover, new taxes took a heavy toll on indigenous communities, which bore the brunt of all forms of taxation and suffered from the corruption and brutality of tax collectors. Riots and protest movements met with harsh repression.

Political conflicts beyond the colonies also helped drive aspirations for independence. The French Revolution and the Napoleonic Wars, which involved France's occupation of Spain and Britain's domination of the seas, isolated Spain from Latin America. As Spain's control over its Latin American colonies diminished, foreign traders, especially from the United States, swarmed into Spanish-American ports. In 1796 the Madrid government made exceptions to its trade restrictions for countries not engaged in the Napoleonic Wars, such as the United States, thus acknowledging Spain's inability to supply the colonies with needed goods and markets.

Racial, ethnic, and class privileges also fueled discontent. The Creoles — people of Spanish or other European descent born in the Americas (see page 583) — resented the economic and political dominance of the peninsulares (puh-nihn-suh-LUHR-ayz), as the colonial officials and other natives of Spain or Portugal were called. In 1800 there were about thirty thousand peninsulares and 3.5 million Creoles. Peninsulares controlled the rich export-import trade, intercolonial trade, and mining industries and increasingly replaced Creoles in administrative positions. The Creoles wanted to free themselves from Spain and Portugal and to rule the colonies themselves. They had little interest in improving the lot of the Indians, the mestizos of mixed Spanish and Indian background, or the mulattos of mixed Spanish and African heritage.

As in Saint-Domingue, a racial backlash against the growing numbers and social prominence of people of mixed racial origin occurred in the last quarter of the eighteenth century. In 1776 King Charles III outlawed marriages between whites and any person with Indian or African blood. The cabildos (municipal councils) of cities like Lima, Caracas, and Buenos Aires issued ordinances prohibiting nonwhites from joining guilds, serving in the militia, and mixing with whites in public.

A final factor contributing to rebellion was cultural and intellectual ideas. One set of such ideas was the Enlightenment thought of Montesquieu, Voltaire, and Rousseau, which had been trickling into Latin America for decades (see Chapter 19). North American ships calling at South American ports introduced the subversive writings of Thomas Paine and Thomas Jefferson. In 1794 the Colombian Antonio Nariño translated and published the French Declaration of the Rights of Man and of the Citizen. (Spanish authorities sentenced him to ten years in an African prison, but he lived to become the father of Colombian independence.) By 1800 the Creole elite throughout Latin America was familiar with liberal Enlightenment political thought and its role in inspiring colonial revolt.

Another important set of ideas consisted of indigenous traditions of justice and political rule, which often looked back to an idealized precolonial past. During the eighteenth century these ideas served as a rallying point for Indians and non-Indians alike, roused by anger against the Spanish. As Spain was increasingly reviled as cruel and despotic, indigenous culture and history were celebrated. Creoles took advantage of indigenous symbols, but this did not mean they were prepared to view Indians and mestizos as equals.

Resistance, Rebellion, and Independence

The mid-eighteenth century witnessed frequent Andean Indian rebellions against increased taxation and other impositions of the Bourbon crown. In 1780, under the leadership of a descendant of the Inca rulers who took the name Tupac Amaru II, a massive insurrection exploded. Indian chieftains from the Cuzco region (Map 22.3) gathered a powerful force of Indians and people of mixed race. Rebellion swept across highland Peru, where many Spanish officials were executed. Creoles joined forces with Spaniards and Indian nobles to crush the rebellion, shocked by the radical social and economic reforms promised by its leaders. A hundred thousand Indians were killed and vast amounts of property destroyed. The government was obliged to concede to some of the rebels' demands by abolishing the repartimiento system, which required Indians to buy goods solely from tax collectors, and establishing assemblies of local representatives in Cuzco.

As news of the rebellion of Tupac Amaru II trickled northward, it helped stimulate the 1781 Comuneros Revolt in the New Granada viceroyalty (see Map 22.3). In this uprising, an Indian and mestizo peasant army commanded by Creole captains marched on Bogotá to protest high taxation and state monopolies on liquor and tobacco. Dispersed by the ruling Spanish, who made promises they did not intend to keep, the revolt in the end did little to improve the Indians' lives.

These two revolts (and the many smaller riots and uprisings that broke out through the eighteenth century) shook authorities, but their ties to the independence movements that followed are indirect. Led from below, these uprisings did not question monarchical rule or the colonial relationship between Spain and Spanish America. Instead two events outside of Spanish America did more to shape the ensuing struggle for independence. First, the revolution on Saint-Domingue and the subsequent independence of the nation of Haiti in 1804 convinced Creole elites, many of whom were slaveholders, of the dangers of slave revolt and racial warfare (see Map 22.2). Their

Before independence

Spanish colonies

- Viceroyalty of New Spain
- Viceroyalty of New Granada
- Viceroyalty of Peru and Audiencia of Chile
- Viceroyalty of Rio de la Plata

Portuguese colonies

- Viceroyalty of Brazil
- ✕ Silver mine

Effective frontier of Spanish settlement

40°N

NEW FRANCE
(Conquered by England, 1760)

ENGLISH COLONIES
(Independence declared, 1776)

COAHUILA

Gulf of Mexico

VICEROYALTY OF NEW SPAIN

BAJIO LEÓN (1535)

Guadalajara ✕ Zacatecas

Mexico City ✕ Guanajuato

Veracruz

20°N

FLORIDA
(Ceded to England, 1763–1783)

Havana

HAITI [SAINT-DOMINGUE]
(Ceded to France, 1697)

PUERTO RICO

BRITISH HONDURAS   JAMAICA   SANTO DOMINGO
(Conquered by England, 1655)

Guatemala

Caribbean Sea

ATLANTIC OCEAN

Caracas

0°   Equator

Bogotá

VICEROYALTY OF NEW GRANADA
(Separated from Viceroyalty of Peru, 1717, 1739)

Quito

GUIANA

Amazon R.

VICEROYALTY OF PERU
(1590s)

Lima   Cuzco

PACIFIC OCEAN

La Paz

Chuquisaca
(La Plata; Sucre)

VICEROYALTY OF BRAZIL
(1720)

Salvador

Potosí

20°S

ANDES

São Paulo   Rio de Janeiro
(Capital, 1763)

VICEROYALTY OF RIO DE LA PLATA
(Separated from Viceroyalty of Peru, 1776)

Santiago

AUDIENCIA OF CHILE
(Retained by Viceroyalty of Peru, 1776)

Buenos Aires   Montevideo

N   W   E   S

40°S

Claimed but not settled by Spain

Islas Malvinas
(Falkland Islands)

0   500   1,000 miles
0   500   1,000 kilometers

Cape Horn

120°W   100°W   80°W   60°W   40°W   20°W

MAP 22.3   Latin America in ca. 1780 (above) and 1830 (opposite) By 1830 almost all of Central America, South America, and the Caribbean islands had won independence. Note that the many nations that now make up Central America were unified when they first won independence from Mexico. Similarly, modern Venezuela, Colombia, and Ecuador were still joined in Gran Colombia.

In 1830

1811 Year independence gained

Colony

OREGON COUNTRY (Joint U.S.-British occupation)

BRITISH NORTH AMERICA (CANADA) (Gr. Br.)

ATLANTIC OCEAN

UNITED STATES 1783

San Antonio

MEXICO 1821

Gulf of Mexico

Mexico City
Veracruz

BAHAMA IS. (Gr. Br.)

Havana
CUBA (Spain)

HAITI 1804

PUERTO RICO (Spain)

BRITISH HONDURAS (Gr. Br.)
Guatemala City
GUATEMALA

JAMAICA (Gr. Br.)

Caribbean Sea

UNITED PROVINCES OF CENTRAL AMERICA 1823–1839

Panama

Caracas
VENEZUELA
Socorro
Bogotá

TRINIDAD (Gr. Br.)
BR. GUIANA (Gr. Br.)
DUTCH GUIANA (Neth.)
FRENCH GUIANA (France)

GRAN COLOMBIA 1819–1830

Equator
Galápagos Islands

Quito
ECUADOR

PACIFIC OCEAN

Lima
PERU 1824

EMPIRE OF BRAZIL 1822

Salvador

La Paz
BOLIVIA 1825
Sucre

Rio de Janeiro
São Paulo

PARAGUAY 1811
UNITED PROVINCES OF THE RIO DE LA PLATA 1816

URUGUAY 1828

N
W E
S

Santiago
CHILE 1817

ARGENTINA
Buenos Aires

Montevideo

PATAGONIA (Disputed between Argentina and Chile)

0   500   1,000 miles
0   500   1,000 kilometers

120°W   100°W   80°W   60°W   40°W   20°W

Islas Malvinas (Falkland Islands)

40°N

20°N

0°

20°S

40°S

plans and strategies would henceforth be shaped by their determination to avoid a similar outcome in Spanish America.

Second, in 1808 Napoleon Bonaparte deposed Spanish king Ferdinand VII and placed his own brother on the Spanish throne (see page 671). The Creoles in Latin America claimed that the removal of the legitimate king shifted sovereignty to the people — that is, to themselves. Like the patriots in British North America, the Creoles who led the various movements for independence had no desire for a radical redistribution of property or a new social order. They merely rejected the authority of the Spanish crown. Cabildos in cities like Buenos Aires and Caracas took power into their own hands, ostensibly on behalf of Ferdinand, the deposed king.

The great hero of the movement for independence was Simón Bolívar (1783–1830), who was born into a wealthy land- and slave-owning family and went on to become a very able general. Under his leadership, a regional congress in Caracas declared the independence of the United States of Venezuela in July 1811 and quickly drafted a constitution guaranteeing freedom of the press and racial equality. The republic failed after only one year, but Bolívar continued to fight royalist forces for the next eight years, with assistance from the newly formed Haitian republic. His victories over Spanish armies won him the presidency of the new republic of Gran Colombia (formerly the New Granada viceroyalty) in 1819.

Bolívar dreamed of a continental union and in 1826 summoned a conference in Panama City of the American republics he had liberated, which included the future nations of Venezuela, Colombia, Ecuador, Peru, and Bolivia. The meeting achieved little, however. The territories of Gran Colombia soon splintered (see Map 22.3), and a sadly disillusioned Bolívar went into exile, saying, "America is ungovernable."

Under Spain, Mexico had been united with Central America as the Viceroyalty of New Spain. In 1808, after Napoleon's coup, the Spanish viceroy assumed control of the government of New Spain from its capital in Mexico City. Meanwhile, groups of rebels plotted to overthrow royalist power. Under the leadership of two charismatic priests, poor Creoles and indigenous peasants rose up against the Spanish. This movement from below fell to royalist forces, but in 1821 a new movement commanded by Creole elites succeeded in winning independence from Spain.

Triumph of Bolívar Bolívar was treated as a hero everywhere he went in South America. (akg-images)

Although Creole officers dominated rebel armies, their success depended on a rank and file largely composed of nonwhites. These included many blacks and free people of color, who had come to dominate the colonial militias. In Mexico many indigenous people also fought for the patriots, but elsewhere Indians were often indifferent to independence or felt their status was more secure with the royal government than with the Creoles.

In the 1830s regional separatism resulted in New Spain's breakup into five separate countries. The failure of political union in New Spain and Gran Colombia isolated individual countries, prevented collective action, and later paved the way for the political and economic intrusion of the United States and other powers. Spain's Caribbean colonies of Puerto Rico and Cuba remained loyal, in large part due to fears that slave revolt would spread from neighboring Haiti.

Brazil followed a different path to independence. When Napoleon's troops entered Portugal, the royal family fled to Brazil and made Rio de Janeiro the capital of the Portuguese Empire. The new government immediately lifted the old mercantilist restrictions and opened Brazilian ports to the ships of all friendly nations. The king returned to Portugal in 1821, leaving his son Pedro in Brazil as regent. Under popular pressure, Pedro proclaimed Brazil's independence in 1822, issued a constitution, and even led resistance against Portuguese troops. He accepted the title Emperor Pedro I (r. 1822–1831). Even though Brazil was a monarchy, Creole elites dominated society as they did elsewhere in Latin America. The reign of Pedro I's successor, Pedro II (r. 1831–1889), witnessed the expansion of the coffee industry, the beginnings of the rubber industry, and massive immigration.

The Aftermath of Revolution in the Atlantic World

The Atlantic revolutions shared many common traits. They had common origins in imperial competition, war debt, social conflict, and Enlightenment ideals. Over the course of revolution, armed struggle often took on the form of civil war, in which the participation of ordinary people—sans-culottes, slaves, free people of color, mestizos, and Indians—played a decisive role. Perhaps their most important similarity was in the democratic limitations of the regimes these revolutions created and the frustrated aspirations they bequeathed to subsequent generations.

For the most part, the elite liberals who led the revolutions were not democrats and had no intention of creating regimes of economic or social equality. The constitutions they wrote generally restricted voting rights and the capacity to be elected to government to landowners and middle-class men. Indigenous people may have gained formal equality as citizens, yet they found that the actual result was the removal of the privileged status they had negotiated with their original conquerors. Thus they suffered the loss of rights over their land and other resources. Moreover, none of the postrevolutionary constitutions gave women a role in political life.

The issue of slavery, by contrast, divided the revolutions. The American Revolution was led in part by slaveholding landowners, who were determined to retain slavery in its aftermath, while the more radical French republic abolished it throughout the French empire (a measure soon reversed by Napoleon). The independent nation of Haiti was built on the only successful slave revolt in history, but the need for revenue from plantation agriculture soon led to the return of coercive labor requirements, if not outright slavery. In Latin America, independence speeded the abolition of slavery, bringing an immediate ban on the slave trade and gradual emancipation from the 1820s to the 1850s. Still, Cuba and Brazil, which had enormous slave populations, did not end slavery until 1886 and 1888, respectively.

The aftermaths of the Atlantic revolutions brought extremely different fortunes to the new nations that emerged from them. France returned to royal rule with the restoration of the Bourbon monarchy in 1815. A series of revolutionary crises ensued in the nineteenth century as succeeding generations struggled over the legacies of monarchicalism, republicanism, and Bonapartism. It was not until 1871 that republicanism finally prevailed (see Chapter 24). The transition to an independent republic was permanent and relatively smooth in the United States, where war was brief and limited, colonial assemblies had long practiced self-governance, and manufacturing and trade recovered quickly with renewed ties with Britain. Nevertheless, the unresolved conflict over slavery would lead to catastrophic civil war in 1860.

The newly independent nations of Latin America had difficulty achieving political stability when the wars of independence ended. The economic lives of most Latin American countries were disrupted during the years of war. Mexico and Venezuela in particular suffered great destruction of farmland and animals. Between 1836 and 1848 Mexico lost half its territory to the United States, and other countries, too, had difficulty defending themselves from their neighbors. The Creole leaders of the revolutions had little experience in government, and the wars left a legacy of military, not civilian, leadership.

Chapter Summary

From 1775 to 1825 a wave of revolution swept through the Atlantic world. Its origins included long-term social and economic changes, Enlightenment ideals of liberty and equality, and the costs of colonial warfare. British efforts to raise taxes after the Seven Years' War aroused violent protest in the American colonies. In 1776 the Second Continental Congress issued the Declaration of Independence, and by 1783 Britain had recognized the independence of the thirteen colonies. Following ratification of a new constitution, Congress passed ten amendments to safeguard individual liberties but denied equal rights to women and nonwhites.

In 1789 delegates to the Estates General defied royal authority to declare themselves a National Assembly, which promulgated France's first constitution in 1791. Led by the Jacobin Club, the Assembly waged war on Austria and Prussia and proclaimed France a republic. From the end of 1793, under the Reign of Terror, the Revolution pursued internal and external enemies ruthlessly and instituted economic controls to aid the poor. The weakness of the Directory government after the fall of Robespierre enabled charismatic general Napoleon Bonaparte to claim control of France. Napoleon's relentless military ambitions allowed him to spread French power through much of Europe but ultimately led to his downfall.

After a failed uprising by free men of color, slaves rose in revolt in the French colony of Saint-Domingue in August 1791. Their revolt, combined with the outbreak of war and the radicalization of the French Revolution, led to the enfranchisement of free men of color, the emancipation of slaves who fought for France, and ultimately the abolition of slavery throughout the colony in late 1793. Like Napoleon Bonaparte,

Toussaint L'Ouverture was an unknown soldier who claimed glory and power, only to endure exile and defeat. After his exile, his forces won independence for the new Haitian nation in 1804.

Latin American independence movements drew strength from Spain's unpopular policies. External events—the outbreak of the Haitian Revolution and Napoleon's seizure of the Spanish throne—accelerated the path toward revolt. Under the leadership of Simón Bolívar, the United States of Venezuela claimed independence in 1811. Led by Creole officers but reliant on nonwhite soldiers, rebel armies successfully fought Spanish forces over the next decade. Despite Bolívar's efforts to build a unified state, in the 1830s New Spain split into five separate countries. In Brazil the royal regent proclaimed independence in 1822 and reigned as emperor of the new state.

Notes

1. Quoted in L. Gershoy, *The Era of the French Revolution, 1789–1799* (New York: Van Nostrand, 1957), p. 150.
2. Cited in Wim Klooster, *Revolutions in the Atlantic World: A Comprehensive History* (New York: New York University Press, 2009), p. 74.
3. T. Blanning, *The French Revolutionary Wars, 1787–1802* (London: Arnold, 1996), pp. 116–128.
4. Donald Sutherland, *France, 1789–1815: Revolution and Counterrevolution* (New York: Oxford University Press, 1986), p. 420.
5. John K. Thornton, "'I Am the Subject of the King of Congo': African Political Ideology and the Haitian Revolution," *Journal of World History* 4.2 (Fall 1993): 181–214.
6. Quoted in Laurent Dubois, *Avengers of the New World: The Story of the Haitian Revolution* (Cambridge, Mass.: Harvard University Press, 2004), p. 97.
7. See B. Keen and M. Wasserman, *A Short History of Latin America* (Boston: Houghton Mifflin, 1980), pp. 109–115.

CONNECTIONS

The Atlantic world formed an essential context for a great revolutionary wave in the late eighteenth and early nineteenth centuries. The movement of peoples, commodities, and ideas across the Atlantic Ocean in the eighteenth century created a world of common debates, conflicts, and aspirations. Moreover, the high stakes of colonial empire heightened competition among European states, leading to a series of wars that generated crushing costs for overburdened treasuries. For both the British in their North American colonies and the French at home, the desperate need for new taxes weakened government authority and opened the door to revolution. In turn, the ideals of the French Revolution inspired slaves and free people of color in Saint-Domingue to rise up and claim the promise of liberty, equality, and fraternity for people of all races.

The chain reaction did not end with the liberation movements in Spanish America that followed the Haitian Revolution. Throughout the nineteenth and early twentieth centuries periodic convulsions occurred in Europe, the Americas, and elsewhere as successive generations struggled over political rights first proclaimed by late-eighteenth-century revolutionaries. Meanwhile, as dramatic political events unfolded, a parallel economic revolution was gathering steam. This was the Industrial Revolution, originating around 1780 and accelerating through the end of the eighteenth century (see Chapter 23). After 1815 the twin forces of industrialization and democratization would combine to transform Europe and the world.

Chapter Review

MAKE IT STICK

✓ **LearningCurve**
Go online and use LearningCurve to retain what you've read.

IDENTIFY KEY TERMS

Identify and explain the significance of each item below.

Treaty of Paris (p. 657)

Declaration of Independence
(p. 659)

Antifederalists (p. 660)

Estates General (p. 662)

National Assembly (p. 663)

Jacobin Club (p. 665)

Mountain (p. 665)

Girondists (p. 665)

sans-culottes (p. 665)

Reign of Terror (p. 666)

Thermidorian reaction (p. 667)

Napoleonic Code (p. 669)

Grand Empire (p. 671)

Continental System (p. 671)

Creoles (p. 680)

peninsulares (p. 680)

REVIEW THE MAIN IDEAS

Answer the focus questions from each section of the chapter.

1. What were the factors behind the age of revolution in the Atlantic world? (p. 654)

2. Why and how did American colonists forge a new, independent nation? (p. 658)

3. How did the events of 1789 result in a constitutional monarchy in France, and what were the consequences? (p. 662)

4. How did Napoleon Bonaparte assume control of France and much of Europe, and what factors led to his downfall? (p. 668)

5. How did slave revolt on colonial Saint-Domingue lead to the creation of the independent nation of Haiti in 1804? (p. 673)

6. Why and how did the Spanish and Portuguese colonies of North and South America shake off European domination and develop into national states? (p. 677)

MAKE CONNECTIONS

Analyze the larger developments and continuities within and across chapters.

1. What were major differences and similarities among the British North American, French, Haitian, and Spanish American Revolutions?

⏏LaunchPad
ONLINE DOCUMENT PROJECT

The Rights of Which Men?
How did the French Revolution affect France's Caribbean colonies?

Examine reactions of slaves and free men of color to the French Revolution, and then complete a quiz and writing assignment based on the evidence and details from this chapter.

See inside the front cover to learn more.

CHRONOLOGY

1715–1774	• Reign of Louis XV in France
1743–1803	• Life of Toussaint L'Ouverture
1756–1763	• Seven Years' War
1763	• Treaty of Paris
1774–1792	• Reign of Louis XVI in France
1775	• Thomas Paine publishes *Common Sense*
1775–1783	• American Revolution
1789–1799	• French Revolution
1790	• Edmund Burke publishes *Reflections on the Revolution in France*
1791–1804	• Haitian Revolution
1799–1814	• Reign of Napoleon Bonaparte in France

23

LearningCurve
After reading the chapter, go online and use LearningCurve to retain what you've read.

The Revolution in Energy and Industry

1760–1850

WHILE THE REVOLUTIONS OF THE ATLANTIC WORLD WERE OPENING A new political era, another revolution was beginning to transform economic and social life. The Industrial Revolution began in Great Britain around 1780 and soon began to influence continental Europe and the United States. Quite possibly only the development of agriculture during Neolithic times had a comparable impact and significance in world history. Non-European nations began to industrialize after 1860.

Industrialization profoundly modified human experience. It changed patterns of work, transformed the social structure, and eventually altered the international balance of political power in favor of the most rapidly industrialized nations, especially Great Britain. What was revolutionary about the Industrial Revolution was not its pace or that it represented a sharp break with the previous period. On the contrary, the Industrial Revolution built on earlier developments, and the rate of progress was slow. What was remarkable about the Industrial Revolution was that it inaugurated a period of sustained economic and demographic growth that has continued to the present. Although it took time, the Industrial Revolution eventually helped ordinary people in the West gain a higher standard of living.

The Industrial Revolution in Britain

Why did the Industrial Revolution begin in Britain, and how did it develop between 1780 and 1850?

The Industrial Revolution began in Great Britain, the nation created by the formal union of Scotland, Wales, and England in 1707. The transformation in industry was something new in history, and it was unplanned. It originated from a unique combination of possibilities and constraints in late-eighteenth-century Britain. With no models to copy and no idea of what to expect, Britain pioneered not only in industrial technology but also in social relations and urban living.

Why Britain?

Perhaps the most important debate in economic history focuses on why the Industrial Revolution originated in western Europe, and Britain in particular, rather than in other parts of the world, such as Asia. Historians continue to debate this issue, but the best answer seems to be that Britain possessed a unique set of possibilities and constraints—abundant coal, high wages, a relatively peaceful and centralized government, well-developed financial systems, innovative culture, highly skilled craftsmen, and a strong position in empire and global trade—that spurred its people to adopt a capital-intensive, machine-powered system of production. The long-term economic advantages of this system were not immediately apparent, and its adoption by the British was more a matter of circumstance than a planned strategy.

Thus a number of factors came together over the long term to give rise to the Industrial Revolution in Britain. The Scientific Revolution and the Enlightenment fostered a new worldview that embraced progress and the role of research and experimentation in understanding and mastering the natural world. Britain's intellectual culture emphasized the public sharing of knowledge, including that of scientists and technicians from other countries. The British Royal Society of Arts, for example, sponsored prizes for innovations in machinery and agriculture and played a pivotal part in the circulation of "useful knowledge."

In the economic realm, the seventeenth-century expansion of rural industry produced a surplus of English woolen cloth. Exported throughout Europe, English cloth brought commercial profits and high wages to the detriment of traditional producers in Flanders and Italy. By the eighteenth century the expanding Atlantic economy and trade with India and China were also serving Britain well. The mercantilist colonial empire Britain aggressively built, augmented by a strong position in Latin America and in the transatlantic slave trade, provided raw materials like cotton and a growing market for British manufactured goods (see Chapter 19). Strong demand for British manufacturing meant that British workers earned high wages compared to the rest of the world's laborers.

Agriculture also played an important role in bringing about the Industrial Revolution. English farmers were second only to the Dutch in productivity in 1700, and they were continually adopting new methods of farming (see page 577). The result, especially before 1760, was a period of bountiful crops and low food prices. Because of increasing efficiency, landowners were able to produce more food with a smaller workforce. By the mid-eighteenth century, on the eve of the Industrial Revolution, less than half of Britain's population worked in agriculture. The enclosure movement had deprived many small landowners of their land, leaving the landless poor to work as hired agricultural laborers or in rural industry. These groups created a pool of potential laborers for the new factories.

Abundant food and high wages in turn meant that the ordinary English family no longer had to spend almost everything it earned just to buy bread. Thus the family could spend more on manufactured goods—a razor for the man or a shawl for the woman. They could also pay to send their children to school. Britain's populace enjoyed high levels of literacy and numeracy (knowledge of mathematics) compared to the rest of Europe. Moreover, in the eighteenth century the members of the average British family—including women and girls—were redirecting their labor away from unpaid work for household consumption and toward work for wages that they could spend on goods, a trend reflecting the increasing commercialization of the entire European economy.

Britain also benefited from rich natural resources and a well-developed infrastructure. In an age when it was much cheaper to ship goods by water than by land, no part of England was more than fifty miles from navigable water. Beginning in the 1770s a canal-building boom enhanced this advantage. Rivers and canals provided easy movement of England and Wales's enormous deposits of iron and coal, resources that would be critical raw materials in Europe's early industrial age. The abundance of coal combined with high wages in manufacturing placed Britain in a unique position among the nations of the world: its manufacturers had extremely strong incentives to develop technologies to draw on the power of coal to increase workmen's productivity. In regions with lower wages, such as India and China, the costs of mechanization outweighed potential gains in productivity.

A final factor favoring British industrialization was the British state and its policies, especially in the formative decades of industrial change. Despite its rhetoric in favor of "liberty," Britain's parliamentary system taxed its population aggressively. The British state collected twice as much per capita as the supposedly "absolutist" French monarchy and spent the money on a navy to protect imperial commerce and on an army that could be used to quell uprisings by disgruntled workers. Starting with the Navigation Acts under Oliver Cromwell (see Chapter 18), the British state also adopted aggressive tariffs, or duties, on imported goods to protect its industries.

All these factors combined to initiate the Industrial Revolution, a term first coined by awed contemporaries in the 1830s to describe the burst of major inventions and technical changes they had witnessed in certain industries. This technical revolution went hand in hand with an impressive quickening in the annual rate of industrial growth in Britain. Whereas industry had grown at only 0.7 percent between 1700 and 1760 (before the Industrial Revolution), it grew at the much higher rate of 3 percent between 1801 and 1831, when industrial transformation was in full swing.[1]

Technological Innovations and Early Factories

The pressure to produce more goods for a growing market and to reduce the labor costs of manufacturing was directly related to the first decisive breakthrough of the Industrial Revolution: the creation of the world's first machine-powered factories in the British cotton textile industry. Technological innovations in the manufacture of cotton cloth led to a new system of production and social relationships. This was not the first time in European history that large numbers of people were systematically put to work in a single locale; the military arsenals of Venice are one example of a much older form of "factory." The crucial innovation in Britain was the introduction of machine power into the factory and the organization of labor around the functioning of a highly productive machine.

The putting-out system that developed in the seventeenth-century textile industry involved a merchant who loaned, or "put out," raw materials to cottage workers who processed the raw materials in their own homes and returned the finished products to the merchant. There was always a serious imbalance in textile production based on cottage industry: the work of four or five spinners was needed to keep one weaver steadily employed. Cloth weavers constantly had to try to find more thread and more spinners. During the eighteenth century the putting-out system grew across Europe, but most extensively in Britain. The growth of demand only increased pressures on the supply of thread.

Many a tinkering worker knew that devising a better spinning wheel promised rich rewards. It proved hard to spin the traditional raw materials—wool and flax—with improved machines, but cotton was different. Cotton textiles had first been imported into Britain from India by the East India Company as a rare and delicate luxury for the upper classes. In the eighteenth century a lively market for cotton cloth emerged in West Africa, where the English and other Europeans traded it in exchange for slaves. By 1760 a tiny domestic cotton industry had emerged in northern England based on imported raw materials, but it could not compete with cloth produced by workers in India and other parts of Asia. At this time, Indian cotton textiles dominated the world market, due to their workers' mastery over design and dyeing techniques, easy access to raw materials, and relatively low wages. International competition thus drove English entrepreneurs to invent new technologies to bring down labor costs.

After many experiments over a generation, a gifted carpenter and jack-of-all-trades, James Hargreaves, invented his cotton-spinning jenny about 1765. At almost the same moment, a barber-turned-manufacturer named Richard Arkwright invented (or possibly pirated) another kind of spinning machine, the water frame. These breakthroughs produced an explosion in the infant cotton textile industry in the 1780s, when it was increasing the value of its output at an unprecedented rate of about 13 percent each year. By 1790 the new machines were producing ten times as much cotton yarn as had been made in 1770.

Hargreaves's **spinning jenny** was simple, inexpensive, and powered by hand. In early models from six to twenty-four spindles were mounted on a sliding carriage, and each spindle spun a fine, slender thread. The machines were usually worked by women, who moved the carriage back and forth with one hand and turned a wheel to supply power with the other. Now it was the male weaver who could not keep up with the vastly more efficient female spinner.

Arkwright's **water frame** employed a different principle. It quickly acquired a capacity of several hundred spindles driven by waterpower. The water frame required large specialized mills located beside rivers and factories that employed as many as one thousand workers from the very beginning. It did not completely replace cottage industry, however, for the water frame could spin only a coarse, strong thread, which was then put out for respinning on hand-powered cottage jennies. Around 1790 a

Woman Working a Spinning Jenny   The loose cotton strands on the slanted bobbins shown in this illustration of Hargreaves's spinning jenny passed up to the sliding carriage and then on to the spindles in back for fine spinning. The worker, almost always a woman, regulated the sliding carriage with one hand, and with the other she turned the crank on the wheel to supply power. By 1783 one woman could spin a hundred threads at a time. (© Mary Evans Picture Library/The Image Works)

hybrid machine invented by Samuel Crompton proved capable of spinning very fine and strong thread in large quantities. Gradually, all cotton spinning was concentrated in large-scale factories.

These revolutionary developments in the textile industry allowed British manufacturers to produce vast quantities of both fine and coarse cotton thread. At first, the machines were too expensive to build and did not provide enough savings in labor to be adopted in continental Europe or elsewhere. Where wages were low and investment capital more scarce, there was little point in adopting mechanized production until significant increases in the machines' productivity, and a drop in the cost of manufacturing them, occurred in the first decades of the nineteenth century.[2]

Families using cotton in cottage industry were freed from their constant search for adequate yarn from scattered part-time spinners, since all the thread needed could be spun in the cottage on the jenny or obtained from a nearby factory. The income of weavers, now hard-pressed to keep up with the spinners, rose markedly until about 1792. For a brief period, they were among the highest-earning workers in England. As a result, large numbers of agricultural laborers became handloom weavers, while mechanics and capitalists sought to invent a power loom to save on labor costs. This

Edmund Cartwright achieved in 1785. But the power looms of the factories worked poorly at first and did not fully replace handlooms until the 1820s.

Working conditions in the early cotton factories were so poor that adult workers were reluctant to work in them. Factory owners often turned to orphans and abandoned children instead. By placing them in "apprenticeship" with factory owners, parish officers charged with caring for such children saved money. The owners gained workers over whom they exercised almost the authority of slave owners. Apprenticed as young as five or six years of age, boys and girls were forced by law to labor for their masters for as many as fourteen years. Housed, fed, and locked up nightly in factory dormitories, the young workers labored thirteen or fourteen hours a day, six days a week, for little or no pay. Harsh physical punishment maintained brutal discipline. To be sure, poor children typically worked long hours in many types of demanding jobs, but the wholesale coercion of orphans as factory apprentices constituted exploitation on a truly unprecedented scale.

The creation of the world's first machine-powered factories in the British cotton textile industry in the 1770s and 1780s, which grew out of the putting-out system of cottage production, was a major historical development. Both symbolically and substantially, the big new cotton mills marked the beginning of the Industrial Revolution in Britain. By 1831 the largely mechanized cotton textile industry accounted for fully 22 percent of the country's entire industrial production.

The Steam Engine Breakthrough

Human beings have long used their toolmaking abilities to construct machines that convert one form of energy into another. In the medieval period, Europeans began to adopt water mills to grind grain and windmills to pump water and drain swamps. More efficient use of water and wind in the sixteenth and seventeenth centuries enabled them to accomplish more. Nevertheless, even into the eighteenth century, Europe, like other areas of the world, relied mainly on wood for energy, and human beings and animals performed most work. This dependence meant that Europe and the rest of the world remained poor in energy and power.

By the eighteenth century wood was in ever-shorter supply in Britain. Processed wood (charcoal) was mixed with iron ore in blast furnaces to produce pig iron, crude iron molded into ingots called "pigs" that could be processed into steel, cast iron, or wrought iron. The iron industry's appetite for wood was enormous, and by 1740 the British iron industry was stagnating. Vast forests enabled Russia in the eighteenth century to become the world's leading producer of iron, much of which was exported to England. As wood became ever more scarce, the British looked to coal (combustible rock composed of fossilized organic matter) as an alternative. They had first used coal in the late Middle Ages as a source of heat. By 1640 most homes in London were heated with coal, and it was also used in industry to provide heat for making beer, glass, soap, and other products. The breakthrough came when industrialists began to use coal to produce mechanical energy and to power machinery.

To produce more coal, mines had to be dug deeper and deeper and were constantly filling with water. Mechanical pumps, usually powered by animals walking in circles at the surface, had to be installed. Animal power was expensive and bothersome. In an attempt to overcome these disadvantages, Thomas Savery in 1698 and Thomas

James Nasmyth's Mighty Steam Hammer   Nasmyth's invention was the forerunner of the modern pile driver, and its successful introduction in 1832 epitomized the rapid development of steam-power technology in Britain. In this painting by the inventor himself, workers manipulate a massive iron shaft being hammered into shape at Nasmyth's foundry near Manchester. (Universal History Archive/UIG/The Bridgeman Art Library)

Newcomen in 1705 invented the first primitive steam engines. Both engines burned coal to produce steam that drove the water pumps. Although both models were extremely inefficient, by the early 1770s many of the Savery engines and hundreds of the Newcomen engines were operating successfully in English and Scottish mines.

In 1763 a gifted young Scot named James Watt (1736–1819) was drawn to a critical study of the steam engine. Watt worked at the University of Glasgow as a skilled craftsman making scientific instruments. Scotland's Enlightenment emphasis on practicality and social progress had resulted in its universities becoming pioneers in technical education. In 1763 Watt was called on to repair a Newcomen engine being used in a physics course. After a series of observations, Watt saw that the Newcomen engine's waste of energy could be reduced by adding a separate condenser. This splendid invention, patented in 1769, greatly increased the efficiency of the steam engine.

To invent something is one thing; to make it a practical success is quite another. Watt needed skilled workers, precision parts, and capital, and the relatively advanced nature of the British economy proved essential. A partnership in 1775 with Matthew Boulton, a wealthy English industrialist, provided Watt with adequate capital and exceptional skills in salesmanship that equaled those of the renowned pottery king,

Josiah Wedgwood. (See "Individuals in Society: Josiah Wedgwood," page 698.) Among Britain's highly skilled locksmiths, tinsmiths, and millwrights, Watt found mechanics who could install, regulate, and repair his sophisticated engines. From ingenious manufacturers such as the cannonmaker John Wilkinson, Watt was gradually able to purchase precision parts. This support allowed him to create an effective vacuum in the condenser and regulate a complex engine. In more than twenty years of constant effort, Watt made many further improvements. By the late 1780s the firm of Boulton and Watt had made the steam engine a practical and commercial success in Britain.

The coal-burning steam engine of Watt and his followers was the Industrial Revolution's most fundamental advance in technology. For the first time in history, humanity had, at least for a few generations, almost unlimited power at its disposal. For the first time, inventors and engineers could devise and implement all kinds of power equipment to aid people in their work. Steam power began to replace waterpower in cotton-spinning mills during the 1780s, contributing greatly to that industry's phenomenal rise. Steam also took the place of waterpower in flour mills, in the malt mills used in breweries, in the flint mills supplying the pottery industry, and in the mills exported by Britain to the West Indies to crush sugarcane.

The British iron industry was also radically transformed. Originally, the smoke and fumes resulting from burning coal meant that it could not be substituted for charcoal in smelting iron. Starting around 1710, ironmakers began to use coke — a smokeless and hot-burning fuel produced by heating coal to rid it of impurities — to smelt pig iron. After 1770 the adoption of steam-driven bellows in blast furnaces allowed for great increases in the quantity of pig iron produced by British ironmakers. In the 1780s Henry Cort developed the puddling furnace, which allowed pig iron to be refined with coke.

Strong, skilled ironworkers — the puddlers — "cooked" molten pig iron in a great vat, raking off globs of refined iron for further processing. Cort also developed steam-powered rolling mills, which were capable of spewing out finished iron in every shape and form. The economic consequence of these technical innovations was a great boom in the British iron industry. In 1740 annual British iron production was only 17,000 tons. With the spread of coke smelting and the impact of Cort's inventions, production had reached 260,000 tons by 1806. In 1844 Britain produced 3 million tons of iron. Once scarce and expensive, iron became the cheap, basic, indispensable building block of the British economy.

Steam-Powered Transportation

The coal industry had long used plank roads and rails to move coal wagons within mines and at the surface. Rails reduced friction and allowed a horse or a human being to pull a heavier load. Thus, once a rail capable of supporting a heavy locomotive was developed in 1816, all sorts of experiments with steam engines on rails went forward.

The first steam locomotive was built by Richard Trevithick after much experimentation. George Stephenson acquired glory for his locomotive named *Rocket*, which sped down the track of the just-completed Liverpool and Manchester Railway at a maximum speed of 35 miles per hour, without a load, in 1829. The line from Liverpool to Manchester was a financial as well as a technical success, and many private companies

INDIVIDUALS IN SOCIETY • Josiah Wedgwood

As the making of cloth and iron was revolutionized by technical change and factory organization, so, too, were the production and consumption of pottery. Acquiring beautiful tableware became a craze for eighteenth-century consumers, and continental monarchs often sought prestige in building royal china works. But the grand prize went to Josiah Wedgwood, who wanted to "astonish the world."

The twelfth child of a poor potter, Josiah Wedgwood (1730–1795) grew up in the pottery district of Staffordshire in the English Midlands, where many tiny potteries made simple earthenware utensils for sale in local markets. Having grown up as an apprentice in the family business inherited by his oldest brother, Wedgwood struck off on his own in 1752. Soon manager of a small pottery, Wedgwood learned that new products recharged lagging sales. Studying chemistry and determined to succeed, Wedgwood spent his evenings experimenting with different chemicals and firing conditions.

In 1759, after five years of tireless efforts, Wedgwood perfected a beautiful new green glaze. Now established as a master potter, he opened his own factory and began manufacturing teapots and tableware finished in his green and other unique glazes, or adorned with printed scenes far superior to those being produced by competitors. Wedgwood's products caused a sensation among consumers, and his business quickly earned substantial profits. Subsequent breakthroughs, including ornamental vases imitating classical Greek models and jasperware for jewelry, contributed greatly to Wedgwood's success.

Competitors were quick to copy Wedgwood's new products and sell them at lower prices. Thus Wedgwood and his partner, Thomas Bentley, sought to cultivate an image of superior fashion, taste, and quality in order to develop and maintain a dominant market position. They did this by first capturing the business of the trendsetting elite. In one brilliant coup the partners first sold a very large cream-colored dinner set to Britain's queen, which they quickly christened "Queen's ware" and sold as a very expensive, must-have luxury to English aristocrats. Equally brilliant was Bentley's suave expertise in the elegant London showroom selling Wedgwood's imitation Greek vases, which became the rage after the rediscovery of the cities of Pompeii and Herculaneum in the mid-eighteenth century.

Above all, once Wedgwood had secured his position as the luxury market leader, he was able to successfully extend his famous brand to the growing middle class,

were organized to build more rail lines. Within twenty years they had completed the main trunk lines of Great Britain (Map 23.1). Other countries were quick to follow, with the first steam-powered trains operating in the United States in the 1830s and in Brazil, Chile, Argentina, and the British colonies of Canada, Australia, and India in the 1850s.

The arrival of the railroad had many significant consequences. It dramatically reduced the cost and uncertainty of shipping freight over land. Previously, markets had tended to be small and local; as the barrier of high transportation costs was lowered, capturing an enormous mass market for his "useful ware." Thus, when sales of a luxury good grew "stale," Wedgwood made tasteful modifications and sold it to the middling classes for twice the price his competitors could charge. This unbeatable combination of mass appeal and high prices brought Wedgwood great fame all across Europe and enormous wealth.

A workaholic with an authoritarian streak, Wedgwood contributed substantially to the development of the factory system. In 1769 he opened a model factory on a new canal he had promoted. With two hundred workers in several departments, Wedgwood exercised tremendous control over his workforce, imposing fines for many infractions, such as being late, drinking on the job, or wasting material. He wanted, he said, to create men who would be like "machines" that "cannot err." Yet Wedgwood also recognized the value in treating workers well. He championed a division of labor that made most workers specialists who received ongoing training. He also encouraged employment of family groups, who were housed in company row houses with long, narrow backyards suitable for raising vegetables and chickens. Paying relatively high wages and providing pensions and some benefits, Wedgwood developed a high-quality labor force that learned to accept his rigorous discipline and carried out his ambitious plans.

QUESTIONS FOR ANALYSIS

1. How and why did Wedgwood succeed?
2. Was Wedgwood a good boss or a bad one? Why?
3. How did Wedgwood exemplify the new class of factory owners?

ᗷLaunchPad
ONLINE DOCUMENT PROJECT

How were social and economic change connected in nineteenth-century England? Read sources on early industrial manufacturing, and then complete a quiz and writing assignment based on the evidence and details from this chapter.

See inside the front cover to learn more.

markets became larger and even nationwide. Larger markets encouraged larger factories with more sophisticated machinery in a growing number of industries. Such factories could make goods more cheaply and gradually subjected most cottage workers and many urban artisans to severe competitive pressures. In all countries, the construction of railroads created a strong demand for unskilled labor and contributed to the growth of a class of urban workers.

The railroad also had a tremendous impact on cultural values and attitudes. The last and culminating invention of the Industrial Revolution, the railroad dramatically

MAP 23.1 The Industrial Revolution in Great Britain, ca. 1850 Industry concentrated in the rapidly growing cities of the north and the center of England, where rich coal and iron deposits were close to one another.

revealed the power and increased the speed of the new age. Racing down a track at 16 miles per hour or by 1850 at a phenomenal 50 miles per hour was a new and awesome experience. Some great painters, notably Joseph M. W. Turner (1775–1851) and Claude Monet (1840–1926), succeeded in expressing this sense of power and awe. So did the massive new train stations, the cathedrals of the industrial age. Leading railway engineers such as Isambard Kingdom Brunel and Thomas Brassey, whose tunnels pierced mountains and whose bridges spanned valleys, became public idols — the astronauts of their day.

The steam engine also transformed water travel. French engineers completed the first steamships in the 1770s, and the first commercial steamships came into use in North America several decades later. The *Clermont* began to travel the waters of the Hudson River in New York State in 1807, shortly followed by ships belonging to brewer John Molson on the St. Lawrence River. The steamship brought the advantages of the railroad — speed, reliability, efficiency — to water travel.

Industry and Population

In 1851 London hosted an industrial fair called the Great Exhibition in the newly built Crystal Palace. More than 6 million visitors from all over Europe marveled at the gigantic new exhibition hall set in the middle of a large, centrally located park. The building was made entirely of glass and iron, both of which were now cheap and abundant. Sponsored by the British royal family, the exhibition celebrated the new era of industrial technology and the kingdom's role as world economic leader.

Britain's claim to be the "workshop of the world" was no idle boast, for it produced two-thirds of the world's coal and more than half of its iron and cotton cloth. More generally, in 1860 Britain produced a remarkable 20 percent of the entire world's output of industrial goods, whereas it had produced only about 2 percent of the world total in 1750.[3] As the British economy significantly increased its production of manufactured goods, the gross national product (GNP) rose roughly fourfold at constant prices between 1780 and 1851. At the same time, the population of Britain boomed, growing from about 9 million in 1780 to almost 21 million in 1851. Thus growing numbers consumed much of the increase in total production.

Rapid population growth in Great Britain was key to industrial development. More people meant a more mobile labor force, with a wealth of young workers in need of employment and ready to go where the jobs were. Sustaining the dramatic increase in population, in turn, was only possible through advances in agriculture and industry. Based on the lessons of history, many contemporaries feared that the rapid growth in population would inevitably lead to disaster. In his *Essay on the Principle of Population* (1798), Thomas Malthus (1766–1834) examined the dynamics of human populations. He argued:

> There are few states in which there is not a constant effort in the population to increase beyond the means of subsistence. This constant effort as constantly tends to subject the lower classes of society to distress, and to prevent any great permanent melioration of these conditions.[4]

Since, in his opinion, population would always tend to grow faster than the food supply, Malthus concluded that the only hope of warding off such "positive checks" to population growth as war, famine, and disease was "prudential restraint." That is, young men and women had to limit the growth of population by marrying late in life. But Malthus was not optimistic about this possibility. The powerful attraction of the sexes would cause most people to marry early and have many children.

Economist David Ricardo (1772–1823) spelled out the pessimistic implications of Malthus's thought. Ricardo's depressing iron law of wages posited that because of the pressure of population growth, wages would always sink to subsistence level. That is, wages would be just high enough to keep workers from starving.

Malthus, Ricardo, and their followers were proved wrong in the long run. However, until the 1820s, or even the 1840s, contemporary observers might reasonably have concluded that the economy and the total population were racing neck and neck, with the outcome very much in doubt. There was another problem as well. Perhaps workers, farmers, and ordinary people did not get their rightful share of the new wealth. Perhaps only the rich got richer, while the poor got poorer or made no progress. We will turn to this great issue after situating the process of industrialization in its European and global context.

Industrialization in Europe and the World

How did countries in Europe and around the world respond to the challenge of industrialization after 1815?

As new technologies and a new organization of labor began to revolutionize production in Britain, other countries took notice and began to emulate its example. With the end of the Napoleonic Wars, the nations of the European continent quickly adopted British inventions and achieved their own pattern of technological innovation and economic growth. By the last decades of the nineteenth century, western European countries as well as the United States and Japan had industrialized their economies to a considerable, albeit varying, degree.

Industrialization in other parts of the world proceeded more gradually, with uneven jerks and national and regional variations. Scholars are still struggling to explain these variations as well as the dramatic gap that emerged for the first time in history between Western and non-Western levels of economic production. These questions are especially important because they may offer valuable lessons for poor countries that today seek to improve their material condition through industrialization and economic development. The latest findings on the nineteenth-century experience are encouraging. They suggest that there were alternative paths to the industrial world and that there was and is no need to follow a rigid, predetermined British model.

National and International Variations

Comparative data on industrial production in different countries over time help give us an overview of what happened. One set of data, the work of a Swiss scholar, compares the level of industrialization on a per capita basis in several countries from 1750 to 1913. These data are far from perfect, but they reflect basic trends and are presented in Table 23.1 for closer study.

Table 23.1 presents a comparison of how much industrial product was produced, on average, for each person in a given country in a given year. All the numbers are expressed in terms of a single index number of 100, which equals the per capita level of industrial goods in Great Britain and Ireland in 1900. Every number in the table is thus a percentage of the 1900 level in Britain and is directly comparable with other numbers. The countries are listed in roughly the order that they began to use large-scale, power-driven technology.

TABLE 23.1   Per Capita Levels of Industrialization, 1750–1913

	1750	1800	1830	1860	1880	1900	1913
Great Britain	10	16	25	64	87	100	115
Belgium	9	10	14	28	43	56	88
United States	4	9	14	21	38	69	126
France	9	9	12	20	28	39	59
Germany	8	8	9	15	25	52	85
Austria-Hungary	7	7	8	11	15	23	32
Italy	8	8	8	10	12	17	26
Russia	6	6	7	8	10	15	20
China	8	6	6	4	4	3	3
India	7	6	6	3	2	1	2

Note: All entries are based on an index value of 100, equal to the per capita level of industrialization in Great Britain in 1900. Data for Great Britain include Ireland, England, Wales, and Scotland.

Source: P. Bairoch, "International Industrialization Levels from 1750 to 1980," *Journal of European Economic History* 11 (Spring 1982): 294, U.S. Journals at Cambridge University Press. Reprinted by permission.

What does this overview tell us? First, one sees in the first column that in 1750 all countries were fairly close together, including non-Western areas such as China and India. Both China and India were extremely important players in early modern world trade; both were sophisticated, technologically advanced, and economically powerful up to 1800. However, the column headed 1800 shows that Britain had opened up a noticeable lead over all countries by 1800, and that gap progressively widened as the British Industrial Revolution accelerated through 1830 and reached full maturity by 1860.

Second, the table shows that Western countries began to emulate the British model successfully over the nineteenth century, with significant variations in the timing and in the extent of industrialization. Belgium, achieving independence from the Netherlands in 1831 and rich in iron and coal, led in adopting Britain's new technology, and it experienced a truly revolutionary surge between 1830 and 1860. France developed factory production more gradually and did not experience "revolutionary" acceleration in the growth of overall industrial output. Slow but steady economic growth in France was overshadowed by the spectacular rise of Germany and the United States after 1860 in what has been termed the "Second Industrial Revolution." In general, eastern and southern Europe began the process of industrialization later than northwestern and central Europe. Nevertheless, these regions made real progress in the late nineteenth century, as growth after 1880 in Austria-Hungary, Italy, and Russia suggests. This meant that all European states as well as the United States managed to raise per capita industrial levels in the nineteenth century.

These increases stood in stark contrast to the decreases that occurred at the same time in many non-Western countries, most notably in China and India, as Table 23.1 shows. European countries industrialized to a greater or lesser extent even as most of the non-Western world stagnated. Japan, which is not included in this table, stands out as an exceptional area of non-Western industrial growth in the second half of the nineteenth century. After the forced opening of the country to the West in the 1850s, Japanese entrepreneurs began to adopt Western technology and manufacturing methods, resulting in a production boom by the late nineteenth century (see Chapter 26). Differential rates of wealth- and power-creating industrial development, which heightened disparities within Europe, also greatly magnified existing inequalities between Europe and the rest of the world (see Chapter 25).

Industrialization in Continental Europe

Throughout Europe the eighteenth century was an era of agricultural improvement, population increase, expanding foreign trade, and growing cottage industry. Thus, when the pace of British industry began to accelerate in the 1780s, continental businesses began to adopt the new methods as they proved their profitability. British industry enjoyed clear superiority, but at first the European continent was close behind. During the period of the revolutionary and Napoleonic Wars, from 1793 to 1815, however, western Europe experienced tremendous political and social upheaval that temporarily halted economic development. With the return of peace in 1815, however, western European countries again began to play catch-up.

They faced significant challenges. In the newly mechanized industries, British goods were being produced very economically, and these goods had come to dominate

MAP 23.2   Continental Industrialization, ca. 1850 Although continental countries were beginning to make progress by 1850, they still lagged far behind Britain. For example, continental railroad building was still in an early stage, whereas the British rail system was essentially complete (see Map 23.1). Coal played a critical role in nineteenth-century industrialization, both as a power source for steam engines and as a raw material for making iron and steel.

world markets. In addition, British technology had become so advanced that very few engineers or skilled technicians outside England understood it. Moreover, the technology of steam power had grown much more expensive. It involved large investments in the iron and coal industries and, after 1830, required the existence of railroads. Continental business people had great difficulty amassing the large sums of money the new methods demanded, and laborers bitterly resisted the move to working in factories. All these factors slowed the spread of mechanization (Map 23.2).

Nevertheless, western European nations possessed a number of advantages that helped them respond to these challenges. First, most had rich traditions of putting-out enterprise, merchant capitalism, and skilled urban trades. These assets gave their firms the ability to adapt and survive in the face of new market conditions. Second, continental capitalists did not need to develop their own advanced technology. Instead, they could "borrow" the new methods developed in Great Britain, as well as the engineers and some of the financial resources they lacked. European countries such as

France and Russia also had a third asset that many non-Western areas lacked in the nineteenth century: they had strong, independent governments that did not fall under foreign political control. These governments would eventually use the power of the state to promote industry and catch up with Britain.

Most continental businesses adopted factory technology slowly, and handicraft methods lived on. Indeed, continental industrialization usually brought substantial but uneven expansion of handicraft industry in both rural and urban areas for a time. Artisan production of luxury items grew in France as the rising income of the international middle class created increased foreign demand for silk scarves, embroidered needlework, perfumes, and fine wines. Focusing on artisanal luxury production made sense for French entrepreneurs given their long history of dominance in that sector. Rather than being a "backward" refusal to modernize, it represented a sound strategic choice that allowed the French to capitalize on their know-how and international reputation for high-quality goods.

Agents of Industrialization

Western European success in adopting British methods took place despite the best efforts of the British to prevent it. The British realized the great value of their technical discoveries and tried to keep their secrets to themselves. Until 1825 it was illegal for artisans and skilled mechanics to leave Britain; until 1843 the export of textile machinery and other equipment was forbidden. Many talented, ambitious workers, however, slipped out of the country illegally and introduced the new methods abroad.

One such man was William Cockerill, a Lancashire carpenter. He and his sons began building cotton-spinning equipment in French-occupied Belgium in 1799. In 1817 the most famous son, John Cockerill, built a large industrial enterprise in Liège in southern Belgium, which produced machinery, steam engines, and then railway locomotives. He also established modern ironworks and coal mines. Cockerill's plants in the Liège area became a center for gathering and transmitting industrial information from across Europe. Many skilled British workers came to work for Cockerill, bringing the latest industrial advances from Britain, and some went on to found their own companies throughout Europe.

Thus British technicians and skilled workers were a powerful force in the spread of early industrialization. A second agent of industrialization consisted of talented European entrepreneurs such as Fritz Harkort (1793–1880), a pioneer in the German machinery industry. Serving in England as a Prussian army officer during the Napoleonic Wars, Harkort was impressed with what he saw. Harkort set up shop building steam engines in the Ruhr Valley, on the western border with France. In spite of problems obtaining skilled workers and machinery, Harkort succeeded in building and selling engines. However, his ambitious efforts also resulted in large financial losses for himself and his partners. His career illustrates both the great efforts of a few important business leaders to duplicate the British achievement and the difficulty of the task.

National governments played an even more important role in supporting industrialization in continental Europe than in Britain. Tariff protection was one such support, and it proved to be important. The French, for example, responded to a flood of cheap British goods in 1815, after the Napoleonic Wars, by laying high taxes on

A German Ironworks, 1845   The Borsig ironworks in Berlin mastered the new British method of smelting iron ore with coke. Germany, especially the state of Prussia, was well endowed with both iron and coal, and the rapid exploitation of these resources after 1840 transformed a poor agricultural country into an industrial powerhouse. (Stiftung Stadtmuseum/ akg-images)

imported goods. Customs agreements emerged among some German states starting in 1818, and in 1834 a number of states signed a treaty creating a customs union, or *Zollverein*. The treaty allowed goods to move between member states without tariffs, while erecting a single uniform tariff against other nations.

After 1815 continental governments also bore the cost of building roads, canals, and railroads to improve transportation. Belgium led the way in the 1830s and 1840s. Built rapidly as a unified network, Belgium's state-owned railroads stimulated the development of heavy industry and made the country an early industrial leader. In France the state shouldered all the expense of acquiring and laying roadbed, including bridges and tunnels. In short, governments helped pay for railroads, the all-important leading sector in continental industrialization.

Finally, banks, like governments, also played a larger and more creative role on the continent than in Britain. Previously, almost all banks in Europe had been private. Because of the possibility of unlimited financial loss, the partners of private banks tended to be conservative and were content to deal with a few rich clients and a few big merchants. They generally avoided industrial investment as being too risky.

In the 1830s two important Belgian banks pioneered in a new direction. They received permission from the growth-oriented government to establish themselves as corporations enjoying limited liability. That is, if the bank went bankrupt, stockholders would lose only their original investments in the bank's common stock, and they could not be forced to pay for additional losses out of other property they owned.

Limited liability helped these banks attract investors. They mobilized impressive resources for investment in big companies, became industrial banks, and successfully promoted industrial development. Similar corporate banks became important in France and Germany in the 1850s and 1860s. Usually working in collaboration with governments, corporate banks established and developed many railroads and many companies working in heavy industry, which were also increasingly organized as limited liability corporations.

The combined efforts of skilled workers, entrepreneurs, governments, and industrial banks meshed successfully between 1850 and the financial crash of 1873. In Belgium, France, and the German states key indicators of modern industrial development—such as railway mileage, iron and coal production, and steam engine capacity—increased at average annual rates of 5 to 10 percent. As a result, rail networks were completed in western Europe and much of central Europe, and the leading continental countries mastered the industrial technologies that had first been developed in Great Britain. In the early 1870s Britain was still Europe's most industrial nation, but a select handful of countries were closing the gap.

The Global Picture

The Industrial Revolution did not extend outside of Europe prior to the 1860s, with the exception of the United States and Japan, both early adopters of British practices. In many countries, national governments and pioneering entrepreneurs did make efforts to adopt the technologies and methods of production that had proved so successful in Britain, but they fell short of transitioning to an industrial economy. For example, in Russia the imperial government brought steamships to the Volga River and a railroad to the capital, St. Petersburg, in the first decades of the nineteenth century. By mid-century ambitious entrepreneurs had established steam-powered cotton factories using imported British machines. However, these advances did not lead to overall industrialization of the country, most of whose people remained mired in rural servitude. Instead Russia confirmed its role as provider of raw materials, especially timber and grain, to the hungry West.

Egypt, a territory of the Ottoman Empire, similarly began an ambitious program of modernization after a reform-minded viceroy took power in 1805. This program included the use of imported British technology and experts in textile manufacture and other industries (see page 786). These industries, however, could not compete with lower-priced European imports. Like Russia, Egypt fell back on agricultural exports, such as sugar and cotton, to European markets.

Such examples of faltering efforts at industrialization could be found in many other places in the Middle East, Asia, and Latin America. Where European governments maintained direct or indirect control, they acted to maintain colonial markets as both sources of raw materials and consumers for their own products, rather than encouraging the spread of industrialization. Such regions could not respond to low-cost imports by raising tariffs, as the United States and western European nations had done, because they were controlled by imperial powers that did not allow them to do so. In India millions of poor textile workers lost their livelihood because they could not compete with industrially produced British cotton. The British charged stiff import duties on Indian cottons entering the kingdom, but prohibited the Indians from doing

Press for Packing Indian Cotton, 1864   British industrialization destroyed a thriving Indian cotton textile industry, whose weavers could not compete with cheap British imports. India continued to supply raw cotton to British manufacturers. (English wood engraving, 1864/The Granger Collection, NYC—All rights reserved.)

the same to British imports. The arrival of railroads in India in the mid-nineteenth century served the purpose of agricultural rather than industrial development.

Latin American economies were disrupted by the early-nineteenth-century wars of independence (see Chapter 22). As these countries' economies recovered in the mid-nineteenth century, they increasingly adopted steam power for sugar and coffee processing and for transportation. Like elsewhere, this technology first supported increased agricultural production for export and only later drove domestic industrial production. As in India, the arrival of cheap British cottons destroyed the pre-existing textile industry that had employed many people.

The rise of industrialization in Britain, western Europe, and the United States thus caused other regions of the world to become increasingly economically dependent. Instead of industrializing, many territories underwent a process of deindustrialization or delayed industrialization. In turn, relative economic weakness made them vulnerable to the new wave of imperialism undertaken by industrialized nations in the second half of the nineteenth century (see Chapters 25 and 26).

As for China, it did not adopt mechanized production until the end of the nineteenth century, but continued as a market-based, commercial society with a massive rural sector and industrial production based on traditional methods. Regions of China experienced slow economic growth, while others were stagnant. In the 1860s and 1870s, when Japan was successfully adopting industrial methods, the Chinese government showed similar interest in Western technology and science. However, China faced widespread uprisings in the mid-nineteenth century, which drained attention and resources to the military; moreover, after the Boxer Rebellion of 1898–1900 (see page 809), Western powers forced China to pay massive indemnities, further reducing its capacity to promote industrialization. With China poised to surpass the United States in economic production by 2020, scholars wonder whether the ascension of Europe and the West from 1800 was merely a brief interruption in a much longer pattern of Asian dominance.

New Patterns of Working and Living

How did work evolve during the Industrial Revolution, and how did daily life change for working people?

Having first emerged in the British countryside in the late eighteenth century, factories and industrial labor began migrating to cities by the early nineteenth century. As factories moved from rural to urban areas, their workforce evolved as well, from pauper children to families to men and women uprooted from their traditional rural communities. Many women, especially young single women and poor women, continued to work, but married women began to limit their participation in the workforce when possible. For some people, the Industrial Revolution brought improvements, but living and working conditions for the poor stagnated or even deteriorated until around 1850, especially in overcrowded industrial cities.

Work in Early Factories

The first factories of the Industrial Revolution were cotton mills, which began functioning in the 1770s along fast-running rivers and streams and were often located in sparsely populated areas. Cottage workers, accustomed to the putting-out system, were reluctant to work in the new factories even when they received relatively good wages. In a factory, workers had to keep up with the machine and follow its relentless tempo. Moreover, they had to show up every day, on time, and work long, monotonous hours under the constant supervision of demanding overseers, and they were punished if they broke the work rules. For example, if a worker was late to work or accidentally spoiled material, the employer deducted fines from the weekly pay. Employers frequently beat children and adolescents for their infractions.

    Cottage workers were not used to that way of life. All members of the family worked hard and long, but in spurts, setting their own pace. They could interrupt their work when they wished. Women and children could break up their long hours of spinning with other tasks. On Saturday afternoon the head of the family delivered the week's work to the merchant manufacturer and got paid. Saturday night was a time of relaxation and drinking, especially for men.

    Also, early factories resembled English poorhouses, where totally destitute people went to live at public expense. Some poorhouses were industrial prisons, where the inmates had to work in order to receive their food and lodging. The similarity between large brick factories and large stone poorhouses increased the cottage workers' fear of factories and their hatred of factory discipline. It was cottage workers' reluctance to work in factories that prompted early cotton mill owners to turn to pauper children.

Mill owners contracted with local officials to employ large numbers of such children, who had no say in the matter. Attitudes began to change in the last decade of the eighteenth century, as middle-class reformers publicized the brutal toil imposed on society's most vulnerable members.

Working Families and Children

By the 1790s the early labor pattern was rapidly changing. The use of pauper apprentices was in decline, and in 1802 it was forbidden by Parliament. Many more textile factories were being built, mainly in urban areas, where they could use steam power rather than waterpower and attract a workforce more easily than in the countryside. People came from near and far to work in the cities, as factory workers and as laborers, builders, and domestic servants. Collectively, these wage laborers came to be known as the "working class," a term first used in the late 1830s.

In some cases, workers accommodated to the system by carrying over familiar working traditions. Some came to the mills and the mines as family units, as they had worked on farms and in the putting-out system. The mill or mine owner bargained with the head of the family and paid him or her for the work of the whole family. In cotton mills, children worked for their mothers or fathers, collecting scraps and "piecing" broken threads together. In mines, children sorted coal and worked the ventilation equipment. Their mothers hauled coal in the tunnels below the surface, while their fathers hewed with pick and shovel at the face of the seam.

Ties of kinship were particularly important for newcomers, who often traveled great distances to find work. Many urban workers in Great Britain were from Ireland. They were forced out of rural Ireland by population growth and deteriorating economic conditions from 1817. Their numbers increased dramatically during the desperate years of the potato famine, from 1845 to 1851. As early as 1824 most of the workers in the Glasgow cotton mills were Irish; in 1851 one-sixth of the population of Liverpool was Irish. Like many other immigrant groups held together by ethnic and religious ties, the Irish worked together, formed their own neighborhoods, and maintained their cultural traditions.

In the early decades of the nineteenth century, however, technical changes made it less and less likely that workers could continue to labor in family groups. As control and discipline passed into the hands of impersonal managers and overseers, adult workers began to protest against inhuman conditions on behalf of their children. Some enlightened employers and social reformers in Parliament agreed that more humane standards were necessary, and they used widely circulated parliamentary reports to influence public opinion. For example, Robert Owen (1771–1858), a successful textile manufacturer, testified in 1816 before an investigating committee on the basis of his experience. He argued that employing children under ten years of age as factory workers was "injurious to the children, and not beneficial to the proprietors."[5] Workers also provided graphic testimony at such hearings as the reformers pressed Parliament to pass corrective laws.

These efforts resulted in a series of British Factory Acts from 1802 to 1833 that progressively limited the workday of child laborers and set minimum hygiene and safety requirements. The **Factory Act of 1833** installed a system of full-time professional inspectors to enforce the provisions of previous acts. Children between ages nine and thirteen could work a maximum of eight hours per day, not including two hours for education. Teenagers aged fourteen to eighteen could work up to twelve hours, while those under nine were banned from employment. The Factory Acts constituted significant progress in preventing the exploitation of children. One unintended drawback of restrictions on child labor, however, was that they broke the pattern of whole families working together in the factory, because efficiency required standardized shifts for all workers. After 1833 the number of children employed in industry declined rapidly.

The Sexual Division of Labor

With the restriction of child labor and the collapse of the family work pattern in the 1830s came a new sexual division of labor. By 1850 the man was emerging as the family's primary wage earner, while the married woman found only limited job opportunities. Generally denied good jobs at high wages in the growing urban economy, wives were expected to concentrate on their duties at home.

This new pattern of **separate spheres** had several aspects. First, all studies agree that married women from the working classes were much less likely to work full-time for wages outside the house after the first child arrived, although they often earned small amounts doing handicrafts at home and taking in boarders. Second, when married women did work for wages outside the house, they usually came from the poorest families, where the husbands were poorly paid, sick, unemployed, or absent. Third, these poor married or widowed women were joined by legions of young unmarried women, who worked full-time but only in certain jobs, of which textile factory work, laundering, and domestic service were particularly important. Fourth, all women were generally confined to low-paying, dead-end jobs. Evolving gradually, but largely in place by 1850, the new sexual division of labor in Britain constituted a major development in the history of women and of the family.

Several factors combined to create this new sexual division of labor. First, the new and unfamiliar discipline of the clock and the machine was especially hard on married women of the laboring classes. Factory discipline conflicted with child care in a way that labor on the farm or in the cottage had not. A woman operating earsplitting spinning machinery could mind a child of seven or eight working beside her (until such work was outlawed), but she could no longer pace herself through pregnancy or breast-feed her baby on the job. Thus a working-class mother had strong reasons to stay home, if she could afford it. Caring for babies was a less important factor in areas of continental Europe, such as northern France and Scandinavia, where women relied on paid wet nurses instead of breast-feeding their babies.

Second, running a household in conditions of urban poverty was an extremely demanding job in its own right. There were no supermarkets or public transportation. Shopping and feeding the family constituted a never-ending challenge. Taking on a brutal job outside the house — a "second shift" — had limited appeal for the average married woman from the working class. Thus many women might well have accepted the emerging division of labor as the best available strategy for family survival in the industrializing society.[6]

Third, to a large degree the young, generally unmarried women who did work for wages outside the home were segregated from men and confined to certain "women's jobs" because the new sexual division of labor replicated long-standing patterns of gender segregation and inequality. In the preindustrial economy, a small sector of the labor market had always been defined as "women's work," especially tasks involving needlework, spinning, food preparation, child care, and nursing. This traditional sexual division of labor took on new overtones, however, in response to the factory system. Previously, at least in theory, young people worked under a watchful parental eye. The growth of factories and mines brought unheard-of opportunities for girls and boys to mix on the job, free of familial supervision. Such opportunities led to more unplanned pregnancies and fueled the illegitimacy explosion that had begun in the late eighteenth century and that gathered force until at least 1850. Thus segregation of jobs by gender was partly an effort by older people to help control the sexuality of working-class youths.

Investigations into the British coal industry before 1842 provide a graphic example of this concern. The middle-class men leading the inquiry professed horror at the sight of girls and women working without shirts, which was a common practice because of the heat, and they quickly assumed the prevalence of licentious sex with the male miners, who also wore very little clothing. In fact, most girls and married women worked for related males in a family unit that provided considerable protection and restraint. Yet many witnesses from the working class also believed that the mines were inappropriate and dangerous places for women and girls. Some miners stressed particularly the danger of sexual aggression for girls working past puberty. As one explained, "I consider it a scandal for girls to work in the pits. Till they are 12 or 14 they may work very well but after that it's an abomination. . . . The work of the pit does not hurt them, it is the effect on their morals that I complain of."[7] The **Mines Act of 1842** prohibited underground work for all women and girls as well as for boys under ten.

A final factor encouraging working-class women to withdraw from paid labor was the domestic ideals emanating from middle-class women, who had largely embraced the "separate spheres" ideology. Middle-class reformers published tracts and formed societies to urge poor women to devote more care and attention to their homes and families.

Living Standards for the Working Class

Although the evidence is complex and sometimes contradictory, most historians now agree that overall living standards for the working class did not rise substantially until the 1840s at least. British wages were always high compared to those in the rest of Europe, but the stresses of war with France from 1792 to 1815 led to a decline in the average British worker's real wages and standard of living. These difficult war years, marked by unemployment and high inflation, lent a grim color to the new industrial system. Factory wages began to rise after 1815, but these gains were modest and were offset by a decline in married women's and children's participation in the labor force, meaning that many households had less total income than before. Moreover, many people still worked outside the factories as cottage workers or rural laborers, and in those sectors wages declined. Thus the increase in the productivity of industry did not lead to an increase in the purchasing power of the British working classes. Only after 1830, and especially after 1840, did real wages rise substantially, so that the average worker earned roughly 30 percent more in real terms in 1850 than in 1770.[8]

Up to that point, the harshness of labor in the new industries probably outweighed their benefits as far as working people were concerned. With industrialization, workers toiled longer and harder at jobs that were often more grueling and more dangerous.

In England nonagricultural workers labored about 250 days per year in 1760 as compared to 300 days per year in 1830, while the normal workday remained an exhausting eleven hours throughout the entire period.[9]

As the factories moved to urban areas, workers followed them in large numbers, leading to an explosion in the size of cities, especially in the north of England. Life in the new industrial cities, such as Manchester and Glasgow, was grim. Given extremely high rates of infant mortality, average life expectancy was around only twenty-five to twenty-seven years, some fifteen years less than the national average.[10] Migrants to the booming cities found expensive, hastily constructed, overcrowded apartments and inadequate sanitary systems.

Another way to consider the workers' standard of living is to look at the goods they purchased, which also suggest stagnant or declining living standards until the middle of the nineteenth century. One important area of improvement was in the consumption of cotton goods, which became much cheaper and could be enjoyed by all classes. Now millions of poor people could afford to wear cotton slips and underpants as well as cotton dresses and shirts. However, in other areas, food in particular, the modest growth in factory wages was not enough to compensate for rising prices. Accordingly, parish statistics show no gains in life expectancy or infant survival until the middle of the nineteenth century.

From the 1840s onward, matters improved considerably as wages made substantial gains and the prices of many goods dropped. A greater variety of foods became available, including the first canned goods. Some of the most important advances were in medicine. Smallpox vaccination became routine, and surgeons began to use anesthesia in the late 1840s. By 1850 trains and steamships had revolutionized transportation for the masses, while the telegraph made instant communication possible for the first time in human history. Gaslights greatly expanded the possibilities of nighttime activity. Gas lighting is one of the most important examples of a direct relationship between the scientific advances of the eighteenth century—in this case, chemistry—and the development of new technologies of the Industrial Revolution.

In addition to the technical innovations that resulted from industrialization, other, less tangible, changes were also taking place. As young men and women migrated away from their villages to seek employment in urban factories, many close-knit rural communities were destroyed. Village social and cultural traditions disappeared without new generations to carry them on. Although many young people formed new friendships and appreciated the freedoms of urban life, they also suffered from the loneliness of life in the anonymous city. The loss of skills and work autonomy, along with the loss of community, must be included in the assessment of the Industrial Revolution's impact on the living conditions of the poor.

Relations Between Capital and Labor

How did the changes brought about by the Industrial Revolution lead to new social classes, and how did people respond to the new structure?

In Great Britain industrial development led to the creation of new social groups and intensified long-standing problems between capital and labor. A new class of factory owners and industrial capitalists arose. These men and women and their families strengthened the wealth and size of the middle class, which had previously been made up mainly of merchants and professional people. The demands of modern industry regularly brought the interests of the middle-class industrialists into conflict with those of the people who worked for them—the working class. As observers took note of these changes, they raised new questions about how industrialization affected social relationships. Meanwhile, enslaved labor in European colonies contributed to the industrialization process in multiple ways.

The New Class of Factory Owners

Early industrialists operated in a highly competitive economic system. As the careers of James Watt and Fritz Harkort illustrate, there were countless production problems, and success and large profits were by no means certain. Manufacturers therefore waged a constant battle to cut their production costs and stay afloat. Much of the profit had to go back into the business for new and better machinery.

Most early industrialists drew upon their families and friends for labor and capital, but they came from a variety of backgrounds. Many, such as Harkort, were from well-established merchant families with rich networks of contacts and support. Others, such as Watt, Wedgwood, and Cockerill, were of modest means, especially in the early days. Artisans and skilled workers of exceptional ability had unparalleled opportunities. Members of ethnic and religious groups who had been discriminated against in the traditional occupations controlled by the landed aristocracy jumped at the new chances

Ford Maddox Brown, *Work*   This midcentury painting provides a rich and realistic visual representation of the new concepts of social class that had become common by 1850. (Birmingham Museums and Art Gallery, Birmingham, UK/The Bridgeman Art Library)

and often helped each other. Scots, Quakers, and other Protestant dissenters were tremendously important in Britain; Protestants and Jews dominated banking in Catholic France.

As factories and firms grew larger, opportunities declined, at least in well-developed industries. It became harder for a gifted but poor young mechanic to start a small enterprise and end up as a wealthy manufacturer. Expensive, formal education became more important for young men as a means of success and advancement. In Britain by 1830 and in France and Germany by 1860, leading industrialists were more likely to have inherited their well-established enterprises, and they were financially much more secure than their struggling parents had been.

Just like working-class women, the wives and daughters of successful businessmen also found fewer opportunities for active participation in Europe's business world. Rather than contributing as vital partners in a family-owned enterprise, as so many middle-class women had done before, these women were increasingly valued for their ladylike gentility. By 1850 some influential women writers and most businessmen assumed that middle-class wives and daughters should steer clear of work in offices and factories. Rather, a middle-class lady was expected to concentrate on her proper role as wife and mother, preferably in an elegant residential area far removed from ruthless commerce and the volatile working class.

Responses to Industrialization

From the beginning, the British Industrial Revolution had its critics. Among the first were the romantic poets. William Blake (1757–1827) called the early factories "satanic mills" and protested against the hard life of the London poor. William Wordsworth (1770–1850) lamented the destruction of the rural way of life and the pollution of the land and water. Some handicraft workers—notably the **Luddites**, who attacked factories in northern England in 1811 and later—smashed the new machines, which they believed were putting them out of work. Doctors and reformers wrote of problems in the factories and new towns, while Malthus and Ricardo concluded that workers would earn only enough to stay alive.

This pessimistic view was accepted and reinforced by Friedrich Engels (1820–1895), the future revolutionary and colleague of Karl Marx (see Chapter 24). After studying conditions in northern England, this young son of a wealthy Prussian cotton manufacturer published in 1844 *The Condition of the Working Class in England*, a blistering indictment of the capitalist classes. "At the bar of world opinion," he wrote, "I charge the English middle classes with mass murder, wholesale robbery, and all the other crimes in the calendar." The new poverty of industrial workers was worse than the old poverty of cottage workers and agricultural laborers, according to Engels. The culprit was industrial capitalism, with its relentless competition and constant technical change. Engels's extremely influential charge of capitalist exploitation and increasing worker poverty was embellished by Marx and later socialists (see Chapter 24).

Analysis of industrial capitalism, often combined with reflections on the French Revolution, led to the development of a new overarching interpretation—a new paradigm—regarding social relationships. Briefly, this paradigm argued that individuals were members of separate classes based on their relationship to the means of production, that is, the machines and factories that dominated the new economy. As owners of expensive industrial machinery and as dependent laborers in their factories, the two main groups of society had separate and conflicting interests. Accordingly, the comfortable, well-educated "public" of the eighteenth century came increasingly to be defined as the middle class ("middle" because they were beneath the small group of aristocracy at the top of society who claimed to be above industrial activity), and the "people" gradually began to perceive themselves as composing a modern working class. And if the new class interpretation was more of a deceptive simplification than a fundamental truth for some critics, it appealed to many because it seemed to explain what was happening. Therefore, conflicting classes existed, in part, because many individuals came to believe they existed and developed an awareness that they belonged to a particular social class—what Karl Marx called **class-consciousness**.

Meanwhile, other observers believed that conditions were improving for the working people. In his 1835 study of the cotton industry, Andrew Ure (yoo-RAY) wrote that conditions in most factories were not harsh and were even quite good. Edwin Chadwick, a government official well acquainted with the problems of the working population, concluded that the "whole mass of the laboring community" was increasingly able "to buy more of the necessities and minor luxuries of life."[11] Nevertheless, those who thought, correctly, that conditions were stagnating or getting worse for working people were probably in the majority.

The Early Labor Movement in Britain

Not everyone worked in large factories and coal mines during the Industrial Revolution. In 1850 more British people still worked on farms than in any other single occupation. The second-largest occupation was domestic service, with more than 1 million household servants, 90 percent of whom were women. Thus many old, familiar jobs outside industry lived on.

Within industry itself, the pattern of artisans working with hand tools in small shops remained unchanged in many trades, even as others were revolutionized by technological change. For example, the British iron industry was completely dominated by large-scale capitalist firms by 1850. Many large ironworks had more than one thousand people on their payrolls. Yet the firms that fashioned iron into small metal goods, such as tools, tableware, and toys, employed on average fewer than ten wageworkers who used handicraft skills. The survival of small workshops gave many workers an alternative to factory employment.

Working-class solidarity and class-consciousness developed in small workshops as well as in large factories. In the northern factory districts, anticapitalist sentiments were frequent by the 1820s. Commenting in 1825 on a strike in the woolen center of Bradford and the support it had gathered from other regions, one newspaper claimed with pride that "it is all the workers of England against a few masters of Bradford."[12] Modern technology and factory organization had created a few versus the many.

Such sentiments ran contrary to the liberal tenets of economic freedom championed by eighteenth-century thinkers like Adam Smith. Liberal economic principles were embraced by statesmen and middle-class business owners in the late eighteenth century and continued to gather strength in the early nineteenth century. In 1799 Parliament passed the **Combination Acts**, which outlawed unions and strikes. In 1813 and 1814 Parliament repealed an old law regulating the wages of artisans and the conditions of apprenticeship. As a result of these and other measures, certain skilled artisan workers, such as bootmakers and high-quality tailors, found aggressive capitalists ignoring traditional work rules and trying to flood their trades with unorganized women workers and children to beat down wages.

The capitalist attack on artisan guilds and work rules was bitterly resented by many craftworkers, who subsequently played an important part in Great Britain and in other countries in gradually building a modern labor movement. The Combination Acts were widely disregarded by workers. Printers, papermakers, carpenters, tailors, and other such craftsmen continued to take collective action, and societies of skilled factory workers also organized unions. Unions sought to control the number of skilled workers, to limit apprenticeship to members' own children, and to bargain with owners over wages.

They were not afraid to strike; there was, for example, a general strike of adult cotton spinners in Manchester in 1810. In the face of widespread union activity, Parliament repealed the Combination Acts in 1824, and unions were tolerated, though not fully accepted, after 1825.

The next stage in the development of the British trade-union movement was the attempt to create a single large national union. This effort was led not so much by working people as by social reformers such as Robert Owen. Owen, a self-made cotton manufacturer (see page 710), had pioneered in industrial relations by combining firm discipline with concern for the health, safety, and hours of his workers. After 1815 he experimented with cooperative and socialist communities, including one in New Harmony, Indiana. Then in 1834 Owen organized one of the largest and most visionary of the early national unions, the Grand National Consolidated Trades Union.

When Owen's and other grandiose schemes collapsed, the British labor movement moved once again after 1851 in the direction of craft unions. The most famous of these was the Amalgamated Society of Engineers, which represented skilled machinists. These unions won real benefits for members by fairly conservative means and thus became an accepted part of the industrial scene.

British workers also engaged in direct political activity in defense of their interests. After the collapse of Owen's national trade union, many working people went into the Chartist movement, which sought political democracy. The key Chartist demand — universal manhood suffrage — became the great hope of millions of people. Workers were also active in campaigns to limit the workday in factories to ten hours and to permit duty-free importation of wheat into Great Britain to secure cheap bread. Thus working people developed a sense of their own identity and played an active role in shaping the new industrial system. They were neither helpless victims nor passive beneficiaries.

The Impact of Slavery

Another mass labor force of the Industrial Revolution was composed of the millions of enslaved men, women, and children who toiled in European colonies in the Caribbean and in North and South America. Historians have long debated the extent to which revenue from slavery contributed to Britain's achievements in the Industrial Revolution.

Most now agree that profits from colonial plantations and slave trading were a small portion of British national income in the eighteenth century and were probably more often invested in land than in industry. Nevertheless, the impact of slavery on

Britain's economy was much broader than direct profits alone. In the mid-eighteenth century the need for items to exchange for colonial cotton, sugar, tobacco, and slaves stimulated demand for British manufactured goods in the Caribbean, North America, and West Africa. Britain's dominance in the slave trade also led to the development of finance and credit institutions that would help early industrialists obtain capital for their businesses.

The British Parliament abolished the slave trade in 1807 and freed all slaves in British territories in 1833, but by 1850 most of the cotton processed by British mills was supplied by the coerced labor of slaves in the southern United States. Thus the Industrial Revolution cannot be detached from the Atlantic world and the misery of slavery it included.

Chapter Summary

As markets for manufactured goods increased both domestically and overseas, Britain was able to respond with increased production, largely because of its stable government, abundant natural resources, and flexible labor force. The first factories arose as a result of technical innovations in spinning cotton, thereby revolutionizing the textile industry. The demand for improvements in energy led to innovations and improvements in the steam engine, which transformed the iron industry, among others. In the early nineteenth century transportation of goods was greatly enhanced with the adoption of steam-powered trains and ships.

After 1815 continental European countries gradually built on England's technical breakthroughs. Entrepreneurs set up their own factories and hired skilled urban workers from local areas along with English immigrants experienced in the new technologies. Newly established corporate banks worked in conjunction with government interventions in finance and tariff controls to promote railroads and other industries. Beginning around 1850 Japan and the United States also began to rapidly industrialize, but generally the Industrial Revolution spread more slowly outside of Europe, as many countries were confined to producing agricultural goods and other raw materials to serve European markets. As a result, the gap between the industrialized West and the rest of the world widened.

The rise of modern industry had a profound impact on society, beginning in Britain in the late eighteenth century. Industrialization led to the growing size and wealth of the middle class and the rise of a modern industrial working class. Rigid rules, stern discipline, and long hours weighed heavily on factory workers, and improvements in the standard of living came slowly, but they were substantial by 1850. Married women withdrew increasingly from wage work and concentrated on child care and household responsibilities. The era of industrialization also fostered new attitudes toward child labor, encouraged protective factory legislation, and called forth a new sense of class feeling and an assertive labor movement. Slave labor in European colonies contributed to the rise of the Industrial Revolution by increasing markets for European goods, supplying raw materials, and encouraging the development of financial systems.

Notes

1. N. F. R. Crafts, *British Economic Growth During the Industrial Revolution* (Oxford: Oxford University Press, 1985), p. 32.
2. John Allen, *The British Industrial Revolution* (Cambridge: Cambridge University Press, 2009), pp. 1–2.

3. P. Bairoch, "International Industrialization Levels from 1750 to 1980," *Journal of European Economic History* 11 (Spring 1982): 269–333.

4. Quoted in J. Bowditch and C. Ramsland, eds., *Voices of the Industrial Revolution* (Ann Arbor: University of Michigan Press, 1961), p. 55, from Thomas Malthus, *Essay on the Principle of Population*, 4th ed. (1807).

5. Quoted in E. R. Pike, *"Hard Times": Human Documents of the Industrial Revolution* (New York: Praeger, 1966), p. 109.

6. See especially J. Brenner and M. Rama, "Rethinking Women's Oppression," *New Left Review* 144 (March–April 1984): 33–71, and sources cited there.

7. J. Humphries, ". . . 'The Most Free from Objection' . . . : The Sexual Division of Labor and Women's Work in Nineteenth-Century England," *Journal of Economic History* 47 (December 1987): 941; Pike, *"Hard Times,"* p. 266.

8. Joel Mokyr, *The Enlightened Economy: An Economic History of Britain, 1700–1850* (New Haven: Yale University Press, 2009), pp. 460–461.

9. H.-J. Voth, *Time and Work in England, 1750–1830* (Oxford: Oxford University Press, 2000), pp. 268–270; also pp. 118–133.

10. Mokyr, *The Enlightened Economy*, p. 455.

11. Quoted in W. A. Hayek, ed., *Capitalism and the Historians* (Chicago: University of Chicago Press, 1954), p. 126.

12. Quoted in D. Geary, ed., *Labour and Socialist Movements in Europe Before 1914* (Oxford: Berg, 1989), p. 29.

13. Kenneth Pomeranz, *The Great Divergence: China, Europe, and the Making of the Modern World Economy* (Princeton, N.J.: Princeton University Press, 2000).

CONNECTIONS

For much of its history, Europe lagged behind older and more sophisticated civilizations in China and the Middle East. There was little reason to predict that the West would one day achieve world dominance. And yet by 1800 Europe had broken ahead of the other regions of the world in terms of wealth and power, a process historians have termed "the Great Divergence."[13]

One important prerequisite for the rise of Europe was its growing control over world trade, first in the Indian Ocean in the sixteenth and seventeenth centuries and then in the eighteenth-century Atlantic world. Acquisition of New World colonies— itself the accidental result of explorers seeking direct access to the rich Afroeurasian trade world—brought Europeans new sources of wealth and raw materials as well as guaranteed markets for their finished goods. A second crucial factor in the rise of Europe was the Industrial Revolution, which dramatically increased the pace of production and distribution while reducing their cost, thereby allowing Europeans to control other countries first economically and then politically. Britain dominated this process at first, but was soon followed by other European nations. By the middle of the nineteenth century the gap between Western industrial production and standards of living and those of the non-West had grown dramatically, bringing with it the economic dependence of non-Western nations, meager wages for their largely impoverished populations, and increasingly aggressive Western imperial ambitions (see Chapter 25). In the late nineteenth century non-Western countries began to experience their own processes of industrialization. Today's world is witnessing a surge in productivity in China, India, and other non-Western nations, with uncertain consequences for the global balance of power.

Chapter Review

MAKE IT STICK

✓ LearningCurve
Go online and use LearningCurve to retain what you've read.

IDENTIFY KEY TERMS

Identify and explain the significance of each item below.

Industrial Revolution (p. 692)

spinning jenny (p. 693)

water frame (p. 693)

steam engines (p. 696)

Rocket (p. 697)

Crystal Palace (p. 700)

iron law of wages (p. 701)

tariff protection (p. 705)

Factory Act of 1833 (p. 710)

separate spheres (p. 711)

Mines Act of 1842 (p. 712)

Luddites (p. 715)

class-consciousness (p. 716)

Combination Acts (p. 716)

REVIEW THE MAIN IDEAS

Answer the focus questions from each section of the chapter.

1. Why did the Industrial Revolution begin in Britain, and how did it develop between 1780 and 1850? (p. 691)

2. How did countries in Europe and around the world respond to the challenge of industrialization after 1815? (p. 701)

3. How did work evolve during the Industrial Revolution, and how did daily life change for working people? (p. 709)

4. How did the changes brought about by the Industrial Revolution lead to new social classes, and how did people respond to the new structure? (p. 713)

MAKE CONNECTIONS

Analyze the larger developments and continuities within and across chapters.

1. Why did Great Britain take the lead in industrialization, and when did other countries begin to adopt the new techniques and organization of production?

2. How did the achievements in agriculture and rural industry of the late seventeenth and eighteenth centuries (Chapter 19) pave the way for the Industrial Revolution of the late eighteenth century?

3. How would you compare the political revolutions of the late eighteenth century (Chapter 22) with the Industrial Revolution? Which seems to you to have created the most important changes, and why?

LaunchPad

Inventing a New Workforce
How were social and economic change connected in nineteenth-century England?

Read sources on early industrial manufacturing, and then complete a quiz and writing assignment based on the evidence and details from this chapter.

See inside the front cover to learn more.

CHRONOLOGY

ca. 1765	• Hargreaves invents spinning jenny; Arkwright creates water frame
1769	• Watt patents modern steam engine
ca. 1780–1850	• Industrial Revolution and accompanying population boom in Great Britain
1799	• Combination Acts passed in England
1805	• Egypt begins process of modernization
1810	• Strike of Manchester, England, cotton spinners
1824	• British Combination Acts repealed
1829	• Stephenson's *Rocket*, first important railroad
1830s	• Industrial banks promote rapid industrialization of Belgium
1833	• Factory Act passed in England
1834	• Creation of a *Zollverein* (customs union) among many German states
1842	• Mines Act passed in England
1844	• Engels, *The Condition of the Working Class in England*
1850s	• Japan begins to adopt Western technologies; industrial gap widens between the West and the rest of the world
1851	• Great Exhibition held at Crystal Palace in London
1860s	• Germany and the United States begin to rapidly industrialize

24

✓ **LearningCurve**
After reading the chapter, go online and use LearningCurve to retain what you've read.

Ideologies of Change in Europe

1815–1914

THE MOMENTOUS TRANSFORMATIONS WROUGHT BY THE POLITICAL and economic revolutions of the late eighteenth and early nineteenth centuries left a legacy of unfinished hopes and dreams for many Europeans: for democracy, liberty, and equality and for higher living standards for all. These aspirations would play out with unpredictable and tumultuous consequences over the course of the nineteenth century. After 1815 the powers that defeated Napoleon united under a revived conservatism to stamp out the spread of liberal and democratic reforms. But the political and social innovations made possible by the unfinished revolutions proved difficult to contain.

In politics, powerful ideologies—liberalism, nationalism, and socialism—emerged to oppose conservatism. All played critical roles in the political and social battles of the era and the great popular upheaval that eventually swept across Europe in the revolutions of 1848. These revolutions failed, however, and gave way to more sober—and more successful—nation building in the 1860s. Redrawing the political geography of central Europe and uniting first Italy and then Germany, European political leaders and middle-class nationalists also began to deal effectively with the challenges of the emerging urban society. One way they did so was through nationalism—mass identification with a nation-state that was increasingly responsive to the needs of its people. At the same time, the triumph of nationalism promoted bitter rivalries between states and peoples, spurred a second great wave of imperialism, and in the twentieth century brought an era of tragic global conflict.

A Conservative Peace Gives Way to Radical Ideas

How did the allies fashion a peace settlement in 1815, and what radical ideas emerged between 1815 and 1848?

The eventual eruption of revolutionary political and economic forces was by no means certain as the Napoleonic era ended in 1815. Quite the contrary. After finally defeating Napoleon, the conservative aristocratic monarchies of Russia, Prussia, Austria, and Great Britain—known as the Quadruple Alliance (see Chapter 22)—reaffirmed their determination to hold France in line. But many other international questions remained, and the allies agreed to meet at the Congress of Vienna to fashion a general peace settlement. The great challenge for political leaders in 1814 and 1815 was to construct a settlement that would last and not sow the seeds of another war. By carefully managing the European balance of power and embracing conservative restoration, they brokered an agreement that contributed to fifty years without major warfare in Europe (see Map 24.1, page 725).

In the years following the peace settlement, intellectuals and social observers sought to harness the radical ideas of the revolutionary age to new political movements. Many rejected conservatism, a political philosophy that stressed retaining traditional values and institutions, including hereditary monarchy and a strong landowning aristocracy. Radical thinkers developed and refined alternative visions—alternative ideologies—and tried to convince society to act on them.

The Political and Social Situation After 1815

With the French agreeing to the restoration of the Bourbon dynasty (see Chapter 22), the four allies of the Quadruple Alliance—Russia, Prussia, Austria, and Great Britain—were lenient toward France after Napoleon's abdication. The first Peace of Paris gave France the boundaries it possessed in 1792, which were larger than those of 1789, and France did not have to pay any war reparations.

When the Quadruple Alliance, along with representatives of minor powers, met together at the Congress of Vienna, they agreed to raise a number of barriers against renewed French aggression. The Low Countries—Belgium and Holland—were united under an enlarged Dutch monarchy capable of opposing France more effectively. Prussia received considerably more territory along France's eastern border to stand as a "sentinel on the Rhine" against renewed French aggression. In these ways, the Quadruple Alliance combined leniency toward France with strong defensive measures.

In their moderation toward France, the allies were motivated by self-interest and traditional ideas about the balance of power. To the peacemakers, especially to Klemens von Metternich (1773–1859), Austria's foreign minister, the balance of power meant an international equilibrium of political and military forces that would discourage aggression by any combination of states or, worse, the domination of Europe by any single state. The Quadruple Alliance members, therefore, agreed to meet periodically to discuss their common interests and to consider appropriate measures to maintain peace in Europe. This agreement marked the beginning of the European "congress system," which lasted long into the nineteenth century.

LA BALANCE   POLÍTIQUE .

Adjusting the Balance   The Englishman on the left uses his money to counterbalance the people that the Prussian and the fat Metternich are gaining in Saxony and Italy. Alexander I sits happily on his prize, Poland. This cartoon captures the essence of how the educated public thought about the balance-of-power diplomacy resulting in the Treaty of Vienna. (*"La Balance Politique,"* 1815, colored etching/Deutsches Historisches Museum, Berlin, Germany/© DHM/The Bridgeman Art Library)

Conservatism After 1815

The peace settlement's domestic side was much less moderate. In 1815, under Metternich's leadership, Austria, Prussia, and Russia formed the Holy Alliance, dedicated to crushing the ideas and politics of the revolutionary era within their borders and across Europe. Metternich's policies dominated the entire German Confederation of thirty-eight independent German states, which the Vienna peace settlement had created (Map 24.1). It was through the German Confederation that Metternich had the repressive Karlsbad Decrees issued in 1819. These decrees required the member states to root out radical ideas in their universities and newspapers, and a permanent committee was established to investigate and punish any liberal or radical organizations.

Adhering to a conservative political philosophy, Metternich believed that human nature was prone to error, excess, and self-serving behavior and that strong governments were needed to protect society from its worst instincts. Born into the landed nobility, Metternich zealously defended his caste and its privileges. The nobility was one of Europe's most ancient institutions, and conservatives regarded tradition as the basic source of human institutions. Like many European conservatives of his time, Metternich believed that liberalism, as embodied in revolutionary America and France, had been responsible for a generation of war with untold bloodshed and suffering. He

MAP 24.1 Europe in 1815 In 1815 Europe contained many different states, but after the defeat of Napoleon international politics was dominated by the five Great Powers: Russia, Prussia, Austria, Great Britain, and France. (The number rises to six if one includes the Ottoman Empire.)

blamed liberal revolutionaries for stirring up the lower classes, which he believed desired nothing more than peace and quiet.

Another belief that Metternich opposed, which was often allied with liberalism, was nationalism, the idea that each national group had a right to establish its own independent government. The Habsburgs' Austrian Empire was a dynastic state dominated by Germans but containing many other national groups, including Magyars (Hungarians), Czechs, Italians, Poles, Ukrainians, Slovenes, Croats, Serbs, and Romanians. This multinational state was both strong and weak. It was strong because of its large population and vast territories, but weak because of its many and potentially dissatisfied nationalities. In these circumstances, Metternich opposed both liberalism and nationalism, for Austria could not accommodate those ideologies and remain a powerful empire. Metternich's antinationalist efforts were supported by the two great multinational empires on Austria's borders, Russia and the Ottoman Empire.

Liberalism and the Middle Class

The principal ideas of liberalism — liberty and equality — were by no means defeated in 1815. (This form of liberalism is often called "classical liberalism" and should not be confused with modern American liberalism, which usually favors government programs to meet social needs and to regulate the economy.) First realized in the American Revolution and then achieved in part in the French Revolution, liberalism demanded representative government and equality before the law. The idea of liberty also meant specific individual freedoms: freedom of the press, freedom of speech, freedom of assembly, and freedom from arbitrary arrest. In Europe only France, with Louis XVIII's Constitutional Charter, and Great Britain, with its Parliament and historic liberties of English men and women, had realized much of the liberal program in 1815. Even in those countries, liberalism had only begun to succeed.

Liberalism faced more radical ideological competitors in the early nineteenth century. Opponents of liberalism especially criticized its economic principles, which called for unrestricted private enterprise and no government interference in the economy. This philosophy was popularly known as the doctrine of laissez faire (lay-say FEHR).

Scottish philosopher Adam Smith posited the idea of a free economy in 1776 in opposition to mercantilism and its attempt to regulate trade. Smith argued that freely competitive private enterprise would give all citizens a fair and equal opportunity to do what they did best and would result in greater income for everyone. In early-nineteenth-century Britain this economic liberalism was embraced most enthusiastically by business groups and thus became a doctrine associated with business interests.

In the early nineteenth century liberal political ideals also became more closely associated with narrow class interests. Early-nineteenth-century liberals favored representative government, but they generally wanted property qualifications attached to the right to vote and to serve in Parliament. In practice this meant limiting the vote and the right to serve to well-to-do males.

As liberalism became increasingly identified with the middle class after 1815, some intellectuals and foes of conservatism felt that liberalism did not go nearly far enough. Inspired by memories of the French Revolution, they called for replacing monarchical rule with republics, for democracy through universal male suffrage, and for greater economic and social equality. These democrats and republicans were more radical than the liberals, and they were more willing to endorse violence to achieve goals. As a result, liberals and radical republicans could join forces against conservatives only up to a point.

The Growing Appeal of Nationalism

Nationalism was a radical new ideology that emerged in the years after 1815 — an idea destined to have an enormous influence in the modern world. In 1808, in an address to a German audience in French-occupied Berlin, the German philosopher Johann Gottlieb Fichte called on all Germans "to have that organic unity in which no member regards the fate of another as the fate of a stranger."[1] Fichte and other early advocates of the "national idea" argued that the members of what we would call today an ethnic group had their own spirit and their own cultural unity, which were manifested especially in a common language, history, and territory. In fact, such cultural unity was more a dream than a reality as local dialects abounded, historical memory divided the inhabitants of the different states as much as it unified them, and a variety of ethnic groups shared the territory of most states.

Nevertheless, many European nationalists sought to make the territory of each people coincide with well-defined boundaries in an independent nation-state. It was this political goal that made nationalism so explosive in central and eastern Europe after 1815, when there were either too few states (Austria, Russia, and the Ottoman Empire) or too many (the Italian peninsula and the German Confederation), and when different peoples overlapped and intermingled.

Scholars have struggled to understand how the nationalist vision, often fitting poorly with existing conditions and having the potential for tremendous upheaval, was so successful in the long run. The nationalist vision triumphed partly because the development of complex industrial and urban society required better communication between individuals and groups.[2] The need for communication promoted the development of a standardized national language that was spread through mass education, creating at least a superficial cultural unity. Nationalism also came into being as a result of the ardent writings and speeches of nationalists themselves, which helped to spread the new idea of the nation as a natural community that should possess control over its destiny as a sovereign state. Those who believed in the new ideology thus helped create "imagined communities," which bound inhabitants through the abstract concept of an all-embracing national identity. Nationalists and leaders brought citizens together with emotionally charged symbols and ceremonies, such as ethnic festivals and flag-waving parades that celebrated the imagined nation of spiritual equals.[3]

Between 1815 and 1850 most people who believed in nationalism also believed in either liberalism or radical democratic republicanism. A common faith in the creativity and nobility of the people was perhaps the single most important reason for the linking of these two concepts. Liberals and especially democrats saw the people as the ultimate source of all good government. They agreed that the benefits of self-government would be possible only if the people were united by common traditions that transcended class and local interests. Thus individual liberty and love of a free nation overlapped greatly.

Yet early nationalists also stressed the differences among peoples, and they developed a strong sense of "we" and "they"; the "they" was often viewed as the enemy. Thus, while European nationalism's main thrust was liberal and democratic, below the surface lurked ideas of national superiority and national mission that eventually led to aggression and conflict against supposedly inferior peoples in Africa and Asia, and to the great world wars of the twentieth century.

The Birth of Socialism

Socialism, a second radical doctrine after 1815, began in France. Early French socialists shared a sense of disappointment that political revolution in France had ended with the restoration of the Bourbon monarchy. They were also alarmed by the rise of laissez faire and the emergence of modern industry, which they saw as fostering inequality and selfish individualism. There was, they believed, an urgent need for a further reorganization of society to establish cooperation and a new sense of community.

Early French socialists felt an intense desire to help the poor, whose conditions had not been improved by industrial advances, and they preached greater economic equality between the rich and the poor. Inspired by the economic planning implemented in revolutionary France (see Chapter 22), they argued that the government should rationally organize the economy to control prices and prevent unemployment. Socialists also believed that government should regulate private property or that private property should be abolished and replaced by state or community ownership.

One of the most influential early socialist thinkers was Henri de Saint-Simon (1760–1825). Saint-Simon optimistically proclaimed the tremendous possibilities of industrial development: "The age of gold is before us!" In his view the key to progress was proper social organization that required the "parasites" — the royal court, the aristocracy, lawyers, churchmen — to give way, once and for all, to the "doers" — the leading scientists, engineers, and industrialists. The doers would carefully plan the economy, guide it forward, and improve conditions for the poor.

Charles Fourier (1772–1837), another influential French thinker, envisaged a socialist utopia of self-sufficient communities. An early proponent of the total emancipation of women, Fourier also called for the abolition of marriage, free unions based only on love, and sexual freedom. Some socialist thinkers embraced the even more radical ideas of anarchism. In his 1840 pamphlet *What Is Property?* Pierre-Joseph Proudhon (1809–1865), a self-educated printer, famously argued that "property is theft!" Property, he claimed, was profit that was stolen from the worker, who actually produced all wealth.

Up to the 1840s France was the center of socialism, as it had been the center of revolution in Europe, but in the following decades the German intellectual Karl Marx (1818–1883) would weave the diffuse strands of social thought into a distinctly modern ideology. Marx had studied philosophy at the University of Berlin before turning to journalism and economics. In 1848 the thirty-year-old Karl Marx and the twenty-eight-year-old Friedrich Engels (see page 715) published *The Communist Manifesto*, which became the guiding text of socialism.

Marx's work united sociology, economics, philosophy, and history in an impressive synthesis. He learned from British political economists like Adam Smith and David Ricardo to apply social-scientific analysis to economic problems, though he pushed their ideas in radical directions. Deeply influenced by the French socialists, Marx dismissed their appeals to the middle class and the state to help the poor as naïve. Instead he argued that middle-class interests and those of the industrial working class were inevitably opposed to each other. According to the *Manifesto*, the "history of all previously existing society is the history of class struggles." In Marx's view, one class had always exploited the other, and, with the advent of modern industry, society was split more clearly than ever before: between the middle class — the bourgeoisie — and the modern working class — the proletariat.

Just as the bourgeoisie had triumphed over the feudal aristocracy in the French Revolution, Marx predicted that the proletariat would conquer the bourgeoisie in a new revolution. While a tiny majority owned the means of production and grew richer, the ever-poorer proletariat was constantly growing in size and in class-consciousness. Marx believed that the critical moment when class conflict would result in revolution was very near, as the last lines of *The Communist Manifesto* make clear:

> Germany . . . is on the eve of a bourgeois revolution, that is bound to be . . . the prelude to an immediately following proletarian revolution. . . .
>
> Let the ruling classes tremble at a Communist revolution. The proletarians have nothing to lose but their chains. They have a world to win. WORKING MEN OF ALL COUNTRIES, UNITE!

Marx drew on the arguments of Smith and Ricardo, who taught that labor was the source of all value. He went on to argue that profits were really wages stolen from the workers. Moreover, Marx incorporated Friedrich Engels's account of the terrible oppression of the new class of factory workers in England. Thus Marx pulled together powerful ideas and insights to create one of the great secular religions out of the intellectual ferment of the early nineteenth century.

Reforms and Revolutions, 1815–1850

Why did revolutions triumph briefly throughout most of Europe in 1848, and why did they fail?

As liberal, nationalist, and socialist forces battered the conservatism of 1815, social and economic conditions continued to deteriorate for many Europeans, adding to the mounting pressures. In some countries, such as Great Britain, change occurred gradually and largely peacefully, but in 1848 radical political and social ideologies combined with economic crisis to produce revolutionary movements that demanded an end to repressive government. Between 1815 and 1848 many European countries, including France, Austria, and Prussia, experienced variations on this basic theme.

Social and Economic Conflict

The slow and uneven spread of industrialization in Europe after 1815 (see Chapter 23) meant that the benefits of higher productivity were not felt by many. In Great Britain, the earliest adopter of industrial methods, living standards did not rise until the 1840s, and this trend took longer to spread to the continent, where only a few industries in a few regions had adopted steam power up to 1850. Most of the continent remained agricultural, and the traditional social hierarchy, dominated by a landowning aristocracy, persisted. In the early nineteenth century the pressures of a rapidly growing population, the adoption of new forms of agriculture, and the spread of exploitative rural industry destabilized these existing patterns. Conditions were deteriorating, and contemporaries had no way to understand that decades later the full-scale adoption of industrialization would lead to higher wages and a rise in standards of living.

Many of the social conflicts that ensued resembled those of the eighteenth century. Peasants resented the demands of their noble landlords and state tax collectors. Many lost access to collective land due to enclosure and the adoption of more efficient farming techniques. The growing number of cottage workers resisted exploitation by merchant capitalists, and journeymen battled masters in urban industries. Serfdom still existed in the Hungarian provinces of the Austrian Empire, Prussian Silesia, and Russia.[4]

What transformed these conflicts was the political ideologies born from the struggles and unfulfilled hopes of the French Revolution — liberalism, nationalism, and socialism—as well as the newly invigorated conservatism that stood against them. These ideologies helped turn economic and social conflicts into the revolutions of 1848.

Liberal Reform in Great Britain

The English parliamentary system guaranteed basic civil rights, but only about 8 percent of the population could vote for representatives to Parliament. By the 1780s there was growing interest in some sort of reform, but the French Revolution threw the British aristocracy that still dominated Parliament into a panic. After 1815 the British government put down popular protests over unemployment and the high cost of grain caused by the Napoleonic Wars with repressive legislation and military force.

By the early 1830s the social and economic changes created by industrialization began to be felt in politics. In 1832 continuous pressure from the liberal middle classes and popular unrest convinced the king and the House of Lords that they needed to act. The Reform Bill of 1832 moved British politics in a more democratic direction by giving new industrial areas increased representation in the House of Commons and by increasing the number of voters by about 50 percent. For the first time, comfortable middle-class urban groups, the main beneficiaries of industrialization, as well as some substantial farmers, received the vote. Two years later, the New Poor Law called for the growing number of unemployed and indigent families to be placed in harsh workhouses rather than receiving aid from local parishes to remain in their own homes. With this act, Britain's rulers sought to relieve middle-class taxpayers of the burden of poor relief and to encourage unemployed rural workers to migrate to cities and take up industrial work. Because workhouses were usually segregated by sex, the act caused the breakup of many poor families.

Thus limited democratic reform was counterbalanced by harsh measures against the poor, both linked to the new social and economic circumstances of the Industrial Revolution. Many working people protested their exclusion from voting and the terms of the New Poor Law. Between 1838 and 1848 they streamed into the Chartist movement (see page 717), which demanded that all men should be able to vote and stand for office and that all members of Parliament (MPs) be paid (so that men without a private fortune could hold office). In 1847 the ruling conservative party, known as the Tories, sought to appease working people with the Ten Hours Act, which limited the workday for women and young people in factories to ten hours. Tory aristocrats continued to champion legislation regulating factory conditions in order to compete with the middle class for working-class support.

This competition meant that the parliamentary state functioned well in eliciting support from its people and thereby managed unrest without the outbreak of revolution. Conciliating the middle and working classes did not mean relinquishing the government's authority, however. To ensure its control, the government maintained a heavy police presence throughout Great Britain, especially in Ireland. Another factor favoring Great Britain's largely peaceful evolution in the nineteenth century was the fact that living standards had begun to rise significantly by the 1840s, as the benefits of industrialization finally began to be felt. Thus England avoided the violence and turmoil of the revolutions of 1848 that shook continental Europe.

The people of Ireland did not benefit from these circumstances. Long ruled as a conquered people, the population was mostly composed of Irish Catholic peasants who rented their land from a tiny minority of Protestant landowners, many of whom resided in England. Ruthlessly exploited and growing rapidly in numbers, the rural population around 1800 lived under abominable conditions. The novelist Sir Walter Scott wrote:

> The poverty of the Irish peasantry is on the extreme verge of human misery; their cottages would scarce serve for pig styes even in Scotland; and their rags seem the very refuse of a sheep, and are spread over their bodies with such an ingenious variety of wretchedness that you would think nothing but some sort of perverted taste could have assembled so many shreds together.[5]

A compassionate French traveler agreed, writing that Ireland was "pure misery, naked and hungry. . . . I saw the American Indian in his forests and the black slave in his chains, and I believed that I was seeing the most extreme form of human misery; but that was before I knew the lot of poor Ireland."[6]

In spite of terrible conditions, Ireland's population doubled from 4 million to 8 million between 1780 and 1840, fueled in large part by the calories and nutritive qualities of the potato. However, the potato crop failed in 1845, 1846, 1848, and 1851 in Ireland and throughout much of Europe. Blight attacked the young plants, and the tubers rotted. Many suffered in Europe, but in Ireland, where dependency on the potato was much more widespread, the result was starvation and death. The British government, committed to laissez-faire economic policies, reacted slowly and utterly inadequately. One and a half million died, while another million fled between 1845 and 1851, primarily to the United States and Great Britain. The Great Famine, as this tragedy came to be known, intensified anti-British feeling and promoted Irish nationalism.

Revolutions in France

Louis XVIII's Constitutional Charter of 1814 was essentially a liberal constitution. It protected economic and social gains made by the middle class and the peasantry in the French Revolution, recognized intellectual and artistic freedom, and created a parliament with upper and lower houses. The charter was anything but democratic, however. Only a tiny minority of males had the right to vote for the legislative deputies who, with the king and his ministers, made the nation's laws.

Louis's conservative successor, Charles X (r. 1824–1830), wanted to re-establish the old order in France. To rally French nationalism and gain popular support, he exploited a long-standing dispute with Muslim Algeria, a vassal state of the Ottoman Empire. In June 1830 a French force of thirty-seven thousand troops crossed the Mediterranean and took the capital of Algiers. The French continued to wage war against Algerian resistance until 1847, when they finally subdued the country. Bringing French and other European settlers to Algeria and expropriating large amounts of Muslim-owned land, the conquest of Algeria marked the rebirth of French colonial expansion.

Charles profited from early success in Algeria to repudiate the Constitutional Charter in 1830. After three days of uprisings in Paris, which sparked a series of revolts by frustrated liberals and democrats across Europe, Charles fled. His cousin Louis Philippe (r. 1830–1848) accepted the Constitutional Charter of 1814 and assumed the title of the "king of the French people." Still, the situation in France remained fundamentally unchanged. The vote was extended only from 100,000 to 170,000 citizens. Political and social reformers and the poor of Paris were bitterly disappointed.

During the 1840s this sense of disappointment was worsened by bad harvests and the slow development of industrialization, which meant that living conditions for the majority of the working classes were deteriorating rather than improving. Similar conditions prevailed across continental Europe, which was soon rocked by insurrections: in northern Austria in 1846, in Switzerland in 1847, and in Naples in January 1848. In February full-scale revolution broke out in France, and its shock waves ripped across the continent.

Louis Philippe, whose reign was labeled the "bourgeois monarchy" because it served the interests of wealthy elites, had refused to approve social legislation or consider electoral reform. Frustrated desires for change, high-level financial scandals, and crop failures in 1845 and 1846 united diverse groups of the king's opponents, including merchants, intellectuals, shopkeepers, and workers. In February 1848, as popular revolt broke out, barricades went up, and Louis Philippe abdicated.

The revolutionaries quickly drafted a democratic, republican constitution for France's Second Republic, granting the right to vote to every adult male. Revolutionary compassion and sympathy for freedom were expressed in the freeing of all slaves in French colonies, the abolition of the death penalty, and the establishment of national workshops for unemployed Parisian workers.

The Triumph of Democratic Republics   This French illustration offers an opinion of the initial revolutionary breakthrough in 1848. The peoples of Europe, joined together around their respective national banners, are achieving republican freedom, which is symbolized by the Statue of Liberty and the discarded crowns. The woman wearing pants at the base of the statue—very radical attire—represents feminist hopes for liberation. (Lithograph by Frederic Sorrieu [1807–ca. 1861]. Musée de la Ville de Paris, Musée Carnavalet, Paris, France/Giraudon/The Bridgeman Art Library)

Yet there were profound differences within the revolutionary coalition in Paris. The socialism promoted by radical republicans frightened not only the liberal middle and upper classes but also the peasants, many of whom owned land. When the French masses voted for delegates to the new Constituent Assembly in late April 1848, they elected 500 monarchists and conservatives, only about 270 moderate republicans, and just 80 radicals or socialists. After the elections this clash of ideologies—of liberal capitalism and socialism—became a clash of arms. When the government dissolved the national workshops in Paris, workers rose in a spontaneous insurrection. Working people fought with courage, but the government had the army and the support of the French countryside. After three terrible "June Days" and the death or injury of more than ten thousand people, the republican army stood triumphant in a sea of working-class blood and hatred.

The revolution in France thus ended in failure. The February coalition of the middle and working classes had in four short months become locked in mortal combat. In place of a generous democratic republic, the Constituent Assembly completed a constitution featuring a strong executive. This allowed Louis Napoleon, nephew of Napoleon Bonaparte, to win a landslide victory in the December 1848 election based on promises to lead a strong government in favor of popular interests.

President Louis Napoleon at first shared power with a conservative National Assembly. But in 1851 Louis Napoleon dismissed the Assembly and seized power in a coup d'état. A year later he called on the French to make him hereditary emperor, and 97 percent voted to do so in a national plebiscite. Louis Napoleon then ruled France's Second Empire as Napoleon III, initiating policies favoring economic growth and urban development to appease the populace. In 1870, on the eve of a disastrous war with Prussia (see page 739), the emperor was still seeking with some success to reconcile a strong national state with universal male suffrage and an independent National Assembly.

The Revolutions of 1848 in Central Europe

Throughout central Europe, social conflicts were exacerbated by the economic crises of 1845 to 1846. News of the upheaval in France in 1848 provoked the outbreak of revolution. Drawing on the great traditions of 1789, liberals demanded written constitutions, representative government, and greater civil liberties from authoritarian regimes. When governments hesitated, popular revolts followed. Urban workers and students allied with middle-class liberals and peasants. In the face of these coalitions, monarchs made hasty concessions. Soon, however, popular revolutionary fronts broke down as they had in France.

Compared with the situation in France, where political participation by working people reached its peak, revolts in central Europe tended to be dominated by social elites. They were also more sharply divided between moderate constitutionalists and radical republicans. The revolution in the Austrian Empire began in 1848 in Hungary, when nationalistic Hungarians demanded national autonomy, full civil liberties, and universal suffrage. When Viennese students and workers also took to the streets and peasant disorders broke out, the Habsburg emperor Ferdinand I (r. 1835–1848) capitulated and promised reforms and a liberal constitution. The coalition of revolutionaries was not stable, however. When the monarchy abolished serfdom, the newly free peasants lost interest in the political and social questions agitating the cities.

The revolutionary coalition was also weakened and ultimately destroyed by conflicting national aspirations. In March the Hungarian revolutionary leaders pushed through an extremely liberal, almost democratic, constitution. But the Hungarian revolutionaries also sought to create a unified Hungarian nation. The minority groups that formed half the population — the Croats, Serbs, and Romanians — objected that such unification would hinder their own political autonomy and cultural independence. Likewise, Czech nationalists based in Bohemia and the city of Prague came into conflict with German nationalists. Thus nationalism within the Austrian Empire enabled the monarchy to play off one ethnic group against the other.

The monarchy's first breakthrough came in June when the army crushed a working-class revolt in Prague. In October the predominantly peasant troops of the regular Austrian army attacked the student and working-class radicals in Vienna and retook the city. Thus the determination of Austria's aristocracy and the loyalty of its army were the final ingredients in the triumph of reaction and the defeat of revolution.

When Ferdinand I abdicated in favor of his young nephew, Franz Joseph (see page 756), only Hungary had yet to be brought under control. Another determined conservative, Nicholas I of Russia (r. 1825–1855), obligingly lent his iron hand. In June 1849, 130,000 Russian troops poured into Hungary and subdued the country. For a number of years the Habsburgs ruled Hungary as a conquered territory.

After Austria, Prussia was the largest and most influential kingdom in the German Confederation. Prior to 1848, middle-class Prussian liberals had sought to reshape Prussia into a liberal constitutional monarchy, which would lead the confederation's thirty-eight states into a unified nation. The agitation following Louis Philippe's fall in France combined with economic crisis encouraged Prussian liberals to press their demands. When artisans and factory workers in Berlin exploded in revolt in March 1848 and joined with middle-class liberals against the monarchy, Prussian king Frederick William IV (r. 1840–1861) caved in. On March 21 he promised to grant Prussia a liberal constitution and to merge Prussia into a new national German state.

Elections were held across the German Confederation for a national parliament, which convened to write a federal constitution for a unified German state. Members of the new parliament completed drafting a liberal constitution in March 1849, which ignored calls for more radical measures from workers and socialists, and elected King Frederick William of Prussia emperor of the new German national state. By early 1849, however, Frederick William had reasserted his royal authority, contemptuously refusing to accept the "crown from the gutter." When Frederick William tried to get the small monarchs of Germany to elect him emperor on his own terms, with authoritarian power, Austria balked. Supported by Russia, Austria forced Prussia to renounce all its unification schemes in late 1850. The German Confederation was re-established. Attempts to unite the Germans — first in a liberal national state and then in a conservative Prussian empire — had failed completely.

Thus, across Europe, the uprisings of 1848, which had been inspired by the legacy of the late-eighteenth-century revolutionary era, were unsuccessful. Reform movements splintered into competing factions, while the forces of order proved better organized and more united, on both a domestic and international level. The revolutions did succeed, nonetheless, in bringing about the abolition of serfdom in the regions they touched.

Nation Building in Italy, Germany, and Russia

How did strong leaders and nation building transform Italy, Germany, and Russia?

Louis Napoleon's triumph in 1848 and his authoritarian rule in the 1850s provided Europe's victorious forces of order with a new political model. To what extent might the expanding urban middle classes and even portions of the working classes rally to a strong and essentially conservative national state that also promised change? This was one of the great political questions in the 1850s and 1860s. In central Europe a resounding answer came with the national unification of Italy and Germany.

The Russian empire also experienced profound political crises in this period, but they were unlike those in Italy or Germany because Russia was already a vast multinational state built on long traditions of military conquest and absolutist rule by elites from the dominant ethnic group—the Russians. It became clear to Russian leaders that they had to embrace the process of **modernization**, defined narrowly as the changes that enable a country to compete effectively with the leading countries at a given time.

Cavour, Garibaldi, and the Unification of Italy

Italy had never been a united nation prior to 1850. A battleground for the Great Powers after 1494, Italy was reorganized in 1815 at the Congress of Vienna. Austria received the rich northern provinces of Lombardy and Venetia. Sardinia and Piedmont fell under the rule of an Italian monarch, and Tuscany shared north-central Italy with several smaller states. The papacy ruled over central Italy and Rome, while a branch of the Bourbons ruled Naples and Sicily. Metternich was not wrong in dismissing Italy as "a geographical expression" (Map 24.2).

After 1815 the goal of a unified Italian nation captivated many Italians, but there was no agreement on how it could be achieved. In 1848 the idealistic nationalist Giuseppe Mazzini hailed efforts to form a democratic Italian republic. Like the other revolutions of 1848, Mazzini's failed, crushed by Austrian forces. Temporarily driven from Rome during the upheavals of 1848, a frightened Pope Pius IX (pontificate 1846–1878) turned against most modern trends, including national unification. At the same time, Victor Emmanuel, king of independent Sardinia, retained the moderate liberal constitution granted under duress in March 1848. To the Italian middle classes, Sardinia (see Map 24.2) appeared to be a liberal, progressive state ideally suited to drive Austria out of northern Italy and achieve the goal of national unification.

Sardinia had the good fortune of being led by Count Camillo Benso di Cavour. Cavour came from a noble family and embraced the economic doctrines and business activities associated with the prosperous middle class. Cavour's national goals were limited and realistic. Until 1859 he sought unity only for the states of northern and perhaps central Italy in a greatly expanded kingdom of Sardinia.

In the 1850s Cavour worked to consolidate Sardinia as a liberal constitutional state capable of leading northern Italy. He worked out a secret diplomatic alliance with Napoleon III, and in July 1858 he goaded Austria into attacking Sardinia. The combined Franco-Sardinian forces were victorious, but Napoleon III decided on a compromise peace with the Austrians in July 1859 to avoid offending French Catholics

MAP 24.2   The Unification of Italy, 1859–1870 The leadership of Sardinia-Piedmont, nationalist fervor, and Garibaldi's attack on the Kingdom of the Two Sicilies were decisive factors in the unification of Italy.

by supporting an enemy of the pope. Sardinia would receive only Lombardy, the area around Milan. Cavour resigned in protest.

Popular revolts and Italian nationalism salvaged Cavour's plans. While the war against Austria raged in the north, dedicated nationalists in central Italy had risen and driven out their rulers. Nationalist fervor seized the urban masses, and the leaders of the nationalist movement called for fusion with Sardinia. Cavour returned to power in early 1860, and the people of central Italy voted overwhelmingly to join a greatly enlarged kingdom of Sardinia. Cavour had achieved his original goal of a north Italian state (see Map 24.2).

For superpatriots such as Giuseppe Garibaldi (1807–1882), the job of unification was still only half done. A poor sailor's son, Garibaldi personified the romantic revolutionary nationalism of 1848. Having led a unit of volunteers to several victories over Austrian troops in 1859, Garibaldi emerged in 1860 as an independent force in Italian politics. (See "Individuals in Society: Giuseppe Garibaldi," page 738.)

Secretly supported by Cavour, Garibaldi conceived a bold plan to "liberate" the Kingdom of the Two Sicilies. Landing on the shores of Sicily in May 1860, Garibaldi's guerrilla band captured the imagination of the Sicilian peasantry, which rose in rebellion. Outwitting the royal army, Garibaldi captured Palermo, crossed to the mainland, and prepared to attack Rome and the pope. But Cavour quickly sent Sardinian forces to occupy most of the Papal States (but not Rome) and to intercept Garibaldi. When Garibaldi and Victor Emmanuel rode through Naples to cheering crowds, they symbolically sealed the union of north and south, of monarch and people.

The new kingdom of Italy, which did not include Venice until 1866 or Rome until 1870, was a parliamentary monarchy under Victor Emmanuel, neither radical nor democratic. Only a small minority of Italian males could vote. Despite political unity, the propertied classes and the common people were divided. A great social and cultural gap separated the progressive industrializing north from the stagnant agrarian south.

Bismarck and German Unification

In the aftermath of 1848 the German states, particularly Austria and Prussia, were locked in a political stalemate, each seeking to block the power of the other within the German Confederation. At the same time, powerful economic forces were undermining the political status quo. Modern industry was growing rapidly within the German customs union, or *Zollverein*, founded in 1834 to stimulate trade. By 1853 all the German states except Austria had joined the customs union, and a new Germany excluding Austria was becoming an economic reality. Rising prosperity from the rapid growth of industrialization after 1850 gave new impetus to middle-class liberals.

By 1859 liberals had assumed control of the parliament that emerged from the upheavals of 1848 in Prussia. The national uprising in Italy in 1859, however, convinced Prussia's tough-minded William I (r. 1861–1888) that political change and even war with Austria or France were possible. William I pushed to raise taxes and increase the defense budget to double the army's size. The Prussian parliament, reflecting the middle class's desire for a less militaristic society, rejected the military budget in 1862, and the liberals triumphed in new elections. King William then called on Count Otto von Bismarck to head a new ministry and defy the parliament.

The most important figure in German history between Martin Luther and Adolf Hitler, Otto von Bismarck (1815–1898) was above all a master of politics. Born into the Prussian landowning aristocracy, Bismarck loved power, but he was also extraordinarily flexible and pragmatic in pursuing his goals. When Bismarck took office as chief minister in 1862, he declared that government would rule without parliamentary consent. He lashed out at the middle-class opposition: "The great questions of the day will not be decided by speeches and resolutions . . . but by blood and iron." Bismarck had the Prussian bureaucracy continue to collect taxes even though the parliament refused to approve the budget, and he reorganized the army. For their part, the voters of Prussia continued to express their opposition by sending large liberal majorities to the parliament from 1862 to 1866.

In 1866 Bismarck launched the Austro-Prussian War with the intent of expelling Austria from German politics. The war lasted only seven weeks, as the reorganized Prussian army defeated Austria decisively at the Battle of Sadowa in Bohemia. Bismarck

INDIVIDUALS IN SOCIETY • Giuseppe Garibaldi

When Giuseppe Garibaldi visited England in 1864, he received the most triumphant welcome ever given to any foreigner. Honored and feted by politicians and high society, he also captivated the masses. An unprecedented crowd of a half-million people cheered his carriage through the streets of London. These ovations were no fluke. In his time, Garibaldi was probably the most famous and most beloved figure in the world.* How could this be?

A rare combination of wild adventure and extraordinary achievement partly accounted for his demigod status. Born in Nice, Garibaldi went to sea at fifteen and sailed the Mediterranean for twelve years. At seventeen his travels took him to Rome, and he was converted in an almost religious experience to the "New Italy, the Italy of all the Italians." As he later wrote in his bestselling *Autobiography*, "The Rome that I beheld with the eyes of youthful imagination was the Rome of the future—the dominant thought of my whole life."

Sentenced to death in 1834 for his part in a revolutionary uprising in Genoa, Garibaldi barely escaped to South America. For twelve years he led a guerrilla band in Uruguay's struggle for independence from Argentina. "Shipwrecked, ambushed, shot through the neck," he found in a tough young woman, Anna da Silva, a mate and companion in arms. Their first children nearly starved in the jungle while Garibaldi, clad in his long red shirt, fashioned a legend as a fearless freedom fighter.

After he returned to Italy in 1848, the campaigns of his patriotic volunteers against the Austrians in 1848 and 1859 mobilized democratic nationalists. The stage was set for his volunteer army to liberate Sicily against enormous odds, astonishing the world and creating a large Italian state. Garibaldi's achievement matched his legend.

A brilliant fighter, the handsome and inspiring leader was an uncompromising idealist of absolute integrity. He never drew personal profit from his exploits, continuing to milk his goats and rarely possessing more than one change of cloth-

---

*Denis Mack Smith, *Garibaldi: A Great Life in Brief* (New York: Alfred A. Knopf, 1956), pp. 136–147; Denis Mack Smith, "Giuseppe Garibaldi," *History Today*, August 1991, pp. 20–26.

---

forced Austria to withdraw from German affairs and dissolved the existing German Confederation. The mainly Protestant states north of the Main River were grouped in the new North German Confederation, led by an expanded Prussia (Map 24.3). Each state retained its own local government, but the federal government—William I and Bismarck—controlled the army and foreign affairs.

To make peace with the liberal middle class and the nationalist movement, Bismarck asked the Prussian parliament to approve after the fact all the government's "illegal" spending between 1862 and 1866. Overawed by Bismarck's achievements, middle-class liberals now jumped at the chance to cooperate, opting for national unity and military glory over the battle for truly liberal institutions. Bismarck also followed Napoleon III's example by creating a legislature with members of the lower house ing. When Victor Emmanuel offered him lands and titles after his great victory in 1860, even as the left-leaning volunteers were disbanded and humiliated, Garibaldi declined, saying he could not be bought off. Returning to his farm on a tiny rocky island, he denounced the government without hesitation when he concluded that it was betraying the dream of unification with its ruthless rule in the south. Yet even after a duplicitous Italian government caused two later attacks on Rome to fail, his faith in the generative power of national unity never wavered. Garibaldi showed that ideas and ideals count in history.

Above all, millions of ordinary men and women identified with Garibaldi because they believed that he was fighting for them. They recognized him as one of their own and saw that he remained true to them in spite of his triumphs, thereby ennobling their own lives and aspirations. Welcoming runaway slaves as equals in Latin America, advocating the emancipation of women, introducing social reforms in the south, and pressing for free education and a broader suffrage in the new Italy, Garibaldi the national hero fought for freedom and human dignity. The common people understood and loved him for it.

QUESTIONS FOR ANALYSIS

1. Why was Garibaldi so famous and popular?
2. Nationalism evolved and developed in the nineteenth century. How did Garibaldi fit into this evolution? What kind of a nationalist was he?

▷LaunchPad
ONLINE DOCUMENT PROJECT

How did Italian nationalists respond to unification? Examine evidence from the period following Italian unification, and then complete a quiz and writing assignment based on the evidence and details from this chapter.

See inside the front cover to learn more.

elected by universal male suffrage, allowing him to bypass the middle class and appeal directly to the people if necessary. The constitutional struggle in Prussia was over, and the German middle class was respectfully accepting the monarchical authority and aristocratic superiority that Bismarck represented.

The final act in the drama of German unification followed quickly with a patriotic war against France. The apparent issue—whether a distant relative of Prussia's William I might become king of Spain—was only a diplomatic pretext. By 1870, alarmed by their powerful new neighbor on the Rhine, French leaders had decided on a war to teach Prussia a lesson.

As soon as war against France began in 1870, Bismarck had the wholehearted support of the south German states. The Germans by this point had outpaced France

MAP 24.3 The Unification of Germany, 1866–1871 This map shows how Prussia expanded and a new German Empire was created through two wars, the Austro-Prussian War of 1866 and the Franco-Prussian War of 1870–1871.

on many fronts—population, industrialization, railroads, military preparations—and they quickly defeated Louis Napoleon's armies at Sedan on September 1, 1870. Three days later French patriots in Paris proclaimed yet another French republic and vowed to continue fighting. But after five months, in January 1871, a starving Paris surrendered, and France accepted Bismarck's harsh peace terms. By this time the south German states had agreed to join a new German Empire. As in the 1866 constitution, the Prussian king and his ministers had ultimate power in the new German Empire, and the lower house of the legislature was elected by universal male suffrage.

The Franco-Prussian War released an enormous surge of patriotic feeling in Germany. The new German Empire had become Europe's most powerful state, and most Germans were enormously proud, blissfully imagining themselves the fittest and best of the European species. Semi-authoritarian nationalism and a "new conservatism," which was based on an alliance of the propertied classes and sought the active support of the working classes, had triumphed in Germany.

The Modernization of Russia

In the 1850s Russia was a poor agrarian society with a rapidly growing population. Almost 90 percent of the population lived off the land, and serfdom was still the basic social institution. Then the Crimean War of 1853 to 1856 arose from the breakdown of the balance of power established at the Congress of Vienna, European competition over influence in the Middle East, and Russian desires to expand into European territories held by the Ottoman Empire. In this war of massive modern weaponry and staggering casualties, France and Great Britain, aided by Sardinia and the Ottoman Empire, inflicted a humiliating defeat on Russia.

Russia's military defeat showed that it had fallen behind the industrializing nations of western Europe. Russia needed railroads, better armaments, and military reorganization if it was to maintain its international position. Moreover, the war had caused hardship and raised the specter of massive peasant rebellion. Military disaster thus forced the new tsar, Alexander II (r. 1855–1881), and his ministers along the path of rapid social change and general modernization.

The first and greatest of the reforms was the freeing of the serfs in 1861. The emancipated peasants received, on average, about half of the land, which was to be collectively owned by peasant villages. The prices for the land were high, and collective ownership limited the possibilities of agricultural improvement and migration to urban areas. Thus the effects of the reform were limited. More successful was reform of the legal system, which established independent courts and equality before the law. The government also relaxed censorship and partially liberalized policies toward Russian Jews.

Russia's greatest strides toward modernization were economic rather than political. Rapid, government-subsidized railroad construction to 1880 enabled agricultural Russia to export grain and thus earn money for further industrialization. Industrial suburbs grew up around Moscow and St. Petersburg, and a class of modern factory workers began to take shape. Russia began seizing territory in far eastern Siberia, on the border with China; in Central Asia, north of Afghanistan; and in the Islamic lands of the Caucasus.

In 1881 an anarchist assassinated Alexander II, and the reform era came to an abrupt end. Political modernization remained frozen until 1905, but economic modernization sped forward in the massive industrial surge of the 1890s. The key leader was Sergei Witte (suhr-GAY VIH-tuh), the energetic minister of finance. Under Witte's leadership, the government doubled Russia's railroad network by the end of the century and promoted Russian industry with high protective tariffs.

By 1900 a fiercely independent Russia was catching up with western Europe and expanding its empire in Asia. By 1903 Russia had established a sphere of influence in Chinese Manchuria and was eyeing northern Korea. When the diplomatic protests of equally imperialistic Japan were ignored, the Japanese launched a surprise attack on

Russian forces in Manchuria in February 1904. After Japan scored repeated victories, to the amazement of self-confident Europeans, Russia was forced in September 1905 to accept a humiliating defeat.

Military disaster in East Asia brought political upheaval at home. On January 22, 1905, workers peacefully protesting for improved working conditions and higher wages were attacked by the tsar's troops outside the Winter Palace. Over one hundred were killed and around three hundred wounded. This event, known as Bloody Sunday, set off a wave of strikes, peasant uprisings, and troop mutinies across Russia. The revolutionary surge culminated in October 1905 in a paralyzing general strike, which forced the government to capitulate. The tsar, Nicholas II (r. 1894–1917), issued the **October Manifesto**, which granted full civil rights and promised a popularly elected Duma (DOO-muh; parliament) with real legislative power.

Under the new constitution, Nicholas II retained great powers and the Duma had only limited authority. The middle-class liberals, the largest group in the newly elected Duma, were badly disappointed, and efforts to cooperate with the tsar's ministers soon broke down. In 1907 Nicholas II and his reactionary advisers rewrote the electoral law so as to increase greatly the weight of the propertied classes. When elections were held, the tsar could count on a loyal majority in the Duma. On the eve of World War I, Russia was partially modernized, a conservative constitutional monarchy with an agrarian but industrializing economy.

Urban Life in the Age of Ideologies

What was the impact of urban growth on cities, social classes, families, and ideas?

After 1850, as identification with the nation-state was becoming a basic organizing principle in Europe, urban growth rushed forward with undiminished force. By 1900 western Europe was urban and industrial as surely as it had been rural and agrarian in 1800. Rapid urban growth in the nineteenth century worsened long-standing overcrowding and unhealthy living conditions, lending support to voices calling for revolutionary change. To prevent unrest and promote a strong, healthy population capable of competing with other nations, government leaders, city planners, reformers, and scientists urgently sought solutions to these challenges. Over the long term, success in improving the urban environment and the introduction of social welfare measures encouraged people to put their faith in a responsive national state.

Urban Development

Since the Middle Ages, European cities had been centers of government, culture, and large-scale commerce. They had also been congested, dirty, and unhealthy. Industrialization greatly worsened these conditions. The steam engine freed industrialists from dependence on the energy of fast-flowing streams and rivers so that by 1800 there was every incentive to build new factories in cities, which had better shipping facilities and a large and ready workforce. Therefore, as industry grew, overcrowded and unhealthy cities expanded rapidly.

In the 1820s and 1830s people in Britain and France began to worry about the condition of their cities. Except on the outskirts, each town or city was using every scrap of land to the full extent. Parks and open areas were almost nonexistent, and narrow houses were built wall to wall in long rows. Highly concentrated urban populations lived in extremely unsanitary conditions, with open drains and sewers flowing alongside or down the middle of unpaved streets. "Six, eight, and even ten occupying one room is anything but uncommon," wrote a Scottish doctor for a government investigation in 1842.

The urban challenge—and the growth of socialist movements calling for radical change—eventually brought an energetic response from a generation of reformers. The most famous early reformer was Edwin Chadwick, a British official. Chadwick was a follower of radical British philosopher Jeremy Bentham (1748–1832), whose approach to social issues, called utilitarianism, had taught that public problems ought to be dealt with on a rational, scientific basis and in a way that would yield the "greatest good for the greatest number." Chadwick became convinced that disease and death actually caused poverty by increasing unemployment and depriving children of parents to provide for them. He also believed that cleaning up the urban environment would prevent disease.

Collecting detailed reports from local officials and publishing his findings in 1842, Chadwick concluded that the stinking excrement of communal outhouses could be carried off by water through sewers at less than one-twentieth the cost of removing it by hand. In 1848 Chadwick's report became the basis of Great Britain's first public health law, which created a national health board and gave cities broad authority to build modern sanitary systems. Such sanitary movements won dedicated supporters in the United States, France, and Germany from the 1840s on. By the 1860s and 1870s European cities were making real progress toward adequate water supplies and sewerage systems, and city dwellers were beginning to reap the reward of better health.

Early sanitary reformers were handicapped by the prevailing miasmatic theory of disease—the belief that people contract disease when they breathe foul odors. In the 1840s and 1850s keen observation by doctors and public health officials suggested that contagion spread through physical contact with filth and not by its odors, thus weakening the miasmatic idea. An understanding of how this occurred came out of the work of Louis Pasteur (1822–1895), who was named professor of chemistry in 1854 and subsequently developed the **germ theory** of disease. At the request of local brewers, Pasteur investigated fermentation and found that the growth of living organisms in a beverage could be suppressed by heating it—a process that became known as pasteurization. By 1870 the work of Pasteur and others had demonstrated that specific living organisms—germs (which we now divide into bacteria, viruses, fungi, and protozoa)—caused specific diseases and that those organisms could be controlled. These discoveries led to the development of a number of effective vaccines. Surgeons also applied the germ theory in hospitals, sterilizing not only the wound but everything else—hands, instruments, clothing—that entered the operating room.

The achievements of the bacterial revolution coupled with the public health movement saved millions of lives, particularly after about 1890. In England, France, and Germany death rates declined dramatically, and the awful death sentences of the past—diphtheria, typhoid, typhus, cholera, yellow fever—became vanishing diseases in the industrializing nations.

More effective urban planning after 1850 also improved the quality of urban life. France took the lead during the rule of Napoleon III (r. 1848–1870), who believed national health insurance, unemployment benefits, old-age pensions, and a host of other social measures. The state was integrating the urban masses socially as well as politically.

On the eve of World War I, however, the unanswered question of Ireland brought Great Britain to the brink of civil war. The terrible Irish famine of the 1840s and early 1850s had fueled an Irish revolutionary movement. The English slowly granted concessions but refused to give Ireland self-government. In 1910 Irish nationalists in the British Parliament supported the Liberals in their battle for the People's Budget. In 1913 Liberals accordingly gave them enough support to pass a bill granting Ireland self-government, or home rule.

The Irish Catholic majority in the southern counties ardently desired home rule. Irish Protestants in the northern counties of Ulster, however, vowed to resist it, fearing they would fall under the control of the majority Catholics. Unable to resolve the conflict as World War I started in August 1914, the British government postponed indefinitely the whole question of Irish home rule.

The dilemma of conflicting nationalisms in Ireland helps one appreciate how desperate the situation in the Austro-Hungarian Empire had become by the early twentieth century. Following the savage defeat of the Hungarian republic (see page 734), Hungary was ruled as a conquered territory, and Emperor Franz Joseph (r. 1848–1916) and his bureaucracy tried hard to centralize the state and Germanize the language and culture of the different nationalities.

Following its defeat by Prussia in 1866, a weakened Austria was forced to establish the so-called dual monarchy. The empire was divided in two, and the nationalistic Magyars gained virtual independence for Hungary. The two states were joined only by a shared monarch and common ministries for finance, defense, and foreign affairs. Still, the disintegrating force of competing nationalisms continued unabated, and the Austro-Hungarian Empire was progressively weakened and eventually destroyed by the conflicting national aspirations of its different ethnic groups. It was these ethnic conflicts in the Balkans, the "powder keg of Europe," that touched off the Great War in 1914 (see Chapter 28).

Jewish Emancipation and Modern Anti-Semitism

Revolutionary changes in political principles and the triumph of the nation-state brought equally revolutionary changes in Jewish life in western and central Europe. Beginning in France in 1791, Jews gradually gained their civil rights, although progress was slow and uneven. In the 1850s and 1860s liberals in Austria, Italy, and Prussia pressed successfully for legal equality. In 1871 the constitution of the new German Empire abolished all restrictions on Jewish marriage, choice of occupation, place of residence, and property ownership. Exclusion from government employment and discrimination in social relations remained, however, in central Europe.

The process of emancipation presented Jews with challenges and opportunities. Traditional Jewish occupations, such as court financial agent, village moneylender, and peddler, were undermined by free-market reforms, but careers in business, the professions, and the arts were opening to Jewish talent. By 1871 a majority of Jews in western and central Europe had improved their economic situations and entered the middle classes. Most Jews identified strongly with their respective nation-states and considered themselves patriotic citizens.

Vicious anti-Semitism reappeared after the stock market crash of 1873, beginning in central Europe. Drawing on long traditions of religious intolerance, ghetto exclusion, and periodic anti-Jewish riots and expulsions, this hostility also drew on modern supposedly scientific ideas about Jews as a separate race (see page 750). Modern anti-Semitism whipped up resentment against Jewish achievement and Jewish "financial control," while fanatics claimed that the Jewish race posed a biological threat to the German people. Anti-Semitic beliefs were particularly popular among conservatives, extremist nationalists, and people who felt threatened by Jewish competition.

Anti-Semites also created modern political parties. In Austrian Vienna in the early 1890s, Karl Lueger (LOO-guhr) and his "Christian socialists" won striking electoral victories. Lueger, the popular mayor of Vienna from 1897 to 1910, combined fierce anti-Semitic rhetoric with his support of municipal ownership of basic services. He appealed especially to the German-speaking lower middle class—and to an unsuccessful young artist named Adolf Hitler. In response to spreading anti-Semitism, a Jewish journalist named Theodor Herzl (1860–1904) turned from German nationalism to advocate Jewish political nationalism, or Zionism, and the creation of a Jewish state.

Before 1914 anti-Semitism was most oppressive in eastern Europe, where Jews also suffered from terrible poverty. In the Russian empire, where there was no Jewish emancipation and 4 million of Europe's 7 million Jewish people lived in 1880, officials used anti-Semitism to channel popular discontent away from the government. In 1881–1882 a wave of violent pogroms commenced in southern Russia. The police and the army stood aside for days while peasants assaulted Jews and looted and destroyed their property. Official harassment continued in the following decades, and some Russian Jews turned toward self-emancipation and the vision of a Zionist settlement in the Ottoman province of Palestine. Large numbers also emigrated to western Europe and the United States.

The Socialist Movement

Socialism appealed to large numbers of working men and women in the late nineteenth century, and the growth of socialist parties after 1871 was phenomenal. Neither Bismarck's repressive laws nor his social welfare measures checked the growth of the German Social Democratic Party. By 1912 the party, which espoused Marxist principles, had millions of followers and was the Reichstag's largest party. Socialist parties also grew in other countries, and Marxist socialist parties were linked together in an international organization. In 1864 Karl Marx played an important role in founding the socialist International Working Men's Association, also known as the First International. Marx presided over its annual meetings, which he used to spread the doctrine of socialist revolution.

The First International collapsed in 1872 over disputes about the use of violence to achieve revolution, but in 1889 socialist leaders came together to form the Second International, which lasted until 1914. Every three years delegates from the different parties met to interpret Marxist doctrines and plan coordinated action. Yet socialism was not as radical and revolutionary in these years as it sometimes appeared. As socialist parties grew and attracted large numbers of members, they looked more and more toward gradual change and steady improvement for the working class and less and less toward revolution. Workers themselves were progressively less inclined to follow radical programs for several reasons. As workers gained the right to vote and won real benefits, their attention focused more on elections than on revolutions. Workers were also not immune to nationalistic patriotism, even as they loyally voted for socialists. Nor were workers a unified social group. Perhaps most important of all, workers' standard of living rose steadily after 1850, and the quality of life improved substantially in urban areas. Thus workers tended to become militantly moderate: they demanded gains, but they were less likely to take to the barricades in pursuit of them.

The growth of labor unions reinforced this trend toward moderation. In the early stages of industrialization, modern unions were considered subversive bodies and were generally prohibited by law. In Great Britain new unions that formed for skilled workers after 1850 avoided radical politics and concentrated on winning better wages and hours for their members through collective bargaining and compromise. After 1890 unions for unskilled workers developed in Britain.

German unions were not granted important rights until 1869, and until the Anti-Socialist Laws were repealed in 1890 the government frequently harassed them as socialist fronts. But after most legal harassment was eliminated, union membership skyrocketed from only about 270,000 in 1895 to roughly 3 million in 1912. Genuine collective bargaining, long opposed by socialist intellectuals as a "sellout," was officially recognized as desirable by the German Trade Union Congress in 1899.

The German trade unions and their leaders were thoroughgoing revisionists. Revisionism was an effort by various socialists to update Marxist doctrines to reflect the realities of the time. The socialist Eduard Bernstein (1850–1932) argued in his *Evolutionary Socialism* in 1899 that Marx's predictions of ever-greater poverty for workers had been proved false. Therefore, Bernstein suggested, socialists should reform their doctrines and win gradual evolutionary gains for workers through legislation, unions, and further economic development. The Second International denounced these views as heresy. Yet the revisionist gradualist approach continued to gain the tacit acceptance of many German socialists, particularly in the trade unions.

Moderation found followers elsewhere. In France the great socialist leader Jean Jaurès (1859–1914) formally repudiated revisionist doctrines in order to establish a unified socialist party, but he remained at heart a gradualist. Questions of revolutionary versus gradualist policies split Russian Marxists.

Socialist parties in other countries had clear-cut national characteristics. Russians and socialists in the Austro-Hungarian Empire tended to be the most radical. In Great Britain the socialist but non-Marxist Labour Party formally committed to gradual reform. In Spain and Italy anarchism, seeking to smash the state rather than the bourgeoisie, dominated radical thought and action.

In short, socialist policies and doctrines varied from country to country. Socialism itself was to a large extent "nationalized." This helps explain why almost all socialist leaders supported their governments when war came in 1914.

Chapter Summary

In 1814 the victorious allied powers sought to restore peace and stability in Europe. Led by Metternich of Austria, the conservative powers used intervention and repression as they sought to prevent the spread of subversive ideas and radical changes in politics. After 1815 ideologies of liberalism, nationalism, and socialism all developed to challenge the new order. The growth of these forces culminated in the liberal and nationalistic revolutions of 1848. Monarchies panicked and crumbled in the face of popular uprisings, yet few revolutionary goals were realized. Instead a resurgence of conservative forces crushed revolution across Europe. In the second half of the nineteenth century Italy and Germany became unified nation-states for the first time in history, while Russia undertook a modernization program that culminated in popular uprising and a constitutional monarchy after 1905, in which the tsar retained great power.

Living conditions in rapidly growing industrial cities declined until the mid-nineteenth century, when governments undertook major urban development programs, including new systems of sewerage, water supply, and public transportation. Major changes in the class structure and family life occurred, as the home was celebrated as a domestic oasis, the separate spheres ideology strengthened, and the class structure became more complex and diversified. The prestige of science grew tremendously, and scientific discoveries, such as Darwin's theory of natural selection, challenged the traditional religious understanding of the world. In the realm of literature and the arts, the romantic movement reinforced the spirit of change. Romanticism gave way to realism in the 1840s, reflecting Western society's growing faith in science and evolutionary thinking, but also a sympathy with the plight of the poor.

Western society became increasingly nationalistic as well as urban and industrial in the late nineteenth century. Nation-states became more responsive to the needs of their people, and they enlisted widespread support as political participation expanded, educational opportunities increased, and social security systems took shape. Even socialism became increasingly national in orientation, gathering strength as a champion of working-class interests in domestic politics. Yet even though nationalism served to unite peoples, it also drove them apart and contributed to the tragic conflicts of the twentieth century.

Notes

1. J. G. Fichte, *Addresses to the German Nation*, trans. R. F. Jones and G. H. Turnbull (Chicago: Open Court Publishing Company, 1922), p. 4.
2. E. Gellner, *Nations and Nationalism* (Oxford: Basil Blackwell, 1983), pp. 19–39.
3. B. Anderson, *Imagined Communities: Reflections on the Origins and Spread of Nationalism*, rev. ed. (London: Verso, 1991).
4. Jonathan Sperber, *The European Revolutions, 1848–1851*, 2d ed. (Cambridge: Cambridge University Press, 2005), pp. 40–47.
5. Quoted by G. O'Brien, *The Economic History of Ireland from the Union to the Famine* (London: Longmans, Green, 1921), p. 21.
6. Ibid., pp. 23–24.
7. J. McKay, *Tramways and Trolleys: The Rise of Urban Mass Transport in Europe* (Princeton, N.J.: Princeton University Press, 1976), p. 81.
8. "*La Citoyenne* in the World: Hubertine Auclert and Feminist Imperialism," *French Historical Studies* 31.1 (Winter 2009): 63–84.

Colonial presence, 1914

British
French
German
Italian
Portuguese
Belgian
Spanish
Independent African states
Afrikaner republic

SPANISH MOROCCO
Madeira Is. (Portugal)   Tangier
Canary Is. (Spain)   Casablanca
IFNI   MOROCCO   TUNISIA
RIO DE ORO   ALGERIA
Algiers
Tripoli   *Mediterranean Sea*
Cyrene
LIBYA
EGYPT
Cairo
Aswan
ARABIA
Tropic of Cancer
Red Sea
20°N

S A H A R A

FRENCH WEST AFRICA
GAMBIA
PORTUGUESE GUINEA
Senegal R.
L. Chad
Niger R.
Omdurman   ERITREA
Khartoum
FRENCH SOMALILAND
Adowa
SIERRA LEONE   Freetown
IVORY COAST   GOLD COAST
Monrovia   LIBERIA
NORTHERN NIGERIA
S. NIGERIA
ANGLO-EGYPTIAN SUDAN
Fashoda
BRITISH SOMALILAND
ETHIOPIA
ITALIAN SOMALILAND
TOGOLAND
Fernando Po (Spain)
KAMERUN
SPANISH GUINEA
FRENCH EQUATORIAL AFRICA
Uele R.
Congo R.
São Tomé (Portugal)
ATLANTIC OCEAN
CABINDA
CONGO FREE STATE
L. Tanganyika
L. Victoria
BRITISH EAST AFRICA
Mombasa
Zanzibar (Gr. Br.)
GERMAN EAST AFRICA
INDIAN OCEAN
Equator   0°

ANGOLA
NORTHERN RHODESIA
L. Nyasa (L. Malawi)
NYASALAND
SOUTHERN RHODESIA   MOZAMBIQUE
MADAGASCAR
20°S
GERMAN SOUTHWEST AFRICA   BECHUANALAND
Tropic of Capricorn
TRANSVAAL
ORANGE FREE STATE   SWAZILAND
NATAL   Isandhlwana
UNION OF SOUTH AFRICA
BASUTOLAND
Cape Town

0   250   500 miles
0   250   500 kilometers

Colonial presence, 1878
ALGERIA
EGYPT
SENEGAL
SAHARA
Nile R.
Niger R.
Congo R.
ANGOLA
MOZAMBIQUE
ORANGE FREE STATE (Afrikaner)
TRANSVAAL (Afrikaner)
CAPE COLONY   NATAL

MAP 25.1   The Partition of Africa The European powers carved up Africa after 1880 and built vast political empires.

publications of Protestant missionaries such as David Livingstone from Scotland and the fiery eyewitness accounts of the Catholic White Fathers missionary society (named for their white robes), antislavery activists learned of the horrors of slave raids and the suffering of thousands of innocent victims sold within Africa and through East African ports. The public was led to believe that European conquest and colonization would end this human tragedy by bringing, in Livingstone's famous phrase, "Commerce, Christianity, and Civilization" to Africa.

King Leopold II (r. 1865–1909) of Belgium also played a crucial role. His agents signed treaties with African chiefs and planted Leopold's flag along the Congo River. In addition, Leopold intentionally misled leaders of the other European nations to gain their support by promising to promote Christianity and civilization in his proposed Congo Free State. By 1883 Europe had caught "African fever," and the race for territory was on. To lay down some rules for this imperialist competition, French premier Jules Ferry and German chancellor Otto von Bismarck arranged a European conference on Africa in Berlin in 1884–1885. The Berlin Conference, to which Africans were not invited, established the principle that European claims to African territory had to rest on "effective occupation" in order to be recognized by other states. This meant that Europeans would push relentlessly into interior regions from all sides and that no single European power would be able to claim the entire continent. A nation could establish a colony only if it had effectively taken possession of the territory through signed treaties with local leaders and had begun to develop it economically. The representatives at the conference recognized Leopold's rule over the Congo Free State.

In addition to developing rules for imperialist competition, participants at the Berlin Conference also promised to stop black and Islamic slave dealers and to bring Christianity and civilization to Africa:

> All the Powers exercising sovereign rights or influence in the aforesaid territories bind themselves to watch over the preservation of the native tribes, and to care for the improvement of the conditions of their moral and material well-being, and to help in suppressing slavery, and especially the slave trade.
>
> They shall, without distinction of creed or nation, protect and favour all religious, scientific or charitable institutions and undertakings created and organized for the above ends, or which aim at instructing the natives and bringing home to them the blessings of civilization.[6]

In truth, however, these ideals ran a distant second to, and were not allowed to interfere with, the nations' primary goal of commerce—holding on to their old markets and exploiting new ones.

The Berlin Conference coincided with Germany's emergence as an imperial power. In 1884 and 1885 Bismarck's Germany established protectorates over a number of small African kingdoms and societies in Togoland, Kamerun, southwest Africa, and, later, East Africa (see Map 25.1). In acquiring colonies, Bismarck cooperated with France's Jules Ferry against the British. The French expanded into West Africa and also formed a protectorate on the Congo River. Meanwhile, the British began enlarging their West African enclaves and pushed northward from the Cape Colony and westward from the East African coast.

The British also moved southward from Egypt, which they had seized in 1882 (see page 787), but were blocked in the eastern Sudan by fiercely independent Muslims, who had felt the full force of Islamic revival. In 1881 a pious Sudanese leader, Muhammad Ahmad (1844–1885), proclaimed himself the "Mahdi" (a messianic redeemer of Islam) and led a revolt against foreign control of Egypt. In 1885 his army massacred a British force and took the city of Khartoum, forcing the British to retreat to Cairo. Ten years later a British force returned, building a railroad to supply arms and reinforcements as it went. In 1898 these troops, under the command of Field Marshal Horatio Hubert Kitchener, met their foe at Omdurman, where Sudanese Muslims armed with spears charged time and time again, only to be cut down by the recently invented machine gun. In the end eleven thousand brave but poorly armed Muslim fighters lay dead. Only twenty-eight Britons had been killed. Their commander received the title of "Lord Kitchener of Khartoum."

All European nations resorted to some violence in their colonies to retain control, subdue the population, appropriate land, and force African laborers to work long hours at physically demanding, and often dangerous, jobs. In no colony, however, was the violence and brutality worse than in Leopold II's Congo Free State. Rather than promoting Christianity and civilization as Leopold had promised, the European companies operating in the Congo Free State introduced slavery, unimaginable savagery, and terror. Missionaries and other religious leaders were not even allowed into the colony, to prevent them from reporting the horrors they would witness there.

Profits in the Congo Free State came first from the ivory trade, but in the 1890s, after many of the Congo's elephant herds had been decimated, a new cash crop arose to take ivory's place. In the mid-1880s a northern Irishman named John Dunlop

Brutality in the Congo   No Africans suffered more violent and brutal treatment under colonial rule than those living in Belgian king Leopold II's Congo Free State. When not having their hands, feet, or heads cut off as punishment, Africans were whipped with *chicottes*, whips made of dried hippopotamus hide. Some Congolese were literally whipped to death. (© TopFoto/ The Image Works)

developed a process to make inflatable rubber tires for his son's tricycle. Other scientific developments soon followed, and new uses for rubber were found, causing a worldwide boom in the demand for raw rubber. As it happened, more than half of the Congo Free State possessed wild rubber vines growing thickly in the equatorial rain forest. By the mid-1890s rubber had surpassed ivory as the colony's major income producer, and the companies Leopold allowed to make profits in the Congo soon could not get enough of it. Violence and brutality increased exponentially as the European appetite for rubber became insatiable. Europeans and their well-armed mercenaries terrorized entire regions, cutting off hands, feet, and heads and wiping out whole villages to send the message that Africans must either work for the Europeans or die. The African blood that was shed is recalled in the colony's frightening nickname—the "red rubber colony." In the first years of the nineteenth century, human rights activists such as Edmund Morel exposed the truth about the horrific conditions in the Congo Free State, and in 1908 Leopold was forced to turn over his private territory to Belgium as a colony, the Belgian Congo.

Southern Africa in the Nineteenth Century

The development of southern Africa diverged from the rest of sub-Saharan Africa in important ways. Whites settled in large numbers, modern capitalist industry took off, and British imperialists had to wage all-out war.

In 1652 the Dutch East India Company established a supply station at Cape Town for Dutch ships sailing between Amsterdam and Indonesia. The healthy, temperate climate and the sparse Khoisan population near the Cape promoted the colony's gradual expansion. When the British took possession of the Cape Colony during the Napoleonic Wars, there were about twenty thousand free Dutch citizens and twenty-five thousand African slaves, with substantial mixed-race communities on the northern frontier of white settlement. After 1815 powerful African chiefdoms, Dutch settlers— first known as Boers, and then as **Afrikaners**—and British colonial forces waged a complicated three-cornered battle to build strong states in southern Africa.

While the British consolidated their rule in the Cape Colony, the talented Zulu king Shaka (r. 1818–1828) was revolutionizing African warfare and creating the largest and most powerful kingdom in southern Africa in the nineteenth century. Drafted by age groups and placed in highly disciplined regiments, Shaka's warriors perfected the use of a short stabbing spear in deadly hand-to-hand combat. The Zulu armies often destroyed their African enemies completely, sowing chaos and sending refugees fleeing in all directions. Shaka's wars led to the creation of Zulu, Tswana, Swazi, Ndebele, and Sotho states in southern Africa. By 1890 these states were largely subdued by Dutch and British invaders, but only after many hard-fought frontier wars.

Between 1834 and 1838 the British abolished slavery in the Cape Colony and introduced color-blind legislation (whites and blacks were equal before the law) to protect African labor. In 1836 about ten thousand Afrikaner cattle ranchers and farmers, resentful of equal treatment of blacks by British colonial officials and missionaries after the abolition of slavery, began to make their so-called Great Trek northward into the interior. In 1845 another group of Afrikaners joined them north of the Orange River. Over the next thirty years Afrikaner and British settlers, who often fought and generally detested each other, reached a mutually advantageous division of southern

Africa. The British ruled the strategically valuable colonies of Cape Colony and Natal (nuh-TAL) on the coast, and the Afrikaners controlled the ranch-land republics of Orange Free State and the Transvaal in the interior. The Zulu, Xhosa, Sotho, Ndebele, and other African peoples lost much of their land but remained the majority—albeit an exploited majority.

The discovery of incredibly rich deposits of diamonds in 1867 near Kimberley, and of gold in 1886 in the Afrikaners' Transvaal Republic around modern Johannesburg, revolutionized the southern African economy, making possible large-scale industrial capitalism and transforming the lives of all its peoples. The extraction of these minerals, particularly the deep-level gold deposits, required big foreign investment, European engineering expertise, and an enormous labor force. Thus small-scale white and black diamond and gold miners soon gave way to powerful financiers, particularly Cecil Rhodes (1853–1902). Rhodes came from a large middle-class British family and at seventeen went to southern Africa to seek his fortune. By 1888 Rhodes's firm, the De Beers mining company, monopolized the world's diamond industry and earned him fabulous profits. The "color bar" system of the diamond fields gave whites—often English-speaking immigrants—the well-paid skilled positions and put black Africans in the dangerous, low-wage jobs far below the earth's surface. Whites lived with their families in subsidized housing. African workers lived in all-male prison-like dormitories, closely watched by company guards. Southern Africa became the world's leading gold producer, pulling in black migratory workers from all over the region (as it does to this day).

The mining bonanza whetted the appetite of British imperialists led by the powerful Rhodes, who was considered the ultimate British imperialist. He once famously observed that the British "happen to be the best people in the world, with the highest ideals of decency and justice and liberty and peace, and the more of the world we inhabit, the better for humanity."[7] Between 1888 and 1893 Rhodes used missionaries and his British South Africa Company, chartered by the British government, to force African chiefs to accept British protectorates, and he managed to add Southern and Northern Rhodesia (modern-day Zimbabwe and Zambia) to the British Empire.

Southern Rhodesia is one of the most egregious examples of Europeans misleading African rulers to take their land. In 1888 the Ndebele (or Matabele) king, Lobengula (1845–1894), ruler over much of modern southwestern Zimbabwe, met with three of Rhodes's men, led by Charles Rudd, and signed the Rudd Concession. Lobengula believed he was simply allowing a handful of British fortune hunters a few years of gold prospecting in Matabeleland. Lobengula had been misled, however, by the resident London Missionary Society missionary (and Lobengula's supposed friend), the Reverend Charles Helm, as to the document's true meaning and Rhodes's hand behind it. Even though Lobengula soon repudiated the agreement, he opened the way for Rhodes's seizure of the territory.

In 1889 Rhodes's British South Africa Company received a royal charter from Queen Victoria to occupy the land on behalf of the British government. Though Lobengula died in early 1894, his warriors fought Rhodes's private army in the First and Second Matabele Wars (1893–1894, 1896–1897); however, they were decimated by British Maxim guns. By 1897 Matabeleland had ceased to exist, replaced by the British-ruled settler colony of Southern Rhodesia. Before his death, Lobengula asked Reverend Helm, "Did you ever see a chameleon catch a fly? The chameleon gets behind the fly and remains motionless for some time, then he advances very slowly and gently, first putting forward one leg and then the other. At last, when well within reach, he darts his tongue and the fly disappears. England is the chameleon and I am that fly."[8]

The Transvaal goldfields still remained in Afrikaner hands, however, so Rhodes and the imperialist clique initiated a series of events that sparked the South African War of 1899–1902 (also known as the Anglo-Boer War), Britain's greatest imperial campaign on African soil. The British needed 450,000 troops to crush the Afrikaners, who never had more than 30,000 men in the field. Often considered the first "total war," this conflict witnessed the British use of a scorched-earth strategy to destroy Afrikaner property, and concentration camps to detain Afrikaner families and their servants, thousands of whom died of illness. Estimates of Africans who were sometimes forced and sometimes volunteered to work for one side or the other range from 15,000 to 40,000 for each side. They did everything from scouting and guard duty to heavy manual labor, driving wagons, and guarding the livestock.

The long and bitter war divided whites in South Africa, but South Africa's blacks were the biggest losers. The British had promised the Afrikaners representative government in return for surrender in 1902, and they made good on their pledge. In 1910 the Cape Colony, Natal, the Orange Free State, and the Transvaal formed a new self-governing Union of South Africa. After the peace settlement, because whites — 21.5 percent of the total population in 1910 — held almost all political power in the new union, and because Afrikaners outnumbered English-speakers, the Afrikaners began to regain what they had lost on the battlefield. South Africa, under a joint British-Afrikaner government within the British Empire, began the creation of a modern segregated society that culminated in an even harsher system of racial separation, or apartheid, after World War II.

Colonialism's Impact After 1900

By 1900 much of Africa had been conquered — or, as Europeans preferred to say, "pacified" — and a system of colonial administration was taking shape. In general, this system weakened or shattered the traditional social order and challenged accepted values.

The self-proclaimed political goal of the French and the British — the principal colonial powers — was to provide good government for their African subjects, especially after World War I. "Good government" meant, above all, law and order. It meant strong, authoritarian government, which maintained a small army and built up an African police force to put down rebellion, suppress ethnic warfare, and protect life and property. Good government required a modern bureaucracy capable of taxing and governing the population. Many African leaders and their peoples had chosen not to resist the invaders' superior force, and others stopped fighting and turned to other, less violent means of resisting colonial rule. Thus the goal of law and order was widely achieved.

Colonial governments demonstrated much less interest in providing basic social services. Education, public health, hospital, and other social service expenditures increased after the Great War but still remained small. Europeans feared the political implications of mass education and typically relied instead on the modest efforts of state-subsidized mission schools. Moreover, they tried to make even their poorest

A Missionary School A Swahili schoolboy leads his classmates in a reading lesson in Dar es Salaam in German East Africa before 1914, as portraits of Emperor William II and his wife look down on the classroom. Europeans argued that they were spreading the benefits of a superior civilization with schools like this one, which is unusually well built and well furnished because of its strategic location in the capital city. (ullstein bild/The Granger Collection, NYC—All rights reserved.)

colonies pay for themselves. Thus government workers' salaries normally absorbed nearly all tax revenues.

Economically, the colonial goal was to draw the African interior into the world economy on terms favorable to the dominant Europeans. The key was railroads linking coastal trading centers to outposts hundreds of miles in the interior. Cheap, dependable transportation facilitated easy shipment of raw materials out and manufactured goods in. Most African railroads, generally direct lines from sources of raw materials in the interior to coastal ports, were built after 1900; fifty-two hundred miles were in operation by 1926, when attention turned to building roads for trucks. Railroads and roads had two other important outcomes: they allowed quick troop movements to put down local unrest, and they allowed many African peasants to earn wages for the first time.

The focus on economic development and low-cost rule explains why colonial governments were reluctant to move decisively against slavery within Africa. Officials feared that an abrupt abolition of slavery where it existed would disrupt production and lead to costly revolts by powerful slaveholding elites, especially in Muslim areas. Thus colonial regimes settled for halfway measures designed to satisfy humanitarian groups in Europe and also make all Africans, free or enslaved, participate in a market economy and work for wages. Even this cautious policy emboldened many slaves to run away, thereby facilitating a rapid decline of slavery within Africa.

Colonial governments also often imposed head or hut taxes. Payable only in labor or European currency, these taxes compelled Africans to work for their white overlords. Africans despised no aspect of colonialism more than forced labor, widespread until about 1920. In some regions, particularly in West Africa, African peasants continued to respond freely to the new economic opportunities by voluntarily shifting to export crops on their own farms. Overall, the result of these developments was an increase in wage work and production geared to the world market and a decline in nomadic herding and traditional self-sufficient farming of sustainable crops.

In sum, the imposition of bureaucratic Western rule and the gradual growth of a world-oriented cash economy after 1900 had a revolutionary impact on large parts of Africa. The experiences of the Gold Coast and British East Africa, two very different African colonies, dramatically illustrate variations on the general pattern.

The British established the beginnings of the Gold Coast colony in 1821. Over the remainder of the century they extended their territorial rule inland from the coast and built up a fairly complex economy. This angered the powerful Asante kingdom in the interior, which had been expanding its rule toward the coast. After a series of Anglo-Asante wars beginning in 1824, British troops finally forced the Asante kingdom to accept British protectorate status in 1902. The large territory the British then controlled is essentially today's nation of Ghana.

Precolonial trade along the Gold Coast was vigorous and varied, with expanding exports of feathers, ivory, rubber, and palm oil. Into this sophisticated economy the British subsequently introduced cocoa bean production in 1878 for the world's chocolate. Output rose spectacularly from a few hundred tons in the 1890s to 305,000 tons in 1936. Independent peasants and energetic African businessmen and businesswomen were mainly responsible for this enormous growth. Creative African entrepreneurs even built their own roads, and they sometimes reaped large profits. Gold production remained in African hands until the 1890s, when European companies began acquiring mines and extracting gold using modern techniques. Gold revenues went to the mining companies and the colonial government.

The Gold Coast also showed the way politically and culturally. The westernized black elite — relatively prosperous and well-educated lawyers, professionals, and journalists — and business people took full advantage of opportunities provided by the fairly enlightened colonial regime. The black elite was the main presence in the limited local elections permitted by the British, for few permanent white settlers ventured to hot and densely populated West Africa. Some members of this black elite became passionate nationalists, such as Kwame Nkrumah, and in 1957 gained independence for the Gold Coast as Ghana (see page 988).

Across the continent in British East Africa (modern Kenya), events unfolded differently. In West Africa Europeans had been establishing trading posts since the 1400s and had carried on a complex slave trade for centuries. In East Africa there was very little European presence, other than some Portuguese, until after the scramble for Africa in the 1880s. Once the British started building their strategic railroad from the Indian Ocean across British East Africa in 1901, however, foreigners from Great Britain and India moved in to exploit the more welcoming environment. Indian settlers became shopkeepers, clerks, and laborers in the towns. British settlers dreamed of turning the cool, beautiful, and fertile East African highlands into a "white man's country" like Southern Rhodesia or the Union of South Africa. They dismissed the local population of peasant farmers as barbarians, fit only to toil as cheap labor on their large estates and plantations. British East Africa's blacks thus experienced much harsher colonial rule than did their fellow Africans in the Gold Coast, and they had to fight a long and violent war before gaining Kenyan independence in 1963.

The New Imperialism, 1880–1914

What were the causes and consequences of European empire building after 1880?

Western expansion into Africa and Asia reached its apex between about 1880 and 1914. In those years the leading European nations sent streams of money and manufactured goods to both continents and also rushed to create or enlarge vast overseas political empires. This frantic activity differed sharply with the limited economic penetration of non-Western territories between 1816 and 1880, which, albeit by naked military force, had left a China or a Japan "opened" but politically independent (see Chapter 26). By contrast, late-nineteenth-century empires recalled the old European colonial empires of the seventeenth and eighteenth centuries and led contemporaries to speak of the **new imperialism**.

Characterized by a frenzied rush to plant the flag over as many people and as much territory as possible, the most spectacular manifestation of the new imperialism was the seizure of almost all of Africa. Less striking but equally important was Europe's extension of political control in Asia. The British expanded from their base in India, and in the 1880s the French took Indochina (modern Vietnam, Cambodia, and Laos). India and China also experienced a profound imperialist impact (see Chapter 26).

Causes of the New Imperialism

Many factors contributed to the West's late-nineteenth-century rush for territory in Africa and Asia, and controversies continue to rage over interpretation of the new imperialism. Despite complexity and controversy, however, basic causes are clearly identifiable.

Economic motives played an important role in the extension of political empires, especially of the British Empire. By the 1870s France, Germany, and the United States were rapidly industrializing. For a century Great Britain had been the "workshop of the world," the dominant modern industrial power. Now it was losing its industrial leadership, as its share of global manufacturing output dropped from 33 percent to just 14 percent between 1870 and 1914, and facing increasingly tough competition in foreign markets. In this changing environment of widening economic internationalism, the world experienced one of the worst economic depressions in history, the Long Depression (originally called the Great Depression until the 1930s Great Depression supplanted it; see pages 929–935), which lasted from 1873 to 1879. To protect home industries, America and Europe (except for Britain and the Netherlands) raised tariff barriers, abandoning the century-long practice of free trade and laissez-faire capitalism (see page 726). Unable to export their goods and faced with excess production, market saturation, and high unemployment, Britain, the other European powers, and the United States turned to imperial expansion, seeking African and Asian colonies to sell their products and acquire cheap raw materials. The Long Depression was arguably the single most important spark touching off the age of new imperialism.

Economic gains from the new imperialism proved limited, however, before 1914. The new colonies were too poor to buy much, and they offered few immediately profitable investments. Nonetheless, colonies became important for political and diplomatic reasons. Each leading European country considered them crucial to national security, military power, and international prestige.

Colonial rivalries reflected the increasing aggressiveness of Social Darwinian theories of brutal competition among races (see page 750). As one prominent English economist argued in 1873, the "strongest nation has always been conquering the weaker . . . and the strongest tend to be best."[9] Thus European nations, considered as racially distinct parts of the dominant white race, had to seize colonies to prove their strength and virility. Moreover, since racial struggle was nature's inescapable law, the conquest of "inferior" peoples was just. Social Darwinism and harsh racial doctrines fostered imperialist expansion.

So, too, did the industrial world's unprecedented technological and military superiority. Three developments were crucial. First, the rapidly firing machine gun, so lethal at Omdurman in Sudan, was an ultimate weapon in many unequal battles. Second, newly discovered **quinine** effectively controlled malaria attacks, which had previously decimated Europeans in the tropics whenever they left breezy coastal enclaves and dared to venture into mosquito-infested interiors. Third, the introduction of steam power (see page 695) strengthened the Western powers in two ways. Militarily, they could swiftly transport their armies by sea or rail where they were most needed. Economically, steamships with ever-larger cargoes now made round-trip journeys to far-flung colonies much more quickly and economically. Small steamboats could travel back and forth along the coast and also carry goods up and down Africa's great rivers, as portrayed in the classic American film *The African Queen*. Likewise, freight cars pulled by powerful steam engines — immune to disease, unlike animals and humans — replaced the thousands of African porters hitherto responsible for carrying raw materials from the interior to the coast. Never before — and never again after 1914 — would the technological gap between the West and the non-Western regions of the world be so great.

Domestic political and class conflicts also contributed to overseas expansion. Conservative political leaders often manipulated colonial issues in order to divert popular attention from domestic problems and to create a false sense of national unity. Imperial propagandists relentlessly stressed that colonies benefited workers as well as capitalists, and they encouraged the masses to savor foreign triumphs and imperial glory.

Finally, special-interest groups in each country were powerful agents of expansion. Shipping companies wanted lucrative subsidies. White settlers wanted more land. Missionaries and humanitarians wanted to spread religion and stop the slave trade. Military men and colonial officials foresaw rapid advancement and high-paid positions in growing empires. The actions of such groups pushed the course of empire forward.

A "Civilizing Mission"

Imperialists did not rest the case for empire solely on naked conquest and a Darwinian racial struggle or on power politics and the need for navy bases on every ocean. They developed additional arguments to satisfy their consciences and answer their critics.

To rationalize their actions, Europeans and Americans argued they could and should "civilize" supposedly primitive non-Western peoples. According to this view, Africans and Asians would benefit from Western educations, modern economies, cities, advanced medicine, and higher living standards and eventually might be ready for self-government and Western democracy.

Another argument was that imperial government protected colonized peoples from ethnic warfare, the slave trade within Africa, and other forms of exploitation by white settlers and business people. Thus the French spoke of their sacred "civilizing mission." In 1899 Rudyard Kipling (1865–1936), who wrote extensively on Anglo-Indian life and was perhaps the most influential British writer of the 1890s, exhorted Westerners to unselfish service in distant lands (while warning of the high costs involved) in his poem "The White Man's Burden":

> Take up the White Man's Burden —
> Send forth the best ye breed —
> Go bind your sons to exile
> To serve your captives' need,
> To wait in heavy harness,
> On fluttered folk and wild —
> Your new-caught, sullen peoples
> Half-devil and half-child.[10]

Kipling's poem, written in response to America's seizure of the Philippines after the Spanish-American War, and his concept of a **white man's burden** won wide acceptance among American imperialists. This principle was an important factor in the decision to rule, rather than liberate, the Philippines after the Spanish-American War (see page 853). Like their European counterparts, these Americans believed their civilization had reached unprecedented heights, enabling them to bestow unique benefits on all "less advanced" peoples.

Imperialists also claimed that peace and stability under European or American dominion permitted the spread of Christianity. In Africa Catholic and Protestant missionaries competed with Islam south of the Sahara, seeking converts and building schools. Many Africans' first real contact with Europeans and Americans was in mission schools. Some peoples, such as the Ibo in Nigeria, became highly Christianized. Such successes in black Africa contrasted with the general failure of missionary efforts in the Islamic world and in much of Asia.

Critics of Imperialism

Imperial expansion aroused sharp, even bitter, critics. One forceful attack was delivered in 1902, after the unpopular South African War, by radical English economist J. A. Hobson (1858–1940) in his *Imperialism*, a work that influenced Russian socialist leader Vladimir Lenin (see Chapter 28) and others. Hobson contended that the rush to acquire colonies resulted from the economic needs of unregulated (by governments) capitalism. Moreover, Hobson argued, the quest for empire diverted popular attention away from domestic reform and the need to reduce the great gap between rich and poor at home. These and similar arguments had limited appeal because most people fervently believed imperialism was economically profitable for the homeland. Both Hobson and public opinion were wrong, however. Most British and European investors put the bulk of their money in the United States, Canada, Russia, and other industrializing countries. Sub-Saharan Africa accounted for less than 5 percent of British exports in 1890, and British investments in Africa flowed predominantly to the mines in southern Africa. Thus, while some sectors of the British economy did profit from imperial conquests, and trade with these conquests was greater just before the Great War than in 1870, overall profits from imperialism were marginal at best.

Hobson and many Western critics struck home, however, with their moral condemnation of whites imperiously ruling nonwhites. Kipling and his kind were lampooned as racist bullies whose rule rested on brutality, racial contempt, and the Maxim machine gun. Polish-born novelist Joseph Conrad (1857–1924), in *Heart of Darkness* (1902), castigated the "pure selfishness" of Europeans in "civilizing" Africa. The novel's main character, once a liberal European scholar, is corrupted by power in Africa and turns into a savage brute.

Critics charged Europeans with applying a degrading double standard and failing to live up to their own noble ideals. At home Europeans had won or were winning representative government, individual liberties, and a certain equality of opportunity. In their empires Europeans imposed military dictatorships on Africans and Asians, forced them to work involuntarily, and discriminated against them shamelessly. Only by renouncing imperialism and giving captive peoples the freedom idealized in Western society would Europeans be worthy of their traditions.

African and Asian Resistance

To African and Asian peoples, Western expansion represented a profoundly disruptive assault with many consequences. Everywhere it threatened traditional ruling classes, economies, and ways of life. Christian missionaries and European secular ideologies challenged established beliefs and values. African and Asian societies experienced crises of identity, although the details of each people's story varied substantially.

Initially African and Asian rulers often responded by trying to drive the unwelcome foreigners away, as in China and Japan (see Chapter 26). Violent antiforeign reactions exploded elsewhere again and again, but the industrialized West's superior military technology almost invariably prevailed. In addition, Europeans sought to divide and conquer by giving special powers and privileges to some individuals and groups from among the local population, including traditional leaders such as chiefs, landowners, and religious figures, and Western-educated professionals and civil servants, including police officers and military officers. These local elites recognized the imperial power realities in which they were enmeshed, and manipulated them to maintain or gain authority over the masses. Some concluded that the West was superior in certain ways and that they needed to reform and modernize their societies by copying some European achievements. By ruling indirectly through a local elite (backed by the implied threat of force), a political model referred to as hegemony, a relatively small number of Europeans could maintain control over much larger populations without constant rebellion and protest. European empires were won by force, but they were maintained by cultural as well as military and political means.

Nevertheless, imperial rule was in many ways an imposing edifice built on sand. Acceptance of European rule was shallow and weak among the colonized masses. They were often quick to follow determined charismatic personalities who came to oppose the Europeans. Such leaders always arose, both when Europeans ruled directly, or indirectly through native governments, for at least two basic reasons.

First, the nonconformists—the eventual anti-imperialist leaders—developed a burning desire for human dignity. They felt such dignity was incompatible with, and impossible under, foreign rule. Second, potential leaders found in the Western world the necessary ideologies and justification for their protest, such as liberalism, with its credo of civil liberty and political self-determination. They echoed European and American anti-imperialists in demanding that the West live up to its own ideals. Above all, they found themselves attracted to the nineteenth-century Western ideology of nationalism, which asserted that every people had the right to control their own destiny (see Chapter 24). After 1917 anti-imperialist revolt found another weapon in Lenin's version of Marxist socialism.

The Islamic Heartland Under Pressure

How did the Ottoman Empire and Egypt try to modernize themselves, and what were the most important results?

Stretching from West Africa into southeastern Europe and across Southwest Asia to the East Indies, Islamic civilization competed successfully with western Europe for centuries. Beginning in the late seventeenth century, however, the rising absolutist states of Austria and Russia began to challenge the greatest Muslim state, the vast Ottoman Empire, and gradually to reverse Ottoman rule in southeastern Europe. In the nineteenth century European industrialization and nation building further altered the long-standing balance of power, and Western expansion eventually posed a serious challenge to Muslims everywhere.

Ruling elites both in the Ottoman Empire and in Egypt, a largely independent Ottoman province, led the way in trying to survive against constant European political, cultural, and military pressure. The ongoing European military threat required, first of all, wrenching army reforms along Western lines in order to defend and preserve the state. These military reforms then snowballed into a series of innovations in education, which had a powerful cultural impact on Ottoman and Egyptian elites.

Efforts to defend against Western expansion and adapt to a rapidly changing world brought about momentous transformations that were profound and paradoxical. On the one hand, the Ottoman Empire and Egypt achieved considerable modernization along Western lines. On the other hand, these impressive efforts came about too slowly to offset the West's growing power and imperial appetite. The Islamic heartland in Southwest Asia and North Africa increasingly fell under foreign control.

Decline and Reform in the Ottoman Empire

Although the Ottoman Empire began a slow decline after Suleiman the Magnificent in the sixteenth century, the relationship between the Ottomans and the Europeans in about 1750 was still one of roughly equal strength. This parity began to change quickly and radically, however, in the later eighteenth century, as the Ottomans fell behind western Europe in science, industrial skill, and military technology.

A transformation of the army was absolutely necessary to battle the Europeans more effectively and enhance the sultanate's authority within the empire. There were two primary obstacles to change, however. First, Ottoman military weakness reflected the decline of the sultan's "slave army," the so-called janissary corps (see page 494).

With time, the janissaries — boys and other slaves raised in Turkey as Muslims, then trained to serve in the Ottoman infantry's elite corps — became a corrupt and privileged hereditary caste. They zealously pursued their own interests and refused any military innovations that might undermine their high status. Second, the empire was no longer a centralized military state. Instead local governors were becoming increasingly independent, pursuing their own interests and even seeking to establish their own governments and hereditary dynasties.

The energetic sultan Selim III (r. 1789–1807) understood these realities, but when he tried to reorganize the army, the janissaries refused to use any "Christian" equipment. In 1807 they revolted and executed Selim in a palace revolution, one of many that plagued the Ottoman state. Selim's successor, the reform-minded Mahmud II (r. 1808–1839), proceeded cautiously, picking loyal officers and building his dependable artillery corps. In 1826 his council ordered the janissaries to drill in the European manner. As expected, the janissaries revolted and charged the palace, where they were mowed down by the waiting artillery.

The destruction and abolition of the janissaries cleared the way for building a new army, but it came too late to stop the rise of Muhammad Ali, the Ottoman governor in Egypt. In 1831 his French-trained forces occupied the Ottoman province of Syria and appeared ready to depose Mahmud II. The Ottoman sultan survived, but only by begging Britain, Russia, and Austria for help. They intervened and negotiated a peace settlement. The Ottomans were saved again in 1839, after their forces were routed trying to drive Muhammad Ali from Syria. In the last months of 1840 Russian diplomatic efforts, British and Austrian naval blockades, and threatened military action convinced Muhammad Ali to return Syria to the Ottomans. European powers preferred a weak and dependent Ottoman state to a strong and revitalized Muslim entity under a dynamic leader such as Muhammad Ali.

In 1839, realizing their precarious position, liberal Ottoman statesmen launched an era of radical reforms, which lasted with fits and starts until 1876 and culminated in a constitution and a short-lived parliament. Known as the Tanzimat (literally, "regulations" or "orders"), these reforms were designed to remake the empire on a western European model. The new decrees called for Muslim, Christian, and Jewish equality before the law and in business, security of life and property, and a modernized administration and military. New commercial laws allowed free importation of foreign goods, as British advisers demanded, and permitted foreign merchants to operate freely throughout an economically dependent empire. Under heavy British pressure, slavery in the empire was drastically curtailed, though not abolished completely. Of great significance, growing numbers among the elite and the upwardly mobile embraced Western education, adopted Western manners and artistic styles, and accepted secular values to some extent.

Intended to bring revolutionary modernization such as that experienced by Russia under Peter the Great (see page 549) and by Japan in the Meiji era (see page 810), the Tanzimat achieved only partial success. The Ottoman state and society failed to regain its earlier power and authority for several reasons. First, implementation of the reforms required a new generation of well-trained and trustworthy officials, and that generation did not exist. Second, the liberal reforms failed to halt the growth of nationalism among Christian subjects in the Balkans (see below and Chapter 28), which resulted in crises and defeats that undermined all reform efforts. Third, the Ottoman initiatives did not

Pasha Halim Receiving Archduke Maximilian of Austria   As this painting suggests,
Ottoman leaders became well versed in European languages and culture. They also mastered
the game of power politics, playing one European state against another and securing the
Ottoman Empire's survival. The black servants on the right may be slaves from the Sudan.
(Painting by Peter Johann Nepomuk Geiger, 1850, oil on canvas/Miramare Palace, Trieste, Italy/De Agostini Picture
Library/Gianni Dagli Orti/The Bridgeman Art Library)

curtail the appetite of Western imperialism, and European bankers gained a usurious
stranglehold on Ottoman finances. In 1875 the Ottoman state had to declare partial
bankruptcy and place its finances in the hands of European creditors.

Finally, the elaboration—at least on paper—of equal rights for citizens and religious communities failed to create greater unity within the state. Religious disputes
increased, worsened by the Great Powers' relentless interference. This development
embittered relations between religious communities, distracted the government from
its reform mission, and split Muslims into secularists and religious conservatives. Many
conservative Muslims detested the religious reforms, which they considered an irrever-
ent departure from Islamic tradition and holy law. These Islamic conservatives became
the most dependable supporters of Sultan Abdülhamid II (r. 1876–1909), who abandoned the model of European liberalism in his long and repressive reign.

Meanwhile, the threat of Europe's Great Powers gradually conquering the Ottoman Empire and dividing up its vast territories became quite real. At the beginning
of the nineteenth century, while Ottoman forces were caught up in the Napoleonic
Wars in Egypt, Serbian nationalists rebelled and forced the Ottomans to grant Serbia

local autonomy in 1816. The Greeks revolted against Ottoman rule in 1821 and won their national independence in 1830. As the Ottomans dealt with these uprisings by their Christian subjects in Europe, they failed to defend their Islamic provinces in North Africa. In 1830 French armies began their long and bloody conquest of the Arabic-speaking province of Algeria. By 1860 two hundred thousand French, Italian, and Spanish colonists had settled among the Muslim majority, whose number had been reduced to about 2.5 million by the war against the French and related famines and epidemics.

Finally, during the Russo-Turkish War (1877–1878), absolutist Russia and a coalition of Balkan countries pushed southward into Ottoman lands and won a decisive victory. At the Congress of Berlin in 1878, the European Great Powers and the Ottoman Empire met to formally recognize Bulgarian, Romanian, Serbian, and Montenegrin independence. The Ottomans also lost territory to the Russians in the Caucasus, Austria-Hungary occupied the Ottoman provinces of Bosnia-Herzegovina and Novi Pazar, and Great Britain took over Cyprus. The Ottoman Empire, now labeled the "sick man of Europe" in the European press, left the meeting significantly weakened and humiliated.

The combination of declining international power and conservative tyranny eventually led to a powerful resurgence of the modernizing impulse among idealistic Turkish exiles in Europe and young army officers in Istanbul. These fervent patriots, the so-called **Young Turks**, seized power in the 1908 revolution, overthrowing Sultan Abdülhamid II. They made his brother Mehmed V (r. 1909–1918) the figurehead sultan and forced him to implement reforms. Though they failed to stop the rising tide of anti-Ottoman nationalism in the Balkans, the Young Turks did help prepare the way for the birth of modern secular Turkey after the defeat and collapse of the Ottoman Empire in World War I (see pages 867–868).

Egypt: From Reform to British Occupation

The ancient land of the pharaohs had been ruled by a succession of foreigners from 525 B.C.E. to the Ottoman conquest in the early sixteenth century. In 1798, as France and Britain prepared for war in Europe, the young French general Napoleon Bonaparte invaded Egypt, thereby threatening British access to India, and occupied the territory for three years. Into the power vacuum left by the French withdrawal stepped an extraordinary Albanian-born Turkish general, Muhammad Ali (1769–1849).

Appointed Egypt's governor by Sultan Salim III in 1805, Muhammad Ali set out to build his own state on the strength of a large, powerful army organized along European lines. In 1820–1822 the Egyptian leader conquered much of the Sudan to secure slaves for his army, the first of thousands of African slaves brought to Egypt during his reign. Because many slaves died in Egyptian captivity, Muhammad Ali turned to drafting Egyptian peasants. He also reformed the government and promoted modern industry. (See "Individuals in Society: Muhammad Ali," page 784.) For a time Muhammad Ali's ambitious strategy seemed to work, but it eventually foundered when his armies occupied Syria and he threatened the Ottoman sultan, Mahmud II. In the face of European military might and diplomatic entreaties, Muhammad Ali agreed to peace with his Ottoman overlords and withdrew. In return he was given unprecedented hereditary rule over Egypt and Sudan. By his death in 1849, Muhammad Ali had

INDIVIDUALS IN SOCIETY • Muhammad Ali

The dynamic leader Muhammad Ali stands across the history of modern Egypt like a colossus. Yet the essence of the man remains a mystery, and historians vary greatly in their interpretations of him. Sent by the Ottomans, with Albanian troops, to oppose the French occupation of Egypt in 1799, Muhammad Ali maneuvered skillfully after the French withdrawal in 1802. In 1805 he was named pasha, or Ottoman governor, of Egypt. Only the Mamluks remained as rivals. Originally an elite corps of Turkish slave soldiers, the Mamluks had become a semifeudal military ruling class living off the Egyptian peasantry. In 1811 Muhammad Ali offered to make peace, and he invited the Mamluk chiefs and their retainers to a banquet in Cairo's Citadel. As the unsuspecting guests processed through a narrow passage, his troops opened fire, slaughtering all the Mamluk leaders.

After eliminating his foes, Muhammad Ali embarked on a program of radical reforms. He reorganized agriculture and commerce, reclaiming most of the cultivated land for the state domain, which he controlled. He also established state agencies to monopolize, for his own profit, the sale of agricultural goods. Commercial agriculture geared to exports to Europe developed rapidly, especially after the successful introduction of high-quality cotton in 1821. Canals and irrigation systems along the Nile were rebuilt and expanded.

Muhammad Ali used his growing revenues to recast his army along European lines. He recruited French officers to train the soldiers. As the military grew, so did the need for hospitals, schools of medicine and languages, and secular education. Young Turks and some Egyptians were sent to Europe for advanced study. The ruler boldly financed factories to produce uniforms and weapons, and he prohibited the importation of European goods so as to protect Egypt's infant industries. In the 1830s state factories were making one-fourth of Egypt's cotton into cloth. Above all, Muhammad Ali drafted Egyptian peasants into the military for the first time, thereby expanding his army to one hundred thousand men. It was this force that conquered the Ottoman province of Syria, threatened the sultan in Istanbul, and triggered European intervention. Grudgingly recognized by his Ottoman overlord as Egypt's hereditary ruler in 1841, Muhammad Ali nevertheless had to accept European and Ottoman demands to give up Syria and abolish his monopolies and protective tariffs. The old ruler then lost heart; his reforms languished, and his factories disappeared.

In the attempt to understand Muhammad Ali and his significance, many historians have concluded that he was a national hero, the "founder of modern Egypt."

established a strong and virtually independent Egyptian state within the Ottoman Empire.

To pay for a modern army and industrialization, Muhammad Ali encouraged the development of commercial agriculture geared to the European market, which had profound social implications. Egyptian peasants had been poor but largely self-sufficient, growing food on state-owned land allotted to them by tradition. Offered the possibility

His ambitious state-building projects—hospitals, schools, factories, and the army—were the basis for an Egyptian reawakening and eventual independence from the Ottomans' oppressive foreign rule. Similarly, state-sponsored industrialization promised an escape from poverty and Western domination, which was foiled only by European intervention and British insistence on free trade.

A growing minority of historians question these views. They see Muhammad Ali primarily as an Ottoman adventurer. In their view, he did not aim for national independence for Egypt, but rather "intended to carve out a small empire for himself and for his children after him."* Paradoxically, his success, which depended on heavy taxes and brutal army service, led to Egyptian nationalism among the Arabic-speaking masses, but that new nationalism was directed against Muhammad Ali and his Turkish-speaking entourage. Continuing research into this leader's life will help resolve these conflicting interpretations.

QUESTIONS FOR ANALYSIS

1. Which of Muhammad Ali's actions support the interpretation that he was the founder of modern Egypt? Which actions support the opposing view?

2. After you have studied Chapter 26, compare Muhammad Ali and the Meiji reformers in Japan. What accounts for the similarities and differences?

---

*K. Fahmy, *All the Pasha's Men: Mehmed Ali, His Army, and the Making of Modern Egypt* (Cambridge: Cambridge University Press, 1997), p. 310.

▷LaunchPad
ONLINE DOCUMENT PROJECT

How did reformers address the challenges facing the Ottoman Empire in the nineteenth century? Read excerpts from Ottoman reformers, and then complete a quiz and writing assignment based on the evidence and details from this chapter.

See inside the front cover to learn more.

of profits from export agriculture, high-ranking officials and members of Muhammad Ali's family began carving large private landholdings out of the state domain, and they forced the peasants to grow cash crops for European markets. Landownership became very unequal. By 1913, 12,600 large estates owned 44 percent of the land, and 1.4 million peasants owned only 27 percent. Estate owners also "modernized" agriculture, to the detriment of the peasants' well-being.

Muhammad Ali's modernization policies attracted growing numbers of Europeans to the banks of the Nile. In 1863, when Muhammad Ali's grandson Ismail began his sixteen-year rule as Egypt's khedive (kuh-DEEV), or prince, the port city of Alexandria had more than fifty thousand Europeans. By 1900 about two hundred thousand Europeans lived in Egypt, accounting for 2 percent of the population. Europeans served as army officers, engineers, doctors, government officials, and police officers. Others worked in trade, finance, and shipping. Above all, Europeans living in Egypt combined with landlords and officials to continue steering commercial agriculture toward exports. As throughout the Ottoman Empire, Europeans enjoyed important commercial and legal privileges and formed an economic elite.

Ismail (r. 1863–1879) was a westernizing autocrat. Educated at France's leading military academy, he dreamed of using European technology and capital to modernize Egypt and build a vast empire in northeastern Africa. He promoted cotton production, and exports to Europe soared. Ismail also borrowed large sums, and with his support the Suez Canal was completed by a French company in 1869, shortening the voyage from Europe to Asia by thousands of miles. Cairo acquired modern boulevards and Western hotels. As Ismail proudly declared, "My country is no longer in Africa, we now form part of Europe."[11]

Major cultural and intellectual changes accompanied the political and economic ones. The Arabic of the masses, rather than the conqueror's Turkish, became the official language, and young, European-educated Egyptians helped spread new skills and ideas in the bureaucracy. A host of writers, intellectuals, and religious thinkers responded to the novel conditions with innovative ideas that had a powerful impact in Egypt and other Muslim societies.

Three influential figures who represented broad families of thought were especially significant. The teacher and writer Jamal al-Din al-Afghani (1838/39–1897) preached Islamic regeneration and defense against Western Christian aggression. Regeneration, he argued, required the purification of religious belief, Muslim unity, and a revolutionary overthrow of corrupt Muslim rulers and foreign exploiters. The more moderate Muhammad Abduh (1849–1905) also sought Muslim rejuvenation and launched the modern Islamic reform movement, which became very important in the twentieth century. Abduh concluded that Muslims should adopt a flexible, reasoned approach to change, modernity, science, social questions, and foreign ideas and not reject these out of hand.

Finally, the writer Qasim Amin (1863–1908) represented those who found inspiration in the West in the late nineteenth century. In his influential book *The Liberation of Women* (1899), Amin argued forcefully that superior education for European women had contributed greatly to the Islamic world's falling far behind the West. The rejuvenation of Muslim societies required greater equality for women:

> History confirms and demonstrates that the status of women is inseparably tied to the status of a nation. Where the status of a nation is low, reflecting an uncivilized condition for that nation, the status of women is also low, and when the status of a nation is elevated, reflecting the progress and civilization of that nation, the status of women in that country is also elevated.[12]

Egypt changed rapidly during Ismail's rule, but his projects were reckless and enormously expensive. By 1876 the Egyptian government could not pay the interest

Egyptian Travel Guide Ismail's efforts to transform Cairo were fairly successful. As a result, European tourists could more easily visit the country that their governments dominated. Ordinary Europeans were lured to exotic lands by travel books like this colorful "Official Guide" to an exhibition on Cairo held in Berlin. (Private Collection/Archives Charmet/The Bridgeman Art Library)

on its colossal debt. Rather than let Egypt go bankrupt and repudiate its loans, France and Great Britain intervened politically to protect the European investors who held the Egyptian bonds. To guarantee the Egyptian debt would be paid in full, they forced Ismail to appoint French and British commissioners to oversee Egyptian finances. This meant that Europeans would determine the state budget and in effect rule Egypt.

Foreign financial control evoked a violent nationalistic reaction among Egyptian religious leaders, intellectuals, and army officers. In 1879 they formed the Egyptian Nationalist Party with Colonel Ahmed Arabi as their leader. Continuing diplomatic pressure, which forced Ismail to abdicate in favor of his weak son, Tewfiq (r. 1879–1892), resulted in bloody anti-European riots in Alexandria in 1882. Several Europeans were killed, and Tewfiq and his court had to seek refuge on British ships. The British fleet then bombarded Alexandria, and a British expeditionary force decimated Arabi's forces and occupied all of Egypt. British armies remained in Egypt until 1956.

Initially the British maintained the façade of the khedive's government as an autonomous province of the Ottoman Empire, but the khedive was a mere puppet. The British consul, General Evelyn Baring, later Lord Cromer, ruled the country after 1883. Baring was a paternalistic reformer. He initiated tax reforms and made some improvements to conditions for peasants. Foreign bondholders received their interest payments, while Egyptian nationalists chafed under foreign rule.

The Expanding World Economy

What were the global consequences of European industrialization between 1800 and 1914?

The Industrial Revolution created, first in Great Britain and then in continental Europe and North America, a growing and dynamic economic system. Over the course of the nineteenth century that system expanded and transformed economic relations across the face of the earth. As a result, the world's total income grew as never before, and international trade boomed. Western nations used their superior military power to force non-Western nations to open their doors to Western economic interests. Consequently, the largest share of the ever-increasing gains from trade flowed to the West, resulting in a stark division between rich and poor countries.

The Rise of Global Inequality

From a global perspective, the ultimate significance of the Industrial Revolution was that it allowed those world regions that industrialized in the nineteenth century to increase their wealth and power enormously in comparison with those that did not. A gap between the industrializing regions (Europe, North America, Japan) and the nonindustrializing regions (mainly Africa, Asia, and Latin America) opened and grew steadily throughout the nineteenth century. Moreover, this pattern of uneven global development became institutionalized, built into the structure of the world economy. Thus evolved a world of economic haves and have-nots, with the have-not peoples and nations far outnumbering the haves.

In 1750 the average living standard was no higher in Europe as a whole than in the rest of the world. By 1914 the average person in the wealthiest countries had an income four or five times as great (and in Great Britain nine or ten times as great) as an average person's income in the poorest countries of Africa and Asia. The rise in average income and well-being reflected the rising level of industrialization in Great Britain and then in the other developed countries before World War I.

The reasons for these enormous income disparities, which are poignant indicators of disparities in food and clothing, health and education, life expectancy, and general material well-being, have generated a great deal of debate. One school of interpretation stresses that the West used science, technology, capitalist organization, and even its critical worldview to create its wealth and greater physical well-being. An opposing school argues that the West used its political, economic, and military power to steal much of its riches through its rapacious colonialism in the nineteenth and twentieth centuries.

These issues are complex, and there are few simple answers. As noted in Chapter 23, the wealth-creating potential of technological improvement and more intensive capitalist organization was great. At the same time, the initial breakthroughs in the late eighteenth century rested in part on Great Britain's having already used political force to dominate a substantial part of the world economy. In the nineteenth century other industrializing countries joined with Britain to extend Western dominion over the entire world economy. Unprecedented wealth was created, but the lion's share of that new wealth flowed to the West and its propertied classes and to a tiny indigenous elite of cooperative rulers, landowners, and merchants.

The World Market

World trade was a powerful stimulus to economic development in the nineteenth century. In 1913 the value of world trade was about twenty-five times what it had been in 1800, even though prices of manufactured goods and raw materials were lower in 1913 than in 1800. In a general way, this enormous increase in international commerce summed up the growth of an interlocking world economy centered in Europe.

Great Britain played a key role in using trade to tie the world together economically. In 1815 Britain already possessed a colonial empire, with India, Canada, Australia, and other scattered areas remaining British possessions after American independence. The technological breakthroughs of the Industrial Revolution encouraged British manufacturers to seek export markets around the world. After Parliament repealed laws restricting grain importation in 1846, Britain also became the world's leading importer of foreign goods. Free access to Britain's market stimulated the development of mines and plantations in Africa and Asia.

The conquest of distance facilitated the growth of trade. The earliest railroad construction occurred in Europe and in America north of the Rio Grande; railroads were built in other parts of the globe after around 1860. By 1920 about a quarter of the world's railroads were in Latin America, Asia, Africa, and Australia. Wherever railroads were built, they drastically reduced transportation costs, opened new economic opportunities, and called forth new skills and attitudes.

Much of the railroad construction undertaken in Africa, Asia, and Latin America connected seaports with inland cities and regions, as opposed to linking and developing cities and regions within a country. Thus railroads dovetailed with Western economic interests, facilitating the inflow and sale of Western manufactured goods and the export and development of local raw materials.

Steam power also revolutionized transportation by sea. Long used to drive paddle wheelers on rivers, particularly in Russia and North America, steam power finally began to supplant sails on the world's oceans in the late 1860s. Lighter, stronger, cheaper steel replaced iron, which had replaced wood. Passenger and freight rates tumbled, and the shipment of low-priced raw materials from one continent to another became feasible.

The revolution in land and sea transportation helped European settlers seize vast, thinly populated territories and produce agricultural products and raw materials for sale in Europe. Improved transportation enabled Asia, Africa, and Latin America to export not only the traditional tropical products—spices, dyes, tea, sugar, coffee—but also new raw materials for industry, such as jute, rubber, cotton, and peanut and coconut oil.

Intercontinental trade was enormously facilitated by the Suez Canal and the Panama Canal (see page 855). Of great importance, too, was large and continual investment in modern port facilities, which made loading and unloading cheaper, faster, and more dependable. Finally, transoceanic telegraph cables inaugurated rapid communications among the world's financial centers and linked world commodity prices in a global network.

The growth of trade and the conquest of distance encouraged Europeans to make massive foreign investments beginning about 1840, but not in European colonies or protectorates in Asia and Africa. About three-quarters of total European investment went to other European countries, the United States and Canada, Australia and New Zealand, and Latin America. Here booming, industrializing economies offered the most profitable investment opportunities. Much of this investment was peaceful and mutually beneficial for lenders and borrowers. The victims were Native Americans, Australian Aborigines, New Zealand Maoris, and other native peoples who were displaced and decimated by the diseases, liquor, and weapons of an aggressively expanding Western society (see Chapter 27).

The Great Global Migration

What fueled migration, and what was the general pattern of this unprecedented movement of people?

A poignant human drama was interwoven with this worldwide economic expansion: millions of people left their ancestral lands in one of history's greatest migrations, the so-called **great migration**. In the early eighteenth century the world's population entered a period of rapid growth that continued unabated through the nineteenth and twentieth centuries. Europe's population (including Asiatic Russia) more than doubled during the nineteenth century, from approximately 188 million in 1800 to roughly 432 million in 1900.

Between 1750 and 1900 Asia's population followed the same general trend. The population of China, by far the world's most populous country in the middle of the eighteenth century, increased from about 143 million in 1741 to a little more than 400 million in the 1840s, although total numbers grew more slowly in the turbulent late nineteenth century. Since African and Asian populations increased more slowly than those in Europe, Europeans and peoples of predominantly European origin jumped from about 22 percent of the world's total in 1850 to a high of about 38 percent in 1930.

Rapid population growth led to relative overpopulation in area after area in Europe and was a driving force behind emigration and Western expansion. Millions of country folk moved to nearby cities, and the more adventuresome went abroad, in search of work and economic opportunity. Some governments encouraged their excess populations to emigrate, even paying part of their expenses. Wars, famine, poverty, and, particularly in the case of Russian and eastern European Jews, bigotry and discrimination were also leading causes for emigrants to leave their ancestral homelands. More than 60 million people left Europe over the course of the nineteenth century, primarily for the rapidly growing "areas of European settlement"—North and South America, Australia, New Zealand, and Siberia (see Chapter 27). European emigration crested in the first decade of the twentieth century, when more than five times as many men and women departed as in the 1850s.

The European migrant was most often a small peasant landowner or a village craftsman whose traditional way of life was threatened by too little land, estate agriculture, and cheap factory-made goods. Determined to maintain or improve their precarious status, the vast majority of migrants were young and often unmarried. Many European migrants returned home after some time abroad. One in two migrants to Argentina and probably one in three to the United States eventually returned to their native lands.

Ties of family and friendship played a crucial role in the movement of peoples. Over several years a given province or village might lose significant numbers of its inhabitants to migration. These then settled together in rural enclaves or tightly knit urban neighborhoods in foreign lands thousands of miles away. Very often a strong individual—a businessman, a religious leader—blazed the way, and others followed, forming a **migration chain**.

A spirit of revolt, adventure, and independence spurred many young European men and women to emigrate. In Sweden and Norway, in Jewish Russia and Italy, these

Steerage Passengers, 1902
Conditions for steerage passengers traveling from Europe to the Americas were cramped, as evidenced by this photo from 1902. (Private Collection/Peter Newark American Pictures/The Bridgeman Art Library

young people felt frustrated by the small privileged classes that often controlled both church and government and resisted demands for change and greater opportunity. Migration slowed when the economic situation improved at home, particularly as countries industrialized and many more occupational opportunities became available. People also stayed put when they began to win basic political and social reforms, such as the right to vote and social security.

A substantial number of Asians—especially Chinese, Japanese, Indians, and Filipinos—also responded to population pressure and rural hardship with temporary or permanent migration. At least 3 million Asians moved abroad before 1920. Most went as indentured laborers to work under incredibly difficult conditions on the plantations or in the gold mines of Latin America, southern Asia, Africa, California, Hawaii, and Australia (see Chapter 26). White estate owners often used Asians to replace or supplement black Africans after the suppression of the Atlantic slave trade.

Asian migration would undoubtedly have been much greater if planters and mine owners desiring cheap labor had had their way. But usually they did not. Asians fled the plantations and gold mines as soon as possible, seeking greater opportunities in trade and towns. Here, however, they came into conflict with white settlers, who demanded a halt to Asian immigration. By the 1880s Americans and Australians were building **great white walls**—discriminatory laws designed to keep Asians out.

The general policy of "whites only" in the lands of large-scale European settlement meant that Europeans and people of European ancestry reaped the main benefits of the great migration. By 1913 people in Australia, Canada, and the United States all had higher average incomes than did people in Great Britain, still Europe's wealthiest nation. This, too, contributed to Western dominance in the increasingly lopsided world.

Within Asia and Africa the situation was different. Migrants from south China frequently settled in Dutch, British, and French colonies of Southeast Asia, where they established themselves as peddlers and small shopkeepers (see Chapter 26). These "overseas Chinese" gradually emerged as a new class of entrepreneurs and officeworkers. Traders from India and modern-day Lebanon performed the same function in much of sub-Saharan Africa after European colonization in the late nineteenth century. Thus in some parts of Asia and Africa the business class was both Asian and foreign, protected and tolerated by Western imperialists who found these business people useful.

Chapter Summary

Following Europe's Industrial Revolution in the late eighteenth and early nineteenth centuries, European demands for raw materials and new markets reoriented Africa's economy. The transatlantic slave trade declined dramatically as Africans began producing commodities for export. This legitimate trade in African goods proved profitable and led to the emergence of a small black middle class. Islam revived and expanded until about 1870.

After 1880 a handful of Western nations seized most of Africa and parts of Asia and rushed to build authoritarian empires. The reasons for this empire building included trade rivalries, competitive nationalism in Europe, and self-justifying claims of a civilizing mission. European nations' unprecedented military superiority enabled them to crush resistance and impose their will.

The Ottoman Empire and Egypt prepared to become modern nation-states in the twentieth century by introducing reforms to improve the military, provide technical and secular education, and expand personal liberties. They failed, however, to defend themselves from Western imperialism. The Ottoman Empire lost territory but survived in a weakened condition. Egypt's Muhammad Ali reformed the government and promoted modern industry, but Egypt went bankrupt and was conquered and ruled by Britain. Western domination was particularly bitter for most Muslims because they saw it as profaning Islam and taking away their political independence.

Population pressures at home and economic opportunities abroad caused millions of European emigrants to resettle in the sparsely populated areas of European settlement in North and South America, Australia, and Asiatic Russia. Some migrants were escaping oppression, though migration generally slowed when the economic situation improved at home or when social or political reform occurred. Migration from Asia was much more limited, mainly because European settlers raised high barriers to prevent the settlement of Asian immigrants.

Notes

1. P. Lovejoy, *Transformations in Slavery: A History of Slavery in Africa*, 2d ed. (Cambridge: Cambridge University Press, 2000), p. 142.
2. Ibid., p. 179.
3. Quoted in J. Iliffe, *Africans: The History of a Continent* (Cambridge: Cambridge University Press, 1995), p. 169.
4. Lovejoy, *Transformations in Slavery*, p. 15.
5. R. Oliver, *The African Experience* (New York: Icon Editions, 1991), pp. 164–166.
6. Quoted in H. Wheaton, *Elements of International Law* (London: Stevens & Sons, 1889), p. 804.
7. Quoted in Bernard Porter, *The Lion's Share: A Short History of British Imperialism, 1850–1970* (London: Longman, 1975), p. 134.

8. Quoted in Anthony Thomas, *Rhodes* (New York: St. Martin's Press, 1996), p. 194.

9. Walter Bagehot, *Physics and Politics, or Thoughts on the Application of the Principle of "Natural Selection" and "Inheritance" to Political Society* (New York: D. Appleton, 1873), pp. 43, 49.

10. Rudyard Kipling, *The Five Nations* (London, 1903).

11. Quoted in Earl of Cromer, *Modern Egypt* (London, 1911), p. 48.

12. Qasim Amin, *The Liberation of Women and The New Woman* (The American University of Cairo Press, 2000), p. 6.

CONNECTIONS

By the end of the nineteenth century broader industrialization across Europe increased the need for raw materials and markets, and with it came a rush to create or enlarge vast political empires abroad. The new imperialism was aimed primarily at Africa and Asia, and in the years before 1914 the leading European nations not only created empires abroad, but also continued to send massive streams of migrants, money, and manufactured goods around the world. (The impact of this unprecedented migration is taken up in the next two chapters.) This political empire building contrasted sharply with the economic penetration of non-Western territories between 1816 and 1880, which had left China and Japan "opened" but politically independent, as Chapter 26 will show.

European influence also grew in the Middle East. Threatened by European military might, modernization, and Christianity, Turks and Arabs tried to implement reforms that would assure their survival and independence but also endeavored to retain key aspects of their cultures, particularly Islam. Although they made important advances in the modernization of their economies and societies, their efforts were not enough to overcome Western imperialism. With the end of World War I and the collapse of the Ottoman Empire, England and France divided much of the Middle East into colonies and established loyal surrogates as rulers in other, nominally independent, countries. Chapter 29 will take up the story of these developments.

Easy imperialist victories over weak states and poorly armed non-Western peoples encouraged excessive pride and led Europeans to underestimate the fragility of their accomplishments. Imperialism also made nationalism more aggressive and militaristic. As European imperialism was dividing the world after the 1880s, the leading European states were also dividing themselves into two opposing military alliances. As Chapter 28 will show, when the two armed camps stumbled into war in 1914, the results were disastrous. World War I set the stage for a new anti-imperialist struggle in Africa and Asia for equality and genuine independence (see Chapters 32 and 33).

Chapter Review

MAKE IT STICK

✓ **LearningCurve**
Go online and use LearningCurve to retain what you've read.

IDENTIFY KEY TERMS

Identify and explain the significance of each item below.

palm oil (p. 764)

jihad (p. 766)

Sokoto caliphate (p. 766)

Berlin Conference (p. 769)

protectorate (p. 769)

Afrikaners (p. 771)

new imperialism (p. 776)

quinine (p. 777)

white man's burden (p. 778)

Tanzimat (p. 781)

Young Turks (p. 783)

great migration (p. 790)

migration chain (p. 790)

great white walls (p. 791)

REVIEW THE MAIN IDEAS

Answer the focus questions from each section of the chapter.

1. What were the most significant changes in Africa during the nineteenth century, and why did they occur? (p. 764)

2. What were the causes and consequences of European empire building after 1880? (p. 776)

3. How did the Ottoman Empire and Egypt try to modernize themselves, and what were the most important results? (p. 780)

4. What were the global consequences of European industrialization between 1800 and 1914? (p. 787)

5. What fueled migration, and what was the general pattern of this unprecedented movement of people? (p. 790)

MAKE CONNECTIONS

Analyze the larger developments and continuities within and across chapters.

1. Explain the transitions in Africa from the slave trade to legitimate trade to colonialism in the late eighteenth and nineteenth centuries. How was Europe's Industrial Revolution related to these transitions?

2. Europeans had been visiting Africa's coasts for four hundred years before colonizing the entire continent in thirty years in the second half of the nineteenth century. Why hadn't they colonized Africa earlier, and what factors allowed them to do it then?

LaunchPad
ONLINE DOCUMENT PROJECT

Reform Movements in the Late Ottoman Empire
How did reformers address the challenges facing the Ottoman Empire in the nineteenth century?

Read excerpts from Ottoman reformers, and then complete a quiz and writing assignment based on the evidence and details from this chapter.

See inside the front cover to learn more.

CHRONOLOGY

1805–1849	• Muhammad Ali modernizes Egypt
1808–1839	• Mahmud II rules Ottoman state and enacts reforms
1809	• Uthman dan Fodio founds Sokoto caliphate
1830	• France begins conquest of Algeria
1839–1876	• Western-style reforms (Tanzimat) in Ottoman Empire
1860s	• Transatlantic slave trade declines rapidly
1869	• Completion of Suez Canal
1875	• Ottoman state declares partial bankruptcy; European creditors take over
1876	• Europeans take financial control in Egypt
1879–1882	• Ahmed Arabi leads revolt against foreign control of Egypt
1880	• Western and central Sudan unite under Islam
1880–1900	• Most of Africa falls under European rule
1880–1914	• Height of new imperialism in Asia and Africa
1884–1885	• Berlin Conference
1899	• Kipling, "The White Man's Burden"; Amin, *The Liberation of Women*
1899–1902	• South African War
1902	• Conrad, *Heart of Darkness*; Hobson, *Imperialism*
1908	• Young Turks seize power in Ottoman Empire

✓ LearningCurve
After reading the chapter, go online
and use LearningCurve to retain what
you've read.

26

Asia and the Pacific in the Era of Imperialism

1800–1914

DURING THE NINETEENTH CENTURY THE SOCIETIES OF ASIA UNDER-
went enormous changes as a result of population growth, social unrest,
and the looming presence of Western imperialist powers. At the beginning
of the century Spain, the Netherlands, and Britain had colonies in the Philippines, modern Indonesia, and India, respectively. By the end of the century
much more land—most of the southern tier of Asia, from India to the Philippines—had been made colonies of Western powers. Most of these colonies
became tied to the industrializing world as exporters of agricultural products
or raw materials, including timber, rubber, tin, sugar, tea, cotton, and jute.
The Western presence brought benefits, especially to educated residents of
major cities, where the colonizers often introduced modern public health,
communications, and educational systems. Still, cultural barriers between the
colonizers and the colonized were huge, and the Western presence rankled.
The West relied on force to conquer and rule, and it treated non-Western
peoples as racial inferiors.

Not all the countries in Asia were reduced to colonies. Although Western
powers put enormous pressures on China and exacted many concessions
from it, China remained politically independent. Much more impressively,
Japan became the first non-Western nation to use an ancient love of country
to transform itself and thereby meet the many-sided challenge of Western
expansion. Japan emerged from the nineteenth-century crisis stronger than
any other Asian nation, becoming the first non-Western country to industrialize successfully. By the end of this period Japan had become an imperialist
power itself, making Korea and Taiwan its colonies.

India and the British Empire in Asia

In what ways did India change as a consequence of British rule?

Arriving in India on the heels of the Portuguese in the seventeenth century, the British East India Company outmaneuvered French and Dutch rivals and was there to pick up the pieces as the Mughal Empire decayed during the eighteenth century (see pages 513–514). By 1757 the company had gained control over much of India. During the nineteenth century the British government replaced the company, progressively unified the subcontinent, and harnessed its economy to British interests.

Travel and communication between Britain and India became much faster, safer, and more predictable in this period. Clipper ships with their huge sails cut the voyage from Europe to India from six to three months. By the 1850s steamships were competing with clipper ships, and they made ocean travel more predictable. After the 1869 opening of the Suez Canal, which connected the Mediterranean and Red Seas, the voyage by steamship from England to India took only three weeks. After cables were laid on the ocean floor in the 1860s, telegrams could be sent from England to India. Whereas at the beginning of the nineteenth century someone in England had to wait a year or more to get an answer to a letter sent to India, by 1870 it took only a couple of months—or, if the matter was urgent, only a few hours by telegraph. Faster travel and communication aided the colonial government and foreign merchants, but they did not keep Indians from resenting British rule.

The Evolution of British Rule

In 1818 the British East India Company controlled territory occupied by 180 million Indians—more people than lived in all of western Europe and fifty times the number of people the British had lost in 1783 when the thirteen American colonies successfully overthrew British colonial control. In India the British ruled with the cooperation of local princely allies, whom they could not afford to offend. To assert their authority, the British disbanded and disarmed local armies, introduced simpler private property laws, and enhanced the powers of local princes and religious leaders, both Hindu and Muslim. The British administrators, backed by British officers and native troops, were on the whole competent and concerned about the welfare of the Indian peasants. Slavery was outlawed and banditry suppressed, and new laws designed to improve women's position in society were introduced. Sati (widow suicide) was outlawed in 1829, legal protection of widow remarriage was extended in 1856, and infanticide (disproportionately of female newborns) was banned in 1870.

The last armed resistance to British rule occurred in 1857. By that date the British military presence in India had grown to include two hundred thousand Indian sepoy troops and thirty-eight thousand British officers. The sepoys were well trained and armed with modern rifles. In 1857 groups of them, especially around Delhi, revolted in what the British called the **Great Mutiny** and the Indians called the **Great Revolt**. The sepoys' grievances were many, ranging from the use of fat from cows (sacred to Hindus) and pigs (regarded as filthy by Muslims) to grease rifle cartridges to high tax rates and the incorporation of low-caste soldiers into the army. The insurrection spread rapidly throughout northern and central India before it was finally crushed, primarily by native troops from other parts of India loyal to the British. Thereafter, although

British and Sikh Leaders at Lahore   The Sikh kingdom in the Punjab fell to the British in a brief war in 1845–1846. This painting depicts the British and Sikh representatives who negotiated the resulting treaty, which gave Britain control of the region. (© The Trustees of the British Museum/Art Resource, NY)

princely states were allowed to continue, Britain ruled India much more tightly. Moreover, the British in India acted more like an occupying power and mixed less with the Indian elite.

After 1858 India was ruled by the British Parliament in London and administered by a civil service in India, the upper echelons of which were all white. In 1900 this elite consisted of fewer than 3,500 top officials for a population of 300 million. In 1877 Queen Victoria adopted the title empress of India, and her image became a common sight in India.

The Socioeconomic Effects of British Rule

The impact of British rule on the Indian economy was multifaceted. In the early stages, the British East India Company expanded agricultural production, creating large plantations. Early crops were opium to export to China (see page 806) and tea to substitute for imports from China. India gradually replaced China as the leading exporter of tea to Europe. During the nineteenth century India also exported cotton fiber, silk, sugar, jute, coffee, and other agricultural commodities to be processed elsewhere. Clearing land for tea and coffee plantations, along with massive commercial logging operations, led to extensive deforestation.

To aid the transport of goods, people, and information, the colonial administration invested heavily in India's infrastructure. By 1855 India's major cities had all been linked by telegraph and railroads, and postal service was being extended to local villages. By 1870 India had the fifth-largest rail network in the world—4,775 miles, carrying more than 18 million passengers a year. By 1900 the rail network had increased fivefold to 25,000 miles, and the number of passengers had increased tenfold to 188 million. By then over 370,000 Indians worked for the railroads. Irrigation also received attention, and by 1900 India had the world's most extensive irrigation system.

At the same time, Indian production of textiles suffered a huge blow. Britain imported India's raw cotton but exported machine-spun yarn and machine-woven cloth, displacing millions of Indian hand-spinners and hand-weavers. By 1900 India was buying 40 percent of Britain's cotton exports. Not until 1900 were small steps taken toward industrializing India. Local businessmen set up textile mills in Bombay, and the Tata family started the first steel mill in Bihar in 1911. By 1914 about a million Indians worked in factories.

Although the economy expanded, the poor did not see much improvement in their standard of living. Tenant farming and landlessness increased with the growth in plantation agriculture. Increases in production were eaten up by increases in population, which, as noted, had reached approximately 300 million by 1900. There was also a negative side to improved transportation. As Indians traveled more widely on the convenient trains, disease spread, especially cholera, which is transmitted by exposure to contaminated water. Pilgrims customarily bathed in and drank from sacred pools and rivers, worsening this problem. New sewerage and water supply systems were installed in Calcutta in the late 1860s, and the death rate there decreased, but in 1900 four out of every one thousand residents of British India still died of cholera each year.

The British and the Indian Educated Elite

The Indian middle class probably gained more than the poor from British rule, because they were the ones to benefit from the English-language educational system Britain established in India. Missionaries also established schools with Western curricula, and 790,000 Indians were attending some 24,000 schools by 1870. High-caste Hindus came to form a new elite profoundly influenced by Western thought and culture.

By creating a well-educated, English-speaking Indian elite and a bureaucracy aided by a modern communication system, the British laid the groundwork for a unified, powerful state. Britain placed under the same general system of law and administration the various Hindu and Muslim peoples of the subcontinent who had resisted one another for centuries. It was as if Europe, with its many states and varieties of Christianity, had been conquered and united in a single great empire. University graduates tended to look on themselves as Indians more than as residents of separate states and kingdoms, a necessary step for the development of Indian nationalism.

Some Indian intellectuals sought to reconcile the values of the modern West and their own traditions. Rammohun Roy (1772–1833), who had risen to the top of the native ranks in the British East India Company, founded a college that offered instruction in Western languages and subjects. He also founded a society to reform traditional customs, especially child marriage, the caste system, and restrictions on widows. He espoused a modern Hinduism founded on the *Upanishads* (oo-PAH-nih-shadz), the ancient sacred texts of Hinduism.

The more that Western-style education was developed in India, the more the inequalities of the system became apparent to educated Indians. Indians were eligible to take the examinations for entry into the elite Indian Civil Service, the bureaucracy that administered the Indian government, but the exams were given in England. Since few Indians could travel such a long distance to take the test, in 1870 only 1 of the 916 members of the service was Indian. In other words, no matter how Anglicized educated Indians became, they could never become the white rulers' equals. The top jobs, the best clubs, the modern hotels, and even certain railroad compartments were sealed off to brown-skinned men and women. Most of the British elite considered the jumble of Indian peoples and castes to be racially inferior. For example, when the British Parliament in 1883 was considering a bill to allow Indian judges to try white Europeans in India, the British community rose in protest and defeated the measure. As Lord Kitchener, one of the most distinguished British military commanders in India, stated:

> It is this consciousness of the inherent superiority of the European which has won for us India. However well educated and clever a native may be, and however brave he may prove himself, I believe that no rank we can bestow on him would cause him to be considered an equal of the British officer.[1]

The peasant masses might accept such inequality as the latest version of age-old class and caste hierarchies, but the well-educated, English-speaking elite eventually could not. They had studied not only Milton and Shakespeare but also English traditions of democracy, liberty, and national pride.

In the late nineteenth century the colonial ports of Calcutta, Bombay, and Madras, now all linked by railroads, became centers of intellectual ferment. In these and other cities, newspapers in English and in regional languages gained influence. Lawyers trained in English law began agitating for Indian independence. By 1885, when a group of educated Indians came together to found the Indian National Congress, demands were increasing for the equality and self-government that Britain enjoyed and had already granted white-settler colonies such as Canada and Australia. The Congress Party called for more opportunities for Indians in the Indian Civil Service and reallocation of the government budget from military expenditures to the alleviation of poverty. The party advocated unity across religious and caste lines, but most members were upper-caste, Western-educated Hindus.

Defending British possessions in India became a key element of Britain's foreign policy during the nineteenth century and led to steady expansion of the territory Britain controlled in Asia. The kingdom of Burma, to India's east, also was trying to expand, which led the British to annex Assam (located between India and Burma) in 1826, then all of Burma by 1852. Burma was then administered as a province of India. British trade between India and China went through the Strait of Malacca, making that region strategically important. Britain had taken over several Dutch territories in this region, including Java, during the Napoleonic occupation of the Netherlands (Map 26.1). After returning them to the Netherlands in 1814, Britain created its own base in the area at Singapore, later expanding into Malaya (now Malaysia) in the 1870s and 1880s. In both Burma and Malaya, Britain tried to foster economic development, building railroads and promoting trade. Burma became a major exporter of timber and rice, Malaya of tin and rubber. So many laborers were brought into Malaya for the expanding mines and plantations that its population came to be approximately one-third Malay, one-third Chinese, and one-third Indian.

Competition for Southeast Asia

Why were most but not all Southeast Asian societies reduced to colonies?

At the beginning of the nineteenth century only a small part of Southeast Asia was under direct European control. Spain administered the Philippines, and the Dutch controlled Java. By the end of the century most of the region would be in foreign hands.

The Dutch East Indies

Although Dutch forts and trading posts in the East Indies dated back to the seventeenth century, in 1816 the Dutch ruled little more than the island of Java. Thereafter they gradually brought almost all of the 3,000-mile-long archipelago under their political authority. In extending their rule, the Dutch, like the British in India, brought diverse peoples with different languages and distinct cultural traditions into a single political entity (see Map 26.1). Thus they inadvertently created the foundations of modern-day Indonesia—the world's fourth-most-populous nation.

Taking over the Dutch East India Company in 1799, the Dutch government modified the company's loose control of Java and gradually built a modern bureaucratic state. Javanese resistance to Dutch rule led to the bloody Java War (1825–1830). In 1830, after the war, the Dutch abolished the combination of tribute from rulers and forced labor from peasants that they had used to obtain spices, and they established instead a particularly exploitive policy called the Culture System. Under this system, Indonesian peasants were forced to plant a fifth of their land in export crops, especially coffee and sugar, to turn over to the Dutch as tax. The Culture System proved highly profitable for the Dutch and brought Dutch shipping and intercontinental commerce back to life.

At the end of the nineteenth century the Dutch began to encourage Western education in the East Indies. The children of local rulers and privileged elites, much like their counterparts in India, encountered new ideas in Dutch-language schools. They began to question the long-standing cooperation of local elites with Dutch colonialism, and they searched for a new national identity. Thus anticolonial nationalism began to take shape in the East Indies in the early twentieth century, and it would blossom after World War I.

Mainland Southeast Asia

Unlike India and Java, mainland Southeast Asia had escaped European rule during the eighteenth century. In 1802 the Nguyen Dynasty came to power in Vietnam, putting an end to thirty years of peasant rebellion and civil war. For the first time in the country's history, a single Vietnamese monarchy ruled the entire country. Working through a centralizing scholar bureaucracy fashioned on the Chinese model, the Nguyen

Territories held by Western powers

- Great Britain
- France
- Netherlands
- United States
- Russian empire
- Japan and its territories
- Independent states
- 1842 — Date of colonization or occupation
- ┼┼┼┼ Major railroad

1,000 miles
1,000 kilometers
500
500
0
0

◀ **MAP 26.1** **Asia in 1914** India remained under British rule, while China precariously preserved its political independence. The Dutch Empire in modern-day Indonesia was old, but French control of Indochina was a product of the new imperialism.

(gwihn) Dynasty energetically built irrigation canals, roads and bridges, and impressive palaces in Hue (hway), the new capital city. Construction placed a heavy burden on the peasants drafted to do the work, and this hardship contributed to a resurgence of peasant unrest.

Roman Catholic missionaries from France posed a second, more dangerous threat to Vietnam's Confucian ruling elite. The king and his advisers believed that Christianity would undermine Confucian moral values and the unity of the Vietnamese state. In 1825 King Minh Mang (r. 1820–1841) outlawed the teaching of Christianity, and soon his government began executing Catholic missionaries and Vietnamese converts. As many as thirty thousand Vietnamese Christians were executed in the 1850s. In response, in 1859–1860 a French naval force seized Saigon and three surrounding provinces in southern Vietnam, making that part of Vietnam a French colony. In 1884–1885 France launched a second war against Vietnam and conquered the rest of the country. Laos and Cambodia were added to form French Indochina in 1887. In all three countries the local rulers were left on their thrones, but France dominated and tried to promote French culture.

After the French conquest, Vietnamese patriots continued to resist the colonial occupiers. After Japan's victory over Russia in 1905 (see page 814), a new generation of nationalists saw Japan as a model for Vietnamese revitalization and freedom. They went to Japan to study and planned for anticolonial revolution in Vietnam.

In all of Southeast Asia, only Siam succeeded in preserving its independence. Siam was sandwiched between the British in Burma and the French in Indochina. Siam's very able King Chulalongkorn (r. 1868–1910) took advantage of this situation to balance the two competitors against each other and to escape the smothering embrace of both. Chulalongkorn had studied Greek and Latin and Western science and kept up with Western news by reading British newspapers from Hong Kong and Singapore. He outlawed slavery and implemented modernizing reforms that centralized the government so that it could more effectively control outlying provinces coveted by the imperialists. Independent Siam gradually developed a modern centralizing state similar to those constructed by Western imperialists in their Asian possessions.

The Philippines

The United States became one of the imperialist powers in Asia when it took the Philippines from Spain in 1898. When the Spanish established rule in the Philippines in the sixteenth century, the islands had no central government or literate culture; order was maintained by village units dominated by local chiefs. Under the Spanish, Roman Catholic churches were established, and Spanish priests able to speak the local languages became the most common intermediaries between local populations, who rarely could speak Spanish, and the new rulers. The government of Spain encouraged Spaniards to colonize the Philippines through the encomienda system (see page 476):

INDIVIDUALS IN SOCIETY • José Rizal

In the mid-seventeenth century a Chinese merchant immigrated to the Philippines and married a woman who was half Chinese, half Filipino. Because of anti-Chinese animosity, he changed his name to Mercado, Spanish for "merchant."

Mercado's direct patrilineal descendant, José Rizal (1861–1896), was born into a well-to-do family that leased a plantation from Dominican friars. Both of his parents were educated, and he was a brilliant student himself. In 1882, after completing his studies at the Jesuit-run college in Manila, he went to Madrid to study medicine. During his ten years in Europe he not only earned a medical degree in Spain and a Ph.D. in Germany but he also found time to learn several European languages and make friends with scientists, writers, and political radicals.

While in Europe, Rizal became involved with Filipino revolutionaries and contributed numerous articles to their newspaper, La Solidaridad, published in Barcelona. Rizal advocated making the Philippines a province of Spain, giving it representation in the Spanish parliament, replacing Spanish friars with Filipino priests, and making Filipinos and Spaniards equal before the law. He spent a year at the British Museum doing research on the early phase of the Spanish colonization of the Philippines. He also wrote two novels.

The first novel, written in Spanish, was fired by the passions of nationalism. In satirical fashion, it depicts a young Filipino of mixed blood who studies for several years in Europe before returning to the Philippines to start a modern secular school in his hometown and to marry his childhood sweetheart. The church stands in the way of his efforts, and the colonial administration proves incompetent. The novel ends with the hero being gunned down after the friars falsely implicate him in a revolutionary conspiracy. Rizal's own life ended up following this narrative surprisingly closely.

In 1892 Rizal left Europe, stopped briefly in Hong Kong, and then returned to Manila to help his family with a lawsuit. Though he secured his relatives' release from jail, he ran into trouble himself. Because his writings were critical of the power of the church, he made many enemies, some of whom had him arrested.

Spaniards who had served the Crown were rewarded with grants giving them the exclusive right to control public affairs and collect taxes in a specific locality of the Philippines. A local Filipino elite also developed, aided by the Spanish introduction of private ownership of land. Given the great distance between Madrid and Manila, the capital of the Philippines, the local governor general, appointed by Spain, had almost unlimited powers over the courts and the military. Manila developed into an important entrepôt in the galleon trade between Mexico and China, and this trade also attracted a large Chinese community, which handled much of the trade within the Philippines.

Spain did not do much to promote education in the Philippines. In the late nineteenth century, however, wealthy Filipinos began to send their sons to study abroad, and a movement to press Spain for reforms emerged among those who had been abroad.

He was sent into exile to a Jesuit mission town on the relatively primitive island of Mindanao. There he founded a school and a hospital, and the Jesuits tried to win him back to the church. He kept busy during his four years in exile, not only teaching English, science, and self-defense, but also maintaining his correspondence with scientists in Europe. When a nationalist secret society rose in revolt in 1896, Rizal, in an effort to distance himself, volunteered to go to Cuba to help in an outbreak of yellow fever. Although he had no connections with the secret society and was on his way across the ocean, Rizal was arrested and shipped back to Manila.

Tried for sedition by the military, Rizal was found guilty. When handed his death certificate, Rizal struck out the words "Chinese half-breed" and wrote "pure native." He was publicly executed by a firing squad in Manila at age thirty-five, making him a martyr of the nationalist cause.

QUESTIONS FOR ANALYSIS

1. How did Rizal's comfortable family background contribute to his becoming a revolutionary?

2. How would Rizal's European contemporaries have reacted to his opposition to the Catholic Church?

LaunchPad
ONLINE DOCUMENT PROJECT

How did Filipinos and Americans respond to Spanish and American imperialism? Examine documents about the Philippines during the Spanish-American War, and then complete a quiz and writing assignment based on the evidence and details from this chapter.

See inside the front cover to learn more.

When the Spanish cracked down on critics, a rebellion erupted in 1896. (See "Individuals in Society: José Rizal," above.)

In 1898 war between Spain and the United States broke out in Cuba (see page 853), and in May the American naval officer Commodore George Dewey sailed into Manila Bay and sank the Spanish fleet anchored there. Dewey called on the Filipino rebels to help defeat the Spanish forces, but when the rebels declared independence, the U.S. government refused to recognize them, despite protests by American anti-imperialists. U.S. forces fought the Filipino rebels, and by the end of the insurrection in 1902 the war had cost the lives of five thousand Americans and about two hundred thousand Filipinos. In the following years the United States introduced a form of colonial rule that included public works and economic development projects, improved education and medicine, and, in 1907, an elected legislative assembly.

China Under Pressure

Was China's decline in the nineteenth century due more to internal problems or to Western imperialism?

In 1800 most Chinese had no reason to question the concept of China as the central kingdom. No other country had so many people; Chinese products were in great demand in foreign countries; and the borders had recently been expanded. A century later China's world standing had sunk precipitously. In 1900 foreign troops marched into China's capital to protect foreign nationals, and more and more Chinese had come to think that their government, society, and cultural values needed to be radically changed.

The Opium War

Seeing little to gain from trade with European countries, the Qing (Manchu) emperors, who had been ruling China since 1644 (see page 630), permitted Europeans to trade only at the port of Guangzhou (Canton) and only through licensed Chinese merchants. Initially, the balance of trade was in China's favor. Great Britain and the other Western nations used silver to pay for tea, since they had not been able to find anything the Chinese wanted to buy. By the 1820s, however, the British had found something the Chinese would buy: opium. Grown legally in British-occupied India, opium was smuggled into China, where its use and sale were illegal. Huge profits and the cravings of addicts led to rapid increases in sales, from 4,500 chests a year in 1810 to 10,000 in 1830 and 40,000 in 1838. At this point it was China that suffered a drain of silver, since it was importing more than it was exporting.

To deal with this crisis, the Chinese government dispatched Lin Zexu to Guangzhou in 1839. He dealt harshly with Chinese who purchased opium and seized the opium stores of British merchants. Lin even wrote to Queen Victoria: "Suppose there were people from another country who carried opium for sale to England and seduced your people into buying and smoking it; certainly your honorable ruler would deeply hate it and be bitterly aroused."[2] When Lin pressured the Portuguese to expel the uncooperative British from their trading post at Macao, the British settled on the barren island of Hong Kong.

Although for years the little community of foreign merchants had accepted Chinese rules, by 1839 the British, the dominant group, were ready to flex their muscles. British merchants wanted to create a market for their goods in China and get tea more cheaply by trading closer to its source in central China. They also wanted a European-style diplomatic relationship with China, with envoys and ambassadors, commercial treaties, and published tariffs. With the encouragement of their merchants in China, the British sent an expeditionary force from India with forty-two warships, many of them leased from the major opium trader, Jardine, Matheson, and Company.

With its control of the seas, the British easily shut down key Chinese ports and forced the Chinese to negotiate. Dissatisfied with the resulting agreement, the British sent a second, larger force, which took even more coastal cities, including Shanghai. This **Opium War** was settled at gunpoint in 1842. The resulting treaties opened five ports to international trade, fixed the tariff on imported goods at 5 percent, imposed an indemnity of 21 million ounces of silver on China to cover Britain's war expenses, and ceded the island of Hong Kong to Britain. Through the clause on **extraterritoriality**, British subjects in China became answerable only to British law, even in disputes with Chinese. The treaties also had a "most-favored nation" clause, which meant that whenever one nation extracted a new privilege from China, it was extended automatically to Britain.

The treaties satisfied neither side. China continued to refuse to accept foreign diplomats at its capital in Beijing, and the expansion of trade fell far short of Western expectations. Between 1856 and 1860 Britain and France renewed hostilities with China. Seventeen thousand British and French troops occupied Beijing and set the emperor's summer palace on fire. Another round of harsh treaties gave European merchants and missionaries greater privileges and forced the Chinese to open several more cities to foreign trade. Large areas in some of the treaty ports were leased in perpetuity to foreign powers.

Internal Problems

China's problems in the nineteenth century were not all of foreign origin. By 1850 China, for centuries the world's most populous country, had more than 400 million people. As the population grew, farm size shrank, forests were put to the plow, and surplus labor suppressed wages. When the best parcels of land were all occupied, conflicts over rights to water and tenancy increased. Hard times also led to increased female infanticide, as families felt that they could not afford to raise more than two or three children and saw sons as necessities. A shortage of marriageable women resulted, reducing the incentive for young men to stay near home and do as their elders told them. Some became bandits, others boatmen, carters, sedan-chair carriers, and, by the end of the century, rickshaw pullers.

These economic and demographic circumstances led to some of the most destructive rebellions in China's history. The worst was the **Taiping Rebellion** (1851–1864), in which some 20 million people lost their lives, making it one of the bloodiest wars in world history.

The Taiping (TIGH-ping) Rebellion was initiated by Hong Xiuquan (hong show-chwan) (1814–1864), a man from south China who had studied for the civil service examinations but never passed. His career as a religious leader began with visions of an old golden-bearded man and a middle-aged man who addressed him as younger brother and told him to annihilate devils. After reading a Christian tract given to him by a missionary, Hong interpreted his visions to mean he was Jesus's younger brother. He soon gathered followers, whom he instructed to destroy idols and ancestral temples, give up opium and alcohol, and renounce foot binding and prostitution. In 1851 he declared himself king of the Heavenly Kingdom of Great Peace (Taiping), an act of open insurrection.

By 1853 the Taiping rebels, as Hong's followers were known, had moved north and established their capital at the major city of Nanjing, which they held on to for a decade. From this base they set about creating a utopian society based on the equalization of landholdings and the equality of men and women. Christian missionaries quickly concluded that the Christian elements in Taiping doctrines were heretical, and they did not help the rebels. To suppress the Taipings, the Manchus had to turn to Chinese scholar-officials, who raised armies on their own, revealing that the Manchus were no longer the mighty warriors they had been when they had conquered China two centuries earlier.

The Self-Strengthening Movement

After the various rebellions were suppressed, forward-looking reformers began addressing the Western threat. Under the slogan "self-strengthening," they set about modernizing the military along Western lines, establishing arsenals and dockyards. Recognizing that guns and ships were merely the surface manifestations of the Western powers' economic strength, some of the most progressive reformers also initiated new industries, which in the 1870s and 1880s included railway lines, steam navigation companies, coal mines, telegraph lines, and cotton spinning and weaving factories. These were the same sorts of initiatives that the British were introducing in India, but China lagged behind, especially in railroads.

These measures drew resistance from conservatives, who thought copying Western practices was compounding defeat. A highly placed Manchu official objected that "from ancient down to modern times" there had never been "anyone who could use mathematics to raise a nation from a state of decline or to strengthen it in times of weakness."[3] Yet knowledge of the West gradually improved with more translations and travel in both directions. Newspapers covering world affairs began publication in Shanghai and Hong Kong. By 1880 China had embassies in London, Paris, Berlin, Madrid, Washington, Tokyo, and St. Petersburg.

Despite the enormous effort put into trying to catch up, China was humiliated yet again at the end of the nineteenth century. First came the discovery that Japan had so successfully modernized that it posed a threat to China. Then in 1894 Japanese efforts to separate Korea from Chinese influence led to the brief Sino-Japanese War in which China was decisively defeated even though much of its navy had been purchased abroad at great expense. In the peace negotiations, China ceded Taiwan to Japan, agreed to a huge indemnity (compensation for war expenses), and gave Japan the right to open factories in China. China's helplessness in the face of aggression led to a scramble among the European powers for concessions and protectorates in China. At the high point of this rush in 1898, it appeared that the European powers might actually divide China among themselves, the way they had recently divided Africa.

Republican Revolution

China's humiliating defeat in the Sino-Japanese War in 1895 led to a renewed drive for reform. In 1898 a group of educated young reformers gained access to the twenty-seven-year-old Qing emperor. They warned him of the fate of Poland (divided by the European powers in the eighteenth century; see pages 574–576) and regaled him with the triumphs of the Meiji reformers in Japan. They proposed redesigning China as a constitutional monarchy with modern financial and educational systems. For three months the emperor issued a series of reform decrees. But the Manchu establishment and the empress dowager, who had dominated the court for the last quarter century, felt threatened and not only suppressed the reform movement but imprisoned the emperor as well. Hope for reform from the top was dashed.

Hong Kong Tailors　In 1872 the newspaper *Shenbao* was founded in Shanghai, and in 1884 it added an eight-page weekly pictorial supplement. Influenced by the pictorial press then popular in Europe, it depicted both news and human interest stories, both Chinese and foreign. This scene shows a tailor shop in Hong Kong where Chinese tailors use sewing machines and make women's clothes in current Western styles. To Chinese readers, men making women's clothes and placing them on bamboo forms would have seemed as peculiar as the style of the dresses. (From *Dianshizhai huabao*, a Shanghai picture magazine, 1885 or later/Visual Connection Archive)

A period of violent reaction swept the country, reaching its peak in 1900 with the uprising of a secret society that foreigners dubbed the **Boxers**. The Boxers blamed China's ills on foreigners, especially the missionaries who traveled throughout China telling the Chinese that their beliefs were wrong and their customs backward. After the Boxers laid siege to the foreign legation quarter in Beijing, a dozen nations including Japan sent twenty thousand troops to lift the siege. In the negotiations that followed, China had to accept a long list of penalties, including cancellation of the civil service examinations for five years (punishment for gentry collaboration) and a staggering indemnity of 450 million ounces of silver, almost twice the government's annual revenues.

After this defeat, gradual reform lost its appeal. More and more Chinese were studying abroad and learning about Western political ideas, including democracy and revolution. The most famous was Sun Yatsen (1866–1925). Sent by his peasant family to Hawaii, he learned English and then continued his education in Hong Kong. From 1894 on, he spent his time abroad organizing revolutionary societies and seeking financial support from overseas Chinese. He joined forces with Chinese student revolutionaries studying in Japan, and together they sparked the **1911 Revolution**, which brought China's long history of monarchy to an end in 1912, to be replaced by a republic modeled on Western political ideas. China had escaped direct foreign rule but would never be the same.

Japan's Rapid Transformation

How was Japan able to quickly master the challenges posed by the West?

During the nineteenth century, while China's standing in the world plummeted, Japan's was rising. European traders and missionaries first arrived in Japan in the sixteenth century, but in the early seventeenth century, in part because of the remarkable success of Catholic missionaries (see page 639), the Japanese government expelled them. During the eighteenth century Japan much more effectively than China kept foreign merchants and missionaries at bay. It limited trade to a single port (Nagasaki), where only the Dutch were allowed, and forbade Japanese to travel abroad. Because Japan's land and population were so much smaller than China's, the Western powers never expected much from Japan as a trading partner and did not press it as urgently. Still, the European threat was part of what propelled Japan to modernize.

The "Opening" of Japan

Wanting to play a greater role in the Pacific, the United States decided to force the Japanese to share their ports and behave as a "civilized" nation. In 1853 Commodore Matthew Perry steamed into Edo (now Tokyo) Bay and demanded diplomatic negotiations with the emperor. Some Japanese samurai (members of the warrior class) urged resistance, but senior officials knew what had happened in China and how defenseless their cities would be against naval bombardment. Under threat of **gunboat diplomacy**, and after consulting with the daimyo (major lords), the officials signed a treaty with the United States that opened two ports and permitted trade.

Japan at this time was a complex society. The emperor in Kyoto had no effective powers. For more than two hundred years real power had been in the hands of the Tokugawa shogun in Edo (see pages 637–639). The country was divided into numerous domains, each under a daimyo. Each daimyo had under him samurai, who had hereditary stipends and privileges, such as the right to wear a sword. Peasants and merchants were also legally distinct classes, and in theory social mobility from peasant to merchant or merchant to samurai was impossible. After two centuries of peace, there were many more samurai than were needed to administer or defend the country, and many lived very modestly. They were proud, however, and felt humiliated by the sudden American intrusion and the unequal treaties that the Western countries imposed. Some began agitating against the shogunate under the slogan "Revere the emperor and expel the barbarians."

When foreign diplomats and merchants began to settle in Yokohama after 1858, radical samurai reacted with a wave of antiforeign terrorism and antigovernment assassinations. The Western response was swift and unambiguous. Much as the Western powers had sent troops to Beijing a few years before, they now sent an allied fleet of American, British, Dutch, and French warships to demolish key Japanese forts, further weakening the power and prestige of the shogun's government.

The Meiji Restoration

In 1867 a coalition of reform-minded daimyo led a coup that ousted the Tokugawa Shogunate. The samurai who led this coup declared a return to direct rule by the emperor, which had not been practiced in Japan for more than six hundred years. This emperor was called the Meiji (MAY-jee) emperor and this event the **Meiji Restoration**, a great turning point in Japanese history.

The domain leaders who organized the coup, called the Meiji Oligarchs, moved the boy emperor to Tokyo castle (previously the seat of the shogun, now the imperial palace). They used the young sovereign to win over both the lords and the commoners. During the emperor's first decade on the throne, the leaders carried him around in hundreds of grand imperial processions so that he could see his subjects and they him. The emerging press also worked to keep its readers informed of the young emperor's actions and their obligations to him. Real power remained in the hands of the oligarchs.

The battle cry of the Meiji reformers had been "strong army, rich nation." How were these goals to be accomplished? In an about-face that is one of history's most remarkable chapters, the determined but flexible leaders of Meiji Japan dropped their antiforeign attacks. Convinced that they could not beat the West until they had mastered the secrets of its military and industrial might, they initiated a series of measures to reform Japan along modern Western lines. One reformer even proposed that "Japan must be reborn with America its mother and France its father."[4] In 1868 an imperial declaration promised that "deliberative assemblies shall be widely established and all matters decided by public discussion" and that "knowledge shall be sought throughout the world so as to strengthen the foundations of imperial rule."[5] Within four years a delegation was traveling the world to learn what made the Western powers strong. Its members examined everything from the U.S. Constitution to the factories, shipyards, and railroads that made the European landscape so different from Japan's.

Japan under the shoguns had been decentralized, with most of the power over the population in the hands of the many daimyo. By elevating the emperor, the oligarchs were able to centralize the government. In 1871 they abolished the domains and merged the domain armies. Following the example of the French Revolution, they dismantled the four-class legal system and declared everyone equal. This amounted to stripping the samurai (7 to 8 percent of the population) of their privileges. First the samurai's stipends were reduced; then in 1876 the stipends were replaced by one-time grants of income-bearing bonds. Most samurai had to find work or start businesses, as the value of the bonds declined with inflation. Furthermore, samurai no longer were to wear their swords, long the symbols of their status. Even their monopoly on the use of force was eliminated: the new army recruited commoners along with samurai. Not surprisingly, some samurai rose up against their loss of privileges. In one extreme case, the rebels refused to use guns in a futile effort to retain the mystique of the sword. None of these uncoordinated uprisings made any difference.

Several leaders of the Meiji Restoration, in France on a fact-finding mission during the Franco-Prussian War of 1870–1871, were impressed by the active participation of French citizens in the defense of Paris. This contrasted with the indifference of most Japanese peasants during the battles that led to the Meiji Restoration. For Japan to survive in the hostile international environment, they concluded, ordinary people had to be trained to fight. Consequently, a conscription law, modeled on the French law, was issued in 1872. Like French law, it exempted first sons. To improve the training of soldiers, the new War College was organized along German lines, and German instructors were recruited to teach there. Young samurai were trained to form the new professional officer corps. The success of this approach was demonstrated first in 1877, when the professionally led army of draftees crushed a major rebellion by samurai.

Many of the new institutions established in the Meiji period reached down to the local level. Schools open to all were rapidly introduced beginning in 1872. Teachers were trained in newly established teachers' colleges, where they learned to inculcate discipline, patriotism, and morality. Another modern institution that reached the local level was a national police force. In 1884 police training schools were established in every prefecture, and within a few years one- or two-man police stations were set up throughout the country. These policemen came to act as local agents of the central government. They not only dealt with crime but also enforced public health rules, conscription laws, and codes of behavior.

In time these new laws and institutions brought benefits, but at the local level they were often perceived as oppressive. Protests became very common against everything from conscription and the Western calendar to the new taxes to pay for the new schools.

In 1889 Japan became the first non-Western country to adopt the constitutional form of government. Prefectural assemblies, set up in the 1870s and 1880s, gave local elites some experience in debating political issues. The constitution, however, was handed down from above, drafted by the top political leaders and issued in the name of the emperor. A commission sent abroad to study European constitutional governments had come to the conclusion that the German constitutional monarchy would provide the best model for Japan, rather than the more democratic governments of the British, French, and Americans. Japan's new government had a two-house parliament, called the Diet. The upper house of lords was drawn largely from former daimyo and nobles, and the lower house was elected by a limited electorate (about 5 percent of the adult male population in 1890). Although Japan now had a government based on laws, it was authoritarian rather than democratic. The emperor was declared "sacred and inviolable." He had the right to appoint the prime minister and cabinet. He did not have to ask the Diet for funds because wealth assigned to the imperial house was entrusted to the Imperial Household Ministry, which was outside the government's control.

Cultural change during the Meiji period was as profound as political change. For more than a thousand years China had been the major source of ideas and technologies introduced into Japan, ranging from the writing system to Confucianism and Buddhism, tea and silk, and chopsticks and soy sauce. But in the late nineteenth century China, beset by Western pressure, had become an object lesson on the dangers of stagnation rather than a model to follow. The influential author Fukuzawa Yukichi began urging Japan to pursue "civilization and enlightenment," by which he meant Western civilization. Fukuzawa advocated learning Western languages and encouraged Japan to learn from the West in order to catch up with it. Soon Japanese were being told to conform to Western taste, eat meat, wear Western-style clothes, and drop customs that Westerners found odd, such as married women blackening their teeth.

Industrialization

The leaders of the Meiji Restoration, wanting to strengthen Japan's military capacity, promoted industrialization. The government paid large salaries to attract foreign experts to help with industrialization, and Japanese were encouraged to go abroad to study science and engineering.

Japan's First Skyscraper Meiji Japan's fascination with things Western led to the construction of Western-style buildings. Japan's first elevator made possible this twelve-story tower built in Tokyo in 1890. Situated in the entertainment district, it was filled with shops, theaters, bars, and restaurants. ("Pavilion Above the Clouds," Sugoroku 1890, Utagawa Kunimasa IV [1848–1920]/Mead Art Museum, Amherst College, MA, USA/The Bridgeman Art Library)

The government played an active role in getting railroads, mines, and factories started. Japan's coal mines had produced only 390,000 tons in 1860, but by 1900 this output had risen to 5 million tons. Early on, the Japanese government decided to compete with China in the export of tea and silk to the West. Introducing the mechanical reeling of silk gave Japan a strong price advantage in the sale of silk, and Japan's total foreign trade increased tenfold from 1877 to 1900. The next stage was to develop heavy industry. The huge indemnity exacted from China in 1895 was used to establish the Yawata Iron and Steel Works. The third stage of Japan's industrialization would today be called import substitution. Factories such as cotton mills were set up to help cut the importation of Western consumer goods. By 1912 factory output accounted for 13 percent of the national product, even though only 3 percent of the labor force worked in factories, mostly small ones with fewer than fifty workers.

Most of the great Japanese industrial conglomerates known as *zaibatsu* (zigh-BAHT-dzoo), such as Mitsubishi, got their start in this period, often founded by men with government connections. Sometimes the government set up plants that it then sold to private investors at bargain prices. Successful entrepreneurs were treated as patriotic heroes.

As in Europe, the early stages of industrialization brought hardship to the countryside. Farmers often rioted as their incomes failed to keep up with prices or as their tax burdens grew. Workers in modern industries were no happier, and in 1898 railroad workers went on strike for better working conditions and overtime pay. Still, rice production increased, death rates dropped as public health was improved, and the population grew from about 33 million in 1868 to about 45 million in 1900.

Japan as an Imperial Power

During the course of the Meiji period, Japan became an imperial power, making Taiwan and Korea into its colonies. Taiwan had been a part of China for two centuries; Korea had been an independent country with a unified government since 668. The conflicts that led to Japanese acquisition of both of them revolved around Korea.

The Chosŏn Dynasty had been on the throne in Korea since 1392. Chinese influence had grown over this period as the Korean elite enthusiastically embraced Confucian teachings and studied for Chinese-style civil service examinations. In the second half of the nineteenth century Korea found itself caught between China, Japan, and Russia, each trying to protect or extend its sphere of influence. Westerners also began demanding that Korea be "opened." Korea's first response was to insist that its foreign relations be handled through Beijing. Matters were complicated by the rise in the 1860s of a religious cult, the Tonghak movement, that had strong xenophobic elements. Although the government executed the cult founder in 1864, this cult continued to gain support, especially among impoverished peasants. Thus, like China in the same period, the Korean government faced simultaneous internal and external threats.

In 1871 the U.S. minister to China took five warships to try to open Korea, but left after exchanges of fire resulted in 250 Koreans dead without any progress in getting the Korean government to make concessions. Japan tried next and in 1876 forced the Korean government to sign an unequal treaty and open three ports to Japanese trade. On China's urging, Korea also signed treaties with the European powers in an effort to counterbalance Japan.

Over the next couple of decades reformers in China and Japan tried to encourage Korea to adopt its own self-strengthening movement, but Korean conservatives, including the queen (serving as regent for the child-king), did their best to undo reform efforts. In 1894, when the religious cult rose in a massive revolt, both China and Japan sent military forces, claiming to come to the Korean government's aid. They ended up fighting each other instead in what is known as the Sino-Japanese War (see page 808). With Japan's decisive victory, it gained Taiwan from China and was able to make Korea a protectorate. Japan also arranged the assassination of the Korean queen in 1895.

As already noted, five years later Japan participated with the European powers in occupying Beijing to suppress the Boxer Rebellion. In this period Japan was competing aggressively with the leading European powers for influence and territory in China, particularly in the northeast (Manchuria). There Japanese and Russian imperialism met and collided. In 1904 Japan attacked Russian forces and, after its 1905 victory in the bloody **Russo-Japanese War**, emerged with a valuable foothold in China—Russia's former protectorate over Port Arthur (see Map 26.1).

Japan also steadily gained more control over Korea. In 1907, when the Korean king proved less than fully compliant, the Japanese forced him to abdicate in favor of his feebleminded son. Korean resistance to Japan's actions was suppressed in bloody fighting, and in 1910 Korea was formally annexed as a province of Japan.

Japan's victories over China and Russia changed the way European nations looked at Japan. Through negotiations Japan was able to eliminate extraterritoriality in 1899 and gain control of its own tariffs in 1911. Within Japan, the success of the military in raising Japan's international reputation added greatly to its political influence.

The Pacific Region and the Movement of People

What were the causes and consequences of the vast movement of people in the Pacific region?

The nineteenth century was marked by extensive movement of people into, across, and out of Asia and the broad Pacific region. Many of these migrants moved from one Asian country to another, but there was also a growing presence of Europeans in Asia, a consequence of the increasing integration of the world economy (see pages 790–792). Families were more likely to join colonial officers in Asia as travel and foreign residences grew more comfortable. Europeans had died at a high rate in tropical zones because of diseases they were not immune to; in the nineteenth century the survival rate improved as doctors found new treatments. (Native peoples who had not yet had extensive contact with outsiders continued to die in large numbers from Eurasian diseases.)

By the end of the century hundreds of thousands of British soldiers and civil servants lived in British colonies from India to Hong Kong and Malaya. In countries not under colonial rule missionaries and traders were the most prominent long-term foreign residents. Missionaries opened schools and hospitals and were active in spreading Western learning. In China by 1905 about 300 fully qualified physicians were doing medical missionary work, and 250 mission hospitals and dispensaries served about 2 million patients. Missionary hospitals in Hong Kong ran a medical school, which trained hundreds of Chinese as physicians.

Settler Colonies in the Pacific: Australia and New Zealand

The largest share of the Europeans who moved to the Pacific region in the nineteenth century went to the settler colonies in Australia and New Zealand. In 1770 the English explorer James Cook mapped the coast of New Zealand and then went on to Australia, which he declared suitable for settlement. Eight years later Cook was the first European to visit Hawaii. All three of these places in time became destinations for migrants.

As discussed in Chapter 12, between 200 and 1300 C.E., Polynesians settled numerous islands of the Pacific, from New Zealand in the south to Hawaii in the north and Easter Island in the east. Thus most of the lands that explorers like Cook encountered were occupied by societies with chiefs, crop agriculture, domestic animals such as chickens and pigs, excellent sailing technology, and often considerable experience in warfare. Australia had been settled millennia earlier by a different population. When Cook arrived in Australia, it was occupied by about three hundred thousand Aborigines who lived entirely by food gathering, fishing, and hunting. Like the Indians of Central and South America, the people in all these lands fell victim to Eurasian diseases and died in large numbers. By 1900 there were only ninety thousand Aborigines in Australia.

Australia was first developed by Britain as a penal colony. In May 1787 a British fleet of eleven ships packed with one thousand felons and their jailers began an eight-month voyage to Australia. Up until the penal colony system was abolished in 1869, a total of 161,000 convicts were transported to Australia. Convicts became free when their sentences expired or were remitted. Few returned to England.

Governor Phillip and his successors urged the Colonial Office to send free settlers to Australia, not just prisoners. After the end of the Napoleonic Wars in 1815, a steady stream of people relocated. Raising sheep proved suitable to Australia's climate, and wool exports steadily increased, from 75,400 pounds in 1821, to 2 million pounds in 1830, to 24 million pounds in 1845. To encourage migration, the government offered free passage and free land to immigrants. By 1850 Australia had five hundred thousand inhabitants. The discovery of gold in Victoria in 1851 quadrupled that number in a few years. Although the government charged prospectors a very high license fee, men and women from all parts of the globe flocked to Australia to share in the fabulous wealth. The gold rush also provided the financial means for cultural development. Public libraries, museums, art galleries, and universities opened in the thirty years after 1851. These institutions dispensed a distinctly British culture, though a remote and provincial version.

Not everyone in Australia was of British origin, however. In Victoria in 1857 one adult male in seven was Chinese. "Colored peoples" (as all nonwhites were called in Australia) adapted more easily than the British to the warm climate and worked for lower wages. Thus they proved essential to the country's economic development in the nineteenth century. Chinese and Japanese built the railroads and ran the shops in the towns and the market gardens nearby. Filipinos and Pacific Islanders did the hard work in the sugarcane fields. Afghans and their camels controlled the carrying trade in some areas. But fear that colored labor would lower living standards and undermine Australia's distinctly British culture led to efforts to keep Australia white.

Australia gained independence in stages. In 1850 the British Parliament passed the Australian Colonies Government Act, which allowed the four most populous colonies—New South Wales, Tasmania, Victoria, and South Australia—to establish colonial legislatures, determine the franchise, and frame their own constitutions. In 1902 Australia became one of the first countries in the world to give women the vote. By then Australia had about 3.75 million people.

Maori Chief, 1885
This photograph depicts Chief Wahanui of the Ngati Maniapoto tribe with his family and friends. The chief had fought in the Maori wars against the British in 1864–1865. Twenty years later, he and his family had adopted many elements of Western material culture.
(The Great Ngatimaniopoto Chief Wahanui with family and friends at his house in Alexandria, 7 June 1885 [albumen print], Alfred Burton [1834–1914]/Private Collection/ © Michael Graham-Stewart/ The Bridgeman Art Library)

By 1900 New Zealand's population had reached 750,000, only a fifth of Australia's. One major reason more people had not settled these fertile islands was the resistance of the native Maori people. They quickly mastered the use of muskets and tried for decades to keep the British from taking their lands.

Foreign settlement in Hawaii began gradually. Initially, whalers stopped there for supplies, as they did at other Pacific Islands. The diseases they introduced took a heavy toll on the population, measles alone killing a fifth of the population in the 1850s. Missionaries and businessmen came next, and soon other settlers followed, both whites and Asians. A plantation economy developed centered on sugarcane. In the 1890s leading settler families overthrew the native monarchy, set up a republic, and urged the United States to annex Hawaii, which it did in 1898.

Asian Emigration

Like Europeans, Asians left their native countries in unprecedented numbers in the nineteenth century (Map 26.2). As in Europe, both push and pull factors prompted people to leave home. Between 1750 and 1900 world population grew rapidly, in many places tripling. China and India were extremely densely populated countries— China with more than 400 million people in the mid-nineteenth century, India with more than 200 million. Not surprisingly, these two giants were the leading exporters of people in search of work or land. On the pull side were the new opportunities created by the flow of development capital into previously underdeveloped areas. In many of the European colonies in Asia the business class came to consist of both Asian and European migrants, the Asians protected and tolerated by the Western imperialists who found them useful. Asian diasporas formed in many parts of the world, with the majority in Asia itself, especially Southeast Asia.

For centuries Chinese from the southern coastal provinces ventured out, and by the nineteenth century they formed key components of mercantile communities throughout Southeast Asia, from Siam south to Java and east to the Philippines. Chinese often assimilated in Siam and Vietnam, but they rarely did so in Muslim areas such as Java, Catholic areas such as the Philippines, and primitive tribal areas such as northern Borneo. In these places distinct Chinese communities emerged, usually dominated by speakers of a single Chinese dialect.

With the growth in trade that accompanied the European imperial expansion, Chinese began to settle in the islands of Southeast Asia in larger numbers. After Singapore was founded by the British in 1819, Chinese rapidly poured in, soon becoming the dominant ethnic group. In British-controlled Malaya, some Chinese built great fortunes in the tin business, while others worked in the mines. There the Chinese community included old overseas families, Malay-speakers who had long lived in the Portuguese city of Malacca, and a much larger number of more recent immigrants, most of whom spoke Cantonese or other southern dialects. Chinese also settled in the Spanish-controlled Philippines and in Dutch-controlled Indonesia, but there they suffered repeated persecutions. In Borneo early in the nineteenth century, the Dutch expropriated the mines that the Chinese had worked for generations. Elsewhere, however, the Dutch made use of the Chinese. In Java, for instance, Chinese merchants were used as tax collectors. Moreover, after the Dutch conquered southern Sumatra in 1864, Chinese were recruited to work in the sugar and tobacco plantations.

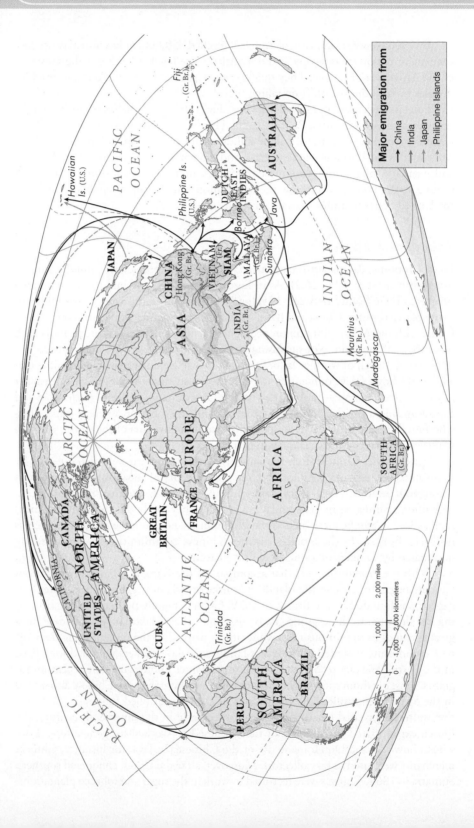

◀ **MAP 26.2** **Emigration Out of Asia, 1820–1914** As steamships made crossing oceans quicker and more reliable, many people in Asia left their home countries to find new opportunities elsewhere. European imperialism contributed to this flow, especially by recruiting workers for newly established plantations or mines. Many emigrants simply wanted to work a few years to build their savings and planned to return home. Often, however, they ended up staying in their new countries and forming families there.

By 1900 more than five hundred thousand Chinese were living in the Dutch East Indies.

Discovery of gold in California in 1848, Australia in 1851, and Canada in 1858 encouraged Chinese to book passage to those places. In California few arrived soon enough to strike gold, but they quickly found other work. Thousands laid railroad tracks, and others took up mining in Wyoming and Idaho. In 1880 more than a hundred thousand Chinese men and three thousand Chinese women were living in the western United States.

Indian entrepreneurs were similarly attracted by the burgeoning commerce of the growing British Empire. The bulk of Indian emigrants were **indentured laborers**, recruited under contract. The rise of indentured labor from Asia was a direct result of the outlawing of the African slave trade in the early nineteenth century by Britain and the United States. Sugar plantations in the Caribbean and elsewhere needed new sources of workers, and planters in the British colonies discovered that they could recruit Indian laborers to replace blacks. By 1870 more than half a million Indians had migrated to Mauritius (in the southern Indian Ocean, east of Madagascar) and to the British Caribbean, especially Trinidad. After the French abolished slavery in 1848, they recruited workers from India as well, with nearly eighty thousand Indians making the trip to the French Caribbean over the next half century. Later in the century many Indians emigrated to British colonies in Africa, the largest numbers to South Africa. Indentured Indian laborers built the railroad in East Africa. Malaya, Singapore, and Fiji also received many emigrants from India.

Indentured laborers secured as substitutes for slaves were often treated little better than slaves both on the ships that delivered them and on the plantations and in the mines where they worked. After abuses of this sort were exposed, the Indian colonial government established regulations stipulating a maximum indenture period of five years, after which the migrant would be entitled to passage home. Even though government "protectors" were appointed at the ports of embarkation, exploitation of indentured workers continued largely unchecked. Still, many of the migrants voluntarily stayed on after their indenture (others remained because they could not afford passage home).

In areas outside the British Empire, China offered the largest supply of ready labor. Starting in the 1840s contractors arrived at Chinese ports to recruit labor for plantations and mines in Cuba, Peru, Hawaii, Sumatra, South Africa, and elsewhere. In the 1840s, for example, the Spanish government actively recruited Chinese laborers for the plantations of Cuba. These workers were placed under eight-year contracts, were paid about twenty-five cents a day, and were fed potatoes and salted beef. Between 1853 and 1873 more than 130,000 Chinese laborers went to Cuba, the majority spending their lives as virtual slaves.

Canadian Immigration Certificate   This certificate proved that the eleven-year-old boy in the photograph had a legal right to be in Canada, as the $500 head tax required for immigration of Chinese had been paid. The head tax on Chinese immigrants introduced in 1885 started at $50, but it was raised to $100 in 1900 and to $500 in 1903. Equal to about what a laborer could earn in two years, the tax succeeded in its goal of slowing the rate of Asian immigration to Canada. (Head tax certificate for Jung Bak Hun, issued January 3, 1919/© Government of Canada. Reproduced with the permission of the Minister of Public Works and Government Services Canada [2013]/Library and Archives Canada/Canada. Department of Employment and Immigration fonds/RG76-D-2-g, Vol. 712, C.I.5 certificate #88103)

Chinese laborers did not have the British government to protect them and seem to have suffered even more than Indian workers. Some of the worst abuses were in Peru, where nearly a hundred thousand Chinese had arrived by 1875, lured by promoters who promised them easy riches. Instead they were set to laying railroad tracks or working on cotton plantations or in dangerous guano pits. Those who tried to flee were forced to work in chains.

India and China sent more people abroad than any other Asian countries during this period, but they were not alone. As Japan started to industrialize, its cities could not absorb all those forced off the farms, and people began emigrating in significant numbers, many to Hawaii and later to South America. Emigration from the Philippines also was substantial, especially after it became a U.S. territory in 1898.

Asian migration to the United States, Canada, and Australia—the primary destinations of European emigrants—would undoubtedly have been greater if it had not been so vigorously resisted by the white settlers in those regions. On the West Coast of the United States, friction between Chinese and white settlers was fed by racist rhetoric that depicted Chinese as opium-smoking heathens. In 1882 Chinese were barred from becoming American citizens, and the immigration of Chinese laborers was suspended. In 1888 President Grover Cleveland declared the Chinese "impossible of assimilation with our people, and dangerous to our peace and welfare."[6] Australia also put a stop to Asian immigration with the Commonwealth Immigration Restriction Act of 1901, which established the "white Australia policy" that remained on the books until the 1970s.

Most of the Asian migrants discussed so far were illiterate peasants or business people, not members of traditional educated elites. By the beginning of the twentieth century, however, another group of Asians was going abroad in significant numbers: students. Indians and others in the British colonies usually went to Britain, Vietnamese and others in the French colonies to France, and so on. Chinese eager to master modern learning most commonly went to Japan, but others went to Europe and the United States, as did Japanese students. Most of these students traveled abroad to learn about Western science, law, and government in the hope of strengthening their own countries. On their return they contributed enormously to the intellectual life of their societies, increasing understanding of the modern Western world and also becoming the most vocal advocates of overthrowing the old order and driving out the colonial masters.

Among the most notable of these foreign-educated radicals were Mohandas Gandhi (1869–1948) and Sun Yatsen (see page 914). Sun developed his ideas about the republican form of government while studying in Hawaii and Hong Kong. Gandhi, after studying law in Britain, took a job in South Africa, where he became involved in trying to defend the interests of the Indians who lived and worked there. He started a periodical, *Indian Opinion*, in which he gradually elaborated his idea of passive resistance. In 1909 he wrote:

> Passive resistance is a method of securing rights by personal suffering; it is the reverse of resistance by arms. When I refuse to do a thing that is repugnant to my conscience, I use soul-force. For instance, the Government of the day has passed a law which is applicable to me. I do not like it. If by using violence I force the Government to repeal the law, I am employing what may be termed body-force. If I do not obey the law and accept the penalty for its breach, I use soul-force. It involves sacrifice of self.[7]

The Countries of Asia in Comparative Perspective

What explains the similarities and differences in the experiences of Asian countries in this era?

The European concept of Asia encourages us to see commonalities among the countries from India east. Although to Westerners it may seem natural to think about Japan and Indonesia as part of the same region, the world looked very different from the perspective of the peoples of these countries. The concept of Asia is handy, but we should be careful not to let it keep us from recognizing the very real differences in the historical experiences of the countries we label "Asian."

At the start of the nineteenth century the societies in this region varied much more than those of any other part of the world. In the temperate zones of East Asia, the old established monarchies of China, Japan, and Korea were all densely populated and boasted long literary traditions and traditions of unified governments. They had ties to each other that dated back many centuries and shared many elements of their cultures. South of them, in the tropical and subtropical regions, cultures were more diverse. India was just as densely populated as China, Japan, and Korea, but politically and culturally less unified, with several major languages and dozens of independent rulers reigning in kingdoms large and small, not to mention the growing British presence. In both India and Southeast Asia, Islam was much more important than it was in East Asia, although there was a relatively small Muslim minority in China. All the countries with long written histories and literate elites were at a great remove from the thinly populated and relatively primitive areas without literate cultures and sometimes even without agriculture, such as Australia and some of the islands of the Philippines and Indonesia.

The nineteenth century gave the societies of Asia more in common in that all of them in one way or another had come into contact with the expanding West (an experience that linked them to societies across the Middle East, Africa, and Latin America as well). Still, the Western powers did not treat all the countries the same way. Western powers initially wanted manufactured goods from the more developed Asian societies, especially Indian cotton textiles and Chinese porcelains. At the beginning of the nineteenth century Britain had already gained political control over large parts of India and was intent on forcing China to trade on terms more to its benefit. It paid virtually no attention to Korea and Japan, not seeing in them the same potential for profit. The less developed parts of Asia also attracted increasing Western interest, not because they could provide manufactured goods, but because they offered opportunities for Western development, much as the Americas had earlier.

The West that the societies of Asia faced during the nineteenth century was itself rapidly changing, and the steps taken by Western nations to gain power in Asia naturally also changed over time. Western science and technology were making rapid advances, which gave European armies progressively greater advantages in weaponry. The Industrial Revolution made it possible for countries that industrialized early, such as Britain, to produce huge surpluses of goods for which they had to find markets; this development shifted their interest in Asia from a place to buy goods to a place to sell goods. Britain had been able to profit from its colonization of India, and this profit both encouraged it to consolidate its rule and invited its European rivals to look for their own colonies. For instance, rivalry with Britain led France to seek colonies in Southeast Asia not only for its own sake but also as a way to keep Britain from extending its sphere of influence any farther.

There were some commonalities in the ways Asian countries responded to pressure from outside. In the countries with long literary traditions, often the initial response of the established elite was to try to drive the unwelcome foreigners away. This was the case in China, Japan, and Korea in particular. Violent antiforeign reactions exploded again and again, but the superior military technology of the industrialized West almost invariably prevailed. After suffering humiliating defeats, some Asian leaders insisted on the need to preserve their cultural traditions at all costs. Others came to the opposite conclusion that the West was indeed superior in some ways and that they would have to adopt European ideas or techniques for their own purposes. This can be seen both among Indians who acquired education in English and in many of the Meiji reformers in Japan. The struggles between the traditionalists and the westernizers were often intense. As nationalism took hold in the West, it found a receptive audience among the educated elites in Asia. How could the assertion that every people had the right to control its own destiny not appeal to the colonized?

Whether they were colonized or not, most countries in Asia witnessed the spread of new technologies between 1800 and 1914. Railroads, telegraphs, modern sanitation, and a wider supply of inexpensive manufactured goods brought fundamental changes in everyday life not only to lands under colonial rule, such as India and Vietnam, but also, if less rapidly, to places that managed to remain independent, such as China and Japan. In fact, the transformation of Japan between 1860 and 1900 was extraordinary. By 1914 Japan had urban conveniences and educational levels comparable to those in Europe.

Chapter Summary

In the nineteenth century the countries of Asia faced new challenges. In India Britain extended its rule to the whole subcontinent, though often the British ruled indirectly through local princes. Britain brought many modern advances to India, such as railroads and schools. Slavery was outlawed, as was widow suicide and infanticide. Resistance to British rule took several forms. In 1857 Indian soldiers in the employ of the British rose in a huge revolt, and after Britain put down this rebellion it ruled India much more tightly. Indians who received English education turned English ideas of liberty and representative rule against the British and founded the Indian National Congress, which called for Indian independence.

In Southeast Asia by the end of the nineteenth century most countries, from Burma to the Philippines, had been made colonies of Western powers, which developed them as exporters of agricultural products or raw materials including rubber, tin, sugar, tea, cotton, and jute. The principal exception was Siam (Thailand), whose king was able to play the English and French off against each other and institute centralizing reforms. In the Philippines more than three centuries of Spanish rule ended in 1898, but Spain was replaced by another colonial power: the United States.

In the nineteenth century China's world standing declined as a result of both foreign intervention and internal unrest. The government's efforts to suppress opium imports from Britain led to military confrontation with the British and to numerous concessions that opened China to trade on Britain's terms. Within its borders, China faced unprecedented population pressure and worsening economic conditions that resulted in uprisings in several parts of the country. These rebellions proved very difficult to suppress. Further humiliations by the Western powers led to concerted efforts to modernize the military and learn other secrets of Western success, but China never quite caught up. Inspired by Western ideas of republican government, revolutionaries tried to topple the dynasty, finally succeeding in 1911–1912.

Japan was the one Asian country to quickly transform itself when confronted by the military strength of the West. It did this by overhauling its power structure. The Meiji centralized and strengthened Japan's power by depriving the samurai of their privileges, writing a constitution, instituting universal education, and creating a modern army. At the same time they guided Japan toward rapid industrialization. By the early twentieth century Japan had become an imperialist power with colonies in Korea and Taiwan.

The nineteenth century was also a great age of migration. Citizens of Great Britain came east in large numbers, many to join the Indian civil service or army, others to settle in Australia or New Zealand. Subjects of Asian countries also went abroad, often leaving one Asian country for another. Asian students traveled to Europe, Japan, or the United States to continue their educations. Millions more left in search of work. With the end of the African slave trade, recruiters from the Americas and elsewhere went to India and China to secure indentured laborers. In other cases, ambitious young men who heard of gold strikes or other chances to get rich funded their own travels. Asian diasporas formed in many parts of the world.

By the turn of the twentieth century the countries in the Asia and Pacific region varied greatly in wealth and power. There are several reasons for this. The countries did not start with equivalent circumstances. Some had long traditions of unified rule; others did not. Some had manufactured goods that Western powers wanted; others offered raw materials or cheap labor. The timing of the arrival of Western powers also made a difference, especially because Western military superiority increased over time. European Great Power rivalry had a major impact, especially after 1860. Similarities in the experiences of Asian countries are also notable and include many of the benefits (and costs) of industrialization seen elsewhere in the world, such as modernizations in communication and transportation, extension of schooling, and the emergence of radical ideologies.

Notes

1. Quoted in K. M. Panikkar, *Asia and Western Dominance: A Survey of the Vasco da Gama Epoch of Asian History* (London: George Allen & Unwin, 1959), p. 116.
2. Ssu-yu Teng and J. K. Fairbank, *China's Response to the West: A Documentary Survey* (New York: Atheneum, 1971), p. 26.
3. Ibid., p. 76, modified.
4. Quoted in J. W. Hall, *Japan, from Prehistory to Modern Times* (New York: Delacorte Press, 1970), p. 289.
5. R. Tsunoda, W. T. de Bary, and D. Keene, eds., *Sources of Japanese Tradition*, vol. 2 (New York: Columbia University Press, 1964), p. 137.
6. Quoted in J. D. Spence, *The Search for Modern China* (New York: W. W. Norton, 1990), p. 215.
7. Homer A. Jack, ed., *The Gandhi Reader: A Sourcebook of His Life and Writings* (Bloomington: Indiana University Press, 1956), p. 112.

CONNECTIONS

The nineteenth century brought Asia change on a much greater scale than did any earlier century. Much of the change was political—old political orders were ousted or reduced to tokens by new masters, often European colonial powers. Old elites found themselves at a loss when confronted by the European powers with their modern weaponry and modern armies. Cultural change was no less dramatic as the old elites pondered the differences between their traditional values and the ideas that seemed to underlie the power of the European states. In several places ordinary people rose in rebellion, probably in part because they felt threatened by the speed of cultural change. Material culture underwent major changes as elites experimented with Western dress and architecture and ordinary people had opportunities to travel on newly built railroads. Steamships, too, made long-distance travel easier, facilitating the out-migration of people seeking economic opportunities far from their countries of birth.

In the Americas, too, the nineteenth century was an era of unprecedented change and movement of people. Colonial empires were being overturned there, not imposed as they were in Asia in the same period. The Americas were on the receiving end of the huge migrations taking place, while Asia, like Europe, was much more an exporter of people. The Industrial Revolution brought change to all these areas, both by making available inexpensive machine-made products and by destroying some old ways of making a living. Intellectually, in both Asia and the Americas the ideas of nationalism and nation building shaped how people, especially the more educated, thought about the changes they were experiencing.

Chapter Review

MAKE IT STICK

☑ LearningCurve
Go online and use LearningCurve to retain what you've read.

IDENTIFY KEY TERMS

Identify and explain the significance of each item below.

Great Mutiny / Great Revolt (p. 797)
Indian Civil Service (p. 800)
Indian National Congress (p. 800)
Java War (p. 801)
Nguyen Dynasty (p. 801)
Opium War (p. 806)
extraterritoriality (p. 807)

Taiping Rebellion (p. 807)
Boxers (p. 809)
1911 Revolution (p. 809)
gunboat diplomacy (p. 810)
Meiji Restoration (p. 811)
Russo-Japanese War (p. 814)
indentured laborers (p. 819)

REVIEW THE MAIN IDEAS

Answer the focus questions from each section of the chapter.

1. In what ways did India change as a consequence of British rule? (p. 797)
2. Why were most but not all Southeast Asian societies reduced to colonies? (p. 801)
3. Was China's decline in the nineteenth century due more to internal problems or to Western imperialism? (p. 806)
4. How was Japan able to quickly master the challenges posed by the West? (p. 810)
5. What were the causes and consequences of the vast movement of people in the Pacific region? (p. 815)
6. What explains the similarities and differences in the experiences of Asian countries in this era? (p. 821)

MAKE CONNECTIONS

Analyze the larger developments and continuities within and across chapters.

1. How quickly was Asia affected by the Industrial Revolution in Europe? Explain your answer.
2. How do the experiences of European colonies in Asia compare to those in Africa (Chapter 25)?
3. How does China's response to the challenge of European pressure compare to that of the Ottoman Empire (Chapter 25) during the same period?

⮡LaunchPad
ONLINE DOCUMENT PROJECT

Imperialism in the Philippines
How did Filipinos and Americans respond to Spanish and American imperialism?

Examine documents about the Philippines during the Spanish-American War, and then complete a quiz and writing assignment based on the evidence and details from this chapter.

See inside the front cover to learn more.

CHRONOLOGY

1825	• King Minh Mang outlaws teaching of Christianity in Vietnam
1830	• Dutch institute Culture System in Indonesia
1839–1842	• Opium War
1851–1864	• Taiping Rebellion in China
1853	• Commodore Perry opens Japanese ports to foreign trade
1857	• Great Mutiny / Great Revolt by Indian sepoys against British rule
1858	• British Parliament begins to rule India
1859–1885	• Vietnam becomes a colony of France
1867	• Meiji Restoration in Japan
1869	• Suez Canal opens
1872	• Universal public schools established in Japan
1885	• Foundation of Indian National Congress
1894–1895	• Japan defeats China in Sino-Japanese War and gains control of Taiwan
1898	• United States takes control of Philippines from Spain
1900	• Boxer Rebellion in China
1904	• Japan attacks Russia and starts Russo-Japanese War
1910	• Korea becomes a province of Japan
1912	• China's monarchy is replaced by a republic

27

✓ **LearningCurve**
After reading the chapter, go online and use LearningCurve to retain what you've read.

The Americas in the Age of Liberalism

1810–1910

THE INDEPENDENCE OF NEW NATIONS IN THE AMERICAS USHERED in an era of striking change and stubborn continuities. With the exception of Haiti, which experienced a profound social revolution, other American nations gained independence with their colonial social order mostly intact. In the United States, Cuba, and Brazil slavery endured until the second half of the nineteenth century, far longer than in Spanish America. In Spanish America land remained concentrated in the hands of colonial elites. The resulting poverty and marginalization of rural workers continued, and by the end of the nineteenth century these conditions had intensified in many regions. As new nations consolidated, the patterns of where and how people lived changed profoundly. Territorial expansion displaced most of the indigenous communities that had withstood the colonial era. By 1900 millions of immigrants from Europe, the Middle East, and Asia had settled in the Americas.

New political systems and governing institutions emerged quickly in the United States, Canada, and Brazil, while in much of the rest of the continent political rivals struggled to share power. Liberal, constitutional republicanism emerged as the most common form of government. But there were exceptions, such as the monarchy that ruled Brazil for much of the century and the parliamentary system tied to Britain that developed in Canada. Across the Caribbean, Britain, France, Denmark, and the Netherlands retained their colonies. Spain struggled to suppress movements for independence in Cuba and Puerto Rico.

One of the greatest indicators of success for new nations in the Americas was the way in which they entered the global economy. Canada remained tied to an economically ascendant British Empire, and the United States managed to nurture internal markets and assume an influential place in both Atlantic and Pacific trade. Across Latin America, new nations with weak internal markets and often poorly consolidated political systems struggled to accumulate capital or industrialize.

New Nations

How and why did the process of nation-state consolidation vary across the Americas?

The American nations that gained their independence between 1783 and 1825 (see Chapter 22) faced similar challenges, but they responded with different strategies. At the moment of their independence, none of the nations of the Americas had consolidated what would become their national territory. Across the continent, independent indigenous societies resisted or negotiated their often-violent incorporation into the new nations. Some of these groups sustained their autonomy until the twentieth century.

The consolidation of new nations often took place violently. In countries such as Mexico and Argentina new governments failed to establish the trust needed for political stability. In the United States tensions and disagreements that had simmered since independence culminated in the Civil War, while in Cuba nationalists fought a long struggle for independence from Spain. While the political framework most commonly adopted was liberal republicanism, independent Brazil remained a monarchy until 1889. Independent Canada adopted a parliamentary system and retained a symbolic role for the British monarch.

Liberalism and Caudillos in Spanish America

The nations that gained independence from the Spanish Empire in the Americas drew upon ideological currents that circulated in the Atlantic in the age of revolution in order to establish new frameworks of government and social organization (see Chapter 22). The dominant ideology of the era was liberalism, inspired by the founders of the United States, ideologues of the French Revolution, and economic thinkers in Britain, as well as the liberal faction that fought Spain's Peninsular War (1808–1814) and succeeded in establishing its 1812 Constitution. Liberal ideology guided politics, economics, and society. Liberals sought to create representative republics with strong central governments framed by constitutions that defined and protected individual rights, in particular the right to freely own and buy and sell private property. Beginning with the United States, colonies that became independent nations in the Americas all adopted liberal constitutions.

The U.S. Constitution, in its earliest form, is an example of classic liberalism: it defined individual rights, but those individual rights were subordinated to property rights. Slaves were considered property rather than individuals with constitutional rights.

Only property owners could vote, only men could own property, and the new government did not recognize the property of Indians. Though liberalism offered a seemingly fair political and social framework, it mainly served and protected oligarchs — the small number of individuals and families who had monopolized political power and economic resources since the colonial era. Liberalism preserved slavery, created tools that allowed the wealthy and powerful to continue to concentrate landownership in the countryside, gave industrialists a free hand over their workers, and concentrated political power in the hands of those who held economic power.

By the end of the nineteenth century liberalism commingled with other ideologies such as Social Darwinism and scientific racism (see pages 749–750). Oligarchs combined liberalism with Social Darwinism to consolidate and justify their control over economic activity and political affairs. This combination also inspired the imperial ambitions of the United States toward Mexico and the Circum-Caribbean, the region that includes the Antilles as well as the lands that bound the Caribbean Sea in Central America and northern South America.

Though liberalism provided the political and economic framework that replaced colonialism, nations of the Americas took different approaches. The United States deferred questions about centralized federal power over local state authority, as well as the legality of slavery, until its Civil War (1861–1865). After the North prevailed, economic growth under its liberal economic model accelerated, causing titanic business and industrial empires to form and stimulating the immigration of millions of people to provide cheap labor for the booming industrial economy. In Spanish America wars of independence left behind a weak consensus about government, which led to long cycles of civil war across many countries.

The lack of a shared political culture among powerful groups in Spanish America created a crisis of confidence. Large landowners held great local power that they refused to yield to politicians in a distant capital. Political factions feared that if a rival faction

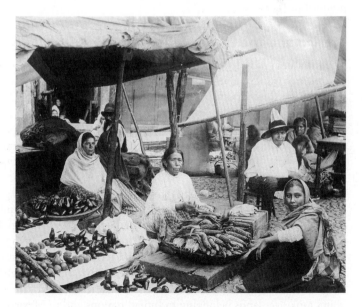

Market Vendors in Mexico
Women sell produce at a market in San Luis Potosí, Mexico, around 1910. (© ullstein—Haeckel-Archiv/The Image Works)

won power, it would not abide by the rules and limits framed by the constitution, or that a rival would use its governing authority to crush its opponents. The power vacuum that resulted was often filled by caudillos, strong leaders who came to power and governed through their charisma and leadership abilities rather than on the basis of a functioning political system. This form of leadership is known as **caudillismo**.

In Argentina, Juan Manuel de Rosas was one such caudillo who ruled much of the country from 1829 to 1852. Caudillos commanded loyal and armed followers, and Rosas pitched his followers against the Unitarian Party that had pressed for the creation of a strong liberal state. An ally of Rosas reflected on the differences between liberals and supporters of the caudillo. He contrasted what he saw as the arrogance of the Unitarians' modernizing liberal project, based on foreign ideology, with what he defined as more authentic local traditions of "Old School" rural landowners:

> Among the Unitarians there was greater talent, more men with new ideas, a greater affinity for the theories and spirit of the times, more brilliance and eloquence; the Unitarians also . . . lived more stylishly. But they were dominated by a disagreeable spirit — that of exclusivism; and their liberal doctrines contrasted sharply with their pronounced and obnoxious intolerance. From every pore they exuded a pigheaded pride, and extreme fatuousness incompatible with true knowledge. Their airs of insulting condescension had rendered them totally unpopular. . . . They were mannered men with imitative customs, whose parody of Europe offended local values and habits. . . . [Rosas's supporters] were, with few exceptions, pure Creoles, stuck in the routine of the Old School. . . . For them everything else smelled of foreignness.[1]

The rule of a caudillo, anchored in his charisma and the loyalty of his followers, often provided temporary stability amid the struggles between liberals and conservatives, but caudillos cultivated their own prestige at the expense of building stable political institutions.

Mexico and the United States

The rumblings of independence first stirred Mexico in 1810. A century later, in 1910, the country was engulfed in the first great social upheaval of the twentieth century, the Mexican Revolution. In the century between these events, Mexico declined politically and economically from its status as the most prosperous and important colony of the Spanish Empire. It lost most of its national territory as Central American provinces broke away and became independent republics and as the United States expanded westward and captured, purchased, or otherwise wrangled away Mexico's northern lands.

Mexicans experienced political stabilization and economic growth again in the second half of the nineteenth century when liberal leaders, especially the dictator Porfirio Díaz (r. 1876–1910), imposed order and attracted foreign investment. But as Díaz himself is said to have remarked, "Poor Mexico, so far from God, so close to the United States."[2] The United States pursued territorial expansion under the doctrine of **manifest destiny**, by which the United States would absorb all the territory spanning from its original Atlantic states to the Pacific Ocean. In the process, the United States took over lands belonging to Indian nations and to Mexico. And as the United

States grew economically, investors from the United States drove railroad construction and land speculation in Mexico that stripped lands away from peasants, who rose up in the 1910 revolution.

Mexico's woes after independence resulted mainly from the inability of its political leaders to establish a consensus about how to govern the new nation. The general who led the war against Spain, Agustín de Iturbide, resisted liberal pressure for a republican constitution and proclaimed himself emperor in 1822. When he was deposed a year later, the country's southern provinces broke away, forming the new nations of Guatemala, Honduras, Nicaragua, El Salvador, and Costa Rica. For the next three decades, power in Mexico rested in the hands of regional caudillos and local bosses. The presidency changed hands frequently as rival factions competed against each other. Antonio López de Santa Anna, the most powerful of Mexico's caudillos, held the presidency ten times between 1833 and 1854 — three separate times in 1833 alone.

By contrast, the United States established a clearer vision of government based on the shared principles and difficult compromises written into the 1789 Constitution. Deep differences of opinion remained over questions such as the power of the federal government relative to state governments, which played out in debates about the future of slavery and of westward expansion. These differences created regional tensions that lasted well into the early nineteenth century and culminated in the Civil War (1861–1865).

Economically, the United States remained integrated into the expanding and industrializing British Empire, so U.S. merchants retained access to Atlantic markets and credit. But the United States faced deepening regional differences: in the first half of the nineteenth century the North's economy and population grew faster than the South's, and the North became the center of immigration, banking, and industrialization. In the South slavery and tenant farming kept much of the population at the economic margins and weakened internal markets. Slavery also inhibited immigration, since immigrants avoided settling in areas where they had to compete for work with unfree labor.

The dichotomy between the economies of the U.S. North and South repeated itself in the difference between the economies of the United States and Latin America. The Spanish imperial economy imploded in the course of the Napoleonic invasion, followed by the Peninsular War in which different factions in Spain, claiming to act in their deposed king's name, fought their French occupiers (1808–1814). Latin American economies were organized around the export of agricultural and mineral commodities like sugar and silver, not around internal markets as in the United States, and these export economies were disrupted by the independence process.

The fate of the major silver mine in Mexico illustrates the challenges presented by independence. La Valenciana in central Mexico was the site of the greatest private investment in the colony and was the most productive silver mine in the world. It was one of the first places where the steam engine, developed by Scottish inventor James Watt, was used to pump water out of shafts and to allow the mine to drill well below the water table. The machinery was destroyed during the wars of independence (1810–1821), and the flooded mine ceased operation. Neither private investors nor the new government had the capital necessary to reactivate the mine after independence. Without the private profits, wages, and taxation that mining produced, Mexico's economy withered and its credit networks collapsed.

Mexico entered a vicious cycle: without capital and economic activity, tax revenues evaporated, public administration disintegrated, and the national government became unmanageable. In turn, the lack of political stability drove investors away. The consequences are striking when measured against the experience of the United States. In 1800 Mexico produced half the goods and services that the United States did; by 1845 production had dropped to only 8 percent. Per capita income fell by half. At independence in 1821, Mexico had a population of 6.2 million, while the United States had 3.9 million. In 1900 Mexico's population had barely doubled to 13.6 million, while the U.S. population increased nearly twenty times, reaching 76 million.[3]

Politically and economically weakened after independence, Mexico was vulnerable to expansionist pressure from the United States. At independence, Mexico's northern territories included much of what is today the U.S. Southwest and West, stretching from Texas to California. These northern territories attracted the interest of U.S. politicians, settlers, and land speculators. In the 1820s settlers from the U.S. South petitioned the Mexican government for land grants in the province of Texas, in return for which they would adopt Mexican citizenship. The U.S. government encouraged these settlers to declare the independence of Texas in 1836. The Battle of the Alamo (1836) was a rare Mexican victory in the failed effort by caudillo Santa Anna to retake the province.

After Texas and Florida became U.S. states in 1845, President James Polk expanded the nation's border westward, precipitating the Mexican-American War (1845–1847). U.S. forces captured Mexico City, where at the last site of resistance, the military fort at Chapultepec, young Mexican cadets jumped to their death rather than surrender. In the Treaty of Guadalupe Hidalgo (1848), Mexico ceded half its territory, including California, Nevada, Arizona, New Mexico, and parts of Colorado and Utah, to the United States. With the U.S. acquisition of Florida from Spain in 1819 and the conquest of Mexican territory, many Latinos—U.S. citizens or residents of Latin American origin or descent—became U.S. citizens not because they moved to the United States but because the United States moved to them.

Liberal Reform in Mexico

In 1853 Mexican president Santa Anna unintentionally ushered in a new era of liberal political consolidation and economic reform by triggering a backlash against his sale of territory along the northern border to the United States. In the Gadsden Purchase, Santa Anna sold Mexican land that U.S. engineers eyed as the route for a transcontinental railroad in exchange for $10 million that he mostly pocketed. Many Mexicans saw his act as a betrayal of the nation and threw their support behind a new generation of liberal leaders. Beginning with the presidency of Ignacio Comonfort (pres. 1855–1858), these liberals carried out sweeping legal and economic changes called *La Reforma*, or "the reform."

Liberal reformers sought to make all individuals equal under the law and established property ownership as a basic right and national goal. The first major step in La Reforma was the Juárez Law (1855), which abolished old legal privileges for military officers and members of the clergy. The law was written by Minister of Justice Benito Juárez, an Indian from Oaxaca whose first language was Zapotec. Juárez began life as a farmer but earned a law degree and became the most important force in consolidating Mexico's political system in the decades after independence. An even more consequential measure, the Lerdo Law (1856), banished another legacy of colonialism: "corporate lands," meaning lands owned by groups or institutions, such as the Catholic Church, rather than by individual property owners. Since the beginning of the colonial era, the Catholic Church had been a major rural landowner, and liberals saw those landholdings as backward and inefficient. They wanted to redistribute church-owned lands among farmers who would own them as private parcels and who would profit from working them efficiently.

These liberal reforms triggered a backlash from conservative landowners and the church. When liberals enshrined these laws and other reforms in a new constitution ratified in 1857, the Catholic Church, which faced the loss of its lands as well as the loss of legal protections for the clergy, threatened to excommunicate anyone who swore allegiance to it. Conservatives revolted, triggering a civil war called the Wars of Reform (1857–1861). Liberal forces led by Benito Juárez defeated the conservatives, who then conspired with French emperor Napoleon III to invite a French invasion of Mexico. Napoleon III saw an opportunity to re-establish France's American empire. His propaganda gave currency to the term "Latin America," which the propagandists used to assert that France had a natural role to play in Mexico because of a common "Latin" origin.

The French army invaded Mexico in 1862. It faced little resistance other than the defense mounted by a young officer named Porfirio Díaz, who blocked the invaders' advance through the city of Puebla on their way to Mexico City. The May 5 Battle of Puebla became enshrined as a national holiday (now also observed in the United States as "Cinco de Mayo"). Having expelled the Juárez government from Mexico City, Mexican conservatives and Napoleon III installed his Austrian cousin Maximilian of Habsburg as emperor of Mexico. In many respects, Maximilian was a good candidate for emperor: he was descended from Charles V, the Spanish emperor in whose name Cortés had conquered the Aztec Empire and claimed Mexico. He was politically able and quickly learned Spanish. But Mexico had been an independent nation for too long for a European power to install a foreign monarch.

The deposed Juárez led a guerrilla war against the French troops backing Maximilian. When the U.S. Civil War ended in 1865, the U.S. government sought to root out France's influence on its border. The United States threw its support behind Juárez and pressured Napoleon III to remove French troops, and surplus Civil War armaments flooded across the border into Mexico. Juárez's nationalists prevailed, restored Mexico's republic, and executed Maximilian. Conservatives had been completely discredited: they had conspired with another country to install a foreign leader through a military invasion.

We can compare Benito Juárez, who governed the restored republic until 1876, with Abraham Lincoln. Both rose from humble rural origins to become able liberal lawyers. They both proved to be agile political and military leaders who prevailed in civil wars in which a liberal political philosophy triumphed over conservative opposition. The decade between the Wars of Reform that began in 1857 and Juárez's restoration of the republic in 1867 can also be compared to the U.S. Civil War: both were watersheds in which questions of political philosophy and governing authority that had lingered since national independence were violently resolved.

Brazil: A New World Monarchy

Brazil gained independence in 1822 as a monarchy ruled by Emperor Pedro I, the son and heir of Portuguese emperor João IV (Pedro I eventually abdicated the Brazilian throne and returned to Portugal as its emperor). In other words, when Pedro I rode up Ipiranga Hill, raised his sword, and proclaimed "Independence or death!" the newly independent country was ruled by the same people who had governed it that morning. Nonetheless, this act marked the culmination of a process that began in 1808, when Napoleon's armies crossed the Pyrenees from France to invade the Iberian Peninsula. Napoleon toppled the Spanish crown, but the Portuguese royal family, many of the government's bureaucrats, and most of the aristocracy fled aboard British warships to Portugal's colony, Brazil. This would be the first and only time a European empire would be ruled from one of its colonies.

Before the seat of Portuguese power relocated to Brazil, colonial policies had restricted many activities in Brazil in order to keep the colony dependent and subordinate to Portugal. It was only with the arrival of the imperial court that Brazil gained its first printing press, library, and military and naval academies, as well as schools for engineering, medicine, law, and the arts. The first comprehensive university in Brazil was not founded until 1922, nearly four centuries after the first universities were established in Mexico and Peru, and three centuries later than in the United States. (The first university was established during the commemoration of the centenary of independence, in order to be able to award an honorary degree to a visiting European dignitary.)

With the flight of the emperor to Brazil in 1808 and the declaration of independence by his son in 1822, Brazil achieved something that had eluded Spanish-American nations: it retained the unifying symbol of the monarchy and continued to build upon the infrastructure of colonial administration, even if that infrastructure had been more rudimentary than in the Spanish colonies. A liberal constitution adopted in 1824 lasted until a republican military coup in 1889. It established a two-chamber parliamentary system and a role for the emperor as a guide and intermediary in political affairs. Pedro I was not adept in this role and abdicated in 1831, leaving behind a regency governing in the name of his five-year-old son, Pedro II. In 1840, at the age of fourteen, Pedro II declared himself an adult and assumed the throne. His rule, which lasted forty-nine years, provided the country with unusual political stability that helped keep Brazil from dividing into separate nations, as occurred in Spanish America, and avoided the internal strife that characterized the United States during that period.

The nature of Brazil's independence nonetheless constrained its growth in the nineteenth century. Portugal had been economically and militarily dependent on Britain, and Britain transferred this dependency onto Brazil. The British treaty recognizing Brazilian independence compelled the Brazilian state to assume the debts owed by Portugal: the British government presumed that without revenue from Brazil, the Portuguese crown could not honor the debts. Britain negotiated with Brazil a "Friendship Treaty" that allowed British industrial goods to enter the country with very low tariffs and granted British citizens in Brazil the right to be tried by British rather than Brazilian judges. The flood of cheap British imports inhibited Brazilian industrialization. British economic and political influence, as well as the special privileges enjoyed by British citizens in Brazil, were examples of **neocolonialism**, the influence that

European powers and the United States exerted over politically and economically weaker countries after they gained their independence.

Slavery and Abolition

Why did slavery last longer in the United States, Brazil, and Cuba than in the other republics of the Americas? How did patterns of resistance shape slavery and abolition?

Across the former colonies of Spanish America, the abolition of slavery quickly followed independence. Abolitionist pressure from Britain ended slavery in its Caribbean colonies in 1834, and the British navy suppressed the Atlantic slave trade. But slavery endured well into the nineteenth century in the United States, Cuba, and Brazil. In each of these countries the question of abolition became entwined with the disputes over the nature of government and authority—federal unionism versus states' rights in the United States, independence for Cuba, and monarchy versus republicanism in Brazil.

Slave Societies in the Americas

Africans and their descendants were enslaved in every country of the Americas, from Canada to Chile. The experiences in slavery and freedom for Africans and African Americans, broadly defined here as the descendants of slaves brought from Africa anywhere in the New World, varied considerably. Several factors shaped their experiences: the nature of slave regimes in different economic regions, patterns of manumission (individual slaves gaining their freedom), and the nature of abolition (the ending of the institution of slavery). Their experiences were also shaped by the density of the slave trade in the crescent stretching from Brazil northward through the Caribbean and across the U.S. South. In some regions Africans and African Americans constituted the majority of the population, while in other regions they were a minority whose proportion of the population was further diluted by subsequent European immigration. But even in regions with few enslaved people, they formed part of an African diaspora in the Americas that faced common challenges, such as formal and informal restrictions on social mobility, education, and intermarriage.

The settlement of Africans as slaves was the most intense in areas that relied on plantation agriculture. Plantations were an unusual kind of farming: they were typically enormous tracts of land dedicated to cultivating a single crop—especially sugar, coffee, tobacco, and cotton—on a scale so great that plantation regions usually supplied distant global markets. Cotton from Alabama was spun by looms in New England or Britain; sugar from Brazil was added to cups of coffee (also from Brazil) in European salons. The massive scale of this kind of agriculture, along with the practice of importing African labor to sustain it, originated in the sugar region of northeastern Brazil under the Portuguese. African slaves played many other roles as well. From Buenos Aires to Boston, slavery was also widespread in port cities, fed by easy access to the slave trade and the demand for street laborers such as porters. And across the Americas, slaves—especially slave women—were forced into domestic service, a role that conferred social prestige on their masters, but which also added sexual abuse to the miseries that slaves endured.

companies to identify land that was not being cultivated (often land that communities allowed to lay fallow as they rotated crops) so it could be surveyed and auctioned off. The abuse of these laws by land speculators with ties to the regime, along with intimidation and violence, had devastating consequences: by 1910, 80 percent of rural peasants had no land. The increase in land values paradoxically reduced production: speculators from the United States bought large tracts of land not to farm but to hold as investments. Mexico, the country where maize had been developed, now had to import it from the United States.

The Porfiriato and its liberal ideology favored the needs of foreign investors over its own citizens. Most of Mexico's 1910 population of 12 million remained tied to the land. The expansion of railroads into that land made it valuable, and liberal reforms provided the tools to transfer that value from peasants to capitalists. Given Mexico's proximity to the United States, that process was swifter and more intense than elsewhere in Latin America, and it led to the first great social upheaval of the twentieth century, the Mexican Revolution that erupted in 1910.

Liberal Consolidation in South America

As in the United States and Mexico, the process of liberal nation-state consolidation in South America took place through military conflict. The War of the Triple Alliance, or Paraguay War (1865–1870), in which Paraguay fought Brazil, Argentina, and Uruguay, played a similar role to Mexico's Wars of Reform and the U.S. Civil War in consolidating liberalism in South America. In 1865 Paraguayan leader Francisco Solano López declared war against the three neighboring countries after political competition between Argentina and Brazil threatened Paraguay's use of Uruguay's Atlantic port in Montevideo. Landlocked Paraguay depended on Montevideo as a shipping point for its imports and exports. Paraguay fought a five-year war against much larger neighbors until it was defeated in 1870. Paraguay's perseverance can be ascribed to the intensive training of Solano López's army, as well as the relative inability of the governments of Argentina and Brazil to mobilize armies and resources.

The war was devastating for Paraguay, which lost more than half its national population, including most adult men. But victory, too, was traumatic for Argentina and Brazil, where soul-searching took place about the conduct of the war: Argentines and Brazilians asked themselves why it had taken five years to defeat a much smaller neighbor. The war prompted debates about the need for economic modernization and the reform of national governments.

In Brazil, where Emperor Pedro II's calls for volunteers to enlist in the army fell on deaf ears, the army enlisted slaves who, if they served honorably and survived, would be granted freedom. What did it mean when the free citizens of a nation would not mobilize to defend it, and when a nation prevailed only through the sacrifices borne by its slaves? For many, especially military officers who were veterans of the conflict, the lesson was that being a monarchy that relied on slavery made Brazil a backward nation. Veteran officers and liberal opponents of the war formed a movement to create a liberal republic and abolish slavery. These republicans overthrew monarchy in 1889 and installed a liberal regime that lasted until 1930.

In Argentina, after the war with Paraguay, a succession of liberal leaders beginning with Domingo Sarmiento (pres. 1868–1874) also pressed modernizing reforms intended to establish the political authority of the capital, Buenos Aires, over the rest of Argentina; take possession of frontier regions; institute universal public education; and strengthen economic production. Economic measures in Argentina were the most far-reaching and drew on the experience of the United States in settling its western frontier as a model. In a military campaign called the Conquest of the Desert (1878–1885), Argentine troops seasoned by war with Paraguay took control of the lands of Mapuche Indians in the southern region of Patagonia and opened new lands for sale to ranchers. The wars were accompanied by ambitious railroad construction that linked inland areas to the coast to transport goods, the introduction of barbed wire fencing that intensified ranching capabilities, and the development of new strains of cattle and wheat that increased production. The Conquest of the Desert and the government's land distribution policies transformed Argentina's countryside into highly productive ranch lands and farmlands whose exports competed directly with the ranches of the North American West.

Latin America Re-enters the World Economy

The wars of independence in Spanish America interrupted the Atlantic and Pacific trade networks that had sustained the region's colonial economies. Amid the political instability that followed independence, investment dried up and trade networks collapsed. Civil war and rule by caudillos delayed the consolidation of liberal regimes in Spanish America. In the first decades of independence, Latin America's economic integration with the world decreased. For rural peasants and indigenous communities, this was a benefit in disguise: the decline of trade made lands less valuable. The rents landowners could charge tenant farmers decreased, making it easier for peasants to gain access to land.

By the second half of the nineteenth century Latin American elites reached a compromise that combined liberal political ideas about the way national government should be structured with liberal economic policies that favored large landowners. Political stability and economic growth returned. Foreign investment intensified. By the turn of the twentieth century Latin American countries were firmly tied to the world economy. Indigenous and rural communities paid a high price for this return to economic growth: as the value of agricultural exports increased, so did the value of land. Governments, foreign investors, and large landowners seized lands through war, legal action, or coercion at a dizzying rate.

As Latin American governments stabilized, they consolidated control of national territory in part by eliminating, subjugating, or displacing indigenous communities. Through this process, Latin American governments opened new lands for private ownership much as the United States did along its expanding frontier, but with very different results. In the United States the 1862 Homestead Act made over 500 million acres available for settlement, often on lands forced from Indian communities. The Homestead Act had two objectives: to promote white settlement of western territories to integrate those territories into the nation, and to make those regions economically dynamic by creating an extensive class of small farmers.

After the Conquest of the Desert in the 1870s and 1880s, the Argentine government sold off lands it took from indigenous communities. The land was inexpensive, but because it was sold in such large parcels, the few who could purchase it did

INDIVIDUALS IN SOCIETY • Henry Meiggs, Promoter and Speculator

All throughout the Americas in the nineteenth century, opportunities beckoned. Henry Meiggs, born in upstate New York in 1811, responded to several of them, building and losing fortunes in Brooklyn, San Francisco, Chile, and Peru. Meiggs, with only an elementary school education, began work at his father's shipyard. He soon started his own lumber business and did well until he lost everything in the financial panic of 1837. He rebuilt his business, and when gold was discovered in California in 1848, he filled a ship with lumber and sailed around Cape Horn to San Francisco, where he sold his cargo for $50,000, twenty times what he had paid for it. He then entered the lumber business, organizing crews of five hundred men to fell huge California redwoods and bring them to his steam sawmills. As his business flourished, he began speculating in real estate, which led to huge debts when the financial crisis of 1854 hit. In an attempt to save himself and his friends, Meiggs forged warrants for more than $900,000; when discovery of the fraud seemed imminent, he sailed with his wife and children for South America.

Although at one point Meiggs was so strapped for cash that he sold his watch, within three years of arriving in Chile, he had secured his first railway contract, and by 1867 he had built about 200 miles of rail lines in that country. In 1868 he went to Peru, which had less than 60 miles of track at the time. In the next nine years he would add 700 more.

Meiggs was not an engineer, but he was a good manager. He recruited experienced engineers from abroad and arranged the purchase of foreign rolling stock, rails, and ties, acting as a promoter and developer. Much of the funding came from international investors in Peruvian bonds.

The most spectacular of the rail lines Meiggs built was Peru's Callao-Lima-Oroya line, which crosses the Andes at about seventeen thousand feet above sea level, making it the highest standard-gauge railway in the world. Because water was scarce in many areas along the construction site, it had to be transported up to workers, who were mostly local people. Dozens of bridges and tunnels had to be built, and casualties were high. Eight hundred people were invited to the banquet that marked the beginning of work on the Oroya Railway. Meiggs drummed up

so by mortgaging existing landholdings. Though Domingo Sarmiento, too, had imagined the creation of a class of small farmers, the result was the opposite: more than 20 million acres were sold to just 381 landowners who created vast estates known as latifundios. In contrast, the Brazilian Land Law of 1850 restricted landownership by prohibiting anyone from gaining title to land by settling it, as the Homestead Act allowed. The law was a response to pressure from Britain to end the slave trade: planters used the law to keep slaves or free workers on their plantations by preventing them from setting out to farm on their own.[4]

Liberal economic policies and the intensification of foreign trade concentrated land in the hands of wealthy exporters. Governments represented the interests of large landowners by promoting commodity exports and industrial imports, following the enthusiasm at the event by calling the locomotive the "irresistible battering ram of modern civilization."

In Peru Meiggs became known for his extravagance and generosity, and some charged that he bribed Peruvian officials on a large scale to get his projects approved. He was a good speaker and loved to entertain lavishly. In one example of his generosity, he distributed thousands of pesos and soles to the victims of the earthquake of 1868. He also contributed to the beautification of Lima by tearing down an old wall and putting a seven-mile-long park in its place.

Always the speculator, in 1877 Meiggs died poor, his debts exceeding his assets. He was beloved, however, and more than twenty thousand Peruvians, many of whom had labored on his projects, attended his funeral at a Catholic church in Lima.

QUESTIONS FOR ANALYSIS

1. What accounts for the changes in fortune that Meiggs experienced?

2. Were the Latin American governments that awarded contracts to Meiggs making reasonable decisions?

3. Should it matter whether Meiggs had to bribe officials to get the railroads built? Why or why not?

ᑭ LaunchPad
ONLINE DOCUMENT PROJECT

How did investors like Henry Meiggs fit into the larger context of Latin American nation building? Read descriptions of Latin America's past and visions of its future, and then complete a quiz and writing assignment based on the evidence and details from this chapter.

See inside the front cover to learn more.

liberal economic principle of comparative advantage (that countries should export what they could produce the most efficiently and import what other countries could produce more cheaply and efficiently). Brazil became the world's largest exporter of coffee and experienced a brief but intense boom in rubber production. Argentina's conquests on the frontier and economic modernization made it one of the most efficient and profitable exporters of grains and beef. Chile and Peru served the international market for fertilizers by exporting nitrates and bat guano.

These export booms depended on imported capital and technology. In the Circum-Caribbean this came mostly from investors in the United States, while in South America it often came from Britain. (See "Individuals in Society: Henry Meiggs, Promoter and Speculator," above.)

British capital and technology built Argentina's network of railroads and refrigerated meatpacking plants. Chile's nitrate-mining industry was expanded through the War of the Pacific (1879–1883), a conflict in which Chile seized territory in bordering Peru and Bolivia. In the process, Bolivia lost its access to the Pacific and became a landlocked nation. The war and its outcomes revealed British influence as well: the Chilean government issued bonds bought by British investors in order to finance the war. The bonds were repaid with concessions for mining the nitrate-rich lands that Chile conquered from Bolivia. In 1878 British companies controlled 13 percent of nitrate mining. By 1890 they controlled 90 percent.

The rise in the quantity and value of primary commodity exports concentrated wealth in the hands of oligarchs. Large landowners, such as Brazilian coffee planters, relied on cheap labor provided by slaves until 1888 and, increasingly, by tenant farmers and free laborers who worked for little pay. The exported coffee produced by these workers garnered profits so great that although coffee planters were the main slaveholders, they could afford to give up slavery and pursue immigrant labor from Europe. In the late nineteenth century planters united to create colonization companies in southern European cities that promoted and subsidized immigration to Brazil. The planters combined economic liberalism with Social Darwinism: they believed that free workers were more efficient than slave laborers and that white workers were more productive than black ones.

Immigration

What factors shaped immigration patterns to the Americas? How did immigrants shape—and how were they shaped by—their new settings?

During the late nineteenth and early twentieth centuries unprecedented numbers of people from Europe, Asia, and the Middle East settled across North and South America. The largest wave of immigrants—some 28 million between 1860 and 1914—settled in the United States. Another 8 million had settled in Argentina and Brazil by 1930. This cycle of immigration was a product of liberal political and economic reforms that abolished slavery, established stable political systems, and created a framework for integrating immigrants as factory and farm laborers.

Immigration to Latin America

In 1852 the Argentine political philosopher Juan Bautista Alberdi published *Bases and Points of Departure for Argentine Political Organization*, in which he argued that the development of his country depended on immigration. Indians and blacks, Alberdi maintained, lacked basic skills, and it would take too long to train them. Thus he pressed for massive immigration from northern Europe and the United States:

> Each European who comes to our shores brings more civilization in his habits, which will later be passed on to our inhabitants, than many books of philosophy. . . . Do we want to sow and cultivate in America English liberty, French culture, and the diligence of men from Europe and from the United States? Let us bring living pieces of these qualities.[5]

Alberdi's ideas, guided by the aphorism "to govern is to populate," won immediate acceptance and were even incorporated into the Argentine constitution, which declared, "The Federal government will encourage European immigration." Other Latin American countries adopted similar policies promoting immigration to achieve similar goals.

Coffee barons in Brazil, *latifundiarios* (owners of vast estates) in Argentina, or investors in nitrate and copper mining in Chile made enormous profits that they reinvested in new factories. Latin America had been tied to the Industrial Revolution in Britain and northern Europe from the outset as a provider of raw materials and as a consumer of industrial goods. In the major exporting countries of Argentina, Brazil, and Mexico, domestic industrialization now began to take hold in the form of textile mills, food-processing plants, and mechanized transportation such as modern ports and railroads.

By the turn of the twentieth century, industrial parks had emerged in Mexico City, Veracruz, Buenos Aires, Rio de Janeiro, and São Paulo. In 1907 Brazil had an industrial working class of 150,000. By 1914 Argentina's numbered 400,000. In Brazil and Argentina these workers were mainly European immigrants. The workers proved unexpectedly contentious: they brought with them radical ideologies that challenged liberalism, particularly anarchism and anarcho-syndicalism, a version of anarchism that advocated placing power in the hands of labor unions. These workers clashed with bosses and political leaders who rejected the idea that workers had rights. The authorities suppressed worker organizations such as unions, and they resisted implementing labor laws such as a minimum wage, restrictions on child labor, the right to strike, or factory safety regulations. Workers had little political voice — the first Latin American country to grant universal male suffrage, Argentina, only did so in 1912.

Although Europe was a significant source of immigrants to Latin America, so were Asia and the Middle East. For example, in the late nineteenth and early twentieth centuries large numbers of Japanese arrived in Brazil, most settling in São Paulo state. By 1920 Brazil had the largest Japanese community in the world outside of Japan. From the Middle East, Lebanese, Turks, and Syrians also entered Brazil. Between 1850 and 1880, 144,000 South Asian laborers went to Trinidad, 39,000 to Jamaica, and smaller numbers to the islands of St. Lucia, Grenada, and St. Vincent, mostly as indentured servants under five-year contracts. Perhaps one-third returned to India, but the rest stayed, saved money, and bought small businesses or land. Cuba, the largest of the Caribbean islands (about the size of the state of Pennsylvania), had received 500,000 African slaves between 1808 and 1865. When slavery was abolished in 1886, some of the work in the sugarcane fields was done by Chinese indentured servants, who followed the same pattern as the South Asian migrants who had gone to Trinidad. Likewise, the abolition of slavery in Mexico led to the arrival of thousands of Chinese bonded servants.

Thanks to the influx of new arrivals, Buenos Aires, São Paulo, Mexico City, Montevideo, Santiago, and Havana experienced spectacular growth. By 1914 Buenos Aires in particular had emerged as one of the most cosmopolitan cities in the world, with a population of 3.6 million. As Argentina's political capital, the city housed its government bureaucracies and agencies. The meatpacking, food-processing, flour-milling, and wool industries were concentrated there as well. Half of all overseas tonnage passed through the city, which was also the heart of the nation's railroad network. Elegant shops near the Plaza de Mayo catered to the expensive tastes of the elite upper classes that constituted about 5 percent of the population. By contrast, the thousands of immigrants who toiled twelve hours a day, six days a week, on docks and construction sites and in meatpacking plants were crowded into the city's one-room tenements, furnished with a few iron cots, a table and chairs, and maybe an old trunk.

Immigrants brought wide-ranging skills that helped develop industry and commerce. In Argentina, Italian and Spanish settlers stimulated the expansion of cattle ranching, meat processing, wheat farming, and the shoe industry. In Brazil, Swiss immigrants built the cheese business, Italians gained a leading role in the coffee industry, and Japanese farmers made the country self-sufficient in rice production. In Peru, Italians became influential in banking and the restaurant business, while the French dominated dressmaking as well as the jewelry and pharmaceutical businesses. Chinese laborers built Peruvian railroads, and in sections of large cities such as Lima, the Chinese dominated the ownership of shops and restaurants.

The vast majority of migrants were unmarried males; seven out of ten people who landed in Argentina between 1857 and 1924 were single males between thirteen and forty years old. There, as in other larger South American countries, many of those who stayed married native-born women who were often of mixed indigenous or African ancestry.

Immigration to the United States

After the Civil War ended in 1865, the United States underwent an industrial boom powered by exploitation of the country's natural resources. The federal government turned over vast amounts of land and mineral resources to private industrialists for development. In particular, railroad companies — the foundation of industrial expansion — received 130 million acres. By 1900 the U.S. railroad system was 193,000 miles long, connected every part of the nation, and represented 40 percent of the railroad mileage in the world, and it was all built by immigrant labor.

Between 1860 and 1914, 28 million immigrants came to the United States. Though many became rural homesteaders, industrial America developed on the sweat and brawn of immigrants. Chinese, Scandinavian, and Irish immigrants laid railroad tracks. At the Carnegie Steel Corporation, Slavs and Italians produced one-third of the world's total steel supply in 1900. As in South America, immigration fed the growth of cities. In 1790 only 5.1 percent of Americans were living in centers of twenty-five hundred or more people. By 1860 this figure had risen to 19.9 percent, and by 1900 almost 40 percent of the population lived in cities. Also by 1900, three of the largest cities in the world were in the United States — New York City with 3.4 million people, Chicago with 1.7 million, and Philadelphia with 1.4 million.

Working conditions for new immigrants were often deplorable. Industrialization had created a vast class of workers who depended entirely on wage labor. Employers paid women and children much less than men. Some women textile workers earned as little as $1.56 for seventy hours of work, while men received from $7 to $9 for the same work. Because business owners resisted government efforts to install costly safety devices, working conditions in mines and mills were frightful. In 1913 alone, even after some safety measures had been instituted, twenty-five thousand people died in

Immigrants in Hawaii   Fruit store owned and run by Chinese immigrants in Honolulu, Hawaii, around 1905. (The Art Archive at Art Resource, NY)

industrial accidents. Between 1900 and 1917 seventy-two thousand railroad workers died on the job. Workers responded to these conditions with strikes, violence, and, gradually, unionization.

Immigrants faced more than economic exploitation: they were also subjected to harsh ethnic stereotypes and faced pressure to culturally assimilate. An economic depression in the 1890s increased resentment toward immigrants. Powerful owners of mines, mills, and factories fought the organization of labor unions, fired thousands of workers, slashed wages, and ruthlessly exploited their workers. Workers in turn feared that immigrant labor would drive salaries lower. Some of this antagonism sprang from racism, some from old Protestant suspicions of Roman Catholicism, the faith of many of the new arrivals. Long-standing anti-Semitism against Jewish immigrants from eastern Europe intensified, while increasingly violent agitation against Asians led to race riots in California and finally culminated in the Chinese Exclusion Act of 1882, which denied Chinese laborers entrance to the country. Japanese immigration to the United States was restricted in 1907, so later Japanese immigrants settled in South America, especially Brazil.

Immigrants were received very differently in Latin America, where oligarchs encouraged immigration from Europe, the Middle East, and Japan because they believed these "whiter" workers were superior to native-born, often racially mixed workers. They hoped immigration would whiten their nations. By contrast, in the United States the descendants of northern European Protestants developed prejudices and built social barriers out of their belief that Catholic Irish, southern and eastern European, or Jewish immigrants were not white enough.

◀ **MAP 27.2**   **The Dominion of Canada, 1871**   Shortly after the Dominion of Canada came into being as a self-governing nation within the British Empire in 1867, new provinces were added. Vast areas of Canada were too sparsely populated to achieve provincial status. Alberta and Saskatchewan did not become part of the Dominion until 1905; Newfoundland was added only in 1949.

Immigration to Canada

Canada was sparsely populated in the nineteenth century relative to other areas of the Americas. Provinces of the British colony gained governing autonomy after 1840 and organized a national government, the Dominion of Canada, in 1867 (Map 27.2). British authorities agreed to grant the provinces political independence in order to avoid the disruption and loss of influence that followed U.S. independence, and in return the Dominion retained a symbolic role for the British monarchy. By 1900 Canada still had only a little over 5 million people (as compared to 13.6 million in Mexico and 76 million in the United States). As in the United States and Latin America, native peoples were pushed aside by Canada's development plans, and their population dropped by half or more during the century, many succumbing to the newcomers' diseases. By 1900 there were only about 127,000 indigenous people left in Canada. French Canadians were the largest minority in the population, and they remained different in language, law, and religion.

Russian Immigrant Women in Saskatchewan   These women were Doukhobors, members of a Christian religious sect who came to Canada from Russia seeking religious freedom from tsarist persecution. While most of the men took railroad jobs, the women planted the vast plains with rye, wheat, oats, and flax. Their farms and orchards flourished, and the Doukhobors played an important role in the development of western Canada. (Saskatchewan Archives Board, photo no. R-B 1964)

◀ **MAP 28.2**   **The First World War in Europe** The trench war on the western front was concentrated in Belgium and northern France, while the war in the east encompassed an enormous territory.

Then two nationalist wars, the first and second Balkan wars in 1912 and 1913, finally destroyed the centuries-long Ottoman presence in Europe. This sudden but long-expected event elated Balkan nationalists but dismayed Austria-Hungary's leaders, who feared that Austria-Hungary might next be broken apart.

Within this tense context, Serbian nationalist Gavrilo Princip assassinated Archduke Franz Ferdinand, heir to the Austro-Hungarian throne, and his wife, Sophie, on June 28, 1914, during a state visit to the Bosnian capital of Sarajevo. Austria-Hungary's leaders held Serbia responsible and on July 23 presented Serbia with an unconditional ultimatum that included demands amounting to Austrian control of the Serbian state. When Serbia replied moderately but evasively, Austria began to mobilize and declared war on Serbia on July 28.

Of prime importance in Austria-Hungary's fateful decision was Germany's unconditional support. Kaiser William II and his chancellor, Theobald von Bethmann-Hollweg, realized that war between Austria and Russia was likely, for Russia could not stand by and watch the Serbs be crushed. Yet Bethmann-Hollweg hoped that while Russia (and its ally France) might go to war, Great Britain would remain neutral.

Anticipating a possible conflict, Europe's military leaders had been drawing up comprehensive war plans and timetables for years, and now these, rather than diplomacy, began to dictate policy. On July 28, as Austrian armies bombarded Belgrade, Tsar Nicholas II ordered a partial mobilization against Austria-Hungary but almost immediately found this was impossible. Russia had assumed a war with both Austria and Germany, and it could not mobilize against one without mobilizing against the other. Therefore, on July 29 Russia ordered full mobilization and in effect declared general war. The German general staff had also prepared for a two-front war. Its Schlieffen plan, first drafted in 1905, called for first knocking out France with a lightning attack through neutral Belgium to capture Paris before turning on a slower-to-mobilize Russia. On August 3 German armies invaded Belgium. Great Britain declared war on Germany the following day. In each country the great majority of the population rallied to defend its nation and enthusiastically embraced war in August 1914.

Stalemate and Slaughter

When the Germans invaded Belgium in August 1914, everyone believed "the boys will be home by Christmas." The Belgian army defended its homeland, however, and then fell back to join a rapidly landed British army corps near the Franco-Belgian border. Instead of quickly capturing Paris in a vast encircling movement, German soldiers were advancing slowly along an enormous front in the scorching August heat. On September 6 the French attacked the German line at the Battle of the Marne. For three days France threw everything into the attack. At one point the French government desperately requisitioned all Paris taxis to rush reserves to the frontline troops. Finally the Germans fell back. France had been miraculously saved (Map 28.2).

The two stalled armies now dug in behind rows of trenches, mines, and barbed wire to protect themselves from machine-gun fire. A "no-man's land" of one hundred to three hundred yards lay between the two combatants. Eventually an unbroken line of parallel zigzag trenches stretched over four hundred miles from the Belgian coast to the Swiss frontier. By November 1914 the slaughter on the western front had begun in earnest. For four years battles followed the same plan: after ceaseless heavy artillery shelling to "soften up" the enemy, young soldiers went "over the top" of the trenches in frontal attacks on the enemy's line.

German writer Erich Remarque, who fought on the western front, described a typical attack in his great novel *All Quiet on the Western Front* (1929):

> We see men living with their skulls blown open; we see soldiers run with their two feet cut off. . . . Still the little piece of convulsed earth in which we lie is held. We have yielded no more than a few hundred yards of it as a prize to the enemy. But on every yard there lies a dead man.[3]

The human cost of trench warfare was staggering, while territorial gains were minuscule. The massive French and British offensives during 1915 never gained more than three miles of blood-soaked earth from the enemy. In the Battle of the Somme in summer 1916, the British and French gained an insignificant 125 square miles at a cost of 600,000 dead or wounded. The Germans lost 500,000 men. That same year

Henri de Groux, *The Assault, Verdun*   An eerie portrayal by Belgian artist Henri de Groux (1867–1930) of French troops moving forward in a thick haze of smoke and perhaps clouds of diphosgene, a poisonous gas first used by the Germans at Verdun on June 22, 1916. (Musées des Deux Guerres Mondiales, Paris, France/The Bridgeman Art Library)

the unsuccessful German campaign against Verdun cost 700,000 lives on both sides. The slaughter was made even greater by new weapons of war—including chemical gases, tanks, airplanes, flamethrowers, and the machine gun. British poet Siegfried Sassoon (1886–1967) wrote of the Somme offensive, "I am staring at a sunlit picture of Hell."[4] The year 1917 was equally terrible.

On the eastern front, there was slaughter but not suicidal trench warfare. With the outbreak of war, the "Russian steamroller," as the imperial army was known, immediately moved into eastern Germany but suffered appalling losses against the Germans at the Battles of Tannenberg and the Masurian Lakes in August and September 1914 (see Map 28.2). German and Austrian forces then reversed the Russian advances of 1914 and forced the Russians to retreat deep into their own territory in the 1915 eastern campaign. A staggering 2.5 million Russians were killed, wounded, or taken prisoner.

These changing tides of victory and hopes of territorial gains brought neutral countries into the war. Italy, a member of the Triple Alliance since 1882, declared its neutrality in 1914, charging that Austria had launched a war of aggression. Then in May 1915 Italy joined the Triple Entente of Great Britain, France, and Russia in return for promises of Austrian territory. In September Bulgaria joined the Triple Alliance in order to settle old scores with Serbia.

The War Becomes Global

In October 1914 the Ottoman Empire joined with Austria and Germany, by then known as the Central Powers. The Young Turks (see page 903) were pro-German because the Germans had helped reform the Ottoman armies before the war and had built important railroads, like the one to Baghdad. A German alliance permitted the Turks to renounce the limitations on Ottoman sovereignty imposed by Europeans in the nineteenth century and also to settle old grievances with Russia, the Turks' historic enemy.

The entry of the Ottoman Turks pulled the entire Middle East into the war and made it truly a global conflict. While Russia attacked the Ottomans in the Caucasus, the British protected their rule in Egypt. In 1915, at the Battle of Gallipoli, British forces tried to take the Dardanelles and Constantinople from the Ottoman Turks but were badly defeated. Casualties were high on both sides and included thousands of Australians and New Zealanders. Deeply loyal to the mother country, Australia sent 329,000 men and vast economic aid to Britain during the war. Over 100,000 New Zealanders also served in the war, almost a tenth of New Zealand's entire population, and they suffered a 58 percent casualty rate—one of the highest of any country. Nearly 4,000 native New Zealand Maori soldiers also fought at Gallipoli and on the western front. Ormond Burton, a highly decorated New Zealand infantryman who served in Gallipoli and then in France, later observed that "somewhere between the landing at Anzac [a cove on the Gallipolian peninsula] and the end of the battle of the Somme, New Zealand very definitely became a nation."[5]

The British had more success inciting Arabs to revolt against their Turkish overlords. The foremost Arab leader was Hussein ibn-Ali (1856–1931), who governed much of the Ottoman Empire's territory along the Red Sea, an area known as the Hejaz (see Map 29.1, page 902). In 1915 Hussein won vague British commitments for an independent Arab kingdom. The next year he revolted against the Turks, proclaiming himself king of the Arabs. He joined forces with the British under T. E. Lawrence, who in 1917 led Arab tribesmen and Indian soldiers in a successful guerrilla war against the Turks on the Arabian peninsula. In the Ottoman province of Iraq, Britain occupied Basra in 1914 and captured Baghdad in 1917. In 1918 British armies, aided by imperial forces from Egypt, India, Australia, and New Zealand, totally smashed the old Ottoman state. Thus war brought revolutionary change to the Middle East (see pages 901–905).

Japan, allied with the British since 1902, joined the Triple Entente on August 23, 1914, and began attacking German-controlled colonies and territories in the Pacific. Later that year Japan seized Germany's holdings on the Shandong (Shantung) Peninsula in China and in 1915 forced China to accept Japanese control of Shandong and southern Manchuria. China had declared its neutrality in 1914, which infuriated Chinese patriots and heightened long-standing tensions between China and Japan.

War also spread to colonies in Africa and East Asia. Instead of revolting as the Germans hoped, French and British colonial subjects generally supported the Allied powers. Colonized peoples provided critical supplies and fought in Europe, Africa, and the Ottoman Empire. They also helped local British and French commanders seize Germany's colonies around the globe. More than a million Africans and Asians served in the various armies of the warring powers, with more than double that number serving as porters to carry equipment. Some of the most famous and bravest of these colonial troops were the Senegalese Tirailleurs (colonial riflemen). Drawn from Senegal and French West Africa, over 140,000 fought on the western front, and 31,000 of them died there.

Many of these men joined up to get clothes (uniforms), food, and money for enlisting. Others did so because colonial recruiters promised them better lives when they returned home. Most were illiterate and had no idea of why they were going or what they would experience. One West African infantryman, Kande Kamara, later wrote:

> We black African soldiers were very sorrowful about the white man's war. . . . I didn't really care who was right—whether it was the French or the Germans—I went to fight with the French army and that was all I knew. The reason for war was never disclosed to any soldier. . . . We just fought and fought until we got exhausted and died.[6]

The war had a profound impact on these colonial troops. Fighting against and killing Europeans destroyed the impression, encouraged in the colonies, that the Europeans were superhuman. New concepts like nationalism and individual freedoms—ideals for which the Europeans were supposedly fighting—were carried home to become rallying cries for future liberation struggles.

A crucial turning point in the expanding conflict came in April 1917 when the United States declared war on Germany. American intervention grew out of the war at sea and sympathy for the Triple Entente. At the beginning of the war Britain and France established a naval blockade to strangle the Central Powers. No neutral cargo ship was permitted to sail to Germany. In early 1915 Germany launched a counter-blockade using the new and deadly effective submarine. In May a German submarine sank the British passenger liner *Lusitania* (which, besides regular passengers, was secretly and illegally carrying war materials to Britain). More than a thousand people died, including 139 U.S. citizens. President Woodrow Wilson protested vigorously. Germany was forced to restrict its submarine warfare for almost two years or face almost certain war with the United States.

Early in 1917 the German military command—confident that improved submarines could starve Britain into submission before the United States could come to its rescue—resumed unrestricted submarine warfare. This was a reckless gamble. The United States declared war on Germany and eventually tipped the balance in favor of the Triple Entente.

The Home Front

How did total war affect the home fronts of the major combatants?

The war's impact on civilians was no less massive than on the men crouched in trenches. Total war mobilized entire populations, led to increased state power, and promoted social equality. It also led to dissent and a growing antiwar movement.

Mobilizing for Total War

In August 1914 most Europeans greeted the outbreak of hostilities enthusiastically, believing their own nation was in the right and defending itself from aggression. Yet by mid-October generals and politicians realized that victory required more than patriotism. Combatant countries desperately needed men and weapons. Change had to come, and fast, to keep the war machine from sputtering to a stop.

The change came through national unity governments that began to plan and control economic and social life in order to wage **total war**. Governments imposed rationing, price and wage controls, and even restrictions on workers' freedom of movement. These total-war economies blurred the old distinction between soldiers on battlefields and civilians at home. The ability of central governments to manage and control highly complicated economies increased and strengthened their powers, often along socialist lines.

Germany went furthest in developing a planned economy to wage total war. Soon after war began, the Jewish industrialist Walter Rathenau convinced the German government to set up the War Raw Materials Board to ration and distribute raw materials. Under Rathenau's direction, every useful material from foreign oil to barnyard manure was inventoried and rationed. Food was also rationed. Moreover, the board successfully produced substitutes, such as synthetic rubber and synthetic nitrates, for scarce war supplies. Following the terrible Battles of Verdun and the Somme in 1916, military leaders forced the Reichstag to accept the Auxiliary Service Law, which required all males between seventeen and sixty to work only at jobs considered critical to the war effort. Women also worked in war factories, mines, and steel mills.

As mature liberal democracies, France, Great Britain, and the United States were much less authoritarian in August 1914 than autocratic Russia, Germany, and Austria-Hungary. France and Great Britain also mobilized economically for total war less rapidly and less completely than Germany, as they could import materials from their colonies and from the United States. When it became apparent that the war was not going to end quickly, however, the Western Allies all passed laws giving their governments sweeping powers over all areas of the nation's daily life—including industrial and agricultural production, censorship, education, health and welfare, the curtailment of civil liberties, labor, and foreign aliens.

In June 1915, for example, a serious shortage of shells led the British to establish a Ministry of Munitions that organized private industry for war production, controlled profits, allocated labor, fixed wage rates, and settled labor disputes. By December 1916 the state largely directed, planned, and regulated the British economy. The Espionage Act of June 1917 and the Sedition Act of May 1918 allowed the United States government to keep groups like labor unions, political parties, and ethnic organizations under surveillance. Welfare systems were also adopted in most belligerent countries. Many of these laws were revoked at war's end. Still, they set precedents and were turned to again during the economic depressions of the 1920s and 1930s and World War II.

The Social Impact of War

The social impact of total war was no less profound than the economic impact, though again there were important national variations. The military's insatiable needs—nearly every belligerent power resorted to conscription to put soldiers in the field—created a tremendous demand for workers at home. This situation—seldom, if ever, seen before 1914—brought about momentous changes.

One such change was increased power and prestige for labor unions. Unions cooperated with war governments in return for real participation in important decisions. This entry of labor leaders into policymaking councils paralleled the entry of socialist leaders into the war governments.

Women's roles also changed dramatically. In every belligerent country, large numbers of women left home and domestic service to work in industry, transportation, and offices. A former parlor maid reportedly told her boyfriend as he prepared to leave for France:

> While you are at the front firing shells, I am going into a munitions factory to make shells. The job will not be as well paid as domestic service, it will not be as comfortable as domestic service; it will be much harder work, but it will be my bit, and every time you fire your gun you can remember I am helping to make the shells.[7]

Moreover, women became highly visible—not only as munitions workers but as bank tellers, mail carriers, and even police officers. Women also served as nurses and doctors at the front. (See "Individuals in Society: Vera Brittain," page 872.) In general, the war greatly expanded the range of women's activities and changed attitudes toward women. Although at war's end most women were quickly let go and their jobs were given back to the returning soldiers, their many-sided war effort caused Britain, Germany, and Austria to grant them the right to vote immediately after the war.

Recent scholarship has shown, however, that traditional views of gender—of male roles and female roles—remained remarkably resilient and that there was a significant conservative backlash in the postwar years. Even as the war progressed, many men, particularly soldiers, grew increasingly hostile toward women. Some were angry at mothers, wives, and girlfriends for urging them to enlist and fight in the horrible war. Suggestive posters of scantily clad women were used to remind men of the rewards they would receive for enlisting and fighting, while soldiers with wives and girlfriends back home grew increasingly convinced that they were cheating on them. Others worried that factory or farm jobs had been taken by women and there would be no work when they returned home. Men were also concerned that if women received the vote at war's end, they would vote themselves into power. These concerns, as well as anxiety over women losing their femininity, are reflected in a letter from Private G. F. Wilby, serving in East Africa, to his fiancée in London, Ethel Baxter, in August 1918:

> Whatever you do, don't go in Munitions or anything in that line — just fill a Woman's position and remain a woman. . . . I want to return and find the same loveable little woman that I left behind — not a coarse thing more of a man than a woman.[8]

War promoted social equality, blurring class distinctions and lessening the gap between rich and poor. Greater equality was reflected in full employment, rationing according to physical needs, and a sharing of hardships. Society became more uniform and more egalitarian.

Growing Political Tensions

During the war's first two years, belief in a just cause and patriotic nationalism united soldiers and civilians behind their various national leaders. Each government employed censorship and propaganda to maintain popular support.

By spring 1916, however, cracks were appearing under the strain of total war. In April Irish nationalists in Dublin unsuccessfully rose up against British rule in the Easter Rebellion. Strikes and protest marches over inadequate food flared up on every home front. In April 1917 nearly half the French infantry divisions mutinied for two months after suffering enormous losses in the Second Battle of the Aisne. Later that year there was a massive mutiny of Russian soldiers supporting the revolution.

The Central Powers experienced the most strain. In October 1916 a young socialist assassinated

"Never Forget!" This 1915 French poster with a passionate headline dramatizes Germany's brutal invasion of Belgium in 1914. The "rape of Belgium" featured prominently — and effectively — in anti-German propaganda. (© Mary Evans Picture Library/The Image Works)

INDIVIDUALS IN SOCIETY ◆ Vera Brittain

Although the Great War upended millions of lives, it struck Europe's young people with the greatest force. For Vera Brittain (1893–1970), as for so many in her generation, the war became life's defining experience, which she captured forever in her famous autobiography, *Testament of Youth* (1933).

Brittain grew up in a wealthy business family in northern England, bristling at small-town conventions and discrimination against women. Very close to her brother Edward, two years her junior, Brittain read voraciously and dreamed of being a successful writer. Finishing boarding school and beating down her father's objections, she prepared for Oxford's rigorous entry exams and won a scholarship to its women's college. Brittain also fell in love with Roland Leighton, an equally brilliant student from a literary family and her brother's best friend. All three, along with two more close friends, Victor Richardson and Geoffrey Thurlow, confidently prepared to enter Oxford in late 1914.

When war suddenly approached in July 1914, Brittain shared with millions of Europeans a thrilling surge of patriotic support for her government, a prowar enthusiasm she later played down in her published writings. She wrote in her diary that her "great fear" was that England would declare its neutrality and commit the "grossest treachery" toward France.* She seconded Roland's decision to enlist, agreeing with her sweetheart's glamorous view of war as "very ennobling and very beautiful." Later, exchanging anxious letters in 1915 with Roland in France, Vera began to see the conflict in personal, human terms. She wondered if any victory or defeat could be worth Roland's life.

Struggling to quell her doubts, Brittain redoubled her commitment to England's cause and volunteered as an army nurse. For the next three years she served with distinction in military hospitals in London, Malta, and northern France, repeatedly torn between the vision of noble sacrifice and the reality of human tragedy. She lost her sexual inhibitions caring for mangled male bodies, and she longed to consummate her love with Roland. Awaiting his return on leave on Christmas Day in 1915, she was greeted instead with a telegram: Roland had been killed two days before.

Roland's death was the first of the devastating blows that eventually overwhelmed Brittain's idealistic patriotism. In 1917 first Geoffrey and then Victor died from gruesome wounds. In early 1918, as the last great German offensive covered the floors of her war-zone hospital with maimed and dying German prisoners, the

---

*Quoted in the excellent study by P. Berry and M. Bostridge, *Vera Brittain: A Life* (London: Virago Press, 2001), p. 59; additional quotations are from pp. 80 and 136.

Austria's chief minister. Conflicts among nationalities grew, and both Czech and Yugoslav leaders demanded autonomous democratic states for their peoples. By 1917 German political unity was also collapsing, and prewar social conflicts were re-emerging. A coalition of Socialists and Catholics in the Reichstag called for a compromise "peace bone-weary Vera felt a common humanity and saw only more victims. A few weeks later brother Edward—her last hope—died in action. When the war ended, she was, she said, a "complete automaton," with "my deepest emotions paralyzed if not dead."

Returning to Oxford and finishing her studies, Brittain gradually recovered. She formed a deep, restorative friendship with another talented woman writer, Winifred Holtby, published novels and articles, and became a leader in the feminist campaign for gender equality. She also married and had children. But her wartime memories were always there. Finally, Brittain succeeded in coming to grips with them in *Testament of Youth*, her powerful antiwar autobiography. The unflinching narrative spoke to the experiences of an entire generation and became a runaway bestseller. Above all, perhaps, Brittain captured the ambivalent, contradictory character of the war, in which millions of young people found excitement, courage, and common purpose but succeeded only in destroying their lives with their superhuman efforts and futile sacrifices. Becoming ever more committed to pacifism, Brittain opposed England's entry into World War II.

QUESTIONS FOR ANALYSIS

1. What were Brittain's initial feelings toward the war? How and why did they change as the conflict continued?

2. Why did Brittain volunteer as a nurse, as many women did? How might wartime nursing have influenced women of her generation?

3. In portraying the ambivalent, contradictory character of World War I for Europe's youth, was Brittain describing the contradictory character of all modern warfare? Explain your answer.

LaunchPad
ONLINE DOCUMENT PROJECT

What words and images did governments use to recruit women to serve in World War I? Examine several recruitment posters aimed at women, and then complete a quiz and writing assignment based on the evidence and details from this chapter.

See inside the front cover to learn more.

without annexations or reparations," something conservatives and military leaders found unthinkable. Thus Germany, like its ally Austria-Hungary and its enemy France, began to crack in 1917. But it was Russia that collapsed first and saved the Central Powers—for a time.

The Russian Revolution

What factors led to the Russian Revolution, and what was its outcome?

The 1917 Russian Revolution, directly related to the Great War, opened a new era with a radically new prototype of state and society that changed the course of the twentieth century.

The Fall of Imperial Russia

Imperial Russia in 1914 was still predominantly a rural and nonurbanized society. Russia came late to industrialization (see page 741), and, although rapidly expanding, industrialization was still in its early stages. Peasants made up perhaps 80 percent of the population, although by 1914 a large number of these did seasonal work in the cities. To prevent peasant unrest, Prime Minister Pyotr Stolypin (stal-EE-pihn) instituted agrarian reforms between 1906 and 1911 to replace the communal system of peasant land use with one that encouraged individual, private landownership. Stolypin hoped to create a class of politically conservative, capitalist farmers — an agrarian bourgeoisie. The permanent urban working class remained small, and many of these were simply commuters from the countryside. Besides the royal family and the nobility, Russian society consisted of the bourgeoisie (the elite, educated upper and middle classes, such as liberal politicians, propertied and professional classes, military officer corps, and landowners) and the proletariat (the popular masses, such as the urban working class, and rank-and-file soldiers and sailors). These two factions contended for power when the tsar abdicated in 1917.

Like their allies and their enemies, Russians embraced war with patriotic enthusiasm in 1914. At the Winter Palace, while kneeling throngs sang "God Save the Tsar," Tsar Nicholas II (r. 1894–1917) vowed never to make peace as long as the enemy stood on Russian soil. For a moment Russia was united, but soon the war began to take its toll.

Unprecedented artillery barrages quickly exhausted Russia's supplies of shells and ammunition, and better-equipped German armies inflicted terrible losses — 1.5 million casualties and nearly 1 million captured in 1915 alone. Russian soldiers were sent to the front without rifles; they were told to find their arms among the dead. The Duma, Russia's lower house of parliament, and *zemstvos* (zemst-vohs), local governments, led the effort toward full mobilization on the home front. These efforts improved the military situation, but overall Russia mobilized less effectively for total war than did the other warring nations.

Although limited industrial capacity was a serious handicap in a war against highly industrialized Germany, Russia's real problem was leadership. Under the constitution resulting from the 1905 revolution (see page 742), the tsar retained complete control over the bureaucracy and the army. A kindly, slightly dull-witted man, Nicholas distrusted the moderate Duma and rejected popular involvement. As a result, the Duma, whose members came from the elite classes, and the popular masses became increasingly critical of the tsar's leadership and the appalling direction of the war. In response, Nicholas (who had no military background) traveled to the front in September 1915 to lead Russia's armies — and thereafter received all the blame for Russian losses.

His departure was a fatal turning point. His German-born wife, Tsarina Alexandra, took control of the government and the home front. She tried to rule absolutely in her husband's absence with an uneducated Siberian preacher, Rasputin, as her most trusted adviser. Rasputin gained her trust by claiming he could stop the bleeding of her hemophiliac son, Alexei, heir to the throne. On November 1, 1916, opposition party leader Pavel Milyukov, speaking before the Duma, recounted the government's failures and demanded, "Is this stupidity or is it treason?"[9] In a desperate attempt to right the situation, three members of the high aristocracy murdered Rasputin in December 1916. In this atmosphere of unreality, the government slid steadily toward revolution.

Large-scale strikes, demonstrations, and protest marches were now commonplace, as were bread shortages. On March 8, 1917, a women's bread march in Petrograd (formerly St. Petersburg) started riots, which spread throughout the city. While his ministers fled the city, the tsar ordered that peace be restored, but discipline broke down, and the soldiers and police joined the revolutionary crowd. The Duma declared a provisional government on March 12, 1917. Three days later, Nicholas abdicated.

The Provisional Government

The **March Revolution** was joyfully accepted throughout the country. A new government formed in May 1917, with the understanding that an elected democratic government, ruling under a new constitution drafted by a future Constituent Assembly, would replace it when circumstances permitted. After generations of authoritarianism, the provisional government established equality before the law; freedom of religion, speech, and assembly; the right of unions to organize and strike; and other classic liberal measures. But the provisional government represented the elite faction of the Russian population, as opposed to the popular masses. Many members were westernized Russians, who looked admiringly at the West for models of modernization, industrialization, and government. There were some socialists among them, but these rejected social (that is, Communist) revolution.

The provisional government soon made two fatal decisions that turned the people against the new government. First, it refused to confiscate large landholdings and give them to peasants, fearing that such drastic action in the countryside would only complete the disintegration of Russia's peasant army. Second, the government decided that the continuation of war was still the all-important national duty and that international alliances had to be honored. Neither decision was popular. The peasants believed that when the tsar's autocratic rule ended, so too did the nobles' title to the land, which was now theirs for the taking. The army believed that the March Revolution meant the end of the war.

From its first day, the provisional government had to share power (dual power) with a formidable rival that represented the popular masses—the **Petrograd Soviet** (or council) of Workers' and Soldiers' Deputies. Modeled on the revolutionary soviets of 1905, the Petrograd Soviet comprised two to three thousand workers, soldiers, and socialist intellectuals. This counter-government, or half government, issued its own radical orders, further weakening the provisional government. Most famous of these was Army Order No. 1, issued in March 1917, which stripped officers of their authority and gave power to elected committees of common soldiers.

Order No. 1 led to a total collapse of army discipline. Peasant soldiers began "voting with their feet," to use Lenin's graphic phrase. They returned to their villages to get a share of the land that peasants were seizing from landowners, either through peasant soviets (councils) or by force, in a great agrarian upheaval. Through the summer of 1917, the provisional government, led from July by the socialist Alexander Kerensky, became increasingly more conservative and authoritarian as it tried to maintain law and order and protect property (such as nobles' land and factories). The government was being threatened from one side by an advancing German army and from the other by proletarian forces, urban and rural alike, shouting "All power to the soviets!" and calling for an even more radical revolution.

Lenin and the Bolshevik Revolution

Most traditional accounts of the two Russian revolutions in 1917 written through the twentieth century by both anti-Soviet Russian and Western scholars present a Russia that in March successfully overthrew the tsar's autocratic rule and replaced it with a liberal, Western-style democracy. Then in November a small group of hard-core radicals, led by Vladimir Lenin, somehow staged a second revolution and installed an atheistic Communist government. More recently, however, and especially since the Soviet archives were opened in the 1990s following the dissolution of the Soviet Union, a different picture is emerging. Scholars are recognizing that the second revolution had widespread popular support and that Lenin was often following events as much as leading them.

Born into the middle class, Vladimir Ilyich Lenin (1870–1924) became an enemy of imperial Russia when his older brother was executed for plotting to kill the tsar in 1887. As a law student Lenin studied Marxist doctrines with religious ferocity. Exiled to Siberia for three years because of socialist agitation, Lenin lived in western Europe after his release for seventeen years and developed his own revolutionary interpretations of Marxist thought (see page 728).

Three interrelated ideas were central for Lenin. First, he stressed that only violent revolution could destroy capitalism. Second, unlike the socialist members of the provisional government, Lenin believed that a socialist revolution was possible even in a country like Russia. According to classical Marxist theory, a society must have reached the capitalist, industrial stage of development before its urban workers, the proletariat, can rise up and overthrow the owners of the means of production, the bourgeoisie, and create a Communist society. Because Russia was only just ending the feudal stage of economic development and entering the industrial stage, socialists and Marxists fiercely disagreed as to whether Russia was ready for a Communist revolution. Lenin thought that although the industrial working class was small, the peasants, who made up the bulk of the army and navy, were also potential revolutionaries. Third, Lenin believed that at a given moment revolution was determined more by human leadership than by vast historical laws. He called for a highly disciplined workers' party, strictly controlled by a dedicated elite of intellectuals and full-time revolutionaries like him. This "vanguard of the proletariat" would not stop until revolution brought it to power.

Lenin's ideas did not go unchallenged by other Russian Marxists. At a Social Democratic Labor Party congress in London in 1903, Lenin demanded a small, disciplined, elitist party; his opponents wanted a more democratic party with mass

Lenin and His Supporters   Vladimir Lenin (center) with two other major figures of the Russian Revolution, Joseph Stalin (left) and Mikhail Kalinin (right). After Lenin's death in January 1924, Stalin moved to seize power and ruled the Soviet Union until his death in 1953. Kalinin was one of Lenin's earliest followers and then supported Stalin in the power struggle after Lenin's death. He was one of the few "old Bolsheviks" to survive Stalin's purges and received a large state funeral following his death from natural causes in 1946. (Photo by Keystone-France/Gamma-Keystone via Getty Images)

membership. The Russian Marxists split into two rival factions. Because his side won one crucial vote at the congress, Lenin's camp became known as **Bolsheviks**, or "majority group"; his opponents were Mensheviks, or "minority group."

In March 1917 Lenin and nearly all the other leading Bolsheviks were living in exile abroad or in Russia's remotest corners. From neutral Switzerland Lenin opposed the war as a product of imperialistic rivalries and saw it as an opportunity for socialist revolution. After the March Revolution, the German government provided safe passage for Lenin across Germany and back into Russia, hoping he would undermine Russia's sagging war effort. They were not disappointed. Arriving in Petrograd on April 16, Lenin attacked at once, issuing his famous April Theses. To the Petrograd Bolsheviks' great astonishment, he rejected all cooperation with what he called the "bourgeois" provisional government — he didn't wanted "dual power." He called for exactly what the popular masses themselves were demanding: "All power to the soviets!" and "Peace, Land, Bread!" Bolshevik support increased through the summer, culminating in mass demonstrations in Petrograd on July 16–20 (known as the July Days) by soldiers, sailors, and workers. Lenin and the Bolshevik Central Committee had not planned these demonstrations and were completely unprepared to support them. Nonetheless, the provisional government labeled Lenin and other leading Bolsheviks traitors and ordered them arrested. Lenin had to flee to Finland.

Meanwhile, however, the provisional government itself was collapsing. The coalition between liberals and socialists was breaking apart as their respective power bases — bourgeoisie and proletariat — demanded they move further to the right or left. Prime Minister Kerensky's unwavering support for the war lost him all credit with the army, the only force that might have saved him and democratic government in

Russia. In early September an attempted right-wing military coup failed as Petrograd workers organized themselves as Red Guards to defend the city and then convinced the coup's soldiers to join them. Although the workers' actions were organized by local unions and factories—the Bolshevik leaders had no hand in stopping the coup—the Bolsheviks gained more support nevertheless. The Bolsheviks were untainted by any association with the provisional government or the bourgeoisie and were seen as the only party completely committed to a proletarian revolution. Lenin, from his exile in Finland, now called for an armed Bolshevik insurrection before the Second All-Russian Congress of Soviets met in early November.

In October the Bolsheviks gained a fragile majority in the Petrograd Soviet. Lenin did not return to Russia until mid-October and even then remained in hiding. It was Lenin's supporter Leon Trotsky (1879–1940), an independent radical Marxist and later the commander of the Red Army, who brilliantly executed the Bolshevik seizure of power. On November 6 militant Trotsky followers joined with trusted Bolshevik soldiers to seize government buildings and arrest provisional government members. That evening Lenin came out of hiding and took control of the revolution. The following day revolutionary forces seized the Winter Palace, and Kerensky capitulated. At the Congress of Soviets, a Bolshevik majority declared that all power had passed to the soviets and named Lenin head of the new government.

The Bolsheviks came to power for three key reasons. First, by late 1917 democracy had given way to anarchy as the popular masses no longer supported the provisional government. Second, in Lenin and Trotsky the Bolsheviks had a truly superior leadership who were utterly determined to provoke a Marxist revolution. Third, the Bolsheviks appealed to soldiers, urban workers, and peasants who were exhausted by war and eager for socialism.

Dictatorship and Civil War

The Bolsheviks' true accomplishment was not taking power but keeping it and conquering the chaos they had helped create. Lenin was able to profit from developments over which he and the Bolsheviks had no control. Since summer 1917 an unstoppable peasant revolution had swept across Russia, as peasants divided among themselves the estates of the landlords and the church. Thus Lenin's first law, which supposedly gave land to the peasants, actually merely approved what peasants were already doing. Lenin then met urban workers' greatest demand with a decree giving local workers' committees direct control of individual factories.

The Bolsheviks proclaimed their regime a "provisional workers' and peasants' government," promising that a freely elected Constituent Assembly would draw up a new constitution. However, when Bolshevik delegates won fewer than one-fourth of the seats in free elections in November, the Constituent Assembly met for only one day, on January 18, 1918, after which it was permanently disbanded by Bolshevik soldiers acting under Lenin's orders.

Lenin then moved to make peace with Germany, at any price. That price was very high. Germany demanded the Soviet government surrender all its western territories (which contained a third of old Russia's population) in the Treaty of Brest-Litovsk (BREHST lih-TAWFSK), in March 1918. With Germany's defeat eight months later, the treaty was nullified, but it allowed Lenin time to escape the disaster of continued war and pursue his goal of absolute political power for the Bolsheviks—now renamed Communists—within Russia.

The war's end and the demise of the democratically elected Constituent Assembly revealed Bolshevik rule as a dictatorship. "Long live the [democratic] soviets; down with the Bolsheviks" became a popular slogan. Officers of the old army organized so-called White opposition to the Bolsheviks in southern Russia, Ukraine, Siberia, and west of Petrograd and plunged the country into civil war from November 1917 to October 1922. The Whites came from many political factions and were united only by their hatred of the Bolsheviks—the Reds. White armies attacked the Red Army from the east (Siberia), the south, and the northwest. By October 1919 it appeared they might triumph as they closed in on Lenin's government (which made its capital in Moscow from March 1919), but they did not. Eventually 125,000 Reds and 175,000 Whites and Poles were killed before the Red Army under Trotsky's command captured Vladivostok in October 1922 and brought the civil war to an end.

The Bolsheviks' Red Army won for several reasons. Strategically, they controlled the center, while the disunited Whites attacked from the fringes. Moreover, the Whites' poorly defined political program failed to unite all of the Bolsheviks' foes under a progressive democratic banner. Most important, the Communists developed a better army, against which the divided Whites were no match.

The Bolsheviks also mobilized the home front. Establishing War Communism— the application of the total-war concept to a civil conflict—they seized grain from peasants, introduced rationing, nationalized all banks and industry, and required everyone to work. Although these measures contributed to a breakdown of normal economic activity, they also served to maintain labor discipline and to keep the Red Army supplied.

Revolutionary terror also contributed to the Communist victory. The old tsarist secret police was re-established as the Cheka, which hunted down and executed thousands of real or supposed foes, including the tsar and his family. During the so-called Red Terror of 1918–1920, the Cheka sowed fear, silenced opposition, and executed an estimated 250,000 "class enemies."

Finally, foreign military intervention in the civil war ended up helping the Communists. The Allies sent troops to prevent war materiel that they had sent to the provisional government from being captured by the Germans. After the Soviet government nationalized all foreign-owned factories without compensation and refused to pay foreign debts, Western governments began to support White armies. While these efforts did little to help the Whites' cause, they did permit the Communists to appeal to the ethnic Russians' patriotic nationalism.

The War's Consequences

What were the global consequences of the First World War?

In spring 1918 the Germans launched their last major attack against France. It failed, and Germany was defeated. Austria-Hungary and the Ottoman Empire broke apart and ceased to exist. The armistice came in November, and in January 1919, as civil war spread in Russia and chaos engulfed much of eastern Europe, the victorious Western Allies came together in Paris hoping to establish a lasting peace.

Laboring intensively, the Allies soon worked out peace terms with Germany, created the peacekeeping League of Nations (see page 881), and reorganized eastern Europe and southwest Asia. The 1919 peace settlement, however, failed to establish a lasting peace or to resolve the issues that had brought the world to war. World War I and the treaties that ended it shaped the course of the twentieth century, often in horrible ways. Surely this was the ultimate tragedy of the Great War that cost $332 billion and left 10 million people dead and another 20 million wounded.

The End of the War

Peace and an end to the war did not come easily. Victory over revolutionary Russia had temporarily boosted sagging German morale, and in spring 1918 the German army under General Ludendorff attacked France once more. German armies came within thirty-five miles of Paris before they were stopped in July at the Second Battle of the Marne, where 140,000 fresh American soldiers saw action. Adding 2 million men in arms to the war effort by August, the late but massive American intervention decisively tipped the scales in favor of Allied victory.

By September British, French, and American armies were advancing steadily on all fronts. On October 4 the German emperor formed a new, more liberal German government to sue for peace. As negotiations over an armistice dragged on, the frustrated German people rose up. On November 3 sailors in Kiel (keel) mutinied, and throughout northern Germany soldiers and workers established revolutionary councils on the Russian soviet model. Austria-Hungary surrendered to the Allies the same day. With army discipline collapsing, Kaiser William abdicated and fled to Holland. Socialist leaders in Berlin proclaimed a German republic on November 9 and agreed to tough Allied terms of surrender. The armistice went into effect on November 11, 1918.

Germany's 1918 November Revolution resembled Russia's 1917 March Revolution. In both countries a popular uprising toppled an authoritarian monarchy, and moderate socialists took control of the government. But when Germany's radical socialists tried to seize power, the moderate socialists called on the army to crush the attempted coup. Thus Germany had a political revolution, but without a Communist second installment.

The Paris Peace Treaties

Seventy delegates from twenty-seven nations attended the opening of the Paris Peace Conference at the Versailles Palace on January 18, 1919. They then adjourned to different sites around Paris to negotiate the various treaties that would end the war. By August 1920 five major treaties with the defeated powers had been agreed upon: the Treaty of Saint-Germain (Austria); the Treaty of Neuilly (Bulgaria); the Treaty of Trianon (Hungary); the Treaty of Sèvres, subsequently revised by the Treaty of Lausanne in 1923 (Ottoman Empire / Republic of Turkey); and the famous Treaty of Versailles, which laid out peace terms with Germany and also included the Covenant of the League of Nations and an article establishing the International Labour Organization. The conference also yielded a number of minor treaties, unilateral declarations, bilateral treaties, and League of Nations mandates (Map 28.3). The delegates met with great expectations. A young British diplomat later wrote that the victors "were journeying

MAP 28.3 **Territorial Changes in Europe After World War I** The Great War brought tremendous changes to eastern Europe. Empires were shattered, new nations were established, and a dangerous power vacuum was created by the relatively weak states established between Germany and Soviet Russia.

to Paris . . . to found a new order in Europe. We were preparing not Peace only, but Eternal Peace."[10]

This idealism was strengthened by President Wilson's January 1918 peace proposal, the Fourteen Points. Wilson stressed national self-determination and the rights of small countries and called for the creation of a **League of Nations**, a permanent international organization designed to protect member states from aggression and avert future wars.

The real powers at the conference were the United States, Great Britain, and France. Germany and Russia were excluded, and Italy's role was limited. Almost immediately the three Allies began to quarrel. President Wilson insisted that the first order of business be the League of Nations. Wilson had his way, although Prime Ministers Lloyd George of Great Britain and, especially, Georges Clemenceau of France were unenthusiastic. They were primarily concerned with punishing Germany.

The "Big Three" were soon in a stalemate over Germany's fate. Although personally inclined to make a somewhat moderate peace with Germany, Lloyd George felt pressured for a victory worthy of the sacrifices of total war. As Rudyard Kipling summed up the general British feeling at war's end, the Germans were "a people with the heart of beasts."[11] Clemenceau also wanted revenge and lasting security for France, which, he believed, required the creation of a buffer state between France and Germany, Germany's permanent demilitarization, and vast German reparations. Wilson, supported by Lloyd George, would hear none of this.

In the end, Clemenceau agreed to a compromise. He gave up the French demand for a Rhineland buffer state in return for a formal defensive alliance with the United States and Great Britain. Both Wilson and Lloyd George also promised their countries would come to France's aid if attacked. Thus Clemenceau appeared to win his goal of French security, as Wilson had won his of a permanent international organization.

The **Treaty of Versailles** was the first step toward re-establishing international order, though it was an order that favored the victorious Allies. Germany's colonies were given to France, Britain, and Japan as League of Nations mandates. Germany's territorial losses within Europe were minor: Alsace-Lorraine was returned to France, and parts of Germany were ceded to the new Polish state (see Map 28.3). The treaty limited Germany's army to one hundred thousand men and allowed no new military fortifications in the Rhineland.

More harshly, the Allies declared that Germany (with Austria) was responsible for the war and therefore had to pay reparations equal to all civilian damages caused by the war. These much-criticized "war-guilt" and "reparations" clauses expressed inescapable popular demands for German blood. The actual reparations figure was not set, however, leaving open the possibility that it might be set at a reasonable level in the future when tempers had cooled.

When presented with the treaty, the German government protested vigorously, but there was no alternative. On June 28, 1919, in the great Hall of Mirrors at Versailles (where Germany had forced France to sign the armistice ending the Franco-Prussian War), German representatives of the ruling moderate Social Democrats and the Catholic Party signed the treaty.

The other Paris treaties also had far-reaching consequences for the course of the twentieth century. In eastern Europe, Poland regained its independence (see Map 19.1, page 576), and the independent states of Austria, Hungary, Czechoslovakia, and a larger Romania were created out of the Austro-Hungarian Empire (see Map 28.3). A greatly expanded Serbian monarchy united Slavs in the western Balkans and took the name Yugoslavia.

Controversially, Britain and France extended their power in the Middle East, taking advantage of the breakup of the Ottoman Empire. Despite strong French objections, Hussein ibn-Ali's son Faisal (1885–1933) attended the Paris Peace Conference, but his efforts to secure Arab independence came to nothing. President Wilson wanted to give the Arab case serious consideration, but Wilson's and the Arabs' opposition was brushed aside. As League of Nations mandates, the French received Lebanon and Syria, and Britain took Iraq and Palestine. Palestine was to include a Jewish national homeland first promised by Britain in 1917 in the Balfour Declaration (see page 903). Only Hussein's Arab kingdom of Hejaz received independence. These Allied acquisitions, although officially League of Nations mandates, were one of the most imperialistic elements of the peace settlement. Another was mandating Germany's holdings in China to Japan (see page 899). Germany's African colonies were mandated to Great Britain, France, South Africa, and Belgium. The mandate system left colonial peoples in the Middle East, Asia (see Chapter 29), and Africa bitterly disappointed and demonstrated that the age of Western and Eastern imperialism lived on.

American Rejection of the Versailles Treaty

The 1919 peace settlement was not perfect, but for war-shattered Europe it was an acceptable beginning. The remaining problems could be worked out in the future. Moreover, Allied leaders wanted a quick settlement for another reason: they detested Lenin and feared his Bolshevik Revolution might spread.

It came as a major shock, therefore, when the United States quickly reverted to its prewar preferences for isolationism and the U.S. Senate rejected the Versailles treaty. Republican senators led by Henry Cabot Lodge believed the treaty gave away Congress's constitutional right to declare war. In failing health, Wilson rejected all attempts at compromise. His obstinacy ensured the treaty would never be ratified in any form and that the United States would never join the League of Nations. Moreover, the Senate refused to ratify Wilson's defensive alliance with France and Great Britain. Using U.S. action as an excuse, Great Britain also refused to ratify its defensive alliance with France. Betrayed by its allies, France stood alone, and the great hopes of early 1919 had turned to ashes by year's end.

The Search for Peace and Political Stability, 1919–1929

How did leaders deal with the political dimensions of uncertainty and try to re-establish peace and prosperity in the interwar years?

The Versailles settlement had established a shaky truce, not a solid peace, and the pursuit of real and lasting peace in the first half of the interwar years proved difficult for many reasons. Germany hated the Treaty of Versailles. France was fearful and isolated. Britain was undependable, and the United States had turned its back on Europe's problems. Eastern Europe was in ferment, and no one could predict Communist Russia's future. Moreover, the international economic situation was poor and was greatly complicated by war debts and disrupted patterns of trade. Yet for a time, from 1925 to late 1929, it appeared that peace and stability were within reach.

Germany and the Western Powers

Germany held the key to lasting peace, but plagued by Communist uprisings, reactionary plots, and popular disillusionment with losing the war, Germany's moderate socialists and their liberal and Catholic supporters faced an enormous challenge. They needed time (and luck) if they were to establish a peaceful and democratic republic. Progress in this direction required understanding yet firm treatment of Germany by the victorious Western Allies. Yet nearly all Germans and many other observers immediately and for decades after believed the Versailles treaty represented a harsh dictated peace and should be revised or repudiated as soon as possible. Many right-wing Germans, including Adolf Hitler, believed there had been no defeat; instead they believed German soldiers had been betrayed (*Dolchstoss*—"stabbed in the back") by liberals, Marxists, Jews, and other "November criminals" who had surrendered in order to seize power.

Historians have recently begun to reassess the treaty's terms, however, and many scholars currently view them as relatively reasonable. They argue that, given Germany's efforts and losses in the war, Germans would not have been satisfied with any treaty imposed on them, and that much of German anger toward the Allies, as well as much of Hitler's appeal, was based more on perception than reality. With the collapse of Austria-Hungary, the dissolution of the Ottoman Empire, and the revolution in Russia, Germany emerged from the war an even stronger power in eastern Europe than before, and economically stronger and more populated than France or Great Britain. Without the costs of funding a military, Germany could direct more of the national budget to reconstruction and reparation payments. Moreover, when contrasted with the extremely harsh Treaty of Brest-Litovsk that Germany had forced on Lenin's Russia, and the peace terms Germany intended to impose on the Allies if they won the war, the Versailles treaty was far from being a vindictive and crippling peace. Had it been, Germany could hardly have become the economic and military juggernaut that it was only twenty years later.

This is not to say, however, that France did not seek some degree of revenge on Germany for both the Franco-Prussian War (see page 740) and the Great War. Most of the war on the western front had been fought on French soil. The expected reconstruction costs and the amount of war debts owed to the United States were staggering. Thus the French believed that heavy German reparations were an economic necessity that could hold Germany down indefinitely and would enable France to realize its goal of security.

The British soon felt differently. Prewar Germany had been Great Britain's second-best market, and after the war a healthy, prosperous Germany appeared to be essential to the British economy. In addition, the British were suspicious of France's army—the largest in Europe—and the British and French were at odds over their League of Nations mandates in the Middle East.

While France and Britain drifted in different directions, the Allied reparations commission completed its work. In April 1921 it announced that Germany had to pay the enormous sum of 132 billion gold marks ($33 billion) in annual installments of 2.5 billion gold marks. The young German republic—known as the Weimar Republic—made its first payment in 1921. Then in 1922, wracked by rapid inflation and political assassinations and motivated by hostility and arrogance as well, the Weimar Republic announced its inability to pay more and proposed a reparations moratorium for three years.

The British were willing to accept a moratorium, but the French were not. Led by their prime minister, Raymond Poincaré (1860–1934), they decided they had to either call Germany's bluff or see the entire peace settlement dissolve to France's great disadvantage. So in January 1923 French and Belgian armies occupied the Ruhr district, industrial Germany's heartland, creating the most serious international crisis of the 1920s.

Strengthened by a wave of patriotism, the German government ordered the people of the Ruhr to stop working and to nonviolently resist French occupation. The French responded by sealing off not only the Ruhr but also the entire Rhineland from the rest of Germany, letting in only enough food to prevent starvation.

By summer 1923 France and Germany were engaged in a great test of wills. French armies could not collect reparations from striking workers at gunpoint. But French occupation was paralyzing Germany and its economy. Needing to support the striking Ruhr workers and their employers, the German government began to print money to pay its bills. Prices soared, and German money rapidly lost all value. In 1919 one American dollar equaled nine German marks; by November 1923 it took over 4.2 trillion German marks to purchase one American dollar. Many retired and middle-class people saw their savings wiped out. Catastrophic inflation cruelly mocked the old middle-class virtues of thrift, caution, and self-reliance. Many Germans felt betrayed. They hated and blamed the Western governments, their own government, big business, the Jews, the workers, and the Communists for their misfortune. The crisis left them psychologically prepared to follow radical right-wing leaders, including Adolf Hitler and the new Nazi Party.

In August 1923, as the mark's value fell and political unrest grew throughout Germany, Gustav Stresemann (1878–1929) became German chancellor. Stresemann adopted a compromising attitude. He called off the peaceful resistance campaign in the Ruhr and in October agreed in principle to pay reparations, but asked for a re-examination of Germany's ability to pay. Poincaré accepted. Thus, after five years of hostility and tension, Germany and France, with British and American help, decided to try compromise and cooperation.

Hope in Foreign Affairs

In 1924 an international committee of financial experts headed by American banker Charles G. Dawes met to re-examine reparations. The resulting Dawes Plan (1924) was accepted by France, Germany, and Britain. Germany's yearly reparations were reduced and linked to the level of German economic prosperity. Germany would also receive large loans from the United States to promote German recovery, as well as to pay reparations to France and Britain, thus enabling those countries to repay the large sums they owed the United States.

This circular flow of international payments was complicated and risky, but it worked for a while. Germany experienced a spectacular economic recovery. With continual inflows of American capital, Germany paid about $1.3 billion in reparations in 1927 and 1928, enabling France and Britain to pay the United States. Thus the Americans belatedly played a part in the general economic settlement that facilitated the worldwide recovery of the late 1920s.

This economic settlement was matched by a political settlement. In 1925 European leaders met in Locarno, Switzerland. Germany and France solemnly pledged to accept their common border, and both Britain and Italy agreed to fight either France or Germany if one invaded the other. Stresemann also agreed to settle boundary disputes with Poland and Czechoslovakia by peaceful means, and France promised those countries military aid if Germany attacked them. For years a "spirit of Locarno" gave Europeans a sense of growing security and stability in international affairs.

Other developments also strengthened hopes for international peace. In 1926 Germany joined the League of Nations, and in 1928 fifteen countries signed the Kellogg-Briand Pact, initiated by French prime minister Aristide Briand and American secretary of state Frank B. Kellogg. The signing nations "condemned and renounced war as an instrument of national policy." The pact fostered the cautious optimism of the late 1920s and also encouraged the hope that the United States would accept its international responsibilities.

Hope in Democratic Government

European domestic politics also offered reason for hope. During the Ruhr occupation and the great inflation, Germany's republican government appeared ready to collapse. In 1923 Communists momentarily entered provincial governments, which frightened Europe's leaders, who worried that Communist Bolsheviks would carry the revolution to the West. In November an obscure politician named Adolf Hitler proclaimed a "national socialist revolution" in a Munich beer hall. Hitler's plot to seize government control was poorly organized and easily crushed. Hitler was sentenced to prison, where he outlined his theories and program in his book **Mein Kampf** (*My Struggle*, 1925). Throughout the 1920s Hitler's National Socialist Party attracted support from only a few fanatical anti-Semites, ultranationalists, and disgruntled former servicemen.

The moderate businessmen who tended to dominate the various German coalition governments believed that economic prosperity demanded good relations with the Western powers, and they supported parliamentary government at home. Elections were held regularly, and as the economy boomed, republican democracy appeared to have growing support among a majority of Germans. There were, however, sharp political divisions in the country. Many unrepentant nationalists and monarchists populated the right and the army. Members of Germany's Communist Party received directions from Moscow, and they accused the Social Democrats of betraying the revolution. The working classes were divided politically, but a majority supported the socialist, but nonrevolutionary, Social Democrats.

France's situation was similar to Germany's. Communists and socialists battled for the workers' support. After 1924 the democratically elected government rested mainly in the hands of moderate coalitions, and business interests were well represented. France's great accomplishment was rapid rebuilding of its war-torn northern region, and good times prevailed until 1930.

Britain, too, faced challenges after 1920. The great problem was unemployment, which hovered around 12 percent throughout the 1920s. The state provided unemployment benefits and supplemented those payments with subsidized housing, medical aid, and increased old-age pensions. These and other measures kept living standards from seriously declining, defused class tensions, and pointed the way to the welfare state Britain established after World War II.

Thus the wartime trend toward greater social equality continued, helping maintain social harmony. Relative social harmony was accompanied by the rise of the Labour Party. Committed to moderate, "revisionist" socialism (see page 758), the Labour Party under Ramsay MacDonald (1866–1937) governed the country in 1924 and 1929–1935. Labour moved toward socialism gradually and democratically, so that the middle classes were not overly frightened as the working classes won new benefits.

The British Conservatives under Stanley Baldwin (1867–1947) showed the same compromising spirit on social issues, and Britain experienced only limited social unrest in the 1920s and 1930s. In 1922 Britain granted southern, Catholic Ireland full autonomy after a bitter guerrilla war, thereby removing another source of prewar friction. Thus developments in both international relations and domestic politics gave the leading democracies cause for cautious optimism in the late 1920s.

The Age of Anxiety

In what ways were the anxieties of the postwar world expressed or heightened by revolutionary ideas in modern thought, art, and science and in new forms of communication?

Many people hoped that happier times would return after the war, along with the familiar prewar ideals of peace, prosperity, and progress. These hopes were in vain. The First World War and the Russian Revolution had mangled too many things beyond repair. Great numbers of men and women felt themselves increasingly adrift in an age of anxiety and continual crisis.

Uncertainty in Philosophy and Religion

Before 1914 most people in the West still believed in Enlightenment philosophies of progress, reason, and individual rights. As the century began, progress was a daily reality, apparent in the rising living standard, the taming of the city, the spread of political rights to women and workers, and the growth of state-supported social programs. Just as there were laws of science, many thinkers felt, there were laws of society that rational human beings could discover and wisely act on.

Even before the war, however, the particularly influential German philosopher Friedrich Nietzsche (NEE-chuh) (1844–1900) called such faith in reason into question. In the first of his *Untimely Meditations* (1873), he argued that ever since classical Athens, the West had overemphasized rationality and stifled the passions and animal instincts that drive human activity and true creativity. Nietzsche went on to ridicule Western society's values. He believed that reason, democracy, progress, and respectability were outworn social and psychological constructs that suffocated self-realization and excellence. Rejecting religion, Nietzsche claimed that Christianity embodied a "slave morality" that glorified weakness, envy, and mediocrity. Little read during his lifetime, Nietzsche attracted growing attention in the early twentieth century.

The First World War accelerated the revolt against established philosophical certainties. Logical positivism, often associated with Austrian philosopher Ludwig Wittgenstein (VIHT-guhn-shtighn) (1889–1951), rejected most concerns of traditional philosophy—from God's existence to the meaning of happiness—as nonsense and argued that life must be based on facts and observation. Others looked to **existentialism** for answers. Highly diverse and even contradictory, existential thinkers were loosely united in a search for moral values in an anxious and uncertain world. Often inspired by Nietzsche, they did not believe that a supreme being had established humanity's fundamental nature and given life its meaning. In the words of the famous French existentialist Jean-Paul Sartre (ZHAWN-pawl SAHR-truh) (1905–1980), "Man's existence precedes his essence. . . . To begin with he is nothing. He will not be anything until later, and then he will be what he makes of himself."[12]

In contrast, the loss of faith in human reason and in continual progress led to a renewed interest in Christianity. After World War I several thinkers and theologians began to revitalize Christian fundamentals, stressing human beings' sinful nature, the need for faith, and the mystery of God's forgiveness. As a result, religion became much more relevant and meaningful than it had been before the war, and intellectuals increasingly turned to religion between about 1920 and 1950. Sometimes described as Christian existentialists because they shared the loneliness and despair of atheistic existentialists, these believers felt this shift was one meaningful answer to terror and anxiety. In the words of a famous Roman Catholic convert, English novelist Graham Greene, "One began to believe in heaven because one believed in hell."[13]

The New Physics

By the late nineteenth century science, specifically Newtonian science (see page 561), was one of the main pillars supporting Western society's optimistic and rationalistic worldview. Unchanging natural laws seemed to determine physical processes and permit useful solutions to more and more problems. All this was comforting, especially to people no longer committed to traditional religious beliefs. And all this was challenged by the new physics.

An important first step toward the new physics was the British physicist J. J. Thomson's 1897 discovery of subatomic particles, which proved that atoms were not stable and unbreakable. The following year Polish-born physicist Marie Curie (1867–1934) and her French husband, Pierre (1859–1906), discovered radium and demonstrated that it constantly emits subatomic particles and thus does not have a constant atomic weight. Building on this, German physicist Max Planck (1858–1947) showed in 1900 that subatomic energy is emitted in uneven little spurts, which Planck called "quanta," and not in a steady stream, as previously believed.

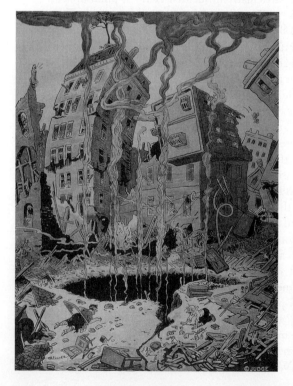

In 1905 the German-Jewish genius Albert Einstein (1879–1955) further undermined Newtonian physics. His theory of special relativity postulated that time and space are relative to the observer's viewpoint and that only the speed of light is constant for all frames of reference in the universe. In addition, Einstein's theory stated that matter and

Unlocking the Power of the Atom Many of the fanciful visions of science fiction came true in the twentieth century, although not exactly as first imagined. This 1927 cartoon satirizes a professor who has split the atom and has unwittingly destroyed his building and neighborhood in the process. In the Second World War scientists harnessed the atom in bombs and decimated faraway cities and their inhabitants. (© Mary Evans Picture Library/The Image Works) energy are interchangeable and that even a particle of matter contains enormous levels of potential energy.

The 1920s opened the "heroic age of physics," in the apt words of one of its leading pioneers, Ernest Rutherford (1871–1937). In 1919 Rutherford first split the atom. Breakthrough followed breakthrough, but some discoveries raised new doubts about reality. In 1927 German physicist Werner Heisenberg theorized his "uncertainty principle," whereby any act of measurement in quantum physics is affected by, and blurred by, the experimenter. Thus, if experiments in an exact science like physics can be distorted by human observation, what other areas of human knowledge are similarly affected? Is ultimate truth unknowable?

By 1944 seven subatomic particles had been identified, the most important of which was the neutron. The neutron's capacity to pass through other atoms allowed for even more intense experimental bombardment of matter, leading to chain reactions of unbelievable force. The implications of the new theories and discoveries were disturbing to millions of people in the 1920s and 1930s. The new universe was strange and troubling, and, moreover, science appeared distant from human experience and human problems.

Freudian Psychology

With physics presenting an uncertain universe so unrelated to ordinary human experience, questions about the power and potential of the human mind assumed special significance. The findings and speculations of psychologist Sigmund Freud (1856–1939) were particularly disturbing.

Before Freud, most psychologists assumed that human behavior resulted from rational thinking by the conscious mind. By analyzing dreams and hysteria, Freud developed a very different view of the human psyche. Freud concluded that human behavior was governed by three parts of the self: the id, ego, and superego. The irrational unconscious, which he called the id, was driven by sexual, aggressive, and pleasure-seeking desires and was locked in constant battle with the mind's two other parts: the rationalizing conscious—the ego—which mediates what a person can do, and ingrained moral values—the superego—which specify what a person should do. Thus for Freud human behavior was a product of a fragile compromise between instinctual drives and the controls of rational thinking and moral values. The danger for individuals was that unacknowledged drives might overwhelm the control mechanisms, leading to sexual repression, guilt, neurotic fears, and even violence.

Freudian psychology and clinical psychiatry had become an international movement by 1910, but only after 1918 did they receive popular attention. Many misinterpreted Freud as saying that the first requirement for mental health was an uninhibited sex life. After World War I this popular interpretation reflected and encouraged growing sexual experimentation.

Twentieth-Century Literature

Western literature was also influenced by the general intellectual climate of pessimism, relativism, and alienation. Nineteenth-century novelists had typically written as all-knowing narrators, describing realistic characters in an understandable, if sometimes harsh, society. In the twentieth century many writers adopted the limited, often confused viewpoint of a single individual. Like Freud, these novelists focused on the complexity and irrationality of the human mind.

Some novelists used the stream-of-consciousness technique with its reliance on internal monologues to explore the psyche. The most famous stream-of-consciousness novel is *Ulysses*, published by Irish novelist James Joyce (1882–1941) in 1922. Into an account of a single day in the life of an ordinary man, Joyce weaves an extended ironic parallel between his hero's aimless wanderings through Dublin's streets and pubs and the adventures of Homer's hero Ulysses on his way home from Troy. Abandoning conventional grammar and blending foreign words, puns, bits of knowledge, and scraps of memory together in bewildering confusion, the language of *Ulysses* was intended to mirror modern life itself.

Creative writers rejected the idea of progress; some even described "anti-utopias," nightmare visions of things to come. In 1918 Oswald Spengler (1880–1936) published *The Decline of the West*, in which he argued that Western civilization was in its old age and would soon be conquered by East Asia. Likewise, T. S. Eliot (1888–1965) depicted a world of growing desolation in his famous poem *The Waste Land* (1922). Franz Kafka's (1883–1924) novels *The Trial* (1925) and *The Castle* (1926) portrayed helpless individuals crushed by inexplicably hostile forces.

Modern Architecture, Art, and Music

Like scientists and intellectuals, creative artists rejected old forms and old values after the war. **Modernism** in architecture, art, and music meant constant experimentation and a search for new kinds of expression.

The United States, with its rapid urban growth and lack of rigid building traditions, pioneered in the new architecture. In the 1890s the Chicago School of architects, led by Louis H. Sullivan (1856–1924), used cheap steel, reinforced concrete, and electric elevators to build skyscrapers and office buildings lacking almost any exterior ornamentation. The buildings of Frank Lloyd Wright (1867–1959), another visionary American architect, were renowned for their sometimes-radical design, their creative use of wide varieties of materials, and their appearance of being part of the landscape.

In Europe architectural leadership centered in German-speaking countries. In 1919 Walter Gropius (1883–1969) merged the schools of fine and applied arts at Weimar into a single interdisciplinary school, the Bauhaus. Throughout the 1920s the Bauhaus, with its stress on **functionalism** and good design for everyday life, attracted enthusiastic students from all over the world.

Art increasingly took on a nonrepresentational, abstract character. New artistic styles grew out of a revolt against French impressionism, which was characterized by an overall feeling, or impression, of light falling on a real-life scene before the artist's eyes, rather than an exact copy of objects. Though individualistic in their styles, "post-impressionists" and "expressionists" were united in their desire to depict unseen inner worlds of emotion and imagination. Artists such as the Dutch expressionist Vincent van Gogh (1853–1890) painted the moving vision of the mind's eye. Paul Gauguin (1848–1903), a French expressionist, moved to the South Pacific, where he found inspiration in Polynesian forms, colors, and legends.

In 1907 in Paris the famous Spanish painter Pablo Picasso (1881–1973), along with Georges Braque, Marcel Duchamp, and other artists, established cubism—an

Eiffel Tower, 1926   The works of the French artist Robert Delaunay (1885–1941) represent most of the major art styles of the early twentieth century, including modernism, abstraction, futurism, fauvism, cubism, and Orphism. His early renderings of the Eiffel Tower (1909–1912), the iconic symbol of urbanization, the machine age, and, as a radio tower, limitless communication, possess features drawn from several of these styles. His later paintings of the Eiffel Tower, such as the one shown here, draw on a much wider palette of brilliant colors, reflecting aspects of a style known as Orphism, with which he is most closely identified. (*Eiffel Tower*, 1926, oil on canvas by Robert Delaunay [1885–1941]/Private Collection/Photo © Christie's Images/The Bridgeman Art Library)

artistic approach concentrated on a complex geometry of zigzagging lines and sharply angled overlapping planes. Since the Renaissance, artists had represented objects from a single viewpoint and had created unified human forms. In his first great cubist work, *Les Demoiselles d'Avignon* (1907), Picasso's figures resemble large wooden African masks, presenting a radical new view of reality with a strikingly non-Western depiction of the human form. The influence of carved African masks on Picasso reflected the growing importance of non-Western artistic traditions in Europe in the early twentieth century.

The ultimate stage in the development of abstract, nonrepresentational art occurred around 1910. Artists such as the Russian-born Wassily Kandinsky (1866–1944) turned away from nature completely. "The observer," said Kandinsky, "must learn to look at [my] pictures . . . as form and color combinations . . . as a representation of mood and not as a representation of *objects*."[14]

Radicalization accelerated after World War I. The most notable new developments were New Objectivity (*Sachlichkeit* in German), Dadaism, and surrealism. New Objectivity emerged from German artists' experiences in the Great War and the Weimar Republic. Paintings by artists like George Grosz and Otto Dix were provocative, emotionally disturbing, and harshly satirical. Dadaism attacked all accepted standards of art and behavior, delighting in outrageous conduct. After 1924 many Dadaists were attracted to surrealism. Surrealists, such as Salvador Dalí (1904–1989), painted fantastic worlds of wild dreams and complex symbols.

Developments in modern music were strikingly parallel to those in painting. Attracted by the emotional intensity of expressionism, composers depicted unseen inner worlds of emotion and imagination. The pulsating, dissonant rhythms and the dancers' earthy representation of lovemaking in the ballet *The Rite of Spring* by composer Igor Stravinsky (1882–1971) nearly caused a riot when first performed in Paris in 1913.

Likewise, modernism in opera and ballet flourished. Led by Viennese composer Arnold Schönberg (SHUHN-buhrg) (1874–1951), some composers turned their backs on long-established musical conventions. As abstract painters arranged lines and color but did not draw identifiable objects, so modern composers arranged sounds without creating recognizable harmonies. Accustomed to the harmonies of classical and romantic music, audiences generally resisted modern atonal music.

Movies and Radio

Cinema and radio became major industries after World War I, and standardized commercial entertainment began to replace the traditional arts and amusements of people in villages and small towns. Moving pictures were first shown as a popular novelty in naughty peep shows and penny arcades in the 1890s, especially in Paris. The first movie houses, dating from an experiment in Los Angeles in 1902, showed short silent action films.

During the First World War the United States became the dominant force in the rapidly expanding silent-film industry, and Charlie Chaplin (1889–1978), an Englishman working in Hollywood, was unquestionably the king of the silver screen. In his enormously popular role as a lonely tramp, complete with baggy trousers, battered derby, and an awkward, shuffling walk, Chaplin symbolized the "gay spirit of laughter in a cruel, crazy world."[15] Chaplin also demonstrated that in the hands of a genius the new medium could combine mass entertainment and artistic accomplishment.

Motion pictures also became powerful tools of indoctrination, especially in countries with dictatorial regimes. Lenin encouraged the development of Soviet film making, and beginning in the mid-1920s a series of epic films, the most famous of which were directed by Sergei Eisenstein (1898–1948), dramatized the Communist view of Russian history. In Germany Hitler, who rose to power in 1933, turned to a talented woman film maker, Leni Riefenstahl (1902–2003), for a masterpiece of documentary propaganda, *Triumph of the Will*, based on the 1934 Nazi Party rally at Nuremberg. Her film was a brilliant and all-too-powerful depiction of Germany's Nazi rebirth (see Chapter 30).

Whether foreign or domestic, motion pictures became the main entertainment of the masses worldwide until after the Second World War. Featuring glittering stars such as Ginger Rogers and Fred Astaire and the fanciful cartoons of Mickey Mouse, motion pictures offered ordinary people a temporary escape from the hard realities of international tensions, uncertainty, unemployment, and personal frustrations.

Radio also dominated popular culture after the war. The work of Guglielmo Marconi (1874–1937) in 1901 and the development of the vacuum tube in 1904 permitted the transmission of speech and music. Only in 1920, however, were the first major public broadcasts made in Great Britain and the United States. Every major country quickly established national broadcasting networks. In the United States these were privately owned and financed by advertising, as was LOR Radio Argentina, which became the first formal radio station in the world when it made its first broadcast in August 1920. In Europe, China, Japan, India, and elsewhere the typical pattern was direct government control. By the late 1930s more than three-fourths of the households in both democratic Great Britain and dictatorial Germany had at least one cheap, mass-produced radio. Radio was well suited for promoting patriotism and spreading political propaganda. Radios were revolutionary in that they were capable of reaching all of a nation's citizens at once, offering them a single perspective on current events, and teaching them a single national language and pronunciation. Dictators such as Mussolini and Hitler controlled the airwaves and could reach enormous national audiences with their frequent, dramatic speeches. In democratic countries politicians such as President Franklin Roosevelt and Prime Minister Stanley Baldwin effectively used informal "fireside chats" to bolster support.

Chapter Summary

Nationalism, militarism, imperialism, and the alliance system increased political tensions across Europe at the end of the nineteenth century. Franz Ferdinand's assassination in 1914 sparked a regional war that soon became global, as imperialistic ties brought countries and colonies around the world into the conflict. Four years of stalemate and slaughter followed. Entire societies mobilized for total war, and government powers greatly increased. Women earned greater social equality, and labor unions grew. Many European countries adopted socialism as a realistic economic blueprint.

Horrible losses on the eastern front led to Russian tsar Nicholas II's abdication in March 1917. A provisional government controlled by moderate social democrats replaced him but refused to withdraw Russia from the war. A second Russian revolution followed in November 1917, led by Lenin and his Communist Bolshevik Party. The Bolsheviks established a radical regime, smashed existing capitalist institutions, and posed an ongoing challenge to Europe and its colonial empires.

The "war to end war" brought only a fragile truce. Over American protests, France and Great Britain sought revenge on Germany. The Versailles treaty took away Germany's colonies, limited its army and navy, and demanded admittance of war guilt and exorbitant war reparations. Separate treaties redrew the maps of Europe and the Middle East. Allied wartime solidarity faded, and Germany remained unrepentant, setting the stage for World War II. Globally, the European powers refused to extend self-determination to their colonies, instead creating a mandate system that sowed further discontent among colonized peoples.

World War I caused political and economic disruption across Europe. In the 1920s moderate political leaders sought to create an enduring peace and rebuild prewar prosperity through compromise. By decade's end they seemed to have succeeded: Germany experienced an economic recovery, France rebuilt its war-torn regions, and Britain's Labour Party expanded social services. Ultimately, however, these measures were short-lived.

The war's horrors, particularly the industrialization of war that slaughtered millions, shattered Enlightenment ideals and caused widespread anxiety. In the interwar years philosophers, artists, and writers portrayed these anxieties in their work. Movies and the radio initially offered escape but soon became powerful tools of indoctrination and propaganda.

Notes

1. Erich Maria Remarque, *All Quiet on the Western Front*, trans. A. W. Wheen (New York: Fawcett, 1996), p. 13.
2. Winston Churchill, *The World Crisis, 1911–1918* (New York: Free Press, 2005), p. 96.
3. Remarque, *All Quiet*, pp. 134–135.
4. Siegfried Sassoon, *The Memoirs of George Sherston: Memoirs of an Infantry Officer* (New York: Literary Guild of America, 1937), p. 74.

5. Quoted in Keith Sinclair, *The Growth of New Zealand Identity, 1890–1980* (Auckland, N.Z.: Longman Paul, 1987), p. 24.

6. Svetlana Palmer and Sarah Wallis, eds., *Intimate Voices from the First World War* (New York: William Morrow, 2003), p. 221.

7. Ethel Alec-Tweedie, *Women and Soldiers*, 2d ed. (London: John Lane, 1918), p. 29.

8. Janet S. K. Watson, "Khaki Girls, VADS, and Tommy's Sisters: Gender and Class in First World War Britain," *The International History Review* 19 (1997): 49.

9. Melissa Kirschke Stockdale, *Paul Miliukov and the Quest for a Liberal Russia, 1880–1918* (Ithaca, N.Y.: Cornell University Press, 1996), p. 235.

10. Quoted in H. Nicolson, *Peacemaking 1919* (New York: Grosset & Dunlap Universal Library, 1965), pp. 8, 31–32.

11. Quoted ibid., p. 24.

12. Quoted in John Macquarrie, *Existentialism* (New York: Penguin Books, 1972), p. 15.

13. G. Greene, *Another Mexico* (New York: Viking Press, 1939), p. 3.

14. Quoted in A. H. Barr, Jr., *What Is Modern Painting?* 9th ed. (New York: Museum of Modern Art, 1966), p. 25.

15. R. Graves and A. Hodge, *The Long Week End: A Social History of Great Britain, 1918–1939* (New York: Macmillan, 1941), p. 131.

CONNECTIONS

The Great War has continued to influence global politics and societies nearly a century after the guns went silent in November 1918. To understand the origins of many modern world conflicts, one must study first the intrigues and treaties and the revolutions and upheavals that were associated with this first truly world war.

The war's most obvious consequences were felt in Europe, where three empires collapsed and new states were created out of the ruins. Old European antagonisms and mistrust made the negotiation of fair and just treaties ending the war impossible, despite the best efforts of an outsider, American president Wilson, to make this a war to end all wars. In Chapter 30 we will see how the conflict contributed to a worldwide depression, the rise of totalitarian dictatorships, and a Second World War more global and destructive than the first. In the Middle East the five-hundred-year-old Ottoman Empire came to an end, allowing France and England to carve out mandated territories—including modern Iraq, Palestine/Israel, and Lebanon—that remain flash points for violence and political instability in the twenty-first century. Nationalism, the nineteenth-century European ideology of change, took root in Asia, partly driven by Wilson's promise of self-determination. In Chapter 29 the efforts of various nationalist leaders—Atatürk in Turkey, Gandhi in India, Mao Zedong in China, Ho Chi Minh in Vietnam, and others—to throw off colonial domination will be examined, as well as the rise of ultranationalism in Japan, which led it into World War II and to ultimate defeat.

America's entry into the Great War placed it on the world stage, a place it has not relinquished as a superpower in the twentieth and twenty-first centuries. Russia, too, eventually became a superpower, but this outcome was not so clear in 1919 as its leaders fought for survival in a vicious civil war. By the outbreak of World War II Joseph Stalin had solidified Communist power, and the Soviet Union and the United States would play leading roles in defeating totalitarianism in Germany and Japan. But at war's end, as explained in Chapter 31, the two superpowers found themselves opponents in a Cold War that lasted for much of the rest of the twentieth century.

Chapter Review

MAKE IT STICK

 LearningCurve
Go online and use LearningCurve to retain what you've read.

IDENTIFY KEY TERMS

Identify and explain the significance of each item below.

militarism (p. 861)

Triple Entente (p. 862)

trench warfare (p. 866)

total war (p. 869)

March Revolution (p. 875)

Petrograd Soviet (p. 875)

Bolsheviks (p. 877)

War Communism (p. 879)

League of Nations (p. 881)

Treaty of Versailles (p. 882)

Dawes Plan (p. 885)

Mein Kampf (p. 886)

existentialism (p. 887)

id, ego, superego (p. 889)

modernism (p. 890)

functionalism (p. 890)

REVIEW THE MAIN IDEAS

Answer the focus questions from each section of the chapter.

1. What were the long-term and immediate causes of World War I, and how did the conflict become a global war? (p. 861)

2. How did total war affect the home fronts of the major combatants? (p. 869)

3. What factors led to the Russian Revolution, and what was its outcome? (p. 874)

4. What were the global consequences of the First World War? (p. 879)

5. How did leaders deal with the political dimensions of uncertainty and try to re-establish peace and prosperity in the interwar years? (p. 883)

6. In what ways were the anxieties of the postwar world expressed or heightened by revolutionary ideas in modern thought, art, and science and in new forms of communication? (p. 887)

MAKE CONNECTIONS

Analyze the larger developments and continuities within and across chapters.

1. The war between Austria and Serbia should have been a small regional conflict in one corner of Europe. How did nationalism, militarism, and the new imperialism contribute to its expansion into a global conflict?

2. How might someone transported in time from 1900 to 1925 have been shocked and surprised at the changes that had occurred in that short time?

⤷LaunchPad

ONLINE DOCUMENT PROJECT

Calling Young Women to War
What words and images did governments use to recruit women to serve in World War I?

Examine several recruitment posters aimed at women, and then complete a quiz and writing assignment based on the evidence and details from this chapter.

See inside the front cover to learn more.

CHRONOLOGY

1914	• Assassination of Archduke Franz Ferdinand; Ottoman Empire joins Central Powers; German victories on the eastern front; Japan joins the Triple Entente and seizes German holdings in China
1914–1918	• World War I
1915	• Italy joins the Triple Entente; German submarine sinks the *Lusitania*; Japan expands into southern Manchuria
1916	• Battles of Verdun and the Somme; Irish Easter Rebellion; German Auxiliary Service Law requires seventeen- to sixty-year-old males to work for war effort; Rasputin murdered
1916–1918	• Growth of antiwar sentiment throughout Europe
1917	• United States declares war on Germany; Bolshevik Revolution in Russia
1917–1922	• Civil war in Russia
1918	• Treaty of Brest-Litovsk; revolution in Germany
1919	• Treaty of Versailles; Freudian psychology gains popularity; Rutherford splits the atom; Bauhaus school founded
1920s	• Existentialism, Dadaism, and surrealism gain prominence
1923	• French and Belgian armies occupy the Ruhr
1924	• Dawes Plan
1926	• Germany joins League of Nations
1928	• Kellogg-Briand Pact

Nationalism in Asia

1914–1939

FROM ASIA'S PERSPECTIVE THE FIRST WORLD WAR WAS LARGELY A European civil war that shattered Western imperialism's united front, underscored the West's moral bankruptcy, and convulsed prewar relationships throughout Asia. Most crucially, the war sped the development of modern Asian nationalism. Before 1914 the nationalist gospel of anti-imperialist political freedom and racial equality had already won converts among Asia's westernized, educated elites. In the 1920s and 1930s it increasingly won the allegiance of the masses. As in nineteenth-century Europe, nationalism in Asia between 1914 and 1939 became a mass movement with potentially awesome power.

The modern nationalism movement was never monolithic. In Asia especially, where the new and often narrow ideology of nationalism was grafted onto old, rich, and complex civilizations, the shape and eventual outcome of nationalist movements varied enormously. Between the outbreaks of the First and Second World Wars, each Asian country developed a distinctive national movement rooted in its own unique culture and history. Each nation's people created their own national reawakening, which reinvigorated thought and culture as well as politics and economics. And as in Europe, nationalist movements gave rise in Asia to conflict both within large, multiethnic states and between independent states.

The Asian nationalist movement witnessed the emergence of two of the true giants of the twentieth century. Mohandas Gandhi in India and Mao Zedong in China both drew their support from the peasant masses in the

897

two most populous countries in the world. Gandhi successfully used campaigns of peaceful nonviolent resistance to British colonial rule to gain Indian independence. Mao, on the other hand, used weapons of war and socialist promises of equality to defeat his westernized nationalist opponents and establish a modern Communist state.

The First World War's Impact on Nationalist Trends

Why did modern nationalism develop in Asia between the First and Second World Wars, and what was its appeal?

In the late nineteenth and early twentieth centuries the peoples of Asia adapted the European ideology of nationalism to their own situations. In some cases, such as in Vietnam and India, they sought genuine freedom from foreign imperialism. The Turks and Japanese sought to avoid European colonialism by modernizing and industrializing so they would be the equals of the West. In China there was a limited colonial presence. There different leaders arose who, after overthrowing the ancient monarchy, fought a long civil war to determine what form a modern China would take. The First World War profoundly affected these aspirations by altering relations between Asia and Europe. For four years Asians watched Kipling's haughty bearers of "the white man's burden" (see page 778) vilifying and destroying each other. Japan's defeat of imperial Russia in 1905 (see page 742) had shown that an Asian power could beat a European Great Power; now for the first time Asians saw the entire West as divided and vulnerable.

Asian Reaction to the War in Europe

The Great War was a global conflict, but some peoples were affected more significantly than others. The Japanese and Ottoman Turks were directly involved, fighting with the Allies and Central Powers, respectively. The Chinese, who overthrew their emperor in 1911, were more concerned with internal events and the threat from Japan than they were with war in Europe. In British India and French Indochina the war's impact was unavoidably greater. Total war required the British and the French to draft their colonial subjects into the conflict, uprooting hundreds of thousands of Asians to fight the Germans and the Ottoman Turks.

An Indian or Vietnamese soldier who fought in France and came in contact there with democratic and republican ideas, however, was less likely to accept foreign rule when he returned home. The British and the French therefore had to make rash promises to gain the support of these colonial peoples and other allies during the war. In India the British were forced in 1917 to announce a new policy of self-governing institutions in order to counteract Indian popular unrest fanned by wartime inflation and heavy taxation. French representatives suggested to Syrian nationalists in 1917 that Syria would have self-government after the war. British leaders promised Europe's Jewish nationalists a homeland in Palestine, while promising Arab nationalists independence from the Ottoman Empire. After the war the nationalist genie the colonial powers had called on refused to slip meekly back into the bottle.

U.S. President Wilson's war aims also raised the hopes of peoples under imperial rule. In January 1918 Wilson proposed his Fourteen Points (see page 881), whose key idea was national self-determination for the peoples of Europe and the Ottoman Empire. Wilson recommended in Point 5 that in all colonial questions "the interests of native populations be given equal weight with the desires of European governments," and he seemed to call for national self-rule. This subversive message had enormous appeal for educated Asians, fueling their hopes of freedom.

The Mandates System

After winning the war, the Allies tried to re-establish or increase their political and economic domination of their Asian and African colonies. Although fatally weakened, Western imperialism remained very much alive in 1918, partly because President Wilson was no revolutionary. At the Paris Peace Conference he compromised on colonial questions in order to achieve some of his European goals and create the League of Nations. Also, Allied statesmen and ordinary French and British citizens quite rightly believed that their colonial empires had contributed to their ultimate victory over the Central Powers. They would not give up such valuable possessions voluntarily. If pressed, Europeans said their administration was preparing colonial subjects for eventual self-rule, but only in the distant future.

The compromise at the Paris Peace Conference between Wilson's vague, moralistic idealism and the European preoccupation with "good administration" was a system of League of Nations mandates over Germany's former colonies and the old Ottoman Empire. Article 22 of the League of Nations Covenant, which was part of the Treaty of Versailles, assigned territories "inhabited by peoples incapable of governing themselves" to various "developed nations." "The well-being and development of such peoples" was declared "a sacred trust of civilization." The **Permanent Mandates Commission**, whose members came from European countries with colonies, was created to oversee the developed nations' fulfillment of their international responsibility. Thus the League elaborated a new principle—development toward the eventual goal of self-government—but left its implementation to the colonial powers themselves.

The mandates system demonstrated that Europe was determined to maintain its imperial power and influence. Bitterly disappointed patriots throughout Asia saw France, Great Britain, and other nations—industrialized Japan was the only Asian state to obtain mandates—as grabbing Germany's colonies as spoils of war and extending the existing system of colonial rule in Muslim North Africa into the territories of the old Ottoman Empire. Yet Asian patriots did not give up. They preached national self-determination and struggled to build mass movements capable of achieving freedom and independence.

In this struggle Asian nationalists were encouraged by Soviet communism. After seizing power in 1917, Lenin declared that the Asian inhabitants of the new Soviet Union were complete equals of the Russians with a right to their own development. (In actuality this equality hardly existed, but the propaganda was effective nonetheless.) The Communists also denounced European and American imperialism and pledged to support revolutionary movements in colonial countries, even when they were primarily national independence movements led by middle-class intellectuals instead of by revolutionary workers. Foreign political and economic exploitation was the immediate enemy, they said, and socialist revolution could wait until Western imperialism had been defeated. The example, ideology, and support of Soviet communism exerted a powerful influence in the 1920s and 1930s, particularly in China and French Indochina (see page 922).

Nationalism's Appeal

There were at least three reasons for the upsurge of nationalism in Asia. First and foremost, nationalism provided the most effective means of organizing anti-imperialist resistance both to direct foreign rule and to indirect Western domination. Second, nationalism called for fundamental changes and challenged old political and social practices and beliefs. As in Russia after the Crimean War, in Turkey after the Ottoman Empire's collapse, and in Japan after the Meiji Restoration, the nationalist creed after World War I went hand in hand with acceptance of modernization by the educated elites. Modernization promised changes that would enable old societies to compete effectively with the world's leading nations. Educated elites thus used modernization to contest the influence and power of conservative traditionalists. Third, nationalism offered a vision of a free and prosperous future, and provided an ideology to ennoble the sacrifices the struggle would require.

Nationalism also had a dark side. As in Europe (see page 726), Asian nationalists developed a strong sense of "we" and "they." "They" were often the enemy. European imperialists were just such a "they," and nationalist feeling generated the will to destroy European empires and challenge foreign economic domination. But, as in Europe, Asian nationalism also stimulated bitter conflicts and wars between peoples, in three different ways.

First, as when the ideology of nationalism first developed in Europe in the early 1800s (see pages 726–727), Asian (and African) elites were often forced to create a national identity in colonies that Europeans had artificially created, or in multiethnic countries held together by authoritarian leaders but without national identities based on shared ethnicities or histories. Second, nationalism stimulated conflicts between relatively homogeneous peoples in large states, rallying, for example, Chinese against Japanese and vice versa. Third, nationalism often heightened tensions between ethnic or religious groups within states, very much like what occurred in the multiethnic Austro-Hungarian and Ottoman Empires before 1914. In nearly all countries there were ancient ethnic and religious differences and rivalries. Imperial rulers of colonial powers (like the British and French) and local authoritarian rulers (like the Austrian emperor, the Russian tsar, and the Chinese emperor) exploited these ethnic and religious differences to "divide and conquer" the peoples in their empires. They favored one ethnic or religious group over another or used a police or army unit formed from one group to put down rebellion by another group. Such tactics enabled the imperial power to keep the people divided as they fought among themselves rather than uniting against their rulers. When the rigid imperial rule ended, the different national, religious, or even ideological (Communists versus capitalists) factions turned against each other, each seeking to either seize control of or divide the existing state, and to dominate the enemy "they" within its borders. This habit of thinking in terms of "we" versus "they" was, and still is, a difficult frame of mind to abandon, and these divisions made it difficult for nationalist leaders to unite people under a common national identity.

Nationalism's appeal in Asia was not confined to territories under direct European rule. The extraordinary growth of international trade after 1850 had drawn millions of Asian peasants and shopkeepers into the Western-dominated world economy, disrupting local markets and often creating hostility toward European businessmen. Moreover, Europe and the United States had forced even the most solid Asian states, China and Japan, to accept unequal treaties (see page 807) and humiliating limitations on their sovereignty. Thus the nationalist promise of genuine economic independence and true political equality with the West appealed as powerfully in old but weak states like China as in colonial territories like British India.

Nationalist Movements in the Middle East

How did the Ottoman Empire's collapse in World War I shape nationalist movements in the Middle East?

The most flagrant attempt to expand Western imperialism occurred in the Middle East, or, more accurately, in southwest Asia — the vast expanse that stretches eastward from the Suez Canal and Turkey's Mediterranean shores across the Tigris-Euphrates Valley and the Persian (Iranian) Plateau to the Arabian Sea and the Indus Valley (Map 29.1). There the British and the French successfully encouraged an Arab revolt in 1916 and destroyed the Ottoman Empire. Europeans then sought to replace Turks as principal rulers throughout the region, even in Turkey itself. Turkish, Arab, and Persian nationalists, as well as Jewish nationalists arriving from Europe, reacted violently. They struggled to win dignity and nationhood, and as the Europeans were forced to make concessions, they sometimes came into sharp conflict with each other, most notably in Palestine.

The Arab Revolt

Long subject to European pressure, the Ottoman Empire failed to reform and modernize in the late nineteenth century (see pages 780–783). Declining international stature and domestic tyranny led to revolutionary activity among idealistic exiles and young army officers who wanted to seize power and save the Ottoman state. These patriots, the so-called Young Turks, succeeded in the 1908 revolution, and subsequently they were determined to hold together the remnants of the vast multiethnic empire. Defeated by Bulgaria, Serbia, and Greece in the Balkan war of 1912 and stripped of practically all territory in Europe, the Young Turks redoubled their efforts in southwest Asia. The most important of their possessions were Syria — consisting of modern-day Lebanon, Syria, Israel, the West Bank, the Gaza Strip, and Jordan — and Iraq. The Ottoman Turks also claimed the Arabian peninsula but exercised only loose control there.

For centuries the largely Arab populations of Syria and Iraq had been tied to their Ottoman rulers by their common faith in Islam (though there were Christian Arabs as well). Yet beneath the surface, ethnic and linguistic tensions simmered between Turks and Arabs.

Young Turk actions after 1908 made the embryonic "Arab movement" a reality. The majority of Young Turks promoted a narrow Turkish nationalism. They further centralized the Ottoman Empire and extended the sway of Turkish language and culture. In 1909 the Turkish government brutally slaughtered thousands of Armenian

MAP 29.1   The Partition of the Ottoman Empire, 1914–1923 By 1914 the Ottoman Turks had been pushed out of the Balkans, and their Arab provinces were on the edge of revolt. That revolt erupted in the First World War and contributed greatly to the Ottomans' defeat. When the Allies then attempted to implement their plans, including independence for the Armenian people, Mustafa Kemal arose to forge in battle the modern Turkish state.

Christians, a prelude to the wholesale massacre of more than a million Armenians during the First World War. Meanwhile, Arab discontent grew.

During World War I the Turks freely aligned themselves with the Central Powers—Germany and Austria-Hungary (see page 867). As a result, the Young Turks drew all of the Middle East into what had been up to that point a European war. Arabs opposed to Ottoman rule found themselves allied with the British, who encouraged the alliance with vague promises of an independent Arab kingdom. After decisive British victories on the Arab peninsula in 1917 and 1918, Arabs rejoiced, and many patriots expected a large, unified Arab state to rise from the dust of the Ottoman collapse. Within two years, however, Arab nationalists felt bitterly betrayed by Great Britain and its allies, and this bitterness left a legacy of distrust and hatred toward the West.

Arab bitterness was partly directed at secret wartime treaties between Britain and France to divide and rule the old Ottoman Empire. In the 1916 **Sykes-Picot Agreement**, Britain and France secretly agreed that France would receive modern-day Lebanon, Syria, and much of southern Turkey, and Britain would receive Palestine, Jordan, and Iraq. The Sykes-Picot Agreement contradicted British (and later Wilsonian) promises concerning Arab independence after the war and left Arab nationalists feeling cheated and betrayed.

A related source of Arab frustration was Britain's wartime commitment to a Jewish homeland in Palestine. The **Balfour Declaration** of November 1917, made by the British foreign secretary Arthur Balfour, declared:

> His Majesty's Government views with favour the establishment in Palestine of a national home for the Jewish People, and will use their best endeavors to facilitate the achievement of this object, it being clearly understood that nothing shall be done which may prejudice the civil and religious rights of existing non-Jewish communities in Palestine, or the rights and political status enjoyed by Jews in any other country.[1]

As a careful reading reveals, the Balfour Declaration made contradictory promises to European Jews and Middle Eastern Arabs. The last phrase in the final sentence is a guarantee that Jews in England or France, for example, would not automatically lose their citizenship and rights in those countries if there were an independent Jewish state.

Some British Cabinet members believed the Balfour Declaration would appeal to German, Austrian, and American Jews and thus help the British war effort. Others sincerely supported the Zionist vision of a Jewish homeland (see page 757), but also believed that Jews living in this homeland would be grateful to Britain and thus help maintain British control of the Suez Canal.

In 1914 Jews made up about 11 percent of the predominantly Arab population in the Ottoman territory that became, under British control, Palestine. The "national home for the Jewish People" mentioned in the Balfour Declaration implied to the Arabs—and to the Zionist Jews as well—some kind of Jewish state that would be incompatible with majority rule. Moreover, a state founded on religious and ethnic exclusivity was out of keeping with both Islamic and Ottoman tradition, which had historically been more tolerant of religious diversity and minorities than had the Christian monarchs and nation-states of Europe.

After Faisal bin Hussein's failed efforts at the Paris Peace Conference to secure Arab independence (see page 882), Arab nationalists met in Damascus as the General Syrian Congress in 1919 and unsuccessfully called again for political independence. Ignoring Arab opposition, the British mandate in Palestine formally incorporated the Balfour Declaration and its commitment to a Jewish national home. In March 1920 Faisal's followers met again as the Syrian National Congress and proclaimed Syria independent, with Faisal as king. A similar congress declared Iraq an independent kingdom.

Western reaction to events in Syria and Iraq was swift and decisive. A French army stationed in Lebanon attacked Syria, taking Damascus in July 1920. Faisal fled, and the French took over. Meanwhile, the British put down an uprising in Iraq with bloody fighting and established effective control there. Western imperialism appeared to have replaced Turkish rule in the Middle East (see Map 29.1).

The Turkish Revolution

Days after the end of the First World War, French and then British troops entered Constantinople to begin a five-year occupation of the Ottoman capital. A young English official wrote that he found the Ottoman Empire "utterly smashed." The Turks were "worn out" from the war, and without bitterness they awaited the construction of a "new system."[2] The Allies' new system was blatant imperialism, which proved harsher for the defeated Turks than for the Arabs now free from Turkish rule. A treaty forced on the helpless sultan dismembered Turkey and reduced it to a puppet state. Great Britain and France occupied parts of Turkey, and Italy and Greece claimed shares as well. There was a sizable Greek minority in western Turkey, and Greek nationalists cherished the "Great Idea" of a modern Greek empire modeled on long-dead Christian Byzantium. In 1919 Greek armies carried by British ships landed on the Turkish coast at Smyrna, met little resistance from the exhausted Turkish troops, and advanced into the interior. Turkey seemed finished.

But Turkey produced a great leader and revived to become an inspiration to the entire Middle East. Mustafa Kemal (1881–1938), considered the father of modern Turkey, was a military man sympathetic to the Young Turk movement. Kemal had distinguished himself in the Great War by directing the successful defense of the Dardanelles against British attack. After the armistice, he watched with anguish the Allies' aggression and the sultan's cowardice. In early 1919 he began working to unify Turkish resistance.

The sultan, bowing to Allied pressure, initially denounced Kemal, but the cause of national liberation proved more powerful. The catalyst was the Greek invasion and attempted annexation of much of western Turkey. A young Turkish woman described feelings she shared with countless others:

> After I learned about the details of the Smyrna occupation by Greek armies, I hardly opened my mouth on any subject except when it concerned the sacred struggle. . . . I suddenly ceased to exist as an individual. I worked, wrote and lived as a unit of that magnificent national madness.[3]

Refusing to acknowledge the Allied dismemberment of their country, the Turks battled on through 1920 despite staggering defeats. The next year the Greeks advanced almost to Ankara, the nationalist stronghold in central Turkey. There Mustafa Kemal's forces took the offensive and won a great victory. The Greeks and their British allies sued for peace. The resulting **Treaty of Lausanne** (1923) abolished the hated capitulations, which since the sixteenth century had given Europeans special privileges in the Ottoman Empire (see page 506), and recognized a truly independent Turkey. Turkey lost only its former Arab provinces (see Map 29.1).

Mustafa Kemal believed Turkey should modernize and secularize along Western lines. His first moves, beginning in 1923, were political. Drawing on his prestige as a war hero, Kemal called on the National Assembly to depose the sultan and establish a republic. He had himself elected president and moved the capital from cosmopolitan Constantinople (now Istanbul) to Ankara in the Turkish heartland. Kemal savagely crushed the demands for independence of ethnic minorities within Turkey like the Armenians and the Kurds, but he realistically abandoned all thought of winning back lost Arab territories. He then created a one-party system—partly inspired by the Bolshevik example—in order to work his will.

Kemal's most radical changes pertained to religion and culture. For centuries most believers' intellectual and social activities had been regulated by Islamic religious authorities. Profoundly influenced by the example of western Europe, Mustafa Kemal set out, like the philosophes of the Enlightenment, to limit religious influence in daily affairs, but, like Russia's Peter the Great, he employed dictatorial measures rather than reason and democracy to reach his goal. Kemal decreed a revolutionary separation of church and state. Secular law codes inspired by European models replaced religious courts. State schools replaced religious schools and taught such secular subjects as science, mathematics, and social sciences.

Mustafa Kemal also struck down many entrenched patterns of behavior. Women, traditionally secluded and inferior to males in Islamic society, received the right to vote. Civil law on a European model, rather than the Islamic code, now governed marriage. Women could seek divorces, and no man could have more than one wife at a time. Men were forbidden to wear the tall red fez of the Ottoman era

Mustafa Kemal Surnamed Atatürk, meaning "father of the Turks," Mustafa Kemal and his supporters imposed revolutionary changes aimed at modernizing and westernizing Turkish society and the new Turkish government. Dancing here with his adopted daughter at her high-society wedding, Atatürk often appeared in public in elegant European dress—a vivid symbol for the Turkish people of his radical break with traditional Islamic teaching and custom. (Hulton Archive/Getty Images)

as headgear; government employees were ordered to wear business suits and felt hats, erasing the visible differences between Muslims and "infidel" Europeans. The old Arabic script was replaced with a new Turkish alphabet based on Roman letters, which facilitated massive government efforts to spread literacy after 1928. Finally, in 1935, family names on the European model were introduced. Before this, while Jewish and Christian citizens of the empire had used surnames, Muslim Turks had not. Muslims had generally used a simple formulation of "son of" with their father's name. The National Assembly granted Mustafa Kemal the surname Atatürk, which means "father of the Turks."

By his death in 1938, Atatürk and his supporters had consolidated their revolution. Government-sponsored industrialization was fostering urban growth and new attitudes, encouraging Turks to embrace business and science. Poverty persisted in rural areas, as did some religious discontent among devout Muslims. But like the Japanese after the Meiji Restoration, the Turkish people had rallied around the nationalist banner to repulse European imperialism and were building a modern secular nation-state.

Modernization Efforts in Persia and Afghanistan

In Persia (renamed Iran in 1935) strong-arm efforts to build a unified modern nation ultimately proved less successful than in Turkey. In the late nineteenth century Persia had also been subject to extreme foreign pressure, which stimulated efforts to reform the government as a means of reviving Islamic civilization. In 1906 a nationalistic coalition of merchants, religious leaders, and intellectuals revolted. The despotic shah was forced to grant a constitution and establish a national assembly, the **Majlis**. Nationalist hopes ran high.

Yet the 1906 Persian revolution was doomed to failure, largely because of European imperialism. Without consulting Iran, Britain and Russia in 1907 divided the country into spheres of influence. Britain's sphere ran along the Persian Gulf; the Russian sphere encompassed the whole northern half of Persia (see Map 29.1). Thereafter Russia intervened constantly. It blocked reforms, occupied cities, and completely dominated the country by 1912. When Russian power collapsed in the Bolshevik Revolution, British armies rushed into the power vacuum. By bribing corrupt Persians, Great Britain in 1919 negotiated a treaty allowing the installation of British "advisers" in every government department.

The Majlis refused to ratify the treaty, and the blatant attempt to make Persia a British satellite aroused the national spirit. In 1921 reaction against the British brought to power a military dictator, Reza Shah Pahlavi (1877–1944), who proclaimed himself shah in 1925 and ruled until 1941.

Inspired by Turkey's Mustafa Kemal, the patriotic, religiously indifferent Reza Shah had three basic goals: to build a modern nation, to free Persia from foreign domination, and to rule with an iron fist. The challenge was enormous. Persia was a vast, undeveloped country of deserts, mountain barriers, and rudimentary communications. The rural population was mostly poor and illiterate, and among the Persian majority were sizable ethnic minorities with their own aspirations. Furthermore, Iran's powerful religious leaders hated Western (Christian) domination but were equally opposed to a more secular, less Islamic society.

To realize his vision of a strong Persia, the energetic shah created a modern army, built railroads, and encouraged commerce. He won control over ethnic minorities such as the Kurds in the north and Arab tribesmen on the Iraqi border. He reduced the privileges granted to foreigners and raised taxes on the powerful Anglo-Persian Oil Company, which had been founded in 1909 to exploit the first great oil strike in the Middle East. Yet Reza Shah was less successful than Atatürk.

Because the European-educated elite in Persia was smaller than the comparable group in Turkey, the idea of re-creating Persian greatness on the basis of a secularized society attracted relatively few determined supporters. Many powerful religious leaders turned against Reza Shah, and he became increasingly brutal, greedy, and tyrannical, murdering his enemies and lining his pockets. His support of Hitler's Nazi Germany (discussed in Chapter 30) also exposed Persia's tenuous and fragile independence to the impact of European conflicts.

Afghanistan, meanwhile, was nominally independent in the nineteenth century, but the British imposed political restrictions and constantly meddled in the country's affairs. In 1919 the violently anti-British emir Amanullah Khan (1892–1960) declared war on the British government in India and won complete independence for the first time. Amanullah then decreed revolutionary modernizing reforms designed to hurl his primitive country into the twentieth century. He established modern, secular schools for both boys and girls, and adult education classes for the predominantly illiterate population. He did away with seclusion and centuries-old dress codes for women, abolished slavery, created the country's first constitution in 1923, restructured and reorganized the economy, and established a legislative assembly and secular (rather than Islamic) court system. The result was tribal and religious revolt, civil war, and retreat from reform. Islam remained both religion and law. A powerful but primitive patriotism enabled Afghanistan to win political independence from the West, but not to build a modern society.

Amanullah's efforts to modernize Afghanistan were similar to Mustafa Kemal's in Turkey and Shah Pahlavi's in Persia. Most of Kemal's reforms took root and remain in place today. Shah Pahlavi's reforms have a mixed history, as Persia/Iran became increasingly modern and westernized through the mid-twentieth century, particularly in the urban areas. After the Islamic revolution of 1979, however, Iran became much more conservative socially, while remaining a modern industrialized nation (see pages 1013–1015). In Afghanistan most of Amanullah's reforms were abandoned when he was forced to abdicate in 1929.

Gradual Independence in the Arab States

French and British mandates established at gunpoint forced Arab nationalists to seek independence by gradual means after 1920. Arab nationalists were indirectly aided by Western taxpayers who wanted cheap — that is, peaceful — empires. As a result, Arabs won considerable control over local affairs in the mandated states, except Palestine, though the mandates remained European satellites in international and economic affairs.

In Iraq the British chose Faisal bin Hussein, whom the French had deposed in Syria, as king. Faisal obligingly gave British advisers broad behind-the-scenes control. The king also accepted British ownership of Iraq's oil fields, consequently giving the

West a stranglehold on the Iraqi economy. Given the severe limitations imposed on him, Faisal (r. 1921–1933) proved to be an able ruler, gaining his people's support and encouraging moderate reforms. In 1932 he secured Iraqi independence at the price of a restrictive long-term military alliance with Great Britain.

Egypt had been occupied by Great Britain since 1882 (see page 787) and had been a British protectorate since 1914. Following intense nationalist agitation after the Great War, Great Britain in 1922 proclaimed Egypt formally independent but continued to occupy the country militarily and control its politics. In 1936 the British agreed to restrict their troops to their bases in the Suez Canal Zone.

The French compromised less in their handling of their mandated Middle East territories. Following the Ottoman Empire's collapse after World War I, the French designated Lebanon as one of several ethnic enclaves within a larger area that became part of the French mandate of Syria. They practiced a policy of divide and rule and generally played off ethnic and religious minorities against each other. Maronite Catholic Christians made up the majority of Lebanon's population, but there were also significant numbers of Muslims and Druzes. In 1926 Lebanon became a separate republic but remained under the control of the French mandate. Arab nationalists in Syria finally won promises of Syrian independence in 1936 in return for a friendship treaty with France.

In short, the Arab states gradually freed themselves from Western political mandates but not from Western military threats or from pervasive Western influence. Since large Arab landowners and urban merchants increased their wealth and political power after 1918, they often supported the Western hegemony, from which they benefited greatly. Radical nationalists, on the other hand, recognized that Western control of the newly discovered Arab oil fields was proof that economic independence and genuine freedom had not yet been achieved.

Arab-Jewish Tensions in Palestine

Relations between the Arabs and the West were complicated by the tense situation in the British mandate of Palestine, and that situation deteriorated in the interwar years. Both Arabs and Jews denounced the British, who tried unsuccessfully to compromise with both sides. Arab nationalist anger, however, was aimed primarily at Jewish settlers. The key issue was Jewish migration from Europe to Palestine.

A small Jewish community had survived in Palestine ever since the dispersal of the Jews in Roman times. But Jewish nationalism, known as Zionism, took shape in Europe in the late nineteenth century under Theodor Herzl's leadership (see page 757). Herzl believed only a Jewish state could guarantee Jews dignity and security. The Zionist movement encouraged some of the world's Jews to settle in Palestine, but until 1921 the great majority of Jewish emigrants preferred the United States.

After 1921 the situation changed radically. An isolationist United States drastically limited immigration from eastern Europe, where war and revolution had kindled anti-Semitism. Moreover, the British began honoring the Balfour Declaration despite Arab protests. Thus Jewish immigration to Palestine from turbulent Europe in the interwar years grew rapidly, particularly after Adolf Hitler became German chancellor in 1933. In the 1930s German and Polish persecution created a mass of Jewish refugees. By

1939 Palestine's Jewish population had increased almost fivefold since 1914 and accounted for about 30 percent of all inhabitants.

Jewish settlers in Palestine faced formidable difficulties. Although much of the land purchased by the Jewish National Fund was productive, the sellers of such land were often wealthy absentee Arab landowners who cared little for their Arab tenants' welfare. When the new Jewish owners replaced those long-time Arab tenants with Jewish settlers, Arab farmers and intellectuals burned with a sense of injustice. Moreover, most Jewish immigrants came from urban backgrounds and preferred to establish new cities like Tel Aviv or to live in existing towns like Haifa or Jerusalem, where they competed with the Arabs. The land issue combined with economic and cultural friction to harden Arab protest into hatred.

The British gradually responded to Arab pressure and tried to slow Jewish immigration. This effort satisfied neither Jews nor Arabs, and by 1938 the two communities were engaged in an undeclared civil war. Jewish and Arab armed militias attacked each other, and both attacked British police and military forces. Massacres were committed by both Arabs and Jews, viewed by one side as necessary for the freedom struggle, and by the other side as terrorist acts.

On the eve of the Second World War, the frustrated British proposed an independent Palestine with the number of Jews permanently limited to only about one-third of the total population. Zionists felt themselves in grave danger of losing their dream of an independent Jewish state.

Nevertheless, in the face of adversity Jewish settlers from many different countries gradually succeeded in forging a cohesive community in Palestine. Hebrew, for centuries used only in religious worship, was revived as a living language in the 1920s–1930s to bind the Jews in Palestine together. Despite its slow beginnings, rural development achieved often remarkable results. The key unit of agricultural organization was the **kibbutz** (kih-BOOTS), a collective farm on which each member shared equally in the work, rewards, and defense. An egalitarian socialist ideology also characterized industry, which grew rapidly. By 1939 a new but old nation was emerging in the Middle East.

Toward Self-Rule in India

What role did Gandhi and his campaign of militant nonviolence play in leading India to independence from the British?

The nationalist movement in British India grew out of two interconnected cultures, Hindu and Muslim. While the two joined together to challenge British rule, they also came to see themselves as fundamentally different. Nowhere has modern nationalism's power both to unify and to divide been more strikingly demonstrated than in India.

British Promises and Repression

Indian nationalism had emerged in the late nineteenth century (see page 799), and when the First World War began, the British feared revolt. Instead Indians supported the war effort. About 1.2 million Indian soldiers and laborers voluntarily served in Europe, Africa, and the Middle East. The British government in India and the native Indian princes sent large supplies of food, money, and ammunition. In return, the British opened more good government jobs to Indians and made other minor concessions.

As the war in distant Europe ground on, however, inflation, high taxes, food shortages, and a terrible influenza epidemic created widespread suffering and discontent. The prewar nationalist movement revived stronger than ever, and moderates and radicals in the Indian National Congress Party (see page 800) joined forces. Moreover, in 1916 Hindu leaders in the Congress Party hammered out an alliance — the **Lucknow Pact** — with India's Muslim League. The League was founded in 1906 to uphold Muslim interests, as, under British rule, the once-dominant Muslim minority had fallen behind the Hindu majority. The Lucknow Pact forged a powerful united front of Hindus and Muslims and called for putting India on equal footing with self-governing British dominions like Canada, Australia, and New Zealand.

The British response to the Lucknow Pact was mixed. E. S. Montagu, the secretary of state for India, made the unprecedented announcement on August 20, 1917, that British policy called for the "gradual development of self-governing institutions with a view to the progressive realization of responsible government in India."[4] But the proposed self-government was much more limited than that granted the British dominions. In late 1919 the British established a dual administration: part Indian and elected, part British and authoritarian. Such uncontroversial activities as agriculture and health were transferred from British to Indian officials who were accountable to elected provincial assemblies. More sensitive matters like taxes, police, and the courts remained solely in British hands.

Old-fashioned authoritarian rule also seriously undermined whatever positive impact this reform might have had. Despite the unanimous opposition of the elected Indian members, the British in 1919 rammed the repressive Rowlatt Acts through India's Imperial Legislative Council. These acts indefinitely extended wartime "emergency measures" designed to curb unrest and root out "conspiracy." The result was a wave of rioting across India.

Under these tense conditions a crowd of some ten thousand gathered to celebrate a Sikh religious festival in an enclosed square in the Sikh holy city of Amritsar in the northern Punjab province. Unknown to the crowd, the local English commander, General Reginald Dyer, had banned all public meetings that very day. Dyer marched his native Gurkha troops into the square and, without warning, ordered them to fire into the unarmed mass at point-blank range until the ammunition ran out. Official British records of the Amritsar Massacre list 379 killed and 1,137 wounded, but these figures remain hotly contested as being too low. Tensions flared, and India stood on the verge of more violence and repression and, sooner or later, terrorism and guerrilla war. That India took a different path to national liberation was due largely to Mohandas K. Gandhi (1869–1948), the most influential Indian leader of modern times.

The Roots of Militant Nonviolence

By the time of Gandhi's birth in 1869, the Indian subcontinent was firmly controlled by the British. Part of the country was ruled directly by British (and subordinate Indian) officials, answerable to the British Parliament in London. In each of the so-called protected states, the native prince — usually known as the maharaja — remained the titular ruler, although he was bound to the British by unequal treaties and had to accept the "advice" of the British resident assigned to his court.

Gandhi grew up in one of the small protected states north of Bombay. Gandhi's father was the well-to-do head of a large extended family. Gandhi's mother was devoted but undogmatic in religious matters, and she exercised a strong influence on her son. After his father's death, Gandhi went to study law in England, where he passed the English bar. Upon returning to India, he decided in 1893 to try a case for some wealthy Indian merchants in the British colony of Natal (part of modern South Africa). It was a momentous decision.

In Natal Gandhi took up the plight of the expatriate Indian community. White plantation owners had been importing thousands of poor Indians as indentured laborers on five-year renewable contracts since the 1860s. When Gandhi arrived there were more Indians than whites in Natal. Some of these Indians, after completing their contracts, remained in Natal as free persons and economic competitors. In response, the Afrikaner (of Dutch descent) and British settlers passed brutally discriminatory laws. Poor Indians had to work on plantations or return to India. Rich Indians, who had previously had the vote in Natal, lost that right in 1896. Gandhi undertook his countrymen's legal defense, and in 1897 a white mob almost lynched the "coolie lawyer."

Meanwhile, Gandhi was searching for a spiritual theory of social action. He studied Hindu and Christian teachings and gradually developed a weapon for the poor and oppressed that he called **satyagraha** (suh-TYAH-gruh-huh). Gandhi conceived of satyagraha, loosely translated as "soul force," as a means of striving for truth and social justice through love and a willingness to suffer the oppressor's blows, while trying to convert him or her to one's views of what is true and just. Its tactic was active nonviolent resistance.

As the undisputed leader of South Africa's Indians before the First World War, Gandhi put his philosophy into action. When South Africa's white government severely restricted Asian immigration and internal freedom of movement, Gandhi organized a nonviolent mass resistance campaign. Thousands of Indian men and women marched in peaceful protest and withstood beatings, arrest, and imprisonment.

In 1914 South Africa's exasperated whites agreed to many of the Indians' demands. They passed a law abolishing discriminatory taxes on Indian traders, recognized the legality of non-Christian marriages, and permitted the continued immigration of free Indians. Satyagraha — militant nonviolence in pursuit of social justice — proved a powerful force in Gandhi's hands.

Gandhi's Resistance Campaign in India

In 1915 Gandhi returned to India. His reputation had preceded him: the masses hailed him as a mahatma, or "great soul" — a Hindu title of veneration for a man of great knowledge and humanity. Drawing on his South African experience because he knew Indians could not compete militarily against the British, Gandhi in 1920 launched a national campaign of nonviolent resistance to British rule. Denouncing British injustice and even violence (such as the Amritsar Massacre the year before), he urged his countrymen to boycott British goods, jobs, and honors (such as honorary titles like baron, rai, diwān, and khan, and other awards). He told peasants not to pay taxes or buy

English goods, primarily cloth, or the heavily taxed liquor. Gandhi electrified the Indian people, initiating a revolution in Indian politics.

The nationalist movement had previously touched only the tiny, prosperous, Western-educated elite. Now both the illiterate masses of village India and the educated classes heard Gandhi's call for militant nonviolent resistance. It particularly appealed to the masses of Hindus who were not members of the warrior caste or the so-called military races and who were traditionally passive and nonviolent. The British had regarded ordinary Hindus as cowards. Gandhi told them that they could be courageous and even morally superior:

> What do you think? Wherein is courage required — in blowing others to pieces from behind a cannon, or with a smiling face to approach a cannon and be blown to pieces? Who is the true warrior — he who keeps death always as a bosom-friend, or he who controls the death of others? Believe me that a man devoid of courage and manhood can never be a passive resister.[5]

Gandhi made the Indian National Congress into a mass political party, welcoming members from every ethnic group and cooperating closely with the Muslim minority.

In 1922 some Indian resisters turned to violence, murdering twenty-two policemen. Savage riots broke out, and Gandhi abruptly called off his campaign, observing that he had "committed a Himalayan blunder in placing civil disobedience before those who had never learnt the art of civil disobedience."[6] Arrested for fomenting rebellion, Gandhi served two years in prison. Upon his release Gandhi set up a commune, established a national newspaper, and set out to reform Indian society and improve the lot of the poor. He welcomed the outcaste untouchables (a caste composed of people who worked in occupations deemed unclean or "polluting"), worked to help child widows who were denied the right to remarry and suffered discrimination, and promoted native cottage industry production. For Gandhi moral improvement, social progress, and the national movement went hand in hand. Above all, Gandhi nurtured national identity and self-respect. He also tried to instill in India's people the courage to overcome their fear of their colonial rulers and to fight these rulers with nonviolence.

The 1920–1922 resistance campaign left the British severely shaken, but the commission formed in 1927 to consider further steps toward self-rule included no Indian members. In the meantime, Gandhi had served two years (1922–1924) of a six-year sentence for sedition, and in his absence the Indian National Congress had splintered into various factions. Indian resentment of British rule was intense and growing throughout the 1920s, and Gandhi spent the years after his release from prison quietly trying to unite the different factions. In 1929 the radical nationalists, led by the able and aristocratic Jawaharlal Nehru (1889–1964), pushed through the National Congress a resolution calling for virtual independence within a year. The British stiffened in their resolve against Indian independence, and Indian radicals talked of a bloody showdown.

Into this tense situation Gandhi masterfully reasserted his leadership, taking a hard line toward the British but insisting on nonviolent methods. He organized a massive resistance campaign against the tax on salt, which gave the British a veritable monopoly on the salt that was absolutely necessary for survival in India's heat and

Gandhi on the Salt March, June 1930
A small, frail man, Gandhi possessed enormous courage and determination. His campaign of nonviolent resistance to British rule inspired the Indian masses and mobilized a nation. Here he is shown walking on his famous march to the sea to protest the English-Indian government's monopoly on salt production. (akg-images)

humidity. As Gandhi shrewdly realized, the tax affected every Indian family. From March 12 to April 6, 1930, Gandhi led fifty thousand people in a spectacular march to the sea, where he made salt in defiance of the law. A later demonstration at the British-run Dharasana salt works resulted in many of the 2,500 nonviolent marchers being beaten senseless by policemen in a brutal and well-publicized encounter. Over the next months the British arrested Gandhi and sixty thousand other protesters for making and distributing salt. But the protests continued, and in 1931 the frustrated and unnerved British released Gandhi from jail and sat down to negotiate with him, as an equal, over Indian self-rule. Negotiations resulted in a new constitution, the Government of India Act, in 1935, which greatly strengthened India's parliamentary representative institutions and gave Indians some voice in the administration of British India. Although there was little Indian involvement in the drafting of the act, and it was never fully implemented, it served as a blueprint for the constitutions of India and Pakistan when they gained independence soon after World War II.

Despite his best efforts, Gandhi failed to heal a widening split between Hindus and Muslims. Indian nationalism, based largely on Hindu symbols and customs, increasingly disturbed the Muslim minority. Tempers mounted, and both sides committed atrocities. By the late 1930s Muslim League leaders were calling for the creation of a Muslim nation in British India, a "Pakistan," or "land of the pure." As in Palestine, the rise of conflicting nationalisms in India based on religion would lead to tragedy (see pages 976–978).

Nationalist Struggles in East and Southeast Asia

How did nationalism shape political developments in East and Southeast Asia?

Because of the efforts of the Meiji reformers, nationalism and modernization were well developed in Japan by 1914 (see pages 810–812). Japan competed politically and economically with the world's leading nations, building its own empire and proclaiming its special mission in Asia. Initially China lagged behind, but after 1912 the pace of nationalist development began to quicken.

In the 1920s the Chinese nationalist movement managed to reduce the power and influence both of the warlords who controlled large territories in the interior and of the imperialist West, by weakening the effects of the "unequal treaties" (see page 806) and promoting extensive modernization. These achievements were soon undermined, however, by an internal civil war followed by war with an expanding Japan. Nationalism also flourished elsewhere in Asia, scoring a major victory in the Philippines.

The Rise of Nationalist China

The 1911 Revolution led by Sun Yatsen (1866–1925) overthrew the Qing Dynasty, and after four thousand years of monarchy the last Chinese emperor, Puyi (1906–1967), abdicated in February 1912 (see page 809). Sun Yatsen proclaimed China a republic and thereby opened an era of unprecedented change for Chinese society. Before the revolution many progressive Chinese realized that fundamental technological and political reforms were necessary to save the Chinese state, but most hoped to preserve the traditional core of Chinese civilization and culture. The fall of the ancient dynastic system shattered such hopes. If the emperor himself was no longer sacred, what was?

In 1912 Sun Yatsen turned over leadership of the republican government to the other central figure in the revolution, a seasoned and cunning military man, Yuan Shigai (Yüan Shih-k'ai). Called out of retirement to save the dynasty, Yuan (1859–1916) betrayed the Qing Dynasty's Manchu leaders and convinced the revolutionaries that he could unite the country peacefully and prevent foreign intervention. Once elected president of the republic, however, Yuan concentrated on building his own power. In 1913 he used military force to dissolve China's parliament and ruled as a dictator. China's first modern revolution had failed.

The extent of the failure became apparent only after Yuan's death in 1916, when the central government in Beijing almost disintegrated. For more than a decade thereafter, power resided in a multitude of local military leaders, the so-called warlords. Their wars, taxes, and corruption created terrible suffering.

Foreign imperialism intensified the agony of warlordism. Japan's expansion into Shandong and southern Manchuria during World War I (see page 868) angered China's growing middle class and enraged China's young patriots. On May 4, 1919, five thousand students in Beijing exploded against the decision of the Paris Peace Conference to leave the Shandong Peninsula in Japanese hands. This famous incident launched the May Fourth Movement, which opposed both foreign domination and warlord government.

The May Fourth Movement, which was both strongly pro-Marxist and passionately anti-imperialist, looked to the October 1917 Bolshevik Revolution in Russia as a model for its own nationalist revolution. In 1923 Sun Yatsen decided to ally his Nationalist Party, or Guomindang, with Lenin's Communist Third International and the newly formed Chinese Communist Party. The result was the first of many so-called national liberation fronts, in keeping with Lenin's blueprint for temporarily uniting all anti-conservative, anti-imperialist forces in a common revolutionary struggle.

Sun, however, was no Communist. In his *Three Principles of the People*, elaborating on the official Nationalist Party ideology — nationalism, democracy, and people's livelihood — nationalism remained of prime importance:

> Compared to the other peoples of the world we have the greatest population and our civilization is four thousand years old; we should be advancing in the front rank with the nations of Europe and America. But the Chinese people have only family and clan solidarity, they do not have national spirit. . . . If we do not earnestly espouse nationalism and weld together our four hundred million people into a strong nation, there is a danger of China's being lost and our people being destroyed. If we wish to avert this catastrophe, we must espouse nationalism and bring this national spirit to the salvation of the country.[7]

Democracy, in contrast, had a less exalted meaning. Sun equated it with firm rule by the Nationalists, who would improve people's lives through land reform and welfare measures.

Sun planned to use the Nationalist Party's revolutionary army to crush the warlords and reunite China under a strong central government. When Sun unexpectedly died in 1925, Jiang Jieshi (traditionally called Chiang Kai-shek) (1887–1975), the young Japanese-educated director of the party's army training school, took his place. In 1926 and 1927 Jiang led Nationalist armies in a successful attack on warlord governments in central and northern China. In 1928 the Nationalists established a new capital at Nanjing. Foreign states recognized the Nanjing government, and superficial observers believed China to be truly reunified.

In fact, national unification was only skin-deep. China remained a vast agricultural country plagued by foreign concessions, regional differences, and a lack of modern communications. Moreover, the uneasy alliance between the Nationalist Party and the Chinese Communist Party had turned into a bitter, deadly rivalry. Justifiably fearful of Communist subversion of the Nationalist government, Jiang decided in April 1927 to liquidate his left-wing "allies" in a bloody purge. Chinese Communists went into hiding and vowed revenge.

China's Intellectual Revolution

Nationalism was the most powerful idea in China between 1911 and 1929, but it was only one aspect of a complex intellectual revolution, generally known as the **New Culture Movement**, that hammered at traditional Chinese thought and custom, advocated cultural renaissance, and pushed China into the modern world. The New Culture Movement was founded around 1916 by young Western-oriented intellectuals in Beijing, some of whom were later involved in the May Fourth Movement in 1919. These intellectuals fiercely attacked China's ancient Confucian ethics, which subordinated subjects to rulers, sons to fathers, and wives to husbands. As modernists, they provocatively advocated new and anti-Confucian virtues: individualism, democratic equality, and the critical scientific method. They also promoted the use of simple, understandable written language as a means to clear thinking and mass education. China, they said, needed a whole new culture, a radically different worldview.

Many intellectuals thought the radical worldview China needed was Marxist socialism. It, too, was Western in origin, "scientific" in approach, and materialist in

The Fate of a Chinese Patriot
On May 30, 1925, Shanghai police opened fire on a group of Chinese demonstrators who were protesting unfair labor practices and wages and the foreign imperialist presence in their country. The police killed nine people and wounded many others, touching off nationwide and international protests and attacks on foreign offices and businesses. This political cartoon shows the fate of the Chinese patriots at the hands of warlords and foreign imperialists. (Library of Congress, LC-USZ62-99451)

its denial of religious belief and Confucian family ethics. But while liberalism and individualism reflected the bewildering range of Western thought since the Enlightenment, Marxist socialism offered the certainty of a single all-encompassing creed. As one young Communist intellectual exclaimed, "I am now able to impose order on all the ideas which I could not reconcile; I have found the key to all the problems which appeared to me self-contradictory and insoluble."[8]

Though undeniably Western, Marxism provided a means of criticizing Western dominance, thereby salving Chinese pride. Chinese Communists could blame China's pitiful weakness on rapacious foreign capitalistic imperialism. Thus Marxism, as modified by Lenin and applied by the Bolsheviks in the Soviet Union, appeared as a means of catching up with the hated but envied West. For Chinese believers, it promised salvation soon.

Chinese Communists could and did interpret Marxism-Leninism to appeal to the masses—the peasants. Mao Zedong (Mao Tse-tung) in particular quickly recognized the impoverished Chinese peasantry's enormous revolutionary potential. A member of a prosperous, hard-working peasant family, Mao (1893–1976) converted to Marxist socialism in 1918. He began his revolutionary career as an urban labor organizer. In 1925 protest strikes by Chinese textile workers against their Japanese employers unexpectedly spread from the big coastal cities to rural China, prompting Mao (like Lenin in Russia) to reconsider the peasants (see page 878). Investigating the rapid growth of radical peasant associations in Hunan province, Mao argued passionately in a 1927 report:

> The force of the peasantry is like that of the raging winds and driving rain. It is rapidly increasing in violence. No force can stand in its way. The peasantry will tear apart all nets which bind it and hasten along the road to liberation. They will bury beneath them all forces of imperialism, militarism, corrupt officialdom, village bosses and evil gentry.[9]

Mao's first experiment in peasant revolt — the Autumn Harvest Uprising of September 1927 — was not successful, but Mao learned quickly. He advocated equal distribution of land and broke up his forces into small guerrilla groups. After 1928 he and his supporters built up a self-governing Communist soviet, centered at Ruijin (Juichin) in southeastern China, and dug in against Nationalist attacks.

China's intellectual revolution also stimulated profound changes in popular culture and family life. After the 1911 Revolution Chinese women enjoyed increasingly greater freedom and equality. Foot binding was outlawed and attacked as cruel and uncivilized. Arranged marriages and polygamy declined. Women gradually gained unprecedented educational and economic opportunities. Thus rising nationalism and the intellectual revolution interacted with monumental changes in Chinese family life. (See "Individuals in Society: Ning Lao, a Chinese Working Woman," page 918.)

From Liberalism to Ultranationalism in Japan

The nearly total homogeneity of the Japanese population (98.5 percent ethnic Japanese) was a major factor in the Meiji reformers' efforts to build a powerful, nationalistic, modern state and resist Western imperialism (see page 810). Their spectacular success deeply impressed Japan's fellow Asians. The Japanese, alone among Asia's peoples, had mastered modern industrial technology by 1910 and had fought victorious wars against both China and Russia. The First World War brought more triumphs. In 1915 Japan easily seized Germany's Asian holdings and retained most of them as League of Nations mandates. The Japanese economy expanded enormously. Profits soared as Japan won new markets that wartime Europe could no longer supply.

In the early 1920s Japan made further progress on all fronts. Most Japanese nationalists believed that Japan had a semidivine mission to enlighten and protect Asia, but some were convinced that they could achieve their goal peacefully. In 1922 Japan signed a naval arms limitation treaty with the Western powers and returned some of its control over the Shandong Peninsula to China. These conciliatory moves reduced tensions in East Asia. At home Japan seemed headed toward genuine democracy. The electorate expanded twelvefold between 1918 and 1925 as all males over twenty-five won the vote. Two-party competition was intense. Japanese living standards were the highest in Asia. Literacy was universal.

Japan's remarkable rise was accompanied by serious problems. Japan had a rapidly growing population but scarce natural resources. As early as the 1920s Japan was exporting manufactured goods in order to pay for imports of food and essential raw materials. Deeply enmeshed in world trade, Japan was vulnerable to every boom and bust. These economic realities broadened support for Japan's colonial empire. Before World War I Japanese leaders saw colonial expansion primarily in terms of international prestige and national defense. They believed that control of Taiwan, Korea, and Manchuria provided an essential "outer ring of defense" to protect the home islands from Russian attack and Anglo-American imperialism. Now, in the 1920s, Japan's colonies also seemed essential for markets, raw materials, and economic growth.

Japan's rapid industrial development also created an imbalanced "dualistic" economy. The modern sector consisted of a handful of giant conglomerate firms, the zaibatsu, or "financial combines." Zaibatsu firms like Mitsubishi employed thousands of workers and owned banks, mines, steel mills, cotton factories, shipyards, and trading companies,

INDIVIDUALS IN SOCIETY • Ning Lao, a Chinese Working Woman

The voice of the poor and uneducated is often muffled in history. Thus *A Daughter of Han*, a rare autobiography of an illiterate working woman as told to an American friend, Ida Pruitt, offers unforgettable insights into the evolution of ordinary Chinese life and family relations.

Ning Lao was born in 1867 to poor parents in the northern city of Penglai on the Shandong Peninsula. Her foot binding was delayed to age nine, since she "loved so much to run and play." She described the pain when the bandages were finally drawn tight: "My feet hurt so much that for two years I had to crawl on my knees."* Her arranged marriage at age fourteen was a disaster. She found that her husband was a drug addict ("in those days everyone took opium to some extent") who sold everything to pay for his habit. Yet "there was no freedom then for women," and "it was no light thing for a woman to leave her house" and husband. Thus Ning Lao endured her situation until her husband sold their four-year-old daughter to buy opium. Taking her remaining baby daughter, she fled.

Taking off her foot bandages, Ning Lao became a beggar. Her feet began to spread, quite improperly, but she walked without pain. And the beggar's life was "not the hardest one," she thought, for a beggar woman could go where she pleased. To better care for her child, Ning Lao became a servant and a cook in prosperous households. Some of her mistresses were concubines (secondary wives taken by rich men in middle age), and she concluded that concubinage resulted in nothing but quarrels and heartache. Hot tempered and quick to take offense and leave an employer, the hard-working woman always found a new job quickly. In time she became a peddler of luxury goods to wealthy women confined to their homes.

The two unshakable values that buoyed Ning Lao were a tough, fatalistic acceptance of life—"Only fortune that comes of itself will come. There is no use to seek for it"—and devotion to her family. She eventually returned to her husband, who had mellowed, seldom took opium, and was "good" in those years. She reflected, "But I did not miss him when he died. I had my newborn son and I was happy. My house was established. . . . Truly all my life I spent thinking of my family." Her life-

---

*Ida Pruitt, *A Daughter of Han: The Autobiography of a Chinese Working Woman* (New Haven, Conn.: Yale University Press, 1945), p. 22. Other quotations are from pages 83, 62, 71, 182, 166, 235, and 246.

---

all of them closely interrelated. Zaibatsu firms wielded enormous economic power and dominated the other sector of the economy, an unorganized multitude of peasant farmers and craftsmen. The result was financial oligarchy, corruption of government officials, and a weak middle class.

Behind the façade of party politics, the old and new elites—the emperor, high government officials, big businessmen, and military leaders—were jockeying savagely for the real power. Cohesive leadership, which had played such an important role in Japan's modernization by the Meiji reformers, had ceased to exist. By far the most serious challenge to peaceful progress was fanatical nationalism. As in Europe, ultralong devotion was reciprocated by her son and granddaughter, who cared for her well in her old age.

Ning Lao's remarkable life story encompasses both old and new Chinese attitudes toward family life. Her son moved to the capital city of Beijing, worked in an office, and had only one wife. Her granddaughter, Su Teh, studied in missionary schools and became a college teacher and a determined foe of arranged marriages. She personified the trend toward greater freedom for Chinese women.

Generational differences also highlighted changing political attitudes. When the Japanese invaded China and occupied Beijing in 1937, Ning Lao thought that "perhaps the Mandate of Heaven had passed to the Japanese . . . and we should listen to them as our new masters." Her nationalistic granddaughter disagreed. She urged resistance and the creation of a new China, where the people governed themselves. Leaving to join the guerrillas in 1938, Su Teh gave her savings to her family and promised to continue to help them. One must be good to one's family, she said, but one must also work for the country.

QUESTIONS FOR ANALYSIS

1. Compare the lives of Ning Lao and her granddaughter. In what ways were they different and similar?

2. In a broader historical perspective, what do you find most significant about Ning Lao's account of her life? Why?

⯈LaunchPad
ONLINE DOCUMENT PROJECT

How did China's conflicts with the Western powers and Japan affect its people? Read the excerpts from Ning Lao's autobiography, and then complete a quiz and writing assignment based on the evidence and details from this chapter.

See inside the front cover to learn more.

nationalism first emerged in Japan in the late nineteenth century but did not flower fully until the First World War and the 1930s.

Though their views were often vague, Japan's ultranationalists shared several fundamental beliefs. They were violently anti-Western. They rejected democracy, big business, and Marxist socialism, which they blamed for destroying the older, superior Japanese practices they wanted to restore. Reviving old myths, they stressed the emperor's godlike qualities and the samurai warrior's code of honor, obedience, and responsibility. Despising party politics, they assassinated moderate leaders and plotted armed uprisings to achieve their goals. Above all else, the ultranationalists preached

Japanese Suffragists   In the 1920s Japanese women pressed for political emancipation in demonstrations like this one, but they did not receive the right to vote until 1946. Like these suffragists, some young Japanese women adopted Western fashions. Most workers in modern Japanese textile factories were women. (Time Life Pictures/Getty Images)

foreign expansion. Like Western imperialists shouldering "the white man's burden," Japanese ultranationalists thought their mission was a noble one. "Asia for the Asians" was their anti-Western rallying cry. As the famous ultranationalist Kita Ikki wrote in 1923, "Our seven hundred million brothers in China and India have no other path to independence than that offered by our guidance and protection."[10]

The ultranationalists were noisy and violent in the 1920s, but it took the Great Depression of the 1930s to tip the scales decisively in their favor. The worldwide depression, which had dire consequences for many countries (see Chapter 30), hit Japan like a tidal wave in 1930. Exports and wages collapsed; unemployment and raw suffering soared. Starving peasants ate the bark off trees and sold their daughters to brothels. The ultranationalists blamed the system, and people listened.

Japan Against China

Among those who listened with particular care were young Japanese army officers in Manchuria, the underpopulated, resource-rich province of northeastern China controlled by the Japanese army since its victory over Russia in 1905. Many junior Japanese officers in Manchuria came from the peasantry and were distressed by the stories of rural suffering they heard from home. They also knew the Japanese army's budget and prestige had declined in the prosperous 1920s.

The rise of Chinese nationalism worried the young officers most. This new political force, embodied in the Guomindang unification of China, challenged Japanese control over Manchuria. In response, junior Japanese officers in Manchuria, in cooperation with top generals in Tokyo, secretly manufactured an excuse for aggression in late 1931. They blew up some Japanese-owned railroad tracks near the city of Shenyang (Mukden) and then, with reinforcements rushed in from Korea, quickly occupied all of Manchuria in "self-defense."

In 1932 Japan proclaimed Manchuria an independent state and installed Puyi, the last Qing emperor, as puppet emperor. When the League of Nations condemned its aggression in Manchuria, Japan resigned in protest. Japanese aggression in Manchuria proved that the army, though reporting directly to the Japanese emperor, was an independent force subject to no outside control.

The Japanese puppet state named Manchukuo in northeast China became the model for the subsequent conquest and occupation of China and then Southeast Asia. Throughout the 1930s the Japanese worked to integrate Manchuria, along with Korea and Taiwan, into a large, self-sufficient economic bloc that provided resources, markets, and investment opportunities safe from Western power in East Asia. While exporting raw materials, state-sponsored Japanese companies in Manchuria also built steel mills and heavy industry to supply vital military goods. At home, newspapers and newsreels glorified Japan's efforts and mobilized public support for colonial empire.

For China the Japanese conquest of Manchuria was disastrous. Japanese aggression in Manchuria drew attention away from modernizing efforts. The Nationalist government promoted a massive boycott of Japanese goods but lost interest in social reform. Above all, the Nationalist government after 1931 completely neglected land reform and the Chinese peasants' grinding poverty.

As in many poor agricultural societies throughout history, Chinese peasants paid roughly half of their crops to their landlords as rent. Landownership was very unequal. One study estimated that a mere 4 percent of families, usually absentee landlords living in cities, owned fully half the land. Poor peasants and farm laborers—70 percent of the rural population—owned only one-sixth of the land. As a result, peasants were heavily in debt and chronically underfed. A contemporaneous Chinese economist spelled out the revolutionary implications: "It seems clear that the land problem in China today is as acute as that of eighteenth-century France or nineteenth-century Russia."[11] Mao Zedong agreed.

Having abandoned land reform, partly because they themselves were often landowners, the Nationalists under Jiang Jieshi devoted their energies between 1930 and 1934 to great campaigns of encirclement and extermination of the Communists' rural power base in southeastern China. In 1934 they closed in for the kill, but, in one of the most incredible sagas of modern times, the main Communist army broke out, beat off attacks, and retreated 6,000 miles in twelve months to a remote region on the northwestern border. Of the estimated 100,000 men and women who began the Long March, only 8,000 to 10,000 reached the final destination in Yan'an.

There Mao built up his forces once again, established a new territorial base, and won local peasant support in five unprecedented ways. First, Mao's forces did not pillage and rape across the countryside as imperialist and warlord armies had always done. Second, Mao set up schools, albeit for Marxist education, so the nearly universally illiterate peasants could learn to read and write. Third, Mao established health clinics to provide the peasants with basic medical care. Fourth, Mao's armies, rather than stealing the peasants' produce, put down their weapons and helped the peasants plant and harvest their crops. Fifth, Communist courts tried the warlords and landlords for crimes against the peasants, who for the first time in Chinese history received economic and social justice.

In Japan politics became increasingly chaotic. In 1937 the Japanese military and the ultranationalists were in command. Unable to force China to cede more territory in northern China, they used a minor incident near Beijing as a pretext for a general attack. This marked the beginning of what became World War II in Asia, although Japan issued no declaration of war. The Nationalist government, which had just formed a united front with the Communists, fought hard, but Japanese troops quickly took Beijing and northern China. Taking the great port of Shanghai after ferocious combat, the Japanese launched an immediate attack up the Yangzi River.

Foretelling the horrors of World War II, the Japanese air force bombed Chinese cities and civilian populations with unrelenting fury. Nanjing, the capital, fell in December 1937. Entering the city, Japanese soldiers went berserk and committed dreadful atrocities over seven weeks. They brutally murdered an estimated 200,000 to 300,000 Chinese civilians and unarmed soldiers, and raped 20,000 to 80,000 Chinese women. The "Rape of Nanjing" combined with other Japanese atrocities to outrage world opinion. The Western powers denounced Japanese aggression but, with tensions rising in Europe, took no action.

By late 1938 Japanese armies occupied sizable portions of coastal China. But the Nationalists and the Communists had retreated to the interior, and both refused to accept defeat. In 1939, as Europe edged toward another great war, China and Japan were bogged down in a savage stalemate. This undeclared war—called by historians the Second Sino-Japanese War (1937–1945)—provided a spectacular example of conflicting nationalisms.

Striving for Independence in Southeast Asia

The tide of nationalism was also rising in Southeast Asia. Like their counterparts in India, China, and Japan, nationalists in French Indochina, the Dutch East Indies, and the Philippines urgently wanted genuine political independence and freedom from foreign rule. In both French Indochina and the Dutch East Indies they ran up against an imperialist stone wall. The obstacle to Filipino independence came from America and Japan.

The French in Indochina, as in all their colonies, refused to export the liberal policies contained in the stirring words of their own Declaration of the Rights of Man and of the Citizen: liberty, equality, and fraternity (see page 655). This uncompromising attitude stimulated the growth of an equally stubborn Communist opposition under Ho Chi Minh (1890–1969), which despite ruthless repression emerged as the dominant anti-French force in Indochina.

In the East Indies—modern Indonesia—the Dutch made some concessions after the First World War, establishing a people's council with very limited lawmaking power. But in the 1930s the Dutch cracked down hard, jailing all the important nationalist leaders. Like the French, the Dutch were determined to hold on.

In the Philippines, however, a well-established nationalist movement achieved greater success. As in colonial Latin America, the Spanish in the Philippines had been indefatigable missionaries. By the late nineteenth century the Filipino population was 80 percent Catholic. Filipinos shared a common cultural heritage and a common racial

Uncle Sam as Schoolmaster

In this cartoon that first appeared on the cover of *Harper's Weekly* in August 1898, unruly students identified as a "Cuban Ex-patriot" and a "Guerilla" are being disciplined with a switch by a stern Uncle Sam as he tries to teach them self-government. The gentleman to the left reading a book is José Miguel Gómez, one of Cuba's revolutionary heroes, while the Filipino insurrectionist Emilio Aguinaldo is made to wear a dunce cap and stand in the corner. The two well-behaved girls to the right represent Hawaii and Puerto Rico. (The Granger Collection, NYC—All rights reserved.)

origin. Education, especially for girls, was advanced for Southeast Asia, and already in 1843 a higher percentage of people could read in the Philippines than in Spain itself. Economic development helped to create a westernized elite, which turned first to reform and then to revolution in the 1890s. As in Egypt and Turkey, long-standing intimate contact with Western civilization created a strong nationalist movement at an early date.

Filipino nationalists were bitterly disillusioned when the United States, having taken the Philippines from Spain in the Spanish-American War of 1898, ruthlessly beat down a patriotic revolt and denied the universal Filipino desire for independence. The Americans claimed the Philippines was not ready for self-rule and might be seized by Germany or Britain if it could not establish a stable, secure government. As the imperialist power in the Philippines, the United States encouraged education and promoted capitalistic economic development. And as in British India, an elected legislature was given some real powers. In 1919 President Wilson even promised eventual independence, though subsequent Republican administrations saw it as a distant goal.

As in India and French Indochina, demands for independence grew. One important contributing factor was American racial attitudes. Americans treated Filipinos as inferiors and introduced segregationist practices borrowed from the American South. American racism made passionate nationalists of many Filipinos. However, it was the Great Depression that had the most radical impact on the Philippines.

As the United States collapsed economically in the 1930s, the Philippines suddenly appeared to be a liability rather than an asset. American farm groups lobbied for protection from cheap Filipino sugar. To protect American jobs, labor unions demanded an end to Filipino immigration. Responding to public pressure, in 1934 Congress made the Philippines a self-governing commonwealth and scheduled independence for 1944. Sugar imports were reduced, and immigration was limited to only fifty Filipinos per year.

Chapter Review

MAKE IT STICK

 LearningCurve
Go online and use LearningCurve to retain what you've read.

IDENTIFY KEY TERMS

Identify and explain the significance of each item below.

Permanent Mandates Commission
(p. 899)
Sykes-Picot Agreement (p. 903)
Balfour Declaration (p. 903)
Treaty of Lausanne (p. 905)
Majlis (p. 906)
kibbutz (p. 909)

Lucknow Pact (p. 910)
satyagraha (p. 911)
May Fourth Movement (p. 914)
New Culture Movement (p. 915)
zaibatsu (p. 917)
Long March (p. 921)

REVIEW THE MAIN IDEAS

Answer the focus questions from each section of the chapter.

1. Why did modern nationalism develop in Asia between the First and Second World Wars, and what was its appeal? (p. 898)

2. How did the Ottoman Empire's collapse in World War I shape nationalist movements in the Middle East? (p. 901)

3. What role did Gandhi and his campaign of militant nonviolence play in leading India to independence from the British? (p. 909)

4. How did nationalism shape political developments in East and Southeast Asia? (p. 913)

MAKE CONNECTIONS

Analyze the larger developments and continuities within and across chapters.

1. In what ways were Japan's and China's reactions to European imperialism similar, and in what ways were they different?

2. Compare and contrast Indian and Turkish nationalism in response to European imperialism.

3. Besides modernizing their society and industrializing their economy, the Japanese also adopted ideologies from the West that would heavily influence their domestic and foreign policies in the first half of the twentieth century. What were these ideologies? Give examples of how they were important.

⯈LaunchPad

ONLINE DOCUMENT PROJECT

Foreign Intervention in China
How did China's conflicts with the Western powers and Japan affect its people?

Read the excerpts from Ning Lao's autobiography, and then complete a quiz and writing assignment based on the evidence and details from this chapter.

See inside the front cover to learn more.

CHRONOLOGY

1904–1905	• Russo-Japanese War ends in Russia's defeat
1916	• Sykes-Picot Agreement divides Ottoman Empire; Lucknow Pact forms alliance between Hindus and Muslims in India; New Culture Movement in China begins
1917	• Balfour Declaration establishes Jewish homeland in Palestine
1919	• Amritsar Massacre in India; May Fourth Movement in China; Treaty of Versailles; Afghanistan achieves independence
1920	• King of Syria deposed by French; Gandhi launches campaign of nonviolent resistance against British rule in India
1920s–1930s	• Large numbers of European Jews immigrate to Palestine; Hebrew becomes common language
1923	• Sun Yatsen allies Nationalist Party with Chinese Communists; Treaty of Lausanne ends war in Turkey; Mustafa Kemal begins to modernize and secularize Turkey
1925	• Reza Shah Pahlavi proclaims himself shah of Persia and begins modernization campaign
1927	• Jiang Jieshi, leader of Chinese Nationalist Party, purges his Communist allies
1930	• Gandhi leads Indians on march to the sea to protest the British salt tax
1931	• Japan occupies Manchuria
1932	• Iraq gains independence in return for military alliance with Great Britain
1934	• Mao Zedong leads Chinese Communists on Long March; Philippines gains self-governing commonwealth status from United States
1937	• Japanese militarists launch attack on China; Rape of Nanjing

30

✓ LearningCurve
After reading the chapter, go online and use LearningCurve to retain what you've read.

The Great Depression and World War II

1929–1945

THE YEARS OF ANXIETY AND POLITICAL MANEUVERING IN EUROPE
that followed World War I were made much worse when a massive economic depression spread around the world following the American stock market crash of October 1929. An increasingly interconnected global economy now collapsed. Free-market capitalism appeared to have run its course. People everywhere looked to new leaders for relief, some democratically elected, many not. In Europe on the eve of the Second World War, liberal democratic governments were surviving only in Great Britain, France, the Low Countries, the Scandinavian nations, and neutral Switzerland. Worldwide, in countries such as Brazil, Japan, the Soviet Union, and others, as well as in Europe, dictatorships seemed the wave of the future.

The mid-twentieth-century era of dictatorship is a highly disturbing chapter in the history of civilization. The key development was not only the resurgence of authoritarian rule but also the rise of a particularly ruthless brand of totalitarianism that reached its fullest realization in the Soviet Union, Nazi Germany, and Japan in the 1930s. Stalin, Hitler, and Japan's military leaders intervened radically in society and ruled with unprecedented severity. Hitler's desire for eastward territorial expansion was partially racially motivated (against the Slavs and Jews, whom he considered inferior). His sudden attack on Poland in 1939 started World War II. Hitler's successes encouraged the Japanese to expand their stalemated Chinese campaign into a vast Pacific war by attacking Pearl Harbor in Hawaii and advancing into Southeast Asia. By war's end, millions had died on the battlefields and in the bombed-out cities. Millions more died in the Holocaust, in Stalin's Soviet Union from purges and forced imposition of communism, and during Japan's quest to create an "Asia for Asians."

The Great Depression, 1929–1939

What caused the Great Depression, and what were its consequences?

Like the Great War, the Great Depression must be spelled with capital letters. Beginning in 1929 an exceptionally long and severe economic depression struck the entire world with ever-greater intensity, and recovery was uneven and slow. Only the Second World War brought it to an end.

The social and political consequences of prolonged economic collapse were enormous and were felt worldwide. Economic depression was a major factor in Japan's aggressive empire building and militarism in the 1930s. Elsewhere in Asia, as well as in Latin America and Africa, agricultural depression devastated millions of peasants and small farmers. Western markets for raw materials dried up, and prices collapsed. Urban workers faced pay cuts and high unemployment. In West Africa anticolonial nationalism attracted widespread support for the first time in the 1930s, setting the stage for strong independence movements after World War II.

In Europe and the United States the depression shattered the fragile political stability of the mid-1920s. Mass unemployment made insecurity a reality for millions of ordinary people. In desperation, people looked for new leaders who would "do something." They willingly supported radical attempts to deal with the crisis by both democratic leaders and dictators. Leaders espousing alternatives to free-market capitalism, such as fascism and communism, gained massive popular support.

The Economic Crisis

Though economic activity was already declining moderately in many countries by early 1929, the U.S. stock market crash in October of that year really started the Great Depression. The American stock market boom, which had seen stock prices double between early 1928 and September 1929, was built on borrowed money. Two factors explain why. First, the wealth gap (or income inequality) between America's rich and poor reached its greatest extent in the twentieth century in 1928–1929. One percent of Americans then held 70 percent of all America's wealth. (Similar wealth gaps were present in other countries as well.) This meant the other 99 percent of Americans had to divide up the remaining 30 percent of wealth for all their purchases. Eventually, with not enough money to go around, the 99 percent had to borrow to make even basic purchases — as a result, the cost of farm credit, installment loans, and home mortgages skyrocketed. Then a point was reached where the 99 percent could borrow no more, so they stopped buying.

Second, wealthy investors and speculators, as they accumulated more and more wealth, took increasingly greater investment risks. One such popular risk was to buy stocks by paying only a small fraction of the total purchase price and borrowing the remainder from their stockbrokers or from banks — about $4 out of every $10 in bank loans went to buy stocks. Even people of more modest means speculated in this way, believing, as had been true throughout the "Roaring Twenties," that the market would just keep going up. Such buying "on margin" was extremely dangerous. When prices started falling, the hard-pressed margin buyers started selling to pay their debts. The result was a financial panic. Countless investors and speculators were wiped out in a matter of days or weeks, and the New York stock market's crash started a domino effect that hit most of the world's major stock exchanges.

The financial panic in the United States triggered a worldwide financial crisis. Throughout the 1920s American bankers and investors had lent large sums to many countries, and as panic spread, New York bankers began recalling their short-term loans. Frightened citizens in Europe, Australia, Canada, several countries in Latin America, and elsewhere began to withdraw their bank savings, leading to general financial chaos. The recall of American loans also accelerated the collapse in world prices, as business people dumped goods in a frantic attempt to get cash to pay what they owed.

The financial chaos led to a drastic decline in production in country after country. Between 1929 and 1933 world output of goods fell by an estimated 38 percent. Countries now turned inward and tried to go it alone. Many followed the American example, in which protective tariffs were raised to their highest levels ever in 1930 to seal off shrinking national markets for American producers only.

Although historians' opinions differ, two factors probably best explain the relentless slide to the bottom from 1929 to early 1933. First, the international economy lacked leadership able to maintain stability when the crisis came. Neither the seriously weakened British nor the United States — the world's economic leaders — stabilized

Louisville Flood Victims, 1937   During the Great Depression, Louisville, Kentucky, was hit by the worst flood in its history. The famous documentary photographer Margaret Bourke-White captured this image of African American flood victims lining up for food. Not only does the billboard message mock the Depression-era conditions, but the smiling white family appears to be driving its car through the line of people, drawing attention to America's race and class differences. (Margaret Bourke-White/Time-Life Pictures/Getty Images)

the international economic system in 1929. Instead Britain and the United States cut back international lending and erected high tariffs.

Second, in almost every country, governments cut their budgets and reduced spending instead of running large deficits to try to stimulate their economies. That is, governments needed to put large sums of money into the economy to stimulate job growth and spending. After World War II such a "counter-cyclical policy," advocated by the British economist John Maynard Keynes (1883–1946), became a well-established weapon against depression. But in the 1930s orthodox economists generally regarded Keynes's prescription with horror.

Mass Unemployment

The need for large-scale government spending was tied to mass unemployment. The 99 percent's halt in buying contributed to the financial crisis, which led to production cuts, which in turn caused workers to lose their jobs and have even less money to buy goods. This led to still more production cuts, and unemployment soared. In Britain unemployment had averaged 12 percent in the 1920s; between 1930 and 1935 it averaged more than 18 percent. In Germany 25 percent and in Australia 32 percent of the people were out of work in 1932. The worst unemployment was in the United States. In the 1920s unemployment there had averaged only 5 percent; in 1933 it soared to about 33 percent of the entire labor force: 14 million people were out of work. This was the only time in American history when more people left America than immigrated in—including thousands of Mexican Americans who suffered increasing hostility, accused of stealing jobs from those who considered themselves to be "real Americans," and perhaps a hundred thousand Americans who migrated to the Soviet Union, attracted by communism's promises of jobs and a new life.

Mass unemployment created great social problems. Poverty increased dramatically, although in most industrialized countries unemployed workers generally received some meager unemployment benefits or public aid that prevented starvation. Millions of unemployed people lost their spirit, and homes and ways of life were disrupted in countless personal tragedies. In 1932 workers in Manchester, England, appealed to their city officials—a typical appeal echoed throughout the Western world:

> We tell you that thousands of people . . . are in desperate straits. We tell you that men, women, and children are going hungry. . . . We tell you that great numbers are being rendered distraught through the stress and worry of trying to exist without work. . . .
>
> If you do not do this—if you do not provide useful work for the unemployed—what, we ask, is your alternative? Do not imagine that this colossal tragedy of unemployment is going on endlessly without some fateful catastrophe. Hungry men are angry men.[1]

Only strong government action could deal with the social powder keg preparing to explode.

The New Deal in the United States

The Great Depression and the response to it marked a major turning point in American history. Herbert Hoover (U.S. pres. 1929–1933) and his administration initially reacted to the stock market crash and economic decline with dogged optimism but limited action. When the financial crisis struck Europe with full force in summer 1931 and boomeranged back to the United States, banks failed and unemployment soared. In 1932 industrial production fell to about 50 percent of its 1929 level.

In these desperate circumstances Franklin Delano Roosevelt (U.S. pres. 1933–1945) won a landslide presidential victory in 1932 with promises of a "New Deal for the forgotten man." Roosevelt's basic goal was to preserve capitalism by reforming it. Rejecting socialism and government ownership of industry, Roosevelt advocated forceful federal government intervention in the economy. His commitment to national relief programs marked a profound shift from the traditional stress on family support and local community responsibility.

As in Asia, Africa, and Latin America, American farmers were hard hit by the Great Depression, and agricultural recovery became a top priority. Roosevelt's decision to leave the gold standard and devalue the dollar was designed to raise American prices and save farmers. Innovative programs, such as the 1933 Agricultural Adjustment Act, aimed to raise prices and farm income by limiting production. For a while, these measures worked.

Roosevelt then attacked mass unemployment, by creating over a hundred new federal agencies. These launched a vast range of public works projects so the federal government could directly employ as many people as financially possible. The most famous agency was the Works Progress Administration (WPA), set up in 1935. The WPA employed one-fifth of the entire U.S. labor force at some point in the 1930s, and these workers constructed public buildings, bridges, and highways.

Following the path blazed by Germany's Bismarck in the 1880s (see page 737), the U.S. government in 1935 established a national social security system with old-age pensions and unemployment benefits. The 1935 National Labor Relations Act declared collective bargaining to be U.S. policy, and union membership more than doubled. In general, between 1935 and 1938 government rulings and social reforms chipped away at the privileges of the wealthy and tried to help ordinary people.

Despite undeniable accomplishments in social reform, the New Deal was only partly successful as a response to the Great Depression. At the height of the recovery in May 1937, 7 million workers were still unemployed (down from a high of 15 million in 1933). A reduction in federal government spending only worsened the economic situation, causing a recession in 1937–1938. Unemployment was still a staggering 10 million when war broke out in Europe in 1939. The New Deal brought fundamental reform, but it never did pull the United States out of the depression; only the Second World War did that.

The European Response to the Depression

The American stock market's collapse in October 1929 set off a chain of economic downturns that hit Europe, particularly Germany and Great Britain, the hardest. Postwar Europe had emerged from the Great War deeply in debt and in desperate need of investment capital to rebuild. The United States became the primary creditor and financier. Germany borrowed, for example, to pay Britain war reparations, and then Britain took that money and repaid its war debts and investment loans to America. When the American economy crashed, the whole circular system crashed with it.

Of all the Western democracies, the Scandinavian countries under socialist leadership responded most successfully to the challenge of the Great Depression. When the economic crisis struck in 1929, Sweden's socialist government pioneered the use of large-scale deficits to finance public works projects and thereby maintain production and employment. Scandinavian governments also increased social welfare benefits, from old-age pensions and unemployment insurance to subsidized housing and maternity allowances. All this spending required a large bureaucracy and high taxes. Yet both private and cooperative enterprise thrived, as did democracy. Some observers considered Scandinavia's welfare socialism an appealing middle way between what they considered to be sick capitalism and cruel communism or fascism.

In Britain, Ramsay MacDonald's Labour government (1929–1931) and, after 1931, the Conservative-dominated coalition government followed orthodox economic theory. The budget was balanced, but unemployed workers received barely enough welfare support to live. Nevertheless, the economy recovered considerably after 1932, reflecting the gradual reorientation of the British economy. After abandoning the gold standard in 1931 and establishing protective tariffs in 1932, Britain concentrated increasingly on the national, rather than the international, market. Old export industries, such as textiles and coal, continued to decline, but new industries, such as automobiles and electrical appliances, grew. These developments encouraged British isolationism and often had devastating economic consequences for Britain's far-flung colonies and dominions, particularly Australia, Canada, New Zealand, and India, which depended heavily upon reciprocal trade with Great Britain and the United States.

The Great Depression came late to France as it was relatively less industrialized and more isolated from the world economy. But once the depression hit, it stayed. Decline was steady until 1935, and a short-lived recovery never restored production or employment to predepression levels. Economic stagnation both reflected and heightened an ongoing political crisis, as liberals, democratic socialists, and Communists fought for control of the French government with conservatives and the far right. The latter groups agitated against parliamentary democracy and turned to Mussolini's Italy and Hitler's Germany for inspiration. At the same time, the Communist Party and many workers looked to Stalin's Russia for guidance. Moderate republicanism's vital center was sapped from both sides.

Frightened by the growing popularity of Hitler- and Mussolini-style right-wing dictatorships at home and abroad, the Communist, Socialist, and Radical Parties in France formed an alliance — the **Popular Front** — for the May 1936 national elections. Following its clear victory, the Popular Front government made the only real attempt to deal with France's social and economic problems of the 1930s. Inspired by Roosevelt's New Deal, the Popular Front launched a far-reaching program of social and economic reform. Popular with workers and the lower middle class, these measures were quickly sabotaged by rapid inflation, rising wages, a decline in overseas exports, and cries of socialist revolution from frightened conservatives. Wealthy people sneaked their money out of the country, labor unrest grew, and France entered a severe financial crisis. Politically, the Popular Front lost many left-wing supporters when it failed to back the republican cause in the Spanish Civil War, while Hitler and Mussolini openly armed and supported Franco's nationalists (see page 949). In June 1937, with the country hopelessly divided, the Popular Front collapsed.

Worldwide Effects

The Great Depression's magnitude was unprecedented, and its effect rippled well beyond Europe and the United States. As many countries and colonies in Africa, Asia, and Latin America were nearly totally dependent on one or two commodities—such as coffee beans, rubber, tin, or cocoa—for income, the implementation of protectionist trade policies by the leading industrial nations had devastating effects.

The Great Depression hit the vulnerable commodity economies of Latin America especially hard. Long dependent on foreign markets, Latin America saw its commodity prices and exports collapse as Europe and the United States drastically reduced purchases and raised tariffs to protect domestic products. Chile was arguably the hardest-hit country in the world, as 80 percent of government revenues came from the production and export of nitrate and copper, products that were now in low demand. Brazil burned millions of bags of coffee beans for which there was no longer a market. With foreign sales plummeting, Latin American countries could not buy the industrial goods they needed from abroad. The global depression provoked a profound shift toward economic nationalism after 1930, as popularly based governments worked to reduce foreign influence and gain control of their own economies and natural resources. These efforts were fairly successful. By the late 1940s factories in Argentina, Brazil, and Chile could generally satisfy domestic consumer demand for the products of light industry. But as in Hitler's Germany, the deteriorating economic conditions in Brazil, Guatemala, Nicaragua, Honduras, El Salvador, Argentina, and elsewhere also gave rise to dictatorships, some of them modeled along European Fascist lines (990–994).

The Great Depression marked a decisive turning point in the development of African nationalism. For the first time, educated Africans faced widespread unemployment. African peasants and small business people who had been drawn into world trade, and who sometimes profited from booms, also felt the agony of the decade-long bust, as did urban workers. In some areas the result was unprecedented mass protest. The Gold Coast (modern Ghana) cocoa holdups of 1930–1931 and 1937–1938 are the most famous examples (see page 987).

While Asians were somewhat affected by the Great Depression, the consequences varied greatly by country or colony and were not as serious generally as they were elsewhere. That being said, where the depression did hit, it was often severe. The price of rice—Asia's staff of life and main cash crop—fell by two-thirds between 1929 and 1932. Also crippling to the region's economies was Asia's heavy dependence on raw material exports, such as rubber and tin from Malaya for automobile production. With debts to local moneylenders fixed in value and taxes to colonial governments hardly ever reduced, many Asian peasants in the 1930s struggled under crushing debt and suffered terribly.

In China industrial production increased substantially after the Qing Dynasty collapsed in 1911, while the 1919 May Fourth Movement, which encouraged a boycott of foreign goods, caused foreign imports to drop through the 1920s. When the Great Depression reached China in the early 1930s, it hit the rural economy the hardest. China's economy depended heavily on cash-crop exports and these declined dramatically, while cheap foreign agricultural goods—such as rice and wheat—were dumped in China. Agricultural prices in 1932 were only 41 percent of 1921 prices, and rural incomes fell by over 50 percent between 1931 and 1934. While Chinese industrial production dropped off after 1931, it quickly recovered so that by 1936 it had recovered to pre-1931 levels. Much of this growth was in the military sector, as China tried to catch up with the West and also prepare for war with Japan. Still, China's main concerns during the 1930s (see Chapter 29) were a civil war between Communist and Nationalist armies, and Japan's invasion and occupation of large areas of the country.

In Japan the terrible suffering caused by the Great Depression caused ultranationalists and militarists to call for less dependence on global markets and the expansion of a self-sufficient empire. Such expansion began in 1931 when Japan invaded Chinese Manchuria, which became a major source of the raw materials needed to feed Japanese industrial growth (see Chapter 29). Japan recovered more quickly from the Great Depression than any other major industrial power because of prompt action by the civilian democratic government, but the government and large corporations continued to be blamed for the economic downturn. By the mid-1930s this lack of confidence, combined with the collapsing international economic order, Europe's and America's increasingly isolationist and protectionist policies, and a growing admiration for Nazi Germany and its authoritarian, militaristic model of government, had led the Japanese military to topple the civilian authorities and dictate Japan's future.

Authoritarian States

What was the nature of the new totalitarian dictatorships, and how did they differ from conservative authoritarian states and from each other?

Both conservative and radical totalitarian dictatorships arose in Europe in the 1920s and the 1930s. Although they sometimes overlapped in character and practice, they were profoundly different in essence.

Conservative Authoritarianism

The traditional form of antidemocratic government in world history was conservative authoritarianism. Like Russia's tsars and China's emperors, the leaders of such governments relied on obedient bureaucracies, vigilant police departments, and trustworthy armies to control society. They forbade or limited popular participation in government, and often jailed or exiled political opponents. Yet they had neither the ability nor the desire to control many aspects of their subjects' lives. As long as the people did not try to change the system, they often enjoyed considerable personal independence.

After the First World War, conservative authoritarianism revived, especially in Latin America. Conservative dictators also seized power in Spain and Portugal, and in the less-developed eastern part of Europe, where by 1938 only Czechoslovakia remained true to liberal political ideals. There were several reasons for this development. These lands lacked strong traditions of self-government, and many new states, such as Yugoslavia, were torn by ethnic conflicts. Dictatorship appealed to nationalists and military leaders as a way to repress such tensions and preserve national unity. Large landowners and the church were still powerful forces in these predominantly agrarian areas and often looked to dictators to protect them from progressive land reform or Communist agrarian upheaval. Although some of the conservative authoritarian regimes (particularly Spain) adopted certain Fascist characteristics in the 1930s, they were concerned more with maintaining the status quo than with mobilizing the masses or forcing society into rapid change or war.

a "revolution from above,"[5] as he so aptly termed it, to transform Soviet society along socialist lines. Stalin and the Communist Party used constant propaganda, enormous sacrifice, and unlimited violence and state control to establish a dynamic, modern totalitarian state in the 1930s.

From Lenin to Stalin

By spring 1921 Lenin and the Bolsheviks had won the civil war, but they ruled a shattered and devastated land. Facing economic disintegration, the worst famine in generations, riots by peasants and workers, and an open rebellion by previously pro-Bolshevik sailors at Kronstadt, Lenin changed course. In March 1921 he announced the **New Economic Policy (NEP)**, which re-established limited economic freedom in an attempt to rebuild agriculture and industry. Peasant producers could sell their surpluses in free markets, as could private traders and small handicraft manufacturers. Heavy industry, railroads, and banks, however, remained wholly nationalized.

The NEP was successful both politically and economically. Politically, it was a necessary but temporary compromise with the Soviet Union's overwhelming peasant majority, the only force capable of overturning Lenin's government. Economically, the NEP brought rapid recovery. In 1926 industrial output surpassed prewar levels, and peasants were producing almost as much grain as before the war.

As the economy recovered, an intense power struggle began in the Communist Party's inner circles, for Lenin left no chosen successor when he died in 1924. The principal contenders were Stalin and Leon Trotsky. Stalin was a good organizer but had no experience outside Russia. Trotsky, who had planned the 1917 takeover (see page 878) and created the Red Army, appeared to have all the advantages. Yet Stalin won because he gained the party's support, the only genuine source of power in the one-party state.

With cunning Stalin gradually achieved absolute power between 1922 and 1927. He used the moderates to crush Trotsky and then turned against the moderates and destroyed them as well. Stalin's final triumph came at the party congress of December 1927, which condemned all deviation from the general party line as formulated by Stalin.

The Five-Year Plans

The 1927 party congress marked the end of the NEP and the beginning of socialist five-year plans. The first five-year plan had staggering economic objectives. In just five years, total industrial output was to increase by 250 percent and agricultural production by 150 percent. By 1930 economic and social change was sweeping the country in a frenzied effort to modernize, much like the Industrial Revolution in Europe in the 1800s (see Chapter 23), and dramatically changing the lives of ordinary people, sometimes at great personal cost. One worker complained, "The workers . . . made every effort to fulfill the industrial and financial plan and fulfilled it by more than 100 percent, but how are they supplied? The ration is received only by the worker, except for rye flour, his wife and small children receive nothing. Workers and their families wear worn-out clothes, the kids are in rags, their naked bellies sticking out."[6]

Stalin unleashed his "second revolution" because, like Lenin, Stalin and his militant supporters were deeply committed to socialism as they understood it. Stalin was also driven to catch up with the advanced and presumably hostile Western capitalist nations. To a conference of managers of socialist industry in February 1931, Stalin famously declared:

> It is sometimes asked whether it is not possible to slow down the tempo a bit, to put a check on the movement. No, comrades, it is not possible! The tempo must not be reduced! . . . To slacken the tempo would mean falling behind. And those who fall behind get beaten. But we do not want to be beaten. No, we refuse to be beaten! . . . We are fifty or a hundred years behind the advanced countries. We must make good this distance in ten years. Either we do it, or we shall be crushed.[7]

Domestically, there was the peasant problem. For centuries peasants had wanted to own the land, and finally they had it. Sooner or later, the Communists reasoned, the peasants would become conservative capitalists and threaten the regime. Stalin therefore launched a preventive war against the peasantry to bring it under the state's absolute control.

That war was **collectivization**—the forcible consolidation of individual peasant farms into large, state-controlled enterprises. Beginning in 1929 peasants were ordered to give up their land and animals and become members of collective farms. As for the kulaks, the better-off peasants, Stalin instructed party workers to "break their resistance, to eliminate them as a class."[8] Stripped of land and livestock, many starved or were deported to forced-labor camps for "re-education."

Since almost all peasants were poor, the term *kulak* soon meant any peasant who opposed the new system. Whole villages were often attacked. One conscience-stricken colonel in the secret police confessed to a foreign journalist:

> I am an old Bolshevik. I worked in the underground against the Tsar and then I fought in the Civil War. Did I do all that in order that I should now surround villages with machine guns and order my men to fire indiscriminately into crowds of peasants? Oh, no, no![9]

Forced collectivization led to disaster. Many peasants slaughtered their animals and burned their crops in protest. Nor were the state-controlled collective farms more productive. Grain output barely increased, and collectivized agriculture made no substantial financial contribution to Soviet industrial development during the first five-year plan.

In Ukraine Stalin instituted a policy of all-out collectivization with two goals: to destroy all expressions of Ukrainian nationalism, and to break the Ukrainian peasants' will so they would accept collectivization and Soviet rule. Stalin began by purging Ukraine of its intellectuals and political elite, labeling them reactionary nationalists and enemies of socialism. He then set impossibly high grain quotas—up to nearly 50 percent of total production—for the collectivized farms. This grain quota had to be turned over to the government before any peasant could receive a share. Many scholars and dozens of governments and international organizations have declared Stalin's and the Soviet government's policies a deliberate act of genocide. As one historian observed:

> Grain supplies were sufficient to sustain everyone if properly distributed. People died mostly of terror-starvation (excess grain exports, seizure of edibles from the starving, state refusal to provide emergency relief, bans on outmigration, and forced deportation to food-deficit locales), not poor harvests and routine administrative bungling.[10]

frightened. If people were arrested only for specific misdemeanors, all the others would feel safe and so become ripe for treason."[11] In all, at least 8 million people were arrested, and millions of these were executed. Those not immediately executed were sent to gulags—labor camps from which few escaped. Many were simply worked to death as they provided convict labor for Stalin's industrialization drive in areas of low population. Between January 1937 and January 1939 the number of camp inmates rose from 0.5 million to nearly 1.5 million.

Stalin recruited 1.5 million new members to replace those purged. Thus more than half of all Communist Party members in 1941 had joined since the purges. Products of this second revolution of the 1930s, these new members sought the opportunities and rewards party membership offered. This new generation of Stalin-formed Communists served the leader effectively until his death in 1953 and then governed the Soviet Union until the early 1980s.

Stalin's mass purges remain baffling, for most historians believe those purged posed no threat and confessed to crimes they had not committed. Some historians have challenged the long-standing interpretation that blames the great purges on Stalin's cruelty or madness. They argue that Stalin's fears were exaggerated but genuine and were shared by many in the party and in the general population who were bombarded daily with propaganda. Investigations and trials snowballed into a mass hysteria, a new witch-hunt.[12] Historians who have accessed recently opened Soviet archives, however, continue to hold that Stalin was intimately involved and personally directed the purges, abetted by amenable informers, judges, and executioners. Oleg Khlevniuk, a Ukrainian historian familiar with these archives, writes, "Theories about the elemental, spontaneous nature of the terror, about a loss of central control over the course of mass repression, and about the role of regional leaders in initiating the terror are simply not supported by the historical record."[13] In short, a ruthless and paranoid Stalin found large numbers of willing collaborators for crime as well as for achievement.

Mussolini and Fascism in Italy

How did Italian fascism develop?

Mussolini's Fascist movement and his seizure of power in 1922 were important steps in the rise of dictatorships between the two world wars. Mussolini and his supporters were the first to call themselves "Fascists." His dictatorship was brutal and theatrical, and it contained elements of both conservative authoritarianism and modern totalitarianism.

The Seizure of Power

In the early twentieth century Italy was a liberal state with civil rights and a constitutional monarchy. On the eve of the First World War, the parliamentary regime granted universal male suffrage. But there were serious problems. Poverty was widespread, and many peasants were more attached to their villages and local interests than to the national state. Moreover, the papacy, many devout Catholics, conservatives, and landowners remained opposed to the middle-class lawyers and politicians who ran the country largely for their own benefit. Church-state relations were often tense. Class differences were also extreme, and by 1912 the Socialist Party's radical wing led the powerful revolutionary socialist movement.[14]

World War I worsened the political situation. Having fought on the Allied side almost exclusively for purposes of territorial expansion, the parliamentary government disappointed Italian nationalists with Italy's modest gains at the Paris Peace Conference. Workers and peasants also felt cheated: to win their support during the war, the government had promised social and land reform, which it failed to deliver after the war.

The Russian Revolution inspired and energized Italy's revolutionary socialist movement, and radical workers and peasants began occupying factories and seizing land in 1920. These actions scared and mobilized the property-owning classes. Thus by 1921 revolutionary socialists, antiliberal conservatives, and frightened property owners were all opposed — though for different reasons — to the liberal parliamentary government.

Into these crosscurrents of unrest and fear stepped Benito Mussolini (1883–1945). Mussolini began his political career as a Socialist Party leader and radical newspaper editor before World War I. Expelled from the Italian Socialist Party for supporting the war, and wounded on the Italian front in 1917, Mussolini returned home and began organizing bitter war veterans into a band of Fascists — from the Italian word for "a union of forces."

At first Mussolini's program was a radical combination of nationalist and socialist demands, including territorial expansion, workers' benefits, and land reform for peasants. As such, it competed directly with the well-organized Socialist Party and failed to attract followers. Mussolini realized his violent verbal assaults on rival Socialists won him growing support from conservatives and the frightened middle classes. He now began to shift gears and to exalt nation over class, such as in this 1921 speech in which he ridicules and dismisses the Marxist interpretation of history:

> We deny the existence of two classes, because there are many more than two classes. We deny that human history can be explained in terms of economics. We deny your internationalism. That is a luxury article which only the elevated can practice, because peoples are passionately bound to their native soil.[15]

Mussolini and his private army of **Black Shirts** also turned to physical violence. Few people were killed, but Socialist newspapers, union halls, and local Socialist Party headquarters were destroyed. A skillful politician, Mussolini convinced his followers they were opposing the "Reds" while also making a real revolution of the little people against the established interests.

With the government breaking down in 1922, partly because of the chaos created by his Black Shirt bands, Mussolini stepped forward as the savior of order and property, demanding the existing government's resignation and his own appointment by the king. In October 1922 thirty thousand Fascists marched on Rome, threatening the king and demanding he appoint Mussolini prime minister. Victor Emmanuel III (r. 1900–1946), forced to choose between Fascists or Socialists, asked Mussolini to form a new cabinet. Thus, after widespread violence and a threat of armed uprising, Mussolini seized power "legally."

The Regime in Action

In 1924 Mussolini declared his desire to "make the nation Fascist"[16] and imposed a series of repressive measures. Press freedom was abolished, elections were fixed, and the government ruled by decree. Mussolini arrested his political opponents, disbanded all independent labor unions, and put dedicated Fascists in control of Italy's schools. He created a Fascist youth movement, Fascist labor unions, and many other Fascist organizations. He trumpeted his goal in a famous slogan of 1926: "Everything in the state, nothing outside the state, nothing against the state."[17] By year's end Italy was a one-party dictatorship under Mussolini's unquestioned leadership.

Mussolini was only primarily interested, however, in personal power. Rather than destroy the old power structure, he remained content to compromise with the conservative classes that controlled the army, the economy, and the state. He never tried to purge these classes or even move very vigorously against them. He controlled labor but left big business to regulate itself, profitably and securely. There was no land reform.

Mussolini also drew increasing support from the Catholic Church. In the **Lateran Agreement** of 1929, he recognized the Vatican as a tiny independent state and agreed to give the church heavy financial support. The pope in return urged Italians to support Mussolini's government.

Like Stalin and Hitler, Mussolini favored a return of traditional roles for women. He abolished divorce and told women to stay at home and produce children. In 1938 women were limited by law to a maximum of 10 percent of the better-paying jobs in industry and government. Despite these policies, Italian women appear not to have changed their attitudes or behavior in any important way under Fascist rule.

Mussolini's government passed no racial laws until 1938 and did not persecute Jews savagely until late in the Second World War, when Italy was under Nazi control. Nor did Mussolini establish a truly ruthless police state. Only twenty-three political prisoners were condemned to death between 1926 and 1944. Mussolini's Fascist Italy, though repressive and undemocratic, was never really totalitarian.

Hitler and Nazism in Germany

Why were Hitler and his Nazi regime initially so popular, and how did their actions lead to World War II?

The most frightening dictatorship developed in Nazi Germany. A product of Hitler's evil genius as well as of Germany's social and political situation, the Nazi movement shared some of the characteristics of Mussolini's Italian Fascist model. But Nazism asserted an unlimited claim over German society and proclaimed the ultimate power of its aggressive leader, Adolf Hitler. Nazism's aspirations were truly totalitarian.

The Roots of Nazism

Nazism grew out of many complex concepts, of which the most influential were extreme nationalism and racism. These ideas captured the mind of the young Adolf Hitler (1889–1945) and evolved into Nazism.

The son of an Austrian customs official, Hitler spent his childhood in small towns in Austria. He did poorly in high school and dropped out at age sixteen. He then headed to Vienna, where he was exposed to extreme Austro-German nationalists who believed Germans to be a superior people and central Europe's natural rulers. They advocated union with Germany and violent expulsion of "inferior" peoples from the Austro-Hungarian Empire.

From these extremists Hitler eagerly absorbed virulent anti-Semitism, racism, and hatred of Slavs. He developed an unshakable belief in the crudest distortions of Social Darwinism (see page 750), the superiority of Germanic races, and the inevitability of racial conflict. The Jews, he claimed, directed an international conspiracy of finance capitalism and Marxist socialism against German culture, German unity, and the German race. Anti-Semitism and racism became Hitler's most passionate convictions.

Hitler greeted the Great War's outbreak as a salvation. The struggle and discipline of serving as a soldier in the war gave his life meaning, and when Germany suddenly surrendered in 1918, Hitler's world was shattered. Convinced that Jews and Marxists had "stabbed Germany in the back," he vowed to fight on.

In late 1919 Hitler joined a tiny extremist group in Munich called the German Workers' Party, which promised a uniquely German "national socialism" that would abolish the injustices of capitalism and create a mighty "people's community." By 1921 Hitler had gained absolute control of this small but growing party, now renamed the National Socialist German Worker's Party, or Nazi Party. A master of mass propaganda and political showmanship, Hitler worked his audiences into a frenzy with wild attacks on the Versailles treaty, the Jews, war profiteers, and Germany's Weimar Republic.

In late 1923 Germany under the Weimar Republic was experiencing unparalleled hyperinflation and seemed on the verge of collapse (see page 884). In 1925 the old Great War field marshal Paul von Hindenburg (1847–1934) became the second president of the young democratic Germany. Hitler, inspired by Mussolini's recent victory, attempted an armed uprising in Munich. Despite the failure of the poorly organized plot and Hitler's arrest, Nazism had been born.

Hitler's Road to Power

At his trial Hitler violently denounced the Weimar Republic and attracted enormous publicity. From the unsuccessful revolt, Hitler concluded he had to gain power legally through electoral competition. During his brief prison term he dictated *Mein Kampf* (*My Struggle*), in which he expounded on his basic ideas on race and anti-Semitism, the notion of territorial expansion based on "living space" for Germans, and the role of the leader-dictator, called the *Führer* (FYOUR-uhr).

In the years of relative prosperity and stability between 1924 and 1929, Hitler concentrated on building his Nazi Party. The Nazis remained a small splinter group until the 1929 Great Depression shattered economic prosperity. By the end of 1932 an incredible 43 percent of the labor force was unemployed. Industrial production fell by one-half between 1929 and 1932. No factor contributed more to Hitler's success than this economic crisis. Hitler began promising German voters economic as well as political and international salvation.

Hitler rejected free-market capitalism and advocated government programs to promote recovery. He pitched his speeches to middle- and lower-middle-class groups and to skilled workers. As the economy collapsed, great numbers of these people "voted their pocketbooks"[18] and deserted the conservative and moderate parties for the Nazis.

Young People in Hitler's Germany   This photo from 1930 shows Hitler admiring a young boy dressed in the uniform of Hitler's storm troopers, a paramilitary organization of the Nazi Party that supported Hitler's rise to power in the 1920s and early 1930s. Only a year after the founding of the storm troopers in 1921, Hitler began to organize Germany's young people into similar paramilitary groups in an effort to militarize all of German society. The young paramilitaries became the Hitler Youth, who eventually numbered in the millions. (Popperfoto/Getty Images)

In the 1930 election the Nazis won 6.5 million votes and 107 seats, and in July 1932 they gained 14.5 million votes — 38 percent of the total — and became the largest party in the Reichstag.

Hitler and the Nazis appealed strongly to German youth. Hitler himself was only forty in 1929, and he and most of his top aides were much younger than other leading German politicians. "National Socialism is the organized will of the youth,"[19] proclaimed the official Nazi slogan. In 1931 almost 40 percent of Nazi Party members were under thirty, compared with 20 percent of Social Democrats. National recovery, exciting and rapid change, and personal advancement made Nazism appealing to millions of German youths.

Hitler also came to power because of the breakdown of democratic government. Germany's economic collapse in the Great Depression convinced many voters that the country's republican leaders were stupid and corrupt. Disunity on the left was another nail in the republic's coffin. The Communists refused to cooperate with the Social Democrats, even though the two parties together outnumbered the Nazis in the Reichstag.

Finally, Hitler excelled in shadowy backroom politics. In 1932 he succeeded in gaining support from key people in the army and big business who thought they could use him to their own advantage. Many conservative and nationalistic politicians thought similarly. Thus in January 1933 President von Hindenburg legally appointed Hitler, leader of Germany's largest party, as German chancellor.

The Nazi State and Society

Hitler quickly established an unshakable dictatorship. When the Reichstag building was partly destroyed by fire in February 1933, Hitler blamed the Communist Party. He convinced President von Hindenburg, in poor health and displaying signs of senility, to sign dictatorial emergency acts that abolished freedom of speech and assembly and most personal liberties. He also called for new elections in an effort to solidify his political power.

When the Nazis won only 44 percent of the votes, Hitler outlawed the Communist Party and arrested its parliamentary representatives. Then on March 23, 1933, the Nazis forced through the Reichstag the so-called **Enabling Act**, which gave Hitler absolute dictatorial power for four years.

Hitler and the Nazis took over the government bureaucracy, installing many Nazis in top positions. Hitler next outlawed strikes and abolished independent labor unions, which were replaced by the Nazi Labor Front. Professional people — doctors and lawyers, teachers and engineers — also saw their independent organizations swallowed up in Nazi associations. Publishing houses and universities were put under Nazi control, and students and professors publicly burned forbidden books. Modern art and architecture were ruthlessly prohibited. Life became violently anti-intellectual. As the cynical Joseph Goebbels, later Nazi minister of propaganda, put it, "When I hear the word 'culture' I reach for my gun."[20] By 1934 a brutal dictatorship characterized by frightening dynamism and total obedience to Hitler was already largely in place.

In June 1934 Hitler ordered his elite personal guard — the SS — to arrest and shoot without trial roughly a thousand long-time Nazi storm troopers. Shortly thereafter army leaders surrendered their independence and swore a binding oath of "unquestioning obedience" to Adolf Hitler. The SS grew rapidly. Under Heinrich Himmler (1900–1945), the SS took over the political police (the Gestapo) and expanded its network of concentration camps.

From the beginning, German Jews were a special object of Nazi persecution. By late 1934 most Jewish lawyers, doctors, professors, civil servants, and musicians had been banned from their professions. In 1935 the infamous Nuremberg Laws classified as Jewish anyone having three or more Jewish grandparents and deprived Jews of all rights of citizenship. By 1938 roughly one-quarter of Germany's half million Jews had emigrated, sacrificing almost all their property in order to leave Germany.

In late 1938 the attack on the Jews accelerated, changing from social, political, and economic bigotry and persecution to physical violence, incarceration, and murder. On November 9 and 10, 1938, the Nazis initiated a series of well-organized attacks against Jews throughout Nazi Germany and some parts of Austria. This infamous event is known as Kristallnacht, or Night of Broken Glass, after the broken glass that littered the streets following the frenzied destruction of Jewish homes, shops, synagogues, and neighborhoods by German civilians and uniformed storm troopers. U.S. consul David Buffum reported of the Nazis in Leipzig:

> The most hideous phase of the so-called "spontaneous" action, has been the wholesale arrest and transportation to concentration camps of male German Jews between the ages of sixteen and sixty. . . . Having demolished dwellings and hurled most of the effects to the streets, the insatiably sadistic perpetrators threw many of the trembling inmates into a small stream that flows through the Zoological Park, commanding horrified spectators to spit at them, defile them with mud and jeer at their plight.[21]

Many historians consider this night the beginning of Hitler's Final Solution against the Jews (see page 953), and after this event it became very difficult for Jews to leave Germany.

Some Germans privately opposed these outrages, but most went along or looked the other way. Although this lack of response reflected the individual's helplessness in a totalitarian state, it also reflected the strong popular support Hitler's government enjoyed.

Hitler's Popularity

Hitler had promised the masses economic recovery — "work and bread" — and he delivered. The Nazi Party launched a large public works program to pull Germany out of the depression. Work began on highways, offices, sports stadiums, and public housing. In 1935 Germany turned decisively toward rearmament. Unemployment dropped steadily, and by 1938 the Nazis boasted of nearly full employment. The average living standard increased moderately. Business profits rose sharply. For millions of Germans economic recovery was tangible evidence that Nazi promises were more than show and propaganda.

For ordinary German citizens, in contrast to those deemed "undesirable" (Jews, Slavs, Gypsies, Jehovah's Witnesses, Communists, and homosexuals), Hitler's government offered greater equality and more opportunities. In 1933 class barriers in Germany were generally high. Hitler's rule introduced changes that lowered these barriers. For example, stiff educational requirements favoring the well-to-do were relaxed. The new Nazi elite included many young and poorly educated dropouts, rootless lower-middle-class people like Hitler who rose to the top with breathtaking speed. More generally, the Nazis tolerated privilege and wealth only as long as they served party needs.

Yet few historians today believe that Hitler and the Nazis brought about a real social revolution. The well-educated classes held on to most of their advantages, and only a modest social leveling occurred in the Nazi years. Significantly, the Nazis shared with the Italian Fascists the stereotypical view of women as housewives and mothers. Only when facing labor shortages during the war did they reluctantly mobilize large numbers of German women for office and factory work.[22] Not all Germans supported Hitler, and a number of German groups actively resisted him after 1933. Tens of thousands of political enemies were imprisoned, and thousands were executed. In the first years of Hitler's rule, the principal resisters were trade-union Communists and Socialists, groups smashed by the expansion of the SS system after 1935. Catholic and Protestant churches produced a second group of opponents. Their efforts were directed primarily at preserving genuine religious life, however, not at overthrowing Hitler. Finally, in 1938 and again during the war, some high-ranking army officers, who feared the consequences of Hitler's reckless aggression, plotted, unsuccessfully, against him.

Aggression and Appeasement, 1933–1939

After Germany's economic recovery and Hitler's success in establishing Nazi control of society, he turned to the next item on his agenda: aggressive territorial expansion. He camouflaged his plans at first, for the Treaty of Versailles limited Germany's army to only a hundred thousand men. Thus, while Hitler loudly proclaimed his peaceful intentions, Germany's withdrawal from the League of Nations in October 1933 indicated its determination to rearm. When in March 1935 Hitler established a general military draft and declared the "unequal" Versailles treaty disarmament clauses null and void, leaders in Britain, France, and Italy issued a rather tepid joint protest and warned him against future aggressive actions.

But the emerging united front against Hitler quickly collapsed. Britain adopted a policy of appeasement, granting Hitler everything he could reasonably want (and more) in order to avoid war. British appeasement, which practically dictated French policy, had the support of many powerful British conservatives who, as in Germany, underestimated Hitler. They believed that Soviet communism was the real danger and that Hitler could be used to stop it. The British people, still horrified by the memory, the costs, and the losses of the First World War, generally supported pacifism rather than war. Some British leaders at the time, however, such as Winston Churchill, bitterly condemned appeasement as peace at any price. After the war, British appeasement came to be viewed as "the granting from fear or cowardice of unwarranted concessions in order to buy temporary peace at someone else's expense."[23] Beginning in the 1990s some historians have argued that British leaders had no real choice but to appease Hitler in the 1930s, because neither Great Britain nor France was prepared psychologically or militarily to fight another war.[24] In March 1936 Hitler suddenly marched his armies into the demilitarized Rhineland, brazenly violating the Treaties of Versailles and Locarno. France would not move without British support, and Britain refused to act. As Britain and France opted for appeasement and the Soviet Union watched all developments suspiciously, Hitler found powerful allies. In October 1935 the bombastic Mussolini attacked the independent African kingdom of Ethiopia. The Western powers and the League of Nations condemned Italian aggression, but Hitler supported Italy energetically. In October 1936 Italy and Germany established the so-called Rome-Berlin Axis. Japan, which wanted support for its occupation of Manchuria (see page 921), also joined the Axis alliance.

At the same time, Germany and Italy intervened in the Spanish Civil War (1936–1939), where their support helped General Francisco Franco's Fascist movement defeat republican Spain. Republican Spain's only official aid in the fight against Franco came from the Soviet Union.

In late 1937 Hitler moved forward with his plans to crush Austria and Czechoslovakia as the first step in his long-contemplated drive to the east for living space. By threatening Austria with invasion, Hitler forced the Austrian chancellor in March 1938 to put local Nazis in control of the government. The next day German armies moved in unopposed, and Austria became two provinces of Greater Germany.

Simultaneously, Hitler demanded that the pro-Nazi, German-speaking territory of western Czechoslovakia—the Sudetenland—be turned over to Germany. Democratic Czechoslovakia was prepared to defend itself, but appeasement triumphed again. In September 1938 British prime minister Arthur Neville Chamberlain (1869–1940) flew to Germany three times in fourteen days. In these negotiations Chamberlain and the French agreed with Hitler that the Sudetenland should be ceded to Germany immediately. Returning to London from the Munich Conference, Chamberlain told cheering crowds that he had secured "peace with honour . . . peace for our time."[25] Sold out by the Western powers, Czechoslovakia gave in.

Hitler's armies occupied the remainder of Czechoslovakia in March 1939. This time, there was no possible rationale of self-determination for Nazi aggression, because Hitler had seized the Czechs and Slovaks as captive peoples. When Hitler used the question of German minorities in Danzig as a pretext to confront Poland, Chamberlain declared that Britain and France would fight if Hitler attacked his eastern neighbor. Hitler did not take these warnings seriously and pressed on.

Through the 1930s Hitler had constantly referred to ethnic Slavs in the Soviet Union and other countries as *Untermenschen* (inferior people), and relations between the two countries had grown increasingly tense. War between Germany and the Soviet Union seemed inevitable, and, indeed, Stalin believed that Great Britain and France secretly hoped the Nazis and Bolsheviks would destroy each other. In an about-face that stunned the world, especially fervent Communists everywhere, sworn enemies Hitler and Stalin signed a nonaggression pact in August 1939. Each dictator promised to remain neutral if the other became involved in war. An attached secret protocol divided eastern Europe into German and Soviet zones "in the event of a political and territorial reorganization."[26] Stalin agreed to the pact for three reasons: he distrusted Western intentions, he needed more time to build up Soviet industry and military reserves, and Hitler offered territorial gain.

For Hitler, everything was now set. He told his generals on the day of the non-aggression pact, "My only fear is that at the last moment some dirty dog will come up with a mediation plan."[27] On September 1, 1939, the Germans attacked Poland from three sides. Two days later, Britain and France, finally true to their word, declared war on Germany. The Second World War had begun.

The Second World War, 1939–1945

How did Germany and Japan build empires in Europe and Asia, and how did the Allies defeat them?

World war broke out because Hitler's and Japan's ambitions were essentially unlimited. Nazi soldiers scored enormous successes in Europe until late 1942, establishing a vast empire of death and destruction. Japan attacked the United States in December 1941 and then moved to expand its empire throughout Asia and the Pacific Ocean. Eventually, the mighty coalition of Britain, the United States, and the Soviet Union, which Winston Churchill called the Grand Alliance, overwhelmed the aggressors in manpower and military strength. Thus the Nazi and Japanese empires proved short-lived.

Hitler's Empire in Europe, 1939–1942

Using planes, tanks, and trucks in the first example of a **blitzkrieg**, or "lightning war," Hitler's armies crushed Poland in four weeks. The Soviet Union quickly took its share agreed to in the secret protocol—the eastern half of Poland and the Baltic states of Lithuania, Estonia, and Latvia. In the west French and British armies dug in; they expected another war of attrition and economic blockade. But in spring 1940 the Nazi lightning war struck again. After occupying Denmark, Norway, and Holland, German motorized columns broke through southern Belgium and into France.

As Hitler's armies poured into France, aging marshal Henri-Philippe Pétain, a national hero of the Great War, formed a new French government—the so-called Vichy (VIH-shee) government—and accepted defeat. Initially many French supported Pétain, who they believed would stand up for them against the Germans, but as the war progressed Pétain increasingly collaborated with the Nazis. By July 1940 Hitler ruled practically all of western continental Europe; Italy was an ally, the Soviet Union a friendly neutral (Map 30.1). Only Britain, led by Winston Churchill, remained unconquered.

To prepare for an invasion of Britain, Germany first needed to gain control of the air. In the Battle of Britain, which began in July 1940, German planes attacked British airfields and key factories, dueling with British defenders high in the skies. In September Hitler began indiscriminately bombing British cities to break British morale. British aircraft factories increased production, and Londoners defiantly dug in. By September Britain was winning the air war, and Hitler abandoned his plans for an immediate German invasion of Britain.

Hitler now allowed his lifetime obsession of creating a vast eastern European empire for the "master race" to dictate policy. In June 1941 Germany broke the Nazi-Soviet nonaggression pact and attacked the Soviet Union. By October Leningrad was practically surrounded, Moscow was besieged, and most of Ukraine had been conquered. But the Soviets did not collapse, and when a severe winter struck German armies outfitted in summer uniforms, the invaders were stopped.

Although stalled in Russia, Hitler ruled an enormous European empire stretching from the outskirts of Moscow to the English Channel. He now began building a New Order based on the guiding principle of Nazi totalitarianism: racial imperialism. Within the New Order, the Dutch, Norwegians, Swedes, and Danes received preferential treatment, for the Germans believed they were racially related to the German "Aryan" master race. The French, an "inferior" Latin people, occupied the middle

London Bomb Shelter, 1940   Hitler believed that his relentless terror bombing of London — the "blitz" — could break the will of the British people. He was wrong. The blitz caused enormous destruction, but Londoners went about their business with courage and calm determination, as this unforgettable image of people being entertained in a bomb shelter in the Tube (subway) suggests. (© Bettmann/Corbis)

Germans repulsed, Dec. 1941

Siege of Stalingrad, Aug. 21, 1942– Jan. 31, 1943

Siege of Leningrad, Sept. 1941–Jan. 1944

Moscow
Oct. 1941–Jan. 1942
Stalingrad
Yalta
SOVIET UNION
Tula
Smolensk
Russian front, Nov. 1942
Kursk
July–Aug. 1943
Dnieper
Aug.–Dec.
1943
Kiev
Russian front, Dec. 1941
UKRAINE
Black Sea

FINLAND
Helsinki
Russian front, spring 1944
LITHUANIA
LATVIA
ESTONIA
Riga
BELARUS
Pinsk
ROMANIA
Bucharest
Sofia
BULGARIA

SWEDEN
Stockholm
Baltic Sea
Siege, Sept. 1939
Uprising, Aug.–Sept. 1944
POLAND
Kraków
Warsaw
Posen
SLOVAKIA
HUNGARY
Budapest
SERBIA
CROATIA
GREECE
Athens
ANKARA
TURKEY
Battle for Crete,
May 20–June 1
1941
Crete (Gr.)

SYRIA
(Fr. Mandate)
IRAQ
(Br.
Mandate)
TRANS-
JORDAN
(Br. Mandate)
SAUDI
ARABIA
LEBANON
(Fr. Mandate)
PALESTINE
(Br. Mandate)
Cyprus
(Gr. Br.)
El Alamein
autumn 1942
EGYPT
Mediterranean Sea

NORWAY
Oslo
DENMARK
Copenhagen
Germany
surrenders,
May 8, 1945
Berlin
GERMANY
Vienna
Russian front, Feb. 1945
Adriatic Sea
ITALY
Rome
Salerno
Sept. 1943
Monte Cassino
May 1944
Italian front
Feb. 1945
Sicily
July 1943
Sicily
Malta
(Gr. Br.)
LIBYA (It.)

North
Sea
NETHERLANDS
London
BELGIUM
Battle of
Paris the Bulge
Dec. 1944
Western front, Feb. 1945
SWITZERLAND
Bologna
Corsica
Sardinia
Allies invade Sicily and
Italy, July–Sept. 1943
TUNISIA
(Fr.)
Axis troops
evacuated,
May 1943

NORTHERN
IRELAND
GREAT
BRITAIN
IRELAND
Dunkirk
FRANCE
Vichy
VICHY
FRANCE
Axis troops occupy
Vichy France,
Nov. 10 and 11, 1942
Invasion of Normandy,
June 6, 1944
Battle of Britain,
fall 1940

ATLANTIC
OCEAN
SPAIN
Madrid
SPANISH
MOROCCO
Casablanca
Nov. 1942
MOROCCO
(Fr.)
Lisbon
PORT.
GIBRALTAR
(Gr. Br.)
ALGERIA
(Vichy France)
Joined Allies,
Nov. 1942

400 miles
400 kilometers
200
200
0

Axis powers and their allies

Occupied by Germany and its allies

Allied powers and their allies

Neutral nations

Boundary of Greater Germany

✶ Major battle

◄ **MAP 30.1   World War II in Europe and Africa, 1939–1945** The map shows the extent of Hitler's empire at its height, before the Battle of Stalingrad in late 1942 and the subsequent advances of the Allies until Germany surrendered on May 7, 1945.

position. At the bottom of the New Order were the harshly treated "subhumans," Jews and Slavs.

Hitler envisioned a vast eastern colonial empire where enslaved Poles, Ukrainians, and Russians would die or be killed off while Germanic peasants would resettle the abandoned lands. Himmler and the elite SS corps, supported by military commanders and German policemen, implemented a program of destruction in the occupied territories to create a "mass settlement space" for Germans. Many Poles, captured Communists, Gypsies, and Jehovah's Witnesses were murdered in cold blood.

The Holocaust

Finally, the Nazi state condemned all European Jews to extermination in the Holocaust. After Warsaw fell in 1939, the Nazis forced Jews in the occupied territories to move to urban ghettos, while German Jews were sent to occupied Poland. After Germany attacked Russia in June 1941, forced expulsion spiraled into extermination. Himmler's SS killing squads and regular army units compelled Soviet Jews to dig giant pits, then stand on the edge of these mass graves and be cut down by machine guns. In late 1941 Hitler and the Nazi leadership, in some still-debated combination, ordered the SS to speed up planning for "the final solution of the Jewish question."[28] Throughout the Nazi empire Jews were systematically arrested, packed like cattle onto freight trains, and dispatched to extermination camps.

Arriving at their destination, small numbers of Jews were sent to nearby slave labor camps, where they were starved and systematically worked to death. (See "Individuals in Society: Primo Levi," page 954.) Most victims were taken to "shower rooms," which were actually gas chambers. For fifteen to twenty minutes terrible screams and gasping sobs arose from men, women, and children choking to death on poison gas. Then, only silence. Special camp workers quickly yanked the victims' gold teeth from their jaws, and the bodies were cremated. By 1945 about 6 million Jews had been murdered.

Who was responsible for this terrible crime? After the war historians laid the guilt on Hitler and the Nazi leadership, arguing that ordinary Germans had little knowledge of the extermination camps, or that those who cooperated had no alternative given the brutality of Nazi terror and totalitarian control. Beginning in the 1990s studies appeared revealing a much broader participation of German people in the Holocaust and popular indifference (or worse) to the Jews' fate.[29] In most occupied countries local non-German officials also cooperated in the arrest and deportation of Jews.

Only a few exceptional bystanders did not turn a blind eye. Catholic and Protestant church leaders protested rarely. Thus some scholars have concluded that the key for most Germans (and most people in occupied countries) was that they felt no personal responsibility for Jews and therefore were not prepared to help them. This meant that many individuals, who were sympathetic to Nazi racist propaganda and were also influenced by peer pressure and brutalizing wartime violence, were psychologically prepared to perpetrate ever-greater crimes, from mistreatment to arrest to mass murder.

INDIVIDUALS IN SOCIETY • Primo Levi

Most Jews deported to Auschwitz were murdered as soon as they arrived, but the Nazis made some prisoners into slave laborers, and a few of these survived. Primo Levi (1919–1987), an Italian Jew, became one of the most influential witnesses to the Holocaust and its death camps.

Like many in Italy's small Jewish community, Levi's family belonged to the urban professional classes. The young Primo Levi graduated in 1941 from the University of Turin with highest honors in chemistry. Since 1938, when Italy introduced racial laws, he had faced growing discrimination, and two years after graduation he joined the antifascist resistance movement. Quickly captured, he was deported to Auschwitz with 650 Italian Jews in February 1944. Stone-faced SS men picked only ninety-six men and twenty-nine women to work in their respective labor camps. Levi was one of them.

Nothing had prepared Levi for what he encountered. The Jewish prisoners were kicked, punched, stripped, branded with tattoos, crammed into huts, and worked unmercifully. Hoping for some sign of prisoner solidarity in this terrible environment, Levi found only a desperate struggle of each against all and enormous status differences among prisoners. Many stunned and bewildered newcomers, beaten and demoralized by their bosses—the most privileged prisoners—collapsed and died. Others struggled to secure their own privileges, however small, because food rations and working conditions were so abominable that ordinary Jewish prisoners perished in two to three months.

Sensitive and noncombative, Levi found himself sinking into oblivion. But instead of joining the mass of the "drowned," he became one of the "saved"—a complicated surprise with moral implications that he would ponder all his life. As Levi explained in *Survival in Auschwitz* (1947), the usual road to salvation in the camps was some kind of collaboration with German power.* Savage German criminals were released from prison to become brutal camp guards; non-Jewish political prisoners competed for jobs entitling them to better conditions; and, especially troubling for Levi, a small number of Jewish men plotted and struggled for the power of life and death over other Jewish prisoners. Though not one of these Jewish bosses, Levi believed that he himself, like almost all survivors, had entered the "gray zone" of moral compromise. Only a very few superior individuals, "the

---

*Primo Levi, *Survival in Auschwitz: The Nazi Assault on Humanity*, rev. ed. 1958 (London: Collier Books, 1961), pp. 79–84, and *The Drowned and the Saved* (New York: Summit Books, 1988). These powerful testimonies are highly recommended.

Japan's Asian Empire

By late 1938, 1.5 million Japanese troops were bogged down in China, holding a great swath of territory but unable to defeat the Nationalists and the Communists (see pages 920–922). In 1939, as war broke out in Europe, the Japanese redoubled their ruthless efforts in China to crush peasant support for the Nationalists and the Communists, demonstrating that the Nazis held no monopoly on racism and brutalizing wartime stuff of saints and martyrs," survived the death camps without shifting their moral stance.

For Levi, compromise and salvation came from his profession. Interviewed by a German technocrat for the camp's synthetic rubber program, Levi performed brilliantly in scientific German and savored his triumph as a Jew over Nazi racism. Work in the warm camp laboratory offered Levi opportunities to pilfer equipment that could then be traded to other prisoners for food and necessities. Levi also gained critical support from three saintly prisoners who refused to do wicked and hateful acts. And he counted "luck" as essential for his survival: in the camp infirmary with scarlet fever in February 1945 as advancing Russian armies prepared to liberate the camp, Levi was not evacuated by the Nazis and shot to death like most Jewish prisoners.

After the war Primo Levi was forever haunted by the nightmare that the Holocaust would be ignored or forgotten. Always ashamed that so many people whom he considered better than himself had perished, he wrote and lectured tirelessly to preserve the memory of Jewish victims and guilty Nazis. Wanting the world to understand the Jewish genocide in all its complexity so that never again would people tolerate such atrocities, he grappled tirelessly with his vision of individual choice and moral compromise in a hell designed to make the victims collaborate and persecute each other.

QUESTIONS FOR ANALYSIS

1. Describe Levi's experience at Auschwitz. How did camp prisoners treat each other? Why?
2. What does Levi mean by the "gray zone"? How is this concept central to his thinking?
3. Will a vivid historical memory of the Holocaust help prevent future genocide? Why or why not?

▷LaunchPad
ONLINE DOCUMENT PROJECT

What choices did Holocaust survivors face? Listen to testimonies from Holocaust survivors, and then complete a quiz and writing assignment based on the evidence and details from this chapter.

See inside the front cover to learn more.

violence. Implementing a savage policy of "kill all, burn all, destroy all," Japanese troops committed shocking atrocities, including the so-called Rape of Nanjing. During Japan's war in China—the second Sino-Japanese War (1937–1945)—the Japanese are estimated to have killed 4 million Chinese people.

In August 1940 the Japanese announced the formation of a self-sufficient Asian economic zone. Although they spoke of liberating Asia from Western imperialism and of "Asia for the Asians," their true intentions were to eventually rule over a vast

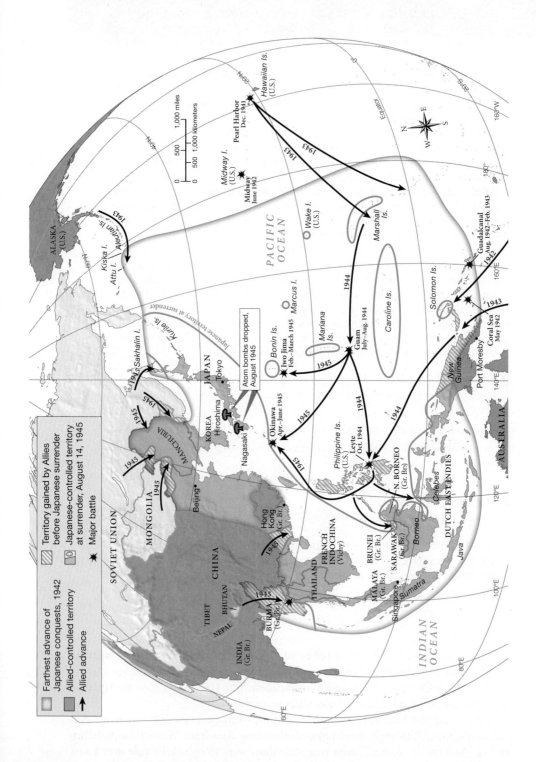

◀ **MAP 30.2**   **World War II in the Pacific**   Japanese forces overran an enormous amount of territory in 1942, which the Allies slowly recaptured in a long, bitter struggle.

Japanese empire. Ultranationalists moved to convince Japan's youth that Japan had a sacred liberating mission in Asia, glorified the virtues of honor and sacrifice, and demanded absolute devotion to the semidivine emperor.

For the moment, however, Japan needed allies. In September 1940 Japan signed a formal alliance (the Axis alliance) with Germany and Italy, and Vichy France granted the Japanese domination over northern French Indochina—from where the Japanese could block Allied military aid and fuel from reaching southern China. The United States, upset with Japan's occupation of Indochina and fearing embattled Britain would collapse if it lost its Asian colonies, froze scrap iron sales to Japan and applied further economic sanctions in October.

As 1941 opened, Japan's leaders faced a critical decision. Japan remained dependent on the import of several essential materials, the most important of which was oil. In 1941 the United States was the world's largest oil producer and supplied over 90 percent of Japan's oil needs. Japan had only a year and a half's worth of military and economic oil reserves, which the war in China and the Japanese military and merchant navies were quickly drawing down. The Netherlands' colonial possessions in Indonesia (Netherlands East Indies) could supply all of Japan's oil, rubber, and tin needs, but the Japanese feared an attack there would bring American reprisal. On July 26, 1941, President Roosevelt embargoed all oil exports to Japan and froze its assets in the United States. Japan now had to either recall its forces from China or go to war before running out of oil. It chose war.

On December 7, 1941, Japan launched a surprise attack on the U.S. fleet in Pearl Harbor in the Hawaiian Islands. Japan hoped to cripple its Pacific rival, gain time to build a defensible Asian empire, and eventually win an ill-defined compromise peace.

The Japanese attack was a complete surprise but a limited success. The Japanese sank or crippled every American battleship, but by chance all the American aircraft carriers were at sea and escaped unharmed. Hours later the Japanese destroyed half of the American Far East Air Force stationed at Clark Air Base in the Philippines. Americans were humiliated by these unexpected defeats, which soon overwhelmed American isolationism and brought the United States into the war.

Hitler immediately declared war on the United States. Simultaneously, Japanese armies successfully attacked European and American colonies in Southeast Asia. Small but well-trained Japanese armies defeated larger Dutch and British armies to seize the Netherlands East Indies and the British colonies of Hong Kong, Malaya, and Singapore. After American forces surrendered the Philippines in May 1942, Japan held a vast empire in Southeast Asia and the western Pacific (Map 30.2).

The Japanese claimed they were freeing Asians from Western imperialism, and they called their empire the Greater East Asian Co-Prosperity Sphere. By promising to create a mutually advantageous union for Asia's long-term development, the Japanese tapped currents of nationalist sentiment. Most local populations were glad to see the Western powers go, but Asian faith in "co-prosperity" and support for Japan steadily declined as the war progressed. Although the Japanese set up anticolonial governments and promised genuine independence, real power always rested with Japanese military commanders and their superiors in Tokyo. The "independent" governments established in the Philippines, French Indochina, Burma, and the Netherlands East Indies were basically shams. Moreover, the Japanese never treated local populations as equals, and the occupiers exploited local peoples for Japan's wartime needs. They cut wages, imposed supply quotas on raw materials, and drafted local people for military and labor service.

The Japanese often exhibited great cruelty toward prisoners of war and civilians. After the fall of Hong Kong in December 1941, for example, wounded prisoners were murdered, and there was a mass rape of nurses. Elsewhere Dutch, Indonesian, and perhaps as many as two hundred thousand Korean women were forced to provide sex for Japanese soldiers as "comfort women." Recurring cruel behavior aroused local populations against the invaders.

The Grand Alliance

While the Nazis and the Japanese built their empires, Great Britain (the greatest colonial power), the United States (the greatest capitalist power), and the Soviet Union (the greatest Communist power) joined together in an unlikely military pact called the Grand Alliance. The vagaries of war, rather than choice, brought them together. Stalin had been cooperating with Hitler before Germany attacked Russia in June 1941, and the United States entered the war only after the Japanese attack on Pearl Harbor in December.

Grand Alliance leaders Stalin and Roosevelt agreed to a **Europe first policy** as proposed by Winston Churchill (Chamberlain's successor as British prime minister). Only after defeating Hitler would the Allies mount an all-out attack on Japan. To encourage mutual trust, the Allies adopted the principle of the unconditional surrender of Germany and Japan, and no unilateral treaties (as Russia had signed with Germany in World War I). This policy cemented the Grand Alliance because it denied Germany and Japan any hope of dividing their foes.

The Grand Alliance's military resources were awesome. The United States possessed a unique capacity to wage global war with its large population and mighty industry, which it harnessed in 1943 to outproduce not only the Axis powers but also the rest of the world combined.[30] The British economy was totally and effectively mobilized, and the country became an important staging area for the war in Europe. As for the Soviet Union, so great was its strength that it might well have defeated Germany without Western help. In the face of the German advance, whole factories and populations were successfully evacuated to eastern Russia and Siberia. There war production was reorganized and expanded, and the Red Army was increasingly well supplied and well led. Above all, Stalin drew on the massive support of the people for what the Soviets called the "Great Patriotic War of the Fatherland."

The War in Europe, 1942–1945

Halted at the gates of Moscow and Leningrad in 1941, the Germans renewed their offensive against the Soviet Union in 1942 and attacked Stalingrad in July. The Soviet armies counterattacked, quickly surrounding the entire German Sixth Army of 300,000 men. By late January 1943 only 123,000 soldiers were left to surrender. Hitler, who had refused to allow a retreat, suffered a catastrophic defeat. In summer 1943 the larger, better-equipped Soviet armies took the offensive and began to push the Germans back (see Map 30.1).

To match the Allied war effort, Germany had applied itself to total war in 1942 and had enlisted millions of German women and millions of prisoners of war and slave laborers to work in the war industry. Between early 1942 and July 1944 German war production tripled in spite of heavy Anglo-American bombing. Terrorized at home and frightened by the prospect of unconditional surrender, the Germans fought on with suicidal stoicism.

Not yet prepared to attack Germany directly through France, the Western Allies engaged in heavy fighting in North Africa (see Map 30.1). The French Vichy government allowed Germany to transport war materials and aircraft through Syria to Iraq to use against the British. In June–July 1941 the British invaded Syria and Lebanon. In autumn 1942 British forces defeated German and Italian armies at the Battle of El Alamein (el a-luh-MAYN) in Egypt. Shortly thereafter an Anglo-American force took control of the Vichy French colonies of Morocco and Algeria.

Having driven the Axis powers from North Africa by spring 1943, Allied forces invaded Italy. War-weary Italians deposed Mussolini, and the new Italian government accepted unconditional surrender in September 1943. Italy, it seemed, was liberated. But German commandos rescued Mussolini in a daring raid and made him head of a puppet government. German armies seized Rome and all of northern Italy. The Allies' Italian campaign against German forces lasted another two years and involved, in terms of infantry dead and wounded, the most costly battles of the war in western Europe. The German armies in Italy finally surrendered on April 29, 1945. Two days earlier Mussolini—dressed in a German military uniform and trying to escape with the retreating German forces—had been captured by partisan forces, and he was executed the next day.

On June 6, 1944, American and British forces under General Dwight Eisenhower landed on the beaches of Normandy, France, in history's greatest naval invasion. More than 2 million men and almost 0.5 million vehicles pushed inland and broke through the German lines. In March 1945 American troops crossed the Rhine and entered Germany.

The Soviets, who had been advancing steadily since July 1943, reached the outskirts of Warsaw by August 1944. On April 26, 1945, the Red Army met American forces on the Elbe River in Germany. The Allies had closed their vise on Nazi Germany and overrun Europe. As Soviet forces fought their way into Berlin, spawning unimaginable scenes of carnage, destruction, and brutality, Hitler committed suicide in his bunker on April 30. On May 7 the remaining German commanders capitulated.

The War in the Pacific, 1942–1945

While gigantic armies clashed on land in Europe, the greatest naval battles in history decided the fate of the war in Asia. In April 1942 the Japanese devised a plan to take Port Moresby in New Guinea and also destroy U.S. aircraft carriers in an attack on Midway Island (see Map 30.2). Having broken the secret Japanese code, the Americans skillfully won a series of decisive naval victories. First, in the Battle of the Coral Sea in May 1942, an American carrier force halted the Japanese advance on Port Moresby and relieved Australia from the threat of invasion. Then, in the Battle of Midway in June 1942, American pilots sank all four of the attacking Japanese aircraft carriers and established overall naval equality with Japan in the Pacific.

Badly hampered in the ground war by the Europe first policy, the United States gradually won control of the sea and air as it geared up its war industry. By 1943 the United States was producing one hundred thousand aircraft a year, almost twice as many as Japan produced in the entire war. In July 1943 the Americans and their Australian allies opened an "island-hopping" campaign toward Japan. Pounding Japanese forces on a given island with saturation bombing, Allied units would then hit the beaches and secure victory in vicious hand-to-hand combat. By 1944 hundreds of American submarines were hunting in "wolf packs," decimating shipping and destroying economic links in Japan's far-flung, overextended empire.

The Pacific war was brutal — a "war without mercy" — and atrocities were committed on both sides.[31] Aware of Japanese atrocities in China and the Philippines, the U.S. Marines and Army troops seldom took Japanese prisoners after the Battle of Guadalcanal in August 1942, killing even those rare Japanese soldiers who offered to surrender. American forces moving across the central and western Pacific in 1943 and 1944 faced unyielding resistance, and this resistance hardened soldiers as American casualties kept rising. A product of spiraling violence, mutual hatred, and dehumanizing racial stereotypes, the war without mercy intensified as it moved toward Japan.

In June 1944 U.S. bombers began a relentless bombing campaign of the Japanese home islands. In October 1944 American forces under General Douglas MacArthur landed on Leyte Island in the Philippines. The Japanese believed they could destroy MacArthur's troops and transport ships before the main American fleet arrived. The result was the four-day Battle of Leyte Gulf, the greatest battle in naval history, with 282 ships involved. The Japanese lost 13 large warships, including 4 aircraft carriers, while the Americans lost only 3 small ships. The Japanese navy was practically finished.

In spite of massive defeats, Japanese troops continued to fight with courage and determination. Indeed, the bloodiest battles of the Pacific war took place on Iwo Jima in February 1945 and on Okinawa in June 1945. American commanders believed that an invasion of Japan might cost 1 million American casualties and possibly 10 to 20 million Japanese lives. In fact, Japan was almost helpless, its industry and cities largely destroyed by intense American bombing. As the war in Europe ended in April 1945, Japanese leaders were divided. Hardliners argued that surrender was unthinkable; Japan had never been invaded or lost a war. A peace faction sought a negotiated end to the war, seeking help from the Soviet Union to mediate a diplomatic settlement between Japan and the United States and Great Britain. In archives made available after the Soviet Union's collapse, it is clear that Stalin led the Japanese on by giving them false hope of a diplomatic solution. In truth, Stalin was stalling for time to move his military forces from Europe to Asia, making plans to seize Japanese occupied territories in China and Korea.

On July 26 Truman, Churchill, and Stalin issued the Potsdam Declaration, which demanded unconditional surrender. The declaration left unclear whether the Japanese emperor would be treated as a war criminal. The Japanese, who considered Emperor Hirohito a god, sought clarification and amnesty for him. The Allies remained adamant that the surrender be unconditional. The Japanese felt compelled to fight on.

A Hiroshima Survivor Remembers Yasuko Yamagata was seventeen when she saw the brilliant blue-white "lightning flash" that became a fiery orange ball consuming everything that would burn. Thirty years later Yamagata painted this scene, her most unforgettable memory of the atomic attack. An incinerated woman, poised as if running with her baby clutched to her breast, lies near a water tank piled high with charred corpses. (GE15-05 drawn by Yasuko Yamagata, Hiroshima Peace Memorial Museum)

On August 6 and 9, 1945, the United States dropped atomic bombs on Hiroshima and Nagasaki in Japan. Mass bombing of cities and civilians, one of the terrible new practices of World War II, had led to the final nightmare—unprecedented human destruction in a single blinding flash. Also on August 9, Soviet troops launched an invasion of the Japanese puppet state of Manchukuo (Manchuria, China). Japan's leaders knew they could not stop a Soviet invasion of the Japanese islands from the west, as they had only prepared for an Allied invasion from the south. To avoid a Soviet invasion and further atomic bombing, the Japanese announced their surrender on August 14, 1945. The Second World War, which had claimed the lives of more than 50 million soldiers and civilians, was over.

Chapter Summary

The 1929 American stock market crash triggered a Great Depression, which caused the international economy to collapse and affected millions worldwide. Western democracies expanded their powers and responded with relief programs. Authoritarian and Fascist regimes arose to replace some capitalist democracies, which many perceived as outdated. Only World War II ended the depression.

The radical totalitarian dictatorships of the 1920s and 1930s were repressive, profoundly antiliberal, and exceedingly violent. Mussolini set up the first Fascist government, a one-party dictatorship, but it was never truly a totalitarian state on the order of Hitler's Germany or Stalin's Soviet Union.

In the Soviet Union Stalin launched a socialist "revolution from above," to modernize and industrialize the U.S.S.R. He set staggering industrial and agricultural goals and replaced private lands with (often forced) collectivization. Mass purges of the

Communist Party in the 1930s, leading to the imprisonment and deaths of millions, allowed Stalin to replenish the Communist Party with young loyalists.

Hitler and the Nazi elite rallied support by recalling the humiliation of World War I and the terms of the Versailles treaty, condemning Germany's leaders, building on racist prejudices against "inferior" peoples, and warning of a vast Jewish conspiracy to harm Germany and the German race. The Great Depression caused German voters to turn to Hitler for relief. After he declared the Versailles treaty disarmament clause null and void, British and French leaders tried appeasement. On September 1, 1939, his unprovoked attack on Poland forced the Allies to declare war, starting World War II.

Nazi armies first seized Poland and Germany's western neighbors and then turned east. Here Hitler planned to build a New Order based on racial imperialism over the Jews, Slavic peoples, and others. In the Holocaust that followed, millions of Jews and other "undesirables" were systematically exterminated. In Asia the Japanese created the Greater East Asian Co-Prosperity Sphere. This was a sham, as "Asia for the Asians" meant nothing but Japanese domination and control. After Japan attacked Pearl Harbor, the United States entered the war. In 1945 the Grand Alliance of the United States, Britain, and the Soviet Union defeated the outproduced and outmanned Germans and Japanese.

Notes

1. Quoted in S. B. Clough et al., eds., *Economic History of Europe: Twentieth Century* (New York: Harper & Row, 1968), pp. 243–245.
2. E. Halévy, *The Era of Tyrannies* (Garden City, N.Y.: Doubleday, 1965), pp. 265–316, esp. p. 300.
3. Carl J. Friedrich and Zbigniew K. Brzezinski, *Totalitarian Dictatorship and Autocracy*, 2d ed. (Cambridge, Mass.: Harvard University Press, 1965), pp. 21–23.
4. I. Kershaw, *The Nazi Dictatorship: Problems and Perspectives of Interpretation*, 2d ed. (London: Edward Arnold, 1989), p. 34.
5. See Robert C. Tucker, *Stalin in Power: The Revolution from Above, 1928–1941* (New York: W. W. Norton, 1992).
6. Lewis Siegelbaum and Andrei Sokolov, *Stalinism as a Way of Life: A Narrative in Documents* (New Haven, Conn.: Yale University Press, 2000), pp. 38–39.
7. Joseph Stalin, "Speech to First All-Congress Conference of Managers of Socialist Industry, February 4, 1931," in Joseph Stalin, *Leninism* (London: George Allen & Unwin, 1940), pp. 365–366.
8. Robert Service, *Stalin: A Biography* (Cambridge, Mass.: Harvard University Press, 2005), p. 266.
9. Quoted in I. Deutscher, *Stalin: A Political Biography*, 2d ed. (New York: Oxford University Press, 1967), p. 325, fn. 1.
10. Steven Rosefielde, *Red Holocaust* (New York: Routledge, 2010), p. 259, fn. 12.
11. Malcolm Muggeridge, *Chronicles of Wasted Time. Chronicle 1: The Green Stick* (New York: William Morrow, 1973), pp. 234–235.
12. M. Malia, *The Soviet Tragedy: A History of Socialism in Russia, 1917–1991* (New York: Free Press, 1995), pp. 227–270; see also the controversial work by historian John Archibald Getty, *Origins of the Great Purges: The Soviet Communist Party Reconsidered, 1933–1938* (New York: Cambridge University Press, 1985).
13. Oleg V. Khlevniuk, *Master of the House: Stalin and His Inner Circle* (New Haven, Conn.: Yale University Press, 2009), p. xix.
14. R. Vivarelli, "Interpretations on the Origins of Fascism," *Journal of Modern History* 63 (March 1991): 41.
15. Ion Smeaton Munro, *Through Fascism to World Power: A History of the Revolution in Italy* (London: Alexander Maclehose, 1933), p. 120.
16. Christopher Seton-Watson, *Italy from Liberalism to Fascism, 1870–1925* (London: Methuen, 1967), p. 661.
17. Ibid.
18. W. Brustein, *The Logic of Evil: The Social Origins of the Nazi Party, 1925–1933* (New Haven, Conn.: Yale University Press, 1996), pp. 52, 182.
19. Karl Dietrich Bracher, *The German Dictatorship: The Origins, Structure, and Effects of National Socialism*, trans. Jean Steinberg (New York: Praeger, 1970), p. 146.

20. Quoted in R. Stromberg, *An Intellectual History of Modern Europe* (New York: Appleton-Century-Crofts, 1966), p. 393.
21. Quoted in R. Moeller, *The Nazi State and German Society: A Brief History with Documents* (Boston: Bedford/ St. Martin's, 2010), p. 108.
22. See Claudia Koonz, *Mothers in the Fatherland: Women, the Family, and Nazi Politics* (New York: St. Martin's Press, 1987).
23. D. N. Dilks, "Appeasement Revisited," *University of Leeds Review* 15 (1972): 28–56.
24. See Frank McDonough, *Neville Chamberlain, Appeasement, and the British Road to War* (Manchester: Manchester University Press, 1998).
25. Winston Churchill, *The Second World War: The Gathering Storm* (Boston: Houghton Mifflin, 1948), p. 318.
26. Izidors Vizulis, *The Molotov-Ribbentrop Pact of 1939: The Baltic Case* (New York: Praeger, 1990), p. 16.
27. Anthony Read, *The Devil's Disciples: Hitler's Inner Circle* (New York: W. W. Norton, 2004), pp. 571–572.
28. Jeremy Noakes and Geoffrey Pridham, eds., "Message from Hermann Göring to Reinhard Heydrich, 31 July, 1941," in *Documents on Nazism, 1919–1945* (New York: Viking Press, 1974), p. 486.
29. See, for example, Christopher Browning, *Ordinary Men: Reserve Police Battalion 101 and the Final Solution in Poland* (New York: HarperCollins, 1992); Robert Gellately, *Backing Hitler: Consent and Coercion in Nazi Germany* (Oxford: Oxford University Press, 2001); Ian Kershaw, *Hitler, the Germans, and the Final Solution* (New Haven, Conn.: Yale University Press, 2008).
30. H. Willmott, *The Great Crusade: A New Complete History of the Second World War* (New York: Free Press, 1989), p. 255.
31. J. Dower, *War Without Mercy: Race and Power in the Pacific War* (New York: Pantheon, 1986).

CONNECTIONS

 If anyone still doubted the interconnectedness of all the world's inhabitants following the Great War, those doubts faded as events on a truly global scale touched everyone as never before in the 1930s and 1940s. First a Great Depression shook the financial foundations of the wealthiest capitalist economies and the poorest producers of raw materials and minerals. Another world war followed, bringing global death and destruction at a magnitude beyond the imaginations of even Great War survivors. At war's end, as we shall see in Chapter 31, the world's leaders revived Woodrow Wilson's idea of a League of Nations and formed the United Nations in 1946 to prevent such tragedies from ever reoccurring.

Although the United Nations was an attempt to bring nations together, the postwar world became more divided than ever. Chapter 31 will describe how two new superpowers—the United States and the Soviet Union—emerged from World War II to engage one another in the Cold War for nearly the rest of the century. Then in Chapters 32 and 33 we will see how less developed nations in Asia, Africa, and Latin America emerged after the war. Many of them did so by turning the nineteenth-century European ideology of nationalism against its creators, breaking the bonds of colonialism.

Today we want to believe that the era of totalitarian dictatorship was a terrible accident—that Stalin's slave labor camps, Hitler's gas chambers, and Japan's Rape of Nanjing "can't happen again." But the cruel truth is that horrible atrocities continue to plague the world in our time. The Khmer Rouge inflicted genocide on its people in Cambodia, and civil war has led to ethnically motivated atrocities in Bosnia, Rwanda, Burundi, and Sudan, recalling the horrors of the Second World War. Today's dictators, however, are losing control over access to information—historically a cornerstone of dictatorial rule—and are being challenged and even overthrown by citizens with cell phones, cameras, and Internet connections.

Chapter Review

MAKE IT STICK

 LearningCurve
Go online and use LearningCurve to retain what you've read.

IDENTIFY KEY TERMS

Identify and explain the significance of each item below.

New Deal (p. 932)
Popular Front (p. 933)
totalitarianism (p. 936)
fascism (p. 937)
five-year plan (p. 937)
New Economic Policy
   (NEP) (p. 938)

collectivization (p. 939)
Black Shirts (p. 943)
Lateran Agreement
   (p. 944)
Nazism (p. 944)
Enabling Act (p. 947)
blitzkrieg (p. 950)

New Order (p. 951)
Holocaust (p. 953)
Europe first policy
   (p. 958)

REVIEW THE MAIN IDEAS

Answer the focus questions from each section of the chapter.

1. What caused the Great Depression, and what were its consequences? (p. 929)
2. What was the nature of the new totalitarian dictatorships, and how did they differ from conservative authoritarian states and from each other? (p. 935)
3. How did Stalin and the Communist Party build a totalitarian order in the Soviet Union? (p. 937)
4. How did Italian fascism develop? (p. 942)
5. Why were Hitler and his Nazi regime initially so popular, and how did their actions lead to World War II? (p. 944)
6. How did Germany and Japan build empires in Europe and Asia, and how did the Allies defeat them? (p. 950)

MAKE CONNECTIONS

Analyze the larger developments and continuities within and across chapters.

1. Compare the effects of the Great Depression on the peoples and economies of Europe, Latin America, and East Asia. How did governments in these regions and their citizens respond to this economic cataclysm?
2. Which ideologies of change from nineteenth-century Europe (Chapter 24) contributed to the outbreak of World War II? What new ideologies arose at this time that led the world to war?

LaunchPad

ONLINE DOCUMENT PROJECT

Remembering the Holocaust
What choices did Holocaust survivors face?

Listen to testimonies from Holocaust survivors, and then complete a quiz and writing assignment based on the evidence and details from this chapter.

See inside the front cover to learn more.

CHRONOLOGY

1921	• New Economic Policy in Soviet Union
1922	• Mussolini seizes power in Italy
1924–1929	• Buildup of Nazi Party in Germany
1925	• Hitler, *Mein Kampf*
1927	• Stalin comes to power in Soviet Union
1928	• Stalin's first five-year plan
1929	• Start of collectivization in Soviet Union; Lateran Agreement
1929–1939	• Great Depression
1931	• Japan invades Manchuria
1932–1933	• Famine in Ukraine
1933	• Hitler appointed chancellor in Germany; Nazis begin control of state and society
1935	• Mussolini invades Ethiopia; creation of U.S. Works Progress Administration as part of New Deal
1936	• Start of great purges under Stalin; Spanish Civil War begins
1936–1937	• Popular Front government in France
1939	• Germany occupies Czech lands and invades Poland; Britain and France declare war on Germany, starting World War II
1940	• Japan signs formal alliance with Germany and Italy; Germany defeats France; Battle of Britain
1941	• Germany invades Soviet Union; Japan attacks Pearl Harbor; United States enters war
1941–1945	• The Holocaust
1944	• Allied invasion at Normandy
1945	• Atomic bombs dropped on Japan; World War II ends

31

✓ LearningCurve
After reading the chapter, go online and use LearningCurve to retain what you've read.

Decolonization, Revolution, and the Cold War

1945–1968

THE TRIUMPHANT VICTORY OF THE ALLIES IN 1945 SOON REVEALED a startling reality: war-torn nations were in shambles, entire economies were destroyed, and hundreds of thousands of people had been displaced. Physical rebuilding took place in the main battleground areas of Europe and Asia, but the war profoundly changed the entire world. Hopes of world peace quickly faded when the differences in economic and political ideologies that the Allies had set aside during wartime reasserted themselves and developed into a tense but nonviolent conflict known as the Cold War, which lasted more than four decades.

As people in Asia and Africa pushed back against centuries of Western expansion and demanded national self-determination and racial equality, new nations emerged and nearly every colonial territory gained formal independence between 1945 and the early 1960s. A revolution in China consolidated Communist rule and initially followed the Soviet model, but then veered in new directions. Rather than form an allied Communist front, China and the Soviet Union became economic and political rivals.

Amid the growing tensions of the global Cold War, remarkable growth and economic prosperity occurred in the postwar era. Europe once again dug itself out from under the rubble of war and, with U.S. aid, experienced an amazing recovery. The United States converted its wartime economy to peacetime production. The Soviet Union sought to protect itself from future attacks from the west by occupying eastern Europe and establishing Communist dictatorships there. In eastern European countries forced to ally with and follow the Soviet political and economic model, citizens who rose up to demand reforms faced repeated repression by Soviet forces.

966

The World Remade

How did the Cold War and decolonization shape the postwar world?

The bitter rivalry between the United States and the Soviet Union divided postwar Europe and became a **Cold War** — not an outright military confrontation between nations, but a long, tense standoff. As the Cold War took shape, three events separated by barely two years foreshadowed the changes that would take place in the world following the Second World War: the independence of India and Pakistan in 1947; the establishment of the state of Israel in 1948; and the Communist revolution in China in 1949. All had their roots in the decades preceding the Second World War — and even predating the First World War. Yet each was also profoundly influenced by the war and its outcomes. In turn, these events reflected tendencies that became dominant in the postwar period: decolonization, revolution, and renewed political and economic competition.

The Cold War and the Division of Europe

The Cold War originated in disputes over the political outcome of the war. During talks among the three major powers — the United States, Britain, and the Soviet Union — held toward the end of the war, Soviet leader Joseph Stalin, who had lived through two German invasions, insisted that control of eastern Europe was the best way to guarantee military security from Germany. Where U.S. president Franklin Roosevelt had been inclined to accommodate these demands, his successor, Harry Truman, demanded free elections throughout eastern Europe. Stalin refused. Philip Mosely, a founder of the academic discipline of Soviet studies in the United States, recalled Stalin stating at the 1945 Potsdam Conference that "any freely elected government would be anti-Soviet and that we cannot permit."[1]

Truman refused to negotiate with Stalin, bolstered by the fact that the United States was the only country that possessed atomic weapons at the end of the war. Soviet actions deepened the rift with the United States. Just as the U.S. sense of security came from having a monopoly on the atomic bomb, Stalin pursued security for the Soviet Union by militarily occupying eastern Europe and imposing obedient governments. These countries were considered Soviet satellites — nations whose politics and economics were dictated by the Soviet Union. They provided a buffer that shielded the Soviet Union from the threat of western European aggression of the kind the Soviet Union had faced in the Second World War and that Russia had faced in the First World War.

President Truman misread these occupations as a campaign for world domination. Communist movements beyond Stalin's occupation zone in Greece and China fed these fears. In October 1945 Truman declared that the United States would never recognize governments established by force, establishing the **Truman Doctrine**, aimed at "containing" communism to areas already occupied by the Soviet army by providing military and economic support to governments threatened by Communist control. (His reference to regimes imposed by force applied only to Europe and countries threatened by communism, not to European colonial domination in Asia and Africa.)

To prevent the spread of communism, Truman asked Congress for military aid for Greece and Turkey. Soon after, Secretary of State George C. Marshall proposed a broader package of economic and food aid — the **Marshall Plan** — to help Europe rebuild. Stalin refused Marshall Plan assistance for all of eastern Europe, where he had established Soviet-style Communist dictatorships. The Soviet Union's aid and support for the overthrow of the democratically elected Czechoslovakian government in February 1948 and its replacement by a Communist government shocked the U.S. Congress into action, and on April 2, 1948, it voted for the Marshall Plan.

On July 24, 1948, Stalin blocked all road traffic through the Soviet zone of Germany to Berlin. The Western allies responded with an airlift of millions of tons of provisions to the West Berliners. After 324 days the Soviets backed down: containment seemed to work. In 1949 the United States formed an anti-Soviet military alliance of Western governments: the North Atlantic Treaty Organization (**NATO**). Stalin countered by tightening his hold on his satellites, later united in the Warsaw Pact. Europe was divided into two hostile blocs. British prime minister Winston Churchill warned that an "iron curtain has descended across the Continent."[2]

The Soviet Union, with its massive army arrayed across eastern Europe, and the United States, with its industrial strength and atomic weapons, emerged from the war as **superpowers** whose might dwarfed that of other countries. Superpower status reached an awkward balance after the Soviet Union developed its own atomic weapons in 1949. Both nations pitched themselves into a military and geopolitical confrontation that stopped short of outright war: the Cold War (Map 31.1).

A deep ideological divide defined the rivalry between the United States and the Soviet Union. The United States saw itself as the defender of a "free world" governed by liberal principles such as free markets, private property, and individual rights pro-

Berlin Airlift   Residents of Berlin watch a U.S. Air Force cargo plane land with supplies to support West Berliners during the Soviet blockade (1948–1949). (Courtesy CSU Archives/The Everett Collection)

MAP 31.1 Cold War Europe in the 1950s Europe was divided by an "iron curtain" during the Cold War. None of the Communist countries of eastern Europe were participants in the Marshall Plan.

tected by democratic constitutions. The Soviet Union defined itself as the defender of the rights of workers and peasants against their exploiters, the rights of colonial peoples against their colonizers, and economic development based on rational production and equitable distribution. The Cold War sharpened the distinctions between these models, creating opposing paths that the superpowers pressured other countries to follow.

Each of these ideologies offered much that was attractive, be it individual rights or the promise of equality, but both superpowers fell short of the ideals they espoused. This was true within the superpowers themselves, but even more so in the pressures they applied on other nations. Each country dealt harshly with dissenters or distributed the freedoms it promised selectively — the rights the United States celebrated were violently denied to racial and ethnic minorities, while the Soviet Union imposed conformity and compliance on its citizens and made eastern European countries into puppet states whose citizens could not choose their leaders or their countries' directions. Both superpowers engaged in unsavory behavior in their efforts to assert and expand their spheres of influence over other countries.

The United Nations

The Cold War was not just a confrontation between the United States and the Soviet Union, but also an effort to avoid war. Similar efforts after the Second World War to assure peace and stability through international cooperation culminated in 1945 when representatives of fifty nations met in San Francisco to draft a charter for a new intergovernmental organization called the United Nations. Like that of its predecessor, the League of Nations (see Chapter 28), the immediate goal of the United Nations was to mediate international conflicts in order to preserve peace. But in 1945 the founders of the United Nations foresaw a more ambitious role for the new body than the League of Nations had played: beyond conflict resolution, the UN would support the decolonization of territories under foreign rule; promote economic development; and expand access to health care, protection for workers, environmental conservation, and gender equity.

The United Nations was divided into two bodies: a General Assembly that met annually and included all nations that signed the UN Charter; and a Security Council made up of the five main regional powers, each of which held veto power over the council's decisions, making it a body that in effect only functioned through unanimous consent. Roosevelt's vision for the members of the Security Council included the United States, the Soviet Union, the United Kingdom, China, and Brazil. Given the intensity of U.S. influence in Latin America (see Chapter 27), British and Soviet leaders feared the Brazilian seat would simply be a second vote for the United States, so they insisted that France instead be the fifth member of the Security Council. After the Chinese Revolution in 1949, the government of Taiwan held China's seat until the United Nations transferred it to the People's Republic of China in 1971.

The UN gave critical support to decolonization efforts. Its charter defended the right of self-determination, and it served as a forum for liberation movements to advocate for their claims, negotiate the terms of independence, or define new national boundaries. The UN also provided a platform for opponents of colonialism to condemn those colonial powers that resisted their calls for self-determination. In addition, UN member nations volunteered military forces to serve around the world as peacekeepers. These forces, still in use today, are not involved in combat, but their presence has at different times provided a buffer to ease violent disputes, and they have served as observers to ensure that agreements were being met or that abuses were not being committed in conflict areas.

In its early years, the United Nations mediated Indonesia's demand for independence from the Netherlands, which fought a four-year war to reoccupy the former colony. The UN deployed peacekeepers in the newly created border between India and Pakistan, and it helped determine the terms under which Britain relinquished control of Palestine and Jordan, as well as the terms for the creation of Israel in 1948. In the 1950s and 1960s its advocacy for decolonization became more forceful as more colonial peoples sought independence. In 1960 alone, eighteen African nations were seated at the UN, forming part of an "Afro-Asian bloc" committed to completing the decolonization process and advancing postcolonial economic development.

The Politics of Liberation

The term *Third World* emerged in the 1950s when many thinkers, journalists, and politicians viewed Africa, Asia, and Latin America as a single entity, different from both the capitalist, industrialized "First World" and the Communist, industrialized "Second World." The Cold War rivalry between the United States and the Soviet Union reinforced this "three-bloc" perspective, which staked out separate camps for the superpowers and created a third general category for everyone else. Despite differences in history and culture, most so-called Third World countries in Africa, Asia, and Latin America were poor and economically underdeveloped — meaning less industrialized — during the Cold War era, and thus are also referred to as "nonindustrial" or "industrializing" nations. They also shared many characteristics that encouraged the development of a common consciousness about their marginalization and ideologies for defining their future.

The roots of many liberation movements in these countries went back well before the Second World War and often as far back as the nineteenth century. In the 1920s and 1930s colonial powers dampened these movements through repression and limited reforms. After the Second World War weakened the colonial powers, nationalist movements in the colonies became more insistent. As nations fought against colonial rule, their quest for liberation took many forms. Economically, they pursued national industrialization and development to end dependence on industrialized nations. Politically, they sought alliances within the industrializing world to avoid the neocolonial influences of more powerful nations. Intellectually, they reacted against the white supremacism prevalent not just in Nazi Germany, but also among European colonial powers and the United States.

Liberation movements that arose in former colonies worldwide proposed an alternative, anti-imperial and antiracist worldview as they responded to historic injustices and to the structures of the Cold War order. As countries faced intense pressure to align themselves ideologically and economically with either the United States or the Soviet Union, few could resist the pressure or the incentives those powers brought to bear. But it is helpful for us to think of the world after 1945 not as one divided between East and West, between the Soviet Union and the United States, but as a world of societies pulled in many different directions at the same time. This world was shaped by radical revolutions, reform movements, and conservative reactions. The possibilities for change seemed immense.

Nonindustrialized nations tried to operate independently from the two superpowers in a variety of ways. In 1955 leaders of twenty-nine recently independent nations in Asia and Africa met in Bandung, Indonesia, to create a framework for political and economic cooperation to help them emerge from colonialism without having to resubordinate their nations either to their former colonizers or to pressures from the Cold War superpowers. The participants outlined principles for rejecting pressure from the superpowers and supporting decolonization. In 1961 nations participating in the Bandung Conference met in Yugoslavia, where Marxists who had come to power in the struggle against Nazi Germany zealously guarded their independence from the Soviet Union, to form a Non-Aligned Nations Movement.

Dependency and Development Theories

In 1948 the United Nations established the Economic Commission for Latin America (ECLA) in Santiago, Chile, to study economic development. Under the direction of Argentine economist Raúl Prebisch, ECLA produced one of Latin America's most influential intellectual contributions of the twentieth century: a diagnosis of reasons why Latin America, like other less industrialized regions of the world, remained economically and technologically dependent on Europe and the United States, along with prescriptions for remedying that dependency. These ideas formed what became known as **dependency theory**.

According to dependency theory, countries in Latin America, Africa, and Asia were trapped in the position of borrowers of capital and technology, and producers of primary commodities such as agricultural and mineral goods. Since western Europe and the United States industrialized in the nineteenth century, they secured a lasting economic advantage magnified by colonialism and neocolonialism, which reorganized production and consumption around the world for their benefit.

According to this analysis, the prosperity of Europe and the United States was built on the impoverishment of other regions of the world because the products that industrialized countries made were worth more than the agricultural or mineral exports of other nations. For instance, in 2013 one would need to harvest 70 million pounds of coffee to purchase a Boeing 737 aircraft, while Boeing's shareholders and workers could afford enough coffee to stay awake for a very long time. This inequality in the market value of goods increased over time as the relative value of commodities such as coffee or copper decreased relative to the value of manufactured goods like automobiles or technologically advanced goods like computer software.

How could this pattern be broken? Could a country that grew coffee become a country that manufactured jets? This question would be asked many times around the world in the second half of the twentieth century, and it would be answered in many ways.

One approach was **modernization theory**, championed by U.S. economist Walt Whitman Rostow. He suggested that societies passed through phases of development from primitive to modern, and that adopting the political, economic, or cultural practices of places like the United States was the best remedy for poverty. Modernization theory shaped foreign aid programs: the U.S. government deployed armies of experts around the world to advise governments and communities in areas ranging from revising legal codes to digging wells. These technicians often did not understand local conditions, believing that the American way was the only way. Regardless of their intentions, or the abundance of funding that backed them, these projects were often riddled with unintended negative consequences, and many people began to mistrust these experts.

To peoples emerging from colonialism, dependency theory offered a more appealing path. Newly independent nations faced enormous pressure for economic development. Rural poverty pushed millions into cities where good jobs were scarce. Cities and the countryside alike had insufficient schools and health care. Dependency theorists rejected liberalism because they believed free-market capitalism reinforced these problems by inhibiting the accumulation of wealth in dependent regions. Instead they favored state intervention to remake national economies so that resources would be distributed more equitably. Prebisch advocated a practice that became common in much of the world: import substitution industrialization (ISI). Under ISI policies, countries imposed trade barriers to keep certain foreign products out and provided subsidies to develop domestic industries that could make the same goods. Dependency theorists like Brazilian Marxist economists Celso Furtado and Fernando Henrique Cardoso suggested that even ISI was not enough, and that deeper social reforms were needed, such as the redistribution of farmlands from large landowners to rural workers, as well as state control of major industries and banks.

The governments that attempted land redistribution or the nationalization of foreign firms often faced a fierce backlash by landowners, foreign corporations, and political conservatives. In many cases, reformist governments were deposed in military coups supported by the United States. The U.S. reaction against reformers in countries like Guatemala, where the elected government was overthrown in a coup organized by the United States in 1954, pushed reformers in other countries into more radical and defiant approaches. In Cuba a revolutionary movement led by Fidel Castro took power in 1959. Castro's regime executed a deep social and economic transformation of Cuba, including the redistribution of land and urban properties. This pressure from the United States pushed revolutionary Cuba into an alliance with the Soviet Union. The Argentine military strategist who worked closely with Castro, Che Guevara, became an icon of radical revolutionary liberation. Guevara wrote a widely read handbook for would-be insurgents, *Guerilla Warfare*. He built his ideas for social change into a revolutionary theory, Guevarism, which suggested that private property and wage labor were forms of exploitation that could be overthrown by free workers volunteering their labor to help liberate others.

One of the most influential areas where the idea of liberation crystallized was a movement within the Catholic Church called liberation theology. The movement emerged in Latin America amid reforms of church doctrine carried out by Pope John XXIII

Liberation Theology Participants at a meeting of ecclesiastical base communities in Brazil gather under a banner reading "Altar of Martyrs: Your Blood Nourishes Our Base Communities." This 1986 meeting, eighteen years after the Medellín Conference, shows the lasting impact of liberation theology in Latin America. (© Bernard Bisson/Sygma/Corbis) (pontificate 1958–1963), who called on clergy to engage more directly with the contemporary world—a world characterized by poverty, exclusion, and often dictatorship. In 1968 the Latin American Council of Bishops gathered in Medellín, Colombia, and invoked dependency theory as it called on clergy to exercise a "preferential option for the poor," by working toward "social justice," including land redistribution, the recognition of peasants' and labor unions, and denouncing economic dependency and neocolonialism.

Drawing on dependency theory and sometimes verging on revolutionary Marxism, priests attracted to liberation theology challenged governments, fought against landowners and business owners they saw as oppressors, and formed community organizations, or ecclesiastical base communities, where the residents of poor neighborhoods could gather to discuss their problems and devise solutions. After the 1970s, Popes John Paul II (pontificate 1978–2005) and Benedict XVI (pontificate 2005–2013) suppressed liberation theology and silenced its most outspoken thinkers. Advocates of liberation theology greeted the naming of a pope from Latin America, Francis, in 2013 as a return to the focus on fighting poverty and social exclusion within the Catholic Church.

Interpreting the Postcolonial Experience

Many intellectuals who came of age during and after the struggle for political emancipation embraced a vision of solidarity among peoples oppressed by colonialism and racism. Some argued that genuine freedom required a total rejection of Western values in addition to an economic and political break with the former colonial powers. Frantz Fanon (1925–1961) expressed these views in his powerful study of colonial peoples, *The Wretched of the Earth* (1961).

According to Fanon, a French-trained black psychiatrist from the Caribbean island of Martinique, decolonization is always a violent and totally consuming process whereby one "species" of men, the colonizers, is completely replaced by an absolutely different species—the colonized, the wretched of the earth. During decolonization the colonized masses mock colonial values, "insult them, and vomit them up" in a psychic purge. Fanon believed that throughout Africa and Asia the former imperialists and their local collaborators—the "white men with black faces"—remained the enemy:

> During the colonial period the people are called upon to fight against oppression; after national liberation, they are called upon to fight against poverty, illiteracy, and underdevelopment. The struggle, they say, goes on. . . . We are not blinded by the moral reparation of national independence; nor are we fed by it. The wealth of the imperial countries is our wealth too. . . . Europe is literally the creation of the Third World. The wealth which smothers her is that which was stolen from the underdeveloped peoples.[3]

Fanon's passionate, angry work became a sacred text for radicals attacking imperialism and struggling for liberation.

As countries gained independence, some writers looked beyond wholesale rejection of the industrialized powers. They, too, were anti-imperialist, but they were often also activists and cultural nationalists who celebrated the rich histories and cultures of their peoples. Many did not hesitate to criticize their own leaders or fight oppression and corruption.

The Nigerian writer Chinua Achebe (1930–2013) rendered these themes with sharp insight. Achebe sought to restore his people's self-confidence by reinterpreting the past. For Achebe, the "writer in a new nation" had first to embrace the "fundamental theme" that Africans had their own culture before the Europeans came and that it was the duty of writers to help Africans reclaim their past.

In his 1958 novel *Things Fall Apart*, Achebe brings to life the men and women of an Ibo village at the beginning of the twentieth century, with all their virtues and frailties. Woven into the story are the proverbs and wisdom of a sophisticated people and the beauty of a vanishing world:

> [The white man] says that our customs are bad; and our own brothers who have taken up his religion also say that our customs are bad. How do you think we can fight when our own brothers have turned against us? The white man is very clever. He came quietly and peaceably with his religion. We were amused at his foolishness and allowed him to stay. Now he has won our brothers, and our clan can no longer act like one. He has put a knife on the things that held us together and we have fallen apart.[4]

In later novels Achebe portrayed the postindependence disillusionment of many writers and intellectuals, which reflected trends in many developing nations in the 1960s and 1970s: the rulers seemed increasingly corrupted by Western luxury and estranged from the rural masses. From the 1970s onward, Achebe was active in the struggle for democratic government in Nigeria.

Novelist V. S. Naipaul, born in Trinidad in 1932 of Indian parents, also castigated governments in the developing countries for corruption, ineptitude, and self-deception. Another of Naipaul's recurring themes is the poignant loneliness and homelessness of people uprooted by colonialism and Western expansion.

For peoples emerging from colonial domination, or confronting the poverty and social exclusion that was commonplace outside of industrialized nations, the postwar challenge of liberation was not simply political and economic, but also cultural and spiritual. The middle decades of the twentieth century saw a broad awakening of voices among peoples who had been rendered voiceless by their marginalization.

Nationalism in South Asia and the Middle East

How did religion and the legacies of colonialism affect the formation of new nations in South Asia and the Middle East after World War II?

As Europe moved toward greater economic unity in the postwar era, nationalist independence movements in former colonies dramatically reversed centuries of overseas imperial expansion. The three South Asian countries created through independence from Britain and subsequent partition, India, Pakistan, and Bangladesh, reflected the dominant themes of national renaissance and modernization that characterized the end of colonialism, but ethnic and religious rivalries greatly complicated their renewal and development.

Throughout the vast *umma* (world of Islam), nationalism became a powerful force after 1945, stressing modernization and the end of subordination to Western nations. The nationalists who guided the formation of modern states in the Arab world struggled to balance Cold War pressures from the United States and the Soviet Union, as well as the tension between secular modernization and Islam. In many cases, these pressures resulted in the formation of one-party dictatorships that became corrupt and failed to alleviate poverty. The longer experience with secular modernization in Turkey, which dated to the aftermath of the First World War, shielded it from many of the difficulties faced by other Muslim nations. At the heart of this world, Jewish nationalists founded the state of Israel following the Second World War. The Zionist claim to a homeland came into sharp, and often violent, conflict with the rights and claims of the Palestinian people displaced by the creation of Israel.

Independence in India, Pakistan, and Bangladesh

World War II accelerated the drive toward Indian independence begun by Mohandas Gandhi (see page 910). In 1942 Gandhi called on the British to "quit India" and threatened another civil disobedience campaign. He and the other Indian National Congress Party leaders were soon after arrested and were jailed for much of the war. Thus India's wartime support for Britain was substantial but not always enthusiastic. Meanwhile, the Congress Party's prime rival skillfully seized the opportunity to increase its influence.

The Congress Party's rival was the **Muslim League**, led by the English-educated lawyer Muhammad Ali Jinnah (1876–1948). Jinnah feared Hindu domination of an independent Indian state led by the Congress Party. Asserting the right of Muslim areas to separate from the Hindu majority, Jinnah called on the British government in March 1940 to grant the Muslim and Hindu peoples separate national states:

> The Hindus and Muslims have two different religions, philosophies, social customs, literatures. They neither inter-marry, nor dine together, and indeed, they belong to two different civilizations which are based mainly on conflicting ideas and conceptions. . . . To yoke together two such nations under a single State, one as a numerical minority and the other as majority, must lead to growing discontent and final destruction of any fabric that may be so built up for the government of such a State.[5]

Gandhi regarded Jinnah's two-nation theory as untrue and as promising the victory of hate over love.

Britain agreed to speedy independence for India after 1945, but conflicts between Hindu and Muslim nationalists led to murderous clashes in 1946. When it became clear that Jinnah and the Muslim League would accept nothing less than an independent state of Pakistan, India's last colonial viceroy, Louis Mountbatten, mediated a partition that created a predominantly Hindu nation and a predominantly Muslim nation. On August 14, 1947, India and Pakistan gained political independence from Britain as two separate nations (Map 31.2).

Massacres and mass expulsions followed independence. Perhaps a hundred thousand Hindus and Muslims were slaughtered, and an estimated 5 million became refugees. Congress Party leaders were completely powerless to stop the wave of violence. "What is there to celebrate?" exclaimed Gandhi in reference to independence, "I see nothing

MAP 31.2   The Partition of British India, 1947 Violence and fighting were most intense where there were large Hindu and Muslim minorities—in Kashmir, the Punjab, and Bengal. The tragic result of partition, which occurred repeatedly throughout the world in the twentieth century, was a forced exchange of populations and greater homogeneity on both sides of the border.

but rivers of blood."[6] Gandhi labored to ease tensions between Hindus and Muslims, but in the aftermath of riots in January 1948, he was killed by a Hindu gunman who resented what he saw as Gandhi's appeasement of Muslims.

After the ordeal of independence, relations between India and Pakistan remained tense. Fighting over the disputed area of Kashmir, a strategically important northwestern border state with a Muslim majority annexed by India, lasted until 1949 and broke out again in 1965–1966, 1971, and 1999 as tensions continued.

Jawaharlal Nehru (1889–1964) and the Indian National Congress Party ruled India for a generation and introduced major social reforms. Hindu women gained legal equality, including the right to vote, to seek divorce, and to marry outside their castes. The constitution abolished the untouchable caste. In practice, less discriminatory attitudes toward women and untouchables evolved slowly—especially in rural villages, where 85 percent of the people lived.

The Congress Party leadership pursued nationalist, state-driven economic development, but population growth of about 2.4 percent per year consumed much of the increased output of economic expansion. The relocation of millions during the partition of India and Pakistan exacerbated poverty. The Congress Party maintained neutrality in the Cold War, distancing itself from both the United States and the Soviet Union. Instead India became one of the most avid advocates of a "third force" of non-aligned nations that aimed for economic and cultural cooperation. This effort culminated in the Afro-Asian Conference in Bandung, Indonesia, in 1955 (see page 971).

At independence, Pakistan was divided between eastern and western provinces separated by more than a thousand miles of Indian territory, as well as by language, ethnic background, and social custom. The Bengalis of East Pakistan constituted a majority of Pakistan's population as a whole, but were neglected by the central government, which remained in the hands of West Pakistan's elite after Jinnah's death. In 1971 the Bengalis revolted and won their independence as the new nation of Bangladesh after a violent civil war. Bangladesh, a secular parliamentary democracy, struggled to find political and economic stability amid famines that resulted from monsoon floods, tornadoes, and cyclones in the vast, low-lying, and intensely farmed Ganges Delta.

Arab Socialism in the Middle East

In the postwar period, new Arab states in the Middle East emerged from a long cycle of colonial rule. For centuries the region had been dominated by the Ottoman Empire. After the First World War, France and Britain claimed protectorates in the former Ottoman territories of Iraq, Syria, Lebanon, and Jordan. Britain had already claimed Egypt as a protectorate in 1914, and France controlled Algeria. These new nations, along with other countries gaining independence from the southern Mediterranean to the Persian Gulf, embraced **Arab socialism**—a modernizing, secular, and nationalist project of nation building aimed at economic development, a strong military, and Pan-Arab unity that would deter imperial impulses from Europe or the superpowers. Arab socialism focused on modernization and state formation rather than ideological Marxism.

Arab socialism held particular significance for women in Middle Eastern societies. It cast aside religious restrictions on women's fashions, education, occupations, and public activities. In countries like Egypt and Iraq, Western dress, the openness of education, and access to professions enjoyed by urban, typically affluent women symbolized an embrace of modernity, although senior posts in government, the professions, and business were still dominated by men.

In 1952 army officers overthrew Egypt's monarchy and expelled the British military force that the king had allowed to occupy the country. The movement's leader, Gamal Abdel Nasser (1918–1970), built a nationalist regime aimed at eradicating the vestiges of European colonialism (such as British and French control of the Suez Canal), as well as creating an economic transformation through land redistribution and state support for industrialization. Applying the principles of Arab socialism, Nasser pursued the secularization of Egyptian society and equal opportunity for women and men, and created an extensive social welfare network.

Nasser's National Charter called for the nationalization of railroads, mines, ports, airports, dams, banks, utilities, insurance companies, and heavy industries. In the countryside the size of landholdings was limited and large estates broken up. As Nasser declared, "When we started this revolution, we wanted to put an end to exploitation. Hence our struggle to put capital at the service of man, and to put land at the service of man, instead of leaving man at the service of the feudalist who owns the land." His main development goal was constructing the Aswan Dam on the Nile River, which generated electricity for industrialization in northern Egypt while allowing southern Egypt to control seasonal flooding of the river to increase agricultural production.[7]

In 1956 Nasser took a symbolic and strategic step toward nationalizing Egypt's economy when he ordered the army to take control of the Suez Canal, still held by Britain and France. A coalition of British, French, and Israeli forces invaded to retake the canal. The Soviet Union offered support to Egypt. To prevent Soviet intervention and a Soviet-Egyptian alliance, the United States negotiated a cease-fire that granted Egypt control of the Suez Canal against the wishes of the British and French governments. Alongside control of the canal, Nasser's other main economic accomplishment was building the Aswan Dam to provide electricity and control Nile River flooding. Nasser negotiated the funding and technical expertise for building the dam with both the United States and the Soviet Union, eventually settling on Soviet aid. The Suez crisis and the construction of the Aswan Dam were examples of a nationalist leader like Nasser successfully playing the superpowers against each other.

Nationalist military officers in other Arab countries emulated Nasser's public political profile and socialist developmental projects. In countries like Syria and Iraq, these nationalists formed the Pan-Arab socialist Ba'ath Party. For members of national Ba'ath parties, Nasser's Egypt served as a model for developing a strong state governed by a single ruling party that channeled nationalist and development aspirations. Syria briefly merged with Egypt from 1958 until 1961, forming the United Arab Republic. Ba'athist military officers who resented Nasser's control of Syria revolted against Egypt and established a new national Syrian government dominated by the Ba'ath Party. In Iraq the Ba'ath Party formed part of the military movement that in 1958 overthrew the British-backed monarchy, leading to a long reign by Ba'athist leaders that ended when a U.S. military invasion toppled Saddam Hussein in 2003.

The Arab-Israeli Conflict

Before the Second World War, Arab nationalists were loosely united in their opposition to the colonial powers and to Jewish migration to Palestine. Palestinian Arabs, as well as Arabs in new states forming as British and French domination of the Middle East crumbled in the aftermath of the Second World War, strenuously opposed Jewish settlement in Palestine (see pages 908–909). The British announced in early 1947 their intention to withdraw from Palestine in 1948. The difficult problem of a Jewish homeland was dumped in the lap of the United Nations. In November 1947 the UN General Assembly passed a plan to partition Palestine into two separate states—one Arab and one Jewish. The Jews accepted, and the Arabs rejected, the partition of Palestine.

By early 1948 an undeclared civil war raged in Palestine. When the British mandate ended on May 14, 1948, the Jews proclaimed the state of Israel. Arab countries immediately attacked the new Jewish state, but Israeli forces drove off the invaders and conquered more territory. Roughly nine hundred thousand Palestinian refugees fled or were expelled from old Palestine. The war left an enormous legacy of Arab bitterness toward

Israel and its political allies, Great Britain and the United States. In 1964 a loose union of Palestinian refugee groups opposed to Israel joined together, under the leadership of Yasir Arafat (1929–2004), to form the Palestine Liberation Organization (PLO).

Nationalist leaders in neighboring Syria and Egypt cultivated political support at home through fierce opposition to Israel and threats to crush it militarily. This tension repeatedly erupted into war. On June 1, 1967, when Syrian and Egyptian armies massed on Israel's borders, the Israeli government decided to go to war, launching surprise air strikes that destroyed most of the Egyptian, Syrian, and Jordanian air forces. Over the next five days Israeli armies defeated Egyptian, Syrian, Jordanian, and Palestinian forces and took control of the Sinai Peninsula and the Gaza Strip from Egypt, the West Bank and East Jerusalem from Jordan, and the Golan Heights from Syria. In the Six-Day War (also known as the 1967 Arab-Israeli War), Israel proved itself to be the pre-eminent military force in the region, and it expanded the territory under its control threefold.

After the war Israel began to build large Jewish settlements in the Gaza Strip and the West Bank, home to millions of Palestinians. On November 22, 1967, the UN Security Council adopted Resolution 242, which contained a "land for peace" formula by which Israel was called upon to withdraw from the occupied territories, and in return the Arab states were to withdraw all claims to Israeli territory, cease all hostilities, and recognize the sovereignty of the Israeli state. The tension between rival territorial claims persisted.

Revolution and Resurgence in East and Southeast Asia

How did the Cold War shape reconstruction, revolution, and decolonization in East and Southeast Asia?

In Asia Japan's defeat ended the Second World War, but other conflicts continued: nationalists in territories colonized by European nations intensified their struggle for independence, and in China Nationalist and Communist armies that had cooperated to expel the Japanese invaders now confronted each other in a renewed civil war. In 1949 Communist forces under Mao Zedong triumphed and established the People's Republic of China. The Nationalist government retreated to the island of Taiwan, where it remained a Republic of China independent of the Communist mainland. The Communist victory in China shaped the nature of Japan's reconstruction, as its U.S. occupiers determined that an industrially and economically strong Japan would serve as a counterweight to Mao. U.S. fear of the spread of communism drew the country into conflicts in Korea and Vietnam, intensifying the stakes in the decolonization struggle across East and Southeast Asia.

The Communist Victory in China

When Japan surrendered to the Allies in August 1945, Communists and Nationalists both rushed to seize evacuated territory. In the last months of World War II, the Soviet Union occupied large areas of Manchuria previously held by the Japanese. When the

Soviet troops left in March 1946, they allowed the Chinese Communists to seize control of key industrial areas in the north, including stockpiles of weapons left behind by the Japanese. Communists and Nationalists had fought each other before the Second World War, but had put aside their struggle to resist Japanese invasion. With the war over, the Nationalists and Communists resumed their conflict. By 1948 the Nationalist forces disintegrated before the better-led, more determined Communists. The following year Nationalist leader Jiang Jieshi and 2 million mainland Chinese fled to Taiwan, and in October 1949 Mao Zedong proclaimed the People's Republic of China.

Communism triumphed in China for many reasons. Mao Zedong and the Communists had avoided pitched battles and concentrated on winning peasant support and forming a broad anti-Japanese coalition. By reducing rents, promising land redistribution, enticing intellectuals, and spreading propaganda, they emerged in peasant eyes as the true patriots, the genuine nationalists.

Between 1949 and 1954 the Communists consolidated their rule. They seized the vast landholdings of a minority of landlords and rich peasants and distributed the land to 300 million poor peasants. This land reform was extremely popular and widely publicized through propaganda campaigns. Meanwhile, as Mao admitted in 1957, mass arrests led to eight hundred thousand "class enemies" being summarily executed; the true figure is probably much higher. Millions more were deported to forced-labor camps. All visible opposition from the old ruling groups was thus destroyed.

Mao and the party looked to the Soviet Union for inspiration in the early 1950s. China adopted collective agriculture and Soviet-style five-year plans to promote rapid industrialization. Russian specialists built many Chinese factories, and the Soviets provided considerable economic aid. The first five-year plan was successful, as economic growth followed the Communists' social revolution. In the cultural and intellectual realms, too, the Chinese followed the Soviet example. Basic civil and political rights, which the Nationalists had seriously curtailed, were abolished. Temples and churches were closed. Soviet-style puritanism took hold, as the Communists quickly eradicated prostitution and drug abuse, which they had long regarded as marks of exploitation and national decline. They enthusiastically promoted Soviet Marxist ideas concerning women and the family. Full equality, work outside the home, and state-supported child care became primary goals.

In 1958 China broke from the Marxist-Leninist course of development and began to go its own way. Mao proclaimed a **Great Leap Forward** in which industrial growth would be based on small-scale backyard workshops and steel mills run by peasants living in gigantic self-contained communes. The intended great leap produced an economic disaster, as land in the countryside went untilled when peasants turned to industrial production. As many as 30 million people died in famines that swept the country in 1960–1961, one of the greatest human disasters in world history. When Soviet premier Nikita Khrushchev criticized Chinese policy in 1960, Mao condemned him and his Russian colleagues as detestable "modern revisionists." The Russians cut off economic and military aid, splitting the Communist world apart.

Mao lost influence in the party after the Great Leap Forward fiasco and the Sino-Soviet split, but in 1965 he staged a dramatic comeback. Fearing that China was becoming bureaucratic, capitalistic, and "revisionist" like the Soviet Union, Mao launched the **Great Proletarian Cultural Revolution**. He sought to purge the party and to recapture the revolutionary fervor of the guerrilla struggle (see pages 915–917). The army and the nation's young people responded enthusiastically, organizing themselves into radical cadres called **Red Guards**. Students denounced their teachers and practiced rebellion in the name of revolution. Mao's thoughts, through his speeches and writings, were collected in the *Little Red Book*, which became scripture to the Red Guards. Here the young Red Guards learned the underlying maxim of Mao's revolution: "Every communist must grasp the truth, 'Political power grows out of the barrel of a gun.'"[8]

The Red Guards sought to erase all traces of "feudal" and "bourgeois" culture and thought. Ancient monuments and countless works of art, antiques, and books were destroyed. Party officials, professors, and intellectuals were exiled to remote villages to purify themselves with heavy labor. Universities were shut down for years. Thousands of people died, many of them executed, and millions more were sent to rural forced-labor camps. The Red Guards attracted enormous worldwide attention and served as an extreme model for the student rebellions in the West in the late 1960s.

Conflict in Korea

As tensions rose in Europe, the Cold War spread to Asia. In 1945 Korea, like Germany, was divided into Soviet and American zones of occupation, which in 1948 became Communist North Korea and anticommunist South Korea (see Map 31.3, page 986). When the Communists triumphed in China in late 1949, many fearful Americans saw new evidence of a powerful worldwide Communist conspiracy. When the Russian-backed Communist forces of North Korea invaded South Korea in spring 1950, President Truman sent U.S. troops to lead a twenty-nation UN coalition force to stop what he interpreted as a coordinated Communist effort to dominate Asia.

The Korean War (1950–1953) was bitterly fought, but ended in a stalemate with little more than symbolic gains for either side. The well-equipped North Koreans conquered most of the peninsula, but the South Korean, American, and UN troops rallied and drove their foes north to the Chinese border. At that point China intervened and pushed the South Koreans and Americans back south. In 1953 a fragile truce was negotiated, and the fighting stopped. Thus the United States extended its policy of containing communism to Asia, but drew back from invading Communist China and possibly provoking nuclear war.

Mao and the Communists entered the Korean conflict to prove that China was once again a Great Power and to challenge what they saw as U.S. capitalist imperialism. The Chinese army's ability to fight the United States and its allies to a bloody standstill on the Korean peninsula mobilized the masses and increased Chinese self-confidence. For its part, the U.S. government demonstrated a willingness to wage war against the spread of communism and to guarantee the autonomy of its ally, South Korea. Fighting a war in Korea did not prevent the Chinese from also expanding their territory in the west: in 1950 they invaded the region of Tibet and declared Chinese sovereignty over the country in 1951.

Japan's American Reconstruction

When American occupation forces landed in the Tokyo-Yokohama area after Japan's surrender in August 1945, they found only smokestacks and large steel safes standing amid miles of rubble in what had been the heart of industrial Japan. Japan, like Germany, was formally occupied by all the Allies, but real power resided in Amer-

Baseball in Japan   Though baseball arrived in Japan in the late nineteenth century, it increased in popularity during U.S. occupation. This photo from 1950 shows children in their baseball uniforms, with a U.S. Jeep in the background. (Courtesy CSU Archives/ The Everett Collection)

ican hands. U.S. general Douglas MacArthur exercised almost absolute authority. MacArthur and the Americans had a revolutionary plan for defeated Japan, introducing reforms designed to make Japan a free, democratic society along American lines.

Japan's sweeping American revolution began with demilitarization and a systematic purge of convicted war criminals and wartime collaborators. The American-dictated constitution of 1946 allowed the emperor to remain the "symbol of the State." Real power resided in the Japanese Diet, whose members were popularly elected. A bill of rights granted basic civil liberties and freed all political prisoners, including Communists. Article 9 of the new constitution abolished the Japanese armed forces and renounced war. The American occupation left Japan's powerful bureaucracy largely intact and used it to implement fundamental social and economic reforms. The occupation promoted the Japanese labor movement, introduced American-style antitrust laws, and "emancipated" Japanese women, granting them equality before the law. The occupation also imposed revolutionary land reform that strengthened the small independent farmers who became staunch defenders of postwar democracy.

America's efforts to remake Japan in its own image were powerful but short-lived. As Mao's forces prevailed in China, American leaders began to see Japan as a potential ally, not as an object of social reform. The American command began purging leftists and rehabilitating prewar nationalists. The Japanese prime minister during much of the occupation and early post-occupation period was Shigeru Yoshida. Yoshida had served as Japanese ambassador to Italy and the United Kingdom; with his pro-British and pro-American sympathies, he was the ideal leader in Western eyes for postwar Japan. He channeled all available resources to the rebuilding of Japan's industrial infrastructure, while he left the military defense of the country to the American occupying forces.

The occupation ended in 1952. Under the treaty terms Japan regained independence, and the United States retained its vast military complex in Japan. Japan became the chief Asian ally of the United States in its efforts to contain the spread of communism in East Asia.

The Vietnam War

French Indochina experienced the bitterest struggle for independence in Southeast Asia. With financial backing from the United States, France tried to reimpose imperial rule there after the Communist and nationalist guerrilla leader Ho Chi Minh (1890–1969) declared an independent republic in 1945. French forces were decisively defeated in the 1954 Battle of Dien Bien Phu. At the subsequent international peace conference, French Indochina gained independence. Laos and Cambodia became separate states, and Vietnam was temporarily divided into separately governed northern and southern regions pending elections to select a single unified government within two years. The South Vietnamese government refused to hold the elections, and civil war between it and the Communist Democratic Republic of Vietnam, or North Vietnam, broke out.

Cold War fears and U.S. commitment to the ideology of containment drove the United States to get involved in Vietnam. The administration of President Dwight D. Eisenhower (elected in 1952) refused to sign the Geneva Accords that temporarily divided the country, and provided military aid to help the south resist North Vietnam. Eisenhower's successor, John F. Kennedy, increased the number of American "military advisers." In 1964 President Lyndon Johnson greatly expanded America's role in the Vietnam conflict, declaring, "I am not going to be the President who saw Southeast Asia go the way China went."[9]

The American strategy was to "escalate" the war sufficiently to break the will of the North Vietnamese and their southern allies without resorting to "overkill," which might risk war with the entire Communist bloc. South Vietnam received massive military aid. Large numbers of American forces joined in combat. The United States bombed North Vietnam with ever-greater intensity. But there was no invasion of North Vietnam or naval blockade of its ports.

Most Americans initially saw the war as part of a legitimate defense against communism, but the combined effect of watching the results of the violent conflict on the nightly television news and experiencing the widening dragnet of a military draft spurred a growing antiwar movement on U.S. college campuses. In 1965 student protesters joined forces with old-line socialists, New Left intellectuals, and pacifists in antiwar demonstrations in fifty American cities. By 1967 a growing number of critics had denounced the American presence in Vietnam as an intrusion into a complex and distant civil war. The north's Tet Offensive in January 1968, a major attack on South Vietnamese cities, failed militarily but shook Americans' confidence in their government's ability to manage the conflict. Within months President Johnson announced he would not stand for re-election, and he called for negotiations with North Vietnam.

Elected in 1968, President Richard Nixon sought to disengage America gradually from Vietnam. He intensified the continuous bombardment of the enemy while simultaneously pursuing peace talks with the North Vietnamese. He also began a slow process of withdrawal from Vietnam in a process called "Vietnamization," which transferred the burden of the war to the South Vietnamese army. He cut American forces there from 550,000 to 24,000 in four years. Nixon finally reached a peace agreement with North Vietnam in 1973 that allowed the remaining American forces to complete their withdrawal in 1975.

Despite tremendous military effort in the Vietnam War by the United States, the Communists proved victorious in 1975 and created a unified Marxist nation. After more than thirty-five years of battle, the Vietnamese Communists unified their country in 1975 and engaged in the process of nation building that had been delayed by decades of war against colonial rule and the U.S. effort to force a political and economic model on the country as part of its doctrine of containment of communism. Millions of Vietnamese civilians faced reprisals for aligning with the United States, including Hmong and Degar peoples (such as the Mnong) and other ethnic minorities. They first fled to refugee camps elsewhere in Southeast Asia and later settled as refugees in the United States. (See "Individuals in Society: Sieng, a Mnong Refugee in an American High School," page 1052.)

Decolonization in Africa

What factors influenced decolonization in Africa after World War II?

By 1964 most of Africa had gained independence (Map 31.3). Only Portugal's colonies and white-dominated southern Africa remained beyond the reach of African nationalists. The rise of independent states in sub-Saharan Africa came about as a reaction against Western imperialism and through the growth of African nationalism.

Africans who sought independence wanted a complete break from the colonial mold: they wanted to create nations that were free of economic exploitation and could realize their own national aims for the first time. Many new leaders saw socialism as the best way to sever colonial ties and erase exploitation within their new borders. But institutional barriers left over from the colonial era hampered liberation efforts: new nations inherited inefficient colonial bureaucracies, economic systems that privileged the export of raw materials, and colonial educational systems intended to build servants of empire. The range of actions available to new leaders was narrowed by former colonizers' efforts to retain their economic influence and by the political and ideological divisions of the Cold War. Efforts by new leaders could easily run afoul of powerful foreign businesses, the United States, or the Soviet Union.

The Growth of African Nationalism

African nationalism resembled similar movements in Asia and the Middle East in its reaction against European colonialism, but there were two important differences. First, because the imperial system and Western education did not solidify in Africa until after 1900 (see pages 773–775), national movements came of age in the 1920s and reached maturity after 1945. Second, Africa's multiplicity of ethnic groups, coupled with colonial boundaries that often bore no resemblance to existing ethnic geography, greatly complicated the development of political—as distinct from cultural— nationalism. Was a modern national state based on ethnic or clan loyalties? Was it to be a continent-wide union of all African peoples? Would the multiethnic territories carved out by European empires become the new African nations? Such questions were not fully addressed until after 1945.

The first nationalist impetus came from the United States and the Caribbean. The most renowned participant in this "black nationalism" was W. E. B. Du Bois (1868– 1963). The first African American to receive a Ph.D. from Harvard, Du Bois was a brilliant writer and historian who was a cofounder of the National Association for the

◀ **MAP 31.3   Decolonization in Africa and Asia, 1947 to the Present** After the
Second World War, countries colonized by Britain, France, the Netherlands, and the United
States gained their independence. In cases such as Vietnam and Indonesia, independence came
through armed struggles against colonizers who were reluctant to leave. Most African territories
achieved statehood by the mid-1960s as European empires passed away, unlamented.

Advancement of Colored People (NAACP) in the United States and organized Pan-
African congresses in Paris during the Paris Peace Conference in 1919 and in Brussels
in 1921. **Pan-Africanists** sought black solidarity and, eventually, a vast self-governing
union of all African peoples. Jamaican-born Marcus Garvey (1887–1940) was the
most influential Pan-Africanist, rallying young, educated Africans to his call of "Africa
for the Africans."

In the 1920s a surge of anticolonial nationalism swept educated Africans in French
and British colonies. African intellectuals in Europe formulated and articulated *négri-
tude*, or blackness: racial pride, self-confidence, and joy in black creativity and the
black spirit. This westernized African elite pressed for better access to government jobs,
modest steps toward self-government, and an end to humiliating discrimination. They
claimed the right to speak for ordinary Africans and denounced the government-
supported chiefs for subordinating themselves to white colonial leaders.

The mass protests that accompanied the deprivations of the Great Depression, in
particular the **cocoa holdups** of 1930–1931 and 1937–1938, fueled the new nationalism. Cocoa dominated the British colonial economy in the Gold Coast (which became
Ghana). As prices plummeted after 1929, cocoa farmers refused to sell their beans to
the British firms that fixed prices and monopolized exports. Now farmers organized
cooperatives to cut back production and sell their crops directly to European and
American chocolate manufacturers. The cocoa holdups mobilized the population
against the foreign companies and demonstrated the power of mass organization and
protest.

The repercussions of the Second World War in Africa greatly accelerated the
changes begun in the 1930s. Many African soldiers who served in India had been
powerfully impressed by Indian nationalism. As African mines and plantations strained
to meet wartime demands, towns mushroomed into cities where ramshackle housing,
inflation, and shortages of consumer goods created discontent and hardship.

Western imperialism also changed. The principle of self-government was written
into the United Nations charter and was supported by Great Britain's postwar Labour
government. Thus the key issue for Great Britain's various African colonies was their
rate of progress toward self-government. The British and the French were in no rush.
But a new type of African leader was emerging. Impatient and insistent, these spokes-
men for modern African nationalism were remarkably successful. These postwar African
leaders formed an elite by virtue of their advanced European or American education,
and they were profoundly influenced by Western thought. But compared with the
interwar generation of educated Africans, they were more radical and had humbler
social origins. Among them were former schoolteachers, union leaders, government
clerks, lawyers, and poets.

Postwar African nationalists pragmatically accepted prevailing colonial boundaries
to avoid border disputes and achieve freedom as soon as possible. Sensing a loss of

power, traditional rulers sometimes became the new leaders' worst political enemies. Skillfully, the new leaders channeled postwar hope and discontent into support for mass political organizations that offset this traditional authority. These organizations staged gigantic protests and became political parties.

Ghana Shows the Way

The most charismatic of this generation of African leaders was Kwame Nkrumah (KWA-may ihn-CROO-mah) (1909–1972). Nkrumah spent ten years studying in the United States, where he was influenced by European socialists and Marcus Garvey. He returned to the Gold Coast after the Second World War and entered politics. Under his leadership the Gold Coast—which he renamed "Ghana"—became the first sub-Saharan state to emerge from colonialism.

Nkrumah came to power by building a radical party that appealed particularly to modern groups—veterans, merchant women, union members, urban toughs, and cocoa farmers. He and his party injected the joy and enthusiasm of religious revivals into their rallies and propaganda: "Self-Government Now" was their credo, secular salvation their promise. Rejecting halfway measures—"We prefer self-government with danger to servitude in tranquility"—Nkrumah and his Convention People's Party staged strikes and riots.

After he was arrested in 1950, the "Deliverer of Ghana" campaigned from jail and saw his party win a smashing victory in the 1951 national elections. Called from prison to head the transitional government, Nkrumah and his nationalist party defeated westernized moderates and more traditional political rivals in free elections. By 1957 Nkrumah had achieved worldwide fame and influence as Ghana became independent. After Ghana's breakthrough, independence for other African colonies followed rapidly. The main problem in some colonies, such as Algeria, was the permanent white settlers, not the colonial officials. Wherever white settlers were numerous, as in Kenya and Rhodesia, they fought to preserve their privileged position.

The Opening of Parliament in Ghana As part of an ancient ritual, two medicine men pour out sacred oil and call on the gods to bless the work of the Second Parliament and President Kwame Nkrumah, standing on the right. The combination of time-honored customs and modern political institutions was characteristic of African states after they secured independence. (AP Photo)

French-Speaking Regions

Decolonization took a different course in French-speaking Africa. The events in the French North African colony of Algeria in the 1950s and early 1960s help clarify France's attitude toward its sub-Saharan African colonies.

France tried hard to retain Algeria, where predominantly Arabic-speaking and Muslim nationalists were emboldened by Egyptian president Gamal Nasser's successful revolution in 1952 and by France's defeat and loss of its colonies in Indochina in 1954. But Algeria's large, and mostly Catholic, European population—known as the pieds-noirs (black feet) because its members wore black shoes instead of sandals—was determined to keep Algeria part of France. In November 1954 Algeria's anticolonial movement, the National Liberation Front (FLN), began a bitter war for independence. After the FLN won and created an independent Algerian state in 1962, an estimated 900,000 of the 1.25 million Europeans and indigenous Jews fled.

The long and violent anticolonial war in Algeria, following Indochina's military victory, sharply divided France and undermined its political stability. As a result, it was difficult for France to respond to nationalists in its other African colonies until Charles de Gaulle returned to power in 1958. Seeking to maximize France's influence over the future independent nations, de Gaulle devised a divide-and-rule strategy. He divided the French West Africa and French Equatorial Africa federations into thirteen separate governments, thus creating a "French commonwealth." Plebiscites were called in each territory to ratify the new arrangement. An affirmative vote meant continued ties with France; a negative vote signified immediate independence and a complete break with France.

De Gaulle's gamble was shrewd. The educated black elite—as personified by the influential poet-politician Léopold Sédar Senghor, who now led Senegal's government—identified with France and dreaded an abrupt separation. They also wanted French aid to continue. France, in keeping with its ideology of assimilation, had given the vote to its educated colonial elite after the Second World War, and about forty Africans held French parliamentary seats after 1946. For these reasons, French Africa's leaders tended to be moderate in their pursuit of independence.

In Guinea, however, a young nationalist named Sékou Touré (1922–1984) led his people to overwhelmingly reject the new constitution in 1958. Echoing Ghana's Nkrumah, Touré laid it out to de Gaulle face-to-face: "We have to tell you bluntly, Mr. President, what the demands of the people are. . . . We have one prime and essential need: our dignity. But there is no dignity without freedom. . . . We prefer freedom in poverty to opulence in slavery."[10]

Though peoples that had been colonized by France and Britain often found paths for independence, those of other regions of Africa struggled with the colonial policies of European nations less prepared to acknowledge the wave of decolonization. Portugal's dictatorship sought to simply ride out the pressure for decolonization: it hoped to keep its colonies, such as Angola and Mozambique, in perpetuity. To ensure this, the Portuguese regime intensified white settlement and repression of nationalist groups.

Belgium, a long-time practitioner of colonial paternalism coupled with harsh, selfish rule in its enormous Congo colony (see page 769), had always discouraged the development of an educated elite. When Belgium abruptly decided to grant independence in 1959 after intense riots, the fabric of Congo's government broke down. Independence was followed by violent ethnic conflict, civil war, and foreign intervention. The mineral-rich nation stabilized under the U.S.-backed dictatorship of Mobutu Sese Seko, who renamed the country Zaire. Mobutu's corruption deepened poverty as the tremendous wealth generated from mining went into the hands of foreign companies and Mobutu's family and cronies.

Revolutionary Pathways in Latin America

Why did populism emerge as such a powerful political force in Latin America?

In the decades after the Second World War, Latin American nations struggled to find a political balance that integrated long-excluded groups such as women, workers, and peasants in the face of growing anxiety and resistance by liberal oligarchs. Populist politicians rose to power by building a base of support among the urban and rural poor. They often combined charisma with promises of social change, particularly through national economic development that would create more and better job opportunities. The populists' nationalist economic projects and appeals to the masses were often met with unease by traditional economic and political power holders as well as the United States, which viewed their policies as a step toward communism. In many cases, the conservative reaction against populists led the armed forces to seize power. Revolutionary leader Fidel Castro carved an alternative path in Cuba. Castro went beyond the reforms advocated by populists and sought an outright revolutionary transformation of Cuban society.

Economic Nationalism in Mexico

Although Spain's Central and South American colonies and Portuguese Brazil won political independence in the early nineteenth century, the new nations struggled to achieve genuine economic independence. Latin American countries had developed as producers of foodstuffs and raw materials exported to Europe and the United States in return for manufactured goods and capital investment. This exchange brought considerable economic development but exacted a heavy price: neocolonialism (see page 834). Latin America became dependent on foreign markets, products, and investments. The Great Depression further hampered development and provoked a shift toward **economic nationalism**, a systematic effort by nationalists to end neocolonialism and to free their national economies from U.S. and western European influences.

Economic nationalism and industrialization were especially successful in the largest countries in Latin America: Mexico, Brazil, and Argentina. In Mexico the 1917 constitution created in the aftermath of the 1910 Mexican Revolution was a radically nationalistic document that called for universal suffrage, land reform, labor rights, and strict control of foreign capital. Progress toward these goals was modest until 1934, when the charismatic leader Lázaro Cárdenas became president as the candidate of the Institutional Revolutionary Party (PRI), which monopolized power until the end of the century (see Chapter 32). Under Cárdenas millions of acres of large estates were divided among small farmers or were returned undivided to Indian communities. State-supported Mexican businessmen built many small factories to meet domestic needs. In 1938 Cárdenas nationalized the petroleum industry. The 1930s also saw the flowering of a distinctive Mexican culture that proudly celebrated cultural mixture and intermarriage between Indians, Africans, and Europeans.

The presidents who followed Cárdenas used the state's power to promote industrialization, and the Mexican economy grew consistently through the 1970s. During the years of the "Mexican miracle," the economy grew 3 to 4 percent annually. This was a time of rapid urbanization as well, with people leaving rural areas for jobs in factories or for lower-paying service jobs, such as maids and janitors. While the country's economic health improved, social inequities remained. The upper and middle classes reaped the lion's share of the benefits of this economic growth.

Populism in Argentina and Brazil

Argentina and Brazil's postwar economic development was shaped by a rising cadre of populist politicians who channeled aspirations into votes through direct popular appeals and economic nationalism. Earlier liberal politicians had dismissed the electoral potential of the working class and denied it the right to vote. But as pressure for universal voting rights intensified, first for men then for women, large numbers of Latin Americans who had never been given a political voice gained it, beginning with universal male suffrage in Argentina in 1912 and Mexico in 1917. Women gained the right to vote across Latin America in the decades that followed, beginning with Ecuador in 1929 and Brazil in 1932. Though in most cases voters still needed to be literate to vote, universal literacy efforts and male and female suffrage increased the electoral base of Latin American countries by millions. To appeal to these voters, populist candidates promised schools and hospitals, higher wages, and nationalist projects that would create more industrial jobs.

At the turn of the century Argentina's economy prospered through its liberal export boom (see Chapter 27), but industrialization followed only haltingly and the economy faltered. Populist Juan Perón, an army colonel, was elected president in 1946 with support of Argentina's unions. Juan Perón was charismatic, but his wife, Eva, known by her nickname Evita, was even more so, and played a vital role in promoting Perón. Once in power, Perón embarked on an ambitious scheme to transform Argentina's economy: the government would purchase all of the country's agricultural exports in order to negotiate their sale abroad at a higher price. He would reinvest the profits in industry and raise worker wages to stimulate demand.

Perón's scheme worked in the immediate postwar period, when European agricultural production had not yet recovered and the international price of Argentina's exports was high. But when commodity prices declined, Perón reduced government payments to farmers, who ceased to bring their harvests to market. In the coming decades Argentina never returned to the high rates of economic growth it enjoyed at the beginning of the century. Many blamed Perón for distorting the economy for his own political gain. Others saw Perón's efforts as halting a worse decline: Argentina's economy had long been dependent on Britain, and as Britain's capacity to import declined, so did Argentina's fortunes.

INDIVIDUALS IN SOCIETY • Eva Perón

When Eva Perón died of cancer at age thirty-three on July 26, 1952, the state radio broadcaster sadly announced that "today at 20:25 Eva Perón, Spiritual Leader of the Nation, entered immortality." Argentina went into official mourning; although Perón had never held an official political office, she was accorded a state funeral. Immediately after her death her corpse was embalmed, with the intention of putting it on public display forever in a planned memorial larger than the Statue of Liberty.

Often called Evita (the Spanish diminutive of Eva), she was one of five illegitimate children born near Buenos Aires to Juan Duarte and Juana Ibarguren. Duarte returned to his legitimate wife and children when Eva was a year old, leaving Juana and her children destitute and dependent on Juana's sewing for their existence. As they grew older all the children had to work, but Eva apparently also dreamed of becoming an actress.

At fifteen Eva Duarte moved to the cosmopolitan city of Buenos Aires. Although she had little formal education and no connections, she possessed beauty and charisma, and soon she joined a professional theater group with which she toured nationally. She also modeled, appeared in a few movies, and then obtained regular employment as a character on a radio series. By 1943, although only twenty-three years old, she was one of the highest-paid actresses in the country.

In 1943 Eva met widowed Colonel Juan Perón, then secretary of labor and social welfare in the military government that had seized power that year. Juan Perón had grand ambitions, intending to run for president. Eva Duarte became his partner and confidante, and she won him support among the Argentine masses. In 1945 Juan Perón and Eva Duarte married.

A year later Perón won the presidency. Eva had gone out on the campaign trail and organized support for her husband from *los descamisados* (the shirtless ones), her name for Argentina's poor. When Perón assumed the presidency, Eva, though not officially appointed, became the secretary of labor. Having come from a childhood of poverty herself, she now worked tirelessly for the poor, for the working classes, and with organized labor. She instituted a number of social welfare measures and promoted a new Ministry of Health, which resulted in the creation of new hospitals and disease-treatment programs. In 1948 she established the Eva Perón Welfare Foundation, which grew into an immense semiofficial welfare agency, helping the poor throughout Argentina and even contributing to victims of natural disasters in other countries.

Despite these economic setbacks, Perón initially remained highly popular, buoyed by the popular appeals made by Evita. (See "Individuals in Society: Eva Perón," above.)

After Evita died of cancer in 1952, much of the magic slipped away. Amid the stagnating economy even Perón's union supporters faltered, and he responded harshly to press criticism. In 1955 the armed forces deposed Perón, and he fled to exile in

From early on, Eva Perón had supported women's suffrage, and in September 1947 Argentine women won the right to vote. Eva then formed the Female Perónist Party, which by 1951 had five hundred thousand members. Thousands of Argentine women have credited Eva's example as a reason for their involvement in politics. In 1951 she seemed ready to run for vice president beside her husband. The huge base of women, the poor, and workers assured them victory. Her declining health, however, forced her to turn down the nomination. Juan Perón won the election by over 30 percent, but when Eva died the following year, his authoritarian rule and bad economic policies lost him support, and a military junta forced him into exile.

Eva Perón's life story is an amazing one, but what happened following her death is just as extraordinary. Before the massive monument intended to hold her embalmed body could be built, the military seized power, and her body disappeared. Seventeen years later the generals finally revealed that it was in a tomb in Milan, Italy. Juan Perón, living in Spain with his third wife, had the body exhumed and brought to Spain, where he kept it in his house. Perón returned to Argentina in 1973 and won the presidential election, but died the following year. His wife, Isabelita Perón, succeeded him as president. Juan and Eva's bodies were briefly displayed together at his funeral and then, finally, buried.

Source: Nicholas Fraser and Marysa Navarro, *Evita: The Real Life of Eva Perón* (New York: Norton, 1976).

QUESTIONS FOR ANALYSIS

1. Why do you think Eva Perón was adored by the Argentine people when she died?
2. What were some of the welfare and government programs that Eva Perón promoted?

LaunchPad
ONLINE DOCUMENT PROJECT

What were the political implications of Eva Perón's public presentation of herself? Examine photos of Eva Perón, and then complete a quiz and writing assignment based on the evidence and details from this chapter.

See inside the front cover to learn more.

Spain. The military ruled Argentina for the next three years, conducting a process of "de-Perónization." They banned Perón's party and even forbade mention of his name. But Perón remained the most popular politician in the country. Presidential candidates could not win without discreetly winning the exiled Perón's endorsement, and this veiled support for Perón by civilian leaders prompted repeated military interventions.

The 1955–1958 military government was the first of several, including a dictatorship that ruled from 1966 to 1973.

In Brazil, reacting against the economic and political liberalism through which coffee planters dominated the country, the armed forces installed a state governor, Getúlio Vargas, as president in 1930. Vargas initiated democratic reforms, but veered into a nationalist dictatorship known as the "New State" (1937–1945), inspired by European fascism. Despite his harsh treatment of opponents, he was popular with the masses and was elected to a new term as president in 1950, now reinvented as a populist who promised nationalist economic reforms that would favor industrial workers. The armed forces and conservatives mistrusted Vargas's appeals to workers and organized to depose him in 1954. Before they could act, Vargas killed himself.

Vargas's two periods in power saw rapid industrialization, the legalization of labor unions, and the institution of a minimum wage. Juscelino Kubitschek, elected in 1955, continued to build upon Vargas's populism and nationalism. Between 1956 and 1960 Kubitschek's government borrowed heavily from abroad to promote industry and build the futuristic new capital of Brasília in the midst of a wilderness. Kubitschek's slogan was "Fifty Years' Progress in Five."

By the late 1950s economic and social progress seemed to be bringing more democratic politics to Brazil and other Latin American countries. The Cuban Revolution, which in 1959 put Cuba on a course to radical Marxism, shook these expectations. Across Latin America conservative leaders, fearing redistribution of their wealth, and military officers, who were often trained by the U.S. armed forces and identified ideologically with the United States, took control of governments to block the further spread of communism. In 1961 leftist populist João Goulart became Brazil's president. Goulart sought social and economic reforms, including the redistribution of land and limits on the profits multinational corporations could take out of the country. In 1964 a military coup backed by the United States deposed Goulart. The armed forces held power for the next twenty-one years.

Communist Revolution in Cuba

Cuba remained practically an American colony until the 1930s, when a series of rulers with socialist and Communist leanings seized and lost power. Cuba's political institutions were weak and its politicians corrupt. In March 1952 Fulgencio Batista (1901–1973) staged a coup with American support and instituted a repressive authoritarian regime that favored wealthy Cubans and multinational corporations. Though Cuba was one of Latin America's most prosperous countries, tremendous differences remained between rich and poor.

The Cuban Revolution led by Fidel Castro (b. 1927) began in 1953. Castro's second-in-command, the legendary Argentine revolutionary Ernesto "Che" Guevara (1928–1967), and a force of guerrilla rebels finally overthrew the Cuban government on New Year's Day 1959. Castro had promised a revolution that pursued land reform, nationalized industries, and imposed limits on rent to help the urban poor. Affluent Cubans began fleeing to Miami. The U.S. Eisenhower administration slashed Cuban import quotas and began planning to depose Castro. In April 1961 U.S. president John F. Kennedy carried out the plans created by Eisenhower to use Cuban exiles to topple Castro, but when the invasion force landed ashore at the Bay of Pigs, the Cuban revolutionary army, commanded directly by Castro, repelled them in an embarrassment to the United States.

Castro had not come to power as a Communist: his main aim had been to regain control of Cuba's economy and politics from the United States. But U.S. efforts to overthrow him and to starve the Cuban economy drove him to form an alliance with the Soviet Union, which agreed to place nuclear missiles in Cuba to protect against another U.S. invasion. When Kennedy demanded the missiles be removed, the military and diplomatic brinksmanship of the 1962 Cuban missile crisis ensued. In 1963 the United States placed a complete commercial and diplomatic embargo on Cuba that has remained in place ever since.

Castro now declared himself a Marxist-Leninist and relied on Soviet military and economic support, though Cuba retained a revolutionary ethos that differed from the rest of the Soviet bloc. Castro was committed to spreading revolution to the rest of Latin America, and Guevara participated in revolutionary campaigns in the Congo and Bolivia before being assassinated by U.S.-trained Bolivian forces in 1967. Within Cuba activists swept into the countryside and taught people who were illiterate. Medical attention and education became free and widely accessible. The Cuban Revolution inspired young radicals across Latin America to believe in the possibility of swift revolution and brisk reforms to combat historic inequalities. But these reforms were achieved at great cost and through the suppression of political dissent. Castro declared in 1961, "Inside of the revolution anything, outside the revolution, nothing."[11] Political opponents were jailed or exiled. Meanwhile, reforms were improvised with ideological objectives rather than economic logic, which often resulted in productive inefficiency and scarcity of foodstuffs and other goods.

The Limits of Postwar Prosperity

Why did the world face growing social unrest in the 1960s?

In the 1950s and 1960s the United States and the Soviet Union, as well as both western and eastern Europe, rebounded economically from the combined strains of the Great Depression and the Second World War. The postwar return of prosperity increased living standards and expanded education, health, and leisure opportunities for many. But these decades of economic growth did not resolve underlying tensions and conflicts. In the Soviet Union and eastern Europe reforms could not undo the harsh dictatorial grip of the socialist system and Communist parties. In western Europe a process of political and economic integration softened but could not fully offset the loss of overseas empires and the damage inflicted by war. In the United States, while an economic boom broadened the middle class, millions confronted racism and segregation, and growing popular opposition to Cold War military interventions such as the war in Vietnam increasingly dominated national politics.

The Soviet Union Struggles to Move Beyond Stalin

Though the "Great Patriotic War of the Fatherland" had fostered Russian nationalism and a relaxation of totalitarian terror, Stalin's new rivalry with the United States provided him with an excuse to re-establish a harsh dictatorship. He purged thousands of returning soldiers and ordinary civilians in 1945 and 1946, and he revived the terrible forced-labor camps of the 1930s. Culture and art were purged of Western influences, Orthodox Christianity again came under attack, and Soviet Jews were accused of being pro-Western and anti-socialist.

Stalin reasserted control of the government and society through the reintroduction of five-year plans to cope with the enormous task of economic reconstruction. Once again, Soviet central planners favored heavy and military industry over consumer goods, housing, and collectivized agriculture. Stalin exported this system to eastern Europe. Rigid ideological indoctrination, attacks on religion, and a lack of civil liberties were soon facts of life in the region's one-party states. Only Yugoslavia's Josip Tito (1892–1980), the popular resistance leader and Communist Party chief, could resist Soviet domination successfully because there was no Russian army in Yugoslavia.

In 1953 the aging Stalin died. Even as his heirs struggled for power, they realized that reforms were necessary because of the widespread fear and hatred of Stalin's political terrorism. They curbed secret police powers and gradually closed many forced-labor camps. Change was also necessary for economic reasons. Agriculture was in bad shape, and shortages of consumer goods discouraged hard work. Moreover, Stalin's foreign policy had led directly to a strong Western alliance, isolating the Soviet Union.

The Communist Party leadership was badly split on just how much change to permit. Reformers, led by Nikita Khrushchev (1894–1971), argued for major innovations and won. Khrushchev spoke out in a "secret speech" against Stalin and his crimes at a closed session of the Twentieth Party Congress in 1956:

> It is clear that . . . Stalin showed in a whole series of cases his intolerance, his brutality, and his abuse of power. Instead of proving his political correctness and mobilizing the masses, he often chose the path of repression and physical annihilation, not only against actual enemies, but also against individuals who had not committed any crimes against the party and the Soviet Government.[12]

The liberalization of the Soviet Union—labeled **de-Stalinization** in the West—was genuine. Khrushchev eased foreign policy, declaring that "peaceful coexistence" with capitalism was possible. The government relaxed controls over heavy industry and the military and shifted some resources from these areas to consumer goods, improving standards of living substantially throughout the booming 1960s. De-Stalinization created ferment among writers and intellectuals who hungered for cultural freedom. The writer Aleksandr Solzhenitsyn (1918–2008) created a sensation when his *One Day in the Life of Ivan Denisovich* was published in the Soviet Union in 1962. Solzhenitsyn's novel portrayed life in a Stalinist concentration camp in grim detail and was a damning indictment of the Stalinist past.

De-Stalinization stimulated rebelliousness in the eastern European satellites. Poland won greater autonomy in 1956 after extensive protests forced the Soviets to allow a new Communist government. Led by students and workers, the people of Budapest, Hungary, installed a liberal Communist reformer as their new chief in October 1956. The rebellion was short-lived. After the new government promised free elections and renounced Hungary's military alliance with Moscow, the Soviet army invaded and crushed the revolution, killing around 2,700 protesters. When the United States did not come to their aid, Hungarians and most eastern European reformers concluded that their only hope was to strive for small domestic gains while obediently following Russia in foreign affairs.

In August 1961 the East German government began construction of a twenty-seven-mile wall between East and West Berlin. It also built a ninety-mile-long barrier between the three allied sectors of West Berlin and East Germany, thereby completely cutting off West Berlin. Officially the wall was called the "Anti-Fascist Protection Wall." In reality the Berlin Wall prevented East Germans from "voting with their feet" by defecting to the West.

By late 1962 party opposition to Khrushchev's policies had gained momentum. De-Stalinization was seen as a dangerous threat to party authority. Moreover, Khrushchev's policy toward the West was erratic and ultimately unsuccessful. In 1962 Khrushchev ordered missiles with nuclear warheads installed in Fidel Castro's Communist Cuba, triggering the military standoff known as the Cuban missile crisis. After a tense diplomatic crisis Khrushchev backed down and removed the missiles. Two years later, Communist Party leaders removed Khrushchev in a bloodless coup. After Leonid Brezhnev (1906–1982) and his supporters took over in 1964, they talked quietly of Stalin's "good points," stopped further liberalization, and launched a massive arms buildup, determined never to suffer Khrushchev's humiliation in the face of American nuclear superiority.

Western Europe's Postwar Challenge

If in 1945 much of western Europe was devastated by the war, the years immediately following were often bleaker: the continent faced mass unemployment, shortages of food and fuel, physical destruction of many cities and much infrastructure, and the dislocation of millions of people. But in the decades that followed, western Europe's political recovery was unprecedented. Democratic governments took root throughout western Europe and thrived in an atmosphere of civil liberties and individual freedom. Progressive Catholics and their Christian Democratic political parties were particularly influential. In Italy Alcide De Gasperi (1881–1954) and in Germany Konrad Adenauer (1876–1967) took power, rejecting the fascism of their predecessors and placing their faith in democracy and cooperation. Socialists and Communists active in the resistance against Hitler returned with renewed prestige, especially in France and Italy. In the immediate postwar years welfare measures such as family allowances, health insurance, and increased public housing were enacted throughout much of Europe.

The Cold War prevented the allies occupying Germany from finding a political settlement, resulting in a partition between a Soviet-controlled German Democratic Republic (East Germany) and a Federal Republic of Germany (West Germany). Under its first postwar chancellor, Konrad Adenauer, West Germany recovered from near total devastation in World War II and became the leading economic power in Europe. A fierce opponent of communism, Adenauer brought Germany firmly into the Western capitalist camp. He forged close ties with the United States and restored relations with Great Britain and France. Under his direction, Germany became a leading member of NATO and fully supported efforts at European unity. He also initiated dialogues with leaders of Europe's Jewish community and with Israel to encourage a reconciliation of the Jewish and German peoples following the Holocaust.

Greek Guest Workers in Germany   Thousands of Greeks immigrated to Germany after the signing of a guest worker (*Gastarbeiter*) agreement between Greece and Germany in 1961. In the 1950s and 1960s the Greek government encouraged workers, such as these Greek women working in a bottling factory in Hamburg in 1963, to emigrate because of a weak economy and high unemployment. Unlike some guest workers from countries in North Africa and the Middle East, the Greeks have generally integrated smoothly into German society. An estimated 350,000 Greeks were living in Germany in 2011. (bpk, Berlin, Germany/Art Resource, NY)

European nations followed different paths to postwar recovery. West Germany balanced a free-market economy with an extensive social welfare network, while France resorted to central planning, using nationalized banks to funnel money into key industries. But amid the destruction and uncertainty brought by two world wars caused by Europeans and fought in Europe, many Europeans believed that only unity could forestall future European conflicts.

The experience of close cooperation among European states for Marshall Plan aid led European leaders to pursue economic unity. On May 9, 1950 (now celebrated as Europe Day), French foreign minister Robert Schuman proposed an international organization to control and integrate all European steel and coal production. France, West Germany, Italy, Belgium, the Netherlands, and Luxembourg joined together in 1952 for this purpose. In 1957 the six nations of the Coal and Steel Community signed the Treaty of Rome, creating the European Economic Community, popularly known as the **Common Market**. The treaty's primary goal was a gradual reduction of all tariffs among the six in order to create a single market almost as large as that of the United States.

The Common Market was a great success, encouraging hopes of rapid progress toward political as well as economic union. In the 1960s, however, a resurgence of more traditional nationalism in France led by Charles de Gaulle, French president from 1958 to 1969, frustrated these hopes. Viewing the United States as the main threat to genuine French (and European) independence, he withdrew all French military forces from NATO and developed France's own nuclear weapons. De Gaulle also thwarted efforts by Denmark, Ireland, Norway, and the United Kingdom to join the Common Market. (All but Norway were finally admitted after de Gaulle left office.)

Migrant laborers, mainly from southern Italy, North Africa, Turkey, Greece, and Yugoslavia, also shaped western European societies and drove their economic recovery. Tens of millions of migrant workers made it possible for western European economies to continue to grow beyond their postwar labor capacity. This was especially important in Germany, where they filled gaps left by the loss of a large proportion of the adult male population during the war. Governments at first labeled the migrants as "guest workers" to signal their temporary status, though in practice many chose to remain in their new homes. As their communities became more settled, migrants faced a backlash from majority populations and came to resent and resist their treatment as second-class citizens.

America's Economic Boom and Civil Rights Revolution

The Second World War ended the Great Depression in the United States, bringing about a great economic boom that decreased unemployment and increased living standards dramatically. By the end of the war, the United States had the strongest economy and held several advantages over its past commercial rivals: its industry and infrastructure had not been damaged by war. In the first decades following the war, U.S. manufactured goods saturated markets around the world that had previously been dominated by Britain, France, and Germany.

Postwar America experienced a genuine social revolution as well: after a long struggle African Americans began to experience major victories against the deeply entrenched system of segregation and discrimination. This civil rights movement advanced on several fronts. The NAACP challenged school segregation in the courts. In 1954 it won a landmark decision in the Supreme Court, which ruled in *Brown v. Board of Education* that "separate educational facilities are inherently unequal." Blacks challenged inequality by using Gandhian methods of nonviolent peaceful resistance. In describing his principles for change, the civil rights leader Martin Luther King, Jr. (1929–1968), said that "Christ furnished the spirit and motivation, while Gandhi furnished the method." He told the white power structure, "We will not hate you, but we will not obey your evil laws."[13]

With African American support in key Northern states, Democrat Lyndon Johnson won the 1964 presidential election in a liberal landslide. A brilliant negotiator, Johnson secured enactment of the 1964 Civil Rights Act, which prohibited discrimination in public services and on the job, and the 1965 Voting Rights Act, which prohibited discrimination in voting. In the mid-1960s President Johnson began an "unconditional war on poverty." With the support of Congress, Johnson's administration created a host of antipoverty projects, such as medical care for the poor and aged (Medicaid and Medicare), free preschools for poor children (Head Start), and community-action programs. Thus the United States promoted the kind of fundamental social reform that had succeeded in western Europe after the Second World War.

The World in 1968

In 1968 pressures for social change boiled over into protests worldwide. The preceding two decades offered the world an example of how much people could change as decolonization swept much of the world. Radical revolutionary struggles stretched from Cuba to the remaining colonies in Africa and the war in Southeast Asia. The architecture of white supremacism and racial segregation was being dismantled in the United States. In turn, in industrialized and industrializing regions of the world, the generation raised in the aftermath of the Second World War saw great economic growth and a rapid rise in consumer culture and popular media.

Young protesters drew upon recent history to appreciate how much could be achieved and looked at their world to see how much more was needed. Students across Latin America and western Europe, Czechoslovaks weary of the harshness of Soviet domination, activists for civil rights and women's rights in the United States, along with opponents of the U.S. war in Vietnam, all took loudly to the streets. The world seemed to be at a tipping point between the goals of conservative defenders of the existing social and political order and those of a young generation energized by the possibility of radical and swift change.

In Czechoslovakia the "Prague Spring"—a brief period of liberal reform and loosening of political controls—unfolded as reformers in the Czechoslovakian Communist Party gained a majority and replaced a long-time Stalinist leader with Alexander Dubček (DOOB-chehk), whose new government launched dramatic reforms. Dubček and his allies called for "socialism with a human face," which meant rolling back many of the economic, political, and civil rights restrictions imposed by Stalin. He restored freedom of speech and freedom of the press. Communist leaders in the Soviet Union and other eastern European states feared that they would face similar demands for reform from their own citizens. Protests against the excesses of Communist rule erupted in Poland and Yugoslavia.

In France, students went on strike over poor university conditions. When government forces punished those protesters harshly, a much larger and more radical wave of student protests erupted. The students were soon joined by a general strike carried out by France's labor unions. The intensity of the strikes captured the angst of the generation that had been raised in postwar Europe. For many of them, their governments' postwar socialist reforms were incomplete and the time was now ripe for more far-ranging change—if not outright revolution. Similar student movements erupted across western Europe.

In Latin America students rose in protest as well. In Argentina students in the industrial city of Córdoba went on strike against the military dictatorship that had been in place since 1966. Joined by factory workers, the protesters took control of the city in an event known as the Cordobazo. In Brazil a national student strike challenged the military dictatorship that had been in power since 1964. In Mexico City, where the Olympic games were scheduled to be held, students used the international visibility of the event to protest the heavy-handed regime of the PRI. In each case the students challenged the authoritarian excesses of their regimes, but they were also animated by the example offered by Cuba, which suggested that directly confronting the political regime could bring revolutionaries to power, and that once in power, they could quickly transform their societies.

In the United States protests against the Vietnam War and against the military draft erupted on college campuses nationwide. These protests marked an increase in popular mobilization in a country where civil rights marches in the South now extended to protests against discrimination and police violence in cities like Boston and Chicago. Protesters around the world were aware of each other, and their sense that they participated in a worldwide movement against the abuses of the established order empowered them. Their actions echoed Che Guevara's call for "two, three or many Vietnams" of resistance against imperialism.

In 1968 the intensification of protests may have suggested that social movements worldwide were on the verge of opening the floodgates to a wave of radical change, but the opposite was more true. Protesters and reformers faced violent reactions from the powerful political and economic groups they challenged. If 1968 seemed to be the peak of young radicals' aspirations for social transformation, this was because it also marked the intensification of the reaction against their efforts. Conservatives reacted against more than the protests of 1968: they sought to slow or sometimes reverse the dramatic changes that had taken place in the postwar era.

In October 1968 Soviet troops and tanks flooded into Czechoslovakia, crushing the Prague Spring and unseating Dubček. Supporters of the Prague Spring faced harsh persecution. In Cuba, where revolutionary dreams of liberation were increasingly subsidized by the Soviet Union, Castro was obligated to support the Soviet crackdown, ruefully declaring: "We accept the bitter necessity which demanded the sending of troops to Czechoslovakia."[14]

Around the world, protests were followed by violent crackdowns. The images of Soviet tanks enforcing the crackdown in Prague blurred with the Mexican government's shooting of student protesters in Tlatelolco. The Argentine army and paramilitary groups launched a violent campaign to retake the city of Córdoba from protesters. In Brazil, the military regime reacted to protests by imposing a harsh new national security law that made even criticizing the government an offense punishable by jail sentences handed out by military tribunals. In the United States, assassins killed Martin Luther King, Jr., and other civil rights leaders. Chicago police attacked antiwar demonstrators outside the Democratic National Convention. In 1967 Che Guevara was assassinated by Bolivian troops trained and led by the U.S. government. Around the world, revolutionary violence was met with increasingly violent repression.

Chapter Summary

The decades after the Second World War were an era of rebuilding. In Europe, the Soviet Union, and Japan rebuilding literally meant clearing the rubble from wartime devastation and building back what had been destroyed. In Germany and Japan in particular, rebuilding meant charting a new political and economic path that would lead both countries away from the kinds of global conflicts that nationalist fervor had fueled.

For the United States and the Soviet Union, rebuilding had other meanings. For both countries, it meant building a military and ideological complex with which to confront each other in the Cold War. This involved building rival networks of military and economic alliances, participating in a nuclear arms race, and making a renewed investment in military industry and technology instead of undertaking the sustained demobilization following the Second World War. In each country individually, rebuilding took other forms: in the Soviet Union it meant seeking the means to reform the system of political terror and coercion through which Stalin had ruled; in the United States it meant struggling to overcome the structures of white supremacism and other forms of racial discrimination that divided society and oppressed millions of citizens — not only African Americans, but other ethnic and racial minorities as well.

In Asia, Africa, and the Middle East, rebuilding meant dismantling European colonialism to reconstitute independent states or to build new independent states. Here the idea of rebuilding took on its deepest meaning: learning how to replace not just colonial institutions but colonial mentalities, patterns of production, forms of education, and ways of relating to each other with new versions that were not dictated by colonizers. Intellectuals and artists strove to decolonize the mind as politicians worked to decolonize the state in a process that proved slow and difficult.

In Latin America rebuilding meant finding the means to overcome patterns of social exclusion — especially of rural workers — that were legacies of its colonial experience, as well as finding a political formula that could integrate long-excluded groups. It also meant finding the means to build industry and develop economically, overcoming the patterns of dependency and underdevelopment diagnosed by Latin American intellectuals and social scientists.

In the end, the decades after 1945 showed how much was possible through mass movements, advancing industrialization, and political self-determination. But the balance of these years also showed how much more work remained to overcome poverty, underdevelopment, and neocolonialism.

Notes

1. Philip E. Mosely, "Hopes and Failures: American Policy Toward East Central Europe, 1941–1947," *Review of Politics* 17.4 (October 1955): 461–485, 481.
2. Winston Churchill, "Sinews of Peace" (the Iron Curtain Speech), delivered at Westminster College in Fulton, Missouri, March 5, 1946, in Robert Rhodes James, ed., *Winston S. Churchill: His Complete Speeches, 1897–1963*. Vol. 7: *1943–1949* (New York: Chelsea House, 1974), p. 7509.
3. Frantz Fanon, *The Wretched of the Earth*, trans. Constance Farrington (New York: Grove Press, 1968), pp. 43, 93–94, 97, 102.
4. Chinua Achebe, *Things Fall Apart* (London: Heinemann, 2000), pp. 124–125.
5. Syed Sharifuddin Pirzada, ed., *Foundations of Pakistan: All-India Muslim League Documents*. Vol. 2: *1924–1947* (Karachi: National Publishing House, 1970), p. 338.
6. Quoted in K. Bhata, *The Ordeal of Nationhood: A Social Study of India Since Independence, 1947–1970* (New York: Atheneum, 1971), p. 9.
7. Cited in Sami Hanna and George Gardner, *Arab Socialism: A Documentary Survey* (Leiden: Brill, 1969), p. 106.
8. Mao Zedong, *Quotations from Chairman Mao Tsetung* (Peking: Foreign Language Press, 1972), p. 61.
9. Quoted in S. E. Morison et al., *A Concise History of the American Republic* (New York: Oxford University Press, 1977), p. 735.
10. Quoted in R. Hallett, *Africa Since 1875: A Modern History* (Ann Arbor: University of Michigan Press, 1974), pp. 378–379.
11. Quoted in Samuel Farber, *Cuba Since the Revolution of 1959: A Critical Assessment* (Chicago: Haymarket Books, 2011), p. 22.

12. *Congressional Record: Proceedings and Debates of the 84th Congress, 2nd Session* (May 22, 1956–June 11, 1956), C11, Part 7 (June 4, 1956), pp. 9389–9403.

13. Regarding Gandhi's methods: see M. L. King, Jr., *Stride Toward Freedom: The Montgomery Story* (New York: Perennial Library, 1964), p. 67. Regarding evil laws: quoted in Morison et al., *A Concise History of the American Republic*, p. 697.

14. "Castro Comments on Czechoslovak Crisis," Havana Domestic TV, August 24, 1968, http://lanic.utexas .edu/project/castro/db/1968/19680824.html.

CONNECTIONS

The great transformations experienced by peoples around the world following the Second World War can best be compared to the age of revolution in the late eighteenth and early nineteenth centuries (see Chapter 22). In both eras peoples rose up to undertake the political, economic, social, and cultural transformation of their societies, and in both eras history seemed to accelerate as a quick succession of events had impacts across the globe. As in the age of revolution, which saw the independence of the United States and most of Spanish America as well as the Haitian and French Revolutions, people swept aside old notions of authority tied to kings and empires. In Asia the Chinese Revolution and the independence of India and Pakistan marked the accelerating pace of liberation movements that dismantled European colonialism and ushered in new political ideologies and economic systems.

Liberation movements spanning the globe sought not only to end imperial domination and remove social boundaries imposed by white racism, but also to make deeper changes in how peoples perceived themselves and their societies. As radical and new as these ideas were, they nonetheless owed much to the Enlightenment ideals about liberal individual rights that were promoted by the ideologues of the French and American Revolutions.

Though the social revolutions in countries like China and Cuba and the independence movements across Africa, Asia, and the Middle East brought unprecedented deep and fast changes, they were only the first steps in remaking societies that had been created by centuries of colonialism. Uprooting the legacies of colonialism—in the form of poverty, continued domination of economies by foreign powers, limited industrialization, and weak states—remained a daunting challenge that societies continued to face in the future.

Chapter Review

MAKE IT STICK

 LearningCurve
Go online and use LearningCurve to retain what you've read.

IDENTIFY KEY TERMS

Identify and explain the significance of each item below.

Cold War (p. 967)

Truman Doctrine (p. 967)

Marshall Plan (p. 967)

NATO (p. 968)

superpowers (p. 968)

dependency theory (p. 972)

modernization theory (p. 972)

import substitution industrialization (ISI) (p. 973)

liberation theology (p. 973)

Muslim League (p. 976)

Arab socialism (p. 978)

Palestine Liberation Organization (PLO) (p. 980)

Great Leap Forward (p. 981)

Great Proletarian Cultural Revolution (p. 981)

Red Guards (p. 982)

Pan-Africanists (p. 987)

cocoa holdups (p. 987)

pieds-noirs (p. 989)

National Liberation Front (p. 989)

economic nationalism (p. 990)

populists (p. 991)

de-Stalinization (p. 996)

Common Market (p. 998)

Civil Rights Act (p. 999)

REVIEW THE MAIN IDEAS

Answer the focus questions from each section of the chapter.

1. How did the Cold War and decolonization shape the postwar world? (p. 967)

2. How did religion and the legacies of colonialism affect the formation of new nations in South Asia and the Middle East after World War II? (p. 975)

3. How did the Cold War shape reconstruction, revolution, and decolonization in East and Southeast Asia? (p. 980)

4. What factors influenced decolonization in Africa after World War II? (p. 985)

5. Why did populism emerge as such a powerful political force in Latin America? (p. 990)

6. Why did the world face growing social unrest in the 1960s? (p. 995)

MAKE CONNECTIONS

Analyze the larger developments and continuities within and across chapters.

1. What effect did the Cold War have on the process of decolonization?

┣━LaunchPad

ONLINE DOCUMENT PROJECT

Gender Roles and Populism in Argentina

What were the political implications of Eva Perón's public presentation of herself?

Examine photos of Eva Perón, and then complete a quiz and writing assignment based on the evidence and details from this chapter.

See inside the front cover to learn more.

CHRONOLOGY

1945	• United Nations established
1946–1955	• Populist Juan Perón leads Argentina
1947	• Independence of India
1948	• Marshall Plan aid in Europe; independence of Israel
1949	• Chinese Revolution; formation of NATO
1949–present	• Harsh restrictions against religion and speech in China
1950–1953	• Korean War
1953–1964	• Khrushchev implements policy of de-Stalinization in the Soviet Union
1956	• Nasser nationalizes Suez Canal Company; Soviet invasion of Hungary
1957	• Formation of Common Market
1957–1964	• Decolonization in sub-Saharan Africa
1957–1975	• War between North and South Vietnam
1959	• Cuban Revolution
1960	• Brazil's new capital, Brasília, inaugurated
1961	• Building of Berlin Wall
1962	• Cuban missile crisis
1964–1965	• Civil Rights Act and Voting Rights Act passed in United States
1965	• Great Proletarian Cultural Revolution in China
1967	• Six-Day War in Israel

32

Liberalization

1968–2000s

IN THE 1970S TWO CURRENTS RAN AGAINST EACH OTHER IN MUCH of the world. The radicalism of liberation in decolonization, revolutions, and mass social movements continued. Women's movements achieved important successes in pressing for reproductive rights and equity in education, employment, and compensation, both in the West and in nationalist regimes around the world. The most dramatic phase of decolonization in Africa and black civil rights mobilization in the United States had succeeded, but the hard work of making new nations function, or of achieving racial equality, continued.

But alongside this current ran a different one whose influence was not easily apparent in the early 1970s but was undeniable by the 1990s: liberalization. Liberal political and economic ideology experienced a resurgence. After the Second World War, the United States had championed liberal economic policies and global free trade, but this objective ran against the desires of other countries to protect and promote their own industrialization and economic development. In the last decades of the century, the U.S. drive for global liberalization of trade experienced greater success, while reform movements in the Eastern bloc and in Latin America pursued human rights and political liberalization.

Oil Shocks and Liberalization

What were the short-term and long-term consequences of the OPEC oil embargo?

In 1973 war erupted again between Israel and its neighbors Egypt and Syria. The conflict became known both as the Yom Kippur War because it coincided with the Jewish religious holiday of atonement, and as the Ramadan War because it occurred during the Muslim month of fasting. Armed with advanced weapons from the Soviet Union, Egyptian and Syrian armies came close to defeating Israel before the U.S. government airlifted sophisticated arms to Israel. Israel counterattacked, reaching the outskirts of both Cairo and Damascus before the fighting ended.

Arab oil-exporting countries retaliated against U.S. support for Israel by imposing an embargo on oil sales to countries that had aided Israel during the war. The embargo caused a worldwide disruption in oil supplies that had consequences around the world. The United States, western Europe, and Japan faced recession and inflation. In Latin America the oil crisis began a cycle of government borrowing from abroad that culminated in a crippling debt crisis. The embargo and changing oil prices created a boom-and-bust cycle for oil-exporting countries like Mexico and Nigeria.

Amid the oil embargo, the war in Vietnam, and political conflict within the United States, U.S. political and economic influence as a global superpower seemed to decline. The inability of the United States to defeat North Vietnam or to force a political solution to the conflict made the postwar atomic superpower seem increasingly powerless. President Richard Nixon further eroded the moral and political credibility of the U.S. government when he became enmeshed in the Watergate scandal, an illegal surveillance operation and subsequent cover-up during the 1972 presidential campaign that led to his resignation.

The OPEC Oil Embargo

In 1960 oil-exporting countries formed a cartel called OPEC (the Organization of the Petroleum Exporting Countries) in order to coordinate production and raise prices. They aimed to increase national revenue to support economic development. Until the early 1970s OPEC had failed to control the market for oil. But in 1973 OPEC countries agreed to an embargo, withholding oil sales to the United States and western Europe in response to U.S. support for Israel in the Yom Kippur War.

Since oil is a commodity that is traded globally, it remained available in Europe and the United States despite the embargo. But the embargo disrupted the market and caused panic. The price of oil increased almost overnight from $3 to $12 per barrel, quadrupling energy costs. OPEC's ability to disrupt the world economy, and the U.S. government's powerlessness to reverse the disruption, suggested a new world order. Brazil's military leaders, for example, distanced themselves from their traditional alliance with the United States and built relations with OPEC countries. Fearing reprisal from Arab countries, Brazil quietly halted exports to Israel, while promoting arms sales and engineering services to Libya and Iraq. As Brazil's foreign minister told U.S. secretary of state Henry Kissinger, "If you could supply us with a million barrels of oil a day, perhaps this shift would not be so abrupt."[1]

Oil prices remained high and peaked again in the second oil shock of 1979 as a result of the Iranian revolution, which ousted the secular government and brought religious leaders to power. In the United States soaring energy costs sapped economic growth and also triggered inflation, making prices rise at a time when earning power was diminished, a combination dubbed stagflation. Europe and Japan, heavily dependent on oil imports, resorted to bicycle and mass transit use to reduce their energy needs, as well as intense development of nuclear power generation.

In the decade after the first oil shock, OPEC countries such as Saudi Arabia deposited their huge profits in large international banks, particularly in the United States, which in turn reinvested these deposits as loans that governments around the world used to finance development projects. This money, which began as oil profits and circulated the world as bank loans, was known as **petrodollars**. In this economic cycle, the higher prices that consumers around the world paid for fuel generated profits for oil exporters that they invested in large banks. In turn, these banks loaned this capital out to foreign governments. Many industrializing countries faced both high energy costs and heavy debts amassed through petrodollar loans.

In the United States, as stagflation and the 1979 second oil shock drove rising inflation, the Federal Reserve Bank raised interest rates. Increased interest rates in the United States made it more expensive to borrow money, which slowed economic activity and led to an economic recession. The recession diminished consumer demand for goods, which reduced inflation. But the United States was not the only country to experience this recession: countries that exported to the United States faced reduced demand for their goods, and countries that borrowed from U.S. banks found that the interest on their debts increased as well. In industrializing nations the rapid increase in interest on their heavy debts became a crippling burden, triggering a global crisis. Countries facing soaring debts and interest rates became dependent on U.S. assistance to restructure unsustainable loans, and the U.S. government was able to impose neoliberal free-market reforms for the first time.

Beginning in the 1980s neoliberal policies increasingly shaped the world economy. **Neoliberalism** promoted free-market policies and the free circulation of capital across national borders. Debtor countries needed to continue to borrow in order to pay the interest on the debts they held, and their ability to secure loans now depended on their adherence to a set of liberal principles known as the **Washington Consensus**: policies that restricted public spending, lowered import barriers, privatized state enterprises, and deregulated markets.

The forces unleashed by the Yom Kippur War and the OPEC oil embargo of 1973 at first tipped the scale in favor of less industrialized nations, but by the 1980s the scale had swung back as debt and liberalization shifted power back to the most economically powerful countries, in particular the United States. The experiences of Mexico and Nigeria reflect the effects of the boom-and-bust cycle ignited by the oil embargo. In both cases, the oil boom of the 1970s fueled long-standing projects for development and industrialization. But as boom turned to bust, both countries were left with enduring challenges: ethnic and religious divisions continued to undermine Nigeria, while Mexico's one-party state struggled to retain power as it yielded to liberalizing pressure from the United States.

Mexico Under the PRI

By the 1960s Mexico was a democracy that functioned like a dictatorship. The Institutional Revolutionary Party (PRI) held absolute power to a degree rivaled only by the Communist parties of countries like China and the Soviet Union. PRI candidates held nearly every public office. The PRI controlled both labor unions and federations of businessmen. More than a party, it was a vast system of patronage. Even at the landfills where the most desperately poor scavenged through trash, a PRI official with a beach chair and umbrella sat watch and collected a cut of their meager earnings. Mexico's road from the nationalist economic project that emerged from the 1910 revolution to the liberal reforms of the 1960s and 1970s is also the story of the PRI.

The PRI claimed the legacy of the Mexican Revolution: it was the party of land reform, universal public education, industrialization, and state ownership of the country's oil reserves. But these claims were undermined when PRI politicians ordered the deadly crackdown on student protesters in 1968 (see page 1000). The party that had defined itself as the agent of progress and change became the reactionary party preserving a corrupt order.

In 1970 the PRI chose and elected as president populist Luis Echeverría, who sought to reclaim the mantle of reform by nationalizing utilities and increasing social spending. Echeverría and his successor, José López Portillo, embarked on massive development projects financed through projected future earnings of the state oil monopoly PEMEX. Amid inflation, corruption, and the decline of oil prices and demand during the global recession of the 1980s, the Mexican government stopped payments on its foreign debt, nationalized the banks, and steeply devalued the peso. As Mexico fell into the debt crisis, it was compelled to embrace the Washington Consensus, which meant restricted spending, opening trade borders, and privatization.

Several dramatic events discredited the PRI, beginning with the 1968 Tlatelolco massacre and followed by the debt crisis and the painful liberal reforms. The PRI was further undermined by its inept and corrupt response to a devastating earthquake that struck Mexico City in 1986. Two years later the PRI faced its first real presidential election challenge. Cuauhtémoc Cárdenas, who was the son of populist Lázaro Cárdenas and was named after the last Aztec ruler, ran against PRI candidate Carlos Salinas de Gortari. On election night, as the vote counting favored Cárdenas, the government declared that the computers tabulating the votes had crashed and declared Gortari the winner. The PRI-controlled congress ordered the ballots burned afterward. The PRI now governed through simple fraud. In its last years holding power, the PRI pursued liberalization of the economy, negotiating a free-trade agreement with the United States and Canada, the North American Free Trade Agreement (NAFTA), which went into effect in 1994.

The debt crisis forced the PRI government to abandon the nationalist development project created in the decades after the 1910 revolution and to embrace economic liberalism, but the experience with neoliberalism proved equally corrupt. Mexico continued to face economic crises such as a 1994 financial panic. As the PRI's power slipped and as Mexico's trade with the United States intensified, violent drug cartels proliferated, especially in Mexico's northern border states, and competed for the lucrative drug trade into the United States.

Nigeria, Africa's Giant

Nigeria's boom-and-bust oil economy aggravated the challenges of nation building after independence. The British imposed the name "Nigeria" on a region of many ancient kingdoms and hundreds of ethnic groups (see Map 31.3, page 986). After the country gained independence from Britain in 1960, Nigeria's key constitutional question was the relationship between the central government and its ethnically distinct regions. Under the federal system created after independence, each region had a dominant ethnic group and a corresponding political party. After independence Nigeria's ethnic rivalries intensified, and in 1967 they erupted in the Biafran war in which the Igbo ethnic group in southeastern Nigeria fought unsuccessfully to form a separate nation. The war lasted three years and resulted in famine that left millions dead.

The wealth generated by oil exports in the 1970s had contradictory effects on Nigerian society. On one hand, a succession of military leaders who held power after a 1966 coup grew increasingly corrupt throughout the 1970s. When the dictator General Murtala Muhammad (1938–1976) sought to eradicate corruption, fellow officers assassinated him. On the other hand, oil wealth allowed the country to rebuild after the Biafran war. By the mid-1970s Nigeria had the largest middle and professional classes on the continent outside of South Africa, where the minority white population had exploited black South African labor and the country's mineral wealth to its own economic benefit. Nigeria's oil boom in the 1970s resembled Mexico's experience: the expectation of future riches led to growing indebtedness, and when global demand and oil prices collapsed amid the global recession of the early 1980s, Nigeria faced a corrosive debt crisis.

Oil in Nigeria A Nigerian woman ferries fuel drums across Warri Harbor, near an abandoned oil tanker. Nigeria's oil has brought great profits to some, but boom-and-bust cycles and corruption keep wealth out of the hands of most Nigerians. (© George Steinmetz/Corbis)

Oil wealth allowed Nigeria to develop one innovative solution to its ethnic divisions: the construction of a modernist new capital, Abuja, modeled on Brazil's project in Brasília (see page 994). Located in the center of the country at the confluence of major regional and ethnic boundaries, Abuja symbolized equal representation in government. Urban planning reflected both the reality of ethnic divisions and the objective of integration: residential areas were divided by ethnicity, but shopping and services were located between them to encourage commingling.

Except for an early period of civilian rule, Muslim army officers ruled Nigeria until 1998, when the brutal military dictator General Sani Abacha suddenly died. Nigerians adopted a new constitution in 1999, and that same year they voted in free elections and re-established civilian rule. Elections in 2003 ended thirty-three years of military rule. Subsequent elections in 2007 marked the first civilian-to-civilian transfer of power. Across the country and at the local level, ethnic tensions remained. Since 2000 ethnic riots have left thousands dead in the predominantly Muslim northern Nigerian states. Much of the violence can be attributed to conflicts between Muslims and non-Muslim groups that resented the introduction of shari'a (Islamic law) in the state of Zamfara in 1999. Since then, another eleven northern Nigerian states have adopted shari'a, spurring resentment from the non-Muslim populations in these states.

War and Revolution in the Middle East

How did war and revolution reshape the Middle East?

The 1973 Yom Kippur War had a lasting effect not only on the combatants—Egypt, Syria, and Israel—but across the Middle East. Egypt and Syria had again been defeated, but Israelis also felt more vulnerable after the war. The intensity of the global economic disruption caused by the oil embargo empowered oil-exporting nations like Saudi Arabia, Libya, and Iraq. The Middle East faced deepening divisions, which added to the conflict between Israel and its neighbors. The region was reshaped by the increasing wealth of oil producers relative to other Arab states, and rising Islamic militancy led to revolution in Iran, as well as a spreading religious challenge to the rule of secular, modernizing dictatorships in countries like Egypt.

The Palestinian-Israeli Conflict

After the 1973 war, the United States recognized the need to become more actively involved in the Middle East. Peacemaking efforts by U.S. president Jimmy Carter led to the Camp David Accords in 1979, which normalized relations between Israel and its neighbors Egypt and Jordan. The accord included the return of the Sinai Peninsula to Egypt—the first successful realization of the UN "land for peace" formula. With the prospect of border wars between Israel and its neighbors diminished, political attention turned to the conflict between Israel and Palestinian nationalist organizations. Tensions between Syria and Israel shifted from their border into Lebanon, where Syria backed the militia Hezbollah, or Party of God. Hezbollah condemned the 1978 and 1982 Israeli invasions of Lebanon aimed at eradicating the Palestine Liberation Organization's control of southern Lebanon, and had as one of its stated objectives the complete destruction of the state of Israel.

In 1987 young Palestinians in the occupied territories of the Gaza Strip and the West Bank began the intifada, a prolonged campaign of civil disobedience against Israeli soldiers. Inspired increasingly by Islamic fundamentalists, the Palestinian uprising eventually posed a serious challenge not only to Israel but also to the secular Palestine Liberation Organization (PLO), long led from abroad by Yasir Arafat. The result was an unexpected and mutually beneficial agreement in 1993 between Israel and the PLO. Israel agreed to recognize Arafat's organization and start a peace process that granted Palestinian self-rule in Gaza and called for self-rule throughout the West Bank in five years. In return, Arafat renounced violence and abandoned the demand that Israel must withdraw from all land occupied in the 1967 war.

The peace process increasingly divided Israel. In 1995 a right-wing Jewish extremist assassinated Prime Minister Yitzhak Rabin. In 1996 a coalition of opposition parties won a slender majority, charging the Palestinian leadership with condoning anti-Jewish terrorism. The new Israeli government limited Palestinian self-rule where it existed and expanded Jewish settlements in the West Bank. On the Palestinian side, dissatisfaction with the peace process grew. Between 1993 and 2000 the number of Jewish settlers in the West Bank doubled to two hundred thousand, and Palestinian per capita income declined by 20 to 25 percent.

Failed negotiations between Arafat and Israel in 2000 unleashed an explosion of violence between Israelis and Palestinians known as the Second Intifada. In 2003 the Israeli government began to build a barrier around the West Bank, which met with opposition from Israelis and Palestinians alike.

The death of Yasir Arafat, the PLO's long-time leader, in November 2004 marked a turning point in the Israeli-Palestinian conflict. Mahmoud Abbas, Arafat's pragmatic successor, found little room for negotiation. In January 2006 Hamas, a Sunni Muslim political party, won 72 of the 136 seats in the Palestinian legislature, seizing control from Abbas and the PLO. Considered by Israel to be a terrorist organization, Hamas had gained widespread support from many Palestinians for the welfare programs it established in the West Bank and Gaza Strip.

Immediately after the Hamas victory, Israel, the United States, and the European Union suspended aid to the Palestinian Authority, the governing body of the West Bank and Gaza Strip established by the 1994 peace agreement. Since then, economic and humanitarian conditions for Palestinians living in the Gaza Strip have deteriorated. In 2010, 63 percent of the 1.5 million citizens of Gaza lived below the United Nations–defined poverty line. When a "Gaza freedom flotilla" attempted to break an Israeli blockade around Gaza in May 2010, the Israeli navy intercepted the flotilla and raided the ships. Nine activists were killed, eight of whom were Turkish, straining relations between the two countries. Under pressure, Israel eased its blockade in 2010, allowing more humanitarian goods and food aid into Gaza, but the movement of people to and from Gaza remained restricted.

Egypt: Arab World Leader

From the time of Gamal Nasser's seizure of power in 1956 to the mid-1970s, Egypt, due to its large military, its anti-imperialist rhetoric, and its support for Arab unity, was recognized as the leader of the Arab world. In 1977 Egypt's president, Anwar Sadat (1918–1981), negotiated a peace settlement with Israel known as the Camp David

Accords. Each country gained: Egypt got back the Sinai Peninsula, which Israel had taken in the 1967 Six-Day War, and Israel obtained peace and normal relations with Egypt. Israel also kept the Gaza Strip, taken from Egypt in 1967 and home to about 1 million Palestinians. Some Arab leaders denounced Sadat's initiative as treason.

After Sadat was assassinated by Islamic radicals in 1981, Egyptian relations with Israel deteriorated, but Egypt and Israel maintained their fragile peace as Sadat's successor, Hosni Mubarak, took office. Mubarak was a consistent supporter of Israel and a mediator for peaceful relations between Israel and the Arab world. In return for helping to stabilize the region, the United States gave Egypt billions of dollars in development, humanitarian, and military aid. Domestically, this aid failed to yield economic development, and Mubarak ruled with an increasingly dictatorial hand. Many of the government's critics charged that massive fraud and corruption funneled Egypt's wealth to a privileged few. Over 40 percent of Egyptians lived in poverty.

Human rights under Mubarak's thirty years in office were no better. Emergency law, in place since 1967, legalized censorship, suspended limited freedom of expression and assembly, allowed for the establishment of a special security court, and gave the government the right to arrest people without charge and detain prisoners indefinitely. Mubarak used the emergency law to create a wholly separate justice system in order to silence all opposition and punish, torture, and kill anyone perceived as a threat to his rule. Demonstrations, political organizations, and even financial donations that were not approved by the government were banned under the law. Thousands of people were arrested. In May 2010 the parliament approved the law's extension for another two years.

In December 2010 demonstrations broke out in Tunisia against the twenty-three-year authoritarian rule of President Zine Ben Ali, leading to his downfall on January 14, 2011. This populist revolt soon spread across North Africa and the Middle East, including to the streets of Cairo and other cities in Egypt as Egyptians of all ages united in revolt against Mubarak's dictatorial rule. After three weeks of increasingly large demonstrations, coordinated through Facebook, Twitter, and other electronic communications networks, Mubarak stepped down as president in 2011 and was arrested soon after. Libya, located between Tunisia and Egypt, also witnessed an uprising against its dictatorial leader of forty-two years, Muammar Gaddafi. Gaddafi struggled violently to remain in power, but was deposed and killed amid European and U.S. air strikes. That same year, a lengthy and intense civil war erupted in Syria, pitting opponents of ruler Bashar al-Assad against an army equipped and trained to oppose Israel.

The "Arab Spring" uprisings that swept the Middle East shook a political order that had rested in the hands of the armed forces and pursued secular, nationalist objectives. The deposed leaders were the ideological descendants of Nasser, though their regimes had come to rely more on force than on modernizing social reform. The reaction against these regimes was often religious and culturally conservative. The political transitions resulting from this upheaval tended to pit secular and religious factions against each other amid debates over the nature of government and social change.

Revolution and War in Iran and Iraq

In oil-rich Iran foreign powers competed for political influence in the decades after the Second World War, and the influence of the United States in particular helped trigger a revolutionary backlash. In 1953 Iran's prime minister, Muhammad Mossadegh

(1882–1967), tried to nationalize the British-owned Anglo-Iranian Oil Company, forcing the pro-Western shah Muhammad Reza Pahlavi (r. 1941–1979) to flee to Europe. But Mossadegh's victory was short-lived. Loyal army officers, with the help of the American CIA, quickly restored the shah to his throne.

Pahlavi set out to build a powerful modern nation to ensure his rule, and Iran's gigantic oil revenues provided the necessary cash. The shah undermined the power bases of the traditional politicians — large landowners and religious leaders — by means of land reform, secular education, and increased power for the central government. Modernization surged forward, accompanied by widespread corruption and harsh dictatorship. The result was a violent reaction against modernization and secular values: an Islamic revolution in 1979 aimed at infusing strict Islamic principles into all aspects of personal and public life. Led by the Islamic cleric Ayatollah Ruholla Khomeini, the fundamentalists deposed the shah and tried to build their vision of a true Islamic state.

Iran's revolution frightened its neighbors. Iraq, especially, feared that Iran — a nation of Shi'ite Muslims — would succeed in getting Iraq's Shi'ite majority to revolt against its Sunni leaders. In September 1980 Iraq's ruler, Saddam Hussein (1937–2006), launched a surprise attack against Iran. Hussein emerged from the tradition of Ba'athist secular nationalism within the armed forces. With their enormous oil revenues and powerful armed forces, Iran and Iraq — Persians and Arabs, Islamists and nationalists — clashed in an eight-year conflict that killed hundreds of thousands of soldiers on both sides before ending in a modest victory for Iran in 1988.

Saddled with the costs of war, Hussein eyed Kuwait's great oil wealth. In August 1990 he ordered his forces to overrun his tiny southern neighbor and proclaimed its annexation to Iraq. To Hussein's surprise, his troops were driven out of Kuwait by an American-led, United Nations–sanctioned military coalition, which included Arab forces from Egypt, Syria, and Saudi Arabia. The United Nations Security Council imposed economic sanctions on Iraq as soon as it invaded Kuwait, and these sanctions continued after the Persian Gulf War to force Iraq to destroy its stockpiles of chemical and biological weapons. Through the agreement that ended the war in 1991, United Nations inspectors supervised the destruction of many such weapons. The United States charged Iraq with deceiving UN inspectors and engaging in ongoing weapons development. An American-led invasion of Iraq in 2003 began the Second Persian Gulf War and overthrew Saddam Hussein's regime. The invasion led to a lengthy U.S. occupation and a violent insurgency against U.S. military forces, which remained in Iraq until 2011.

As secular Iraq staggered, the Iran revolutionary regime seemed to moderate. Following the constitution established by Ayatollah Khomeini, executive power in Iran was divided between a Supreme Leader and twelve-member Guardian Council selected by high Islamic clerics, and a popularly elected president and parliament. A reform movement pressed for relaxation of strict Islamic decrees and elected a moderate, Muhammad Khatami (b. 1943), as president in 1997 and again in 2001. The Supreme Leader, controlling the army and the courts, vetoed Khatami's reforms and jailed some of the religious leadership's most vocal opponents.

In 2005 dubious election returns gave the presidency to conservative populist Mahmoud Ahmadinejad (b. 1956). He engaged in brinksmanship over the development of a nuclear weapons program, called for Israel's destruction, and backed the Hamas Party in the Gaza Strip and Hezbollah in Lebanon. Ahmadinejad won re-election in 2009 after a bitterly contested challenge from moderates. The government suppressed a "green revolution" of protests that broke out after news of the election results, proving itself more able to stifle public unrest than were the leaders unseated by the Arab Spring. In 2013 opposition groups came together to support the election of Hassan Rouhani, a centrist cleric who promised civil rights reforms and has made overtures to the West in the hopes of relieving economic sanctions in return for negotiating an end to Iran's nuclear weapons program.

Latin America: Dictatorship, Debt, and Democratization

What effect did the Cold War and debt crisis have on Latin America?

After the Cuban Revolution in 1959, the United States formed alliances with conservative groups and the armed forces in much of Latin America to prevent communism from gaining further ground in the region. The United States financed and armed military dictatorships to suppress any dissent that might lead to communism and to secure U.S. influence in the region. Many elected governments were toppled in military coups that brought right-wing military dictatorships to power with U.S. military and financial support. The United States provided military regimes in Guatemala, El Salvador, and Nicaragua with everything from economic assistance to training in torture techniques. In South America, U.S. influence was less direct, though Cold War tensions intensified the repression meted out by military regimes in countries like Chile, Argentina, and Brazil.

Civil Wars in Central America

Central America experienced the greatest violence in Latin America during the Cold War. Many Latin American governments had long supported the interests of U.S. companies like United Fruit, which grew export crops and relied on cheap labor. In the second half of the twentieth century nationalists in Central America sought economic development that was less dependent on the United States and U.S. corporations, and groups of peasants and urban workers began to press for political rights and improved living standards. Through the lens of the Cold War, Central American conservatives and the United States government saw these nationalists, peasants, and workers as Communists who should be suppressed. In turn, many workers and peasants radicalized and formed Marxist revolutionary movements. The result of this conflict, and of U.S. support for right-wing governments, officers, and paramilitary groups, was hundreds of thousands of deaths.

In Guatemala reformist president Jacobo Arbenz was deposed in a military coup organized by the CIA in 1954. Subsequent Guatemalan leaders backed by the U.S. government violently suppressed peasant movements, resulting in the likely death of over two hundred thousand mostly indigenous people. In 2013 former dictator José Efraín Ríos-Montt was convicted of genocide against Maya communities, though the Guatemalan Constitutional Court annulled the conviction.

El Salvador and Nicaragua, too, faced civil wars. In 1979 the Sandinista movement overthrew dictator Anastasio Somoza Debayle. The Sandinistas, who conducted a

The Dirty War in Argentina

The Argentine military either held power or set the political rules for decades after it deposed populist Juan Perón in 1955 (see page 993). By 1973 the armed forces conceded that their efforts to "de-Perónize" the country had failed. They allowed Perón to return, and he was again elected president, with his third wife, María Estela, known as Isabelita, as vice president. Soon after the election, Juan Perón died. Isabelita Perón, the first woman to become president in Latin America, faced daunting circumstances: Marxist groups such as the Montoneros waged a guerrilla war against the regime, while the armed forces and death squads waged war on them.

In March 1976 a military junta took power and announced a Process of National Reorganization. Influenced by French military theorists who had been stung by their defeats in guerrilla wars in Vietnam and Algeria, the generals waged a "dirty war," seeking to kill and "disappear" people whom they considered a destructive "cancer" on the nation. As one general declared, "First we will kill all the subversives, then we will kill their collaborators, then their sympathizers, then . . . those who remain indifferent, and finally we will kill the timid."[3] Argentine military forces killed between fourteen thousand and thirty thousand of their fellow citizens during the dirty war.

A handful of mothers whose children had disappeared began appearing in the Plaza de Mayo in front of the presidential palace holding pictures of their missing children and carrying signs reading "Where are they?" A growing organization of the Mothers of the Plaza de Mayo was soon joined by the Grandmothers, who demanded the whereabouts of children born to women who were detained and disappeared while pregnant. These mothers were only kept alive until they gave birth. Their children were placed with adoptive families tied to the police or armed forces. Unlike in Chile and Brazil, in Argentina senior Catholic clergy did not advocate for human rights or the protection of dissidents. Instead Argentine bishops praised the coup and defended the military regime until it ended in 1983.

In 1982, emboldened by its success in eradicating its opposition, the Argentine junta occupied a set of islands off its southern coast that were claimed by Britain. Known in Britain as the Falklands and in Argentina as the Malvinas, the islands were home to a small British settlement. Britain resisted the invasion and the Falklands/ Malvinas War resulted in a humiliating defeat for the Argentine junta. After the war the junta abruptly called for elections, and a civilian president took office in 1983.

The new president, Raúl Alfonsín, faced a debt crisis similar to Mexico's that resulted from the junta's failed effort to implement Chilean-style free-market reforms. He also had to figure out how to mete out justice for the crimes committed by the junta, whose members were tried and convicted. Their convictions created a backlash in the armed forces: mid-ranking officers revolted out of fear that they, too, would be prosecuted, and they forced the government to halt prosecutions. Alfonsín could not find a way out of the debt crisis and struggled to establish the rule of law in the aftermath of the dictatorship. He was succeeded by Carlos Menem, who tried a different approach. Menem pardoned the junta members and embarked on free-market reforms, privatizing businesses and utilities and reducing trade barriers. Investment flooded in, and Argentina seemingly put the past to rest.

As the capacity to attract foreign investment through privatization ran out by the end of the century, Argentina faced economic crisis again. In 2001, amid a run on banks and a collapse of the Argentine peso, the country had five different presidents in a single month. Eventually, the economy stabilized during the presidency of Néstor Kirchner, succeeded by his wife, Cristina Fernández de Kirchner. Néstor Kirchner, who died in 2010 while Cristina Fernández de Kirchner was president, prosecuted those responsible for violence during the dirty war again. The Kirchners' governments retried and convicted members of the junta and also prosecuted people further down the ranks of the police and the armed forces.

Development and Dictatorship in Brazil

Brazil's military dictatorship, in power since 1964, pursued a different economic model than Chile's and Argentina's. Though Brazil's generals began with liberal reforms, they moved to a nationalist project of industrialization and infrastructure development that resembled some of the prescriptions of dependency theorists: increased state control of industry, restrictions on imports, and heavy investments in energy and transportation infrastructure. They initially experienced great success, realizing an "economic miracle" with annual growth rates averaging 11 percent between 1968 and 1973. This growth depended on cheap imported oil and harsh political repression. When the oil embargo threatened to cripple the country's accelerating industrialization, the generals borrowed heavily from abroad to subsidize fuel costs and conducted costly alternative energy projects to substitute oil with hydroelectric dams and ethanol made from sugarcane.

The Brazilian cycle of borrowing petrodollars to subsidize oil imports and development projects was ruinous for the country. By the end of the 1970s Brazil had the largest foreign debt in the developing world. When the second oil shock hit in 1979, and as the U.S. government raised interest rates, making Brazil's debt more expensive to manage, the country entered what became known as a "lost decade" of recession and inflation. Many workers earned less in 1989 than they had in 1980, and income inequalities increased.[4] The "economic miracle" of the 1970s had provided a favorable political environment for the dictatorship because many Brazilians credited the generals for their increased standard of living. In the 1980s the economic crisis set the tone for a transition to democracy: as the generals made painful cuts to public services and as Brazilians faced crippling inflation and recession, people overwhelmingly turned against military rule and supported redemocratization. When the first civilian president took office in 1985, inflation stood at 235 percent per year and the foreign debt at $95 billion (compared to $3.2 billion when the military took power). Inflation peaked at 3,375 percent before being tamed by the introduction of a new currency linked to the U.S. dollar, coupled with high interest rates.

As in Chile, Brazil's transition to democracy was shaped by liberalization. Business groups, which had grown uneasy with the dictatorship's borrowing and central planning, joined forces with human rights advocates to return the "rule of law," rather than arbitrary rule by generals. Unlike in Chile, the debt left behind by Brazil's military leaders drove liberal economic reforms. In order to sustain its debt payments, the Brazilian government accepted the Washington Consensus, reducing public spending and opening the economy to imports and foreign investment. Within this changed climate, in 1994 Brazilians elected Fernando Henrique Cardoso, the former Marxist sociologist and architect of dependency theory (see page 972). Cardoso carried out the deepest and most sustained liberal reforms Brazil had seen since the 1930s, privatizing many state enterprises, reducing protections for domestic industry against foreign competition, and keeping interest rates high to control inflation. Inflation remained low, but Brazilians faced a high cost of living, and high interest rates reduced lending to businesses and suppressed economic growth.

Resistance to White Rule in Southern Africa

How did white-minority rule end in southern Africa?

The racially segregated system of apartheid in South Africa was part of a larger region of white-minority rule that included Portuguese Angola and Mozambique, the government of Ian Smith in Rhodesia, and South African control of the former German colony of Namibia. In the 1970s the buffer of neighboring white-minority governments around South Africa crumbled. Independent Marxist regimes in Angola and Mozambique denounced apartheid and supported black militants in South Africa. South Africa invaded Angola in 1975 to try to install a puppet government. The two countries remained in almost constant conflict between 1977 and 1988 as Angolan forces backed by Cuban troops made South Africa's incursions into a long and violent conflict. In Namibia, the South West Africa People's Organization (SWAPO) fought for independence from South Africa. Domestic and foreign pressure brought a political transition to majority rule in Namibia and South Africa in the 1990s.

Portuguese Decolonization and Rhodesia

At the end of World War II Portugal was the poorest country in western Europe and was ruled by a dictatorship, but it still claimed an immense overseas empire that included Angola, Mozambique, Guinea-Bissau, and Cape Verde. Since the 1920s Portuguese dictator António Salazar (1889–1970) had relied on forced labor in Angola's diamond mines to finance his regime. To alleviate poverty in Portugal, Salazar also promoted colonial settlement in Angola and Mozambique, where the white population rose from seventy thousand in 1940 to over five hundred thousand in 1970.

Salazar was determined to resist decolonization, insisting that Portuguese territories were "overseas provinces," whose status he compared to Alaska and Hawaii's relationship to the United States before statehood. Unlike other European colonial leaders, Salazar refused to consider ending colonial rule. Without government support for independence, nationalists in Portugal's colonies resorted to armed insurrections. By the early 1970s independence movements in Cape Verde, Guinea-Bissau, and Mozambique all fought guerrilla wars against the Portuguese army and colonial militias. Angola had three separate guerrilla movements. The human toll was immense, and Portuguese officers returning from the colonies deposed the dictator in 1974. Guinea-Bissau and Cape Verde became independent that same year; Angola and Mozambique gained independence a year later. The nationalist movements that took power were all Marxist. Their radicalism was a product of their long struggle against oppression, inequality, and lack of access to their countries' resources, and Marxism provided a blueprint for building new states, aided by support from other Marxist regimes in Africa, eastern Europe, and Asia.

The end of colonialism in Angola and Mozambique shifted the political landscape of southern Africa. Mozambique helped rebels fighting white-minority rule in Rhodesia, while the South African government saw independent Angola as a threat to apartheid and to its control over Namibia. The bloc of white-minority rule had been shattered. But after more than a decade of war for independence, neither Angola nor Mozambique would soon find peace.

The new government of Mozambique faced a guerrilla movement financed by Rhodesia. As Angola became independent, it faced immediate invasions from Zaire (encouraged by the United States) and South Africa. The new president of Angola, Agostinho Neto (1922–1978), requested military aid from Cuba, which airlifted troops that repelled both invasions and kept the regime in place. Until the late 1980s tens of thousands of Cuban troops faced off with the South African Defense Forces and mercenary armies to defend the government of Angola.

In the British colony of Rhodesia white settlers were a small minority of the population — barely 5 percent — who declared independence on their own in order to avoid sharing power with the black majority. In 1965 they established a white-minority government under farmer and politician Ian Smith. The new Rhodesian state faced international condemnation for its treatment of black citizens, including the first economic sanctions imposed by the United Nations. Under white rule, Rhodesian laws created the illusion that the regime was not racist, though the objective of the legal and political system was to exclude blacks. Blacks and whites voted on separate ballots, with the weight of their vote proportionate to the amount of taxes each group paid. Since whites controlled the economy and the tax base, this meant they controlled the government. The Rhodesian army and police dealt violently with black political activists who challenged white rule.

The Zimbabwe African People's Union (ZAPU), a political party that fought for majority rule in Rhodesia, was banned and fought a guerrilla war against the white regime. Rebuffed by the United States and Britain, ZAPU received training and equipment from China and the Soviet Union. When Mozambique gained independence in 1974, its government allowed ZAPU and other guerrilla groups to use neighboring Mozambican territory as a staging ground to launch attacks on Rhodesia, making it impossible for the Ian Smith government to endure. Negotiations between the Rhodesian government, Britain, and the rebel forces fighting for majority rule led to an open election in 1980 that ZAPU leader Robert Mugabe won easily. The transition to majority rule went through an unusual political process: since Britain had never relinquished its colonial rule over Rhodesia, the Smith government ceded control to Britain, which in turn granted independence to the newly elected government in 1980. The new Mugabe government renamed the country Zimbabwe after an ancient city-state that predated colonial rule.

Other peoples and nations in Africa or with historical connections to Africa through the slave trade supported the transition to majority rule. Activists in the United States, Europe, and Latin America and the Caribbean had campaigned against the white-minority governments in Rhodesia and South Africa. They now celebrated an important victory. Bob Marley and the Wailers performed at Zimbabwe's independence festivities.

South Africa Under Apartheid

In 1948 the ruling South African National Party created a racist and segregationist system of discrimination known as **apartheid**, meaning "apartness" or "separation." The population was divided into four legally unequal racial groups: whites, blacks, Asians, and racially mixed "coloureds." South Africa was the most highly industrialized country in Africa at this time. Good jobs in the cities were reserved for whites, who lived in luxurious modern central neighborhoods. Blacks were restricted to precarious outlying townships plagued by poverty, crime, and mistreatment from white policemen.

By the 1950s black South Africans and their allies mounted peaceful protests. A turning point came in 1960, when police in the township of Sharpeville fired at demonstrators and killed sixty-nine black demonstrators. The main black nationalist organization—the **African National Congress (ANC)**—was outlawed but sent some of its leaders abroad to establish new headquarters. Other ANC members, led by a young lawyer, Nelson Mandela (1918–2013), stayed in South Africa to mount armed resistance. In 1962 Mandela was captured, tried for treason, and sentenced to life imprisonment.

In the 1970s the South African government fell into the hands of "securocrats," military and intelligence officers who directed the state's resources into policing apartheid and dominating South Africa's neighbors by force. They adopted a policy known as the "total strategy," which intensified repression of black activists at home and launched military strikes against ANC and SWAPO camps operating in neighboring countries. At the United Nations, African leaders denounced the South African government, and activists in countries around the world pressured their governments to impose economic sanctions against the South African regime. South Africa's white leaders responded with a program of cosmetic reforms in 1984 to improve their international standing. The 3 million coloureds and the 1 million South Africans of Asian descent gained limited parliamentary representation, but no provision was made for any representation of the country's 22 million blacks.

The reforms provoked a backlash. In the segregated townships young black militants took to the streets, clashing with heavily armed white security forces. Between 1985 and 1989 five thousand people died and fifty thousand were jailed without charges because of the political unrest. Across the border with Angola, South African troops engaged in escalating conflicts with Angolan, ANC, SWAPO, and Cuban forces. Mounting casualties and defeat in major battles shook white South Africans' confidence.

Isolated politically, besieged by economic sanctions, and defeated on the battlefield, South African president Frederik W. de Klerk opened a dialogue with ANC leaders in 1989. He lifted the state of emergency imposed in 1985, legalized the ANC, and freed Mandela in February 1990, in time for him to attend Namibia's independence ceremony. Mandela suspended the ANC's armed struggle and negotiated an agreement with de Klerk calling for universal suffrage, which meant black-majority rule. The accord also guaranteed the civil and economic rights of minorities, including job security for white government workers.

In May 1994 Mandela was elected president of South Africa by an overwhelming majority. Heading the new "government of national unity," which included de Klerk as vice president, Mandela and the South African people set about building a multiracial

Student Demonstrations Against Apartheid   Police fire tear gas at anti-apartheid protesters in 1989 at Witwatersrand University in Johannesburg. (Ulli Michel/Reuters/Landov)

democracy. The government established a Truth and Reconciliation Commission modeled on the commission impaneled in Chile to investigate abuses under Pinochet. The commission let black victims speak out, and it offered white perpetrators amnesty in return for fully confessing their crimes. Seeking to sustain the economy built through South Africa's industrialization and to avoid white flight, Mandela repudiated his Marxist beliefs and reassured domestic and foreign investors of his commitment to liberalization.

Political Change in Africa Since 1990

Democracy's rise in South Africa was part of a trend toward elected civilian rule that swept through sub-Saharan Africa after 1990. The end of the Cold War that followed the breakup of the Soviet Union in 1990 transformed Africa's relations with Russia and the United States. Both superpowers had treated Africa as a Cold War battleground, and both had given large-scale military and financial aid to their allies to undermine rivals. Communism's collapse in Europe brought an abrupt end to Communist aid to Russia's African clients. Since the world was no longer divided between allies of the United States and of the Soviet Union, U.S. support for pro-Western dictators, no matter how corrupt or repressive, declined as well. But the decrease in support for dictators left a power vacuum in which ethnic conflicts intensified, with often-disastrous results.

For instance, in the early 1990s the United States cut off decades of support for the anticommunist General Mobutu Sese Seko (1930–1997), who seized power in 1965 in Zaire (the former Belgian Congo, renamed the Democratic Republic of the Congo in 1997) and looted the country. Opposition groups toppled the dying tyrant in 1997, and a civil war ensued that left an estimated 5.4 million dead by 2007. Hundreds of thousands more have died in the years since, making it the world's deadliest conflict since World War II.

The agreement by national independence leaders across the continent to respect colonial borders prevented one kind of violence, but resulted in another. In countries whose national boundaries had been created by colonial powers irrespective of historic divisions, political parties were often based on ethnicity and kinship. The armed forces, too, were often dominated by a single ethnic group. At times, ethnic strife boiled over into deep violence, such as the genocides of ethnic Hutus by Tutsis in Burundi in 1972 and by Tutsis of Hutus in 1993 and 1994 in Rwanda, which left hundreds of thousands dead. In Kenya disputes about the legitimacy of the 2007 re-election of Mwai Kibaki left hundreds dead before the National Accord and Reconciliation Act in 2008 ended the violence. A test of the alternative to preserving national boundaries came amid efforts to ease tensions that had created famine and hardship in Sudan. In 2011, 98 percent of the electorate in southern Sudan voted to break away and form a new country, South Sudan. The early promise of peace after separation has been challenged by increased ethnic and political violence in South Sudan.

Amid these conflicts, political and economic reform has occurred in other African nations where years of mismanagement and repression had delegitimized one-party rule. Above all, the strength of the democratic opposition rested on a growing class of educated urban Africans. Postindependence governments enthusiastically expanded opportunities in education, especially higher education. In Cameroon, for example, the number of students graduating from the national university jumped from 213 in 1961 to 10,000 in 1982 and 41,000 in 1992.[5] The growing middle class of educated professionals — generally pragmatic, moderate, and open to new ideas — chafed at the ostentatious privilege of tiny closed elites and pressed for political reforms that would democratize social and economic opportunities. Thus after 1990 sub-Saharan Africa accompanied the global trend toward liberalization and human rights.

Growth and Development in Asia

How have East and South Asian nations pursued economic development, and how have political regimes shaped those efforts?

China, Japan, and the countries that became known as the "Asian Tigers" (South Korea, Hong Kong, Singapore, and Taiwan) experienced fantastic economic growth in the last decades of the twentieth century. The Chinese Communist Party managed a transition in which it maintained tight political control amid liberalization and economic growth. Japan's economy stagnated in the 1990s and struggled to recover amid growing competition from its neighbors. In South Asia tensions between India and Pakistan persisted.

China's Economic Resurgence

Amid the Cultural Revolution of 1965–1969, Chairman Mao and the Red Guards mobilized the masses, shook up the Communist Party, and created greater social equality (see pages 981–982). But the Cultural Revolution also created chaos and a general crisis of confidence, especially in the cities. Intellectuals, technicians, and purged party officials launched a counterattack on the radicals and regained much of their influence by 1969. This shift opened the door to a limited but lasting reconciliation between China and the United States in 1972.

After Mao's death in 1976, Chinese leader Deng Xiaoping (1904–1997) and his supporters initiated the "Four Modernizations": agriculture, industry, science and technology, and national defense. China's 800 million peasants experienced the greatest change from what Deng called China's "second revolution." Rigid collectivization had failed to provide the country with adequate food. Deng allowed peasants to farm in small family units rather than in large collectives and to "dare to be rich" by producing crops of their choice. Peasants responded enthusiastically, increasing food production by more than 50 percent by 1984.

The successful use of free markets in agriculture encouraged further experimentation. Foreign capitalists were allowed to open factories in southern China and to export their products around the world. Private enterprise was permitted in cities, where snack shops and other small businesses sprang up. China's Communist Party also drew on the business talent of "overseas" Chinese in Hong Kong and Taiwan who understood world markets and sought cheap labor. The Chinese economy grew rapidly between 1978 and 1987, and per capita income doubled in these years.

Most large-scale industry remained state owned, however, and cultural change proceeded slowly. Above all, the Communist Party zealously preserved its monopoly on political power. When the worldwide movement for political liberalization took root in China in the 1980s, the government banned demonstrations and slowed economic reform. Inflation soared to more than 30 percent a year. The economic reversal, the continued lack of political freedom, and the conviction that Chinese society was becoming more corrupt led idealistic university students to spearhead demonstrations in 1989.

More than a million people streamed into Beijing's central Tiananmen Square in support of the students' demands. The government declared martial law and ordered the army to clear the students. Masses of courageous citizens blocked the soldiers' entry into the city for two weeks, but in the early hours of June 4, 1989, tanks rolled into Tiananmen Square. At least seven hundred students died as a wave of repression, arrests, and executions descended on China. As communism fell in eastern Europe and the Soviet Union broke apart, China's rulers felt vindicated. They believed their action had preserved Communist power, prevented chaos, and demonstrated the limits of reform.

China became politically Communist and economically capitalist. In 2001 China joined the World Trade Organization, completing its immersion in the liberal global economy. From 1978, when Deng Xiaoping began economic reforms, through 2012, the Chinese economy grew at an average annual rate of over 9 percent, and foreign trade at an average of 16 percent. Average per capita income in China doubled every ten years, and in March 2011 China replaced Japan as the world's second-largest

Tiananmen Square, 1989   Protesters in Tiananmen Square surround a towering figure of
the Goddess of Democracy built by Chinese art students. The statue was eventually destroyed
by Chinese soldiers. (© Peter Turnley/Corbis)

economy, surpassed only by that of the United States. After 2012 China's economic
growth slowed to near 7 percent—a high rate, but one that has strained the capacity
of the government to pursue economic development and that has diminished Chinese
imports, slowing the economies of trading partners like Brazil.

"Japan, Inc." and the "Asian Tigers"

Japan's postwar economic recovery, like Germany's, proceeded slowly at first. But during the Korean War, the Japanese economy took off and grew with spectacular speed.
Japan served as a base for American military operations during the war, and billions
of dollars in military contracts and aid poured into the Japanese economy. Between
1950 and 1970 Japan's economic growth averaged a breathtaking 10 percent a year.
By the 1960s Japan had the third-largest economy in the world. In 1986 Japan's average per capita income exceeded that of the United States for the first time.

Japan's emergence as an economic superpower fascinated outsiders. Many Asians
and Africans looked to Japan for the secrets of successful modernization, but some of
Japan's Asian neighbors again feared Japanese exploitation. In the 1970s and 1980s
some Americans and Europeans bitterly accused **"Japan, Inc."** of an unfair alliance
between government and business and urged their own governments to retaliate.

In Japan's system of managed capitalism, the government protected its industry
from foreign competition, decided which industries were important, and then made
loans and encouraged mergers to create powerful firms in those industries. The govern-

ment rewarded large corporations and encouraged them to develop extensive industrial and financial activities. Workers were hired for life, and employees' social lives revolved around the company. (Discrimination against women remained severe: their wages and job security were strikingly inferior to men's.) But the 1990s saw Japan's economy stagnate amid the bursting of a speculative bubble that crippled banks and led to record postwar unemployment as the country faced competition from industrializing neighbors in Asia.

The "Asian Tigers," named for their economic development, replicated the rapid industrialization that characterized Japan. Both South Korea and Taiwan were underdeveloped countries in the early postwar years — poor, small, agricultural, densely populated, and lacking natural resources. They also had suffered from Japanese imperialism and from destructive civil wars with Communist foes.

They each pursued development through a similar series of reforms. First, land reform allowed small farmers to become competitive producers as well as consumers. Second, governments stimulated business through lending, import barriers, and control of labor. Third, nationalist leaders (Park Chung Hee in South Korea and Jiang Jieshi in Taiwan) maintained stability at the expense of democracy. When Park was assassinated in 1979, South Korea faced an even more authoritarian regime until democracy was established at the end of the 1980s. By the late 1990s South Korea had one of the largest economies in the world, leading in shipbuilding and electronics.

In 1949, after Jiang Jieshi had fled to Taiwan with his Nationalist troops and around 2 million refugees, he re-established the Republic of China (ROC) in exile. Over the next fifty years Taiwan created one of the world's most industrialized economies, becoming a leader in electronic manufacturing and design. Mainland China continued to claim Taiwan, considering it part of "One China." Hong Kong, which was returned to Chinese control by Britain in 1997, became a Special Administrative Region (SAR), as did the former Portuguese colony Macau, under a "one country, two systems" formula of partial autonomy.

Development Versus Democracy in India and Pakistan

Jawaharlal Nehru's daughter, Indira Gandhi (no relation to Mohandas Gandhi) (1917–1984), a member of the Indian National Congress Party that led national politics in the decades after independence, became prime minister of India in 1966. She dominated Indian political life for a generation. In 1975 she subverted parliamentary democracy and proclaimed a state of emergency. The state of emergency gave her extensive powers and restricted citizens' civil liberties. Gandhi applied her expanded powers across a broad range of areas, including combating corruption, quelling labor unrest, and jailing political opponents. She also threw the weight of the government behind a campaign of mass sterilization to reduce population growth. More than 7 million men were forcibly sterilized in 1976. Many believed that Gandhi's emergency measures marked the end of liberal democracy, but in 1977 Gandhi called for free elections. She suffered a spectacular electoral defeat, largely because of the vastly unpopular sterilization campaign and her subversion of democracy. Her successors fell to fighting among themselves, and in 1980 she returned to power in an equally stunning electoral victory.

Separatist ethnic nationalism plagued Indira Gandhi's last years in office. Democratic India remained a patchwork of religions, languages, and peoples, always threatening to further divide the country along ethnic or religious lines. Most notable were the 15 million Sikhs of the Punjab in northern India (see Map 31.2, page 977), with their own religion, distinctive culture, and aspirations for greater autonomy for the Punjab. By 1984 some Sikh radicals were fighting for independence. Gandhi cracked down hard and was assassinated by Sikhs in retaliation. Violence followed as Hindu mobs slaughtered over a thousand Sikhs throughout India.

One of Indira Gandhi's sons, Rajiv Gandhi, was elected prime minister in 1984 by a landslide sympathy vote. Rajiv Gandhi departed from his mother's and the Congress Party's socialism and prepared the way for Finance Minister Manmohan Singh to introduce market reforms, capitalist development, and Western technology and investment from 1991 onward. These reforms were successful, and since the 1990s India's economy has experienced explosive growth.

Though the Congress Party held power in India almost continuously after 1947, in the 1990s Hindu nationalists increasingly challenged the party's grip on power. These nationalists argued that India was based, above all, on Hindu culture and religion and that these values had been undermined by the Western secularism of the Congress Party and the influence of India's Muslims. The Hindu nationalist party, known as the BJP, finally gained power in 1998. The new government immediately tested nuclear devices, asserting its vision of a militant Hindu nationalism. In 2004 the United Progressive Alliance (UPA), a center-left coalition dominated by the Congress Party, regained control of the government and elected Manmohan Singh as prime minister. Under Narendra Modi, credited with the rapid economic growth of Gujarat state, the BJP returned to power after a sweeping electoral victory in 2014.

After Pakistan announced that it had developed nuclear weapons in 1998, relations between Pakistan and India worsened. In 2001 the two nuclear powers seemed poised for conflict until intense diplomatic pressure from the United States and other nations brought them back from the abyss of nuclear war. In 2005 both sides agreed to open business and trade relations and to try to negotiate a peaceful solution to the Kashmir dispute (see page 977). Tensions again increased in 2008 when a Pakistan-based terrorist organization carried out a widely televised shooting and bombing attack across Mumbai, India's largest city, killing 164 and wounding over 300.

In the decades following the separation of Bangladesh, Pakistan alternated between civilian and military rule. General Muhammad Zia-ul-Haq, who ruled from 1977 to 1988, drew Pakistan into a close alliance with the United States that netted military and economic assistance. Relations with the United States chilled as Pakistan pursued its nuclear weapons program. In Afghanistan, west of Pakistan, Soviet military occupation lasted from 1979 to 1989. Civil war followed the Soviet withdrawal, and in 1996 a fundamentalist Muslim group, the Taliban, seized power. The Taliban's leadership allowed the terrorist organization al-Qaeda to base its operations in Afghanistan. It was from Afghanistan that al-Qaeda conducted acts of terrorism like the attack on the U.S. World Trade Center and the Pentagon in 2001. Following that attack, the United States invaded Afghanistan, driving the Taliban from power and seeking to defeat al-Qaeda and its leader, Osama bin Laden.

When the United States invaded Afghanistan in 2001, Pakistani dictator General Pervez Musharraf (b. 1943) renewed the alliance with the United States, and Pakistan

Fall of the Berlin
stands atop the part
Berlin Wall flashing
sign as he and thous
Berliners celebrate th
Berlin Wall in Novem
a year the wall was
munism collapsed, a
ended. (Lionel Cironnea

leaders into legalizir
allowing free electi
some seats in the Po
Solidarity won ever
A month later Tade
(1927–2013), the edi
weekly newspaper, w
first noncommunist
in eastern Europe in
    Czechoslovakia
lution followed the c
in Poland and led to tl
of Communist lead
movement for dem
of massive street pro
dents and intellectu
in the election of Vác
slahf HAH-vuhl) as
page 1032.)
    Only in Romani
(chow-SHEHS-koo)
an armed uprising. A
and executed by a m
    Amid growing r
tions for early 1990.
that separated Hunga
to refugees from East
slovakia and Hungai
East Germany. East G
1989, before being sv
negotiated an econoi
    Two factors con
First, in the first weel
roughly half the cour
Almost all returned

received billions of dollars in U.S. military aid. But U.S. combat against radical groups that imposed their vision of Islam through war or terrorist acts (including the Taliban and al-Qaeda) drove militants into regions of northwest Pakistan, where they undermined the government's already-tenuous control. Cooperation between Pakistan and the United States in the war was often strained, but never more so than when U.S. Special Forces killed al-Qaeda leader Osama bin Laden on May 1, 2011. He had been hiding for years in a compound several hundred yards away from a major Pakistani military academy outside of the capital, Islamabad.

In 2007 Musharraf attempted to reshape the country's Supreme Court by replacing the chief justice with one of his close allies, bringing about calls for his impeachment. Benazir Bhutto (1953–2007), who became the first female elected head of a Muslim state when she was elected prime minister in 1988, returned from exile to challenge Musharraf's increasingly repressive military rule. She was assassinated while campaigning. After being defeated at the polls in 2008, Musharraf resigned and went into exile in London to avoid facing impeachment and possible corruption and murder charges. Asif Ali Zardari (b. 1955), Benazir Bhutto's husband, won the presidency by a landslide in the elections that followed.

The End of the Cold War

How did decolonization and the end of the Cold War change Europe?

In the late 1960s and early 1970s the United States and the Soviet Union pursued a relaxation of Cold War tensions that became known as **détente** (day-TAHNT). The policy of détente reached its high point in 1975 when the United States, the Soviet Union, Canada, and all European nations (except Albania and Andorra) signed the Helsinki Accords. These nations agreed that Europe's existing political frontiers could not be changed by force, and they guaranteed the human rights and political freedoms of their citizens. Détente stalled when Brezhnev's Soviet Union invaded Afghanistan to save an unpopular Marxist regime. President Jimmy Carter reacted with alarm at the spread of Soviet influence, much like predecessors John F. Kennedy and Harry Truman.

Carter's successor, Ronald Reagan (U.S. pres. 1981–1989), further re-ignited the Cold War by calling the Soviet Union the "evil empire" and deploying nuclear arms in western Europe. Reagan found conservative allies in British prime minister Margaret Thatcher and German chancellor Helmut Kohl. In the 1980s they gave indirect support to ongoing efforts to liberalize Communist eastern Europe. But as Reagan, Thatcher, and Kohl rekindled the Cold War, the Soviet Union underwent a cycle of reform that culminated in the release of Soviet control over eastern Europe and the dismantling of the Soviet Union and its Communist state.

The Limits of Reform in the Soviet Union and Eastern Europe

After their 1968 military intervention in Czechoslovakia, Soviet leaders worked to restore order and stability. Free expression and open protest disappeared throughout their satellite nations. Dissidents were blacklisted or imprisoned in jails or mental institutions. Although the economic crisis of the 1970s slowed the rate of improvement,

a rising standard
Communist Part
sought access to
Beneath this app
revolution. The v
scientists, manag
education that cr
Educated people
ranging from pol
When Mikha
the Soviet system
democratic face."
the economy. This
more autonomy f
private cooperativ
gradually eroded.
or **glasnost**, introc
had long characte
and marked a sigr
Democratiza
Union since 1917
minority was elect
ratization encoura
especially in the Ba
Gorbachev had en
demands continue
Finally, Gorba
Soviet troops fron
Gorbachev repudia
of eastern Europe'
eastern Europe, ov
port for democrati
almost overnight.
Poland led the
break with the Car
vigorous church, t
aged the economy,
Paul II (pontificate
and country and th
the economic crisis
In August 1980
vah-LEHN-suh) (b
Communist leader
resting Solidarity's
and strong popular
to the brink of eco

INDIVIDUALS IN SOCIETY • Václav Havel

On the night of November 24, 1989, the revolution in Czechoslovakia reached its climax. Three hundred thousand people had poured into Prague's historic Wenceslas Square to continue the massive protests that had erupted a week earlier after the police savagely beat student demonstrators. Now all eyes were focused on a high balcony. There an elderly man with a gentle smile and a middle-aged intellectual wearing jeans and a sports jacket stood arm in arm and acknowledged the cheers of the crowd. "Dubček-Havel," the people roared. "Dubček-Havel!" Alexander Dubček, who represented the failed promise of reform communism in the 1960s (see page 1000), was symbolically passing the torch to Václav Havel, who embodied the uncompromising opposition to communism that was sweeping the country. That very evening, the hard-line Communist government resigned, and soon Havel was the unanimous choice to head a new democratic Czechoslovakia. Who was this man to whom the nation turned in 1989?

Born in 1936 into a prosperous, cultured, upper-middle-class family, the young Havel was denied admission to the university because of his class origins. Loving literature and philosophy, he gravitated to the theater, became a stagehand, and emerged in the 1960s as a leading playwright. His plays were set in vague settings, developed existential themes, and poked fun at the absurdities of life and the pretensions of communism. In his private life, Havel thrived on good talk, Prague's lively bar scene, and officially forbidden rock 'n' roll.

In 1968 the Soviets rolled into Czechoslovakia, and Havel watched in horror as a tank commander opened fire on a crowd of peaceful protesters in a small town. "That week," he recorded, "was an experience I shall never forget."* The free-spirited artist threw himself into the intellectual opposition to communism and became its leading figure for the next twenty years. The costs of defiance were enormous. Purged and blacklisted, Havel lifted barrels in a brewery and wrote bitter satires that could not be staged. In 1977 he and a few other dissidents publicly protested Czechoslovakian violations of the Helsinki Accords on human rights, and in 1989 this Charter '77 group became the inspiration for Civic Forum, the democratic coalition that toppled communism. Havel spent five years in prison and was constantly harassed by the police.

*Quoted in M. Simmons, *The Reluctant President: A Political Life of Václav Havel* (London: Methuen, 1991), p. 91.

hopes of unity and change. Second, West German chancellor Helmut Kohl reassured American, Soviet, and European leaders that they need not fear a reunified Germany. Kohl and Gorbachev signed a historic agreement in July 1990 in which united Germany affirmed its peaceful intentions. Within the year, East and West Germany merged into a single nation under West Germany's constitution and laws.

Eastern European countries pursued liberalization, but electoral politics suffered from intense battles between presidents and parliaments, and from weak political parties. The elderly suffered from the loss of pensions and social welfare programs after

Havel's thoughts and actions focused on truth, decency, and moral regeneration. In 1975, in a famous open letter to Czechoslovakia's Communist boss, Havel wrote that the people were indeed quiet, but only because they were "driven by fear. . . . Everyone has something to lose and so everyone has reason to be afraid." Havel saw lies, hypocrisy, and apathy undermining and poisoning all human relations in his country: "Order has been established—at the price of a paralysis of the spirit, a deadening of the heart, and a spiritual and moral crisis in society."†

Yet Havel saw a way out of the Communist quagmire. He argued that a profound but peaceful revolution in human values was possible. Such a revolution could lead to the moral reconstruction of Czech and Slovak society, where, in his words, "values like trust, openness, responsibility, solidarity and love" might again flourish and nurture the human spirit. Havel was a voice of hope and humanity who inspired his compatriots with a lofty vision of a moral postcommunist society. As president of his country from 1989 to 2003, Havel continued to speak eloquently on the great questions of our time.

QUESTIONS FOR ANALYSIS

1. Why did Havel oppose Communist rule? How did his goals differ from those of Dubček and other advocates of reform communism?

2. Havel has been called a "moralist in politics." Is this a good description of him? Why or why not?

---

†Quoted ibid., p. 110.

▷LaunchPad
ONLINE DOCUMENT PROJECT

How did people in Czechoslovakia overturn the existing social and political order? Explore the efforts of dissidents to produce a peaceful revolution, and then complete a quiz and writing assignment based on the evidence and details from this chapter.

See inside the front cover to learn more.

the end of communism, but the young often enjoyed greater economic opportunities. Many former Communist Party officials became wealthy as they gained control of state enterprises that were privatized. Regional inequalities persisted. Capital cities such as Warsaw, Prague, and Budapest concentrated wealth, power, and opportunity; provincial centers stagnated; and industrial areas declined.

The great postcommunist tragedy was Yugoslavia, whose federation of republics and regions had been held together under Josip Tito's Communist rule. After Tito's death in 1980, power passed increasingly to the republics. Rising territorial and ethnic tensions were intensified by economic decline and charges of ethnically inspired massacres during World War II. The revolutions of 1989 accelerated the breakup of Yugoslavia. Serbian president Slobodan Milošević (SLOH-buh-dayn muh-LOH-suh-vihch) (1941–2006) attempted to grab land from other republics and unite all Serbs in a "greater Serbia." His ambitions led to civil wars that between 1991 and 2001 engulfed Kosovo, Slovenia, Croatia, and Bosnia-Herzegovina. In 1999 Serbian aggression prompted NATO air strikes, led by the United States, against the Serbian capital of Belgrade as well as against Serbian military forces until Milošević relented. Milošević was voted out of office in 2000. The new Serbian government extradited him to a United Nations war crimes tribunal in the Netherlands to stand trial for crimes against humanity as peace was restored to the former Yugoslav republics.

Recasting Russia Without Communism

Amid anticommunist upheavals in eastern Europe, the Soviet Union itself transitioned away from Communist Party rule. In February 1990 the Soviet Communist Party was defeated in local elections throughout the country. Gorbachev responded by asking Soviet citizens to ratify a new constitution that abolished the Communist Party's monopoly on political power and expanded the power of the Congress of People's Deputies. Gorbachev's eroding power and unwillingness to risk a popular election for the presidency strengthened his rival, Boris Yeltsin (1931–2007), the former mayor of Moscow. Yeltsin embraced the democratic movement, and in May 1990, as leader of the Russian parliament, he announced that Russia would declare its independence from the Soviet Union. In June 1991 Yeltsin was elected president of the Russian Federation within the Soviet Union, placing him in direct confrontation with Gorbachev, who wanted to keep the Soviet Union together amid carefully managed reforms.

In August 1991 Gorbachev survived an attempted coup by Communist Party hardliners and their allies in the armed forces who wanted to preserve Communist Party power and the multinational Soviet Union. Not only did their coup attempt fail but it also hastened the end of the Soviet Union. Yeltsin emerged as a popular hero for his dramatic resistance to the coup attempt. At one point, he climbed atop a tank deployed by the coup conspirators in front of the Russian Federation Parliament, from which he delivered a rousing speech in which he called for a general strike in resistance to the coup.

In the aftermath of the attempted military takeover, an anticommunist revolution swept the Russian Federation as the Communist Party was outlawed and its property confiscated. Yeltsin and his liberal allies declared Russia independent and withdrew from the Soviet Union. All the other Soviet republics followed suit. Gorbachev agreed to their independence, and the Soviet Union ceased to exist on December 25, 1991 (Map 32.1). The newly independent post-Soviet republics faced painful challenges, including the need to quickly build new political systems and the urgency of economic reforms meant to turn socialist economies into economies that functioned on free-market principles.

As Boris Yeltsin presided over newly independent Russia, he sought to create economic conditions that would prevent a return to communism. Following the example of some postcommunist governments in eastern Europe, Yeltsin opted for breakneck liberalization. This shock therapy, which followed methods similar to radical free-market policies in Chile and other parts of Latin America, freed prices on 90 percent of all Russian goods, with the exception of bread, vodka, oil, and public transportation. The government also launched a rapid privatization of industry and turned thousands of factories and mines over to new private companies. Yeltsin and his advisers believed shock therapy would re-ignite production and bring prosperity after a brief period of hardship. The results were quite different. Prices soared and production collapsed.

Rapid economic liberalization had harsh consequences for Russia. Powerful state industrial monopolies became powerful private monopolies that cut production and raised prices in order to maximize profits. The managerial elite worked with organized crime to cower would-be rivals, preventing the formation of new firms. A new capitalist elite acquired great wealth and power, while the vast majority of people fell into poverty. Managers, former officials, and financiers who netted large shares of the old state monopolies stood at the top of Russian society. The quality of public services and health care declined to the point that the average male life expectancy dropped from sixty-nine years in 1991 to fifty-nine years in 2007. In 2003 Russia's per capita income was lower than at any time since 1978, essentially erasing the economic progress gained over the past twenty-five years.

The election of Yeltsin's handpicked successor, President Vladimir Putin (b. 1952), in 2000 ushered in a new era of "managed democracy." Putin's stress on public order and economic reform was popular, even as he became progressively more authoritarian. Significant restrictions were placed on media freedoms, regional elections were abolished, and the distinction between judicial and executive authority collapsed. Putin consolidated the power and authority of the state around himself and his closest advisers, closing off the development of democratic pluralism and an independent legal system in Russia.

Putin's illiberal tendencies were also evident in his brutal military campaign against Chechnya (CHEHCH-nyuh), a tiny republic of 1 million Muslims in southern Russia (see Map 32.1, inset) that in 1991 declared its independence. Up to two hundred thousand Chechen civilians are estimated to have been killed between 1994 and 2011. Many more became refugees. Chechen resistance to Russian domination continued, often in the form of attacks such as a suicide bombing at Moscow's airport in 2011 that killed scores of travelers.

Putin's increasingly authoritarian rule drew criticism from many quarters, both within and outside Russia. Unable to run for re-election in 2008, Putin handpicked a successor, Dmitry Medvedev, to be president, and took the position of Russian prime minister for himself. He remained the main power broker and returned to the presidency in 2012. Liberal reforms doomed much of Russia's industry, and its economy depended increasingly on oil and natural gas exports. Despite its weakened economy, Russia retained the world's second-largest nuclear arsenal, as well as a powerful vote (and veto) in the United Nations Security Council.

In the aftermath of the dissolution of the Soviet Union, political and ethnic divisions threatened peace and stability among the post-Soviet republics. Rival claims between the Republic of Georgia and the Russian Federation over the territory of

◀ **MAP 32.1   Russia and the Successor States** After the attempt in August 1991 to depose Gorbachev failed, an anticommunist revolution swept the Soviet Union. Led by Russia and Boris Yeltsin, the republics that formed the Soviet Union declared their sovereignty and independence. Eleven of the fifteen republics then formed a loose confederation called the Commonwealth of Independent States, but the integrated economy of the Soviet Union dissolved into separate national economies, each with its own goals and policies.

South Ossetia led to war in 2008 in which Russian forces quickly defeated their Georgian rivals and established the pro-Russian autonomy of the region. In Ukraine, in 2014 pro-Western protesters toppled a president who refused to sign agreements with the European Union. In the aftermath of the uprising, Russian forces occupied the Ukrainian province of Crimea along the Black Sea and backed secessionist movements in ethnically Russian regions of Ukraine. Russia's seizure of Crimea undermined the terms under which the Soviet Union had dissolved into separate republics, provoking unease among other new states such as the Baltic republics.

Integration and Reform in Europe

Building on integration efforts in the 1940s and 1950s established through NATO and the Common Market (see page 998), at the end of the twentieth century European nations moved toward greater unity. With military and trade integration in place, France and Germany took the lead in pushing for a monetary union among Common Market members. The European Union (EU), established in 1993, allowed for the free movement of people and goods among its original twelve member countries; created a common currency, the euro (2002); and formed a European Parliament that established regulations and pooled infrastructure and education investments. This integration was a response to the Cold War, and it provided a logic for rebuilding a continent that had devastated itself through two world wars and wished to avoid another. But it was also a response to the end of European overseas empires.

The loss by western European countries of their colonies in Africa and Asia was a major incentive to unify within Europe because it dramatically shifted their access to markets and resources. For five centuries overseas empires not only provided the engine for economic development at home but also shaped international relations as well as intellectual currents ranging from abolitionism to scientific racism and even Marxism. Empires provided raw materials and markets that produced industrialization. For France, colonies in the Mediterranean, Africa, and Southeast Asia served, at least in principle, as a counterweight to Germany's might. Empires in Africa and Asia allowed Britain and Portugal to remain "proudly alone," in the words of Portuguese dictator Salazar.[6] As the cycle of colonialism ended, nations that had related to each other with the crutch of overseas empires now needed to forge new relationships directly with one another—the first time they had ever done so since the cycle of colonialism accompanied the process of nation-state formation. The result was an unprecedentedly close degree of economic and political integration.

For eastern Europe, integration with western European countries was a means of ending Soviet domination. As the Cold War barriers between eastern and western

Europe fell after 1989, eastern European countries became some of the most avid participants in the process of economic and institutional integration. Much as integration created the logic for rebuilding Germany and reimagining nations without empires attached to them, European economic integration provided a blueprint for reforming economies and institutions in countries transitioning away from Soviet models, and the collapse of Communist regimes brought the apparent triumph of liberal democracy. For the first time since before the French Revolution, almost all of Europe followed the same general political model.

European leaders embraced, or at least accepted, a neoliberal, free-market vision of capitalism. The most radical economic changes had been implemented in the 1980s by Margaret Thatcher (1925–2013) in Britain, who drew inspiration from Pinochet's Chile. Other governments also introduced austerity measures to slow the growth of public spending and the welfare state. Many individuals suffered under the impact of these reductions in public spending and social welfare, and the threat of unemployment — or underemployment in dead-end jobs — shaped the outlook of a whole generation. Harder times meant that more women entered or remained in the workforce after they married.

In the 1990s Germany and France continued to lead the push for integration. French president François Mitterrand (1916–1996) and German chancellor Helmut Kohl (b. 1930) pursued a monetary union of European Community members, and the Maastricht Treaty of 1992 created a single EU currency, the euro. In 1993 the European Community rechristened itself the European Union (EU).

The success of the euro encouraged the EU to accelerate plans for an ambitious enlargement to the east. On May 1, 2004, the EU started admitting eastern European countries. By 2007 the EU had twenty-seven member states, including most of eastern Europe, and a population of nearly 500 million. Future candidates for membership include Croatia, Macedonia, former parts of the Soviet Union, and Turkey (Map 32.2).

The movement toward union raised profound questions about the meaning of European unity and identity. Would the EU remain an exclusive Western club, or would it expand to include the postcommunist nations of eastern Europe? If some of them were included, how could Turkey, a secular nation with a Muslim majority, be denied its long-standing request for membership? Turkey had been a member of NATO since 1952 and had labored to meet membership requirements.

A proposed EU constitution binding EU member states even closer together was scheduled to go into effect in 2007. First, however, it needed to be approved by voters in all member countries. In 2005 voters in France and Holland voted overwhelmingly against the constitution and threw the entire process into confusion. The rejected constitution was replaced with the Treaty of Lisbon in 2007. The new treaty kept most of the reforms contained in the original European constitution, but it revised the political structure of the EU bureaucracy. By November 2009 all members had approved it, and the Lisbon treaty came into force on December 1, 2009, unifying what had been a profoundly divided, war-torn continent just fifty years earlier.

The economic crisis that began in 2008 tested the European Union and the euro. Countries that had adopted the euro currency had to meet stringent fiscal standards and imposed budget cuts and financial austerity. The resulting reductions in health

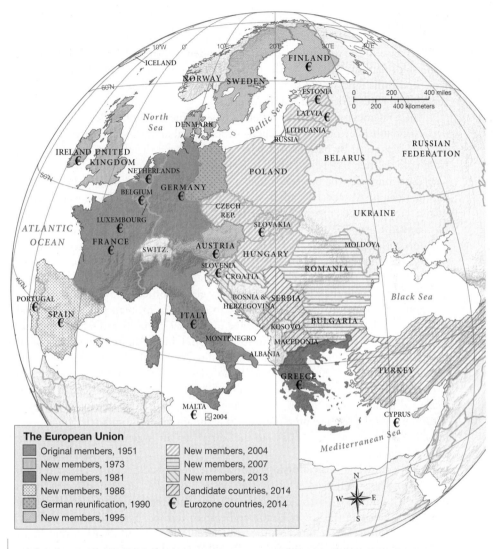

MAP 32.2 The European Union, 2014 No longer divided by ideological competition and the Cold War, much of today's Europe has banded together in a European Union.

care and social benefits hit ordinary citizens hard. A global economic recession magnified these difficulties. National governments could no longer expand their own monetary supplies to promote recovery, and governments were forced to slash budgets to meet debt obligations. Economic austerity brought ruinous economic cycles that crippled Greece, Portugal, Spain, and Italy. The consequences of liberalization in Europe resembled the consequences elsewhere: economic growth was greater, but economic hardships were deeper.

Chapter Summary

In 1976 most of the world was governed by undemocratic regimes. This included the Soviet-bloc nations, China, North and South Korea, Indonesia, the Philippines, Vietnam, and India (and would soon include Pakistan), as well as almost all countries in the Middle East, Africa, and South America.

These regimes came in many different types: some were controlled by Communist parties and others by right-wing military officers loyal to the United States. There were dictatorships ruled by nationalist leaders who had been the champions of liberation from colonial rule like Félix Houphouët-Boigny of the Ivory Coast. More common were the strongmen who unseated independence leaders, such as Suharto (1921–2008) of Indonesia or Ahmed Hassam al-Bakr (1914–1982) in Iraq. There were dictators whose families owned much of a nation's resources, like Anastasio Somoza Debayle of Nicaragua or Jean-Claude "Bébé Doc" Duvalier (b. 1951) in Haiti. Some of these dictators created an illusion of governing democratically, but they restricted opposition or required one-party rule. In other cases, countries had sham democracies, as in Rhodesia and South Africa, where only the small white minority could hold power, or in Mexico, where the PRI dominated every elected office.

Some dictatorships created the space to engage in utopian projects to remake nations. South Korea's Park Chung Hee (1917–1979) or Brazil's Ernesto Geisel (1907–1996) pursued aggressive industrialization. Chile's Augusto Pinochet pursued radical free-market reforms, while Tanzania's Julius Nyerere (1922–1999) implemented socialist collective farming, both of which caused wrenching hardship for their citizens. Even when such dictatorships succeeded in their goals, they did so at enormous costs measured in debt and inflation, famine and malnutrition, the tattering of public institutions, and the reliance on repression to maintain order. From Soviet gulags—the infamous political prison camps—to the "dirty war" in Argentina, violence replaced political dialogue.

By the mid-1980s dictatorships around the world had begun to fall, and democratic transitions followed. During the 1980s most of Latin America returned to democracy, and in 1989 the fall of the Berlin Wall began a wave of political and economic change in the Soviet Union and eastern Europe. The end of the Cold War division of Europe accelerated a process of integration and unification that had its roots in reconstruction after the Second World War and the process of decolonization that dismantled European empires. Alongside political transitions, a wave of economic liberalization, often promoted by the United States, swept the world. Trade and economic activity increased as a result of liberalization, but it also created growing gaps between rich and poor.

Notes

1. *Jornal do Brasil*, March 14, 1976, quoted in Roberto Jorge Ramalho Cavalcanti, "O presidente Ernesto Geisel e o estabelecimento do retorno à democracia ao Brasil pós Regime Militar de 1964," *Governo e Politica*, November 7, 2010, http://www.webartigos.com/artigos/artigo-o-presidente-ernesto-geisel-e-o-estabelecimento-do-retorno-a-democracia-ao-brasil-pos-regime-militar-de-1964/51497/.

2. CIA Director Richard Helms, notes on Nixon's plan for Chile, September 15, 1970, accessed October 14, 2012, http://www2.gwu.edu/~nsarchiv/NSAEBB/NSAEBB8/docs/doc26.pdf.

3. Quoted in Jonathan C. Brown, *A Brief History of Argentina*, 2d ed. (New York: Facts on File, 2010), p. 243.

4. Paulo Eduardo de Andrade Baltar, "Estagnação da economia, abertura e crise do emprego urbano no Brasil," *Economia e Sociedade* 6 (1996): 86.

5. D. Birmingham and P. Martin, eds., *History of Central Africa: The Contemporary Years Since 1960* (London: Routledge, 1998), p. 59.

6. David Corkill, *The Development of the Portuguese Economy: A Case Study of Europeanization* (London: Routledge, 1999), p. 2.

CONNECTIONS

The experiences of people living under authoritarian regimes varied greatly. Many supported the regimes from which they drew privileges or found a reassuring sense of order. Others avoided political questions and stayed out of trouble. But even they were marked by authoritarianism: censorship and propaganda meant that official pronouncements lacked credibility, so rumors, some true and others wild, became their basic currency of exchange.

Many, however, resisted the regimes. For some, a closed political system meant the only tools available were armed resistance. Guerrilla movements against authoritarian regimes were common, though the imbalance in their resources meant they mostly met with violent ends at the hands of security forces. Another form of resistance proved more effective: nonviolent, and ostensibly nonpolitical, resistance was harder for regimes to repress. Mothers asking for the whereabouts of missing children or quilting the scenes of their grief in Argentina and Chile, or workers organizing an independent union in Poland, found ways to challenge their regimes.

The most successful resistance was often opposition that was not explicitly ideological, such as the defense of human rights, or the establishment of the rule of law that would restrict a regime's arbitrary power. These pressures had a similar effect when applied to right-wing or socialist dictatorships alike: they were liberalizing. As dictatorships in Latin America, East Asia, and eastern Europe moved toward multiparty democracy, and as the Soviet bloc disintegrated, those countries shared a historical moment in which liberal economic and political reforms swept the world.

Chapter Review

MAKE IT STICK

 LearningCurve
Go online and use LearningCurve to retain what you've read.

IDENTIFY KEY TERMS

Identify and explain the significance of each item below.

petrodollars (p. 1008)

neoliberalism (p. 1008)

Washington Consensus (p. 1008)

intifada (p. 1012)

junta (p. 1016)

apartheid (p. 1022)

African National Congress (ANC)
(p. 1022)

Tiananmen Square (p. 1025)

"Japan, Inc." (p. 1026)

détente (p. 1029)

perestroika (p. 1030)

glasnost (p. 1030)

Solidarity (p. 1030)

European Union (EU) (p. 1037)

REVIEW THE MAIN IDEAS

Answer the focus questions from each section of the chapter.

1. What were the short-term and long-term consequences of the OPEC oil embargo? (p. 1007)
2. How did war and revolution reshape the Middle East? (p. 1011)
3. What effect did the Cold War and debt crisis have on Latin America? (p. 1015)
4. How did white-minority rule end in southern Africa? (p. 1020)
5. How have East and South Asian nations pursued economic development, and how have political regimes shaped those efforts? (p. 1024)
6. How did decolonization and the end of the Cold War change Europe? (p. 1029)

MAKE CONNECTIONS

Analyze the larger developments and continuities within and across chapters.

1. How did transitions to democracy and free markets around the world draw on earlier ideologies?
2. How did the impact of oil shocks resemble previous economic crises?
3. What similarities do you see in social movements that advocated for democracy and for majority rule around the world?

LaunchPad

ONLINE DOCUMENT PROJECT

Václav Havel: Planning a Nonviolent Revolution
How did people in Czechoslovakia overturn the existing social and political order?

Explore the efforts of dissidents to produce a peaceful revolution, and then complete a quiz and writing assignment based on the evidence and details from this chapter.

See inside the front cover to learn more.

CHRONOLOGY

1973	• Yom Kippur War; OPEC oil embargo
1979	• Islamic revolution in Iran; second oil shock
1980	• Rhodesian white-minority rulers surrender power and the nation is renamed Zimbabwe
1980–1988	• Iran-Iraq War
1982	• Falklands (or Malvinas) War leads to the collapse of the Argentine junta
1985	• Glasnost leads to greater freedom of speech and expression in the Soviet Union
1987	• Palestinian intifada
1989	• Collapse of Berlin Wall; "NO" campaign in Chile; Tiananmen Square protests suppressed in China
1989–1991	• Fall of communism in Soviet Union and eastern Europe
1990–1991	• Persian Gulf War
1991	• Congress Party in India embraces Western capitalist reforms
1991–2001	• Civil war in Yugoslavia
1993	• Formation of the European Union
1994	• North American Free Trade Agreement goes into effect between Canada, Mexico, and the United States
1994	• Nelson Mandela elected president of South Africa
2003–2011	• Second Persian Gulf War
2007	• Hamas seizes control of Gaza Strip from Palestinian Authority
2009–2014	• Popular uprisings and protests across the Middle East

✓ LearningCurve
After reading the chapter, go online
and use LearningCurve to retain what
you've read.

The Contemporary World in Historical Perspective

THE APPROACHES TO THE HISTORY OF WORLD SOCIETIES IN THE
preceding chapters give us critical thinking skills to help interpret the contemporary world. Through this lens, we can understand contemporary
events and debates as rooted in history and also see those events as
subjects of study that we can analyze using the same tools we employ
for interpreting the past.

Since the end of the Cold War, many nations around the world have
undergone transitions from dictatorship to democracy, and a growing
number of nations have pursued free trade. These new experiences have
been shaped by past struggles, and they have intensified global connections, aided by revolutions in communications and information technology.
Amid these changes, stubborn regional and political conflicts remain in
many parts of the world, and the experiences of poverty and marginalization continue to be widespread. But this is also a world in which, as in
the past, humans have had the ability to shape, adapt, and transform the
problems they confront.

The End of History?

Does the contemporary world reflect the "end of history"?

In 1989, as the Berlin Wall fell and the Soviet system disintegrated, a historian wrote a provocative article called "The End of History?" in which he argued that the collapse of the Soviet system meant the triumph of liberalism as a political and economic philosophy. Amid the transitions from dictatorship to democracy in Latin America, and the transition away from socialism and Communist Party control in Russia and eastern Europe, political leaders embraced liberalism as the ideology of government and of economics. This was the "triumph of the West, of the Western *idea* . . . in the total exhaustion of viable systematic alternatives to Western liberalism."[1] Was liberalism the ultimate stage of human political and economic development?

Around the world at the turn of the twenty-first century, liberalism certainly emerged as the dominant political and economic philosophy. But there have been limits to liberalism's reach and its effectiveness as a solution to political and economic problems. For instance, economic liberalism has tended to increase social inequality and the disparity of wealth between nations and regions in ways that are not sustainable. As a result, the rise of liberalism has been met by a growing range of social activism aimed at reducing social inequality; gender, ethnic, and racial marginalization; and the environmental costs of economic development.

The tension between liberalism and activism is one example of the kinds of contradictory and competing pressures that shape the contemporary world. For instance, the earth's growing population has increased demands for food production, prompting a revolution in agricultural sciences. Although new technologies have helped meet the world's demand for food, the diversion of water resources and the expansion of farming at the expense of forests remind us that new technologies often bring unintended costs. Similarly, the end of the Cold War has been met not with peace but with regional conflicts around the world. And with the intensification of communications, increase in travel, and the spread of technology, capital and liberal ideology have been met with conservative, often religious reactions in different regions of the world. Some of the most intense reactions have come from militant fundamentalist movements in the Middle East and Africa. Increasingly, those conflicts have had a global impact as militants pursue their causes in the United States and Europe.

Complexity and Violence in a Multipolar World

When the Cold War ended, the global alignment between supporters of the United States, supporters of the Soviet Union, and countries that tried to remain unaligned yielded to new regional relationships in which many middle powers exerted increased influence. Increasingly assertive middle powers, countries with significant economic influence either in relation to their neighbors or in broader trade networks, jockeyed for regional leadership, sometimes bringing them into conflict. Brazil, a rapidly industrializing country with 200 million people and vast territory and resources, emerged as the dominant nation-state in South America. Mexico, both highly industrialized and economically integrated with the United States, emerged as the leader of the Spanish-speaking Americas. France and Germany re-emerged as central economic powers in Europe. Nigeria and South Africa became the leading powers in sub-Saharan

Africa. Turkey, Egypt, and Israel were also regional powers in the Middle East. Iran and Iraq fought for dominance in the Persian Gulf. China, India, and Japan all became leading regional powers, and several other Asian countries—notably South Korea, Indonesia, and Pakistan—were determined to join them.

While the end of the Cold War reduced superpower pressures that intensified regional conflicts, other factors continued to feed conflicts around the world. In the 1990s civil wars in Bosnia, Kosovo, Rwanda, and Afghanistan killed over a million people and sent hundreds of thousands of refugees running for their lives. Since 2000 new and continuing wars have caused millions more deaths and new refugees, particularly in Syria, Sierra Leone, Liberia, the Democratic Republic of the Congo, Mali, Uganda, Afghanistan, Burundi, Somalia, Iraq, Sudan, and Angola. Rivalries between ethnic groups often lie at the heart of the civil wars that produce so many deaths and refugees. Ethnic competition can lead to demands for ethnic autonomy or political independence.

An Expanding Atomic Age

After the bombing of Hiroshima and Nagasaki in 1945 (see page 961), the United States briefly held a monopoly on atomic weapons. Since then, a growing number of nations have developed nuclear arms, which they use as a deterrent against attack and as a means to increase their international leverage and prestige.

The Cold War arms race resulted in intense competition for the development of increasingly powerful atomic weapons, and it also meant massive spending in the United States, the Soviet Union, and Europe on the development of other weapons, ranging from ballistic missile systems to jets, tanks, and all manner of other weapons. While the superpowers and their closest allies sought to restrict access to nuclear weapons, they sold huge numbers of conventional arms to other nations.

Amid the Cold War arms race, atomic tests brought fear that radiation would enter the food chain and cause leukemia, bone cancer, and genetic damage. Concerned scientists called for a ban on atomic bomb testing. In 1963 the United States, Great Britain, and the Soviet Union reached an agreement, eventually joined by more than 150 countries, to ban nuclear tests in the atmosphere. In 1970 more than sixty countries signed the Treaty on the Non-Proliferation of Nuclear Weapons, designed to halt the spread of nuclear weapons to states that did not yet have them and to reduce stockpiles of existing bombs held by the nuclear powers. It seemed that the nuclear arms race might yet be reversed.

This outcome did not come to pass. French and Chinese leaders disregarded the test ban and by 1968 had developed their own nuclear weapons, although they later signed the nonproliferation treaty. India also developed nuclear weapons and in 1974 exploded an atomic device. Meanwhile, the nuclear arms race between the Soviet Union and the United States was so intense that after the 1960s both sides sought ways of slowing it and negotiated shared limits to their nuclear arsenals. The Strategic Arms Limitation Talks (SALT), which took place between 1969 and 1979, limited the rate at which the two superpowers produced nuclear warheads, and in 1991 the United States and Russia negotiated the first Strategic Arms Reduction Treaty (START I), which eventually removed about 80 percent of existing strategic nuclear weapons. The New START treaty, signed by U.S. president Barack Obama and Russian president

Dmitry Medvedev in 2010, required the two countries to further reduce the number of their nuclear warheads by one-third.

India developed its atomic capability partly out of fear of China, but India's nuclear test in 1974 in turn frightened Pakistan, which pursued its own nuclear weapons. In 1998 both India and Pakistan tested nuclear devices within weeks of each other, confirming their status as the world's sixth and seventh acknowledged nuclear powers, after the United States, Russia, the United Kingdom, France, and China. Other nations discreetly pursued nuclear arms without publicly stating that they possessed them.

In the 1950s Israel began developing nuclear weapons, and it is generally believed to have had an arsenal of nuclear weapons since the 1970s, though Israel has never publicly confirmed this. Israel's apparent nuclear superiority was threatening to Arab states that for decades had tried to vanquish Israel. When Iraq attempted, with help from France, to develop nuclear capability in the 1980s, Israel responded by attacking and destroying the Iraqi nuclear reactor in June 1981.

The risks associated with the proliferation of nuclear weapons helped mobilize the international community and contributed to positive developments through the 1980s and 1990s. Between 1983 and 2003 Argentina, Romania, Brazil, South Africa, and Libya all agreed to abandon their nuclear weapons programs. Several of the former Soviet republics that possessed nuclear arsenals, including Ukraine, Belarus, and Kazakhstan, returned their nuclear weapons to Russia. International agencies monitored exports of nuclear material, technology, and missiles that could carry atomic bombs. These measures encouraged confidence in global cooperation and in the nonproliferation treaty, which was extended indefinitely in 1995. The treaty has been signed by 190 countries as of 2014.

Despite these efforts, nuclear proliferation has continued. In 2003 the United States accused Iran of seeking to build nuclear weapons, and ongoing diplomatic efforts, sanctions, and other punitive measures by France, Germany, Britain, China, the United States, and Russia have failed to induce Iran to limit its nuclear program. There is also the threat that enriched nuclear materials will fall into the hands of terrorist organizations or that countries possessing nuclear weapons technology would share it with other nations. In 2004 the father of Pakistan's nuclear weapons program, Abdul Qadeer Khan, was charged by a Pakistani military court with sharing nuclear weapons expertise and technology with Iran, Libya, and North Korea.

In the new century long-standing tensions between North Korea and the United States, which had never signed a peace treaty to end the 1950–1953 Korean War, intensified over North Korea's pursuit of nuclear weapons and ballistic missile technology that would allow it to launch atomic weapons at South Korea and Japan. As each side accused the other of failing to live up to its agreements, North Korea tested its first nuclear device in 2006. A year later, North Korea agreed to shut down its major nuclear facility at Yŏngbyŏn in exchange for thousands of tons of fuel oil from the West and the release of $25 million in frozen North Korean funds. In 2009, however, North Korea ended all diplomatic talks, expelled all nuclear inspectors, and conducted a nuclear test. In the years that followed, North Korean authorities have engaged in nuclear brinkmanship not seen since the Cold War.

For nations still pursuing the development of nuclear weapons, and for some of the nations that recently developed them, nuclear diplomacy has played a primary role in shaping their relations with the world.

Al-Qaeda and Afghanistan

In the Middle East and Central Asia, conflicts that had involved the superpowers continued beyond the Cold War. The 1979 Soviet invasion of Afghanistan, as well as the Iranian revolution, which was followed by the Iran-Iraq War, led to enduring political upheaval that continued to draw the United States into violent conflicts in the twenty-first century.

In Afghanistan rebel groups supported by the United States fought the Soviet armed forces occupying the country and forced a humiliating Soviet withdrawal in 1989. In 1996, after years of civil war, a puritanical Islamic movement called the Taliban filled the military and political vacuum left by the Soviet Union. The Taliban pursued a radical religious transformation of Afghan society, in particular by imposing harsh restrictions on women, who were forbidden from attending schools or universities and were subjected to limits on their employment and activities outside the home. The Taliban government provided safe haven in Afghanistan for a terrorist organization called al-Qaeda, which included militants who had fought in Afghanistan against the Soviet occupation. In the 1990s, led by Osama bin Laden (1957–2011), al-Qaeda attacked U.S. diplomatic and military targets in Africa and the Middle East.

On September 11, 2001, al-Qaeda carried out its most notorious act: its militants hijacked four passenger planes in the United States. They flew two of them into the World Trade Center buildings in New York City and a third into the Pentagon in

Washington, D.C. A fourth, believed to be targeting the White House or the U.S. Capitol, crashed into a field in rural Pennsylvania. These terrorist attacks killed almost three thousand people. Though the U.S. government had repeatedly attacked al-Qaeda in the 1990s, it had failed to destroy it. Now the U.S. government demanded that the Taliban government in Afghanistan surrender the al-Qaeda leadership it hosted. When the Taliban refused, the United States formed a military coalition including NATO members as well as Russia, Pakistan, and rebel groups in Afghanistan. The coalition mounted an invasion, deposed the Taliban, and pursued al-Qaeda.

After the U.S.-led coalition deposed the Taliban in 2001 and installed

New York, September 11, 2001
Pedestrians race for safety as the World Trade Center towers collapse after being hit by jet airliners. (Amy Sanetta/AP Photo)

a new government in Afghanistan, it faced a protracted guerrilla war against Taliban forces that controlled rural areas. The Taliban drew upon Afghanistan's long experience in resisting foreign military incursions such as the Soviet and earlier British invasions. Having displaced the Taliban, U.S.-led forces decimated al-Qaeda camps in Afghanistan, but terrorist acts continued. The conflict in Afghanistan spread to Pakistan, where some members of al-Qaeda found refuge, and acts of terrorism increased around the world in the years following the invasion of Afghanistan.

Through years of war, the United States and allied governments devastated al-Qaeda's leadership and reduced its reach, but local groups acting in conflicts in the Middle East and Africa continued to act under al-Qaeda's name. Militants with loose ties to al-Qaeda set off multiple bombs in a Madrid train station on March 11, 2004, killing 191 and wounding over 1,800. In London on July 7, 2005, terrorist bombs killed 56 people and injured more than 700. At least three of the bombers were British citizens of Pakistani descent with unclear links to al-Qaeda. A suicide bomber who may have had links to al-Qaeda has also been blamed for the 2007 assassination of Pakistani presidential candidate Benazir Bhutto. In 2011 U.S. intelligence services identified bin Laden's hideout in Pakistan in a compound located near the country's main military academy in Abbottabad. In a night raid, U.S. forces killed bin Laden.

U.S. military action against al-Qaeda and the Taliban spilled over into another conflict in the Middle East when the U.S. government invaded Iraq in 2003. The 2003 invasion of Iraq re-ignited a conflict that dated to Iraq's invasion of Kuwait in 1990 to seize its oil wealth. The 1990 invasion prompted a military response initiated and led by the United States. The Persian Gulf War became the largest joint military action undertaken by the United Nations since the Korean War. UN forces, among which the United States was the most prominent, expelled the invading Iraqi army but stopped short of removing Iraqi leader Saddam Hussein from power. Over the decade that followed, Iraq faced international economic sanctions along with constant political and military pressure from the United States to surrender its chemical and biological weapons stockpiles.

After 2001, amid the U.S. invasion of Afghanistan, U.S. president George W. Bush accused Iraq of rebuilding its nuclear, chemical, and biological weapons programs. To build domestic support for an invasion, the U.S. government also falsely implied that there were connections between Iraq and al-Qaeda. Bush asserted that the United States had the right to wage a pre-emptive war to depose Iraqi ruler Saddam Hussein, even though Iraq, impoverished by a decade of economic sanctions, gave no indication of plans to attack any other country. In 2002 UN inspectors found no weapons of mass destruction. France, Russia, China, Germany, and a majority of the smaller states argued for continued weapons monitoring, and France threatened to veto any resolution authorizing an invasion of Iraq. Rather than risk this veto, the United States and Britain claimed that earlier Security Council resolutions provided sufficient authorization and invaded Iraq in 2003.

A coalition of U.S.-led forces quickly defeated the Iraqi military, and in the power vacuum that ensued, armed groups representing all three main factions in Iraq—Sunni Muslims, Shi'ite Muslims, and Kurds—carried out daily attacks on Iraqi military and police, government officials, religious leaders, and civilians. Estimates of Iraqi deaths since the beginning of the war in 2003 and the U.S. withdrawal in 2011 ranged from 100,000 to over 1 million. The Iraq War and its subsequent toll split the West and spurred debate in the United States. In 2008 Democratic presidential candidate Barack Obama campaigned on a pledge to bring American troops home. Though the U.S. military occupation ended in 2011, the violence continued. Paradoxically, though the connection between al-Qaeda and the government of Saddam Hussein implied by President Bush did not exist, the violent environment of postwar Iraq became a place where militant groups that identified with al-Qaeda proliferated.

Global Circulation and Exchange

How have migration and the circulation of capital and technology continued to shape the world?

Much of the history in this textbook is driven by the circulation of peoples over great distances. Migration continues to be one of the great engines of history, though its experience exposes one of the major contradictions in the way liberalization has been conducted: governments have pressed for the free circulation of goods and capital, but have sought to limit the movement of people across borders.

Migration

National immigration policies vary considerably. In Europe the process of integration has meant that European Union member countries permit the free movement of citizens from other EU nations. But in many other cases, restrictions on migration have increased even as barriers to trade and investment have fallen.

The border between the United States and Mexico reflects many of the challenges of contemporary migrations. Since long before a border existed between the United States and Mexico, migrants have circulated throughout North America, but as the United States conquered land that had belonged to Mexico in the nineteenth century (see Chapter 27), it restricted the movement of migrants northward across the border. At the beginning of the twenty-first century the U.S. government began building a wall at its border with Mexico, further restricting the circulation of people even as the United States and Mexico implemented a free-trade agreement that made it easier for goods and capital to cross the border.

Similar trade agreements, coupled with similar restrictions on migration, exist between the United States and many Central American and Caribbean nations. The United States is by far the leading source of foreign investment in those countries. And the United States has participated in military conflicts in all of those countries over the past century, often multiple times. Still, within the United States, the most intense public discussions about Latin America surround the restriction of migration.

In many cases, restrictions on immigration have increased in countries where national economic growth has slowed. For instance, as Japanese industry boomed in the 1980s, the country welcomed descendants of Japanese emigrants who had settled in South America in the first half of the century. Because these migrants were culturally and linguistically different from natives, Japanese citizens considered them *dekasegi*, or "temporary guest workers," who had no right to citizenship despite their ancestry. As manufacturing and economic growth stagnated in the 1990s, this circuit of migration to Japan dwindled. During the same period millions of people, first from South Korea and then Vietnam, Cambodia, and Laos, whose countries had experienced great upheavals in conflicts involving the United States found legal refuge in the United States. (See "Individuals in Society: Sieng, a Mnong Refugee in an American High School," page 1052.)

Though pursuit of economic opportunity and flight from persecution are the major factors that drive international migration, other factors shape the creation of migratory circuits. A migratory circuit is a deep connection created between two regions through an initial experience of migration that results in a greater circulation of people. These migratory circuits have often followed experiences of violence. For instance, many immigrants settling in European countries like Britain or France migrated from regions that those countries dominated as colonies. In turn, circuits of migration to the United States have often followed U.S. military actions, such as wars in Southeast Asia and Korea or military interventions in Latin America. It remains to be seen whether U.S. military action in Iraq and Afghanistan will eventually yield the same result.

Migrants usually become ethnic, religious, or linguistic minorities in the countries where they settle, and they commonly face discrimination. Sometimes this discrimination is expressed in violence and oppression, such as that experienced by contemporary Zimbabwean workers in South Africa. In turn, discrimination and social pressures have also triggered violent reactions from ethnic minorities, such as riots in the Paris suburbs in 2007 and Stockholm in 2013 to protest discrimination experienced by Middle Eastern and North African migrants, or the radicalization of some Muslim migrants in Britain. When migrants lack legal standing, as is the case for millions in the United States, they can fall prey to criminal organizations or be exploited by employers.

Migrants don't just cross national borders; they also move within countries, most often from the countryside to the city. In countries with high degrees of rural poverty combined with a significant amount of urban industrialization, this current of migration often leads to sprawling, overcrowded urban areas.

Urbanization

Cities in Africa, Asia, and Latin America expanded at an astonishing pace after 1945. Many doubled or even tripled in size in a single decade (Table 33.1). In 1920 three out of every four of the world's urban inhabitants were concentrated in Europe

TABLE 33.1 Urban Population as a Percentage of Total Population in the World and in Eight Major Areas, 1925–2025

AREA	1925	1950	1975	2000	2025 (EST.)
World Total	21%	28%	39%	50%	63%
North America	54	64	77	86	93
Europe	48	55	67	79	88
Soviet Union	18	39	61	76	87
East Asia	10	15	30	46	63
Latin America	25	41	60	74	85
Africa	8	13	24	37	54

Note: Little more than one-fifth of the world's population was urban in 1925. In 2000 the total urban proportion in the world was about 50 percent. According to United Nations experts, the proportion should reach two-thirds by about 2025. The most rapid urban growth will occur in Africa and Asia, where the move to cities is still in its early stages.

INDIVIDUALS IN SOCIETY • Sieng, a Mnong Refugee in an American High School

n 2008, at a large urban high school in the U.S. South, Sieng, a seventeen-year-old Mnong refugee, recited the Pledge of Allegiance in his JROTC class. His aspiration to join the U.S. Marine Corps was an act of belonging that bridged both his life in the United States and his sense of his family and its history.

The Mnong are among a diverse group of ethnic minorities, known broadly as Montagnards, whose communities stretch across the central highlands of Vietnam. They are also a religious minority in Vietnam—many had converted to Christianity. During the Vietnam War, many Mnong provided military service alongside the United States, particularly with the U.S. Army Special Forces. After the war ended in 1975, the Mnong faced persecution, and over time many fled the country, joining the current of refugees who resettled in camps in Thailand, Malaysia, the Philippines, and later Cambodia. Sieng's family left Vietnam when he was a child in the late 1990s. He recalled his journey:

> We had a hard time in Vietnam, so we had to leave. We didn't have no choice because we had no food, and no land. And [the Vietnamese government] wanted my dad and took my grandpa. So we left in the night and went through the jungle. We walked and walked and got lost. So me and my dad tried to find the way and we found a house. Some people let us sleep there and also gave us food. Then we got to a [refugee] camp in Cambodia and stayed there for a year. I didn't have school in Vietnam, and I didn't have school at the camp. Then we came here.

Arriving in the United States at the age of sixteen, Sieng was not literate in Mnong, Vietnamese, or English, the language of his new school. Sieng aspired to become a Marine so he could help other refugees and his family. He explained, "A man needs to take care of the family too, and that's what I want to do. The Marines will help me take care of my family."

For Sieng, being a refugee instilled a sense of pride, a sense of what he and his family had overcome in coming to the United States, and a sense of what he desired for the future. As the oldest male child, Sieng was, in his words, "second in command" in the home while his father worked the third shift at a shipping facility. In the United States Sieng was an ethnic minority and a refugee with limited

and North America; by 2000 more than 60 percent of the world's urban population was concentrated in Africa, Asia, and Latin America. In 1950 there were only eight megacities (5 million or more inhabitants), and only two were in developing countries. Of the fifty-nine megacities anticipated to exist by 2015, forty-eight will be outside North America and Europe.

What caused this urban explosion? First, the overall population growth in the developing nations was critical. Urban residents gained substantially from a medical revolution that provided improved health care but only gradually began to reduce the size of their families. Second, more than half of all urban growth came from rural migration. Manufacturing jobs in the developing nations were concentrated in cities. In 1980 half of all the industrial jobs in Mexico were located in Mexico City.

English skills. He was misunderstood. A classmate in a world history class asked him where he was from in Mexico, and the question made him indignant:

> I am a *refugee*, not an immigrant! I am *Mnong*, not Vietnamese! But people call me Spanish. Some kids once asked me to say something in Spanish. . . . And Mexican students think I'm Chinese. They say, *"Hey Chino! Hey Chino!"* I get mad when they do this because I am more like American. My grandpa worked with Americans [in the war].

In a diverse school, amid other immigrants and ethnic minorities, Sieng found comfort in his identity as a refugee, reflecting on his family's past, its connection to the United States, and his role facilitating its journey, as he confronted a new environment, struggling to be understood.

Source: Liv T. Dávila, "Performing Allegiance: An Adolescent Refugee's Construction of Patriotism in JROTC," *Educational Studies* 39.5 (2014), in press. Reprinted by permission of Taylor & Francis LLC (http://www.tandfonline.com).

QUESTIONS FOR ANALYSIS

1. What aspects of Sieng's experience reflect broader patterns of migration?
2. How does Sieng's experience as a refugee shape his identity?
3. What role does JROTC play in Sieng's sense of belonging?

▷LaunchPad
ONLINE DOCUMENT PROJECT

What are the key issues surrounding immigration reform? Examine documents related to the debate over U.S. immigration reform, and then complete a quiz and writing assignment based on the evidence and details from this chapter.

See inside the front cover to learn more.

Newcomers have streamed to cities even when industrial jobs have been scarce, seeking any type of employment. Sociologists call this phenomenon urbanization without industrialization. Many migrants were pushed into cities. As large landowners found it more profitable to produce export crops, their increasingly mechanized operations reduced the need for agricultural laborers. Ethnic or political unrest in the countryside can also push migrants into cities. These push factors have been particularly strong in Latin America, with its neocolonial pattern of large landowners and foreign companies that exported food and raw materials. Many young people left home for the city to work in construction or domestic service, while many others found informal work.

Most of the exploding numbers of urban poor earned precarious livings in a **bazaar economy** comprised of petty traders and unskilled labor. In the bazaar economy, which

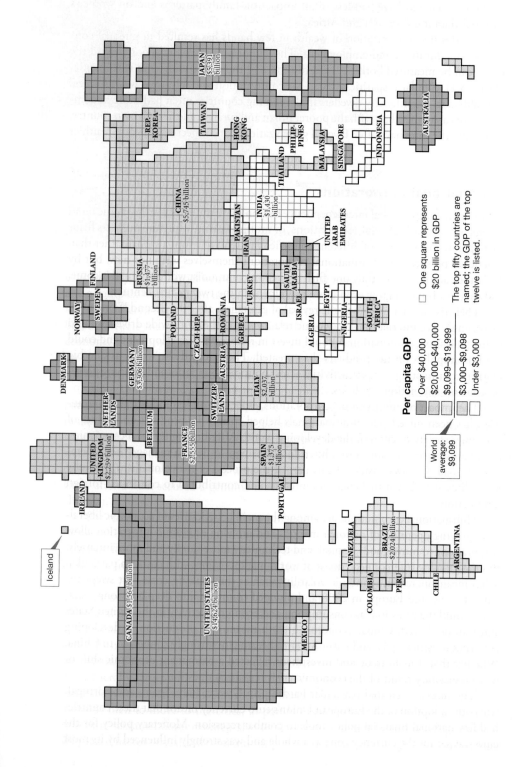

Per capita GDP

Over $40,000
$20,000–$40,000
$9,099–$19,999
$3,000–$9,098
Under $3,000

World average: $9,099

☐ One square represents $20 billion in GDP

☐ The top fifty countries are named; the GDP of the top twelve is listed.

◀ **MAP 33.1   The Global Distribution of Wealth, ca. 2010** This size-comparison map, arranged according to global wealth distribution, vividly illustrates the gap in wealth between the Northern and Southern Hemispheres. The two small island nations of Japan and the United Kingdom have more wealth than all the nations of the Southern Hemisphere combined, although wealth creation in India and Brazil has advanced significantly. The wealthiest countries are also the most highly urbanized. As market capitalism expands in China, Vietnam, and other Asian countries and in Latin America and Africa, the relative-size ratios on the map will continue to change and evolve. Tiny Iceland, whose GDP is less than $20 billion, nevertheless has one of the highest per capita GDPs in the world.

powerful economies, Germany and France, which resisted expanding the monetary supply to relieve the most afflicted economies in the Eurozone. The tension between the economic policymaking of Germany and France and the deep economic crisis in southern Europe threatened European economic unity. This would be a basic test of the European Union: could a shared economic and political system meet the challenges faced by individual nations?

Social Movements

What challenges did social reformers address at the turn of the twenty-first century?

Just as nineteenth-century social reformers embraced the cause of ending slavery, modern social reformers have sought to end global inequality, racism, and sexism and to improve human and civil rights for all. Social movements played a critical role in the victory of the democratic movements in Latin America and Europe and the end of the apartheid system in South Africa (see page 1022).

As movements for human rights and social reform gained ground in the 1960s and 1970s, activists increasingly looked beyond national borders to form alliances. Movements for women's rights, nuclear disarmament, environmental protection, and addressing climate change all became both local and global efforts. For example, the global anti-apartheid movement kept pressure on nations to apply economic and political sanctions on the white-minority regime in South Africa. But at the same time, the anti-apartheid movement served as a means to address local problems. For instance, in Brazil anti-apartheid activism helped draw attention to the country's own racial inequalities, while in the United States anti-apartheid activism on college campuses helped students organize movements concerned with other issues such as gender equality.

The 1977 Nestlé boycott exemplified the kinds of success such movements could achieve as well as their limitations. Critics charged that the Swiss company's intense marketing of powdered baby formula in poor countries or regions with little access to clean water posed a risk to children. These critics argued that Nestlé profited from the death of children by coaxing mothers away from breast-feeding, which provided the best nutrition, and toward formula that would likely be mixed with contaminated water, or diluted by mothers who couldn't afford enough formula to use the recommended amounts. Activists called on consumers around the world to boycott Nestlé products.

At first, Nestlé dismissed the boycott and sought to discredit the movement. The president of the company's Brazilian division declared that "the US Nestlé Co has advised me that their research indicates that this [boycott] is actually an indirect attack on the free world's economic system."[2] Condemnation of Nestlé mounted. In a 1978 hearing, U.S. senator Ted Kennedy asked a Nestlé executive: "Can a product which requires clean water, good sanitation, adequate family income and a literate parent to follow printed instructions be properly and safely used in areas where water is contaminated, sewage runs in the streets, poverty is severe and illiteracy is high?"[3] The executive answered evasively.

In 1981 the UN World Health Organization responded to the campaign by developing a set of voluntary standards, the International Code of Marketing of Breast-Milk Substitutes, regulating the marketing of infant formula in poorer countries where access to clean water was precarious. In 1984 Nestlé agreed to follow the standards. The movement succeeded, but its success raised questions: multinational corporations operate beyond the reach of single governments, and often operate in regions with weak regulatory or investigatory structures, or in countries where repressive political systems shield them from scrutiny. As a result, it is hard to hold them accountable when their conduct is unethical. At the same time, social movements and nongovernmental organizations also acted outside the realm of public accountability.

Environmentalism

In the eighteenth century governments became increasingly concerned about forests as the great demand for lumber to build ships nearly destroyed the forests of Britain, Europe, the eastern United States, and later India. To protect forests, the United States created the first national park in the nineteenth century. The modern environmental movement began with concerns about chemical waste, rapid consumption of energy and food supplies, global deforestation, and threats to wildlife. By the 1970s citizens had begun joining together in nongovernmental organizations to pursue preservation or restoration of the natural environment.

The environmental movement is actually several different movements, each with its own agenda. American biologist and writer Rachel Carson was an early proponent of the environmental health movement. In *Silent Spring* (1962), she warned of the dangers of pesticides and pollution:

> Along with the possibility of the extinction of mankind by nuclear war, the central problem of our age has therefore become the contamination of man's total environment with such substances of incredible potential for harm—substances that accumulate in the tissues of plants and animals and even penetrate the germ cells to shatter or alter the very material of heredity upon which the shape of the future depends.[4]

Carson and others were concerned about the harmful effects of chemicals, radiation, pollution, waste, and urban development on the environment and on human health. Environmentalists like Carson acted out of concern that all living things were connected and that damage to one part of an ecological system could have consequences across that ecosystem.

The conservation movement, represented in the United States by the Sierra Club and the Audubon Society, seeks to protect the biodiversity of the planet and emphasizes the spiritual and aesthetic qualities of nature. The ecology movement consists of different groups with somewhat similar agendas, ranging from politically active green parties to the nongovernmental organization Greenpeace. These organizations are concerned about global warming, pollution, the use of nuclear energy and nuclear weapons, genetically modified food, recycling, preserving endangered species, sustainable agriculture, protecting ancient forests, and environmental justice, or the effort to address disproportionately high adverse human health or environmental effects of pollution and industrial facilities among minority, low-income populations.

Environmentalists today are especially concerned about **global warming**, the increase of global temperatures over time caused by the buildup of carbon in the atmosphere that captures heat. As a result of global warming, average temperatures have increased worldwide in recent decades, a trend that most scientists expect will intensify without curbs on carbon emissions. The decade from 2000 to 2010 was the warmest in recorded history. Scientists believe that man-made climate change began with the Industrial Revolution in the eighteenth century. The subsequent release of hydrocarbons produced through the burning of fossil fuels—coal, oil, natural gas—has caused a greenhouse effect that traps these gases and heats up earth's atmosphere. Paradoxically, industrialization and increased consumption in the developing world meant diminished global inequalities but intensified global carbon emissions.

Effects of global warming over the next century include a catastrophic rise in sea levels that threatens to put many coastal cities and islands underwater; ecosystem changes that may threaten various species of plants and animals; extreme and abnormal weather patterns; destruction of the earth's ozone layer, which shields the planet from harmful solar radiation; and a decline in agricultural production. International concerns over global warming resulted in a 1997 agreement, the Kyoto Protocol, which amended the United Nations Framework Convention on Climate Change. Countries that ratify the Kyoto Protocol agree to reduce their emissions of carbon dioxide and five other

Global Warming
In the twenty-first century development pressures meet growing concern about climate change.
(Joel Pett Editorial Cartoon used with the permission of Joel Pett and the Cartoonist Group)

greenhouse gases. As of April 2014, 191 countries had ratified it. The most notable exception was the United States. The United Nations and environmental activists have continued to pursue an international environmental accord that can bring all nations into a shared effort to combat climate change.

Lesbian, Gay, and Transgender Rights

In the United States and western Europe the growing focus on liberal individual freedoms since the 1960s has opened social space for same-sex unions and affinities, which had long been suppressed by religious and cultural strictures. By the early 1970s a global gay rights movement championed the human rights of lesbian, gay, and transgendered people. The movement intensified in the 1980s as it became clear that governments neglected medical research and treatment for people sick with AIDS, which they dismissed as a "gay disease." The organization ACT UP's advocacy campaign for AIDS research created a powerful symbol using the words "Silence = Death" beneath a pink triangle to represent the AIDS crisis. A journalist who wrote about AIDS in the 1980s described his reaction to the ACT UP symbol:

> When I first saw the [ACT UP] poster, I didn't really know what it was. . . . I recognized the triangle as the symbol of homosexual victimization by the Nazis, but this triangle pointed up. Did it suggest supremacy? And the phrase itself, with its diabolical math, lodged in my imagination. Did it suggest conspiracy? Because of the word "death" I supposed it was about AIDS; had I noticed the tiny type at the bottom, which for a time included the instruction "Turn anger, fear, grief into action," perhaps I would have been sure.[5]

By the 1990s gay rights activists had broadened their efforts to challenge discrimination in employment, education, and public life. In 1995 Canada became the first country to allow same-sex marriage. In the ensuing years many European countries followed suit. But the legalization of same-sex marriage was not only a Western achievement: by 2013 Argentina, South Africa, Ecuador, and Uruguay had legalized same-sex

Equal Marriage in Argentina Latin America's first same-sex marriage occurred in Tierra del Fuego, Argentina, in 2009. (Tierra del Fuego Government/ Reuters/Landov)

marriage, while many other nations provided legal protections for families that stopped shy of marriage. Argentina led the way in legal support for transgendered people and made sexual reassignment surgery a legal right in 2012.

The movement toward recognition of same-sex marriage reflects the connection between liberalization and human rights: beyond dignifying discriminated minorities, marriage rights give same-sex families legal equality to manage property rights and financial activities, such as the ability to inherit a home or jointly purchase insurance. Human rights successes in Latin America or Europe have widened the disparity in the experiences of lesbian, gay, or transgendered people in many other regions of the world. Parts of the Middle East, Africa, and Asia enforce religious strictures against same-sex relationships that include imprisonment or death.

Women's Right to Equality

The 1995 United Nations Fourth World Conference on Women, held in Beijing, China, called on the world community to take action in twelve areas of critical concern to women: poverty, access to education and training, access to health care, violence against women, women and war, economic inequality with men, political inequality with men, creation of institutions for women's advancement, lack of respect for women's rights, stereotyping of women, gender inequalities and the environment, and violation of girl children's rights.[6] These are concerns that all women share, although degrees of inequality vary greatly from one country to another.

The **feminization of poverty**, the disproportionate number of women living in extreme poverty, applies to even the wealthiest countries, where two out of every three poor adults are women. There are many causes for this phenomenon. Because women are primarily responsible for child care in many cultures, they have less time and opportunity for work. Male labor migration increases the number of households headed by women and thus the number of families living in poverty. Job restrictions, discrimination, and limited access to education reduce women's employment options, except in the "informal economy" of domestic service, prostitution, and street vending. Birthrates are higher among poor women, particularly among adolescents, who make up many of the estimated 585,000 women who die every year during pregnancy and childbirth. The poorest women usually suffer most from government policies, usually legislated by men, which restrict their access to reproductive health care and family planning.

Women have made gains in the workplace, making up 38 percent of the nonfarm-sector global workforce in the early 2000s, as compared to 35 percent in 1990. But segregated labor markets remain the rule, with higher-paying jobs reserved for men. In the farm sector, women produce more than half of all the food and up to 80 percent of subsistence crops grown in Africa. Because this is informal labor and often unpaid, these women laborers are denied access to loans, and many cannot own the land they farm.

Social class continues to be a major divider of women's opportunities. Over the course of the twentieth century women from more affluent backgrounds experienced far greater gains in access to education, employment, and political representation than women in poverty did. In the aftermath of decolonization and state formation, women emerged as heads of state in Bangladesh, India, Israel, and Pakistan. A wave of democratic political transitions in the 1980s yielded women heads of state in the Philippines and Nicaragua. In the years following democratic transitions, the same occurred in Panama, Chile, Argentina, Brazil, Indonesia, and Liberia.

Children: The Right to Childhood

In 1989 the United Nations General Assembly adopted the Convention on the Rights of the Child, which spelled out a number of rights that are due every child. These include civil and human rights and economic, social, and cultural rights. It is not difficult to see why such a document was necessary. Globally, a billion children live in poverty — one in every two children in the world. The convention also addresses other concerns, including the fact that children make up half the world's refugees, and the problems of child labor and exploitation, sexual violence and sex trafficking, police abuse of street children, HIV/AIDS orphans, lack of access to education, and lack of access to adequate health care. The convention has been ratified by more countries than any other human rights treaty — 193 countries as of 2014. The United States and Somalia remain the only two United Nations member nations that have not ratified it.

As the twenty-first century began, nearly a billion people — mostly women denied equitable access to education — were illiterate. Increasing economic globalization has put pressure on all governments to improve literacy rates and educational opportunities; the result has been reduced gender inequalities in education. While the percentage of illiterate adults in 2010 who were women was 64 percent, the percentage of girls among illiterate children was 60 percent, with the greatest gains in literacy occurring in South Asia and the Middle East.

Mexico pioneered a new approach to combating poverty that has been implemented in a growing number of countries. Conditional cash transfer, or CCT, provides a stipend to families who meet certain goals, such as keeping their children in school. This approach addresses poverty directly, while enlisting families to work toward its long-term solution by increasing education levels, which will broaden opportunities for new generations. Mexico's Oportunidades (Opportunities) CCT was followed by Brazil's

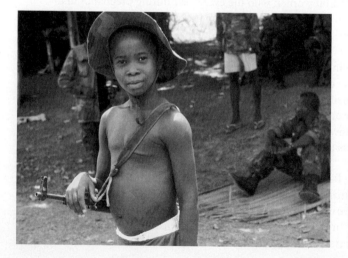

Child Soldier in Sierra Leone   This eleven-year-old boy with a rifle slung over his shoulder is a member of the Sierra Leone army and stands guard at a checkpoint during his country's civil war. Tens of thousands of boys and girls under eighteen have been used by the militaries in more than sixty countries since 2000. (Brennan Linsley/AP Photo)

Bolsa Famila (Family Scholarship) and by similar projects in many other countries in Latin America. Versions of the program have been introduced across Asia and the Middle East, including in Bangladesh, where a CCT program promotes the education of girls.

Science and Technology: Changes and Challenges

How have science and technology kept pace with population change?

Since 1950 the world's population has increased from 2.5 billion people to over 7 billion. This population growth has been matched by increasing demand for food and has placed growing strains on natural resources. Advances in agriculture and medicine have helped offset this challenge, while technological innovations in areas such as transportation and communications have increased the complexity of interactions among the world's growing population.

Intensified Agriculture and the Green Revolution

As the world's population grew in the second half of the twentieth century, food production strained to keep pace, prompting a greater emphasis on rural development and agricultural sciences. Before 1939 the countries of Asia, Africa, and Latin America had collectively produced more grain than they consumed. After 1945, as their populations soared, they began importing food from countries like the United States. Although crops might fail in poor countries, starvation seemed a thing of the past. In 1965, when India was urged to build up its food reserves, one top Indian official expressed a widespread attitude: "Why should we bother? Our reserves are the wheat fields of Kansas."[7] The official was proved wrong when devastating famines gripped India in 1966 and 1967.

That close brush with mass starvation created widespread alarm that population growth was outpacing food production. The American scientist Paul Ehrlich envisioned a grim future in his 1968 bestseller *The Population Bomb*, which warned of a population crisis:

> The battle to feed all of humanity is over. In the 1970s the world will undergo famines — hundreds of millions of people are going to starve to death in spite of any crash programs embarked upon now. At this stage nothing can prevent a substantial increase in the world death rate.[8]

Ehrlich was not the first scientist to make such dire predictions, and like Thomas Malthus before him (see page 701), he failed to understand the adaptability of farmers and agricultural technology to keep pace with population growth.

Technological improvements countered such nightmarish visions and offered hope. Plant scientists set out to develop new genetically engineered seeds to suit particular growing conditions. The first breakthrough came in Mexico in the 1950s when an American-led team developed new strains of high-yield wheat. These varieties enabled farmers to double their yields, though the plants demanded greater amounts of fertilizer and water for irrigation. Mexican wheat production soared. Thus began the transformation of agriculture in some poor countries — the so-called **green revolution**.

In the 1960s American-backed scientists in the Philippines developed a new hybrid "miracle rice" that required more fertilizer and water but yielded more and grew much faster than ordinary rice. It permitted the revolutionary introduction of year-round farming on irrigated land, allowing farmers to plant two to four crops a year rather than one. Asian scientists developed similar hybrid strains of rice to meet local conditions.

As they applied green revolution technologies, many Asian countries experienced rapid increases in grain production. Farmers in India increased production more than 60 percent in fifteen years. By 1980 thousands of new grain bins dotted the Indian countryside, symbols of the agricultural revolution and the country's newfound ability to feed all of its population. China followed with its own highly successful version of the green revolution.

The green revolution offered new hope to industrializing nations, though its benefits often flowed to large landowners and export farms that could afford the necessary investments in irrigation and fertilizer. Experiences in China and other Asian countries showed, however, that even peasant families with tiny farms could gain substantially. Indeed, the green revolution's greatest successes occurred in Asian countries with broad-based peasant ownership of land. However, few of the poorest villagers benefited from the technological revolution in equipment because they rarely owned land or had enough capital to invest in new agricultural technology to increase their yields. This helps explain why in Latin America, where 3 to 4 percent of the rural population owned 60 to 80 percent of the land, the green revolution spread slowly beyond Mexico, where land had been redistributed after the 1910 revolution.

As the practice of planting genetically engineered crops to increase production grew in the late twentieth and early twenty-first centuries, many feared that such foods would have still-unknown harmful effects on the human body. Several European and other countries banned imports of genetically modified corn and soybeans from the United States, where the practice was most common. The loss of biodiversity was also of growing concern. When one or two genetically engineered seeds replaced all the naturally occurring local seeds in an area, food security was threatened. With a shrinking diversity of plants and animals, farmers find it more difficult to find alternatives if the dominant hybrid seed in use becomes susceptible to a particular disease or pest or if a significant climate change occurs.

Slowing Population Growth

By the 1970s and 1980s population growth in the industrialized countries had begun to fall significantly. By the 1990s some European leaders were expressing concern that low birthrates threatened national economies by reducing the labor force, the tax base, and the number of consumers. Between 1970 and 1975 China registered the fastest five-year birthrate decline in recorded history. Other countries, especially in Latin America and East Asia, experienced declines in fertility. In 1970 the average Brazilian woman had close to 6 children; by 2005 she had 1.9. In 1970 the average woman in Bangladesh had more than 7 children; in 2005 she had 3.1. Fertility in most of the developing world could fall below the replacement level (2.1 children per woman) before 2100. There were several reasons for this decline in fertility among women in the developing world. As fewer babies died of disease or malnutrition, families needed fewer births to guarantee the survival of the number of children they wanted. Better living conditions, urbanization, and more education encouraged women to have fewer children.

In the early 1960s the introduction of the birth control pill allowed women to take control of their own fertility. Family planning was now truly possible. In the early twenty-first century, more than half of the world's couples practiced some form of birth control, up from one in eight just forty years earlier. However, male chauvinists, religious leaders, and conservative government leaders in many Catholic and Muslim countries restricted access to birth control methods and abortion because they felt that these violated their core beliefs. Birth control and abortion were most accepted in North America, Protestant regions in Europe, the Soviet Union, and East Asia, which explains why these regions had the lowest birthrates and population growth; however, the issue remains controversial.

The most recent estimates are that the world's population will grow by a further 50 percent between 2000 and 2050, when it will reach about 9 billion. Over the next century it is then expected to level off at about 10 billion.

The Medical Revolution

The medical revolution began in the late 1800s with the development of the germ theory of disease (see page 743) and continued rapidly after World War II. Scientists discovered vaccines for many of the most deadly diseases. Jonas Salk's development of the polio vaccine in 1952 was followed by the first oral polio vaccine (1962) and vaccines for measles (1964), mumps (1967), rubella (1970), chicken pox (1974), and hepatitis B (1981). According to the United Nations World Health Organization, medical advances reduced deaths from smallpox, cholera, and plague by more than 95 percent worldwide between 1951 and 1966.

Following independence, Asian and African countries increased the small numbers of hospitals, doctors, and nurses they had inherited from colonial regimes. In addition, local people were successfully trained as paramedics to staff rural outpatient clinics that offered medical treatment, health education, and prenatal and postnatal care. Many paramedics were women, who traditionally addressed health problems that involved childbirth and infancy.

Medical advances significantly lowered death rates and lengthened life expectancies worldwide. Children became increasingly likely to survive their early years, although infant and juvenile mortality remained far higher in poor countries than in rich ones. By 1980 the average inhabitant of the developing countries could expect to live about fifty-four years, although life expectancy at birth varied from forty to sixty-four years depending on the country. In industrialized countries, life expectancy at birth averaged seventy-one years. In 1979 the World Health Organization announced that smallpox had been eradicated worldwide. By this time, surgical transplants of organs such as hearts, lungs, and kidneys had become routine. In 2003 scientists working on the Human Genome Project announced that they had successfully identified, mapped,

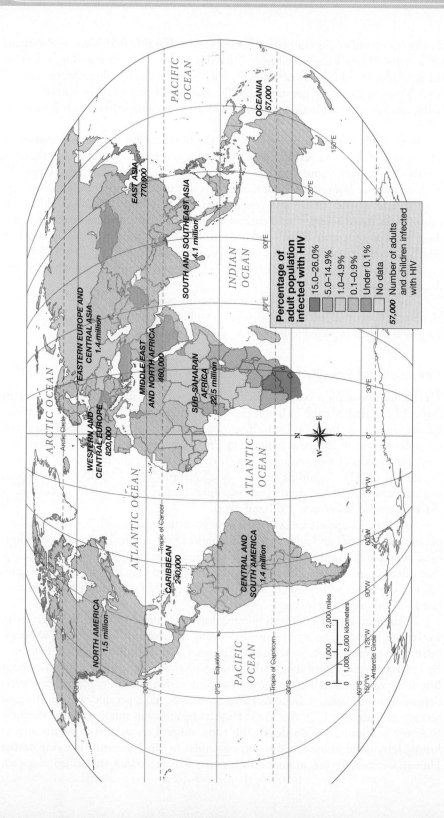

◀ **MAP 33.2** **People Living with HIV/AIDS Worldwide, ca. 2010** As this map illustrates, Africa has been hit the hardest by the HIV/AIDS epidemic. It currently has fifteen to twenty times more identified cases than any other region of the world. AIDS researchers expect that in the coming decade, however, Russia and South and East Asia will overtake and then far surpass Africa in the number of infected people. (Source: Data from World Health Organization, www.whosea.org)

and sequenced the entire genome, or hereditary genetic information, of human beings, opening new pathways to address illness.

The medical benefits of scientific advances have been limited by unequal access to health care, which is more readily available to the wealthy than to the poor. Between 1980 and 2000 the number of children under the age of five dying annually of diarrhea dropped by 60 percent through the global distribution of a cheap sugar-salt solution mixed in water. Still, over 1.5 million children worldwide continue to die each year from diarrhea, primarily in poorer nations. Deaths worldwide from HIV/AIDS, malaria, and tuberculosis were concentrated in the world's poorest regions, while tuberculosis remained the leading killer of women worldwide.

Tuberculosis (TB) claims millions of lives every year, even though it is a curable disease. Malaria kills a million people a year worldwide, 90 percent of them in Africa. In 2007 the Population Division of the United Nations calculated that 36 million persons globally were infected with HIV, the virus that causes AIDS, and that AIDS was the world's fourth-leading cause of death. About 90 percent of all persons who die from AIDS and 86 percent of those currently infected with HIV live in sub-Saharan Africa (Map 33.2). In Africa HIV/AIDS is most commonly spread through heterosexual sex. Widespread disease and poverty are also significant factors in that Africans already suffering from other illnesses such as malaria or tuberculosis are less resistant to HIV and have less access to health care for treatment.

Another critical factor contributing to the spread of AIDS in Africa is the continued political instability of many countries—particularly those in the corridor running from Uganda to South Africa. This region was the scene of brutal civil and liberation wars that resulted in massive numbers of refugees, a breakdown in basic health-care services, and the destruction of family and cultural networks. The people living in this area in the countries of Uganda, Rwanda, Burundi, Zaire/Congo, Angola, Zimbabwe, Mozambique, and South Africa have been decimated by HIV/AIDS. South Africa currently has the largest number of HIV/AIDS cases in the world. In 2010 around 10 percent of the South African population, about 5.6 million people, were living with HIV/AIDS. Of these, over 330,000 were children under fifteen years of age. An estimated 310,000 South Africans died of AIDS in 2009. Since 2001 relatively inexpensive AIDS drugs that are widely available in the West have been dispensed freely to many of those infected in Africa and Asia, but the availability of these drugs has generally failed to keep up with the need.

A Digital Revolution

On any given day, a reader of this textbook is likely to receive an e-mail message from someone claiming to be the widow of a deposed dictator offering to share her ill-gotten riches in return for the reader's cooperation or banking information. Millions of such messages are transmitted daily around the world. Their proliferation rides upon a swift and profound change in information and communications technologies.

The invention of moving pictures, the telephone, and other communications technologies between 1875 and 1900 prepared the way for a twentieth-century era of mass communications. In parallel, new information-processing technologies began with development of adding and calculating machines and culminated in the development of the first computers during the Second World War. As computing and communications technologies converged, they created the "information age." The global availability and affordability of radios and television sets in the 1950s introduced a second communications revolution that followed the first revolution brought by telegraph and telephone. The transistor radio penetrated the most isolated hamlets of the world. Governments embraced radio broadcasting as a means to project their power, disseminate propaganda, and broaden education. Though initially less common, television use expanded into nearly every country during the 1960s and 1970s, even if there was only one television in a village.

Governments recognized the power of the visual image to promote their ideologies or leaders, and a state television network became a source of national pride. In countries like Brazil, television transmission towers that rose up in the 1960s became monuments to modernity and development. Around the world, governments controlled the introduction of color television to symbolize progress. The Argentine military junta introduced color broadcasting to the nation for the 1978 soccer World Cup, transmitting games that took place within earshot of the detention centers where it waged its "dirty war." Television became a powerful disseminator of culture: U.S. television programming reached around the world. Mexican television programs dominated Spanish-speaking regions. Brazilian soap operas gained loyal followers from the Soviet Union to Angola.

The third, and perhaps greatest, communications revolution occurred with the first Apple personal computers in 1976, followed by the introduction of cell phones in 1985. The use of mass communications and the pace of technological development in communications have exploded since then. Cell phones allowed individuals and nations in the developing world to bypass traditional telephone lines, installation, and other obstacles. Africa now has over 85 million cell phone users. Cell phones have become among the most widely owned communications tools worldwide.

Despite the ubiquity of cell phones, the Internet, or World Wide Web, has had the greatest impact on human communication. First made available to the general public in 1994, the Internet and e-mail allow people to communicate instantly anywhere with an Internet connection. The possibilities for global access to information and knowledge are seemingly infinite. Authoritarian governments have realized the threat that the Internet and social media platforms like Facebook and Twitter pose to their power and control. The governments of China and North Korea, for example, have spent millions of dollars trying to restrict information traveling in and out of their countries over the Internet, while the governments of the United States and other nations have spent even more to develop ways to monitor that information. Even as expanding means of communication through cell phones, computers, and their networks have made censorship more difficult to enforce, they have made it even harder to keep information or communications private.

The intensity of innovation in communications and information technology created new business giants. Apple, Microsoft, Google, and IBM are entities that stand at the forefront of the contemporary world, and they absorb and distribute enormous amounts of capital. Their combined revenue in 2012 was $335.5 billion, larger than the GDP of Nigeria. Apple's revenue alone was larger than the GDP of Hungary or any of 125 other countries.[9]

The success of these technology companies and the proliferation of computer, cellular telephone, and Internet use are remarkable changes, but they also deepen a stubborn continuity: deep socioeconomic inequalities between countries and within countries. For instance, when Windows XP was released in 2001, a Nigerian cocoa laborer would have had to save his or her entire year's earnings to buy the Home Edition.[10] The unevenness of both the production and consumption of computer technology has resulted in a digital divide, meaning the gap in access to Internet, computer, and telecommunications resources. This gap is the greatest between nations like the United States, western European countries, and Japan and nations in Africa and South or Southeast Asia. The digital divide also exists between the wealthy and poor, as well as between urban and rural areas within countries. As the Internet becomes more integral to business, education, and government, communities with no or limited access face growing disadvantages.

Chapter Summary

The end of the Cold War confrontation between superpowers has resulted in a world in which regional tensions endure and sometimes become international conflicts. Consequently, in a way similar to its actions in the Cold War era, the United States after 1990 continued to be involved in military conflicts far from home in regions ranging from the Balkans to Libya, Iraq, and Afghanistan. These conflicts have also spurred arms races that have led to the emergence of new nuclear powers in South Asia and East Asia.

The transitions to economic and political liberalism in the former Soviet bloc and in Latin America were particularly dramatic expressions of the rise of liberalism worldwide, which included the economic and political integration of Europe and the emergence of China as an economic superpower. Growing interconnectedness of world markets has meant increased economic volatility, such as the global financial market crisis of 2008. Cycles of economic growth and crisis, as well as contradictory experiences of integration and regional conflict, are tensions of the modern world rooted in historical experiences.

Notes

1. Francis Fukuyama, "The End of History?" *The National Interest*, Summer 1989, p. 3.
2. Quoted in Judith Richter, *Holding Corporations Accountable: Corporate Conduct, International Codes, and Citizen Action* (London: Zed Books, 2002), p. 55.
3. Quoted in Simon Robinson, "Nestlé Baby Milk Substitute and International Marketing: A Case History," in *Case Histories in Business Ethics*, ed. Chris Megone and Simon Robinson (New York: Routledge, 2002), p. 141.
4. Rachel Carson, *Silent Spring* (1962; repr., New York: Houghton Mifflin, 1994), pp. 1–3, 7–8.
5. Jesse Green, "When Political Art Mattered," *New York Times*, December 7, 2003, http://www.nytimes.com/learning/teachers/featured_articles/20031208monday.html.

6. United Nations, "Critical Areas of Concern," *Report of the Fourth World Conference on Women* (New York: United Nations Department for Policy Coordination and Sustainable Development, 1995), ch. 1, annex II, ch. 3, pp. 41–44, http://www.un.org/esa/gopher-data/conf/fwcw/off/a—20.en. See also Population Reference Bureau, *Women of Our World 2005* (Washington, D.C.: Population Reference Bureau, 2005) for the latest data and ten-year follow-up to the Beijing meeting.

7. Quoted in L. R. Brown, *Seeds of Change: The Green Revolution and Development in the 1970s* (New York: Praeger, 1970), p. 16.

8. Paul Ehrlich, *The Population Bomb* (New York: Ballantine, 1968), p. 11.

9. The World Bank, "GDP (Current US$)," 2014, http://data.worldbank.org/indicator/NY.GDP.MKTP .CD?order=wbapi_data_value_2012+wbapi_data_value+wbapi_data_value-last&sort=desc.

10. James Gockowski and S. Oduwole, *Labor Practices in the Cocoa Sector of Southwest Nigeria with a Focus on the Role of Children* (Ibadan, Nigeria: International Institute of Tropical Agriculture, 2003), p. 23.

CONNECTIONS

A joke about baseball umpires captures the ways we read history. At the umpires' convention, a lifetime achievement award is presented to a venerable umpire who refereed the 1947 World Series. Accepting the award, the elderly umpire addressed the audience: "I call it like it *is*." The crowd cheered wildly. The presiding umpire thanked him but added, "I call it like I *see* it." Again, the crowd howled and cheered. After he spoke, the rookie umpire of the year addressed the gathering and, with deference to his senior colleagues, declared, "It's *nothing* until I call it."

This joke reminds us that the present shapes the ways we ask questions about the past. Understanding of the past also shapes our questions about the present and the future. Our history of world societies shows that the forces that shape the world we live in have deep roots: globalization reaches back for centuries. Current armed conflicts are based on historic tensions often rooted in ethnic differences or legacies of colonialism. The gaps between rich and poor countries, and between the rich and poor within countries, have sometimes been diminished by advances in science and technology or by reforms in social policy. But science, technology, and public policy also deepen those inequalities, as uneven industrialization and the digital divide reflect.

We find these competing tensions throughout history, and we find them often recurring over time and place: our relationship with the past is one of continuity and change. The study of history allows us to frame questions about complex, competing, and often-contradictory experiences. Asking these questions sharpens our focus on not only the past but also the present. We are shaped by history. But we also make it.

Chapter Review

MAKE IT STICK

 LearningCurve
Go online and use LearningCurve to retain what you've read.

IDENTIFY KEY TERMS

Identify and explain the significance of each item below.

middle powers (p. 1045)

megacities (p. 1052)

bazaar economy (p. 1053)

multinational corporations (p. 1055)

global warming (p. 1059)

feminization of poverty (p. 1061)

green revolution (p. 1064)

digital divide (p. 1069)

REVIEW THE MAIN IDEAS

Answer the focus questions from each section of the chapter.

1. Does the contemporary world reflect the "end of history"? (p. 1045)

2. How have migration and the circulation of capital and technology continued to shape the world? (p. 1050)

3. What challenges did social reformers address at the turn of the twenty-first century? (p. 1057)

4. How have science and technology kept pace with population change? (p. 1063)

MAKE CONNECTIONS

Analyze the larger developments and continuities within and across chapters.

1. Why hasn't the end of the Cold War been followed by an easing of regional conflicts?

2. How do socioeconomic inequalities in the twenty-first-century world resemble the gaps between rich and poor in earlier eras?

3. How do contemporary technological and scientific developments reflect historical change and continuity?

⏻LaunchPad
ONLINE DOCUMENT PROJECT

The Immigration Debate
What are the key issues surrounding immigration reform?

Examine documents related to the debate over U.S. immigration reform, and then complete a quiz and writing assignment based on the evidence and details from this chapter.

See inside the front cover to learn more.

CHRONOLOGY

1950s	• Beginning of green revolution
1969–1979	• Strategic Arms Limitation Talks (SALT) between the Soviet Union and United States
1970	• Treaty on the Non-Proliferation of Nuclear Weapons
1981	• UN World Health Organization International Code of Marketing of Breast-Milk Substitutes
1989	• United Nations Convention on the Rights of the Child
1994	• Zapatista Army for National Liberation insurrection in Chiapas, Mexico
1997	• Chemical Weapons Convention goes into effect, banning the production of chemical weapons; Kyoto Protocol on global warming
2000–2010	• Warmest decade in recorded history
2001	• Al-Qaeda attacks on World Trade Center and U.S. Pentagon
2001	• U.S. invasion and occupation of Afghanistan
2003	• U.S.-led coalition invades Iraq; Human Genome Project completes sequencing of human genome

Index

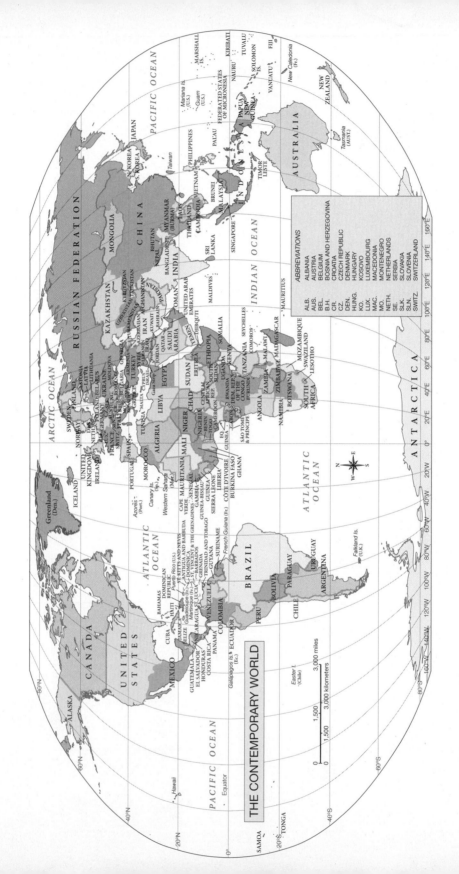

THE CONTEMPORARY WORLD